Essential Readings in Sport and Exercise Psychology

Daniel Smith, PhD
Cerritos College

Michael Bar-Eli, PhD
Ben-Gurion University of the Negev

Editors

HUMAN KINETICS

Library of Congress Cataloging-in-Publication Data

Essential readings in sport and exercise psychology / [edited by] Daniel Smith, Michael Bar-Eli.
p. cm.
Includes bibliographical references and index.
ISBN-13: 978-0-7360-5767-7 (hard cover)
ISBN-10: 0-7360-5767-6 (hard cover)
1. Sports--Psychological aspects. 2. Exercise--Psychological aspects. I. Smith, Daniel, 1952- II. Bar-Eli, Michael.
GV706.4.E77 2007
796'.01--dc22
2006038972

ISBN-10: 0-7360-5767-6
ISBN-13: 978-0-7360-5767-7

Acquisitions Editor: Myles Schrag; **Managing Editor:** Maureen Eckstein; **Assistant Editor:** Heather Tanner; **Copyeditor:** Jan Feeney; **Proofreaders:** Kathy Bennett and Jim Burns; **Indexer:** Gerry Lynn Shipe; **Permission Manager:** Dalene Reeder; **Graphic Designer:** Nancy Rasmus; **Graphic Artist:** Denise Lowry; **Photo Manager:** Laura Fitch; **Cover Designer:** Robert Reuther; **Photographs (cover) from left to right:** © Human Kinetics, © Human Kinetics, © Stockbyte; **Photographs (interior):** © Human Kinetics; **Art Manager:** Kelly Hendren; **Illustrator:** Al Wilborn; **Printer:** Thomson-Shore, Inc.

Printed in the United States of America 10 9 8 7 6 5 4 3 2 1

Human Kinetics
Web site: www.HumanKinetics.com

United States: Human Kinetics, P.O. Box 5076, Champaign, IL 61825-5076
800-747-4457
e-mail: humank@hkusa.com

Canada: Human Kinetics, 475 Devonshire Road Unit 100, Windsor, ON N8Y 2L5
800-465-7301 (in Canada only)
e-mail: orders@hkcanada.com

Europe: Human Kinetics, Stanningley, Leeds LS28 6AT, United Kingdom
+44 (0) 113 255 5665
e-mail: hk@hkeurope.com

Australia: Human Kinetics, 57A Price Avenue, Lower Mitcham, South Australia 5062
08 8372 0999
e-mail: liaw@hkaustralia.com

New Zealand: Human Kinetics, Division of Sports Distributors NZ Ltd., P.O. Box 300 226 Albany, North Shore City, Auckland
0064 9 448 1207
e-mail: info@humankinetics.co.nz

To my wife, Wendy, and my children, Spencer, Clark, and Torrey, for their love and unwavering support over the years

–Daniel Smith

To my son Asaph, with deep love

–Michael Bar-Eli

Contents

Part IV Understanding Group Processes 165

Part V Enhancing Performance 209

Part VI Enhancing Health and Well-Being 315

Preface

Essential Readings in Sport and Exercise Psychology is intended for anyone with a passion for sport psychology, from the first-year sport psychology student to the experienced professional. This book is a compilation of the essential readings in sport psychology. We asked ourselves as well as many of the most renowned people in sport psychology to determine what book chapters and journal articles are truly *essential*. Each reading is preceded by an introduction by the editors. We recommend that you read each introduction because it highlights important concepts, ties some readings to others, offers cogent summaries, and raises challenging questions.

Growth of a Dynamic Field

Since the 1920s, sport psychology has experienced tremendous growth, which is due to the influences of Coleman Griffith, Carl Diem, and A.Z. Puni. Today hundreds of sport psychology courses are taught in colleges and universities around the world. Numerous researchers investigate issues globally. Many national and international academic organizations are devoted to the field. Fitness, strength, and exercise researchers have embraced the field of exercise psychology, which has become a subdiscipline of sport psychology. Close to a hundred sport psychology researchers worldwide have also embraced this developing field.

Since Puni, Griffith, Diem, and a few advocates began asking important questions in their own corners of the globe more than 75 years ago, the field has gone through several distinct eras and now boasts thousands of students, instructors, and practitioners worldwide. They connect at annual conferences, read one another's work in a variety of journals, and help athletes and exercisers of all ages lead fuller lives on and off the field. Now is the time for

Timeline of Representative Events in Emergence of Psychology: 1800s

1862 — Wilhelm Wundt teaches course titled *Psychology as a Natural Science*

1874 — Wundt publishes *Principles of Physiological Psychology*

1875 — William James teaches course titled *The Relationships Among the Physiology and the Psychology* at Harvard University

1879 — Wundt establishes first psychological laboratory at the University of Leipzig (Germany)

1881 — First doctoral degree granted in experimental psychology at the University of Leipzig

1883 — First American psychology laboratory established by G. Stanley Hall at Johns Hopkins University

1884 — First sport/exercise psychology case study on effects of hypnosis on muscular endurance (Rieger)

1886 — First doctorate in American psychology awarded at Johns Hopkins University

1887 — Term *philosophy* dropped from titles of several early journals to separate experimental psychology from philosophy

1887 — James M. Cattell first designated professor of psychology in U.S. at University of Pennsylvania

1889 — First psychology laboratory established in Canada at University of Toronto

1889 — First International Congress of Psychology

1890 — James publishes *Principles of Psychology*

1890 — Cattell publishes "Mental Tests and Measurements" in *Mind*

1892 — American Psychology Association founded by G. Stanley Hall

these essential readings to be identified and included in one text. The readings come from some of the most prominent figures in the field of sport psychology. They have been included in a variety of literature reviews and used as references in numerous sport psychology lectures. With these readings compiled together, one can begin to understand what issues the field has grappled with and how it has evolved.

In some cases a reading was deemed essential for its historical significance; in other cases, it was due to the discovery of new knowledge or a new perspective on an important concept. For example, in reading 26 "Three Myths About Applied Consultancy Work", Hardy refutes three well-established premises accepted by sport psychology consultants for years. In reading 22, "The Arousal-Performance Relationship Revisited," Landers revisits the arousal–performance relationship as it applies to skilled performance. Many of these readings help us develop a new perspective on the field. For example, in reading 6, "The Trait Psychology Controversy," Morgan relates the trait psychology controversy specifically to sport. In reading 45, Martens' "Science, Knowledge, and Sport Psychology" questions even how and why we study what we do.

Most of the readings help us discover new knowledge. The readings that provide us with new research instruments enable us to measure central concepts. These include reading 8, "A Multidimensional Theory of Competitive State Anxiety," by Martens, Burton, Vealey, Bump, and Smith; reading 19, "Dimensions of Leader Behavior in Sports: Development of a Leadership Scale," by Chelladurai and Saleh; reading 27, "Imagery Use by Athletes: Development of the Sport Imagery Questionnaire," by Hall, Mack, Paivio, and Hausenblas; and reading 28, "Reliability and Validity of The Attentional and Interpersonal Style (TAIS) Inventory Concentration Scales," by Nideffer. These readings represent the field's essential knowledge base.

Selecting the Essential Readings

The daunting task was determining which readings were most essential. Our desire to alleviate as much subjectivity as possible led us to compile a list 80 potential readings.

Timeline of Events That Foreshadowed Sport and Exercise Psychology: 1885-1920

1885 — William Anderson leads formation of Association for the Advancement of Physical Education

1891 — First kinesiology laboratory established in U.S. at Harvard University by George Fitz

1893 — Harvard becomes first U.S. university to confer degree in physical education

1895 — Fitz published study on reaction time in *Psychological Review*

1898 — Francis Kellor writes "A Psychological Basis for Physical Culture" in *Education*

1898 — Norman Triplett publishes first research on social psychology of sport

1899 — E.W. Scripture reports case study findings on character development through sport participation

1899 — Anderson publishes experiments on mental practice and transfer of learning

1903 — G.T. Patrick publishes "Psychology of Football" in *American Journal of Psychology*

1904 — Mary Calkins of Wellesley College elected first female president of the American Psychology Association (although denied a PhD from Harvard because she was a woman)

1904 — Luther Gulick organizes an Academy of Physical Education to promote scientific work

1905 — Effects of exercise on depression published by S.I. Franz and G.V. Hamilton

1908 — G. Stanley Hall advocates physical education for the sake of mental and moral culture

1910 — First master's degree offered in physical education (Teacher's College, Columbia University)

1911 — L.P. Ayres publishes social facilitation study in *American Physical Education Review*

1912 — G.E. Howard writes "Social Psychology of the Spectator" in *American Journal of Sociology*

1914 — Cummins (1914) studies effects of basketball practice on motor reaction, attention, and suggestibility

1916 — Margaret Washburn publishes *Movement and Mental Imagery*

(continued)

We sent the list of 80 readings to 137 sport psychology professionals in 25 countries; 67 of the individuals chose to participate in this selection process. We then asked the professionals to vote on the essential readings based on the ones that had the most impact on the field, had been used most by those professionals, and set the direction for future research. We recognized that there was some subjectivity in the selection of these readings. Each of us informally discussed these readings with various professionals in the field. Dan Smith was at a university in Asia at the time and had spent more than 20 years in North American universities. He was thus able to get both an Asian and North American perspective. Miki Bar-Eli was at a university in Israel and had numerous European contacts; thus he was able to secure a European perspective. In addition, we encouraged each professional to add to this list any additional readings he or she deemed essential in case any readings had been overlooked. The 80 readings were subdivided into 8 topical areas. Each professional voted for 50 of the 80 options. The top 50 voted readings have been included in this book. We strived to make the selection process as democratic as possible. One concern was that the scope of readings within a single topical area might be narrow; however, the selected readings provide adequately diverse topics within each area and thus we are confident that no important topics were left out.

In our process of seeking permission from the original publishers of these readings, we were successful in securing permission for all but three of the original 50 selections. In each of these three cases, the author of the article or chapter was asked to substitute a similar reading on the same topic. While we regret not being able to include the original selections, the replacement readings provide either more contemporary or more comprehensive looks at the same topic. In one case (reading 28), Robert Nideffer suggested that the reading be replaced with an unpublished manuscript. This was

Timeline of Events Influencing Sport and Exercise Psychology: 1920-1939 *(continued)*

1920 — Carl Diem establishes sport psychology laboratory at Deutsche Sporthochschule in Berlin

1924 — First PhD offered in physical education (Teacher's College, Columbia University)

1924 — Floyd Allport publishes *Social Psychology*

1925 — A.Z. Puni establishes sport psychology laboratory in Leningrad (St. Petersburg)

1925 — Coleman Griffith establishes first sport psychology laboratory in North America

1925 — Griffith writes "Psychology and Its Relation to Athletic Competition"

1926 — Griffith publishes *Psychology of Coaching*

1926 — C.L. Vaux proposes physiological explanations for why exercise relieves depression

1928 — Griffith publishes *Psychology and Athletics*

1930 — Clarence Ragsdale of University of Wisconsin writes *The Psychology of Motor Learning*

1930 — Charles McCloy publishes "Character Building Through Physical Education"

1930 — First publication of *Research Quarterly*

1930 — American Academy of Physical Education officially chartered

1931 — Mabel Lee first female president of the American Physical Education Association

1932 — Dorothy Yates publishes *Psychological Racketeers,* describing her work with boxers

1935 — Paul Schilder publishes book that first defines concept of body image

1936 — Muzafer Sherif publishes *The Psychology of Social Norms*

1937 — Gordon Allport publishes *Personality: A Psychological Interpretation*

1938 — Henry Murray publishes *Explorations in Personality*

1938 — Griffith hired as sport psychology consultant by the Chicago Cubs

allowed since it was determined that the manuscript was of tremendous value to the field because it answers some historical criticisms of the Attentional and Interpersonal Style inventory in a timely fashion (see introduction to reading 28). Part V, "Enhancing Performance," contains more readings than any other part because much of the early research in sport psychology focused on performance enhancement. The field has diversified, but performance enhancement remains one of the leading research areas.

It was important to the authors for this book to have a global perspective. The 67 professionals who voted hailed from many countries: Australia, Belgium, Canada, China, Finland, Germany, Greece, Ireland, Israel, New Zealand, Netherlands, Qatar, Russia, Singapore, Sweden, Switzerland, Taiwan, Turkey, the United Kingdom, and the United States. The readings also include publications from a variety of countries; these readings might not be readily assessable in all parts of the world.

All readings are in English, despite the fact that English was not the first language of a few of these professionals. We recognize that several non-English-speaking countries support professional sport psychology organizations and have excellent academic journals in other languages. These non-English readings were not considered since many professionals would not have been familiar with them. The author affiliations listed are the affiliation on each author at the time the reading was published.

To fit 50 readings into a reasonably sized book, the editors abridged each reading. This was one of the most difficult parts of the process. The abridgement process took the form of deletion of repeated text in introductions and ending summaries and deletion of art and tables unless those elements were deemed critical to the reading or not described in the body of the reading. If you would like to see the readings in their entirety, you can refer to the original sources.

Timeline of Events Influencing Sport and Exercise Psychology: 1965-1979

- 1965 — First World Congress of Sport Psychology
- 1966 — Bruce Ogilvie and Thomas Tutko write *Problem Athletes and How to Handle Them*
- 1967 — First North American Society for the Psychology of Sport and Physical Activity conference
- 1967 — Ulric Neisser publishes *Cognitive Psychology*
- 1969 — First Canadian Society for Psychomotor Learning and Sport Psychology conference
- 1969 — First European sport psychology federation established (FEPSAC)
- 1969 — William Morgan writes "Physical Fitness and Emotional Health: A Review"
- 1970 — *International Journal of Sport Psychology* begins publication
- 1970 — Frederick Baekeland identifies exercise dependence in exercise deprivation
- 1972 — Dorothy Harris publishes *Women in Sport: A National Research Conference*
- 1972 — Bernard Weiner publishes *Theories of Motivation: From Mechanism to Cognition*
- 1973 — Walter Mischel publishes "Toward a Cognitive Social Learning Reconceptualization of Personality"
- 1974 — Richard Alderman writes *Psychological Behavior in Sport*
- 1975 — Rainer Martens writes *Social Psychology and Physical Activity*
- 1977 — George Engel presents biopsychosocial model of disease
- 1977 — Albert Bandura publishes his original article on self-efficacy in *Psychological Review*
- 1978 — Carole Oglesby writes *Women in Sport: From Myth to Reality*
- 1979 — *Journal of Sport Psychology* begins publication
- 1979 — Martens publishes "About Smocks and Jocks" in the *Journal of Sport Psychology*

(continued)

Organizing the Readings

Essential Readings in Sport and Exercise Psychology is divided into eight thematic parts that are roughly aligned with the parts in the sport psychology text *Foundations of Sport and Exercise Psychology* (Weinberg and Gould, 2007). Weinberg and Gould's book has been influential in promoting a basic understanding of the themes in the field. The authors determined which part was most appropriate for each reading. It is logical to have "Understanding the Historical Foundations" as part I. Part VIII, "Understanding Professional Issues," is less obvious in its placement and does not appear in *Foundations of Sport and Exercise Psychology* but should be included in a collection such as this. It includes readings supporting sometimes-controversial professional issues that have been batted around for years. A good example is the issue of certification, including who should be certified, how the certification process should be implemented, and what the certified individual should be called. This issue is addressed in readings 46, 47, and 50.

We hope that this volume brings out the creativity and growth in the field and shows how the field will continue to evolve. We also hope that it represents a global perspective of sport psychology and that the objective nature of the selection process alleviates individual bias. Finally, we hope that you develop an appreciation for the field of sport psychology through your study of these essential readings. Overall they represent the most exciting, innovative, and diverse theoretical orientations and research perspectives in sport psychology today. We encourage feedback from professionals for future editions, since we have every reason to believe that the field will continue to grow at a more rapid pace.

Timeline of Events Influencing Sport and Exercise Psychology: 1980-1992 *(continued)*

- 1979 — Raymond Harrison and Deb Feltz write "The Professionalization of Sport Psychology." Twenty published articles followed regarding professionalization: 1980-1992
- 1981 — C.H. Folkins and Wes Sime (1981) publish review on exercise and mental health
- 1981 — Steve Danish and Bruce Hale propose human development framework for interventions
- 1983 — USOC establishes guidelines/registry for provision of sport psychology services
- 1983 — Dan Landers publishes "Whatever Happened to Theory Testing in Sport Psychology?"
- 1983 — Brad Hatfield and Landers write "Psychophysiology—A New Direction for Sport Psychology"
- 1983 — Maureen Weiss and Brenda Bredemeier publish "Developmental Sport Psychology"
- 1984 — William Straub and Jean Williams publish *Cognitive Sport Psychology*
- 1985 — USOC hires Shane Murphy as first full-time sport psychologist
- 1985 — Association for the Advancement of Applied Sport Psychology is established
- 1987 — Division 47 (Exercise & Sport Psychology) of APA is established
- 1987 — *The Sport Psychologist* begins publication
- 1987 — Rainer Martens writes "Science, Knowledge, and Sport Psychology"
- 1988 — *Journal of Sport Psychology* becomes *Journal of Sport & Exercise Psychology*
- 1988 — Rod Dishman publishes *Exercise Adherence: Its Impact on Public Health*
- 1989 — *Journal of Applied Sport Psychology* begins publication
- 1989 — Michael Greenspan and Feltz publish review of psychological interventions with athletes
- 1991 — AAASP offers "certified consultant" designation in sport and exercise psychology
- 1992 — Joe Willis and Linda Campbell publish the textbook *Exercise Psychology*

Adapted, by permission, from R.S. Vealey, 2006, "Smocks and jocks outside the box," *Quest* 58(1): 128-159. © NAKPEHE.

Acknowledgments

The authors express their appreciation to the following individuals who assisted in the selection of the essential readings. Without their input, this book of essential readings would not have been possible:

Bruce Abernethy
Mark H. Anshel
Frank C. Bakker
Michael Bar-Eli
Jürgen Beckmann
Bonnie G. Berger
Stuart J. H. Biddle
Boris Blumenstein
Brenda Light Bredemeier
Britton W. Brewer
Kevin Burke
Albert V. Carron
Richard Cox
Likang Chi
Dave Collins
Steven J. Danish
Deborah L. Feltz
Hartmut Gabler
Wade Gilbert
Richard Gordon
J. Robert Grove
Dieter Hackfort
Craig R. Hall
Yuri L. Hanin
Stephanie J. Hanrahan
Bradley D. Hatfield
Keith P. Henschen
Thelma S. Horn
Susan A. Jackson
Gregory S. Kolt
Ronnie Lidor
Richard A. Magill
Herbert W. Marsh
Rainer Martens
Penny McCullagh
Aidan Moran
Nanette Mutrie
Athanasios Papaioannon
David Pargman
Dale G. Pease
Cynthia Pemberton
Albert J. Petitpas
Michael L. Sachs
Tara K. Scanlan
Thomas Schack
Roland Seiler
Gangyan Si
John M. Silva III
Daniel Smith
Frank L. Smoll
Natalia Stambulova
William F. Straub
Bernd Strauss
Gershon Tenenbaum
Peter C. Terry
Yannis Theodorakis
Sefik Tiryaki
Hung Tsung-Min
Yves Vanden Auweele
Judy L. Van Raalte
Diane M. Wiese-Bjornstal
Maureen R. Weiss
Jean M. Williams
Craig A. Wrisberg
David Yukelson
Leonard Zaichkowsky
LiWei Zhang

PART I

Understanding the Historical Foundations

The five readings in part I helped establish the historical foundation for the field of sport and exercise psychology. They are essential because of their historical significance. One cannot effectively investigate any scholarly discipline without studying those who established the field. These readings set the direction for the field and influenced it for many years to come. For example, Triplett's work led to early emphasis on social facilitation research. Yerkes and Dodson established the need to draw on research from the parent discipline of psychology and relate it to sport. Griffith gave sport psychology its individual identity and first established it as a field of study. Martens steered us back to an applied orientation after the field had strayed into mostly basic and theoretical research. Without these early influences, the direction the field has taken would be quite different.

Part I begins with Triplett's 1898 investigation of paced bicycle racing. This is the first research article in the field. The second reading is important to all of performance psychology since it includes Yerkes and Dodson's inverted-U hypothesis specifying the relationship between performance and arousal. The third reading, by Griffith in 1926, is a chapter from the first sport psychology book, *The Psychology of Coaching*. Many refer to Griffith as the father of sport psychology for his pioneering work. In 1970, Kroll and Lewis reviewed the work of Griffith during his storied career in their *Quest* journal article. Finally, in 1979, Martens turned the world of sport psychology upside down by advocating new applied research methodologies and by voicing his displeasure with traditional laboratory research methods.

1 The Dynamogenic Factors in Pacemaking and Competition

NORMAN TRIPLETT
Indiana University

It is often difficult to determine when a scientific discipline is born. Usually, historians of science choose a particular event and consider it as the one in which the discipline under consideration was founded.

In Triplett's days (the 1890s), people who defined themselves as psychologists or physical educators began to explore the psychological facets of motor and sport and exercise behavior. Norman Triplett was an enthusiastic bicycle racing fan who also happened to be an active psychologist at Indiana University. In this dual function, he became interested in the question of why cyclists sometimes ride faster when they race in pairs or groups than when they ride alone. To answer this question, Triplett conducted an experimental investigation, which can be viewed as quite complex even now—not to mention in the 1890s!

Triplett's study, in which he investigated the effects of others on cyclists' performance, has become a milestone in two scientific disciplines—sport and exercise psychology and social psychology. This investigation is mentioned in almost every introductory sport psychology and social psychology textbook as being the first research study ever conducted in each of these disciplines. It has affected studies on how the presence of an audience affects performance (i.e., the social facilitation phenomenon) and other important questions related to group dynamics in and outside sport and exercise, such as the effects of group size on performance.

This paper gives some facts resulting from a study in dynamogenic stimulation carried on in the Psychological Laboratory of Indiana University and their application to explain the subject of Pacemaking and Competition.

The definition of these races may be given as follows: The unpaced race against time is an effort by a single individual to lower the established record. No pacemaker is used; the only stimulation of the rider being the idea of reducing his own or some other man's former time. The paced race against time is also a single effort to make a record. It differs only in the fact that a swift multicycle, such as a tandem or "quod" "makes the pace" for the rider. If he has well trained pacers and is skillful in changing crews as they come on, so as to avoid losing speed, the paced man may reduce the mark for the distance ridden. The two kinds of efforts described are not really races but are called so for convenience. Both are run with a flying start.

The third or paced competition race is a real race. Here, besides keeping up with the pacemaker, is the added element of beating the other contestants. No records are given for the unpaced competition race. This race will, however, be referred to in the course of this paper. It is often called a "loafing" race from the fact that the riders hang back and try to make pacemakers of each other, well knowing that a contestant starting out to make the pace can not win.

Value to Be Given These Records

In presenting these records it is with the feeling that they have almost the force of a scientific experiment. There are, it is computed, over 2,000 racing wheelmen, all ambitious to make records. The figures as they stand today have been evolved from numberless contests, a few men making records which soon fall to some of the host who are pressing closely behind. Reductions now made, however, are in general small in amount. Were all the men engaged in racing to make an effort to reduce the time in the kinds of races named, it is probable that the records already made would stand or be but very little reduced while the present leaders and their closest competitors would again assert their superiority, each in his own style of race. Regarding the faster time of the paced races, as derived from the records, it may be asked whether the difference is due to pacing or to the kind of men who take part; and whether the argument ascribing the difference noted to pacing or competition should have less validity from the fact that different men hold the records in the different races. Men fast at one kind of racing are found to be comparatively slow at another. It is for this reason, perhaps, that Michael refuses to meet any one in an unpaced contest. The racer finds by experience that race in which he is best fitted to excel and specializes in that. The difference in time, therefore, between the paced and unpaced race, as shown by the records, is a measure of the difference between the experts in the two classes of racers. It seems probable that the same amount of difference exists relatively between the averages of the classes they represent. A striking practical proof that the difference between the paced and unpaced trials noted in the records is due to pacing, is found in the paced and unpaced time of some individual racers, given later, in which the difference in time corresponds closely to that of the records. The fact may be mentioned, too, that wheelmen themselves generally regard the value of a pace to be from 20 to 30 seconds in the mile.

Adapted from N. Triplett, 1898, "The dynamogenic factors in pacemaking and competition," *American Journal of Psychology* 9: 507-553.

Discussion of Records

It has been stated that the value of a pace is believed by racing men to be worth to the racer from 20 to 30 seconds in the mile, depending on the individual. The difference between the paced and unpaced race against time is, it is seen from these figures, somewhat greater.

	Average time per mile		Gain over unpaced	Gain per cent over unpaced	Gain per cent competition over paced
	Min.	Sec.	Sec.		
25 miles unpaced against time,	2	29.9			
25 miles paced against time	1	55.5	34.4	22.9	
25 miles paced competition,	1	50.35	39.55	26.4	3.5

The paced record from the 3rd to the 10th mile inclusive, is held by Michael. His average gain per mile over Senn, the unpaced champion, is 34 seconds. From the 11th mile upward, a different man, Lesna, holds the paced records. Evidently the pace is not worth so much to him for his average gain per mile is only 29.7 seconds, and a portion of this apparent gain is really due to the increasing exhaustion of the unpaced man, Senn.

That the ability to follow a pace varies with the individual is well known. As a rule the rider who is fast with a pace is slow without it,—and the converse is believed to be true. This is the reason why the same man can never hold records in both paced and unpaced races. Walter Sanger is one of the fastest unpaced riders on the track, but he can ride only a few seconds better with the very best pacemakers, while Michael, whose ability as a "waiter" is almost marvellous, would fall a comparatively easy victim, his rivals think, in an unpaced race. Success in paced racing presupposes a well trained force of pacers. The last named rider has confessedly enjoyed greater advantages than his competitors in this respect.

The regularity with which he rides is seen in his paced record from 3 to 10 miles. His average rate for these 8 miles was 1 min. 53 sec. with a mean variation of less than .8 second. Other evidences of the constancy of the gain from a pace may be seen through all the records, the time for:

20 miles professional, unpaced is	49 min.	20.0 sec.
25 miles professional, paced is	49 min.	8.4 sec.
20 miles amateur, unpaced is	52 min.	17.0 sec.
25 miles amateur, paced is	51 min.	57.2 sec.
80 miles professional, unpaced is	3 hr. 54 min.	53.0 sec.
100 miles professional, paced is	3 hr. 52 min.	14.0 sec.

Showing in these cases a gain in favor of the pace of practically 25%. However, ratios between records made by different men, even though they are the product of many riders and entitled to great consideration, have not the absolute certainty that the paced and unpaced time of the same man would have. Data on this point is difficult to obtain, however, as trackmen seldom follow both kinds of racing but specialize in that for which they are best fitted. The best times for one mile of two prominent racers who are good at both games have, however, been secured and are here given.

Arthur Gardiner, one mile, unpaced	2 min.	3.8 sec.
Arthur Gardiner, one mile, paced by 2 quods,	1 min.	39.6 sec.
Earle Kiser, one mile, unpaced	2 min.	10.0 sec.
Earle Kiser, one mile, paced	1 min.	42.0 sec.

The gain, in the case of the first, of the paced over the unpaced, is 24.2 seconds, nearly 20 per cent. The second gains 28 seconds, nearly 22 per cent., or within nine-tenths of one per cent. of the difference between the official paced and unpaced records made by different men.

Dr. E. B. Turner, F. R. C. S., England, in 1889, began a scientific study of the Physiology of Pacing and Waiting races, lasting over three years. He was a racing man himself and in his investigations made many tests on himself and others. Some figures showing the difference in time made by him at different distances, paced and unpaced, are given. In comparing them with the records of to-day it must be remembered that the wheel then used was heavy and fitted with cushion tires so that the time made in trials is slow as compared with the time made with the modern pneumatic wheel, and in consequence the value of the pace expressed in per cent., appears small. It is seen that as between distances paced and unpaced, his average gain per mile for the different trials varies all the way from 11.8 seconds to 20 seconds.

The upper curve of the chart shows the records made in paced competition races. Here, besides beating the record, the racer is intent on defeating his rivals. This race is started from the tape and in consequence is slightly slower for the first two or three miles than the time in the paced race against time with flying start. Thereafter the better time made witnesses to the power and lasting effect of the competitive stimulus. For 25 miles the time in this race averages 5.15 seconds per mile, or 3.5 per cent. faster than the paced race against time. From the 3rd to the 10th mile the same man, Michael, holds the record in both races. His time in the competition miles averages over 5 seconds faster than his paced miles against time. The fact that the same racing crews were used in both races suggests that in the latter race they also were responsive to the competition stimulus.

In his treatise on the "Physiology of Waiting and Pacemaking in Speed Competitions," Dr. Turner asserts that the causes operating to produce the differences noted between paced and unpaced races are directly due to the physiological effects of bodily and mental exercise. Stated briefly: the man who in a given distance does the greater amount of muscular work burns up the greater amount of tissue and in consequence his blood is more loaded with waste products and he excretes more urea and uric acid than the man who does a less amount in the same time. This excretion of nitrogenous products as shown by his experiments is directly proportional to the amount of work done. The blood, surcharged with the poisonous matter, benumbs the brain and diminishes its power to direct and stimulate the muscles, and the muscles themselves, bathed by the impure blood, lose largely their contractile power. He asserts further, that phosphoric acid is the principal product of brain work, and that carbonic acid, lactic acid and uric acid are excreted in greater quantities during brain work. Therefore, the man racing under conditions to produce brain worry will be most severely distressed.

The production of phosphoric acid by brain work is, however, in dispute. Some observers have found the phosphates diminished, whilst others have found them present in larger quantities during intellectual labor. As James says it is a hard problem from the fact that the only gauge of the amount is that obtained in excretions which represent other organs as well as the brain. Dr. Turner's tables of results bear him out, however, in the assertion that a less amount of waste matter was excreted on days when little or no exercise was taken, a greater amount when pacers were used, and the greatest amount when he made his own pace.

Basing his position on these physiological facts he states his thesis thus: "Given two men of equal calibre, properly trained and racing on a fair course, it is impossible (bar falls and similar accidents) for one of them to lead, make fast running and win the race; and the easier the track, the lighter and better the machines ridden, and the faster the time of the race—the longer the distance by which the one following will win." This is known by every rider and accounts for the "loafing" in unpaced competition races, as no man, unless decidedly superior to his competitors, dares to set the pace.

Theories Accounting for the Faster Time of Paced and Competition Races

Of the seven or eight not wholly distinct theories which have been advanced to account for the faster time made in paced as compared with unpaced competitive races and paced races against time as against unpaced races against time, a number need only be stated very briefly. They are grouped according to their nature and first are given two mechanical theories.

Suction Theory

Those holding to this as the explanation assert that the vacuum left behind the pacing machine draws the rider following, along with it. Anderson's ride of a mile a minute at Roodhouse, Ill., with the locomotive as pacemaker, is the strongest argument in its favor. Those maintaining this theory believe that the racer paced by a tandem is at a disadvantage as compared with the racer paced by a quod or a larger machine, as the suction exerted is not so powerful.

The Shelter Theory

This is closely related to the foregoing. Dr. Turner accepts it as a partial explanation of the aid to be gained from a pace, holding that the pacemaker or the leading competitor serves as a shelter from the wind, and that "a much greater amount of exertion, purely muscular, is required from a man to drive a machine when he is leading than when he is following, on account of the resistance of the air, and the greater the amount of wind blowing the greater the exertion, and conversely, the greater the shelter obtained the less the exertion."

This is the theory held, in general, by racers themselves. One of the champion riders of the country recently expressed this common view in a letter, as follows: "It is true that some very strong unpaced riders do not have any sort of success in paced racing. The only reason I can give for this is just simply that they have not studied the way to follow pace so as to be shielded from the wind. No matter which way it blows there is always a place where the man following pace can be out of the wind."

Encouragement Theory

The presence of a friend on the pacing machine to encourage and keep up the spirits of the rider is claimed to be of great help. The mental disposition has been long known to be of importance in racing as in other cases where energy is expended. It is still as true as in Virgil's time that the winners "can because they think they can."

The Brain Worry Theory

This theory shows why it is difficult for the leader in an unpaced competition race to win. For "a much greater amount of brain worry is incurred by making the pace than by waiting" (following). The man leading "is in a fidget the whole time whether he is going fast enough to exhaust his adversary; he is full of worry as to when that adversary means to commence his spurt; his nervous system is generally strung up, and at concert pitch, and his muscular and nervous efforts act and react on each other, producing an everincreasing exhaustion, which both dulls the impulse-giving power of the brain and the impulse-receiving or contractile power of the muscles."

Theory of Hypnotic Suggestions

A curious theory, lately advanced, suggests the possibility that the strained attention given to the revolving wheel of the pacing machine in front produces a sort of hypnotism and that the accompanying muscular exaltation is the secret of the endurance shown by some long distance riders in paced races. Notice that Michael was able to make the last mile of his great 30 mile competition race the fastest of all and one of the fastest ever ridden.

The Automatic Theory

This is also a factor which favors the waiting rider, and gives him a marked advantage. The leader, as has been noted, must use his brain to direct every movement of his muscles. As he becomes more distressed it requires a more intense exertion of will power to force his machine through the resisting air. On the other hand, the "waiter" rides automatically. He has nothing to do but hang on. "His brain having inaugurated the movement leaves it to the spinal cord to continue it and only resumes its functions when a change of direction or speed is necessary."—(Lagrange.) When he comes to the final spurt, his brain, assuming control again, imparts to the muscles a winning stimulus, while the continued brain work of the leader has brought great fatigue.

These facts seem to have a large foundation in truth. The lesser amount of fatigue incurred in paced trials is a matter of general knowledge. It is a common experience with wheelmen, and within that of the writer, that when following a lead on a long ride the feeling of automatic action becomes very pronounced, giving the sensation of a strong force pushing from behind. Of course the greater the distance ridden the more apparent becomes the saving in energy from automatic riding, as time is required to establish the movement. It may be remembered, in this connection, that while the average gain of the paced over the unpaced record is 34.4 seconds, the difference between them for the first mile is only 23.8 seconds.

As between the pacer and the paced, every advantage seems to rest with the latter. The two mechanical factors of suction and shelter, so far as they are involved, assist the rider who follows. So the psychological theories, the stimulation from encouragement, the peculiar power induced by hypnotism, and the staying qualities of automatic action, if of help at all, directly benefit the paced rider. The element of disadvantage induced by brain action, on the contrary, belongs more especially to the rider who leads.

The Dynamogenic Factors

The remaining factors to be discussed are those which the experiments on competition, detailed in the second part hereof, attempt to explain. No effort is made to weaken the force of the foregoing factors in accounting for the better time of paced races in comparison with unpaced races of the same type, but the facts of this study are given to throw whatever additional light they may.

This theory of competition holds that the bodily presence of another rider is a stimulus to the racer in arousing the competitive instinct; that another can thus be the means of releasing or freeing nervous energy for him that he cannot of himself release; and, further, that the sight of movement in that other by perhaps suggesting a higher rate of speed, is also an inspiration to greater effort. These are the factors that had their counterpart in the experimental study following; and it is along these lines that the facts determined are to find their interpretation.

Other Forms of Racing

A few brief statements, mostly quoted from Dr. Turner's treatise, are given to show the value of a pacemaker in other forms of racing: "Foot racing differs from cycle racing in that it involves a much greater muscular effort. At each stride the whole body must be lifted and projected seven feet or more. The exertion is much the same whether the competitor makes his own pace or follows." So the "leader" and "waiter" commence their final spurt under more equal conditions than those which obtain in a cycle race, and a much smaller degree of superiority in the leading man enables him to run the spurt out of his opponent and win.

In ice skating the conditions are closely similar to those in wheel races, and a pacemaker is of nearly as much use as on the cycle track.

In a boat race the crews do not wait behind each other, but struggle for the lead, and when they have obtained it "wait in front." The reasons for this are good:

1. If a boat be clear in front it may take its opponent's water and wash it.
2. The crew leading can see the others and regulate its pace accordingly.
3. The actual physical labor involved in propelling a boat is very great, and therefore the laws of exercise already treated of apply.
4. The length of a racing eight is 50 feet or more, and the time necessary to pass is too great to permit of waiting.

For similar reasons there is not the slightest advantage in waiting in a swimming race.

In horse racing a pacemaker is of use, but is not the overwhelming advantage it is in cycle racing. A good horse can run out an inferior, just as a good man can on foot; but in big races a stable companion is generally started to make running, when the favorite is a good stayer, in order that he may have a fast run race, without being put to the disadvantage of himself making the pace. This is especially true of distance races.

Kolb, from his study of the respiration and pulse curves resulting from a maximum effort in the various kinds of races, asserts that in cycling and skating, where great speed is attained by the use of special groups of muscles, it is the pulse rate that is largely increased, while in boat racing, running, wrestling and heavy gymnastics, the respiration is chiefly affected. If this claim is established it may furnish a reason why the pacemaker or competitor has greatest value in cycle and skating races. In these, where the ratio between power and speed is high, the outflow of nervous energy necessary in spurting has large expression. In the other class, while the energy made available by the competitive instinct, is probably the same, it is limited in its results by the respiratory need.

Part II

From the laboratory competitions to be described, abstraction was made, of nearly all the forces above outlined. In the 40 seconds the average trial lasted, no shelter from the wind was required, nor was any suction exerted, the only brain worry incident was that of maintaining a sufficiently high rate of speed to defeat the competitors. From the shortness of the time and nature of the case, generally, it is doubtful if any automatic movements could be established. On the other hand, the effort was intensely voluntary. It may be likened to the 100 yard dash — a sprint from beginning to end.

Description of Apparatus

The apparatus for this study consisted of two fishing reels whose cranks turned in circles of one and three-fourths inches diameter. These were arranged on a Y shaped frame work clamped to the top of a heavy table. The sides of this frame work were spread sufficiently far apart to permit of two persons turning side by side. Bands of twisted silk cord ran over the well lacquered axes of the reels and were supported at C and D, two meters distant, by two small pulleys. The records were taken from the course A D. The other course B C being used merely for pacing or competition purposes. The wheel on the side from which the records were taken communicated the movement made to a recorder, the stylus of which traced a curve on the drum of a kymograph. The direction of this curve corresponded to the rate of turning, as the greater the speed the shorter and straighter the resulting line.

Method of Conducting the Experiment

A subject taking the experiment was required to practice turning the reel until he had become accustomed to the machine. After a short period of rest the different trials were made with five-minute intervals between to obviate the possible effects of fatigue.

A trial consisted in turning the reel at the highest rate of speed until a small flag sewed to the silk band had made four circuits of the four-meter course. The time of the trial was taken by means of a stop-watch. The direction of the curves made on the drum likewise furnished graphic indications of the difference in time made between trials.

Limits of Error

Frequent trials of the machinery showed very small errors. In each regular trial the flag travelled 16 meters. For ten test trials the average number of turns of the reel necessary to send it over this course was found to be 149.87, with a mean variation of .15, showing that the silk band did not slip to any appreciable extent. If 40 seconds be taken as the average time of a trial (which is not far wrong), .15 of a turn will be made in .04 second.

Care was also exercised to have the kymograph maintain, so far as possible a uniform rate of turning. When fully wound up it would run for nearly three hours. The actual running time in taking the six trials of a subject was about 4 minutes, or 40 seconds per trial. In testing, the drum was rotated during 4 minutes. The time necessary to repeat this amount of rotation was found, by trials, to be 4 minutes and 3 seconds, thus showing a retardation in each trial of about one-eightieth of the former trial as shown on the drum. The direct time of trials was taken with a stop-watch. It is from records thus taken that the tables given are composed. The drum curves, however, are important as giving a graphic representation of whatever changes occurred during the progress of the trial. The stylus, responding immediately to every change in rate of turning, gives clearly: indications of the force of competition, of the effects of adverse stimulation, fatigue, and other phenomena. The tendency of the retardation of the drum would be to diminish all these effects by one-eightieth—an amount not appreciable to the eye.

Statement of Results

In the course of the work the records of nearly 225 persons of all ages were taken. However, all the tables given below, and all statements made, unless otherwise specified, are based on the records of 40 children taken in the following manner: After the usual preliminaries of practice, six trials were made by each of 20 subjects in this order: first a trial alone, followed by a trial in competition, then another alone, and thus alternating through the six efforts, giving three trials alone and three in competition. Six trials were taken by 20 other children of about the same age, the order of trials in this case being the first trial alone, second alone, third a competition trial, fourth alone, fifth a competition, and sixth alone.

By this scheme, a trial of either sort, after the first one, by either of the two groups, always corresponds to a different trial by the opposite group. Further, when the subjects of the two groups come to their fourth and sixth trials, an equal amount of practice has been gained by an equal number of trials of the same kind. This fact should be remembered in any observation of the time made in trials by any group.

During the taking of the records, and afterwards in working them over, it was seen that all cases would fall into two classes:

First. Those stimulated—

1. to make faster time in competition trials,
2. in such a way as to inhibit motion.

Second. The small number who seemed little affected by the race.

The three tables which follow are made up from the records of the 40 subjects mentioned. The classification was in general determined by the time record as taken by the watch.

The first table gives the records of 20 subjects who, on the whole, were stimulated positively. The second table contains 10 records of subjects who were overstimulated. The third table shows the time of 10 subjects who give slight evidence of being stimulated.

The probable error used in the tables is that for a single observation:

$$r = .6745 - \sqrt{\frac{\sum v2,}{n-1}}$$

Its magnitude is large from the nature of the case. To ascertain how large this should properly be, the individual differences of the subjects of Group A in table 1.1 were eliminated in the following manner: The average of the six trials made by each subject was taken as most fairly representing him. With this as a basis the six trials were reduced to percentages—thus doing away with peculiarities due to age and disposition. By this means the probable errors of this group for the six trials in order were 2.57, 1.43, 1.81, 2.24, 1.11, 1.55. A similar reduction should be made in the probable error of all the tables.

In the tables, A represents a trial alone, C a trial in competition. The 20 subjects given in Group A and Group B, of table 1.1, in nearly all cases make marked reductions in the competition trials. The averages show large gains in these trials and small gains or even losses for the succeeding trials alone. The second trial for Group A is a competition, for Group B a trial alone. The gain between the first and second trials of the first group is 5.6 seconds, between the first and second trials of the second group, 2.52 seconds. The latter represents the practice effect—always greatest in the first trials, the former the element of competition plus the practice. The third trial in Group A—a trial alone—is .72 seconds slower than the preceding race trial. The third trial in Group B—a competition—is 4.48 seconds faster than the preceding

Table 1.1 Subjects Stimulated Positively

Group A							
	Age	A	C	A	C	A	C
Violet F.	10	54.4	42.6	45.2	41.0	42.0	46.0
Anna P.	9	67.0	57.0	55.4	50.4	49.0	44.8
Willie H.	12	37.8	38.8	43.0	39.0	37.2	33.4
Bessie V.	11	46.2	41.0	39.0	30.2	33.6	32.4
Howard C.	11	42.0	36.4	39.0	41.0	37.8	34.0
Mary M.	11	48.0	44.8	52.0	44.6	43.8	40.0
Lois P.	11	53.0	45.6	44.0	40.0	40.6	35.8
Inez K.	13	37.0	35.0	35.8	34.0	34.0	32.6
Harvey L.	9	49.0	42.6	39.6	37.6	36.0	35.0
Lora F.	11	40.4	35.0	33.0	35.0	30.2	29.0
Average	11	47.48	41.88	42.6	39.28	38.42	36.3
P.E.		6.18	4.45	4.68	3.83	3.74	3.74
Gains			5.6	.72	3.32	.86	2.12
Group B							
	Age	A	A	C	A	C	A
Stephen M.	13	51.2	50.0	43.0	41.8	39.8	41.2*
Mary W.	13	56.0	53.0	45.8	49.4	45.0	43.0*
Bertha A.	10	56.2	49.0	48.0	46.8	41.4	44.4
Clara L.	8	52.0	44.0	46.0	45.6	44.0	45.2
Helen M.	10	45.0	45.6	35.8	46.2	40.0	40.0
Gracie W.	12	56.6	50.0	42.0	39.0	40.2	41.4
Dona R.	15	34.0	37.2	36.0	41.4	37.0	32.8
Pearl C.	13	43.0	43.0	40.0	40.6	33.8	35.0
Clyde G.	13	36.0	35.0	32.4	33.0	31.0	35.0
Lucile W.	10	52.0	50.0	43.0	44.0	38.2	40.2
Average	11.7	48.2	45.68	41.2	42.78	39.0	39.82
P.E.		5.6	4.0	3.42	3.17	2.89	2.84
Gains			2.52	4.48	1.58	3.78	.82

* Left handed

trial alone. The fourth trials in these two groups are on an equality, as regards practice, from an equal number of trials of the same kind. In the first case the gain over the preceding trial is 3.32 seconds. In the latter there is a loss of 1.58 seconds from the time of the preceding competition trial. In like manner there is an equality of conditions in regard to the sixth trial of these groups, and again the effect of competition plainly appears, the competition trial gaining 2.12 seconds, and the trial alone losing .82 seconds with respect to the preceding trial. These are decided differences.

The 10 subjects whose records are given in table 1.2 are of interest. With them stimulation brought a loss of control. In one or more of the competition trials of each subject in this group the time is very much slower than that made in the preceding trial alone. Most frequently this is true of the first trial in competition, but with some was characteristic of every race. In all, 14 of the 25 races run by this group were

Table 1.2 Subjects Stimulated Adversely

Group A							
	Age	A	C	A	C	A	C
Jack R.	9	44.2	44.0	41.8	48.0	44.2	41.0
Helen F.	9	44.0	51.0	43.8	44.0	43.0	41.2
Emma P.	11	38.4	42.0	37.0	39.6	36.6	32.0
Warner J.	11	41.6	43.6	43.4	43.0	40.0	38.0
Genevieve M.	12	36.0	36.0	32.6	32.8	31.2	34.8
Average	10.4	40.84	43.32	39.72	41.48	39.0	37.4
P.E.		2.41	3.57	3.25	3.85	3.55	2.52
Group B							
	Age	A	A	C	A	C	A
Hazel M.	11	38.0	35.8	38.2	37.2	35.0	42.0
George B.	12	39.2	36.0	37.6	34.2	36.0	33.8
Mary B.	11	50.0	46.0	43.4	42.0	48.0	36.8
Carlisle B.	14	37.0	35.4	35.0	33.4	36.4	31.4
Eddie H.	11	31.2	29.2	27.6	27.0	26.8	28.8
Average	11.8	39.08	36.48	36.36	34.76	34.4	34.56
P.E.		4.61	4.07	3.89	3.71	5.33	3.45

Table 1.3 Subjects Little Affected by Competition

Group A							
	Age	A	C	A	C	A	C
Albert P.	13	29.0	28.0	27.0	29.0	27.0	28.6
Milfred V.	17	36.4	29.0	29.4	30.2	30.2	32.2
Harry V.	12	32.0	32.0	32.6	32.6	32.6	31.6
Robert H.	12	31.4	31.4	32.2	35.4	35.0	32.4
John T.	11	30.2	30.8	32.8	30.6	32.8	31.8
Average	13	31.8	30.24	30.8	31.56	31.5	31.3
P.E.		1.9	1.13	1.71	1.7	2.06	1.05
Group B							
	Age	A	A	C	A	C	A
Lela T.	10	45.0	37.4	36.8	36.0	37.2	38.0
Lura L.	11	42.0	39.0	38.0	37.0	37.0	38.0
Mollie A.	13	38.0	30.0	28.0	30.0	30.2	29.6
Anna F.	11	35.0	31.8	32.4	30.0	32.0	30.4
Ora R.	14	37.2	30.0	29.0	27.8	28.4	26.8
Average	11.8	39.44	33.64	32.84	32.16	32.96	32.16
P.E.		3.11	2.88	3.03	2.75	2.69	3.71

equal or slower than the preceding trial alone. This seems to be brought about in large measure by the mental attitude of the subject. An intense desire to win, for instance, often resulting in over-stimulation. Accompanying phenomena were labored breathing, flushed faces and a stiffening or contraction of the muscles of the arm. A number of young children of from 5 to 9 years, not included in our group of 40, exhibited the phenomena most strikingly, the rigidity of the arm preventing free movement and in some cases resulting in an almost total inhibition of movement. The effort to continue turning in these cases was by a swaying of the whole body.

This seems a most interesting fact and confirmatory of the probable order of development of the muscles as given by Dr. Hall and others. In the case of those sufficiently developed to have the fast forearm movement, fatigue or overstimulation seemed to bring a recurrence to the whole arm and shoulder movement of early childhood, and if the fatigue or excitement was sufficiently intense, to the whole body movement, while younger children easily fell into the swaying movement when affected by either of the causes named.

It reminds one of the way in which fatigue of a small muscle used in ergographic work, will cause the subject to attempt to draw on his larger muscles, or, of the man who moves to the city and acquires the upright carriage and springing step of the city-bred man, who, when greatly fatigued, insensibly falls into the old "clodhopper" gait. This tendency to revert to earlier movements and also old manners of speech, as Höpfner has shown in his "Fatigue of School Children," is common, when, for any reason, the centers of control are interfered with. It may be said, therefore, that in the work under consideration the chief difference between this group and the large group in table 1.1, was a difference in control; the stimulation inhibiting the proper function of the motor centers in the one case, and reinforcing it in the other. This, at least, seemed apparent from the characteristics exhibited by the two classes. Observation of the subjects of this class under trial, and careful scrutiny of their graphic records, show how decided gains were sometimes lost by the subject "going to pieces" at the critical point of the race, not being able to endure the nervous strain. Yet there exists no sharp line of division between subjects stimulated to make faster time and those affected in the opposite way. In some instances the nervous excitement acted adversely in every race trial, while in others, a gain in control, enabled the subject to make a material reduction in the last competition. A. B., one of three adults affected adversely, is an athletic young man, a fine tennis and hand-ball player, and known to be stimulated in contests of these kinds. It was noticed that in his competition trials time was lost because of his attempt to take advantage of the larger muscles of the arm and shoulder. After many trials and injunctions to avoid the movement he gained sufficient control to enable him to reduce the time in the competitions.

A. V., an adult of nervous organization, went half through his race with a great gain over his trial alone, but seeing his antagonist pushing him closely, broke down and lost the most of the gain made in the first half. The time of the trial alone was 38.6 seconds, that of the competition was 37.2 seconds. A comparison of the time in which the halves of the trials were made was computed in the following way: On the ordinate of the graph is measured the distance the stylus travels across the drum during 150 turns of the reel—the number in a trial. The distance on the abscissa between the ordinates running through the ends of the curve of any trial gives the time of the trial.

Parallel abscissas were drawn at the extremities of the curves, and a third one-half way between them. Half of the turns made in a trial were thus on each side of this middle line, and the times in which these turns were made were proportional to the segments of this line made by the curve intersecting it. By this means it was found that A. V. made the first 75 turns in his competition trial in 15 seconds, the second half in 22.2 seconds. By the same means, each half of the preceding trial alone was 19.3 seconds—an exception to the rule that the last half is slower because of fatigue.

Other curves when worked out in this way gave similar results. The time record, therefore, it must be seen, is not always a true index to the amount of stimulation present. Had the trials consisted of but half as many turns the effect of competition as it appears in the tables would have been shown much more constantly. table 1.2 would have been a smaller group if indeed any necessity existed for retaining it.

A comparison of the time made by the different groups shows that the subjects of table 1.1 are much slower than those of table 1.2, and that a still greater difference exists between this group and the subjects found in table 1.3. It may be said that they are slower because of greater sluggishness of disposition, and that the reductions made are largely a result of the subjects warming up. This, indeed, may be a part of the cause for it, but as the larger reductions coincide with the competition trials this cannot be held to completely account for it. A glance over the individual records discovers some facts which furnish a plausible partial explanation, when taken in connection with the following fact. The age at which children acquire control of the wrist movements, a large factor in turning the reel with speed, was found to be about 11 years in general, although a few of 9 and 10 years had this power. Now, of the 20 subjects composing table 1.1, 7 are 10 years of age or younger, while two others, age 13, are left-handed and being compelled to use the right hand are slow in consequence. So, here are 9 subjects, a number nearly equal to the group in table 1.2 or table 1.3, who had a reason for being slow. Were these omitted from the count, the time of the initial trial would be found not to vary materially from that of table 1.2.

Besides the lack of muscular development of the younger subjects mentioned above, many of the subjects of table 1.1 seemed not to have proper ideals of speed.

The desire to beat, if it did nothing else, brought them to a sense of what was possible for them. The arousal of their competitive instincts and the idea of a faster movement, perhaps, in the contestant, induced greater concentration of energy.

The subjects in table 1.3, are a small group who seemed very little affected by competition. They made very fast time, but they are older than the average; their muscular control was good, and they had the forearm movements. Practice gains while somewhat apparent at first in some cases, are, on the whole, less in amount. Their drum records show fewer fluctuations and irregularities, and less pronounced fatigue curves at the end.

There seems to be a striking analogy between these subjects and those racing men who are fast without a pace, but can do little or no better in a paced or competition race.

Observations on the Work

Energy Fluctuations. Among the many personal differences shown by the various subjects, nervous peculiarities were of great interest. A number exhibited the marked periodicity of energy discovered by Dr. Lombard, and described by him in the American Journal of Psychology. It was especially prominent in the cases of L. P. and H. F., both bright children of an exceedingly nervous temperament, a rapid period being succeeded by one of apparent fatigue, thus alternating to the end of the trial. It was noticeable both in trials alone and in competition. In both subjects the phenomenon became less marked in the course of the trials. Both were much affected by the stimulation. The first making gains in her races, the second, almost helpless from nervous agitation in her first competition, does better in the second, and succeeds in making a substantial reduction in her third race, although a large part of the gain made in the first half of the trial is lost in the second.

Kolb in his "Physiology of Sport" asserts that in every physical contest involving a maximum effort there will be fluctuations of energy, and says that all oarsmen are familiar with the "hills" in the boat race, one being encountered in the second minute, the other at the end of the sixth minute. Long distance runners also experience the ebb and flow of strength markedly.

Effects from Age. It seems probable that one who is amenable to the stimulation of competition in childhood will be susceptible during his whole life; like the race horse that retains his desire to run long after the ability is lacking. The age at which the instinct develops was not ascertained. Two boys of 5 years possessed it to a marked degree. The one defeated in their race, according to his mother, felt badly about it all day. Adult subjects displayed the same differences of stimulation as in the case of children. It might be inferred from the records taken that the effect is greatest in early life and diminishes with advancing years. The practice effect, however, is greatest among the young, as they do not have the skill in the use of the hand that comes later. With adults, owing to their greater muscular control, practice counts for much less. So it was that the latter more surely made reductions in their competition trials, but smaller ones.

People differ greatly, as was noted, in the degree in which they are stimulated, but for the same individual it seems to be a constant force.

Two girls who were trained till the gain from practice was a small matter, in a ten days' trial showed remarkable uniformity in making reductions in their race trials. From the shortness of the period, in these cases, half the usual number of turns, and the skill acquired, the reductions were, however, small in amount. The averages for the ten days are as follows:

	A	C	A	C	A	C
Bessie V.	15.8	14.9	15.3	14.65	15.3	14.55
Helen F.	18.45	17.75	18.52	17.22	18.02	16.77

Each subject had 30 competitions. Out of this number the time for the first subject was reduced in 24 or four-fifths of the entire number. It was equal to the preceding trial in two cases. The second was faster in her race trials in 25 of the 30 or five-sixths of all, and in two cases equalled the preceding record. Of the three remaining trials, the pain from a blister on the hand caused one to be made in slower time.

In the race trials of the 40 subjects a portion of the reduction when made might in some cases be attributed to encouraging remarks. For instance, the racer would be told to "keep on, you are ahead," or "just one more round," in order to steady him. In the extended trial of the two subjects under discussion, however, some preliminary words to arouse the desire to beat were used, but after the start not a word was spoken. Whatever effect appeared was purely that of competition.

Sex Differences

Some small differences were found in the motor rate between the sexes, corresponding in general to the results exhibited in Dr. W. L. Bryan's study of "Motor Ability." For this grouping, the averages only for which are given, all cases were taken in which a trial alone was succeeded by a trial in competition.

At 10 years of age the boys begin faster than the girls, but both sexes are practically together on the competition trial. The greater speed of the boys, as Dr. Bryan has pointed out, is largely a result of their greater knack or skill in doing things, attributable to their more active life.

At 11 the boys are distinctly ahead, and, as noted before, a year's time has brought a large increase in speed, as at about this age a free use of the wrist movement is gained. At 12 the boys are slower than at 11, and have no advantage over the girls. A difference appears again at 13 in favor of the boys. In the case of adults a slight margin of difference on the side of the males is seen.

With this table the mean variation was used.

Table 1.4

	Males			Females		
Age	Cases	A	C	Cases	A	C
10	5	41.88	41.6	13	46.83	41.4
		4.34	5.52		3.76	2.98
11	14	35.76	34.36	25	40.3	37.89
		4.37	5.1		5.2	4.47
12	14	38.1	35.7	19	38.39	35.77
		3.92	2.75		6.11	4.0
13	7	34.1	32.94	15	39.65	36.24
		7.13	4.81		5.3	5.1
Adults	45	31.35	29.0	14	32.77	29.24
		3.17	3.29		2.8	2.56

As to the amount of stimulation the odds are apparently with the female sex. The proportion of girls influenced by competition is greater. Of the 40 subjects, 14 or 36.6 per cent. were boys, 26 or 63.4 per cent. were girls. In the group of those who were susceptible and influenced positively were 28.6 per cent. of the boys and 61.5 per cent. of the girls. In the group influenced negatively were 35.7 per cent. of the boys and 19.2 per cent. of the girls, and in the group not influenced 35.7 per cent. of the boys and 19.2 per cent. of the girls were found. These figures are deduced from the grouping made on the basis of the time record. An inspection of the graphs indicates that six in table 1.3 were somewhat stimulated, although it is not made evident from the watch record. Were these subjects, consisting of 5 girls and 1 boy, to be transferred to their proper table the result would show that 100 per cent. of the girls and 71 per cent. of the boys showed stimulation.

The gross amount of the effect of competition is also greater in girls. When they were stimulated and had control they made greater gains than the boys and when over-stimulated their losses were greater than those made by the boys. The 16 girls of table 1.1 gained the average sum of 10 seconds in their competition trials, while the four boys of this group gained an average sum of 8.15 seconds. In table 1.2 the 5 girls lost 3 seconds each, in the course of their competition trials, while the 5 boys lost less than 1 second each.

Influences Affecting the Time of Succeeding Trials Alone

It is a well-known fact, that some wheelmen, who in private practice can go very fast, fail to distinguish themselves when the real race is run in the presence of the public. The weakening effect of nervous agitation has been ascribed as the cause. On the other hand, Manouvrier, in his dynamometric studies found that his subject increased the energy of his movement when spectators were present. This is a common observation. The boy can turn better handsprings when wishing to impress the girls with a sense of his accomplishments. The football team plays better ball under the stimulation of the home crowd. Other examples could be instanced showing how people respond to various social stimulations.

In the records of the 40 subjects found in the three groups discussed above, there are 80 cases wherein a competition trial is followed by a trial alone. Of these, 45 were made in faster time than the preceding competition trial. Several facts seem to contribute to this result.

First, greater facility in turning naturally follows from the practice gained in former trials. In general, spectators were not permitted during the trials alone, but in a few cases visitors were present. The effect of this would be to stimulate the subject in a trial alone. Then, too, the competition element entered into the trials alone and it was found advisable in some cases to keep from the subject the time made, as there was a constant desire to beat his own or his friend's records, and thus make all the trials competitive. The competition feeling seemed present all the time. It is felt, therefore, that succeeding trials alone are not really non-competitive trials.

In addition, the competition trial was a pattern for after trials, giving a higher ideal of speed and a hint of what was possible for the subject. Féré remarks that it was his own experience, and that of a majority of experimenters in dynamometrie, "that the second trial was in general stronger than the first, the first trial having the effect of reinforcing the idea of the movement." The same thing seems peculiarly true of the kind of work under discussion. The subject comes to a succeeding trial alone with a reinforced image of the movement. The over-excitement of the former race is gone, but somewhat of its stimulating effect, it may be, remains and in consequence more than half of the cases equal or exceed the former competitive trial.

Part III

The Idea of Movement

We are led to believe that in the laboratory competitions detailed in Part II of this article, besides the bodily presence of a competitor, the idea of his movement, whether gained from sight or sound, had a stimulating effect on the racer. Some subjects followed with the eyes the course of the flags during the race and directed their exertions accordingly. Others seemed to be spurred on by the sound of the other machine, gaining some idea of the speed from the noise it made. Either seemed to possess equal power as a stimulus.

A favorite psychological principle with Féré, whose "Sensation et Mouvement" describes the most important work done in the field of Dynamogeny, is that "the energy of a movement is in proportion to the idea of that movement." He gives an experiment illustrating the subject as follows:

"If we ask the subject to look attentively at the movements of flexion, which we make with our hand, at the end of a few minutes he declares that he has the sensation of the same movement being made in his own hand, even though it may be entirely unmoved. And soon, indeed, his hand begins irresistibly to execute rhythmic movements of flexion. Or, if instead of letting the experiment come to this point, the subject is stopped at the moment where he commences to have the sensation of movement, and a dynamometer is placed in his hand, it is shown that the energy of his effort is increased one-fourth to one-half." Before the experiment the normal dynamometric force of the right hand was 23 kg., of the left, 15 kg. After seeing the experimenter make 20 flexions, the pressure for the subject's right hand was 46 kg., or double the former record. The left hand showed a slightly diminished force. An attempt was made to verify Féré's work with the ergograph. The subject was required to make maximum finger lifts corresponding to the beats of a metronome. After a series of lifts, the signal was given by the operator raising the index finger as if with the effort of lifting. Of 12 subjects tried, 8 made an increase when taking the time from the finger. The amount of increase seemed to be in proportion to the attention bestowed on the lifted finger of the operator. Two, who noticeably gave little attention to the straining of the finger except as a mere signal for lifting, made no gain whatever. Five maximum lifts of E. J., immediately preceding the substitution of the finger movement, averaged 17.2 millimeters in height, with a mean variation of .6 m. m. The first five efforts made at the sight of the finger movement averaged 19.1 m. m., mean variation .7 m. m., a gain of 11 per cent. P. M. G., toward the end of an exhaustion curve, of which the last five lifts averaged 7.2 m. m., made five lifts, taking the cue from the finger, of an average height of 11.4 m. m., after which the energy of his efforts again began to decrease.

Effect of a Higher Rate on Counting

An experiment on vocalization was made wherein a higher rate was suggested to the subject.

Ten subjects took the work described below on six successive days. Each was required to count aloud from 1 to 20 and repeat, as rapidly as articulation permitted, for 5 seconds. Three trials were made. The operator now counted at a faster rate and asked the subject to follow that rate. Three trials of this kind were made. This may be called Programme A.

Programme B differed from this merely in the one particular that the operator did no counting, but the three preliminary trials alone were followed instead by three similar trials alone—the intervals between trials, however, remaining the same.

Five subjects began with Programme A and five with Programme B, alternating each day, so that in the course of the six days each person had three experiences with each programme. The average sum counted by each subject during the series of trials is given below. Dividing by nine will give the average number counted in a single trial of that kind.

Table 1.5 Programme A and B

Cases	Programme	No. alone	After a higher rate is given	Alone. No rate given	Gain
10	A	288.4	307.6		19.2
10	B	287.0		288.5	1.5

The difference between the averages of the first two columns, 19.2, is the average gain of the ten subjects after they have had given them the idea of a faster rate of counting. Under this programme each individual makes a gain, under the other, where no higher rate is given, seven make smaller gains, three lose, and the average gain is but 1.5.

The principle of ideomotor action has wide application in human life. In the cases cited the observance of motion in another became a stimulus to greater effort. It may, however, have the opposite effect. A correspondence of rhythm of movement seems necessary to make it of aid. Two boys jumping together, or one following immediately at the sight of the other's jump, will not cover the distance possible in jumping alone, because the swaying of the body, and swinging of the arms, not being synchronous or rhythmic become a distraction. So one soon becomes fatigued when walking with a person out of step.

Concluding Statement

From the above facts regarding the laboratory races we infer that the bodily presence of another contestant participating simultaneously in the race serves to liberate latent energy not ordinarily available. This inference is further justified by the difference in time between the paced competition races and the paced races against time, amounting to an average of 5.15 seconds per mile up to 25 miles. The factors of shelter from the wind, encouragement, brain worry, hypnotic suggestion, and automatic movement, are common to both, while the competitors participate simultaneously in person only in the first.

In the next place the sight of the movements of the pacemakers or leading competitors, and the idea of higher speed, furnished by this or some other means, are probably in themselves dynamogenic factors of some consequence.

2 The Relation of Strength of Stimulus to Rapidity of Habit-Formation

ROBERT M. YERKES AND JOHN D. DODSON
Harvard Psychological Laboratory

There is really no need to explain to anyone familiar with sport and exercise psychology why this reading is included in this book. Psychology has long suggested that the relationship between sensory stimulation (arousal) and human performance varies systematically in the form of an inverted-U function. The basic idea is that human task performance is at first enhanced by arousal, stimulation, or pressure; this would imply that performance is likely to be low if arousal is low (e.g., if the task to be performed is repetitive or boring). But as the level of arousal increases, performance is likely to improve. However, the subject will eventually reach a point at which the level of arousal will become so high that it is experienced not as stimulation but rather as an overwhelming condition. At that point, heightened arousal will gradually hinder performance so that performance will continuously decrease.

This principle of decreased performance with heightened arousal was first presented to psychology by Yerkes and Dodson in this article. Despite the fact that the investigation was conducted with mice (a fact often disregarded), the suggested curvilinear relationship between arousal and performance was soon applied to humans. Actually, Yerkes was a famous psychologist at the beginning of the 20th century. At the outbreak of World War I, he—as president of the American Psychological Association—and a group of psychologists worked with the U.S. Army to create intelligence tests for the placement of army recruits, thereby setting the stage for future mass testing efforts in industrial psychology. However, it seems that he gained his eternal glory through the investigation of heightened arousal, which is known as the Yerkes-Dodson law.

The Yerkes-Dodson law is used today in many domains of general psychology, such as organizational behavior, motivation, and the study of stress and anxiety. In sport and exercise psychology it enjoys wide acceptance among researchers and practitioners as well. Despite the fact that it has received fairly consistent empirical support, it has also received a considerable amount of criticism. As of today, the relationships between arousal and performance seem to be more complex than the simple form of an inverted U; but at the same time, many of the current models proposed in this exciting area of research do acknowledge some kind of relationship between arousal and performance, which is curvilinear in nature. In this way, even the most recent theories that take sport and exercise psychology beyond the simple inverted-U hypothesis do not disregard this classic concept.

In connection with a study of various aspects of the modifiability of behavior in the dancing mouse a need for definite knowledge concerning the relation of strength of stimulus to rate of learning arose. It was for the purpose of obtaining this knowledge that we planned and executed the experiments which are now to be described.

The habit whose formation we attempted to study quantitatively, with respect to the strength of the stimulus which favored its formation, may be described as the white-black discrimination habit. Of the mice which served as subjects in the investigation it was demanded that they choose and enter one of two boxes or passage-ways. One of the boxes was white; the other black. No matter what their relative positions, the subject was required to choose the white one. Attempts to enter the black box resulted in the receipt of a disagreeable electric shock. It was our task to discover (1) whether the strength of this electric stimulus influences the rapidity with which dancers acquire the habit of avoiding the black passage-way, and if so, (2) what particular strength of stimulus is most favorable to the acquisition of this habit.

As a detailed account of the important features of this white-black visual discrimination habit in the dancer has already been published,[1] a brief description of our method of experimentation will suffice for the purposes of this paper.

This apparatus consisted of a wooden box 94 cm. long; 30 cm. wide; and 11.5 cm. deep (inside measurements), which was divided into a nest-box, an entrance chamber, and two electric boxes, together with alleys which connected these boxes with the nest-box. The doorways between the electric boxes and the alleys were 5 by 5 cm. On the floor of each electric box were the wires of an interrupted circuit which could be completed by the experimenter, by closing the key whenever the feet of a mouse rested upon any two adjacent wires in either of the boxes. In this circuit were an electric battery and a Porter inductorium. One of these electric boxes bore black cards, and the other white cards

---

Adapted from R.M. Yerkes and J.D. Dodson, 1908, "The relation of strength of stimulus to rapidity of habit-formation," *Journal of Comparative Neurology and Psychology,* 18, 459-482.

[1]Yerkes, Robert M. The dancing mouse. New York: The Macmillan Company. See especially p. 92, et seq. 1908.

similarly arranged. Each box bore two cards. One was at the entrance on the outside of the box and the other on the inside. The latter consisted of three sections of which two constituted linings for the sides of the box and the third a cover for a portion of the open top of the box. In no case did these inside cards extend the entire length of the electric boxes. The white and black cards were readily interchangeable, and they never were left on the same electric box for more than four consecutive tests. In case a mouse required more than twenty-five series of tests (250 tests), the same set of changes was repeated, beginning with series 1.

The way in which this apparatus was used may be indicated by a brief description of our experimental procedure. A dancer was placed in the nest-box by the experimenter, and thence it was permitted to pass into the entrance chamber. The experimenter then placed a piece of cardboard between it and the doorway and gradually narrowed the space in which the animal could move about freely by moving the cardboard toward the electric boxes. This, without in any undesirable way interfering with the dancer's attempts to discriminate and choose correctly, greatly lessened the amount of random activity which preceded choice. When thus brought face to face with the entrances to the boxes the mouse soon attempted to enter one of them. If it happened to select the white box it was permitted to enter, pass through, and return to the nest-box; but if, instead, it started to enter the black box the experimenter by closing the key, upon which his finger constantly rested during the tests, caused it to receive an electric shock which as a rule forced a hasty retreat from the black passage-way and the renewal of attempts to discover by comparison which box should be entered.

Each of the forty mice experimented with was given ten tests every morning until it succeeded in choosing the white box correctly on three consecutive days, that is for thirty tests. A choice was recorded as wrong if the mouse started to enter the black box and received a shock; as right if, either directly or after running from one entrance to the other a number of times, it entered the white box. Whether it entered the white electric box or the black one, it was permitted to return to the nest-box by way of the white box before another test given. Escape to the nest-box by way of the black box was not permitted. A male and a female, which were housed in the same cage between experiments, were placed in the experiment box together and given their tests.

Almost all of the mice used were between six and eight weeks old at the beginning of their training. The exact age of each, together with its number, is stated in table 2.1. This table shows also the general classification of our experiments. They naturally fall into three sets. These are designated by the roman numerals I, II, and III in the table, and will throughout the paper be referred to as the experiments of set I, set II and set III. As is suggested by the heading "condition of discrimination," at the top of the first vertical column of table 2.1, these sets of experiments differ from one another first of all as to condition of visual discrimination or, more explicitly stated, in the amount by which the two electric boxes differed from one another in brightness. For set I this difference was medium, in comparison with later conditions, and discrimination was therefore of medium difficultness. For set II the difference was great, and discrimination was easy. For set III the difference was slight, and discrimination was difficult. It is clear, then, that the series of words, medium, great, slight, in the table refers to the amount by which the electric boxes differed in brightness, and the series medium, easy, difficult, to the demand made upon the visual discriminating ability of the mice.

For the sake of obtaining results in this investigation which should be directly comparable with those of experiments on the modifiability of behavior in the dancer which have been conducted during the past three years, it was necessary for us to use the same general method of control-

Table 2.1 Age in Days, at the Beginning of Training, of Each Mouse, With a Statement of the Conditions of Training

Condition of discrimination	Strength of stimulus	Males		Females	
		Number	Age in days	Number	Age in days
Medium	Weak 125 ± 10	128	50	127	50
		134	50	133	43
Set I	Medium 300 ± 25	192	47	191	47
		194	47	193	47
Medium	Strong 500 ± 50	130	36	129	36
		132	44	131	37
Great	135	268	52	267	52
		274	50	269	52
	195	266	50	263	50
		418	48	265	50
Set II	255	260	43	259	43
		262	43	261	43
	375	396	48	189	41
		398	48	195	41
Easy	420	280	40	279	40
		412	74	281	43
Slight	135	290	44	199	53
	195	288	45	223	25
Set III	255	286	42	285	42
Difficult	375	284	42	283	42

ling the visual conditions of the experiment that had previously been used. This we decided to do, notwithstanding the fact that we had before us methods which were vastly superior to the old one with respect to the describability of conditions and the accuracy and ease of their control. To any experimenter who wishes to repeat this investigation with other animals we should recommend that, before recourse is had to the use of cardboards for the purpose of rendering the boxes distinguishable, thorough tests be made of the ability of the animal to discriminate when the boxes are rendered different in brightness by the use of a screen which excludes a measurable amount of light from one of them. We have discovered that the simplest and best method of arranging the conditions for such experiments with the dancer as are now to be described is to use two electric boxes which are alike in all respects and to control the amount of light which enters one of them from the top. It is easy to obtain satisfactory screens and to measure their transmitting capacity. We regret that the first use which we wished to make of our results in this investigation forced us to employ conditions which are relatively complicated and difficult to describe.

For the sake of the scientific completeness of our paper, however, and not because we wish to encourage anyone to make use of the same conditions, we shall now describe as accurately as we may the conditions of visual discrimination in the several sets of experiments.

The cards at the entrances to the electric boxes were the same in all of the experiments. Each card (the black and the white) was 11.5 cm. in height and 5.4 cm. in width, with a hole 3.5 by 3.5 cm. in the middle of its lower edge. These entrance cards were held in place by small metal carriers at the edges of the electric boxes. The area of white surface exposed to the view of a mouse as it approached the entrances to the electric boxes was 49.85 sq. cm. and the same amount of black surface was exposed. The white cardboard reflected 10.5 times as much light as the black cardboard.

Special conditions of set I. The inside length of each electric box was 28.5 cm. the width 7 cm. and the depth 11.5 cm. The inside cards extended from the inner edge of the front of each box a distance of 13.5 cm. toward the back of the box. Consequently there was exposed to the view of the mouse a surface 13.5 cm. by 11.5 cm. (the depth of the box and of the cardboard as well) on each side of the box. The section of cardboard at the top measured 13.5 cm. in length by 6.5 cm. in width. The total area of the white (or black) cardboard exposed on the inside of an electric box was therefore $13.5 \times 11.5 \times 2$ (the sides) + 13.5×6.5 (the top) = 398.25 sq. cm. If to this we add the area of the entrance card we obtain 448.10 sq. cm. as the amount of surface of cardboard carried by each electric box.

But another condition, in connection with the amount of cardboard present, determined the difference in the brightness of the boxes, namely, the amount of open space between the end of the inner cardboards and the end of the experiment box. The larger this opening the more light entered each box. In the case of the experiments of set I this uncovered portion of each electric box was 15 cm. long by 7 cm. wide; its area, therefore, was 105 sq. cm.

Special conditions of set II. Both the outer and the inner cardboards were precisely the same in form and arrangement as in the case of set I, but in order that discrimination might be rendered easier, and the time required for the acquisition of the habit thus shortened, a hole 8.7 cm. long by 3.9 cm. wide was cut in the middle or top section of the white cardboard. This greatly increased the amount of light in the white electric box. The difference in the brightness of the boxes was still further increased by a reduction of the space between the end of the cardboard and the end of the box from 15 cm. to 2 cm. or, in terms of area, from 105 sq. cm. to 14 sq. cm. This was accomplished by cutting 13 cm. from the rear end of the experiment box. For the experiments of set II the black box was much darker than it was for those of set I, whereas the white box was not markedly different in appearance.

Special conditions of set III. The experiments of this set were conducted with the visual conditions the same as in set II, except that there was no hole in the white cardboard over the electric box. This rendered the white box much darker than it was in the experiments of set II, consequently the two boxes differed less in brightness than in the case of set II, and discrimination was much more difficult than in the experiments of either of the other sets.

In the second column of table 2.1 the values of the several strengths of electrical stimuli used in the investigation are stated. To obtain our stimulus we used a storage cell, in connection with gravity batteries, and with the current from this operated a PORTER inductorium. The induced current from the secondary coil of this apparatus was carried by the wires which constituted an interrupted circuit on the floor of the electric boxes. For the experiments of set I the strengths of the stimuli used were not accurately determined, for we had not at that time discovered a satisfactory means of measuring the induced current. These experiments therefore served as a preliminary investigation whose chief value lay in the suggestions which it furnished for the planning of later experiments. The experiments of sets II and III were made with a Porter inductorium which we had calibrated, with the help of Dr. E. G. Martin of the Harvard Medical School, by a method which he has recently devised and described.[2]

On the basis of the calibration measurements which we made by Martin's method a curve was plotted. From this curve it is possible to read directly in "units of stimulation" the value of the induced current, which is yielded by a primary current of one ampere for any given position

[2]Martin, E. G. A quantitative study of faradic stimulation. I. The variable factors involved. *Amer. Jour. of Physiol.* vol. 22. pp. 61–74. 1908. II. The calibration of the inductorium for break shocks. *Ibid.*. pp. 116–132.

of the secondary coil. With the secondary coil at 0, for example, the value of the induced current is 350 units; with the secondary at 5.2 centimeters on the scale of the inductorium, its value is 155 units; and with the secondary at 10, its value is 12 units. The value of the induced current for a primary current greater or less than unity is obtained by multiplying the reading from the calibration curve by the value of the primary current. The primary current used for the experiments of sets II and III measured 1.2 amperes, hence the value of the stimulating current which was obtained when the secondary coil stood at 0 was 350 × 1.2 = 420 units of stimulation.

As conditions for the experiments of set I, we chose three strengths of stimuli which we designated as weak, medium, and strong. The weak stimulus was slightly above the threshold of stimulation for the dancers. Comparison of the results which it yielded with those obtained by the use of our calibrated inductorium enable us to state with a fair degree of certainty that its value was 125 ± 10 units of stimulation. The strong stimulus was decidedly disagreeable to the experimenters and the mice reacted to it vigorously. Its value was subsequently ascertained to be 500 ± 50 units. For the medium stimulus we tried to select a value which should be about midway between these extremes. In this we succeeded better than we could have expected to, for comparison indicated that the value was 300 ± 25 units. Fortunately for the interpretation of this set of results, the exact value of the stimuli is not important.

By the use of our calibrated inductorium and the measurement of our primary current, we were able to determine satisfactorily the stimulating values of the several currents which were used in the experiments of sets II and III. The primary current of 1.2 amperes, which was employed, served to actuate the interrupter of the inductorium as well as to provide the stimulating current. The interruptions occurred at the rate of 65 ± 5 per second. We discovered at the outset of the work that it was not worth while to attempt to train the dancers with a stimulus whose value was much less than 135 units. We therefore selected this as our weakest stimulus. At the other extreme a stimulus of 420 units was as strong as we deemed it safe to employ. Between these two, three intermediate strengths were used in the case of set II, and two in the case of set III. Originally it had been our intention to make use of stimuli which varied from one another in value by 60 units of stimulation, beginning with 135 and increasing by steps of 60 through 195, 255, 315, 375 to as nearly 425 as possible. It proved to be needless to make tests with all of these.

We may now turn to the results of the experiments and the interpretation thereof. Before the beginning of its training each mouse was given two series of tests in which the electric shock was not used and return to the nest-box through either the white or the black box was permitted. These twenty tests (ten in series A and ten in series B) have been termed preference tests, for they served to reveal whatever initial tendency a dancer possessed to choose the white or the black box. On the day following preference series B, the regular daily training series were begun and they were continued without interruption until the dancer had succeeded in choosing correctly in every test on three consecutive days.

Results of the experiments of set I. The tests with the weak stimulus of set I were continued for twenty days, and up to that time only one of the four individuals in training (no. 128) had acquired a perfect habit. On the twentieth day it was evident that the stimulus was too weak to furnish an adequate motive for the avoidance of the black box and the experiments were discontinued.

A few words in explanation of the tables are needed at this point. In all of the tables of detailed results the method of arrangement which is illustrated by table 2.2 was employed. At the top of the table are the numbers of the

Table 2.2 The Results of the Experiments of Set I, Stimulus Weak (125 ± 10 Units)

	Males			Females			General
Series	No. 128	No. 134	Average	No. 127	No. 133	Average	average
A	6	7	6.5	4	5	4.5	5.50
B	5	5	5.0	6	4	5.0	5.00
1	3	5	4.0	4	4	4.0	4.00
2	6	6	6.0	6	7	6.5	6.25
3	5	4	4.5	2	5	3.5	4.00
4	4	5	4.5	6	4	5.0	4.75
5	3	7	5.0	3	5	4.0	4.50
6	2	5	3.5	4	4	4.0	3.75
7	3	4	3.5	4	7	5.5	4.50
8	2	2	2.0	2	3	2.5	2.25
9	5	5	5.0	3	3	3.0	4.00
10	1	2	1.5	4	2	3.0	2.25
11	0	3	1.5	3	5	4.0	2.75
12	1	1	1.0	3	2	2.5	1.75
13	1	2	1.5	2	2	2.0	1.75
14	1	1	1.0	0	3	1.5	1.25
15	1	3	2.0	1	3	2.0	2.00
16	0	0	0.0	1	0	0.5	0.25
17	0	1	0.5	0	0	0.0	0.25
18	0	0	0.0	2	1	1.5	0.75
19		1	0.5	2	1	1.5	1.00
20		3	1.5	2	3	2.5	2.00

mice which were trained under the conditions of stimulation named in the heading of the table. The first vertical column gives the series numbers, beginning with the preference series A and B and continuing from I to the last series demanded by the experiment. In additional columns appear the number of errors made in each series of ten tests, day by day, by the several subjects of the experiments; the average number of errors made by the males in each series; the average number of errors made by the females; and, finally, the general average for both males and females. In table 2.2, for example, it appears that male no. 128 chose the black box in preference to the white 6 times in series A, 5 times in series B, 3 times in series I, 6 times in series 2. After series 15 he made no errors during three consecutive series. His training was completed, therefore, on the eighteenth day, as the result of 180 tests. We may say, however, that only 150 tests were necessary for the establishment of a perfect habit, for the additional thirty tests, given after the fifteenth series, served merely to reveal the fact that he already possessed a perfect habit. In view of this consideration, *we shall take as a measure of the rapidity of learning in these experiments the number of tests received by a mouse up to the point at which errors ceased for at least three consecutive series.*

Precisely as the individuals of table 2.2 had been trained by the use of weak stimulus, four other dancers were trained with a medium stimulus. The results appear in table 2.3. All of the subjects acquired a habit quickly. Comparison of these results with those obtained with the weak stimulus clearly indicated that the medium stimulus was much more favorable to the acquirement of the white-black visual discrimination habit.

In its results the strong stimulus proved to be similar to the weak stimulus. All of the mice in this case learned more slowly than did those which were trained with the medium strength of stimulus.

The general result of this preliminary set of experiments with three roughly measured strengths of stimulation was to indicate that neither a weak nor a strong electrical stimulus is as favorable to the acquisition of the white-black habit as is a medium stimulus. Contrary to our expectations, this set of

Table 2.3 The Results of the Experiments of Set I, Stimulus Medium (300 ± 25 Units)

	Males			Females			General
Series	No. 192	No. 194	Average	No. 191	No. 193	Average	average
A	4	8	6.0	3	7	5.0	5.50
B	6	6	6.0	4	6	5.0	5.50
1	4	4	4.0	4	5	4.5	4.25
2	3	3	3.0	4	2	3.0	3.00
3	4	5	4.5	5	6	5.5	5.00
4	3	4	3.5	6	3	4.5	4.00
5	2	4	3.0	5	7	6.0	4.50
6	2	0	1.0	2	2	2.0	1.50
7	2	2	2.0	0	3	1.5	1.75
8	1	0	0.5	1	0	0.5	0.50
9	0	2	1.0	0	0	0.0	0.50
10	0	0	0.0	0	0	0.0	0.00
11	0	0	0.0	0		0.0	0.00
12		0	0.0				0.00

Table 2.4 The Results of the Experiments of Set I, Stimulus Strong (500 ± 50 Units)

	Males			Females			General
Series	No. 130	No. 132	Average	No. 129	No. 131	Average	average
A	7	6	6.5	5	1	3.0	4.75
B	6	4	5.0	4	4	4.0	4.50
1	3	5	4.0	5	5	5.0	4.50
2	3	1	2.0	3	3	3.0	2.50
3	5	3	4.0	3	3	3.0	3.50
4	3	2	2.5	2	3	2.5	2.50
5	2	2	2.0	2	4	3.0	2.50
6	3	1	2.0	2	2	2.0	2.00
7	3	0	1.5	2	4	3.0	2.25
8	4	0	2.0	1	2	1.5	1.75
9	3	2	2.5	2	1	1.5	2.00
10	2	3	2.5	1	1	1.0	1.75
11	1	1	1.0	2	0	1.0	1.00
12	1	2	1.5	0	0	0.0	0.75
13	1	1	1.0	2	2	2.0	1.50
14	0	0	0.0	2	2	2.0	1.00
15	2	0	1.0	0	1	0.5	0.75
16	0	0	0.0	0	2	1.0	0.50
17	0		0.0	0	1	0.5	0.25
18	0		0.0		2	1.0	0.50
19					1	0.5	0.25
20					1	0.5	0.25
21					0	0.0	0.00
22					0	0.0	0.00
23					0	0.0	0.00

experiments did not prove that the rate of habit-formation increases with increase in the strength of the electric stimulus up to the point at which the shock becomes positively injurious. Instead an intermediate range of intensity of stimulation proved to be most favorable to the acquisition of a habit *under the conditions of visual discrimination of this set of experiments.*

In the light of these preliminary results we were able to plan a more exact and thoroughgoing examination of the relation of strength of stimulus to rapidity of learning. Inasmuch as the training under the conditions of set I required a great deal of time, we decided to shorten the necessary period of training by making the two electric boxes very different in brightness, and the discrimination correspondingly easy. This we did, as has already been explained, by decreasing the amount of light which entered the black box, while leaving the white box about the same. The influence of this change on the time of learning was very marked indeed.

With each of the five strengths of stimuli which were used in set II two pairs of mice were trained, as in the case of set I. The detailed results of these five groups of experiments are presented in tables 2.5 to 2.9. Casual examination of these tables reveals the fact that in general the rapidity of learning is this set of experiments increased as the strength of the stimulus increased. The weakest stimulus (135 units) gave the slowest rate of learning; the strongest stimulus (420 units), the most rapid.

The results of the second set of experiments contradict those of the first set. What does this mean? It occurred to us that the apparent contradiction might be due to the fact that discrimination was much easier in the experiments of set II than in those of set I. To test this matter we planned to use in our third set of experiments a condition of visual discrimination which should be extremely difficult for the mice. The reader will bear in mind that for set II the difference in brightness of the electric boxes was great; that for set III it was slight; and for set I, intermediate or medium.

Table 2.5 The Results of the Experiments of Set II, Stimulus 135 Units

	Males			Females			General
Series	No. 268	No. 274	Average	No. 267	No. 269	Average	average
A	9	7	8.0	8	7	7.5	7.75
B	8	6	7.0	4	6	5.0	6.00
1	6	4	5.0	6	4	5.0	5.00
2	2	3	2.5	2	4	3.0	2.75
3	2	4	3.0	4	6	5.0	4.00
4	1	4	2.5	0	1	0.5	1.50
5	0	3	1.5	2	2	2.0	1.75
6	0	2	1.0	0	0	0.0	0.50
7	0	1	0.5	1	1	1.0	0.75
8		0	0.0	0	0	0.0	0.00
9		0	0.0	0	0	0.0	0.00
10		0	0.0	2	0	1.0	0.50
11				1		0.5	0.25
12				1		0.5	0.25
13				0		0.0	0.00
14				0		0.0	0.00
15				1		0.5	0.25
16				0		0.0	0.00
17				0		0.0	0.00
18				0		0.0	0.00

Table 2.6 The Results of the Experiments of Set II, Stimulus 195 Units

	Males			Females			General
Series	No. 266	No. 418	Average	No. 263	No. 265	Average	average
A	6	6	6.0	6	4	5.0	5.50
B	6	7	6.5	8	3	5.5	6.00
1	6	7	6.5	5	7	6.0	6.25
2	5	1	3.0	1	1	1.0	2.00
3	3	5	4.0	1	4	2.5	3.25
4	2	2	2.0	2	1	1.5	1.75
5	1	1	1.0	0	2	1.0	1.00
6	2	1	1.5	1	0	0.5	1.00
7	1	1	1.0	0	0	0.0	0.50
8	1	0	0.5	0	0	0.0	0.25
9	0	0	0.0	0		0.0	0.00
10	0	0	0.0				0.00
11	0		0.0				0.00

For the experiments of set III only one pair of dancers was trained with any given strength of stimulus. The results, however, are not less conclusive than those of the other sets of experiments because of the smaller number of individuals used. The data of tables 2.10 to 2.13 prove conclusively that our supposition was correct. The varying results of the three sets of experiments are explicable in terms of the conditions of visual discrimination. In set III both the weak and the strong stimuli were less favorable to the acquirement of the habit than the intermediate stimulus of 195 units. It should be noted that our three sets of experiments indicate that the greater the brightness difference of the electric boxes the stronger the stimulus which is most favorable to habit-formation (within limits which have not been determined). Further discussion of the results and attempts to interpret them may be postponed until certain interesting general features of the work have been mentioned.

The behavior of the dancers varied with the strength of the stimulus to which they were subjected. They chose no less quickly in the case of the strong stimuli than in the case of the weak, but they were less careful in the former case and chose with less deliberation and certainty. There are characteristic differences in the curves of learning yielded by weak, medium, and strong stimuli. These three curves were plotted on the basis of the average number of errors for the mice which were trained in the experiments of set I. Curve *W* is based upon the data of the last column of table 2.2, curve *M*, upon the data in the last column of table 2.3; and curve *S* upon the data of the last column of table 2.4. In addition to exhibiting the fact that the medium stimulus yielded a perfect habit much more quickly than did either of the other stimuli, there is a noteworthy difference in the forms of the curves for the weak and the strong stimuli. Curve *W* (weak stimulus) is higher throughout its course than is curve *S* (strong stimulus). This means that fewer errors are made from the start under the condition of strong stimulation than under the condition of weak stimulation.

Although by actual measurement we have demonstrated marked difference in sensitiveness to the electric shock among our mice, we are convinced that these differences do not invalidate the conclusions which we are about to formulate in the light of the results that have been presented. Determination of the threshold electric stimulus for twenty male and twenty female dancers proved that the males respond to a stimulus which is about 10 per cent less than the smallest stimulus to which the females respond.

Table 2.14 contains the condensed results of our experiments. It gives, for each visual condition and strength of stimulus, the number of tests required by the various individuals for the acquisition of a perfect habit; the average number of tests required by the males, for any given visual and electrical conditions; the same for the females; and the general averages. Although the numbers of the mice are not inserted in the table they may readily be learned if anyone wishes to identify a particular individual, by referring to the tables of detailed results. Under set I, weak stimulus, for example, table 2.14 gives as the records of the two males used 150 and 200 + tests. By referring to table 2.2, we discover that male no. 128 acquired his habit as a result of 150 tests, whereas male no. 134 was imperfect at the end of 200 tests. To indicate the latter fact the plus sign is added in table 2.14. Of primary importance for the solution of the

Table 2.7 The Results of the Experiments of Set II, Stimulus 255 Units

	Males			Females			General
Series	No. 260	No. 262	Average	No. 259	No. 261	Average	average
A	5	5	5.0	5	6	5.5	5.25
B	7	6	6.5	5	5	5.0	5.75
1	6	7	6.5	9	3	6.0	6.25
2	4	7	5.5	4	3	3.5	4.50
3	1	4	2.5	3	1	2.0	2.25
4	0	2	1.0	4	0	2.0	1.75
5	0	2	1.0	0	2	1.0	1.00
6	0	0	0.0	0	1	0.5	0.25
7		0	0.0	0	1	0.5	0.25
8		0	0.0		1	0.5	0.25
9					0	0.0	0.00
10					0	0.0	0.00
11					0	0.0	0.00

Table 2.8 The Results of the Experiments of Set II, Stimulus 375 Units

	Males			Females			General
Series	No. 396	No. 398	Average	No. 189	No. 195	Average	average
A	6	6	6.0	6	7	6.5	6.25
B	5	3	4.0	5	6	5.5	4.75
1	6	6	6.0	4	5	4.5	5.25
2	5	1	3.0	5	3	4.0	3.50
3	5	3	4.0	8	2	5.0	4.50
4	0	4	2.0	3	1	2.0	2.00
5	0	3	1.5	1	4	2.5	2.00
6	0	0	0.0	0	0	0.0	0.00
7		1	0.5	0	0	0.0	0.25
8		0	0.0	0	0	0.0	0.00
9		1	0.5				0.25
10		0	0.0				0.00
11		0	0.0				0.00
12		0	0.0				0.00

Table 2.9 The Results of the Experiments of Set II, Stimulus 420 Units

	Males			Females			General
Series	No. 280	No. 412	Average	No. 279	No. 281	Average	average
A	5	5	5.0	4	6	5.0	5.00
B	6	6	6.0	6	4	5.0	5.50
1	5	5	5.0	5	5	5.0	5.00
2	4	5	4.5	1	0	0.5	2.50
3	2	5	3.5	2	4	3.0	3.25
4	1	3	2.0	0	2	1.0	1.50
5	0	3	1.5	0	1	0.5	2.00
6	0	0	0.0	0	0	0.0	0.00
7	0	0	0.0		0	0.0	0.00
8		0	0.0		0	0.0	0.00

Table 2.10 The Results of the Experiments of Set III, Stimulus 135 Units

	Males	Females	General
Series	No. 290	No. 199	average
A	6	4	5.0
B	4	7	5.5
1	4	6	5.0
2	5	2	3.5
3	3	6	4.5
4	4	2	3.0
5	7	4	5.5
6	4	4	4.0
7	7	7	7.0
8	7	5	6.0
9	4	4	4.0
10	4	2	3.0
11	4	1	2.5
12	5	3	4.0
13	3	2	2.5
14	2	4	3.0
15	4	3	3.5
16	3	0	1.5
17	2	2	2.0
18	0	2	1.0
19	1	1	1.0
20	3	3	3.0
21	1	1	1.0
22	1	0	0.5
23	2	0	1.0
24	1	0	0.5
25	3		1.5
26	1		0.5
27	1		0.5
28	0		0.0
29	0		0.0
30	2		1.0

Table 2.11 The Results of the Experiments of Set III, Stimulus 195 Units

	Males	Females	General
Series	No. 288	No. 223	average
A	4	4	4.0
B	7	8	7.5
1	5	7	6.0
2	3	6	4.5
3	5	6	5.5
4	6	3	4.5
5	6	7	6.5
6	4	4	4.0
7	5	3	4.0
8	2	2	2.0
9	0	0	0.0
10	3	1	2.0
11	2	1	1.5
12	1	0	0.5
13	1	0	0.5
14	0	0	0.0
15	0		0.0
16	0		0.0

problem which we set out to study are the general averages in the last column of the table. From this series of averages we have constructed curves that very clearly and briefly present the chiefly significant results of our investigation of the relation of strength of electrical stimulus to rate of habit-formation, and they offer perfectly definite answers to the questions which were proposed for solution.

The ordinates represent stimulus values, and the abscissæ number of tests. The roman numerals *I*, *II*, *III*, designate, respectively, the curves for the results of set I, set II, and set III. Dots on the curves indicate the strengths of

Table 2.12 The Results of the Experiments of Set III, Stimulus 255 Units

Series	Males	Females	General average
	No. 286	No. 285	
A	4	7	5.5
B	4	5	4.5
1	5	6	5.5
2	3	3	3.0
3	2	3	2.5
4	5	5	5.0
5	2	4	3.0
6	2	3	2.5
7	3	2	2.5
8	1	1	1.0
9	1	2	1.5
10	2	1	1.5
11	2	3	2.5
12	3	0	1.5
13	2	0	1.0
14	0	1	0.5
15	3	1	2.0
16	1	0	0.5
17	0	0	0.0
18	0	0	0.0
19	0		0.0
20			
21			
22			
23			
24			
25			
26			

Table 2.13 The Results of the Experiments of Set III, Stimulus 375 Units

Series	Males	Females	General average
	No. 284	No. 283	
A	4	7	5.5
B	3	4	3.5
1	6	6	6.0
2	3	2	2.5
3	4	3	3.5
4	4	2	3.0
5	2	5	3.5
6	3	2	2.5
7	6	5	5.5
8	4	2	3.0
9	1	1	1.0
10	1	2	1.5
11	1	2	1.5
12	3	1	2.0
13	1	1	1.0
14	1	1	1.0
15	1	0	0.5
16	1	1	1.0
17	0	1	0.5
18	0	1	0.5
19	0	1	0.5
20		0	0.0
21		2	1.0
22		0	0.0
23		2	1.0
24		0	0.0
25		0	0.0
26		0	0.0

stimuli which were employed. Curve I for example, shows that a strength of stimulus of 300 units under the visual conditions of set I, yielded a perfect habit with 80 tests.

From the data of the various tables we draw the following conclusions:

1. In the case of the particular habit which we have studied, the rapidity of learning increases as the amount of difference in the brightness of the electric boxes between which the mouse is required to discriminate is increased. The limits within which this statement holds have not been determined. The higher the curves stand from the base line, the larger the number of tests represented by them. Curve II is lowest, curve I comes next, and curve III is highest. It is to be noted that this is the order of increasing difficultness of discrimination in the three sets of experiments.

2. The relation of the strength of electrical stimulus to rapidity of learning or habit-formation depends upon the difficultness of the habit, or, in the case of our experiments, upon the conditions of visual discrimination.

3. When the boxes which are to be discriminated between differ very greatly in brightness, and discrimination is easy, the rapidity of learning increases as the strength of the electrical stimulus is increased from the threshold of stimulation to the point of harmful intensity. This is indicated by curve II. Our results do not represent, in this instance, the point at which the rapidity of learning begins to decrease, for we did not care to subject our animals to injurious stimulation. We therefore present this conclusion tentatively, subject to correction in the light of future research. Of its correctness we feel confident because of the results which the other sets of experiments

Table 2.14 The Number of Tests Required by the Mice for the Acquisition of a Perfect Habit of Discrimination

Set	Stimulus	Males		Average	Females		Average	General average
I	Weak	150	200+	175+	200+	200+	200+	187+
	Medium	80	90	85	80	70	75	80
	Strong	150	130	140	140	200	170	155
II	135	40	70	55	150	70	110	82.5
	195	80	70	75	60	50	55	65
	255	30	50	40	40	80	60	50
	375	30	90	60	50	50	50	55
	420	40	50	45	30	50	40	42.5
III	135	300+			210			255
	195	130			110			120
	255	160			150			155
	375	160			230			195

gave. The irregularity of curve II, in that it rises slightly for the strength 375, is due, doubtless, to the small numbers of animals used in the experiments. Had we trained ten mice with each strength of stimulus instead of four the curve probably would have fallen regularly.

4. When the boxes differ only slightly in brightness and discrimination is extremely difficult the rapidity of learning at first rapidly increases as the strength of the stimulus is increased from the threshold, but, beyond an intensity of stimulation which is soon reached, it begins to decrease. Both weak stimuli and strong stimuli result in slow habit-formation. A stimulus whose strength is nearer to the threshold than to the point of harmful stimulation is most favorable to the acquisition of a habit. Curve III verifies these statements. It shows that when discrimination was extremely difficult a stimulus of 195 units was more favorable than the weaker or the stronger stimuli which were used in this set of experiments.

5. As the difficultness of discrimination is increased the strength of that stimulus which is most favorable to habit-formation approaches the threshold. Curve II, curve I, curve III is the order of increasing difficultness of discrimination for our results, for it will be remembered that the experiments of set III were given under difficult conditions of discrimination; those of set I under medium conditions; and those of set II under easy conditions. As thus arranged the most favorable stimuli, so far as we may judge from our results, are 420, 300, and 195. This leads us to infer that an easily acquired habit, that is one which does not demand difficult sense discriminations or complex associations, may readily be formed under strong stimulation, whereas a difficult habit may be acquired readily only under relatively weak stimulation. That this fact is of great importance to students of animal behavior and animal psychology is obvious.

Attention should be called to the fact that since only three strengths of stimulus were used for the experiments of set I, it is possible that the most favorable strength of stimulation was not discovered. We freely admit this possibility, and we furthermore wish to emphasize the fact that our fifth conclusion is weakened slightly by this uncertainty. But it is only fair to add that previous experience with many conditions of discrimination and of stimulation, in connection with which more than two hundred dancers were trained, together with the results of comparison of this set of experiments with the other two sets, convinces us that the dancers would not be likely to learn much more rapidly under any other condition of stimulation than they did with a strength of 300 ± 25 units of stimulation.

Naturally we do not propose to rest the conclusions which have just been formulated upon our study of the mouse alone. We shall now repeat our experiments, in the light of the experience which has been gained, with other animals.

3 Getting Ready to Coach

COLEMAN GRIFFITH
University of Illinois

This reading is essential because of its historical significance. One cannot effectively investigate any scholarly discipline without first studying those who established the field. The author, Coleman Griffith, is sometimes referred to as the "father of sport psychology." As an associate professor of educational psychology at the University of Illinois in 1925, he established an athletic research laboratory to study men while they engaged in various forms of athletic competition. This laboratory had three directional foci: toward the discovery of pure psychological fact and theory, toward the discovery of fact about human behavior that has a bearing on athletic skill and athletic mindedness, and toward increasing the effectiveness of coaching methods. Dr. Griffith became one of the first advocates for applied research methods since he went directly to the playing fields to observe psychological processes.

This reading is the first chapter in his book The Psychology of Coaching, which was published in 1926. This is the first book dedicated entirely to applied sport psychology. In addition to being a faculty member at the University of Illinois, Dr. Griffith consulted with the university football team. After his athletic research laboratory closed in 1932, he consulted with the Chicago Cubs.

It is surprising how timeless the concepts are in Dr. Griffith's book. He begins by emphasizing that a coach is a teacher first. The coach teaches skills and builds character and is a physiologist and psychologist. Specifically Griffith recommends that the coach be familiar with muscular work, metabolism, respiration, fatigue, and rest. Griffith's background in motor learning is evident when he expounds on the laws of learning and the skill acquisition process. He states that humans move from skill to skill because of forces and the operation of principles. Although phrased a little differently, these concepts are studied today in the areas of exercise physiology, motor learning, and sport psychology.

Introduction

Too many people are of the opinion that the coach is merely an appendage of the play instinct, that his main business is to supervise play-grounds and teach youngsters the formal and technical aspects of organized games. This notion is inadequate not because it is wrong but because it comprehends only a small part of his total task.

The Coach Is a Teacher

The first of the many things we may say about the coach is this: In every sense of the word he is a teacher. Few of his colleagues on the high school or college faculty have a larger task of teaching than he. Students may spend a whole semester on mathematics or history or language, and acquire a very moderate degree of knowledge and of verbal skill; while in less than half the time they attain levels of verbal and manual skill on the football field or basketball floor which are rarely approached in the classroom. It would be a remarkable class indeed that, in six weeks, acquired as much skill handling a French vocabulary as is acquired by the same men, perhaps, in handling a baseball or a football under a large number of variable and critical conditions.

The coach is aided, of course, by the vital energies which make us play. If teachers of mathematics or of history or of language could tap the same energies, their problem of instruction would be very different from what it is; but this use of play tendencies in athletic instruction should not blind us to the fact that the coach does share a vast amount of information and he must develop enormous degrees of skill and that he is, therefore, in these respects, a teacher.

The Coach as a Character-Builder

The coach is more than a teacher; he is a character-builder; he molds personalities. All teachers should have this fact in mind, and many of them do; but the coach has unique opportunities in this sort of craftsmanship.

History, language, physics and chemistry do not have so immediate and personal a reference to youngsters as do games. Society approves of science and art as being good forms of knowledge for the advancement of culture; and also because they may be turned to account in early adulthood as a means to a livelihood. Play, however, has a direct biological value to growing youngsters. The chance to play not only satisfies immediate desires but enables the youth or maiden to secure benefits that are wholesome and pleasing. The man who enters into the play life of young people has, then, a unique opportunity to make himself effective in controlling that life and adding to it traits that might not otherwise be acquired.

It is a common thing for a youngster to make his coach a confidant where his father and his mother will not serve. Moreover, young people are hero-worshipers. An effective

Adapted from C. Griffith, 1926, *The psychology of coaching* (New York: Simon and Schuster), 1-18.

coach will be obeyed and imitated where other teachers are endured.

For these reasons the coach is more than an instructor. He is a *teacher* in the ancient sense of the word. He holds the power to impress himself upon the growing personalities of boys and girls. He gives them instruction and facts, he tells them how to develop skill; but he may also mold their character and lead them into those traits and virtues which make them men and women of parts instead of men and women having thin minds, lean characters and weak wills.

Old and New Objectives in Coaching

Huge muscles and brute strength were the old objectives; fine skill is the aim of the modern coach. Ferocity and viciousness were the attitudes of the old athlete; high spirited sportsmanship and mental staying power or morale are the virtues of the modern athlete.

Save as we recognize these new objectives there is really no excuse for the existence of a coaching profession. Unless we can make others believe in them we must listen to others convince us that a saw and a wood pile, a sewer ditch, a broom, or a corn row, will give us all the exercise and physical training we need. This is correct if *physical* training is our main objective. It is far beside the mark if *mental alertness, morale,* and *sportsmanship* are the objectives.

Unless we go to war at least once in every generation or unless our young men can continually open up new frontiers, we shall have no sure way of acquiring physical ruggedness and morale except upon the athletic field. We learn languages, history, art, and science in the classroom; but not morale. We acquire certain habits of neatness and persistence in school life; but a genuine fighting frame of mind tempered by sportsmanship and good will is one of the first products of athletic competition.

Must We Always Win?

At the present time a coach must win games or lose his job. This is a pathetic state of affairs and it is due more to the alumni of schools, to Rotary and Kiwanis Clubs and to the "Barber-shop Board of Strategy," than to the students. The alumni do not come into the same intimate contact with the coach as do the students. The only standard by which they can measure the success of the coach is the standard of victory. The Rotary and Kiwanis Clubs are eager for the advertising value of victories. The students, however, are often aware of the virtues of the coach in making men, in reconstructing personalities, and in raising the sportsmanship of the team and of the college. The defeats which such a coach suffers may be tempered by his real contributions to the mental and physical well-being of the students who actually live on the campus.

The chief aim of competition is not victory. Victory is desirable; but if it is made an end in itself we are tempted to use every means, fair or foul, for gaining it. There is a reason why we say that in love and war everything is fair. The maiden *must* be won, the war *must* issue victory; and thus it happens that romance and military history are marred by many wrongs.

In competition the game is the thing. Competition is merely a formal way of exercising play tendencies which are as old as life. The athletic field should be a place where, under the energies of the play instinct and under the rules of the game, we can find a way to exercise our mental and physical skills in spite of hurt, exhaustion or emotion. The making of virile men is the aim of competition, not the winning of victories, much less the winning of prizes, and the like. We do strive for prizes because we are urged by the instinct to play. Take away the prizes and we would still play; take away the instinct and we would have little interest in the prizes.

Athletics for the Modern World

If we are mindful of these new objectives in coaching we must have athletics for all after the fashion of the greatest athletes in history, *viz.,* the Greeks. There was nothing mean or little about Hellenic sportsmanship; and there must be nothing mean or small about our modern games if we are to put to scorn the critics of athletics and if we are to draw as many dividends as we ought, from our instinctive desire to play. The coach may go ahead if he chooses, fighting for championships, and lauding large muscles; but if he chooses that ideal, the time may come when he will be without a profession and without a job. On the other hand, he may see his profession as a means of training good judgment, alertness, skill, steadiness, courage, and ideals of sportsmanship; and if this is his goal his profession will be subject to no man's scorn.

The Preparation of a Coach

The first and perhaps the most essential step in preparing to coach has been taken when a man has gained a profound respect for the profession and an earnest regard for the opportunities it offers of becoming a construction engineer in the realms of human personality. But there are many more ways in which the coach must prepare himself. We may list three fields in which he ought to be more or less proficient, *viz.,* (a) he should be an athlete, (b) he should be a physiologist and (c) he should know something about psychology.

The Coach as an Athlete

The men who do the best jobs of teaching mathematics are mathematicians. They have studied their subjects, they have a special liking for the subject and they have tried to do a little independent research in the field. Their teaching is effective in proportion as it is the outcome of a large background of information and interest.

In the same way a coach should be an athlete. He should have tried, at least, to "make a team." It isn't necessary that he should have been the "star" or even one of the best men on the team; but unless he has been in the game he will have no sympathetic appreciation of the tasks he will set for his own students. He has gained something of value if he has had only the bitter experience of working for two or three years on the second or the third team without being awarded a letter; he will know better how to give every man his chance, and how to be a friend to the man who loses out.

It goes without saying that a coach should know the tactics of the game he teaches. Modern football is an intricate game and some men spend years in studying football formations and plays. Every game has its rules and principles and the coach must know these of course; but book knowledge, knowledge of diagrams, is one thing; and actual playing knowledge is another. We mean to say, then, that a prospective coach ought to have played his game before he tries to teach it.

The Coach as a Physiologist

If the coach is first of all an athlete he should be, secondly, a physiologist. That is, he should know something about that portion of physiology which has to do with muscular work, metabolism, respiration, fatigue, and rest. The coach who goes out to handle boys whose lungs are delicate, whose muscles are tender, whose bones are soft and whose hearts have more eagerness than endurance, without knowing something of the physiology of these organs is just as great a criminal. Knowledge of this kind is imperative when the coach has to act as his own trainer, and at critical moments, as his own physician.

There is no need that the coach be an expert in physiological research. There is, however, a need that he know more physiology than he will recall from his high school training. He handles human bodies at work and he ought, therefore, to know a few of the properties and capacities and some of the limitations of these bodies.

The Coach as a Psychologist

There was a time—not long past—when a coach who knew his game and his physiology was thought to be sufficiently well equipped to enter the profession. It is becoming clearer every day, however, that the most successful coaches are psychologists of no small ability. They may never have studied psychology as a science and they would hardly be at home in a psychological laboratory; but they have acquainted themselves with some of the pertinent facts about human behavior and their success in their profession rests in no small measure upon this knowledge.

As we have said above competition is becoming more and more a matter of skill, of alertness, of judgment, of cleverness, of sportsmanship, and less and less a matter of brute strength, win at any cost, bullheadedness. Where this is not so, competition stands in serious peril of being eliminated. Where it is so there are men and women who will support it to an increasing degree. Where mental strength and determination are preferred to muscles and weight, there psychology becomes a part of the equipment of a modern coach. Where morale is more of an objective in coaching than animal pugnacity the science of mind must be counted in.

What Is Psychology?

Psychology is the experimental study of certain kinds of human behavior. If an automobile runs into us and we are thrown a dozen feet away we are behaving—behaving as any physical object behaves; but this is not psychology. When, however, we see the automobile coming and by skillful dodging avoid the machine, we are acting in a way that is of interest to a psychologist.

Psychology is particularly interested in those forms of human behavior which display or seem to be a product of, or are commonly believed to be related to, mentality. When we act as though we had profited from our past experience, that is, when we are said to remember or to have learned, we offer ourselves as objects of investigation to a psychologist. When we appear to behave with respect to some objects while disregarding others (attention and inattention) we arouse the curiosity of a psychologist. So with all forms of behavior which are supported by or are in any way related to mentality.

The batter *selects* the ball he wants to hit, the runner *elects* to steal second if he can, the pitcher *tries* to *outwit* the batter, the half-back *dodges* one man and *straight-arms* another, the quarter-back *outwits* the opposing team, one boxer *outlasts* another, every athlete *remembers* the rules of the game; all are choosing, deciding, recognizing, recalling, resolving, perceiving, feeling fit or feeling low; all are at times angry, dismayed, hopeful, and what not! The forms of human experience and behavior suggested by these words constitute the province of psychology.

Psychology is a science. We don't sit down in a chair to speculate as to how men ought to behave under different situations. We go directly to situations in which men are acting and with a critical eye ask, Why? Better yet we take men into a laboratory so that we may ask them to perform under conditions which we can control. Most people misunderstand the laboratory of experimental psychology by supposing that uncanny and mysterious things go on there. This is nonsense. Let us assume that we desire to know how to learn to shoot baskets with the greatest skill and the least expenditure of time. We should go to the laboratory only because there we could try many different ways of throwing, standing, resting or working without being interfered with by other people and other events. Psychology is a science because it makes *experimental* studies in the fields of human behavior and human experience.

What Psychology Should a Coach Know?

Many of the specific facts which a coach should know have been described in the present author's book on Psychology and Athletics. These facts have been drawn from many sources and they are too numerous to mention now. There are, however, certain general principles which must be mentioned here for successful coaching depends upon them just as intimately as it does on a knowledge of many detailed facts. These general principles are (a) the fact of individual differences between men, (b) the original nature of man, (c) the meaning of law in psychology and (d) the natural insurgence and playfulness of youth.

The Psychology of Individual Differences

The Bible is an historical authority for the statement that there are five-talent men, two-talent men and one-talent men. Modern psychology gives abundant proof of this statement and a recognition of its truthfulness is a key to the understanding of a great many problems. Later on we shall make a list of some of the more important ways in which men differ from one another; here we are interested only in making ourselves realize the fact that men do differ. If we were to teach as though every man were a five-talent man we would fall far short of successful instruction for we would be setting problems which will never be solved by a considerable portion of the youngsters under us. On the contrary, if we were to teach as though every man were a two-talent or a one-talent man we should never be able to utilize the abilities that come in such large measure in a few men. Successful coaching, like successful teaching, means making every man realize his full capacities, giving every man tasks coordinate with his talent, making each one a successful man in *his* contribution to teamwork.

The Original Nature of Man

We totally misapprehend life unless we know what life is apart from what it becomes after training. Each member of the human family begins his career with an original nature, with original incentives to action, sometimes even with inherited *ways* of acting; and upon these foundations the skills of later life are erected. Among the incentives to behavior which we do not have to learn is the tendency to play. All of the theories of the origin of play agree on this one point, *viz.,* that the play spirit is an original, unlearned disposition, supported by all the energy of growing life and reflected in every aspect of our being. In health or in sickness (save extreme sickness), in rest or in fatigue, at noon or at night, a child or an animal is always ready to play. Children—even adults—do not force themselves to play; it is done spontaneously and for its own sake, that is, without regard to any profits, prizes, or other external rewards that may come from it. We play because we *want* to; we work because we *have* to.

The play spirit was, is, and should be kept the foundation of all athletic competition. A game is merely a formal way of directing or controlling play energies. We might at high school or in college devote ourselves to play *in general;* but it has been found convenient to throw up more or less artificial conditions around the play spirit and so to confine our instinctive energies to a football, a baseball, or a basketball game. Unless we catch this point we will proceed as if these sports were something other than a spirit of play which has been given concrete expression under formal rules to which we can all agree—perhaps a spectacle for economic gain, or competition for personal prestige. There is no one so silly as to think that we should enter a game without playing under the rules; but, after all, the rules are merely boundaries within which we elect, for the time being, to expend our play energies.

Are There Any Special Athletic Instincts?

The questions are often asked: Is there a football instinct? A base-running instinct? An instinct to swim? So far as anyone has been able to discover there are no such instincts. That is, by original nature we do not run bases well. Our ancestors did not transmit to us any special aptitude for sizing up an offensive play in football. There is no instinctive support for a unique "football sense." There is the urge to play; there are rules within the limits of which we propose to play, and there is long practice which enables us to play well. If we have practiced enough we may appear to act just as quickly and just as skillfully as we would do if we were acting instinctively. Habits have been called *second nature* because we do them unthinkingly; but a habit or a skill in running bases does not become an instinct because it becomes second nature.

Learning is a Remarkable Process

Learning is the most remarkable fact in the universe of living creatures. Consider the infant, on the one hand, with no skill of any sort, and an adult, on the other hand, with the skill to use his vocal cords in thousands of different ways, with the ability to use his fingers (writing, piano playing, etc.,) in ten of thousands of different ways, and with the dexterity to coordinate his arms and hands and feet in skills beyond number. That process by which we move from the complete awkwardness and bare consciousness of infancy to the extraordinary skill and keen mentality of adulthood is the process of learning.

In spite of our common beliefs to the contrary, the process need not be a haphazard affair, nor a wild adventure in which we stumble from one habit to another. It is, as a matter of fact, an orderly process describable in terms of certain laws and principles called the *laws of learning.* We may move on from fact to fact and from skill to skill because of the existence of forces and the operation of principles that are just as inescapable as the forces and principles discovered in other sciences of nature. The stars in their courses proceed no more regularly than does a human learner through the various stages of acquiring a skill.

A generous part of the learning process in young men and women comes directly under the guidance of the coach. He teaches his boys all the technical skills that belong to the various sports; but he teaches them also a variety of skills that will be of service in other affairs of the human family. Basket-shooting, batting, punting, and serving at tennis, are all technical skills useful primarily in the several sports; but athletic competition provides also for training in eye-hand coordination, for steadiness under emotion and in the face of critical moments, for courage under pain, for loyalty and sportsmanship in the place of anger and jealousy, and for many other habits and skills that go down on the credit side of a young man's general character.

Athletic competition is not a matter of special instincts. It is a matter of skills set at work under the urge of the play spirit. It is important, then, that a coach know something about the laws and principles of learning and their relation to original nature. We may blunder along and get out of human nerve and flesh a semblance of skill or of fine character or of generous personality; but if we take our tasks seriously we will become familiar with the laws and the vagaries of the learning process with the hope of making our coaching as effective as it can be made.

The Meaning of Natural Law in Psychology

We owe to philosophy and to religion the idea that a man can always do as he pleases, that he is a perfectly free agent, independent of his heredity, and of his training, the captain of his own soul, the god of his own mental universe. A sober study of human beings as they actually live has, however, wholly changed this idea. We know now that our mental lives are law-abiding, just as law-abiding as are our nervous systems. We do not know all these laws and we shall study a great many years before we can predict human behavior with very much success; but there is every reason to believe that laws of mentality do exist even though they be exceedingly complex.

This fact takes on meaning for a coach when he begins to see himself as an architect or a construction engineer in the realms of human personality. He may make or break the boys under him. He may make them great athletes but poor gentlemen, or he may make them great in both respects. If life didn't obey laws, if we grew into adulthood carrying with us only our own choices, the way we coached our boys would make little difference. We might coach as we pleased and relieve ourselves of responsibility by saying "My boys can do as they choose; they alone are responsible for the men they will be."

The sad part of the matter is that they can't do as they choose. As infants their habits of dressing, eating, and speaking were formed before they knew anything to the contrary. As boys the life and actions of parents, teachers and above all, the coach, impress their lives far more indelibly than the ink has impressed this paper. As we grow we acquire habits, habits of the skillful sort for use on the athletic field; but we acquire under the direction of our neighbors and teachers habits of feeling, prevailing modes of thinking, definitive types of personal and social action. The mental world is an orderly world and we do not know how to remake that world—or even help to make it in the first place—if we do not know the laws and principles by means of which order is wrought into it.

A coach who is interested only in the technical aspects of games will not see this point at all. Such a man is only half a coach. He will make a cunning machine out of a boy but he will not make a superb human being out of him. Personalities are built very much as skills are acquired and what the world wants from high schools and colleges are clean, straight-hitting, alert men—not mannikins.

Knowledge of Youth

A coach will be successful in proportion as he keeps young in his own spirit and keeps everlastingly before him the fervent longings and desires of the boys and young men he has to teach. Adults tend after a season to harden, to lose the perspective of their younger days, to crystallize, to fall out of sympathy with the vagaries and wistfulness of their own adolescence. To move wholly out of the days of youth into the harder, more critical, more unemotional days of maturity is to become an ineffective agent in handling boys and young men.

Youth is a passing scene only with respect to the individual. In our group life youth will always play its part. And what a part it is! Plastic, soft, emotional, jealous, eager, enthusiastic, prejudiced, full of abandon, tireless, insurgent—all this and more is youth! And out of the chaotic emotions, ambitions, fears and depressions of youth the coach must do his part to erect a sober personality. A brimming cup of life brought to a state where it is self-contained–that is one of the tasks of the coach.

That coach is a lucky man who can remember his own youth. He is an unlucky man if he has crossed the years between youth and maturity and has no eyes for his past. Without such a vision his tasks and the demands he places upon his boys are conceived with respect to his own adult world and not with respect to the world of youth. Boys will not warm up to a pure, unadulterated man. A man who is nothing but man will never really live with his boys. A relation of this kind is contrary to all that real teaching and real coaching means. To know youth and to live with it on its own level is to become a tremendously effective instrument in the molding of youth.

Conclusion

We have meant to say the following things in this chapter.

1. The coach is a teacher because he must intelligently share with the men on the squad all he knows about plays

and formations, signal systems, types of skill, strategy, and the rules of the game.

2. The coach is more than a teacher for he has the power to make or to break the character of the boys he teaches.

3. The great objective in coaching is the attainment of a fighting mind activating a skillful and efficient body, first in the games on the athletic field, but finally in the game of life.

4. The coach must prepare himself (a) by having confidence in the dignity of his profession, (b) by knowing the sport he is to teach, (c) by knowing human bodies, and (d) by knowing something about the life of the intellect.

5. As he deals with his men the coach must always have before him the knowledge that men differ widely from one another in ability. He must have due respect for the tremendous process called learning and for the laws and principles to which all mental life is obedient.

6. And finally, the coach must have a living sympathy for the insurgency of youth.

4 America's First Sport Psychologist

WALTER KROLL AND GUY LEWIS
University of Massachusetts

This reading by Kroll and Lewis is a review of Coleman Griffith's legacy. Their label of "father of sport psychology" was an honorable reference to Griffith, which is still used today.

Griffith's research interests included psychomotor skills, learning, and personality. He developed numerous tests and pieces of research apparatus. However, most of these apparatus would be considered in the motor learning and control domain today. He was the first to recognize the need to educate coaches and athletes about psychological aspects of performance enhancement. He interviewed elite coaches, such as Knute Rockne, and elite athletes, such as Red Grange, to study what made them successful from a motivation perspective. His background in laboratory research was extensive, but that did not deter him from branching out into applied methodologies. He was the first in sport psychology to implement case study research, predominantly with an interview format.

Since Griffith was a "prophet without disciples," it was especially important to reestablish his legacy. It is rare for any academic discipline to be traced to a single individual. This is a unique aspect of applied sport psychology.

The first American to engage in formal study of the psychological aspects of sport was Coleman Roberts Griffith, and his accomplishments were of sufficient importance to earn for him the title of "Father of Sports Psychology." Griffith began his investigation at the University of Illinois in 1918 when he conducted a "series of informal observations" on some of the psychological factors involved in basketball and football.[1] Two years later, he began to test football players with a Sanborn reaction-timer.[2]

These studies impressed and excited the imagination of George Huff, Director of Athletics, University of Illinois, and Director of the Department of Physical Welfare, forerunner of the present College of Physical Education. Huff formulated a plan to provide support for a research facility and staff. He proposed to have the Athletic Association assume responsibility for the cost of equipment and the salaries of clerical and professional staff, provided the University would make space available for a laboratory. On September 15, 1925, the Board of Trustees approved the plan, and shortly thereafter Griffith officially became Director of the Athletic Research Laboratory.[3] The facility consisted of two rooms located in the gymnasium: one of 550 square feet was designated the psychological laboratory; the other of 500 square feet, the physiological laboratory. Included was a workshop and a rat colony from Wistar Institute.[4] Griffith was delighted with the set-up. He later wrote: "few other psychological laboratories devoted to a single group of psychological problems are better equipped than this laboratory for research in athletics."[5] In it, according to the commission he received from Huff, Griffith was to study problems in the psychology and physiology of athletic activities, but, in so doing, he was not to ignore making contributions to "pure psychological and physiological science."[6]

Griffith devoted most of his energy to investigating three content areas: psychomotor skills; learning; and, to a lesser extent, personality variables. To pursue knowledge about these areas, he developed a number of tests and many pieces of special apparatus. These included: (1) apparatus for reaction time to muscular load; (2) test of baseball ingenuity; (3) test of muscular tension and relaxation; (4) tests of four different types of serial reaction times; (5) tests for steadiness, muscular coordination, and learning ability; (6) tests for reaction time to light, sound, and pressure; (7) test for measuring flexibility of coordination; (8) test for measurement of muscular sense; and (9) test of mental alertness developed especially for athletes.[7]

The complexity of the questions the psychologist had to ask about sport were so engrossing and answers so elusive that he used every known means and all available opportunities to gather information. Valuable, but not as important to Griffith as objective data gathered in a scientific setting, were the insights gained from carefully studying both the athletes in competitive situations and the verbal responses received to precisely worded questions during interviews. Griffith, especially curious about the triggering of the automatic skill response, used the result of an interview held with Harold "Red" Grange during the 1924 Michigan-Illinois game to illustrate that successful athletes had the capacity to effectively react to stimuli without assistance from the conscious. Grange scored four touchdown runs before the first 12 minutes of the contest had elapsed, and, before the game ended, he added one more. Yet, when questioned by Griffith, Grange was unable to recall a single detail in any of the feats.[8]

Adapted, by permission, from W. Kroll and G. Lewis, 1970, "America's first sport psychologist," *Quest* 13: 1-4. © NAKPEHE.

Through correspondence with Knute Rockne, he was able to gather additional subjective evidence relative to his theory of the role of motivation in sport. Rockne agreed with Griffith's point of view, and, to illustrate the point, once wrote: "I do not make any effort to key them up, except on rare, exceptional occasions. I keyed them up for the Nebraska game this year, which was a mistake, as we had a reaction the following Saturday against Northwestern. I try to make our boys take the game less seriously than, I presume, some others do. . . ."[9]

Recognizing the need to make known to coaches ways in which knowledge could be applied to teaching sports. Griffith produced a number of articles and two books. He was a frequent contributor to the *Athletic Journal.* In these articles he dealt with a wide range of practical topics such as mental stance and errors in the basketball free throw.[10] In 1926, he published the first of his two classics in sports psychology, *Psychology of Coaching.* He followed this with *Psychology and Athletics* two years later. A book he failed to complete was tentatively titled Psychology of Football. Eighteen chapters of this unpublished work are housed with the Griffith Papers in the Archives of the University of Illinois Library.

At the University of Illinois, he taught a course in sports psychology and assisted graduate students with their research. The first stage in the development of the course came when he offered a special section in introductory psychology to athletes. This section was supplanted in the fall of 1923 by a totally new course called Psychology and Athletics in which Griffith sought to make a serious psychological analysis of all phases of athletic competition.[11] He made available the resources of the laboratory to those graduate students who wished to investigate specific topics. The first theses dealing with the psychological aspects of sport and physical activity were completed during his tenure as director.[12]

Griffith's work as Director of the Athletic Research Laboratory came to an end in 1932. The Athletic Association, faced with declining revenues, decided to economize by withdrawing financial support from the project. Griffith resigned his position and America's first research laboratory in sports psychology closed its doors.[13]

Once his responsibilities as Director of the Athletic Research Laboratory came to an end, Griffith turned his energies primarily to his duties as professor of educational psychology, an appointment that began in 1921, and to service to the University of Illinois. He did, however, conduct an extensive research project for the Chicago National League Ball Club in 1938.[14] The same year the Athletic Research Laboratory closed he was named Director of the Bureau of Institutional Research, and from 1944 to 1953 he was Provost of the University.

An extremely productive researcher and writer, Griffith published more than 40 articles; they appeared in the most prestigious journals in psychology and education. He was especially interested in the effects of rotation upon equilibrium and nystagmus. Among the studies reported were: "Concerning the Effects of Repeated Rotation upon Nystagmus"; "The Decrease of After-Nystagmus During Repeated Rotation"; "Experimental Study of Dizziness"; "The Organic Effects of Repeated Bodily Rotation"; "An Experimental Study of Equilibration in the White Rat"; and "Are Permanent Disturbances of Equilibration Inherited?" In addition to the two books in sports psychology, Griffith was the author of: *General Introduction to Psychology* (1928); *An Introduction to Applied Psychology* (1934); *Introduction to Educational Psychology* (1935); *Psychology Applied to Teaching and Learning* (1939); and *Principles of Systematic Psychology* (1943).

Griffith was born at Guthrie Center, Iowa, May 22, 1893. He received an A.B. degree from Greenville College in 1915 and a Ph.D. from the University of Illinois in 1920. With the exception of the academic year 1915-16, when he served as an instructor in psychology at Greenville College, his professional affiliation was with the University of Illinois. After retiring in 1953, he continued active in professional matters until his death in February 1966. In December, 1964, at the first meeting devoted to an examination of "The Body of Knowledge in Physical Education" by the Western Conference of Physical Education Directors, he presented a paper titled "Sport and the Culture."[15] During his career he received numerous honors and distinctions from professional psychological and educational societies, and, in 1946, Greenville College bestowed upon him the LL.D. degree. Physical education associations, however, have failed to recognize the importance of his contributions.

The reason that such outstanding accomplishments have not been given a prominent place in the annals of the profession is wholly or in part due to the striking void between the period in which Griffith was productive and that of contemporary research in the psychology of sport. Impetus, then, for the recent surge of interest in psychological studies came from a source other than Griffith. In the absence of connective links between the beginning and the present, the designation "Father" suggested on the basis of original contributions to the field of study may not be a fitting one. However, due to the significance of his pioneer work and the obvious failure of physical educators to claim the legacy offered by America's first sports psychologist, Griffith should properly be remembered as a prophet without disciples.

References

1. Griffith, Coleman. "A Laboratory for Research in Athletics." Research Quarterly, 1, (October, 1930), 35.
2. Ibid.
3. Seidler, Armond H. "A History of the Professional Training in Physical Education for Men at the University of Illinois." M.S. thesis, University of Illinois, 1948, pp. 51 and 52.
4. Griffith, op. cit., pp. 36 and 37.

5. Ibid., p. 37
6. Ibid., p. 37
7. Ibid., pp. 39 and 40
8. Tape of an interview of Dr. H. E. Kenney (former student and later colleague of Griffith's) conducted by Dr. Larry Locke on September 25, 1969. In possession of Dr. Locke and housed at the University of New Mexico.
9. Letter from Knute Rockne (signature initialed F. M.) to Coleman Griffith, December 13, 1924, Box 1, General Correspondence, Coleman R. Griffith Papers, University Archives, University of Illinois Library.
10. For example, Athletic Journal titles in 1929 were: "Stance," "Mental Stance," "Recent Changes in Basketball Tactics from the Point of View of Psychology."
11. Griffith, op. cit., pp. 35 and 36.
12. Letter from C. O. Jackson to Walter Kroll, November 9, 1968, verified fact that Griffith had directed Jackson's thesis, "The Effect of Fear on Muscular Coordination." King J. McCristal in a letter to Walter Kroll, October 22, 1968, stated that Griffith directed his thesis, "An Experimental Investigation of Foot Rhythms Involved in Gymnastic and Tap Dancing." The studies were reported in the Research Quarterly in 1933.
13. Seidler, op. cit., p. 56.
14. "General Reports, Experimental Laboratories, Chicago National League Ball Club, January 1, 1938-January 1, 1939," Box 13, Coleman R. Griffith Papers, University Archives, University of Illinois Library.
15. Zeigler, Earle F., and McCristal, King J. "A History of the Big Ten Body-of-Knowledge Project in Physical Education." Quest, IX (Winter, 1967), 80.

5 About Smocks and Jocks

RAINER MARTENS
University of Illinois at Urbana-Champaign

This classic reading by Rainer Martens had a profound effect on the type of research methods implemented in sport psychology. Martens expressed his displeasure with traditional laboratory experimental research and instead advocated multivariate, long-term field investigations, thus suggesting that sport psychologists trade their smocks for "jocks."

It is interesting to note that only one of the top researchers in the field could credibly advocate such a profound change. Martens had a great deal of experience with traditional research methods and an extensive publication record. Thus his commitment to and understanding of this type of research methodology could not be questioned. However, some thought that this reading could be detrimental to the field by diverting from basic and theoretical research. In the opponents' view, the field was not yet ready to take this giant step. The fact that this reading appeared in the first issue of the Journal of Sport Psychology certainly influenced future applied research. As this type of research expanded, the formulation of two more applied journals, The Sport Psychologist and the Journal of Applied Sport Psychology, became necessary for meeting this increased demand.

Martens took the leap himself into applied research, and the next four doctoral students he mentored focused on applied research as well. Damon Burton studied goal setting; his subject pool was the University of Illinois swim team. Robin Vealey studied self-confidence; she used a variety of athletes in her subject pool. Linda Bump also studied a variety of athletes in her research on interpersonal skills. Dan Smith implemented an extensive imagery training program with the University of Illinois men's basketball team, which led to his full-time appointment as sport psychologist for the University of Illinois athletic department. Martens and these four doctoral students integrated their research into a program they termed psychological skills training (PST). This PST program was presented at the annual conference of the North American Society for the Psychology of Sport and Physical Activity (NASPSPA) in 1984. This created a rift in the organization because some sport psychology researchers were reluctant to follow the applied route. This, in turn, led to the formation of a new academic organization in sport psychology, the Association for the Advancement of Applied Sport Psychology (AAASP), by John Silva and others in 1986. Thus, this reading had a profound effect on the growth of applied sport psychology.

The dissatisfaction with the existing scientific paradigm of social psychology, and its adoption in sport psychology, is discussed. Although many metapsychological issues are raised, attention focuses on the inadequacies of laboratory experimental research. As a partial solution in the development of a new paradigm, it is suggested that sport psychologists trade their smocks for "jocks," turning their efforts to multivariate, long-term field research.

I see new exciting horizons for sport psychology—better research on more significant issues, stimulating and useful clinical developments, and improved cooperation between scientist/clinician and athlete/coach. But I have not always held such an optimistic perspective. My optimism has arisen only after an analysis of my own past research and much of the sport psychology research completed in the last 15 years. Here is what I have found wanting with this research and why I am optimistic about the future.

For me, there have been gaps greater than tolerable between my aspirations and realizations, both with respect to theoretical synthesis and applicability to important problems in sport. I am concerned about the failures in replicability. I have doubts about the snapshot model of linear causation so fundamental to laboratory experimentation; doubts indeed that the categories of ANOVA—with its neatly isolated independent and dependent variables—can provide a useful model of what goes on in the personal and social world of sport. I have misgivings about the use of deception, and more generally, with the manipulations used in laboratory studies. In fact, I have grave doubts about the utility of laboratory research for most of sport psychology. And, I am disturbed about the gulf between those who do sport psychology research and those who interpret sport psychology research to practitioners.

Just when I was convinced something was seriously wrong with me for having such doubts and concerns, I learned about the "great crisis" in social psychology. Social psychologists for the past 5 or 6 years have been engaging in intensive soul searching, discussing such issues as (a) whether social psychological research is merely a recording of history, (b) the need for a new research paradigm, (c) the direction that the field is and should be moving, and (d) the relevance of the research to the social problems of

---

Adapted, by permission, from R. Martens, 1979, "About smocks and jocks," *Journal of Sport Psychology* 1: 94-99.

This paper was presented at the Canadian Psycho-motor Learning and Sport Psychology Symposium, Toronto, Ontario, November 2, 1978.

the day. These fundamental questions about the science of psychology have paralleled my concerns within the field of sport psychology.

Arising first from an analysis of my personal research, and then from my reading on the crisis in social psychology, my faith has been seriously shaken in logical positivism,[1] operationalism as specified by behaviorism, and laboratory experimentation. These principles of research, the very canons of science, are being doubted by an increasing number of behavioral scientists, including me. I know it is sacrilegious to think that the principles so hallowed in the "hard" sciences cannot satisfactorily be used to explain human behavior, and such hearsay surely deserves excommunication from the kingdom of science.

I have been reticent to discuss these concerns with others in sport psychology. When making reference to some of these issues with colleagues I have sensed an uneasiness to discuss it, an almost I-don't-want-to-think-about-it attitude. You see, these concerns are the very pillars of our faith upon which the practice of our science is built. If we were to find these canons of science to be wanting, what would we do?

Yet somehow I doubt that I am alone in my concern about these issues. I suspect more than a few sport psychologists have dared to risk some introspective analysis, flirting dangerously with such thoughts as: Am I participating in a big intellectual and academic game in which, in the "name of the game," problems are being manufactured rather than formulated, methodological tools are being used because they have the "good scientific stamp of approval" rather than because they have been logically and theoretically derived from a problem, and that unification is to be achieved at any cost, even at the understanding of a problem?

Have you not wondered why sport psychology, as we know it, has had little to no influence on the world of sport? It is not because the coaches and athletes are unreceptive to information from our field; indeed they are eager for such information. It is, unfortunately, because our insights have not been challenging, the issues studied have not been critical, and our data are not convincing to the *vital* issues in sport. Thus, experiential knowledge and common sense, have been more appealing, and usually more beneficial, than knowledge from sport psychology research. But, of course, such knowledge also is sometimes erroneous.

Changing Paradigms

The literature on the crisis in social psychology (e.g., Gergen, 1973, 1976; Helmreich, 1975; McGuire, 1973; Schlenkar, 1974) is excellent reading to stimulate thinking about the metapsychology of sport. Personally I believe that the prevailing paradigm of social psychology, which many of us in sport psychology have borrowed, is inadequate for understanding human behavior. This paradigm directs us to select our hypotheses for their relevance to broad theoretical formulations and then to test them by *laboratory* manipulational experiments. I believe that a radically new paradigm is needed—in Kuhn's terms, a scientific revolution.

But here is where I begin to have difficulty. While it is clear that a new paradigm is needed, I do not know, nor it seems, does anyone else know fully how to create this new paradigm. Indeed it is doubtful that this new paradigm will suddenly be created. Instead it will evolve gradually, emerging from continued modification of the existing paradigm.

Compared to my earlier research, I have incorporated what I think are some of these modifications into my own recent research. I would like to describe some of these changes, suggesting that they are characteristic of an emerging paradigm which has special significance to sport psychology.

The most significant change in my research is the switch from laboratory to field settings. Rather than testing my notions on randomly recruited college sophomores corralled into laboratories, I am observing and describing behavior and probing for cognitions of people who actually are participating in sport. In fact, I no longer have a laboratory at the University of Illinois; my laboratory is the playing fields, gymnasia, and natatoriums everywhere. I have replaced my smock with a jock when necessary, to observe and understand the real world of sport.

I would judge my recent research to have more relevance to sport. Much of it is more applied, but even some of what I consider to be basic research is more relevant to sport than my previous research. The hypotheses I now investigate are formulated for their relevance to sport, but at the same time are formulated with a consideration of existing theory and a view to constructing theory specific to sport. I do believe that socially relevant, applied, field-based research need not be divorced from theory.

I now use a wider array of methods in my research. My loss of faith in the canons of positivism and operationalism, which restrict inquiry into only those areas capable of technical manipulation, has freed me to investigate phenomena that I felt in the past were impossible to study. Part of this new freedom emanates from my rediscovery that much of what man does is determined by his thoughts. And thus, I am enthusiastic about the reception being given the cognitive orientation in psychology. I applaud the radical proposal of dialectical social psychology which states that we should treat people, for scientific purposes, as if they were human beings, capable not only of reacting to, but also interacting with and at times, even changing their environment.

Such a view of people as active agents produces a greater acceptance of self-report information. Such a view places

[1]Logical positivism asserts the primacy of observation in assessing the truth of statements of fact and holding that metaphysical and subjective arguments not based on observable data are meaningless.

greater significance on the observation of behavior as it occurs naturally within the social context of sport. Sport psychology will surely be a healthier field when we recognize that the internal psychological processes that occur when people engage in sport must be understood within the social context of sport. Thus, rather than making war with sport sociologists, we must make love. (Perhaps friends is good enough.)

If we continue to follow the traditional path so deeply cut by our graduate programs, the major journals of our related fields, and our borrowed research paradigm, it will result in a sport psychology of predictive impotence and theoretical irrelevance. Certainly today sport psychology trades more on promise than on performance, but I think that promise is great if we will undertake some change. I would like to briefly elaborate on how I think sport psychology can become a more relevant science.

More Attention Needs to Be Given to Theory Building

We have been so eager to test theories of the larger field of psychology in order to confirm our scientific respectability that we have not adequately observed, described, and theorized about our own thing—*sport!* We have been so enamored with our operational definitions, clever manipulations, and high powered statistics that we are in danger of losing sight of the phenomenon these instruments were designed to illuminate. We clearly need to spend more time observing behavior in sport and building our own theories unique to sport. Then we can test them!

Less Attention Needs to Be Given to Laboratory Research

I am not opposed to laboratory research; there is a place and time for it. I just think it has occupied too big a place and been used before we have adequately identified the important variables of sport psychology. Consequently, we have often taken less relevant variables into the laboratory. It has produced a tremendous amount of chaff and few golden kernels; it threatens to suffocate us under a paper avalanche of little worth.

I am sure we all recognize the weaknesses of descriptive, observational methods; of self-report data. But I am not sure we all know the inadequacies of the laboratory study. Here are a few.

1. I have grave doubts that isolated psychological studies which manipulate a few variables, attempting to uncover the effects of X on Y, can be cumulative to form a coherent picture of human behavior. I sense that the elegant control achieved in laboratory research is such that all meaning is drained from the experimental situation. The external validity of laboratory studies is at best limited to predicting behavior in other laboratories.

2. The populations sampled in laboratory research most often continue to be unrepresentative of those to whom we wish to make application. We all acknowledge this failing, but for pragmatic reasons, continue the practice of unrepresentative sampling.

3. Somehow there continues to be an implicit assumed equivalence of laboratory to life situations, even though we know better. We, of course, never create the richness of social situations in the laboratory; in fact we strive not to because we want to gain control over the situation. Thus, laboratory research almost always forces a kind of reductionism, reducing a multivariate universe to a bivariate to trivariate model usually factorial in design. Such models frequently may isolate significant effects, but account for negligible amounts of variance.

4. Laboratory studies also frequently lead to an erroneous specification of causality. We assume if we manipulate X and it significantly affects Y, then X caused Y to change. Laboratory studies, however, usually impose a directional model of causality. In unconstrained natural settings Y may also cause X, or X and Y may cause changes in each other.

The Why of It All

After only 6 weeks of studying sport psychology, one of my students asked me the question: Why do sport psychologists spend so little time studying SPORT? Can you answer that question or these? Why have we done so little *applied* research? And so little *field* research?

One reason I believe is that there is an attitude that applied research conducted in the field is nonscientific. Others consider this type of research to be unresponsive to theory, assuming that theory development and testing can proceed only through research that is conducted in artificial and contrived settings. But it seems to me to be the contrary. I think there is a greater probability that the best theories of sport psychology will grow from field research on applied problems. Involvement with practical problems in sport should be a never-failing source of theoretical ideas and knowledge of fundamental psychological relationships in sport. Indeed, applied field research in sport psychology need not be restricted to a methodology uniformed by theoretical concerns.

To be sure, I am not saying that field research is the complete and final solution to the serious problems facing behavioral scientists in constructing new or modified paradigms for the study of human behavior. But I do believe it is an important step in the right direction, especially for the field of sport psychology as it currently functions.

To get at the complexities of human behavior in sport, much of our field research will need to be large-scale, long-term, and multivariate. Our new paradigm will consist of theoretical models of cognitive and social systems of sport in their true multivariate complexity, involving a great deal of parallel processing, bidirectional relationships, and feedback circuits. Such theoretical models will emerge from and be tested through field methods, and will thus merge practical and theoretical relevance. Yet I am well aware of the problems inhibiting the undertaking of such research—lack of money, existing university reward systems, and the mobility of the population, to name a few. But the outcome of such research will be a healthy diversity in the subject matter of our field. While research will likely be more difficult to do, while it will be problematical, and occasionally a pain in the ass, I also feel it will be more valid, much more useful, and surely more fun to do. For me, the asking of more sport relevant questions and attempting to answer them through field research, has aborted much of my disenchantment with the sport psychology of the past.

References

Crase, D. Has physical education achieved a scholarly dimension? *Journal of Physical Education and Recreation,* October 1978, pp. 21–22.

Gergen, K.J. Social psychology as history. *Journal of Personality and Social Psychology,* 1973, 26, 309–320.

Gergen, K.J. Social psychology, science and history. *Personality and Social Psychology Bulletin,* 1976, 2, 373–383.

Helmreich. R. Applied social psychology: The unfulfilled promise. *Personality and Social Psychology Bulletin,* 1975, 1, 548–560.

McGuire, W.J. The yin and yang of progress in social psychology: Seven Koans. *Journal of Personality and Social Psychology,* 1973, 26, 446–456.

Schlenkar, B.R. Social psychology and science. *Journal of Personality and Social Psychology*, 1974, 29, 1–15.

PART II

Understanding Individual Differences Among Sport Participants

The readings in part II address some important issues related to personal factors (i.e., personality characteristics, emotions, and various individual orientations) that affect our understanding of sport and exercise behavior.

Morgan's (1980) article addresses some of the major concerns raised against using traits as predictors of athletic behavior and proposes measures intended to promote the efficacy of the trait approach in sport and exercise settings. Morgan put a special emphasis on the Profile of Mood States (POMS) and the iceberg profile. In 1995, Rowley, Landers, Kyllo, and Etnier applied the quantitative review method of meta-analysis in order to examine whether the iceberg profile discriminated between successful and less successful athletes. Some have questioned the sport-specific applicability of the POMS inventory and others have been tremendous advocates for its use. The study conducted by Martens, Burton, Vealey, Bump, and Smith (1990) introduced the classic Competitive State Anxiety Inventory-II (CSAI-II). This has become one of the most-used inventories in sport psychology research, sparking interest in the components and applicability of sport-specific competitive state anxiety. Hanin's (1997) article summarizes his extensive work on the (individual) zone of optimal functioning (IZOF), which addresses the longitudinal influence that anxiety and other emotional states have on the performance of individual athletes. The determination of which states most positively affect performance has long been of interest to practitioners. Duda's (1992) chapter presents an important motivational issue, the goal perspective approach, putting an emphasis on the famous Task and Ego Orientation in Sport Questionnaire (TEOSQ). It has long been proposed that successful athletes take a task and not an ego orientation to adversity. Finally, Tenenbaum and Bar-Eli (1995) not only reviewed the research on personality in sport but also substantially contributed to the understanding of intellectual capabilities required for successful athletic activity within the framework of an extensive review on (sport) intelligence research. This summarized much of the previous research on how intellect affects performance.

6 The Trait Psychology Controversy

WILLIAM P. MORGAN
University of Wisconsin-Madison

In psychology, the question of which primary source—the person or the situation—accounts for the apparent variance in human behavior has long been debated. Whereas the proponents of the first approach advocated stable, intraorganismic constructs as the main determinants of behavior, proponents of the second approach emphasized situational factors as the main source of behavioral variance. In the late 1970s, interactionism, that is, a synthesis between these two views, became the zeitgeist of personality psychology. Some researchers even proceeded further toward the so-called transactional approach to personality.

In essence, these historical developments reflected the patterns observed for general personality research in psychology. In the 1950s and 1960s, sport psychology was characterized mainly by research on the person or the situation. However, toward the mid-1970s, the interactional perspective became the preferred paradigm in research on sport personality. It was argued that the proponents of the situational approach sometimes overreacted to the person paradigm and, therefore, it would be advisable to concurrently study the effects of intrapersonal factors and environmental effects on human behavior. As a consequence, the interactional approach has increased in use from the 1970s onward. In particular, during the second half of the 1970s, the trait approach in sport personality decreased markedly, whereas interactional approaches, especially the cognitively oriented ones, showed a marked increase in use during this time. Morgan, one of the leading proponents of the trait approach in sport psychology, tried to address some of the major concerns that had been raised against the efficacy of traits in predicting human athletic behavior in the decade that preceded the publication of this seminal article. He argued that the failure to find consistent differences in personality traits was due to several problems, such as inadequate operationalization of variables, the use of small samples, poor sampling procedures, inappropriate statistics (univariate as opposed to multivariate designs), disregard for response distortion, and misuse of theory. Morgan admits that traits alone cannot predict sport behavior and athletic success, but he proposes some measures to promote the efficacy of the trait approach in sport psychology. Among others, Morgan discusses in this context the Profile of Mood States (POMS) and the iceberg profile, which have been so often associated with his name.

The trait psychology controversy has existed in academic psychology for many years, and it has represented a central issue for workers in the young field of sport psychology as well. The perceived efficacy of trait psychology has clearly varied as a function of time, context, and author. That is to say, the history of psychology suggests that trait psychology has received enormous support at certain points in time, while at other times it has been viewed as essentially worthless. In other words, the spirit of the time or *zeitgeist* has been characterized by a sine wave function in academic psychology. These periodic oscillations have also characterized activity in the field of sport psychology with the exception that the curve has been displaced to the right such that a lag time of about five or ten years has characterized the response pattern in sport psychology.

This displacement effect has probably been due to a number of factors, and it is fairly representative of the entire field of sport psychology, not simply the personology area. Most work in the field of sport psychology has been atheoretical, and the limited theoretical work has involved the adoption of models and theories from academic psychology—hence, the associated lag time. The classic writings of Henry (1960) and Schmidt (1975) represent notable exceptions to this generalization. The lag time effect is probably best explained by the observation that most "sport psychologists" in North America do not appear to be psychologists.

Recent discussions of the trait psychology issue within academic psychology have been presented by Hogan, DeSoto, & Solano (1977), Mischel (1977), and Zuckerman (1979), and related papers in sport psychology have been authored by Kane (1978), Martens (1975), Morgan (1978a), Rushall (1975), and Singer, Harris, Kroll, Martens, & Sechrest (1977). These authors employ the term "trait" in a similar manner at times, while at other times the meaning or *context* in which the term trait is employed seems to differ substantially. It appears, for example, that authors such as Hogan et al. (1977) and Mischel (1977) employ the term trait within the same context that it has been employed for many years in academic psychology. Martens (1975) employs the term trait in the same manner and proceeds to argue that general trait theory be replaced with "trait specific" measures (Martens, 1977). A lucid discussion of *narrow* versus *broad* trait measurement has recently been presented by Zuckerman (1979), and the overall theoretical view advanced by Zuckerman is supported with empirical evidence.

The view that trait theory fluctuates as a function of time, context, and author is supported in various ways.

Adapted with permission from *Research Quarterly for Exercise and Sport*, Vol. 51, pp. 50-76, Copyright 1980 by the American Alliance for Health, Physical Education, Recreation and Dance, 1900 Association Drive, Reston, VA 20191.

Even during periods when the *zeitgeist* has been characterized by the peak (positive) or base (negative) of the sine curve function, certain authors have argued the converse in a largely contextual manner. An excellent illustration of this matter has been presented by Loy and Donnelly (1976) who depict the common dimensions of personality traits operationalized as (1) somatotype, (2) sensation-seeking, (3) augmentation-reduction, and (4) extroversion. In other words, operationalization of these constructs has been carried out in different ways and within different theoretical frameworks, but the construct, across theories, seems to reflect a common trait. Furthermore, Loy and Donnelly have reported that the need for stimulation motive (*n Stim*) "is expressed by individuals in terms of particular behaviors and in terms of general life-styles" (p. 84). These authors also emphasize that a review of existing research clearly supports "the existence of a need for stimulation that varies among individuals" (p. 84). This particular paper convincingly presents a strong case for trait psychology in general, and the "need for stimulation motive" in particular, at a point in time when many workers in the field of sport psychology have rejected trait psychology.

Why do different authors, writing about the same topic (trait psychology), arrive at seemingly diverse conclusions? Time and context are partial explanations for such controversy, but these are not sufficient explanations. Even when the prevailing *zeitgeist* has been a pro-trait, some psychologists have spoken out strongly against trait theory. Conversely certain psychologists adamantly support trait theory during anti-trait periods. In other words, the trait psychology sine wave peaks and falls, and these period oscillations are easily documented.

The central driving force responsible for any given sport psychology *zeitgeist* in Canada and the United States at present is the North American Society for the Psychology of Sport and Physical Activity (NASPSPA). The earliest workers in North America (Henry, 1941) relied on trait psychology, and this persisted through the 1950s (Johnson, Hutton, & Johnson, 1954). While trait personology continued to represent the dominant approach through the 1960s (Cooper, 1969; Morgan, 1972), a general awareness of the limitations inherent in trait theory began to emerge in the late 1960s (Kenyon, 1970). Awareness of these limitations led many sport psychologists to propose that trait theory be abandoned (Kroll, 1976; Martens, 1975; Rushall, 1970, 1975; Singer et al., 1977). Other authors such as Bird (1979), Kane (1964, 1970, 1978), Morgan (1972, 1974, 1978a), and Williams (1978) have proposed that traits were of value in predicting behavior in sport settings. A discussion of the credulous-skeptical argument in sport personology appears in Straub's edited volume (Morgan, 1978a). The debate which has persisted in sport psychology over the past ten years reflects, perhaps for different reasons, the same debate that has characterized the issue of trait personology in academic psychology (Hogan et al., 1977, Mischel, 1977).

Martens' (1975) original proposal that trait psychology be abandoned served as the impetus for much of the current work in sport psychology. Martens (1975, 1977), however, is not opposed to the use of traits per se, but rather to the use of certain kinds of traits. Martens' (1975) paper, and the report of a subsequent task force (Singer et al., 1977) proposing that sport psychology be abandoned, has been largely misunderstood. Implicit in these recommendations was the understanding that inventories designed to measure specific traits were needed in sport psychology in place of existing measures designed to assess broad or general traits. Publication of the Sport Competition Anxiety Test (SCAT) represents an attempt to fill this presumed need (Martens, 1977). At any rate, development of the SCAT indicates that Martens supports the use of selected trait measures. This position is also related to Zuckerman's (1979) recent paper which makes a distinction between "broad" and "narrow" trait measures. Zuckerman's research demonstrates that narrow trait measures are generally better predictors of behavior than are broad trait measures. State measures performed just prior to performance, however, are even better predictors than narrow trait measures (Zuckerman, 1979). Needless to say, it would be rather foolish, as well as less accurate, to predict state responses from trait measures, if one were able to assess measures in the milieu of interest.

A State of Confusion

Despite advances in personality psychology (Zuckerman, 1979), and sport psychology in particular (Martens, 1977), there continues to be controversy and confusion in sport psychology. At least two distinct personology camps, the skeptical and credulous, have emerged over the past ten years. Sport psychologists from the skeptical camp have argued that *trait* theory in general, and Cattellian theory in particular, be rejected or abandoned in favor of sport specific theories and inventories. This particular camp has selectively adopted and rejected the Mischellian and Cattellian positions respectively. In the case of the credulous camp, however, the converse has occurred.

The controversy which has prevailed is best viewed as a "state of confusion," and it has stemmed in large measure from (1) a general failure to adequately operationalize the dependent and independent variables, (2) atheoretical as opposed to theoretical inquiry, (3) misuse rather than use of existing theory and psychological measures, (4) use of the first order factors alone in some studies, higher order factors in others, and both first and higher order factors in others, (5) utilization of either state or trait models alone rather than state-trait models, (6) a total disregard for the problem of response distortion, (7) failure to conceptualize behavior in a psychophysiological context, and (8) a preference for the study of large groups in a superficial manner rather than in-depth examination of individuals.

One additional problem has related to the nature of training programs in the field of sport psychology. Indeed, rather than list training as a ninth problem, it might be more appropriate to argue that training is, in fact, *the* problem, and the eight problems listed above are actually symptoms. That is to say, the major problem or reason for the prevailing controversy and confusion may simply reflect the nature of academic training received by sport psychologists.

The *zeitgeist* in contemporary sport psychology suggests that trait psychology should be abandoned because available theories and instruments have not been useful in predicting behavior. This movement is somewhat unfortunate since an extensive literature suggests that trait psychology is often of limited value in a univariate sense, and general trait measures consistently enhance overall prediction when included in multivariate models which incorporate psychologic states and physiologic parameters. Members of the NASPSPA cartel may view this position as an undesired effort to resurrect trait psychology, but the author proposes that trait psychology has been alive and well in many sectors of academic psychology right along. Subsequent sections of the present paper will consider earlier reviews, methodologic issues in sport personology, the use of perceptual and cognitive traits, and several recommendations for future directions in sport psychology.

Earlier Reviews

Several reviews dealing with the personality structure of athletes have been published during the past decade. These papers have dealt with comparisons of (1) athletes and nonathletes, (2) athletes of differing ability levels, and (3) athletes from different sport groups.

Most of the research reviewed in these articles and chapters have relied on trait theory in a classical or general sense when evaluating group differences. These reviews have led some authors to conclude that differences in personality traits have consistently been observed (Kane, 1970, 1978; Morgan, 1972, 1976, 1978a, 1979; Williams, 1978). While these differences have been consistent across reviews, they have also been uniformly of a small magnitude. Other reviewers have been led to the conclusion that differences in psychological traits do not exist for three comparisons cited above (Kroll, 1970, 1976; Martens, 1975; Rushall, 1970, 1975; Singer et al., 1977). Rushall (1970), for example, has concluded that "personality is not a significant factor in sport performance" (p. 164). In describing the failure of certain reviewers to find consistent differences between athletes and nonathletes Kroll (1976) has emphasized that "progress may not be made until (a) the use of available standardized psychological inventories be minimized in favor of the development of specific athletic inventories, and (b) the trait psychology approach be abandoned in favor of an interactional paradigm" (p. 35).

Kroll's position is supported in large measure by Martens, Rushall, and Singer et al. One exception is that Martens proposed not only adoption of an interactional paradigm but use of sport-specific trait measures (Martens, 1975, 1977). In other words, Martens rejects general trait theory in favor of narrow or specific trait measures.

Why have some reviewers arrived at the conclusion that general trait measures are capable of discriminating between athletes and nonathletes, athletes of differing ability levels, and athletes from divergent sport groups, while an equal number of reviewers have argued that such measures cannot discriminate between such groups? There are undoubtedly many explanations that might be advanced to account for the credulous-skeptical argument (Morgan, 1978a) that has characterized the sport personology literature. Two of the more apparent problems in this area of inquiry have related to (1) methodological issues surrounding the research upon which subsequent reviews were based and (2) a tendency to include certain types of research in these reviews and exclude other types of research. These two issues will now be reviewed.

Methodological Issues

In an earlier review it was noted that numerous methodological problems have characterized research in the area of sport personology (Morgan, 1972b). Through the early part of the 1970s (1) published research was atheoretical and it seldom was pursued within a conceptual framework, (2) when *theoretical* positions were adopted (e.g., Cattellian) research findings were invariably discussed within an atheoretical context, (3) little or no concern was evidenced relative to rigorous definition of the dependent or independent variables, (4) sampling procedures and the associated problems of volunteerism and optimal sample size were seldom considered, (5) state-trait models were almost totally nonexistent, (6) there was seldom if ever any reference to the use of informed consent policies which suggests not only ethical problems but the substantive problem of response distortion where coercive tactics prevail, and (7) there was a decision not to employ response distortion scales (i.e., fake good, fake bad, random, "sabotage," etc.) in sport personology. When one considers the extensive list of methodological problems associated with research in the area of sport personology, it is surprising that any positive evidence at all has emerged. In other words, the above types of problems are known to inflate experimental error and decrease the likelihood of obtaining statistically significant results.

Another approach has been emphasized by Martens (1975) who has stated: "Thus the first step toward improving the quality of research in sport personology is not the correction of methodological or interpretive errors, although these two must be corrected, but is the adoption of a viable experimental paradigm for studying personality" (p. 22). Adoption of a viable experimental paradigm has come to imply different meanings for various investigators. It has led sport psychologists such as Kroll (1979) and Martens (1977) to develop psychological tools for use in sport settings.

At the same time, however, other sport psychologists such as Dishman, Ickes, & Morgan (in press) and Nideffer

(1978) have developed general trait measures which have been reported to be effective in both athletic and nonathletic settings. Nideffer has reported, for example, that the Test of Attentional and Interpersonal Style (TAIS) has been effective in predicting both a specific sport behavior (e.g., "choking") and behavior of nonathletes in various settings. Dishman et al. (in press) have reported that a general trait scale designed to measure "self-motivation" has been effective in predicting adherence patterns of women rowers involved in an intense training program as well as those of men involved in cardiac rehabilitation and adult fitness programs. These divergent findings and views in the field of sport psychology are comparable to those which exist in other subfields within psychology (Hogan et al., 1977; Mischel, 1977; Zuckerman, 1979). Perhaps Zuckerman is right:

> Psychologists, like Marxists, physicists, lawyers, and other scholastics, love a good intellectual fight. It is in the sensation-seeking nature of the beast. Nothing is duller then a group of pedants nodding over tea and the eternal truths. How much more exciting it is to challenge cherished notions like the Newtonian universe, God, free will, man's rationality, the conscious mind, the unconscious mind, personality, and its favorite son the trait. (p. 43)

Cattellian theory has been the most frequently employed personality theory in sport psychology, and this has resulted in an extensive literature based upon research involving Cattell's 16-Personality Factor (16PF) Inventory. Furthermore, the recommendation that trait theory be abandoned has been based largely upon research resulting from the use of this inventory. It is emphasized once again, however, that this research has been characterized by extensive methodological problems. Furthermore, the research by Irvine and Gendreau (1974), O'Dell (1971), and Winder, O'Dell, & Karson (1975) demonstrates that the 16PF is easily faked. Forms C and D of the 16PF contain a Motivational Distortion scale, but these forms have rarely been utilized by sport psychologists. Forms A and B of the 16PF have been employed most frequently, and these forms do not contain distortion scales. For this reason Karson and O'Dell (1976) developed specific scales for evaluation of (1) faking good, (2) faking bad, and (3) random answering on Forms A and B of the 16PF. The research they described reveals that response distortion must be considered when evaluating personality research involving the 16PF.

Since research in the field of sport personology has not traditionally considered the problem of response distortion, it is quite conceivable that the equivocal nature of much of this literature stems from the use of invalid profiles. This problem has been reviewed in more detail in a related paper (Morgan, 1978a). Nagle, Morgan, Hellickson, Serfass, & Alexander (1975) employed 12 psychological states and traits in an attempt to predict which of 40 candidates would earn a berth on the 1972 Olympic Wrestling Team. The best predictor to emerge following a stepwise multiple regression analysis was the lie scale of the Eysenck Personality Inventory. The lie scale alone accounted for 34% of the variance. This finding suggests that the efficacy of trait psychology (narrow or broad) in predicting behavior is governed by a variety of methodological problems, and response distortion is one in particular that should not be ignored. The extent to which narrow (specific) trait measures are superior to broad (general) trait measures can be readily tested, but the efficacy of the given models and theories can only be determined in settings where methodological problems are either eliminated or minimized.

Existing Trait Research

It is customary when preparing a review of existing research in a particular area to "sift and winnow" available reports, commenting critically as one proceeds, and then attempt to arrive at a reasoned conclusion. It is not appropriate to only select those reports favorable to one's hypothesis (i.e., traits are useful or traits are worthless). Such an approach, however, will be taken in the present section for several reasons. First, well over 75% of the papers to be cited have not been considered in the reviews prepared by anti-trait theorists in sport psychology; these reports have been selectively omitted in the skeptical reviews. Second, detailed accounts of the meager evidence supporting the anti-trait *zeitgeist* have appeared earlier.

One of the first investigators to demonstrate that athletes differ from nonathletes on selected psychological traits was Henry (1941) who compared track athletes, physical education majors, student pilots, and students enrolled in weight lifting. The track athletes and pilots were found to be less hypochondriacal and introverted than the weight lifters and more neurasthenic than the physical education majors. These findings were supported in part by Thune (1949) who later compared 100 YMCA weight lifters with 100 YMCA athletes who did not participate in weight lifting. The weight lifters were less outgoing, lacked self-confidence, and exhibited more concern with body build. The weight lifters also manifested a desire "to be strong, healthy, and dominant, to be more like other men" (p. 305). The reports by Henry and Thune were based upon self-report questionnaires of an objective nature.

The findings of Henry (1941), Thune (1949), and Harlow (1951) are interesting for several reasons. First, the dependent measures in these investigations differed, the samples and geographical locales were different, a period of ten years separated the first and last investigation, and yet, similar conclusions were reached. The findings suggest that behavior, selection of a particular physical activity, was associated with selected personality traits, and one of the investigations demonstrated the relationship to be of a casual nature—that is, masculine inadequacy and compensatory development of physique (Harlow, 1951). A second reason why these findings support trait theory (person variables) are of interest is that they have been selectively omitted from skeptical reviews.

The Sixteen Personality Factor (16PF) was administered to incoming students at the United States Military Academy by Werner (1960). The personality profiles of entering cadets who had earned varsity letters in high school were compared with those cadets who had not been involved in high school athletics. These two groups were found to differ on 8 of the 16 variables. In a later study by Werner and Gottheil (1966) the 16PF was administered to freshman cadets classified as former high school athletes and nonathletes, and the two groups were found to differ on 7 of the 16 personality variables, which supports Werner's earlier report. The athletes and nonathletes in both investigations differed on factors A and H of the 16PF which are regarded as stable traits, and this suggests that observed differences in athletes and nonathletes probably existed from the outset. This hypothesis was tested by Werner and Gottheil who administered the 16PF to both groups again at the time of graduation and found the initial differences to still exist even though the former nonathletes had participated in "Academy athletics" for the intervening four-year period.

The Minnesota Multiphasic Personality Inventory (MMPI) was administered to high school athletes who had won letters in selected varsity sports, and their personality structure was compared with that of nonathletes from the same population by Slusher (1964). The athletes and nonathletes were found to differ on all of the MMPI scales except the hypomania and validity scales. Certain of the MMPI scales such as depression are responsive to various treatments, including physical activity, and therefore, it is not possible to evaluate whether or not involvement in sport was responsible for the observed differences. The important point is, however, that the athlete and nonathlete samples differed significantly on all but two of the MMPI variables.

Additional cross-sectional research by Schendel (1965) supports the observations of Slusher. In Schendel's study the California Psychological Inventory (CPI) was administered to athletes and nonathletes in grades 9 and 12 as well as college. The ninth grade, twelfth grade, and college athletes and nonathletes differed on 8, 4 and 9 of the CPI variables respectively. This study supports the view that athletes and nonathletes differ on selected personality traits, and it also suggests that such differences exist from the outset. This hypothesis was subsequently confirmed by Schendel (1970) in a longitudinal study.

If one is willing to grant that black and white children are generally raised in different socioeconomic settings (i.e., environment), the research of Hunt (1969) has particular relevance to the present discussion. Hunt administered the Gordon Personal Profile to black athletes and nonathletes as well as white athletes and nonathletes. The black and white athlete groups were found to possess similar personality profiles as did the nonathlete groups. The athletes, however, were found to differ significantly from the nonathletes, which suggests that the observed personality differences between such subgroups are independent of environmental forces.

Further support for the view that athletes and nonathletes differ on personality traits is provided by the research of Fletcher and Dowell (1971) who administered the Edwards Personal Preference Schedule (EPPS) to 950 males in the first year of college. These subjects were classified into groups who had participated in high school athletics and those who had not. The former athletes and nonathletes were found to differ on the dominance, aggression, and order scales of the EPPS.

In an attempt to evaluate the gravitation versus change hypothesis for explaining personality differences between athletes and nonathletes, Lukehart and Morgan (Note 1) administered the Junior Eysenck Personality Inventory (JEPI) to 33 junior high school boys who had never participated in organized athletics. The testing was carried out during the summer prior to the beginning of seventh grade and tryouts for the interscholastic football team. Twenty-one of these subjects elected to participate on the football team and 11 did not. Those subjects who elected to participate in football were significantly more extroverted than those who did not. The JEPI was administered to both groups at the conclusion of the season, and the initial difference persisted. Neither group changed on this particular personality trait as expected, and this pilot investigation supports a gravitation explanation of trait differences observed in athletes and nonathletes.

Further support for the view that personality differences between athletes and nonathletes are largely due to initial differences come from the work of Yanada and Hirata (1970). These investigators administered the Tokyo University Personality Inventory (TPI) to athletes in sport clubs at Tokyo University. Students who continued in their sport clubs were found to be less neurotic and depressive and more hypomanic than those students who discontinued.

It may be that low trait anxiety and neuroticism are prerequisites for success in athletics, and anxious or neurotic individuals simply avoid or drop out of athletics. At any rate, world-class wrestlers have been found to score lower than the population mean on a standard measure of neuroticism (Morgan, 1968), and college wrestlers have been found to score significantly lower than the population mean on anxiety (Morgan & Hammer, 1974). It has also been reported by Morgan and Costill (1972) that experienced marathon runners scored significantly lower than the population mean on depression and anxiety. More recent research by Morgan and Pollock (1977) demonstrates that elite runners, wrestlers, and rowers scored significantly lower than the population mean on trait anxiety, tension, and depression, and higher on psychic vigor. While not statistically significant in every case, these elite athletes were found to score lower on state anxiety, fatigue, confusion, neuroticism, and conformity (lie scale) and higher on extroversion and somatic perception.

Most of the research carried out in the field of sport personology has dealt with the male athlete. The limited research performed with female athletes, however, suggests that personality patterns of female athletes tend to differ from those of female nonathletes in much the same way that male athletes and nonathletes have been found to differ. Furthermore, personality differences between female athletes of differing ability levels tend to be comparable to those observed for male athletes. A recent review paper dealing entirely with the personality of the female athlete has been written by Williams (1978).

In one of the first publications dealing with female athletes it was reported by Peterson, Weber, and Trousdale (1967) that elite performers in team sports differed from those in individual sports on personality structure. The groups were found to differ on 7 of the 16 personality variables measured by the 16PF. Athletes from the individual sports were found to be more introverted than those from team sports, and both groups were characterized by emotional stability. The athletes from individual sports were also found to be more dominant and aggressive, adventurous, sensitive, imaginative, radical, self-sufficient, and resourceful and less sophisticated than the team sport athletes. Both groups were found to be more intelligent, conscientious, persevering, and aggressive than females of similar educational background and age.

A similar investigation was performed by Malumphy (1968) who administered the 16PF to female athletes who participated in sports classified as team, individual, team-individual, and subjectively judged. These athletes were found to differ from a random sample of nonathletes on a number of 16PF variables which is in agreement with the report of Peterson et al. (1967). The athlete groups were found to differ on a number of 16PF variables as well. One surprising observation was that individual sport athletes were found to be more extroverted than athletes from team and team-individual sports. Also, the team sport athletes were found to be less extroverted than the nonathlete sample (Malumphy, 1968). These findings are in disagreement with those of Peterson et al. (1967) as well as published literature involving the male athlete.

The apparent contradiction might be explained in several ways. First of all, Malumphy's study involved 77 female athletes and a random selection of 43 nonathletes from five state universities, and only one of the athletes could be regarded as world class. Peterson et al. evaluated elite female performers who had participated in the 1964 Olympics or played on nationally ranked AAU teams. Also, these elite athletes were compared with published norms in the study by Peterson et al.

The 16PF and the EPPS were administered to 30 female fencers who participated in the 1968 National Championships by Williams, Hoepner, Moody, & Ogilvie (1970). The successful and unsuccessful fencers were found to differ on dominance, but this was probably due to chance since the groups were similar on the remaining 38 variables. It was found, however, that these fencers differed from established norms on a number of the 16PF and EPPS variables. These fencers tended to be reserved, self-sufficient, autonomous, assertive, and aggressive, and they scored below the norm on nurturance and affiliation. There were actually 60 fencers involved in this tournament, and 45 of the participants volunteered to participate in the study. Fifteen of these volunteers did not actually follow through with their commitment. It is known that volunteers, pseudo-volunteers, and nonvolunteers differ on a number of psychological traits (Morgan, 1972b). Therefore, it is possible that failure to identify psychological differences between fencers of varying ability level in this study may have been mediated by a volunteerism effect.

It has been reported by Dayries and Grimm (1970) that female athletes engaged in intercollegiate basketball, volleyball, tennis, and track and field possess personality traits that are similar to Edwards' normative group. The 21 athletes evaluated in this study completed the Edwards Personal Preference Schedule (EPPS), and they were found to differ on two of the 15 personality traits, which led these investigators to conclude that as a group the women athletes could not be differentiated from the normative group. It should be noted that Edwards' normative group consisted of 749 college women who were enrolled in liberal arts classes at various colleges and universities. The athletes in the present sample (N = 21) represented ten academic disciplines, four sport groups, and a single institution. Furthermore, since means and standard deviations were not presented in the manuscript, it is difficult to accept the authors' position that the "women athletes could not be well differentiated from the normal group of college women" (p. 230). It is also probable that the normative group contained some athletes.

In a similar investigation the EPPS was administered to 21 women participating in team sports and 21 women involved in individual sports by Wendt and Patterson (1974). These investigations reported that no significant differences were found on any of the 15 personality variables measured by the EPPS. This report is difficult to interpret for several reasons. First of all, there is no reference to a statistical analysis, and therefore, the meaning of "no significant differences" is not clear. Second, mean data are presented for the two groups, but there are no variance estimates or associated probabilities. Third, the means presented for the two groups differ in all 15 cases. This report and the report by Dayries and Grimm (1970) suggest that the EPPS may not be a useful tool in attempting to discriminate between athletes and nonathletes or athletes from different subgroups. The sampling, design, and statistical problems associated with these studies, however, suggest that the apparent absence of significant differences should be viewed cautiously.

A comparison of personality traits of college female athletes and nonathletes has been reported by O'Connor and Webb (1976). These investigators administered Forms

A and B of the 16PF to 41 athletes involved in four intercollegiate sports and a control group of 14 nonparticipants. The results were totaled for the two tests, and the data were analyzed by means of a multivariate stepwise discriminant procedure. There is evidence that reliability (Cattell's dependability coefficient) improves when both forms are used. This procedure, while recommended (Karson & O'Dell, 1976), is seldom followed in sport psychology. O'Connor and Webb also employed raw test scores in their statistical analyses as recommended. Sport psychologists often convert raw scores to sten scores prior to conducting statistical analyses, and this reduces discriminant power. The five groups studied by O'Connor and Webb were found to differ on 4 of the 16 factors, but the sport groups tended to be more alike than unalike. The overall findings were generally in disagreement with earlier investigations involving female athletes. The control group in this study consisted of 14 female volunteers, and "only three of the subjects in this group had competed in any interscholastic athletics" (p. 205). The results of this investigation should be viewed with caution because of the sampling procedure employed, and the potential impact of volunteerism (Morgan, 1972a) is not addressed.

The personality traits of female athletes involved in individual sports (N = 30) and team sports (N = 30) have been compared to those of nonathletes (N = 30) by Stoner and Bandy (1977). The EPPS was administered to the three groups, and it was found that the two athlete groups did not differ on any of the 15 traits measured by the EPPS. These findings are in agreement with those of Wendt and Patterson (1974) who also used the EPPS. The athlete and nonathlete groups, however, were found to differ on 4 of the 15 EPPS scales. The nonathletes were observed to "have a higher need for intraception, change, and heterosexuality than subjects in team sports and participants in team sports have a higher need for deference" (p. 334). The nonparticipants were also found to have a higher "need for interception and change than individual sport females" (p. 334). These findings are in disagreement with those of Dayries and Grimm (1970), but it should be kept in mind that Edwards' normative group was used for comparative purposes by Dayries and Grimm.

These investigations of female athletes from different sport groups are difficult to interpret. There is clearly a potential problem relating to sampling procedure in all of the investigations reviewed. An earlier report by Lakie (1962) is particularly instructive in this regard. Lakie administered the Omnibus Personality Inventory (OPI) to 230 male athletes representing a state university, a private university, and two state colleges. These athletes were members of intercollegiate teams in basketball, football, tennis, golf, track, and wrestling. When the athletes from the four schools were grouped according to sport there were no differences in personality noted. Significant differences between sports were observed, however, when analyses were performed within schools. It was also found that certain sport groups not only differed from other sport groups at their respective schools, but they were found to also differ from the same sport groups at other institutions! These findings led Lakie (1962) to suggest: "Thus it may be that unique groups found in this study and other studies may be persons of similar characteristics being attracted to, or recruited for, specific athletic programs" (p. 572). Lakie's findings indicate that sampling procedures and inferences are linked in a very direct way. The comparison of small groups of athletes and nonathletes at a given institution restricts the development of meaningful inferential statements.

Comparisons of college athletes and nonathletes, or athletes from different sport groups, did not appear to be consistent in the literature dealing with females. This lack of consistency disappears, however, when the personality characteristics of the successful or elite female athlete are evaluated. Williams (1978), for example, has reported that low personality variation has been reported within specific sports, such as fencing, ice hockey, track, and lacrosse. It has also been reported by Williams that a random selection of girls and women involved in lacrosse has revealed that "players at all levels were characterized as more reserved, intelligent, independent, aggressive, and experimenting than the normative population" (p. 252). Since these characteristics existed across age levels, it appears that self-selection into sports may occur as a function of initial personality type. Williams states that selected personality traits are frequently associated with the elite female athlete and specifically, that "the successful female competitor generally tends to be more assertive, dominant, self-sufficient, independent, aggressive, intelligent, reserved, achievement oriented, and to have average to low emotionality" (p. 253).

It is also emphasized by Williams that longitudinal studies will be needed in order to accept or reject the "cause and effect" versus "gravitation" view of the above personality stereotype. Williams points out, however, that the "enduring and stable nature of personality traits would suggest that females have gravitated toward sport as a result of these personality traits rather than sport participation having altered the personality of the athlete" (p. 254).

A recent investigation by Bird (1979) offers support for Williams' proposal. A demographic questionnaire and the Children's Personality Questionnaire (CPQ) were administered to a select group (N = 17) of 8- to 11-year-old girls who participated in body-contact ice hockey. A comparison group of 44 boys, 8- to 11-year-old, who played competitive hockey in the same locale was also tested. The data were analyzed by means of a multivariate discriminant analysis, and the boys were found to be similar to their normative population. The girls, however, differed from the boys and their normative population. The girls were found to score significantly higher than the normative population on Factors F (enthusiastic) and I (tough-minded). The girls differed significantly from the boys on five factors, and tough-minded vs tender-minded scale (I) accounted for the greatest amount of the variance. The girls scored higher on Factor I, and this factor along with Factors F, O, A, and D, accounted for 64% of the variance between the two samples. Bird proposed that these girls, because of their age, were probably different prior to playing hockey, and concluded that the demonstrated self-selection lends credence to the hypothesis that "persons with certain personality configurations gravitate toward activities which they find most satisfying" (p. 972). This view is in agreement with the exploratory findings of Lukehart and Morgan (Note 1) involving young boys who elect to become involved in interscholastic football.

The preceding review indicates that athletes, males and females alike, have been observed to possess personality traits which often differ from those of nonathletes. There is also a trend for athletes from divergent sport groups to differ psychologically, but these differences have not been as consistent as those noted for comparisons of athletes and nonathletes. There has been an extensive debate in sport psychology concerning the extent to which athletes of differing ability level within a sport possess similar or different personality structures. The prior review dealing with the personality traits of female athletes suggests that successful competitors possess unique personality traits. Similar research involving the male athlete will now be reviewed.

In one of the earliest investigations dealing with ability levels, LaPlace (1954) administered the MMPI to 49 major league players and 64 minor league baseball players. The major league players served as the successful group, and these athletes were found to score significantly lower than the minor league players on the schizophrenia and psychopathic deviate scales of the MMPI. The successful players possessed better adjustment than the unsuccessful players, as expected. These observed differences may have existed prior to each group's entrance into professional baseball, or they may reflect the overall impact of differential success patterns.

The Eysenck Personality Inventory (EPI) was administered to participants in the 1966 World Tournament approximately 24 hours prior to initiation of competition, and athletes with high lie scores as measured by the EPI were not included in the analysis (Morgan, 1968). Success in the tournament was significantly correlated ($r = .50$) with extroversion in this study. In other words, the introverted wrestlers did not perform as well as the extroverted wrestlers. Critics of trait theory often point out correlations of this magnitude are of little predictive value. This, of course, is true since a correlation of .50 only accounts for 25% of the variance. A counter argument is that a personality trait such as extroversion, when employed in concert with other psychological states and traits and/or physiological parameters, will contribute significantly to prediction effectiveness.

In an earlier review Kane (1964) reported that athletic ability was correlated with stable and extroverted personality structure as opposed to neuroticism and introversion. Kane also reported that among those athletes of high physical ability the only ones to achieve high performance standards under competitive conditions are those who score high on the trait of extroversion. This study supports the efficacy of utilizing multidimensional models in attempting to predict athletic performance.

A personality theory designed to measure enduring personality traits should be effective in predicting behavior in various settings, and Eysenckian theory seems to possess this ability. Its effectiveness has been demonstrated in nonathletic settings as well as the athletic situations described by Kane (1964) and Morgan (1968). The relationship between swimming ability and personality, for example, has been investigated by Whiting and Stembridge (1965) who administered the Maudsley Personality Inventory (MPI) and the Junior Maudsley Personality Inventory (JMPI) to college and 11-12 year old males respectively. The MPI and the JMPI are predecessors of the EPI and the JEPI mentioned earlier. Comparisons of personality structure were made between students who had previously received swimming instruction, but were still able to swim (i.e., persistent nonswimmers), and those students who had never received prior swimming instruction. The persistent nonswimmers in the college sample were significantly more introverted than the other nonswimmers. The boys classified as persistent nonswimmers were significantly more introverted and neurotic than the other nonswimmers in their age group. These findings are in agreement with derivations and predictions from Eysenckian theory. These findings were replicated by Behrman (1967) who defined "persistent nonswimmers" as "nonlearners." The nonlearners in Behrman's investigation were found to be introverted and neurotic. These investigations demonstrate the effectiveness of a general trait theory (Eysenckian) to predict behavior in a learning situation. The accuracy of such prediction would probably be facilitated if physiologic parameters such as body density, percent body fat, or lean body mass were included in the equation. At any rate, these investigations demonstrate the potential application of a trait theory in both athletic and physical education settings.

It should be noted at this point that all trait theories have not been effective in predicting behavior or in discriminating between athletes of differing ability levels. Kroll (1967, 1970), Kroll and Carlson (1967), and Rushall (1970) have presented evidence indicating that Cattell's 16PF has not been effective in discriminating between athletes differing in ability level. One possible explanation for the failure of these investigators to demonstrate personality differences between such criterion groups relates to their decision not to employ distortion scales of the type recommended for use with the 16PF (Karson & O'Dell, 1976).

A second possible explanation for the negative results frequently reported in 16PF research relates to the preference of investigators for use of first order factors. Kane (1970), for example, found that groups differing in physical ability were comparable when 16PF analyses were limited to first order factors. Kane's analysis of the second order factors from the 16PF, however, revealed that a relationship between physical ability and personality did exist.

It is of interest that extroversion was the most important and consistent second order factor observed in Kane's research. This finding provides indirect support for Eysenckian theory since the extroversion score yielded by the EPI is comparable to the extroversion construct derived as a second order factor from Cattell's 16PF. This research further supports the view that general trait theory is useful in discriminating between athletes of different ability levels.

A mental health model has been found to be effective in predicting success in athletics, and the model specifies that psychopathology and success are inversely proportional. The converse, success and positive mental health, are viewed as directly proportional. The actual extent to which this model has been accurate in predicting success and failure has been outlined in several papers (Morgan, 1978a, 1979; Morgan & Johnson, 1977; Morgan & Pollock, 1977). The model predicts that an athlete who is neurotic, anxious, depressed, schizoid, introverted, confused, fatigued, and scores low on psychic vigor will tend to be unsuccessful in comparison to an athlete who is characterized by the absence of such traits. While such a model does not appear to be very provocative, it should be recalled that many sport psychologists argue that trait theory is not effective in predicting behavior. The mental health model, however, possesses theoretical parsimony. It is based upon an extensive body of knowledge from both clinical and sport psychology, its efficacy is easily tested, and preliminary research suggests that it is effective in predicting performance in selected sport settings. An overview of the model's empirical support follows.

In the first investigation the MMPI was administered to 81 University of Wisconsin wrestlers during the first week of school. The wrestlers represented five successive freshman classes, and the varsity careers of these 81 wrestlers were evaluated four years later in order to psychologically characterize the successful and unsuccessful athletes from the outset of their respective competitive careers. A stepwise discriminant function analysis, based upon the initial MMPI profiles, revealed that psychological differences existed from the outset. Those wrestlers who went on to enjoy successful careers (2-3 varsity letters) were found to possess more desirable mental health in comparison with those who were unsuccessful (0-1 varsity letter).

It was possible to evaluate the 40 candidates for the 1972 U.S. Olympic Wrestling Team prior to the final wrestle-off which consisted of a round-robin tournament held over a three day period. Selected psychological states and traits were evaluated in these candidates on the evening preceding the first day of the tournament (Nagle et al., 1975). A stepwise discriminant function analysis yielded a multiple R of 0.67, and the conformity scale of the Eysenck Personality Inventory (EPI) was found to be the strongest predictor followed by tension. Tension, along with depression, anger, fatigue, and confusion, was evaluated by means of the Profile of Mood States (POMS).

The 16 finalists for the 1976 U.S. Olympic Team were also evaluated with the same psychological inventories prior to the final wrestle-offs. Two of the wrestlers who actually earned berths on the 1976 U.S. Wrestling Team elected not to participate in the study. Hence, the successful and unsuccessful groups consisted of eight wrestlers. All of the differences favored the successful group in terms of positive mental health. Lower anxiety and higher psychic vigor in the successful wrestlers were the most notable distinctions. These findings support the view that positive mental health is a correlate of success in athletics, and this observation holds even with the homogeneous setting of an Olympic camp.

Data from the Profile of Mood States (POMS) for the 1972 and 1976 U.S. Olympic Wrestling Teams were compared. It will be noted that these teams are remarkably similar on each variable. The author has previously referred to this profile as the "iceberg profile" since these elite athletes score below the 50th T-Score (surface) on tension, depression, fatigue, and confusion, and above the 50th T-Score (surface) on vigor in comparison with published norms for individuals of comparable age and educational background. The unsuccessful wrestlers in these trials were found to score at or near the 50th T-Score by comparison. It should be emphasized that the iceberg profile describing these elite wrestlers was found to exist at the outset of a three-day tournament designed to select the final team members. Since such a setting is presumably stressful, it is noteworthy that these elite performers were characterized by positive affect.

In a related investigation the MMPI was administered to 50 college oarsmen during the first week of their freshman year. The athletic records of these rowers were identified four years later in order to permit psychological characterization of the successful (2-3 varsity letters) and unsuccessful (0-1 varsity letter) rowers from the outset of their respective careers. The successful group was found to possess more favorable scores on each of the eight clinical scales of the MMPI (Morgan & Johnson, 1978). These findings offer further support for the view that successful athletes possess more desirable psychological traits than do unsuccessful athletes and furthermore, these differences appear to exist from the outset of each group's career.

It was possible to further test the efficacy of the mental health model with elite rowers. Fifty-seven candidates for the 1975 U.S. Heavyweight Rowing Team were evaluated psychologically prior to the initiation of final training and selection for the 1974 team. The initial selection process consisted of eliminating 41 of these candidates and retaining 16 for the intensive training program scheduled to follow. Using data derived from the earlier MMPI study involving rowers, an attempt was made to predict success and failure. These predictions were made in a blind setting, and comparisons with actual selections were not made until the selection process was completed. The details of this prediction procedure are outlined in a recent paper (Morgan, 1979). The prediction model was accurate in 41 of the 57 cases, and 10 of the 16 finalists were correctly identified in advance. The clinical predictions were performed a priori, and they did not differ from a post hoc statistical analysis. In other words, the a priori (clinical) and post hoc (statistical) models were equally accurate (i.e., 70%). The accuracy of this prediction model was also confirmed in a subsequent camp involving the 1974 U.S. Lightweight Rowing Team. Both heavyweight and lightweight teams were found to possess the iceberg profile previously described for elite wrestlers (Morgan & Johnson, 1977).

Subsequent research involving elite distance runners (Morgan & Pollock, 1977) reveals that the iceberg profile also characterizes this sport group. The psychological profiles for these elite distance runners, along with those for elite rowers and wrestlers were compared. It will be noted that these elite athletes were more alike than unalike. These elite performers scored significantly lower than the general population on trait anxiety (Morgan, 1979; Morgan & Pollock, 1977), and this probably explains their low scores on tension when exposed to the stress characteristic of an Olympic selection camp.

It is noteworthy that a broad measure of trait anxiety (STAI) permits one to predict a state-like property such as tension (POMS). While these elite athletes were observed to score above the population mean on the extroversion variable, they were not significantly more extroverted than the published norm. It is also of importance to note that these elite distance runners were remarkably similar to the elite wrestlers on the extroversion variable (Morgan & Pollock, 1977) which contradicts the earlier work of Morgan (1968) and Morgan and Costill (1972). Since the same instrumentation was employed in these investigations, and since athletes of comparable caliber were involved, it is possible that the personality structure of the distance runner has changed over the past decade. At any rate, the common view that distance runners tend to score low on extroversion is not supported by the recent work of Morgan and Pollock.

The research reviewed in this section reveals that athletes differ from nonathletes on a variety of psychological states and traits, and these differences become most noticeable when the elite performer is considered. There is less agreement concerning differences in the psychological characteristics of athletes differing in ability level. Again, however, psychological differences are consistently demonstrated where response distortion is considered, and the data are analyzed by means of multivariate as opposed to univariate procedures. This research, however, consistently leaves 50-75% of the variance in performance or group discrimination unexplained. It would not be appropriate, therefore, to rely on a state, trait, or state-trait model (narrow or broad) alone in attempting to predict behavior. It is quite obvious that numerous physiological variables, for example, play a profound role in sport performance. It is also possible that additional psychological models may be useful in accounting for a significant portion of the unexplained variance. More specifically, it appears that cognitive, perceptual, or perceptual-cognitive models may prove to be equally or more effective, and this possibility is explored in the following section.

Perception and Cognition

Sport psychologists have always been concerned with "perceptual" variables to some extent, and this probably stems from the crucial role of perception in motor behavior. There has been very little attention paid to "cognitive" variables, however, and this is unfortunate since cognition obviously plays an important role in sport and physical activity. There is evidence that applications from the field of cognitive psychology may have relevance in the study of sport psychology. Mahoney and Avener (1977), for example, studied 13 male gymnasts during the final trials for the U.S. Olympic team. The final qualifying meet was designed to select the six gymnasts and one alternate for the 1976 U.S. Olympic team. The 13 gymnasts completed a standardized questionnaire 48 hours prior to the final selection. The questionnaire was designed to measure various aspects of personality, strategies employed in competition and training, and self-concept. Selected items dealt with the frequency of dreams about gymnastics, use of mental imagery, and "the kinds of private monologues they experienced during competition" (p. 136). Those gymnasts who earned berths on the Olympic team were found to differ from those who did not on measures of dream frequency, self-verbalizations, and certain forms of mental imagery. It was also found that the two groups manifested different anxiety patterns as well as different cognitive strategies in their attempts to cope with competitive stress. The successful performers were more anxious prior to competition, but this pattern was reversed during the crucial moments of competition.

Mahoney and Avener also conducted verbal interviews and found that the successful gymnasts tended "to use their anxiety as a stimulant to better performance" (p. 140). These investigators proceeded to raise questions of whether or not training and practice in "internal" imagery might improve athletic performance. This approach to the study of sport psychology makes the assumption that athletes are "cognitively active" during the precompetitive and competitive settings. Furthermore, without invoking trait theory (narrow or broad), this investigation demonstrates that behavior is correlated with cognition. Behavior is mediated to a large degree by one's perception, but whether or not traits mediate perception upon which cognition is based remains uncertain. It is clear, however, that perception can be "redefined" or "reinterpreted" by means of selected cognitive strategies. Several selected perceptual-cognitive issues will be considered in this section.

Perceptual Styles

It has been reported by Ryan and Kovacic (1966) that a significant relationship exists between an individual's pain tolerance and selection of athletic activity. In this investigation athletes who participated in contact sports (e.g., football and wrestling) were found to possess greater pain tolerance than did athletes who participated in noncontact sports (e.g., golf and tennis). Furthermore, the noncontact athletes were found to possess greater pain tolerance than did nonathletes. These observations led to the hypothesis that differences in augmentation-reduction, a perceptual trait, might account for the differences. This hypothesis was based on the view that certain "types" seem to consistency *reduce*, whereas others are found to consistently *augment* the intensity of their perceptions (Petrie, 1960). According to Ryan and Foster (1967) individuals who consistently reduce the intensity of their perceptions following stimulation are more extroverted, mesomorphic, and tolerant of pain, and judge time as passing more slowly than do augmenters. These investigators have also noted that the reducer's characteristics are often associated with involvement in athletics. Indeed, mesomorphy along with the ability to tolerate pain or discomfort appears to be a prerequisite for success in many sports.

The report by Ryan and Kovacic (1966) demonstrates that pain tolerance of contact athletes was significantly higher than that of noncontact athletes who in turn scored higher on pain tolerance than did nonathletes. Differences of this nature might reflect (1) the effect of involvement in sport, or (2) initial differences that resulted in reducers gravitating toward contact sports. The theoretical conceptualization of perceptual style advanced by Petrie (1960) would support the latter argument since augmentation-reduction is viewed as a trait. The gravitation argument in sport has been described in earlier papers (Morgan, 1972b), and this view has received support for both female (Bird, 1979; Williams, 1978) and male (Kane, 1978; Nideffer, 1978) athletes.

In terms of the augmentation-reduction issue in particular, Ryan and Foster (1967) have presented additional evidence in support of the trait or gravitational view. Their research involved a comparison of contact athletes (football, wrestling) noncontact athletes (golf, tennis, track), and nonathletes. These groups judged a standard bar of 1.5 inch width to be 1.67 (contact athletes), 1.69 (noncontact athletes), and 1.66 (nonathletes) inches prior to stimulation. Following 300 seconds of stimulation the contact athletes estimated the bar to be .258 inches less, the noncontact athletes judged it to be .213 inches less, and the nonathletes judged the bar's width to be essentially the same (i.e., .095 inches less). These differences were statistically significant ($p < .01$), and they support the view that contact athletes are perceptual reducers.

It would be predicted that the contact athletes in the above study would score higher on pain tolerance for two reasons. First, earlier research by Ryan and Kovacic (1966) demonstrated higher pain tolerance in contact athletes, and second, one characteristic of the reducer is high pain tolerance. In the study by Ryan and Foster (1967) a plastic, aluminum-tipped football cleat was fitted to the anterior border of the tibia midway between the ankle and knee. A standard blood pressure cuff was placed around the leg at this point, and it was then inflated with the effect that the cleat created pressure on the tibia. The subject signaled when he could no longer tolerate the experience, and pain tolerance was measured in millimeters of mercury registered on the sphygmomanometer. The pain tolerance for the contact athletes averaged 286 mmHg and this value was significantly higher than the mean response for the noncontact athletes (231 mmHg), which in turn was higher than the mean pain tolerance for the nonathlete group (208 mmHg). Ryan and Foster (1967) stated: "The results of this study clearly support Petrie's theory of a generalized tendency for certain individuals to consistently reduce or diminish their perception of stimulation and for others to consistently augment or enlarge perceptions" (p. 475).

The research findings of Ryan and Kovacic (1966) and Ryan and Foster (1967) are significant for several reasons. First, their research has been carried out within a theoretical framework, and very little research in sport psychology has utilized a theoretical approach. Second, their work involves one of the few attempts in sport psychology to perform an extension and replication of initial research. It should also be noted that the replication was not only successful, but represented a logical extension of the first experiment. Third, the results support the efficacy of employing trait measures in sport psychology; that is, certain individuals were consistently found to behave in a predictable way (reduce or augment). A fourth reason why their research should be regarded as significant is that those authors who have adopted a skeptical view in sport personology do not cite the work of Ryan and Kovacic or Ryan and Foster. This is rather surprising since their work involving pain tolerance and augmentation-reduction represents, without question, two of the most significant experiments in the field of sport psychology. It is conceivable that this research has been ignored by skeptical authors simply because it supports the trait psychology view. It is also possible that skeptical authors are simply unaware of this research. While errors of omission are often regarded as not being as serious as those of commission, the effect of such errors appears to be comparable.

The reports of Petrie, Ryan and Kovacic, and Ryan and Foster indicate that perception of painful stimuli is mediated in part by the individual's perceptual style; that is, perceptual reducers possess greater pain tolerance than do perceptual augmenters. It has also been reported that the perceptual trait known as field dependence-independence plays a role in the perception of pain. Sweeney and Fine (1965), for example, have reported that pain tolerance is greater in field independent subjects. It has also been reported that extroverts possess greater pain tolerance than do introverts, and neurotic individuals score lower on pain tolerance than do stable individuals (Lynn & Eysenck, 1961). It is noteworthy, therefore, that Kane (1964, 1970, 1978) has demonstrated that extroversion and stability are two personality traits that play a role in athletic performance.

The research reviewed in this section reveals that individuals who possess the traits known as perceptual reduction, field independence, extroversion, and stability consistently score higher on measures of pain tolerance than do individuals classified as perceptual augmenters, neurotics, introverts, or field dependent. It is often argued, however, that person variables of this type only account for a small portion of the total variance and this argument has often been extended in one of two directions in sport psychology. Straub (1977), for example, discusses the relative efficacy of the person, situation, and interaction of person by situation models, and the predominant theme seems to support an interactionism approach. Kane (1978) has pointed out that such an approach was actually proposed many years ago, and it reflects the essence of Lewinian field theory. Another prominent argument has been that general traits such as extroversion, neuroticism, and trait anxiety be replaced by traits that are specific to sport. This point of view has been advanced by authors such as Martens (1977) and Rushall (1975).

Morgan and Horstman (1978) performed a series of experiments using the pain stimulator developed by Forgione and Barber (1971), in an attempt to evaluate the extent to which selected psychological states, traits, and the interaction of states and traits could be used in predicting pain perception. Psychophysical judgments were obtained from volunteer test subjects every 15 seconds during a 2 minute period in which a 3,000 gm. force was presented on the periosteum of the left forefinger's second digit. The test-retest correlations ranged from .65 to .84 for this procedure, indicating that it possessed "trait-like" qualities. In the first experiment, it was found that perception of pain was significantly correlated with psychological traits such as extroversion, field dependence, and trait anxiety. The multiple correlations ranged from .57 to .72 indicating that psychological traits (i.e., person variables) accounted for 32-52% of the variance in predicting perception of pain.

Sport psychologists who are opposed to the use of general traits point out that such models leave 50-70% of the variance unexplained, and therefore, situation-specific instruments must be employed to account for more of the unexplained variance. An equally tenable argument is that personality variables, trait or state (general or narrow), should not be expected to account for more than 30 to 50% of the variance since other variables such as birth order, ethnic origin, and athleticism have all been reported to influence perception of pain.

A second experiment was conducted by Morgan and Horstman (1978) in an attempt to cross-validate the above observations. Significant multiple regressions ranging from .62 to .68 were observed, but psychological states (e.g., depression and vigor) as well as traits (e.g., extroversion) entered the prediction equations. The important point is that general or broad measures were able to account for 38-46% of the variance. These findings presumably have relevance to the field of sport psychology since perception and tolerance of pain appears to influence involvement in athletics (Ryan & Kovacic, 1966; Ryan & Foster, 1967).

Cognitive Strategies

Rather than study traits, narrow or broad, it might be more fruitful to evaluate the cognitive processes of athletes as they actually perform. This can be accomplished by means of hypnotic age regression (Morgan, 1980), visuo-motor behavior rehearsal (Suinn, 1978), or conscious recall in the waking state (Mahoney & Avener, 1977). It seems reasonably clear, for example, that endurance performance is governed by both an individual's physical capacity, as well as his or her willingness to tolerate pain and discomfort. The finishers in a marathon (42.2 km), for example, often have times ranging from 2 hours and 12 minutes to 4 or 5 hours. These observations indicate that individuals differ substantially in their capacity, and a certain portion of the observed difference is undoubtedly due to their willingness to tolerate the discomfort associated with running such distances. It is also known that successful marathon runners perform at approximately 75% of their maximal aerobic power (MAP), and the actual range is about 64-90% of maximum (Morgan & Pollock, 1977).

The decision to perform at a rate of 85% of one's MAP versus 65%, however, represents more than mere willingness. It is known, for example, that some runners produce large amounts of lactate while running at 75% of their MAP, whereas others are able to run the 42.2 km at a pace averaging 90% of their MAP, and little lactate accumulation occurs in these runners (Milvy, 1977). In other words, the decision to compete at 65% vs 90% of one's MAP involves more than willingness alone. This decision is largely mediated by physiologic traits rather than psychologic traits, narrow or general. It has been noted, however, that substantial differences exist in the perceptual-cognitive styles of runners, and these observations will now be reviewed.

The predominant cognitive strategy employed by many marathon runners studied by Morgan (1978b) was found to be dissociative in nature. That is, a large number of marathoners cope with the pain and discomfort arising during marathons by imagining that they are not actually running. In other words, rather than pay attention to the sensory feedback received from the working muscles, lungs, and so on, the runner purposely attempts not to attend to such information.

This particular cognitive strategy presumably assists the runner in coping with pain and discomfort. In many respects this involves a form of self-hypnosis, and it is associated with both benefits and risks. First, by means of dissociating sensory input the runner may be able to negotiate a difficult segment of a race, and it is possible that performance gains as high as 30% can result (Morgan, 1978b). This process, however, can lead to bone fractures, heat stress, heat exhaustion, and complete mental disorientation involving visual, auditory, and kinesthetic hallucinations. In other words, adoption of a dissociation strategy must be viewed in terms of a cost-benefit ratio.

It is of considerable theoretic and practical importance that elite or world-class marathoners do not characteristically employ a dissociation strategy during competition. Elite runners have been found to employ a cognitive strategy known as association (Morgan & Pollock, 1977). In other words, rather than purposely cutting himself or herself off from sensory input, the elite runner attempts to constantly monitor respiration, temperature, heaviness in the calves and thighs, neck and shoulder tightness, and so on. Rather, than diverting attention from his or her body by "playing mind games," the elite runner pays close attention to all relevant sensory input, and a conscious effort is made to "stay loose," "relax," not "tie up," and so on.

A comparison of outstanding college runners with elite, world-class runners revealed that the two groups differed substantially in their physiological responses while running at 10 mph on a treadmill, but their effort sense or perceived exertion did not differ (Morgan & Pollock, 1977). The two groups were performing at approximately 68% (elite) and 82% (college runners) of their MAP at this pace. While running at this speed the college runner had an exercise heart rate that was approximately 15 bpm higher ($p < .001$), and this group's ventilatory minute volume exceeded that of the elite runner by an average value of approximately 20 liters/min ($p < .001$). In other words, the college runners were performing far more work, but they judged it to be no more effortful than did the elite runners. It is also noteworthy that these elite runners were found to consume significantly less oxygen than the college runners at a given treadmill speed. These differences were small but statistically significant. Extension of such differences across 150 minutes, however, could be physiologically significant as well. It is also quite possible that consciously attempting to relax (i.e., not "tie up") may represent the basis for this difference.

Use of a dissociation strategy carries with it the possibility of trauma (e.g., bone fractures, heat stress). While this strategy can result in performance gains at times, it can also result in performance decrements. The runner who chooses to dissociate essentially adopts a "buy-now-pay-later" model, whereas the associator operates in a "buy-now-pay-now" mode. Hence the associator is not confronted with the payment of debts throughout the run, but rather, he or she negotiates the course in an economical steady state. The dissociator by contrast runs unevenly and is found to (1) overextend, (2) slow down and repay the debt, (3) overextend, and so on, in a cyclic pattern. This is clearly not the most economical mode.

But why do elite runners associate? Is this a trait they possess from the outset of their career? Can nonelite dissociators be taught to associate? If dissociators begin to associate during competition will they become more successful? The answers to these questions await further research, and these questions are all readily testable. It is also well documented that some of the crucial ingredients for success in the marathon such as maximal aerobic power, somatotype, and muscle fiber type are governed in large measure by genetic influences (Milvy, 1977). In other words, it may be that elite runners associate because they can afford the "luxury" of this cognitive style whereas mediocre runners cannot, and hence must dissociate.

It appears that study of perceptual styles or adoption of models based upon cognitive psychology offers far more promise for the future than trait psychology does, and this view is intended to hold for both narrow (specific) and broad (general) measures. One of the unfortunate by-products of the "person-situation-interaction" argument in sport psychology has been that it has impaired the orderly progress of this young, perhaps embryonic, field.

At any rate, it is not time to completely abandon trait psychology (broad or narrow); it is time to move forward, adopt new research strategies, and use trait psychology if it has a place. Selected personality traits clearly influence the performance of complex physical activities in stressful situations (Morgan, Note 2). The extent to which personality traits are effective in predicting performance in hostile environments, however, is usually governed by the question being asked.

Summary

The efficacy of trait theory in predicting behavior has been debated by sport psychologists for the past decade. On the occasion of the Second International Congress of Sport Psychology held in 1968, for example, Kane[1] (1970) presented data in support of the view that personality traits "can account for approximately 20% of the variance in sports participation rating among both men (R = 0.44) and women (R – 0.44)" (p. 137). It was reported by Rushall (1970) at this same congress that "personality is not a significant factor in sport performance" (p. 164). During the

[1]Kane's presentation has obviously influenced sport psychologists in a differential manner. Those of us who attended the Second International Congress of Sport Psychology will recall that a prominent sport psychologist from the U.S. periodically turned the lights on and off during Kane's presentation because his allotted time had presumably expired. It will also be recalled that Kane fell off the back of the stage during one of these episodes, and his response to the audience following his recovery was "And, for my second act . . .!" This presentation, in more ways than one, reinforced the importance of neuroticism-stability and extroversion-introversion in the mediation of behavior, and it is unfortunate that the written and spoken word often possess different impacts.

decade that followed, several sport psychologists presented evidence in support of Kane's position whereas an equal number have argued that Rushall's view is correct.

The present review has involved an attempt to describe the nature of this controversy. The controversy is best explained at a methodological level, and it appears reasonable to conclude that sport psychologists who have adopted the skeptical or credulous position are equally wrong. That is, various personality traits have consistently been observed to account for 20% to 45% of the variance in sport performance. In other words, to argue that trait theory should be abandoned (skeptical view) is no more appropriate than arguing that trait theory is a precise predictor of behavior in sport settings (credulous view).

It is probably time to discontinue the argument about the value of trait theory in predicting behavior. Trait theory is clearly of limited value where one is interested in the description, explanation, and prediction of behavior. If continued progress is to be made in sport psychology, however, it will be necessary to employ other models that may or may not rely on broad traits. Any dependent variable that accounts for 20-45% of the variance should theoretically be useful in predicting behavior if utilized in concert with other dependent measures.

In addition to employing narrow (specific) versus broad (general) traits, it is also clear that a multidimensional model consisting of psychological states and physiological variables will consistently account for more of the unexplained variance. It is also apparent that models which incorporate cognitive-perceptual variables, states or traits, possess useful explanatory dimensions.

In order for advances in the field of sport psychology to occur it is imperative that investigators pay careful attention to various methodological issues of the type identified in the early portion of this review. Another important problem has been identified by Shaver (1979) who noted that a large portion of educational research is performed by graduate students, and the "majority of educational researchers never report more than one study" (p. 6). Replication is almost nonexistent in sport psychology, and much of our existing research has been reported by investigators whom Shaver has labeled as "one-study researchers." Systematic, on-going research efforts must become the rule rather than the exception if sport psychology is to advance. The essential element of almost every major advance in science has been replication.

Several years ago Dunnette (1966) published a paper titled "Fads, Fashions, and Folderol in Psychology." This title could be changed to read "in sport psychology" and the remedy for the controversy and confusion in sport psychology would then be available. Dunnette advocated a "more systematic study of lawful relationships *before* interpretations are attempted" (p. 350). A second recommendation advanced by Dunnette was the stating and systematic testing of multiple hypotheses, and this view derives from Platt's *Strong Inference* (Platt, 1965). Dunnette concluded this stimulating paper with a plea for "fewer disputes, a spirit of more open cooperation, greater innovation in the generation and testing of working hypotheses, greater care and precision in the development of theoretical formulations, and increased rigor . . ." (p. 351). This plea should have currency for the contemporary scholar in sport psychology.

It has also been proposed by Bass (1974) that good technology may be a prerequisite for the advancement of science. There does not appear to be a sound technology in sport psychology at present, and this will not change unless replication becomes a way of life. It is emphasized by Bass that good scientific *theory* (the shadow) may be one of the most practical methods for advancing *technology* (the substance). Bass qualifies this view, however, by noting that "nothing may be as impractical as bad theory" (p. 870). The few theories adopted by sport psychologists have tended to be bad theories. They have been bad in the sense that they were not intended for use in sport psychology. Hence, it is little wonder that they have not been effective. The field of sport psychology, with a few exceptions, has lacked theoretical inquiry as well as an established technology. If the sport psychologist does not build a technology (the substance) it is unlikely that good theories will emerge. Technology and theory, therefore, should not be viewed as mutually exclusive, but rather, they should be thought of as interdependent. Kane (1978) has noted that our understanding of behavior in sport settings will not be enhanced "by the facile shifting of theoretical perspectives to accommodate all the contemporary moods and 'minitheories' in psychology" (p. 236). This appears, unfortunately, to be precisely what has often occurred in sport psychology.

Most investigators have played some role in development of the methodology they are employing, and this results in ego-involvement. Indeed, because of this ego-involvement it is difficult to even question the utility of one's methodology. It is also very difficult to break free of accepted beliefs in order to gain perspective (Platt, 1964; Shaver, 1979). In other words, it is hard to break out of an established *zeitgeist*, and yet, that is precisely what is needed in sport psychology. A technology must be established; replication must become a way of life; complex multivariate analyses should continue, but we must also become tolerant of the "single-subject" study of behavior; methodological rigor must become routine; our work must be guided by theory, but we must not lock ourselves into static or premature theory; and finally, the questions we ask should govern the methodology we adopt—we must not permit our methodology to structure the questions we ask.

We must all consider "dropping-out" of our respective camps, "lay back," gain perspective, and strive toward the development of community in sport psychology where scholars attempt to share ideas about description, explanation, and prediction of behavior in sport settings. It is never easy to break out of a *zeitgeist*, but the spirit of the times must change before sport psychology can advance.

Reference Notes

1. Lukehart, R., & Morgan, W. P. *The effect of a season of interscholastic football on the personality of junior high school males.* Paper presented at the Annual Convention of the American Association for Health, Physical Education, and Recreation, Boston, 1969.
2. Morgan, W. P. *Psychological problems associated with the use of industrial respirators: A review.* Technical Report, Respirator Test Section, Los Alamos Scientific Laboratory, Los Alamos, 1979.

References

Bass, M.D. The substance and the shadow. *American Psychologist,* 1974, *33*, 870-886.

Behrman, R. M. Personality differences between nonswimmers and swimmers. *Research Quarterly,* 1967, *38,* 163-171.

Bird, E. I. Multivariate personality analysis of two children's hockey teams. *Perceptual and Motor Skills,* 1979, *48,* 967-973.

Cooper, L. Athletics, activity, and personality: A review of the literature. *Research Quarterly,* 1969, *40,* 17-22.

Dayries, J. L., & Grimm, R. L. Personality traits of women athletes as measured by the Edwards Personal Preference Schedule. *Perceptual and Motor Skills,* 1970, *30,* 229-230.

Dishman, R. K., Ickes, W., & Morgan, W. P. Self-motivation and adherence to habitual physical activity. *Journal of Applied Social Psychology* (in press).

Dunnette, M. D. Fads, fashions, and folderol in psychology. *American Psychologist,* 1966, *21,* 343-352.

Fletcher, R., & Dowell, L. Selected personality characteristics of high school athletes and nonathletes. *Journal of Psychology,* 1971, 77, 39-41.

Forgione, A. G., & Barber, T. X. A strain gauge stimulator. *Psychophysiology,* 1971, *8*, 102-106.

Harlow, R. G. Masculine inadequacy and compensatory development of physique. *Journal of Personality,* 1951, *19,* 312-323.

Henry, F. M. Personality differences in athletes, physical education, and aviation students. *Psychological Bulletin,* 1941, *38*, 745.

Henry, F. M. Increased response latency for complicated movements and a "memory drum" theory of neuromotor reaction. *Research Quarterly,* 1960, *31,* 448-458.

Hogan, R., DeSoto, C. B., & Solano, C. Traits, tests, and personality research. *American Psychologist,* 1977, *32,* 255-264.

Hunt, D. H. A cross racial comparison of personality traits between athletes and nonathletes. *Research Quarterly,* 1969, *40,* 704-707.

Irvine, M. J., & Gendreau, P. Detection of the fake "good" and "bad" response on the sixteen personality factor inventory in prisoners and college students. *Journal of Consulting and Clinical Psychology,* 1974, *42,* 465-466.

Johnson, W. R., Hutton, D. C., & Johnson, G. B. Personality traits of some champion athletes as measured by two projective tests: The Rorschach and H-T-P. *Research Quarterly,* 1954, *25,* 484-485.

Kane, J. E. Psychological correlates of physique and physical abilities. In E. Jokl & E. Simon (Eds.), *International research in sport and physical education.* Springfield, Ill.: Charles C Thomas, 1964. Pp. 85-94.

Kane, J. E. Personality and physical abilities. In G. S. Kenyon (Ed.), *Contemporary psychology of sport.* Chicago: Athletic Institute, 1970.

Kane, J. E. Personality research: The current controversy and implications for sports studies. In W. F. Straub (Ed.), *Sport psychology: An analysis of athlete behavior.* Ithaca: Mouvement Publications, 1978. Pp. 228-240.

Karson, S., & O'Dell, J. W. *A guide to the clinical use of the 16PF.* Champaign: Institute for Personality and Ability Testing, 1976.

Kenyon, G. S. (Ed.). *Contemporary psychology of sport: Proceedings of the Second International Congress.* Chicago: Athletic Institute, 1970.

Kroll, W. Sixteen personality factor profiles of collegiate wrestlers. *Research Quarterly,* 1967, *38,* 49-57.

Kroll, W. Personality assessments of athletes. In L. E. Smith (Ed.), *Psychology of motor learning.* Chicago: Athletic Institute, 1970. Pp. 349-367.

Kroll, W. Reaction to Morgan's paper: Psychological consequences of vigorous physical activity and sport. In M. G. Scott (Ed.), *The Academy papers.* Iowa City: American Academy of Physical Education, 1976.

Kroll, W. The stress of high performance athletics. In P. Klavora & J. V. Daniel (Eds.), *Coach, athlete, and the sport psychologist.* Champaign: Human Kinetics Publishers, 1979.

Kroll, W., & Carlson, R. B. Discriminant function and hierarchical grouping analysis of karate participants' personality profiles. *Research Quarerly,* 1967, *38,* 405-411.

Lakie, W. L. Personality characteristics of certain groups of intercollegiate athletes. *Research Quarterly,* 1962, *33,* 566-573.

LaPlace, J. P. Personality and its relationship to success in professional baseball. *Research Quarterly,* 1954, *25,* 313-319.

Loy, J. W., & Donnelly, P. Need for stimulation as a factor in sport involvement. In T. Craig (Ed.), *The humanistic and mental health aspects of sports, exercise, and recreation.* Chicago: American Medical Association, 1976. Pp. 80-89.

Lynn, R., & Eysenck, H. J. Tolerance for pain, extraversion, and neuroticism. *Perceptual and Motor Skills,* 1961, *12,* 161-162.

Mahoney, M. J., & Avener, M. Psychology of the elite athlete: An exploratory study. *Cognitive Therapy and Research,* 1977, *1,* 135-141.

Malumphy, T. M. Personality of women athletes in intercollegiate competition. *Research Quarterly,* 1968, *39,* 610-620.

Martens, R. The paradigmatic crisis in American sport personology. *Sportwissenschaft,* 1975, *5*, 9-24.

Martens, R. *Sport competition anxiety test.* Champaign: Human Kinetics Publishers, 1977.

Milvy, P. (Ed.). *The marathon: Physiological, medical, epidemiological, and psychological studies.* Annals of the New York Academy of Science, (Volume 301), 1977.

Mischel, W. On the future of personality measurement. *American Psychologist,* 1977, *32*, 246-254.

Morgan, W. P. Personality characteristics of wrestlers participating in the world championships. *Journal of Sports Medicine and Physical Fitness,* 1968, *8*, 212-216.

Morgan, W. P. Basic considerations. In W. P. Morgan (Ed.), *Ergogenic aids and muscular performance.* New York: Academic Press, 1972. Pp. 3-31. (a)

Morgan, W. P. Sport psychology. In R. N. Singer (Ed.), *The psychomotor domain: Movement behavior.* Philadelphia: Lea & Febiger, 1972. Pp. 193-228. (b)

Morgan, W. P. Selected psychological considerations in sport. *Research Quarterly,* 1974, *45,* 374-390.

Morgan, W. P. Sport personology: The credulous-skeptical argument in perspective. In W. F. Straub (Ed.), *Sport psychology: An analysis of athlete behavior.* Ithaca: Mouvement Publications, 1978. Pp. 218-227. (a)

Morgan, W. P. Mind of the marathoner. *Psychology Today,* 1978, *11,* 38-49. (b)

Morgan, W. P. Prediction of performance in athletics. In P. Klavora & J. V. Daniel (Eds.), *Coach, athlete, and the sport psychologist.* Champaign: Human Kinetics Publishers, 1979. Pp. 173-186.

Morgan, W. P. Hypnosis and sports medicine. In G. Burrows & L. D. Dennerstein (Eds.), *Handbook of hypnosis and psychosomatic medicine.* Amsterdam, Netherlands: Elsevier/North Holland Biomedical Press, 1980.

Morgan, W. P., & Costill, D. L. Psychological characteristics of the marathon runner. *Journal of Sports Medicine and Physical Fitness,* 1972, *12,* 42-46.

Morgan, W. P., & Hammer, W. M. Influence of competitive wrestling upon state anxiety. *Medicine and Science in Sports,* 1974, *6,* 58-61.

Morgan, W. P., & Horstman, D. H. Psychometric correlates of pain perception. *Perceptual and Motor Skills,* 1978, *47,* 27-39.

Morgan, W. P., & Johnson, R. W. Psychologic characterization of the elite wrestler: A mental health model. *Medicine and Science in Sports,* 1977, *9,* 55-56.

Morgan, W. P., & Johnson, R. W. Psychological characteristics of successful and unsuccessful oarsmen. *International Journal of Sport Psychology,* 1978, *11,* 38-49.

Morgan, W. P., & Pollock, M. L. Psychologic characterization of the elite distance runner. *Annals of the New York Academy of Science,* 1977, *301,* 382-403.

Nagle, F. J., Morgan, W. P., Hellickson, R. O., Serfass, R. C., & Alexander, J. F. Sporting success traits in Olympic contenders. *Physician and Sportsmedicine,* 1975, *3,* 31-34.

Nideffer, R. M. The relationship of attention and anxiety to performance. In W. F. Straub (Ed.), *Sport psychology: An analysis of athlete behavior.* Ithaca: Mouvement Publications, 1978. Pp. 163-167.

O'Connor, K. A., & Webb, J. L. Investigation of personality traits of college female athletes and nonathletes. *Research Quarterly,* 1976, *47,* 203-210.

O'Dell, J. W. Methods for detecting random answers on personality questionnaires. *Journal of Applied Psychology,* 1971, *55,* 380-383.

Peterson, S. L., Weber, J. C., & Trousdale, W. W. Personality traits of women in team sports vs. women in individual sports. *Research Quarterly,* 1967, *38,* 686-690.

Petrie, A. Some psychological aspects of pain and the relief of suffering. *Annals of the New York Academy of Sciences,* 1960, *86,* 13-27.

Platt, J. R. Strong inference. *Science,* 1964, *146,* 347-353.

Rushall, B. S. An evaluation of the relationship between personality and physical performance categories. In G. S. Kenyon (Ed.), *Contemporary psychology of sport.* Chicago: Athletic Institute, 1970.

Rushall, B. S. Alternative dependent variables for the study of behavior in sport. In D. M. Landers (Ed.), *Psychology of sport and motor behavior II.* College Park: Pennsylvania State University, 1975.

Ryan, E. D., & Foster, R. Athletic participation and perceptual augmentation and reduction. *Journal of Personality and Social Psychology,* 1967, *6,* 472-476.

Ryan, E. D., & Kovacic, C. R. Pain tolerance and athletic participation. *Perceptual and Motor Skills,* 1966, *22,* 383-390.

Schendel, J. Psychological differences between athletes and nonparticipants in athletics at three educational levels. *Research Quarterly,* 1965, *36,* 52-67.

Schendel, J. S. The psychological characteristics of high school athletes and nonparticipants in athletics: A three-year longitudinal study. In G. S. Kenyon (Ed.), *Contemporary psychology of sport.* Chicago: Athletic Institute, 1970. Pp. 79-96.

Schmidt, R. A. A schema theory of discrete motor learning. *Psychological Review,* 1975, *82,* 225-260.

Shaver, J. P. The productivity of educational research and the applied basic research distinction. *Educational Researcher,* 1979, *8,* 3-9.

Singer, R. N., Harris, D., Kroll, W., Martens, R., & Sechrest, L. Psychological testing of athletes. *Journal of Physical Education and Recreation,* 1977, *48,* 30-32.

Slusher, H. S. Personality and intelligence characteristics of selected high school athletes and nonathletes. *Research Quarterly,* 1964, *38,* 539-545.

Stoner, S., & Bandy, M. A. Personality traits of females who participate in intercollegiate competition and nonparticipants. *Perceptual and Motor Skills,* 1977, *45,* 332-334.

Straub, W. F. Approaches to personality assessment of athletes: Personologism, situationism, and interactionism. In C. O. Dotson, V. L. Katch, & J. Schick (Eds.), *Research and practice in physical education.* Champaign: Human Kinetics Publishers, 1977.

Suinn, R. M. Psychology and sports performance: Principles and applications. In W. F. Straub (Ed.), *Sport psychology: An analysis of athlete behavior.* Ithaca: Mouvement Publications, 1978, Pp. 20-28.

Sweeney, D. R., & Fine, B. J. Pain reactivity and field dependence. *Perceptual and Motor Skills,* 1965, *21,* 757-758.

Thune, A. R. Personality of weight lifters. *Research Quarterly,* 1949, *20,* 296-306.

Wendt, D. T., & Patterson, T. W. Personality characteristics of women in intercollegiate competition. *Perceptual and Motor Skills,* 1974, *38,* 861-862.

Werner, A. C. *Physical education and the development of leadership characteristics of cadets at the United States Military Academy.* Unpublished doctoral dissertation, Springfield College, 1960.

Werner, A. C., & Gottheil, E. Personality development and participation in college athletics. *Research Quarterly,* 1966, *37,* 126-131.

Whiting, H. T. A., & Stembridge, D. E. Personality and the persistent nonswimmer. *Research Quarterly,* 1965, *36,* 348-356.

Williams, J. M. Personality characteristics of the successful female athlete. In W. F. Straub (Ed.), *Sport psychology: An analysis of athlete behavior.* Ithaca: Mouvement Publications, 1978. Pp. 249-255.

Williams, J. M., Hoepner, B. J., Moody, D. L., & Ogilvie, B. C. Personality traits of champion level female fencers. *Research Quarterly,* 1970, *41,* 446-453.

Winder, P., O'Dell, J. W., & Karson, S. New motivational distortion scales for the 16PF. *Journal of Personality Assessment,* 1975, *39,* 532-537.

Yanada, H., & Hirata, H. Personality traits of students who dropped out of their athletic clubs. *Proceedings of the College of Physical Education,* University of Tokyo, 1970, No. 5.

Zuckerman, M. Traits, states, situations, and uncertainty. *Journal of Behavioral Assessment,* 1979, *1,* 43-54.

7 Emotions and Athletic Performance: Individual Zones of Optimal Functioning Model

YURI L. HANIN
Research Institute for Olympic Sports, Jyväskylä, Finland

In the former Eastern Bloc, sport psychologists often had an opportunity not available to their colleagues in the West: that of working with many elite athletes. For several reasons, much of the knowledge gained by these sport psychologists was not exposed in the West, partially because of the nondemocratic political systems in which these people operated, and partly because of language barriers. One of the exceptions to this state of affairs was the work of the Russian sport psychologist Yuri Hanin.

Hanin was influenced by ideas presented by eminent Soviet psychologists, such as Vygotsky, Rubinstein, and Leontjev, who were not well known in the West in the late 1970s. However, he developed his approach mainly with a strong reference to the naturalistic reality of top athletes in elite sport. Hanin criticized the inverted-U hypothesis by arguing that it is unlikely that only one optimal arousal state exists that corresponds with the best performances of different athletes across contests. He used Spielberger's State-Trait Anxiety Inventory (STAI) to operationalize arousal and conducted systematic retrospective multiple-field observations of athletes' state anxiety and performance levels. He found that each top athlete had a typical zone of state anxiety in which his or her best performance occurred; in contrast, poor performance occurred outside this zone. Hanin defined this zone as an athlete's mean precompetitive state anxiety score on the STAI, plus or minus 4 points (i.e., approximately 0.5 SD), and labeled it zone of optimal functioning (ZOF).

Soon, the ZOF concept became popular in sport psychology, mainly because it enabled the sport psychology practitioner to use a practical tool that could quite easily provide criteria and reference points for diagnosis and evaluation of athletes' precompetitive state anxiety with a relatively high ecological validity. The ZOF started to gain empirical support and was further developed in several directions and not only by Hanin. Toward the mid-1990s, the European Federation of Sport Psychology (FEPSAC) decided to launch a new journal of its own, starting with a yearbook. In the first volume of this European Yearbook of Sport Psychology (later to become FEPSAC's official journal, Psychology of Sport and Exercise), Hanin, now living in Finland, published this article. He not only summarized his previous research but also extended his original concept further to explain the relationships between performance and various emotions. Toward the mid-1990s he revised his original term, turning it into individual zone of optimal functioning (IZOF), with a reference not only to anxiety but to many emotional states measured ideographically and longitudinally. This article is widely cited and has inspired much research on the IZOF, emotions, and performance in sport.

The present paper examines the key issues related to emotion–performance relationships in sports. It is argued that reality-grounded models reflecting specific conditions of sports setting and athletic performance are needed. A case of the individual zones of optimal functioning (IZOF) model is presented as a conceptual framework for the qualitative and quantitative analysis of individual subjective emotional experiences related to athletic performance. Several aspects including the issues of multidimensionality of emotions, the content of positive and negative affect (PNA), and the in–out of the zone concept are examined. Furthermore, step-wise idiographic assessment procedures to identify individually optimal and dysfunctional PNA patterns using standardised and individualised scales are briefly described. Empirical evidence in support of the basic assumptions of the IZOF model as applied to precompetition anxiety and PNA is reviewed and tentative functional interpretations of PNA-performance relationships are suggested. And, finally, implications and a number of future directions of IZOF research into subjective experiences enhancing or impairing athletic performance are specified.

It is well documented that emotion or affect (considered as synonymous in the present paper) is an important component of total human functioning. Emotion is now recognised to be critically important to understanding many of the core phenomena in virtually every major subdiscipline of psychology (Davidson & Cacioppa, 1992) including clinical, developmental, educational, social and sport psychology. Performance related emotions represent an important aspect of one's involvement in sport (Vallerand, 1983). Furthermore, in elite sports emotions can either enhance or impair individual or team performance, especially under conditions of competitive stress (see Hanin, 1978, 1983, 1995, for a review). However, little systematic research was conducted into positive and negative emotions and there

Adapted, by permission, from Y.L. Hanin, 1997, "Emotions and athletic performance: Individual zones of optimal functioning model," *European Yearbook of Sport Psychology* 1: 29-72.

was a clearly negative bias in sport psychology literature. For instance, most of sport psychology research during the last two decades focused on establishing the shape of anxiety–performance relationships using the models borrowed from non sport settings (Gould & Krane, 1992; Hackfort & Schwenkmezger, 1993; Hanin, 1986, 1993; Jones, 1995; Klavora, 1979; Kleine, 1990; Landers & Boutcher, 1986; Morgan & Elickson, 1989; Raglin, 1992; Spielberger, 1989; Weinberg, 1990). Apparently, the major problem in anxiety–performance research is the same as in sport psychology in general.

> . . . Sport psychology is theory poor. . . . We have been so eager to test theories of the larger field of psychology in order to confirm our scientific respectability that we have not adequately observed, described, and theorized about our own thing—SPORT. We clearly need to spend more time observing behavior in sport and building our own theories unique to sport. . . (Martens, 198a, p.51)

Interestingly, the main emphasis in European sport psychology from the very beginning was more on the applied issues and the needs of elite athletes and coaches than on theory testing. For instance, in Russia, emotions, pre-start states, emotional stability, psychological readiness, and psychological preparation for the competition were among the "hot" research topics back in the 1960-70s (Chernikova, 1962; Gagayeva, 1960; Gissen, 1973; Kiselev, 1967; Puni, 1959, 1969; Rodionov, 1968; Vlatkin, 1974). However, two recent FEPSAC Congress in Cologne (Nitsch & Seller, 1993) and in Brussels (Vanfraechem-Raway & Vanden Auweele, 1995) indicate a renewed interest in both theory and applications of positive and negative emotions in sport.

The Individualized Zones of Optimal Functioning (IZOF) Model

Scope and Basic Assumptions

The IZOF model represents an extension of earlier research and theoretical statements by Hanin (1978, 1986, 1989) initially focused on the relationship between individually optimal anxiety and performance in top Russian athletes (see for review, Hanin, 1995). During the last decade the validity and practical utility of the IZOF approach as applied to precompetition anxiety has been extensively tested cross-culturally (Gould, Tuffey, Hardy, & Lochbaum, 1993; Krane, 1993; Morgan, O'Connor, Ellickson, & Bradley, 1988; Pons, 1994; Prapavessis & Grove, 1991; Raglin, Morgan, & Wise, 1990; Salminen, Liukkonen, Hanin, & Hyvönen, 1995; Turner & Raglin, 1996). Recently the IZOF model has been extended to the analysis of functionally optimal and dysfunctional patterns of positive and negative emotions in elite athletes representing different sports (Hamill, 1996; Hanin, 1993, 1994, 1995; Hanin & Syrjä, 1995 a, b; 1996; Johnson, Anderson, AhYee, & Makua, 1995; Liukkonen, 1995; Pesonen, 1995; Saamio, 1995; Syrjä, 1993, Syrjä, Hanin, & Pesonen, 1995; Syrjä, Hanin, & Tarvonen, 1995; Tarvonen, 1995).

The IZOF model was developed in the naturalistic setting of elite sports and combines the within- and between-individual analysis of the structure and function of subjective experiences affecting athletic performance. The model is basically designed to describe and predict the effect of positive and negative emotions upon performance and to provide an explanation of the emotion–performance relationships. Although intended to have general applicability, it is most relevant to high achievement setting with a special emphasis on consistent performance up to one's potential under conditions of stress. This enhancement-oriented focus in the IZOF model emphasizes the role of optimal and dysfunctional effect of both positive and negative emotions on performance process. Furthermore, the dynamics of each athlete's subjective experiences are always examined via the within-individual contrasts between individually best and poor performance patterns.

Conceptually the IZOF model is based on several ideas and principles developed in general, social, educational, and sport psychology. The main among them are the notion of the unity of consciousness, psyche and activity (Rubinstein, 1946), the activity theory (Leontjev, 1975), the conceptualisation of nature of subjective emotional experiences (Vygotsky, 1926) and the role of cognitive appraisals in person-environment interactions (Lazarus, 1991,1993). In the extended IZOF model several issues are critical to understanding the emotion–performance relationships. These include the conceptualisation of multidimensionality of performance affect, and emotion content and the in–out-of-the zone notion as applied to optimal and dysfunctional emotions, both positive and negative. These aspects will be briefly reviewed and empirical evidence to support them will be provided in the sections that follow.

The Multidimensionality of Subjective Emotional Experiences There is a growing consensus among sport psychologists that the unidimensional approach to arousal/anxiety–performance relationship is ineffective and oversimplistic (Fazey & Hardy, 1988; Gould & Krane, 1992; Hardy, 1990; Jones, 1995; Landers, 1994; Weinberg, 1989, 1990). Thus, several investigators addressed the issue of multidimensionality, for instance, in stress and anxiety research. Table 7.1 presents a selected summary of various components of anxiety (ranging from 2 to 5) that were proposed under different labels.

Furthermore, there has been considerable inconsistency and confusion in the sport psychology literature in the use of arousal-related terms. Consequently, Gould and Krane (1992) proposed a conceptual model in an attempt to integrate arousal construct terminology. However, it was still not clear what the basic dimensions (necessary and sufficient) to

Table 7.1 Current conceptions of mutidimensional anxiety

Author, year	Description and a number of component labels
In non-sports setting:	
Alpert & Haber (1960)	facilitating, debilitating (2)
Liebert & Morris (1967)	worry, emotionality (trait) (2)
Schwartz, Davidson, & Goleman (1978)	cognitive, somatic (2)
Spielberger, Gorsuch, & Lushene (1970)	state-trait, anxiety-present, anxiety-absent (4)
Endler & Magnusson (1976)	interpersonal, physical danger, ambiguity (novel), daily routines (4)
In sports setting:	
Martens (1977)	competition anxiety (trait) (1)
Smith, Smoll, & Schutz (1990)	cognitive, somatic (trait) (2)
Martens, Vealey, & Burton (1990)	cognitive, somatic, self-confidence (state) (3)
Jones (1991, 1995)	intensity, frequency, direction (3)
Hanin (1986, 1989, 1992, 1993, 1995)	form, intensity, time content, context (5)

describe anxiety and other emotions in sports were. Moreover, the logical foundation to identify these dimensions of positive and negative emotions was missing.

As a possible solution to this difficult conceptual and methodological problem, the ideas of the systems approach as applied to psychology might be appropriate (Allport, 1960; Ananjev, 1968; Lomov, 1984; Schedrovitsky, 1964; Bertalanffy, 1952). Specifically, the *method of bases* proposed for the systems description of complex phenomena was instrumental (Ganzen, 1984, Ganzen & Yurchenko, 1981). In the systems description, a multitude of elements of the object under investigation is contrasted with the elements of the basis (the logical foundation). Ganzen, having analysed the descriptions of different objects and phenomena, proposed that "spatiality, time, information and energy were the basic characteristics of any object that typically functions as their integrator" (1984, p. 44). These separate concepts (space, time, energy, information, and a substrate) were suggested as a conceptual basis (*penta*-basis or a five-element foundation) to integrate existing concepts and empirical research findings. The penta-basis as a framework and a "stable foundation" for the description, makes it also possible to examine if the description of the phenomenon is complete. Additionally, it is possible to better organise the components, to compare different descriptions, and, consequently, to discover the similarity in the objects or phenomena of different nature (Ganzen, 1984, p. 41-42). This approach has been theoretically substantiated and empirically validated in the systems descriptions of psychological subdisciplines, general characteristics of nervous system and in the description of human personality and individuality (Ganzen, 1984). In sports setting, the penta-basis and the idea of systems description were used in the longitudinal study of communication patterns in top sport teams (Hanin, 1985, 1992), in sports career research (Stambulova, 1994), and in the systematic investigation of performance-induced emotions (Hanin, 1993, 1994, 1995).

In the IZOF model the penta-basis includes *form* (substrate), *intensity* (energy), *time, context* (space), and *content* (information) dimensions. As applied to performance affect, the five basic dimensions are briefly characterized as follows:

1. Form includes such modalities or components as cognitive, affective, motivational, bodily somatic, motor-behavioural, performance-operational, and communicative/interactive (see also Burton, 1990; Davis & West, 1991). Subjective emotional experiences are represented in the affective component of total human functioning that is closely related with other modalities of performance related psychobiosocial state.

2. Intensity, as a quantitative characteristic of affect is expressed either in objective or in subjective metrics and typically consists of individual and total scores on selected modalities. Intensity is typically the most studied dimension in stress, anxiety and emotional research.

3. Temporal dimension reflects the dynamics of affect before, during, and after the performance of a single or repeated short- or long-duration tasks (Fenz & Epstein, 1967; Gould, Petlichkoff, & Weinberg, 1984; Hanin, 1978, 1983, 1993; Jones, 1991; Karteroliotis, & Gill, 1987).

4. Context as an environmental characteristic includes situational, interpersonal, intra-group antecedents or consequences that determine the intensity and consent of emotions in sport (Hanin, 1977; 1980; 1985; 1989; 1992; Hanin & Bulanova, 1979; Hanin & Kopysov, 1977; Iso-Ahola, 1995; McCann, Murphy, & Raedeke, 1992; Prapavessis & Carron, 1996).

5. Content as a qualitative and informational characteristic includes such categories of emotional experiences as positive-negative (Russell, Weiss, & Mendelsohn, 1989; Watson & Tellegen, 1985; Young, 1959), functionally optimal-dysfunctional (Hanin, 1978, 1993, 1994), facilitating-debilitating (Alpert & Haber, 1960; Jones, 1991, 1995).

It is noteworthy that although the PNA content is critical for the functional interpretation of the performance-emotion relationships, it is still the least studied dimension in sport psychology (Bejek & Hagtvet, 1996; Hanin, 1992, 1993). One reason for this situation seems to be related to the predominantly nomothetic approach to the study of emotions. Thus, when standardised scales with researcher-generated items are used, the content of emotions (single or global affect) is usually "fixed" or taken for granted. In the section that follows, the conceptualisation of the PNA content in the IZOF model will be briefly discussed.

The Content of Emotions in Athletic Performance The content of emotions in the IZOF model is conceptualised within the framework of two factors: (a) hedonic tone and (b) emotion effect upon athletic performance. Hedonic tone (pleasure-displeasure or positivity-negativity) is the major concept in the content dimension of emotions that emerged in many contexts (see Lazarus & Folkman, 1984; Russell et al., 1989; Young, 1959, for review). For instance, in the area of stress-related emotions, Folkman and Lazarus (1989) argued that the content and intensity of anticipation (challenge or threat) and outcome (benefit or harm) emotions were determined by the appraisals of person-environment interactions. Moreover, empirical studies indicate that positive-negative is a fundamental dimension in situational momentary emotion (Russell, 1979; Russell et al., 1989; Watson, Clark, & Tellegen, 1988; Watson & Tellegen, 1985). Positive and negative emotions are relatively independent and polarisation usually occurs during strong emotions in which a person feels either positive or negative (Diener & Emmons, 1985; Lorr, McNair, & Fisher, 1982; Warr, Barter, & Brownbridge, 1983). Nevertheless, it is possible at times to feel "mixed emotions" that include both specific positive and negative elements (Diener & Iran-Nejad, 1986).

Much debate, however, occurs over whether positivity and negativity are bipolar or unipolar. For instance, it has been suggested that positive and negative affect can be characterised as "*descriptively bipolar* but *affectively unipolar* dimensions" to emphasise that only the high end of each dimension represents affective involvement (Zevon & Tellagen, 1982, p. 112). There is also some confusion in the existing PNA scales: typically the low end of positive affect includes negative emotions and the low end of negative emotions includes positive items (Watson & Tellegen, 1985; Watson et al., 1988). Thus, in assessments positive and negative emotions are bipolar and are treated as the opposite poles of one continuum. In the IZOF model, it is proposed that positive and negative emotions are unipolar descriptors of individual subjective experiences. In other words, each emotion is assessed separately and varies from high to low in intensity on just one continuum.

The second important factor to categorise the emotion content is the *effect of emotion* upon performance. This notion is not new and has been around in psychology for some time under different labels: most *favourable* stimulus (Yerkes & Dodson, 1908), *optimal* arousal (Bertyne, 1960; Hebb, 1955; Malmo, 1959; Schlosberg, 1954), *facilitating-debilitating* anxiety (Alpert & Haber, 1960; Jones, 1991, 1995). Initially, optimal effects were simply implied and the main concern, for instance, in test anxiety research and in clinical psychology was on alleviating debilitative consequences of high anxiety. In elite sports, however, it was for quite some time increasingly clear that state anxiety does not necessarily impair athletic performance and can in some circumstances for some athletes, enhance it (Aleksejev, 1969; Gissen, 1973; Hanin, 1978, 1986; Jones, 1995; Mahoney & Avener, 1977; Orlick, 1990; Parfitt & Hardy, 1993; Schilling, 1979; Uneståhl, 1986; Vanek & Cratty, 1968).

In early test anxiety literature Alpert and Haber (1960) were among the first to address the question of whether test anxiety will facilitate, debilitate, or have no effect upon performance. They proposed the "direction of effect" dimension operationalised in two independent constructs of facilitating and debilitating anxiety as *response tendencies* in test situations. The Achievement Anxiety Test (AAT) with two separate subscales as trait specific measures of facilitating and debilitating anxiety was constructed: a facilitating scale of nine items based on a prototype of the item—"Anxiety helps me to do better during examinations and tests"; and a debilitating scale of 10 items based on a prototype of the item—"Anxiety interferes with my performance during examinations and tests." Empirical evidence clearly indicated that "facilitating anxiety added significantly to the prediction of grade-point average when it was combined with a measure of debilitating anxiety" (Alpert & Haber, 1960, p. 215).

In sports setting, the concept of facilitating-debilitating anxiety with some modification was applied by Jones and associates (see Jones, 1995 for review). These investigators used a single item bipolar direction scale to rate the degree to which the situationally experienced intensity of each symptom on the Martens' et al., (1990) Competitive State Anxiety Inventory (CSAI-2) was either facilitative or debilitative to subsequent performance. The response scale ranged from –3 (very debilitating) to +3 (very facilitative) so that possible direction scores on the CSAI-2 subscales ranged from –27 to +27. Thus, the major emphasis in this approach was on situational interpretation on anxiety symptoms intensity.

A different strategy in the evaluation of anxiety effect upon athletic performance was proposed by Hanin (1978, 1986, 1989). In unpublished study of Olympic level divers and rowers preparing for the Montreal Olympics (Hanin, 1975), athletes' current and recalled pre-competition levels of anxiety using the Russian version of the STAI was assessed. The main emphasis, however, was the analysis of past successful performances and experiences of these highly skilled athletes. Thus, the key question was not whether anxiety was facilitative or debilitative but how much precompetition anxiety was optimal or useful for each individual. A total score on the STAI state anxiety subscale provided an individualised level of optimal anxiety intensity which served as a tentative criterion to evaluate current anxiety levels in subsequent performance situations for each athlete. The concept of zones of optimal functioning was then proposed as a tentative optimal range of intensity scores predicting the high probability of individually successful performance. Empirical findings provided support for the approach and the methodology of assessing optimal levels and zones of individually optimal anxiety (see later and Hanin, 1978, 1986, 1989, 1995 for review).

The notion of emotion effect, as applied to positive and negative affect in athletic performance, was further developed. Specifically, it was proposed that *functionally optimal* and *dysfunctional* impact of positive and negative emotions upon athletic performance should be considered as two separate concepts. Although "success" and "failure" performance outcomes seem to represent the opposite poles on the same continuum, qualitatively these performance process categories are clearly discontinuous. In other words, there exists not one, but two continua indicating a range of occurrences between success and non-success and between failure and non-failure (cf. Kelmar, 1990, Hanin, 1993, 1994, 1995).

Consequently, the emotion content in the IZOF model is conceptualised within the framework of two closely related but independent factors: "positivity-negativity" and "optimality-dysfunctionality". Four global affect categories derived from these two factors include (a) pleasant, functionally optimal emotions (P+), (b) unpleasant, functionally optimal emotions (N+), (c) pleasant, dysfunctional emotions (P–), and (d) unpleasant, dysfunctional (N–) emotions. In other words, both positive and negative emotions of different intensity can be either functionally optimal, helpful (P+, N+), or dysfunctional, harmful (P–, N–) for the individual's performance. It is also assumed that these four basic categories of emotions are relevant for the description of athletes' emotional experiences before, during or after performance.

Considering clearly idiographic emphasis of the IZOF model, a prototype perspective was taken (Cantor, Mischel, & Schwartz, 1982; Fehr & Russell, 1984). It was argued that athlete-generated items within the four emotion content (P+, N+, P–, N–) categories will reflect athletes' real-life subjective experiences. In other words, individual emotion prototypes will be quite adequate in representing individually relevant and meaningful content of performance-induced emotions. These prototypes could be contrasted at the individual, interindividual and group levels across the basic content categories for the same and different tasks and sport events (see below).

The In–Out of the Zone Concept The in–out of the zone concept within the IZOF model is used in the assessment, prediction and optimization of individual's performance. The in–out of the zone concept reflects the cyclic nature of athletic performance and has been derived from the empirical data obtained in naturalistic setting of elite sports.

As initially applied to precompetition anxiety, it was proposed that each athlete has an individually optimal intensity level (high, moderate and low) and a range or zone of optimal anxiety. Successful performance, particularly in short-duration tasks, occurs when current precompetition anxiety is near or within these individually optimal zones. When precompetition anxiety falls outside the zones, i.e. is higher and lower, the quality of individual performance usually deteriorates. Therefore, the in–out of the zone notion served an individualised criterion and a guiding principle in the description and prediction of anxiety–performance relationships irrespective of whether a single or multidimensional scores of anxiety were used.

At this point, however, the extended in–out of the zone concept is used also to describe separate and joint effects of both positive and negative emotions (Hanin, 1993, 1994, 1995). Specifically, the individual zone of optimal intensity is identified for each functionally optimal emotion, whereas the individual zone of dysfunctional intensity is identified for each dysfunctional emotion in other words, there are zones of optimal function in some emotions (P+N+) within which the probability of successful performance is highest. Additionally, there are also dysfunctional zones in other emotions (P–N–) within which the probability of poor performance is the highest. Optimal and dysfunctional intensity levels can be low, moderate or high and vary for the same and different emotions across different athletes (Hanin & Syrjä, 1995a, b; Syrjä, Hanin, & Pesonen, 1995; Syrjä, Hanin, & Tarvonen, 1995). Moreover, it is argued that functionally optimal and dysfunctional effects occur separately and or jointly only when these emotions are near or within these previously established individual zones. In other words, the total effect of positive and negative emotions on performance appears to be determined by the interaction of optimal and dysfunctional effects. Consequently, although functionally optimal emotions are important predictors of successful performance, they alone may not be sufficient, if potential detrimental effect of dysfunctional emotions is not considered. The notion of a zone, therefore, as applied to a wide range of positive and negative emotions, seems quite appropriate since both optimal and dysfunctional effects are considered separately and jointly.

The in–out of the zone notion was applied to predict individually successful performance in the case of a top Finnish javelin thrower. Based on recalls of previously successful and poor performances a tentative individualised PNA scale was developed for this athlete. Then the specific intensity zones for optimal and dysfunctional emotions were identified using Borg's (1982) Category Ratio (CR-10) scale (see later). This athlete has a clearly unique PNA profile in that emotion items and optimal and dysfunctional zones for each of the P+, N+, P–, N– categories are idiosyncratic. His optimal positive emotions were eager, sure, and determined, whereas optimal negative emotions were tense and furious. Negative dysfunctional emotions were feeling too slack, lazy, unwilling and tired, whereas positive dysfunctional emotions included the feelings of too much complacency: calm, nice, content, and pleasant. As revealed via past-performance recall of 12 self-rated successful throws, this athlete had consistently similar profiles on most of the PNA items. Specifically, he was clearly inside his previously established optimal zones and outside his dysfunctional zones. Moreover, the obtained PNA profiles indicate similarity and consistency of emotion patterns related to successful performance and interaction effects between functionally optimal (N+P+) and dysfunctional (N–P–) emotions.

Methodological Issues

Analysis of emotion patterns in the IZOF model is based on the notion that skilled athletes are aware of and able to report their subjective emotional experiences related to individually significant performance. Therefore, an individualised technique of recall, actual, and anticipatory self-report measures (Hanin, 1978, 1986, 1989) was used to test empirically the basic assumptions of the IZOF model in the field setting. Specifically, in recall athletes rated their emotional states based on the experiences in most successful ("best ever") or poor ("worst ever") performance situations. In prediction, the athletes rated their anticipated feelings based on their perception of the up-coming performance situation and past experiences in similar situations. In all cases, both standardised and individualised self-report scales were used in recalls, predictions and actual assessments.

Idiographic Assessment of Anxiety Using Standardized Scales Although the emphasis in the IZOF model is on within-individual analysis rather than on inter-individual comparisons, only instructions are individualised when standardised (nomothetic) scales are used for assessments in research and applications. For instance, the studies of precompetition anxiety were idiographic to the extent that individual levels of optimal anxiety were identified for each athlete. A strong nomothetic element was still retained, since an identical set of researcher-generated anxiety items was presented to all subjects and their content was implicitly treated as having the same meaning across all athletes. However, research, initially using Spielberger et al. (1970) State-Trait Anxiety Inventory (STAI), has shown that skilled athletes were accurate in recalling their anxiety before successful and unsuccessful competitions. Significant correlations in the range of .75 to .89 were found between actual and recalled levels of precompetition anxiety with up to 3 or 4 month interval between the assessments (Hanin, 1978, 1986, 1989, 1995; Imlay, Carda, Stanbrough, & O'Connor, 1995; Raglin & Morris, 1994; Raglin & Turner, 1993). Even higher accuracy was found in two-day recalls in female ($r = .97$) and male ($r = .96$) track and field athletes and it was not influenced by their relative success (Harger & Raglin, 1994). Research contrasting anticipated and actual self-ratings also demonstrated that skilled athletes in different sports were able to predict accurately their anticipated emotions and performance. Significant correlations in the range of 0.49 to 0.98 were found between anticipatory and actual measures of precompetition anxiety. The time interval between the anticipatory and actual assessments was from 24 hours to 2-3 weeks (Hanin, 1986; Raglin et al., 1990; Salminen et al., 1995). Thus, the findings from these studies using standardised scales demonstrate quite acceptable accuracy of recalls and predictions in skilled athletes at the group level. However, accuracy of recall/predictions at the individual level should be estimated for each individual athlete on a wide range of emotions (items) using individualised PNA scales with athlete-generated items (Hanin, 1993; Hanin & Syrjä, 1996).

Assessments Using the Individualised PNA Scales In the extended IZOF model a new method was needed that would provide a tool for analysing individually relevant content of emotions. A stepwise recall scaling procedure was used to identify positive and negative emotions that were subjectively meaningful for each subject in terms of the individual's past performance history (Hanin, 1993, 1994). These athlete-generated items were then used to develop an individualised PNA scale that was subsequently refined and further validated in repeated actual, anticipatory, and recall assessments.

In idiographic recall athletes generate individually relevant emotion words that best describe their optimal (helpful) and dysfunctional (harmful) positive and negative emotions. To help athletes to generate individual items, the PNA stimulus list including positive and negative emotions typically experienced in performance was used. The English version of the PNA stimulus list was compiled through selection and revision of items from the 10 global PNA scales described by Watson and Tellegen (1985). These PNA items were then translated into Finnish, and three judges evaluated the item content by selecting the most appropriate synonyms used in current spoken Finnish. The final version of the PNA list included 40 positive emotions and 37 negative emotions. Examples of positive affect items included "active", "calm", "confident", "determined", whereas representative negative affect items were "nervous", "angry", "dissatisfied", "uncertain". At this point paper and pencil and computerized versions of the procedure are available in English, Finnish, Norwegian, Polish, Portuguese, Russian, and Spanish.

Recall scaling includes several steps. First, optimal PNA patterns are identified. Athletes, using the PNA stimulus list, select 4 or 5 positive and then 4 or 5 negative items that best describe their emotions related to individually successful performances in the past. Then dysfunctional PNA patterns are identified by selecting 4 or 5 positive and 4 or 5 negative items that describe their emotions related to individually poor performances. In order to elicit a pattern, repeated experiences on several occasions are emphasised rather than one specific situation. Athletes use the PNA stimulus list to generate individually relevant positive and negative emotion descriptors and can also add emotion words of their own choice.

A separate scale is used alongside each of the emotions selected by individual athletes that related to intensity. The intensity scale asks: "How much of this feeling or emotion is usually helpful (or harmful) for your performances in competition (or in practices)?" Athletes indicate either a level or a range of intensity (minimum and maximum amount of the emotion that was helpful or harmful). The intensity is measured on the Borg's Category Ratio (CR-10) scale (Borg, 1982) based on the range principle and constructed to avoid the ceiling effect. The CR-10 permits ratio comparisons to be made of intensities as well as determinations of direct intensity levels. A standard format of the CR-10 scale (Hanin, 1994; Hanin & Syrjä, 1995 a, b, 1996) was used with the following verbal anchors: 0 = *nothing at all,* 0.5 =, 1 = *very little,* 2 = *little,* 3 = *somewhat,* 4 = *moderately,* 5 = *much,* 7 = *very much,* 10 = *very, very much,* # = *maximal possible* (no verbal anchors were used for 6, 8, and 9).

In the applied setting, first, individualised PNA profiles including optimal (P+N+) and nonoptimal (P–N–) emotions with the intensity ranges on the CR-10 scale are developed for each athlete following the recall procedures described earlier. The PNA profiles are then used as individualised PNA scales for self-ratings of actual, anticipated and recalled emotions before and after performance.

The reliability of the individualised PNA scales intra-individually was established by calculating Cronbach alpha-coefficients in a sample of 17 Olympic-level soccer players (Hanin & Syrjä, 1996). It was found that mean intra-individual alphas ranged from .76 to .90 for different subscales with the highest internal consistency (.90, *SD* = .04) observed in positive and negative optimal (P+N+) items. It was also demonstrated that skilled soccer players were accurate in one-day predictions and immediate post-performance recalls of pre-game affect in international matches using their individualised PNA scales.

Additionally, in an unpublished study by Syrjä (1996) involving 24 Olympic-level soccer players, the PNA content of individualised and standardised scales was contrasted. In the case of positive affect, it was revealed that the amount of overlap (items similar in content) was 0.18 for the STAI. Even lower overlap scores (0.12 and 0.10, respectively) were obtained for PANAS (Positive and Negative Affect Schedule) (Watson & Tellegen, 1985), and POMS (Profile of Mood States) (McNair, Lorr, & Droppleman, 1971). In other words, the content of positive affect athlete-generated items differed from the content of researcher-generated items in standardised scales in 82-90% of all cases. The amount of overlap between individualised negative affect items and STAI, PANAS and POMS items was 0.19, 0.14 and 0.23, respectively. Thus, these standardised scales with researcher-generated items did not assess 77-86% of the individually relevant emotion content. These findings seem to indicate that, for instance, in high achievement and clinical settings, individualised PNA scales might be preferable. However, since the data were obtained using the Finnish language forms of the STAI, PANAS, and POMS, replication studies using with the scales in different languages are warranted.

Performance Measures

Based on the conceptualisation of performance as a task execution process, it is proposed in the IZOF model to clearly distinguish between performance outcome and performance process measures.

Three groups of criteria are currently used for evaluation of performance outcomes: (a) task or activity-oriented, (b) normative or other people-oriented, and (c) individualised or self-oriented criteria. Task (activity-oriented) criteria include a range of results (from the entry to the world record level) achieved on a particular sporting task irrespective of who was the performer. Thus, the dynamics of sports participation and achievement level, for instance, in the world can be described in terms of task criterion. Normative criteria are based on seasonal (or sport career) statistics and include a range of outcome measures achieved by a specified group of performers (top 10 in the world, 10 national best, qualification norm, etc.). Both task and normative criteria reflect inter-individual and or inter-group ranking of outcome measures within or across different groups of athletes. Task and group norms, for instance, for track and field athletes include multi-event IAAF scoring tables and NCAA qualifying standards (Raglin & Turner, 1993; Turner & Raglin, 1996). In contrast, individualised (person-oriented) criteria are based on within-individual statistics and include a range of results achieved by a particular athlete recently or across the whole season or sports career.

All three groups of criteria can be used in evaluating performance outcomes at the group, interindividual and intraindividual levels of analysis. Current outcomes of athletic performance can be expressed as a percentage of achievement specified by the selected criterion (Raglin, 1992, Turner & Raglin, 1996; Imlay et al. 1995) or as z-score transformations (Moles & Kerr, 1996; Yarnold, 1988). However, in the field setting of elite sports it is important that the analysis is not limited to a cross-section of actual outcome measures. Customary and within-individual performance variability (Klavora, 1979; Sonstroem & Bernado, 1982) including sudden up-lifts (Uneståhl, 1986; Orlick, 1990) and drops in individual performance (Bar-Eli, 1985; Bar-Eli, Taoz, Levy-Kolker, & Tennenbaum, 1992; Hardy, 1990) should also be considered. Thus, additional criteria or individual-oriented standards reflecting normal, better and worse than usual conditions of activity (weather, opponents, etc.) and environment might be appropriate (Gould et al., 1984; Martens et al., 1990; Rushall, 1978).

As evidenced in the literature on arousal and performance, most researchers had focused on the end result of movement or skill quantified into some performance outcome measure (Weinberg, 1989, 1990). Both conceptually and technically, the development of performance measures, especially in team sports, still present a challenge for researchers (Courneya & Chelladurai, 1991). Specifically, process-oriented performance measures should be based on the conception focusing on "how individuals organise and integrate their energies in the execution of motor skills" (Weinberg, 1989). Since each individual exhibits a particular style of movement process (task execution), then to better understand the emotion–performance process relationships, it seems necessary to describe movement patterns and processes underlying these patterns. Of special relevance to the study of movement patterns is a biomechanical analysis based on movement data obtained from repeated observations of performance in individual athletes (Yeadon & Challis, 1992). Specifically, elements of technique in individually best performances can be identified by decomposing each movement sequence into single frames and by quantifying the shapes and differences between them (Ferrario, Sforza, Michelion, Mauro, & Miani, 1995).

Only a few studies in sport psychology combined psychological and biomechanical aspects. For instance, Beuter and Duda (1985) examined the impact of arousal on motor behaviour by using kinematic characteristics of a stepping motion (joint angular displacement and velocity) in high and low anxiety states. Furthermore, in previously cited studies by Weinberg and Hunt (1976) and Weinberg (1978) the quality of movement was assessed via EMG markers. Patterns of neuromuscular energy during performance could be useful for substantiating the functional interpretation of emotion effect upon performance.

A promising recent development, based on the principles of Personal Construct Theory (Kelly, 1955) and emanating from applied research and consultancy with elite athletes in Europe, is performance profiling (Butler & Hardy, 1992; Doyle & Parfitt, 1996; Jones, 1995; Vanden Auweele, De Cuyper, Van Mele, & Rzewnicki, 1993). Research in this area, however, with more emphasis on individual-oriented and task-specific profiling of performance process is clearly indicated.

The IZOF Model: Predictions and Empirical Evidence

Anxiety–Performance Relationships

Earlier version of the model describing individually optimal pre-competition anxiety and the ZOF notion was empirically tested in different sports, samples and countries (see for reviews, Gould & Tuffey, 1996; Hanin, 1978, 1983, 1986, 1989; 1995; Morgan & Elickson, 1989; Raglin, 1992). Specifically, it was revealed that (a) individually optimal anxiety varied greatly within and across different samples of athletes representing different sports (Hanin, 1978, 1983, 1986, 1995; Turner & Raglin, 1996); (b) distribution of athletes who reported experiencing low (38.3-48.0%), moderate (22.0-36.7%) and high (25.0-30.0%) levels of anxiety prior to their best performance was consistent across different studies (Hanin, 1978; Hyvönen, 1992; Morgan, O'Connor, Sparling, & Rate, 1987; Salminen et al., 1995); (c) both repeated actual and retrospective assessments were reliable and valid procedures for obtaining ZOFs using the total STAI score or somatic and cognitive subscores (CSAI-2) separately (Dennis, Bartsokas, Lewthwaite, & Palin, 1993; Krane, 1993; Schuijers, 1989) and jointly (Gould et al., 1993); (d) athletes who were inside or close to their optimal zones of anxiety performed better than those outside their optimal zones (Dennis et al., 1993; Gould et al., 1993; Hanin, 1978; Imlay et al., 1995; Krane, 1993; Prapavessis & Grove, 1991; Raglin et al., 1990; Salminen et al., 1995; Scallen, 1993; Turner & Raglin, 1996). It should also be emphasised that the variability in optimal levels of anxiety (distribution percentages) was consistent across athletes who clearly differed in skill, experience and age. Additionally, in several studies (Gould et al., 1993; Prapavessis & Grove, 1991; Raglin & Turner, 1993; Turner & Raglin, 1996) the IZOF model was explicitly contrasted against other theoretical approaches.

Taken together, these studies, testing the practical utility and validity of the IZOF anxiety model, provided a fairly good support for the notion of zones of optimal functioning. However, several limitations, that warrant additional research, have been also identified. For instance, it was found at the group level that in extremely important competition 63-75% of the successful athletes were within the zone and 67-69% of the less successful athletes were outside the zone (Hyvönen, 1992; Imlay et al., 1995; Salminen et al., 1995). Moreover, studies using a three-dimensional measure of anxiety (CSAI-2) revealed that anxiety ZOFs in some cases were asymmetrical (Gould et al., 1993; Krane, 1993; Schuijers, 1989; Woodman, Albinson, & Hardy, 1996). Although, these data are consistent with Hanin's earlier suggestion that a range of +/– 4 points on the STAI should be taken with precaution (Hanin, 1989, 1995), they seem also to indicate that the individualised zones on a wide range of emotions (see below) would be a better predictor of performance than "average" ZOFs based on a total score of anxiety. The findings from Swain's unpublished study using intra-individual design with basketball players provide support for this contention (Swain, 1992 cited in Jones, 1995). Specifically, it was found that "two levels of anxiety intensity in an individual on two occasions were not associated with the same level of performance on both occasions" (Jones, 1995, p. 141). On one hand, similarity of total intensity scores (on the CSAI-2 subscales) on two occasions does not necessarily imply the similarity of ratings for all anxiety items. On the other hand, performance is often dependent upon several extraneous factors outside athlete's control (Gould & Tuffy, 1996; Martens et al., 1990). Moreover, standardised self-report scales and group-oriented performance measures sometimes can be less than effective for idiographic assessments (Hanin & Syrjä, 1996). Finally, the finding that "performer interprets the facilitating/debilitating consequences of anxiety intensity for performance in different ways on different occasions" (Jones, 1995, p. 141) warrants additional research. In fact, was the instability in ratings due to the fact that the athlete was not fully aware of own experiences? Or, were the items on the CSAI-2 scale not entirely relevant for this athlete and did not tap really significant idiosyncratic factors affecting his performance? Whatever is the case, it becomes increasingly clear that, although precompetition anxiety is an important predictor of athletic performance, the effect of other emotions should also be examined (Gill, 1994; Gould & Tuffy, 1996; Hanin, 1993, 1994; Landers, 1994). In the sections that follow empirical evidence in support of the IZOF model extended to positive and negative emotions will be reviewed.

Emotions–Performance Relationships

Research testing the basic assumptions of the extended IZOF model includes two closely related directions. The first direction includes a prototype analysis of emotion patterns (PNA content and intensity) in different athletes across different sports, settings (practices and competitions), and multi-sports tasks. The second research direction attempts to test directly the validity of the extended in–out of the zone concept by examining the interactive effect of optimal and dysfunctional emotions upon athletic performance. In idiographic analysis of PNA patterns and emotion–performance relationships individualised PNA scales described earlier were used.

Optimal and Dysfunctional PNA Patterns in Different Sports Empirical evidence supporting the notion that PNA patterns are individual across athletes and different sports was reported by Hanin (1993, 1994, 1995), Hanin & Syrjä (1995a, 1995b, 1996, 1997) Saamio (1995), Syrjä (1993), Tarvonen (1995). Selected studies briefly reviewing these findings are reported in the section that follows.

Hanin and Syrjä (1995a) studied 46 ice-hockey players (ages 15-17 years) via recall idiographic scaling described earlier to identify PNA content and intensity patterns of subjective emotional experiences related to successful and unsuccessful game performance. It was revealed that each player's idiosyncratic PNA profile always included individually optimal (P+N+) and dysfunctional (P–N–) emotions. Significant differences reflected in the selection of emotions within the previously established four basic PNA content categories were found only at intra- and interindividual level. Additionally, 78.8% of all subjective estimations of the intensity zones were in the range of 0 – 4 points on the Borg's CR-10 scale. Significant differences at the group level were found in the zone ranges for positive (P+ vs. P–, $t = 2.8$, $p < .01$), negative (N+ vs. N–, $t = 7.64$, $p < .01$), and ineffective (P– vs. N–, $t = 4.35$, $p < .01$) emotions. In contrast, the differences in intensity zones were not significant for optimal positive and negative emotions (P+ vs. N+, $t = 1.05$, $p = .296$).

Furthermore, at the group level, different players selected positive and negative emotions as either functionally optimal (20.5%), dysfunctional (25.3%), or both (54.2%). Although the PNA content is functionally idiosyncratic, the same emotions can be optimal for some athlete, but dysfunctional for other athletes within the same and across different sports. These data also revealed a significant "reversal effect" of emotions on performance reflected in the selection of positive dysfunctional emotions and the selection of functionally optimal negative emotions (Hanin, 1993, 1994, 1995; Hanin & Syrjä, 1995a, 1995b). In most cases, both optimal and dysfunctional effects of emotions upon athletic performance were related to their idiosyncratic meaning, intensity, and predominant function.

In the case of positive affect, top nine functionally optimal emotions included energetic, charged, motivated, certain, confident, purposeful, willing, resolute, alert, whereas easy-going, excited, composed, relaxed, overjoyed, fearless, satisfied, exalted, pleasant were most often dysfunctional. In the case of negative affect, top ten functionally optimal emotions were tense, charged, dissatisfied, attacking, vehement, intense, nervous, irritated, provoked, angry, and furious. Among top ten negative dysfunctional emotions were tired, unwilling, uncertain, sluggish, depressed, lazy, distressed, sorrowful, afraid, and exhausted. Additionally, also at the group level, positive optimal emotions (P+) were selected as helpful in 94.1% of cases, whereas positive dysfunctional emotions (P–) were selected as harmful by athletes in 77.5% of all cases. In negative emotions optimal effect (N+) was observed in 85.3%, while dysfunctional effect was found in 93% of all cases. Thus, these findings provide empirical support for the validity of the four global PNA content categories proposed in the IZOF model for the description of performance-induced emotions. Specifically, the fact that content of most frequently selected emotions did not overlap even at the group level seems to indicate that these emotions represent two relatively independent factors. Thus, the orthogonality of the positive-negative and optimal-dysfunctional dimensions of the emotion content has been confirmed, at least, at the descriptive and intuitive levels. However, more research employing, for instance, P-factor analysis is clearly warranted to provide additional support for this hypothesis.

PNA Patterns Across Settings and Tasks Although the main focus of the idiographic analysis of emotion content and intensity has been on sports activity in competitions, recently the PNA patterns across different settings (competitions versus practices) were also examined.

Hanin and Syrjä (1997) investigated via recall optimal and dysfunctional emotions in 12 elite Finnish cross-country skiers across three settings including races, hard work training and in technical skills training. It was revealed that the athletes perceived over 50% of all positive emotions as facilitating their performance in competitions and technical skills training. In the case of negative affect, only 14.2% of items were reported as facilitating in technical skills training. From 20 to 45.7% of positive and negative emotions in different settings had either facilitating or debilitating effect on athletic performance. Moreover, mean intraindividual scores of content overlap between optimal and dysfunctional emotions were quite low both in positive ($M = .08$, R = .00-.28) and in negative ($M = .20$, R = .7-.36) affect.

On the other hand, the mean overlap for emotion words selected by the skiers for competitions and hard work training was moderate ($M = .41$, $SD = .28$, ranging from 0 to 1.00). The mean overlap scores for technical skills training contrasted with hard work training ranging from 0 to .87 ($M = .31$, $SD = .22$). In the case of competitions contrasted with technical skills training, the overlap was, as expected, even lower ($M = .27$, $SD = .23$, ranging from 0 to .71). The Friedman Two-Way ANOVA revealed significant differences among these three pairs of contrasts ($p = .05$). Specifically, relatively greater similiarity in contrasts of words chosen in competition with hard work training compared with technical skills training was found. The lowest overlap in content, as expected, was observed between words chosen for the two types of training. Significant differences in the intensity for similar positive facilitating ($p < .02$) and negative debilitating emotions ($p < .03$) were also revealed by the Friedman Two-Way ANOVA. Additionally, the Wilcoxon test revealed that the optimal positive emotions in competitions were significantly ($p < .02$) more intensive than in hard work training. As expected, the intensity of positive optimal emotions reported for competition was significantly higher (p = <.03) than the intensity reported in the technical skills training. In other PNA categories these differences were not significant at the group level. In within-individual comparisons independent t-tests revealed significant differences ($t = 3.92$, $p < .01$) in the intensity between positive optimal and positive dysfunctional emotions. In the case of negative affect, the intensity of optimal emotions was significantly ($t = 4.5$, $p < .01$) lower than the intensity of dysfunctional emotions.

The results of this investigation provide support for the multidimensional conception of that affect in sports (Hanin, 1993, 1994, 1995) from which the content, intensity and context (setting) dimensions were derived. Results revealed that Olympic-level skiers were able to identify individual patterns of emotions that were helpful and harmful for their performance in three different settings: competitions, hard work training, and technical skills training. The findings from this exploratory study are consistent with the previous IZOF research (Hanin, 1994; Hanin & Syrjä, 1995a, 1995b; Syrjä, Hanin, & Pesonen, 1995) that has found that patterns of optimal and dysfunctional emotions were individual within and across different sports. However, this investigation further extended the IZOF model by demonstrating that optimal and dysfunctional emotions in the same skiers were not only individual but also different across three performance settings. Thus, the data from this study seem to contradict the hypothesis that there exists "the optimal level of arousal for a typical performer for a given activity" (Oxendine, 1970). In contrast to this view, Hanin's multi-setting hypothesis received initial empirical support and seems instrumental in the description of the intraindividual PNA patterns across in competition and practices within the same sport. Although additional research is clearly indicated, however, it is argued that in future studies emotion content and intensity should be examined at least at three different levels. These include sports activity level (in skiing), performance setting level (practices versus competitions), and the task level (specific components of the race). From this perspective, a more differentiated approach to the study of performance affect in such multi-task sports as Nordic combined, biathlon, triathlon, and decathlon might be in order.

PNA–Performance Relationships The in–out of the zone concept, extended to individually optimal and dysfunctional positive and negative emotions, was tested empirically in soccer (Syrjä, Hanin, & Pesonen, 1995; Pesonen, 1995), badminton and squash (Syrjä, Hanin, & Tarvonen, 1995; Tarvonen, 1995).

Syrjä, Hanin, and Pesonen (1995) examined emotion–performance relationships in 27 junior soccer players aged 15-17 years. Recall and current idiographic scaling was used to identify the PNA patterns (content and intensities) of players' repeated emotional experiences in successful and unsuccessful performances in practices and games. The intensities (level and zones) for each emotion and players' performance were estimated on the Borg's CR-10 scale. Individualised PNA scales were used in three games to assess each player's PNA 30 min prior to performance, PNA 5 min post-performance, recalled PNA and performance during the game. Each player's current and recalled PNA measures were contrasted with his PNA profile in 5 practices and 3 games separately. Then deviations from individually optimal and dysfunctional zones for each emotion were calculated across all players who were within the successful (7-10), average (4-6), or poor (0-3) performance ranges in games and practices. The Kruskal-Wallis test revealed that the differences in PNA deviations before and during game performance were significant and in the predicted direction (in 81.0% of all 21 cases). As expected, successful players were closer to their optimal and outside dysfunctional zones. In practices, significant differences in the predicted direction were observed only during but not prior to performance. The results of regression analysis indicated that the joint impact of the negative harmful and positive helpful emotions accounted for 41.8% of variance ($F = 23.0$, $p < .01$), whereas negative harmful emotions alone accounted for 34.0% of variance in game performance ($F = 33.5$, $p < .01$). In practices, 31.6% of variance in performance was explained by joint impact of positive helpful and negative harmful emotions ($F = 20.3$,

$p < .01$), while positive helpful emotions alone explained 26.7% of variance ($F = 32.5, p < .01$).

The Friedman Two-Way ANOVA revealed that PNA intensity before, during and after performance changed over time, however, in a different way in successful and unsuccessful players. In poor performance group, players were outside optimal zones before the game in 88.2% of all cases. They also failed to either enter their optimal PNA zones or to maintain the optimal emotions during performance. In contrast, successful players prior to the game were closer to their optimal PNA zones and outside dysfunctional zones. These players also managed to maintain their optimal PNA until the task was completed. As a result, the PNA in successful players changed less often (37.5%) than in a poor performance group.

Syrjä, Hanin, and Tarvonen (1995) replicated the soccer study in a sample of Finnish squash (N = 17) and badminton (N = 13) players of national and international level. Current pre-performance and recalled (during and after performance) PNA measures in 5 game practices were contrasted with previously established individualised optimal and dysfunctional zones. In squash all differences in PNA deviations in successful and poor performance groups were significant and in the predicted direction, with the exception for negative optimal and positive dysfunctional emotions. As expected, PNA scores in successful players were closer to their optimal zones and outside their dysfunctional zones. Before practices significant differences were founded only for positive optimal and negative dysfunctional emotions, whereas after practices the significant differences were observed for positive optimal, negative dysfunctional, positive and negative dysfunctional, and total deviation scores.

In squash, predicted relationships were observed in 52.4% of all 21 cases. Significant correlations were found between performance and deviations in dysfunctional (P–N–), optimal (P+N+) and total PNA scores. In badminton, significant correlations between performance and PNA deviations post-performance were found only for positive optimal ($p<.01$) and positive and negative optimal emotions ($p=.01$), but not before practices. Significant relationships between PNA deviations and performance level before practices were observed only in 14.4% of all cases. During performance these relationships were significant for deviations in positive optimal emotions, and positive and negative optimal emotions ($p< .01$), as well as for the total deviation score ($p< .05$). The regression analysis indicated that interactive effect of positive and negative optimal emotions during the performance in squash players accounted for 51.2% of variance ($F = 38.9, p< .01$), whereas positive optimal alone accounted for 40.4% of variance ($F = 50.8, p< .01$). In badminton players, 27.2% of variance in performance was explained by interactive effect of positive (optimal and dysfunctional) emotions ($F = 10.1, p< .01$), whereas positive optimal emotions alone explained 21.1% of variance ($F = 14.7, p< .01$). Thus, the PNA deviations from optimal and dysfunctional zones during the activity were in the predicted direction in both successful and unsuccessful performance groups.

PNA intensity changed significantly over time before, during and after performance in both successful and unsuccessful players. Additionally, it was revealed that in general players were better aware of the effect of positive optimal and negative dysfunctional emotions on the performance. In contrast, some players were less aware about the effect of negative optimal and positive dysfunctional emotions upon their performance.

Taken together, these findings indicate that the best predictors of performance before and during practices were positive optimal and negative dysfunctional emotions. During practices PNA-performance relationships were more significant and in the predicted direction than either before or after performance. In general, the study provided clear empirical support for the utility of the in–out of the zone concept to examine the interactive effect of optimal and dysfunctional emotions (both positive and negative).

Functional Interpretation of Emotion–Performance Relationships The interpretation of emotion–performance relationships in the IZOF model is based on the notion of the functional significance of emotion for human behaviour and performance (Oatley & Jenkins, 1992; Simonov, 1970; Rubinstein, 1946). However, since a detailed description of the performance process is still missing, only tentative explanations are suggested at this point.

From the psychobiological perspective, two constructs with their opposites related to energising and organising aspects of emotion have been proposed (Hanin, 1993, 1994, 1995). These include "energy mobilisation" (energy demobilisation) and "energy utilisation" (miss-use of energy). Energy in this context is similar to Martens' notion of psychic energy as "vigour, vitality and intensity with which mind functions" (1987b, p. 92). However, the term energy is used in a more general sense to imply an active force, an intensity of effort, persistence, decisiveness in reaching one's goal. Moreover, in contrast to Martens' approach, a distinction between physical and psychic as well as between positive and negative energy is not made at this point. Instead, the major focus is on the functional meaning of individually relevant emotions, both positive and negative.

Energy mobilisation/utilisation factors have been initially derived from the anecdotal evidence in applied work with top athletes (Hanin, 1978) and the content analysis of subjective functional interpretation of PNA patterns by athletes in different sports (Hanin, 1993, 1994, 1995; Hanin & Syrjä, 1995a, 1995b). In an exploratory longitudinal study, involving 46 young Finnish ice-hockey players (Hanin, 1993; Hanin & Syrjä, 1995a; Syrjä, 1993), athletes first selected individually relevant emotions that best described their feelings in successful and unsuccessful game situations. Then each athlete was asked to recall and explain in his own words how each particular emotion affected his performance. These comments were content analysed to identify the key themes that would reflect the functional meaning of optimal and dysfunctional emotions. In the case of positive and negative optimal emotions, typical descriptions included feeling of being "strong", "powerful", "quick", "vigorous", "energetic", "alert". Apparently these emotions were related to the generation of additional energy and increased effort usually reflecting more active involvement and a better individual performance. The other instrumental and optimal function was efficient energy utilisation reflected in such themes as "smart and timely use of one's resources", "playing accurately", and "being in control of the situation". In the case of positive and negative dysfunctional emotions typical descriptors included feelings of being "too concerned with success", "too arrogant", "taking too much risk", "trying too much", "not careful", "skating becomes difficult", "making silly mistakes", "not enough effort", "lazy". Here, two opposite functional effects resulting in less involvement and impaired individual performance seemed to operate. One effect was manifested in the failure to generate enough energy and typically resulted in less than effective performance or even in giving up the task pre-maturely. The other detrimental effect was observed in the erroneous or inadequate utilisation of energy (inefficient information processing).

Additionally, it was revealed that both energy generation and energy utilisation functions are closely related. For instance, 63.3% of optimal emotions (12 from the total of 19) were mentioned as useful in *both* energy generation and energy utilisation functions. The remaining 4 positive optimal emotions were useful in the utilisation function, whereas 3 negative optimal emotions were instrumental in the energy generation function. In the case of 15 dysfunctional emotions, 86.7% were harmful for *both* energy generation and energy utilisation functions, whereas the remaining two emotions were detrimental only for the utilisation function (Syrjä, 1993). These findings provided preliminary empirical support for the validity of the two proposed functions (and their opposites) as tentative explanations of the emotion effect upon individual athletic performance.

Interestingly, these two aspects of emotion effect upon behaviour were implicitly present in several conceptualisations of emotion and arousal/activation functions (Duffy, 1951, 1962; Neiss, 1988; Oatley & Jenkins, 1992; Thayer, 1978). Duffy (1951) was among the first to propose the concept of energy mobilisation to revise traditional descriptive categories of psychology. She argued that certain phenomena could be fully described by means of a smaller number of more basic categories suggesting that all behaviour shows variation in goal-direction and in intensity, or energy mobilisation. Also important was the contention that energy level and energy direction (the latter concept was never elaborated in detail) were two different aspects of behaviour that may vary independently. However, later Duffy dropped the term "mobilisation", initially proposed as a principle and a conceptual category, and focused on the description of psychological correlates of activation (Duffy, 1962).

In sport psychology literature energising aspects of arousal and behaviour as well as energising intervention techniques were always of interest to researchers and practitioners (Aleksejev, 1969; Gissen, 1973; Il'in, 1980; Landers & Boutcher, 1986; Loehr, 1982; Machac, 1976; Mahoney & Avener, 1977; Martens, 1987b; Sonstroem, 1986; Weinberg & Hunt, 1976; Zaichkowski & Takenaka, 1993). Consequently, the term *mobilisation* was widely used by European sport psychologists who attempted to describe both qualitatively and quantitatively the state of psychological readiness for competition (Puni, 1969; Genov, 1976). However, neither energy mobilisation, nor utilisation of energy was used as exploratory constructs or principles.

In the IZOF model, the term functioning was introduced to emphasise the role of the quality of performance provided by optimal functions of emotions (Hanin, 1993, 1994, 1995). One such function was optimal task involvement manifested in individual's readiness to perform up to one's potential through the active and sustained efforts. This becomes possible through: (a) generating enough energy to initiate and maintain the task execution process with adequate effort level, and (b) efficient utilisation of available resources until the task is successfully completed.* Dysfunctional emotions typically result in too much (or too little) energy generation and in its inefficient, erroneous or inappropriate utilisation (task-irrelevant focus). Thus, optimal and dysfunctional effects of emotions upon the quality of individual performance are manifested in the increase or decrease in the energising (increasing intensity, effort) and energy utilising functions. Based on energy mobilisation (effort intensity)—energy utilisation (efficiency) distinctions, four types of closely related and relatively independent emotion functions can be identified. These include (a) energising or energy mobilising (M+) function, (b) energy de-mobilising (M–) function, (c) energy utilisation or regulation (U+) function, and (d) energy mis-use or de-regulation (U–) function. The four energy functions also provide a framework for the interpretation of separate and interactive effects of positive and negative emotions upon individual performance.

As reported by Syrjä (1993) and Hanin and Syrjä (1995a), positive optimal emotions serve usually mobilising and organising functions, whereas negative optimal emotions are typically more instrumental in energy producing than in energy utilising function. The dysfunctional effect

*Earlier suggested recovery on-the-task (or between-the-tasks) function (Hanin, 1994) was, in fact, a component of the energy ulitisation (mis-use) function.

of positive emotions (for instance, complacency) may result in a reversal of energy generation function. Thus, an athlete prematurely stops working on the task at hand or fails to invest even a minimum effort (energy de-mobilisation). Positive dysfunctional emotions also disturb effective utilisation of available resources due to inefficient effort or less than efficient strategies in information processing. On the other hand, negative dysfunctional emotions trigger erroneous or inappropriate use of energy by distracting available resources to task-irrelevant (performance damaging) aspects of the situation. Additionally, in some cases, motivational effect of negative emotions triggering increased energy and effort (Eysenck & Calvo, 1992; Mahoney & Avener, 1977) may result in the overload of the utilisation and control function.

From the functional effect perspective, the constructs of energy mobilisation-utilisation (and their opposites) seems useful in explaining why in some athletes the optimal emotions are predominantly positive, whereas in other athletes they are negative. For instance, low-anxious athletes are typically "smart users" of available energy and are less distracted by task-irrelevant and energy wasting concerns. In contrast, high-anxious athletes typically generate more energy, especially in stressful or emergency situations, because they are often less efficient in its use. Negative emotions, such as anxiety, are functionally useful for these athletes in that they help to generate additional energy to compensate for the apparent limitation in information processing or the use of energy. Since the quality of athletic performance is related to both the amount of available energy and its efficient use, different athletes can be successful by using different resources. In other words, the same level of performance may be achieved either through the increase of total effort or via skillful utilisation of available resources (efficiency).

The proposed interpretation of emotion effect upon athletic performance seems to be consistent with available anecdotal data and empirical findings. For instance, Weinberg and Hunt (1976) assessed muscle activity using electromyography (EMG) during throwing task in high-anxious and low-anxious subjects. It was revealed that high-anxious subjects were using "more energy than necessary" and expended it over a greater period of time. Later, it was shown also that the high-anxious subjects were less efficient than their low-anxious counterparts in energy expenditure (Weinberg, 1978). However, since both available resources and their control or utilisation are limited capacity functions (Kahneman, 1973), their interaction is the critical factor for successful performance. For instance, excessive or uncontrolled energy production can overload or disturb processing efficiency (Eysenck & Calvo, 1992; Humphreys & Revelle, 1984; Lang, 1984; Simonov, 1970) resulting in impaired performance. It is argued, therefore, that the total emotion impact upon performance can be better predicted, if it is based on the interactive effects of energy-mobilisation and energy-utilisation functions.

Conclusions and Future Directions

Empirical evidence and tentative theoretical formulations provided above make it possible to explicitly acknowledge apparent advantages and limitations of the IZOF model. Several aspects of the IZOF-anxiety model have already been identified (Cox, 1994; Gould & Krane, 1992; Gould & Tuffy, 1996; Hackfort & Schwenkmezger, 1993; Jones, 1995; Morgan & Elickson, 1989; Raglin, 1992; Weinberg, 1990; Zaichkowski & Takenaka, 1993). These reviewers agree that the IZOF model is a novel alternative approach that has aided understanding of the anxiety–performance relationships. Specifically, the IZOF model has the strength of precisely predicting at what anxiety levels individually optimal performance is most probable. All previous IZOF research has been conducted in naturalistic, field setting and has ecological validity (aimed for coaches and athletes). Moreover, the IZOF model takes into consideration individual differences in athletes' emotional responses by advocating idiographic (within-individual) and longitudinal design. Therefore, the necessity of employing systematic monitoring with individual athletes in order to systematically establish, validate, and refine an athlete's IZOF is strongly emphasised. Additionally, the practical utility and validity of the basic assumptions of the model can be directly examined through hypothesis testing using step-wise assessment procedures through recall, current and anticipatory measures. Consequently, from applied perspective, the IZOF model at this stage provides a useful practical tool for the athlete and sport psychologist.

However, some reviewers, examining early IZOF anxiety research (Gould & Krane, 1992; Gould & Tuffy, 1996; Jones, 1995), expressed concern that "no explanation has been forwarded by Hanin or any subsequent IZOF investigators as to why best performance occurs when an athlete is within his or her IZOF and why poor performance is associated with state anxiety outside one's zone" (Gould & Tuffy, 1996, p. 59). Although this call for a more theoretically-oriented approach to the IZOF research sounds intuitively appealing, advancing mechanisms or explanations to account for the phenomena that first were not adequately described, seems pre-mature at best (Gill, 1994; Landers, 1994; Morgan, 1984). Therefore, the main emphasis in the IZOF model from the very beginning was on accurate descriptions of the effect of anxiety and other emotions upon athletic performance in real-life situations of elite sport. Moreover, all predictions were based on the individual-oriented and previously established criteria and the in–out of the zone notion. It was only after the basic assumptions of the model have been tested empirically in different sports, settings, and samples that functional interpretations the emotion–performance relationships were suggested.

These explanations are still tentative due to the lack of individualised performance process measures and the data describing the dynamics of emotion–performance *reciprocal* relationships. For instance, from the psychosocial perspective (Hanin, 1980, 1985, 1992), it would be critical to examine when and how performance as unfolding process (Folkman & Lazarus, 1985) influences the PNA content and intensity. Thus, it can be argued that change or functional reversals in emotion content occurs as a "response to relational meaning of an encounter in terms of a person's perception of the harms and benefits in a particular person-environment relationship" (Lazarus, 1993, p. 13). Available anecdotal data and preliminary findings are consistent with this conceptualisation (Hanin, 1994, 1995; Hanin & Syrjä, 1995b, 1996, 1997; Pesonen, 1995; Saarnio, 1995; Tarvonen, 1995). Specifically, optimal emotions (P+N+) are mainly *anticipatory* (challenge and threat), whereas situationally dysfunctional emotions (P–N–) represent *outcome* (gain and loss) emotions. Since actual performance process is continually appraised, there is an urge for a shift from the anticipatory, active mind-set to the outcome and relatively passive emotional response. The predominate outcome emotion (P–N–) typically results in impaired or faulty energy mobilization, energy utilisation, or both functions, and therefore, a "sudden" drop in performance is highly probable. However, more systematic research is clearly indicated to test empirically the validity of these tentative psychosocial interpretations.

Several new aspects in the IZOF model need to be studied before this approach evolves into a status of well-developed grounded theory.

First, the best performance patterns in different sports should continue to be an important focus of the studies with more emphasis on the process characteristics and movement patterns in different tasks. Additionally, more attention should be given to the systematic study of typical performance and intraindividual variability of performance (Klavora, 1979; Sonstroem, 1986; Sonstroem & Bernardo, 1982), across several competitions, between practices and competitions during the season and across several seasons. More research into less than successful athletic performance, especially the discontinuities of performance is also warranted (Fazey & Hardy, 1988). This direction, as mentioned earlier, should include a detailed description of both unexpected up-lifts and drops in performance that might follow big successes (Bar-Eli et al., 1992; Hardy, 1990; Kreiner-Phillips & Orlick, 1993; Moormann, 1995; Unestähl, 1986). Second, the systematic study of the dynamics of reciprocal relationships between emotions and performance should be emphasised. Specifically, care should be taken to examine how and when performance results in the shifts or reversals (Apter, 1982; Kerr, 1993) in the content and intensity of individual's emotions. However, until the detailed individualised measures of performance process are developed, this direction of research will be a major block in explaining emotion–performance relationships. Third, the relationships between emotions, cognitions, and motivations should be examined so that their interactive effects upon performance could be more fully assessed, predicted, and explained. Apparently, procedures suggested in the IZOF model for the analysis of individually relevant content and intensity in emotions could be also instrumental in the assessment of situational cognitions and motivations. Fourth, the basic functions of subjective emotional experiences related to the energy/effort and efficiency/skill in performance also warrant additional research using individual-, setting, and task-oriented approach. The interdisciplinary focus here might be especially useful and should involve systematic application of physiological markers (Collins, 1995; Hamill, 1996; Landers & Boutcher, 1986; Zaichowski, Hamill, & Dallis, 1994; Zaichkowski & Takenaka, 1993) and kinematic characteristics of movement patterns (Beuter, Duda, & Widule, 1989; Weinberg, 1990). And, finally, future researchers should be more sensitive to advantages and limitations of objective and subjective measures in the assessments of different modalities of performance psychobiosocial states. For instance, all modalities of the form dimension can be assessed using subjective measures, whereas "objective" markers of physiological, psychomotor, performance, and interactive components are usually limited to actual ongoing assessments. Limitations of the existing standardised self-report measures should also be considered. Otherwise, predictive validity of such measures, that sometimes fail to assess individually relevant emotion content, will be less than satisfactory.

This review has examined recent conceptual and methodological developments in the IZOF model extended to positive and negative emotions related to individually successful and poor performance. The existing empirical evidence is encouraging and supports the IZOF model assumptions regarding the multidimensionality of performance psychobiosocial states, a two-factor conceptualisation of emotion content, and validity of idiographic assessments using individualised PNA scales. However, more sophisticated research, both qualitative and quantitative, is needed within each of the future directions that were specified. Additionally, it might be useful to reexamine advantages and limitations of the existing approaches in sport psychology to emotion–performance relationships within the framework of the IZOF model.

References

Aleksejev, A.V. (1969). *Psihoreguilrujutshaja trenlrovka* (Psychoregulation training Mobilization). Part II. Moscow: VNIIFK.

Allport, G. (1960). The open system in personality theory. *Journal of Abnormal and Social Psychology, 61,* 301-310.

Alpert, R., & Haber, R. N. (1960). Anxiety in academic achievement situations. *Journal of Abnormal and Social Psychology, 61,* 207-215.

Anajev, B.G. (1968). Chelovek kak predmet poznanyla (Person as a subject of study). Leningrad: Leningrad University Press.

Apter, M.J. (1982). *The experience of motivation: The theory of psychological reversals.* London: Academic Press.

Bar-Eli, M. (1985). Arousal-performance relationship: a transactional view on performance jags. *International Journal of Sport Psychology, 16,* 193-209.

Bar-Eli, M., Taoz, E., Levy-Kolker, N., & Tennebaum, G. (1992). Performance quality and behavioral violations as crisis indicators in competition. *International Journal of Sport Psychology, 23,* 325-342.

Bejek, K., & Hagtvet, K.A. (1996). The content of pre-competitive state anxiety in top and lower level female gymnasts. *Anxiety, Stress, and Coping, 9,* 19-31.

Bertyne, D.E. (1960). *Conflict, arousal, and curiosity.* New York: McGraw-Hill.

Bertalanffy, L.V. (1952). Theoretical models in biology and psychology. In D. Krech & Klein, G.S. (Eds.), *Theoretical models and personality therapy* (pp. 24-38). Durham, NC: Duke University Press.

Beuter, A., & Duda, J.L. (1985). Analysis of the arousal/motor performance relationship in children using movement kinematics. *Journal of Sport Psychology, 7,* 229-243.

Beuter, A., Duda, J.L., Widule, C.L. (1989). The effects of arousal on joint kinematics and kinetics in children. *Research Quarterly for Exercise & Sport, 13,* 227-238.

Borg, G. (1982). A category scale with ratio properties for intermodal and interindividual comparisons. In H.-G. Geiss & P. Petzold (Eds.), *Psychophysical judgment and the process of perception* (pp. 25-34). Berlin: VEB Deutscher Verlag der Wissenschaften.

Burton, D. (1990). Multimodal stress management in sport: current status and future directions. In J.G. Jones & L. Hardy (Eds.), *Stress and performance in sport* (pp. 171-202). Chichester: John Wiley.

Butler, R.J., & Hardy, L. (1992). The performance profile: theory and application. *The Sport Psychologist, 6,* 253-264.

Cantor, N., Mischel, W., & Schwartz, J.C. (1982). A prototype analysis of psychological situations. *Cognitive Psychology, 14,* 45-77.

Chemikova, O.A. (1962). *Emotsil v sporte* (Emotions in sport). Moscow: Fizkultura i sport.

Collins, D. (1995). Psychophysiology and sport performance. In S.J.H. Biddle (Ed.), *European perspectives on exercise and sport psychology* (pp. 154-178). Champaign, IL: Human Kinetics.

Courneya, K.S., & Chelladurai, P. (1991). A model of performance measures in baseball. *Journal of Sport & Exercise Psychology, 13,* 16-25.

Cox, R.H. (1994). *Sport psychology: concepts and applications* (3rd ed.; pp. 126-128). Dubuque, IA: WCB Brown & Benchmark.

Davidson, R.J., & Cacioppa, J.T. (1992). New developments in the scientific study of emotion: an introduction to the special section. *Psychological Science, 3,* 21-22.

Davis, S., & West, J.D. (1991). A theoretical paradigm for performance enhancement: the multimodal approach. *The Sport Psychologist, 6,* 167-174.

Dennis, K.M., Bartsokas, T., Lewthwaite, R., & Palin, D. (1993). Relationship between CSAI-2 subscales and performance in youth athletes: The zone of optimal function. *Medicine & Science in Sports & Exercise, 25* (Suppl. 5), S155.

Diener, E., & Emmons, R.A. (1985). The independence of positive and negative affect. *Journal of Personality and Social Psychology, 47,* 1105-1117.

Diener E., & Iran-Nejad, A. (1986). The relationship in experience between various types of affect. *Journal of Personality and Social Psychology, 50,* 1031-1038.

Doyle, J., & Parfitt, G. (1996). Performance profiling and predictive validity. *Journal of Applied Sport Psychology, 8,* 160-170.

Duffy, E. (1951). The concept of energy mobilization. *Psychological review, 58,* 30-40.

Duffy, E. (1962). *Activation and behavior.* New York: John Wiley.

Easterbrook, J.A. (1959). The effect of emotion on cue utilization and organization of behavior. *Psychological Review, 66,* 183-201.

Endler, N.S., & Magnusson, D. (1976). Multidimensional aspects of state and trait anxiety: a cross-cultural study of Canadian and Swedish college students. In C.D. Spielberger & R. Diaz-Guerrero (Eds.), *Cross-cultural anxiety.* (pp. 143-172). Washington, D.C.: Hemisphere.

Eysenck, M.W., & Calvo, M. G. (1992). Anxiety and performance: The processing efficiency theory. *Cognition and Emotion, 6,* 409-434.

Fazey, J., & Hardy, L. (1988). *The Inverted-U hypothesis: A catastrophe for sport psychology?* (BASS Monograph No. 1). Leeds: British Association of Sports Sciences & National Coaching Federation.

Fehr, B., & Russell, J.A. (1984). Concept of emotion viewed from a prototype perspective. *Journal of Experimental Psychology: General, 113,* 464-486.

Fenz, W.D., & Epstein, S. (1967). Gradients of physiological arousal in parachutists as a function of an approaching jump. *Psychosomatic Medicine, 29,* 33-51.

Ferrario, V.G., Sforza, C., Michielon, G., Mauro, F., & Miani, A. (1995). Morphological variation analysis: a new method to quantify the repeatability of sport actions. *Coaching & Sport Sciences Journal, 1,* 29-36.

Folkman, S., & Lazarus, R.S. (1985). If it changes it must be a process: study of emotion and coping during three stages of a college examination. *Journal of Personality and Social Psychology, 48,* 150-170.

Gagayeva, G.M. (1960). *Psykhologiya futbola* (Psychology of soccer). Moscow: Fizkultura i sport.

Ganzen, V.A. (1984). *Systemnyje Opisanija v Psikhologii* (Systems descriptions in psychology). Leningrad: Leningrad University Press.

Ganzen, V.A., & Yurchenko, B.N. (1981). Systemnyj podkhod k analizu, opisaniyu i eksperimnetal'nomu issiedovanlyu psikhicheskih sostoyanij cheloveka. (Systems approach to the analysis, description and experimental study of psychological states in humans). *Psykhicheskjie sostoyaniya l Eksperimental'naya i prikladnaya psykhologyla* (Vol. 10, pp. 9-38). Leningrad: Leningrad University Press.

Genov, F. (1976). The nature of mobilization readiness of the sportsmen and the influence of different factors upon its formation. In A.C. Fisher (Ed.), *Psychology of sport: issues and insights* (pp. 145-155). Palo Alto, CA: Mayfield.

Gill, D.L. (1994). A sport and exercise psychology perspective on stress. *Quest, 46,* 20-27.

Gissen, L.D. (1973). *Psihologiya l pshhogigiyena v sporte (iz opyta raboty v komandah po akademicheskol greble)* (Psychology and psychohygiene in sport. A summary of experiences of applied work in rowing teams). Moscow: Fizkultura i sport.

Gould, D., & Krane, V. (1992). The arousal-athletic performance relationship: Current status and future directions. In T.S. Horn (Ed.), *Advances in sport psychology* (pp. 119-141) Champaign, IL: Human Kinetics.

Gould, D., Petlichkoff, L., & Weinberg, R. (1984). Antecedents of temporal changes in and relationships between CSAI-2 subcomponents. *Journal of Sport Psychology, 6,* 289-304.

Gould, D., & Tuffey, S. (1996). Zones of optimal functioning research: A review and critique. *Anxiety, Stress, and Coping, 9,* 53-68.

Gould, D., Tuffey, S., Hardy, L., & Lochbaum, M. (1993). Multidimensional state anxiety and middle distance running performance: an exploratory examination of Hanin's (1980) zones of optimal functioning hypothesis. *Journal of Applied Sport Psychology, 5,* 85-95.

Hackfort, D., & Schwenkmezger, P. (1993). Anxiety. In R.N. Singer, M. Murphey, & L.K. Tennant (Eds.), *Handbook of research on sport psychology* (pp. 328-364). New York: Macmillan.

Hamill, G. (1996). *Psychological and physiological correlates of the individual zones of optimal functioning.* Unpublished Ed.D. Thesis, Boston University.

Hanin, Y.L. (1977). O srochnoj diagnostike sostojanji lichnosti v grupp (On immediate diagnostics of personality's state in the group). *Teoria lI Praktika Fizicheskoj Kultury, 8,* 8-11.

Hanin, Y.L. (1978). A study of anxiety in sports. In W.F. Straub (Ed.), *Sport psychology: An analysis of athlete behavior* (pp. 236-249). Ithaca, NY: Movement Publications.

Hanin, Y.L. (1980). *Psyhologiya obscheniya v sporte* (Psychology of communication in sport). Moscow: Fuzkultura i sport.

Hanin, Y.L. (1983). STAI in sport: problems and perspectives. In E. Apitzsch (Ed.) *Anxiety in sport* (pp. 129-141). Magglingen: FEPSAC.

Hanin, Y.L. (1985). *Psihologiya obshceniya v sovmestnoj deatel'nosti* (Psychology of communication in group activity). Unpublished Rehabilitation Doctor of Psychological Sciences Dissertation. Leningrad: Leningrad University.

Hanin, Y. (1986). The state-trait anxiety research on sports in the USSR. In C.D. Spielberger & R. Diaz-Guerrero (Eds.), *Cross-cultural anxiety* (Vol. 3, pp. 45-64). Washington: Hemisphere.

Hanin, Y.L. (1989). Interpersonal and intragroup anxiety in sports. In D. Hackfort & C.D. Spielberger (Eds.), *Anxiety in sports: An international perspective* (pp 19-28). Washington: Hemisphere.

Hanin, Y.L. (1992). Social psychology and sport: communication processes in top performance teams. *Sport Science Review, 1*(2), 13-28.

Hanin, Y.L. (1993). Optimal performance emotions in top athletes. In S. Serpa, J. Alves, V. Ferreira, & A. Paula-Brito (Eds.), *Sport psychology: An integrated approach. Proceedings from the VIII World Congress of Sport Psychology* (pp. 229-232). Lisbon: ISSP.

Hanin, Y.L. (1994). Optimization of performance emotions: individual scaling of performance emotions. *Top performance: Proceedings of the 1st National congress of elite Finnish coaches* (pp. 94-106). Jyväskylä: KIHU.

Hanin, Y.L. (1995). Individual zones of optimal functioning (IZOF) model: An idiographic approach to performance anxiety. In K. Henschlen & W. Straub (Eds.), *Sport psychology: an analysis of athlete behavior* (pp. 103-119). Longmeadow, MA: Movement Publications.

Hanin, Y.L., & Bulanova, G.V. (1979). Emotsional'noje sostajanie studentov v sportivnyh i uchebnyh gruppah (Emotional state of students in sports and study groups). *Teoria i Praktika Fizicheskoj Kultury, 4,* 45-47.

Hanin, Y.L., & Kopysov, V.S. (1977). Sostojanie sorevnuyuschegosya sportsmena pri obstchenii s razichnymy sekundantami (Athlete's emotional state in communication with different seconds). *Teoria i Praktika Fizicheskoj Kultury, 11,* 37-39.

Hanin, Y.L., & Syrjä, P. (1995a). Performance affect in junior ice hockey players: An application of the individual zones of optimal functioning model. *The Sport Psychologist, 9,* 169-187.

Hanin, Y.L., & Syrjä, P. (1995b). Performance affect in soccer players: An application of the IZOF model. *International Journal of Sports Medicine, 16,* 264-269.

Hanin, Y.L., & Syrjä, P. (1996). Predicted, actual and recalled affect in Olympic-level soccer players: Idiographic assessments on individualized scales. *Journal of Sport and Exercise Psychology, 18,* 325-335.

Hanin, Y.L., & Syrjä, P. (1997). Optimal emotions in elite cross-country skiers. In E. Müller, H. Schwarneder, E. Kornexi, & C. Raschner (Eds.), *Science and skiing* (pp. 408-419). London: E. & F.N. Spon.

Hardy, L. (1990). A catastrophe model of sport in performance. In J.G. Jones & L. Hardy (Eds.), *Stress and performance in sport* (pp. 81-106). Chichester: John Wiley.

Harger, G.J., & Raglin, J.S. (1994). Correspondence between actual and recalled precompetition anxiety in collegiate track and field athletes. *Journal of Sport and Exercise Psychology, 16,* 206-211.

Hebb, O. (1955). Drive and the C.N.S. (Conceptual nervous system). *Psychological Review, 62,* 243-254.

Humphreys, M.S., & Revelle, W. (1984). Personality, motivation, and performance: A theory of the relationship between individual differences and information processing. *Psychological Review, 91,* 153-184.

Hyvönen, A. (1992). Mielialan yhteys kilpailusuorltukseen (Precompetition anxiety and performance). Unpublished Master's Thesis. Jyväskylä University, Jyväskylä.

Il'in, E.P. (1980). *Psihofiziologija flzicheskogo vospitaniya* (Psychophysiology of physical education). Moscow: Prosveschenjie.

Imlay, G.J., Corda, R.D., Stanbrough, M.E., & O'Connor, P.J. (1995). Anxiety and performance: A test of optimal function theory. *International Journal of Sport Psychology, 26,* 295-306.

Iso-Ahola, S.E. (1995). Intrapersonal and interpersonal factors in athletic performance. *Scandinavian Journal of Medicine & Science in Sports, 5,* 191-199.

Johnson, J., Anderson, J., AhYee, M., & Makua, G. (1995, March/April). *Precompetition emotions in elite junior triathletes.* Paper presented at the Western Psychological Association Convention, Los Angeles.

Jones, J.G. (1991). Recent developments and current issues in competitive state anxiety research. *The Psychologist, 4,* 152-155.

Jones, G. (1995). Competitive anxiety in sport. In S.J.H. Biddle (Ed.), *European perspectives on exercise and sport psychology* (pp. 128-153). Champaign, IL: Human Kinetics.

Kahneman, D. (1973). *Attention and effort.* Englewood Cliffs, NJ: Prentice-Hall.

Karteroliotis, C., & Gill, D.L. (1987). Temporal changes in psychological and physiological components of state anxiety. *Journal of Sport Psychology, 9,* 261-274.

Kelly, G.A. (1955). *The psychology of personal construct.* New York: Norton.

Kelmar, J.H. (1990, November). *Measurement of success and failure in small business—dichotomous anachronism.* Paper presented at the 13th Small Firms Policy & Research Conference, 14-16 November 1990, Harrogate, England.

Kerr, J.H. (1993). An eclectic approach to psychological interventions in sport: Reversal theory. *The Sport Psychologist, 7,* 400-418.

Kiselev, Y.Y. (1967). Opyt podgotovki bortsov k preodolenlyu prepyatstvii neozhidanno voznikayuschih v sorevnovanii (Experience of preparation of wrestlers for coping with unexpected competition barriers). In P.A. Rudik, A.C. Puni, & N.A. Khudadov (Eds.), *Psykhologizeskie voprosy sportivnai trenirovki* (pp. 66-71). Moscow: Fiskultura i Sport.

Klavora, P. (1979). Customary arousal for peak performance. In P. Klavora & J.V. Daniel (Eds.), *Coach, athlete, and sport psychologist* (pp. 155-163). Toronto, Canada: University of Toronto.

Kleine, D. (1990). Anxiety and sport performance: A meta-analysis. *Anxiety Research, 2,* 113-131.

Krane, V. (1993). A practical application of the anxiety-athletic performance relationships: The zone of optimal functioning hypothesis. *The Sport Psychologist, 7,* 113-126.

Kreiner-Phillips, K., & Orlick, T. (1993). Winning after winning: The psychology of ongoing excellence. *The Sport Psychologist, 7,* 31-48.

Landers, D.M. (1994). Performance, stress, and health: Overall reaction. *Quest, 46,* 123-135.

Landers, D.M., & Boutcher, S.H. (1986). Arousal-performance relationships. In J.M. Williams (Ed.), *Applied sport psychology* (pp. 164-184). Palo Alto, CA: Mayfield Publishing.

Lang, P.J. (1984). Cognition in emotion: Concept and action. In C. Izard, J. Kagan, & R. Zajonc (Eds.), *Emotions, cognition and behavior* (pp. 192-226). New York: Cambridge University Press.

Lazarus, R.S. (1991). Cognition and motivation in emotion. *American Psychologist, 46,* 352-367.

Lazarus, R.S. (1993). From psychological stress to the emotions: A history of changing outlooks. *Annual Review of Psychology, 44,* 1-21.

Lazarus, R.F., & Folkman, S. (1984). *Stress, appraisal, and coping.* New York: Springer.

Leontjev, A.N. (1975). *Deatel'nost. Soznanie. Lichnost* (Activity. Consciousness. Personality) Moscow: Politizdat.

Liebert, R.M., & Morris, L.W. (1967). Cognitive and emotional components of test anxiety: A distinction and some initial data. *Psychological Reports, 20,* 975-978.

Liukkonen, J. (1995). Regulation of performance emotions in sports. In J.T. Viltasaio & U. Kujala (Eds.). *The way to win: Proceedings of the international congress on applied research in sports* (pp. 317-322). Helsinki: The Finnish Society for Research in Sport and Physical Education.

Loehr, J.E. (1982). *Athletic excellence: Mental toughness training for sport.* Denver, CO: Forum.

Lomov, B.F. (1984). *Metodologicheskie i teoreticheskie problemy psyhologii* (Methodological and theoretical problems in psychology). Moscow: Nauka.

Lorr, M., McNair, D., & Fisher, S. (1982). Evidence for bipolar mood states. *Journal of Personality Assessment, 46,* 432-436.

Machac, M. (1976). *Harmonizing of mental states and performance.* Praha: Univerzita Karlova.

Mahoney, M.J., & Avener, M. (1977). Psychology of the elite athlete: An exploratory study. *Cognitive Therapy and Research, 1,* 135-141.

Males, J.R., & Kerr, J.H. (1996). Stress, emotion, and performance in elite slalom canoeists. *The Sport Psychologist, 10,* 17-36.

Malmo, R.B. (1959). Activation: A neuropsychological dimension. *Psychological Review, 66,* 367-385.

Martens, R. (1977). *Sport Competition Anxiety Test.* Champaign, IL: Human Kinetics.

Martens, R. (1987a). Science, knowledge, and sport psychology. *The Sport Psychologist, 1,* 29-55.

Martens, R. (1987b). *Coaches guide to sport psychology.* Champaign, IL: Human Kinetics.

Martens, R., Vealey, R.S., & Burton, D. (1990). *Competitive anxiety in sport.* Champaign, IL: Human Kinetics.

McCann, S.C., Murphy, S.M., & Raedeke, T.D. (1992). The effect of performance setting and individual differences on the anxiety–performance relationships for elite cyclists. *Anxiety, Stress, and Coping, 5,* 177-187.

McNair, D.M., Lorr, M., & Droppleman, L.F. (1971). *Manual for the Profile of Mood States.* San Diego, CA: Educational & Industrial Testing Service.

Moormann, P.P. (1995). Dissociative states as an explanation for sudden collapse of figure skating performance. In R. Vanfraechem-Raway & Y. Vanden Auweele (Eds.), *Proceedings of the IXth European Congress on Sport Psychology: Integrating laboratory and field studies: Part 1* (pp. 175-182). Brussels: FEPSAC/Belgian Federation of Sport Psychology.

Morgan, W.P. (1984). Selected psychological factors limiting performance: A mental health model. In D.H. Clarke & H.M. Eckert (Eds.), *Limits of human performance,* (pp. 70-80). Champaign, IL: Human Kinetics.

Morgan, W.P., & Elickson, K.A. (1989). Health, anxiety, and physical exercise. In D. Hackfort & C.D. Spielberger (Eds.), *Anxiety in sports: an international perspective* (pp. 165-182). New York: Hemisphere.

Morgan, W.P., O'Connor, P.J., Elickson, K.-A., & Bradley, P.W. (1988). Personality structure, mood states, and performance in elite male distance runners. *International Journal of Sport Psychology, 19,* 247-263.

Morgan, W.P., O'Connor, P.J., Sparling, P.B., & Rate, R.R. (1987). Psychological characterization of the elite female distance runners. *International Journal of Sports Medicine, 8* (Suppl.), 124-131.

Neiss, R. (1988). Reconceptualizing arousal: Psychobiological states in motor performance. *Psychological Bulletin, 103,* 345-366.

Nitsch, J.R., & Seller, R. (Eds.). (1993). *Movement and sport. Psychological foundations and effects: Vol. 1. Motivation, emotion, stress.* Sankt Augustin: Academia.

Oatley, K., & Jenkins, J.M. (1992). Human emotions: Function and dysfunction. *Annual Review of Psychology, 43,* 55-85.

Orlick, T. (1990). *In pursuit of excellence.* Champaign, IL: Leisure Press.

Oxendine, J.B. (1970). Emotional arousal and performance. *Quest, 13,* 23-32.

Parfitt, G., & Hardy, L. (1993). The effects of competitive anxiety on memory span and rebound shooting tasks in basketball players. *Journal of Sports Sciences, 11,* 517-524.

Pesonen, T. (1995). *Tuntelden yhteys suoritukseen juniorijalkapallollijoila* (Emotion–performance relationship in junior soccer players). Unpublished Master's Thesis. Jyväskylä University, Jyväskylä, Finland.

Pons, D.C. (1984). *Un estudio sobre la relacion entre ansiedad y rendimiento en jugadores de golf* (A study of relationship between anxiety and performance in golf-players). Unpublished PhD. Thesis, Universitat de Valencia, Valencia.

Prapavessis, H., & Carron, A. (1966). The effect of group cohesion on competitive state anxiety. *Journal of Sport & Exercise Psychology, 18,* 64-74.

Prapavessis, H., & Grove, J.R. (1991). Precompetitive emotions and shooting performance: The mental health and zone of optimal function models. *The Sport Psychologist, 5,* 223-234.

Puni, A.C. (1959). *Ocherki psyhologii sporta* (Essays of Sport psychology) Moscow: Fizkultura i Sport.

Puni, A.C. (1969). *Psikhologicheskaja podgotovka k sorevnovaniyu v sporte* (Psychological preparation for the competition in sport). Moscow: Fizkultura i Sport.

Raglin, J.S. (1992). Anxiety and sport performance. In J.O. Holloszy (Ed.), *Exercise and sports sciences reviews* (Vol. 20, pp. 243-274). Baltimore, MD: Williams & Wilkins.

Raglin, J.S., Morgan, M.P., & Wise, K.J. (1990). Pre-competition anxiety and performance in female high school swimmers: A test of optimal function theory. *International Journal of Sports Medicine, 11,* 171-175.

Raglin, J.S., & Morris, M.J. (1994). Precompetition anxiety in women volleyball players: A test of ZOF theory in a team sport. *British Journal of Sports Medicine, 28,* 47-52.

Raglin, J.S., & Turner, P.E. (1993). Anxiety and performance in track and field athletes: A comparison of the inverted-U hypothesis with zone of optimal function theory. *Personality and Individual Differences, 14,* 163-171.

Rodionov, A.V. (1968). *Psyhologiya sportivnogo poedinka* (Psychology of sports contest). Moscow: Fizkultura i Sport.

Rubinstein, S.L. (1946). *Osnovy obtshej psykhologuii* (Foundations of General Psychology). Moscow: Uchpedgiz.

Rushall, B.S. (1978). Environment specific behavior inventories: Developmental procedures. *International Journal of Sport Psychology, 9,* 97-110.

Russell, J.A. (1979). Affective space is bipolar. *Journal of Personality & Social Psychology, 37,* 345-256.

Russell, J.A., Weiss, A., & Mendelsohn, G.A. (1989). Affect grid: A single-item scale of pleasure and arousal. *Journal of Personality and Social Psychology, 57,* 493-502.

Saamio, J. (1995). *Performance affect in competitive swimmers.* Unpublished Master's Thesis. University of Jyväskylä, Jyväsklylä, Finland.

Salminen, S., Liukkonen, J., Hanin, Y., & Hyvönen, A. (1995). Anxiety and athletic performance of Finnish athletes: An application of the zone of optimal functioning model. *Personality and Individual Differences, 19,* 725-729.

Scallen, S. (1993). Collegiate swimmers and the zone of optimal functioning theory. *Journal of Sport and Exercise Psychology,* Suppl. NASPSPA Conference Abstracts, *15,* S 68.

Schedrovitsky, G.P. (1964). *Problemy metodologii systemnogo issledovanlya* (Methodological problems of the systems research). Moscow: Uchpedgiz.

Schilling, G. (1979). Aufgaben der Sportpsychologie. In H. Gabler, H. Ebersprächer, E. Hahn, J. Kern, & G. Schilling (Eds.), *Praxis der Psychologie im Leistungssport* (pp. 23-25). Berlin: Bartels & Wertnitz.

Schlosberg, H. (1954). Three dimensions of emotion. *Psychological Review, 61,* 81-88.

Schwartz, G.E., Davidson, R.J., Goleman, D.J. (1978). Patterning of cognitive and somatic processes in the self-regulation of anxiety: Effects of meditation versus exercise. *Psychosomatic Medicine, 40,* 321-328.

Schuijers, H.P.M. (1989). *Intra-individual pre-event state anxiety and performance in female college gymnastics: A Comparison of Three Models.* Unpublished Ph.D. Thesis, University of Nijmegen, The Netherlands.

Simonov, P.V. (1970). *Teoria otrazhenia l psykhofisologia emotsij* (Reflection theory and psychophysiology of emotions). Moscow: Medgiz.

Smith, R.E., Smoll, F.L., & Schutz, R.W. (1990). Measurement and correlates of sport specific cognitive and somatic trait anxiety: The sport anxiety scale. *Anxiety Research, 2,* 263-280.

Sonstroem, R.J. (1986). An overview of anxiety in sport. In J.M. Silva & R.S. Weinberg (Eds.), *Psychological foundations of sport psychology* (pp. 104-117). Champaign, IL: Human Kinetics.

Sonstroem, R.J., & Bernardo, P. (1982). Intraindividual pregame state anxiety and basketball performance: A re-examination of the inverted-U curve. *Journal of Sport Psychology, 4,* 235-245.

Spielberger, C.D. (1989). Stress and anxiety in sports. In D. Hackfort & C.D. Spielberger (Eds.), *Anxiety in sports: An international perspective* (pp. 3-17). New York: Hemisphere.

Spielberger, C.D., Gorsuch, R.L., & Lushene, R.E. (1970). *Manual for the State-Trait Anxiety Inventory (STAI).* Palo Alto, CA: Consulting Psychologists Press.

Stambulova, N.B. (1994). Developmental sports career investigations in Russia: A post-perestroika analysis. *The Sport Psychologist, 8,* 221-237.

Syrjä, P. (1993). *Suaoritustunteet juniorijaakiekkoilljoila.* (Performance emotions in junior ice-hockey players). Unpublished Master's Thesis, University of Jyväskylä, Jyväskylä, Finland.

Syrjä, P., Hanin, Y., & Pesonen, T. (1995). Emotion and performance relationships in soccer players. In R. Vanfraechem-Raway & Y. Vanden Auweele (Eds.), *Proceedings of the IXth European Congress on Sport Psychology: Integrating laboratory and field studies, Part 1* (pp. 191-197). Brussels: FEPSAC/Belgian Federation of Sport Psychology.

Syrjä, P., Hanin, Y., & Tarvonen (1995). Emotion and performance relationships in squash and badminton players. In R. Vanfraechem-Raway & Y. Vanden Auweele (Eds.), *Proceedings of the IXth European Congress on Sport Psychology: Integrating laboratory and field studies, Part 1* (pp. 183-190). Brussels: FEPSAC/Belgian Federation of Sport Psychology.

Tarvonen, S. (1995). *Suoritustunteiden ja suorituksen valinen yhteys squash- ja suikapaliopelaajilla* (Emotion–performance relationships in squash and badminton plahyers). Unpublished Masters Thesis. Jyväskylä University, Jyväskylä, Finland.

Thayer, R.E. (1978). Toward a psychological theory of multidimensional activation (arousal). *Motivation and Emotion, 2,* 1-34.

Turner, P.E., & Raglin, J.S. (1996). Variability in precompetition anxiety and performance in college track and field athletes. *Medicine & Science in Sports & Exercise, 28,* 378-385.

Unestähl, L.-E. (1986). The ideal performance. In L.-E. Unestähl (Ed.), *Sport psychology in theory and practice* (pp. 21-38). Örebro: Veje Publishers.

Vallerand, R.J. (1983). On emotion in sport: Theoretical and social psychological perspectives. *Journal of Sport Psychology, 5,* 197-215.

Vanden Auweele, Y., De Cuyper, B., Van Mele, V., & Rzewnicki, R. (1993). Elite performance and personality: From description and prediction to diagnosis and intervention. In R.N. Singer, M. Murphey, & L.K. Tennant (Eds.), *Handbook of research on sport psychology* (pp. 257-289). New York: Macmillan.

Vanek, M., & Cratty, B.J. (1968). *Psychology and the superior athlete.* London: The Macmillan.

Vanfraechem-Raway, R., & Vanden Auweele, Y. (Eds.). (1995). *Proceedings of the IXth European Congress on Sport Psychology: Integrating laboratory and field studies, Part 1.* Brussels: FEPSAC/Belgian Federation of Sport Psychology.

Vlatkin, B.A. (1974). *Diagnostika I regulirovanie pshycheskogo sostaoniya sportsmena v sorevnovaniya* (Diagnostics and regulation of athlete's psychic stress in competition). Perm, Russia: Perm Pedagogical Institute.

Vygotsky, L.S. (1926). *Pedagogicheskaja psyhologiya* (Pedagogical psychology). Moscow: Rabotnik Prosveschenija.

Warr, P., Barter, J., & Brownbridge, G. (1983). On the independence of positive and negative affect. *Journal of Personality and Social Psychology, 44,* 644-651.

Watson, D., Clark, L.A., & Tellegen, A. (1988). Development and validation of brief measures of positive and negative affect: The PANAS scales. *Journal of Personality and Social Psychology, 54,* 1063-1070.

Watson, D., & Tellegen, A. (1985). Towards a consensual structure of mood. *Psychological Bulletin, 98,* 219-235.

Weinberg, R.S. (1978). The effects of success and failure on patterning of neuromuscular energy. *Journal of Motor Behavior, 10,* 53-61.

Weinberg, R.S. (1989). Anxiety, arousal, and motor performance: theory, research, and applications. In D. Hackfort & C.D. Spielberger (Eds.), *Anxiety in sports: An international perspective* (pp. 95-112). New York: Hemisphere.

Weinberg, R.S. (1990). Anxiety and motor performance: Where to from here? *Anxiety Research, 2,* 227-242.

Weinberg, R.S., & Hunt, V.V. (1976). The interrelationships between anxiety, motor performance, and electromyography. *Journal of Motor Behavior, 8,* 219-224.

Woodman, T., Albinson, J., & Hardy, L. (1996). An investigation of the zone of optimal functioning (ZOF) hypothesis within a multidimensional framework. In P. Marconnet, J. Gaulard, I. Margaritis, & F. Tessler (Eds.), *First Annual Congress of the ECSS. Frontiers in Sport Science. The European Perspective.* Book of Abstracts (pp. 66-67). Nice-France: University of Nice Sophia-Antipolis.

Yarnold, P.R. (1988). Classical test theory methods for repeated measures N = 1 research designs. *Education and Psychological Measurement, 48,* 913-919.

Yeadon, M.R., & Challis, J.H. (1992). *Future directions for performance related research in sport biomechanics.* London, UK: The Sports Council.

Yerkes, R.M., & Dodson, J.D. (1908). The relation of strength of stimulus to rapidity of habit-formation. *Journal of Comparative Neurology & Psychology, 18,* 459-482.

Young, P.T. (1959). The role of affective processes in learning and motivation. *Psychological Review, 66,* 104-125.

Zaichkowski, L., Hamill, G., & Daltis, B. (1994, October). *Physiological correlates of the zone of optimal functioning.* Poster session of the annual meeting of the Association for the Advancement of Applied Sport Psychology. Lake Tahoe, NV.

Zaichkowski, L., & Takenaka, K. (1993). Optimizing arousal level. In R.N. Singer, M. Murphey, & L.K. Tennant (Eds.), *Handbook of research on sport psychology* (pp. 511-527). New York: Macmillan.

Zevon, M.A., & Tellegen, A. (1982). The structure of mood change: An idiographic/nomothetic analysis. *Journal of Personality and Social Psychology, 43,* 111-122.

Acknowledgment

The research described in this paper was supported by grants from the Finnish Ministry of Education (1992-1997) and the Finnish Olympic Committee (1993-1995).

Appreciation is expressed to the following individuals for their contribution to various phases of the research described in this paper: Pasi Syrjä, Simo Tarvonen, Jarno Liukkonen, Simo Salminen, Jussi Saamio, Tuomas Pesonen, Ari Hyvönen, and Muusa Hanina. Special thanks are extended to athletes who volunteered to participate in this research, and the cooperation of their coaches, Jyrki Heliskoski, Tapio Korjus, Pekka Vänäsöyrinki, and Antti Leppävuari is also acknowledged.

The author also wishes to thank Stuart Biddle, William Morgan, John Raglin, and the reviewers Lew Hardy and Yannis Zervas for their helpful comments on an earlier draft of this paper.

8 A Multidimensional Theory of Competitive State Anxiety

RAINER MARTENS
Human Kinetics Publishers
DAMON BURTON
University of Idaho
ROBIN S. VEALEY
Miami University, Ohio
LINDA A. BUMP
Human Kinetics Publishers
DANIEL E. SMITH
State University of New York-Brockport

This chapter from a section in the book Competitive Anxiety in Sport introduces the Competitive State Anxiety Inventory (CSAI). In the 1960s it was found that situation-specific anxiety scales predicted behavior better than did general anxiety inventories. This led to Martens' (1977) development of the Sport Competition Anxiety Test (SCAT), a sport-specific trait anxiety scale that was determined to be more receptive to changes in the competitive sport environment. Thus Martens, Burton, Rivkin, and Simon (1980) developed the CSAI to assess sport-specific state anxiety.

Since cognitive state anxiety and somatic state anxiety influence behavior differently, it is important to measure both areas in terms of their cause-and-effect relationship and their influence on performance. This cognitive and somatic distinction is also important from a treatment perspective, because intervention techniques differ for each. CSAI II measures these cognitive and somatic components, along with a state self-confidence scale.

It is difficult to select one chapter in this book section by Martens, Burton, Vealey, Bump, and Smith as essential. Also in that section of the book, chapters 9 and 10 discuss the psychometric properties of the CSAI II. Chapters 11 and 12 establish its norms and explore research using this inventory. Finally, chapter 13 discusses conclusions drawn from CSAI II research and potential problems, and it provides future directions. Because of its strong theoretical base and extensive psychometric properties, the CSAI II has become one of the most used research instruments in the field.

Beginning in the 1950s, anxiety researchers measured anxiety with general inventories such as the Taylor (1953) Manifest Anxiety Scale, the IPAT Anxiety Scale (Cattell, 1957), and the General Anxiety Scale (Sarason, et al., 1960). Results with these instruments led researchers to conclude that anxiety was too amorphous to be useful as a predictor of behavior. Indications were that anxiety was both acute and chronic, which led to a major conceptual advance best espoused by Spielberger (1966a). He is credited with articulating the distinction between momentary anxiety states (A-state) and more enduring anxiety traits A-trait). This led Spielberger et al. (1970) to develop the STAI, a significant advance in measurement.

At about the same time, a number of researchers were finding that situation-specific anxiety scales predicted behavior better than did general anxiety inventories. For example, scales were developed to measure test anxiety (Sarason et al., 1960), social evaluation anxiety (Watson & Friend, 1969), and even anxieties about snakes, heights, and darkness (Mellstrom, Cicala, & Zuckerman, 1976). Within sport, Martens (1977) developed SCAT, a sport-specific A-trait inventory, and demonstrated that it predicted A-state in sport better than did Spielberger et al.'s (1970) SAI.

Early research with SCAT suggested that, although a sport-specific A-trait scale was needed, a sport-specific A-state scale would also be useful. Therefore, Martens, Burton, Rivkin, and Simon (1980) modified Spielberger et al.'s SAI by identifying 10 items from the 20-item scale that were most sensitive to changes in a competitive sport environment. This new scale was named the Competitive State Anxiety Inventory (CSAI) because it assesses sport-specific A-state.

Recent theory and research suggest that even with these conceptual developments anxiety may be a more useful construct with even greater conceptual specificity (Davidson, 1978). It is becoming increasingly evident that the prediction of behavior will not succumb to grand and parsimonious theoretical explanations but instead requires theoretical constructs of increasing specificity and hence instruments to measure them.

Endler (1978), for example, asserted that both A-trait and A-state were multidimensional and suggested five components of A-trait: interpersonal ego threat, physical danger, ambiguity, innocuousness, and social evaluation threat. He also cited the research of Sarason (1975a, 1975b) and Wine (1971) in support for a two-component model of A-state. These two components he labeled *cognitive- worry* and *emotional-arousal.* Actually, Liebert and Morris (1967) first introduced these two components in the test anxiety literature. More recently, Davidson and Schwartz (1976)

Adapted, by permission, from R. Martens et al., 1990, A multidimensional theory of competitive state anxiety (CASI II). In *Competitive anxiety in sport,* edited by R. Martens, R. Vealey, and D. Burton (Champaign, IL: Human Kinetics), 119-126.

and Borkovec (1976) have identified two similar components of anxiety that they have labeled *cognitive anxiety* and *somatic anxiety*. In fact, Morris, Davis, and Hutchings (1981), in a review of multidimensional conceptualizations of A-state, indicated that the cognitive-somatic distinction is essentially the same as the worry-emotionality distinction made by Liebert and Morris.

By whatever name, this conceptual distinction led to the construction of at least three inventories to measure cognitive and somatic anxiety. Liebert and Morris (1967) developed the Worry-Emotionality Inventory (WEI), which was later revised by Morris, Davis, and Hutchings (1981); Spielberger, Gonzalez, Taylor, Algaze, and Anton (1978) developed the Test Anxiety Inventory (TAI); and Schwartz, Davidson, and Goleman (1978) developed the Cognitive-Somatic Anxiety Questionnaire (CSAQ). The former is an A-state scale, and the latter two inventories measure A-trait. Thus, the cognitive-somatic distinction has been used for assessing both A-trait and A-state. However, because this chapter presents a multidimensional theory of competitive A-state, the remaining discussion about the cognitive-somatic anxiety distinction will focus on A-state, not A-trait.

The conceptual distinction between cognitive and somatic A-state and the subsequent development of instrumentation to tap these multidimensional components of anxiety initiated the reconceptualization of competitive anxiety and a modification of the CSAI to account for both components of A-state. The remainder of this chapter focuses on the distinction between cognitive and somatic A-state and discusses why this distinction is important in understanding competitive anxiety.

Cognitive and Somatic A-State Defined

Cognitive A-state is closely associated with worry, a mental process pervasive in our society. Morris, Davis, and Hutchings (1981) defined cognitive A-state as "negative expectations and cognitive concerns about oneself, the situation at hand, and potential consequences" (p. 541). In sport, cognitive A-state is most commonly manifested in negative expectations about performance and thus negative self-evaluation, both of which precipitate worry, disturbing visual images, or both.

Somatic A-state refers to the physiological and affective elements of the anxiety experience that develop directly from autonomic arousal. Somatic A-state is reflected in such responses as rapid heart rate, shortness of breath, clammy hands, butterflies in the stomach, and tense muscles.

Significance of the Cognitive-Somatic Distinction

The value in measuring cognitive and somatic A-state rests separately with the conceptual arguments and empirical evidence that these two components are elicited by different antecedents and that they influence behavior differently (Davidson & Schwartz, 1976; Liebert & Morris, 1967). Thus, one person may respond to a stressor with primarily cognitive A-state and another with primarily somatic A-state, or the same person may experience primarily cognitive A-state in one situation and primarily somatic A-state in a different situation. Davidson and Schwartz (1976) offered the example of

> a person who is physically tired and somatically relaxed lies down, unable to fall asleep because his "mind is racing." This individual is manifesting cognitive symptoms of anxiety. Alternatively, somatic anxiety is characteristic of the person who complains of bodily tension and autonomic stress without accompanying cognitive symptoms. Often, beginning meditators report somatic aches and pains and diffuse muscle tension despite the presence of general "cognitive calmness." (Goleman, 1971, p. 402)

Although cognitive and somatic A-state are hypothesized to be conceptually independent, Morris, Davis, and Hutchings (1981) noted that they likely covary in stressful situations because these situations contain elements related to the arousal of each. Borkovec (1976) agreed, but for a different reason. He suggested that each component of anxiety may serve a conditional or a discriminative function for the other component.

For example, if powerful somatic responses have been conditioned to a particular stimulus, these responses may indicate to the person that there is reason to worry. An athlete may have acquired conditioned somatic responses to precontest events such as locker-room preparation, presence on the playing field, an audience in the stands, and precontest warm-up routines. The conditioned somatic responses may then trigger the athlete to begin worrying because he or she is feeling certain somatic symptoms of anxiety. On the other hand, cognitions in the form of negative self-talk and images of failure may trigger a specific pattern of somatic responses. Understanding how these components interact within an individual should help sport psychologists assist athletes in managing anxiety more effectively, and this requires that the cognitive and the somatic components of A-state be measured both reliably and validly.

Independence of Cognitive and Somatic A-State

The original justification for revising the CSAI was based not only on these conceptual arguments but also on extensive scientific evidence that cognitive and somatic A-state are independent and thus warrant separate measurement.

Evidence Based on Correlations, Factor Analyses, and Item Analyses

Liebert and Morris (1967) were the first to investigate this relationship using their WEI. They hoped to demonstrate the theoretical independence of cognitive and somatic A-state by obtaining low to moderate correlations between these two components of anxiety. Unfortunately, they failed to obtain the evidence they sought, as correlations from six studies ranged from .55 to .76 (Deffenbacher, 1977, 1978, 1980; Morris & Liebert, 1970, 1973; Morris & Perez, 1972). Morris, Davis, and Hutchings (1981) revised the WEI and obtained a lower correlation of .48. In two other studies using the revised WEI, the correlations between cognitive and somatic A-state were .43 (Carden, 1979) and .41 (Parks, 1980). Schwartz et al. (1978), using the CSAQ (a trait scale), obtained a correlation of .42 between cognitive and somatic A-trait.

Even these latter correlations indicate modest dependence, but they have been interpreted by researchers in this area as evidence of relative independence. This interpretation appears to be warranted because most situations that are powerful stressors contain stimuli that elicit and maintain both anxiety components.

Evidence for the independence of these two components also comes from factor analyzing and computing item analyses on the anxiety items commonly used in many general anxiety scales. Each of the studies doing so has found statistical support for two major subsets of anxiety items: cognitive and somatic (Barratt, 1972; Buss, 1962; Fenz & Epstein, 1967).

Evidence Based on Different Antecedents of Cognitive and Somatic A-State

Perhaps the most convincing evidence for the conceptual independence of cognitive and somatic A-state is found in the research identifying the different antecedents associated with these two components of anxiety (i.e., construct validity). When differential antecedents of cognitive and somatic A-state are tested for, experimental conditions must be established that elicit high levels of one component of A-state without elevating the other. Thus, if high arousal can be elicited without self-evaluation, then high levels of somatic A-state should be reported without accompanying increments in cognitive A-state. Similarly, different experimental conditions that are highly evaluative but not arousing should primarily elicit cognitive but not somatic A-state.

The extant research investigating cognitive versus somatic A-state has found some support for these predictions. Morris and Liebert (1973) reported that the threat of electric shock with no performance evaluation increased somatic A-state primarily and that failure feedback in the same setting predominantly increased cognitive A-state. Morris, Harris, and Rovins (1981) observed similar results in a social evaluation situation, and Morris, Brown, and Halbert (1977) observed peers exhibiting either cognitive or somatic A-state and found that cognitive and somatic A-state were elicited independently.

Two additional studies demonstrated that performance expectancies held by individuals before evaluation were highly correlated with cognitive but not somatic A-state (Liebert & Morris, 1967; Morris & Liebert, 1970). Moreover, research has confirmed that cognitive and somatic A-state follow different temporal patterns that correspond to predictions for these two components of anxiety. Four studies have shown that somatic A-state increased steadily until the start of an examination and then decreased significantly as the test progressed. Cognitive A-state changed before or during evaluation only when expectation of success was experimentally altered (Doctor & Altman, 1969; Morris & Engle, 1981; Morris & Fulmer, 1976; Smith & Morris, 1976).

However, the research evidence on the independence of cognitive and somatic anxiety is by no means unequivocal. Several studies have manipulated antecedent variables in ways similar to the procedures employed in the studies cited but have failed to obtain the hypothesized results (Deffenbacher & Dietz, 1978; Holroyd, 1978; Holroyd, Westbrook, Wolf, & Badhorn, 1978; Morris & Perez, 1972; Smith & Morris, 1976, 1977). What these studies suggest is that finding experimental conditions that elicit cognitive anxiety but not somatic anxiety or vice versa is difficult. As observed earlier, many situations offer cues that are salient to manifesting both cognitive and somatic anxiety.

Two other sources of evidence for the independence of cognitive and somatic A-state are found in

- the relationship between these anxiety components and performance and
- the research investigating the efficacy of various anxiety treatment methods for individuals who have predominantly cognitive or somatic anxiety.

These two topics have especially significant implications for sport psychologists.

Evidence Based on the Relationship Between Anxiety Components and Performance

Cognitive and somatic A-state should influence performance differently, depending on previous theorizing. Somatic A-state is likely to reach its peak at the onset of competition and to dissipate once the contest begins. Thus, somatic A-state should influence performance less than should cognitive A-state unless the somatic A-state becomes so great that attention is diverted from the task to these internal states or unless certain task demands (e.g., duration or complexity) become highly salient.

On the other hand, cognitive A-state is indicative of negative expectations about success in performing a task, and these expectations are known to have powerful effects on performance (Bandura, 1977; Feltz, Landers, & Raeder,

1979; Rosenthal, 1968; Weinberg, Gould, & Jackson, 1979). Thus, cognitive A-state should be more strongly related to performance than should somatic A-state. Wine (1971, 1980) has marshaled substantial evidence that the mechanism by which cognitive A-state inhibits performance is by disrupting attentional processes. When athletes are worried, they become preoccupied with their own self-evaluation and ruminate about possible failure rather than directing attention to the task at hand.

The research evidence examining the relationship between performance and cognitive-somatic components of A-state is limited, and none has employed sport populations. Morris, Davis, and Hutchings (1981), after reviewing the evidence, concluded that cognitive A-state is more consistently and strongly related to performance. In a set of studies using the motor skills of typing, Morris, Smith, Andrews, and Morris (1975) found that somatic A-state did not interfere with performance but that cognitive A-state did in one of three studies. Somatic A-state was significantly related to performance in several of the studies but always to a less significant degree than was cognitive A-state. Moreover, Deffenbacher (1977) found a complex interaction between cognitive and somatic A-state, suggesting that anxiety may become debilitating only when both components of anxiety are elevated to high levels. Thus, one of the challenges for future researchers is to untangle the possible cause-and-effect relationship between cognitive and somatic A-state as they influence performance.

Evidence Based on the "Matching Hypothesis" of Anxiety Reduction

Borkovec (1976) and Davidson and Schwartz (1976) have each described how cognitive and somatic anxiety reflect two independent systems of response to stressors. Thus, the treatment of anxiety may be more efficacious if the method of treatment is directed at the system most activated by the stressor, a process known as the "matching hypothesis." For example, relaxation therapies, systematic desensitization, implosive therapy, and biofeedback are expected to be better suited to reduce somatic anxiety. Rational emotive therapy, cognitive therapies, thought stopping, and expectancy manipulations should be more effective in reducing cognitive anxiety. However, anxiety-reduction methods directed at one system may indirectly facilitate relaxation through the other system because the systems do interact. Nevertheless, it is hypothesized that the more efficacious approach is to reduce anxiety with a method directed at the type of anxiety being experienced.

The evidence supporting the matching hypothesis is by no means unanimous, although the weight of the evidence tends to support it (Lehrer, Schoicket, Carrington & Woolfolk, 1980; Morris, Davis, and Hutchings, 1981; Ost, Jerremalm, & Johansson, 1981; Schwartz et al., 1978). Morris, Davis, and Hutchings (1981) suggested that cognitive anxiety is more resistant to change than is somatic anxiety and that it requires a more complex cognitive-oriented approach. Although several studies have found cognitive and somatic treatment methods equally effective in reducing cognitive A-state, those studies finding one method more effective used cognitive therapies (Cooley & Spiegler, 1980; Goldfried, Lineham, & Smith, 1978; Hahnloser, 1974; Kaplan, McCordick, & Twitchell, 1979).

Researchers have also examined the relationship between the methods used to reduce cognitive and somatic A-state and subsequent performance, especially on intellectual tasks. Of the five studies in which performance improved, cognitive A-state was significantly reduced, but in four of the studies somatic A-state also was significantly reduced (Deffenbacher, Mathis, & Michaels, 1979; Deffenbacher, Michaels, Michaels, & Daley, 1980; Kirkland & Hollandsworth, 1980; Osarchuk, 1976; Thompson, Griebstein, & Kuhlenschmidt, 1980). However, cognitive A-state accounted for more performance variance than did somatic A-state in each of these studies, although both anxiety components together accounted for less than 10% of the total variance. Interestingly, this finding may be more indicative of the problems associated with measuring performance accurately than with the hypothesis being tested.

Summary

Despite some equivocality, the accumulated evidence clearly supports the value of distinguishing between cognitive and somatic A-state. This distinction has significance for sport psychology in helping us better understand the relationship between anxiety and performance and in the treatment of high A-state.

Currently, many sport psychologists are using progressive relaxation or desensitization therapies to help highly anxious athletes. These techniques may be appropriate if athletes are primarily experiencing somatic anxiety, but if the athlete is experiencing cognitive anxiety, then a cognitive-based relaxation procedure may be more efficacious. Only with sport-specific research and the instrumentation that is needed to conduct this research will answers to these conjectures be gained.

Recognizing and measuring cognitive and somatic A-state within the sport context may also help untangle the relationship between anxiety and sport performance. The past research on the relationship between anxiety and motor performance is equivocal, although evidence does support the inverted-U hypothesis (Martens, 1974; Yerkes & Dodson, 1908). However, it is not at all clear why performance deteriorates when athletes reach high levels of A-state. Some evidence suggests that the increased muscular tension (somatic A-state) causes the deterioration (Weinberg, 1978), but other evidence suggests that it is self-rumination, or turning attention inward rather than on the task (i.e., cognitive A-state), that causes the deterioration (Wine, 1980). Then too it will become necessary to unravel what most likely is the complex cause-and-effect relationship between cognitive and somatic A-state and performance.

9 Motivation in Sport Settings: A Goal Perspective Approach

JOAN L. DUDA
University of Birmingham

Over the past two decades, social cognitive models of motivation that emphasize the significance of personal goals have become increasingly popular. One of the most important approaches to motivation proposed in this context has dealt with goal perspectives. Research on goal perspectives in sport and exercise has been grounded in achievement goal theories in educational psychology put forth in the mid-1980s by Nicholls, Dweck, Maehr, and Ames. Toward the end of the 1980s, sport and exercise psychologists, mainly under the leadership of Joan Duda, began to advocate the importance of testing these notions in the physical achievement domain.

Achievement goals focus on the ways in which people understand differences in achievement. Each of the aforementioned scholars would agree that, in achievement settings, a major motive for individuals to pursue would be to demonstrate competence; therefore, a central feature of achievement strivings would be the salience of ability perceptions. At least two major goal perspectives are said to operate in achievement situations: a self-referenced and mastery-focused and a normatively referenced and comparatively oriented strategy. Variations in goal perspectives are fundamental to the understanding of the differences observed in people's achievement-related affect, cognition, and behavior. It is argued that motivation in achievement settings is affected by the manner in which people construe their ability level and define success and failure, and two primary perspectives toward involvement in achievement situations play a major role in how individuals interpret and react in such settings (task and ego goal perspectives).

Task involvement operates when human action is motivated mainly by task mastery and by the experience of personal improvement, whereas ego involvement is characterized by actions that are motivated mainly by the wish to demonstrate normatively superior competence. In the former case, success and failure are defined in terms of self-referenced perceptions of the person's performance; in the latter case, success is experienced when a person performs better than peers or similarly with less effort. It is predicted that a focus on task-involved goals will lead to maximal motivation regardless of the performer's level of perceived ability, whereas an ego perspective, coupled with doubts about a person's own level of competence, is said to result in negative achievement-related behaviors, such as rescinded effort, impaired performance, and even complete dropout. It should be emphasized that according to the goal perspective approach, whether an individual is in a state of task or ego involvement would be a function not only of dispositional differences but, in keeping with the social-cognitive tradition, also of situational factors. This approach is supported by an impressive body of research conducted in academic achievement settings, including classroom-based field studies and laboratory experiments with cognitive tasks.

In this seminal chapter, Duda provides an extensive review of the work that has adopted this approach of goal perspectives in an attempt to test major motivational issues in sport and exercise contexts. The author describes the research that has been directed toward the measurement of individual differences in goal perspectives (in particular on developing the famous TEOSQ—Task and Ego Orientation in Sport Questionnaire). Then, she presents sport investigations that tested different assumptions embedded in achievement motivation theories derived from the social cognitive approach, with a special reference to various facets of the concept of goal perspectives. Finally, similarities and differences between sport and exercise studies on goal perspectives are reviewed. Taken together with the concluding remarks and the future directions outlined, this chapter constitutes essential reading for every sport and exercise psychologist.

Recent motivation research stemming from a social cognitive perspective has focused on a goal perspective analysis of motivational processes and behavioral patterns. The majority of this work has been directed toward the understanding of academic achievement and has been primarily based on the theoretical contributions of Nicholls (1984a, 1984b, 1989; Duda, 2001), Dweck (1986; Dweck & Elliott, 1983; Dweck & Leggett, 1988; Elliott & Dweck, 1988), Maehr (1984; Maehr & Braskamp, 1986), and Ames (1984a, 1984b; Duda 2001; Ames & Archer, 1988). Although each might have his or her preferred nomenclature, issues of emphasis, and conceptual nuances, commonality exists among their theoretical frameworks with respect to the conception and role of goals in human motivation (see also Roberts in Duda, 2001).

In general, these theorists (Ames, 1984b; Dweck, 1986; Maehr, 1984; Nicholls, 1989) argue that a major focus in achievement settings is to demonstrate competence. More-

Adapted, by permission, from J.L. Duda, 1992, Motivation in sport settings: A goal perspective approach. In *Motivation in sport and exercise*, edited by G. Roberts (Champaign, IL: Human Kinetics), 57-91.

over, the psychological prominence of perceived ability is held to be the distinguishing feature of achievement motivation. When concerned with the study of motivation in nonachievement domains, perceptions of other personal attributes besides intellectual or physical skill and talent (e.g., honesty, kindness) are presumed to take on greater importance.

Contemporary social cognitive approaches to achievement motivation also assume that there are two major goal perspectives operating in achievement contexts. Nicholls (1984a, 1989; Duda, 2001), in particular, proposes that these goal perspectives are orthogonal and relate to how an individual construes his or her level of competence in a particular situation. In the first of these goal perspectives, perceptions of demonstrated competence are self-referenced, and the subjective experience of improving one's performance or mastering the demands of a task are the criteria underlying subjective success. According to Elliott and Dweck (1988, p. 5), the major question for someone who is focused on such a goal is "How can I best acquire this skill or master this task?"

With respect to the second goal perspective, improvement and/or personal mastery is not enough to occasion feelings of high ability. Perceptions of demonstrated competence are normative or other-referenced in this case, and subjective success is dependent on a favorable comparison of one's own ability with that of others. The question of whether an individual's ability is adequate is salient when he or she adopts this second goal perspective (Elliott & Dweck, 1988).

The terms *task involvement* and *ego involvement,* respectively, have been used by Nicholls (1984a, 1984b) to describe these two goal perspectives. These concepts have been introduced in earlier writings on motivation (e.g., Asch, 1952; Ausubel, Novak, & Hanesian, 1978; Crutchfield, 1962). Nicholls (1984a, 1984b) specifically argues that the two major goal perspectives relate to different ways of construing one's level of competence. Drawing from his developmental-based work (Nicholls & Miller, 1984), he suggests that ego and task involvement are based on a more or less differentiated conception of ability.

Other theorists (Ames & Archer, 1988; Elliott & Dweck, 1988) have developed different labels and slightly different conceptualizations of the two types of achievement goals. Dweck (1986; Dweck & Elliott, 1983; Dweck & Leggett, 1988), for example, refers to two classes of achievement goals. The first, learning goals, operate when individuals try to increase their competence and/or understand or master something new. The second type, performance goals, is focused toward gaining positive judgments of one's ability or avoiding negative perceptions of personal competence. Contrary to Nicholls (Duda, 2001), Dweck assumes that these two classes of achievement goals are bipolar rather than independent dimensions.

Ames has adopted the concepts of mastery goals and ability goals in her work (1984b; Ames & Archer, 1988, p. 260). Respectively, the first type of goal perspective entails a "concern with being judged able, and one shows evidence of ability by being successful, by outperforming others, or by achieving success with little effort". The second major goal perspective places an emphasis on "developing new skills. The process of learning itself is valued, and the attainment of mastery is seen as dependent on effort." For the most part, Ames's research tends to focus on the antecedents and consequences of mastery versus ability goal-evoking environments (see Duda, 2001). For the purposes of conceptual clarity and consistency, the terms task and ego involvement will be utilized throughout the present text to represent the two distinct achievement goals.

A third point of convergence in the predominant goal-related theories of achievement motivation is that a person's goal perspective (or state of task or ego involvement) in a particular setting is held to be a function of situational factors and "individual differences in proneness to the different types of involvement . . ." (Nicholls, 1989, p. 95). According to Dweck and Leggett (1988, p. 269), dispositional differences in goal perspective "determine the a priori probability of adopting a particular goal and displaying a particular behavior pattern, and situational factors are seen as potentially altering these probabilities." In situations characterized by interpersonal competition, public evaluation, normative feedback and/or the testing of valued skills, a state of ego involvement is more likely to emerge. On the other hand, environments which place an emphasis on the learning process, participation, individualized skill mastery, and/or problem solving tend to evoke task involvement (Ames & Archer, 1988; Nicholls, 1989). Thus, situations may be considered more or less *task-* or *ego-involving* depending on the demands of the social environment.

In terms of individual differences in goal perspective, people are assumed to vary in task orientation and ego orientation (Maehr & Braskamp, 1986; Nicholls, 1989). It has been suggested that these dispositional goal orientations are independent and are a result of childhood socialization experiences (Nicholls, 1989; Nicholls, Patashnick, and Nolen, 1985).

A final point of agreement in the thinking of Nicholls (1989), Dweck (1986), Ames (1984b), and Maehr (1984) concerns the proposed interrelationships between goal perspectives, motivational processes, and behavior. An important tenet in recent theorizing on achievement motivation is that goals influence how we interpret and respond to achievement events. Specifically, it is suggested that an individual's goal perspective will affect self-evaluations of demonstrated ability, expended effort, and attributions for success and failure. In turn, these cognitions are assumed to impact achievement-related affect, strategies, and subsequent behaviors such as performance, task choice, and persistence (see also Roberts and Ames in Duda, 2001).

Dependent on whether one is task- or ego-involved, different achievement-related patterns are predicted. Task involvement, regardless of the level of perceived competence, is assumed to relate to the choosing of moderately challenging tasks, the exerting of effort, intrinsic interest in the activity, sustained or improved performance, and persistence (particularly following failure). Further, this goal state entails an attributional focus on effort.

In general, the desirable behaviors described are also predicted for ego-involved people—as long as they have high confidence in their level of ability. Perceptions of competence, however, are believed to be particularly fragile in ego involvement (Dweck, 1986). When ego involvement prevails and doubts about one's competence exist, a maladaptive pattern is expected. Such a behavioral pattern is labeled "maladaptive" because it is not conducive to long-term achievement and/or investment in achievement-related environments, however adaptive and rational the behaviors described are when considered in relation to the goal perspective being emphasized. It is assumed that ego involvement coupled with perceptions of low ability will result in the choosing of tasks that are too hard or too easy, in the rescinding of effort or devaluing of the task when success seems improbable, and in performance impairment and a lack of persistence (especially following failure). These predictions are predicated on the assumption that one is concerned with the adequacy of his or her competence when in a state of ego involvement. The attributional focus, in this case, is on ability.

The purpose of this chapter is to review recent work which has adopted a goal-focused approach to the study of motivation in sport. First, research is described which has been directed toward the development of a sport-specific measure of task and ego orientation. Second, sport investigations are presented which have begun to test the assumptions embedded in social cognitive theories of achievement motivation. The studies highlighted in this chapter focus on three major issues, namely the relationship between goal perspectives and cognitive mediators of motivation such as perceived competence, causal attributions, and intrinsic interest; the potential impact of goal perspectives on behavior in sport settings; and the correspondence between goal perspectives and the broader concept of values in the sport domain. Third, similarities and distinctions between recent sport-specific studies and exercise motivation research based on a goal perspective approach are also briefly reviewed. Finally, the chapter concludes with suggestions for future work on the topic of goals and motivation in sport.

Measurement of Individual Differences in Goal Perspective

Past research in the sport domain has indicated that perceptions of demonstrated competence underlie perceptions of goal accomplishment or subjective success and failure (Kimiecik, Allison, & Duda, 1986; Roberts & Duda, 1984). Previous studies, employing both quantitative and qualitative techniques have also suggested that sport participants do base their goals on personal improvement and task mastery as well as the demonstration of superior ability (Duda, 1985, 1986a, 1986b, 1988; Ewing, 1981). In general, the literature provides us with evidence for the existence and salience of task and ego involvement goal states in the specific achievement context of sport.

During the past decade, there has been considerable interest in determining individual differences in orientations to sport achievement (e.g., Gill & Deeter, 1988; Vealey, 1986). In particular, efforts have been directed toward developing measures of the tendency to be task- and ego-involved in the context of competitive sport. For example, based on Maehr and Nicholls's (1980) conceptualization of achievement goals, Ewing (1981; Pemberton, Petlichkoff, & Ewing, 1986) designed her Achievement Orientation Inventory to assess a sport-specific ability orientation and task orientation (as well as a social approval orientation). Balague and Roberts (1989) have recently worked on establishing the validity and reliability of an instrument which measures the emphasis placed on mastery and competitive achievement goals in sport.

Drawing from the scales designed to assess task and ego orientation in the classroom (Nicholls, 1989; Nicholls et al., 1985), John Nicholls and I recently developed the Task and Ego Orientation in Sport Questionnaire, or TEOSQ. When completing the TEOSQ, subjects are requested to think of when they felt most successful in a particular sport and then indicate their agreement with items reflecting task- and ego-oriented criteria. Version I of the TEOSQ contained 15 items and was initially administered to 286 male and female high school sport participants (see Duda, 1989c). Exploratory factor analysis (principal components analysis with both oblique and orthogonal rotations) revealed a two-factor solution with seven items loading on the Task Orientation factor and six items loading on the Ego Orientation factors. (It is interesting to note that the item "I feel most successful when I win," which was contained in Version 1 of the TEOSQ, tended to load on both the Task and Ego Orientation factors.) The two-dimensional factor structure was found to be stable across two subsamples in this initial study and in subsequent research involving samples of youth sport, and high school and college-age sport participants and nonparticipants (Boyd, 1990; Duda & Nicholls, 1989b). Consistent with what has been observed in the assessment of task and ego orientation in the classroom (Nicholls, 1989), the two scales are orthogonal.

In further studies of 10- through 12-year-old children, of adolescents, and of adults (Duda & Nicholls, 1989a; Duda, Olson, & Templin, 1991; White, Duda, & Sullivan, 1991), The Sport Task Orientation and Sport Ego Orientation scales have been found to be internally consistent (alpha = .81 -.86 and .79 -.90, respectively). Neither of the scales significantly correlate with social desirability, and both have acceptable test-retest reliability following a three-week period (r = .68 and .75, respectively). A listing

Table 9.1 Items Contained in the Task and Ego Orientation in Sport Subscales

I feel most successful in sport when . . .	
Task orientation	**Ego orientation**
I learn a new skill and it makes me want to practice more.	I'm the only one who can do the play or skill.
I learn something that is fun to do.	I can do better than my friends.
I learn a new skill by trying hard.	The others can't do as well as me.
I work really hard.	Others mess up and I don't.
Something I learn makes me want to go and practice more.	I score the most points/goals, etc.
A skill I learn really feels right.	I'm the best.
I do my very best.	

of the items contained in the Sport Task and Ego Orientation scales (Version 2) can be found in table 9.1.

To address issues related to concurrent validity, the TEOSQ and Nicholls's (1989) classroom-specific Motivation Orientation Scales were administered to 205 high school students (Duda & Nicholls, 1989b). The presentation of the two instruments was counter-balanced. Significantly high positive correlations emerged between the Sport Task and Ego Orientation scale scores and their counterpart measures in the classroom (r = .67 and .62, respectively).

In a second validity study, we (Duda & Nicholls, 1989a) administered the TEOSQ, the Sport Orientation Questionnaire (SOQ; Gill & Deeter, 1988), and the Competitive Orientation Inventory (COI; Vealey, 1986) to a sample of undergraduate students. A further purpose of this investigation was to attempt to conceptually distinguish the concepts of task and ego orientation from seemingly similar constructs in the sport achievement goal literature.

The SOQ was developed as a "multidimensional, sport-specific measure of individual differences in sport achievement orientation" (Gill & Deeter, 1988, p. 191). The instrument is comprised of three separate but related factors which have been labeled Competitiveness, Win Orientation, and Goal Orientation. According to Gill and Deeter (1988):

> [The competitive factor assesses] the desire to enter and strive for success in sport achievement situations . . . The items . . . reflect a desire to enter sport achievement situations, to strive for success, to work hard, to master skills, and an eagerness to meet competitive challenges . . . The other two factors seem to reflect an orientation to the two major types of outcomes in sport achievement situations, specifically the desire to win in interpersonal competition in sport, and the desire to reach personal goals in sport. (p. 195)

A much stronger positive correlation emerged between the competitiveness and win subscales scores and Sport Ego Orientation than what was observed between these two SOQ subscales and Sport Task Orientation. This result makes conceptual sense since a person high in ego orientation (particularly if she or he has high perceived competence) would be more likely to seek out competitive activities. The process of interpersonal competition is most conducive to judging the adequacy of one's ability relative to others. Further, it is also logical that an ego-oriented individual would tend to focus on competitive outcomes. Winning in interpersonal competition is an overt means to demonstrating superior ability.

An individual high in task orientation, on the other hand, seeks out and values competition only to the extent that this social process allows him or her to try one's best and improve skills. It is "how you play the game" rather than "whether you win or lose" which is most salient to a task-oriented person. In other words, task involvement means that one is primarily focused on the process of task mastery rather than on successful task outcomes. Although a task-oriented person may also be to some degree competitive, the very nature and meaning of the competitive challenge would contrast to what is assumed by an ego-oriented person. Thus, the concept of "competitiveness" seems obscure when analyzed from a goal perspective analysis.

Additionally, due to the ambiguity implicit in the concept of goal orientation, it was also not surprising that both the Sport Task and Ego Orientation scales would significantly and positively correlate with this particular SOQ subscale. In the case of both of these goal perspectives, it is likely that individuals will be concerned with setting goals, with working toward reaching those goals, and with performing to the best of their abilities. However, the critical conceptual distinction between task and ego orientation is how such people tend to construe their ability and judge subjective success (or goal accomplishment) in particular situations. That is, the very nature of the *goal* is different when one is in a state of task or ego involvement, and whether a person is in one of these states or the other is dependent on individual differences in task and ego orientation.

The Competitive Orientation Inventory or COI (Vealey, 1986) was developed to measure individual differences in the tendency to "strive toward achieving a certain type of goal in sport" (p. 222). In Vealey's view, the two goals upon which competitive orientations are based are playing well (performance orientation) and winning (outcome orientation).

The format of the COI requires that the respondent weigh the importance of each goal simultaneously. Specifically, the respondent is requested to indicate his or her degree of satisfaction with 16 possible combinations of different game outcomes (i.e., easy win, close win, close loss, big loss) and levels of performance (i.e., very good, above average, below average, very poor).

As predicted (Duda & Nicholls, 1989b), a significant and positive relationship emerged between outcome orientation and ego orientation. Once again, we would expect the outcome of a contest to be more salient to ego-oriented individuals as winning in sport typifies superior ability. Task orientation was not expected to correlate with outcome orientation, and this prediction was substantiated. It was also predicted that neither task orientation nor ego orientation would significantly relate to the emphasis placed on playing well or performance orientation. As I've pointed out previously (Duda, 1989a), the concept of "playing well" as measured by the COI is conceptually ambiguous. The meaning of playing well and the basis of such a judgment would vary dependent on whether task or ego involvement is prevailing. Moreover, as argued by Nicholls (Duda, 2001), both task- and ego-involved individuals would be concerned with "performance" or the execution of the task at hand.

In general, our initial research on the TEOSQ has indicated that established measures of competitiveness, of orientations to winning, and of the desire to reach personal goals in sport are not psychologically equivalent to task and ego orientation. Further, this research suggests that the determination of the importance placed on playing well in contrast to objective outcome in sport is not synonymous to a person's proneness for task or ego involvement in that context.

Previous classroom-based research has indicated that the assessment of individual differences in task and ego orientation provides us with considerable insight into how students interpret and respond to the academic environment (Nicholls, 1989). A valid and reliable measure of task and ego orientation specific to the sport domain would be invaluable to future studies examining the correlates of goal perspectives in sport. The preliminary psychometric work on the TEOSQ looks promising in this regard.

Goal Perspectives and Motivational Processes in Sport

Research based on a social cognitive perspective of motivation in educational environments has indicated that students' goal perspectives relate to how they cognitively and affectively respond to classroom activities (Ames & Ames, 1981; Ames & Archer, 1988; Dweck & Leggett, 1988). In particular, studies have demonstrated that task and ego involvement impact causal attributions for performance, perceptions of competence, and subsequent intrinsic interest in the academic domain.

The generalizability of this literature to the sport setting has only recently begun to be examined. In ascertaining the potential impact of goal perspectives on motivational processes in sport, two research strategies have been adopted. One approach has been to determine the degree and direction of the relationships between task orientation, ego orientation, and the cognitions or related affects in question. A second strategy has been to manipulate the experimental situation so that it is more or less task- or ego-involving and then study the effect on subjects' subsequent cognitive and affective responses.

Attributions

Previous investigations in the academic context have revealed conceptually consistent relationships between goal perspectives and attributional focus (Ames in Duda, 2001; Ames & Ames, 1981; Nicholls, 1989). In general, this work indicates that ego involvement is linked to an emphasis on ability attributions (and/or downplaying the role of effort in performance), while task involvement corresponds to the employment of effort attributions.

Past sport research examining the attributions underlying goal orientations (e.g., Ewing, 1981; Whitehead, 1986) has supported the educational literature. This is exemplified by one of our recent studies which replicated classroom-based research by Nicholls and his colleagues (Nicholls et al., 1985; Nicholls, Cheung, Lauer, & Patashnick, 1989; Nicholls, Cobb, Wood, Yackel, & Patashnick, 1990). In the latter studies, the correspondence between task and ego orientation and students' beliefs about the causes of success in school was examined. Results indicated that students with a strong task orientation were more likely to believe that success in school stems from working hard, cooperating, being interested in one's work, and trying to understand rather than memorize. Ego orientation, on the other hand, was linked to the belief that success in school comes from being smart, trying to outperform other students, and knowing how to impress the teacher.

In our study (Duda and Nicholls, 1989a) in the sport domain, high school students were requested to complete the TEOSQ and then indicate their agreement with a series of reasons for success in sport. Factor analysis revealed four major beliefs, namely Motivation/Effort (e.g., players succeed if they work hard, try their best, and help each other), Ability (e.g., players succeed if they try to beat others, have the talent, and are naturally competent), Deception (e.g., players succeed if they cheat, know how to impress the coach, and know how to make themselves look better than they are), and External Factors (e.g., players succeed if they are lucky or have the right clothes and equipment). Consistent with what has been found in the classroom setting (Nicholls et al., 1985, 1989, 1990), task orientation was positively correlated with the belief that sport success is a function of motivational factors and hard work. Task orientation negatively related to the view that the ability to cheat and deceive the coach leads to sport success. Ego orientation, in contrast, was positively linked to the belief that being a more talented and skilled player results in sport success.

Our findings suggest that, in the achievement domain of sport, a person's dispositional goal perspective is logically consistent with his or her beliefs about how success is typically caused in the sport context. As proposed by Nicholls (1989; Duda, 2001), the observed patterns of relationships between goals and beliefs constitute individuals' personal theories of sport achievement.

Early work on sport attributions has indicated that causal attributional patterns vary depending on whether individuals are interpreting objectively (i.e., win/loss) or subjectively defend outcomes (McAuley, 1985b; Spink & Roberts, 1980). Further, this research reinforces the point that objective and subjective outcomes are not necessarily synonymous for all sport participants; in short, not everyone holds an ego-involved conception of success and failure in the sport setting. Researchers have only begun to specifically determine the effect of variations in conceptions of success and failure or, in other words, *differences in goal perspective* on performance-related attributions. Two such experimental studies will be described here.

Hall (1990) recently determined the effect of a task- versus ego-involving goal structure and perceived competence on ability and effort attributions among adult men performing a stabilometer task. Low-perceived-ability subjects performing under an ego-involving goal structure reported that they did not try as hard during the early trials as low-perceived-ability subjects in the task-involving situation or high-perceived-ability subjects in either condition. In the ego-involving condition, males with low perceived competence felt that their performance was *less* influenced by demonstrated ability than high-perceived-competence subjects or low-perceived-competence subjects in the task-involving condition. The implication of Hall's (1990) results on subsequent motivation are intriguing. In explicating these findings, it would appear that people who doubt their physical skill and are placed in an ego-involving situation may be more likely to diminish the role of effort and to sever the link between their competence and task performance. The latter might be a precursor to a learned helpless attributional pattern (Dweck & Leggett, 1988). The former, namely downplaying how hard one tried, surely would not lead to long-term achievement. When task-involved, on the other hand, people may be more likely to believe in the potential impact of effortful investment and demonstrated physical skill on performance, regardless of their level of perceived competence. Such an outlook should be conducive to positive achievement strivings over time.

In a field experiment, Duda and Chi (1989) examined the effect of a task- versus ego-involving game condition and objective outcome on performance attributions in basketball among college-age males. Seventy-nine students, who were enrolled in a physical education skill class, were assigned to play a one-on-one basketball game against an opponent of equal skill. In the ego-involving condition, the subjects played a competitive 12-point game. The first player to reach 12 points was declared the winner, and the outcome of the game was reported to the class instructor. To enhance the perceived importance and evaluative nature of the ego-involving condition, a referee was present to "call the game."

In the task-involving game, the subjects were asked to play one-on-one basketball for 10 minutes. They were told that there would be no winner or loser, to try their best, and to work on a specific offensive and defensive skill weakness which was identified by the class instructor. Unknown to the subjects in this condition, the score after 10 minutes of play (i.e., objective outcome) was recorded by an observer.

Immediately following the game, the subjects rated the degree to which they perceived their performance to be a function of how hard they tried, their basketball skill, the opponent's basketball skill, and lucky breaks. The results indicated that more winners than losers believed that their skill level had a greater effect on their performance. More losers than winners felt that their opponent's skill had a greater influence on their performance. The situational manipulation of goal perspective, however, had an impact on effort attributions among objective winners and losers. Specifically, consistent with the results of Hall (1990), losers in the ego-involving game were less likely to attribute their performance to the amount of effort exerted when compared to losers in the task-involving condition or to winners. That is, ego involvement was linked to the tendency to downplay the role or impact of effort when faced with failure (or the possibility of demonstrating inferior ability).

Other results of this study indicated that in the task-involving situation, attributional patterns were best predicted by subjective outcome. Objective outcome (win/loss) was only pertinent to attribution ratings in the ego-involving condition.

In sum, initial sport research suggests that goal perspectives correspond to performance attributions and wider beliefs about the causes of success in a predicted manner. Based on this preliminary work, it appears that an awareness of the goals adopted by sport participants can provide us with an understanding of how they explain and interpret their sport experiences. Certainly much more systematic research on goals and attributions in sport is needed—research which examines short- and long-term variations in attributional patterns as a function of goal perspective, perceived ability, objective and subjective sport outcomes, as well as the subject's history of success and failure in the activity.

Perceived Competence

Although sometimes known as perceived ability, self-efficacy, or confidence in various theoretical circles, the construct of perceived competence has played a central role in previous sport motivation research (Roberts, 1984). The predominant focus in this literature has been to ascertain the psychological and behavioral antecedents and consequences of varying levels of perceived competence in the sport domain (e.g., Feltz in Duda, 2001; Harter, 1978; Roberts, Kleiber, & Duda, 1981). Adopting a goal perspective approach to the study of perceptions of ability, however, underscores the relevance of how one's perceived competence is construed and the effects of such on subsequent feelings of competence.

Because the emphasis is on mastering the task, and perceptions of demonstrated competence are self-referenced, it is assumed that task involvement will foster the development of perceived ability. As pointed out by Elliott and Dweck (1988), the "focus of individuals who pursue learning goals or are *task involved* (whether they believe their ability to be high or low) is on improving ability over time, not on proving current ability" (p. 6). Ego involvement, on the other hand, entails a concern with the adequacy of one's ability level. When ego-involved, perceptions of demonstrated competence mean that one has outperformed others (or performed similarly with less effort). Consequently, it is proposed that ego involvement increases the probability of feeling incompetent (especially in the case of those who already doubt their ability).

Preliminary field studies in sport-related contexts support these predictions. Burton (1989b) determined the effect of a 5-month goal-setting program on self-confidence and post-meet ratings of perceived ability and subjective success among male and female intercollegiate swimmers. The goal-setting training was designed to encourage participants to base their competence on performance rather than outcome goals. Performance goals were focused on the attainment of challenging personal performance standards. Winning was considered to be the primary outcome goal operating in sport. Intercollegiate swimmers from a second university who did not receive goal-setting training served as the control. Swimmers who participated in the goal-setting program demonstrated higher perceived ability and felt more successful following competition than the swimmers who were not trained in personal performance-oriented goal-setting.

Similar findings emerged in a study by Newsham (1989) which examined the impact of a task-oriented physical education program on the perceived ability of elementary school children. The 12-week experimental program was designed to de-emphasize social comparison between the students and to focus the children on meeting personal performance goals. A control group participated in a 12-week traditional physical education class. Newsham found that the students who participated in the mastery-oriented physical education program were significantly higher in perceived sport competence and social acceptance than the controls.

Evidence supporting the predicted relationships between goal perspectives and perceptions of competence has also accrued from experimental research. In his study of the impact of a task- versus ego-involving condition on subjects performing a stabilometer task discussed above, Hall (1990) found that the experimentally-induced goal structure and perceived ability affected subjects' perceptions of competence before, during, and following task performance. Subjects who had low perceived ability and were placed in the ego-involving situation expected to perform worse during early trials than low-perceived ability subjects in the task-involving condition or high-perceived-ability subjects in either condition. Interestingly, if performing under an ego-involving goal structure, even high-perceived-ability subjects began to doubt their ability and to expect that they would do less well during the later trials.

A similar pattern held for perceptions of confidence and demonstrated ability over trials as well as subjects' confidence regarding future success at the conclusion of the experiment. In each case, low perceived ability coupled with an ego-involving goal structure led to further decreases in the subject's sense of competence at the task.

Hall's (1990) research clearly indicates that ego involvement is not conducive to maintaining perceptions of high ability, particularly among individuals whose perceived competence is tenuous at best. Furthermore, this study implies that a declining sense of competence is unlikely when people are task-involved, regardless of their initial level of perceived ability.

In the field experiment described more previously, Duda and Chi (1989) determined the effect of pregame perceived competence, objective outcome, and a task- versus ego-involving game condition on post-performance ratings of perceived ability. In general, findings were consistent with the sport studies to date. The results indicated that, regardless of the objective outcome, low-pregame-perceived-competence subjects who were in the task-involving condition felt more able at the conclusion of a one-on-one basketball game than low-perceived-competence subjects who were in the ego-involving condition. Among the players who were objectively victorious, perceived competence was higher in the task-involving game than in the ego-involving game. Since perceptions of how well one played were not highly correlated with objective outcome in the task-involving condition (in contrast to what was observed in the ego-involving condition), it would appear that the task-involved subjects were using other criteria besides score to judge their post-game level of competence. The determination of the criteria used by people to judge their demonstrated ability in task- versus ego-involving situations is an important area for future inquiry (Ames & Ames, 1981).

In sum, the research to date suggests that task involvement fosters perceptions of ability in sport contexts when contrasted with ego involvement. An abundance of sport-related studies have demonstrated that perceptions of competence are important mediators of both performance (e.g., see Feltz in Duda, 2001) and persistence in the sport domain (Burton & Martens, 1986; Roberts, Kleiber, &

Duda, 1981). Consequently, it would be interesting to examine the stability of the observed effects of goals on perceived competence and the behavioral consequences of the same over time.

Intrinsic Motivation

Contemporary social cognitive theories of achievement motivation suggest that goal perspectives should influence intrinsic motivation in achievement-related activities such as sport. Specifically, it is inferred that task involvement should foster intrinsic interest in an activity. In contrast, ego involvement is assumed to lead to a decrease in intrinsic motivation. According to Nicholls (1989), achievement strivings are experienced as a means to an end (i.e., the demonstration of superior ability) when one is ego involved. He argued that when an individual is task involved, an activity is experienced more as an end in itself. In a state of task involvement, therefore, our task-related strivings are more likely to be intrinsically satisfying. Using a similar line of reasoning, Dweck (1986) suggests that individuals who emphasize performance goals are primarily concerned about goal attainment and showing their superiority. Consequently, she proposes that a focus on performance goals will result in decreased intrinsic interest in an activity and less enjoyment from working hard at a task for its own sake.

These predictions are aligned with the tenets of cognitive evaluation theory (Deci & Ryan, 1980; Plant & Ryan, 1985; Ryan, 1982; Ryan & Deci, 1989). According to Ryan (1982), ego involvement prevails when an individual's self-worth is contingent on good performance. The concept of ego involvement as addressed in cognitive evaluation theory is not exclusively focused on the demonstration of ability (Ryan & Deci, 1989). That is, Ryan and Deci assume that "people can be ego involved in matters of appearance, wealth, gender-consistent behavior, or any other outcome where failing to meet an internal standard is experienced as a threat to self-esteem" (p. 267). Task involvement, in contrast, is considered to be a state in which one's motivation to perform a task is derived from its intrinsic properties. It is argued that ego involvement represents a type of internal control or regulation. This "controlling" feature of ego involvement is assumed to foster an external perceived locus of causality; that is, the focus in this case is on meeting a performance standard rather than on the task at hand. Consequently, ego involvement is predicted to lead to a decrease in intrinsic motivation relative to task involvement.

In general, laboratory experiments have revealed a significant decline in intrinsic interest to engage in cognitive tasks when subjects are placed in evaluative and/or competitive environments, that is, ego-involving situations (Deci & Ryan, 1980; Koestner, Zuckerman, & Koestner, 1987; Plant & Ryan, 1985; Ryan, 1982; Ryan, Mims, & Koestner, 1983). The results of classroom-based studies, which have determined the impact of task- versus ego-involving evaluative feedback on intrinsic interest, are also consistent with theoretical predictions (Butler, 1987, 1988).

Recent sport research has examined the relationship between goal perspectives and intrinsic motivation. In general, this literature has concentrated on determining the possible influence of dispositional goal perspective or situationally induced goals on a variety of indices of intrinsic interest.

The correlations between task and ego orientation (as measured by the TEOSQ) and the degree of satisfaction, interest, and boredom experienced in the sport domain among high school students were determined by Duda and Nicholls (1989b). A significant and positive relationship emerged between task orientation and the tendency to perceive playing sport as interesting and fun. Task orientation, on the other hand, was negatively correlated with the reported experience of boredom in sport. That is, students who were task oriented tended to disagree with such items as "I am usually bored when playing sport," "In sport, I often daydream instead of thinking about what I'm doing," and "When playing sports, I usually wish the game would end quickly."

Jackson (1988) examined the correspondence between goal perspective and the experience of flow in sport. As described by Csikszentmihalyi (1975), *flow* is an intrinsically enjoyable experience that is typically autotelic in nature. In her study of college sport participants, Jackson found a positive relationship between task orientation and the frequency with which flow was experienced in competition. Ego-oriented individuals, particularly if they were low in perceived ability, experienced flow less frequently when competing.

The relationship between intrinsic motivation and individual differences in the proneness to be task- or ego-involved in sport was the focus of a study by Duda, Chi, and Newton (1990). In particular, we requested undergraduate students who were enrolled in a tennis skills class to complete the TEOSQ and the Intrinsic Motivation Inventory (IMI; Plant & Ryan, 1985; Ryan, et al., 1983) specific to the sport of tennis. The IMI assesses overall intrinsic motivation and five of the underlying dimensions of intrinsically motivated behavior (i.e., interest-enjoyment, effort, competence, pressure-tension, and perceived choice). Recent work by McAuley and colleagues (McAuley, Duncan, & Tammen, 1989; McAuley, Duncan, & Wraith, 1989) has provided evidence for the validity and reliability of the IMI when applied to sport and exercise settings.

Simple correlations revealed that task orientation was positively related to enjoyment, effort, and the composite intrinsic motivation score. A significant inverse relationship emerged between ego orientation, enjoyment, and overall intrinsic motivation. A canonical correlation analysis was used to determine the multivariate relationship between the two goal perspectives and the five dimensions of intrinsic motivation. High task orientation and low ego orientation corresponded to greater perceived enjoyment of the tennis class.

Several experimental sport studies have examined the effect of task- versus ego-involving situations on intrinsic interest in the physical domain. Vallerand, Gauvin, and Halliwell (1986), for example, found that young boys spent significantly less time on task in a free-choice period if they were previously assigned to a competitive (i.e., focus placed on beating other children's scores), in contrast to a mastery-oriented (i.e., focus placed on trying one's best), condition.

Orgell and Duda (1990) determined the impact of task- versus ego-involving instructions on intrinsic interest in a sport activity. Male and female undergraduate students who were enrolled in a golf skill class were randomly assigned to one of two experimental conditions. In the task-involving situation, the subjects were requested to engage in a golf putting task which was being developed for future students to practice their skills. The subjects were told that they would not be scored on this task and to try their best at the activity. The subjects in the ego-involving condition were informed that the task had been designed to test putting skills in golf. Further, the subjects were told that their score would be recorded and compared to other students who had previously performed the task.

Intrinsic motivation was operationalized as the time spent engaging in the task during a subsequent 5-minute free-choice period. Results indicated that females spent less time-on-task in the ego-involving ($\bar{X}$ = 102.7 sec) in comparison to the task-involving condition ($\bar{X}$ = 114.4 sec). There was no significant condition effect on the time spent on task among the male subjects. Males spent more time-on-task during the free-choice period than females.

The tendency for evaluative environments to lead to a decreased intrinsic interest among females in particular has emerged in other sport research (Weinberg & Ragan, 1979). Further, given that the females in our study were significantly lower in perceived putting ability than the male subjects, we would expect that an ego-involving situation would be more detrimental to their level of intrinsic motivation.

In a study of Little League players, Boyd (1990) examined the effect of dispositional goal perspective (as measured by the TEOSQ) and win/loss on post-competition affective responses. The subjects in this investigation were members of four winning and four losing baseball teams. The players who were high in ego orientation reported that they enjoyed the game less than players low in ego orientation—regardless of whether they won or lost the contest. High ego-oriented players who lost the game, however, were less satisfied following the contest than high ego-oriented players who won the game. Among the low ego-oriented players, game outcome did not significantly effect their level of satisfaction.

In sum, preliminary correlational and experimental evidence in the sport domain supports recent theoretical predictions concerning the relationship between goal perspectives and intrinsic motivation. It seems that ego involvement can result in decreased intrinsic interest in and enjoyment of a sport activity. However, at the present time, there is more support for the proposition that task involvement tends to nourish intrinsic motivation in sport.

Goal Perspectives and Sport Behavior

The critical test of any theory of motivation is its ability to predict behavior. The behaviors which we assume reflect an individual's state of motivation include exerted effort, task choice, performance, and persistence (Maehr, 1984; Maehr & Braskamp, 1986; Roberts in Duda, 2001).

Effort Exerted

Exerting effort or *behavioral intensity,* particularly in the face of obstacles, has always been considered a hallmark of high motivation. In sport, we often speak in glowing terms of the individual who "hustles" or exerts effort, and we assume that such a person is highly motivated. Few investigations to date have examined the relationship between goal perspectives and the degree to which individuals work hard. In general, the research which has been conducted supports the theoretical predictions of Nicholls (1989), Dweck (1986), and Ames (1984b).

In my 1988 study, I found intramural sport participants who were high in task orientation reported that they practiced more in their free time. In a recent study of the predictors of adherence to athletic injury rehabilitation (Duda, Smart, & Tappe, 1989), task orientation was positively related to the effort exerted by athletes while completing their prescribed exercises. As indicated in the daily ratings provided by the assigned athletic trainer, athletes who were high in task orientation tended to push themselves and work hard during the exercise session. In contrast, low-task-orientation athletes were more likely to "walk through" their exercise protocol.

Trying hard as one performs certain sport-related skills or exercises is certainly a critical ingredient to improvement, to recovery from a setback such as physical injury, or to ultimate performance. Although behavioral intensity is not an easy variable to operationalize, much more work on the interdependence between goals and exerted effort in the physical domain is needed.

Task Choice

Nicholls (1984a, 1989) and Dweck (Dweck & Leggett, 1988; Elliott & Dweck, 1988) make elaborate predictions concerning the ways in which goal perspective and perceived ability impact patterns of task choice. Little sport research has been done on this issue. However, Nicholls (1989) interprets previous studies of risk taking, which used physical tasks to test the risk-taking predictions in Atkinson's (1964) theory of achievement motivation, in accordance with his theoretical framework (e.g., deCharms & Dave, 1965; Hamilton, 1974; Roberts, 1974). Because these investigations entailed the demonstration of a salient skill (i.e., physical ability among males) in a public arena, he suggests that the subjects were probably in a state of ego involvement. Nicholls also argues that the primary independent variable in such risk-taking studies (i.e., group differences in resultant achievement motivation scores) could be considered a measure of perceived ability. Congruent with social cognitive theories of achievement motivation, subjects in these investigations with low resultant motivation chose more extreme (i.e., very easy or very difficult) tasks. High-resultant-motivation subjects, on the other hand, tended to select a challenge of intermediate difficulty. It would appear that the systematic study of the effect of goal perspectives and perceived ability on subsequent task or activity choice is a promising area for future research.

Performance

A paucity of correlational studies specifically focus on the relationship of task and ego orientation to sport performance. Cross-sectional investigations using the SOQ (Gill, 1986; Gill & Deeter, 1988) and the COI (Vealey, 1986), though, have found high achieving sport players to have a higher goal or performance orientation, respectively, than their counterparts who have not demonstrated the same outstanding level of performance.

In a quasi field experiment previously described, Burton (1989b) examined the effect of a goal-setting program on the performance of intercollegiate swimmers. The purpose of this program was to teach the swimmers how to set accurate goals based on personal performance standards rather than outcome. Performance (time and race outcome) was assessed during a midseason dual meet and the league championship. The results indicated that trained swimmers who set accurate personal performance goals demonstrated higher performance when compared to a control group of trained swimmers who set inaccurate goals.

In another goal-setting study, Hall (1990) determined the effect of perceived ability, situational goal perspective, and success/failure feedback on performance. Perceived ability was manipulated by telling the subjects that they had performed well or poorly following a baseline measure of stabilometer performance. The subjects were then randomly assigned to either a task-involving (in which only personal performance feedback was given) or ego-involving (in which personal performance and normative feedback was given) experimental condition. Each subject completed six trials during which he was asked to achieve a goal of 60% improvement over baseline. Bogus feedback (i.e., the subject was told he reached or did not reach the target goal) was given at the conclusion of the second, fourth, and sixth trials. In support of contemporary social cognitive theories of achievement motivation (Ames, 1984b; Dweck & Leggett, 1988; Nicholls, 1989), subjects with low perceived ability who performed in the ego-involving condition displayed lower performance than low-perceived-ability subjects who were assigned to the task-involving condition.

To date, Hall's (1990) investigation has been one of the best experimental tests of the performance predictions embedded in recent goal-related theories of achievement motivation (see also Weinberg in Duda, 2001). Nicholls (1989), however, questions the possibility of producing a high state of task involvement in such laboratory experiments. He also distinguishes between the determination of factors influencing short- versus long-term performance. Laboratory experiments, in his view, tend to be oriented to the prediction of immediate, short-term performance. Nicholls (1989) maintains that the understanding and fostering of lifetime accomplishments (e.g., a scientific breakthrough, a stellar sport career) should be the major concern of motivation theorists. In that regard, he predicts that "task orientation is more likely to maintain the long-term involvement that such significant accomplishments demand" (p. 128).

Although preliminary research in sport-related contexts has been congruent with theoretical predictions concerning the impact of goal perspectives on performance, little is known about the mechanism by which goals influence task accomplishment. In particular, we have evidence at this point in time, in educational (e.g., Miller, 1985) and physical (e.g., Hall, 1990) environments, which reflects the potential performance debilitating effects of ego involvement. The major question which faces us, however, is *why* does this occur?

Nicholls (1989) argues that, in an ego-involving situation, "performance is impaired more by the expectation that failure will indicate one's lack of competence than by the mere expectation of failure to complete a task" (p. 119). He proposes that the expectation of looking incompetent might result in performance impairment in several ways. First, since individuals who are ego involved tend to be very concerned about demonstrating their competence, this goal perspective may push people into forming unrealistic aspirations. This proposition is consistent with the risk-taking literature briefly reviewed above.

Second, ego involvement may be linked to a conscious (or unconscious) willingness to withdraw effort when failure seems imminent. Although recent research has questioned the existence of this behavioral strategy in the academic context (Jagacinski & Nicholls, 1990), preliminary sport studies suggest that reduced effort may be a consequence of ego involvement in the sport domain (Duda & Chi, 1989; Hall, 1990).

An emphasis on ego-involved goals coupled with questions concerning one's level of competence may lead to alienation. That is, it is proposed (Nicholls, 1989) that ego-involved individuals with low perceived competence may eventually devalue or lose interest in an activity, and, consequently, performance will wane. In sport settings, we know that individuals who withdraw from sport often report that they had not been performing well and had lost interest in it (e.g., Burton & Martens, 1986). In research by Hall (1990), low-perceived-ability subjects performing under an ego-involving goal structure placed less importance on doing well on the (stabilometer) task than high-perceived-ability subjects in the same condition or low-perceived-ability subjects in a task-involving condition.

Finally, Nicholls (1989) suggests that ego involvement may result in impaired performance due to the debilitating effects of anxiety. Results of sport studies by Vealey and Campbell (1988) and Duda, Newton, and Chi (1990) are consistent with this hypothesis. In the latter investigation specifically, high precompetition state cognitive and somatic anxiety (and low state confidence) were primarily evident among tennis players who were high in ego orientation and did not expect to win the match.

Persistence

Researchers in the field of sport psychology have demonstrated considerable interest in identifying the predictors of dropping out of sport (Burton & Martens, 1986; Feltz & Petlichkoff, 1983; Gould, Feltz, Horn, & Weiss, 1982; Klint & Weiss, 1986). Drawing from this literature, we know that withdrawal from sport is linked to low perceived competence and less enjoyment of the sport experience.

Roberts (1984) was the first to attempt to assimilate work on dropping out (or a *lack of persistence*) in sport within social cognitive theories of achievement motivation. In particular, he argued that individuals with high ego involvement will not persist in sport if their high ability goals are not met.

To date, the majority of research on goal perspectives and persistence in the sport domain has been correlational in nature. For the most part, these correlational studies have revealed a positive relationship between task orientation and persistence. Aligned with Roberts's (1984) predictions, ego involvement has been negatively linked with continued involvement in sport.

Ewing (1981), in her research on 14- to 15-year-old adolescents, found ability-oriented subjects (or adolescents who were high in ego orientation) to be most likely to have dropped out of sport. In a study of intramural sport participants, recreational participants who were higher in task orientation were found to have continued involvement in their chosen sport for a longer time (Duda, 1988).

The relationship between goal perspectives and participation and persistence in sport among high school students was examined in a second study by Duda (1989b). The students were divided into five groups in this investigation. Group One was presently involved in both interscholastic and recreational sport programs. Group Two participated in organized sport only, and Group Three was comprised of recreational sport only participants. Those students who had dropped out of sport were included in Group Four. Group Five included students who had never been regularly involved in sport. The results indicated that those students who were presently involved in sport endorsed a mastery-based conception of success more than did those who had ceased participation or students who had never been involved. Further, dropouts were found to be most troubled (as indicated in a preference rating) by a sport failure experience in which an individual demonstrated lower ability in relation to his or her peers. This latter finding is consistent with research by Whitehead (1989) who observed dropouts in British sport clubs to be more concerned than youngsters who have persisted about demonstrating superiority over their peers.

A recent study by Weitzer (1989) nicely linked perceptions of competence with goal perspectives in an attempt to predict involvement in physical activity among male and female fourth grade children. The results indicated that boys and girls who emphasized mastery (i.e., task-involved) goals, regardless of their level of perceived ability, tended to participate in physical activities such as sport. Children who stressed outcome (or ego-involving goals) and perceived their competence to be low were less likely to still be active when compared to low ego-oriented children who had high perceived competence.

In a laboratory experiment, Rudisill and her colleagues (Rudisill, Meaney, McDermott, & Jibaja-Rusth, 1990) examined the effect of goal-setting orientations on children's perceived competence and persistence. Nine- through twelve-year-old children were requested to perform three different motor tasks (i.e., throwing for accuracy, standing long jump, sit and reach) under one of four experimental conditions:

1. A task-mastery goal condition in which the children were asked to set performance goals which were 20% higher than their own previous performance
2. A competitive goal condition in which the children were asked to set normatively based goals
3. A self-goal condition in which the children were asked to set their own goals for performance
4. A control group condition in which the children were not instructed to set goals

Persistence was defined as the time the children spent practicing the motor skills during a free-time period following the test trials. Perceived motor skill competence did not significantly change pre- to post-trials as a function of experimental condition. However, consistent with theoretical predictions and previous correlational sport research, children who were assigned to the task-involving mastery group persisted longer at the long jump and flexibility tasks than those assigned to the other three goal-setting conditions.

In an attempt to explain the observed negative relationship between ego involvement and persistence, I have argued that a prevailing ego orientation provides less opportunity for subjective success in competitive sport environments marked by uncertain outcomes and constant challenges to one's ability (Duda, 1989b). As subjective success is based primarily on personal improvement when task-involved, the reproduction of successful sport experiences seems more secure in this case. Consequently, we would expect task involvement to positively correspond to persistence in sport. In support of this argument, Hall (1990) found subjects assigned to an ego-involving condition reporting lower levels of subjective success over performance trials than those assigned to a task-involving condition. Moreover, the research reviewed concerning the differential relationship of task and ego involvement to attributions, perceived competence, and intrinsic motivation in sport is consistent with this thesis. The cognitions and achievement-related experiences associated with ego involvement do not set the stage for long-term investment in an activity. The opposite appears to hold for task involvement.

Goal Perspectives and Views About Sport

Adopting an ecological perspective on social cognition, Nicholls (1989) argues that "different motivational orientations are not just different types of wants or goals. They involve different world views" (p. 102). Specifically, he proposes that an individual's goal perspective tends to be consistent with the person's views or philosophy about the wider purposes of the achievement activity itself, and his or her opinions concerning what is acceptable behavior in that arena. In regard to the former, studies in the academic domain have found that an ego orientation is linked to the belief that education should result in extrinsic ends such as wealth and status. Task orientation, however, corresponded to the view that school should enhance one's commitment to society, understanding of the world, and desire to keep learning (Nicholls et al., 1985; Thorkildsen,1988).

Sport has been assumed to be a vehicle for the socialization of prosocial values (Kleiber & Roberts, 1981). The presumed positive relationship between sport involvement and character development has not been strongly supported in the literature. Drawing from Nicholls's (1989) thinking, an examination of participants' goal perspectives might provide us with a better understanding of the positive or negative attitudes and values which have been linked to the sport experience.

Replicating work done in the academic domain, I (Duda, 1989c) recently examined the relationship between goal perspectives and the perceived wider purpose of sport involvement among high school sports participants. The subjects were administered the TEOSQ and the 60 item Purpose of Sport Questionnaire. The items contained in the latter questionnaire were generated from three sources: relevant questions contained in the Purposes of Schooling Questionnaire (Nicholls, 1989), previous literature on the values and benefits associated with youth sport involvement, and open-ended responses provided by high school students in a pilot investigation. A factor analysis of the sport questionnaire revealed seven beliefs about what sport should accomplish, namely that

1. sport should teach the value of mastery and cooperation;
2. sport should show people how to be physically active for life;
3. sport should make good citizens;
4. sport should make people competitive;
5. sport should help individuals obtain a high status career;
6. sport should enhance self-esteem; and
7. sport should show people how to "get ahead" and increase their social status.

A conceptually coherent relationship emerged between task and ego orientation and the seven purposes of sport. Individuals high in task orientation tended to believe that sport should enhance our cooperative skills and investment in personal mastery. Task orientation negatively related to the view that sport should improve an individual's social status. In total, task orientation was linked to an endorsement of the intrinsic dimensions and prosocial consequences of the sport experience.

A strong ego orientation, on the other hand, corresponded to beliefs about sport reflecting the extrinsic benefits and personal gains aligned with athletic involvement (Duda, 1989c). Specifically, the stronger the ego orientation, the stronger the belief that sport should increase one's sense of self-importance and make one popular. Further, ego orientation positively related to the view that sport should build a competitive spirit and the desire to get ahead in the world, and negatively related to the belief that sport should foster good citizenship. Clearly, the broader conception that sport involvement is a means to some end appears to coincide with an ego-oriented goal perspective in the sport setting.

The premise that an individual's goal perspective will correspond to his or her view of an activity as a means to some outcome or as an end in itself also presupposes a logical relationship between task and ego orientation and what a person would do to achieve his or her goal. In Nicholls's words (1989),

> a preoccupation with winning (beating others) may well be accompanied by a lack of concern about justice and fairness. . . . When winning is everything, it is worth doing anything to win. (p. 133)

In the context of interscholastic sport specifically, I and my colleagues (Duda, Olson, & Templin, 1991) examined the link between goal perspectives and the behaviors perceived as acceptable to secure victory. More specifically, we determined among male and female basketball players the relationship of task and ego orientation (as measured by the TEOSQ) to sportsmanship attitudes and perceptions of the legitimacy of intentionally injurious acts. With respect to the assessment of sportsmanship attitudes, players indicated their degree of approval of three types of behaviors. The first were actions that entailed stretching the rules so that one's team could have an unfair advantage (e.g., allowing an ineligible star player to play, turning up the heat in your gymnasium when playing a faster team, faking an injury to stop the clock). These actions were labeled "unsportsmanshiplike/cheating" behaviors. The second class of behaviors were those that were more strategic in nature (e.g., faking a charge on defense, trying to distract the opposing free throw shooter). The third type of behaviors reflected what we might consider to be good sportsmanship in basketball (e.g., admitting to touching a ball knocked out of bounds, helping an opposing player up from the floor).

Task orientation was negatively related to the endorsement of cheating behaviors. Simple and multivariate analyses also indicated that task orientation corresponded to a greater approval of sportsmanlike actions.

A modified basketball-specific version of the Continuum of Injurious Acts or CIA (Bredemeier, 1985) was also completed to assess the players' legitimacy judgments. The revised CIA consisted of six written scenarios depicting aggressive acts in basketball with intended consequences that become increasingly more serious, that is, nonphysical intimidation, physical intimidation, miss a few minutes, miss the rest of the game, miss the rest of the season, and permanent disability. Following the presentation of each scenario, the players were requested to answer the following question: Is this OK (legitimate) to do if it was necessary in order to win the game? Ego orientation related to higher legitimacy ratings of non-physical intimidation, injuring an opponent so that she or he misses a game, and injuring an opponent so that she or he misses the entire season.

These findings, focused on the relationship between goal perspectives and ratings of the legitimacy of intentionally injurious acts, were replicated among high school and college-level football players (Huston & Duda, 1990). Further, the football players' adopted goal perspectives were found to be a better predictor of legitimacy judgments than competitive level (i.e., high school versus college) or the reported years of involvement in competitive football.

Previous sport research has indicated that values such as the importance of fairness, of playing by the rules, of the gracious acceptance of victory and defeat, and of respect for one's opponent tend to be inversely related to competitive sport involvement (e.g., Allison, 1982; Blair, 1985; Kleiber & Roberts, 1981; Silva, 1983). The studies described here, however, suggest that it is not competitive involvement per se but the goal perspective that is adopted by sport participants that impacts their broader view of what sport is all about. Participants who tend to be ego- or task-involved in sport seem to have very different conceptions of the long-term value of sport involvement and of what is considered acceptable or fair behavior within the sport arena (see Nicholls in Duda, 2001). Based on initial research in this area, it appears that players who are high in ego orientation focus on two questions, namely "What's in it for me?" and "What do I need to do to win?"

Tentative Conclusions

At the present time, the limited research which has been conducted in the sport realm is consistent with the academic literature and the theoretical arguments of Nicholls (1989), Ames (1984b; Ames & Archer, 1988), and Dweck (1986; Dweck & Leggett, 1988). In particular, conceptually coherent relationships have emerged with respect to the interdependencies between goal perspectives and motivational processes, achievement-related behaviors, and values and beliefs in the sport domain.

This consistency in findings across academic and sport environments might be due to the fact that both are clearly achievement situations. In each context, the demonstration of competence, the standards of excellence, and the evaluation of performance are salient and apparent (Roberts, 1984; Scanlan, 1978b). Consequently, one might assume that theories which focus on the motivational dynamics of achievement behavior in the classroom setting might readily generalize to sport. However, results from one of our recent studies suggest an additional reason for the convergence in research findings (Duda & Nicholls, 1989a). Specifically, it appears that goal perspectives and the corresponding beliefs about the causes of success generalize across sport and the classroom.

In this particular study, parallel scales assessing motivational orientation and beliefs about the causes of success in both the classroom and sport were administered to high school students. Each situation-specific motivational orientation assessment included four scales, namely a measure of task orientation, ego orientation, work avoidance, and cooperation. For example, "I feel really successful when I can goof off," and "I feel really successful when my friends and I help each other improve" are typical items reflecting work avoidance and cooperation motivation orientations, respectively. The four context-specific beliefs about the cause of success were motivation/effort, ability, deception, and external factors.

A factor analysis of the scale scores was conducted and four factors emerged. The first indicated that work avoidance was a motivational strategy that transcended situation. The second factor suggested that an emphasis on learning and personal improvement (i.e., task orientation), the belief that success is due to effort, and the importance of helping others generalizes across the two achievement domains. As reflected in the third factor, the salience of outdoing others and the view that success is dependent on superior ability (i.e., ego involvement) also appears not to be situationally dependent. Finally, the fourth factor indicates that the tendency to perceive that deceptive tactics and external factors result in success in the classroom coincides with a similar belief system in sport.

In sum, this preliminary data implies that people operate in accordance with implicit transsituational motivation theories (Dweck & Leggett, 1988). Such theories entail a systematic interplay between goal perspective, cognitive mediators such as attributions, and behavioral patterns. Roberts (Duda, 2001) argues that a convergence of recent social cognitive theories of achievement motivation may provide a strong, conceptual framework for our further understanding of sport and exercise. Our findings (Duda & Nicholls, 1989a) suggest that an understanding of goal perspectives may be at the forefront of the development of a general theory of motivation in achievement contexts.

Goal Perspectives in the Exercise Domain

The possible relevance of variations in goal perspectives to motivational processes and behavior in the exercise context has begun to be considered in recent research (e.g., Kimiecik, 1990). The majority of the work in this area has been conceptually based on the personal investment theory (Maehr & Braskamp, 1986). Personal investment theory is a comprehensive social cognitive theory of motivation which assumes that one's behavioral investment in a situation is a function of the meaning of the situation to the person. *Meaning* is held to be comprised of three interrelated components, namely *personal goals or incentives, sense-of-self characteristics,* and *perceived behavioral options.*

Similar to contemporary social cognitive theories of achievement motivation (Ames, 1984b; Dweck, 1986; Nicholls, 1989), personal investment theory, or PIT, holds that task and ego involvement are two major goal perspectives that individuals can adopt in a particular situation. There are important differences, however, between these former theoretical perspectives and Maehr and Braskamp's (1986) theory of motivation. First, PIT assumes that there are other salient goal perspectives or *personal incentives* which serve as the focus of motivated behavior. Because the PIT is not specific to achievement settings, it acknowledges that people can strive to demonstrate other attributes besides competence (e.g., power incentives). Further, this theoretical perspective recognizes that individuals may emphasize the social consequences (e.g., affiliation or social recognition incentives) of one's involvement in an activity, rather than the experience of learning or beating others.

Second, the theory of personal investment holds that other *sense-of-self variables* besides perceived competence impact an individual's behavioral investment. According to Maehr and Braskamp (1986), a person's tendency to set and to try to achieve goals (i.e., *goal directedness*), degree of *self-reliance*, and sense of *social identity* (or perceived social group membership) are also believed to determine behavioral patterns.

Third, PIT maintains that an individual's *perceived behavioral options* will also affect his or her investment in a particular context. This more situationally based factor refers to whether a person views a specific action as an attractive and realistic alternative. Such a concept is not specifically addressed in contemporary social cognitive theories of achievement motivation (Ames, 1984b; Dweck, 1986; Nicholls, 1989).

Finally, PIT differs from the theoretical perspectives proffered by Ames (1984b), Dweck (1986), and Nicholls (1989) because the theory of personal investment tends to be more descriptive in nature. That is, in its present stage of development, the interrelationships between personal incentives, sense-of-self variables, and behavioral options have not yet been clearly delineated at either a theoretical or empirical level. The PIT predicts that these three dimensions of meaning will predict behavior. How and why personal incentives, perceptions of self, and behavioral options interact to result in different behavioral patterns in specific settings has not yet been systematically addressed.

In contrast to the PIT, other contemporary social cognitive theories of achievement motivation focus on goals as the critical determinant of behavioral variation (Ames, 1984b; Dweck, 1986; Nicholls, 1989). It is assumed that one's goal perspective interacts with perceived competence "to set in motion a sequence of specific (cognitive) processes that influence, in turn, task choice, performance, and persistence" (Elliott & Dweck, 1988, p. 11).

I have been involved with both students and colleagues in a series of studies focused on determining the predictive utility of personal investment theory with respect to exercise behavior. The first major step of this work, of course, entailed the operationalization of the concepts embedded in the PIT specific to the exercise domain. Our recent investigations have involved a variety of populations and exercise-related contexts (Chen & Duda, 1990; Duda, 1989a; Duda & Tappe, 1988, 1989a; Duda, Tappe, & Savage, 1990; Tappe & Duda, 1988; Tappe, Duda, & Ehrnwald, 1990). At this point in our work, two findings stand out: (a) Task involvement, in contrast to ego involvement, seems to be a salient ego perspective in the exercise domain (see also Roberts in Duda, 2001), and (b) consistent to what has been observed in the classroom and sport settings, task involvement has been predictive of positive motivated behaviors (e.g., intensity of participation, persistence). Similar results have been reported by Kimiecik, Jackson, and Giannini (in press) in a study of adult exercisers.

Recent research has indicated that one's degree of task orientation can impact the experience of exercise in and of itself (Duda, Sedlock, Noble, Cohen, & Chi, 1990). Specifically, we determined the effect of a task- versus ego-involving condition on perceived exertion ratings (RPE) and affective response among high task-/low ego-oriented and low task-/high ego-oriented college students. Task and ego orientation was assessed before the start of the experiment by the TEOSQ (Duda & Nicholls, 1989b). The task was a 6-minute submaximal cycle ergometer exercise at an intensity equal to 70% of maximum oxygen uptake. Perceptions of overall exertion were assessed in addition to effort perceptions specific to the legs and cardiorespiratory system using the Borg (1962) scale. Affective response (i.e., how the subject felt at a specific moment in time) was indicated on an 11-point bipolar feeling scale with +5 being extremely positive and -5 being extremely negative (Rejeski, Best, Griffith, & Kenney, 1987). Both the RPE and affective response measures were obtained during the last minute of exercise.

Subjects completed this exercise bout in one of two experimental conditions. In the task-involving condition, subjects were informed that the purpose of the task was to determine individualized physiological responses to the exercise. They were told that they should "try your best" and "try to enjoy the exercise." Subjects assigned to the ego-involving condition, on the other hand, were informed that the exercise was a test of physiological capacity. It was emphasized to these subjects that their responses would be compared to other students of the same age and sex.

The results indicated that high task-/low ego-oriented subjects tended to perceive their exertion level to be lower and reported more positive affect than did low task-/high ego-oriented subjects. Although not statistically significant, it is interesting to point out that the two groups of subjects were best distinguished in the ego-involving condition. That is, in contrast to the task-involving condition, high task-/low ego-oriented subjects tended to perceive that the exercise was less demanding in the ego-involving condition. The reverse was true for subjects who were low task-/high ego-oriented.

It has been proposed in previous work that motivation has an important impact on RPE and affective responses during exercise (Mihevic, 1981; Pandolf, 1983; Rejeski, 1985). In this regard, our preliminary research suggests that if a person emphasizes skill acquisition and improvement (i.e., task involvement) and de-emphasizes social comparison (i.e., ego involvement) during exercise testing, she or he tends to respond to the exercise experience with a more positive outlook. Such an individual seems to report more of a "feel good" response and appears less likely to focus on the discomfort associated with moderately demanding physical activity. Further, based on the lower RPE values obtained from the high task-flow ego-oriented subject, it would appear that she or he could work much harder if necessary. That is, the exercise did not seem to be as fatiguing to such an individual. On the other hand, individuals who are high ego-/low task-oriented and are placed into an ego-involving exercise setting seem to be more aware of the distress associated with physical exertion. In any regard, the potential impact of goal perspective on perceptions during exercise appears to be an intriguing topic for further study.

Future Directions

Initial sport-related research based on contemporary social cognitive theories of achievement motivation provides support for these theories' relevance to the sport domain. Much more work is needed in the sport realm, however, to examine systematically the tenets of these theoretical perspectives. As we forge ahead in such efforts, there are several important directions for future research based on a goal perspective approach to the study of sport behavior. In concluding this chapter, I would like to propose that sport motivation researchers begin to

1. develop ways by which we can assess perceived situational goal perspective and determine the effect of these perceptions on sport participants (see also Ames in Duda, 2001);
2. study specific ways in which practitioners can create a task-involving sport climate (see also Ames in Duda, 2001);
3. examine the socialization processes by which individuals become disposed to being more task- or ego-involved in sport (see also Roberts in Duda, 2001); and
4. investigate the impact of developmental change on goals, conceptions of ability, and related cognitive mediators of behavior (see also Roberts in Duda, 2001).

As emphasized by Nicholls (1989), Ames (1984b), and Dweck (Dweck & Leggett, 1988), the understanding and determination of situational demands as they relate to goal perspectives is an important area of study. Ames and Archer (1988) and Nicholls (1989) have demonstrated that students clearly perceive the goal perspective which is prevailing in a particular classroom. The perceptions of the degree to which a classroom is task- or ego-involving relate to the students' beliefs about success and use of effective learning strategies.

Do athletic participants differentiate sport environments with respect to task- and ego-involving dimensions? If yes, what are the major cues which are used by participants to distinguish the sport climate with respect to the predominant goal perspective (Ames & Archer, 1988)? Such questions would provide the basis for most interesting sport motivation research.

As mentioned, previous classroom-based studies and laboratory experiments have supported the predictions stemming from recent social cognitive theories of achievement motivation (Ames, 1984b; Dweck & Leggett, 1988; Nicholls, 1989). Although this line of work is in its infancy, sport research as highlighted in this chapter has also been consistent with these theoretical perspectives. In general, both bodies of literature seem to point to the significance of task involvement in regard to adaptive motivational processes and behavioral patterns.

Based on this literature then, we are faced with a practical issue that needs our careful attention. If task involvement is so desirable from a motivational standpoint, how can those who are out in the fields, gymnasiums, and ballparks (e.g., coaches and physical education teachers) create and maintain a task-involving sport situation for their players/students? The enhancement of task involvement might be viewed as a particular challenge as the sport world is so overtly competitive and outcome-oriented. To begin to address this issue, there is a need for applied studies that implement and test the practical implications of recent goal-related research in real-life sport settings. An excellent model for such research is the work of Smith and Smoll (Smith, Smoll, & Curti, 1978; Smith, Zane, Smoll, & Coppell, 1983; Smoll & Smith, 1984) on coaching effectiveness within the youth sport context. As has been suggested by Chaumeton and Duda (1988), the behavioral guidelines for effective coaching developed by Smith and Smoll can be considered to be the building blocks for a task-involving environment. It would seem that this type of work would provide sound theoretically-based guidelines for the practitioner in terms of how to foster "equality of motivation" (Nicholls, 1989).

Because there appears to be individual differences in the proneness to be task- or ego-involved in sport (Balague & Roberts, 1989; Duda & Nicholls, 1989b), the issue of how people are socialized to favor one goal orientation over the other also becomes important. Previous classroom (Eccles, Midgley, & Adler, 1984) and sport (Chaumeton & Duda, 1988) research has suggested that both environments are characterized by greater evaluation and emphasis on performance outcomes as children progress through the system (i.e., from grade to grade, or from one competitive sport level to the next). Based on these investigations and other work (e.g., Scanlan, 1978a), this increase in the ego-involving dimensions of the classroom and sport setting should relate to a corresponding increase in ego orientation among students and sport participants, respectively. Recent cross-sectional research in the sport domain by White et al. (1990) is compatible with this premise. They found male and female intercollegiate sport participants to be significantly higher in ego orientation (as measured by the TEOSQ) than college-age recreational sport participants or high school-level competitors.

Of course, when we speak of variations in the self-perceptions and behaviors of children as they continue their involvement in sport, the potential impact of cognitive as well as motoric developmental change must be considered. The relevance of developmental differences in children's conceptions of ability, intelligence, effort, luck, and task difficulty in academic environments has played an important role in the development of contemporary social cognitive theories of achievement motivation (e.g., Dweck, 1986; Nicholls & Miller, 1984; Nicholls, 1989). To date in the sport motivation literature focused on children, however, we have virtually ignored possible age-related changes in psychological processing and physical development, or we have generalized from work conducted in the academic domain (Duda, 1987; Roberts, 1984; Weiss & Bredemeier, 1983). One notable exception to this state of affairs is research by Whitehead and Dalby (1987). Future investigations stemming from a developmental perspective are critical to furthering our knowledge of achievement motivation in sport.

10 Does the Iceberg Profile Discriminate Between Successful and Less Successful Athletes? A Meta-Analysis

ALLAN J. ROWLEY, DANIEL M. LANDERS, L. BLAINE KYLLO, AND JENNIFER L. ETNIER
Arizona State University

The idea that personality states may have a significant influence on sport behavior was presented to sport psychology in the 1920s and 1930s by Coleman Griffith. The notion that athletes' mood states are connected to sport performance substantially affected the work of Morgan, who proposed the mental health model. This model asserts that the presence of positive mood states in athletes will be associated with better performances when compared with the performances of athletes who have mood states that are less positive. In other words, according to the mental health model, positive mental health and athletic success will be directly related; in contrast, psychopathology and success will be inversely related.

Morgan used the Profile of Mood States (POMS) to test his assertions. POMS, which was first presented in the early 1970s, measures six dimensions of subjective mood states and was initially intended to assess moods in psychiatric patients. However, it has also been used extensively in sport personality research, in particular by Morgan and his colleagues. Morgan examined mood states of athletes and nonathletes and compared them by plotting their raw scores on profile sets. It was consistently found that athletes, in particular the successful ones, had a unique profile. According to this concept, successful elite athletes' profiles, reflecting positive mental health, would look like an iceberg because their scores on the subscale of vigor would be above the population's norm, and their scores on the subscales of tension, depression, anger, fatigue, and confusion would be below the population's norms. In contrast, less successful elite athletes would have flat profiles, reflecting negative mental health.

Morgan, as well as his associates and followers, presented empirical research that supported these notions with various athletic samples. In sport psychology, the mental health model has been considered a systematic work with quite convincing empirical evidence, which has contributed substantially to the study of the relationship between state personality and sport performance. However, in the early 1990s, leading sport psychologists, such as Landers, began to criticize and question the general acceptance of the mental health model in light of accumulating, conflicting evidence.

In this article, the team of researchers, led by Landers, examined whether the iceberg profile does indeed distinguish successful athletes from less successful athletes. The authors made use of meta-analysis, a quantitative review method that integrates the findings of many studies conducted on a particular topic and enables the researcher to arrive at general conclusions on that domain. Since the presentation of this statistical method in the late 1970s, Landers and his associates made extensive use of meta-analyses to critically examine some generally accepted models in sport and exercise psychology. Here, not only did they demonstrate how meta-analysis should be used in the field to quantitatively review a basic problem, but they also enabled their readership to develop some fruitful ideas on how to promote research on the mental health model, in light of some important questions to be derived from their critical findings.

The Profile of Mood States (POMS) is commonly used to measure mental health in athletes. Athletes scoring below norms on scales of tension, depression, confusion, anger, and fatigue, and above norms on vigor, are said to possess a positive profile that graphically depicts an iceberg. However, the predictive power of the iceberg profile has recently been questioned. A meta-analysis was conducted on 33 studies comparing the POMS scores of athletes differing in success to estimate the magnitude of the findings. The overall effect size was calculated to be 0.15. Although this value was significantly different from zero, the amount of variance accounted for was less than 1%. The results suggest that across many different sports and levels of performance, successful athletes possess a mood profile slightly more positive than less successful athletes. However, with such a small and nonrobust effect, the utility of the POMS in predicting athletic success is questionable.

Morgan's (1985) mental health model states that "positive mental health enhances the likelihood of success in sport, whereas psychopathology is associated with a greater incidence of failure" (p. 79). In examining the mood states of athletes and nonathletes, Morgan found that athletes, especially successful ones, possessed a unique mood profile which he labeled the *iceberg profile.* This term refers to the graphic picture that raw scores on

Adapted, by permission, from A.J. Rowley et al., 1995, "Does the iceberg profile discriminate between successful and less successful athletes? A Meta-Analysis" *Journal of Sport and Exercise Psychology* 17: 185-199.

the Profile of Mood States (POMS) create when they are plotted on a profile sheet (McNair, Lorr, & Droppleman, 1971/1981), with the test norms representing the "water line." If an athlete scores low on "negative" mood scales (tension, depression, anger, fatigue, confusion) and high on the "positive" vigor scale, the plotted curve resembles an iceberg. Using this terminology, Morgan's hypothesis can be simplified as follows: Successful athletes possess more of an iceberg profile than less successful athletes.

Textbook reviews of personality and sport research have given the mental health model considerable attention. Gill (1986) stated that "Morgan offers the most systematic and strongly supported work on the relationship of personality to success in sport" (p. 31), and Cox (1990) stated that "the research evidence is very convincing that the successful athlete is likely to enjoy positive mental health" (p. 38). Others have described the consistency of Morgan's results as "remarkable" (Eysenck, Nias, & Cox, 1982, p. 19).

Claiming that successful athletes tend to be mentally healthy is not a provocative concept, and surely, psychopathology and success at nearly anything should be inversely correlated. Yet, when examining the mental health model, a question arises as to whether the relationship between mental health and athletic performance is correlated highly enough to make fine-grain distinctions between athletes possessing similar psychological profiles. After all, athletes do not fall into two categories: psychopaths and normals. Mental health is a continuum, and athletes may fall very close to each other in their overall rating of mental health, or they may be very different. The point is, the smallest divisions between levels of mental health are nearly indistinguishable. Can the mental health model detect fine-grain distinctions among successful and less successful athletes with similar mental health profiles? The empirical evidence presented by Morgan (1985) in support of the mental health model, in fact, came from studies examining fairly homogeneous groups of athletes (elite or advanced athletes from relatively few sports) whose profiles were likely to be similar. The results from these studies, in terms of the ability to predict success from these similar profiles, were very impressive.

The general acceptance of the mental health model is based largely on seven of Morgan's early studies that provided convincing research support. In the years following Morgan's early research, however, conflicting evidence has generated criticism and concern as to the usefulness of the mental health model (Landers, 1991; Prapavessis & Grove, 1991). Criticism is leveled at five problem areas in the research: the measures of mental health, the measures of performance, the time span between the measurement of these variables, the interpretation of the findings, and the design methodology.

Although other psychological measures have been used to assess mental health, the POMS has been the inventory of choice because of its success in Morgan's early studies. Morgan (1980b) stated that "of all the psychological tests my colleagues and I have experimented with, we have found the Profile of Mood States (POMS) to be the most highly predictive of athletic success" (pp. 93, 97). However, situational factors, such as completing the POMS before team selection, can influence the results. The validity of the POMS in such environments is questionable because, according to Boyle (1987), "the instrument is highly susceptible to distorting influences such as effects of social desirability and other response sets, inadequate self-insight, and even downright dissimulation, given the obvious item transparency" (p. 353). In fact, undergraduate students were able to "fake good" and produce an iceberg profile when asked to imagine themselves as elite athletes who suspected that POMS data would influence their being selected for a team (Miller & Edgington, 1984).

A second concern with past research is related to the measures of performance that were used. Specifically, successful performance, which the mental health model claims to predict, was never directly assessed in Morgan's research. Instead, success was inferred from placement in a competition or in terms of qualifying for a team (e.g., Morgan & Johnson, 1978; Morgan, O'Connor, Sparling, & Pate, 1987). This definition fails to account for the nonqualifiers and nonplacers who produced career-best performances. As Krane (1992) points out, this use of a between-subjects comparison in terms of performance does not adequately account for how well the athlete actually performs. Thus, the measures of success that have typically been used are not appropriate, nor is it appropriate to rely upon between-subjects comparisons rather than within-subjects analysis. There is a need to incorporate within-subjects analyses rather than between-subjects analyses because precompetitive mood profiles related to successful and unsuccessful performances may vary between individuals. For instance, one athlete may perform quite well when angry, whereas another athlete with the same mood state may perform poorly.

The third criticism of the research in this area is that the time span between the assessment of mental health and performance has been inconsistent (Landers, 1991). Administration of the POMS, a paper-and-pencil measure, is limited to times outside an athlete's precompetition preparatory period and has occurred anywhere from 1 week to 4 years (Morgan & Johnson, 1978) prior to performance. Often, the wording of the instructions for the POMS did not direct athletes to report their moods for the time in which the performance occurred. Additionally, empirical evidence has shown that mood states measured by the POMS are influenced by time of day (Hill & Hill, 1991) and, in swimmers, by level of training intensity (Morgan, Brown, Raglin, O'Connor, & Ellickson, 1987). Therefore, since the mood state likely changes between the time of psychological test administration and the time of performance assessment, the relationship between a "snapshot" of mental health and performance is tenuous at best.

Another criticism of research in this area is that early researchers may have misinterpreted their results. In fact, the initial praise for Morgan's research may have resulted from these faulty interpretations. Prapavessis and Grove (1991) indicated that past researchers have wrongly interpreted correlational findings as causal by assuming that a certain mood profile *produces* good performances. An athlete's outstanding performances and training in the past may cause both a positive mood profile and a successful performance, without the mood state actually causing the performance. Heyman's (1982) reanalysis of a series of articles on the relationship between psychological states and performance support this contention. Heyman (1982) found that athletes exhibiting successful performances had significantly better season records, more experience, and came from superior training programs when compared to unsuccessful athletes. As Heyman concluded "the psychological patterns and cognitions may themselves reflect previous experiences rather than cause or facilitate performance in most of the participants" (p. 299). This evidence supports an overlooked concept in the psychological testing of athletes: the impact of an athlete's physical skills and abilities upon psychological parameters.

The final criticism against studies that have investigated the mental health model is that they have been plagued with methodological problems. In spite of Morgan's consistent results, many of the studies claiming to support the iceberg profile made no statistical comparison to an appropriate control group (Landers, 1991). Rather than compare groups of athletes, researchers have often contrasted an athletic group's scores with POMS norms generated in 1967 by participants in psychological tests and students in psychology classes (e.g., Morgan & Johnson, 1978; Morgan, O'Connor, et al., 1987). As Landers (1991) argued, the normative sample reported in the POMS manual is an inappropriate comparison group for research on athletes. McNair et al. (1971/1981), the authors of the POMS, even cautioned that the normative information "should be considered as very tentative" (p. 19) because the data were obtained from only one university at one point in time.

In fact, since Morgan's early work, few studies have found the iceberg profile to be successful at predicting athletic performance. In a review of research, Landers (1991) discovered that only 53% of the comparisons were in the predicted direction. This percentage is not significantly different from the total that would be expected from chance. Unfortunately, a traditional narrative review of the literature is unable to determine the magnitude of an effect, and Landers (1991) could not conclusively estimate the predictive import of the mental health model. However, Glass's (1977) quantitative review method, meta-analysis, integrates the findings of multiple studies that meet present selection criteria in a particular domain in order to arrive at general conclusions on a topic.

Meta-analyses quantify the results of all relevant, appropriate, and available studies with a standard metric, the effect size (ES), that can later be subjected to statistical analysis. Combining the ESs of many studies is equivalent to combining all of the participants from all of the studies. This then augments the statistical power of the analysis, which is useful in detecting small, significant trends and which allows for the use of multivariate techniques. Meta-analysis, therefore, can provide what traditional reviews cannot: in this case, a replicable, relatively objective, scaled measure of the mental health model's efficacy in discriminating among athletes. None of the methodological concerns with the past research can be corrected through meta-analysis; however, these concerns can be coded so that the impact that they have on the ESs can be examined.

The extent to which mental health, as measured by the POMS, is predictive of athletic performance was tested using meta-analytic techniques. It was hypothesized that, as predicted by Morgan (1985), successful athletes would possess a more positive mood (i.e., iceberg) profile when compared to less successful athletes. Additional a priori hypotheses were proposed with regard to characteristics that could potentially moderate the effects outlined in the original hypothesis. Referring to the mental health model, Morgan (1985) stated that "specific responses will be dependent upon specific stimulus conditions" (p. 71). This suggests that the model's predictive utility may be limited to certain types of activities (Landers, 1991). Therefore, it is hypothesized that the ability of the POMS to predict athletic success will be influenced by the type of activity (endurance or strength) being observed.

Additionally, because mood states change over time (Hill & Hill, 1991) and because the mood of the athlete is thought to influence the athlete's performance capability, it is hypothesized that studies that assess mood immediately before competition will be better predictors of performance than those that assess mood well before competition or after competition.

As evident in previous meta-analyses in sport psychology (Feltz & Landers, 1983; North, McCullagh, & Tran, 1990), published studies have a larger overall ES than unpublished studies. Thus, it is predicted that effects from published studies will be significantly larger than effects from unpublished studies.

Finally, since the POMS is susceptible to distorting influences (Boyle, 1987; Miller & Edgington, 1984), it is hypothesized that the POMS will be less effective as a predictive instrument in environments with strong demand characteristics (i.e., during team selection) because all athletes may respond in a "desirable" manner if they feel that their responses may impact their chances of, for example, making the team. This idea is also supported by Morgan's (1974) caution that studies reporting null findings often do not use lie, guess, or random response scales. Without such safeguards, the truthfulness of the responses may be questioned, and the variability in the responses may be misleadingly small. As such, studies that include any of these distortion scales should produce larger ESs than studies without safeguards.

Method

Selection and Inclusion of Studies

All available literature from 1971 (the copyright date of the POMS) through January 1992 were located using computer databases (PsychLIT, ERIC, Medline and *Dissertation Abstracts International*); *AAHPERD Convention Abstracts of Research Papers; Completed Research in Health, Physical Education, Recreation and Dance; Psychological Abstracts; Social Sciences Citation Index; Current Contents;* and *Microform Publications*. Systematic searches of referenced lists were also conducted to locate studies not located through the computerized data sets.

Glass (1977) has recommended that a priori exclusions of research should be minimized. As such, inclusion criteria were kept broad so that studies included in the analysis had to assess mental health only with the POMS and with at least two groups of athletes (i.e., any individual who is a regular participant in a sport at the time of mood assessment) in the same sport at different levels of success.

A total of 94 studies were located using the search strategies described. However, 8 studies could not be included in the analyses because they did not include sufficient data for the calculation of ESs. Additionally, 52 studies were not included because they did not include any comparison of POMS scores between athletes who differed in success. Finally, one study was excluded because the data were presented in another study included in the analysis. Therefore, 33 studies yielding 411 ESs were subjected to further analysis. These studies are identified in the reference list by an asterisk.

Coding Characteristics

Studies were coded for variables that could potentially moderate the effect of mental health on athletic performance. Publication status referred to whether the study was published in a journal or book or was an unpublished thesis, dissertation, or professional presentation. Participant characteristics included the following:

1. The difference between the groups on the level of expertise (see bulleted list), which was coded as same level, one level different, or two levels different
2. The confidence in the expertise level categorization which was simply coded as questionable (unclear) or valid (clear)
3. The sex of participants, which was coded as men only, women only, or men and women combined

Activity characteristics included the following:

1. Aerobic (training consists of continuous rhythmic movements using major muscle groups) or strength (any activity not meeting the aerobic definition)
2. The operational definition of performance, which was coded as personal best, ranking, selection for team, starters/nonstarters, placement in a race, finishing/not finishing a race, winning/losing, or a subjective measure of performance
3. The confidence in this definition of performance, which was coded as questionable (unclear) or valid (clear)

Methodological characteristics included the following:

1. Time of mood assessment, which was coded as more than 24 hours prior to performance, less than 24 hours prior to performance, or postperformance
2. Presence of a lie scale, which was coded as included or not
3. Presence of demand characteristics (any situation in which athletes were being evaluated for selection to a team) as present or not
4. Differences in physical training state between groups as different or the same
5. Internal validity, as good (0 threats), moderate (1–2 threats), or poor (3 or more threats) based upon the number of threats to internal validity which existed

Effect sizes were calculated for each scale of the POMS (i.e., tension, depression, anger, vigor, fatigue, and confusion). Expertise categories were based upon the following operational definitions:

Elite

- Ranked in the top 10 in the United States
- Member of a national team or professional
- Best marathon: men: under 2.5 hours; women under 2.75 hours
- Best 10K: women: under 35 minutes

Advanced

- Ranked, but not in top 10
- Member of a state team or winner of a state tournament
- College athletes
- High School: member of a national team or nationally ranked
- Black belt in martial arts
- Best marathon: under 4 hours
- Able to run an ultramarathon (50 miles or more)

Intermediate

- High school athletes
- Colored belt in martial arts
- Able to run a marathon, triathlon, or 15 miles per week regularly

Novice

- Ranked as novice
- Regular participant for less than one year at time of assessment

Analyses

ESs were calculated using Hedges and Olkin's (1985) extension of Glass's (1977) original technique. The pooled standard deviation (weighted to correct for sample size bias) was used in ES calculation because it provides a more precise estimate of the population variance (Hedges, 1981). The formula for this calculation is:

$$ES = \frac{M_E - M_C}{SD_P}, \text{ where } SD_P = \sqrt{\frac{(N_E - 1) \cdot SD_E^2 + (N_C - 1) \cdot SD_C^2}{N_E - N_C - 2}},$$

and where M_E = mean of the experimental group; M_C = mean of the control group; SD_P = pooled standard deviation; N_E = number of participants in the experimental group; N_C = number of participants in the comparison group; SD_C = standard deviation of the comparison group. To ensure that ESs in support of the iceberg profile were positive values, the means of the successful group were subtracted from the means of the less successful group for all scales except "vigor," in which the less successful group was subtracted from the more successful group. Because studies with small samples sizes may have a biased effect size (Thomas & French, 1986), each effect size was then multiplied by a correction factor designed to yield an unbiased estimate of effect size (Hedges, 1981). The correction factor is: $c = 1 - [3/(4m - 9)]$ where $m = N_c + N_c - 2$.

Studies that reported more than one set of six ESs (representing the six POMS scales) can pose a threat to the statistical validity of the results. This situation violates the assumption of independence of data points (Bangert-Drowns, 1986). To control for this problem, overall ES was calculated twice. First, all ESs were combined to determine overall ES. Then for the remainder of the analyses only one ES (reflecting the two most extreme success groups) per study was included. The decision to use this particular set of ESs was made to give the mental health model the greatest likelihood of showing an effect. That is, since Morgan (1980a), contends that the relationship between psychological state and performance is linear, greater differences between performance outcome should be reflected in greater differences in POMS scores. Additionally, while effects could be calculated for total mood disturbance scores, these scores represent a sum of the six aspects of the mood scale and thus would not be independent scores. Therefore, these scores were only used in the overall average of effects and were not included in any subsequent analyses.

Results

The overall average ES ($n = 411$) was calculated to be 0.15 ($SD = 0.89$), which indicates that successful athletes possess a mood profile approximately one sixth of standard deviation healthier than less successful athletes. Based on the preceding rationale, which prescribed the elimination of the total mood disturbance score and the use of only one set of ESs for the most extreme groups, the overall ES was 0.19 ($SD = 1.09$, $n = 198$).

Next, three outliers (ESs falling outside of three standard deviations from the mean) were identified and omitted. This did not change the mean ES, but the SD was decreased to 0.71. Following the procedures outlined by Thomas and French (1986), the H-statistic was calculated and found to be significant, $X^2(194) = 817.69$, $p < .05$, with a critical value of 227.21, indicating that ESs were not homogeneous. This lack of homogeneity warranted further examination of moderator variables.

One-way analyses of variance (ANOVAs) were conducted on all of the coded variables to test for significant differences in ESs among the levels of each variable. ANOVAs were used because the distribution of the effects was reasonably close to normal to warrant the use of parametric techniques rather than necessitating the use of nonparametric techniques (Wolf, 1986).

The only moderating variable that was found to significantly impact the ESs was the moderating variable that reflected the confidence the coder had in the value assigned to the performance variable, $F(1, 193) = 5.652$, $p < .05$. The studies in which the categorization was questionable (i.e., in which performance scores were unclear) had larger ESs ($M = 0.51$, $SD = 0.78$, $n = 29$) than did studies in which the categorization was not questionable (i.e., in which performance scores were quite clear) ($M = 0.13$, $SD = 0.69$, $n = 166$).

Discussion

All available research included in the meta-analysis indicated that successful athletes, in general, report POMS scores one sixth of a standard deviation higher than less successful athletes in the same sport ($ES = 0.15$). Despite biasing analyses to allow the mental health model to demonstrate an effect (by using the largest possible set of ESs from each study in the analysis), these results show that POMS scores for successful athletes are less than one fifth ($ES = 0.19$) of a standard deviation higher than POMS scores for unsuccessful athletes. The magnitude of this effect, according to Cohen's (1988) classification, is very small. Of additional concern is the fact that larger effects were found in those studies in which the definition of success was of questionable clarity ($M = 0.51$) as compared to studies in which the definition of success was clear ($M = 0.13$). This does not encourage the use of the mental health model as an instrument to predict performance, or as a dimension for team selection.

The lack of strong support for the POMS in predicting athletic success reflects poorly on the mental health model proposed by Morgan (1985). Given that prediction rates of the model have been reported to range from 70% to 80% (Morgan, 1985) and 70% to 90% (Raglin, Morgan, & Luchsinger, 1990), the ESs generated by the meta-analytic procedures should have been larger. Further, when these ESs are converted to a Pearson's r^2, they account for less than 1% of the variance explained for performance outcome. That is, of all the factors that determine an athlete's performance, precompetitive mood states as measured by the POMS accounted for less than 1%, and the remaining 99% could be explained by other components (e.g., physiological characteristics, biomechanical status, practice, diet, or other psychological variables).

Eight studies were excluded from the analysis due to insufficient data for the calculation of ESs. Four of these studies (DeMers, 1983; Morgan, O'Connor, Ellickson, & Bradley, 1988; Nagle, Morgan, Hellickson, Serfass, & Alexander, 1975; Silva, Shultz, Haslam, Martin, & Murray, 1988) reported that the POMS discriminated between successful and less successful athletes, with the successful athletes possessing a more pronounced iceberg profile. The other four studies found that mood profiles either did not differ between athletes of different levels (Berger & Owen, 1986; Craighead, Privette, Vallianos, & Byrkit, 1986; Durtschi & Weiss, 1986) or that less successful athletes had a more pronounced iceberg profile than did more successful athletes (Riddick, 1984). It appears that, had these studies been included in the analysis, they would not have significantly affected the overall ES.

The results of the present analysis mirror Landers's (1991) traditional review of the mental health model. Landers (1991) identified 14 studies that compared the POMS scores of two groups of athletes representing two levels of performance outcome, and a total of 148 comparisons between successful and less successful athletes were made for the six scales of the POMS. Of these comparisons, only 18% were statistically significant, with 16% of the significant results in the direction predicted by the mental health model. Since the sample sizes of the studies were so small, Landers (1991) conducted a second analysis in which statistical significance was ignored, and the 148 comparisons were divided into those that supported and those that did not support the mental health model. As already mentioned, when examined in this manner 53% of the results supported the mental health model. The present meta-analysis yielded a total of 411 comparisons, with 54% in the predicted direction. The striking similarity of results adds credence to Landers's (1991) conclusion that the findings "fail to clearly support the predictions of the mental health model" (p. 197).

Based on the results of this analysis, future research would benefit from using larger samples. To ensure that adequate statistical power exists (i.e., 0.80), approximately 100 participants are required for 95% confidence in the results (Kraemer & Thiemann, 1987). However, there appears to be little promise in using the POMS and the mental health model in attempts to predict performance in athletes. Although a series of studies with strong research designs may be helpful in demonstrating a larger effect, it is likely to be moderate at best, and the resources may be better spent on more promising endeavors.

However, Morgan and his colleagues have recently shifted their focus to a more "dynamic" mental health model, which proposes a within-subjects approach to predicting individual performance by means of consistent monitoring of the athlete's psychological states across different training conditions (Morgan, O'Connor, et al., 1987). The dynamic mental health model accounts for an athlete's individual differences by tracking his or her unique level of success and mood profiles. As such, each athlete will generate his or her own graphic profile of POMS scores that is consistent with success, which may or may not depict the classic iceberg profile. The dynamic mental health model is likely a more appropriate and effective application of the POMS as it relates to athletic performance.

References

References marked with an asterisk were included in the meta-analysis.

Bangert-Drowns, R.L. (1986). Review of developments in meta-analytic method. *Psychological Bulletin*, 99, 388–399.

*Bell, G.J., & Howe, B.L. (1988). Mood state profiles and motivations of triathletes. *Journal of Sport Behavior,* 11, 66–77.

*Berger, B.G., & Owen D.R. (1983). Mood alteration with swimming: Swimmers really do "feel better." *Psychosomatic Medicine,* 45, 425–433.

Berger, B.G., & Owen, D.R. (1986). Mood alteration with swimming: A reexamination. In L. Vander Velden & J.H. Humphrey (Eds.), *Psychology and sociology of sport: Current selected research* (pp. 97–113). New York: AMS Press.

*Boyce, L.V. (1987). Psychology fitness, personality, and cognitive strategies of marathon runners as related to success and gender [Abstract]. *Completed Research in Health, Physical Education, Recreation, & Dance,* 29, 108.

Boyle, G.P. (1987). A cross-validation of the factor structure of the profile of mood states: Were the factors correctly identified in the first instance? *Psychological Reports,* 60, 343–354.

*Cavanaugh, S.R. (1982). The mood states of selected collegiate athletes during the season of varsity competition (Doctoral dissertation, Brigham Young University). *Dissertation Abstracts International,* 43, 1874A.

Cohen, J. (1988). *Statistical power analysis for the behavioral sciences* (3rd ed.). New York: Academic Press.

Cox, R.H. (1990). *Sport psychology: Concepts and applications* (2nd ed.). Dubuque, IA: Brown.

Craighead, D.J., Privette, G., Vallianos, F., & Byrkit, D. (1986). Personality characteristics basketball players, starters, and non-starters. *International Journal of Sport Psychology,* 17, 110–119.

*Daiss, S., LeUnes, A., & Nation, J. (1986). Mood and locus of control of a sample of college and professional football players. *Perceptual and Motor Skills,* 63, 733–734.

*Daus, A.T., Wilson, J. , & Freeman, W.M. (1986). Psychological testing as an auxiliary means of selecting successful college and professional football players. *Journal of Sports Medicine,* 26, 274–278.

DeMers, G.E. (1983, May-June). Emotional states of high-caliber divers. *Swimming Technique,* pp. 33–35.

Durtschi, S.K., & Weiss, M.R. (1986). Psychological Characteristics of elite and nonelite marathon runners. In D.M. Landers (Ed.), *Sport and elite performers: The 1984 Olympic scientific congress proceedings* (pp. 73–80). Champaign, IL: Human Kinetics.

*Dyer, J.B., & Crouch, J.G. (1987). Effects of running on moods: A time series study. *Perceptual and Motor Skills,* 64, 783–789.

Eysenck, H.J., Nias, D.K.B., & Cox, D.N. (1982). Sport and personality. *Advances in Behavior Research and Therapy,* 4, 1–56.

Feltz, D.L., & Landers, D.M. (1983). The effects of mental practice on motor skill learning and performance: A meta-analysis. *Journal of Sport Psychology,* 5, 25–57.

*Frazier, S.E. (1986). Psychological characteristics of male and female marathon runners of various performance levels (Doctoral dissertation, Indiana University). *Dissertation Abstracts International,* 47, 2076.

*Frazier, S.E. (1988). Mood state profiles of chronic exercisers with differing abilities. *International Journal of Sport Psychology,* 19, 65–71.

*Frazier, S.E., & Nagy, S. (1989). Mood state changes of women as a function of regular aerobic exercise. *Perceptual and Motor Skills,* 68, 283–287.

Gill, D.L. (1986). *Psychological dynamics of sport.* Champaign, IL: Human Kinetics.

Glass, G.V. (1977). Integrating findings: The meta-analysis of research. *Review of Research in Education,* 5, 351–379.

*Gondola, J.C., & Tuckman, B.W. (1983). Extent of training and mood enhancement in women runners. *Perceptual and Motor Skills,* 57, 333–334.

*Gutmann, M.C., Pollock, M.L., Foster, C., & Schmidt, D. (1984). Training stress in Olympic speed skaters: A psychological perspective. *The Physician and Sportsmedicine,* 12(12), 45–57.

*Hagberg, J.M., Mullin, J.P., Bahrke, M., Limburg, J. (1979). Physiological profiles and selected psychological characteristics of national class American cyclists. *Journal of Sports Medicine and Physical Fitness,* 19, 341–346.

*Harris, D. (1985). The relationship between player mood state and performance outcome of a woman's intercollegiate softball team (Master's thesis, Stephen F. Austin State University). *Master's Abstracts International,* 23, 503.

*Hassmen, P., & Blomstrand, E. (1991). Mood change and marathon running: A pilot study using a Swedish version of the POMS test. *Scandinavian Journal of Psychology,* 32, 225–232.

Hedges, L.V. (1981). Distribution theory for Glass' estimator of effect size and related estimators. *Journal of Educational Statistics,* 6, 107–128.

Hedges, L.V., & Olkin, I. (1985). *Statistical methods for meta analysis.* New York: Academic Press.

Heyman, S.R. (1982). Comparisons of successful and unsuccessful competitors: A reconsideration of methodological questions and data. *Journal of Sport Psychology,* 4, 259–300.

Hill, C.M., & Hill, D.W. (1991). Influence of time of day on responses to the Profile of Mood States. *Perceptual and Motor Skills,* 72, 434–439.

Kraemer, H.C., & Thiemann, S. (1987). *How many subjects? Statistical power analysis in research.* Newbury Park, CA: Sage.

Krane, V. (1992). Conceptual and methodological considerations in sport anxiety research: From the inverted-U hypothesis to catastrophe theory. *Quest,* 44, 72–87.

Landers, D.M. (1991). Optimizing individual performance. In D. Druckman & R.A. Bjork (Eds.), *In the mind's eye: Enhancing human performance* (pp. 193–246). Washington, DC: National Academy Press.

*Lindstrom, D.V. (1990). Personality characteristics of ultramarathoners: Finishers vs. nonfinishers (Master's thesis, San Jose State University). *Master's Abstracts International,* 28, 644.

*Mahoney, M.J. (1989). Psychological predictors of elite and non-elite performance in Olympic weightlifting. *International Journal of Sport Psychology,* 20, 1–12.

McNair, D.M., Lorr, M., & Droppleman, L.F. (1981). *Profile of mood states manual.* San Diego: Educational and Industrial Testing Service. (Original work published 1971)

*McGowan, R.W., & Miller, M.J. (1989). Difference in mood states between successful and less successful karate participants. *Perceptual and Motor Skills,* 68, 505–506.

*McGowan, R.W., Miller, M.J., & Henschen, K.P. (1990). Differences in mood states between belt ranks in karate tournament competitors. *Perceptual and Motor Skills,* 71, 147–150.

*Miller, B.P., & Edgington, G.P. (1984). Psychological mood state distortion in a sporting context. *Journal of Sport Behavior,* 7, 91–94.

Morgan, W.P. (1974). Selected psychological considerations in sport. *Research Quarterly,* 45, 374–390.

Morgan, W.P. (1980a). The trait psychology controversy. *Research Quarterly*, 51, 50–76.

Morgan, W.P. (1980b, July). Test of champions: The iceberg profile. *Psychology Today,* pp. 92–99.

*Morgan, W.P. (1985). Selected psychological factors limiting performance: A mental health model. In D.H. Clarke & H.M. Eckert (Eds.), *Limits of human performance* (pp. 70–80). Champaign, IL: Human Kinetics.

Morgan, W.P., Brown, D.R., Raglin, J.S., O'Connor, P.J., & Ellickson, K.A. (1987). Psychological monitoring of overtraining and staleness. *British Journal of Sports Medicine,* 21, 107–114.

*Morgan, W.P., & Johnson, R.W. (1978). Personality characteristics of successful and unsuccessful oarsmen. *International Journal of Sport Psychology,* 9, 119–133.

Morgan, W.P., O'Connor, P.J., Ellickson, K.A., & Bradley, P.W. (1988). Personality structure, mood states, and performance in the elite male distance runners. *International Journal of Sport Psychology,* 19, 247–263.

*Morgan, W.P., O'Connor, P.J., Sparling, P.B., & Pate, R.R. (1987). Psychological characteristics of the elite female distance runner. *International Journal of Sports Medicine,* 8(Suppl.), 124–131.

*Morgan, W.P., & Pollock, M.L. (1977). Psychologic Characterization of the elite distance runner. *Annals of the New York Academy of Sciences,* 301, 383–403.

Nagle, F.J., Morgan, W.P., Hellickson, R.O., Serfass, R.C., & Alexander J.F. (1975). Spotting success traits in Olympic contenders. *The Physician and Sportsmedicine,* 3(12), 31–34.

North, T.C., McCullagh, P., & Tran, Z.V. (1990). Effect of exercise on depression. *Exercise and Sport Science Reviews,* 18, 379–415.

*Poole, C., Henschen, K.P., Shultz, B., Gordon,R., & Hill, J. (1986). A longitudinal investigation of the psychological profiles of elite collegiate female athletes according to performance level. In L. Unestahl (Ed.), *Contemporary sport psychology: Proceedings from the VI World Congress in Sport Psychology* (pp. 65–72). Orebro, Sweden: Veje.

*Prapavessis, H., & Grove, J.R. (1991). Precompetitive emotions and shooting performance: The mental health and zone of optimal functioning models. *The Sport Psychologist,* 5, 223–234.

*Raglin, J.S., Morgan, W.P., & Luchsinger, A.E. (1990). Mood and self-motivation in successful and unsuccessful female rowers. *Medicine and Science in Sports and Exercise,* 22, 849–853.

*Ramadan, J.M. (1984). Selected physiological, psychological, and anthropometric characteristics of Kuwaiti World Cup soccer team (Doctoral dissertation, Louisiana State University). *Dissertation Abstracts International,* 46, 924A.

Riddick, C.C. (1984). Comparative psychological profiles of three groups of female collegians: Competitive swimmers, recreational swimmers, and inactive swimmers. *Journal of Sport Behavior,* 7, 160–174.

*Robinson, D.W., & Howe, B.L. (1987). Causal attribution and mood state relationships of soccer players in a sport achievement setting. *Journal of Sport Behavior,* 10, 137–146.

Silva, J.M., Shultz, B.B., Haslam, R.W., Martin T.P., & Murray, D.F. (1988). Discriminating characteristics of contestants at the United States Olympic wrestling trials. *International Journal of Sport Psychology,* 16, 79–102.

*Silva, J.M., Shultz, B.B., Haslam, R.W., & Murray, D. (1981). A psychophysiological assessment of elite wrestlers. *Research Quarterly,* 52, 348–358.

*Tharion, W.J., Strowman, S.R., & Rauch, T.M. (1988). Profile and changes in moods of ultramarathoners. *Journal of Sport & Exercise Psychology,* 10, 229–235.

Thomas, J.R., & French, K.E. (1986). The use of meta-analysis in exercise and sport: A tutorial. *Research Quarterly for Exercise and Sport,* 57, 196–204.

*Toner, M.K. (1981). The relationship of selected physical fitness, skill, and mood variables to success in female high school basketball candidates (Doctoral dissertation, Boston University). *Dissertation Abstracts International,* 42, 3909A.

*Wilson, V.E., Morley, N.C., & Bird, E.I. (1980). Mood profiles of marathon runners, joggers, and non-exercisers. *Perceptual and Motor Skills,* 50, 117–118.

Wolf, F.M. (1986). *Meta-analysis: Quantitative Methods for Research Synthesis.* Beverly Hills, CA: Sage.

11 Personality and Intellectual Capabilities in Sport Psychology

GERSHON TENENBAUM
University of Southern Queensland

MICHAEL BAR-ELI
Wingate Institute for Physical Education and Sport

The study of individual differences in sport and exercise is first and foremost associated with the concept of personality. Personality researchers are interested in the ways in which people are similar, but they are much more interested in individual uniqueness—that is, in the ways in which people differ. Since the beginning of sport psychology, personality research has been associated with some popular assumptions. For example, it was believed that particular attributes of personality may contribute to success in sport ("winners are born") or that, through sport participation, valued personal characteristics can be developed in humans ("sport builds character"). As a result, a wealth of research was evident in this area, mostly during the 1960s and 1970s. Already in that period, more than a thousand studies have been conducted on personality and sport.

Intelligence was considered an inherent trait in various inventories intended to measure personality in sport. However, the findings drawn from research conducted with the use of such instruments were inconclusive. Therefore, in the 1980s, researchers began to draw more attention to different paradigms and methods, which could probably better account for intelligent behavior related to skilled motor performance. In essence, intelligence is a complex cognitive construct, particularly when applied to a specific field such as athletic performance. In the early 1990s, research in this area was in its relative infancy; therefore, as in the case of personality research, the exact nature of the relationship between intellectual capabilities and motor behavior and performance was still quite unclear.

On the invitation of the editors of the prestigious International Handbook of Personality and Intelligence, Tenenbaum and Bar-Eli undertook the mission of presenting the state of the art in personality and intelligence research in sport psychology to the general psychology readership. After discussing some historical perspectives on personality research in sport, they presented the relationships between personality and motor behavior with regard to variables such as sensation seeking, introversion–extraversion, anxiety, and motivation. Intelligence was discussed with reference to intellectual capabilities required for successful athletic activity, such as information processing, knowledge, experience, decision making, reaction time, timing, memory and recall, vision, sensorimotor processing, attention, anticipation, cognitive styles, and time and space perception. The authors concluded by suggesting the transactional approach as an integrating, ecologically valid paradigm for future research on personality and intelligence in sport and exercise settings.

Historical Perspectives on Personality: From Traits and Dispositions to Interactions and Transactions

More than four decades ago, philosophers Dewey and Bentley (1949) argued that there are three phases in the development of theories in each scientific discipline: (a) self-action, in which objects are regarded as behaving under their own power; (b) interaction, in which objects are regarded as being in a causal interaction where one acts upon another; and (c) process transaction, in which objects are regarded as relating to one another within a system. Within psychology, it has been debated as to which source accounts for most of the variance in human behavior (Houts, Cook, & Shadish, 1986; Kenrick & Funder, 1988; Pervin, 1985). For instance, Ekehammer (1974) differentiated between "personologism" (which advocates stable, intraorganismic constructs as the main determinants of behavioral variance) and "situationism" (which emphasizes situational factors as the main source of behavioral variance). It seemed to Ekehammer that personality psychology was moving toward being governed by interactionism. The latter "can be regarded as the synthesis of personologism and situationism, which implies that neither the person nor the situation per se is emphasized, but the interaction of these two factors is regarded as the main source of behavioral variation" (p. 1026).

Interactionism in fact became the zeitgeist of personality psychology in the late 1970s, especially when combined with cognitive theoretical perspectives (Bern, 1983; Snyder, 1983). Some investigators have proceeded even further in researching personality, toward transactionism. For example, Pervin (1977) stated that too much psychological research had been conducted on the self-action level and suggested that transactionism had a greater potential for investigating complex human behavior, particularly in

---

International handbook of personality and intelligence, 1995, pg. 687-710, Personality and intellectual capabilities in sport psychology, G. Tenenbaum and M. Bar-Eli, © Plenum Press.

applied settings (see also Bandura, 1978; Cronbach, 1957). Interactionism, however, still seems to play a major role in current personality psychology (Vealey, 1992).

Sports personality research was characterized in the 1950s and 1960s mainly by the self-action level. The person-situation debate in the personality literature, however, culminated with the interactional perspective as the preferred paradigm in sports personality research. For example, Martens (1975), reviewing the literature from 1950 to 1973, concluded that the interactional paradigm was the direction that sports personality research should take. Martens based his conclusion on the premise that situationalism was an overreaction to the trait paradigm and that behavior in sports could best be understood by concurrently studying the effects of environmental and intrapersonal variables.

Martens's conclusion did not bring the person-situation debate within sports psychology to an end (Fisher, 1984a; Morgan, 1980a, b; Silva, 1984). Vealey (1989) extended Martens's (1975) review to examine sports personality research from 1974 to 1988. It was found that 55% of the personality literature utilized an interactional approach, compared to 45% that utilized a trait approach. According to Vealey, however, within the interactional category there was a greater trend toward cognitive approaches (35%) as opposed to trait-state approaches (20%). The trait approach in sports personality decreased markedly from 1974 to 1981, whereas the cognitive interactional approach showed a marked increase during this time. The trait-state interactional approach has increased in use from the early 1970s, yet it has not demonstrated the popularity of the trait and cognitive interactional approaches.

In essence, these historical developments reflect the patterns observed for personality research in general psychology. Despite some calls for transactionalism in the sport and exercise domain (Bar-Eli, 1985; Nitsch, 1985), interactionalist approaches still seem to prevail. In this chapter, we will follow these developments. First we discuss the relationship between personality and motor behavior, emphasizing mainly traditional self-acting concepts. Then we emphasize the role of cognitive variables, stressing the relationship between intellectual characteristics and motor behavior. Finally, we briefly introduce some directions for future research in personality within the sports and exercise domain.

Personality and Motor Behavior

Sensation Seeking

The construct of sensation seeking was originally proposed by Zuckerman, Kolin, Price, and Zoob (1964). They argued that some individuals prefer extraordinarily high levels of stimulation to moderate levels. Individuals who rank high in sensation seeking are said to search for experiences that are exciting, risky, and novel. For such persons, "living life on the edge" is a personal orientation and a framework for evaluating the worth of prospective endeavors. Zuckerman et al. (1964) argued that human organisms are not necessarily drive or tension reducers, but rather strive for "optimal stimulation." This notion takes into account large individual differences in the need for stimulus reduction and, hence, the concept of sensation seeking.

Zuckerman originally hypothesized that people differed in levels of cortical arousal, but later, he (e.g., Zuckerman, 1979, 1987) refined his theory to suggest that sensation seekers possess stronger orienting responses than other individuals. An orienting response is an individual's first reaction to a new or unexpected stimulus. It is a tendency toward sensory intake, as opposed to defense responses, which attempt to screen out stimuli. Indeed, stronger orienting responses were revealed among sensation seekers (Neary & Zuckerman, 1976). Sensation seekers also demonstrated a link between sensation seeking, brain-wave response (Zuckerman, Murtaugh, & Siegel, 1974) and the production of endorphins (Johansson, Almay, Knorring, Terenius, & Astrom, 1979).

The sports and exercise literature associated with this concept has concentrated mainly on sporting activities selected by sensation seekers. Research in this area has typically used Zuckerman's Sensation Seeking Scale (SSS; see fifth revision in Zuckerman, 1984), which includes subdimensions of Thrill and Adventure Seeking (TAS), Experience Seeking (ES), Disinhibition (Dis), and Boredom Susceptibility (BS).

The SSS has generally been accepted as a valid assessment tool in sport contexts, particularly with high-risk athletes. Straub (1982), for example, studied 80 male athletes who participated in hang gliding, automobile racing, and bowling. The bowlers scored significantly lower on the total score and two of the four subdimensions when compared with the other two groups. Furthermore, in response to the question "Do you consider your sport to be a high-risk activity?" 67% of the hang gliders, 50% of the auto racers, and none of the bowlers answered positively, though 63% of the hang gliders and 41% of the auto racers reported having been injured at some point in their careers. Similarly, Zuckerman (1983) found auto racers to exhibit unusually high sensation-seeking scores.

Such findings could reflect a need to engage in risky sports activities (Fowler, Knorring, & Oreland, 1980). They could also reflect the fact, however, that sensation seekers are more likely to try a greater number of sports activities (low risk as well as high risk). To clarify this issue, Rowland, Franken, and Harrison (1986) administered Zuckerman's scale to 97 male and 104 female undergraduate students. Their results indicated that persons scoring high on the scale tend to become more involved in more sports, but that persons scoring low are more likely to remain with one sport for a longer period. In addition, Rowland et al. found a positive correlation between sensation seeking and participation in risky sports. These findings indicate that both increased activity and a desire to get involved with high-risk sports characterize the sensation seeker. In other words, sensation-seeking predicts not only the choice but also the degree of involvement in various sports. Thus it seems that arousal levels that would be excessive for most people are only sufficient to keep sensation seekers from boredom.

Introversion-Extraversion

According to Eysenck (e.g., 1967), there are two superordinate trait dimensions (i.e., "second order" factors) in personality introversion-extraversion and neuroticism (emotionality)-stability. These superordinate traits are further subdivided into component traits such as sociability, impulsiveness, activity, liveliness, and excitability, which lead to a person's habitual responses. Eysenck (1967) also suggested a third dimension—psychoticism—strength of superego, which relates to the development of psychopathologies—but this is referred to in the literature far less often than the two other domains.

Eysenck suggested an hereditary biological basis for these superordinate dimensions. Regarding introversion-extraversion, he argued that introverts differ from extraverts in the functioning of the ascending reticular activating system (ARAS), which is responsible for activating/deactivating higher brain portions. Eysenck (1981) later proposed that the base levels of ARAS activation of introverts are higher in comparison to those of extraverts. For this reason, introverts are said to avoid further stimulation, whereas extraverts are induced to seek additional stimulation (because of their lower arousal base levels).

Eysenck's proposal for a neural basis for neuroticism-stability relates to the activity of the limbic system, and the psychoticism-strength of superego is associated with the hormonal system. Extraverts have been found to be more easily conditioned (as well as more highly aroused and reactive) in response to their environment than introverts (Eysenck, 1967; Revelle, Humphreys, Simon, & Gilliland, 1980). Extraverts attend better during short periods, whereas introverts attend more efficiently during the later stages of a prolonged task (e.g., vigilance tasks of prolonged duration; Harkins & Green, 1975). The shorter term attention, learning, and performance of introverts may be inferior to that of extraverts, however, despite the former's ability to attend better and longer. According to Gillespie and Eysenck (1980), the learning process of introverts is more easily disrupted by distractions; in addition, when compared to extraverts, they take longer to respond and are more cautious, and are more likely to be stopped in decision processes conducted during attentive tasks.

The Eysenck Personality Inventory (EPI; Eysenck & Eysenck, 1963) made up of 57 yes-no items purporting to measure introversion-extraversion and neuroticism-stability, was first used in sports research with wrestlers at the 1966 world tournament. Specifically, Morgan (1968) found a significant correlation ($r = .50$) between extraversion and success at that event. Brichin and Kochlan (1970) studied Czech females; they found a significant difference in extraversion scores between 81 accomplished athletes and 86 performers of lesser accomplishment. Delk (1973) found a significant difference between 41 experienced male skydivers and the norms of the EPI manual on extraversion scores. Similar results were reported by Kirkcaldy (1980) regarding German athletes.

Fiegenbaum (1981, cited by Eysenck, Niss, & Cox, 1982) compared high-level long-distance runners with 62 regular joggers and 52 control subjects and found that runners scored higher on extraversion than joggers, who in turn demonstrated higher extraversion than the controls. Eysenck et al. (1982) concluded that athletes, both males and females, tend to be extraverts regardless of their expertise level. As Weingarten (1982) states, "most studies on the personality structure of athletes show an abundance of extraverts" (p. 121).

There are, however, some indications (e.g., Spielman, 1963) that extraverts do not easily tolerate repetitious stimuli for prolonged time periods. One would expect extraverts to be attracted mainly to vivid sports disciplines such as football or basketball, which contain various elements of body contact and intensive stimulation. In contrast, introverts will be more attracted to such relatively monotonous sports as rifle shooting, swimming, cycling or cross-country skiing (Weingarten, 1982). As mentioned above, though, athletes in general tend to be more extraverted in comparison to nonathletes (Eysenck et al., 1982).

In summary, introversion-extraversion seems to be a personality dimension by which top-level athletes can be distinguished from athletes of lower levels, as well as from nonathletes. It remains to be seen, however, whether the typically nontheoretical research in this area will suggest more adequate answers even to practical questions, such as the selection on the basis of this personality dimension (Bakker, Whiting, & van der Brug, 1990). Moreover, much work is needed to illuminate the still-unclear role neuroticism-stability and psychoticism-strength of superego play in the sports and exercise domain.

Anxiety

Spielberger (1989) proposed that anxiety refers to "emotional reactions that consist of a unique combination of: (1) feeling of tension, apprehension, and nervousness; (2) unpleasant thoughts (worries); and (3) physiological changes" (p. 5). This widely accepted definition is interactional in nature, because an anxiety state is caused not only by traits but also by stressors. The latter are viewed as situations that involve some physical and/or subjectively appraised (i.e., psychological) danger or threat (Spielberger, 1989).

Early approaches to anxiety (e.g., Taylor, 1953) conceptualized it as a relatively stable and unchanging construct. Later, researchers such as Cattell (1972) and Spielberger (1972) delineated anxiety into the trait and state components: Whereas trait anxiety represents the relatively stable and unchanging predisposition of a person to perceive situations as threatening, state anxiety is a dynamic variable that relates to the perception of individual and/or environmental factors as stressors.

Early psychometric instruments developed to assess trait anxiety, such as the Taylor Manifest Anxiety Scale (TMAS; Taylor, 1953), have not been widely accepted by sports psychologists. Despite the established construct validity of Spielberger's State-Trait Anxiety Inventory (STAI; Spielberger, Gorsuch, & Lushene, 1970; Spielberger, Gorsuch, Lushene, Vagg, & Jacobs, 1983) and its demonstrated utility in a variety of settings, including sports (Spielberger, 1989), several alternative scales have been developed to evaluate anxiety in this specific context. Martens suggested alternatives such as the Sport Competition Anxiety Test (SCAT; Martens, 1977), the Competitive State Anxiety Scale (CSAI; Martens, Burton, Rivkin, & Simon, 1980), and more recently the Cognitive Somatic Anxiety Questionnaire (CSAI-2; Martens, Vealey, & Burton), which conceives anxiety as a multidimensional construct rather than a global one. Although general measures of anxiety proved to be useful in sport and exercise (Hanin, 1986; Morgan, 1984), the trend of developing sport-specific scales is more noticeable (Raglin, 1992). For example, Ostrow's (1990) directory of psychological tests in the sports and exercise sciences includes 14 sport-specific anxiety tests developed between 1977 and 1990, with only three developed before 1986.

Research on anxiety in sports and exercise has been conducted mainly within the framework of two paradigms—namely, the drive and the inverted-U theories. Hull-Spence's drive concept (Hull, 1983; Spence, 1956) and its relationship to motor performance were extensively reviewed by Martens (1971, 1974). Studies in this area were classified according to the criterion of absence or presence of experimental stressors (e.g., electric shock). The absence of stressors was aimed to examine the drive theory's chronic hypothesis, that high-anxiety individuals will respond with greater drive across all situations. The presence of stressors was intended to test the drive theory's emotional reactivity hypothesis (Spence & Spence, 1966), which stated that differences between high- and low-anxiety persons would become more evident in the presence of stressors.

Martens found only a few studies that supported both hypotheses. Accordingly, he recommended the abandonment of the drive theory, advising alternative trait-state conceptions (Martens, 1972). This recommendation is further strengthened by the difficulty of accurately measuring habit strength in nonlaboratory settings, which are typical to the realm of applied sport and exercise. Moreover, most motor behaviors found in this domain cannot be considered simple, and therefore are problematic to test within the framework of the drive theory (Martens, 1974, 1977).

The inverted-U theory is currently viewed as more accountable to the research of anxiety in sports and exercise (Weinberg, 1989). This theory hypothesizes that performance effectiveness will increase as arousal increases to some optimal point; a further increase in arousal will produce performance decrements. Despite the conceptual differences between the terms *arousal* and *anxiety,* several researchers have used anxiety measures to account for arousal (for reviews, see Raglin, 1992; Weinberg, 1989). For example, Martens and Landers (1970) assigned high, moderate, and low trait anxiety (A-Trait) subjects to a motor tracking task involving three levels of stress. They found that subjects in the moderate stress conditions performed better than subjects in the high or low stress conditions, and that subjects with moderate A-Trait scores outperformed low and high A-Trait subjects.

Klavora (1978) assessed 924 pregame state anxiety (A-State) values of 95 subjects throughout an interscholastic high school basketball season, controlling individual differences in playing ability by asking coaches to evaluate each player's game performance with regard to the player's regular ability. Klavora's results showed that best performance was usually associated with moderate pregame A-State and that worst performance was quite typical for either extremely high or low A-States. Sonstroem and Bernardo (1982) similarly related pregame A-State responses to performance of 30 college varsity players across three games of a basketball tournament, controlling for individual differences in arousal reactivity. The authors found that median anxiety values were significantly associated with best game performance; moreover, 18% of the game performance variance could be explained by a curvilinear relationship with pregame state anxiety. Thus these studies support the inverted-U hypothesis in both the laboratory (Martens & Landers, 1970) and the field (Klavora, 1978; Sonstroem & Bernardo, 1982).

Fiske and Maddi (1961) discussed the role task characteristics play in varying the range of optimal arousal. These authors proposed that as task complexity increases, optimal arousal range will decrease. Oxendine (1970) extended this proposal and developed a hierarchical classification of sports activities based on their complexity (i.e., degree of fine motor control, effort, judgment required for performance). Activities such as weight lifting, sprinting, and football tackling and blocking were contrasted with bowling, field goal kicking, and figure skating. The former sports, demanding gross motor activities, require high arousal levels compared to the latter sports, which demand fine motor activities.

This idea was supported by Weinberg and Genuchi (1980), who found low levels of both competitive A-Trait and A-State to be related to better scores achieved across three days of a golf tournament, with golf being considered a task requiring precision and other fine movements. Other studies conducted to test this hypothesis, though, either failed to support Oxendine's hierarchy of motor tasks (Basler, Fisher, & Mumford, 1976), or even contradicted it (Furst & Tenenbaum, 1984). Despite these and other reservations against Oxendine (Martens et al., 1990; Neiss, 1988), his conceptualization is still considered influential within sports and exercise psychology (Raglin, 1992). Future research should devote more attention to this important issue.

Future studies on anxiety and sport/exercise performance should also inquire the role of individual differences within the framework of the inverted-U theory. Recent reviews (Gould & Krane, 1992; Raglin, 1992) reveal considerable ambiguity and confusion in the understanding of the range of individual differences among athletes. Hence future research efforts should attempt to clarify this issue within the framework of the inverted-U paradigm.

Cognitive mechanisms such as attention seem to play an important role in explaining the arousal/anxiety-performance curvilinear relationship depicted by the inverted-U function. For example, Landers (1978, 1980) suggested that low arousal is associated with uncritical acceptance of irrelevant cues, whereas high arousal is associated with elimination of relevant cues as a result of factors such as perceptual narrowing (Easterbrook, 1959). In contrast, moderate arousal, which increases perceptual selectivity, causes an optimal elimination of task-irrelevant cues, and thus the curvilinear arousal-performance relationship (inverted-U function) can be observed. A full test of this promising theory, however, has never been carried out (Gould & Krane, 1992).

Bar-Eli, Tenenbaum, and Elbaz (1990) used the constructs of anxiety and attention to explain athletes' aggressive behavior during competition. Early theories of anxiety accounted for individual performance differences by the presence or absence of task-irrelevant responses in subjects' behavioral repertories (Sarason, Mandler, & Craighill, 1952). The cognitive-attentional anxiety theory (Wine, 1980, 1982) conceptualized anxiety in terms of cognitive and attentional processes aroused in evaluational settings. According to this approach, cognitive anxiety misdirects attention from task-relevant cues to task-irrelevant self- or social evaluation cues. Although originally related to test anxiety, this theory applies to other situational contexts (Carver & Scheier, 1988), such as sports (Burton, 1988). According to Bar-Eli et al. (1990), as an athlete's anxiety arises in competition, it is accompanied by a higher probability of task-irrelevant behaviors. Because high levels of arousal tend to instigate and magnify aggressive behavior (Caprara, Renzi, D'Augello et al., 1986; Zillman, 1971), however, it is predicted that the more substantial an athlete's deviation from optimal arousal as a result of high anxiety, the higher the probability that he or she will reveal task-irrelevant behaviors, including "hostile" aggression (aggression that is an end rather than a means; Husman & Silva, 1984). This hypothesis has gained strong empirical corroboration in sport disciplines such as team handball (Bar-Eli et al., 1990), basketball (Bar-Eli & Tenenbaum, 1988, 1989a), and tennis (Bar-Eli, Taoz, Levy-Kolker, & Tenenbaum, 1992).

In conclusion, interactional approaches (e.g., Martens et al., 1990) seem to have a great potential for generating considerable research in sports personality with regard to anxiety-behavior relationship (Vealey, 1992). Future research would also have to test various modifications to the inverted-U hypothesis, which have recently been suggested. For example, Hanin's (1989) "zone of optimal functioning" (ZOF) theory appears to be a good candidate for furthering knowledge (Landers, 1989), probably in combination with Morgan's (1985) "mental health" model (Raglin, 1992). Other unidimensional views of arousal/anxiety such as Mahoney's (1979) coping model, or multidimensional views such as the psychic energy model (Martens, 1988), reversal theory (Kerr, 1989), the catastrophe cusp model (Hardy & Parfitt, 1991; Krane, 1992), and the psychological performance crisis model (Bar-Eli & Tenenbaum, 1989b) deserve more empirical research to verify their validity for examining the anxiety construct in sports and exercise. Finally, research incorporating psychobiological states (Hatfield & Landers, 1983; Neiss, 1988) might make a substantial contribution, mainly because of its emphasis on the interaction among cognitive, emotional, and physiological variables. It remains to be seen whether transactional approaches (e.g., Hackfort & Schultz, 1989) will in fact realize the promise of replacing interactional approaches in the more distant future, as would have been predicted by philosophy (Dewey & Bentley, 1949).

Motivation

Motivation research in sports and exercise began from typical self-acting approaches to personality. For example, it was argued that a considerable amount of physical and sports activity can be related to the need to fulfill such motives as competence (White, 1959), stimulation and arousal seeking (Ellis & Scholtz, 1978), perceptual augmentation/reduction (Petrie, 1967; Ryan & Foster, 1967), and affiliation (Alderman, 1976). A similar line of research has continued in the form of investigating motives for participation and withdrawal in youth sports. Petlichkoff (1992) analyzed data from a survey that included more than 10,000 young people from 11 cities across the United States. Her results indicated that (a) participation in organized sports declines sharply as youngsters get older, (b) "fun" is the key reason for involvement, and "lack of fun" is one of the primary reasons for discontinuing; (c) winning plays less of a role than most adults would think; and (d) not all athletes have the same motivations for their involvement. These results are in line with previous findings (for reviews, see Gould & Petlichkoff, 1988; Weiss & Petlichkoff, 1989).

In a series of studies, Scanlan and her associates (reviewed in Scanlan & Simons, 1992) offered the construct of sport enjoyment to account for such findings. This approach views enjoyment as a cornerstone of motivation in sports, in close affiliation with constructs such as perceived competence (Harter, 1981) and intrinsic challenge

(Czikszentmihaly, 1975; Deci & Ryan, 1980). In contrast to previous research, however, Scanlan's research is much more interactional in nature in that it attempts to identify the sources of enjoyment, which are quite often located in a person's environment (Scanlan & Simons, 1992).

Sports are in essence competitive activities. As defined by Martens (1976), sports competition is "a process in which the comparison of an individual's performance is made with some standard in the presence of at least one other person who is aware of the criterion for comparison and can evaluate the comparison process" (p. 14). To explore the role of personality factors within this framework, McClelland-Atkinson's achievement motivation theory received considerable attention in early literature, with sports psychologists making use of traditional tests to measure its constructs (Fineman, 1977).

Following McClelland, Atkinson, Clark, and Lowell (1953), Atkinson (1964, 1974) extended his theory of achievement motivation. In essence, Atkinson's model uses an interactional approach, which formally specifies the role of personality and situational factors as determinants of achievement behavior. Despite the fact that this theory has been the starting point for much of the achievement research to follow, only a few investigations in sports psychology directly tested its predictions with regards to physical-motor tasks (Healey & Landers, 1973; Ostrow, 1976; Roberts, 1972, 1974; Ryan & Lakie, 1965). Moreover, the results of these studies did not always support the predictions of Atkinson's model.

During the 1970s and 1980s, the cognitive approach gave motivation research a substantial impetus, in particular though Weiner's attribution theory (Weiner, 1974, 1986). Weiner's attempt to insert causal attributions into achievement motivation made the situation and its meaning more important; in contrast, individual differences and personality aspects became less important (Maehr, 1989; Roberts, 1992a). The corpus of work on attribution in sports and exercise has grown in both interest and volume (see reviews by Biddle, 1993; McAuley & Duncan, 1990). Although attribution theory has been a potent force in social sports psychology, some of its weaknesses have become evident when motivation research in sports is considered (Biddle, 1993; Roberts, 1992a), probably because of its strong situationistic, self-acting emphasis.

The future of research on motivation in sports seems to lie in the social-cognitive approach. Several theories suggested within this framework have incorporated cognitive, affective, and value-related factors that mediate the process of choice and attainment of achievement goals. Among these theories, self-efficacy (Bandura, 1977, 1986), perceived competence (Harter, 1978, 1981) and various achievement-goal perspectives (Dweck, 1986; Maehr & Braskamp, 1986; Nicholls, 1984, 1989) have played a major role. Based on such approaches, Roberts (1992a) proposed an integrative framework to portray a dynamic process model of motivation, which gives the demonstration of ability a central role. In this model, factors such as goals of action (competitive, mastery), motivational climate (competitive, mastery), perceived ability (high, low, irrelevant) and achievement behavior (adaptive, maladaptive) are considered in order to integrate dynamically ideas delineated in current views of motivation in sports and exercise (Roberts, 1992b). This model is transactional in nature and, as such, leaves many issues open (e.g., the adequate research methods needed for its complete empirical testing; see Tenenbaum & Bar-Eli, 1992). It reflects, however, the way motivation approaches to personality in sport have advanced from self-acting concepts (stressing person or situation) through interactional or social-cognitive approaches to approaches that attempt to conduct future transactional research in this area.

Intellectual Capabilities and Motor Behavior

As depicted in previous sections, testing the personality profile of athletes was quite a popular procedure among sports psychologists, mainly in the 1960s and 1970s. Although intelligence was considered an inherent personality trait within various instruments (e.g., the MMPI or 16PF), the findings drawn from them on athletes' intelligence were inconclusive and sometimes misleading. This result has led researchers to draw attention to other methods and paradigms that more validly account for intelligent behavior related to skilled motor performance.

Intelligence remains a complex cognitive construct that needs further clarification, particularly when it is applied to a specific field such as motor performance. Does skilled motor performance require intelligence? If so, what are the necessary intellectual traits? Furthermore, some motor tasks are performed automatically, particularly in situations involving time pressure. Are such actions dependent on any cognitive construct, or can they be performed skillfully independent of intellectual control? These questions are addressed in this section.

Intelligence and Intellectual Requirements in Sport

Intelligence is the capacity to acquire and apply knowledge. Behavior is considered to be intelligent when people are capable of dealing with old and new demands posed by the environment. Intelligence indicates adaptable behavior based upon the capacity to solve problems, and this behavioral effectiveness is directed by cognitive processes and operations (Combs, 1952; Estes, 1982). Fisher (1984b) further argues that intelligent behavior depends heavily on the richness and variety of perceptions processed at a given moment—that is, the brain's capacity to encode (store and represent) and access (retrieve) information relevant to the task being performed. Because tasks vary with respect to unique characteristics and requirements, it is assumed that the nature and integration of the perceptual-cognitive component required for each task is also unique. Moreover, similar tasks may be performed in different situations; therefore, intelligent behavior is dependent on intellectual capacity, the nature of the task, and the situation in which the task and person interact.

Sports proficiency is in essence intelligence (Fincher, 1976) because it involves encoding of relevant environmental cues, processing them, and choosing an appropriate response. Open motor skills, as well as some closed skills, require making decisions in a continuously changing environment; therefore adaptable behavior is required to perform motor skills proficiently. Thus the classical definition of intelligence fits well into the motor domain, although one should consider both the uniqueness of the environment and motor skills in the general schema. An athlete may arrive at the most appropriate decision while performing a motor task, but execute it inefficiently because of motor immaturity. Therefore it is believed that cognitive skills are necessary but not sufficient for a skilled performance.

It may be concluded that intelligent motor behavior consists of a perceptual style that requires the performer to attend to and concentrate on relevant cues and efficiently process the information, using working and long-term memory mechanisms. This enables the anticipation of upcoming events and formation of internal representations of the external environment in time and space. Finally, an organized, indicative, and controlled movement can be chosen and executed (Marteniuk, 1976).

Information Processing, Knowledge Structures, Experience, and Decision Making

To function efficiently in a dynamic and complex environment with restricted rules requires the athletes to be aware of its complexity and to choose essential cues among many. Thereafter the athlete must identify a cue pattern, activate short-term memory in planning his or her moves, and set up strategies (tactics). These tasks precede any response patterns or retrieval pattern from long-term memory, which are stored so that a preferable solution can be found (Fisher, 1984b).

Several studies examined the motor-perceptual factors that distinguish experienced from inexperienced subjects. It was concluded that experienced subjects utilize the stimuli presented to them more efficiently than inexperienced subjects. Thus the former analyze only necessary information related to performing skills in which time constitutes a determining factor, such as those required in tennis, badminton, and squash (Abernethy & Russell, 1987). Annett and Kay (1956) also maintain that experienced persons examine all the essential information in the early stages of action, whereas the inexperienced person expects information to arrive in the course of events. It follows that experienced players have more time to decide and act.

Encoding information while glancing is usually automatic and dependent on early learning. As one becomes more experienced, qualitative changes in integrative perceptual processing take place without any noticeable change in the encoding processes. Gibson (1969) maintained than an improvement in integration of the information, irrespective of time and space, is actually an increase in sensitivity to the relations among stimuli at the highest level. It is reasonable to assume that experienced athletes integrate information more efficiently than inexperienced ones as a result of more effective matching between newly encoded and stored information (Hochberg, 1982).

According to Abernethy (1987a, b), experience develops more realistic expectations of forthcoming events and, in turn, enhances rapid responses to the occurrence of certain environmental events. Also, the reservoir of options held by the experienced enables skilled judgment as to what is likely to happen in a given situation (Marteniuk, 1976). It seems that experience increases the probability of choosing the correct response, particularly in fast-paced sports. Experience may be perceived not as a chronological variable, but rather as one that confounds a substantial amount of cognitive variables that determine the decision making ability of athletes.

Reaction and Decision Times, Timing Accuracy, and Information Processing

The study of fast-paced ball games (e.g., football, basketball, tennis, hockey) is extensively concerned with reaction time (RT), because the time to detect, process, decide, and respond is very limited. In studies in which the correlation between performance and RT was estimated, the findings are inconsistent. Decision time and choice reaction time (CRT) have been shown to be different in skilled and unskilled athletes (Whiting & Hutt, 1972), and performance quality has been shown to be associated with faster RT (Olsen, 1956). In addition, practice significantly reduces CRT under substantial environmental load compared to CRT under manipulation of information processing load (Conrad, 1962). This reduction in decision time is probably a result of expectations to stimulus-response possibilities, the probability of stimuli to occur, and the sequential dependencies in stimulus presentation (Abernethy, 1987b; Hyman, 1953), all of which facilitate a more rapid response (Abernethy, 1987b).

Abernethy (1991) maintains that in receiving a tennis stroke, a player may have between 500 and 600 ms (if ball speed averages 40-45 ms^{-1}) during which he or she faces uncertainty about the ball direction and speed and must plan an appropriate response. Accordingly, the decision as to what return stroke to play consists of as little as 30 to 50 ms of ball flight information(!). Expert players usually choose the most appropriate strategies among those stored in their long-term repertoire. The research on this topic is concerned mainly with the problem of how much of skilled performance is accounted for by cognitive function (i.e., making the right decisions), motor proficiency (executing the perfect motor skills), or both interactively.

In several sports, the player faces a ball that changes direction on bouncing and then reaches him or her very quickly. It is possible that earlier cues of ball flight and/or other cues are used by experts for more precisely predicting the final location of the ball (Abernethy & Russell, 1984; Adams & Gibson, 1989; McLeod, 1987). The advanced predictions by experts supply them more time to plan the response, so that faster RT is not necessarily required to produce a skillful move. Skilled performers were not found to have faster RTs than less skilled athletes (McLeod & Jenkins, 1991); furthermore, catching performance did not decrease when the last 200 ms of ball flight were not viewed (Lamb & Burwitz, 1988). It may be concluded that differences in accuracy and other task specificities could not be attributed to RT or CRT but rather to other cognitive characteristics.

A number of studies have shown that some people can use information in less than 20 ms (Carlton, 1981). McLeod and Jenkins (1991) argue that although choice RT in fast-paced ball games is reported to be around 200 ms, it is possible that when the stimulus comes from internal sources rather than external ones, RT might be even faster. The time taken to modify an action on the basis of continuously available and changing visual information is much less than that required to initiate an action when new visual information is given (Lee, Young, Reddish, Longh, & Clayton, 1983). Table tennis players were found to time their shots to coincide with certain aspects of ball flight with a standard duration of 8 ms (Bootsma & van Wieringen, 1988). Ski jumpers approaching the lip of the jump could time their upward thrust with a standard deviation of about 10 ms. Several such examples introduced by McLeod and Jenkins (1991) suggest that within the course of action, very fast movements are produced by athletes. It is assumed that skillful performance is very much dependent upon such timing initiations and refinements, rather than RT or CRT per se.

An additional aspect that may be considered a determinant of skilled performance is the *game schema*, a neurological structure in the brain established through long and continuous practice. This structure enables the prediction of similar and familiar events with higher probability than unsimilar and unfamiliar events. Skilled performers may have a clearer schema that may help them to understand, remember, and predict the outcomes of game situations. Consequently their dependence on fast reactions, which are associated with more errors, is reduced (McLeod & Jenkins, 1991).

Whiting (1991) also argues that RT to the onset of visual stimulus is not an influential variant of skilled performance in fast ball games, because actions are not presented in a sudden fashion. Anticipatory skills and the capability to modify continuous actions are more valuable components required in order for an action to be skillful. It is the nature of information processing that mostly contributes to skilled performance, rather than the "hardware" skills.

Recall Capability and Motor Proficiency

In a series of studies (Allard, 1984; Allard, Graham, & Paarsalu, 1980; Allard & Starkes, 1980; Bard & Fleury, 1976; Bard, Fleury, Carriere, & Halle, 1980; Chase & Simon, 1973; Starkes & Deakin, 1984), athletes were asked to scan slides or films and detect, recognize, or recall targets within structured and unstructured situations in sport settings. Chess experts recalled structured but not unstructured (random) chess boards significantly better than their less qualified counterparts following a 5-second exposure (Chase & Simon, 1973). Similar results were obtained with male basketball players (Allard et al., 1980), female field hockey players (Starkes & Deakin, 1984), and volleyball players (Borgeaud & Abernethy, 1987). Although some studies failed to reproduce these results with volleyball players (Allard et al., 1980; Allard & Starkes, 1980), it is believed that long exposure to repeated situations increases the familiarity with the environment and subsequently improves the recall capability of events that occur within this environment.

The relatively few studies carried out on recall of relevant visual information have compared expert athletes to novice or nonathletes after a relatively long exposure (2 to 8 seconds). They have found experts to be superior in the use of strategies that enable the detection of a target within the environmental display (Beitel, 1980; Gentile, Higgins, Miller, & Rosen, 1975), as well as the recall of structured game situations in a variety of sports.

Allard and Starkes (1980) and Starkes and Allard (1983) argue that with time, the organization mechanism is developed to a stage that enables the skilled athlete to better recall the situation and respond appropriately. The findings have shown that the superiority of skilled athletes in recalling specific structured sport situations (but not other situations) is related not to memory capacity but to the use of different encoding and retrieval strategies (Borgeaud & Abernethy, 1987). It was also argued that experts utilize more efficiently the memory representations sensitive to objects in the display (Neisser, 1967; Prinz, 1977, 1979; Prinz & Atalan, 1973).

The studies on recall capability of athletes in the sports domain have not accounted for several variables inherent in real-life situations. In real situations the athlete is required to scan, recall, and process information while performing additional skills (e.g., bouncing a ball, watching the opponents' positions). Parallel actions divert some attention from the playing environment to other sources. Also, athletes are required to attend, recall, process, and respond very fast (i.e., in less than 1 second). The athlete is also exposed to an environment in which the number of stimuli is continually changing in time and complexity. Thus the ecological validity of the findings reported in the literature are to be further examined.

Tenenbaum, Levy-Kolker, Bar-Eli, and Weinberg (1994) studied the recall capability of team handball players while trying to overcome the above-mentioned shortcomings.

Conditions that imposed perceptual constraint and time pressure were as similar as possible to real-game conditions, the display contained many players, attention was partially diverted to a secondary task (bouncing a ball), and exposure duration was short (0.5 vs 1.0 seconds). Surprisingly, in most of the situations, expertise effects were not evident in the recall of either the major features (players and ball) or the minor features (spectators), except for the recall of complex displays. However, skilled athletes do not typically engage in explicit recall of game scenes, but rather use the information based on implicit memory processes during game situations. Also, in real game conditions, perception occurs over time rather than as a result of scanning a frozen image.

Memory Representations and Motor Performance

According to Paillard (1991), the organism-environment interaction enriches the stored representations of the organism's internal and external world events. Cognitive processes refer to the computational transactions that incorporate these stored representations in some kind of internal dialogue. These representations enable the prediction and control of perceptual and motor activities. The perception-action cycle may proceed either directly (via a perceptual schema and an associated motor program already available within an existing sensorimotor unit) or indirectly (through a cognitive computation that enables the recognition of significant features of the situation and the subsequent choice of the appropriate motor strategy).

According to this original view, both perceptual and motor systems trigger the action systems to an optimal level in the speed-accuracy trade-off. If the law of minimal energy expense regulates the bioenergetical and biomechanical requirements of motion, the law of minimal attention may dominate the requirements of information processing in monitoring actions. Therefore, expert behavior may be characterized by a lower charge on the attentional system when the latter encounters overwhelming information within a short time. Nougler, Ripoll, and Stein (1990) found that experts adopt a consistent strategy by avoiding specific expectations as to the behavior of the opponent and attending in a "state of diffuse alertness." Such a state enables one to expect and anticipate forthcoming events and respond very quickly while reducing the frequency of guessing.

Vision, Semantic and Sensorimotor Processing, and Skilled Performance

Based on his previous works in which temporal and spatial occlusion paradigms were applied, Abernethy (1991) concluded that there is an essential link between perceptual skills and the kinematic evaluation of the action being observed by the athlete. Very skilled and less skilled athletes, however, were similar in their visual search strategies. At the same time, information pickup was quite different among experts compared to novices (Abernethy, 1990b).

It is argued that the expert athlete attends to the most important cue, but at the same time scans other cues. The novice athlete attends to and concentrates on one cue, ignoring the others. The research paradigms applied by Abernethy seem to be insufficiently sensitive to the peripheral visual strategies used by athletes when attending to environmental information.

An additional concern, raised by Mestre and Pailhous (1991), is that when an unpredictable perturbation to the ball's kinematic features was introduced within the 200 ms time range before the ball reached the player, experts exhibited stereotyped motor response patterns. Therefore expertise is not dependent on information-pickup superiority. Abernethy's studies lacked the action component that is critical in von Hofsten's (1987) understanding of the perception-action cycle. Mestre and Pailhous (1991) argue that in the expert's action pattern the actual role of "advance" visual cues might be to trigger an action program, whereas "late" cues enable motor adjustments. This line of research may shed more light on the relationship between perceptual properties and intellectual behavior in the course of motor activiation that requires decision making.

Ripoll, Papin, and Simonet (1983) argue that in open-skill sports, vision has two functions: semantic (identifying and interpreting the environment) and sensorimotor (carrying out the response). Consequently, Ripoll (1991) distinguished between two cognitive substances that should be investigated separately and in combination. The first cognitive field of research is "perceiving-acting": how the environmental cues are organized within the neurological system and transferred to the motor system, and whether the nature of processing is direct or inferential. The second cognitive field is "perceiving-understanding": the visual cues used to identify the environment and the operation related to the process of decision making. Whether these two operations work serially or in parallel, are direct or inferential, are automatic or controlled, and are discrete or continuous remains to be determined.

Studies that used the temporal or spatial occlusion paradigms to examine skilled performance have concluded that expert athletes need less information in order to predict forthcoming events and react appropriately (Abernethy, 1990a). Furthermore, the dynamic organization of the environment through the visual system and attending to specific cues within the environment, are those which contribute to skilled performance (Ripoll, 1991).

According to Ripoll (1991), the expert-novice differences are related to the mode of visual scanning, which is synthetic in experts and analytic in novices. Synthetic visual scanning consists of directing one's gaze so that most of the events can be observed and grouped by one visual fixation. When much information and time pressure are inherent within the situation (open skills like those in fast-paced ball games), a synthetic visual strategy is of great advantage for making decisions. Ripoll (1988a) found that volleyball players who correctly solved the problems presented to them used a holistic scanning process in orienting their gaze, independent of the ball or the players' displacements. Thus searching for particular cues is not a sufficient strategy for skilled performance in open, complex, and dynamic situations. It is preferable to fixate on a point in space where most cues are picked up so that a visual pattern can be formed to plan the motor response.

This confirms Chase and Posner's (1965) argument that visual orientation and visual attention are not necessarily related to each other. This argument was experimentally proven by Ripoll, Kerlirzin, Stein, and Reine's (1991) study of boxers of different skill levels. The skilled boxers displayed three times fewer visual fixations than the less skilled boxers. Thus peripheral vision plays the role of alertness in detecting the relevant cues in a long area of the focal vision (Levy-Schoen, 1972) and enables the integration of cues into dynamic patterns that result in fewer fixations of higher duration (Ripoll, 1991).

Future research in this direction should take into account the different nature of various sports. Sports in which time pressure is inherent in the situation but the opponent is pacing the uncertainty (e.g., basketball) should be contrasted with sports in which uncertainty is conveyed by the physical characteristics of the environment, and response is self-paced (skiing, climbing, gliding, etc.).

Dupuy and Ripoll (1989) investigated the visual and sensorimotor behavior of rock climbers. They concluded that the semantic and sensorimotor processes occur in a serial order. Visual cues in the extra personal space are used first to identify the route when the body is immobile; then identification of selected cues and handholds is performed and the appropriate place to reach and catch is selected. Only then is the body displayed. One may conclude that a sensorimotor map is driven from external cues, whereas a semantic map is driven internally by a cognitive map progressively constructed with accumulation of route knowledge. According to Ripoll (1991), in both externally or self-paced situations, the semantic and sensorimotor processing seems to be serially organized. This may be questionable, particularly in situations of substantial time pressure. In such situations decision making is automatic and consists of internal representations that produce responses quite automatically, with no necessity for serial processing.

It is quite reasonable to assume that in order to reach skilled performance in situations inflated with information and constrained heavily by time, the skilled athlete uses heuristic rules to simplify the process of problem solving and decision making (Kahneman, 1973; Norman, 1976). According to Ripoll (1991), these rules consist of synthetic visual behavior, processing general rather than specific information, and eliminating irrelevant cues (thereby focusing on the relevant ones).

Attending to External-Internal Cues and Anticipating Forthcoming Events

In an extensive review of the literature on expert-novice differences in sports, Abernethy (1987b) concluded that the main reasons for the difference in performance between the two skill groups may be attributed to feature detection and pattern recognition of the environment, which leads to advanced anticipatory recognition among experts. This rapid and accurate recognition of the environment develops through many repetitions of similar actions and maneuvers (experience) and guides the sensory system in a manner that enables quick access to knowledge structure, which facilitates anticipation and prediction (Keele, 1982).

Based on studies which have applied a film occlusion paradigm to games such as soccer, ice hockey, volleyball, tennis, cricket, and field hockey, Abernethy (1987a) postulated that advanced identification is of value to the response selection process, particularly under conditions of great temporal stress. These may be viewed as conditions of uncertainty. Also, a summary of field studies supports the notion that experts use shorter viewing times and therefore have more time to select their responses (Abernethy, 1987a).

Investigators such as Buckolz, Prapavesis, and Fairs (1988), Abernethy and Russell (1987), and Abernethy (1990a, b) have shown that expert, intermediate, and novice racquet game players appear to attend to similar advance cues, although experts exhibit superior forecasting accuracy as to the final destination of a ball sequence. It is believed that all interpretation of early ball flight information, from shortly prior to ball-racquet contact and on, is processed quite differently by novice, intermediate, and advanced players. That is, anticipation of the final move becomes more accurate, depending strongly on the player's prior knowledge of similar strokes.

In a study by Tenenbaum, Levy-Kolker, Sade, Libermann, and Lider, 1985) in which the temporal occlusion paradigm to measure anticipatory skills of tennis players was applied, some contradictory results were obtained. Expert tennis players were not found to differ from intermediate-level players in anticipatory skills. Expert and intermediate-level players were superior to their novice counterparts in only about 50% of the situations. Experts were shown to focus attention on several cues simultaneously at very early stages of their opponent's action initiation, whereas less qualified players usually focused attention on one cue at a time. Of vital importance was the finding that under uncertainty conditions (short exposure to event sequence), novice and intermediate-skill players were more confident in their predictive decisions than experts. Shortly before, at and after ball-racquet contact, however, experts were substantially more confident than the others in their anticipatory decisions. This applied to all the strokes that were examined.

The differences in confidence of anticipatory decisions attributed to skill are of much importance to the understanding of perception-performance relationship. Ball-racquet contact is a stage at which final decisions and error correction take place. Therefore, when confidence in the final stages increases and a qualified solution is determined, a qualified action is executed. Here, in our opinion, are the main differences attributed to skill level of the athletes.

Attentional Processes and Motor Performance

Nougier, Stein, and Bonnel (1991) make a theoretical distinction between the orientation of attention (Posner, 1980) and the distribution of attentional resources (Navon & Gopher, 1979). Attention is viewed as a combination of facilitations and inhibitions that occur prior to the processing of a signal. When there is too much information to be attended simultaneously, specific processes are necessary to select the most relevant signals with various characteristics (shape, color, texture, etc.). Concentration, vigilance, and preparation may contribute to the efficiency of the internal processes.

Sport activities contain many stages of uncertainty. The extent of uncertainty is determined by the signal-noise ratio (Coombs, Dawes, & Tversky, 1970). Competitors always attempt to hide their intentions from their rivals. Therefore the more attention is oriented toward the relevant cues, the less uncertain is the environment, and probably the more efficient is the process of decision making (Nougier, Stein, & Bonnel, 1991).

Practice of motor skills and tactical operations enhances the automaticity of the attentional processes so that a smaller number of disturbances occur during competitive performance. Attentional processes, however, can also be optional (voluntary and strategic). That is, the expert athlete may initiate unique strategies that help him or her to attend to the relevant cues in the environment and to the intention of the opponent. Furthermore, the skilled athlete can switch from intentional into automatic processes of attentional orientation when necessary. This has been reported by Nougier, Azemar, Stein, and Ripoll (1989) as a typical behavior of expert athletes.

In situations where environmental information has to be processed, the cost-benefit methodology (Posner & Snyder, 1975) was applied quite efficiently. Faster RT at cued locations was termed as "attentional benefit" (facilitation), whereas slower RT at uncued locations was termed "attentional cost" (inhibition; Posner, 1980; Posner, Snyder & Davidson, 1980). The cost-benefit ratio may determine the attentional effect or flexibility (Keele & Hawkins, 1982). Flexibility of attention was defined as the ability of the subject to quickly disengage, orient, and reengage attention on various locations in space. This was believed to be a strong determinant of high-level performance (Keele & Hawkins, 1982). In sports such as tennis, fencing, and ball games, the shift of attention from one cue to the other helps the athlete to determine the probability of the upcoming event and consequently improve his or her performance by decreasing the costs and increasing the benefits of attentional process (Nougier et al., 1991).

In contrasting expert to nonexpert athletes, Nougier, Ripoll, and Stein (1987, 1990) applied the Posner et al. (1980) paradigm and reported that experts showed reduced costs and benefits (i.e., they were as fast to respond to cued and to uncued locations). Nonexperts were found to exhibit elevated costs and benefits, similar to the regular subjects of Posner et al. (1980). It seems that while performing motor tasks in a skillful manner, athletes learn (consciously or unconsciously) to attend to the relevant signals despite the "noise" that intervenes in their probabilistic choices.

Focal (contracted) and diffuse (expanded) attention modes are also of vital importance in sport. Nougier et al. (1991) and Nideffer (1976) argue that skilled performance requires one of these attentional modalities, depending on the task characteristics. In archery and shooting, focused attention is preferable (Nougier et al., 1987, 1990), whereas diffuse attention is preferable in table tennis, boxing, and fencing (Ripoll, 1988a, b).

Automatization (Kahneman & Treisman, 1984; Shiffrin & Schneider, 1977) and attentional flexibility (Humphreys, 1981; Keele & Hawkins, 1982; Keele & Neill, 1979) are mechanisms that enable the skilled athlete to perform some skills automatically and at the same time attend to and control more complex situations characterized by a high degree of uncertainty. This is done in a more optimal manner, so that the athlete can simultaneously process several tasks (Nougier et al., 1991).

It is still to be determined how attention is distributed in time and space and how the athlete shifts attention from automatic to voluntary modes before and during engagement in a motor task. These questions should be addressed in each sport separately. An additional field of research involves the eye focus–attention–performance relationship. Is eye focus necessary for attending to the environmental cues? Are expert athletes able to shift attention without altering their eye focus? (Umilta, 1991). We may speculate as to how a skilled performer should act in such situations, but we are uncertain at this stage as to the strategies one should adopt to produce optimal performance.

In addition, Umilta (1991) maintains that voluntary orientation of attention is subjected to interference from the concurrent task and is sensitive to expectations and anticipated events. In contrast, automatic orientation of attention cannot be stopped and does not alter with expectations. It is advisable to compare experts to novices in the two attentional orientation types separately. Significant differences are expected to be obtained in the voluntary type of attention, which is more sensitive to knowledge structure and practice of the athlete.

Castiello and Umilta (1990) reported that as the area of the focused attention decreases, processing efficiency for stimuli located within its borders increases. Thus the ability to control the size of the attentional focus may also be related to skilled performance by maximizing processing efficiency at more relevant locations. It should be examined whether skilled performance is related to the ability to split attention to two or more nonadjacent locations. This ability might prove very helpful for efficient processing and consequently improve decision making through a decrease of uncertainty.

Finally, it is quite acceptable that human beings can process a number of stimuli in parallel; however, only one response is chosen (Umilta, 1991). How is this selection performed? Shallice (1988) suggested two selection processes: contention scheduling (CS), and a supervisory attentional system (SAS). CS is automatic and dependent on the activation threshold of a schemata. Schemata are in mutually inhibitory competition for selection; the one which is triggered is selected to be the response. Some refinements in the election process may occur, however, that are not controlled by CS. It seems that the SAS, which has access to the representation of the environment and the organism's intention, facilitates or inhibits particular action schemata and modulates the CS operation. It is argued that the coordination between CS and SAS is of vital importance to decision making and performance processes in many sports. Whether expert athletes have developed special skills that enable them to switch selection of actions from CS to SAS, and vice versa, remains a subject for future research.

Cognitive and Attentional Styles and Motor Performance

Based on extensive research during the 1940s and 1950s, Witkin et al. (1954) argued that individuals vary in their mode of perception along a continuum from field dependence to field independence. According to Witkin, the perceptual style affects performance in situations that require the separation of an embedded object from its surroundings. Indeed, several studies have demonstrated that field-independent subjects process disembedding problems in the analytical manner, whereas field-dependent subjects tend to solve these types of problems in an intuitive manner (Witkin, Dyk, Faterson, Goodenough, & Karp, 1962; Witkin & Goodenough, 1981; Witkin, Goodenough, & Oltman, 1979). These findings were believed to be reproducible in open and closed skills of motor performance. At the moment, however, one cannot unequivocally proclaim that there is a relationship between cognitive style and sport performance (MacGillivary, 1980; McMorris, 1992).

According to Knapp (1964) and Jones (1972), closed skills consist of physical characteristics such as strength, torque, and technique. Open skills—such as those needed in team handball, basketball, and volleyball, in which a variant sequence of events constantly occurs—require the athlete to continually alter his or her perceptual style (i.e., flexibility of cognitive style). Swinnen, Vandenberghe, and Van Asche (1986) assumed that field-dependent examinees are less successful in a nonstructured learning environment because their information-processing technique does not rely on analysis and construction of the environmental information. In contrast, field-independent examinees utilize organizational techniques in cases where the learned environment is not well determined (i.e., is changing). Furthermore, Jones (1972) extended Poulton's (1957) view of generalized skills and argued that a cognitive style of field dependence imposes perceptual disturbances that are crucial for decision making. Field-independent style enables the counteracting of nonessential stimuli in the environment necessary for decision making and focuses attention on essential information.

The failure to establish a clear relationship between cognitive style and motor performance was attributed mainly to the methodology by which cognitive style was determined (MacGillivary, 1980; McMorris & MacGillivary, 1988), as well as to the fact that the nature of the disembedding differs across sport disciplines. One or two standardized tests are not sufficiently sensitive to detect possible differences among athletes in each particular sport (McMorris, 1992). Most sports demand disembedding to be made in a moving environment, whereas the tests failed to accomplish this requirement. Also, the amount of time in which the performer must make his or her decision is much shorter than that allowed in the test, and the frequency and complexity of the disembedding displays in sports are not well represented in the tests. These shortcomings of the tests are the main reasons for not enabling reliable dissemination of field-dependent from field-independent subjects within specific sport environments.

The cognitive style of field dependence-independence is closely related to the concept of attentional style. Relying on the theories of Easterbrook (1959), Heilbrun (1972), and Wachtel (1967), Nideffer (1976) suggested that attention has two dimensions: width and direction. Width is based on a continuum from narrow to broad (number of stimuli), and direction varies from internal to external.

According to Nideffer (1976), in all sports (individual or team), a unique dimensional integration is required for optimal performance. In general, when the situation is more complex and alters rapidly, an exceptionally focused attention is required from the athlete. When the level of decision making necessitates analyzing or planning, the need for a reflective internal attentional style rises. As a result of an incompatible attentional style, athletes may damage performance. In sports such as soccer, basketball, and tennis, the athlete is expected to alter attentional styles both in width and direction, occasionally quite rapidly. It would seem, therefore, that the ability to alter attentional styles voluntarily is a crucial determinant of an athlete's performance. In such other sports as golf and bowling, the athlete is required to sustain attention on one task for a long time, avoiding disturbing stimuli that would lead to improper decisions.

Athletes with fairly external and narrow attentional styles develop one type of action and remain in this state without initiating any decisions posed by the environmental conditions. Nideffer (1979) argued that anxiety limits the ability to move from one attentional style to another. The narrowing of attention was proven to decrease dual-task type performance (Landers, Furst, & Daniels, 1981). Such tasks are typical in ball games and therefore are believed to be influential in decision making in the course of competition that is mentally and physically demanding. Applying Nideffer's attentional style questionnaire (TAIS) to the sports domain proved in some studies (Kirschenbaum & Bale, 1980; Richards & Landers, 1981), but not all (Aronson, 1981; Landers et al., 1981) that attentional style is a valid component which discriminates between expert and novice athletes.

Perception of Time and Space: Essentials for Controlling Motor Actions

Motor actions are performed in space and time. As such, the perception of time within the space is of vital importance in an environment where external objects are moving, sometimes simultaneously with the performance, and deterministic rules of time are also inherent in the context.

To clarify further the space-time interaction, Laurent and Thomson (1991) distinguish between "movement space" (principle speed and direction) and "approach space" (distance). These two functional spaces are observable in subjects' behaviors when they make adjustments in speed and motion while performing motor tasks. Movements need to be synchronized with the structure of the environment and with the events taking place. Therefore visual timing is primarily important in activities that involve hitting, catching, or intercepting objects (cricket, tennis, football, handball, basketball, etc.). Temporal regulation is also essential in a stable environment (e.g., for jumping, running over irregular terrain; Laurent & Thomson, 1991).

It is quite reasonable that spatio-temporal modulation is also related to anticipation. Catching is a task that requires not only perceiving the speed and direction of the ball, but also predicting its final location in order to execute the skilled response appropriately. In life as well as in sports, most visual regulation is prospective in nature (Lee, Lishman, & Thomson, 1982), regulating the future rather than the present. As such, both timing and prospective control are central features of visuo-motor control (Laurent & Thomson, 1991).

Many of the motor skills involve more complex movements than just running, jumping, or catching. When movements are executed first and adjustments are then required, the organization of movement becomes quite complex. Accuracy of action planning and prospective control is required from the skilled athlete to complete his or her task in a skilled manner. The degree to which skilled athletes can control time and space in a prospective manner remains to be determined in the future. Research has shown that it is the temporal relationship between the observer and the obstacle, not the spatial relationship, that accounts for appropriate motor functioning (Laurent, 1987; Laurent & Thomson, 1988; Lee, 1980a, b; Lee et al., 1982). The visuo-motor strategies used to perform skilled movement (and essential for optimal development), however, are still unclear.

Concluding Remarks and Future Directions

Sports and exercise psychology is considered a relatively young scientific discipline. Therefore the research of personality and intellectual capability naturally adopted research paradigms and measurement tools from psychology. Common personality inventories were administered to athletes for descriptive purposes as well as to correlate personality with various behaviors and skill performance. The studies on cognitions and perceptions in sports have used similar paradigms to those applied in other settings. Such strategies failed to draw conclusive generalizations as to the relationship of personality traits and intellectual capabilities to behavior and motor performance.

The uniqueness of the milieu of sports and exercise and the nature of the tasks in which the athlete or performer is engaged call for new directions in the domain of exercise and sports psychology. Personality traits and intellectual capabilities should be examined within the transactional context in which performance and behavior are examined interactively in various tasks and situations.

The transactional approach calls for different research paradigms in the field of sport and exercise with more ecological validity. The psychometric properties of self-report measures of personality traits and states should shift from deterministic approaches to stochastic approaches (e.g., the latent-trait models). Recent developments in this field should also be applied to the field of sports and exercise psychology. Also, the qualitative methods and single case-single subject designs are important approaches that have been neglected in the domain of sports psychology. These applications may contribute much to the understanding of how personality and intellectual capability function in different tasks and situations.

Specific sports personality inventories should be developed. Such inventories may have more potential to distinguish among athletes who differ in personality traits that are relevant to coping with stressful sport demands. Also, specific paradigms are needed to examine possible personality-intellectual capability interactions in sports. For example, simulated decision-making situations may be projected in gradually increasing exposure durations to athletes who differ in anxiety level and attentional flexibility to evaluate their cognitive capacity in such situations. RT and CRT may be added to such paradigms to examine information-processing, encoding, and retrieval processes. Specific paradigms in various sport situations and motor tasks that require cognitive capability when applied interactively with more sensitive methods and tools for measuring personality, have the potential for clarifying how motor tasks are acquired, mastered, and reach perfection.

References

Abernethy, B. (1987a). Anticipation in sport: A review. *Physical Education Review, 10,* 5-16.

Abernethy, B. (1987b). Selective attention in fast ball sports: II. Expert-novice differences. *Australian Journal of Science and Medicine in Sport, 19,* 7-16.

Abernethy, B. (1990a). Anticipation in squash: Differences in advance cue utilization between expert and novice players. *Journal of Sports Sciences, 8,* 17-34.

Abernethy, B. (1990b). Expertise, visual search and information pick-up in squash. *Perception, 19,* 63-77.

Abernethy, B. (1991). Visual search strategies and decision making in sport. *International Journal of Sport Psychology, 22,* 189-210.

Abernethy, B., & Russell, D.G. (1984). Advance cue utilisation by skilled cricket batsmen. *Australian Journal of Science and Medicine in Sport, 16,* 2-10.

Abernethy, B., & Russell, D.G. (1987). The relationship between expertise and visual search strategy in a racquet sport. *Human Movement Science,* 6, 283-319.

Adams, R., & Gibson, A. (1989). Moment of ball release identification by cricket batsmen. *The Australian Journal of Science and Medicine in Sport, 21,* 10-13.

Alderman, R.B. (1976). Incentive motivation in sport: An interpretive speculation of research opportunities. In A. C. Fisher (Ed.). *Psychology of sport* (pp. 205-231). Palo Alto, CA: Mayfield.

Allard, F. (1984). Cognition, expert performance, and sport. In M. Whiting (Ed.), *New paths to sport learning* (pp. 22-26). Ottawa: Coaching Association of Canada.

Allard, F., Graham, S., & Paarsalu, M. E. (1980). Perception in sport: Basketball. *Journal of Sport Psychology, 2,* 14-21.

Allard, F., & Starkes, J. L. (1980). Perception in sport: Volleyball. *Journal of Sport Psychology, 2,* 22-23.

Annett, J., & Kay, H. (1956). Skilled performance. *Occupational Psychology, 30,* 112-117.

Arenson, R. M. (1981). *Attentional and interpersonal factors as discriminators of elite and non-elite gymnasts.* Unpublished doctoral dissertation, Boston University.

Atkinson, J. W. (1964). *An introduction to motivation.* Princeton, NJ: Van Nostrand.

Atkinson, J. W. (1974). The mainsprings of achievement-oriented activity. In J. W. Atkinson & J. O. Raynor (Eds.), *Motivation and achievement* (pp 13-41). New York: Halstead.

Bakker, F. C., Whiting, H. T. A., & van der Brug, H. (1990). *Sport psychology: Concepts and applications.* Chichester, England: Wiley.

Bandura, A. (1977). Self-efficacy: Toward a unifying theory of behavioral change. *Psychological Review, 84,* 191-215.

Bandura, A. (1978). The self system in reciprocal determinism. *American Psychologist, 33,* 344-358.

Bandura, A. (1986). *Social foundation of thought and action: A social cognitive theory.* Englewood Cliffs, NJ: Prentice-Hall.

Bard, C., & Fleury, M. (1976). Analysis of visual search activity during sport problem situation. *Journal of Human Movement Studies, 3,* 214-222.

Bard, C., Fleury, M., Carriere, L., & Halle, M. (1980). Analysis of gymnastics judges' visual search. *Research Quarterly for Exercise and Sport, 51,* 267-273.

Bar-Eli, M. (1985). Arousal-performance relationship: A transactional view on performance jags. *International Journal of Sport Psychology, 16,* 193-209.

Bar-Eli, M., Thox, E., Levy-Kolker, N. & Tenenbaum, G. (1992). Performance quality and behavioral violations as crisis indicators in competition. *International Journal of Sport Psychology, 23,* 325-342.

Bar-Eli, M., & Tenenbaum, G. (1988). Rule- and norm-related behavior and the individual psychological crisis in competitive situations: Theory and research findings. *Social Behavior and Personality, 16,* 187-195.

Bar-Eli, M., & Tenenbaum, G. (1989a). Observations of behavioral violations as crisis indicators in competition. *Sport Psychologist, 3,* 237-244.

Bar-Eli, M., & Tenenbaum, G. (1989b). A theory of individual psychological crisis in competitive sport. *Applied Psychology, 38,* 107-120.

Bar-Eli, M., Tenenbaum, G., & Elbaz, G. (1990). Psychological performance crisis in high arousal situations—diagnosticity of rule violations and performance in competitive team handball. *Anxiety Research, 2,* 281-292.

Basler, M. L., Fisher, A. C., & Mumford, M. L. (1976). Arousal and anxiety correlates of gymnastic performance. *Research Quarterly, 47,* 586-589.

Beitel, P. A. (1980). Multivariate relationship among visual-perceptual attributes and gross-motor tasks with different environmental demands. *Journal of Motor Behavior, 12,* 29-40.

Bem, D. J. (1983). Constructing a theory of the triple typology: Some (second) thoughts on nomothetic and idiographic approaches to personality. *Journal of Personality, 51,* 566-577.

Biddle, S. J. H. (1993). Attribution research and sport psychology. In R. N. Singer, M. Murphy, & L. K. Tennant (Eds.), *Handbook of research on sports psychology.* New York: Macmillan.

Boostma, R., & van Wieringen, P. (1988). Visual control of an attacking forehand drive in table tennis. In O. Meijer & K. Roth (Eds.), *The motor action controversy* (pp. 189-200). Amsterdam: Elsevier.

Borgeaud, P., & Abernethy, B. (1987). Skilled perception in volleyball defense. *Journal of Sport Psychology, 9,* 400-406.

Brichin, M., & Kochian, M. (1970). Comparison of some personality traits of women participating and not participating in sports. *Ceskoslovenska Psychologie, 14,* 309-321.

Buckholz, E., Prapavesis, H., & Fairs, J. (1988). Advanced cues and their use in predicting tennis passing shots. *Canadian Journal of Sports Sciences, 13,* 20-30.

Burton, D. (1988). Do anxious swimmers swim slower? Reexamining the elusive anxiety-performance relationship. *Journal of Sport and Exercise Physiology, 10,* 45-61.

Caprara, G. V., Renzi, P., D'Augelio, D., D'Imperio, G., Rielli, I., & Travaglia, G. (1986). Instigation to aggress and aggression: The role of irritability and emotional susceptibility. *Aggressive Behavior, 12,* 78-83.

Carlton, L. (1981). Processing visual feedback information for movement control. *Journal of Experimental Psychology: Human Perception and Performance, 7,* 1019-1030.

Carver, C. S. & Scheier, M. F. (1988). A control-process perspective on anxiety. *Anxiety Research, 1,* 17-22.

Castiello, U., & Umilta, C. (1990). Size of the attentional focus and efficiency of processing. *Acta Psychologica, 73,* 195-209.

Cattell, R. B. (1972). The nature and genesis of mood states: A theoretical model with experimental measures concerning anxiety, depression, arousal, and other mood states. In C. D. Spielberger (Ed.), *Anxiety: Current trends in theory and research* (pp.115-183). New York: Plenum.

Chase, W. G. & Posner, M. I. (1965). *The effect of auditory and visual confusability on visual memory and search tasks.* Paper presented at the meeting of the Midwestern Psychological Association, Chicago.

Chase, W. G., & Simon, H. A. (1973). Perception in chess. *Cognitive Psychology, 4,* 55-81.

Combs, A. W. (1952). Intelligence from a perceptual point of view. *Journal of Abnormal and Social Psychology, 47,* 662-673.

Conrad, R. (1962). Practice, familiarity, and reading rate for words and nonsense syllables. *Quarterly Journal of Experimental Psychology, 14,* 71-76.

Coombs, C., Dawes, R., & Tversky, A. (1970). *Mathematical psychology.* Englewood Cliffs, NJ: Prentice Hall.

Cronbach, L. J. (1957). The two disciplines of scientific psychology. *American Psychologist, 12,* 671-684.

Csikszentmihaly, M. (1975). *Beyond boredom and anxiety.* San Francisco: Jossey-Bass.

Deci, E. L., & Ryan, R. M. (1980). The empirical exploration of intrinsic motivational processes. In L. Berkowitz (Ed.), *Advances in experimental social psychology* (Vol. 13, pp. 39-80). New York: Academic Press.

Delk, J. (1973). Some personality characteristics of skydivers. *Life Threatening Behavior, 3,* 51-57.

Dewey, J., & Bentley, A. F. (1949). *Knowing and the known.* Boston: Beacon.

Dupuy, C., & Ripoll, H. (1989). Analyse des stratégies visuomotrices en escalade sportive. *Science et Motricité, 7,* 19-26.

Dweck, C. S. (1986). Motivational processes affecting learning. *American Psychologist, 4,* 1040-1048.

Easterbrook, J. A. (1959). The effect of emotion on cue utilization and the organization of behavior. *Psychological Review, 66,* 183-201.

Ekehammar, B. (1974). Interactionism in personality from a historical perspective. *Psychological Bulletin, 81,* 1026-1048.

Ellis, M., & Scholtz, G. (1978). *Activity and play of children.* Englewood Cliffs, NJ: Prentice-Hall.

Estes, W. K. (1982). Learning, memory and intelligence. In R. J. Sternberg (Ed.), *Handbook of human intelligence* (pp. 170-224). New York: Cambridge University Press.

Eysenck, H. J. (1967). *The biological basis of personality.* Springfield, IL: Thomas.

Eysenck, H. J. (1981). *A model for personality.* Berlin: Springer.

Eysenck, H. J., & Eysenck, S. B. G. (1963). *The Eysenck Personality Inventory.* San Diego, CA: Educational and Industrial Testing Service.

Eysenck, H. J., Niss, D. K. B., & Cox, D. N. (1967). Sport and personality. *Behavior Research and Therapy, 4,* 1-56.

Fiegenbaum, T. (1981). *Persoenlichkeltsmerkmales von Langstreckenlauefern* [Personality traits of long-distance runners]. Paper presented at a symposium on sports psychology, Munich.

Fincher, J. (1976). *Human intelligence.* New York: Putnam.

Fineman, S. (1977). The achievement motive construct and its measurement. Where are we now? *British Journal of Psychology, 68,* 1-22.

Fisher, A. C. (1984a). New directions in sport personality research. In J. M. Silva & R. S. Weinberg (Eds.), *Psychological foundations of sport* (pp. 70-80). Champaign, IL: Human Kinetics.

Fisher, A. C. (1984b). Sport intelligence. In W. F Straub & J. M. Williams (Eds.), *Cognitive sport psychology* (pp. 42-50). New York: Sport Science Associates.

Fiske, D. W., & Maddi, S. R. (1961). *Functions of varied experience.* Homewood, IL: Dorsey.

Fowler, C. J., Knorring, L., & Oreland, L. (1980). Platelet monoamine oxidase activity in sensation seekers. *Psychiatric Research, 3,* 273-279.

Furst, D. M., & Tenenbaum, G. (1984). The relationship between worry, emotionality, and sport performance. In D. M. Landers (Ed.), *Sport and elite performance* (pp. 89-96). Champaign, IL: Human Kinetics.

Gentile, A. M., Higgins, J. R., Miller, E. A., & Rosen, B. M. (1975). The structure of motor tasks. In Ç. Bard, M. Fleury, & J. H. Salmela (Eds.), *Movement: Actes du 7 Canadien en appretissage psychomoteur et psychologie du sport* (pp. 11-28). Ottawa: Association of Professionals in Physical Education of Quebec.

Gibson, E. J. (1969). *The ecological approach to visual perception.* Boston: Houghton Mifflin.

Gillespie, C. R. & Eysenck, M. W. (1980). Effects of introversion extraversion on continuous recognition memory. *Bulletin of the Psychonomic Society, 15,* 233-235.

Gould, D., & Krane, V. (1992). The arousal—athletic performance relationship: Current status and future directions. In T. S. Horn (Ed.), *Advances in sport psychology* (pp.113-141). Champaign, IL: Human Kinetics.

Gould, D., & Petlichkoff, L. (1988). Participation motivation and attrition in young athletes. In F. Smoll, R. Magill, & M. Ash (Eds.), *Children in sport* (3rd ed., pp. 161-178). Champaign, IL: Human Kinetics.

Hackfort, D., & Schultz, P. (1989). Competence and valence as determinants of anxiety. In D. Hackfort & C. D. Spielberger (Eds.), *Anxiety in sports* (pp. 29-38). New York: Hemisphere.

Hanin, Y.L. (1986). State-trait research on sports in the USSR. In C. D. Spielberger & R. Diaz-Guerrero (Eds.), *Cross-cultural anxiety* (Vol. 3, pp. 45-64). Washington, DC: Hemisphere.

Hanin, Y. L. (1989). Interpersonal and intragroup anxiety in sports. In D. Hackfort & C.D. Spielberger (Eds.), *Anxiety in sports* (pp. 19-28). New York: Hemisphere.

Hardy, L., & Parfitt, G. (1991). A catastrophe model of anxiety and performance. *British Journal of Psychology, 82,* 163-178.

Harkins, S., & Green, R. G. (1975). Discriminability and criterion differences between extraverts and introverts during vigilance. *Journal of Research on Personality, 9,* 335-340.

Harter, S. (1978). Effectance motivation reconsidered: Toward a developmental model. *Human Development, 21,* 34-64.

Harter, S. (1981). The development of competence motivation in the mastery of cognitive and physical skills: Is there still a place for joy? In G. C. Roberts & D. M. Landers (Eds.), *Psychology of motor behavior and sport—1980* (pp. 3-29). Champaign, IL: Human Kinetics.

Hatfield, B. D., & Landers, D. M. (1983). Psychophysiology: A new direction for sport psychology. *Journal of Sport Psychology, 3,* 243-259.

Healey, R. R., & Landers, D. M. (1973). Effect of need achievement and task difficulty on competitive and noncompetitive motor performance. *Journal of Motor Behavior, 5,* 121-128.

Heilbrun, A. B. (1972). Style of adaptation to perceived aversive maternal control and scanning behavior. *Journal of Consulting and Clinical Psychology, 29,* 15-21.

Hochberg, J. (1982). How big is a stimulus? In J. Beck (Ed.), *Organization and representation in perception* (pp. 191-218). Hillsdale, NJ: Erlbaum.

Houts, A. C., Cook, T.D., & Shadish, W.R. (1986). The person-situation debate: A critical multiplist perspective. *Journal of Personality, 54,* 52-105.

Hull, C.L. (1943). *Principles of behavior.* New York: Appleton.

Humphreys, G. (1981). Flexibility of attention between stimulus dimensions. *Perceptions and Psychophysics, 30,* 291-302.

Husman, B. F., & Silva, J. M. (1984). Aggression in sport: Definitional and theoretical considerations. In J. M. Silva & R. S. Weisberg (Eds.), *Psychological foundation of sport* (pp. 246-260). Champaign, IL: Human Kinetics.

Hyman, R. (1953). Stimulus information as a determinant of time. *Journal of Experimental Psychology, 45,* 188-196.

Johansson, F., Almay, B. G. L., Knorring, L., Terenius, L., & Astrom, M. (1979). Personality traits in chronic pain patients related to endorphin levels in cerebrospinal fluid. *Psychiatry Research, 1,* 231-239.

Jones, M. G. (1972). Perceptual characteristics and athletic performance. In H. T. A Whiting (Ed.), *Readings in sport psychiatry* (pp. 96-115). London: Kimpton.

Kahneman, D. (1973). *Attention and effort.* Englewood Cliffs, NJ: Prentice-Hall.

Kahneman, D., & Treisman, A. (1984). Changing views of attention and automaticity. In R. Parasuraman & D. R. Davies (Eds.). *Varieties of attention* (pp. 29-61). New York: Academic Press.

Keele, S. W. (1982). Component analysis and conceptions of skill. In J. A. S. Kelso (Ed.), *Human motor behavior: An introduction* (pp. 143-159). Hillsdale, NJ: Erlbaum.

Keele, S. W. & Hawkins, H. (1982). Exploration of individual differences relevant to high level skill. *Journal of Motor Behavior, 14,* 3-23.

Keele, S. W., & Neill, T. (1979). Mechanisms of attention. In E. Carterette & M. Friedman (Eds.), *Handbook of perception* (Vol. 9, pp. 3-47). New York: Academic Press.

Kemrick, D. T., & Funder, D. C. (1988). Profiting from controversy: Lessons from the person-situation debate. *American Psychologist, 43,* 23-34.

Kerr, J. H. (1989). Anxiety, arousal and sport performance: An application of reversal theory. In D. Hackfort & C. D. Spielberger (Eds.), *Anxiety in sports* (pp. 137-151). New York: Hemisphere.

Kirkcaldy, B. (1980). An analysis of the relationship between psychophysiological variables connected to human performance and the personality variables extraversion and neuroticism. *International Journal of Sport Psychology, 11,* 276-289.

Kirschenbaum, D. S., & Bale, R. M. (1980). Cognitive-behavioral skills in golf: Brain power golf. In R.M. Suinn (Ed.), *Psychology in sports: Methods and applications* (pp. 334-343). Minneapolis: Burgess.

Klavora, P. (1978). An attempt to derive inverted-U curves based on the relationship between anxiety and athletic performance. In D. M. Landers & R. W. Christina (Eds.), *Psychology of motor behavior and sport.* Champaign, IL: Human Kinetics.

Knapp, B. (1964). *Skill in sport.* London: Routledge & Kegan Paul.

Krane, V. (1992). Conceptual and methodological consideration in sport anxiety research: From the inverted-U hypothesis to catastrophe theory. *Quest, 44,* 72-87.

Lamb, K., & Burwitz, L., (1988). Visual restriction in ball-catching: A re-examination of early findings. *Journal of Human Movement Studies, 14,* 93-99.

Landers, D.M. (1978). Motivation and performance: The role of arousal and attentional factors. In W. Straub (Ed.), *Sport psychology: An analysis of athletic behavior.* Ithaca, NY: Mouvement.

Landers, D. M. (1980). The arousal-performance relationship revisited. *Research Quarterly for Exercise and Sport, 51,* 77-90.

Landers, D. M. (1989). Controlling arousal to enhance sport performance. In G. Tenenbaum & D. Eiger (Eds.), *Proceedings of the Maccabiah-Wingate International Congress: Sport psychology* (pp. 7-27). Netanya, Israel: Wingate Institute.

Landers, D. M., Furst, D. M., & Daniels, F. S. (1981). *Anxiety/attention and shooting ability: Testing the predictive validity of the test of attentional and interpersonal style (TAIS).* Paper presented at the annual meeting of the North American Society for the Psychology of Sport and Physical Activity, Boulder, CO.

Laurent, M. (1987). *Les coordinations visuo-locometrices: Étude comportmentale chez l homme.* Unpublished doctoral dissertation, Université Aix-Marseille II, France.

Laurent, M., & Thomson, J. A. (1988). The role of visual information in control of a constrained locomotor task. *Journal of Motor Behavior, 20,* 17-37.

Laurent, M., & Thomson, J. A. (1991). Anticipation and control of visual-guided locomotion. *International Journal of Sport Psychology, 22,* 251-270.

Lee, D. N. (1980a). The optic flow field: The foundation of vision. *Philosophical Transactions of the Royal Society of London, B290,* 169-179.

Lee, D. N. (1980b). Visuo-motor coordination in space-time. In G. E. Stelmach & J. Requin (Eds.), *Tutorials in motor behavior* (pp. 281-295). Amsterdam: North Holland.

Lee, D.N., Lishman, J., & Thomson, J.A. (1982). Regulation of gait in long jumping. *Journal of Experimental Psychology: Human Perception and Performance, 8,* 448-459.

Lee, D. N., Young, D., Reddish, P., Longh, S., & Clayton, T. (1983). Visual timing in hitting an accelerating ball. *Quarterly Journal of Experimental Psychology, 35,* 333-346.

Levy-Schoen, A. (1972). Rapport entre mouvements des yeux et perception. In H. Hecaen (Ed.), *Neuropsychologie de la perception visuelle* (pp. 76-92). Paris: Masson.

MacGillivary, W.W. (1980). The contribution of perceptual style to human performance. *International Journal of Sport Psychology, 11,* 132-141.

Maehr, M. L. (1989). Thoughts about motivation. In R. Ames & C. Ames (Eds.), *Research on motivation in education: Vol. 3. Goals and cognitions* (pp. 299-315). New York: Academic Press.

Maehr, M. L., & Braskanty, L. A. (1986). *The motivation factor: A theory of personal investment.* Lexington, MA: Lexington Books.

Marteniuk, R.G. (1976). Cognitive information processes in motor short-term memory and movement production. In G. E. Stelmach (Ed.), *Motor control: Issues and trends* (pp. 175-199). New York: Academic Press.

Martens, R. (1971). Anxiety and motor behavior: A review. *Journal of Motor Behavior, 3,* 151-179.

Martens, R. (1972). Trait and state anxiety. In W. P. Morgan (Ed.), *Ergogenic aids and muscular performance* (pp. 35-66). New York: Academic Press.

Martens, R. (1974). Arousal and motor performance. In J. H. Wilmore (Ed.), *Exercise and sport science reviews* (Vol.2. pp. 155-188). New York: Academic Press.

Martens, R. (1975). The paradigmatic crisis in American sport personology. *Sportwissenschaft, 1,* 9-24.

Martens, R. (1976). Competition: In need of a theory. In D. M. Landers (Ed.), *Social problems in athletics* (pp. 9-17). Urbana: University of Illinois Press.

Martens, R. (1977). *Sport competition anxiety test.* Champaign, IL: Human Kinetics.

Martens, R. (1988). *Coaches' guide to sport psychology.* Champaign, IL: Human Kinetics.

Martens, R., Burton, D., Rivkin, R., & Simon, J. (1980). Reliability and validity of the Competitive State Anxiety Scale (CSAI). In C. H. Nadeau, W. C. Halliwell, K. M. Newell, & G. C. Roberts (Eds.), *Psychology of motor behavior and sport—1979* (pp. 91-99). Champaign, IL: Human Kinetics.

Martens, R., & Landers, D.M. (1970). Motor performance under stress: A test of the inverted-U hypothesis. *Journal of Personality and Social Psychology, 16,* 29-37.

Martens, R., Vealey, R. S., & Burton, D. (1990). *Competitive anxiety in sport.* Champaign, IL: Human Kinetics.

McAuley, E., & Duncan, T. (1990). The causal attribution process in sport and physical activity. In S. Graham & V. Folkes (Eds.), *Advances in applied social psychology: V. Applications of attribution theory* (pp. 37-52). Hillsdale, NJ: Erlbaum.

McClelland, D. C., Atkinson, J. W., Clark, R. W., & Lowell, E. L. (1953). *The achievement motive.* New York: Appleton-Century-Crofts.

McLeod, P. (1987). Visual reaction time and high-speed ball games. *Perception, 16,* 49-59.

McLeod, P., & Jenkins, S. (1991). Timing accuracy and decision time in high speed ball games. *International Journal of Sport Psychology, 22,* 279-295.

McMorris, T. (1992). Field independence and performance in sport. *International Journal of Sport Psychology, 23,* 14-27.

McMorris, T., & MacGillivary, W. W. (1988). An investigation into the relationship between field independence and decision making in soccer. In T. Reilly, A. Lees, K. Davids, & W. J. Murphy (Eds.), *Science and football* (pp. 552-557). London: Spon.

Mestre, D., & Pailhous, J. (1991). Expertise in sport as a perceptivo-motor skill. *International Journal of Sport Psychology, 22,* 211-216.

Morgan, W. P. (1968). Personality characteristics of wrestlers participating in the world championships. *Journal of Sports Medicine, 8,* 212-216.

Morgan, W. P. (1980a). Sport personology: The credulous-skeptical argument in perspective. In W. Straub (Ed.), *Sport psychology: An analysis of athlete behavior* (pp. 330-339). Ithaca, NY: Mouvement.

Morgan, W. P. (1980b). The trait psychology controversy. *Research Quarterly for Exercise and Sport, 51,* 50-76.

Morgan, W. P. (1985). Selected psychological factors limiting performance: A mental health model. In D.H. Clarke & H.M. Eckert (Eds.), *Limits of human performance* (pp. 70-80). Champaign, IL: Human Kinetics.

Navon, D., & Gopher, D. (1979). On the economy of the human processing system. *Psychological Review, 86,* 214-255.

Neury, R. S., & Zuckerman, M. (1976). Sensation seeking, trait and state anxiety, and the electrodermal orienting reflex. *Psychophysiology, 13,* 205-211.

Neiss, R. (1988). Reconceptualizing arousal: Psychobiological states in motor performance. *Psychological Bulletin, 103,* 345-366.

Neisser, U. (1967). *Cognitive psychology.* New York: Appleton-Century-Crofts.

Nicholls, J. G. (1984). Achievement motivation: Conceptions of ability, subjective experience, task choice, and performance. *Psychological Review, 91,* 328-346.

Nicholls, J. G. (1989). *The competitive ethos and democratic education.* Cambridge, MA: Harvard University Press.

Nideffer, R. M. (1976). Test of attentional and interpersonal style. *Journal of Personality and Social Psychology, 34,* 394-404.

Nideffer, R. M. (1979). The role of attention in optimal athletic performance. In P. Klavora & J. V. Daniel (Eds.), *Coach, athlete and the sport psychologist* (pp. 99-112). Toronto: University of Toronto.

Nitsch, J.R. (1985). The action-theoretical perspective. *International Review for the Sociology of Sport, 20,* 263-282.

Norman, D.A. (1976). *Memory and attention: An introduction to information processing.* New York: Academic Press.

Nougier, V., Azemar, G., Stein, J. F., & Ripoll, H. (1989). Information processing and attention with expert tennis players according to their age and level of expertise. In C.K. Giam, K.K. Chook, & K. C. Teb (Eds.), *Proceedings of the 7th world congress on Sport Psychology* (p. 237). Singapore: International Society of Sport Psychology.

Nougier, V., Ripoll, H., & Stein, J.F. (1987). Processus attentionnels et practique sportive de haut niveau. In M. Laurent & P. Therme (Eds.), *Recherches en APS II* (pp. 209-221). Aix-Marseille II, France: Centre de Recherche de l'UEREPS.

Nougier, V., Ripoll, H., & Stein, J. F. (1990). Orienting of attention with highly skilled athletes. *International Journal of Sport Psychology, 20,* 205-223.

Nougier, V., Stein, J. F., & Bonnel, A. M. (1991). Information processing in sport and "orienting of attention." *International Journal of Sport Psychology, 22,* 307-327.

Olsen, E. (1956). Relationship between psychological capacities and success in college athletics. *Research Quarterly, 27,* 78-89.

Ostrow, A. C. (1976). Goal-setting behavior and need achievement in relation to competitive motor activity. *Research Quarterly, 47,* 174-183.

Ostrow, A. C. (Ed.). (1990). *Directory of psychological tests in the sport and exercise sciences.* Morgantown, WV: Fitness Information Technology.

Oxendine, J. B. (1970). Emotional arousal and motor performance. *Quest, 13,* 23-32.

Paillard, J. (1991). The cognitive penetrability sensorimotor mechanisms: A key problem in sport research. *International Journal of Sport Psychology, 22,* 244-250.

Pervin, L. A. (1977). The representative design of person-situation research. In D. Magnusson & N. S. Endler (Eds.), *Personality at the crossroads: Current issues in interactional psychology* (pp. 371-384). Hillsdale, NJ: Erlbaum.

Pervin, L. A. (1985). Personality: Current controversies, issues, and directions. *Annual Review of Psychology, 36,* 83-114.

Petlichkoff, L. M. (1992). Youth sport participation and withdrawal: Is it simply a matter of fun? *Pediatric Exercise Science, 4,* 105-110.

Petrie, A. (1967). *Individuality in pain suffering: The reducer and the augmenter.* Chicago: Chicago University Press.

Posner, M. I. (1980). Orienting of attention. *Quarterly Journal of Experimental Psychology, 32,* 3-25.

Posner, M. I., & Snyder, C. (1975). Facilitation and inhibition in the processing of signals. In P. Rabbit & S. Dornic (Eds.), *Attention and performance* (Vol. 5, pp. 669-682). London: Academic Press.

Posner, M. I., Snyder C. R., & Davidson, B. J. (1980). Attention and the detection of signals. *Journal of Experimental Psychology: General, 109,* 160-174.

Poulton, E.C. (1957). On prediction in skilled movements. *Psychological Bulletin, 54,* 467-478.

Prinz, W. (1977). Memory control of visual search. In S. Dornic (Ed.), *Attention and performance* (Vol. 6, pp. 441-462). Hillsdale, NJ: Erlbaum.

Prinz, W. (1979). Integration of information visual search: The Experimental Psychology Society. *Psychological Beitrage, 25,* 57-70.

Prinz, W., & Atalan, D. (1973). Two components and two stages in search performance: A case study in visual search. *Acta Psychologica, 37,* 218-242.

Raglin, J. S. (1992). Anxiety and sport performance. In J. G. Holloszy (Ed.), *Exercise and Sport Sciences Review* (Vol. 20, pp. 243-274). Baltimore, MD: Williams & Wilkins.

Revelle, W., Humphreys, M. S., Simon, L., & Gilliland, K. (1980). The interactive effect of personality, time of day and caffeine: A test of the arousal model. *Journal of Experimental Psychology, 109,* 1-31.

Richards, D. E., & Landers, D. M. (1981). Test of attentional style and interpersonal style scores of shooters. In G. C. Roberts & D.M. Landers (Eds.), *Psychology of motor behavior and sport—1980* (p. 94). Champaign, IL: Human Kinetics.

Ripoll, H. (1988a). Analysis of visual scanning patterns of volleyball players in a problem-solving task. *International Journal of Sport Psychology, 19,* 9-25.

Ripoll, H. (1988b). Stratégies de prise d'informations visuelles dans les taches de résolution de problèmes tactiques en sport. In H. Ripoll & G. Azemar (Eds.), *Éléments de neurosciences du sport* (pp. 329-354). Paris: INSEP.

Ripoll, H. (1991). The understanding-acting process in sport: The relationship between semantic and sensorimotor visual function. *International Journal of Sport Psychology, 22,* 221-243.

Ripoll, H., Kerlirzin, Y., Stein, J.F., & Reine, B. (1991). Visual strategies of boxers (French boxing) in a simulated problem solving situation. In *Proceedings of the sixth European conference on eye movement* (p. 83). Louvain, Belgium: Katholieke University.

Ripoll, H., Papin, J. P., & Simonet, P. (1983). Approche de la function visuelle en sport. *Le Travail Humain, 46,* 163-173.

Roberts, G. C. (1972). Effect of achievement motivation and social environment on performance of a motor task. *Journal of Motor Behavior, 4,* 37-46.

Roberts, G. C. (1974). Effect of achievement motivation and social environment on risk taking. *Research Quarterly, 45,* 42-55.

Roberts, G.C. (1992a). Motivation in sport and exercise: Conceptual constraints and convergence. In G.C. Roberts (Ed.), *Motivation in sport and exercise* (pp. 3-29). Champaign, IL: Human Kinetics.

Roberts, G. C. (Ed.). (1992b). *Motivation in sport and exercise.* Champaign, IL: Human Kinetics.

Rowland, G. L., Franken, R. E., & Harrison, K. (1986). Sensation seeking and participation in sporting activities. *Journal of Sport Psychology, 8,* 212-220.

Ryan, E., & Foster, R. (1967). Athletic participation and perceptual augmentation and reduction. *Journal of Personality and Social Psychology, 6,* 472-476.

Ryan, E., & Lakie, W. (1965). Competitive and noncompetitive performance in relation to achievement motive and manifest anxiety. *Journal of Personality and Social Psychology, 1,* 342-345.

Sarason, S. B., Mandler, G., & Craighill, P. G. (1952). The effect of differential instructions on anxiety and learning. *Journal of Abnormal and Social Psychology, 47,* 561-565.

Scanlan, T. K., & Simons, J. P. (1992). The construct of sport enjoyment. In G. C. Roberts (Ed.), *Motivation in sport and exercise* (pp. 199-215). Champaign, IL: Human Kinetics.

Shallice, T. (1988). *From neuropsychology to mental structure.* Cambridge, England: Cambridge University Press.

Shiffrin, R., & Schneider, W. (1977). Controlled and automatic human information processing: Perceptual learning, automatic attending, and a general theory. *Psychological Review, 84,* 127-190.

Silva, J. M. (1984). Personality and sport performance: Controversy and challenge. In J. M. Silva & R. S. Weinberg (Eds.), *Psychological foundations of sport* (pp. 59-69). Champaign, IL: Human Kinetics.

Snyder, M. (1983). The influence of individuals on situations: Implications for understanding the links between personality and social behavior. *Journal of Personality, 51,* 497-516.

Sonstroem, R. J., & Bernardo, P. B. (1982). Individual pre-game state anxiety and basketball performance: A reexamination of the inverted-U curve. *Journal of Sport Psychology, 4,* 235-245.

Spence, J.T., & Spence, K. W. (1966). The motivational components of manifest anxiety: Drive and drive stimuli. In C. D. Spielberger (Ed.), *Anxiety and behavior* (pp. 291-326). New York: Academic Press.

Spence, K. W. (1956). *Behavior theory and conditioning.* New Haven, CT: Yale University Press.

Spielberger, C. D. (Ed.). (1972). *Anxiety: Current trends in theory and research* (Vol. 1). New York: Academic Press.

Spielberger, C. D. (1989). Stress and anxiety in sports. In D. Hackfort & C. D. Spielberger (Eds.), *Anxiety in sports: An international perspective* (pp. 3-17). New York: Hemisphere.

Spielberger, C. D., Gorsuch, R. L., & Lushene, R. E. (1970). *Manual for the State-Trait Anxiety Inventory (STAI).* Palo Alto, CA: Consulting Psychologists Press.

Spielberger, C. D., Gorsuch, R. L., Lushene, R. E., Vagg, P.R., & Jacobs, G. A. (1983). *Manual for the State-Trait Anxiety Inventory (Form Y).* Palo Alto, CA: Consulting Psychologists Press.

Spielman, J. (1963). *The relation between personality and the frequency and duration of involuntary rest pauses during massed practice.* Unpublished Ph.D. thesis, University of London.

Starkes, J. L., & Allard, F. (1983). Perception in volleyball: The effects of competitive stress. *Journal of Sport Psychology, 5,* 189-196.

Starkes, J. L., & Deakin, J. M. (1984). Perception in sport: A cognitive approach to skilled performance. In W.F. Straub & J.M. Williams (Eds.), *Cognitive sport psychology* (pp. 115-128). New York: Sport Science Associates.

Straub, W.F. (1982). Sensation seeking among high and low-risk male athletes. *Journal of Sport Psychology, 4,* 246-253.

Swinnes, S., Vandenberghe, J., & Van Assche, E. (1986). Role of cognitive style constructs, field dependence-independence, and reflection-impulsivity in skill acquisition. *Journal of Sport Psychology, 8,* 51-69.

Taylor, J. A. (1953). A personality scale of manifest anxiety. *Journal of Abnormal and Social Psychology, 48,* 285-290.

Tenenbaum, G., & Bar-Eli, M. (1992). Methodological issues in sport psychology research. *Australian Journal of Science and Medicine in Sport, 24,* 44-50.

Tenenbaum, G., Levy-Kolker, N., Bar-Eli, M., & Weinberg, R. (1994). Information recall among skilled and novice athletes; The role of display complexity, attentional resources, visual exposure duration, and expertise. *Journal of Sport Sciences, 12,* 529-534.

Tenenbaum, G., Levy-Kolker, N., Sade, S., Liebermann, D., & Liahr, R. (1995). Anticipation and confidence of decisions related to skilled performance. *International Journal of Sport Psychology, 27,* 293-307.

Umilta, C. (1991). Attention in sport: further lines of research. *International Journal of Sport Psychology, 22,* 328-333.

Vealey, R. S. (1989). Sport personology: A paradigmatic and methodological analysis. *Journal of Sport and Exercise Psychology, 11,* 216-235.

Vealey, R. S. (1992). Personality and sport: A comprehensive view. In T.S. Horn (Ed.), *Advances in sport psychology* (pp. 25-59). Champaign, IL: Human Kinetics.

von Hofsten, C. (1987). Catching. In H. Hemer & A. F. Sanders (Eds.), *Perspectives on perception and action* (pp. 33-46). Hillsdale, NJ: Erlbaum.

Wachtel, P. L. (1967). Conceptions of broad and narrow attention. *Psychological Bulletin, 68,* 417-429.

Weinberg, R. S. (1989). Anxiety, arousal and motor performance: Theory, research and applications. In D. Hackfort & C. D. Spielberger (Eds.), *Anxiety in sports* (pp. 95-115). New York: Hemisphere.

Weinberg, R. S., & Genuchi, M. (1980). Relationship between competitive trait anxiety, state anxiety and golf performance: A field study. *Journal of Sport Psychology, 2,* 148-154.

Weiner, B. (1974). *Achievement motivation and attribution theory.* Morristown, NJ: General Learning Press.

Weiner, B. (1986). *An attributional theory of motivation and emotion.* New York: Springer.

Weingarten, G. (1982). Psychological disposition toward athletic activity vesus psychological development through sport. In E. Gerson (Ed.), *Handbook of sport psychology: Vol. 1. Introduction to sport psychology* (pp. 114-128). Netanya, Israel: Wingate Institute.

Weiss, M. R., & Petlichkoff, L. M. (1989). Children's motivation for participation in and withdrawal from sport: Identifying the missing links. *Pediatric Exercise Science, 1,* 195-211.

White, R. (1959). Motivation reconsidered: The concept of competence. *Psychological Review, 66,* 297-334.

Whiting, H. T. A. (1991). Action is not reaction! A reply to McLeod and Jenkins. *International Journal of Sport Psychology, 22,* 296-303.

Whiting, H. T. A, & Hutt, J. W. R. (1972). The effects of personality and ability on speed of decisions regarding the directional aspects of ball flight. *Journal of Motor Behavior, 4,* 89-97.

Wine, J. D. (1980). Cognitive-attentional theory of test anxiety. In I. G. Sarason (Ed.), *Test anxiety: Theory, research and applications* (pp. 349-385). Hillsdale, NJ: Erlbaum.

Wine, J. D. (1982). Evaluation anxiety: A cognitive-attentional construct. In H. W. Krohne & L. Laux (Eds.), *Achievement, stress, and anxiety* (pp. 207-219). Washington, DC: Hemisphere.

Witkin, H.A., Dyk, R.B., Paterson, H.F., Goodenough, D.R., & Karp, S. A. (1962). *Psychological differentiation: Studies of development.* New York: Wiley.

Witkin, H. A., & Goodenough, D. R. (1981). Cognitive style: Essence and origins. *Psychological Issues Monograph No. 51.* New York International University Press.

Witkin, H. A., Goodenough, D. R., & Oltman, P. K. (1979). Psychological differentiation in current status. *Journal of Personality and Social Psychology, 37,* 1127-1145.

Witkin, H. A., Lewis, H. B., Hertzman, M., Machover, K., Meissner, P. B., & Wapner, S. (1954). *Personality through perception: An experimental and clinical study.* Westport, CT: Greenwood.

Zillman, D. (1971). Excitation transfer in communication-mediated aggressive behavior. *Journal of Experimental Social Psychology, 7,* 419-434.

Zuckerman, M. (1979). *Sensation seeking: Beyond the optimal level of arousal.* Hillsdale, NJ: Erlbaum.

Zuckerman, M. (1983). Sensation seeking in sports. *Personality and Individual Differences, 4,* 285-293.

Zuckerman, M. (1984). Experience and desire: A new format for Sensation Seeking Scales. *Journal of Behavioral Assessment, 6,* 101-114.

Zuckerman, M. (1987). A critical look at three arousal constructs in personality theories: Optimal levels of arousal, strength of the nervous system, and sensitivities to signals of reward and punishment. In J. Strelau & H.J. Hysenck (Eds.), *Personality dimensions and arousal* (pp. 217-231). New York: Plenum.

Zuckerman, M., Kolin, E. A., Price, L., & Zoob, I. (1964). Development of a Sensation-Seeking Scale. *Journal of Consulting Psychology, 28,* 477-482.

Zuckerman, M., Murtaugh, T.M., & Siegel, J. (1974). Sensation seeking and cortical augmenting-reducing. *Psychophysiology, 11,* 535-542.

PART III

Understanding Sport and Exercise Environments

Part III focuses on environmental and situational factors that affect athletic behavior, taking into consideration the athlete's intrinsic motivation. Competition and situational factors were evident in Triplett's original study, but environmental issues in sport have become much more sophisticated thanks to these researchers. Smith and Smoll's (1991) article presents some of their classic work on the Coaching Behavior Assessment System (CBAS) and the closely related positive approach to coaching of young athletes, as well as their research concerning the psychosocial influences on adolescents' athletic injuries. The environment in which the young athlete acts is discussed in the chapter by Orlick, McNally, and O'Hara (1978). They systematically analyzed cooperative games and described how their positive impact can be maximized. This prodded some to restructure the youth sport environment to facilitate the physical and psychological development of young athletes. Vallerand and Perrault (1999) investigated the complex relationships between intrinsic and extrinsic sport motivation and proposed a theoretical model that hierarchically integrates many of the factors playing a major role in this context. Intrinsic motivation is substantially affected by one's optimal experiences while performing a task. Ravizza's (1977) pioneering work on peak experience (based on Maslow's humanistic approach) and Jackson's (1995) work on the state of flow (a special case of intrinsic motivation, investigated first by Csikszentmihalyi) have had a profound effect on researchers who have long been trying to determine optimal performance states.

12 Peak Experiences in Sport

KENNETH RAVIZZA
California State University, Fullerton

Any human action can be explained from several different points of view, each of them reflecting a different general approach to psychology. Among these is the phenomenological approach that has focused on a person's view of the world and interpretation of events occurring in his or her environment—that is, on the human subjective experience. Some phenomenological theories, the humanistic ones, emphasize the unique qualities that distinguish people from animals, such as free will, but primarily they stress the drive toward self-actualization. These theories assume that an individual's principal motivational force is the motive toward growth and self-actualization (i.e., the drive to develop one's potential to its fullest and to progress beyond the particular state in which the person is at any particular time).

A leading figure in the development of humanistic psychology was Abraham Maslow. In the 1950s, a fruitful setting for the development of major motivational concepts, Maslow shared the basic humanistic assumption of an existing natural tendency toward actualization and realization of people's potentials. He also suggested the theory of hierarchy of needs, which is still one of the most famous explanations proposed for employee motivation (despite its being heavily attacked, in terms of empirical validity, within organizational psychology). What is, however, more important for our purposes is the fact that Maslow was one of the first humanistic psychologists to attempt to systematically examine peak human experiences across a variety of life dimensions. He defined the term peak experience as a moment of extreme happiness in a person's life. Although infrequently experienced in the lives of most human beings, such moments were viewed by Maslow as important because they can eventually lead to an individual's growth and actualization. In addition, he proposed an extensive list of peak experience factors, including total attention, rich (unity) perceptions, time–space disorientation, and feelings of awe and wonder.

About three decades ago, sport psychology began to reveal an increasing interest in optimal athletic experiences. Assuming that sport psychologists know much less about athletes' positive or optimal experiences than about their negative states (e.g., stress, anxiety, and crisis), several approaches to the study of such positive and optimal experiences in sport have been suggested. Ravizza supports an interdisciplinary approach, exploring different facets of human movement activity. He focused on heightening athletes' awareness of their sport experiences by having athletes reflect on the subjective aspects related to the process of their own sport participation. While attempting to help athletes to increase their awareness through encouraging them to explore the affective domain of their experiences, he decided to examine the specific nature of athletes' peak experiences in terms of Maslow's concept.

Ravizza interviewed athletes and asked them to describe their most joyful moment during their sport participation. He analyzed the contents of these interviews and attempted to check whether the descriptors of these athletes' peak experiences blend with those outlined earlier by Maslow. In general, despite some dissimilarity, athletes' reports indicated many similarities in the qualities of peak experience listed by Maslow. This article, a pioneering examination of an important facet of athletes' optimal experience in sport, has been considered a milestone in understanding positive sport experiences and in enhancing the probability of exploiting their benefits.

The traditional emphasis of research on sports has been to develop techniques to improve physical performance. One result of this emphasis is that the major focus in sport research has been on motor performance. In contrast, the subjective experience of the athlete has been minimized (Kleinman, 1973; Park, 1973). One explanation for this emphasis on motor performance is that athletes' subjective experiences are difficult to measure and to study scientifically. Some progress has been made in studying nonpathological, yet extraordinary, psychological experience (Laski, 1961; Maslow, 1968). The limited research dealing with this aspect of sport reveals that participation provides the athlete with a wide domain of subjective experiences (Leonard, 1975; Metheny, 1968; Slusher, 1967; Thomas, 1967). Some of these studies have focused on specific aspects of the subjective experience of the athlete (Beisser, 1967; Csikszentmihalyi, 1975; Gallwey, 1974; Murphy, 1972, 1973; Raviza, 1973).

The purpose of the present investigation is twofold; first, to use the interview technique to ascertain the personal experiences of athletes; and second, to achieve a general characterization of at least one subjective aspect in sport, those experiences involved in an athlete's "greatest moment" while participating in sport.

Method

Subjects

Sixteen men and four women athletes ranging in age from 19–40 were interviewed. These subjects related experiences in twelve different sports. Eleven of the subjects gave

---

accounts that occurred while participating in team sports (football, volleyball, lacrosse, hockey), while nine respondents referred to experiences that occurred in individual sports (golf, swimming, track and field, jogging, surfing, skiing). Five of these athletes described experiences which took place while participating in informal activities such as recreational and intramural activities, while the remaining fifteen described experiences related to formal activities such as interscholastic, intercollegiate, or international contests. Twelve subjects participated on university level teams, three participated at the Olympic level, and five participated at the intramural or recreational level.

Interview Procedure

Because the athletes previously had seldom shared their subjective experiences about their "greatest moments" in sport with anyone, the interviews were conducted in a relaxed, informal atmosphere. After initial rapport was established, each athlete was asked to discuss his or her "greatest moment" while participating in sport. Occasional open-ended questions were used to stimulate discussion, such as, "How did the world appear to you"?, "How did you feel different than usual"? Maslow (1968) used the interview technique to study similar subjective phenomena which he labeled "peak experiences" in normal adults. The present inquiry provided an opportunity to compare subjective experiences associated with greatest moments while participating in sport with other "peak experiences." With this goal in mind, one intent of the interview was to determine whether or not those qualities Maslow described for peak experience were present in an athlete's experience. To insure that a judgment could be made for each athlete on each quality toward the end of each interview, specific questions were asked about those qualities not spontaneously commented upon earlier.

The tape recordings of each interview were analyzed in detail several times to determine how each athlete characterized his or her subjective experiences. The content of each tape was evaluated in terms of a checklist which was based on pilot interviews with athletes and which reflected the major features of peak experiences described by Maslow (1968).

Table 12.1 Characterization of "Greatest Moment"

Qualities	Percentage of subjects
1. Loss of fear*	100
2. Ability to execute basic skills	100
3. No thinking of performance	95
4. Individual gives full attention (total immersion in activity)*	95
5. Narrow focus of attention	95
6. The experience is perfect*	95
7. Temporary phenomenon	95
8. Feeling of beng Godlike (in control)*	95
9. Self-validating experience*	95
10. Involuntary experience	90
11. Unique experience	90
12. Perception of the universe as integrated and unified*	90
13. Passive perception (effortless)*	90
14. Time-space disorientation*	85
15. Awe and wonder of the experience*	80
16. Transcendence of ordinary self*	80
17. Fusion of the individual*	60
18. Unique being of the individual*	55
19. Rich perception during experience	55
20. Unity of the world*	45
21. Athlete in good physical condition	45
22. Accomplished goal	45
23. Premonition of experience	45
24. Unclassified perception*	45
25. Important to have spectators	20
26. Fusion of dichotomies*	20
27. Awarenes of the absolute*	15
28. Abstract perception*	15
29. Nature of the object in itself*	15
30. Meaning to life in general	15
31. Discussed experience with others	15

*Represents qualities Maslow (1968, pp. 74-96) discussed in relation to peak experiences.

Results

The chief results of this inquiry are summarized in table 12.1. The column at the left lists qualities used by subjects to characterize their experience. The column at the right reflects the percentage of subjects who shared each of the given qualities to characterize their "greatest moment."

Discussion

This investigation indicates that one's greatest moment while participating in sport can be characterized as follows:

"Unique!" A swimmer explained: "This was a whole new experience for me. I never did anything to this degree before. There is no way this could happen twice."

In an involuntary moment, the athlete has no control over its occurrence. A cyclist described: "I am a vehicle for this. I initiate the performance and then the experience takes over."

Short-lived and pleasant, even ecstatic, were adjectives subjects used to express their greatest moments.

Total immersion in the activity without thinking of the details of the motor performance was described. (All subjects had mastered the basic skills required.) A lacrosse player explained: "It is a world within a world . . . focused right there. I am not aware of the external. My concentration was so great I didn't think of anything else."

Subjects reported that they were not aware of their normal selves, but instead were completely absorbed in the activity. This experience appears similar to what some psychologists have referred to as an "ego-transcending experience" into a union with the phenomenon (Maslow, 1968). A skier responded: "I was really blending into the snow, the mountain . . . I wasn't different from the hill. The whole environment was part of me." This experience is also characterized by a feeling of perfection, that is, everything is perfect. With no conscious effort the participant is in total control of the situation with no fears of failure.

Another skier revealed: "Everything was so perfect, everything so right, that it couldn't be any other way. The closest thing I can say about it was that there seemed to be tracks in the snow that my skis were made to fit in. . . . It was no longer me and the hill, but both of us, it was just right, for I belonged there."

A football player describing a block stated: "So many times I put everything into it but nothing happens, but this time I hit him just right and everything went perfectly. It was effortless for me. I hit him and he just flew. Physically, I didn't put as much as usual into it."

The athletes reported a narrow focusing of attention to the immediate activity and a transcendence of the larger situation. For example, some participants whose greatest moments occurred while participating in spectator sports, reported being unaware of the crowd. A football player explained: "I concentrate my whole being on one thing; this was one of the few times I have done this. I am just hitting him [the ball carrier] and nothing else."

This experience stood out from the game itself to such an extent that the athletes generally viewed it as an experience independent of the final outcome of the activity. The experience was self-validating in itself. A volleyball player described: "The experience is in the process while participating. It sometimes happens that the end result may distract from it, but it is still valid."

Finally, each of the athletes reported that although the experience was enjoyable there was little inclination to discuss the experience with others. In fact, for several of the athletes, the interview was their first attempt at describing this experience.

Comparison With Maslow's Peak Experience Qualities

The athletes' reports contained many similarities to Maslow's (1968) description of peak experience. Athletes gave their experiences total attention, resulting in temporary ego loss, union with the experience as a whole, and disorientation in time and space. Some athletes described feeling in total control of the situation which is similar to Maslow's report of the feeling of being Godlike. The experience is reported as being perfect; consequently, the athlete is "passive" in the experience since it is effortless. The usual fears associated with the activity are nonexistent. Another parallel to Maslow's description is the awe and wonder that accompanies the experience and the sense that it is an involuntary and ecstatic phenomenon.

In addition to these similiarities, we also found that certain features of peak experiences listed by Maslow (1968) were not part of an athlete's greatest moments in sport. For example, Maslow referred to how one's attention during the peak experience may be very wide and more of a total attention in breadth of field. This was not the case in sport peak experiences. The athlete's attention was total and accompanied by a narrow focus of attention. There also was not a consciousness of the fusion of dichotomies or the cognitive type of qualities (i.e., abstract thought, awareness of the absolute, nature of object in itself, nonclassifying perception). Thus, the experiences tended to be more of a body experience and less of a cognitive or reflective nature. Although the experiences were invariably reported as intense in nature, few of the athletes viewed them as of pivotal importance to their whole lives, as has been reported with many peak experiences. None of the athletes interviewed reported a life change from this experience.

Implications

Not only is there a motor aspect to sport, but there is also an emotional and cognitive aspect which at times can be quite intense. The inclusion of athletes' subjective experiences along with more traditional sport research will allow for a more complete investigation of the total sport experience than has been previously possible.

During athletes' greatest moments they obtain expanded views of themselves as fully functioning individuals. Sports thus have great payoffs besides winning. One application of these ideas might include guided discussions among coaches and players of these subjective experiences. In this way athletes may begin to become aware of the total sport experience and its full benefits.

References

Beisser, A. *The madness in sports.* New York: Appleton-Century-Crofts, 1967.

Csikszentmihalyi, M. Play and intrinsic rewards. *Journal of Humanistic Psychology.* 1975, 15(3), 41-63.

Gallwey, T. *The inner game of tennis.* New York: Random House, 1974.

Kleinman, S. The significance of human movement: A phenomenological approach. Ellen Gerber (Ed.), *Sport and the body.* Philadelphia: Lea and Febiger, 1973.

Laski, M. *Ecstacy.* London: Crescent Press, 1961.

Leonard, G. *The ultimate athlete.* New York: Viking Press, 1975.

Maslow, A. *Religions, values and peak-experiences.* New York: Viking Press, 1964.

Maslow, A. Lessons from peak-experiences. *Journal of Humanistic Psychology,* 1967, 2, 9-18.

Maslow, A. *Toward a psychology of being* (2nd ed.) New York: Von Nostrand Reinhold Company, 1968.

Maslow, A. *The farther reaches of human nature.* New York: Viking Press, 1971.

Metheny, E. *Movement and meaning.* New York: McGraw-Hill, 1968.

Murphy, M. *Golf in the kingdom.* New York: Viking Press, 1972.

Murphy, M. & Brodie, J. I experience a kind of clarity. *Intellectual Digest,* January 1973, 19-22.

Park, R. Raising the consciousness of sport. *Quest,* 1973, XIX, 78-82.

Ravizza, K. A study of the peak-experiences in sport. Unpublished doctoral dissertation, University of Southern California, 1973.

Slusher, H. *Man, sport, and existence.* Philadelphia: Lea and Febiger, 1967.

Thomas, C. The perfect moment: An authentic perception of the sport experience. Unpublished doctoral dissertation, Ohio State University, 1972.

13 Cooperative Games: Systematic Analysis and Cooperative Impact

T.D. ORLICK, JANE MCNALLY, AND TOM O'HARA
University of Ottawa

Two major classes of situational variables that have a substantial environmental impact on human athletic behavior are competition and cooperation. Competition and cooperation—learned behaviors—are part of many sport and exercise activities. They may have positive and negative effects on one's conduct and performance and can be balanced in order to enable healthy personal development.

Terry Orlick, a Canadian sport psychologist, who is recognized for his work in children's sport, contends that the design of games has an influence on participants' predominant behavioral responses. In this chapter, Orlick and his colleagues conducted a systematic analysis of cooperative games and demonstrated how their cooperative impact can be used to create a social change (i.e., to increase cooperative behavior not only in the game itself but also out of it) in 4-year-old children observed in kindergarten. No less important is the conceptual framework suggested by the researchers, which outlines a component structure of games underlining this study.

The conceptual categories of activities, defined by Orlick and colleagues (competitive means and competitive ends, cooperative means and competitive ends, individual means and individual ends, cooperative means and individual ends, cooperative means and cooperative ends), have become milestones in developing a philosophy of cooperative games. They enable us, in a versatile, adaptive, and economical manner, to balance competitive and cooperative efforts intended to provide young athletes with meaningful and enjoyable athletic experiences.

This chapter represents 3 years of research and reflective thinking directed toward the creation of a cooperative games program. The program was conceived as a means of social change directed towards more humane games and lives. The primary aim of co-op games is to increase cooperative behavior both in and out of games. The games have been designed to provide cooperative success experiences, individual feelings of acceptance, and total involvement.

There have been many stages in arriving at the present frame of reference and there are many more steps ahead. This quest began by analyzing the component structure and emphasis of contemporary games and by assessing what kinds of behaviors they are structured to elicit. It was found that to elicit the desired behaviors (i.e., more cooperative behaviors), it was necessary to restructure games. Old games were adapted and new ones created so that their design was more appropriate for eliciting cooperative behaviors. Many questions had to be answered. Did the games actually work? Did they elicit cooperative behaviors from the participants? Did the games provide success experiences? Was there total involvement? Were the games motivationally viable for the children? Did they hold the child's attention and interest? Did the children like them?

It was, in fact, possible to formulate a series of behaviorally verified cooperative games that kindergarten children enjoyed playing (Orlick, 1976, 1977). A successful co-op games program had been created and we began to examine a question of great personal and social significance. Can we increase children's cooperative behaviors outside of games through a co-op games program?

The remainder of this chapter is devoted to the exploration of this question. The reader is first exposed to some of the different means of cooperative game analysis; then presented with our first study, which focused on the cooperative impact of cooperative games; and, finally, asked to reflect on future directions.

Component Structure of Games

Regardless of its component structure, a game will have some kind of individualistic experience or outcome for the player. Reinforcements or perceived payoffs are experienced by each person even though they may occur in conjunction with others. The important structural distinction relates to how one receives these payoffs—at the expense of others, without reference to others, or by cooperating with others.

The design of a game will largely influence the predominant behavioral response, be it competitive, individualistic, cooperative, or some combination thereof. Consequently, to better understand games and the behavior likely to be elicited by them, each activity can be classified according to its component structure. The following categories have

---

Adapted, by permission, from T. Orlick, J. McNally, and T. O'Hara, 1978, Cooperative games: Systematic analysis and cooperative impact. *Psychological perspectives in youth sports*, edited by F. Smoll and R.E. Smith (New York, NY: Hemisphere Publishing Corporation).

proven to be helpful in classifying the structure of many children's games. Although the categories are neither all-inclusive, nor defined in absolute terms, most activities can be classified according to these paradigms.

1. Competitive Means–Competitive Ends. Everyone is competing against everyone else from the outset to the end. The objective is to beat someone else or everyone else, and the means by which you attempt to do this is by competing against them. Examples are a class race where the first person across the finish line is declared the winner; a group of individuals all fighting to gain sole possession of one ball; to be "King of the Mountain" or "Winner on the Spot."

2. Cooperative Means–Competitive Ends. People engage in cooperation within a group and competition outside the group. Team members are cooperating to beat (or better compete against) another team. An example is any competitive game where teammates help one another in pursuit of a victory and where members of one team share the win and members of the other team share the defeat. In a game like soccer, cooperative means may be evidenced by teammates passing the ball in preparation for a shot on net. In a regular competitive game, cooperative interdependence and input is not always ensured for all team members. To ensure *Cooperative Interdependent Means,* a rule can be introduced in a game like soccer wherein everyone has to play and wherein everyone has to touch the ball (receive a pass and kick a pass) before a shot on net can be taken. This would ensure cooperative interdependence and input from each team member within the competitive goal structure (Cooperative Interdependent Means–Competitive Ends).

3. Individual Means–Individual Ends. One or more people are pursuing an individual goal without cooperative or competitive interaction and without direct evaluative reference to others. Examples are individual movement activities, creative problem solving where there is no incorrect movement response, and trail skiing along a scenic route.

4. Cooperative Means–Individual Ends. Persons are cooperating and helping each other so that each can achieve an individual end. For example, individual athletes can watch one another, give one another feedback or teach one another new skills so that each person can learn, improve, and perform better. The means are shared, the ends are not. To ensure *Cooperative Interdependent Means* and input from each team member, situations can be set up where athletes pair off and watch one another run through routines giving appropriate constructive feedback. Cooperative interdependence could be ensured during a gym class or activity session by having each group member teach all other group members a unique skill (or rule) for which all are individually responsible for knowing.

5. Cooperative Means–Cooperative Ends. Team members are cooperating with each other from the outset to the end, regardless of what team they happen to be on. "Opposing" team members, if they exist, work together to achieve a common goal. The means as well as the ends are shared. Cooperative interdependence is ensured between teams but not necessarily among all team members within a particular group. An example is collective score volleyball where the objective is to keep the ball on the volley as long as possible. To ensure *Cooperative Interdependent Means* as well as Cooperative Ends, a rule could be introduced in volleyball where each person on a particular side must touch the ball within a collective score game, or games such as Cooperative Musical Chairs, Balloon Balance, Collective Blanket Ball, or Log Roll could be played. In these games, everyone is helping one another for everyone's gain.

Games with both cooperative means and cooperative ends are extremely rare in our culture, but, in fact, are the type of game most desirable for the purposes of this research. By redirecting some thought patterns it was possible to devise two subclassifications of games within this major structural category: Cooperative Games with No Losers and Collective Score Games. Nearly all games created or adapted for the experimental cooperative games program for kindergarten children were Co-op Games with No Losers, a few of which are described as follows.[1]

Sample Cooperative Kindergarten Games with No Losers

Cooperative Musical Chairs

Children skip around a row of chairs to music and when the music stops all children must share a chair. Chairs are systematically removed until only one chair remains. The object is to keep every child in the game, even though chairs are being removed. As each chair is removed more children must team up sitting together on parts of chairs, or on top of one another to keep everyone in. Instead of fighting for the sole possession of one chair, kids work together to make themselves part of it.

Turtle

A gym mat acts as the turtle shell, and about eight children get under the shell and make the mat move in one direction.

Caterpillar Over the Mountain

Children get on their hands and knees and hold the ankles of the child in front of them. One giant caterpillar is formed and it moves around the room and over the mountain (a mat draped over a bench).

Beach Ball Balance

Two children are given one beach ball and attempt to hold the ball between them without using their hands. They try

[1]All experimental cooperative games used in this study, as well as many others for different age groups, can be found in Orlick (1977, in press).

to move around the gym or through an obstacle course in this manner. They also see how many different ways they can balance the ball between them and still move around, for example between heads, on side, stomach, back to back and so on.

Numbers and Letters Together

The children find one or two partners and are requested to make one specific number, letter or shape using all their little bodies.

Behavior Observation

Systematic behavior observation can be extremely helpful in evaluating the frequency with which a particular behavior occurs and in assessing behavioral change. It is not our intent to dwell on the methodology of behavior observation, but rather to expose the reader to some behavioral definitions and to a few observational approaches we have attempted in our cooperation research thus far.[2]

For the purpose of our systematic observational analysis, cooperation was based solely on the frequency with which a child interacted in a cooperative way with peers. A cooperative social interaction was defined as any behavior directed toward another child that involved some shared, reciprocal, mutual, or helpful quality. More specifically, cooperative social interaction was delineated as follows.

1. Cooperative Task Behavior—One child shares, assists, or executes a task with another child. The emphasis is upon doing things together, working together for a common goal, alternating responses between children, sharing material, or one child's behaving in a manner explicitly to help another child. For example, two or more children work together to solve a problem or to execute a task; two or more children engage in a cooperative activity in which they respond in turn based on the response of the other child.

2. Cooperative Physical Contact Behavior—(a) one child physically supports or is supported by another child. For example, one child carries another child or helps another child up off the ground or over a barrier. (b) Two or more children engage in physical contact of an affectionate nature by, for example, linking arms, holding hands, placing arms around one another, embracing, kissing, or patting another child on the back.

3. Cooperative Verbal Behavior—Verbal interaction is accepted as meeting the criteria for cooperative social interaction only if it has some definite cooperative quality. For example, one child gives another child instruction on how to do something; one child offers to help or share or agrees to a cooperative request made by another child.

This rather encompassing definition of cooperation manifests itself differently in different games and in different settings. For example, during unstructured free time in the kindergarten classroom, a few specific incidences of cooperative social interaction we have observed include tying another child's shoe lace; handing another child an apron or helping him put it on; lifting a block together for a fort or tower; passing scissors, paint brush, glue, and so on; pushing large blocks together to make a big train. One child says, "Let's push the big train over there," two or three others say "OK," and they proceed to help in the push. One child drags a long board across the room, another child picks up the other end to help carry it; one child holds out a jar of paint for another to use; one child holds a bowl or container while another scoops it full of water; and one child pushes another child in a carriage, in a wagon, or on a truck. Other examples include cleaning up—one child squirts soap for another child or holds the water tap on for another child to use—and building together—one child brings or hands a block to another child, two children place or straighten a block together, or one child steadies the structure for another child (not just independent parallel building on the same structure). A final type of cooperative behavior is peer teaching—one child shows another child how to make a toy barn out of construction paper, "You take it like this and cut around like this" (verbalizing and showing); one child says he is having trouble with a puzzle and another child says, "Here, I'll help you," and proceeds to help him with it.

Cooperative behaviors within games may be specific to that game but still fall within the overall definition of cooperative social interaction previously outlined. For example, in Log Roll (Laughing Logs) the act of rolling together as a unit to move a person across the logs is a cooperative act; whereas, for other games, it may be passing a beach ball, linking arms, making a letter together, tapping a balloon to a partner, helping others fit on a chair, leading a friend through an obstacle course, helping build a tower, freeing friends, carrying a teammate, balancing with a partner, moving a big potato sack together, and so on.

Once observers are familiar with cooperative behavior definitions, it is possible to obtain highly reliable behavioral observations from different observers during classroom free time periods, free play periods in the gym, physical education classes, and newly introduced cooperative games. Regardless of the observation method used, within one or two sessions we have consistently attained over 90% agreement between different observers.

In our cooperative game observations, we focused on obvious, overt, gross levels of behavior. We have only recently begun to attempt to categorize the degree or quality of a particular act. In the work presented herein, if something was defined as a cooperative act, it was recorded as such regardless of the circumstances surrounding the event. It is recognized, however, that differences in degree and quality do exist in such things as cooperation, fun, and

[2]Researchers interested in more on the measurement of behavior are referred to Hall (1974 a,b).

involvement. For example, passing a soccer ball because two opposing players are converging on you is of a different quality than passing off to a teammate, when both have a clear shot at the net. It is also recognized that some behaviors that have a cooperative intent do not necessarily look like cooperative acts. Consequently, some modifications of our behavioral definitions may be warranted where a more highly refined assessment of cooperation is deemed necessary.

Any behavior can be assessed and recorded if it is clearly defined in observable terms. For example, we have tried to get measures of involvement in various games. Involvement indicates *active* participation in pursuit of the ends of the game. This is represented behaviorally in different ways for different games. For example, in Fish Gobbler, if the participants are either running, diving to the floor, linking together with others, or raising their arms and cheering, they are actively involved in the game. One method we have used to assess active involvement is to do a 10-sec scan, if possible early in the game, toward the midpoint of the game, and toward the end of the game. At the beginning of the session, we generally note the number of players in the gym and then, during the scan, count the number of children not actively involved in the game. If for the duration of the scan, all children are running or rolling or bumping or doing whatever the demands of the game may dictate, there is total involvement. According to our definition of involvement, children sitting or standing motionless, waiting for turns, or attending to something unrelated to the game are not actively involved in the game.

Fun is another concept we have tried to observe in games. It was defined as follows: (a) verbal representation—laughter, shouting, cheering, squeals of glee; (b) facial representation—expressions of joy (e.g., beaming smiles, open mouths, wide open eyes); and (c) gestures representing fun in conjunction with the preceding—stomping feet, clapping hands, jumping up and down, slapping one another on the back or arm. It's fun to observe fun.

In many respects, observing games is easier then observing free play in the classroom or gym. One distinct observational advantage of games is that the structure of the game remains relatively stable, as does the frequency of cooperative behavior emitted. To the contrary, the structure and focus of free play activities (particularly in the kindergarten classroom) is continuously changing. One of the main problems that occurs in observing games is that many games do not last long. Sometimes one must get an assessment of cooperation in a game within a few minutes, whereas free play periods can last much longer.

One method we found successful in observing games is to randomly select one person and count the number of cooperative acts that person engages in over a 30-sec period. A second person is then randomly selected and observed for 30 sec. This continues until the game is concluded. The information can then be analyzed to obtain an estimate of average number of cooperative acts engaged in for a particular game or per minute within a particular game. In instances where cooperation is continuous (e.g., Log Roll), the amount of time cooperating in a 30-sec period can be recorded in place of the number of cooperative acts. Another method we have used in games is to do a series of 30-sec scans across the playing area. Following each scan, the observer notes the number of cooperative acts observed and the number of people engaged in cooperative behavior.

People sometimes have experiences or feelings that are not reflected in their overt behavior. Therefore, it is often advisable to get self-report measures in addition to measures of observable behavior.

Assessments of Liking

In our cooperative game analysis, once we know a game can elicit cooperative behavior, it is extremely important to determine whether children like the game and whether they feel happy when playing it. Using "smiley faces" is a quick and comprehensible means of getting some assessment of whether participants of any age like a game. It also gives an assessment of how people feel while playing the particular game. Immediately after the game, the players indicate their feelings by simply marking one of the five faces, which range from very happy to very sad.

The faces are weighted by assigning the value 5 to the happiest face, 4 to the next happiest face, and so on, with 1 being assigned to the saddest face. This procedure provides for calculation of an average level of liking for different games, different ages, and different sexes and can also aid in assessing whether liking increases with repeated exposures. For kindergarten children, we used three faces (happy, in-between, sad) rather than five; and with some retarded groups we used two faces (happy or sad) to ensure comprehension.

A variation of the smiley faces format is the skimetric scale approach wherein players mark how they feel along an 8-cm line between a happy face and a sad face (Orlick, Partington, Scott, & Glassford, 1975). The placing of their mark on the continuum is then measured, giving a score ranging from 0 to 8. We have also used questionnaires and interviews to get more detailed assessments regarding how children feel about playing cooperative games (Orlick, 1977).

Kindergarten Study

The primary purpose of the present study was to determine whether, as a result of a cooperative games program, young children would choose to engage in more cooperative behavior in the kindergarten classroom.

Before beginning the study, our observational procedures were refined and a series of cooperative games were field tested to assess their elicitation of cooperation and overall liking by kindergarten children.

Method

Participants Four intact kindergarten classes from an elementary school in the Carleton School System participated in this study. The school drew primarily from middle-class families living on the outskirts of Ottawa, Ontario. The children attended half-day school sessions (morning and afternoon only). One morning class served as an experimental (cooperative games) group (N = 24), and the other morning class served as a control (traditional games) group (N = 25). Similarly, one of the two afternoon classes served as an experimental group (N = 19) and the other as a control (N = 19). The co-op games group had a total combined sample of 43 (24 boys, 19 girls), and the traditional games group had a total of 44 (20 boys, 24 girls). One teacher had her morning class exposed to cooperative games and her afternoon class exposed to traditional games. Both these classes were held in the same room and were observed during free time in the same room with the same basic options of play materials and activity centers to choose from. In the other kindergarten classroom, one teacher taught the morning class and another teacher taught the afternoon class. The experimental and control children were observed in the same room with the same basic options of play materials and activity centers to choose from.

Baseline measures Two weeks before the introduction of the games program, observers began collecting baseline observation data on cooperative social interaction during free-time periods for experimental and control groups. During the free-time periods, the children participated in self-chosen activities for a period of 30 min in the kindergarten classroom. Preliminary baseline observations were taken on four occasions for each of the four groups of children. These baseline measures were taken early in January 1976, shortly after school resumed following Christmas vacation.

Introduction of games program To control for the possibility that children perform better or appear happier if they are being treated in a special way, all children (experimental and control) were told they were in a special games program. The games programs were introduced to the experimental and control groups by a qualified games teacher from outside the elementary school for an average of two 30–40 min game periods per group, per week, for 8 weeks. The experimental groups engaged in cooperative activities only; whereas, control groups engaged in a combination of traditional competitive games and individual movements activities found in most primary physical education texts. After 8 weeks, the games programs were conducted by the kindergarten teachers for an average of four 30-min game periods per group, per week, for 10 additional weeks.

Postprogram measures After the children had been exposed to 18 weeks of either cooperative or traditional games, poststudy observational data on cooperative social interaction were collected. As with baseline data, these measures were taken during 30-min free time periods in the kindergarten classroom. Observations were taken on four occasions for each of the four groups. These procedures began during the last few days in May and continued into early June 1976.

Observation procedures Observers were completely familiar with the behavioral categories and were trained in the reliable use of the rating schedule before baseline measures were taken. Preliminary observations were made on location to enable the raters to adjust to the idiosyncrasies of the children and the situations. During these prebaseline observations, one or two observers and the principal investigator observed the same child for a selected time period, rated his or her behavior, and then discussed results. Training continued until independent interobserver reliability exceeded 90% agreement. This rarely took more than one or two observation sessions. The percentage of agreement was used as an index of reliability (i.e., number of agreements divided by number of agreements plus disagreements). An agreement was a rating of the same behavior (i.e., cooperative interaction or no cooperative interaction) for the same child, in the same observation interval.

After the behavior categories had been learned, practiced, and discussed, uncertainty regarding coding rarely existed. If an observer was really uncertain about whether a particular behavior was cooperative social interaction, it was coded N (no interaction). It was emphasized that approaching cooperative behavior does not meet the criteria of the behavior itself. In addition, if during an observation interval the child was involved with the teacher or had been told to engage in a specified behavior by an adult, a missed trial (MT) was recorded. Later in that same observation session, an attempt was made to make up the missed trial by again focusing on this particular child.

During recording sessions, observers were instructed to get close enough to the child to hear and see what the child was doing or saying. This posed no reactivity problem, because the kindergarten children were accustomed to having different parent volunteers moving about the room. By the time baseline measures began, the children generally ignored the observers.

All observers participating in this study were *blind observers*; they did not know whether the children they were observing were in an experimental or control group, or the details of the specific treatment condition.

Individual observations (10-sec intervals) During observation sessions, approximately 20 children were engaged in free-time activities in a kindergarten classroom. For observational purposes, one child was singled out and watched for a 10-sec interval and either I (for cooperative interaction) or N (for no cooperative interaction) was recorded next to the child's name on a recording sheet. If any cooperative social interaction occurred within the specified 10-sec time period, an I was recorded next to the child's name. If no cooperation occurred, an N was recorded. If the child cooperated during the 10-sec interval, an I was recorded even though he or she may also have engaged in noncooperative behavior during the same time period. After observing the first child, the observer focused on the second child on the list for a 10-sec period, and then continued until all children had been observed once. This cyclical procedure was repeated until the observation period expired (approximately 30 min).

It was necessary for a primary observer to be able to recognize all children in the study before recording baseline measures. To facilitate this process, Polaroid photographs of each child were studied by the primary observer. Preliminary observations were then conducted on location, and finally a miniature photo album was constructed for each class. Initially these photo albums were carried by the primary observer during recording sessions. A primary observer gathered all data and was periodically joined by a secondary observer for reliability checks. In this case the two observers simultaneously gathered data, but were situated so as not to see the other's data sheet. Each observer had a clipboard and a rating sheet. The primary observer had a stop watch and cued the second observer as to who to observe and when to begin and terminate the recording period. During this study, reliability checks were taken on 15 occasions and averaged slightly above 97% agreement. The range of interobserver agreement extended from 92% to 100%.

Group observations (continuous scans) After posttest measures had been taken via the cyclical 10-sec individual observation interval method, a second set of two blind observers, previously trained and checked for reliability, observed each of the experimental and control groups on three occasions. Their observations were conducted during 30–40-min unstructured free-time periods in the kindergarten classroom. The observers used a continuous observation procedure in which one observer continuously scanned each half of the kindergarten classroom in a slow and methodical manner for any incidents of cooperative behavior. If a cooperative act was observed, the specific act, along with the number of children who cooperated in the act, was recorded. For example, if six children helped lift a bench, then "Lifting bench—6 children" was noted.

Results

Individual observations (10-sec intervals) Baseline measures taken before beginning the games program indicated that the children in experimental and control groups were essentially the same with respect to the percentage of cooperative behavior observed during free activity time in the kindergarten classroom. The percentage of individual 10-sec observation intervals in which children were observed engaging in cooperative behavior during baseline procedures was 10.5% for the combined co-op games group and 10.2% for the combined control groups. After 18 weeks of treatment, the combined co-op games groups had increased their percentage of observable cooperative behavior from 10.5% to 15.5%. This is a direct increase of 5%, representing a 48% proportional increase over the percentage of observable cooperative behavior from 10.2% at the baseline to 11.3% in the posttest. This is a direct increase of 1.1%, which represents an 11% proportional increase over baseline.

Group observations (continuous scans) Continuous observation scans in the kindergarten classroom revealed that after 18 weeks of treatment, the co-op games groups engaged in an average of 43 observable incidents of individuals cooperating per hour; whereas, control groups engaged in an average of 29 observable incidents per hour. Combined co-op games groups averaged 71 incidences of children cooperating over 100 min of observation. Combined control groups averaged 48.5 incidences of children cooperating over 100 min of observation. In short, there were 46% more incidences of children engaging in cooperative behavior observed in the co-op games classes when compared with the traditional games classes. It is clear that on different days, with different blind observers, using different observation techniques, the same trend emerged.

Teachers' informal observations It is worth noting some of the qualitative comments made by the kindergarten teachers toward the end of the 18-week games program.

Sample Comments—Co-op Games Group

Several time kids say they lost something. Every time now, someone else offers to help that one find the missing article, voluntarily. Does this old heart good!

Lloyd spilled a whole jar of purple paint on the floor. Before I got there, there were four kids with sponges, etc., to help him. Amazing!

The most cooperation visible is at clean up time. It constantly amazes me how the majority (all but three or four) team up and help each other. *There is now no discrimination as to whether the mess is theirs or made by someone else.*

These children have learned so well to work in a group that sometimes a job that could be done by one person quickly turns into a 5-minute group effort.

By the end of the co-op games program, peer group sanction for cooperative and helpful behavior seemed to have taken firm hold in co-op games groups. Children who did not help were often encouraged to do so or were told about it in clear terms by their peers and in some cases were not allowed to join in at a play center unless they agreed to help and do their share (see Orlick, 1977).

Although in this particular study we did no systematic pre- and postmeasures in the gym, the teachers' comments indicated that differences between groups were quite evident within this environment, even after 8 weeks of games. This is exemplified by the following comment:

> Today was interesting, it was our first day in the gym since Phase I of the games program finished. I had all the equipment out in five separate centers: (1) large climbing apparatus, (2) hoops, (3) bean bags, (4) tunnel, and (5) balls. They were just there for use as each child saw fit, no instructions. Each group of four or five children was at a center for 4 or 5 minutes and then on to another. This afternoon (Co-op II) the children reacted quite differently from the morning (Control II). They experimented with the bean bags carrying them head to head, etc. The hoop group connected themselves and made a long wiggly creature, and over at the ropes on the climbing equipment, children were taking turns helping another child get up and then pushing him and taking turns. There is noticeably more cooperative play in the afternoon class (Co-op II).

The perceived difference in cooperative orientation between groups was simply stated in a meeting with the kindergarten teachers towards the end of the school year. "Now my kids think of everyone being involved" (Co-op I); "Mine don't do that at all" (Control I); "There's a definite difference in my classes....If there are not enough chairs (in Co-op II), the children will share"; "If there are not enough chairs (in Control II), they'll fight." At this point the teacher who had one class exposed to each of the conditions summed up the feeling of the group: "If you're really interested in better citizens, you can't have a control group." So it came to be in this school the following year—all co-op games, no control group.

Discussion

This introductory study indicates that the incidence of cooperative behavior in the kindergarten classroom can be increased through the implementation of a cooperative games program. Perhaps we can explore some possible reasons for this preliminary finding. Cooperative games provide a series of cooperative experience sessions or practice sessions under a variety of circumstances. The children's cooperative efforts generally result in some form of success or reinforcement, whether the task is moving a mountain (a large wooden structure) or becoming part of a giant caterpillar that crawls over the mountain. When children are expected to cooperate to accomplish a task and are subsequently reinforced for this cooperation, through such things as goal attainment, control over environment, feelings of acceptance, expressions of affection, positive social feedback, satisfaction with self, others, and environment, then we might legitimately expect to find increases in cooperative behavior, at least within similar environments. The diversity of cooperative demands and cooperative responses called for in the co-op games program (including cognitive involvement), along with the varied success experiences, may have increased children's overall repertoire of cooperation behavior that could be drawn on in different settings as well. The possibility that some generalization or internalization of the overall value of cooperation occurred merits consideration. Yet, this must be weighed against possible contingency transfers. The fact that there was an increase in cooperative behavior during unstructured free time in the kindergarten classroom may indicate that there was some transfer in contingencies of reinforcement, once children had been thoroughly seasoned within a cooperation contingent environment. For example, once logical consequences within the games environment had helped children learn to reinforce one another for cooperative behavior, then future expectations and resultant consequences from peers could have set in motion, and maintained, contingencies for new codes of acceptable behavior. Thus, peers would have become both models and mediators of a new response paradigm.

It is also possible that during Phase II of the study (latter 10 weeks), the teachers either transferred reinforcement contingencies from the gym to the classroom or that the children expected them to do so. Consequently, if a child was praised by his teacher for sharing or helping move equipment in the gym, it is conceivable that he would expect a similar kind of reaction or reinforcement from his teacher (or from others) for similar kinds of behaviors elsewhere. This expectation itself could serve to initiate a behavior whether or not the expected reinforcement became a reality. Once the behavior has been emitted, any form of positive consequences may serve to maintain it. Such expectations could be operational, even where the same classroom teacher has an experimental and control group in the gym. Finally, it is possible that the transition from cooperative games in the gym to cooperation in the kindergarten classroom is not as dramatic as it may initially appear, because a great deal of play occurs in both settings, particularly during free-time periods.

It is interesting to note that 8 weeks into the program, when some preliminary behavior observations were taken via 10-sec observation intervals, the co-op games groups did not emerge as more cooperative during free time in the classroom. The classroom teachers, however, had begun to report qualitative changes and cited critical incidents of increased cooperative behavior among the co-op games children. A few examples are listed below.

> A group of eight!! children cleaning the paint center. They had organized themselves into groups—wet wipers and dry wipers and completed the task. Never have seen this before.
>
> Fran comments of the "good games." She hasn't hit anyone for one week now. This was a daily occurrence.

No one has tattled on any of her behaviors for eight school days.

Playing in the sand box. Bobby says to Marc—"Don't grab all the toys, we've got to share." They worked out the problem verbally!! Bobby has never been the verbal type—a good punch has generally been his solution.

When we have story time the children sit in a much smaller group (closer together). There appears to me much less, if any, complaining now about someone bothering another.

The fact that our outside blind observers did not find evidence of these "changes" prompts contemplation of several interesting possibilities:

1. The changes cited by the teachers may have been more of a reflection of their expectations and selective perception of reality than of reality itself.

2. The changes the teachers were observing may not have been strong enough or consistent enough to be picked up by outside observers during individual 10-sec observation intervals.

3. The sensitivity of outside behavior assessors and the behavioral assessments (e.g., the definitions of cooperation and the methods of observation) may not have been refined enough to pick up changes that were in fact occurring.

4. The observation period for outside observers may not have been of a long enough duration to get an adequate sampling of reality.

At that point in time, based on T. D. Orlick's own biased observations and close consultation with the kindergarten teachers who were with the children all day, every day, it was believed that cooperative changes were occurring in the co-op games groups that were not occurring in the control groups. As a result of behavioral scans by Orlick, many borderline cases of cooperative behavior were noted in the co-op games group that were not accepted as meeting the co-op criteria, due to previous instructions to observers (i.e., "if you are uncertain or it is borderline, score it as negative"). These borderline cases were consequently scored the same as clearly noncooperative acts observed in traditional games groups. It appears that the co-op games groups were "pulled over" to this cooperative borderline during Phase II (latter 10 weeks) of the study. It should be noted, however, that during this phase of the study, the teachers, who were now familiar with the games, took over the direction of the games for their own classes; and the games time per week was doubled for the following 10 weeks.

Suggestions for Future Studies

The previous discussion indicates the importance of giving a cooperative games program (or any program aimed at behavior change) enough time to work. It also shows the importance of exploring observational options that provide for a more accurate sampling of reality. The following discussion is addressed to some of these options.

Observational options When following the individual 10-sec interval observation procedure, the more frequently the observer can go through the list of participants, the closer to reality the picture is likely to be for a particular person and for the group. Nevertheless, observers are likely to underestimate the incidence of a low-frequency behavior, such as cooperation in the classroom. An observer may see several cooperative acts occurring, but records only the one engaged in by the particular child under observation for the isolated 10-sec period. It is also sometimes difficult to assess the intent of an act, because an observer may come in and leave in the middle of an activity. In addition, the observer must be able to quickly identify all participants to use this method efficiently, which should be considered by researchers contemplating its use.

By using continuous observation procedures, observers are less likely to underestimate the incidence of low-frequency behaviors like cooperation in the classroom, particularly if different observers are responsible for different sections of the room. A distinct advantage of this method is that observers record any and all cooperative acts seen. In addition, for continuous observation, the ability to identify each child would be necessary only if data were wanted on individuals as well as groups. Consequently, if one opts to do group observations only, it is much less time consuming to train observers. One problem encountered with this method is that an observer would sometimes like to use more time to understand one scene, and yet to do so may require ignoring other scenes.

With additional observation time per child, with more observers using a continuous observation method, or with a permanent visual recording of children's behavior, we would likely have a better picture of reality. In effect, this would allow us to more dramatically demonstrate differences that do in fact exist and to better explore the contingencies associated with competitive and cooperative behavioral responses. How might we operationalize these possibilities?

We could attempt to set up several videotape recorders in different parts of the room and later play them back, focusing on one child at a time. Unfortunately this is not a practical option in the real world (the community schools) within which we work. Even if the cost were not prohibitive, problems such as setting up unobtrusive cameras in different classrooms and in different schools and securing clearance from administrators to do so would be prohibitive. This may be a valid option for campus schools designed for research.

We could attempt to increase the number of observers in the kindergarten classroom. For example, we might have one observer responsible for each play center. However, although the children are accustomed to having outside adults (in the form of parent volunteers) in their kindergarten rooms, more than two or three outside observers tends to become overwhelming.

We could try to restrict a few children at a time to a particular play area (e.g., sand box, blocks center) for observational purposes. This might be a legitimate option—it ensures that the same number of children always have exactly the same play material for the observation time. However, it may restrict natural free play and the element of choice and may pose some confounding motivational problems. The child may simply not want to be there and may in fact decide not to stay, which alters the play setting considerably.

Another observational option that should be given serious consideration is to select a representative number of children from each group (e.g., 5 boys and 5 girls from each classroom) and to use all available observation time to focus only on these children. Potential participants could be equated by sex and then randomly selected, or could be equated by preliminary observations. Each child selected for observation purposes could be continuously observed on an individual basis for a more substantial period of time, as was the case in the present study. For example, one might devote a minimum of 5–10 min per child on five occasions for baseline and for postprogram observations. This would increase accuracy with respect to the frequency of cooperative behaviors engaged in by each child before and after the program. Because each child would have a pre- and postprogram frequency score, this procedure would also better lend itself to appropriate statistical analysis. It is also likely that the quality of cooperative acts could be more easily detected by this individual-focused procedure.

In an attempt to account for some of the qualitative differences that may better reflect cooperative impact, we are now attempting to distinguish helping behavior as a qualitative subcategory of cooperative behavior. To meet the criterion for acceptance as a helping behavior, the act must have a helping orientation or helping quality. A person must be helping (or trying to help) another achieve a goal, or people must be helping (or trying to help) one another achieve a common goal. The intent of the act as well as the act itself is considered. Behavioral events, such as taking turns, holding hands, and linking arms, certainly meet our criteria for cooperation; but they do not necessarily meet the criterion for helping behavior. Only behaviors clearly aimed at helping another are accepted as meeting this criterion. Behaviors either that do not have a helping component or that clearly show lack of helpful intent do not meet the criterion. For example, if one child hands another child an unwanted toy strictly as a diversion so he can keep the desired toy himself, it does not meet the criterion of helpful behavior. By keeping in the forefront, we have been able to attain over 90% agreement between different observers who were assessing kindergarten children's "helping behavior." It is therefore feasible for observers to assess the overall incidence of cooperative behavior, as defined earlier, and to note next to each incident whether the cooperative act had a helping component.

Other methods and measures In addition to considering some of the previously mentioned observational options, the following points might be considered for future studies. Pre- and postprogram measures could be taken during free-play and clean-up time in the gym, on the playground, when getting ready (dressing) for recess, during recess, when moving to and from other rooms, as well as during free time and tidy-up time in the classroom. In this case, the play centers, equipment, and playmates available should be the same for all children for pre- and postmeasures. Some standardized situations could also be set up during pre- and postprogram observations to provide common occasions "to help or not to help." For example, one could spill a container of paint at the painting center; provide enough chairs, enough balls, or enough cookies for only half the children in the class; and then simply see how the children respond. One could also provide two children with a single toy or allow one child the option to have a toy removed from another child by the experimenter. We could also draw on some standardized experimental table games, such as those devised by Madsen and his colleagues (e.g., marble pull games, cooperation board), to assess children's capacity and willingness to respond in a cooperative manner (Kagan & Madsen, 1971; Nelson & Kagan, 1972). Pre- and postprogram measures could be taken via these procedures and instruments.

It would also be interesting to focus on teacher behavior to assess changes in reinforcement contingencies before, during, and after the program; to assess parents' and siblings' perceptions of children's possible cooperative changes in the home; to do observations in an environment other than the school, such as the home or community playground; to interview children to assess their feelings about the overall value of cooperation or sharing; and to ask them about how they might solve some hypothetical problems.

Some other extremely important but untapped areas of potential impact with respect to cooperative games are their effect on: (a) self-esteem, self-acceptance or liking of self, both in and out of games; (b) liking for each other during the games, general liking for classmates outside the games, and overall liking for other people; and (c) overall liking for games and physical activity as well as the extent to which participation occurs in the future. Pre- and postprogram measures along with follow-up measures could be taken in each area.

Concluding Comments

The concept underlying the cooperative kindergames designed for use in this study can easily be replicated, adapted, or expanded for use in other settings. Consequently, whether one is interested in facilitating cooperative social interaction in games, in classrooms, in work, or in politics, or whether one is interested in researching potential effects of specific programs, the co-op games approach can be of value. Co-op games have the potential to serve as a facilitative tool for normal children, as a preventative tool for potential problems, and as a treatment tool for "problem" children. The games and, perhaps more important, the concept behind the games can be adapted for different ages and populations. We are currently working on a co-op games program for preschoolers (ages 3 and 4) and are experiencing some initial success with our field testing. These youngsters are capable of cooperating surprisingly well. Many of their games can be played in the classroom, in the gym, in the community, or even in the home. It might be worthwhile to have preschoolers or kindergarten children take home a few co-op games to teach to their families. We could also consider directing some of our attention to the other end of the age continuum. Clearly, to increase the overall potential for cooperative learning and living, specific strategies can be employed with different groups and in a variety of behavior settings (Orlick, 1977).

References

Hall, R. V. *Managing behavior 1: Behavior modification: The measurement of behavior.* Lawrence, Kan.: H. & H. Enterprises, 1974. (a)

Hall, R. V. *Managing behavior 3: Behavior modification: Applications in school and home.* Lawrence, Kan.: H. & H. Enterprises, 1974. (b)

Kagan, S., & Madsen, M. C. Cooperation and competition of Mexican, Mexican-American and Anglo-American children of two ages under four instructional sets. *Developmental Psychology,* 1971, *5,* 32–39.

Nelson, L. L., & Kagan, S. Competition and the star-spangled scramble. *Psychology Today,* 1972, *6,* 53–56, 91.

Orlick, T. D. The sports environment: A capacity to enhance—a capacity to destroy. In B. S. Rushall (Ed.), *The status of psychomotor learning and sport psychology research.* Dartmouth, Nova Scotia: Sport Science Associates, 1975.

Orlick, T. D. Games of acceptance and psycho-social adjustment. In T. T. Craig (Ed.), *The humanistic and mental health aspects of sports, exercise and recreation.* Chicago: American Medical Association, 1976.

Orlick, T. *Winning through cooperation—Competitive insanity: Cooperative alternatives.* Washington, D.C.: Hawkins & Associates, 1977.

Orlick, T. *The cooperative sports and games book.* New York: Pantheon, in press.

Orlick, T. D., Partington, J. T., Scott, H. A., & Glassford, R. G. The development of the skimetric differential: A childranistic approach. In C. Bard, M. Fleury, & J. Salmela (Eds.), *Mouvement 7.* Quebec: Association des Professionels de Activite Physique de Quebec, 1975.

14 Behavioral Research and Intervention in Youth Sports

RONALD E. SMITH AND FRANK L. SMOLL
University of Washington

In the late 1970s, the expanding sociocultural institution of youth sport constituted a largely unexplored terrain for sport psychologists. This state of affairs dramatically changed toward the end of the 1980s as a result of Smith and Smoll's work on the Coaching Behavior Assessment System (CBAS), later to be extended into the positive approach to coaching.

The major thrust of the collaboration between Smith and Smoll was discovering information on how specific styles of coaching affect children's responses to their athletic experiences. The information was used in developing an intervention program for training coaches. This program was aimed at creating a positive psychosocial environment with a strong reference to the major learning principles associated with the application of positive reinforcement to enhance young athletes' mental well-being and sport outcomes. The researchers specified several links among coaching behaviors and young athletes' perceptions of these behaviors and their evaluative reactions to the coaching behaviors. Furthermore, situational as well as individual differences were identified in coaches and athletes; these factors were found to be influential on the behaviors, perceptions, and evaluative reactions of young athletes.

In this article, Smith and Smoll's model is presented, including its close relations to the CBAS as well as to the results of some relevant research. This article is important because it also addresses another example of these researchers' influential sport-related research—the project that was intended to explore the role of psychosocial factors in adolescents' athletic injuries. As in their coaching research, Smith and Smoll proceeded in a two-stage sequence in which theory and basic research served as a basis for intervention. They proposed an integrated model showing the variables and processes thought to function as mediators of the links between life stress and athletic injuries, and they suggested two foci of potential interventions intended to promote more effective coping behaviors among adolescent athletes.

Not only did these two models and the resulting research and interventions demonstrate how sport environments can be used as a natural laboratory for continually testing and refining hypotheses related to young people's behavior in sport, but they also showed how children and adolescent athletes can benefit from such studies in sport psychology.

The sport environment is an inviting but largely untapped naturalistic laboratory for behavioral research and intervention. We discuss some of the advantages that this environment offers psychological researchers, then illustrate the manner in which basic and applied behavioral research can be carried out in the area of youth sports. Two programs of research and intervention are described. The first involved the use of behavioral assessment to study the effects of coaching behaviors on child athletes and to develop and evaluate a cognitive-behavioral coach training program. The second research program studied the interactive effects of life stress, social support, and cognitive-behavioral coping skills on injury vulnerability in adolescent athletes. Implications of the findings for behavioral intervention programs designed to reduce injury vulnerability are discussed.

In the United States alone, more than 20 million children between the ages of 6 and 18 years participate in nonscholastic sport programs such as Little League Baseball, Pop Warner football, and other community-based programs (Martens, 1986). Millions more participate in interscholastic programs. Sport scientists as well as popular writers have noted that the sport environment provides socialization opportunities and places adaptive demands on participants that parallel those of other important life settings (Martens, 1978; Michener, 1976; Smoll & Smith, 1988). For this reason, organized athletic experiences are regarded as potentially important in child and adolescent development, and participation is believed to have direct relevance to the development of important behaviors such as cooperation, unselfishness, attitudes toward achievement, stress management skills, perseverance, risk-taking, and the abilities to tolerate frustration and delay gratification.

Aside from its significance as a setting in which important developmental processes occur, the sport environment offers a number of significant advantages as a naturalistic laboratory for behavioral research. First, there are few psychological processes that are not relevant to the realm of sport and that cannot be studied there. Learning and performance, motivational, cognitive, and social processes,

---

Adapted, by permission, from R.E. Smith and F.L. Smoll, 1991, "Behavioral research and intervention in youth sports," *Behavior Therapy* 22: 329-344.

stress and coping, adjustment problems, and many other classes of psychological phenomena all occur in the sport environment and can be studied in that setting. Second, the athletic environment is a social system that is relatively circumscribed and largely public. This increases the feasibility of studying meaningful behaviors as they naturally occur by using direct observational techniques, a factor that should enhance the external validity of findings. Finally, sport is a fertile ground for the study of behavioral and cognitive-behavioral intervention programs. Because many athletes are highly committed to their sport and highly motivated to perform well, they typically invest themselves in programs that are designed to enhance performance. This factor can result in a more powerful test of the efficacy of an intervention program than might occur with less motivated subject populations. Moreover, when performance is the outcome measure, overt behavioral measures of unquestioned ecological validity are available to the researcher.

To illustrate some of the ways in which cognitive-behavioral research and intervention can be carried out in sport settings, we summarize two research programs that address significant issues in youth sports. The first involves the study of how specific coaching behaviors affect child athletes and the use of this information as an empirical basis for the development of a cognitive-behavioral training program designed to help coaches create a more positive sport environment for young athletes. The second program evaluates the role of psychosocial factors, including life stress, social support, and psychological coping skills, in adolescent sport injuries and describes the potential application of cognitive-behavioral interventions to reduce injury vulnerability.

Analysis and Modification of Coaching Behaviors

Theoretical model and research paradigm. It goes without saying that adult leaders occupy a critical role in youth sports. The manner in which coaches structure the athletic situation, the goal priorities they establish, the attitudes and values they transmit, and the behaviors they engage in can markedly influence the effects of sport participation on children. The influence of coaches can extend into other areas of the child's life as well, particularly in this era of single-parent families.

Given the social importance of this leadership situation, it is somewhat surprising that only recently have psychologists begun to study coaching behaviors, factors affecting them, and the impact they have on young athletes. Moreover, from a scientific viewpoint, studying leadership behaviors in this context has several attractive features. First, coaches are clearly in a leadership position. Although that position may differ in some as yet undetermined respects from other leadership situations, such as in the military or in business, the commonalities in role demands placed upon these various leaders are probably more notable than are the differences. Second, the sport milieu is sufficiently circumscribed to enable identification of relevant situational variables, and the coach-athlete relationship is typically confined to this setting. Third, coaches engage in a wide range of leadership behaviors that can be observed and measured. Finally, the situation is one that evokes high levels of psychological involvement in both coaches and youngsters (Feltz, 1978; Gould, 1984; Martens & Gould, 1979; Scanlan, 1988). Consequently, the likelihood of identifying meaningful relations between leadership behaviors and athletes' reactions is enhanced.

Our multimethod approach to assessing coach-athlete interactions includes (a) observer codings of overt behaviors, (b) measures of player perception and recall of those same coaching behaviors, and (c) measurement of players' evaluative reactions. It is assumed that the effects of coaching behaviors are mediated by the meaning that players attribute to them. Furthermore, a complex of cognitive and affective processes are involved at this mediational level. These processes are likely to be affected not only by the coach's behaviors, but also by other factors, such as the child's age, normative beliefs and expectations, and by certain personality variables.

In recognition of this, the basic three-element model comprised of overt coaching behaviors, athlete perceptions, and athletes' evaluative reactions has been elaborated to delineate the characteristics and processes that influence adult leadership behaviors and that mediate their effects on children (Smoll & Smith, 1989).

In accordance with the model, we have sought to determine how observed coaching behaviors, athletes' perception and recall of the coach's behaviors, and player attitudes are interrelated. We have also explored the manner in which player and coach individual difference variables might serve as moderator variables and influence the basic behavior-attitude relations.

Behavioral Assessment of Coaches

Several research groups have used behavioral assessment techniques to study the leadership behaviors of youth coaches and the effects of coaching behaviors on young athletes (e.g., Allison & Ayllon, 1980; Buzas & Ayllon, 1981; Komaki & Barnett, 1977; Koop & Martin, 1983; Rushall & Smith, 1979; Shapiro & Shapiro, 1985). To measure leadership behaviors, we developed the Coaching Behavior Assessment System (CBAS) to permit the direct observation and coding of coaches' actions during practices and games (Smith, Smoll, & Hunt, 1977).

The CBAS contains 12 categories divided into two major classes of behaviors. *Reactive* behaviors are responses to immediately preceding athlete or team behaviors, while *spontaneous* behaviors are initiated by the coach and are not a response to a discernible preceding event. Reactive behaviors are responses to either desirable performances, mistakes, or misbehaviors on the part of athletes, while the spontaneous class is subdivided into game-related and game-irrelevant behaviors initiated by the coach. The system thus involves basic interactions between the situation and the coach's behavior. Use of the CBAS in observing and coding coaching behaviors in a variety of sports indicates that the scoring system is sufficiently comprehensive to incorporate the vast majority of overt leader behaviors, that high interrater reliability can be obtained, and that individual differences in behavioral patterns can be discerned (Chaumeton & Duda, 1988; Cruz et al., 1987; Horn. 1984, 1985; Rejeski, Darracott, & Hutslar, 1979; Smith, Zane, Smoll, & Coppel, 1983; Wandzilak, Ansorge, & Potter, 1988).

Coaching Behaviors and Their Effects on Children

Following development of the CBAS, a field study was conducted to establish relations between coaching behaviors and children's reactions to their athletic experience (Smith, Smoll, & Curtis, 1978). Fifty-one male Little League Baseball coaches were observed by trained coders during more than 200 complete games. More than 57,000 individual coaching behaviors were coded into the 12 categories, and a behavioral profile based on an average of 1,100 behaviors was computed for each coach.

Several self-report measures were developed to assess coaches' beliefs, attitudes, and perceptions. These were combined into a questionnaire that the coaches completed at the end of the season. Coaches' self-perception of their behaviors was of primary importance. This was assessed by describing and giving examples of the 12 CBAS behaviors and asking coaches to indicate on a 7-point scale how often they engaged in the behaviors in the situations described.

Postseason data from 542 players were collected during individual interviews and questionnaire administrations carried out in the children's homes. Included were measures of their recall and perception of the coach's behaviors (on the same scales as the coaches had rated their own behavior), their liking for the coach and their teammates, the degree of enjoyment they experienced during the season, and their self-esteem.

Factor analyses of the CBAS data revealed independent behavior dimensions of supportiveness (comprised of Reinforcement and Mistake-Contingent Encouragement), instructiveness (General Technical Instruction and Mistake-Contingent Technical Instruction *versus* General Communication and General Encouragement), and punitiveness (Punishment and Punitive Technical Instruction *versus* organizational behaviors). The first two dimensions correspond closely to the classic leadership styles of relationship orientation and task orientation emphasized in leadership theories such as Fiedler's (1967) Contingency Model, Situational Leadership (Hersey & Blanchard, 1977), and the Vertical Dyad Linkage (VDL) model of Graen and Schiemann (1978) and identified in other research on leadership behavior (e.g., Stogdill, 1959).

Relations between coaches' scores on these behavioral dimensions and player measures indicated that players responded most favorably to coaches who engaged in higher proportions of supportive and instructional behaviors. Players on teams whose coaches created a supportive environment also liked their teammates more. A somewhat surprising finding was that the team's won-lost record was essentially unrelated to how well the players liked the coach and how strongly they wanted to play for the coach in the future. On the other hand, players on winning teams felt that their parents liked the coach more and that the coach liked them more than did players on losing teams. Apparently, winning made little difference to the children, but they knew that it was important to the adults. It is worth noting, however, that winning assumed greater importance beyond age 12, although it continued to be a less important attitudinal determinant than coach behaviors.

Another important issue concerns the degree of accuracy with which coaches perceive their own behaviors. Correlations between CBAS observed behaviors and coaches' ratings of how frequently they performed, the behaviors were generally low and nonsignificant. The only significant correlation occurred for Punishment. In contrast, children's ratings on the same perceived behavior scales correlated much more highly with CBAS measures. It thus appears that coaches have limited awareness of how they behave, and that athletes are more accurate perceivers of actual coach behaviors.

Finally, analysis of the children's attraction responses toward the coaches revealed a significant interaction between coach supportiveness (the tendency of the coach to reinforce desirable performance and effort to respond to mistakes with encouragement rather than punitiveness) and athletes' level of self-esteem (Smith & Smoll, 1990). The low self-esteem children were especially responsive to variations in supportiveness. This finding extends a body of results derived from laboratory studies to a naturalistic setting. These studies suggest that self-enhancement motivation causes people who are low in self-esteem to be especially responsive to variations in supportiveness because of their greater need for positive feedback from others (Dittes, 1959; Shrauger, 1975; Swann, Griffin, Predmore, & Gaines, 1987; Tesser & Campbell, 1983).

Coaching Effectiveness Training

In the second phase of the research, the results from the observational study formed the basis for a cognitive-behavioral intervention program designed to train coaches to provide a more positive and socially supportive athletic environment for their young athletes (Smith, Smoll, & Curtis, 1979). Little League Baseball coaches were randomly assigned to an experimental (training) or to a no-treatment control group. During the preseason intervention program, behavioral guidelines derived from the initial research were presented and modeled by the trainers. In addition to the information-modeling portion of the program, behavioral feedback and self-monitoring procedures were employed in an attempt to increase the coaches' self-awareness of their behaviors and to encourage them to comply with the behavioral guidelines. Behavioral feedback took the form of profiles based on 400-500 behaviors coded during early-season games, and self-monitoring of key target behaviors was carried out by coaches after each of 10 games during the season.

To assess the effects of the experimental program, CBAS data were collected throughout the season and behavioral profiles were generated for each coach. Outcome measures were obtained from the children after the season in individual data-collection sessions in their homes. On both behavioral and player perception measures, the trained coaches differed from the controls in a manner consistent with the coaching guidelines. The trained coaches gave more reinforcement in response to good performance and effort, and they responded to mistakes with more encouragement and technical instruction and with fewer punitive responses. These behavioral differences were, in turn, reflected in their players' attitudes. Although the average won-lost percentages of the two groups of coaches did not differ, the trained coaches were better liked and were rated as better teachers. Additionally, players on their teams liked one another more and enjoyed their sport experience more. In a word, they had more fun. These results are thought to reflect the more socially supportive environment created by the trained coaches. Perhaps most encouraging was the fact that children who played for the trained coaches exhibited a significant increase in general self-esteem as compared with scores obtained a year earlier, while those who played for the untrained coaches showed no significant change.

The results of the program evaluation indicate that cognitive-behavioral methods can be employed to train coaches to relate more effectively to young athletes and that psychological intervention can have a positive impact on a social system that is an important part of the lives of many children. However, a number of important research questions remain. For example, dismantling studies are needed to assess the relative contributions of the various components of the training program, which included didactic instruction, modeling and role playing of desired behaviors, training in self-monitoring of coaching behaviors, and behavioral feedback. Such research could help to establish the necessary and sufficient components of an effective program and could facilitate the development of improved training programs. Likewise, such research can address basic issues of behavior change in a nonclinical population in the same manner that more traditional behavior therapy research does with clinical populations.

We now turn to a second example of sport-related research, this one addressing the role of psychosocial factors in athletic injuries in adolescents. In this project, as in the coaching research, we are proceeding in a two-stage sequence in which the results of basic research serve as the basis for intervention.

Sport Injuries: Psychosocial Factors and Behavioral Interventions

Beginning in the adolescent years, injuries occur with high frequency in athletics. Epidemiological studies indicate that more than 3.5 million athletic injuries occur each year in the United States alone, with injury rates over a season approaching 50-70% in some collision sports like football (Garrick & Requa, 1978; Kraus & Conroy, 1984). While many of the causal factors in athletic injuries are undoubtedly physical or biomechanical in nature, there is mounting evidence that psychosocial factors may also contribute to injury risk. Among the factors that may be involved are stressful life events (Bramwell, Masuda, Wagner, & Holmes, 1975), personality variables such as anxiety, locus of control, self-esteem, and sensation seeking (Bergandi, 1985), and deficits in psychosocial assets such as psychological coping skills and social support (Andersen & Williams, 1988; Smith, Smoll, & Ptacek, 1990; Williams, Tonymon, & Wadsworth, 1986).

Of the psychosocial factors studied to date, life change has received the greatest amount of empirical attention. Bramwell, Masuda, Wagner, and Holmes (1975) modified the Social Readjustment Rating Scale (Holmes & Rahe, 1967) and added items relevant to the athletic environment (e.g., "Problems with the coach," "Significant athletic accomplishments"). Using life change units derived from both positive and negative life changes as the predictor variable in a prospective study of college football players, Bramwell et al. found injury rates of 30%, 50%, and 73%, respectively, in athletes who reported low, moderate, and high levels of life change over the previous year. Using the same life change measure, Cryan and Alles (1983) reported similarly impressive differences in injury rates between groups of football players who differed in life change units. In contrast, recent prospective studies of life change and athletic injuries using improved life event measures that distinguish between positive and negative events have yielded weak and inconsistent results (Passer & Seese, 1983; Williams, Tonymon, & Wadsworth, 1986).

The inconsistent pattern of results obtained in studies of life events and athletic injuries suggests the possibility that, as in the case of other medical and psychological outcomes, certain moderator variables may influence the relation between life events and injury vulnerability. Based on prevailing theories of stress and coping (e.g., Garmezy, 1981; Lazarus & Folkman, 1984) and on research results (e.g., Rosenbaum & Ben-Ari, 1985; Sarason, Sarason, Potter, & Antoni, 1985), we predicted that psychosocial assets such as social support and coping skills would influence the extent to which athletes are affected by stressful life events. In particular, we were interested in the possibility that these two classes of psychosocial assets might operate in combination with one another. Elsewhere, we have suggested that the term *conjunctive* moderation be used to describe instances in which more than one moderator variable must be combined in a particular fashion in order to produce an optimal moderator effect (Smith, Smoll, & Ptacek, 1990). In the present instance, evidence that coping skills and social support operate in a conjunctive manner requires that some combination of these variables (most logically, low levels of both) result in a notable increment in the amount of injury variance accounted for by life event scores over that accounted for when either moderator is considered alone. This approach thus involves searching for interactions among moderator variables themselves in terms of how they affect relations between life stress and injuries.

To study the potential role of life events and other psychosocial variables on athletic injuries, we conducted a prospective study that involved 41 athletic teams in 13 high schools (Smith, Smoll, & Ptacek, 1990). The subjects were 451 male and female high school athletes participating in boys' and girls' varsity basketball, boys' wrestling, and girls' gymnastics. The sports were selected to provide a range of individual, team, contact, and noncontact sports, as well as to expand the life stress-injury data base beyond the sport of football.

Within a prospective research design, the athletes completed a series of questionnaires prior to the beginning of the sport season. Recent positive and negative life events were assessed by means of a modified version of the Adolescent Perceived Events Scale (Compas, Davis, Forsythe, & Wagner, 1987). The subjects also completed a measure of the amount and quality of social support available to them from 20 different individuals, such as parents, coach, teachers, best friend, and from groups, such as their teammates and clubs or religious groups to which they belonged. Self-perceived adequacy of coping skills was assessed by means of the Athletic Coping Skills Inventory (Smith, Smoll, & Ptacek, 1990). This scale consists of 42 behavioral self-report items designed to measure a range of cognitive and behavioral coping skills within a sport context. These include the ability to control arousal and to concentrate and think clearly under stress, the tendency to set specific goals and engage in problem solving strategies, and the ability to relate effectively to authority figures and to profit from corrective feedback.

To provide a measure of injury independent of the subject's retrospective self-report, the coaches of the 41 teams served as paid research assistants for the project and were trained in an injury recording system. Each day during the sport season, coaches indicated on a report form any athletes who were unable to participate fully in practices or competitive events. They also recorded the reason for nonparticipation (injury, illness, or absence for some other reason). Several times each week, the coaches were contacted by phone, and their data were transmitted for later analysis. The total number of days of nonparticipation because of injury over the course of the season served as the injury measure.

Correlations between the various classes of preseason life events and the injury time loss measure yielded no significant relations. Indeed, none of the correlations of positive and negative life events with injury exceeded .10. In a series of moderator variable analyses, we then assessed the role of differences in social support and coping skills, both singly and in combination with one another, on the relations between the life event scores and subsequent injury. Although social support and coping skills were themselves unrelated to injuries, they combined to exert a strong effect on the relation between major negative events and injuries.

High and low groups on each of the moderator variables were formed by selecting subjects from the upper and lower thirds of the distributions. Because social support and coping skills scores were basically uncorrelated ($r = .17$), it was also possible to isolate groups of subjects who fell in the upper or lower thirds on each of the two distributions.

Social support considered alone did not exert a significant moderator effect. Coping skills fared somewhat better; the correlation between negative life events and subsequent injury was significant for athletes who reported low levels of coping skills ($r = .23$, $p < .05$); whereas, no relation existed for subjects who fell within the upper third of the coping skills distribution. However, even in the low coping skills group, life stress accounted for only 5% of the injury time loss variance. The most noteworthy result occurred when possible conjunctive moderator effects of social support *and* coping skills were assessed. Athletes low in both psychosocial assets exhibited the strongest correlation ($r = .47$, $p < .001$) between major negative life events and subsequent injuries. A notable increment in systematic variance occurred, with 22% of the injury variance being accounted for by the life event variable within this low social support/low coping skills group. No other combination of social support and coping skills yielded a statistically significant stress/injury correlation. When we tested this conjunctive moderator effect within groups that were even more extreme in psychosocial assets (subjects in the upper and lower quartiles of the social support *and* coping skills distributions), the correlation between negative events and injuries increased to .55 in the low/low group, accounting for more than 30% of the injury variance. For the other three combinations of social support and coping skills, none of the correlations approached significance.

Our results suggest that only athletes who are low in both classes of psychosocial assets are vulnerable to the impact of negative life events. The 22–30% of injury variance accounted for within this group far exceeds the 1–5% typically accounted for by life events measures in other prospective studies involving objective well-being measures (Rabkin & Streuning, 1976; Schroeder & Costa, 1984). The result is all the more striking in that injuries appear less likely to be influenced by psychological stress than do many illnesses that are not dependent upon the physical/biomechanical factors that undoubtedly play a central role in athletic injuries.

The mechanism whereby stressful events might increase vulnerability to injury is unknown, but two hypotheses have been advanced. One hypothesis is that stress disrupts attentional processes and concentration, resulting in poorer vigilance to cues signaling physical danger (Andersen & Williams, 1988). A second hypothesis is that stress produces physiological arousal that increases general muscular tension and reduces motor coordination and fluidity of movement, thereby increasing risk of injuries (Nideffer, 1983). In relation to these proposed mechanisms, it is worth noting that our coping skills measure contains items that assess the ability to concentrate and avoid distracting thoughts, as well as the ability to control arousal through relaxation and self-instructions. Athletes who lack these psychological skills could be more vulnerable to cognitive and/or physiological mechanisms that increase injury risk. Low levels of perceived social support could serve to increase the threat value of negative life events and of their actual or anticipated consequences, thereby increasing both preoccupation and arousal. Whatever the mechanism involved in the life event-injury relation, our results suggest that only events appraised as major negative ones increased the injury vulnerability of athletes low in these psychosocial assets.

Cognitive-Behavioral Interventions

The data from our prospective study suggest that a certain subgroup of athletes, namely, those low in both social support and psychological coping skills, may be at increased risk for injury if they have experienced recent major stressors. However, our data also showed that if athletes were high in either perceived social support or psychological coping skills, the relation between stress and injury disappeared. Thus, where resiliency (rather than vulnerability) is concerned, we are dealing not with a conjunctive effect of social support and coping skills, but rather with a disjunctive one. That is, an adequate level of *either* of these variables appears to render the athlete resilient to the impact of stressors. The intervention implications of this finding are fairly clear: resiliency should be increased through either an increase in social support, an increase in coping skills, or an increase in both protective factors.

Social support may be viewed as an environmental variable, but its impact on the person typically occurs as part of the process of cognitive appraisal, where its "psychological reality" resides. Coping skills include cognitive, physiological, and behavioral responses that either facilitate meeting the demands introduced by a stressor (problem-focused coping) or help one to control or reduce negative emotional responses evoked by a stressor (emotion-focused coping) (Lazarus & Folkman, 1984).

Social support enhancement within the athletic environment can be brought about in a number of ways. For example, we have already shown that the socially supportive behaviors of athletic coaches can be increased significantly through a relatively brief training program involving didactic presentation and modeling of behavioral guidelines for increasing supportive behaviors and the use of self-monitoring to increase coaches' awareness of how they are behaving. Indeed, we have come to view our coach training program as fundamentally a social support enhancement program. Another promising means of enhancing social support might involve the use of "team building" procedures such as those described by Nideffer (1981), which are designed to increase mutual support among team members. Training coaches to be more supportive and enhancing team cohesion in team sports may serve to increase the amount of social support available to the athlete and thereby enhance resiliency in athletes who fall in the low-support/low coping skills group.

A second approach to injury prevention is to enhance the psychological coping skills of the athletes. A number of cognitive-behavioral programs have already been developed to teach athletes stress-management coping skills such as relaxation, cognitive problem solving, goal-setting, and meditation skills (e.g., Smith, 1980, 1989; Suinn, 1986). The cognitive-affective stress management training program we are using involves training in relaxation to enhance physiological coping with arousal and the use of cognitive restructuring and self-instructional training to enhance cognitive coping skills. These skills are combined into an "integrated coping response" and rehearsed under conditions of induced affect (Smith & Ascough, 1985; Smith & Nye, 1989). Aside from their potential usefulness in increasing resiliency to stress and reducing risk of injury following exposure to stressful life events, the kinds of skills taught in such programs may be expected to generalize across a variety of life situations. Such skills, therefore, have the potential for enhancing performance and adjustment within sport, and helping sport to fulfill its stated goal of helping prepare the child or adolescent athlete to deal more effectively with life demands.

The two research programs we have summarized in this article represent attempts to apply behavioral research and intervention procedures to issues involving child and adolescent athletes. Many other aspects of the athletic environment invite the attention of behavioral and cognitive-behavioral researchers. Already, significant contributions have been made by behavioral researchers in improving athletic performance (e.g., Allison & Ayllon, 1980; Komaki & Barnett, 1977) and in enhancing moral judgment in child athletes using behavioral methods (Bredemeier, Weiss, Shields, & Shewchuk, 1986). More behavioral research and intervention within the naturalistic laboratory of youth sports are needed in the coming years.

References

Allison, M. G., & Ayllon, T. (1980). Behavioral coaching in the development of skills in football, gymnastics, and tennis. *Journal of Applied Behavior Analysis, 13,* 297–314.

Andersen, M. B., & Williams, J. M. (1988). A model of stress and athletic injury. *Journal of Sport and Exercise Psychology, 10,* 294–306.

Bergandi, T. A. (1985). Psychological variables relating to the incidence of athletic injury: A review of the literature. *International Journal of Sport Psychology, 16,* 141–149.

Bramwell, S. T., Masuda, M., Wagner, N. N., & Holmes, T. H. (1975). Psychological factors in athletic injuries: Development and application of the Social and Athletic Readjustment Rating Scale (SARRS). *Journal of Human Stress, 1,* 6–20.

Bredemeier, B. J., Weiss, M. R., Shields, D., & Shewchuk, R. M. (1986). Promoting moral growth in a summer sport camp: The implementation of theoretically grounded instructional strategies. *Journal of Moral Education, 15,* 212–220.

Buzas, H. P., & Ayllon, T. (1981). Differential reinforcement in coaching tennis skills. *Behavior Modification, 5,* 372–385.

Chaumeton, N. R., & Duda, J. L. (1988). Is it how you play the game or whether you win or lose?: The effect of competitive level and situation on coaching behaviors. *Journal of Sport Behavior, 11,* 157–173.

Compas, B. E., Davis, G. E., Forsythe, C. J., & Wagner, B. (1987). Assessment of major and daily stressful events during adolescence: The Adolescent Perceived Events Scale. *Journal of Consulting and Clinical Psychology, 55,* 534–541.

Cruz, J., Bou, A., Fernandez, J. M., Martin, M., Monras, J., Monfort, N., & Ruiz, A. (1987). Avaluacio conductual de les interaccions entre entrenadors i jugadors de basquet escolar. *Apunts Medicina de L'esport, 24,* 89–98.

Cryan, P. D., & Alles, W. F. (1983). The relationship between stress and college football injuries. *Journal of Sports Medicine, 23,* 52–58.

Feltz, D. (1978). Athletics in the status system of female adolescents. *Review of Sport and Leisure, 3,* 98–108.

Fiedler, F. E. (1967). *A theory of leadership effectiveness.* New York: McGraw-Hill.

Garmezy, N. (1981). Children under stress: Perspectives on antecedents and correlates of vulnerability and resistance to psychopathology. In A. I. Rabin, J. Aronoff, A. M. Barclay, & R. A. Zucker (Eds.), *Further explorations in personality* (pp. 196–269). New York: Wiley.

Garrick, J. G., & Requa, R. K. (1978). Injuries in high school sports. *Pediatrics, 61,* 465–473.

Gould, D. (1984). Psychosocial development and children's sports. In J. R. Thomas (Ed.), *Motor development during preschool and elementary years* (pp. 212–235). Minneapolis, MN: Burgess.

Graen, G., & Schiemann, W. (1978). Leader-member agreement: A vertical dyad linkage approach. *Journal of Applied Psychology, 63,* 206–212.

Hersey, P., & Blanchard, K. H. (1977). *Management of organizational behavior.* Englewood Cliffs, NJ: Prentice-Hall.

Holmes, T. H., & Rahe, R. H. (1967). The Social Readjustment Rating Scale. *Journal of Psychosomatic Research, 11,* 213–218.

Horn, T. S. (1984). Expectancy effects in the interscholastic athletic setting: Methodological considerations. *Journal of Sport Psychology, 6,* 60–76.

Komaki, J., & Barnett, F. T. (1977). A behavioral approach to coaching football: Improving the play execution of the offensive backfield on a youth football team. *Journal of Applied Behavior Analysis, 10,* 657–664.

Koop, S., & Martin, G. (1983). Evaluation of a coaching strategy to reduce swimming stroke errors with beginning age-group swimmers. *Journal of Applied Behavior Analysis, 16,* 447–465.

Kraus, J. F., & Conroy, C. (1984). Mortality and morbidity from injuries in sports and recreation. *Annual Review of Public Health, 5,* 163–192.

Lazarus, R. S., & Folkman, S. (1984). *Stress, appraisal, and coping.* New York: Springer.

Martens, R. (1978). *Joy and sadness in children's sports.* Champaign, IL: Human Kinetics.

Martens, R. (1986). Youth sport in the USA. In M. R. Weiss, & D. Gould (Eds.), *Sport for children and youths* (pp. 27–33). Champaign, IL: Human Kinetics.

Martens, R., & Gould, D. (1979). Why do adults volunteer to coach children's sports? In G. C. Roberts, & K. M. Newell (Eds.), *Psychology of Motor Behavior and Sport-1978* (pp. 79–89). Champaign, IL: Human Kinetics.

Michener, J. A. (1976). *Sports in America.* New York: Random House.

Nideffer, R. M. (1981). *The ethics and practice of applied sport psychology.* Ithaca, NY: Mouvement Publications.

Nideffer, R. M. (1983). The injured athlete: Psychological factors in treatment. *Orthopedic Clinics of North America, 14,* 373–385.

Passer, M. W., & Seese, M. D. (1983). Life stress and athletic injury: Examination of positive versus negative events and three moderator variables. *Journal of Human Stress, 9,* 11–16.

Rabkin, J. G., & Streuning, E. L. (1976). Life events, stress, and illness. *Science, 194,* 1013–1020.

Rejeski, W., Darracott, C., & Hutslar, S. (1979). Pygmalion in youth sport: A field study. *Journal of Sport Psychology, 1,* 311–319.

Rosenbaum, M., & Ben-Ari, K. (1985). Learned helplessness and learned resourcefulness: Effect of noncontingent success and failure on individuals differing in self-control skills. *Journal of Personality and Social Psychology, 48,* 198–215.

Rushall, B. S., & Smith, K. C. (1979). The modification of the quality and quantity of behavior categories in a swimming coach. *Journal of Sport Psychology, 1,* 138–150.

Sarason, I. G., Sarason, B. R., Potter, E. H., & Antoni, M. H. (1985). Life events, social support, and illness. *Psychosomatic Medicine, 47,* 156–163.

Scanlan, T. K. (1988). Social evaluation and the competition process: A developmental perspective. In F. L. Smoll, R. A. Magill, & M. J. Ash (Eds.), *Children in sport* (3rd ed., pp. 135–148). Champaign, IL: Human Kinetics.

Schroeder, D. H., & Costa, P. H. (1984). Influence of life event stress on physical illness: substantive effects or methodological flaws? *Journal of Personality and Social Psychology, 46,* 853–863.

Shapiro, E., & Shapiro, S. (1985). Behavioral coaching in the development of skills in track. *Behavior Modification, 5,* 211–224.

Shrauger, J. S. (1975). Responses to evaluation as a function of initial self-perceptions. *Psychological Bulletin, 82,* 581–596.

Smith, R. E. (1980). Development of an integrated coping response through cognitive-affective stress management training. In I. G. Sarason, & C. D. Spielberger (Eds.), *Stress and anxiety* (Vol. 7, pp. 265–280). New York: Hemisphere.

Smith, R. E. (1989). Athletic stress and burnout: Intervention strategies. In D. Hackfort, & C. D. Spielberger (Eds.), *Anxiety in sports: An international perspective* (pp. 217–234). New York: Hemisphere.

Smith, R. E., & Ascough, J. C. (1985). Induced affect in stress management training. In S. Burchfield (Ed.), *Stress: Psychological and physiological interactions* (pp. 359–378). New York: Hemisphere.

Smith, R. E., & Nye, S. L. (1989). Comparison of induced affect and covert rehearsal in the acquisition of stress management coping skills. *Journal of Counseling Psychology, 36,* 17–23.

Smith, R. E., & Smoll, F. L. (1990). Self-esteem and children's reactions to youth sport coaching behaviors: A field test of self-enhancement processes. *Developmental Psychology, 26,* 987–993.

Smith, R. E., Smoll, F. L., & Curtis, B. (1978). Coaching behaviors in Little League Baseball. In F. L. Smoll, & R. E. Smith (Eds.), *Psychological perspectives in youth sports* (pp. 173–201). Washington, DC: Hemisphere.

Smith, R. E., Smoll, F. L., & Curtis, B. (1979). Coach effectiveness training: A cognitive-behavioral approach to enhancing relationship skills in youth sport coaches. *Journal of Sport Psychology, 1,* 59–75.

Smith, R. E., Smoll, F. L., & Ptacek, J. T. (1990). Conjunctive moderator variables in vulnerability and resiliency research: Life stress, social support and coping skills, and adolescent sport injuries. *Journal of Personality and Social Psychology, 58,* 360–370.

Smith, R. E., Zane, N. W. S., Smoll, F. L., & Coppel, D. B. (1983). Behavioral assessment in youth sports: Coaching behaviors and children's attitudes. *Medicine and Science in Sports and Exercise, 15,* 208–214.

Smoll, F. L., & Smith, R. E. (1988). Reducing stress in youth sports: Theory and application. In F. L. Smoll, R. A. Magill, & M. J. Ash (Eds.), *Children in sport* (3rd ed., pp. 229–249). Champaign, IL: Human Kinetics.

Smoll, F. L., & Smith, R. E. (1989). Leadership behaviors in sport: A theoretical model and research paradigm. *Journal of Applied Social Psychology, 19,* 1522–1551.

Stogdill, R. M. (1959). *Individual behavior and group achievement.* New York: Oxford University Press.

Suinn, R. M. (1986). *Seven steps to peak performance: The mental training manual for athletes.* Toronto: Hans Huber.

Swann, W. B., Jr., Griffin, J. J., Predmore, S. C., & Gaines, B. (1987). The cognitive-affective crossfire: When self-consistency confronts self-enhancement. *Journal of Personality and Social Psychology, 52,* 881–889.

Tesser, A., & Campbell, J. (1983). Self-definition and self-evaluation maintenance. In J. Suls, & A. G. Greenwald (Eds.), *Psychological perspectives on the self* (Vol. 2, pp. 1–31). Hillsdale, NJ: Erlbaum.

Wandzilak, T., Ansorge, C. J., & Potter, G. (1988). Comparison between selected practice and game behaviors of youth soccer coaches. *Journal of Sport Behavior, 11,* 78–88.

Williams, J. M., Tonymon, P., & Wadsworth, W. A. (1986). Relation of stress to injury in intercollegiate volleyball. *Journal of Human Stress, 12,* 38–43.

15 Factors Influencing the Occurrence of Flow State in Elite Athletes

SUSAN A. JACKSON
University of Queensland, Australia

In the mid-1970s, Mihaly Csikszentmihalyi presented an innovative approach to enhancing people's intrinsic motivation. Whereas other investigators who studied intrinsic motivation attempted to discover the factors that undermine intrinsic motivation, Csikszentmihalyi examined what makes a particular task intrinsically motivating. Csikszentmihalyi's work on optimal experience focused on the concept of flow, which developed from Maslow's humanistic psychology, in particular his pioneering approach to self-actualization and peak experience.

Flow is an extremely positive psychological state. It occurs when an individual perceives a balance between the challenges associated with a particular situation and his or her capabilities to meet them or to accomplish the demands embedded in that situation. When such a perceived balance is above the person's average balance between skills and challenge, a state of flow is said to be experienced by that person. At that point, the person feels "totally involved," or "on automatic pilot."

When proposing his concept, Csikszentmihalyi investigated several activities that are intensively conducted but usually for little or no external reward (e.g., amateur athletics, rock climbing, or music and dance). Based on this research, he described several flow characteristics or dimensions, such as a balance between challenge and skill, merging of awareness and action, clear goals and feedback, complete concentration on and absorption in the task performed, sense of control, loss of self-consciousness, transformation of time, and an intrinsically rewarding (autotelic) experience. In addition, the identification of antecedent and preventive flow factors and their perceived controllability by the performing person was of utmost importance.

In sport, flow research has been advocated by Susan Jackson, who investigated flow experiences in athletes from a variety of sports. In her research she found the flow characteristics among athletes when they were "hot," "on a roll," "in a groove," or "in the zone"—in other words, when experiencing the holistic sensation characterized by Csikszentmihalyi as flow. Jackson devoted much research effort to the question of how elite athletes achieve flow. In this seminal article, she moved beyond the sheer description of athletic states of flow into the study of factors that affect the probability of occurrence of such states. Using qualitative research methods with elite athletes, Jackson identified a list of significant factors that facilitate, prevent, or disrupt the state of flow. In addition, she thoroughly examined the perceived controllability of flow among athletes and concluded that athletes may have more self-control over experiencing flow than is usually believed. The findings of this study were influential not only in terms of theory (i.e., promoting scientific understanding of flow in sport) but also in terms of application (i.e., enabling athletes and exercisers to enhance the probability of their experiencing flow states during sport participation).

Understanding factors which may influence the occurrence of flow in elite athletes was the goal of the present investigation. Twenty-eight elite level athletes from seven sports were interviewed about the factors they perceived influenced their experience of flow state. Inductive content analyses of athletes' responses to questions about what facilitates, prevents, and disrupts flow, resulted in 10 dimensions that synthesized the 361 themes suggested by the athletes. These themes and dimensions provided insight into factors that may influence whether or not flow occurs in elite athletes. For example, some of the more salient factors influencing whether or not flow occurred included: preparation, both physical and mental; confidence; focus; how the performance felt and progressed; and optimal motivation and arousal level. This study also involved asking elite athletes about the perceived controllability of these factors, and of the state of flow itself. The majority of the athletes interviewed perceived the flow state to be controllable, or potentially within their control. A large percentage of the factors seen to facilitate or prevent flow were perceived as controllable; however, factors seen as disrupting flow were largely seen as uncontrollable.

Flow is a state of optimal experiencing (Csikszentmihalyi, 1990) involving total absorption in a task, and creating a state of consciousness where optimal levels of functioning often occur. Due to the link between flow state and peak performance (Jackson, 1992, 1993; Jackson & Roberts, 1992; Privette & Bundrick, 1991), understanding the factors that may make it more or less likely that flow will occur during an athletic performance is of great interest to the athlete, coach, and sport psychologist. Further, knowing whether these factors are perceived by athletes as being within their control or not, is important information for those involved in helping athletes to prepare for optimal performance. This article describes the findings associated with elite athletes' identification of antecedent and preventive flow factors, and their beliefs about the controllability of such factors.

The Conditions of Flow

How, when, or where do flow experiences occur? Do they just spontaneously happen, or is there a set of circumstances that predispose one to experience flow? Csikszentmihalyi (1990) argues that there are a set of conditions making flow more likely to occur, although he does concur that there is an element of spontaneity in flow occurrences:

> While such events may happen spontaneously, it is much more likely that flow will result either from a structured activity, or from an individual's ability to make flow occur, or both. (Csikszentmihalyi, 1990, p. 71)

Thus, according to Csikszentmihalyi (1990), there are particular activities that are more likely to produce flow, and personal traits that help people achieve flow more easily. Flow-producing activities facilitate concentration and involvement by making the activity as different from everyday reality as possible. Csikszentmihalyi (1990) illustrates this point with a unique perspective on the function of sport. He discusses how in sport competitions participants:

> . . . dress up in eye-catching uniforms and enter special enclaves that set them apart temporarily from ordinary mortals. For the duration of the event, players and spectators cease to act in terms of common sense, and concentrate instead on the peculiar reality of the game. (p.72)

Csikszentmihalyi (1990) describes how every flow activity he studied had the ability to:

> . . . provide a sense of discovery, a creative feeling of transporting the person into a new reality. It pushed the person to higher levels of performance, and led to undreamed-of states of consciousness. (p.74)

It is interesting to note that this quotation implies a link with both what has been termed peak performance and peak experience. A flow activity can achieve such a positive state in a person by virtue of it providing opportunities for action that a person can act upon without becoming bored or anxious. If the demands of an activity are greater than one's skills, anxiety is the result. If, however, skills are greater than the challenges of the situation, boredom results. There is an optimal balance between skills and challenges in a flow activity. A critical qualification of this state of balance is that flow is not dependent on the objective nature of the challenges present, nor on the objective level of one's skills. Csikszentmihalyi (1975) states that whether one is in flow "depends entirely on one's perception of what the challenges and skills are" (p.50). Thus, whether or not flow occurs may depend on an individual's ability to restructure consciousness so as to make flow possible. Csikszentmihalyi (1990) states: "It is not easy to transform ordinary experience into flow, but almost everyone can improve his or her ability to do so." (p.83) A person, within the same objective situation, might move from being bored, to being anxious, to being in a state of flow, all within a couple of moments. It all depends on one's perception of a situation—what a situation means to a person at a particular time.

A study by Jackson (1992) involving in-depth interviews with elite figure skaters provides some information about specific factors influencing the occurrence of flow in sport. Jackson interviewed the skaters about their understanding of factors either helping or preventing flow during performance. Skaters were also asked to identify the perceived controllability of these factors. The main factors found to facilitate flow were: positive mental attitude, positive precompetitive and competitive affect, maintaining appropriate focus, physical readiness, and partner unity (for pairs and dance skaters). Of these factors, only partner unity was perceived as uncontrollable. Factors perceived to prevent or disrupt flow were: physical problems/mistakes, inability to maintain focus, negative mental attitude, and lack of audience response. The audience response factor was perceived to be uncontrollable.

The qualitative data gained from the figure skaters provided a rich source of information about factors influencing the occurrence of flow. The present study was undertaken to further investigate factors influencing the flow state, with a larger and more diverse sample of athletes. In Jackson's (1992) study, factors preventing and factors disrupting flow were grouped together whereas in the present study they are examined independently, allowing for a more fine-grained analysis of what is happening before and during competition that might either take an athlete out of flow, or prevent flow from occurring in the first place. This study also extends Jackson's earlier study by looking more closely at the perceived controllability of flow among elite performers participating in several different sports.

Method

Participants

The participants in this investigation were 28 elite-level athletes (14 females, 14 males). The mean age of the participants was 26 years, with a range of 18 to 35 years. Fourteen of the athletes were Australian and 14 were from New Zealand. Athletes from seven sports (four athletes/sport) were interviewed, namely track and field, rowing, swimming, cycling, triathlon, rugby, and field hockey.

Seventeen of the athletes competed as an individual participant, while 11 competed as part of a team. All athletes were competing at an elite level in their respective sports, having achieved at least a top 10 placement in international competition. Seven World or Olympic medalists, including three World Champions were included in the sample. There were also ten Commonwealth Games medalists among the participants.

Instruments

Interview guide. An interview guide was developed for the purposes of this investigation based on previous flow research (Csikszentmihalyi, 1975; Csikszentmihalyi & Csikszentmihalyi, 1988; Jackson, 1992; Jackson & Roberts, 1992; Privette, 1983; Privette & Bundrick, 1991). The interview covered aspects of the flow experience that went beyond the purposes of this particular article, and are addressed elsewhere (Jackson, 1993). The interview began with the athlete being asked to describe an experience when he/she was in flow. After discussing their flow experience, the athletes were asked a series of questions about flow. These included what the athlete was most aware of during this experience, and the most distinguishing characteristics of the experience. The interview focus broadened to a more general discussion of flow, after which followed the questions specifically addressed by this article: factors athletes perceived helped or hindered them from getting into flow, and the perceived controllability of flow. In addition, athletes were asked about the disruption of flow, and to identify the type of factors that would disrupt flow during a performance. After discussing the factors they believed influenced flow, athletes were asked about the controllability of these factors. Athletes were also asked whether they perceived the flow state in general to be a controllable or uncontrollable state.

Procedures and Analyses

An interview guide was developed and pilot-tested on four athletes for clarity before the athletes forming the present sample were interviewed. All interviews were conducted face-to-face, lasted on average between one to two hours, and were transcribed verbatim in preparation for data analysis. After the transcripts were completed, each interview was read carefully, and salient themes were noted on the transcripts. These themes were later complied into a set of *raw data themes* (quotes or paraphrased quotes) for each of the questions related to the factors influencing flow.

Inductive Content Analysis. The aim of this inductive analysis process is to synthesize specific ideas expressed by individuals into meaningful themes which link similar ideas into a set of integrated concepts. Guiding the process is a search for patterns of similarity across the raw data themes, to group similar themes together, and to progress from the specific to more general across two or more stages. The process involves comparing and contrasting each theme at a particular level with all other themes, uniting themes with similar meaning and separating themes with different meanings.

To record the raw data themes, and to facilitate the inductive analysis process, 3 by 5 index cards were used. One theme was used per card. Athletes' quotations were used to depict the raw data themes, which formed the first level of analysis of the data. This method ensured that the analyses were based directly on what the athletes said, allowing their meaning to come through the process of analysis. The entire quotation was written on one side of an index card, and a summary statement written on the other side of the card. A reliability check was performed on this first step in the inductive content analysis process by having a person otherwise independent of the investigative process read all cards to ensure that summary statements accurately reflected athletes' quotations. Once the list of raw data themes was compiled, an inductive analysis of the data was undertaken in order to generate *higher-order themes* that linked similar raw data themes together into a higher-order concept. A subsequent further inductive analysis was done to link the higher-order themes into themes of even greater generality. These latter themes were labeled *general dimensions,* and represented a further level of abstraction that enabled a larger number of athletes' ideas to be drawn together.

Trustworthiness Procedures. Trustworthiness (Lincoln & Guba, 1985) or credibility (Patton, 1990) of qualitative analyses can be established or enhanced through the use of rigorous techniques and methods for gathering high-quality data that is carefully analyzed (Patton, 1990). The main methods used to help establish data trustworthiness that are relevant to the aspects of the study discussed in this article included use of the following:

(a) *Thick description,* or providing sufficient detail of the data collection and analysis process to allow others to make judgments of quality of the resulting product.

(b) *A reflexive journal,* which is a diary or record of such aspects of the study as scheduling and associated logistics of data collection, personal comments and insights surrounding the collection and analysis of data, and methodological decisions made during the course of the study. The journal is part of the material made available to the auditor, whose role is discussed next.

(c) The involvement of several people in the research process. A *peer debriefer, external, or reliability checker* of the content analysis results, and an *auditor* were involved at various stages of the investigation (Lincoln and Guba, 1985). Briefly, a peer debriefer helps the researcher to explore biases, clarify interpretations and decisions made, and make explicit aspects of the inquiry that might otherwise remain only implicit within the inquirer's mind. An external checker has a similar role, but it is confined to the thematic analyses of the data. In this study, the external checker independently classified raw data themes into the higher-order themes and general dimensions, and his categorizations were compared to those of the investigator. Finally, the auditor examines all documents, data, and interpretations associated with the study. The auditor in this case read the research proposal, samples of the interview transcripts, the reflexive journal, and the final write-up of the study. A letter of attestation is provided by the auditor concerning the process and product of the inquiry, in particular the acceptability of the interpretations and conclusions.

Results

The purpose of this study was to move beyond description of the flow state in elite athletes to analyzing factors that are associated with such athletes getting into, not getting into, or being taken out of flow. Three questions were asked: (1) What helps you to get into a flow state? (2) What prevents you getting into a flow state? (3) What, if anything, disrupts you once you are in flow?

Factors Facilitating Flow

Ten dimensions were formed to represent the factors that help an athlete to get into flow. There were 131 independent raw data themes extracted from the 28 interviews to answer the question as to what factors help an athlete to get into flow. A reliability checker independently classified the raw data themes into the 33 higher order themes, and the higher order themes into the general dimensions. There was 97% agreement at the raw data theme level, and 100% agreement at the higher order theme level. The four raw data themes classified differently to the investigator were discussed, two were moved, one was re-worded, and the checker agreed with keeping the original placement of the fourth theme.

Each dimension is discussed below in relation to the themes from which it was comprised. Dimensions will be discussed in order of percentage of athletes each represented.

Pre-competitive and Competitive Plans and Preparation. This dimension had the equal largest percentage of athletes citing a theme within it (64%), and included the highest percentage of all raw data themes (18.8%). Six higher order themes made up this dimension: *being by self before compete, follow pre-competitive routine, pre-competitive mental preparation, race plan, knowing clearly what to do,* and *being totally prepared.* Clearly, being prepared for the event, and following the pre-competitive routines that helped one to be mentally ready, were important components to setting the stage for flow to occur. Following specific routines, often including mental preparation, was important, so that the athlete felt ready and had a clear idea of what he or she was going to do in the event. Having a specific race plan was also important for some athletes in some events. For example, a runner spoke of how his race plan freed him from worry about his competitors: "With my race plans now, I've thought about every possible thing that can happen . . . so there's no ifs or buts or whats. You're still a bit worried about what other people are doing if you don't have a plan." Knowing everything was in place allowed the athlete to focus on the task and to switch into a more automatic mode of functioning that seems to be part of the flow process. This idea was expressed by a javelin thrower: "The fact that I've done everything possible on my physical and mental side. Every facet is covered . . . that reassures my conscious mind that I've done everything—then I just have to let myself switch off and let it happen."

Confidence and Positive Attitude. Sixty-four percent of the athletes brought up a theme related to confidence or positive attitude, making it the dimension with the equal highest number of athletes mentioning a theme within it. Representing 11.6% of all raw data themes, the five higher order themes in this dimension were: *confidence, believing you can win, positive thinking, blocking negatives,* and *enjoying what doing.* For some athletes, the confidence was in being able to perform well, for others it was in believing one could win. Several of athletes spoke specifically about the challenge-skill balance deemed so important by Csikszentmihalyi (1990). For example, one athlete said: "I think probably the most important is the feeling that I've got the ability to be in that situation."

Optimal Physical Preparation and Readiness. Fifty-seven percent of the athletes spoke of the importance of being physically ready in order to make flow more likely to occur. Eighteen themes, representing 13% of all the raw data themes, were grouped into four higher order themes: *having done the training, be in great physical shape, hydration and good nutrition,* and *being rested/tapered/peaked.* As well as knowing that one had put in the physical work, a theme running through many of the athletes' comments was that good training led to confidence, the previously discussed dimension. For some athletes, making sure that they were well hydrated, rested, or tapered, was essential to being able to get into a flow state. Obviously, the demands of the sport play a role here. The two athletes who specifically mentioned hydration, for example, were both rowers.

Achieving Optimal Arousal Level Before Compete. Representing 57% of the sample, and involving 13% of all raw data themes, this dimension had two higher order themes, *relaxation,* and *getting self energized before compete.* For the majority of the athletes citing themes within this dimension (64%), being relaxed was key, although four did favor a more energized state.

Motivation to Perform. This dimension represented themes relating to being motivated to achieve, to do well, and having reasons for wanting to do well. These themes made up 12.3% of all the raw data themes, and were mentioned by 54% of the sample. Three higher order themes, representing 20 raw data themes, were titled, *having goals, high motivation,* and *challenging situation.* "You have to know it's a race you've set as a goal", said a triathlete, and his comment illustrates what several of the athletes said: the event is an important one to you, and one for which you have set goals.

Performance Feeling Good. Fifty percent of the athletes talked about their performance feeling good as being an important factor for being able to get into flow. This dimension involved two higher order themes, *start well/feel good from the start,* and *movements feeling good,* and contained 8.7% of all raw data themes. Just what feeling good involved depended on the athlete and the sport, but the underlying idea seemed to be that the athlete was receiving feedback from his or her movements that things were in tune, whether it be technique, rhythm, feeling in control of one's body, or ease of movement.

Focus. Being focused was mentioned specifically by 39% of the athletes, and this dimension represented 5.1% of all raw data themes. There were two higher order themes, *focus,* and *release of conscious control.* One athlete summed up well why this dimension of focus was important: "Concentration totally engrosses you in the game, so I guess to achieve flow state you need to have good powers of concentration." Another athlete talked about keeping everything simple in her mind, which would allow her mind to relax. Thus, coming through the athletes' comments is this idea of interdependence between factors that help one to get into flow.

Optimal Environmental and Situational Conditions. For 39% of the athletes, having optimal environmental and/or situational conditions, was important for getting into flow. These conditions included the higher order themes: *good course/event for self, good environmental conditions, good atmosphere, no outside pressures,* and *positive feedback from coach.* Type of sport probably plays a role in how important the environmental/situational conditions are. For example, two rowers said no wind was very important. For a track runner, length of the event played a role, with it being difficult for him to get into flow in the shorter races. As well as sport type, it seems evident that this was an individual difference factor, since only 10 of the athletes mentioned environmental or situational themes.

Positive Team Play and Interaction. For 25% of the athletes, experiencing positive team play and interaction was important for being able to get into flow. Since there were only 11 team sport athletes in the sample, the percentage of all team sport athletes that this dimension represented was calculated. Sixty-four percent of the team sport athletes thought the team was a significant influence on whether or not they attained flow. Three higher order themes, representing 8.7% of all raw data themes, were titled *positive team interaction, team moving as a unit,* and *team/partner focused.* Ideas represented in this dimension included trust between players, a positive feeling on the team, unison of movements, and focus among interacting teammates.

Experience Factor. Two somewhat unique themes were put into this dimension. One, the idea that you had experienced flow before, so you knew what to expect. The other theme was related to being a mature, or experienced competitor, so that one could deal effectively with situations that might prevent, or disrupt flow from occurring.

Factors Preventing Flow

Nine dimensions were inductively formed to represent the factors that prevent an athlete from getting into flow. There were 104 independent raw data themes extracted from the data to answer the question as to what factors prevent an athlete from getting into flow. A reliability checker independently classified the raw data themes into the 33 higher order themes, and the higher order themes into the nine general dimensions. There was 100% agreement at the raw data theme level, and 97% agreement at the higher order theme level. The one higher order theme classified differently to the investigator was discussed, and subsequently moved to a different dimension, where there seemed to be a better fit between ideas expressed in the theme and the new dimension into which it was placed. Each dimension will be discussed below in relation to the themes from which it was comprised. Dimensions are discussed in order of percentage of athletes each represents.

Non-optimal Physical Preparation and Readiness. Seventy-five percent of the athletes mentioned a theme comprising this dimension, making it the dimension with the greatest percentage of athlete representation. There were five higher order themes derived from the raw data themes, which made up 23.1% of all themes in this analysis. These higher order themes were: *not being physically prepared, not feeling good physically, food/ fluid intake problems, fatigue,* and *injury.* If an athlete knew he or she had not done the necessary training to be in good shape for the event, getting into flow was perceived as less likely to occur. Being fatigued from heavy training was also recognized as a factor preventing flow, and finding a balance between too much and not enough training often presented a challenge.

Non-optimal Environmental and Situational Conditions. This dimension, containing 18.3% of all raw data themes, was relevant to 64% of the athletes. Six higher order themes made up this dimension, and were titled: *non-optimal environmental conditions, unwanted crowd response, uncontrollable event influences, external stresses, emotional stress,* and *influence of opponents.* Non-optimal conditions included wind, extremes of temperature, and if conditions were different to what expected. Unwanted crowd response was too much crowd noise for one athlete, and not enough crowd response for another. Uncontrollable event influences included things such as getting a flat tire, or what the type of course was. Stress from work, or relationships, particularly that which caused emotional upset, stood in the way of flow. Finally, the influence of opponents was seen as a factor preventing flow, through not being knowledgeable about their moves, having them directly block your play, or hinder your ability to perform well in a race.

Lacking Confidence/Negative Attitude. Forty-three percent of the athletes mentioned themes that went into this dimension, and these themes made up 10.6% of all raw data themes. *Lacking confidence, non-optimal mental state, negative thinking,* and *not believing you can reach the flow state* were the four higher order themes making up this dimension. How one was feeling about oneself, and one's abilities impacted whether flow could occur, with self-doubt and negative thinking definitely standing in the way.

Inappropriate Focus. This dimension, representing 14.5% of all raw data themes, involved 36% of the sample's responses. Five higher order themes were titled: *losing focus, thinking too much, being over-concerned with what others were doing, worry about what others think of you,* and *worrying about competitors.* Often, the inappropriate focus was due to "being distracted, losing concentration, losing your focus on where you are at that point", and, as this runner continued, "going more to the outcome as opposed to the segment of your plan-losing focus on the plan." Thinking too much was a problem for other athletes, especially when it led one to being over-analytical, or over-concerned with what others were doing, be it teammates or opponents. This "taking on the responsibility of other people", as a track runner put it, took one's focus away from oneself and one's own performance.

Problems with Precompetitive Preparation. Twenty-nine percent of the athletes referred to problems with their precompetitive preparation as being factors preventing flow. The three higher order themes making up this dimension, which included 8.7% of all raw data themes, were: *poor precompetitive preparation, interruptions to precompetitive preparation,* and *distractions before compete.* Not being prepared for the event would be a big stumbling block, as illustrated by this runner's realization that not having a race plan would stand in the way of flow: "If you stand up on the block and just expect it to happen, and haven't thought about what you want to think about, it won't happen." If one's routine was broken, or there was a distraction of some sort, particularly as the time to compete approached, flow would be less likely to occur.

Lacking Motivation to Perform. This dimension, representing 25% of the athletes' responses, was made up of three higher order themes: *no goals, low motivation,* and *lack of challenge.* These themes made up 7.7% of all the raw data themes. Clearly, for the athletes who mentioned it, not having the motivation or commitment to what one was doing would prevent flow state, as evidenced by these comments: "You've got to have 100% commitment", and "It's really hard to get into that state because you can talk to yourself, but if it's not 100% believed, and thought of, and needed, and desired, then you don't get it." Two athletes commented specifically on the deleterious effect of lack of challenge in the situation.

Non-optimal Arousal Level. This dimension also represented 25% of the athletes' responses, however there were fewer themes, with only 3.9% of all raw data themes being represented. *Feeling too relaxed* was a problem for one athlete, making this an independent higher order theme from the other higher order theme, *not being relaxed.* This latter was recognized as a problem by six athletes.

Negative Team Play and Interaction. Twenty-one percent of athletes saw problems with the team play and/or interactions as being something which could prevent flow. The percent of team sport athletes for which this dimension was relevant was 55%. Four higher order themes, involving 7.7% of all raw data themes, grouped the responses in this dimension. These higher order themes were: *team not performing well, partner not focused, negative team interaction,* and *not feeling part of the team.* The team is obviously only a factor in certain sports, and the extent of it's influence depends again on the sport. A team pursuit cyclist saw that the team pace not being smooth would be a major problem; for one hockey player, it was only the people in close proximity to you that could prevent you getting into flow, if they were not performing and working well together. Negative team interactions included negative talk or negative feelings within the team. And if one did not feel part of the team, or trusted by the team, these factors too would prevent flow.

Performance Going Poorly. Eighteen percent of the athletes talked about the deleterious effects of one's performance going poorly, either through having a *poor start,* the *performance not going well,* or *making unforced errors,* the three higher order themes making up this dimension. Making errors, having poor technique, and even very minor changes to position could prevent flow, as illustrated by this track cyclist's comment: "I mean really small, like you might look at a different place on the track or you might move the handlebars just like that a bit and it'll put you off, or really really little things. Wish my mind wouldn't work that fast."

Factors Disrupting Flow

Six dimensions were formed to represent the factors that disrupt an athlete once in flow. Each is discussed below with the 17 higher order and 62 raw data themes from which they were developed. A reliability check gave 94% agreement at the raw data theme level, and 100% agreement at the higher-order theme level. The one raw data theme classified differently to the investigator was discussed and subsequently moved to the higher-order theme suggested by the checker. Dimensions will be discussed in order of percentage of athletes each represented.

Non-optimal Environmental and Situational Influences. This was the largest dimension, containing 56.5% of all raw data themes, and involving 71% of the athletes. Eight higher order themes grouped the raw data themes and included: *mechanical failure; something really funny occurring in game; inappropriate, negative, or no feedback; negative referring decisions; what opposition doing; performance disrupted by competitors; stoppage in play; amount of time left in event;* and *environmental distractions.* Mechanical failure was relevant for the cyclists and triathletes, and involved some problem with their bike. Something really funny occurring in the game was cited by a rugby player as causing momentary lapse out of flow. Problems with feedback could "wake you up", as a rower put it, commenting on the coach doing strange things in his feedback. Receiving a bad call from a referee was a factor for the rugby and field hockey players. Being outperformed by a competitor was disruptive, as were unanticipated turns in play, "like you might be putting all the pressure on the other team and then suddenly they run 80 yards and score a try", said one rugby player. Having competitors physically disrupt your performance was obviously disruptive of flow, examples being getting tripped up, or boxed in, during a track race. Six of the hockey and rugby players mentioned a stoppage in play, such as for an injury or half-time, as being disruptive of flow. For timed events, such as rowing and running, the amount of time left in the event was relevant, for example, a runner commented that he would come out of flow towards the end of the race, "when you're really aware of what everyone is doing, so you're not just focusing on what you're doing." Finally, environmental distractions, such as unfavorable conditions, or sudden noises, would disrupt flow for some athletes.

Problems with Physical Readiness or Physical State. This dimension, involving 25% of the athletes, contained 12.9% of all raw data themes. *Lack of physical preparation/readiness* was a higher order theme containing just one response, while the other higher order theme, *non-optimal physical state,* made up the majority of themes in this dimension. The ideas expressed within this theme included the disruptive effects on flow of pain, feeling sick or fatigued, or getting injured during the performance.

Problems with Team Performance or Interactions. Twenty-one percent of all athletes, and 55% of all team sport athletes had a theme in this dimension, which included 11.3% of all raw data themes. There was just one higher order theme with the same title as the dimension, since the ideas expressed were all of a similar nature. Negative talk, the team not playing well, if you felt uninvolved in the play, or had the unfortunate experience described by a hockey player of "someone on my team that destroys everything you do, that can be quite frustrating.", could all disrupt flow.

Inappropriate Focus. Mentioned by 18% of the athletes, problems with focus during performance accounted for 9.7% of all raw data themes. The two higher order themes were: *loss of focus* and *worrying about others.* Loss of focus could come about through daydreaming, or letting inappropriate thoughts creep in, such as worrying about competitors, or what others are thinking of you.

Performance Errors/Problems. Fourteen percent of the athletes cited performance errors or problems as disrupting flow, with all responses fitting into one higher order theme with the same title as the dimension. For the four athletes who expressed themes in this dimension, disrupters were such occurrences as a fall from one's bike, or making a major unforced error during a rugby game.

Doubting or Putting Pressure on Self. Two athletes (7%) spoke about the disruptive influence of *self-doubt* or *putting pressure on self,* forming two higher order themes of the same names.

The Perceived Controllability of Flow

An additional purpose of this investigation was to examine the perceived controllability of flow. Athletes were asked whether they perceived flow to be controllable, and were also asked to rate each of the help/prevent/disrupt flow factors they derived relative to their controllability. Seventy-nine percent of the athletes perceived flow to be a controllable state, while 21% said they did not think flow was controllable. Quotations illustrating the different perceptions athletes had relative to the controllability of flow are presented below.

For some athletes, flow was very controllable, perhaps programmable, as indicated by this statement by a rower: "I make it happen. It doesn't happen automatically. I make it happen." The athletes who said flow was controllable tended to take responsibility for whether or not flow occurred. For example, a triathlete said:

> I think you can set it up. You can set the scene for it, maybe with all that preparation. It should be something that you can ask of yourself and get into, I think. Through your training and through your discipline.

Several of the athletes said flow was controllable so long as all the factors they had brought up as helping flow were in place. Thus said a rugby player, "As long as none of the ingredients are missed." And a hockey player, "If all those positive factors are going right then there's nothing going to stop me."

For some athletes who perceived flow as controllable, there were qualifiers to whether flow would actually occur. A runner said she had control of flow by having control over most of the factors that helped her to get there, but "just a few things that just happen to you before a race, probably within the last 18 to 24 hours is just crucial to your performance and sometimes you don't have control over that last 24 hours." For a javelin thrower who extensively discussed the struggle between the conscious and subconscious mind, whether flow would occur depended on which part of her mind won out:

> Yeah, it's controllable but it's the battle between your conscious and subconscious, and you've got to tell your conscious mind to shut up and let the subconscious take over, which it will because it's really powerful.

Flow was not a term all athletes were familiar with, nor was the state one that all athletes had consciously thought about, and the interview process became a self-awareness experience for several of the participants. A hockey player, after discussing the factors that she thought would help her get into flow, said, "Yes, I think it's probably more controllable than I realize . . . perhaps I don't have as much control over it as I could." Another hockey player, who initially had trouble with some of the interview questions, gained in her understanding and confidence about flow during the course of the interview. After initially perceiving flow as an uncontrollable event, this player later said, "I think you can control it. Like up until now, I would have said not controlling it, but you probably can control it. Being aware of it and knowing about it, so you can work towards it."

A rower who perceived flow as only partly controllable had this to say:

> I think you can improve the chance of it happening . . . but it is a little bit of magic, like that's why we say that you can't really describe it, or guarantee it or anything. I think it's definitely a little bit setting the stage if you like for trying to make it happen. I think it's what you're looking for all the time.

One athlete, a rugby player said flow was controllable, but sometimes its occurrence was separate to his input:

> For me it's something you can see is almost totally dependent upon my preparation . . . most of the times I achieved that state this year has been through my own controlling it. But sometimes . . . just the pure action of what happened in the game, I had no influence on. And that's what I mean, sometimes you have control over it, but at certain times you don't need to have any input, you're just there and you're taken along with it.

For six of the athletes, flow was not perceived as controllable. Rather, it was just something which just happened. A rugby player said the best one could do to enhance flow occurring was "set the parameters around when it's most likely to occur, but I think it just happens." A rower who was a member of an eight man crew said flow was not controllable due to the team aspect of what he did:

> It all comes back to the team—everybody, all the guys knitted in together and it just rolls along for 5, 10 minutes, half an hour, going very well, but then someone might lose concentration or go off beat or something and then you'd be out of that situation you were just in, and you can't have any control over that.

Interestingly, when I asked this rower if he was in a single sculls event, whether he would perceive the flow state to be controllable, he agreed that he would see it as such.

To summarize the findings about the perceived controllability of flow, the majority of the athletes did see the flow state as within their control to achieve. Further, from the discussions about the controllability of flow, it was evident that being able to control flow was seen as an important ingredient to an athlete's success. A cyclist summed up this idea well: "I believe it *is,* the flow state is a controllable thing. But someone who can ideally or totally control that, has got a lot of power in the sport."

Perceived Controllability of Factors Related to Whether one Gets Into Flow

To further address the question of the perceived controllability of flow, athletes were asked to identify whether each of the factors they put forward in response to the questions about what helps, prevents, or disrupts, flow were controllable or uncontrollable factors. The total number of themes for each analysis is greater than the total number presented when each analysis was discussed separately. This is because every raw data theme was calculated in the present analysis whereas only independent themes were calculated in the totals for the help/prevent/disrupt analyses. Thus, if two or more athletes said the same theme, it was listed as one theme in these earlier analyses. Because some athletes mentioning the same theme differed in whether they saw the factor as controllable or uncontrollable, the total number of themes listed by all athletes was included in the present analysis.

There was a much higher percentage of factors perceived as controllable than uncontrollable. Overall, 67.9% of the 361 factors found across the three questions were perceived as controllable. For the factors that *help* an athlete to get into flow, 82.4% were perceived as controllable. Just under seventy percent of the factors *preventing* flow were perceived as controllable. A change in the trend for most factors to be perceived as controllable was found for the factors *disrupting* flow. Here, 71.6% of the factors were perceived as uncontrollable.

Discussion

The main purpose of this study was to move beyond description of the flow state toward understanding factors which may help an athlete get into flow, as well as those factors which may prevent or disrupt flow from occurring. Ten general dimensions were formed from the raw data themes from 28 elite athletes about what helps flow, nine dimensions from themes about what prevents flow, and seven dimensions from themes about what disrupts flow. There was considerable overlap in the type of ideas expressed in the emerging dimensions, thus the discussion of these results is presented in reference to the ten factors which encompass the 26 dimensions found across the three inductive analyses. In each case, practical suggestions for application are presented.

1. *Motivation to perform.* Being motivated to perform, and to perform well, was important to get into flow, and lacking such motivation prevented flow for some athletes. The challenge-skill balance described by Csikszentmihalyi (1990) may be the most relevant area to focus on to help ensure the athlete is optimally motivated.

2. *Achieving optimal arousal level before performing.* Arousal level before competing was seen by the athletes as a factor influencing whether or not they would get into flow. Optimal arousal level was athlete-specific, a finding well documented in the sport psychology literature (e.g., Gould & Krane, 1992). Again, attention to the challenge-skill balance is a way of helping an athlete gain control over this factor; relaxation training would also be an important means to achieving optimal arousal.

3. *Precompetitive and competitive plans and preparation.* An athlete's preparation for competition was a factor highly relevant to whether or not he or she would get into flow. Following precompetitive routines, and event focus plans, feeling totally prepared, and knowing clearly what to do were important components of preparation. Orlick (1986) provides practical suggestions on the development of these components of psychological preparation for competition.

4. *Optimal physical preparation, readiness, and state.* This factor was relevant to helping, preventing, and disrupting flow. To get into flow, athletes needed to know they had done the training and feel physically ready. Once in the flow state, several athletes said it could be disrupted through problems with physical readiness or physical state, such as experiencing a lot of pain, feeling exhausted, or suffering an injury during the game. The influence of physical preparation on flow may be unique to athletes and others whose activity is of a physical nature. Attention to factors such as rest, training, and nutrition may be important for setting an optimal physical state for flow to occur.

5. *Optimal environmental and situational conditions and influences.* Although this factor was relevant to helping and preventing flow, environmental and situational influences seemed to have the greatest impact on the disruption of the flow state. An athlete's consideration of environmental and situational factors is therefore an important aspect in trying to enhance the likelihood of flow occurring, and to prevent it from being disrupted. Outside assistance from a coach and/or sport psychologist could help the athlete prepare for possible disruptive environmental or situational factors through such means as the use of imagery and refocusing plans (Orlick, 1986).

6. *How performance feels and progresses.* Whether one feels good during performance versus experiencing the performance going poorly impacts flow state. Again, the physical nature of what athletes do probably influences the relevancy of this factor. Helping athletes to be aware of the feeling of their performance is an important first step to gaining control over the performance (Ravizza, 1993). This involves becoming more in tune with one's movements and the impact of one's movements during sports performance.

7. *Focus.* Csikszentmihalyi (1990) refers to concentration on the task at hand as one of "the most frequently mentioned dimensions of the flow experience" (p.58). While focus was a dimension found across the help, prevent and disrupt analyses, it was a little surprising that it did not come through more strongly—it involved responses of between 18–40% of the sample. The eliteness of the sample may have meant that focusing was a taken-for granted skill, and therefore was not recognized as an important an influence on flow state as it may have been by a less elite athlete population. Improving one's ability to appropriately focus during performance comes from the development of specific focus plans (Orlick, 1986) and through attentional control training (Nideffer, 1993).

8. *Confidence and mental attitude.* Confidence came through as an important factor in both the help and prevent flow analyses, and doubting or putting pressure on oneself was perceived as being able to disrupt flow. Confidence seems to be salient to the sport experience no matter what the ability or achievement level of the athlete. After hearing two world champions talk about still having to deal with confidence issues, it became apparent to the investigator that problems with confidence are not something an athlete "grows out of" as they achieve outstanding levels of success. The fact that many of the athletes referred to confidence as being important for them to be able to get into flow may mean that it is the perception of skill rather than the perception of challenge that is the critical component in the challenge-skill balance for elite athletes. The question of sufficient challenge is probably rarely a factor for athletes competing at this level. More critical, it seems is the belief that one can successfully meet the challenge. Skills such as positive self-talk and imagery may be helpful in attempting to heighten athletes' perceived ability, as may performance goal-setting (Burton, 1989).

9. *Team play and interaction.* For certain of the team sport athletes, getting into flow was influenced by the team. At least as important as the team playing well was the presence of positive team interaction. Thus, building team interaction may need to be considered to enhance flow occurring.

10. *Experience factor.* Although only involving two themes, the role of experience may have an influence on the ability of athletes to get into flow, as well as on awareness of things that might prevent or disrupt flow. Research with less elite athletes than those involved in the present investigation is needed to confirm whether this is a significant factor in the experiencing of flow in sport. All athletes can increase their familiarity with their performance through the use of imagery.

When the results of the inductive analyses from this study were compared to those found in previous work with figure skaters (Jackson, 1992), considerable consistency emerged. Confidence, or Positive Mental Attitude, the most important dimension for the skaters, was also one of two most frequently cited dimensions in this study. There is strong support from the psychology and sport psychology literature that confidence is critical to performance and persistence (e.g., Bandura, 1977; Feltz, 1988) and it appears that confidence is also critical to flow. Surprisingly, the other most frequently cited dimension in this study, Pre-Competitive and Competitive Plans/Preparation, did not emerge as a dimension in the skating investigation. The importance of mental plans is a robust finding among applied sport psychology research (e.g., Gould, Eklund, & Jackson, 1992; Orlick & Partington, 1988). Other dimensions not found in Jackson's 1992 study included Performance Feeling Good, and Optimal Environmental and Situational Conditions.

The questions about factors preventing or disrupting flow were grouped together into one question in Jackson's (1992) skating study, and the results indicate that the athletes focused more on the disrupt dimension than the prevent dimension. The themes found in the skating analysis were very similar to those found in the disrupt flow analysis in the present study. And several of the themes found to prevent flow in the present study were not mentioned by the skaters, including Lacking Motivation To Perform, Non-Optimal Arousal Level, and Problems With Precompetitive Preparation. Therefore, the fact that two independent questions were asked in the present study proved to be a strength, since much valuable information was found relating to factors which can prevent flow from occurring.

In comparison to the Jackson (1992) investigation, the fact that a larger and more diverse sample of athletes were interviewed probably influenced the fact that more themes were found in the present study. Seventy-three themes were extracted from the data in the figure skating study, compared to 361 themes in the present study. Therefore, the knowledge base about antecedent and preventive flow factors increased greatly in content and applicability from the analyses of the present investigation.

Although distinct dimensions have been discussed, it should be remembered that flow is a process and so too in all likelihood is getting into flow. Thus, it is most likely that several of the factors presented as influencing whether or not flow occurs interact, rather than operate in isolation. Support for the multidimensional nature of antecedent and preventive flow factors was provided by the finding that each athlete cited themes which fit into several of the antecedent and preventive dimensions. An examination of the proposed dimensions also supports the idea that they can and do interact to influence whether flow occurs. For example, injury/ poor training can affect confidence, which in turn affects one's precompetitive preparation, which affects one's arousal level and so on. Therefore, it is important to consider the totality of antecedent and preventive factors to ensure the chances of flow occurring are optimized.

The Perceived Controllability of Flow

An additional purpose of this investigation was to examine the perceived controllability of flow. The majority of the athletes said they thought flow was a controllable state, that is, a state they could purposefully get into, rather than a state which just happened. The extent of perceived controllability of flow ranged from "it just happens" to "I make it happen". It was not possible to determine what was behind this range of perceptions regarding the controllability of flow. There may have been some difference in the mental skill development and self-awareness between the athletes interviewed that accounted for this range of responses. However, the fact that 79% said they thought flow was controllable is probably related to the high skill level of the sample.

It is interesting to note that while the majority of the factors forwarded as helping and preventing flow were perceived as controllable, the reverse was true for the factors disrupting flow. The fact that most of the factors seen as disrupting flow were perceived as uncontrollable can be seen as lending support to the idea that flow is a potentially controllable state, at least for elite athletes. If most of the disrupting influences are perceived as uncontrollable, then this group of elite athletes seem to be saying that they will remain in flow unless some uncontrollable event occurs to take them out of this state. Support for this idea is given by the finding that over half of the athletes said they were more likely to remain in flow for the duration of their event than to come in and out of this state.

Extending the Knowledge Base About Flow State

Theoretically, anyone can experience flow, if his/her perceived challenges match his/her perceived skills (Csikszentmihalyi, 1990). This study has provided specific information for elite athlete populations regarding how to achieve a challenge-skill balance. The factors just discussed are elements either within the athlete (e.g., motivation, preparation, arousal level, focus) or within the situation (e.g., environmental or relationship issues) that can help determine whether a challenge-skill balance will be achieved for a particular athlete in a particular event. Thus, this study has provided information that illustrates and extends Csikszentmihalyi's formulation about the occurrence of flow by providing examples of influencing factors in athletic situations.

The set of ten factors presented in the discussion, encompassing 26 dimensions and many more lower-level themes, provide specific information on what made it more or less likely that flow would be attained by the athletes in this study. This data provides a base from which future studies can build, and develop understanding, not only of what may influence flow in elite athletes, but also of this how this optimal psychological state occurs in many different situations and across a range of individuals.

The nature of the ten factors which were found in this study to influence the occurrence of flow ranged from the psychological to the physiological to the nutritional to the situational. Thus, whether or not flow occurs was seen by the athletes as depending on a set of situations that create an environment where total absorption in the performance can occur. Importantly, the majority of these factors were seen by the athletes as being within their control. Flow state has often been regarded by athletes and sport psychologists as a special occurrence that one may be "lucky" enough to experience. The findings from this study indicate that athletes may have more self-determination over experiencing flow than typically believed. The possibility of developing training programs for helping athletes and exercisers experience flow is an exciting anticipated outcome of continued research investigating influences on this optimal psychological state.

References

Bandura, A. (1977). Self-efficacy: Towards a unifying theory of behavior change. *Psychological Review, 84,* 191–215.

Burton, D. (1989). Winning isn't everything: Examining the impact of performance goals on collegiate swimmers' cognitions and performance. *The Sport Psychologist, 3,* (2), 105–132.

Csikszentmihalyi, M. (1975). *Beyond boredom and anxiety.* San Francisco: Jossey-Bass.

Csikszentmihalyi, M. (1990). *Flow: The psychology of optimal experience.* New York: Harper & Row.

Csikszentmihalyi, M., & Csikszentmihalyi, I. S. (1988). *Optimal experience: Psychological studies of flow in consciousness.* New York: Cambridge University Press.

Csikszentmihalyi, M. & Le Fevre, J. (1987). Optimal experience in work and leisure. *Journal of Personality and Social Psychology, 56,* (5), 815–22.

Feltz, D. (1988). Self-confidence and sports performance. *Exercise and Sport Science Reviews, 16,* 423–457.

Gould, D., Eklund, R. C., & Jackson, S. A. (1992). 1988 US Olympic Wrestling Excellence I: Mental preparation, precompetitive cognition, and affect. *The Sport Psychologist , 6,* (4), 358–382.

Gould, D., & Krane, V. (1992). The arousal-athletic performance relationship: Current status and future directions. In T. S. Horn (Ed.), *Advances in sport psychology* (pp. 119–142). Champaign, IL: Human Kinetics.

Graef, R., Csikszentmihalyi, M., & Giannino, S. M. (1983). Measuring intrinsic motivation in everyday life. *Leisure Studies, 2,* 155–168.

Jackson, S. A. (1992). Athletes in flow: A qualitative investigation of flow states in elite figure skaters. *Journal of Applied Sport Psychology, 4,* (2), 161–180.

Jackson, S. A. (1993). *Elite athletes in flow: The psychology of optimal sport experience.* (Doctoral dissertation, University of North Carolina at Greensboro, 1992). *Dissertation Abstracts International, 54,* (1), 124-A.

Jackson, S. A., & Roberts, G. C. (1992). Positive performance states of athletes: Toward a conceptual understanding of peak performance. *The Sport Psychologist, 6,* (2), 156–171.

Lincoln, Y. S., & Guba, E. G. (1985). *Naturalistic inquiry.* Newbury Park: Sage.

Martens, R. (1987). Science, knowledge, and sport psychology. *The Sport Psychologist, 1,* (1), 29–55.

Nideffer, R. M. (1993). Concentration and attention control training. In J. M. Williams (Ed.), *Applied sport psychology: Personal growth to peak performance* (2nd ed.) (pp. 243–261). Mountain View, CA: Mayfield.

Orlick, T. (1986). *Psyching for sport.* Champaign, IL: Human Kinetics.

Orlick, T. & Partington, J. (1988). Mental links to excellence. *The Sport Psychologist, 2,* (2), 105–130.

Patton, M. Q. (1990). *Qualitative evaluation and research methods* (2nd ed.). Newbury Park: Sage.

Privette, G. (1983). Peak experience, peak performance, and flow: A comparative analysis of positive human experiences. *Journal of Personality and Social Psychology, 45,* (6), 1361–1368.

Privette, G. & Bundrick, C. M. (1991). Peak experience, peak performance, and flow: Personal descriptions and theoretical constructs. *Journal of Social Behavior and Personality, 6* (5), 169–188.

Ravizza, K. (1993). Increasing awareness for sport performance. In J. M. Williams (Ed.), *Applied sport psychology: Personal growth to peak performance* (2nd ed.). (pp. 148–157). Mountain View, CA: Mayfield.

16 Intrinsic and Extrinsic Motivation in Sport: Toward a Hierarchical Model

ROBERT J. VALLERAND AND STÉPHANE PERREAULT
Université du Quebec à Montréal

In the past three decades, a substantial amount of research in general and in sport and exercise psychology has focused on intrinsic and extrinsic motivation. When a person is engaged in an activity for the pleasures it provides, this person is said to be intrinsically motivated. However, when a person does an activity in order to obtain rewards or to avoid punishment, the person engaged in that activity is viewed as being extrinsically motivated.

Vallerand and his associates have conducted much work on these two specific types of motivation, putting a special emphasis on developing a hierarchical model of them. This model is based on the theory of self-determination suggested by Deci and Ryan during the late 1970s and 1980s. Self-determination is conceived as an intrinsic need to experience freedom of choice in initiating a person's behavior and is usually defined as allowing a person's perceived choices to determine his or her behaviors. Originally Deci and Ryan viewed intrinsic motivation and extrinsic motivation as mutually exclusive. However, this view later shifted toward a conceptualization of a continuum of motivational orientations; current thinking perceives intrinsic and extrinsic motivations on a continuum on which various types of intrinsic and extrinsic motivation are located and viewed as multidimensional.

The model proposed by Vallerand and Perrault hierarchically considers dimensions of motivation as applied to sports. The model differentiates among social factors, mediators (autonomy, competence, and relatedness), motivations (intrinsic, extrinsic, and amotivation), and consequences (affect, cognition, and behavior) at three levels (global, contextual, and situational). It emphasizes the importance of simultaneously examining all these factors. The model allows us not only to integrate various perspectives inherent in the literature on intrinsic and extrinsic motivation, but also to propose new hypotheses to be tested in future research. Indeed, the model has provided some interesting ideas for later research on motivation in physical activity and sport contexts.

The purpose of this chapter is to present a new theoretical model that allows us not only to integrate the various perspectives inherent in the intrinsic/extrinsic motivation literature, but also to propose new and original testable hypotheses. Such a model takes into consideration the variety of ways motivation can be represented in the individual, how these various representations of motivation are related among themselves, as well as to various determinants and consequences. Before we begin the presentation of this new conceptual model, we would like to inform the reader that the model is not only limited to sport but also makes important predictions with respect to other life contexts, such as interpersonal relations and education (see Vallerand, 1997). In this chapter, a number of empirical studies supporting the hierarchical model will be presented to show how the model may lead to a better understanding of motivational phenomena to be found in sport. Although our emphasis will be on how the model can be applied to sport, we will also attempt to show how sport and other life contexts can influence each other.

A Hierachical Model of Intrinsic and Extrinsic Motivation

Let's start with an example that should serve to illustrate some of the issues that the model deals with. John is a 12-year-old adolescent. He is the type of person who does things generally because he likes them. Thus, he goes to school and interacts with other people out of fun. Consequently, such activities generally lead him to experience pleasure and satisfaction. However, contrary to the contexts of school and interpersonal relationships, John plays baseball because he feels he has to. In that context, John feels that other people (including his dad—a former baseball player), and especially his coach, force him to do things he would not choose to do. He feels controlled and experiences very little sense of autonomy. Consequently, his performance is not very good, and he generally derives little satisfaction from his sport involvement. However, in the last 3 weeks, things have started to come around. His regular coach has been away and has been replaced by the assistant coach, who is much less controlling. The new coach allows players to express themselves and to try new things. Players are often allowed to lead the warm-up period, and John likes that. More and more, John feels that he is going to practices and games out of choice and, at times, pleasure. Consequently, his performance has started to improve, and he generally feels happier at the park. This afternoon, in the game, the new coach has just asked John if he wants to try to bunt to advance the runner on first base or would rather go for the hit and run. John indicates that he wants to bunt. John experiences feelings of autonomy

---

because the coach let him decide what to do. He focuses on the pitcher, is fully concentrated on his rhythm, and hits the ball just right, allowing the runner on first to advance to second. Although he is declared out at first, John feels good and is very satisfied with himself. After the game, he also experiences an inclination to play some more. So he throws the ball with teammates and practices different things.

The above example underscores several points with respect to motivation. A first point is that humans are motivationally complex. It is, therefore, not sufficient to talk about motivation in general to describe a person. Rather, we should refer to a collection of motivations that vary in types and levels of generality. In the example, John appeared to be intrinsically motivated toward school and interpersonal relationships, but to be extrinsically motivated toward baseball. Each of these different types of motivation represents a part of John, and if we are to understand this particular individual, we need to take into consideration the different motivations that describe him. Of importance is that these different types of motivation exist within the individual at three levels of generality. For instance, in the example, we indicated that John generally does things because he enjoys them. Overall at the global level, John would, therefore, appear to have an intrinsic-motivation personality that would generally predispose him to be intrinsically motivated toward different contexts. Thus, John was depicted as intrinsically motivated toward school and interpersonal relationships. Finally, at the situational level, that specific day at the park, John was intrinsically motivated to bunt. We feel that it is important to distinguish these different levels as such distinctions should lead to a better understanding of motivational processes.

A second issue of interest is that motivation is not only an intrapersonal phenomenon, but also a social phenomenon. Indeed, other people can have a powerful impact on our motivation, just as John's former coach had on his contextual motivation toward baseball. Although John has an intrinsic-motivation personality, he is nevertheless extrinsically motivated toward baseball. Thus, intrapersonal factors (global motivation) are not the sole influences on motivation. Social factors, and in this case, contextual factors, can play an important role as determinants of (contextual) motivation. The same reasoning applies at the situational level. For instance, the assistant coach's supportive approach to let John decide to bunt or to go for the hit and run seems to have had a positive effect on John's immediate (or situational) motivation at that specific time at the ballpark. It thus appears that both intra- and interpersonal forces can influence global, contextual, and situational motivation at their respective level of generality.

Third, motivation leads to important consequences, and these may occur at the three levels of generality. At the contextual level, they may vary from context to context as a function of the relevant contextual motivation. For instance, John generally experiences positive benefits from his engagement in school and interpersonal activities. Such was not the case in baseball, however, because his motivation was extrinsic in nature. There, he felt unsatisfied with the game, and his performance was low. However, with the change of coach (a change in contextual factors), his motivation shifted from extrinsic to intrinsic. Consequently, his performance started to improve, and he felt much happier playing baseball. At the situational level, it was seen that John's intrinsic motivation allowed him to remain focused during the game, to feel good about himself, and to want to keep on playing later that day at the park. Therefore, motivation does not appear to be an epiphenomenon; it can lead to important outcomes.

Finally, it is believed that instances of situational intrinsic motivation, and associated positive benefits such as those experienced by John at the park that afternoon, serve to facilitate contextual intrinsic motivation. It is thus not surprising that John is now more intrinsically motivated toward baseball: Repeated instances of situational intrinsic motivation like the one at the ballpark have had recursive effects on his contextual motivation toward baseball in general.

As we can see, the model pothat motivation results from an ongoing transaction between the person and the environment. Furthermore, the model also integrates the personality and social psychological traditions of motivation. The model is described below in the forms of five postulates.

Postulate 1—A complete analysis of motivation must include intrinsic and extrinsic motivation and amotivation

The first postulate posits that a complete analysis of motivation must deal with three concepts, namely those of intrinsic motivation (IM), extrinsic motivation (EM), and amotivation (AM). Indeed, much research has supported the existence and the usefulness of these types of motivation.

Intrinsic motivation. In general, IM refers to the fact of doing an activity for itself, and the pleasure and satisfaction derived from participation (e.g., Deci, 1975; Deci & Ryan, 1985a). An example of IM is the athlete who plays soccer because he or she finds it interesting and satisfying to learn more about the game. Although most researchers posit the presence of a global IM construct, a tripartite taxonomy of intrinsic motivation has been postulated by Vallerand and his colleagues (Vallerand, Blais, Brière, & Pelletier, 1989; Vallerand et al., 1992, 1993). These three types of IM can be identified as IM to know, to accomplish things, and to experience stimulation.

Extrinsic motivation. Contrary to IM, EM pertains to a wide variety of behaviors where the goals of action extend beyond those inherent in the activity itself. They are behaviors that are engaged in as a means to an end and not for their own sake. Originally, it was thought that EM referred to behaviors performed in the absence of self-determination and thus could be prompted only by external contingencies. However, more recently, Deci, Ryan, and their colleagues (Deci & Ryan, 1991) have proposed that different types of EM exist, some of which are self-determined and may be performed through choice.

External regulation corresponds to EM as it generally appears in the in the literature. That is, behavior is regulated through external means, such as rewards and constraints. For instance, an individual might say: "I play soccer because my parents force me to."

With *introjected regulation,* the individual begins to internalize the reasons for his or her actions. However, this form of internalization, although internal to the person, is not truly self-determined because it is limited to the internalization of past external contingencies. Thus, the individual might say, "I play soccer because I would feel guilty if I didn't."

To the extent that the behavior becomes valued and judged important for the individual, and especially that it is perceived as chosen by oneself, then the internalization of extrinsic motives becomes regulated through *identification.* The individual might say, for instance: "I choose to play soccer because it is something important for me."

Amotivation. In addition to intrinsic and extrinsic motivation, Deci and Ryan (1985a) have also posited that a third type of motivational construct is important to consider in order to fully understand human behavior. This concept is termed amotivation. Individuals are amotivated when they do not perceive contingencies between outcomes and their own actions. They are neither intrinsically nor extrinsically motivated. They become nonmotivated. Amotivation can be seen in many ways as similar to learned helplessness (Abramson, Seligman, & Teasdale, 1978) because the individual will experience feelings of incompetence and expectancies of uncontrollability. When individuals are amotivated, they perceive their behaviors as caused by forces out of their own control. They feel helpless and start asking themselves why in the world they engage in the activity. Eventually they may stop participating in the activity. Athletes on the verge of burning out may be thought of as experiencing a great deal of amotivation (Smith, 1986).

An increasing amount of research has consistently supported the basic premises of Postulate 1. For instance, results from confirmatory factor analyses on the motivation scales that we and others have developed have consistently supported the presence of IM, EM, and AM in sports (Brière, Vallerand, Blais, & Pelletier, 1995; Li & Harmer, 1996; Pelletier et al., 1995) and in a variety of other contexts (see Vallerand, 1997). In addition, as we will see in a later section, these different types of motivation are related to determinants and consequences as theoretically predicted, thereby providing additional support for their construct validity.

Another important point is that self-determination theory (Deci & Ryan, 1985a) proposes that these different types of motivation represent different levels of self-determination. Thus, from the highest to lowest levels of self-determination, we find intrinsic motivation (IM), identified regulation (ID), introjected regulation (IR), external regulation (ER), and amotivation (AM). These motivations can be aligned on a continuum from AM to IM. Because the various forms of motivation are aligned on a self-determination continuum, it also allows us, for sake of brevity, to use a motivational index integrating all scales. This is called a self-determination index. The more self-determined the index, the more IM and ID, and the less the IR, ER, and AM experienced by the individual. It is this index that has been used in several studies reported herein.

Postulate 2—Intrinsic and extrinsic motivation and amotivation exist at three different levels of generality: the global, contextual, and situational levels

Over the past 15 years or so, much research and theorizing on the self have suggested that self-regulation processes are best represented at different levels in a hierarchy. For instance, Carver and Scheier (1981) proposed a hierarchy of self-regulatory processes. Shavelson and Marsh (1986) also proposed three levels of self-concept, the global, the academic and nonacademic self-concepts, and finally the more specific subject self-concept (e.g., English or math). In line with past research on the self, the second postulate posits that the different types of motivation described above (IM, EM, AM) are represented in the individual at three hierarchical levels of generality. From top to bottom, these are the global, the contextual, and the situational levels.

At the global level, it is proposed that the individual has developed a global and general motivational orientation to interact with the environment in an intrinsic, extrinsic, or amotivated way. The work of Deci and Ryan (1985b) with the General Causality Orientations Scale [GCOS], and of Guay, Blais, Vallerand, and Pelletier (1996), who have developed the Global Motivation Scale, is exemplary of such research. These last researchers have reported among other findings that a global intrinsic orientation is associated with higher levels of life satisfaction as well as global perceptions of competence, autonomy, and relatedness. To the best of our knowledge, no research in sport has been conducted at this level.

Research at the second level of generality, that is at the contextual level, has been particularly popular over the past 15 years. By contexts, we mean a distinct sphere of human activity (Emmons, 1995). Research by Blais, Vallerand, Gasnon, Brière, & Pelletier, (1990b) has shown that the three most important contexts for young adults are education, interpersonal relationships, and leisure, which of course includes sport. In such life contexts, individuals have developed motivational orientations that, although still responsive to the individual's environment, are nevertheless somewhat stable. At this level, individuals' motivational orientations in specific life contexts are assessed and related to various determinants and consequences. The work of Brustad (1988) on the role of parental behavior in the enjoyment of children's sport participation over a season is an example of sport research at the contextual level.

The situational (or state) level represents the third and last level in the hierarchy. Motivation at the situational level refers to the motivation an individual has while he or she is currently engaging in an activity. Motivation at this level of generality has been measured either through a behavioral indicator of how much time the individual spends on the task during a phase subsequent to the experimental phase (the so-called free-choice period; Deci, 1971) or through questionnaires assessing one's interest toward the activity (for a review, see Vallerand & Fortier, 1998). This research has been mainly conducted in the laboratory and has largely focused on the determinants of IM. Thus, research on the effects of rewards, deadlines, performance feedback, and other situational variables on IM, as measured by the time spent on the task or interest toward the activity in that particular setting and at that particular time, have dealt with this level of generality. The work of Orlick and Mosher (1978) on the effects of awards, that of Weinberg and Ragan (1979) on the effects of competition, and of Whitehead and Corbin (1991) on the effects of feedback are exemplary of IM research at the situational level.

In sum, research in the motivation area reveals that motivation exists at three levels of a hierarchy that goes from the global, to the contextual, to the situational levels. It also appears that research in sport has mainly focused on the contextual and situational levels. Furthermore, our recent methodological work has enabled us to develop scales assessing the same motivational constructs at each of the three levels of the hierarchy. Thus, we have developed the Global Motivation Scale (Guay et al., 1996) to assess motivation at the global level. In order to better understand contextual motivation in real-life settings, we have developed scales measuring motivation in education (Vallerand et al., 1989, 1992, 1993), in interpersonal relationships (Blais, Vallerand, Pelletier, & Brière. 1994), and leisure (Pelletier, Vallerand, Blais, Brière, & Green-Demers, 1996). We also developed the Sport Motivation Scale (Brière et al., 1995; Pelletier et al., 1995) because sport is one very important form of leisure. Finally, in order to measure motivation at the situational level, we have developed the Situational Motivation Scale (Guay & Vallerand, 1995, 1997). All of these scales display high levels of reliability and validity (see Vallerand, 1997). Thus, the methodology needed to test novel hypotheses on human motivation within the context of the hierarchical model is now available.

Postulate 3—Motivation at a given level results from two potential sources: (a) social factors and (b) top-down effects from motivation at the proximal level

Postulate 3 deals with the effects of determinants or antecedents on motivation. This third postulate is subdivided into three corollaries.

Corollary 3.1: Motivation at a given level can result from social factors that can be global, contextual, or situational, depending on the level in the hierarchy. By social factors, we refer to both human and nonhuman factors found in our social environment. We distinguish among situational, contextual, and global determinants in the following manner. *Situational factors* refer to variables that are present at a given point in time but not on a permanent basis. For instance, receiving positive feedback at 3:45 of the fourth quarter of a football game represents an example of a situational factor. *Contextual factors* represent variables that are present on a general or recurrent basis in one specific life context (e.g., having a controlling swimming coach) but not in another (e.g., the coach is part of the sport context, but not of the educational context). Finally, *global factors* refer to social factors whose presence is so pervasive that they are present in most aspects of the person's life. A good example of such a global factor is the housing of elite athletes in one location. Being confined to such an environment for an extended period of time may have important consequences on an athlete's global motivation. We feel that it is important to distinguish among the three types of social factors because it then becomes possible to make clearer hypotheses regarding which type of factors should influence motivation at the various levels of the hierarchy. Specifically, social factors should mostly influence motivation at their respective level of the hierarchy.

Recent research has supported this corollary. Research has shown that one type of social factors influences motivation at one level, but not at another level. For example, in a recent study (Vallerand, 1996), we have assessed the effects of a known situational variable, success/failure, on motivation at the situational, context (leisure), and global levels. If our reasoning is correct, failure on the task should have affected only situational motivation (undermining IM especially toward accomplishment and enhancing AM relative to the success condition), but not context (leisure) or global motivation. Results supported this hypothesis.

Corollary 3.2: The impact of social factors on motivation is mediated by perceptions of competence, autonomy, and relatedness. It was posited in Corollary 3.1 that social factors influence motivation. One theoretical perspective that appears to provide a rather complete account of such processes is cognitive evaluation theory (Deci, 1975; Deci & Ryan, 1985a, 1991), a sub-theory of self-determination theory. According to this theory, situational factors affect motivation through their impact on people's perceptions of competence, autonomy, and relatedness. This is because these perceptions relate to fundamental human needs that individuals seek to satisfy. Activities that promote such perceptions will be reengaged in freely because they nurture people's fundamental needs.

The need for competence implies that individuals have a desire to interact effectively with the environment in order to experience a sense of competence in producing desired outcomes and preventing undesired events (Connell & Wellborn, 1991; Deci, 1975; Deci & Ryan, 1985a;

Harter, 1978; White, 1959). On the other hand, the need for autonomy reflects a desire to be the origin of one's own behavior (deCharms, 1968; Deci, 1975, 1980; Deci & Ryan, 1985a). Finally, the need for relatedness (Bowlby, 1988; Harlow, 1958) involves feeling connected (or feeling that one belongs in a given social milieu; see Baumeister & Leary, 1995; Richer & Vallerand, in press; Ryan, 1993, for recent reviews on belongingness and/or relatedness). Thus, according to cognitive evaluation theory, social factors that facilitate individuals' perceptions of competence, autonomy, and relatedness will facilitate their IM and ID, but undermine their IR, ER and AM (see Deci, Vallerand, Pelletier, & Ryan. 1991).

Much research supports cognitive evaluation theory at the situational level. Noteworthy is the work of Vallerand and Reid (1984). In this particular study, participants engaged in the stabilometer task during a pretest and in a posttest during which independent variables were imposed. Participants received positive, negative, or no performance feedback. Following both the pre- and posttest, subjects completed questionnaires assessing perceptions of competence and intrinsic motivation. Change scores were used in a path analysis. In line with cognitive evaluation theory, results showed that the effects of performance feedback on situational intrinsic motivation were mainly mediated by perceptions of competence. In a more recent study by Blanchard and Vallerand (1996), basketball players completed scales measuring perceptions of personal and team performance, as well as situational perceptions of competence, autonomy, and relatedness, and situational motivation during a game. Results from this study also showed that perceptions of autonomy, competence, and relatedness play a mediational role between personal and team performance and self-determined motivation (as assessed by the self-determination index) during the game.

Similar findings have been reported by Cadorette, Blanchard, and Vallerand (1996) at the contextual level. Individuals (*N*=208) involved in a weight-loss program completed scales assessing perceptions of the fitness leader's style (autonomy support) and the ambiance of the fitness center, as well as contextual perceptions of competence, autonomy, and relatedness, and contextual motivation (the SMS) toward exercising and dieting. Cadorette et al. (1996) showed through path analysis that perceptions of competence, autonomy, and relatedness mediated the impact of the fitness leader's style and the ambiance of the center on self-determined motivation toward exercising and dieting.

In sum, although much research still needs to be done on the determinants of motivation, it does appear that perceptions of competence, autonomy, and relatedness at the situational and contextual levels represent key mediators of the effects of various situational, and contextual factors on motivation, respectively. The same logic should apply to the global level, although there is no empirical evidence so far to support this claim in sport. These various mediators should, therefore, be included in a model of human motivation.

Corollary 3.3: In addition to the influence of psychological mediators, motivation at a given level also result from top-down effects from motivation at the proximal level higher up in the hierarchy. The third corollary recognizes the potential top-down impact of motivation at higher levels in the hierarchy on motivation at the next lower level. More specifically, it is proposed that motivation at the proximal level should have stronger effects top-down on motivation at the next lower level than on motivation at a distal level. Thus, contextual motivation should have a stronger impact on situational motivation than does global motivation. Similarly, global motivation should have a strong impact on contextual motivation. For instance, one would expect someone with a global intrinsic-motivation orientation to display an intrinsic motivational orientation in different contexts such as sport. Finally, it is also proposed that self-determined motivation at the higher level will facilitate self-determined levels of motivation at the next level down in the hierarchy. Thus, athletes who display a self-determined motivational profile in contextual motivation toward their sport are likely to display a similar motivational profile at the situational level while playing.

Corollary 3.3 is in line with recent conceptual work on self-regulatory processes that has shown that global properties of the self influence more specific aspects of the self (Brown, 1993; Brown & Dutton, 1995; Sansone & Harackiewicz, 1996). To the best of our knowledge, only two studies have tested Corollary 3.3 in sports and exercise. Thus, in two studies with basketball players, Blanchard, Vallerand, and Provencher (1995) were able to show that contextual motivation toward basketball in general, as assessed either just prior to (Study 1) or several weeks before (Study 2) a game, predicted situational motivation experienced during a basketball game. Here again, the more self-determined the athletes' contextual motivation toward basketball, the more self determined their situational motivation. Overall, the findings from the above two studies indicate that motivation can produce top-down effects on motivation at the next lower level in the hierarchy. Although the results of these two studies are encouraging, more studies are needed to test this hypothesis from an experimental perspective.

In sum, research reviewed in this section provides strong support for Postulate 3 and its corollaries. We have seen that it may prove quite heuristic to distinguish among global, contextual, and situational factors. In addition, the role of perceptions of competence, autonomy, and relatedness as psychological mediators of the social factors-motivation relationship was strongly supported, especially at the situational and contextual levels. Finally, we have also shown that motivation at a higher level in the hierarchy can influence motivation at the next lower level.

Postulate 4—There is a recursive bottom-up relationship between motivation at the proximal level and motivation at the next level up in the hierarchy

The fourth postulate underscores the bidirectional relationship between motivation at the various levels of hierarchy. The purpose of this postulate is to specifically take into consideration motivational changes that may occur over time and how the interplay between the different levels of motivation can account for these.

In order to illustrate more clearly this bidirectional effect, let's take a real life example of a basketball player who participated in the quarter-finals of a high-school basketball tournament. As the leading scorer of the team, the player had to deliver a great performance for his team to have a chance to win the game. Unfortunately, he did not deliver—scored only 16 points—and his team lost by 22 points. Near the end of the game with the team's loss certain, his situational motivation was at its lowest. He did not feel like playing at that moment: He was amotivated. Later that evening he started to think about next season's grueling training camp and boring practices. Then, for the first time in his life, he started wondering if basketball was worth the time investment. Perhaps he had obtained all there was to get from the game. Perhaps it was time to move on. And he did.

How can we explain what this basketball player went through? Let's start explaining his situational motivation near the end of the crucial quarter-final game. He did not play well, and his team lost. These represent two crucial situational factors that had a negative impact on his situational motivation (Corollary 3.1). These factors were so strong that they superseded the impact of the player's intrinsic contextual motivation on his situational motivation and led him to experience a low level of IM and a high level of AM at the situational level (near the end of the game). In turn, this low self-determined situational motivation had a recursive negative effect (Postulate 4) on his contextual motivation toward basketball. With his contextual motivation now being strongly amotivated, the player decided to call it quits (an important behavioral consequence as we will see with Postulate 5).

We have tested the above processes with respect to basketball players. In this study, Blanchard et al. (1995) had basketball players complete the Sports Motivation Scale before a tournament, as well as the Situational Motivation Scale and the Sport Motivation Scale after each of two games of a basketball tournament. Finally, 10 days after the tournament, subjects completed again the Sports Motivation Scale (Pelletier et al., 1995). It was predicted that contextual motivation toward sport (here basketball) would influence situational motivation right after the first game, which in turn would influence subsequent contextual motivation. This cycle was expected to be repeated for the second game. Finally, situational motivation was hypothesized to influence subsequent contextual motivation after the tournament. Results supported the hypothesis. There was a recursive relation between contextual motivation and situational motivation. More specifically, contextual motivation toward basketball influenced situational motivation for Game 1, which in turn influenced subsequent contextual motivation. This cycle was again repeated for Game 2. Finally, situational motivation for game 2 (and also 1) influenced contextual motivation toward basketball 10 days following the tournament. As predicted by the model, the more self-determined the athletes' situational motivation in the tournament, the more self-determined the contextual motivation after the tournament. With respect to our motivational model, as predicted, situational motivation had a recursive effect over time on contextual motivation.

The above reasoning can also be applied to the next level. For example, if for various reasons, an individual displays repeated high levels of IM toward sports, eventually such changes could bring about changes in IM at the global level. This latter hypothesis remains to be empirically tested, however. In sum, not only is there a top-down relation between motivation at higher levels and those below, but there is also a bottom-up effect from lower levels to the next adjacent higher level.

Postulate 5—Motivation leads to important consequences

The fifth and last postulate deals with the consequences of motivation. Although some may object to the use of the term *consequences*, we feel it is appropriate to use such a term for at least two reasons. First, from an intuitive perspective, it seems appropriate to see variables as diverse as attention, satisfaction, and behavioral persistence as being influenced by motivation. For instance, an intrinsically motivated athlete should be more attentive during a game than should one who is amotivated. Second, from an empirical perspective, there is evidence that motivation "causes" some of the consequences mentioned above. For instance, Amabile (1985) has shown that inducing extrinsic motivation in writers led to lower quality poems than those produced in the intrinsic motivation or control conditions. Several other studies provide support for the causal effects of motivation on consequences (Curry, Wagner, & Grothaus, 1991; Lepper & Cordova, 1992). It is thus clear that motivation produces some important consequences.

It would also appear useful to conceive of consequences as being cognitive, affective, and behavioral in nature. Concentration, attention, and memory are examples of cognitive consequences that have been studied in the IM/EM literature. Affective consequences have been particularly popular and include the following: interest, positive emotions, and satisfaction. Finally, choice of behavior, persistence at the task, intensity, task complexity, behavioral intentions, and performance represent examples of behavioral consequences that have been studied in the area. It is important to distinguish among the three general classes of consequences because among other things this distinction should lead to a better prediction of which types of motivation will most strongly affect which types of consequence (see below the corollaries on this issue). Thus, by distinguishing among the three types of consequences, it may eventually become possible to chart the motivation-consequences relationship more precisely.

Corollary 5.1: Consequences are decreasingly positive from intrinsic motivation to amotivation. The first corollary on motivational consequences deals with consequences as a function of the type of motivation. The self-determination continuum proposed by Deci and Ryan (1985a) is especially useful in making predictions about motivational consequences. Because IM, ID, IR, ER, and AM are hypothesized to be on a continuum from high to low self-determination (Deci & Ryan, 1985a), and because self-determination is associated with enhanced psychological functioning (Deci, 1980), one would expect a corresponding pattern of consequences. That is, one might expect IM to have the most positive consequences, followed by identification. On the other hand, one might also expect external regulation and especially AM to be associated with negative consequences. Introjection should lead to consequences inbetween those produced by identification and external regulation.

Much research supports this corollary (see Ryan, 1995; Vallerand. 1993, 1997) in various life contexts including work (Blais, Brière, Lachance, Riddle, & Vallerand, 1993), leisure (Pelletier et al., 1996) education (Vallerand & Bissonnette, 1992), and interpersonal relationships (Blais, Sabourin, Boucher, & Vallerand, 1990a). Research in sport has also supported this corollary. For example, research by Pelletier et al. (1995) has shown that behavioral consequences, such as effort and intentions to continue in sport, are positively correlated with the most self-determined forms of motivation (IM and ID) but negatively with AM (the least self-determined form of motivation). Results from this study also found support for the self-determination continuum by demonstrating that a cognitive consequence (distraction in training) was negatively correlated with IM and ID and positively with AM. Please note that the pattern of correlations is reversed because distraction in training is a negative consequence. Although these results appear promising, much work needs to be done in this area, however.

Corollary 5.2: Motivational consequences exist at the three levels of the hierarchy, and the level of generality of the consequences depends on the level of the motivation that has produced them. The second corollary deals with the level of generality of the consequences. In line with the hierarchical model, it is proposed that motivational consequences exist at the three levels of the hierarchy. The level of generality of the various consequences depends on the level of generality of the motivation that engenders them. Thus, consequences of situational motivation will be experienced at the situational level, such as feelings of satisfaction, levels of attention, and persistence displayed at that specific moment. Similarly, consequences at the contextual level will be of moderate generality (e.g., satisfaction and behavior in sport) and will be specific to the context to which they pertain. Finally, consequences at the global level will be of the highest level of generality (e.g., satisfaction with one's life) and will vary as a function of global motivation.

Results from a recent study by Pelletier, Fortier, Vallerand, and Brière (1997) provide support for the above corollary with respect to motivation and one important consequence at the contextual level in sport, namely dropping out. In this study, 368 competitive swimmers completed various questionnaires including perceptions of autonomy support and control from the coach and the Sport Motivation Scale. In the two following years, the authors determined which swimmers persisted and which dropped out. Results from the structural equation modeling analysis (using LISREL) revealed that amotivation and intrinsic motivation had respectively the most negative and positive impact on persistence over the 2 years. Furthermore, using the different motivations allowed the researchers to show that the impact of external regulation on persistence was negligible the first year but negative the second. On the other hand, the impact of introjected regulation on persistence was positive the first year, but negligible the second.

In sum, research reviewed in this section provides strong support for Postulate 5 and its corollaries in that motivation leads to important consequences. These consequences can be cognitive, affective, and behavioral in nature and take place at three levels of generality in line with the motivation that produces them. Finally, consequences are decreasingly positive as we move from the highest self-determined form of motivation (i.e., IM) to the lowest self-determined form of self-determination (i.e., AM).

Future Sport Research on the Hierarchical Model

Overall, a great deal of sport research supports the postulated links of the model. It therefore appears that the model represents a sound framework to explain current knowledge on sport motivation. In addition, we feel that the hierarchical model can lead to important future research in sport. Here are only a few examples.

First, the interactional effects of social factors and contextual motivation on situational motivation need to be further studied. Research has shown that extrinsic factors, such as trophies and awards, have negative effects on situational motivation (Orlick & Mosher, 1978). However, such research has not taken contextual motivation into consideration. What are the effects of extrinsic factors when the contextual motivation is self-determined? When it is non-self-determined in nature? Future research is needed to answer these questions.

Second, additional work on the psychological mediators is also needed. Researchers to this point have considered perceived competence, autonomy, and relatedness as additive. That is, the higher the individual's perceptions of competence, autonomy, and relatedness, the higher one's self-determined motivation. However, it has been suggested that their effects on motivation may be interactive (Ryan, 1993). For instance, it has been posited that perceptions of competence can primarily influence motivation when one is feeling autonomous (Deci & Ryan, 1985a). Ryan (1993) further posits that perceptions of autonomy and relatedness may even clash, especially for teenagers and young adults. Very little research to date has examined this hypothesis.

Third, research involving motivation at more than one level is needed. More specifically, research needs to deal with the recursive effects of motivation at one level on motivation at the higher level up in the hierarchy. We need to find out about how situational motivation produces the recursive effects on contextual motivation. More specifically, what are the processes through which the recursive motivational effects occur? Does situational motivation affect contextual motivation directly? Or are other variables, such as consequences (e.g., positive or negative effect), responsible for these recursive effects? The same question also applies to the recursive effects from contextual motivation to global motivation.

Fourth, we need to investigate how the different contexts may interact among each other. We see at least two interesting possibilities. First, a conflict effect. In the terminology of the model, athletes who display a self-determined motivational profile in contextual motivation toward their sport are likely to display a similar motivational profile at the situational level while playing. What happens to the link between contextual sport motivation and situational motivation toward a sport activity when another contextual motivation (i.e., education) is primed? For instance, what happens when someone is engaged in a sport task and is reminded that there is an exam tomorrow? How will behavior be influenced by these two contextual motivations (sport vs. education motivation)? Will the individual change from the sport task to the educational activity? If so, what are the psychological processes involved? Are some individuals more inclined than others to experience conflictual motivations?

A second issue deals with two opposing effects, the compensation and the infusion effect (Blanchard, Vallerand, & Provencher, 1996). These occur as a function of motivational changes that take place in one context. For instance, what happens when an individual experiences a loss of intrinsic motivation in one context such as sport? The infusion effect would predict that there should be a ripple effect so that all contexts (e.g., education, interpersonal relationships, sport) will be negatively affected. On the other hand, the compensation effect would predict that the individual should be able to regroup and even experience an increase of intrinsic motivation in another domain. There is evidence that both effects do occur for self-relevant variables such as mental health (Linville, 1987; Sheldon, Ryan, Rawsthorne, & Ilardi, in press). These issues appear as especially important from a sport perspective as they would allow us to focus on the whole individual in sport and not strictly the athlete. Thus, future research is definitely encouraged on this topic.

Finally, we need to replicate some of the present findings with different populations. So far, most of the participants in our sport studies have been athletes at the college level. Although we believe that the present findings would also hold with other populations (e.g., professional athletes), this remains to be empirically tested. This would allow researchers to test the external validity of the hierarchical model.

References

Abramson, L.Y, Seligman, M.E.P., & Teasdale, J.D. (1978). Learned helplessness in humans: Critique and reformulation. *Journal of Abnormal Psychology, 87,* 49–74.

Amabile, T.M. (1985). Motivation and creativity: Effects of motivational orientation on creative writers. *Journal of Personality and Social Psychology, 48,* 393–399.

Baumeister, R.F., & Leary, M.R. (1995). The need to belong: Desire for interpersonal attachments as a fundamental human motivation. *Psychological Bulletin, 117,* 497–529.

Blais, M.R., Brière, N.M., Lachance, L., Riddle, A.S., & Vallerand, R.J. (1993). L'Inventaire des motivations au travail de Blais [The Blais Work Motivation Inventory]. *Revue Québécoise de Psychologie, 14,* 185–215.

Blais, M.R., Sabourin, S., Boucher, C., & Vallerand, R.J. (1990a). Toward a motivational model of couple happiness. *Journal of Personality and Social Psychology, 59,* 1021–1031.

Blais, M.R., Vallerand, R.J., Gagnon, A., Brière, N.M., & Pelletier, L.G. (1990b). Significance, structure, and gender differences in life domains of college students. *Sex Roles, 22,* 199–212.

Blais, M.R., Vallerand, R.J., Pelletier, L.G., & Brière, N.M. (1994). *Construction et validation de l'Inventaire des Motivations Interpersonnelles* [Construction and validation of the Inventory of Interpersonal Motivations]. Unpublished manuscript, Université du Québec à Montréal.

Blanchard, C., & Vallerand, R.J. (1996). *Perceptions of competence, autonomy, and relatedness as psychological mediators of the social factors-contextual motivation relationship.* Unpublished manuscript, Université du Québec à Montréal.

Blanchard, C., Vallerand, R.J., & Provencher, P. (1995, 0ctober). *Une analyse des effets bidirectionnels entre la motivation contextuelle et la motivation situationnelle en milieu natural* [An analysis of the bidirectional effects between contextual and situational motivation in a natural setting]. Paper presented at the annual conference of the Québec Society for Research on Psychology, Ottawa.

Blanchard, C., Vallerand, R.J., & Provencher, P. (1996, August). *Une analyse motivationnelle des mécanismes de compensation et de contagion du soi* [A motivational analysis of the compensation and contagion mechanisms of the self]. Paper presented at the first annual conference on social psychology in the French language, Montreal, Canada.

Bowlby, J. (1988). *A secure base: Parent-child attachment and healthy human development.* New York: Basic Books.

Brière, N.M., Vallerand, R.J., Blais, M.R., & Pelletier, L.G. (1995). Développement et validation d'une mesure de motivation intrinsèque, extrinsèque et d'amotivation en contexte sportif: l'Échelle de motivation dans les sports (EMS) [On the development and validation of the French form of the Sport Motivation Scale]. *International Journal of Sport Psychology, 26,* 465–489.

Brown, J.D. (1993). Self-esteem and self-evaluation: Feeling is believing. In J. Suls (Ed.), *Psychological perspectives on the self* (vol. 4, pp. 27–58). Hillsdale, NJ: Erlbaum.

Brown, J.D., & Dutton, K.A. (1995). *From the top-down: Self-esteem and self-evaluation.* Unpublished manuscript, University of Washington.

Brustad, R.J. (1988). Affective outcomes in competitive youth sports: The influence of intrapersonal and socialization factors. *Journal of Sport and Exercise Psychology, 10,* 307–321.

Cadorette, I., Blanchard, C., & Vallerand, R.J. (1996, October). *Programme d amaigrissement: Influence du centre de comditionnement physique et du style de l entraîneur sur la motivation des participants.* [Weight loss program: Effects of the fitness center and the instructor on participants' motivation]. Paper presented at the annual conference of the Quebec Society for Research in Psychology, Trois-Rivières, Quebec.

Carver, C.S., & Scheier, M.F. (1981). *Attention and self-regulation.* New-York: Springer-Verlag.

Connell, J.P., & Wellborn, J.G. (1991). Competence, autonomy, and relatedness: A motivational analysis of self-esteem processes. In M.R. Gunnar & L.A. Sroufe (Eds.), *The Minnesota symposium on child psychology: Vol. 22. Self-processes in development* (pp. 43–77). Hillsdale. NJ: Erlbaum.

Curry, S.J., Wagner, E.H., & Grotbaus, L.C. (1991). Evaluation of intrinsic and extrinsic motivation interventions with a self-help smoking cessation program. *Journal of Consulting and Clinical Psychology, 59,* 318–324.

deCharms, R.C. (1968). *Personal causation: The internal affective determinants of behavior.* New York: Academic Press.

Deci, E.L. (1971). Effects of externally mediated rewards on intrinsic motivation. *Journal of Personality and Social Psychology, 18,* 105–115.

Deci, E.L. (1975). *Intrinsic motivation.* New York: Plenum.

Deci, E.L. (1980). *The psychology of self-determination.* Lexington, MA: DC Heath.

Deci, E.L., & Ryan, R.M. (l985a). *Intrinsic motivation and self-determination in human behavior.* New York: Plenum.

Deci, E.L., & Ryan, R.M. (l985b). The General Causality Orientations Scale: Self-determination in personality. *Journal of Research In Personality, 62,* 119–142.

Deci, E.L., & Ryan, R.M. (1991). A motivational approach to self: Integration in personality. In R. Dienstbier (Ed.), *Nebraska symposium on motivation: Vol. 38. Perspectives on motivation* (pp. 237–288). Lincoln, NE: University of Nebraska Press.

Deci, E.L., Vallerand, R.J., Pelletier, L.G., & Ryan, R.M. (1991). Motivation and education: The self-determination perspective. *The Educational Psychologist, 26,* 325–346.

Emmons, R.A. (1995). Levels and domains in personality: An introduction. *Journal of Personality, 63,* 341–364.

Guay, F., Blais, M.R., Vallerand, R.J., & Pelletier. L.G. (1996). *The Global Motivation Scale.* Manuscript in preparation, Université du Québec à Montréal.

Guay, F., & Vallerand, R.J. (1995, June). *The Situational Motivation Scale.* Paper presented at the annual convention of the American Psychological Society, New York.

Guay, F., & Vallerand, R.J. (1997). *On the assessment of state intrinsic and extrinsic motivation: The Situational Motivational Scale (SIMS).* Manuscript submitted for publication.

Harlow, H.F. (1958). The nature of love. *American Psychologist, 13,* 673–685.

Harter, S. (1978). Effectance motivation reconsidered: Toward a developmental model. *Human Development, 1,* 34–64.

Koestner, R., Losier, G.F., Vallerand, R.J., & Carducci, D. (1996). Identified and introjected forms of political internalization: Extending self-determination theory. *Journal of Personality and Social Psychology, 70,* 1025–1036.

Lepper, M.R., & Cordova, D.I. (1992). A desire to be taught: Instructional consequences of intrinsic motivation. *Motivation and Emotion, 16,* 187–208.

Li, F., & Harmer, P. (1996). Testing the simplex assumption underlying the sport motivation scale: A structural equation modeling analysis. *Research Quarterly for Exercise and Sport, 67,* 396–405.

Linville, P.W. (1987). Self-complexity as a cognitive buffer against stress-related illness and depression. *Journal of Personality and Social Psychology, 52,* 663–676.

Orlick, T.D., & Mosher, R. (1978). Extrinsic rewards and participant motivation in a sport related task. *International Journal of Sport Psychology, 9,* 27–39.

Pelletier, L.G., Fortier, M. S., Vallerand, R.J., & Brière, N.M. (1997). *Perceived autonomy support, motivation, and persistence in physical activity: A longitudinal investigation.* Unpublished manuscript, University of Ottawa.

Pelletier, L.G., Fortier, M.S., Vallerand, R.J., Tuson, K.M., Brière, N.M., & Blais, M.R. (1995). Toward a new measure of intrinsic motivation, extrinsic motivation, and amotivation in sports: The Sport Motivation Scale (SMS). *Journal of Sport & Exercise Psychology, 17,* 35–53.

Pelletier, L.G., Tuson, K.M., Green-Demers, I., Noels, K., & Beaton, A.M. (in press). Why are we doing things for the environment? The Motivation Towards the Environment Scale (MTES). *Journal of Applied Social Psychology.*

Pelletier, L.G., Vallerand, R.J., Blais, M.R., Brière, N.M., & Green-Demers, I. (1996). Construction et validation d' une mesure de motivation intrinsèque, de motivation extrinsèque et d'amotivation vis-à-vis des activités de loisirs: l'Échelle de motivation vis-à-vis les loisirs (EML) [Construction and validation of the Leisure Motivation Scale). *Loisir et Société, 19,* 559–585.

Richer, S., & Vallerand, R.J. (in press). Construction et validation de l'échelle du sentiment d' appartemamce sociale. (Construction and validation of the Perceived Relatedness Scale). *Revue Européenne de Psychologie Appliquée.*

Ryan, R.M. (1993). Agency and organization: Intrinsic motivation, autonomy and the self in psychological development. In R. Dientsbier (Ed.), *The Nebraska symposium on motivation. Vol. 40,* (pp. 1–56). Lincoln, NE: University of Nebraska Press.

Ryan, R.M. (1995). The integration of behavioral regulation within life domains. *Journal of Personality, 63,* 397–429.

Sansone, C., & Harackiewicz, J.M. (1996). "I don't feel like it": The function of interest in self-regulation. In L. Martin & A. Tesser (Eds.), *Striving and feeling: Interactions between goals and affect* (pp. 203–228). Hillsdale, NJ: Erlbaum.

Shavelson, R.J., & Marsh, H.W. (1986). On the structure of self-concept. In R. Schwarzer (Ed.), *Anxiety and cognitions* (pp. 305–330). Hillsdale, NJ: Erlbaum.

Sheldon, K.M., Ryan, R.M., Rawsthorne, L.J., & Ilardi, B. (in press). "Trait" self and "true" self: Cross-role variation in the Big Five personality traits and its relations with psychological authenticity and subjective well-being. *Journal of Personality and Social Psychology.*

Smith, R. E. (1986). Toward a cognitive-affective model of athletic burnout. *Journal of Sport Psychology, 8,* 36–50.

Vallerand, R.J. (1993). La motivation intrinsèque et extrinsèque en contexte naturel: Implications pour les contextes de l'éducation, du travail, des relations interpersonnelles et des loisirs [Intrinsic and extrinsic motivation in natural contexts; Implications for the education, work, interpersonal relationships, and leisure contexts]. In R.J. Vallerand & E.E. Thill (Eds.), *Introduction à la psychologie de la motivation* [Introduction to the psychology of motivation] (pp. 533–582). Laval, Quèbec: Etudes Vivantes.

Vallerand, R.J. (1996). [On the effects of success/failure on motivation at three levels of generality]. Unpublished raw data.

Vallerand, R.J. (1997). Toward a hierarchical model of intrinsic and extrinsic motivation. In M.P. Zanna (Ed), *Advances in experimental social psychology* (pp. 271–360). New York: Academic Press.

Vallerand, R.J., & Bissonette, R. (1992). Intrinsic, extrinsic, and amotivational styles as predictors of behavior: A prospective study. *Journal of Personality, 60,* 599–620.

Vallerand, R.J., Blais, M.R., Brière, N.M., & Pelletier, L.G, (1989). Construction et validation de l'Echelle de motivation en éducation (EME) [On the construction and validation of the French form of the Academic Motivation Scale] *Canadian Journal of Behavioural Science, 21,* 323–349.

Vallerand, R.J., & Fortier, M. (1998). Measures of intrinsic and extrinsic motivation in sport and physical activity: A rand critique. In J. Duda (Ed.). *Advancements in sport and exercise psychology measurement* (pp. 81–101). Morgantown, WV: Fitness Information Technology.

Vallerand, R.J., Pelletier, L.G., Blais, M.R., Brière, N.M., Senécal, C., & Vallières, E.F. (1992). The Academic Motivation Scale: A measure of intrinsic, extrinsic, and amotivation in education. *Educational and Psychological Measurement, 52,* 1003–1019.

Vallerand, R.J., Pelletier, L.G., Blais, M.R., Brière, N.M., Senécal, C., & Vallières, E.F. (1993). On the assessment of intrinsic, extrinsic, and amotivation in education: Evidence on the concurrent and construct validity of the Academic Motivation Scale. *Educational and Psychological Measurement, 53,* 159–172.

Vallerand, R.J., & Reid, G. (1984). On the causal effect of perceived competence on intrinsic motivation: A test of cognitive evaluation theory. *Journal of Sport Psychology, 6,* 94–102.

Weinberg, R.S., & Ragan. J. (1979). Competition and extrinsic rewards: Effect on intrinsic motivation and attributions. *Research Quarterly, 50,* 494–502.

White, R.W. (1959). Motivation reconsidered: The concept of competence. *Psychological Review, 66,* 297–333.

Whitehead, J.R., & Corbin, C.B. (1991). Youth fitness testing: The effects of percentile-based evaluative feedback on intrinsic motivation. *Research Quarterly for Exercise and Sport, 62,* 225–231.

PART IV

Understanding Group Processes

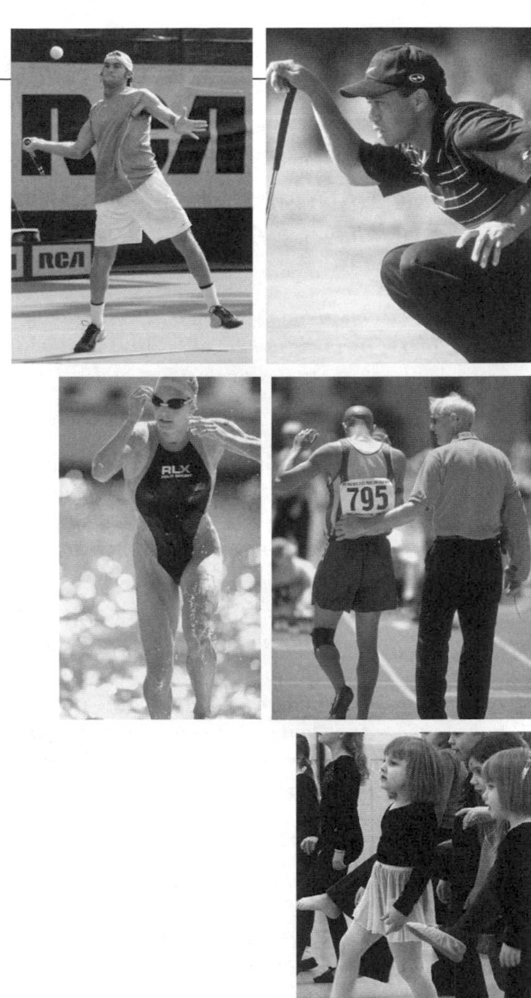

Understanding group processes is important to sport and exercise psychologists because substantial activity in the domain of sport and exercise is conducted in groups. A major issue in this context is group cohesion. Three classic readings in part IV focus on cohesion. Landers and Lüschen's (1974) article is pioneering, because it noted (probably for the first time) that task structure and demands (i.e., the nature of the interactions among group members) should be taken into account when assessing the relationships between cohesion and performance in sport. Many sport practitioners still believe that group cohesiveness is always a positive determinant of success. However, at least after the publication of Gill's (1977) review, it can be concluded that a positive relationship between cohesiveness and performance should not be taken for granted, but that the exact nature of this relationship is dependent on several important mediating variables. To assess cohesion in sport groups, the best existing cohesion measurement instrument, the Group Environment Questionnaire (GEQ), is presented in the article by Carron, Widmeyer, and Brawley (1985). It describes the rationale underlying the GEQ as well as its development. These readings directed a portion of the exercise psychology research to the effects of groups on exercise adherence.

Effective leadership is undoubtedly significant to the success of sport groups. In the article by Chelladurai and Saleh (1980), the development of the leadership scale for sports (LSS), an existing measure of sport leadership behaviors, is presented. Interest in leadership in sport has expanded since this questionnaire has gained popularity and has emphasized the importance of leadership as a performance variable related to sport group achievement. The last article in part IV (Danish, Owens, Green, and Brunelle 1997) is unique in that it deals with an unusual theme in the study of sport groups: the process and impact of disengagement and transition on individuals and teams in sport and how they should be handled.

17 Team Performance Outcome and the Cohesiveness of Competitive Coacting Groups

DANIEL M. LANDERS
University of Illinois

GÜNTHER LÜSCHEN
University of Düsseldorf

Research on cohesion in sport and exercise settings dates back to the early 1950s. For many years, a common belief among sport practitioners and researchers alike was that a positive relationship between cohesiveness and performance exists; that is, group cohesion was said to positively affect athletic success. This popular belief was corroborated by empirical studies conducted in this area. However, leading researchers in this domain were also concerned by some empirical evidence that consistently refuted such a positive relationship.

Dan Landers has gained recognition in sport and exercise psychology through his persistent questioning and thorough examinations of popular beliefs, "truths," and "myths" in this field. To test the possibility that the relationship between cohesion and performance is not always positive, Landers conducted an empirical study with his colleague Günther Lüschen from Germany (an excellent example of international cooperation in the then-young field of sport psychology). These researchers reported a negative relationship between cohesiveness and performance in intramural bowling teams. In this study, team members rated their teammates toward the end of the season on measures of task, communication, and power structure as well as on cohesiveness (interpersonal attraction or group-affect structure). It was found that successful teams had lower interpersonal attraction ratings than unsuccessful teams. This was one of the earliest systematic investigations conducted in sport and exercise psychology (though published in a leading sport sociology journal) that empirically demonstrated such a negative relationship between cohesiveness and team performance in sport and exercise psychology.

To date, one of the most important explanations of the contradictory results between cohesion and performance in athletic groups involves the diversity of task demands that such groups face. Landers and Lüschen were probably the first ones to note that task structure and demands should be taken into account when assessing the relationship between cohesion and performance in sport. They suggested that because of the nature of the group bowling task in their study, rivalry and competition among group members may have improved the individuals' performance at the expense of developing friendships with teammates and may have negatively affected the overall performance of the group. Based on their findings, Landers and Lüschen characterized the nature of interactions among group members along a continuum, from coaction to interaction. Whereas coactive sports (e.g., bowling and golf) require minimal, if any, team interaction and coordination to achieve their goals, interactive sports (e.g., soccer and basketball) require team members to work together and coordinate their actions. According to this reasoning, cohesion would be in a negative (or no) relationship with performance for coactive sports, whereas for interactive sports, this relationship would be positive. This seminal notion is attributed to this pioneering study conducted by Landers and Lüschen, which is considered a classic in sport and exercise psychology.

A question often plaguing investigators is why some competitive teams achieve consistently successful performance outcomes and why others do not. Obviously, the resources, in terms of skills and abilities, that group members bring to the contest are extremely important. This perceived importance has often led to a neglect of other important determinants of team performance outcome, namely group structure and task demands.

The concept of group structure refers to patterned regularities in feeling, perceptions, and actions that characterize aspects of the interactions between members of a group. The structure of task-oriented groups can be described in terms of patterned regularities among group members in regard to interpersonal attraction for one another, as well as communication between group members, power relations, and member perceived contribution to the task. Of these components of group structure only one, interpersonal attraction, has received attention in investigations of sport, primarily as an important force contributing to group cohesiveness (Lott and Lott, 1965). According to Festinger, Schachter and Back (1950) group cohesiveness is defined as the resultant of all forces influencing members to remain in the group. These forces are dependent upon the relative degree of attractiveness of members of the group (social cohesiveness) and activities in which the group engages (task cohesiveness). Since sport performance is voluntary and generally of high salience to the performer, primary attention has focused upon the contribution of social cohesiveness to team performance. In the present study all four structural components were investigated. However, greater theoretical emphasis was attached to the structural component of interpersonal

Adapted, by permission, from D. Landers and G. Lüschen, 1974, "Team performance outcome and the cohesiveness of competitive coacting groups," *International Review of Sport Sociology* 9: 57-71.

attraction because of its frequent use by investigators of team performance.

On a group structural level, it has generally been held that groups whose members indicate high interpersonal attraction and cohesiveness are more effective (Hare, 1964). Although this assumed relationship between group performance outcome and cohesiveness of group members is commonly cited, the empirical findings, underlying such an inductive statement, have been equivocal. In competitive sport settings, for example, a number of investigators have found a positive relationship between performance outcome and team cohesiveness, thus rendering support for the Hare (1964) assertion. Equally provocative, however, are other studies showing the opposite or no relationship, and as a result a state of confusion has persisted. Although the literature on sport is replete with studies examining the association of cohesiveness and team performance outcome, few investigators have attempted to explain the underlying mechanisms for their relationship and then predict *a priori* a specific outcome.

The present investigation sought: (1) to utilize a social psychological model of task demands and explicate its relationship to the contradictory cohesiveness-performance outcome results; and (2) to provide an empirical test of one of the hypotheses derived from an analysis of task demands. Thus conceived, the present investigation represents a radical departure from previous empirical examinations of cohesiveness and team performance outcome.

Task Demands of Group Tasks

The utilization of sport groups has been a popular avenue for testing group performance, perhaps, because sport provides a natural competitive setting in which members of several teams share similar goals. Investigators have restricted their investigations to teams within a given sport, but have at times stated their conclusions as if to encompass different types of competitive team sports. To do this is to overlook the task structure of differing sports as well as processes whereby members adapt in patterned ways to differing task-imposed demands. Without the elucidation of important task requirements among differing team sports, the generality of findings as well as the perusal of scientific explanations is greatly curtailed. Fortunately, recent refinements in the conceptual analysis of the requirements of group tasks have been advanced (Altman and McGrath, 1959; Fiedler, 1967; Glanzer and Glaser, 1959; Shaw, 1963).

Although a profusion of differing terms have been employed in these conceptual analyses of the task demands (i.e., implicit rules) of group tasks, a commonly termed distinction is that of interacting and coacting type groups. The difference between interacting and coacting groups is the way in which group members' efforts are pooled. Interacting groups are dependent on each member's contribution for the completion of the task. For example, in interacting groups with high division-of-labor, the group result is not derivable from the individual efforts by simple summation. Rather the group outcome results from a more complex combination of several individuals' performances since task activities must not only be performed, but also performed at a time, and in a fashion, which are appropriate to the task actions of other members. This latter characteristic has been termed means-interdependence (Thomas, 1957) and, together with the division-of-labor of team members, constitute the essential characteristics found in interacting groups.

These structural demands can have profound effects on components of group structure (e.g., interpersonal attraction). For example, in order to be effective, members of interacting groups must combine their different specialized skills, through interdependent action, to achieve the performance output of the team — a process commonly referred to in sport as team-work. The crucial intervening variable linking the interacting and coacting task dimensions with cohesiveness is *rate of interaction* among team members. Such a relationship is suggested by the findings of Sherif, Harvey, White, Hood, and Sherif (1961) where means-interdependent tasks produced an enhanced rate of interaction and ultimately greater cohesiveness. It is argued here that interacting task groups, which require means-interdependence among team members, facilitate rate of interaction, leading to greater cohesiveness and task performance. Indeed, a perusal of the sport literature indicates that investigations of interacting sport groups, such as basketball teams (Klein and Christiansen, 1966; Martens and Peterson, 1971; Peterson, 1970), football teams (Stogdill, 1963), flag football teams (McIntyre, 1970), and volleyball teams (Vos, Koos and Brinkman, 1967), have shown that successful teams evidenced greater cohesiveness than unsuccessful teams.

In contrast to these interacting groups, the literature on coacting groups has consistently failed to show a positive relationship between cohesiveness and performance outcome for competitive groups in which members independently perform essentially identical functions. McGrath (1962) and Myers (1962), for instance, have shown no significant relationship between team success and cohesiveness of coacting rifle teams. In addition, Lenk (1966) has found an inverse relationship between team success and cohesiveness of world-class German Olympic rowing teams. These shooting and rowing tasks require every member of the group to perform exactly the same function, and although coordination is necessary as in rowing, group members are less reliant on the functions carried out by others for successful completion of their own sub-task.

The foregoing conceptual analysis of important task demands and the empirical evidence reviewed lead to the following hypotheses: (1) for interacting-type teams, a successful team performance outcome effects a greater enhancement of group cohesiveness than unsuccessful team performance outcome; and (2) for coacting-type teams, an unsuccessful team performance effects a greater heightening of cohesiveness than successful performance outcome teams. Using several measures of group structure components and cohesiveness as well as multivariate data analysis techniques similar to those used in other studies (Peterson, 1970; Martens and Peterson, 1971), a test of the second hypothesis for the effects of coacting team performance outcome was examined for four types of sociometric questions which were designed to serve as indicators of group structure (interpersonal attraction, task communication and power relations).

Method

Subjects

The members of fifty-two bowling teams (4-7 members each) participating in an intramural bowling league at the University of Illinois volunteered as participants in the study. Team members bowled without handicaps and knew each other previously since they represented various residential organizations (e.g., fraternities, men's residence halls, and men's independent associations). The teams bowled two-out-of-three games in order to score a victory and competed twice each week for approximately one hour. In spite of the occasional weak opponent, it was necessary for team members to bowl their best since only 16 fraternity and 10 independent bowling teams with the highest total pins could bowl in the final tournament. Teams were motivated to achieve victory in order to obtain trophies and to have their standing in bowling count toward an all sport award given to the residence hall, association, or fraternity achieving the highest cumulative total in all sports during the 1969—1970 school year.

Assessment of Group Structure and Cohesiveness

Team members rated every other teammate on a 9-choice alternative between two polarities for each of six questions designed to determine interpersonal attraction, task, communication, and power interpersonal team relations. For example, to assess interpersonal attraction the following question was asked:

On how much a friendship basis are you with each of your teammates? Record the names of each team member and beneath their names rate the degree to which you like each of them.

JOHN DOE

: : : : : : : : : :

Not at all Very much

Other sociometric questions used to assess task, power, and communication relations among team members were as follows: a) teammates contribution to bowling performance; b) the influence (power) that each team member has on the team as a whole (i.e., decision making, organization, etc.); c) each member's influence (power) on you; d) your amount of verbal communication with each team member on the bowling alley; and e) amount of verbal communication with teammates between bowling sessions.

Measures and Design

From the fifty-two teams, 15 teams highest in total pins with the most wins, and 15 teams lowest in total pins with the fewest wins, were used for comparison. The group mean, derived from each team member's rating of his teammates on each of the six questions, were used as one measure. Although commonly used, these group means many times conceal individual variation within a group (Hollander, 1967, p. 363). Therefore, a second measure, group standard deviations, was also used in order to determine if the group homogeneity on the various sociometric measures differed between the performance outcomes of successful and unsuccessful teams. In addition, this measure provided a check on the equal between-group variance assumption to the analyses performed on the group structure means. One-way univariate analysis of variance (ANOVA) and multivariate ANOVA, step-down F tests, chi square tests of the canonical variate, and discriminant function analyses were the statistical tests used.

Procedure

Through the cooperation of the Division of intramurals, University of Illinois, graduate students under the direction of the investigators administered the questionnaire to all team members in a classroom setting. The testing took place toward the end of the league season before the final tournament.

The win-loss record and the bowling scores for each team were tabulated by the Division of intramurals. The questionnaire data were transferred to IBM cards for analysis.

Results

Correlation Among Group Structure Measures

As would be expected, all correlations among the means of the various group structure measures were significant at the .05 level and 10 were significant at the .01 level. With the exception of how much power the team member thought he had on the team as a whole, all other measures had moderately high (explaining 34% to 46% of the variance) correlations with interpersonal attraction. The two questions used to assess power were also moderately correlated ($r = 0.75$), while the two communication questions, on the bowling alley versus between bowling sessions, were correlated ($p < .01$), but to a much lower degree ($r = 0.48$).

Multivariate Results

In order to test the hypothesis of this study, a single probability, which cannot be obtained from the univariate

ANOVA's needed to be obtained. Since the same subjects rated the several measures, separate univariate ANOVA's are not statistically independent. With several univariate ANOVA's, therefore, no exact probability that at least one of them will exceed some critical level of the null hypothesis can be calculated. Multivariate ANOVA, on the other hand, is based on sample statistics which take into account the correlations between the dependent variables, and have known sampling distributions from which the required probabilities can be obtained (Bock and Haggard, 1968). Significant differences in multivariate ANOVA are considered important primarily as an incentive to further investigate: a) the difference between several levels of the independent variable; and b) the source of the differences in terms of the relative contribution of the six dependent variables.

The multivariate ANOVA on group structure standard deviations was not significant. The multivariate ANOVA on the group structure means, however, was significant. In contrast to the results found with interacting-type sport groups (Peterson, 1970; Martens and Peterson, 1971), the group structure means do not show consistently higher group means for successful teams. In fact, four of the means differences — interpersonal attractions, individual's power on the team, members' power over the individual, and communication between group members on the bowling alley — favored unsuccessful teams. Group members' mean differences for perception of members' task ability and communication among group members between bowling sessions favored the successful teams. These six mean differences, however, do not equally reflect the major source(s) responsible for the significant multivariate *F* found between successful and unsuccessful teams. To locate the major source(s) of the significant difference between groups in terms of the variates which contribute to it, a discriminant function analysis was performed.

A discriminant function analysis determines the linear combination of dependent variables which maximally discriminates in a least-square sense, between members of teams having either a successful or unsuccessful performance outcome. The discriminant coefficients are represented by the latent vector associated with the significant latent root for the successful-unsuccessful group effect. These coefficients are in standard score form which was obtained by multiplying each discriminant coefficient by the within-group standard deviation of the corresponding variate. The standard scores for the largest coefficient indicate that the task and interpersonal attraction structures primarily contributed to the difference between successful and unsuccessful teams. Although the arithmetic signs associated with the task and interpersonal attractions coefficients differ, these signs are arbitrary (Bock and Haggard, 1968).

To further clarify the relationship of the differences between groups on task and interpersonal attraction structure means a step-down *F* test was used. Step down *F* analysis is a sequence of univariate tests of significance on each variable after covarying all preceding variables. The ordering of the variables for the step-down analysis is important since the order in which variables are arranged affects the outcome. The arrangement must be determined *a priori* with the variables believed to be the most discriminating between the performance outcome of successful and unsuccessful teams appearing first. The task variable was ordered first in this study since it was believed that it would be relatively easy for respondents (especially for members of successful teams) to objectively rate teammates' contributions to team effectiveness. Since the member's rating of interpersonal attraction was sometimes of more obvious perceivability among team members than power and communication measures, interpersonal attraction was placed second in the ordering. This variable was then followed by power on the team, power of the team over the individual, communication while bowling, and communication between bowling sessions.

As would be expected from the discriminant function analysis, the step-down *F* test for task and interpersonal attraction measures were significant. The first variable (task) in a step-down analysis is always the same as that found in the univariate analysis. The second variable, interpersonal attraction, and succeeding step-down variables, however, differ from their univariate counterparts since the preceding dependent variables have been covaried out. When the task variable was covaried out, the adjusted interpersonal attraction means for teams having an unsuccessful performance outcome ($X = 7.46$) was significantly higher than for successful teams ($X = 6.92$). Since the task variables were positively correlated ($p < .01$), the adjustment of the interpersonal attraction means, when the task variable was used as a covariate, produced an even greater mean interpersonal attraction difference than was found in the univariate ANOVA. The marginal significance for communication between bowling sessions when all other variables were used as covariates must be regarded with caution due to the high group standard deviations for this particular variable.

Discussion

The results of the multivariate *F* test, which simultaneously considers mean differences in several measures of group structure and cohesiveness, supported the hypothesis of the current study. Discriminant function analysis indicated that the task and interpersonal attraction measures were the greatest contributors to the differences between the performance outcome of successful and unsuccessful teams. The mean differences showed support for the hypothesis of this study in that unsuccessful teams had higher interpersonal attraction ratings than successful teams, particularly when task means are covaried out. The task means, which were a measure of group structure, were in the opposite direction with successful teams rating teammates significantly higher than unsuccessful teams on their contributions to task effectiveness. This task difference, however, was not a test of the cohesiveness hypothesis posed. Furthermore, the findings for the task effect were of lesser theoretical importance since it simply demonstrates a team member's ability to objectively perceive the bowling contributions (e.g., skill ability) of their teammates. It is therefore apparent that members of more successful, as opposed to unsuccessful teams, would give their more highly skilled teammates higher ratings.

The significant differences for the interpersonal attraction measure when task differences are covaried out is of central importance to the hypothesis of the present study. In any field study of the type with its inherent inability to control many relevant variables, a number of readily apparent explanations could be advanced to contest the initially proposed task demands explanation. Three competing explanations which could be forwarded include: (1) the possibility that the results may be an artifact derived from sampling inadequacies or to the specific group structure and cohesiveness measures used; (2) members of unsuccessful bowling teams may have been less task-oriented and more oriented toward affiliation with teammates; and (3) in successful teams greater within-group competition may occur leading to less liking among teammates. The plausibility of these explanations are difficult to dispute unless one examines their consistency with other findings. If we are to accept the findings of other investigators, these explanations would perhaps support some findings but conflict with others. For example, Peterson (1970) and Martens and Peterson (1971) found strikingly dissimilar results utilizing measures and a subject population congruent to those used in the present study. For the second and third explanations to be amenable with the Peterson and Martens data, teams achieving a highly successful, as opposed to unsuccessful performance outcome, should have been less cohesive; however, just the opposite was found. Barring the possibility of sampling inadequacies in either of these studies, the second and third explanations only become consistent with existing literature, and thus more plausible, when the characteristics of the task demands are considered.

As noted previously, rate of interaction among team members is greatly enhanced in interacting-type team sports since the task is such that it requires members reliance upon others to complete their sub-task (e.g., play, score, etc.). Although such a means-interdependence among team members may facilitate higher levels of cohesiveness among teams whose performance outcome is successful, the potential mechanisms underlying findings for coacting-type teams are conceivably quite different when rate of interaction is relatively unspecified by task demands. Coacting group performance not unlike individual sport competition, is seen only as a setting or environment which is influenced by many social situational factors that are intrinsic to the task. Fiedler (1967, p.19), for example, maintains that the coacting team situation many times leads to rivalry and competition among group members, which serves as a motivating force for better individual performance. If such a process was evident, it would tend to increase overall bowling team performance at the expense of developing friendships with teammates.

Since the bowling setting provided an opportunity for relatively unobtrusive data gathering, an attempt was made to conduct a few controlled observations in order to shed additional light on actual group processes. This was done toward the end of the season with two teams that were achieving a successful performance outcome and two other teams that were on their way to having an unsuccessful performance outcome. Of the several group structure measures, communication among members in the bowling setting was the group structure measure chosen for observational rating since it was the easiest to objectively quantify and this measure also had the highest correlation with interpersonal attraction ($r = .68, p < .01$). These observations were independently conducted by two trained assistants who observed the same teams three times in three successive weeks. Verbal and nonverbal communications between members, team members and spectators, and team members and opponents were recorded. The observational findings for actual communication was found to parallel self-ratings, and also were of some relevance to the present discussion. Members of successful teams more often communicated with spectators rather than with one another. On the other hand, teammates comprising teams which were eventually unsuccessful were more communicative to one another while on the bowling alley. Although these observations of team communication can be interpreted as supportive of the rivalry explanation for successful coacting-type teams, such an interpretation, based upon these very limited observations, must be regarded with caution. More research, offering considerably more control than obtained in field studies of this type, is needed before the interaction between task demands and group structure can be more fully comprehended.

References

1. Allport F. H., *Social Psychology,* Boston, Houghton Mifflin, 1924.
2. Altman I. and McGrath J. E., *A conceptual framework for the integration of small group research information,* Arlington, Va., Human Sciences Research, Inc., 1959.
3. Bock R. D. and Haggard E. A., *The use of multivariate analysis of variance in behavioral research,* in Whitla, D. K. (ed.), *Handbook of measurement and assessment in behavioral sciences,* Reading, Mass., Addison-Wesley Publishing Co., 1968.
4. Eitzen S. D., *The effect to group structure on the success of athletic teams,* International Review of Sport Sociology, 1973, 8, pp. 7-17.
5. Festinger L., Schachter S. and Back K., *Social pressures in informal groups,* New York, Harper, 1950.
6. Fiedler F. E., Hartman W. and Rudin S. A., *The relationship of interpersonal perception to effectiveness in basketball*

teams, Urbana, Ill, Bureau of Research and Service, University of Illinois, 1952 (Mineo.), Supl., Tech. Rep. No. 3, Contract N6ori-07135).

7. Fiedler F. E., Hartman W. and Rudin S. A., *Correction and extension of the relationship of interpersonal perception to effectiveness in basketball teams,* Urbana, Ill, Bureau of Research and Service, University of Illinois, 1953 (Mineo.), Tech. Rep. No. 5, Contract N6orl-07135).
8. Fiedler F. E., *A theory of leadership effectiveness,* New York, McGraw-Hill, 1967.
9. Grace H. A., *Conformance and performance,* "Journal of Social Psychology", 1954, 40, pp. 333-335.
10. Glanzer M. and Glaser R., *Techniques for the study of group structure and behavior, I. Analysis of structure,* "Psychological Bulletin", 1959, 56, pp. 317-332.
11. Grusky, O., *The effects of formal structure on managerial recruitment, A study of baseball organization,* "Sociometry", 1963, 26, pp. 345-353.
12. Hare P., *Handbook of small group research,* Glencoe, Ill, The Free Press, 1962.
13. Hollander E. P., *Principles and methods of social psychology,* New York, Oxford University Press, 1967.
14. Klein M. and Christiansen G., *Group composition, group structure and group effectiveness of basketball teams,* in Loy J. W., Jr. and Kenyon G. S. (eds.), "Sport, Culture and Society", *A reader on the sociology of sport,* London, Macmillan, 1969, pp. 397-408.
15. Lanzetta J. T. and Roby T. B., *Group learning and communication as a function of task and structure "demands",* "Journal of Abnormal and Social Psychology", 1957, 55, pp. 121-131.
16. Lenk H., *Top performance despite internal conflict, An antithesis to a functionalistic proposition,* in Loy J. W., Jr. and Kenyon G. S. (eds.), "Sport, Culture and Society", *A reader on the sociology of sport,* London, Macmillan, 1969, pp. 393-397.
17. Lott A. J. and Lott B. R., *Group cohesiveness as interpersonal attraction, A review of relationships with anticedent and consequent variables,* "Psychological Bulletin", 1965, 64, pp. 259-309.
18. Martens R. and Peterson, J. A., *Group cohesiveness as a determinant of success and member satisfaction in team performance,* "International Review of Sport Sociology", 1971, 6, pp. 49-61.
19. McGrath J. E., *The influence of positive interpersonal relations on adjustment and effectiveness in rifle teams,* "Journal of Abnormal and Social Psychology", 1962, 65, pp. 365-375.
20. McIntyre T. D., *A field experimental study of attitude change in four biracial small groups,* Unpublished doctoral study, Pennsylvania State University, 1970.
21. Myers A., *Team composition, success and the adjustment of group members,* "Journal of Abnormal and Social Psychology", 1962, 65, pp. 325-332.
22. Peterson J. A., *Success and residential affiliation as determinants of team cohesiveness,* Unpublished Master's thesis, University of Illinois at Champaign-Urbana, 1970.
23. Shaw M. E., *Scaling group tasks, A method for dimensional analysis,* Technical Report Number 1, Office of Naval Research Contract NR170-266, Nonr-580(11), 1963.
24. Sherif M., Harvey O. J., White B. J., Hood W. R. and Sherif C. W., *Intergroup conflict and cooperation, The Robbers Cave experiment,* Norman, University of Oklahoma, 1961.
25. Steiner I. D., *Models for inferring relationships between group size and potential group productivity,* "Behavioral Science", 1966, 11, pp. 273-283.
26. Stogdill R. M., *Team achievement under high motivation,* "Business Research Monograph", Ohio State University, 1963.
27. Thomas E. J., *Effects of facilitative role interdependence on group functioning,* "Human Relations", 1957, 10, pp. 347-356.
28. Vos, Koos and Brinkman W., *Succes en cohesie in Sportgroepen, (Success and cohesion in sports),* "Sociologische Gios", 1967, 14, pp. 30-40.

18 Cohesiveness and Performance in Sport Groups

DIANE L. GILL
University of Waterloo, Ontario, Canada

Group dynamics has been of great interest to psychologists, especially since World War II. It was believed that understanding small-group processes would enhance the morale of fighting troops. Historically, cohesion has been viewed by many psychologists as the most important topic in small-group research. Accordingly, cohesion has been intensively investigated not only in the military but also in various branches of psychology, such as social, organizational, educational, counseling, and sport and exercise psychology.

The term cohesion refers to everything that binds people to each other and makes them "stick together" (actually, in Latin, cohaesus means to stick together, or cleave). Research on cohesion in sport and exercise settings dates back to the early 1950s, when researchers from social psychology began to examine the relationship of team dynamics (e.g., group cohesion) to team effectiveness in various sports. In the early 1970s, the relatively new discipline of sport psychology started to reveal increasing interest in exploring this domain. In the mid-1970s, enough information was gathered in this area from both social and sport psychological studies to justify an extensive review.

Gill undertook this challenge of studying cohesiveness. She focused her chapter on the relationship between cohesiveness and performance in sport groups, an issue that is until today somewhat misleading, especially for practitioners who are not aware of updated research findings. More specifically, a common belief among sport practitioners is that group cohesiveness is always a positive determinant of success. Gill extensively reviewed the research literature and found that this was not always the case. Some of the findings corroborated the popular belief in a positive relationship between cohesiveness and performance in sport; however, other investigations provided significant refuting evidence. She firmly concluded that a positive relationship between cohesiveness and performance could not be accepted as an empirical fact in light of this substantial negative evidence. To solve this equivocality in the literature on sport cohesiveness, Gill suggested a long list of potential measures on both the conceptual and the methodological levels, including several possible mediating variables.

This chapter can be considered a milestone in this area because it provided an excellent summary of the early literature on sport cohesion, raised an important question for discussion by presenting refuting evidence for a popular and misleading belief, and suggested some solutions that contributed to later developments in this domain.

Most sport cohesiveness research adheres to a conventional investigative paradigm, where field studies quite logically predominate. Cohesiveness is not easily manipulated, and sport-type tasks are not easily performed within laboratories. Furthermore, removing a team, with its own developed level of cohesiveness, from its natural setting destroys any semblance of ecological validity in the cohesiveness-performance relationship. Typical procedures call for administration of a cohesiveness questionnaire to a number of teams at preseason, postseason, or both. The relationship of cohesiveness to team performance, invariably measured as the season win-loss ratio, is then assessed with a correlational analysis. Despite the methodological conformity among sport cohesiveness studies, the findings are far from consistent. For every study finding that cohesiveness is positively related to performance, another reports no relationship, or even a negative relationship between cohesiveness and performance.

The literature examining the cohesiveness-performance relationship within the realm of sport is reviewed in the next section. The studies are listed and the results discussed with little attempt at critical analysis. The remainder of the review chapter discusses the major conceptual issues in the sport cohesiveness literature in an attempt to clarify previous conflicting findings and to provide guidance for future investigations.

The Cohesiveness-Performance Relationship

Positive Evidence

Two early studies often cited in support of a positive cohesiveness-performance relationship were conducted by Klein and Christiansen (1969) and Myers (1962). Klein and Christiansen, like many investigators, examined the cohesiveness-performance relationship within the context of basketball. Members of two eight-member teams were observed during game play for the first stage of the experiment, and for the second stage, seven members of one team participated in different combinations for a series of "three-on-three" games. Players rated the attractiveness of each three-man combination prior to each game. Classifying teams as high or low cohesive, and classifying team

---

Adapted, by permission, from D. Gill, 1977, Cohesiveness and performance in sport groups," *Exercise and Sport Science Reviews* 5: 131-155.

performance as high or low, revealed a positive relationship between team cohesiveness and performance.

Myers (1962) investigated the adjustment of group members (esteem for teammates), rather than cohesiveness per se, with ROTC rifle teams. Sixty three-man teams were formed and divided into competitive and noncompetitive leagues for a 5-week recreational rifle tournament. Competitive teams increased in esteem for teammates from Week 2 to Week 5 more than noncompetitive teams, but that finding is less germane to the current review than the influence of team performance on esteem for teammates. High-success teams increased in esteem for teammates while low-success teams decreased, regardless of the competition condition. Team performance success, then, was positively related to changes in cohesiveness, measured as esteem for teammates. In addition, Myers reported a similar trend in the analysis of perceived acceptance scores. Within the competition condition, perceived acceptance scores of high-success teams were significantly higher than those of low-success teams. Myers concluded that an individual's interpersonal perceptions of his group members is significantly affected by the team's level of success.

Stogdill (1963) investigated the relationship between cohesion and performance under conditions of high motivation or drive. Eight high school football coaches were employed as observers at six Ohio State football games to obtain measures of cohesiveness and drive. Two nine-point ratings, the extent to which the team maintained structure and the extent to which the members coordinated their efforts, were used to assess cohesiveness on every play. Cohesiveness and similarly obtained drive ratings were highly intercorrelated and both correlated with yards gained; Stogdill cited factor analytic results to support his contention that drive, cohesion, and productivity were independent measures. The questionable validity of Stogdill's unique operational measures suggests caution in comparing the results to other cohesiveness studies. Nevertheless, Stogdill concluded that the results supported his theory (presented in greater detail in Stogdill, 1972), namely that under conditions of high drive, cohesiveness and productivity are positively related.

The most notable contribution to the sport cohesiveness literature is the extensive study of intramural basketball teams by Martens and Peterson (Martens & Peterson, 1971; Peterson & Martens, 1972). Over 1200 male college students, who were members of 144 intramural basketball teams, participated in the study. The large number of observations, in comparison to other studies often involving 20 or fewer teams, permits us to place greater faith in the reliability of the Martens and Peterson results. Cohesiveness was assessed both preseason and postseason using the Sport Cohesiveness Questionnaire (Martens & Peterson, 1971). That inventory is multidimensional, including eight separate measures of cohesiveness. The eight individual items fall into three categories: (a) four sociometric measures in which each member rates each other teammate on degree of interpersonal attraction, contribution based on ability, contribution to team satisfaction, and influence or power; (b) two direct individual assessment items, the value of membership on the team and how strong a sense of belonging the respondent felt toward the team; and (c) two direct team assessment items requiring the respondent to evaluate the team as a whole on level of teamwork and how closely-knit the team is. All ratings are made using a nine-point semantic-differential scale.

The first study (Martens & Peterson, 1971) examined preseason cohesiveness as a determinant of success and member satisfaction. On the basis of preseason scores the teams were divided into three levels of cohesiveness with success and satisfaction as dependent variables. Separate analyses of variance using each of the eight measures indicated that three of the four direct assessment items (value of membership, teamwork, and closeness) significantly affected team performance (win percentage). In all cases high cohesive teams won more games than low cohesive teams.

The second study (Peterson & Martens, 1972) examined the cohesiveness-performance relationship from the opposite direction (i.e., the influence of team success on postseason cohesiveness). Teams were classified into three levels of success according to the number of games won, and both univariate and multivariate analyses of variance and covariance were reported. The multivariate analysis of covariance (covarying out preseason cohesiveness) indicated that performance success significantly affected postseason cohesiveness. The univariate covariance analyses also revealed significant success effects for each of the separate postseason cohesiveness measures. In all cases, successful teams were more cohesive than less successful teams.

Arnold and Straub (1972) used the Martens and Peterson (1971) questionnaire with 107 high school basketball players in a 10-team conference. The questionnaire was administered both before and after the season. The top five teams in the conference were classified as successful and the bottom five as less successful. Preseason differences between successful and less successful teams were significant for interpersonal attraction, power, and enjoyment-of-playing ratings, but a multivariate discriminant function comparison, considering all cohesiveness measures simultaneously, failed to reveal significant differences. Analyses of postseason cohesiveness scores revealed that members of successful teams were significantly more cohesive in terms of teamwork and closely-knit ratings than were members of less successful teams. Two of the authors' seven conclusions relate directly to the cohesiveness-performance relationship. First, it was concluded that "At postseason, players who participated on Successful teams were significantly more cohesive than players who played on Less Successful teams" (Arnold & Straub, 1972, p. 350). Second, "Cohesiveness appeared to be a prerequisite for success in varsity high school basketball competition" (Arnold & Straub, 1972, p. 351). It should be noted, however, that the results are more limited than the conclusions suggest.

Widmeyer (1977) has recently adopted the Martens and Peterson (1971) paradigm with some added controls to examine the influence of cohesiveness on intramural basketball performance. Widmeyer formed three-player teams for the study and divided them into separate leagues for men and women and for each of three ability levels. Using factor analysis Widmeyer formed two cohesiveness factors from the individual items of the Martens and Peterson questionnaire. Essentially, the two factors divided the questionnaire into the sociometric items (termed "inferential cohesion" by Widmeyer) and the direct assessment items (direct cohesion). The two cohesion factors were then used in a multiple regression analysis to predict team performance success (win percentage over a 7-10 game season). The multiple regression of performance success on the two cohesion factors was significant, accounting for 19% of the performance variance. The direct cohesion factor, however, accounted for nearly all (18.7%) of this variance. Widmeyer's results, then, supported those of Martens and Peterson in that direct preseason cohesion was positively related to team performance.

Bird (1977), in the one study using only female subjects, investigated the relationship of cohesiveness and leader orientation to intercollegiate volleyball performance. The two most successful and the two least successful teams in each of two separate divisions within the highly competitive Southern California conference (16 teams total) were selected for analysis. Cohesiveness was assessed with a modified version of the Martens and Peterson (1971) questionnaire and a group atmosphere scale. A significant multivariate success effect and subsequent discriminant analysis results indicated that the four successful teams had greater cohesion than the four unsuccessful teams, supporting a positive relationship between cohesiveness and the success of sport teams.

Nixon (1977), like Widmeyer (1977), has recently investigated the cohesiveness-performance relationship with three-man basketball teams, but on a somewhat smaller scale. Cohesiveness was assessed prior to and following each game over a two-week, eight-game season. Prior to each game, players rated the perceived importance of friendliness and perceived amount of friendliness among teammates as measures of interpersonal attraction. An additional pregame rating — the importance of team membership — was deemed cohesiveness and considered separately from interpersonal attraction. A second cohesiveness rating — satisfaction with team membership — was taken after each game, and a final postseason cohesiveness item assessed the desire to become a member of other teams.

Nixon reported no statistical tests of significance, but instead classified teams according to whether they were higher, lower, or equal to their opponents on each measure and compared that classification to game outcome. The data consisted of individual responses, in contrast to the customary practice of deriving team cohesiveness scores when comparing cohesion and team performance. Nixon reported higher postgame cohesiveness for opponents who were winners than for opponents who were losers, and observed that none of the members of the three top teams wanted to leave their teams at postseason while all four members of the last-place team did want to leave. Nixon's observations support a positive relationship between team success and cohesiveness (measured as team satisfaction), but the small sample size, weaknesses in data collection, and the lack of sound statistical procedures cast doubt upon the findings.

Ball and Carron (1976), following a paradigm similar to that of Martens and Peterson (1971) and employing the Sport Cohesiveness Questionnaire, investigated the influence of cohesiveness and participation motivation on team performance in intercollegiate ice hockey. Cohesiveness was assessed early in the season (prior to completion of two league games), at midseason, and at postseason. Midseason teamwork/closeness (direct cohesion) was significantly related to postseason success (total win percentage), and midseason value-of-membership measures significantly discriminated among successful, moderately successful, and unsuccessful teams. The results, however, are difficult to compare with previous research due to the large number of predictor variables included (all measures of both early season and midseason cohesiveness and participation motivation as well as years of experience in the league).

Results of a second study (Carron & Ball, in press) are much clearer in terms of the cohesiveness- performance relationship. A cross-lagged panel correlation design was used to examine the causal direction in the cohesiveness-performance relationship; i.e., does cohesiveness cause performance success or does performance success cause cohesiveness? A single composite cohesiveness score was derived of each of the three times (early season, midseason, and postseason) by averaging the seven items from the Martens and Peterson (1971) questionnaire. The cumulative win-loss ratios at midseason and postseason provided the performance success measures. Performance generally predicted cohesiveness, particularly as indicated by the correlation between midseason performance and postseason cohesiveness ($r = -.77$). (Because low cohesiveness scores indicate greater cohesiveness, the negative correlation indicates a positive relationship.) The correlations between early season cohesiveness and midseason performance ($r = -.23$), midseason cohesiveness and postseason performance ($r = .39$), and early season cohesiveness and postseason performance ($r = .07$) were all nonsignificant.

Negative Evidence

The sport literature cited above corroborates popular belief in a positive cohesiveness-performance relationship; but there is another side to sport cohesiveness research that precludes any decisive statements regarding the cohesiveness-performance relationship. Melnick and Chemers (1974), for example, followed the typical paradigm and investigated cohesiveness within intramural basketball teams using the Sport Cohesiveness Questionnaire and procedures similar to those of Martens and Peterson (1971). Preseason cohesiveness was assessed using the four direct cohesiveness items prior to the first game for each of 21 teams. In contrast to the studies previously discussed, none of the four cohesiveness items correlated significantly with team performance success (correlations ranged from –.10 to .22). Melnick and Chemers, then, failed to find even a trend toward a positive relationship between cohesiveness and performance.

The most widely cited evidence refuting a positive cohesiveness-performance relationship are the negative relationships reported in the earlier studies of Fiedler (1954), Lenk (1969, 1977) and McGrath (1962). Fiedler's study of high school basketball teams involved interpersonal relationships in terms of "assumed similarity" measures. According to Fiedler, assumed similarity scores (derived from subjects' descriptions of themselves and persons with whom they cooperate most and least well) are correlates of liking and warmth in interpersonal relationships. Exploratory data gathered with 14 teams yielded a negative relationship between the assumed similarity measures and the proportion of games won. Seven teams with winning seasons and five teams with losing seasons participated in a second validation study. Fiedler again found a negative relationship between the assumed similarity score of the team's most preferred coworker and team performance. A third study with surveying teams corroborated Fiedler's basic finding that more effective teams tend to be less congenial than less effective teams.

Grace (1954), using data gathered from Fiedler's 14 high school basketball teams, reported that team cooperation, determined from the highest member's rating on cooperativeness, was negatively related to performance. Grace also reported that a wide range of cooperativeness within a team was detrimental to performance and concluded that good performance is a function of the conformance of group members to each other and to the general sample. The reported inverse relationship between cooperativeness and team performance is typically cited as evidence refuting a positive cohesiveness-performance relationship. Despite the frequent citing of the Fiedler (1954) and Grace work, the appropriateness of either assumed similarity or cooperativeness as measures of cohesiveness is highly questionable.

McGrath's (1962) study of interpersonal relations and team effectiveness in rifle teams emanated from the previously discussed study by Myers (1962). On the basis of interpersonal-relationship scores derived from data gathered at the end of Myers' study, McGrath formed teams so that half were comprised of men who gave positive interpersonal rating to former teammates and half were comprised of members who had given low ratings. Initial marksmanship scores did not differ between the two groups, but after six weeks with the new groups the nonpositive groups had significantly better marksmanship scores than the positive groups. The superior performance improvement of less interpersonally oriented teams argues against a positive cohesiveness-performance relationship.

Lenk's (1969, 1977) research was actually a case study report rather than an experimental investigation. Lenk's observations and sociometric data gathered with world-class German rowing teams in the early 1960s revealed poor interpersonal relations and considerable conflict, yet the team became world champions. Quite possibly, extrinsic rewards or goals kept the team together and maintained optimal performance despite the interpersonal conflicts. Lenk cited this example to refute the thesis that top performance can only be achieved with harmonious interpersonal relations. Instead, Lenk contends that even vehement intrateam conflict need not weaken performance at all if the team continues to exist in spite of the conflict.

More recently, Landers and Lüschen (1974) have reported a negative relationship between cohesiveness and team performance with intramural bowling teams. Near the end of the season, team members rated each teammate on interpersonal attraction, task contribution, two communication items, and two power or influence items. Landers and Lüschen thus obtained measures of task, communication, and power structure, as well as the cohesiveness measure (interpersonal attraction or group-affect structure). A multivariate analysis of the six ratings indicated that successful and unsuccessful teams (the top 15 and bottom 15 of 52 teams) were significantly different, with successful teams having *lower* interpersonal attraction ratings than unsuccessful teams. Landers and Lüschen suggested that due to the nature of the group bowling task, rivalry and competition among team members may improve individual performance, and therefore overall team performance, at the expense of developing friendships with teammates.

Summary and Discussion

The negative relationships reported in the immediately preceding section indicate that a positive cohesiveness-performance relationship cannot be accepted as an empirical fact. Furthermore, the positive relationships reported in a number of studies exist only for selected measures or certain aspects of the overall design. In both the Martens and Peterson (1971) and Widmeyer (1977) studies, direct cohesiveness measures predicted team performance, but the sociometric or indirect measures were not related to team performance. The Landers and Crum (1971) results were even more restricted, with only direct group evaluation (not direct individual assessment nor sociometric items) showing a positive relationship to team success. Despite Arnold and Straub's (1972) conclusions that a positive relationship exists, their supporting data are quite sketchy. Successful and less successful teams differed on only three preseason cohesiveness measures and the multivariate comparison failed to yield a significant difference. Only univariate results were reported for postseason cohesiveness, but again, only two measures (teamwork and closeness) significantly differentiated successful and less successful teams. Ball and Carron (1976) likewise found only selected measures (out of more than 20) that predicted team performance success. Their second study (Carron & Ball, in press) suggests that, in fact, cohesiveness did *not* predict performance, although the prediction from performance success to cohesiveness was quite good.

In sum, the sport cohesiveness literature is marked by its equivocality. Some studies (e.g., Bird, 1977; Martens & Peterson, 1971; Peterson & Martens, 1972; Widmeyer, 1977) provide evidence for the intuitively appealing positive relationship between cohesiveness and performance, but other evidence suggests a negative relationship (e.g., Fiedler, 1954; Landers & Lüschen, 1974), or no relationship at all (e.g., Melnick & Chemers, 1974).

The general social psychology cohesiveness literature might logically be consulted to clarify the picture. Neither time, space, nor the scope of this review permits a comprehensive discussion of that general literature. Several authors have reviewed that expansive literature, and the reader is referred to those sources for additional information (see Cartwright, 1968; Collins & Raven, 1969; Lott & Lott, 1965; McGrath & Altman, 1966; Shaw, 1976). The essence of that research, as it relates to the cohesiveness-performance relationship, may be summarized simply. The empirical evidence obtained with such diverse groups as military crews, industrial work groups, and contrived lab groups, reveals both positive and negative relationships; the overall picture is just as equivocal as that painted by the sport cohesiveness literature.

Conceptual Considerations

Cohesiveness research contains more than its share of questionable operational measures, poor sampling procedures, and inappropriate statistical analyses, but methodological deficiencies alone do not account for the lack of conclusive findings. Instead, the conspicuous absence of any theoretical framework and the noticeable lack of conceptual rigor seem to be the primary culprits. Rather than attempting to gather more evidence to tip the scales toward a positive or negative cohesiveness-performance relationship, it may be possible to make more sense of the present literature by viewing it from the vantage point of a conceptual framework. By identifying critical factors and constructs, the role of cohesiveness in the performance of sport teams may be clarified. For the purpose of this review the critical considerations seem to be: (a) the definition and measurement of cohesiveness as a social-psychological construct, (b) the time dimension (or causality) in the cohesiveness-performance relationship, and (c) mediating variables that influence the cohesiveness-performance relationship. These three considerations are discussed as they relate to the sport cohesiveness literature in the remainder of this review.

Definition and Measurement of Cohesiveness

The concept of cohesiveness. A shared definition of cohesiveness as a psychological construct, together with a certain degree of procedural standardization, are essential before any progress in understanding the cohesiveness-performance relationship can be made. Theoretical statements are, however, conspicuous by their absence in the cohesiveness literature. Even today, more than 25 yr after its initial publication, the classic work of Festinger, Schachter, and Back (1950/1963) is the single notable theoretical treatment of group cohesiveness. The absence of theoretical advancement or refinement is amazing considering that the Festinger et al. definition of cohesiveness is too broad for direct use, and that the operational measure in the original study consisted of a single question.

Festinger et al.'s theoretical analysis of cohesiveness was derived from a field study designed to investigate group influence in small social groups rather than cohesiveness per se. Participants in the study were married, veteran, engineering students at MIT who lived in the housing communities of Westgate and Westgate West in the late 1940s. Festinger et al. recognized that the homogeneity of the population could be a limitation, and cautioned against overgeneralization of the results. Successors, however, have generally taken a more cavalier approach and failed to heed such cautions. The housing study was quite broad in scope and a variety of field-study techniques, including observation, interviews, sociometry, and field experimentation, were used. The sole measure of cohesiveness, however, was a single question asking, "What three people in Westgate or Westgate West do you see most of socially?" (Festinger et al., 1950/1963, p. 37). The courts and buildings within the community were treated as social groups, and responses to the above question were used to determine the proportion of in-court choices.

Based on the findings of the housing study, and as direction for subsequent investigations, Festinger and his colleagues proposed a theory of group structure and group standards. Within this theoretical context, the classic and widely quoted definition of cohesiveness was presented as, "the total field of forces which act on members to remain in the group . . ." (Festinger et al., 1950/1963, p. 164). Elaborating on the concept, Festinger et al. identified two classes of forces that contribute to cohesiveness. The first class of forces — the attractiveness of the group in and of itself — refers to the extent to which the group has positive valence. Festinger et al. posited that in informal social groups this attractiveness is most affected by satisfying relationships and friendships with members or interpersonal attraction. The second class of forces, referred to as the "means control" of the group, may further be described as the extent the group mediates goals that are important for members. Festinger et al. concluded, "We may then derive that the more valent a group is and the greater the number and importance of the goals the accessibility to which are in control of the group, the more cohesive the group will be" (Festinger et al., 1950/1963, p. 165).

While Festinger presented a definition and a limited conceptual framework, along with a simplified operational measure, for group cohesiveness, the theory failed to clearly specify forces or sources of attraction, and the concepts seem susceptible to refinement and clarification. Friendship choice as an operational measure is not directly derivable from the theory, and reasons for the imposed operational limitations are not specified. The majority of cohesiveness researchers who followed Festinger have made the same leap from the conceptual definition as stated to interpersonal-attraction choices as the operational measure without justification or consideration of alternatives. Some immediate responses to the work of Festinger and his colleagues did, however, attempt to critically evaluate certain aspects of the cohesiveness theory.

One of the more notable criticisms, by Gross and Martin (1952), challenged Festinger et al.'s operational definition of cohesiveness. The major point of contention was that the nominal definition of cohesiveness (total field of forces) was not adequately represented by the operational definition of interpersonal attraction or the in-group ratio of friendships. Furthermore, interpersonal attraction as a single operational measure was criticized on the empirical grounds that interpersonal attraction and various other operational measures of cohesiveness have low intercorrelations.

Empirical deficiencies in varied cohesiveness measures, which logically should be interrelated if all are tapping the same construct, were illustrated in a study by Eisman (1959) and in a replication by Ramuz-Nienhuis and Van Bergen (1960). Eisman used the following five operational measures of cohesiveness with ongoing university student groups: (a) a sociometric index based on friendship, (b) a direct rating of group attractiveness, (c) the average number of reasons given by group members for belonging to the group, (d) the number of same reasons for group membership given by a majority of the members and (e) the degree of similarity existing among group members with respect to their values. Rank-correlation coefficients yielded no significant inter-relationships among any of the measures. Likewise, the Ramuz-Nienhuis and Van Bergen (1960) replication yielded low intercorrelations.

As Albert (1953) and Eisman (1959) have pointed out, the concept must precede the measurement and the more general and vague the conceptual definition, the more probable are questions of procedure and adequacy of operational definitions. Rather than attempting to refine the operational definition of cohesiveness, it may be more logical to examine the conceptual or nominal definition. Gross and Martin's (1952) paper is most widely quoted for their criticism of operational measures, but a seldom-referenced section of the paper also questions the nominal definition of cohesiveness. Because cohesiveness is a group phenomenon, Gross and Martin insisted that more attention should be directed toward the group or relational aspect of member relations rather than (or in addition to) the individual attractiveness perceptions.

A number of authors advocated attraction-to-group as a conceptual definition of cohesiveness and recommended closer adherence to the group aspect of that concept with operational measures (Enoch & McLemore, 1967; Van Bergen & Koebebakker, 1959). As a matter of fact, Back (1951) in an early study conducted within Festinger et al.'s (1950/1963) theoretical framework, suggested that the Festinger et al., nominal definition could be restated as, "cohesiveness is the attraction of membership in a group for its members" (p. 9). Libo (1953), also operating from Festinger's conceptual framework, similarly emphasized the group aspect of cohesiveness by stating "a totaling of individual needs, preferences, or predispositions which derive from individual personality structure or from interaction with objects other than the group — and which are present regardless of existence of the group — cannot define attraction-to-group" (p. 4-5).

Cohesiveness as a bidimensional construct. Even when investigators accept attraction-to-group as the conceptual definition of cohesiveness, operational procedures vary greatly. One of the most prominent and recurring themes is that cohesiveness, as it has been approached empirically, is not a single unidimensional construct. Instead, cohesiveness appears to be at least a bidimensional construct. Different authors have defined the two dimensions with different terms, but most separate cohesiveness assessed in individual terms, especially interpersonal attraction, from cohesiveness assessed with a more direct group-related approach.

Enoch and McLemore (1967) considered attraction-to-group to have two components: (a) intrinsic attraction and (b) instrumental attraction. Mikalachi (1969) similarly differentiated social cohesion and task cohesion. The most widely referenced work on the bidimensional nature of cohesiveness, however, was done by Hagstrom and Selvin (1965). A factor analysis of 19 cohesiveness items with 20 different living groups of college females identified two separate cohesiveness factors. One factor, termed "sociometric cohesion," essentially represents friendship or interpersonal attraction. The second factor, "social satisfaction," represents an overall group assessment. Conceptually distinguishing between those two types of cohesiveness allows for groups that are not highly attractive as groups, but with a large proportion of members who are mutual friends. Conversely, groups may be highly attractive without having intimate interpersonal ties. Of particular interest to sport psychologists, Hagstrom and Selvin (1965) noted,

> Thus, in strongly task-oriented groups, group effectiveness may be a major determinant of attractiveness, and effectiveness may be

> hindered by too high a degree of sociometric cohesiveness; in such a situation the most satisfied groups might be relatively low in sociometric cohesiveness (p. 40).

Nixon's (1977) theoretical reformulation of cohesiveness advocates a similar conceptual distinction between interpersonal attraction and cohesiveness for sport teams, and several sport-cohesiveness studies provide empirical support for a bidimensional construct. Intercorrelations among the nine individual items of the Sport Cohesiveness Questionnaire (Peterson & Martens, 1972) support the classification of items into two basic categories: (a) direct items requiring the respondent to rate the group as a whole, and (b) sociometric items. All intercorrelations among the four sociometric items (correlation coefficients ranged from .62 to .78) were statistically significant ($p < .01$). Likewise, all direct items correlated significantly ($p < .01$) with each other (correlation coefficients ranged from .44 to .75). Furthermore, not one of the sociometric items correlated significantly with any of the direct items, suggesting that the two types of items represented two separate dimensions of cohesiveness.

Widmeyer's (1977) factor analytic results corroborated the pattern of Peterson and Martens' (1972) intercorrelation matrix. Factor 1 from Widmeyer's analysis, accounting for 62% of the variance, loaded heavily on the five direct items. The three sociometric items loaded heavily on Factor 2, which accounted for the remaining 38% of the variance.

If the sport cohesiveness research is reinterpreted with the interpersonal attraction-cohesiveness distinction in mind, the findings become somewhat less equivocal. A positive relationship between direct cohesiveness measures and performance has typically been reported. The only study using direct measures that failed to yield a positive relationship was that of Melnick and Chemers (1974). Nearly all the reported negative relationships, on the other hand, have involved some type of interpersonal attraction measure (e.g., Landers & Lüschen, 1974; McGrath, 1962). It may be argued that some of these measures are not even of interpersonal attraction. For example, Fielder's (1954) assumed similarity measures seem more akin to his work on leadership than cohesiveness; a cooperativeness index derived from the highest member's rating (Grace, 1954) hardly seems to reflect either cohesiveness or interpersonal attraction.

Interpersonal attraction is surely a phenomenon worthy of investigation, and currently its theoretical and empirical base is stronger than that of cohesiveness. Lott and Lott (1965) have, in fact, advocated interpersonal attraction as a replacement for the construct of cohesiveness. This reviewer takes the opposing view that cohesiveness is a valuable concept distinct from interpersonal attraction, and with greater conceptual and methodological rigor, it can become a viable scientific construct as well.

Cohesiveness measurement in sport. If sport psychologists accept the concept of cohesiveness as attraction-to-group, then the next step is to delineate the meaning of the construct as it relates to sport teams and to develop reliable and valid operational measures. The Sport Cohesiveness Questionnaire (Martens & Peterson, 1971) has been used extensively and it may be the most appropriate instrument available. The questionnaire has good face validity for sport teams, but its reliability, and concurrent and construct validity are unattested. If cohesiveness is a viable construct for sport psychology then it is worthy of more reliable and valid assessment. The initial step probably should be to specify precisely what is to be measured. Based on the evidence, it appears advantageous to define cohesiveness as a sport-specific construct and to restrict its measurement to direct assessment. With those criteria in mind, a sport-cohesiveness scale with appropriate psychometric properties may be developed that will allow sport psychologists to more clearly delineate the concept of cohesiveness and specify its relationship to other social psychological constructs relevant to sport situations.

A carefully developed cohesiveness measure likely would include items such as value-of-membership and closely-knit, which seem to reflect overall attraction-to-group. Teamwork may be something quite different. Several studies have reported their strongest results with the teamwork measure, but to state that teamwork is positively related to team success borders on tautology. Teamwork may reflect attraction-to-group but it appears to include an element of team performance as well. Possibly teamwork is a mediator between cohesiveness and performance rather than a measure of cohesiveness. Potential confusion of cohesiveness and teamwork in the minds of respondents may create problems when asking them to assess cohesiveness directly. Respondents may view cohesiveness in functional rather than affective or attractional terms. That is, team members may assume the team is cohesive if the group performs well as a unit. Only more carefully developed and valid measures and more tightly controlled experimental procedures can determine if this is, in fact, the case. At present, progress is stymied by the time and effort requirements of such rigorous procedures. In lieu of a more valid and comprehensive inventory, the Martens and Peterson (1971) questionnaire is preferable to the use of one or two specific items with no established reliability or validity and no relationship to any other cohesiveness research. In using the Martens and Peterson questionnaire, researchers are advised to analyze the results multivariately because the interrelationships among items have not been established and because no standard procedure for deriving a single overall score exists.

Thus far only questionnaire measures have been discussed, but there is no logical reason why the construct of cohesiveness cannot be assessed in a variety of ways. Sound scientific reasoning suggests that established empirical relationships have greater reliability and generalizability if the constructs are assessed in a variety of ways. Behavioral measures especially seem to offer a number of possibilities.

As a psychological construct cohesiveness may be thought of as a group difference characteristic, analagous to individual-difference characteristics. Cohesiveness should, then, even in its early developing stages, predispose a group to a certain level of cohesiveness behavior.

More specific behaviors, observed over a given period of time, may more clearly differentiate among teams of varying cohesiveness levels. Bakeman and Helmreich (1975) professed the superiority of their cohesiveness measure, based on the accretion of patterns of behavior reliably observed, over typical responses to a one-time questionnaire. The specific behaviors observed by Bakeman and Helmreich—leisure-time conversations—are not necessarily valid for sport teams but, by taking a more innovative view of cohesiveness, sport psychologists may identify specific behavioral criteria that can adequately differentiate among teams of varying cohesiveness levels.

Identifying such behaviors could open a number of research avenues not accessible with more limited measures. Changes in cohesive behavior may be monitored as a team forms and develops; specific cohesive behaviors manifested by teams of differing ages, sexes, or engaged in different activities may be compared; and the relationship of cohesiveness as a group characteristic to immediate group behavior may be examined in a variety of situations. Thus, the role of cohesiveness and immediate situational factors in determining specific group behavior may be approached from an interactionist viewpoint, similar to the interactionist approach in personality psychology.

Discussion to this point has considered only cohesiveness measures, but interest in the cohesiveness-performance relationship suggests attention also be paid to the measurement of performance. Performance is a form of behavior and typical performance measures are relatively unambiguous behavioral observations. Within the cohesiveness literature, however, the measurement of performance has generally been restricted to the season win-loss ratio. The distinction between performance and performance outcome is generally one consideration for performance measurement. As discussed by Widmeyer (1977), and reported in Lowe's (1973) observations of Little League baseball, good performance does not automatically result in good performance outcome; likewise, poor performance does not necessarily lead to a poor performance outcome. In baseball, for example, a well-hit line drive may result in an out, while a poorly hit ball results in a hit. Similarly, a team may play poorly and win or perform well and lose. Sport psychologists should consider more precise measures of performance that may provide greater variation among teams as alternatives to the current performance outcome measures. After sport psychologists have delineated the concept of cohesiveness and devised alternative valid measures of both cohesiveness and performance, the findings of investigations of the cohesiveness-performance relationship may be viewed with more confidence.

Causality

Regardless of the precision and validity of measurement, examination of the cohesiveness-performance relationship is little more than an academic exercise without specification of causality (i.e., does cohesiveness cause performance success, or does successful performance lead to cohesiveness). Sport psychologists have been amazingly cavalier in their approach to causality in the cohesiveness-performance relationship. Failure to consider the time dimension is probably the most flagrant violation of the scientific method in cohesiveness research. A number of investigators have not even specified whether cohesiveness was measured prior to, during, or after performance. Others have specified the times of assessment but have blithely continued to analyze their data and interpret results as though time were irrelevant. Some problems with causal considerations are inevitable due to the interest of sport psychology with the cohesiveness-performance relationship as it occurs in "real-world" sport teams. A number of techniques do exist, however, that may aid in establishing causal predominance in the cohesiveness-performance relationship.

Preseason cohesiveness and team performance. The most common regard for time in sport cohesiveness research is examining the relationship of preseason cohesiveness to subsequent team performance (usually the season win-loss ratio). That paradigm has been followed with mixed results. Martens and Peterson (1971) and Widmeyer (1977) reported positive relationships between direct measures of cohesiveness and performance success. Ball and Carron (1976) reported a positive relationship between midseason teamwork/closeness and the final season win percentage, but preseason cohesiveness and other direct measures were not related to team performance. Arnold and Straub (1912) also reported mixed results. Univariate analyses indicated that the interpersonal attraction, power, and enjoyment-of-playing ratings were related to later performance success, but no other direct preseason measures were related to performance; and the overall multivariate test yielded no significant difference between successful and less successful teams.

Cohesiveness measures that precede team performance in time may imply causality, but the procedures are far from ideal. The possibility that the team's previous history or unassessed confounding variables influenced both preseason cohesiveness and season performance cannot be ruled out. If a team has been in existence in previous years, even if some members have changed, that team may have a history of previous success or lack of success that affects cohesiveness at the time of assessment. On the other hand, assessing the preseason cohesiveness of a newly formed team with no previous history can hardly be expected to yield reliable results. If team members have not had the opportunity to interact as a group, their responses to cohesiveness items are likely to be quite random and unreliable. It would be surprising if such preseason cohesiveness were reliably related to group performance or to any other variable. Most sport teams likely fall between the two extremes. Even newly formed teams have at least a limited history that may influence members' perceptions and expectations as well as future performance. Also, new members and new situational factors at the start of a season create, in effect, a new team situation and render cohesiveness assessments somewhat speculative. To the extent that preseason cohesiveness is unreliable, it is little wonder that the relationship of preseason cohesiveness to later performance success is weak.

Team performance and postseason cohesiveness. Although the relationship of preseason cohesiveness to later performance has been the most common paradigm, some studies have examined the relationship in the opposite direction (i.e., the relationship of performance during a season to postseason cohesiveness). Both Arnold and Straub (1972) and Landers and Crum (1971) reported the successful teams had higher postseason cohesiveness (direct teamwork/closely-knit measures) than less successful teams. Nixon's (1977) findings implied a positive relationship between game outcome and postgame cohesiveness, as well as season performance and postseason cohesiveness. The most compelling evidence for a positive relationship between team success and postseason cohesiveness comes from Peterson and Martens' (1972) extensive study of intramural basketball teams. With preseason cohesiveness covaried out, both univariate and multivariate analyses indicated that highly successful teams were more cohesive (on all measures) than were moderately successful or unsuccessful teams. Covariance analysis (also used by Landers & Crum, 1971) lends more credence to the contention that team success predicts cohesiveness than ANOVA or correlational analyses. Covariance statistically controls for differences among teams that may have existed prior to their performance over the season. Thus, postseason differences in cohesiveness may be attributed to performance success differences with some confidence. Unfortunately, similar covariance analyses have not been applied to control for prior differences in the relationship of preseason cohesiveness to later performance success.

Cross-lagged panel designs. Cross-lagged panel correlation analysis, described in detail by Kenny (1975) and Calsyn (1976), shows promise of shedding light on the causal direction in the cohesiveness-performance relationship. The technique is a quasi-experimental design that provides a method of examining causal relationships among variables that are not easily manipulated in typical experimental designs. To apply it, the two variables (cohesiveness and performance) must each be measured at two points in time. The essential comparison used to establish causal predominance is the cross-lagged differential (i.e., the difference between the correlation of cohesiveness at Time 1 with performance at Time 2 and the correlation of performance at Time 1 with cohesiveness at Time 2).

Bakeman and Helmreich (1975) introduced the cross-lagged panel correlation technique to cohesiveness research with their investigation of aquanaut teams. Both cohesive and performance behaviors were observed and recorded every 6 min over the entire mission for each team. To reduce the data to workable form and to reduce variation, cohesiveness and performance scores were computed for the first segment and the second segment of the mission. Both cohesiveness and performance measures, then, were not one-time assessments, but involved the accretion of patterns of behavior over time. As a first approach to the split-mission data, Bakeman and Helmreich noted that the significant correlation between first-segment performance and second-segment cohesiveness ($r = .72, p < .02$) and the nonsignificant correlation between first-segment cohesiveness and second-segment performance ($r = .13$) strongly suggested a causal flow from performance to cohesiveness. This interpretation was strengthened by examination of partial-correlation coefficients for first-segment performance with second-segment cohesiveness, controlling for first-segment cohesiveness ($r = .86$, $p < .003$) and for first-segment cohesiveness with second-segment performance, controlling for first-segment performance ($r = -.14$, $p > .05$). Bakeman and Helmreich concluded that cohesiveness was not an important determinant of performance, but that good performance may well have been a cause of cohesiveness.

Carron and Ball (in press) have recently applied this approach to sport teams. Cohesiveness was assessed at three points in time (early season, midseason, and postseason) and performance at two points in time (midseason and postseason), but the data most amenable to analyses are the midseason and postseason measures of both cohesiveness and performance. Carron and Ball reported support for a causal relationship from performance to cohesiveness, indicated by the correlation between midseason performance and postseason cohesiveness ($r = -.77, p < .05$), but no support for the view that initial cohesiveness results in later performance success, as indicated by the correlation between midseason cohesiveness and postseason performance ($r = -.39$, $p > .05$). (Because lower cohesiveness scores indicate greater cohesiveness, negative correlations indicate a positive relationship between cohesiveness and performance success.) As with the Bakeman and Helmreich (1975) study, partial-correlation coefficients corroborated the interpretation of the zero-order correlations. The primary statistic for examining causal direction, the cross-lagged differential, was not reported by Carron and Ball. Application of the significance test suggested by both Calsyn (1976) and Kenny (1975) to the Carron and Ball data, however, indicates that the difference between the two cross-lagged correlations (–.77 and –.39) was statistically significant ($z = 2.87$).

Carron and Ball's results imply that the predominant causal direction in the cohesiveness-performance relationship is from performance to cohesiveness, but a number of methodological problems inherent in that study cast doubt upon the interpretation. One major problem is that the cohesive-performance data failed to meet one of the basic assumptions of the analysis, synchronicity. Synchronicity, as discussed by Kenny (1975) and Calsyn (1976), dictates that the two constructs (cohesiveness and performance) be measured at the same point in time. Responses or measures that are aggregated or averaged over an extended period of time pose one threat to synchronicity. Performance measures derived from total season data are not synchronous with cohesiveness measures obtained at a single point in time. Retrospection, another threat to synchronicity, often occurs with cohesiveness measures. Retrospective measures require the subjects to recall behaviors, attitudes, or experiences of the past. In some sense, then, the data obtained at the time of measurement may, in fact, have been generated at some prior time. Due to the empirical finding that variables measured closer in time correlate more highly than those measured further apart in time, violations of the synchronicity assumption invalidate causal interpretations of cross-lagged differentials. The Bakeman and Helmreich cohesiveness and performance measures, although aggregated, were synchronous. Carron and Ball, in contrast, used a cohesiveness measure that, at least to some extent, is retrospective, and performance was not only an aggregate measure, but postseason performance (total-season win percentage) actually included midseason performance. The inability to clearly pinpoint the time of measurement and the nonsynchronous nature of the two measures renders any causal interpretation of the data quite tenuous at best.

The second basic assumption of the analysis, stationarity, means that the causes of the variables are not different at the two points of measurement. The stationarity assumption is especially vulnerable to violation when groups move through different stages over time. The stationarity assumption renders the cross-lagged analysis inappropriate for studying the onset of a causal effect. Thus, attempts to apply it when a team is initially forming, or from season to season, are ill advised.

Although the data collected by Carron and Ball (in press), which is typical of sport cohesiveness data, fails to conform to the assumptions of the cross-lagged technique, the assumptions could be met with appropriately obtained measures. Bakeman and Helmreich (1975) obtained synchronous cohesiveness and performance measures amenable to cross-lagged analysis, and there is no reason why similar data could not be obtained with sport teams. Causal interpretations are only as reliable as the measures upon which they are based. Bakeman and Helmreich's cohesiveness and performance measures were similarly collected behavioral observations over an extended time. Typical sport cohesiveness measures are likely to be of a much different form and much less reliable than performance measures. To give a fair chance to both sides of the causal relationship, cohesiveness and performance measures must be similarly reliable and valid. It may be advisable, then, to employ behavioral measures of cohesiveness as well as performance in studies attempting to establish causal predominance between those two variables.

Circular versus causal models. Some investigators, most notably Cartwright (1968), have suggested that the cohesiveness-performance relationship is circular rather than a relationship of causal predominance. The cross-lagged technique does not easily adapt to a circular model. Positive feedback tends to equate cross-lagged correlations, and a true circular relationship yields no difference between the cross-lagged correlations. An increase in the correlation between the two variables (i.e., cohesiveness and performance) from Time 1 to Time 2 may suggest positive feedback, but only if increased reliability of measurement can be ruled out as a cause of the improved correlation. As Bakeman and Helmreich (1975) noted, circular models are mathematically complex and cumbersome to examine. Instead, Bakeman and Helmreich chose to test the adequacy of two opposed recursive linear models. Their results strongly suggest that a linear model, in which good performance leads to cohesiveness, describes the cohesiveness-performance relationship quite adequately, and provide no evidence for a circular model.

In addition to Bakeman and Helmreich's (1975) direct test of causality, several studies in the sport literature have reported stronger relationships from performance success to cohesiveness than vice versa. Carron and Ball's (in press) study has already been discussed. Nixon (1977) concluded that his results supported a positive relationship from performance success to cohesiveness but provided no evidence for the influence of cohesiveness on performance. The Peterson and Martens (1972) investigation of performance success effects on postseason cohesiveness yielded a much stronger relationship than the Martens and Peterson (1971) study of preseason cohesiveness and performance success. Similarly, the Myers (1962) and McGrath (1962) investigations may be considered together. Myers reported that performance success led to higher cohesiveness in terms of esteem for teammates, but McGrath observed a negative relationship between positive interpersonal relationships and later performance success. Thus, the Bakeman and Helmreich (1975) study and the sport cohesiveness literature strongly imply that causal predominance flows from performance success to cohesiveness; but there is only weak evidence for the often-assumed influence of cohesiveness on team performance. It would be premature, however, to completely discount the circular model until more investigations of causality have been conducted using reliable and valid measures of cohesiveness within sport settings.

The Role of Mediating Variables

Group Norms

Explicit concepts, reliable and valid cohesiveness measures, and regard for causality may elucidate the cohesiveness-performance relationship, but equivocal findings may persist due to the influence of extraneous variables. The influence of one mediating variable, group norms, was recognized early in the history of cohesiveness research as illustrated by the classic study of Schachter, Ellertson, McBride, and Gregory (1951). In that laboratory experiment, high- and low-cohesive groups were formed, and the group norm was manipulated with prewritten notes to induce either greater or lesser productivity on the task of cutting cardboard squares. Subjects in high-cohesive groups complied with the group norm more than members of low-cohesive groups whether the norm was for greater or lesser productivity. Those findings were confirmed in a subsequent lab experiment (Berkowitz, 1954), with military crews (Berkowitz, 1956), and with industrial groups (Mikalachki, 1969; Seashore, 1954). In all cases, high-cohesive groups conformed to the group norm more than less-cohesive groups, whether the group norm was for better or poorer group performance. The empirical evidence, then, implies that highly cohesive groups are likely to outperform less-cohesive groups only if the group norm is for better performance.

In addition to specific norms for immediate performance changes, group norms may operate at a more general level. An investigation of cohesiveness in groups differing in basic orientation (Anderson, 1975) demonstrated that value similarity (typically associated with interpersonal attraction) was associated with cohesiveness in informal social groups, but goal-path clarity (agreement on group task procedures) was more related to cohesiveness in task-oriented groups. Anderson's findings recall the admonishments of Festinger et al. (1950/1963) who limited discussion to informal social groups and did not hesitate to caution against overgeneralization. Anderson's results affirm that the factors that influence (and are influenced by) cohesiveness in task-oriented groups, which undoubtedly include most groups of interest to sport psychology, may be quite distinct from those factors related to cohesiveness in social groups.

The mediating influence of group norms on the cohesiveness-performance relationship has been evidenced in a number of studies, but that mediating effect may not be a compelling concern for sport psychology. All sport teams are essentially task-oriented, and sport groups that adhere to any norms contradicting good group performance are indeed rare. Sport teams may vary in commitment, but generally they represent a restricted range of norms and orientations in comparison to the overall population of groups. Consequently, present methods of assessing group norms or orientations, designed for a wide range of groups, are not likely to differentiate adequately among sport teams. Indeed, studies that have incorporated motivational measures have contributed little to our understanding of the cohesiveness-performance relationship. Ball and Carron (1976), Bird (1977), and Widmeyer (1977) all incorporated measures of participation motivation (i.e., task- vs. affiliation-orientation) into their research. In all cases the cohesiveness-performance relationship was positive but the added consideration of participation motivation failed to alter that relationship appreciably.

Task Characteristics

The crucial role of task characteristics in group dynamics in general, and specifically in the cohesiveness-performance relationship, has recently been acclaimed in several sources. Steiner (1972) emphatically asserted the need to consider task characteristics whenever group performance is of concern. According to Steiner's model, task demands interact with relevant resources possessed by group members to define the optimal or potential productivity of a group on a given task. The degree to which the group's actual performance approaches its potential depends upon the group process which may involve coordination and/or motivation losses. Within Steiner's task typology, group tasks are broadly classified as (a) divisible, which are readily divided into subtasks, or (b) unitary, which make mutual assistance impractical.

Landers (1974) applied Steiner's model and typology to group motor tasks and observed that Steiner's task classification might clarify the equivocal sport cohesiveness literature. Landers noted that a positive relationship between cohesiveness and performance has typically been reported for divisible tasks (e.g., basketball, football), while the negative relationships in the literature most often involve unitary tasks (e.g., rowing, bowling, rifle teams). Landers and Lüschen (1974) elaborated on this point and suggested that the crucial intervening variable linking the interacting and coacting task dimensions with cohesiveness is the rate of interaction among team members. Their results with bowling teams supported that contention in that unsuccessful teams had higher interpersonal attraction ratings than successful teams.

Although Landers' application of a group task dichotomy appears to sort out the cohesiveness research findings, his views are not universally accepted. Widmeyer (1977) suggested that a group task such as rowing, classified as unitary by Landers and as coacting by Landers and Lüschen, requires coordination, and greater cohesiveness can reduce coordination losses. Furthermore, Widmeyer logically argued that the influence of cohesiveness on the performance of tasks that do not require coordination or interaction depends on whether cohesiveness adds or detracts from task motivation. According to Steiner's model, to the extent that cohesiveness reduces motivation losses, cohesiveness should facilitate group performance. Zander (1971) has suggested that when a group is more attractive to its members (cohesive) and when the members are more committed to membership in the group, desire for group success is more likely to develop. Thus, greater task motivation may be expected in more cohesive groups.

Nixon (1977) combined the distinction between interpersonal attraction and cohesiveness with task considerations in his reformulation of cohesiveness theory. Nixon declared that cohesiveness facilitates group performance for both interacting and coacting tasks, supporting the suggestions of Widmeyer (1977) and Zander (1971). On the other hand, Nixon posited a negative relationship between interpersonal attraction and performance for coacting tasks. Presumably, individual performances of coacting team members and resultant team performance are enhanced when members compete against each other. Thus, negative interpersonal relationships may enhance group performance if membership in the team remains attractive (cohesiveness), and if the team can stay together despite the conflict. The empirical evidence for that assertion is not overly compelling. The Lenk (1969) and Landers-Lüschen (1974) results corroborate Nixon's view, but Myers (1962) reported more positive interpersonal relations among members of successful coacting rifle teams than among members of less successful teams.

Recent sport cohesiveness literature, then, suggests that task considerations are more critical for the relationship between interpersonal attraction and group performance than the relationship between cohesiveness and performance. Logically, cohesiveness should enhance group task motivation and therefore facilitate performance. Cohesiveness may also, as Widmeyer (1977) suggested, reduce coordination losses. Thus, cohesiveness might be expected to have a greater effect on the performance of teams with high coordination requirements. Consideration of group task characteristics need not be limited to the dichotomous classification of group tasks as divisible vs. unitary or interacting vs. coacting. It may be advisable to conceive of group tasks as varying along a dimension in terms of cooperation requirements. Sport psychologists would be well advised to consider alternative ways of accounting for task characteristics, or other characteristics of sport groups that may affect the cohesiveness-performance relationship.

Other Mediating Variables

Few mediating variables have received as much attention as group norms and task characteristics, but other factors may affect the cohesiveness-performance relationship. Cohesiveness effects may vary across different activities, and this variance may be due to differences other than the interaction requirements of the tasks. Increasing participation of women in team sports, especially at higher levels of competition, suggests differences in cohesiveness influences on male and female teams as a topic worthy of investigation. Widmeyer (1977) attempted to investigate the mediating influences of ability level, sex, and participation motivation in his study, but the regression of team performance on preseason cohesiveness was not improved by the addition of any of the mediating variables. Cross classification of teams in Widmeyer's study into three ability levels and two sexes may have contributed to the nonsignificant effects. Use of a more powerful design with more observations per category might yield significant mediating effects. Even if ability and sex do not mediate cohesiveness effects, the control of those factors may be important. Widmeyer's division of teams into separate leagues on the basis of ability and sex may have reduced error variance substantially allowing the cohesiveness-performance relationship to emerge.

Further research may uncover additional mediating variables, but rather than arbitrarily adding factors to sport cohesiveness studies it is suggested that the delineation of the conceptual and operational meaning of cohesiveness be accorded top priority. Armed with reliable and valid cohesiveness measures, the systematic investigation of causal implications and further elucidation of variables mediating the cohesiveness-performance relationship may proceed.

References

Albert, R.S. Comments on the scientific function of the concept of cohesiveness. *American Journal of Sociology,* 1953, 59, 231–234.

Anderson, A.B. Combined effects of interpersonal attraction and goal-path clarity on the cohesiveness of task oriented groups. *Journal of Personality and Social Psychology,* 1975, 31, 68–75.

Arnold, G.E., & Straub, W.F. Personality and group cohesiveness as determinants of success among interscholastic basketball teams. In I.D. Williams & L.M. Wankel (Eds.), *Proceedings of the Fourth Canadian Psycho-Motor Learning and Sports Psychology Symposium.* Ottawa: Department of National Health and Welfare, 1972.

Back, K.W. Influence through social communication. *Journal of Abnormal and Social Psychology,* 1951, 46, 9–23.

Bakeman, R., & Helmreich, R. Cohesiveness and performance: Covariation and causality in an undersea environment. *Journal of Experimental Social Psychology,* 1975, 11, 478–489.

Ball, J.R., & Carron, A.V. The influence of team cohesion and participation motivation upon performance success in intercollegiate ice hockey. *Canadian Journal of Applied Sport Sciences,* 1976, 1, 271–275.

Berkowitz, L. Group standards, cohesiveness, and productivity. *Human Relations,* 1954, 7, 509–519.

Berkowitz, L. Group norms among bomber crews: Patterns of perceived crew attitudes, "active" crew attitudes, and crew liking related to air crew effectiveness in Far Eastern combat. *Sociometry,* 1956, 19, 141–153.

Bird, A.M. Development of a model for predicting team performance. *Research Quarterly,* 1977, 48, 24–32.

Calsyn, R.J. Guidelines for using cross-lagged panel correlations. *Representative Research in Social Psychology,* 1976, 7, 105–119.

Carron, A.V., & Ball, J.R. Cause-effect characteristics of cohesiveness and participation motivation in intercollegiate hockey. *International Review of Sport Sociology,* in press.

Cartwright, D. The nature of group cohesiveness. In D. Cartwright & A. Zander (Eds.), *Group dynamics: Research and theory* (3rd ed.). New York: Harper & Row, 1968.

Collins, B.E., & Raven, S.H. Group structure: Attraction, coalitions, communication, and power. In G. Lindzey & E. Aronson (Eds.), *The handbook of social psychology* (Vol. 4). Reading, Massachusetts: Addison-Wesley, 1969.

Eisman, B. Some operational measures of cohesiveness and their interrelations. *Human Relations,* 1959, 12, 183–189.

Enoch, J.R., & McLemore, S.D. On the meaning of group cohesion. *Southwestern Social Science Quarterly*, 1961, 48, 174–182.

Festinger, L., Schachter, S., & Back, K. *Social pressures in informal groups.* Stanford, California: Stanford University Press, 1963. (Originally published, 1950).

Fiedler, F.E. Assumed similarity measures as predictors of team effectiveness. *Journal of Abnormal and Social Psychology,* 1954, 49, 381–388.

Grace, H. Conformance and performance. *Journal of Social Psychology,* 1954, 48, 233–237.

Gross, N., & Martin, W.E. On group cohesiveness. *American Journal of Sociology*, 1952, 57, 533–546.

Hagstrom, W.O., & Selvin, H.C. Two dimensions of cohesiveness in small groups. *Sociometry,* 1965, **28**, 30–43.

Kenny, D.A. Cross-lagged panel correlation: A test for spuriousness. *Psychological Bulletin,* 1975, 82, 887–903.

Klein, M., & Christiansen, G. Group composition, group structure and group effectiveness of basketball teams. In J.S. Loy & G.S. Kenyon (Eds.), *Sport, culture and society.* New York: Macmillan, 1969.

Landers, D.M. Taxonomic considerations in measuring group performance and the analysis of selected group motor performance tasks. In M.G. Wade & R. Martens (Eds.), *Psychology of motor behavior and sport.* Urbana, Illinois: Human Kinetics, 1974.

Landers, D.M., & Crum, T.F. The effect of team success and formal structure on interpersonal relations and cohesiveness of baseball teams. *International Journal of Sport Psychology,* 1971, 2, 88–96.

Landers, D.M., & Lüschen, G. Team performance outcome and cohesiveness of competitive co-acting groups. *International Review of Sport Sociology,* 1974, 2, 57–69.

Lenk, H. Top performance despite internal conflict. In J.W. Loy & G.S. Kenyon (Eds.), *Sport, culture and society.* New York: Macmillan, 1969.

Lenk, H. *Team dynamics.* Champaign, Illinois: Stipes, 1977.

Libo, L.M. *Measuring group cohesiveness.* Ann Arbor: University of Michigan. 1953.

Lott, A.J., & Lott, B.E. Group cohesiveness as interpersonal attraction: A review of relationships with antecedent and consequent variables. *Psychological Bulletin,* 1965, 64, 259–309.

Lowe, R. *Stress, arousal, and task performance of Little League baseball players.* Unpublished doctoral dissertation, University of Illinois at Urbana-Champaign, 1973.

Martens, R., & Peterson, J.A. Group cohesiveness as a determinant of success and member satisfaction in team performance. *International Review of Sport Sociology,* 1971, 6, 49–61.

McGrath, J.E. The influence of interpersonal relations on adjustment and effectiveness in rifle teams. *Journal of Abnormal and Social Psychology,* 1962, 65, 365–375.

McGrath, J.E., & Altman, I. *Small group research: A synthesis and critique of the field.* New York: Holt, Rinehart & Winston, 1966.

Melnick, M.J., & Chemers, M.M. Effects of group social structure on the success of basketball teams. *Research Quarterly,* 1974, 45, 1–8.

Mikalachki, A. *Group cohesion reconsidered.* London, Canada: School of Business Administration, University of Western Ontario, 1969.

Myers, A.E. Team competition, success and the adjustment of group members. *Journal of Abnormal and Social Psychology,* 1962, 65, 325–332.

Nixon, H.L. "Cohesiveness" and team success: A theoretical reformulation. *Review of Sport and Leisure,* 1977, 2, 36–57.

Peterson, J.A., & Martens, R. Success and residential affiliation as determinants of team cohesiveness. *Research Quarterly,* 1972, 43, 62–76.

Ramuz-Nienhius, W., & Van Bergen, A. Relations between some components of attraction-to-group. *Human Relations,* 1960, 13, 271–277.

Schachter, S., Ellertson, N., McBride, D., & Gregory, D. An experimental study of cohesiveness and productivity. *Human Relations,* 1951, 4, 229–238.

Seashore, S.E. *Group cohesiveness in the industrial work group.* Ann Arbor: University of Michigan, 1976.

Shaw, M.E. *Group dynamics: The psychology of small group behavior* (2nd ed.). New York: McGraw-Hill, 1976

Steiner, I.D. *Group process and productivity.* New York: Academic Press, 1972.

Stogdill, R.M. Group productivity, drive, and cohesiveness. *Organizational Behavior and Human Performance,* 1972, 8, 26–43.

Van Bergen, A., & Koekebakker, J. "Group cohesiveness" in laboratory experiments. *Acta Psychologica,* 1959, 16, 81–98.

Widmeyer, W.N. *When cohesiveness predicts performance outcome in sport.* Unpublished doctoral dissertation, University of Illinois, 1977.

Zander, A. *Motives and goals in groups.* New York: Academic Press, 1971.

19 Dimensions of Leader Behavior in Sports: Development of a Leadership Scale

P. CHELLADURAI
University of Western Ontario

S. D. SALEH
University of Waterloo

The concept of leadership is of utmost importance in sport. Despite this fact, until the late 1970s there has been an unfortunate lack of consistent thrust in the study of leadership in sport. Most of the leadership models that had been used came from settings such as the military or industry, in which leadership was intensively investigated. Chelladurai's contribution is pioneering in that it recognized the urgent need to develop a leadership model that would be specific to the domain of sport and physical activity.

Chelladurai argued that effective leadership in sport would be contingent on the characteristics of leaders, group members, and situations. Individual differences among group members and the leader, as well as the characteristics of the situation, would significantly affect the leadership process and its effectiveness. Chelladurai conceptualized leadership in sport as an interactional process. Its effectiveness will depend not only on the characteristics of the leader (e.g., coach) but also on the characteristics of the group members (e.g., athletes) and the constraints of the situation in which the leadership process takes place. He developed a model of leadership effectiveness, which became known as the multidimensional model of sport leadership.

Chelladurai's model inspired substantial empirical research on coaching behavior. Subjects such as leadership style and the antecedents of effective leadership were intensively investigated. Later on, Chelladurai synthesized into his model central theories of leadership from organizational psychology, which emphasized the idea of leader–situation contingency. He then investigated and applied his model in the rapidly developing domain of sport management. As a result, the model became influential in the sport sciences and beyond the narrow borders of sport psychology.

At the heart of this approach lies the leadership scale for sports (LSS), which was developed to measure sport leadership behaviors, including group members' preferences for specific behaviors, their perceptions of their leaders' behavior, and the leaders' perceptions of their own behavior. The LSS was translated into several languages, was tested extensively, and received substantial psychometric support. For all these reasons, the article in which it was presented for the first time to sport psychology can be considered essential in this area.

Three different samples (total $N = 485$) participated in the development and refinement of the Leadership Scale for Sports (LSS). A five-factor solution with 40 items describing the most salient dimensions of coaching behavior was selected as the most meaningful. These factors were named *Training and Instruction, Democratic Behavior, Social Support,* and *Positive Feedback.* Internal consistency estimates ranged from .45 to .93 and the test-retest reliability coefficients ranged from .71 to .82. The relative stability of the factor structure across the different samples confirmed the factorial validity of the scale. The interpretation of the factors established the content validity of the scale. Finally, possible uses of the LSS were pointed out.

To date, most studies of leadership in sports have focused on the personality of the coach (e.g., Sage, 1975), or the coach's decision style—autocratic versus democratic (e.g., Lenk, 1977). Some studies have examined the application of Fiedler's (1967) Contingency Model of Leadership Effectiveness to the sport situation (e.g., Bird, 1977). And, finally, a recent and promising approach has as its focus the analysis of the varying behaviors of the coach which are appropriate to the different athletic situations (Chelladurai & Carron, 1978; Chelladurai & Saleh, 1978). In fact, Chelladurai (1978) has proposed a Multidimensional Model of Leadership which specifies that the effectiveness of leader behavior (i.e., the coaching behavior) is contingent on its congruence with the preferences of the members as well as the dictates of the situational characteristics.

Although theoretical attempts to develop leadership models for sports are worthwhile, the clarity and cogency of any theory cannot be established without adequate leadership instruments. In fact, the elaboration of any theory entails an obligation to measure its constructs or to specify behavioral manifestations which can be adequately measured. Otherwise, theoretical formulations only yield a proliferation in terminology, instead of fulfilling a promise

Adapted, by permission, from P. Chelladurai and S.D. Saleh, 1980, "Dimensions of leader behavior in sports: Development of a leadership scale," *Journal of Sport Psychology* 2: 34-45.

of empirical advance. Although the need for systematic research to identify and describe the dimensions of leader behavior in coaching and the need to develop valid scales to assess coaching behavior have been stressed (e.g., Cratty, 1973), there has been no attempt in this direction.

There have been, of course, a number of leadership behavior instruments used in previous research in other organizational settings—the Leader Behavior Description Questionnaire (Halpin, 1957), the Supervisory Behavior Description Questionnaire (Fleishman, 1957a), the Leadership Opinion Questionnaire (Fleishman, 1957b), and the revised LBDQ-Form XII (Stogdill, 1963). However, it is also necessary to verify whether the dimensions identified in these instruments—initiating structure and consideration—as well as the specific items are relevant to the sports context. The dimensions may not be pertinent because sport-as-an-organization is unique in the following ways: First, in athletics the organizational members spend a disproportionate number of hours in training for a competition of about 1 hour. This is in contrast to the industrial and business situation where the training period is much shorter in duration. A second distinguishing characteristic of team sports is that the organizational rewards, namely winning, is denied to at least one of the contestants. Thus, the members of a team continuously strive for a reward with the realization that they may be deprived of it either through superior performance of the opponents or pure chance. Finally, the relatively brief existence for a team is yet a third distinguishing characteristic. Members of an athletic team are assembled for only about 3 to 6 months.

There have been two studies conducted to identify the salient dimensions of leader behavior in sports. Danielson, Zelhart, and Drake (1975) administered a questionnaire containing 140 items modified from the original Leader Behavior Description Questionnaire (Hemphill & Coons, 1957) to 160 junior and senior high school hockey players. The results of the factor analysis and multidimensional scaling led the authors to conclude that "when perceived coaching behaviors are grouped on the basis of co-occurrence, the number of underlying dimensions is between 8 and 20" (Danielson et al., p. 332). Chelladurai and Saleh (1978), using 160 students enrolled in physical education degree programs at a Canadian University, derived and used a leadership scale consisting of five factors of coaching behavior.

Although these two studies do represent a promising start, unfortunately, neither of the studies presented evidence of the reliability and validity of the scales used. Moreover, the samples were limited and therefore may not give an adequate indication of coaching behavior in different types of sports. The present paper is an attempt to deal with the above mentioned problems by refining the Leadership Scale for Sports (LSS) used by Chelladurai and Saleh (1978). This refinement consisted of determining the reliability and validity of this revised LSS scale.

Method

In the first stage of the development of the LSS (Chelladurai & Saleh, 1978), 160 students (males = 80, females = 80) enrolled in physical education degree programs at a Canadian university responded to a questionnaire containing 99 items chosen and modified from existing leadership scales: Leader Behavior Description Questionnaire (Halpin, 1957), Supervisory Behavior Description Questionnaire (Fleishman, 1957a), Leadership Opinion Questionnaire (Fleishman, 1957b), and Leader Behavior Description Questionnaire-Form XII (Stogdill, 1963). Each item in the LSS was preceded with the phrase, "The coach should . . ."; and five response categories were provided: *always, often, occasionally, seldom,* and *never.*

These data were factor analyzed using the principal factoring with iteration and varimax rotation as outlined by Nie, Hull, Jenkins, Steinbrenner, and Bent (1975). Of the several solutions extracting different numbers of factors, a five-factor solution was found to be the most meaningful. The factors were labeled *Training, Democratic Behavior, Autocratic Behavior, Social Support,* and *Rewarding Behavior.* Items (N = 37) were selected to represent these five dimensions of leader behavior on the basis of their high loading on one factor (.40 or more) and low loadings on any other factor (.30 or less).

Subsequently, it was noted that none of the 99 items in the original pool tapped the behavior of the coach in teaching the skills and strategies of the sport. Although the term "training" connotes a certain degree of teaching, none of the items in the dimension of Training Behavior reflected the teaching behavior of the coach. Hence, in the second stage of development of the LSS, seven more items were included to tap the "instruction" behavior of a coach. Further, because Social Support is a dimension of leader behavior that is close to the traditional "Consideration" (Halpin & Winer, 1957) and because Social Support is a direct correlate of leader's orientation toward interpersonal relations (Fiedler, 1967) six more social support items were included. With the addition of these 13 items, the revised scale was increased to 50 items.

In the revised version, the response categories were quantified in order to present a common frame of reference to all respondents. Accordingly, the response categories of "often," "occasionally," and "seldom" were anchored at 75%, 50%, and 25% of the time, respectively.

The revised questionnaire was then administered to a different sample of 102 physical education students (males = 45, females = 57) and to a male sample of 223 varsity athletes (81 basketball players, 62 wrestlers, 57 track and field athletes, and 23 oarsmen) from different Canadian universities. The physical education students responded to the questionnaire in a class setting. For the athletes, a member of the faculty of physical education (or the athletic department) was contacted and requested to help in the collection of data. The set of questionnaires was sent to the contact who administered, collected, and returned them to the investigator. In most instances the administration was in a group setting, although in the case of a few wrestlers, the questionnaire was directly mailed to their home address.

The physical education students were asked to indicate their preference for specific leader behavior in relation to their favorite sport. The athletes were asked to express their preference in relation to the sport in which they were currently competing. In addition, the athletes responded to a version of the scale in which they recorded their perceptions of the actual behavior of their current coaches. For the preference version, the items were preceded by "I prefer my coach to . . ."; and for the second version, the items were preceded by "My coach . . ." The three sets of data from physical education students' preference, athletes' preference, and athletes' perception were factor analyzed separately. The technique of principal factoring with iteration (Nie et al., 1975) which was used in the original version of the LSS was also used in analyzing the revised scales.

Results and Discussion

Because the second stage of the study was an attempt to confirm the factor structure predicted by the earlier factor analysis, five factors were extracted from each set of data. It must be pointed out that the five factors account for only limited amount of variance in each data set: 41.2% for physical education students' preferences, 39.3% for athletes' preferences, and 55.8% for athletes' perceptions.

From the three solutions certain items were selected to constitute each factor. The criteria for selection of these items were (a) the item should have its highest loading on the same factor in all three solutions, and (b) its loading should be higher than .3 in at least two of the solutions. This procedure resulted in a total of 40 items: 13 items for training and instruction, 9 items for democratic behavior, 5 items for autocratic behavior, 8 items for social support, and 5 items for positive feedback.

Schriesheim and Kerr (1977), in their critical analysis of the existing leadership scales, noted the difficulty of comparing data derived through the four different Ohio State scales even though they are purported to measure the same two dimensions of leader behavior—Initiating Structure and Consideration. This difficulty is caused by the fact that these Ohio State scales contain different sets of items. Our present procedure of selecting the items with the highest loading in all three solutions alleviates this problem and allows for the comparability of data collected from different groups (e.g., physical education majors and athletes) and between preferred and perceived leader behavior.

Internal Consistency and Reliability

As an index of internal consistency, Cronbach's alpha was calculated for each subscale. These coefficients are presented in table 19.1 and are considered acceptable. Though the coefficient was lower for Autocratic Behavior preferred by the athletes (.45) it was adequate for the other two sets of data. It should also be noted that the other coefficients are generally higher in the case of the athletes' perception of leader behavior than in the other two data sets.

Table 19.1 Internal Consistency Estimates (Cronbach's Alpha)

Subscale	Physical education Students (N = 102) Preferred	Athletes (N = 223) Preferred	Athletes (N = 223) Perceived
Training and Instruction	.76	.83	.93
Democratic Behavior	.77	.75	.87
Autocratic Behavior	.66	.45	.79
Social Support	.72	.70	.86
Positive Feedback	.79	.82	.92

For the estimation of test-retest reliability, 53 of the physical education majors responded to the revised questionnaire a second time after an interval of 4 weeks. The composite factor scores (i.e., the sum of the selected items in each factor) were used to calculate the reliability coefficients. These reliability coefficients were adequate and ranged from .71 (Social Support) to .82 (Democratic Behavior).

Factorial Validity

One method of establishing validity of a scale is to administer the scale to different samples and to verify if the factor structure remains stable across these samples (Kerlinger, 1973). Thus, the expectation was that five factors similar to those of the first stage (Chelladurai & Saleh, 1978) would be extracted from the data of the second sample of physical education students and from the two versions of the scale administered to the athletes. The factor structure is very similar across the three analyses—a finding which lends support to the suggestion that the factor structure is stable. The items and factors were also similar to those extracted in the earlier study (Chelladurai & Saleh, 1978).

It should be pointed out that the eigen values and variance of each factor were different among the three solutions. However, the difference in the eigen values and associated variances are to be expected and should not be considered as evidence of instability of factor structure across situations. Since 40 of the 50 items had the highest loadings in the same factors across the three samples, it can be concluded that the factor structure is replicable.

Further Cattell's (1966) Scree test lends support for the present decision to extract five factors. Although the Scree test is somewhat outdated, it provides a rough estimate of the maximum number of factors to be extracted. In general, this test specifies that extraction of factors need not proceed beyond the point where the percentage of variance explained by successive factors levels off. This leveling off occurred after the sixth factor in each of the three solutions. The five-factor solution was preferred since it was more meaningful than the six-factor solution. The eigen values of the factors in each solution exceeded the customary value of 1. It must be noted that factor analysis is a powerful though not the only method of establishing construct validity (Kerlinger, 1973, p. 468).

Content Validity Based on Factor Interpretation

Not only was the five-factor solution stable but it was also found to be meaningful. Each of these factors is described and interpreted below.

Factor 1 — Training and Instruction. The first factor, Training and Instruction, includes 13 items. It reflects one of the important functions of a coach—to improve the performance level of the athlete. The coach trains and instructs the athletes to help them reach their maximum physical potential. He or she is also expected to instruct them in how to acquire the necessary skills and to teach them the techniques and the tactics of the sports. In addition, in the case of team sports, the coach coordinates the activities of the team members.

The Training and Instruction factor in the context of sport is similar to the Competitive Training factor identified by Danielson et al. (1975). It is also similar to the Instrumental Leadership dimension outlined by House and Dessler (1974) which essentially consists of role clarification, coaching, and coordination.

Factor 2 — Democratic Behavior. The factor of Democratic Behavior is composed of nine items. It reflects the extent to which the coach permits participation by the athletes in decision making. These decisions may relate to the setting of group goals and/or the ways in which these goals are to be attained.

Factor 3 — Autocratic Behavior. Autocratic Behavior, a factor with five items, indicates the extent to which a coach keeps apart from the athletes and stresses his or her authority in dealing with them. In such situations, it is expected that the coach would demand strict compliance with his or her decisions.

It is of interest to note that the dimensions of Democratic and Autocratic Behavior refer to the decision style adopted by the leader whereas the other dimensions refer to the substance of the behavior. The emergence of the dimensions of Democratic and Autocratic Behavior is consistent with the distinction made in organizational behavior research between the decision style adopted by the leader and the content of his or her decisions (e.g., House & Dessler, 1974).

Factor 4 — Social Support. Whereas the training and instructing behavior is task oriented and the democratic and autocratic behaviors reflect the decision making approaches adopted by the coach, the Social Support factor (eight items) refers to the extent to which the coach is involved in satisfying the interpersonal needs of the athletes. The coach's behavior may directly satisfy such needs or the coach may create a climate in which the members mutually satisfy their interpersonal needs. It should be noted that social support is provided independently of member performance.

This factor is similar to the Support factor in other leadership scales (Bowers & Seashore, 1966; House & Dessler, 1974). Danielson et al. (1975) in their study of coaching behavior identified a similar dimension which described socially oriented behavior outside the athletic situation.

Factor 5 — Positive Feedback. The factor of Positive Feedback includes five items. Athletic competitions, in general, are zero-sum games in which victory is attainable by only one of the contestants. An athlete, or team may perform at the maximum potential and yet lose a competition. Further, in team sports, contributions by certain positions may go unnoticed and unrecognized. It is therefore important for the coach to express appreciation and to compliment the athletes for their performance and contribution.

Positive feedback from the coach is crucial in maintaining the motivational level of the athletes. Oldham (1976) found that it was one of the motivational strategies that predicted leader effectiveness. The path-goal theory (House & Dessler, 1974) posits that the effectiveness of leadership is related to the extent that the leader provides "rewards necessary for effective and satisfying performance that would otherwise be lacking in the environment" (p. 31). This factor was originally labeled as "Rewarding Behavior" (Chelladurai & Saleh, 1978).

Although Social Support and Positive Feedback are two aspects of the traditional dimension of "Consideration," a distinction must be made between them. Social support behavior is not contingent on individual performance and is provided outside of the athletic context (Danielson et al., 1975) whereas positive feedback behavior depends on the athlete's performance. Positive feedback can be motivational only if it is contingent on performance.

In summary, the LSS consists of one direct task factor (Training and Instruction), two decision-style factors (Democratic and Autocratic Behavior), and two motivational factors (Social Support and Positive Feedback). Although the five selected factors do not explain all of the total variance in the three sets of data,[1] the LSS provides the researcher

[1]An obvious limitation restricting the amount of explained variance in studies of this type is that the number and type of item statements included in the initial pool may not have been completely adequate.

with a valuable tool that has advantages over other proposed factor structures (e.g., Danielson et al., 1975). These dimensions are consistent with the path-goal theory of leadership (House & Dessler, 1974), they are conceptually distinct categories of coaching behavior, and each of the dimensions is relatively reliable. The LSS could be used profitably in the analysis of coaching behavior and its effectiveness. For instance, leadership theory and research suggest that leader behavior should be varied according to the situation and the needs of the individual. The appropriateness of specific coaching behaviors could be assessed by administering the questionnaire to participants in different sports (Chelladurai & Saleh, 1978). The differences in the preferences (or perceptions) expressed by athletes of different teams in a sport could be related to criteria of interest like satisfaction and performance (Chelladurai, 1978). The distinction between the decision style of the leader and the substance of his or her behavior holds promise for the matching of a decision style to specific sports situations (Chelladurai & Haggerty, 1978). Because scales similar to the LSS are used in other fields, it would facilitate comparison with and extensions of research findings from those fields.

References

Bird, A.M. Development of a model for predicting team performance. *Research Quarterly,* 1977, 48, 24–32.

Bowers, D.G., & Seashore, S.E. Predicting organizational effectiveness with a four factor theory of leadership. *Administrative Science Quarterly,* 1966, 11, 238–263.

Cattell, R.B. The meaning and strategic use of factor analysis. In R.B. Cattell (Ed.), *Handbook of multivariate experimental psychology.* Chicago: Rand McNally, 1966.

Chelladurai, P. *A contingency model of leadership in athletics.* Unpublished doctoral dissertation, University of Waterloo, Canada, 1978.

Chelladurai, P., & Carron, A.V. Leadership. *CAHPER Sociology of Sport Monograph Series,* 1978.

Chelladurai, P., & Haggerty, T.R. A normative model of decision styles in coaching. *Athletic Administration,* 1978, 13, 6–9.

Chelladurai, P., & Saleh, S.D. Preferred leadership in sports. *Canadian Journal of Applied Sports Sciences,* 1978, 3, 85–92.

Cratty, B.J. *Psychology in contemporary sport.* Englewood Cliffs, N.J.: Prentice-Hall, 1973.

Danielson, R.R., Zelhart, P.F., & Drake, D.J. Multidimensional scaling and factor analysis of coaching behavior as perceived by high school hockey players. *Research Quarterly,* 1975, 46, 323–334.

Fiedler, F.E. *A theory of leadership effectiveness.* New York: McGraw-Hill, 1967.

Fleishman, E.A. A leader behavior description for industry. In R.M. Stogdill & A.E. Coons (Eds.), *Leader behavior: Its description and measurement.* Columbus: The Ohio State University, Bureau of Business Research, 1957. (a)

Fleishman, E.A. The Leadership Opinion Questionnaire. In R.M. Stogdill & A.E. Coons (Eds.), *Leader behavior: Its description and measurement.* Columbus: The Ohio State University, Bureau of Business Research, 1957. (b)

Halpin, A. W. The leader behavior and effectiveness of aircraft commanders. In R.M. Stogdill & A.E. Coons (Eds.), *Leader behavior: Its description and measurement.* Columbus: The Ohio State University, Bureau of Business Research, 1957.

Halpin, W.W., & Winer, R.J. A factorial study of the leader behavior description. In R.M. Stogdill & A.E. Coons (Eds.), *Leader behavior: Its description and measurement.* Columbus: The Ohio State University, Bureau of Business Research, 1957.

Hemphill, J.K., & Coons, A.E. Development of the leader behavior description questionnaire. In R.M. Stogdill & A.E. Coons (Eds.), *Leader behavior: Its description and measurement.* Columbus: The Ohio State University, Bureau of Business Research, 1957.

House, R.J., & Dessler, G. The path-goal theory of leadership: Some post hoc and a priori tests. In J.G. Hunt & L.L. Larson (Eds.), *Contingency approaches to leadership.* Carbondale, Il.: Southern Illinois University Press, 1974.

Kerlinger, F.N. *Foundations of behavioral research.* New York: Holt, Rinehart, & Winston, 1973.

Lenk, H. Authoritarian or democratic styled coaching? In H. Lenk (Ed.), *Team dynamics.* Champaign, Il.: Stipes, 1977.

Nie, N.H., Hull, C.H., Jenkins, J.G., Steinbrenner, K., & Bent, D.H. *Statistical package for the social sciences* (2nd ed.). New York: McGraw-Hill, 1975.

Oldham, G.R. The motivational strategies used by supervisors: Relationships to effectiveness indicators. *Organizational Behavior and Human Performance.* 1976, 15, 66–86.

Sage, G.H. An occupational analysis of the college coach. In D.W. Ball & J.W. Loy (Eds.), *Sport and social order: Contributions to the sociology of sport.* Reading, Ma: Addison-Wesley, 1975.

Schriesheim, C.A., & Kerr, S. Theories and measures of leadership: A critical appraisal of current and future directions. In J.G. Hunt & L.L. Larson (Eds.), *Leadership: The cutting edge.* Carbondale, Il.: Southern Illinois University Press, 1977.

Stogdill, R.M. *Manual for the Leader Behavior Description Questionnaire—Form XII.* Columbus: The Ohio State University, Bureau of Business Research, 1963.

20 The Development of an Instrument to Assess Cohesion in Sport Teams: The Group Environment Questionnaire

A.V. CARRON
University of Western Ontario

W.N. WIDMEYER AND L.R. BRAWLEY
University of Waterloo

Group dynamics has been recognized as a central branch of social and organizational psychology. The work on groups in social and organizational contexts traces back to the 1930s and 1940s, during which Kurt Lewin, a Jewish refugee from Nazi Germany, presented his ideas to the American public in the English language, among other things, in an attempt to help the United States in their war effort (e.g., by investigating the morale of fighting troops). Lewin had a profound effect on generations of thinkers and researchers concerned with group dynamics. Outside the realm of sport, scientific research on groups has focused on several topics related to group dynamics; these can be found in every textbook on social and organizational psychology. In sport and exercise settings, however, most of these topics are still underresearched. In contrast, group cohesion, traditionally viewed as one of the most important group variables, has been investigated quite extensively in sport and exercise, in particular since the early 1970s.

Generally speaking, the term cohesion relates to all the factors that bind members together and cause them to want to remain in the group. It is the social "glue" that holds people together in groups. However, since the late 1940s and early 1950s, the exact nature of cohesion has been subject to debate; several definitions have been proposed to account for this intriguing concept. This debate has been reflected also in sport and exercise psychology (e.g., in the measurement of cohesion). Cohesion in sport can be measured by sociometry (which has the advantage of showing not only the level of cohesion but also how particular members relate to each other within the group). However, cohesion was also evaluated by other inventories, such as the Sports Cohesiveness Questionnaire (SCQ), Task Cohesiveness Questionnaire (TCQ), and Multidimensional Sport Cohesion Instrument (MSCI), each derived from a different rationale.

Most of these questionnaires were essentially data driven. In contrast, Carron, Widmeyer, and Brawley proceeded from a previous work of the first author and used a theory-driven approach to develop the Group Environment Questionnaire (GEQ). After extensively reviewing the existing literature on group dynamics, they proposed a conceptual model of sport group cohesion that was derived from that literature. This model served them then as a basis for instrument development and validation. The GEQ distinguished between the individual and the group and between task and social dimensions. It was not only conceptually based but also systematically developed in terms of establishing appropriate reliability and validity values. Over the years, it has been used in numerous studies in sport and exercise settings and may therefore be considered the best instrument for measuring cohesion in sport and exercise. In this seminal article, Carron and his associates presented the GEQ for the first time to the scientific community.

The purpose of this paper was fourfold. The first purpose was to demonstrate the need to develop an instrument to assess group cohesion while the second was to outline a conceptual model of group cohesion upon which such an instrument could be based. This model reflected four related constructs which were the a priori basis for developing a large item pool and initial versions of the Group Environment Questionnaire (GEQ). The third purpose was to outline the four projects conducted to obtain construct-related information and to develop an initial version of the GEQ. The final purpose was to outline the two reliability and validity studies conducted with two different sport team samples. The results of these studies revealed that an 18-item version of the GEQ was internally consistent, reliable across studies, and content valid. Factor analyses with oblique rotation revealed preliminary evidence for construct validity. The GEQ is comprised of four scales reflecting the constructs of group integration–task, group integration–social, individual attractions to group–task, and individual attractions to group–social.

The extensive research on cohesion in a wide variety of settings has yielded very equivocal results. These findings have usually been attributed to problems associated with measuring cohesion. The apparent futility of measuring, weighting, and combining all the factors that attract members to a group led most early researchers to treat one factor, namely attraction to the other members, as synonymous with the total factors that attract members to a group. Thus, cohesion was usually assessed by some measure of interpersonal attraction such as reciprocal

Adapted, by permission, from A.V. Carron, 1985, "The development of an instrument to assess cohesion in sport teams: The group environment questionnaire," *Journal of Sport Psychology* 7: 244-266.

sociometric choices (e.g., Deep, Bass, & Vaughan, 1967), social activity of the group (e.g., Horsfall & Arensberg, 1949), group congeniality (e.g., Faunce & Beegle, 1948), cooperativeness versus competitiveness of groups (e.g., Deutsch, 1949), presence or absence of cliques (e.g., Lenk, 1969), similarity of interpersonal perceptions (e.g., Fiedler, Hartman, & Rudin, 1952), and members' perception of group closeness (e.g., Martens & Peterson, 1971). Although the problems associated with this operational definition of cohesion have been discussed by various authors over the years, possibly the strongest criticism of this procedure was advanced by Escovar and Sim (1974). They pointed out that operational measures of cohesion based upon interpersonal attraction (a) underrepresented the concept—there are other factors at work within the group in addition to attraction to other members which keep individuals in a group; (b) fail to account for cohesiveness in situations characterized by negative affect (i.e., dissatisfaction, dissension, hostility); (c) have not been supported empirically—interpersonal attractiveness has not been shown to correlate with other attractiveness measures in groups (Eisman, 1959; Gross & Martin, 1952); and (d) do not totally account for the conditions necessary for group formation.

In investigations in which interpersonal attraction has not been treated as synonymous with group cohesion, researchers have measured such different aspects of group attraction as members' expressed desire to remain in the group (e.g., Schachter, Ellertson, McBride, & Gregory, 1951), members' identification with the group (e.g., Converse & Campbell, 1968), and the value members place on group membership (e.g., Arnold & Straub, 1973). Some investigators have used members' perceptions of group cohesion as the measure of group closeness. These measures include members' perception of group functioning (e.g.,Torrance, 1955) and teamwork (e.g., Martens & Peterson, 1971). Some researchers have assessed the perception of others (e.g., observers' ratings of group integration during group performance; Stogdill, 1963). Still others have examined the similarity of members' interest in the task (e.g., Smith, 1968). Finally, attrition of group members has been used as an indication of low cohesiveness (e.g., Vander Velden, 1971). Most of these measures were devised by the researcher and rarely if ever subjected to psychometric analyses to establish their reliability and validity.

In summary, previous studies of cohesion have been characterized by one or more of the following three major measurement problems: They have utilized some measure of interpersonal attraction, a concept that underrepresents the attractions of groups for their members. They have assessed cohesion by such a wide variety of other measures that findings cannot be compared. They have rarely determined the psychometric soundness of the measures employed.

There is little doubt that the use of different and sometimes inappropriate measures of group cohesion has made it impossible to determine the reliability and/or validity of relationships between cohesion and its suspected antecedents/consequences. Rather than employing patchwork methods to repair existing measures or devising new ones with old problems, it is necessary to go to the root of the measurement issue. Although several reviewers (e.g., Carron, 1980, 1982; Cartwright, 1968; Escovar & Sim, 1974; Evans & Jarvis, 1980; Gill, 1977; Zander, 1979) have suggested that measurement problems stem from the lack of a clear conceptualization of cohesion, rarely have researchers attempted to clarify this construct before measuring it.

Conceptual Framework for the Development of a Group Cohesion Inventory

Cohesion has been defined in a number of ways. One of the most frequently cited is the now classic Festinger, Schachter, and Back (1950) proposal that views cohesion as the total field of forces causing members to remain in the group. One significant aspect of this definition is that it focuses on the individual and forces that attract individuals and cause them to remain with the group. Another significant aspect is their suggestion that cohesion is the result of numerous factors. Subsequently, Gross and Martin (1952) criticized this definition on the grounds that it fails to consider the group as a totality. They preferred to view cohesion as the resistance of the group to disruptive forces.

The need to distinguish between the group and the individual has been one of two major issues dominating the group dynamics literature (e.g., Cattell, 1948; Zander, 1971). For example, Cattell observed that a group can be studied at three different levels—population, structure, and syntality. At the population level the focus is on the individual group members and their needs, aspirations, and motives. At the structure level the focus is on the patterns of interaction within the group. And finally, syntality involves focusing on the group as a whole.

A second major distinction takes into account the task oriented and socially oriented concerns of groups and their members. The study of leadership provides perhaps the best illustration. Certainly every leadership theory, whether it focuses on the traits of leaders or their behaviors, incorporates an assessment of both the task and social dimensions (e.g., Fiedler, 1967; Hersey & Blanchard, 1969).

This first issue, the need to distinguish between the individual and the group, has also been evident in discussions on the nature of group cohesion. For example, as a result of their dissatisfaction with the popular research strategy of summing individual attractions to group (ATG) scores to produce a cohesion index, Van Bergen and Koekebakker (1959) advocated that the concepts of ATG and cohesion be differentiated. They defined ATG as the interaction of motives working on the *individual* to stay in the group and cohesion as the degree of unification of the *group field*. Thus, they identified both an individual concept (ATG) and a group concept (cohesion). Although the latter was not well defined operationally, it recognized cohesion as a group property distinct from ATG, a property reflecting the individual group member.

More recently, Evans and Jarvis (1980) reiterated the ideas of Van Bergen and Koekebakker (1959). They noted that the Van Bergen and Koekebakker definition of cohesion implies "a closeness among members, a similarity in perception of events, and...a bonding together in response to the outside world" (p. 366). Thus, according to Evans and Jarvis, measurement of this closeness/similarity/bonding might rely more on variability rather than a group mean. Evans and Jarvis also noted that, by contrast, ATG is a composite of individual members' feelings about the group in terms of their desire to be accepted and identified as a group member, their personal role involvement with the group, and their involvement with other group members. Thus it might be best assessed by some measure of central tendency.

The second issue discussed above—the need to distinguish between the task and social concerns of groups and their members—has also been considered in discussions on group cohesion. For example, Festinger et al. (1951) considered factors that caused members to remain in the group to be of two types: attractiveness to the group and means control. Enoch and McLemore (1967) considered ATG as intrinsic attraction and instrumental attraction. Anderson (1975) found that ATG (cohesion) became greater in task-oriented groups when they were successful and greater in socially oriented groups when members had similar values. Perhaps Mikalachki (1969) made one of the clearest distinctions when he advocated that cohesiveness be subdivided into task and social components. According to Mikalachki, task cohesion exists when the group coheres around the task it was organized to perform while social cohesion exists when the group coheres around social (nontask) functions. Mikalachki also suggested that these two components of cohesiveness should be considered separately in terms of their antecedents and consequences.

Cohesion: A Conceptual Model

These two important distinctions—the individual versus the group and task versus social concerns—had a major impact on the development of the conceptual model. The model is divided into two major categories: a member's perceptions of the group as a totality and a member's personal attractions to the group. The former category is labeled *group integration,* and the latter, *individual attractions to the group*. Both perceptions help to bind members to their group. Also, the member's perceptions of the group as a unit and their perceptions of the group's attractions for them can be focused on task or social aspects. Thus, four constructs can be identified—*group integration–task, group integration–social, individual attractions to group–task,* and *individual attractions to group–social.* Operationally, members could indicate the extent to which they agree that each of the constructs plays a role in the development and maintenance of group cohesion.

Conceptually, group integration is the category that represents the closeness, similarity, and bonding within the group as a whole—the degree of unification of the *group* field. Individual attractions to group, on the other hand, is the category that represents the interaction of the motives working on the individual to remain in the group—the composite of the *individual* members' feelings about the group, their personal role involvement, and involvement with other group members. Further, the social aspect can be seen as a general orientation toward developing and maintaining social relationships within the group. The task aspect can be seen as a general orientation toward achieving the group's goals and objectives. It is assumed that the four constructs of the conceptualization are correlated. They are related through the perceived interaction of various task and social orientations as viewed through the eyes of the individuals for themselves and their group.

This conceptualization and the questionnaire which ultimately evolved from it must be viewed within the perspective of its delimitations. One of these is that a questionnaire approach is utilized rather than direct behavioral assessments. Another is that individual perceptions are assessed rather than a total group viewpoint. Also, although other aspects of cohesiveness have been discussed in the literature (e.g., normative cohesion), only the four selected constructs are included, that is, the ones thought to account for the greatest variance among groups. And finally, only intragroup perceptions of cohesiveness are tapped; extragroup perceptions are not considered.

These delimitations notwithstanding, the conceptualization and the questionnaire which evolved from it do offer some advantages. One of these is that the antecedents and consequences of cohesiveness are not incorporated into the measurement of cohesion. A second is that cohesion is treated as a multifaceted concept—more than one factor binding members to the group is considered. And finally, the individual perceptions of the group's task and social cohesiveness are considered through two major perspectives: personal ("what am I doing?") and group ("what is the group doing?").

Operationally Defining the Constructs: Phase I—Identification of Constructs and Representation of Content

Although four related constructs had been suggested as aspects of cohesion in the initial conceptual framework, the possibility that group members might perceive cohesiveness as involving other concepts was recognized. Also, in the construction of instruments to assess any construct, the actual representation of the construct (i.e., the semantics and the descriptors used) might be more clearly expressed by the actual subjects than by the investigators. In past research, cohesion instruments have too often been based upon the investigators' rather than the group's ideas. Thus, the intention in the present investigation was to involve group members as active agents in expressing the meaning of the construct of cohesion (cf. Adair, 1973; Russell, 1982; Sherif & Sherif, 1969). To this end then, group members' perceptions of cohesion formed part of the basis for identifying cohesion concepts and the items reflecting the expression of these concepts. In this first phase, four projects were conducted to obtain input, three of which used group members as contributors.

Project 1: Methodology

Each member of an undergraduate class in the social psychology of physical activity interviewed three members from each of two sport teams. The interview questions concerned (a) the personal meaning of cohesion to group members, (b) the behavioral manifestation they could cite to reflect cohesion, (c) the incidents that group members recalled which would denote a low level or absence of cohesion, and (d) factors that contributed to the development of cohesion on the respondents' team. A total of 234 respondents from a variety of different sport teams ($N = 78$) were subjects. University, municipal, and industrial teams from hockey, soccer, baseball, lacrosse, football, track, and swimming were examples of the sports in which athletes were interviewed. More than 1 team in each sport was examined and athletes of both sexes were interviewed. The most consistently appearing responses were tallied, taking care to use the subject's own wording, then coded according to whether responses concerned one of the four constructs (i.e., individual attractions to group–task, individual attractions to group–social, group integration–task, and group integration–social) or concerned another construct altogether.

Project 2: Methodology

The subjects were 63 members of an undergraduate kinesiology class, all of whom had previously competed in team sports. Each subject responded to a series of open-ended questions about why people join groups, leave groups, or stay with groups. A third of the respondents provided self-focused reasons (i.e., "Why did *you*. . . . "), another third provided reasons for their teammates, (i.e., "Why did your *teammates*. . . . "), and a final third gave responses for athletes in general ("Why do *individuals*. . . . "). In this manner, subjects used their own words and their own response rate to describe both personal (i.e., self and group focus) and general factors contributing to individual attractions to group and group integration. The different-person focus provided a range of perceived reasons so that several alternative perceptions, and thus greater potential response variability, could be obtained. Once again, the most frequently appearing responses were tallied and coded as in the first project.

Project 3: Methodology

The subjects were 60 members of intact teams actively involved in ongoing competition. These groups differed in the amount of interaction required to perform their sport. All teams examined were at the university level and involved in the activities of competitive swimming, cross-country running, and cheerleading. The same open-ended questions used in Project 2 were administered. The three sets of questions were randomly distributed so that some members from each group responded to each form of question. Coding proceeded as with Projects 1 and 2.

Project 4: Methodology

A literature search of 29 different articles and studies on the topic of cohesion provided a complement of questions (i.e., operational definitions) that had been previously used to examine the phenomenon. The search covered group dynamics articles published between 1948 to 1982 in the areas of social psychology, sociology, industrial psychology, and sport psychology. These questions were scrutinized for similarity, applicability to sport teams, and frequency of appearance. Coding of the applicable and most frequently appearing questions proceeded as with other projects.

Summary of Phase 1 Projects

All of the responses from the four projects just described were collapsed to form a response pool representing information concerning the four constructs. The responses represented the subjects' own wording of the affective and behavioral manifestations of proposed cohesion-related constructs as well as previously developed items purported to measure the phenomenon. No other responses emerged from the series of projects often enough to require adding constructs to the proposed model.

The resultant pool of affective and behavioral manifestations from subjects and from the group dynamics literature formed a major portion of information used for item development in Phase 2. It is important to note that Phase 1 represents one of the few instances in the development of a cohesion instrument where subjects have been actively involved in providing information for item construction. The use of subjects' as well as investigators' information encourages greater information variability, lessens the possibility of exclusive investigator bias, and encourages item development using language and concepts that subjects can understand (cf. Adair, 1973; Russell, 1982; Sherif & Sherif, 1969).

Instrument Formation: Phase 2— Item Development and Content Validation

The purpose of this phase was twofold. The first purpose was to develop an item pool that would form the basis for the Group Environment Questionnaire (GEQ). The information gleaned from the four projects in Phase I were used to write the items. When this large item pool was reduced to a manageable size, the second purpose of establishing content (face) validity was undertaken.

Methodology: Item Development Project

Four investigators and a senior research assistant used the Phase 1 information and their knowledge of group dynamics to generate an initial large item pool of 354 statements (cf. Guilford, 1954; Nunnally, 1978). Each individual independently wrote items representing each of the four constructs (individual attractions to group–task, individual attractions to group–social, group integration–task, group integration–social). The pool of items concerning each construct was then scrutinized by the five item writers and statements were grouped according to similarity of content. Each of the similar content areas was termed a subarea for a given construct. Several criteria were then used to agree upon the list of items to be included on the first version of the questionnaire. They were (a) frequency of appearance, (b) clarity in writing, (c) amount of ambiguity, (d) use of group members' as opposed to investigator's terminology, and (e) duplication (cf. Guilford, 1954). An agreement of 80% among the investigators was required to retain an item.

In this item-trimming process, care was taken to ensure that no one subarea (e.g., friendship, role clarity, role acceptance) was overrepresented for a given conceptual construct. A bias in representation could have led to erroneous results in subsequent item analyses. As well, care was taken to ensure that each construct's scale had approximately equal numbers of positively and negatively worded items (cf. Nunnally, 1978). Finally, statements were written to ensure an approximately equal representation of affective and behavioral manifestations of individual attractions and group integration.

Methodology: Content Validity Project

Obviously, the item development, refinement, and selection conducted by the five item writers represented a form of content validation. As an additional step toward content validity, the reduced item pool was also sent to five experts in the area of group dynamics from the fields of social psychology, industrial psychology, and sport psychology. Each expert was sent a summary of the conceptual model with instructions to comment on the model and delete or make suggestions about the items representing each construct (cf. Bohrnstedt, 1970). The responses from the five experts were examined and a decision was then made whether to modify, delete, or add items. Experts' responses confirmed the deletion choices of the research team.

Phase 2: Results and Discussion

The GEQ: Version 1

The original 354-item pool contained the following distribution of items representing each construct: individual attractions to group–task, 100 items; individual attractions to group–social, 80 items; group integration–task, 97 items; and group integration–social, 77 items. The process of item deletion by the five researchers reduced this original item pool by 85%. The reduced pool of items ($n = 53$) was then put in questionnaire form. In a manner consistent with the recommendations of Guilford (1954), a Likert-type scale was adopted which varied from strongly disagree (value = 1) to strongly agree (value = 9). In the 53-item questionnaire, the distribution of responses in each of the four construct scales was as follows: individual attractions to group–task; 13 items; individual attractions to group–social, 13 items; group integration–task, 16 items; and group integration–social, 11 items.

The content validity assessments by the five experts were used in conjunction with the preliminary item analysis (Phase 3 of the research) and therefore are discussed with those results. A degree of content validity was assured through the protocol followed by the research team which required 80% agreement across a range of item characteristics.

Social Desirability

Social desirability (SD) is an issue considered by many who develop instruments because of a concern that socially desirable responses can contaminate the validity of the construct of interest. Investigators and authoritative sources often assume that SD instruments or the inclusion of SD scales within the main instrument is a psychometrically sound methodology (e.g., APA, 1974, *Standards for Educational and Psychological Tests*). However, the majority of test developers who accept this view fail to differentiate whether SD is a property of the items/scales or an individual difference variable.

As ingenious as many of the SD devices may be, they are commonly self-reports which fail to differentiate the two aforementioned SD types. McCrae and Costa (1983) have noted that such instruments may lead researchers to identify the honest, cooperative, and conscientious subject as a "liar." Eliminating such subjects may cause the loss of very valuable data. An example in the case of group cohesion might be the highly involved, honest group member who responds to group integration items based upon an invariant perception about his/her group's "highly desirable" behavior. Elimination of his/her responses would not be eliminating an artifact, but rather, substantive data. On the basis of their own and others' data, McCrae and Costa (1983) have noted that instrument scores "corrected" by use of values from popular lie and SD scales decreased, not increased, the main instrument's validity coefficients. This result is opposite to that desired through the use of SD scales.

Based on this rationale, the decision not to use an SD scale in the present questionnaire was anything but arbitrary. As McCrae and Costa have stated, other investigators using known—or worse, their own hastily constructed—lie scales as a methodological benefit might well be doing themselves a disservice.

Reliability of the GEQ: Phase 3—Item Analyses

The purpose of this phase in the test development was to assess the reliability of the questionnaire with respect to a measure of equivalence (i.e., internal consistency) through various item analytic procedures. Two studies were undertaken to accomplish this purpose.

Internal Consistency Issues

Stability and Equivalence. In terms of the reliability of an instrument, consistency can be considered in two categories called measures of stability and of equivalence. Measures of stability or test-retest reliability are time-honored procedures often cited in the literature as one of the indices of an instrument's worth. Unfortunately, most attention is often paid to these estimates even though they have greater limitations than do measures of equivalence (i.e., the internal consistency of items within a scale). Although the test-retest approach is thought to reflect stability, the degree of stability can vary due to between-test time interval, reactivity, or increased probability of the individual's response change over time. Bohrnstedt (1970) has suggested that these problems have turned researchers toward a greater reliance on measures of equivalence.

The previous concerns and suggestions were taken into account in the statistical analyses of the GEQ. The notion of equivalence and its assessment focuses on the internal consistency of a measure. For example, in the GEQ, when items representing a particular scale are summed to yield a score, it is assumed that each item is a relatively unique (i.e., not identical) measure of that scale. Thus, items in the scale are internally consistent with the construct measured by that scale.

In attempting to achieve high internal consistency, both statistical procedures and practical factors were considered. They were (a) increasing reliability by adding/deleting items from a scale; (b) ensuring that each item represented only a single construct; and (c) ensuring that the scale was of a practically administrable length.

Intra- and Interscale Equivalence. The internal consistency approach to equivalence examines the covariance among all items of a scale simultaneously. The statistical indicant generally used to express this reliability is a generalization of the Kuder-Richardson 20 formula (1937) called Cronbach's alpha (1951). The latter statistic is used when items are scored on a continuous measurement scale. Coefficient alpha is calculated for the scale when each item's variance is statistically removed from the total scale. Thus, both an appreciation for an item's relation to a construct and a statistical criterion are gained and used in making a scale reliable and practically shorter.

However, internal consistency within a scale is not sufficient for an instrument having more than one scale. Items should also be correlated with their own scale to a greater extent than with any other scale in the instrument. Items correlating otherwise reduce reliability because of their overlap with the other assessed constructs. Eliminating such items ensures a greater probability of the constructs being relatively unique.

Item Analysis. The processes for determining which items to retain in the various scales of an instrument are called item analysis techniques. The two item analysis techniques described in the previous section were used in reducing the 53-item questionnaire (cf. Phase 2—Results).

The process of item analysis requires not only a pool of subjects large enough to examine item reliability but also a sample representing a broad range of subjects (cf. Nunnally, 1978). An inventory attempting detection of both different aspects and intensity levels of a multifaceted concept requires statements that elicit responses across any population's normal distribution. However, to determine if such statements have the sensitivity to reflect sample differences, one must examine them through the responses of a heterogeneous sample. Improper sampling can cloud the sensitivity of the instrument to detect differences. Unfortunately, heterogeneous sampling is the exception rather than the rule in the sport cohesion literature.

In the case of the present investigation, the unit of analysis was the individual within the group. Inasmuch as groups can be conceived as varying in their stages of development, it seemed wise to sample groups across this continuum.

Study 1 — Method: Item Analysis

Subjects

In this study, athletes ($N = 212$) from a number of teams ($N = 20$) of heterogeneous characteristics were tested. The sample consisted of forming through to well-developed teams (i.e., group tenure ranged from 1 month to 9 years). The teams were interactive, requiring members to integrate their roles in order to accomplish the group task. A variety of sport types was used (i.e., ball hockey, baseball, basketball, ice hockey, rugby, soccer). Teams were from intercollegiate and adult municipal associations. All participants were adult Canadians representing both male ($n = 13$) and female ($n = 7$) teams. Athletes averaged 12 years of playing experience with their sport. The percentage of new members on a given team ranged from 10 to 50% ($M = 20\%$). At the time of assessment, the mean time members had been together that season was 5.8 months. In addition, the teams had participated in an average of 26 competitions during that season. In summary, these teams represented a heterogeneous sample.

Procedure

The GEQ–Version 1 was administered by individual research assistants, who informed teams that they were part of a larger investigation concerning how teams interact. Team members were assured of anonymity (i.e., that no player or coach would see their responses).

Each respondent completed the 53-item GEQ (cf. Phase 2—Results). The GEQ also contained a variety of demographic questions concerning group and member characteristics. These questions not only helped to describe the group but also served to check the heterogeneity of sample characteristics.

Research assistants were given a standard protocol for questionnaire administration. Teams were always assessed before a weekday practice during their regular season. Assessments immediately before or after competitions were avoided so that responses would not be competition-specific.

Results and Discussion

With respect to internal consistency, the two procedures mentioned above provided the statistical bases for item elimination. The first criterion examined was whether an item written to represent one of the four constructs correlated well with its own scale's total score (i.e., intrascale equivalence). Thus, for example, if an item written to measure individual attractions to group–task correlated poorly with the total score for that scale, its internal consistency was questionable and it was considered for elimination from the scale.

The second criterion was whether an item was more related to its own scale than to other scales (i.e., interscale equivalence). For instance, an individual attractions to group–task item that correlated $r = .50$ with its own scale but also correlated $r = .55$ with the scale of individual attractions to group–social was not considered to be internally consistent. This example reflects a case of construct overlap and the item would be considered for elimination from the questionnaire.

While these statistical criteria determined retention or deletion of items, it was necessary to seek a maximum Cronbach's alpha for each of the four scales and simultaneously consider the overall length of the questionnaire. As items were deleted from each scale, the item analysis procedure was reiterated, Cronbach's alpha was recalculated on the basis of the deletion, and item correlations with other scale total scores were recomputed. Four iterations of this process were conducted, reducing the questionnaire from 53 items to 24 while still retaining good internal consistency. It should be noted that any items questioned by the external reviewers in the content validity phase were among those deleted by the item analysis process.

The scales in the reduced version of this GEQ were represented by the following numbers of items: individual attractions to group–task, 7 items; individual attractions to group–social, 5 items; group integration–task, 7 items; group integration–social, 5 items. The respective values for Cronbach's alpha for each of the aforementioned scales were .74, .58, .78, and .61. These results are presented in table 20.1, which also illustrates a matrix of interscale correlations.

The interscale correlations indicate that the scales are moderately related. However, since these relations do not exceed .80, there is no cause for concern about multicollinearity. In fact, they reflect relations suggested by the conceptual model. That is, the scales are assessing constructs that are related but are sufficiently unique not to be considered redundant.

Table 20.1 Internal Consistency of the GEQ: Study 1

	Interscale correlations				Cronbach's alpha
Scales	**ATGT**	**ATGS**	**GIT**	**GIS**	
Individual attractions to group–task (ATGT)	—				.74
ATG–social (ATGS)	.43	—			.58
Group integration–task (GIT)	.54	.32	—		.78
GI–social (GIS)	.35	.32	.39	—	.61

Reliability values are based upon the 24 items selected from the 53-item GEO ($N = 212$). Interscale correlations are calculated by correlating a scale total score (sum of all items in a given scale) with its counterpart for each of the other scales (e.g., the ATGT scale score correlates $r = .54$ with the scale score for GIT).

Although the internal consistency values suggested good reliability in a questionnaire of practical length, it was felt that greater confidence could be placed in these findings if they could be replicated with a different sample. Also, the reliability coefficients just presented for the 24 items reflect relations among items and scales physically embedded in the original 53-item format. Thus, it was concluded that if the scales were reliable, a similar pattern of relations would be evident in another study when the 24-item questionnaire was used.

Study 2 — Method: Item Analysis

The basic purpose of Study 2, then, was to determine the reliability of Version 2 of the GEQ (n items = 24). A second purpose was to determine if the internal consistency values found in Study 1 could be replicated with a different athlete sample.

Subjects

The athletes ($N = 247$) examined were from 26 different teams, heterogeneous in sport type (i.e., basketball, cross-country running, cross-country skiing, curling, figure skating, gymnastics, ice hockey, precision skating, ringette, speed skating, swimming, wrestling). Of these teams, 14 were female and 12 were male. Teams were both interactive, $n = 10$ (i.e., requiring members of different roles to interact to accomplish the group task), and individual, $n = 16$ (i.e., members act individually and their performances sum for a common team outcome) in nature. Teams also varied in their tenure together and in the number of competitions in which they had participated. They were sampled from various intercollegiate and municipal adult leagues in the province of Ontario.

Procedure

Test administration procedures identical to those in Study 1 were followed using the 24-item GEQ. Again, care was taken to ensure that the questionnaire was not administered immediately before or after a competition in order to avoid situation-specific responses.

Results and Discussion: Studies 1 and 2

The values of Cronbach's alpha are quite similar between studies as the scale-by-scale results indicate. Cronbach's alpha for individual attractions to group–task and social and group integration–task and social and group integration–task and social are $r = .65$, .64, .71, and .72, respectively.

Correlations from Study 2 can be compared with those of Study 1. The interscale correlations in Study 2 were slightly lower than those from Study 1. They still reflect the relatedness of the assessed constructs but their size indicates that the measures are relatively unique.

Thus, good internal consistency for the GEQ—Version 2 (hereafter referred to as GEQ) was evident both within and between scales. This consistency was stable across two different samples of sport groups, heterogeneous in their characteristics. It was concluded that the GEQ was reliable from an equivalence perspective and that this equivalence was replicable (cf. Bohrnstedt, 1970). It is important to realize, however, that the reliabilities of any scale are only estimates dependent upon sampling and estimation technique. A greater degree of confidence may be accorded the GEQ than its predecessors because its estimates are reliable within and between studies.

While it is important to demonstrate the reliability of a measuring instrument, it is equally important to examine its validity. This was the purpose of the fourth phase in this instrument's development.

Validity of the GEQ: Phase 4—Factor Analysis

Content Validity

The GEQ had been shown to have good face or content validity (i.e., the degree to which the scale represents the constructs of interest) as mentioned in the Phase 2 discussion. Briefly summarized, the following procedures initially undertaken also contribute to this content validity: (a) broad based literature search, (b) subjects used as active agents in concept definitions, (c) reliance on a conceptual model which provided the rationale for the various scales, (d) assessments of item content made by unbiased experts and the research team, (e) intercorrelations of each item with own and other scale total scores. All of these steps represent logical and statistical procedures that help to ensure content validity (cf. Bohrnstedt, 1970; Kerlinger, 1973).

Construct Validity

Two other types of validity, criterion-related and construct, also require estimation in developing the GEQ. The former mainly concerns the predictive ability of an instrument while the latter concerns the meaning of the instrument—the extent the concepts upon which it is based account for subject responses. A variety of procedures and investigations are required to determine the degree of confidence an investigator has in the "validities" of an instrument (cf. Bohrnstedt, 1970; Campbell & Fiske, 1959; Kerlinger, 1973).

One group of procedures that can be used as a preliminary indicator of construct validity is factor analysis. These data-reduction procedures examine the intercorrelations among items with the notion of collapsing them into a smaller set of variables or constructs. Validity is present when the factors reflect the constructs in the proposed conceptual model. A practical benefit of this procedure in the early stages of test development is that the sample used to achieve the instrument's reduced form (e.g., the 24-item GEQ) can be factor-analyzed. Thus, the investigator can obtain a preliminary indicant as to whether the items on the instrument do represent the proposed conceptual structure. This allows for decision making about further steps toward achieving validity. A factor structure not representing the conceptual model may mean that the instrument, the model, or both need further work. By contrast, preliminary verification of the model may indicate it is worthwhile spending the considerable effort required to conduct predictive studies. The factor analysis in this case was conducted using the 212 team sport athletes sampled in Study 1. The data analyzed were the responses to the 24 items selected for Version 2 of the GEQ.

It should be noted that the factor analytic approach taken in the present investigation represents a theory-driven as opposed to data-driven approach to instrument development. The latter approach proceeds without a conceptual model but with the expectation that a model will emerge. Nunnally (1978) suggests that this avenue of test construction can be viewed as a "shotgun" approach. As emphasized earlier, this approach has been the root of the problems associated with empirical cohesion research. Thus, the opposite approach was taken where preliminary verification of an a priori proposed model was attempted.

Factor Analysis of the GEQ: Method

A variety of factor analytic procedures can be used to determine the structure of a set of variables: The procedure selected is partly dependent upon what the investigator is trying to accomplish. With theory-driven test development, there is an a priori notion of what the underlying factors in the data might be. As well, the theoretical model may also suggest a degree of relatedness among the proposed variables.

Oblique Rotation

In the present investigation, the factor analysis chosen was principal factoring with oblique rotation. The goal of rotation is to achieve the most theoretically meaningful, and if possible the simplest, factor structure (Harris, 1975). The advantage of oblique rotation is that the factor axes need not be orthogonal to each other. The absence of an orthogonality assumption in a factoring approach is probably more realistic when the theoretical constructs under examination are considered related. Gorsuch (1974) noted that if prior evidence suggests these relations are present, oblique rotation is a realistic approach. As previously stated, the interscale correlations in both Studies 1 and 2 illustrated moderate relations between scales. Given this evidence, the choice of oblique rotation seemed logical and appropriate. It also seemed logical to constrain the solution to four factors as proposed in the conceptual model. This is consistent with the choice of procedures which was governed by an a priori set of criteria for determining simple structure (cf. Harris, 1975).

Interpretation Procedures

Although a factor analytic procedure is chosen logically, factor structure may be interpreted in a variety of ways. When the factors are correlated, the contribution of variables (i.e., items in the present case) to the interpretation of factors differs according to the factor matrix examined. The two matrices of chief concern in the oblique solution are the pattern (i.e., pattern coefficients define the grouping of variables) and the structure (i.e., correlations of the variables with the factors). Gorsuch (1974) recommended initial interpretation on the basis of the factor structure matrix. The advantages of this interpretation are that (a) the relation of the variable (item) to the full factor is indicated, and (b) correlation coefficients have more interpretive meaning to the majority of investigators in the sense that their range and the practical importance of that range is known. The relationship of the items to the factors should remain the same regardless of the context of another study and other factors in that study. By contrast, the pattern matrix coefficients can only be interpreted within the context of a given study. Thus, the structure matrix from the oblique rotation was the primary choice for interpretation in the present study.

The salient loadings within a factor help with its interpretation. Once again, however, the investigator is faced with various approaches in assessing what constitutes a sufficiently high loading. There is no single rule to aid in deciding what is a sufficient loading (Gorsuch, 1974). The general approach is to conduct the analysis with a sample of sufficient size so that any variable of interpretive interest is significant. In using this approach, Gorsuch suggested doubling the minimum significant correlation coefficient in the structure matrix to ensure that the loading is high enough to have interpretive meaning. For example, the minimum significant correlation with an n of 100 is $r = .20$. Thus, the doubling guide would suggest that a variable with a minimum loading of .40 is interpretable. However, with a large enough sample, even some doubled correlations would be questionable from an interpretive standpoint. Consequently, a loading of .30 is the criterion generally accepted as a minimum for samples of $n > 175$.

Of course, the size of a structure matrix coefficient is only clearly interpretable if the variables load primarily on one factor. The clearer the strength of the relationship of an item with a single factor, the easier the interpretation. This criterion encourages interpretation in accord with Thurstone's (1947) notion of simple structure.

It should be noted that the item analytic procedures previously discussed are also a form of implicit factor analysis. Thus, elimination of test items by those procedures is not unlike dropping items that do not meet minimum loading criteria in factor analysis. However, the reason for using item as opposed to factor analysis for item deletion is that item analysis has been shown to be a somewhat superior procedure for reliability and validity estimates (Larsen & LeRoux, 1983). It was expected that the majority of the 24 items of the GEQ would meet the loading criterion suggested. Whether the items would relate to the factors for which they were written remained for the factor analysis to determine.

Results and Discussion

The four factors each had an eigenvalue greater than 1.0. The majority of items met the minimum loading criterion of .30. No interpretable factor had less than three items. This solution indicated that in this sample, the GI scales (group integration–task, group integration–social) and the ATG scales (individual attractions to group–task, and individual attractions to group–social) were ranked most to least important, respectively (i.e., as assessed by amount of variance accounted for by factor eigenvalues exceeding 1.0).

What has to be remembered when interpreting a correlated factor model is the purpose of the procedure and what the various correlation loadings represent. Correlations among the factors are based upon the correlation between an item and a factor as well as the factor's relation to the item through other correlated factors. Thus, estimates of an item's contribution to the factor are not exclusive to the factor. It is therefore questionable how the variance accounted for should be interpreted. In this preliminary analysis, what is perhaps more important is the grouping of items within factors. Recall that the primary intent for utilizing factor analysis was to obtain a preliminary indicant of construct validity. Thus, interpretation in terms of the conceptual model was of chief interest.

In considering the structure matrix, four groupings of variables were evident that can be named according to the factors proposed in the conceptual model. For this sample, some of the items in two of the scales (ATG scales) either did not meet the minimum loading criteria or overlapped too much with other factors. Thus, they were not useful in interpretation. However, the majority (n = 19) of the 24 items from the GEQ were satisfactory.

It is also noteworthy that the correlation matrix among factors reflected a degree of relatedness similar to that of the interscale correlations between scales. Much higher or much lower correlations among factors would have been one indication that the rotation used was inappropriate for interpretation.

In summary, results of the exploratory factor analysis revealed a factor structure that would be representative of the constructs proposed in the conceptual model. However, these results also suggested that a third version of the GEQ might be more internally consistent than the second as some of the 24 items did not meet the minimum factor loading criterion. Items from the two individual attractions to group scales were viewed as possible candidates for elimination. Therefore, this same data set (n = 247) was further item-analyzed.

The GEQ: Version 3

Version 2 of the GEQ was examined for one criterion of internal consistency, (i.e., the relation of each item with its own scale; cf. results of Studies 1 and 2). However, the second criterion for inclusion of items in any given scale had not been applied to the 24-item GEQ. Briefly reiterated, each item must be assessed for its relation to its own and other scale total scores. Items relating as well or greater with scales other than their own are not considered internally consistent to the parent scale. Removal of such items from their scale changes the item-to-scale correlations observed in the first iteration of item analysis.

Subsequent iterations are usually conducted. Obviously, when an already refined instrument has been reduced in size, the elimination of various items after two or three iterations must be done cautiously. As well, when items are removed in later steps of the process, an item eliminated at an earlier step may subsequently become more internally consistent and thus "reclaimed" in the scale. The reason the reclaimed item may now correlate best with its own scale is that undesirable items, which were later removed, had originally suppressed the item's contribution to its own scale. The reclaimed item's contribution to internal consistency could only be evaluated given the final list of items retained for all scales.

To summarize, several iterations of item analysis, item elimination, and reclamation occurred. The overall objective was improvement of internal consistency. The final result was Version 3 of the GEQ, an 18-item questionnaire. The number of items retained for each scale was as follows: individual attractions to group–task, 4 items; individual attractions to group–social, 5 items; group integration–task, 5 items; group integration–social, 4 items. The net effect of this process was to increase the internal consistency of the individual attractions to group–task (ATGT) and group integration–social (GIS) scales with no substantive change in individual attractions to group–social (ATGS) or group integration–task (GIT) values. For ATGT, ATGS, GIT, and GIS, the Cronbach's alphas were r = .75, .64, .70, and .76, respectively. Interscale correlations were similar to those of the 24-item GEQ . Thus, Version 3 of the GEQ continued to have good internal consistency after elimination of problem items observed in the previous 24-item version.

General Discussion

The present research project evolved from the view that there is a need within group dynamics in sport to develop a psychometrically sound instrument to assess group cohesion. Based upon this need, it was also felt that the route to such an instrument required a conceptual model of group cohesion. From this, an instrument could evolve in a systematic fashion.

The perceptions of active group members and the group dynamics literature provided the information base for item development. Through a variety of item analytic procedures, an 18-item, four-scale instrument emerged. This instrument, the Group Environment Questionnaire, is (a) practical, (b) reflects good internal consistency and is stable across two independent samples, (c) assesses a wide variety of sport groups having heterogeneous characteristics, (d) is content-valid, and (e) has preliminary psychometric support for its construct validity.

The suggestion is made that the construct validity is preliminary because evidence for that form of validity must come from a variety of investigations and methods (cf. Cook & Campbell, 1979). One factor analytic study alone does not suggest sufficient validation. The factor structure must be replicated across different samples having different characteristics. Further validation research on the GEQ is necessary and is currently under way.

At this stage of instrument development, the GEQ is both similar to and different from other cohesion instruments reported in the sport group literature. The similarities lie in the attempt to measure group members' perceptions of cohesion by self-report. The differences can be grouped into conceptual and psychometric categories. From the conceptual perspective, this instrument is based upon a model concerning group members' perceptions of cohesion (admittedly, other situational factors also contribute to cohesion). By contrast, preceeding instruments neither specify a model nor use it for development.

From a psychometric viewpoint, the form of the GEQ developed to date represents a more concerted attempt to (a) operationalize constructs by independent methods, (b) separate previously confounded perceptions, (c) be generalizable to a large cross-section of sports, (d) have a form of reliability consistent across samples, and (e) satisfy more than one form of validity.

References

Adair, J.G. (1973). *The human subject: The social psychology of the psychological experiment.* Boston, MA: Little, Brown & Co.

American Psychological Association. (1974). *Standards for educational and psychological tests.* Washington, DC: American Psychological Association.

Anderson, A.B. (1975). Combined effects of interpersonal attraction and goal-path clarity on the cohesiveness of task-oriented groups. *Journal of Personality and Social Psychology,* 31, 68–75.

Arnold, G., & Straub, W. (1973). Personality and group cohesiveness as determinants of success among interscholastic basketball teams. In I. Williams & L. Wankel (Eds.), *Proceedings of the Fourth Canadian Psycho-Motor Learning and Sport Psychology Symposium* (pp. 346–353). Ottawa: Dept. of National Health and Welfare.

Bohrnstedt, G.W. (1970). Reliability and validity assessment in attitude measurement. In G.F. Summers (Ed.), *Attitude measurement* (pp. 80–99). Chicago: Rand-McNally.

Campbell, D.T., & Fiske, D.W. (1959). Convergent and discriminant validation by the multitrait-multimethod matrix. *Psychological Bulletin,* 56, 81–105.

Carron, A.V. (1980). *Social psychology of sport.* Ithaca, NY: Mouvement.

Carron, A.V. (1982). Cohesiveness in sport groups: Interpretations and considerations. *Journal of Sport Psychology,* 4, 123–138.

Cartwright, D. (1968). The nature of group cohesiveness. In D. Cartwright & A. Zander (Eds.), *Group dynamics* (pp. 91–109). New York: Harper & Row.

Cattell, R.B. (1948). Concepts and methods in the measurement of group syntality. *Psychological Review,* 55, 48–63.

Converse, P., & Campbell, A. (1968). Political standards in secondary groups. In D. Cartwright & A. Zander (Eds.), *Group dynamics* (pp. 199–211). New York: Harper & Row.

Cook, T.D., & Campbell, D.T. (1979). *Quasi-experimentation: Design and analysis issues for field settings.* Boston: Houghton-Mifflin.

Cronbach, L.J. (1951). Coefficient alpha and the internal structure of tests. *Psychometrika*, 2, 135–138.

Deep, S.D., Bass, B.M., & Vaughan, J.A. (1967). Some effects of business gaming of previous quasi-t group affiliations. *Journal of Applied Psychology,* 51, 426–431.

Deutsch, M. (1949). An experimental study of the effects of cooperation and competition upon group process. *Human Relations,* 2, 199–231.

Eisman, B. (1959). Some operational measures of cohesiveness and their interrelations. *Human Relations,* 12, 183–188.

Enoch, J.R., & McLemore, S.D. (1967). On the meaning of group cohesion. *Southwestern Social Science Quarterly,* 48, 174–182.

Escovar, L.A., & Sim, F.M. (1974). *The cohesion of groups: Alternative conceptions.* Paper presented at the meeting of the Canadian Sociology and Anthropology Association, Toronto.

Evans, N.J., & Jarvis, P.A. (1980). Group cohesion: A review and reevaluation. *Small Group Behavior,* 11, 359–370.

Faunce, D., & Beegle, J. (1948). Cleavages in a relatively homogeneous group of rural growth. *Sociometry,* 11, 207–216.

Festinger, L., Schachter, S., & Back, K. (1950). *Social pressure in informal groups.* New York: Harper & Row.

Fiedler, F.E. (1967). *A theory of leadership effectiveness.* New York: McGraw-Hill.

Fiedler, F., Hartman, W., & Rudin, S. (1952). *The relationship of interpersonal perception to effectiveness in basketball teams.* (Suppl. Tech. Rep. No.3, Contract N6OTI-O7135.) Urbana, IL: Bureau of Records and Service, University of Illinois.

Gill D.L. (1977). Cohesiveness and performance in sport groups. In R.S. Hutton (Ed.), *Exercise and sport science reviews* (Vol. 5, pp. 131–155). Santa Barbara, CA: Journal Publishing.

Gorsuch, R.L. (1974). *Factor analysis.* Philadelphia: W.B. Saunders.

Guilford, J.P. (1954). *Psychometric methods* (2nd ed.). New York: McGraw-Hill.

Gross, N., & Martin, W. (1952). On group cohesiveness. *American Journal of Sociology,* 57, 533–546.

Harris, R.J. (1975). *A primer of multivariate statistics.* New York: Academic Press.

Hersey, P., & Blanchard, K.H. (1969). *Management and organizational behavior.* Englewood Cliffs, NJ: Prentice-Hall.

Horsfall, A.B., & Arensberg, C.M. (1949). Team work and productivity in a shoe factory. *Human Organization,* 8, 13–26.

Kerlinger, F.N. (1973). *Foundations of behavioral research.* New York: Holt, Rinehart & Winston.

Kuder, G.F., & Richardson, M.W. (1937). The theory of the estimation of test reliability. *Psychometrika,* 2, 135–138.

Larson, K.S., & LeRoux, J. (1983). Item analysis versus factor analysis in the development of unidimensional attitude scales. *The Journal of Social Psychology,* 119, 95–101.

Lenk, H. (1969). Top performance despite internal conflict: An antithesis to a functionalistic proposition. In J. Loy Jr. & G. Kenyon (Eds.), *Sport, culture and society: A reader on the sociology of sport.* Toronto: MacMillan.

Martens, R., & Peterson, J. (1971). Group cohesiveness as a determinant of success and member satisfaction in team performance. *International Review of Sport Psychology,* 6, 49–71.

McCrae, R.R., & Costa, P.T. Jr. (1983). Social desirability scales: More substance than style. *Journal of Consulting and Clinical Psychology,* 51, 882–888.

Mikalachki, A. (1969). *Group cohesion reconsidered.* London, Canada: School of Business Administration, University of Western Ontario.

Nunnally, J.C. (1978). *Psychometric theory.* New York: McGraw-Hill.

Russell, D. (1981). The causal dimension scale: A measure of how individuals perceive causes. *Journal of Personality and Social Psychology,* 42, 1137–1145.

Schachter, S., Ellertson, N., McBride, D., & Gregory, D. (1951). An experimental study of cohesiveness and productivity. *Human Relations,* 4, 229–238.

Sherif, M., & Sherif, C.W. (1969). *Social psychology.* New York: Harper & Row.

Smith, G. (1968). *An analysis of the concept of group cohesion in a simulated athletic setting.* Unpublished master's thesis, University of Western Ontario.

Stogdill, R.M. (1963). *Team achievement under high motivation.* Columbus: The Bureau of Business Research, College of Commerce and Administration, The Ohio State University.

Thurstone, L.L. (1947). *Multiple factor analysis.* Chicago: University of Chicago Press.

Torrance, E.P. (1955). Perception of group functioning as a predictor of group performance. *Journal of Social Psychology,* 42, 271–281.

VanBergan, A., & Koekebakker, J. (1959). Group cohesiveness in laboratory experiments. *Acta Psychologica,* 16, 81–98.

Vander Velden, L. (1971). *Relationships among members, team and situational variables and basketball team success: A social-psychological inquiry.* Unpublished doctoral dissertation, University of Wisconsin-Madison.

Zander, A. (1971). *Motives and goals in groups.* New York: Academic Press.

Zander, A. (1979). The psychology of group processes. *Annual Review of Psychology,* 30, 417–451.

21 Building Bridges for Disengagement: The Transition Process for Individuals and Teams

STEVEN J. DANISH, SUSANNA S. OWENS, SCOTT L. GREEN, AND JOHN P. BRUNELLE
Virginia Commonwealth University

Social psychology of sport involves the understanding of group processes, which usually focus on group interactions. Among the traditional issues important to professionals in the field are group and team dynamics, cohesion, leadership, and communication. However, groups and teams are not only formed and functioning but also sometimes dissolved. Danish and his associates maintain that relatively little has been known about athletes' transition processes and about how a team is affected by disengagement. Accordingly, they made a unique attempt to understand the processes and effects of disengagement and transition on individuals and teams in sport and how to handle them.

Danish and colleagues first present some reasons for disengagement. Then they conceptualize their approach by relying on two models of change: Schlossberg's transition model, which places emphasis on three mediating factors of transition (the nature of the transition, the environment in which it occurs, and the qualities of the individual and the team involved); and Danish's own previous work on life-span development. The authors discuss the processes of group development, team transition, and disengagement, placing a special emphasis on the effects of athletes' disengagement on the team. They also provide some examples of a team in transition.

This article is also important from an applied perspective because it offers sport psychologists working in this area some concrete, effective measures through which team transitions after athletes' disengagement can be facilitated. These measures focus on team-building interventions that assist individual athletes and the team in dealing with transition and disengagement, such as clarifying role differentiation, increasing individual awareness of disengagement, facilitating group interaction, and negotiating closure and new group development.

A general discussion for understanding the process and impact of disengagement and transition on individual athletes and teams is presented. Disengagement is presented as a process within athlete and team development. The disengagement of athletes from a team and the impact on the team are examined. Two models of change are described as is a model of group development. Examples of a team in transition are provided and suggestions for sports psychologists' work with athletes and teams in transition are offered. The focus of these suggestions is on work with teams.

In this paper, some of the implications that disengagement has on the athlete and the team are discussed. *Disengagement* is defined as the act of leaving a team and/or sport. It may be planned or unplanned. For athletes participating in team sports, disengagement is both an individual and a group experience. We especially focus on the impact disengagement has on the team in this article.

Transition is the period in which athletes review their identity, roles, and motivation to participate in sport. For teams, this period may result in a review of roles of all the other team members and the identity of the team. Disengagement occurs within a period of transition.

We begin with a discussion of why disengagement occurs in sport. Second, we summarize the perspectives of transition from Schlossberg (1981) and disengagement from a life span development model (Danish, 1981; Danish, D' Augelli, & Ginsberg, 1984; Danish, Galambos, & Laquatra, 1983). Third, the process of group development and the impact an individual athlete's disengagement has on the team are considered. Finally, we discuss implications for counseling and working with teams.

The Reasons Why Disengagement Occurs

Of the many reasons for disengagement, some are normative in that they are initiated by the athlete and are expected; others are non-normative. Non-normative reasons for disengagement are those that are initiated by the team, the sport, or circumstances outside the control of the athlete. In non-normative disengagement, the timing is incongruent with the individual's expectations of when the event *should* occur and is unexpected (Danish, Smyer, & Nowak, 1980). The reasons for disengagement vary as a result of the level at which the athlete competes. Professional athletes may opt for free agency, be released, or be traded to another team. Collegiate and high school athletes may graduate, be cut from the team, drop out of school, or choose to reduce their level of participation to focus on other activities. Recreational athletes may disengage due to family relocation, loss of interest in the sport, or change in responsibilities such as the need to obtain a part-time job. Athletes at any level may retire due to injury, or leave due to problems with the coach(es) or the sport organization. The disengagement experience and transition period will differ, given the unique circumstances of the individual (Baillie & Danish, 1992).

In the past, disengagement at the professional and collegiate levels generally occurred as a result of retirement (e.g., graduation, injury, or being cut from the team). As such, transitions were usually limited to several time periods, often at the beginning and end of seasons. Only when career-ending injuries occurred during the season did a team have to confront in-season transitions.

However, sport has changed. At the professional level, players who stay with the same team for their total career are the exception rather than the rule. At the collegiate level, transferring from one school to another is becoming much more common and will likely increase even more. Thus, a team in transition is a common experience and may even become something for which preparation is required. Given this change, and the example described above of the high school team, transition is better considered a *process* rather than an *event.* This distinction and how it affects the transition a team experiences are discussed in a later section.

To better understand disengagement and transition, we have relied on two models of change. The first model was proposed by Schlossberg (1981); the second is a life-span development model initially described by Baltes, Reese, & Lipsett (1980), and expanded on by Danish and his colleagues (Danish, 1981; Danish, D' Augelli, & Ginsberg, 1984; Danish, Galambos, & Laquatra, 1983; Danish, Petitpas, & Hale, 1992, 1993, in press). It is our belief that these models for transition are applicable to groups (e.g., athletic teams) as well as to individuals. Furthermore, we believe that disengagement can be best understood within the context of transition.

Transition Theory and Life Span Development

Schlossberg's Model of Transition

Schlossberg (1981) stated that transition can "occur if an event or nonevent results in a change in assumptions about oneself and the world and thus requires a corresponding change in one's behavior and relationships" (p. 5).

Schlossberg noted that transition is mediated by three factors: (a) the nature of the transition, (b) the environment before and after the transition occurs, and (c) qualities of the individual.

The Nature of the Transition. Transitions are periods of stress either because life changes are occurring or because predicted changes are not occurring. Schlossberg emphasized that the defining component of transition is the individual's perception that his or her situation is changing. Many transitions occur with a change in an individual's role or identity (Baillie, 1992; Baillie, 1993; Baillie & Danish, 1992). A change in identity may lead to a variety of feelings. On the one hand, some athletes may experience relief as a result of the increased opportunity to focus on their education (Adler & Adler, 1985; Greendorfer & Blinde, 1985). On the other hand, anxiety may be the predominant feeling if the athlete has become so focused on the athletic role that other options have become foreclosed (Chartrand & Lent, 1987; Petitpas & Champagne, 1988). Still other athletes may experience conflicting feelings as indicated by the comments of a female intercollegiate basketball player, who when asked about the impact of her graduation on her feelings toward her sport and team said, "I thought I'd be happy to finish. . . . I had thought about leaving the team during my junior year. But due to my loyalty to the team—I stayed with them. . . . It was like I couldn't leave (my junior year)." This athlete returned, 18 months after graduation, to watch her team play and stated, ". . . last year (after graduation) I went to the games . . . (but) I didn't miss the team until now." When a teammate left the team due to conflicts with the coach, this athlete recalled, "I felt kind of sick . . . betrayed, because she bailed out. We had been together since day one, for the season to have almost been over and then to leave."

It is interesting to note the implication of an unspoken understanding within the team that the athletes would work together. This understanding underlies the sense of betrayal felt by some teammates when a peer chooses to leave. As we have noted above, transitions affect the team as well as the individual. This player's comments also underscore the critical nature of the time within the playing season that the athlete leaves. *Timing* is an important component of life events; events are referred to as either "on time" or "off time" (Danish, Smyer, & Nowak, 1980). As has been previously noted, the degree to which the transition is normative or non-normative, or, in Schlossberg's (1981) words, "internal" or "external", affects the coping response made. Differences exist, both for the individual and the team, in the ease with which a transition is experienced, depending on the characteristics of the transition. Off-time, external transitions are much more difficult to cope with for both an individual and a team.

Eventually, individuals and teams adapt to a transition. Adaptation occurs when an individual or team moves from being totally preoccupied with the transition to integrating the transition into their ongoing functions (Schlossberg, 1981).

The Nature of the Environment. Transitions are influenced by the environment. Schlossberg (1981) divided the environment into three components: (a) the interpersonal,

(b) the institutional, and (c) the physical setting. The interpersonal environment consists of social support, such as significant others, family, and friends. Social support, be it interpersonal or institutional, is seen as a critical variable in how successful an athlete or team copes with a transition (Pearson, 1990; Pearson & Petitpas, 1990). A team that has a growth-oriented atmosphere may more easily adapt to the changes caused by transition.

The institutional setting refers to structures available to the individual or team during the transition. Institutional environments for collegiate athletes include religious or community groups, academic advising, and other university programs.

The third environmental component, the physical setting, can include such factors as the weather or the physical conditions under which a sport is played. The more supportive the environment, the easier the transition is to negotiate for both the individual and team. The nature of the environment may differ for teams. For example, collegiate teams can expect transition to occur as athletes graduate each year. In such teams, transition is to be expected and coaches may be more skilled in negotiating their team through the transition or disengagement process. Further, teams that view transition and disengagement as a short-term process may be able to adapt and return to optimum performance quicker than those teams that view such transition as an event with long-term consequences.

The Qualities of the Individual and the Team. Schlossberg (1981) addressed eight different qualities an individual or team possess that affect transition. The qualities are: (a) psychosocial competence, which we define as the degree to which an athlete or team possesses and utilizes life skills; (b) gender socialization differences, for example, a community center co-ed soccer team may adjust differently to an athlete leaving the team than an all female collegiate team; (c) age (including the individual or team's life experience and development); (d) state of health, in athletes this often refers to injury; (e) ethnicity, the stress of transition may be unique to ethnic groups depending, in part, on the resources available to them for non-sport endeavors; (f) socio-economic status, the cost of disengaging from participation (for professional athletes) or continuing participation (for amateur athletes who must pay for expensive equipment or facilities); (g) value orientation, or an individual's view of life; and (h) past experience with transitions.

The Life Span Development Perspective

We believe that past experience with other transitions is especially important from a life-span development perspective. Danish and D' Augelli (1980) have described a phenomenon they define as "intra-individual similarity" (p.115). Intra-individual similarity is defined as the recognition that a past event or situation is comparable to a present event or situation being experienced. At the cognitive level, the individual knows he or she can deal with the event; at a behavioral level, a behavioral sequence employed successfully in the past is available; and at a psychological level, the event is no longer unique and the properties common to previous events are highlighted. Experience with a past situation enables an athlete or team to use skills that are transferable from one setting to another. Transferable skills are the behaviors we use to bridge the past events and situations to those presently being experienced. Therefore, to the degree that an athlete or team is aware of common elements between disengagement and a similar past situation they have experienced, the transition will be less stressful. For example, a team that loses a player in mid-season has experienced a similar loss at the end of the previous season when older players left and new players arrived. While the timing of the loss is different, awareness of familiar elements in disengagement can aid the transition.

Transitions must be placed within the context of the "life" of the athlete or team. When a transition is placed in this context, an understanding of the life development framework becomes critical. The major assumption of this framework is its emphasis on continuous growth and change. Change disrupts routines and relationships with others and may result in stress. For this reason, such change has been called a *critical life event.* Disengaging from sport is a type of critical life event (Danish, Petitpas, & Hale, 1993).

Although critical life events are often viewed as discrete, they are actually processes, commencing prior to and continuing well after the event. Critical life events, then, have histories; from the time we anticipate them, through their occurrence, and until their aftermath has been determined and assessed (Danish, Smyer, & Nowak, 1980).

Critical life events are not the same as crises. Critical life events may lead to dissatisfaction, little or no change in the life of an individual or team, or serve as a catalyst for increased opportunities and personal growth (Danish, Petitpas & Hale, 1994). The effect of the critical life event is dependent on the resources the individual and team have prior to the event, the level of preparation for the event, and the past history in dealing with similar events. Viewing resources, level of preparation, and past experiences as life skills allows an individual or team to see change as a challenge as opposed to a threat.

So far, we have tried to frame our discussion in terms of how transitions affect both the athlete and the team. To date, most discussions in the literature about transition and disengagement have focused on individual athletes. However, it is important to recognize that when athletes are involved in team sports, their disengagement has an impact on their teammates, as well as the functioning and cohesiveness of the entire team (Lerch, 1982; Rosenberg, 1982).

To understand the dynamics of a team, we must understand its development. Groups, just as individuals, have developmental trajectories that can be detailed across their life-span. In this next section, we focus on some of the literature on group development from a stage theory developed by Tuckman (1965; Tuckman & Jensen, 1977).

Although stage theories, either for individual or group development, provide a convenient categorization system, they tend to oversimplify development. Not all individuals or groups strictly follow the same developmental progression. Some groups may avoid a particular stage; other groups may cycle through a stage for a second time. Thus, it is important to recognize that stage theories act as a heuristic for understanding group development.

The Process of Group Development

Forsyth (1990) defined group development as "patterns of growth and change that occur in groups throughout their life cycle, from formation to dissolution" (p. 76). Tuckman (1965) initially outlined a four stage developmental sequence for small groups. Each stage consisted of two domains. The first domain is a structural-interpersonal component and consists of four segments: (a) testing and dependence, (b) intragroup conflict, (c) development of group cohesion, and (d) functional role-relatedness. The second domain characterizes four developmental tasks associated with each stage: (a) orientation, (b) emotional responses to task demands, (c) open exchange of relevant interpretations, and (d) the emergence of solutions. Tuckman proposed that there was a correspondence between the two domains. The four stages were delineated as "forming", "storming", "norming", and "performing". As part of the description of these stages, brief comments are made about the experiences of the girl's high school basketball team mentioned earlier, as it encountered these stages following the loss of its best player.

In the *forming* stage, the group establishes boundaries for behavior and group interaction and defines its objective. For example, the first workouts in a new season tend to be unpolished as teammates become accustomed to each other, compete for positions, and learn how to communicate. The initial practices following the loss of the point guard were characterized by "forming". The athletes did not know how to communicate, could not run the plays, and performed poorly in their usual position as well as when they tried a new position. It was as if the season was starting all over again.

The *storming* stage is a period where group unity is challenged as group members attempt to differentiate themselves from the others. This stage is represented by emotional resistance as each member experiences conflict due to the demands placed on him or her. This stage is evident just prior to the start of the athletic season when routines are established with regard to practice as team rules are developed and enforced and later during periods when teams are losing. Following several practices when each player's responsibilities were redefined, tension between the player and the coaches and other teammates increased.

In the *norming* stage, conflicts are resolved and a sense of unity forms. The task is the open exchange of relevant interpretations, such as sharing opinions within the group. For athletic teams, norming occurs as a season begins and a common opponent can be identified. In the first game after the high-school player was declared ineligible, the team came from behind to beat an opponent that they could have easily beat earlier in the season. At the end of the first half, the team was 30 points behind. It was during the later stages of this game that unity was formed and the team pulled together to win the game.

In the *performing* stage, the group focuses on problem solving, using group process and relationships to work on tasks and test new ideas. The shift in group activity is toward developing alternatives. Performing in sports is present when a team is able to solve dilemmas within a game or when it is able to rebound successfully from temporary setbacks.

Although the team members in the example performed well given the loss of the player, they never seemed to be able to trust themselves. After seven weeks of play without the former point guard, the team still struggled to reach the performing stage. It was the opinion of the coach that the team's play seemed very rote for the remainder of the season. This suggests that for teams in transition following disengagement, the performing stage is the most difficult to achieve.

Over a decade later, Tuckman and a colleague (Tuckman & Jensen, 1977) added a fifth stage that is especially relevant to the topic of disengagement. Tuckman and Jensen (1977) labelled this final stage "adjourning", but did not identify a related task. The development of this stage was based on a number of models that included a termination stage. For example, Gibbard and Hartman (1973) introduced a life cycle model that recognized the importance of separation in group development. The stage of "adjourning" is addressed in a later section.

There is limited empirical support for Tuckman's model. However it is a useful heuristic to understand athletic team process, in that he outlined development as a function of the interpersonal relationships among members as well as the developmental task relevant to that stage. Teams often function as a social-support network (interpersonal component) and as a group designed to function competitively (task component). Teams are perpetually changing members from one season to the next. The coach, team, and sport psychologist are faced with a new entity each year. Furthermore, in times of transition and disengagement, teams will respond differently given their developmental stage.

Team Transition and Disengagement

In the "adjourning" stage of Tuckman and Jensen's model (1977), the group members adjust to the termination of the total group, or to the disengagement of individuals from the group. While it is much more common for individual athletes to leave a team, in university settings it is becoming more common for "minor" sports teams to be disbanded because of lack of financial support or to reconfigure a gender imbalance among its scholarship athletes.

Forsyth (1990) has made a useful distinction about this final stage, noting that in some groups there is a "planned dissolution." Such a dissolution occurs when the objectives or tasks of the group have been met. A search committee to select a new coach is an example; once the new coach is selected, the group no longer has a purpose. In other groups, a "spontaneous dissolution" occurs. The dropping of a sport eliminates the group's need to function as a team and work together. Competing on an Olympic relay team is another example because once the Olympics are over, the team usually disbands. In recreational sports, the team dissolves at the end of the season. In youth sport, teams frequently change as children leave the team or sport for various reasons. The concept of planned and spontaneous dissolution parallels the normative and non-normative experience in athlete career transitions (Danish, Smyer & Nowak, 1980; Schlossberg, 1981).

The Effect on the Team of Athlete Disengagement

Teams are not often dissolved; although with the cost-cutting measures undertaken by universities, more sports are being eliminated. A situation more likely to occur in sport is the disengagement of individual athletes from the team. To date, most of the literature in athlete transition has focused on the impact of disengagement on the athlete. However, the team on which an athlete competes is also affected. The impact on the team will vary depending on a number of factors including: (a) the stage of group development, (b) the role of the absent teammate, (c) the reason for departure, (d) whether the disengagement was planned or unplanned, and (e) the degree to which the team feels it can continue to play at optimal levels during the time of transition.

Teams experience some feelings of loss when a teammate leaves. Recently, we met with several members of a team in which several athletes either had been traded or sent to a higher level of competition. Additionally, several new players had been added to replace the players who had left. Although such actions are relatively common and expected at this level, the players described the team as having difficulty adjusting because most of the original team had played together for several years. The sense of loss appears to be related to perceptions the team has of an absent athlete's contributions. For example, an absent team leader is missed on the playing field in terms of his or her athletic ability but also in terms of his or her ability to motivate others, disarm conflicts, and maintain a sense of unity.

However, an athlete need not be a team leader to be missed. In small teams, the absence of one member is an important factor. In all groups, each member holds a prescribed role. With the loss of one member, other individuals must assume the missing athlete's role for the transition to be smooth.

Very little research or descriptive literature has considered the impact of an athlete's disengagement on a team. It is our belief that disengagement affects team goals, tasks, and most importantly, team performance. In sum, disengagement affects all aspects of team maintenance. However, the question of "how" the team is affected is pure conjecture. It is recommended that sport psychologists develop models for understanding this process, test their efficacy, and develop interventions that will limit the negative effects of the transition.

Team Building Implications

Danish (1981) emphasized that an understanding of transitional periods is useful when we can use them in the context of an intervention. Understanding the influences that lead an athlete to disengage from a team or the impact of this act on his or her teammates is the first step. We should expand this understanding to develop interventions that will minimize the effects of the disengagement on the team *and* prepare an individual or team for this transition.

Pre-transition intervention is a worthwhile endeavor but is often not supported by the athletic organization (Baillie & Danish, 1992). In fact, interventions to ease a transition are rarely sought by coaches and teams. A brief outline of some of the implications for counseling during transitions is presented. Counseling can either be for the individual or the team; our remarks focus on the team. We refer the reader to Baillie (1993) and Baillie and Danish (1992) for an in-depth discussion of counseling techniques with individual athletes. It is important to emphasize that our counseling approach follows a Life Development Intervention framework which has been discussed in considerable detail elsewhere (Danish, Petitpas, & Hale, 1992, 1993, 1994). Given such a framework, the suggestions by Crook and Robertson (1991) to help the athlete engage in anticipatory socialization (preparation for transitions such as retirement before they occur) is recommended. Furthermore, given that the success of transition is mediated by the skills and deficits of the individual (Danish & D' Augelli, 1980; Schlossberg, 1981), it is useful for sport psychologists to teach skill building. Many life skills interventions can be used for processes such as setting goals, exploring careers, and learning how to seek help and use social support. Finally, sport psychologists should also be sensitive to possible gender and ethnic differences in transition experiences (Coakley, 1983; Schlossberg, 1981).

Interventions for the Team

Initially, it may be useful to ascertain the developmental stage of the team (Tuckman, 1965; Tuckman & Jensen, 1977) as this will affect the ease in which transition takes place. In-season transitions are usually the most difficult. Further, athletes and coaches will benefit from the understanding that the team will change from season to season, regardless of any change in team composition.

As individuals come closer to anticipated disengagement, the perspective of the team will change. This awareness should be conveyed to coaches and athletes. Just as sport psychologists can help an individual by building on his or her personal strengths, they can develop the team's awareness of its individual strengths, emphasizing transferrable skills.

The team will need to understand the contributions made by the disengaging athlete. Rather than a coach or team members prematurely identifying who will assume the role or task of the disengaged member, it is helpful to let the team negotiate this decision. Unexpected team members may "step forward" and assume new responsibilities given a chance. The result of this new configuration may actually be a stronger team.

As a result of these assumptions, we have developed several techniques to facilitate team transition following disengagement of an athlete. Our approach follows four consecutive steps. The steps are: (a) clarify role differentiation, (b) increase individual awareness of disengagement, (c) facilitate group interaction, and (d) negotiate closure and new group development. We will briefly describe the technique(s) for each step.

Clarify Role Differentiation. This step begins by having team members chart the role of each player. This could begin with a schematic diagram of team positions. The objective is to move the team from concrete thinking of the absent athlete's playing role on the team to more effective and group process thinking. By moving the team to a metacognitive type activity, it can begin to think more abstractly about the disengagement and transition process. For example, the team could individually or as a group begin by charting the positions of all team members, highlighting the position of the absent athlete. Next, the sport psychologist could ask the team to draw a different schematic to clarify the role each team member (including the absent athlete) played in constructs such as team unity, team spirit, cooperation, and resolving conflict. It is important for the team to reflect on this activity as it progresses. Such an activity will require that the sport psychologist be able to work with the team to engage itself in this activity. This would require use of counseling skills to build rapport and trust with the team. The sport psychologist would need to focus on two main responsibilities: (a) to clarify the objectives of the activity, and (b) to integrate an understanding of the different athletic and non-athletic qualities each member brings to the team with the qualities of the absent athlete.

Increase Individual Awareness of Disengagement. Once the group has begun to think about the multiple effects an individual has on the working of the team, the next step is to have each member think about how disengagement affected them personally. We have developed a brief questionnaire that can be given to athletes (see table 21.1). The questionnaire is designed to help the athlete cognitively re-frame the transition as personally relevant and to serve as an opportunity for individual growth. Question 7 is designed to encourage athletes to think about their shifting role within the team. As a sport psychologist, one should be prepared to deal with resistance to such activities. Process comments and support of confidentiality will help.

Table 21.1 Questionnaire for team athletes

1. What role did the absent athlete(s) play on your team?
2. How did the absent athlete(s) contribute to the psychological state of the team? What did they bring to the sport?
3. How is their absence going to affect you?
4. What are the negative aspects of this person's absence for you?
5. In what ways will you benefit from their absence?
6. How might your role on the team change now?
7. How committed are you to accepting the responsibility for your new role?
8. If you leave the team, what impact do you think your absence will have?

Facilitate Group Interaction. The third step is to provide the team with opportunities to work together and talk about team interaction. These techniques can also be used to help the team integrate a new teammate into the position formerly held by the absent athlete. Each technique should include time for the sport psychologist to talk with the team about how the activity went, what worked, what did not work, and what the activity meant in terms of helping the team reorient itself.

In activity one, have the team play a completely different team sport. For example, a basketball team could play a game of volleyball or a swim team could play softball. Such an activity could help the team realize new abilities of current members as well as having the opportunity to interact with each other in a different manner.

In activity two, have the team members play their sport but in different positions. People who normally play defense could play offense. The idea is to make the athletes feel somewhat uncomfortable, so that they can break free of prior assumptions and the role of the absent athlete. After this activity, a new player may be better integrated into the team as everyone felt awkward playing.

Negotiate Closure and New Group Development. The key to this part of team building is to provide the team with an open forum to reformulate team goals. The sport psychologist can talk about the disengagement process as a challenge rather than a threat. A new diagram can be created, focusing on current team members.

An emphasis in these techniques is on the sport psychologist's skill in working with a group. Dealing with resistance and engaging the team in trying new activities will most likely be challenging. The open forum format is designed to help the team acknowledge the impact of disengagement, as well as engage in activities that encourage change in group dynamics and reorient the team towards new goals.

Conclusion

Until recently, relatively little was known about the transition process of athletes and we still know very little about how disengagement affects a team. We have attempted to articulate that disengagement is a process marked by a period of transition. Further, disengagement impacts the individual as well as the team. An understanding of transition models (Schlossberg, 1981) and a life span development perspective (Baltes, Reese, & Lipsett, 1980; Danish, 1981; Danish, D' Augelli, & Ginsberg, 1984; Danish, Galambos, & Laquatra, 1983; Danish, Petitpas, & Hale, 1992, 1993, in press) can help psychologists conceptualize disengagement for the individual. Such conceptualization can be generalized from individuals to teams. We have also attempted to offer a strategy and activities that the sport psychologist can use in work with teams. While the effects of disengagement on the athlete and team require further investigation, team building interventions that focus on assisting the individual and team deal with this transition holds promise.

References

Adler, P., & Adler, P. A. (1985). From idealism to pragmatic detachment: The academic performance of college athletes. *Sociology of Education. 58,* 241–250.

Baltes, P., Reese, H. & Lipsett, L. P. (1980). Lifespan developmental psychology. *Annual Review of Psychology. 31,* 65–110.

Baillie, P. H. F. (1992, October). *Career transition in elite and professional athletes: A study of individuals in their preparation for and adjustment to retirement from competitive sports.* Colloquium presented at the seventh annual conference of the Association for the advancement of Applied Sport Psychology, Colorado Springs, CO.

Baillie, P. H. F. (1993). Understanding retirement from sports: Therapeutic ideas for helping athletes in transition. *The Counseling Psychologist, 21,* 399–410.

Baillie, P. H. F., & Danish, S. J. (1992). Understanding the career transition of athletes. *The Sport Psychologist, 6,* 77–98.

Baillie, P. H. F., & Lampron, A. (1992). Retirement from sport: Studies show wide range of experiences and expectations. *Olympinfo, 8,* 4.

Chartrand, J. M., & Lent, R. (1987). Sports counseling: Enhancing the development of the student-athlete. *Journal of Counseling and Development, 66,* 164–167.

Coakley, J. J. (1983). Leaving competitive sport: Retirement or rebirth? *Quest, 35,* 1–11.

Crook, J. M., & Robertson, S. E. (1991). Transitions out of elite sport. *International Journal of Sport Psychology, 22,* 115–127.

Danish, S. J. (1981). Life-span human development and intervention: A necessary link. *Counseling Psychologist, 9,* 40–43.

Danish, S. J., & D' Augelli, A. R. (1980). *Helping skills II: Life Development Intervention.* New York: Human Sciences.

Danish, S. J., D' Augelli, A. R. & Ginsberg, M. R. (1984). Life development intervention: Promotion of mental health through the development of competence. In S. D. Brown & R. W. Lent (Eds.), *Handbook of Counseling Psychology* (pp. 520–544). New York: Wiley.

Danish, S. J., Galambos, N. L. & Laquatra, I. (1983). Life development intervention: Skill training for personal competence. In R. D. Felner, L. A. Jason, J. Moritsugu & S. S. Farber (Eds.), *Preventive psychology: Theory, research, and practice* (pp. 49–66). Elmsford, NY: Pergamon.

Danish, S., Petitpas, A., & Hale, B. (1992). A developmental-educational intervention model of sport psychology. *The Sport Psychologist, 6,* 403–415.

Danish, S., Petitpas, A., & Hale, B. (1993). Life development intervention for athletes: Life skills through sports. *The Counseling Psychologist, 21,* 342–385.

Danish, S., Petitpas, A., & Hale, B. (1994). Psychological interventions with athletes: A life development model. In S. Murphy (Ed.), *Clinical Sport Psychology.* Champaign, IL: Human Kinetics Publishers, Inc.

Danish, S. J., Smyer, M. A., & Nowak, C. A. (1980). Developmental intervention: Enhancing live-event processes. In P. B. Baltes & O. G. Brim, Jr. (Eds.), *Life-span development and behavior* (Vol. 3, pp. 339–366). New York: Academic Press.

Forsyth, D. R. (1990). Chapter Four: Development and Socialization. In D. R. Forsyth, *Group Dynamics* (pp. 75–108). Pacific Grove, CA: Brooks-Cole.

Gibbard, G., & Hartman, J. (1973). The oedipal paradigm in group development: A clinical and empirical study. *Small Group Behavior, 4,* 305–349.

Greendorfer, S. L., & Blinde, E. M. (1985). "Retirement" from intercollegiate sport: Theoretical and empirical considerations. *Sociology of Sport Journal, 2,* 101–110.

Lerch, S. H. (1982). Athlete retirement as social death. In N. Therberge & P. Donnelly (Eds.), *Sport and the sociological imagination* (pp. 259–272). Fort Worth, TX: Texas Christian University Press.

Pearson, R. (1990). *Counseling and social support: Perspectives and practice.* Newbury Park, CA: Sage.

Pearson, R. E., & Petitpas, A. J. (1990). Transitions of athletes: Developmental and preventive perspectives. *Journal of Counseling and Development, 69,* 7–10.

Petitpas, A. L., & Champagne, D. E. (1988). Developmental programming for intercollegiate athletes. *Journal of College Student Development, 29,* 454–460.

Rosenberg, E. (1982). Athletic retirement as social death: Concepts and perspectives. In N. Therberge & P. Donnelly (Eds.), *Sport and the sociological imagination* (pp. 245–258). Fort Worth, TX: Texas Christian University Press.

Schlossberg, N. K. (1981). A model for analyzing human adaptation to transition. *Counseling Psychologist, 9,* 2–18.

Tuckman, B. W. (1965). Developmental sequence in small groups. *Psychological Bulletin 63,* 384–399.

Tuckman, B. W., & Jensen, M. C. (1977). Stages of small-group development revisited. *Group and Organization Studies, 2,* 419–427.

PART V

Enhancing Performance

The 10 readings in this section all relate to various concepts associated with performance enhancement. This topic is by far the most popular subarea in sport psychology. These readings have provided a guide to applied sport psychologists in their work with athletes.

Landers questions the notion that the classic inverted-U hypothesis adequately explains the relationship between arousal and performance, since this relationship may be more appropriately based on attentional selectivity and social facilitation. Landers teams with Feltz in the next reading to review, in a meta-analysis, the previous research on mental practice. They investigated the magnitude of differences between mental practice conditions as well as the probability of finding such differences. This was the first investigation to review a large number of studies (60) in the most popular research area in the domain of performance enhancement.

Gould and Eklund review the application of principles of sport psychology for performance optimization among elite athletes. They also discuss several popular myths circulating about psychological skills training (PST). Since a majority of research to this point had used youth and recreational athletes, the focus on elite athletes was important.

Orlick and McCaffery focus on children's sport participation with the goal of facilitating youngsters' psychological growth, development, and well-being through sport participation. They emphasize that mental training techniques, such as relaxation, should be modified and adapted when implemented in young athletes.

Hardy questions the way applied sport psychology literature is interpreted in relation to three well-established tenets. This forced sport psychologists to reconsider training techniques that had been based on these tenets.

The next two readings supported the psychometric properties and theoretical base for two inventories used extensively in performance enhancement. Hall, Mack, Paivio, and Hausenblas examine the Sport Imagery Questionnaire (SIQ), which has been used as both a research tool for measuring imagery and for identifying how an individual uses imagery for the purpose of facilitating sport training. Nideffer's is the only reading in this publication that is original (i.e., not previously published). It discusses The Attentional and Interpersonal Style (TAIS) inventory. This reading refutes the previous criticism of TAIS and supports the practical value of this commonly used inventory.

Self-confidence (SC) is one of the most-cited factors thought to psychologically affect athletic performance. Feltz organized and presented the theoretical knowledge relevant to SC in sport at the time, which had a profound influence on many researchers in this area.

By the late 1980s psychological skills training (PST) had emerged as a popular application and research topic. Through content analysis, Vealey reviewed all published PST works published between 1980 and 1988. This investigation revealed a major limitation of this research: that the lack of systematically and objectively identified PST characteristics did not allow them to be replicable by other researchers. From these works, she also identified six needs for the future direction of PST.

Finally, Bar-Eli, Tenenbaum, Pie, Btesh, and Almog conducted a field experiment with 346 participants to investigate goal setting (GS). This was one of the first investigations conducted that consistently demonstrated that unattainable, improbable goals produced inferior performance compared with difficult and realistic goals.

22 The Arousal-Performance Relationship Revisited

DANIEL M. LANDERS
Pennsylvania State University

The idea that the relationship between arousal and performance is curvilinear (i.e., the inverted-U hypothesis, or the Yerkes-Dodson law) enjoys wide acceptance among scientists in many areas of psychology (e.g., motivation, stress, anxiety). It has an intuitive appeal to many athletes, coaches, and exercisers. However, a few researchers have felt somewhat uneasy with this state of affairs. Does arousal consistently affect performance in a curvilinear manner? More specifically, does optimal performance always occur at a moderate level of arousal or does this optimal level of arousal depend on the individual or the task?

Landers was not entirely satisfied with the fact that the inverted-U hypothesis does not really explain the relationship between arousal and performance but merely proposes a description of this relationship. Landers argued that a sound theory is required in order to explain this relationship and make corresponding predictions to be examined scientifically. He offered attentional explanations, focusing mainly on previous eminent notions such as Easterbrook's cue utilization and Bacon's attentional selectivity, for how and why performance is affected by arousal to create a curvilinear relationship between these two variables. He also tied his explanations to the important concept of social facilitation.

It is probable that a full test of Landers' predictions has never been made. However, his ideas presented in this article inspired later research conducted on the relationships between arousal and performance, for example, within the psychophysiological framework, also referred to as the psychobiological states approach. Landers is sometimes presented as a critic of the inverted-U hypothesis. But despite his concern about the somewhat simplistic version of the inverted-U concept, he never wanted to "throw the baby out with the bathwater." In other words, Landers argued for improving this idea or taking it forward beyond its rather simple version, but not for abandoning it in favor of other theories that have attempted to replace it completely.

In the scientific literature arousal is used as a motivational construct. According to Murray (1964) motivation is defined as "an internal factor that arouses, directs, and integrates a person's behavior" (p. 7). There are many motivational theories and hypotheses that explain goal-directed behavior but what they have in common is that they conceptualize behavior as varying along two basic dimensions, direction and intensity. The intensity level of behavior is termed arousal. The construct of arousal, which is often used interchangeably with other intensity-related terms such as drive, tension, and activation, refers to the degree of energy release of the organism, which varies on a continuum from deep sleep to high excitement (Duffy, 1957). This energy is sometimes inferred from behavior or self-report measures of behavior, but is more commonly measured centrally by means of an electroencephalogram or by peripheral, autonomic measures such as heart rate and muscle tension.

In the present context, the more general arousal and intensity-related terms are merely used to refer to points along this continuum. When arousal levels are high the individual may experience unpleasant emotional reactions associated with arousal of the autonomic nervous system. This maladaptive condition is often referred to as stress or state anxiety. Each person has a slightly different response to stress depending on their learning histories and the type of situation. These responses can be divided into three general categories: cognitive, behavioral, and, of course, physiological since the latter is directly linked to the arousal construct. Response to stress may include one or more of these component categories. Some individuals, for example, will show autonomic arousal and report intense distress in a competitive situation but will also show no avoidance behavior of the situation. Other individuals may vary in the degree to which they are aware of their heightened arousal, such as victims of high blood pressure who feel healthy and have few complaints.

Explanations for the Arousal-Motor Behavior Relationship

The Inverted-U and Drive-Theory Hypothesis

Before proceeding with a presentation of the model that I advocate, a brief summary of competing explanations is in order. Martens (1974) has provided an extensive review of the two hypotheses that have frequently been used to explain the relationship between arousal and performance. The first is the drive-theory hypothesis and the second is the inverted-U hypothesis.[1] Drive theory, as modified by Spence and Spence (1966), predicts that performance is a

Adapted with permission from *Research Quarterly for Exercise and Sport,* Vol. 51, pp. 77-90, Copyright 1980 by the American Alliance for Health, Physical Education, Recreation and Dance, 1900 Association Drive, Reston, VA 20191.

[1]In actuality, the inverted-U hypothesis is not an explanation for the arousal-performance relationship; it merely posits that this relationship is curvilinear without explaining what internal state or process produces it.

multiplicative function of habit and drive (P = H × D). The theoretical construct of drive is often used synonymously with physiological arousal since the latter is more amenable to scientific measurement. Habit, on the other hand, refers to the hierarchical order or dominance of correct or incorrect responses. According to this theory, one would expect that increases in drive would enhance the probability of the dominant responses being made. When performance errors are frequently made, as in the early stages of skill acquisition, the dominant responses are likely to be incorrect responses. Conversely, when performance errors are infrequent, the dominant response is said to be a correct response. Increases in drive (i.e., arousal) during initial skill acquisition impair performance, but as the skill becomes well learned, increases in arousal facilitate performance.

By comparison, the inverted-U hypothesis predicts that as the subject's arousal level increases from drowsiness to alertness, there is a progressive increase in performance efficiency. But, once arousal increases beyond, for example, alertness to a state of high excitement, there is a progressive decrease in task performance. Thus, this hypothesis suggests that behavior is aroused and directed toward some kind of "balanced" or optimal state.

Notice that the critical difference in the predictions made from these two hypotheses would be for a case when the subject's arousal level was high on a well-learned task. In this situation, drive theory would predict that the quality of performance would be high, whereas the inverted-U would hypothesize it to be low. This distinction is important because, dependent on which hypothesis one accepts, it will lead to different implications for teaching and coaching practice. For example, Oxendine (1970) essentially adopts a position consistent to the drive theory hypothesis for all motor tasks, particularly those involving strength, speed, and endurance. For complex tasks, however, Oxendine (1970) and Coleman (1977) stress that arousal interferes with performance—a position consistent with the inverted-U hypothesis.

Martens (1974) has reviewed the research evidence for the two hypotheses and concluded that:

1. The drive theory hypothesis should be rejected since "it is not testable for motor behavior because of the inability to specify habit hierarchies for motor performance" (p. 182).
2. The evidence essentially provided equivocal support for drive theory.
3. The inverted-U hypothesis supersedes the drive theory hypothesis since arousal levels may not have been of sufficient magnitude to cause a performance decrement in studies finding a positive linear relationship between arousal and performance.
4. The psychophysiological theories of activation and attentional theories, such as Easterbrook's (1959) cue utilization theory, are more viable alternatives for explaining the inverted-U relationship.

While I believe that Martens' review has helped to point researchers in the right direction, recent evidence would now suggest that his reasons for abandoning drive theory were not well founded. In the first place very few, if any, of the motor performance studies he reviewed satisfactorily measured habit strength or subject's arousal level. By including these studies in his review, there was no way to avoid the inescapable conclusion of equivocal results. In order to conduct any review of the arousal-motor performance relationship, it is imperative to determine criteria that would define the conditions under which an adequate test of these hypotheses can be made.

Therefore, to test the inverted-U versus drive-theory hypotheses there must be at least three or more levels of a situational stressor applied, and, in addition to employing a motor task in which habit strength can be operationally defined, there must be corroborative evidence that an experimental exposure is, in fact, stressful. Burkun (1964) suggests the following three criteria for providing corroborative evidence for stress: (1) the performance of subjects assumed to be stressed must be different from a nonstressed-control group, (2) the participants must subjectively report feeling distress in the situation of interest, and (3) there must be an indication of disruption of normal physiological processes. Considering that not one of the motor performance studies reviewed by Martens (1974) satisfied these criteria, it is not appropriate to conclude, based upon the findings of these studies, that drive theory should be abandoned for motor performance.

Martens' conclusion that "habit strength" is not testable for motor performance is equally indefensible. For some motor tasks habit strength can be operationally defined. For example, Hunt and Hillary (1973) used motor mazes, with known floor and ceiling effects, and found results consistent with drive-theory predictions. Likewise, Landers, Brawley, and Hale (1978) found similar results for physical and psychological stressors with the same maze task (see Landers, 1975, for a detailed description of the simple and complex maze tasks). Carron and Bennett (1976), on the other hand, used a choice reaction-time paradigm to develop habit hierarchies. Although these studies show mixed support for drive theory, they do demonstrate rather clearly that for some motor tasks, at least, habit strength can be operationally defined.

Another obstacle in the way of advocating abandonment of drive theory is the overall success this theory has had in the area of social facilitation research. Here it is generally found that the presence of an audience, or individuals working on similar but independent tasks (coaction), perform in a way that is consistent with drive theory predictions. During the initial stages of learning the arousal created by the presence of the audience detrimentally affects performance, but once the task is well learned, performance is facilitated. As recently as 1977, Geen and Gange concluded their extensive review of this literature, with the optimistic appraisal that in spite of numerous competing theories, the drive-theory hypothesis was still the most parsimonious explanation for the research evidence reviewed.

Although the evidence at the time of Martens' review did not support his first two conclusions, the recent research findings do support his last two conclusions. This evidence is derived from studies in which arousal effects on performance have been assessed by means of methodology derived from signal detection theory (see Welford, 1975, for a discussion). This methodology has been employed in three different studies with various types of stressors (Bacon, 1974; Kushnir & Duncan, 1978; Miller & Leibowitz, 1976).

As a case in point, Kushnir and Duncan were able to demonstrate that the effects due to social facilitation are not due to response bias, as would be suggested by the "response dominance" construct in drive theory. What was affected was subjects' sensitivity, or input bias, to the information presented. The problem appears to be a result of improper reception of information rather than inappropriate output after the information has been processed. Thus, the subjects in the alone condition were better able to distinguish between signals and nonsignals than the subjects in the audience condition. These results bring social facilitation research in line with the majority of empirical studies which examine arousal effects on perceptual performance (Broadbent, 1971; Kahneman, 1973).

The results of the Kushnir and Duncan study, and other studies as well (Bacon, 1974; Miller & Leibowitz, 1976), indicate rather directly that response related constructs such as "habit" or "response ceiling" (Broen & Storms, 1961) cannot mediate the arousal-performance relationship. Instead we need to direct our attention to theories which focus on the reception of information.

Elsewhere (Landers, 1978) I have argued that Easterbrook's cue utilization theory, in particular, appears to have heuristic value in understanding the arousal-performance relationship. What has been missing in previous analyses of this relationship (e.g., Oxendine, 1970) is the role that attention plays in most sport skills, including those involving speed, strength, and endurance. In the next section we will examine attention as it relates to arousal and performance.

Attentional Narrowing

One of the commonly reported effects of arousal is its influence on the narrowing of attention. Attention can be directed to a variety of environmental cues, particularly cues detected by the auditory and visual senses. The attentional processes to be discussed appear to function the same for auditory and visual cues (Bacon, 1974).

Although research into the attentional narrowing phenomenon spans many different areas, the methodology is fundamentally the same. Employing the dual-task paradigm, studies on this topic generally show that subjects maintaining performance on a central or primarily important task are less able to respond to peripheral or secondary stimuli under stress. In most studies the central task is generally more demanding of subjects' attention than the peripheral task. In such cases, subjects improved performance on a central task, but decreased performance on a peripheral task when under the influence of such stressors as amphetamines, exercise stress, electric shock, sleep deprivation, incentives, hypoxia, and threat of personal injury (see Landers, 1978). Bacon (1974) maintains that the generalization that emerges from these studies is that arousal effects depend upon the degree of attention the stimuli attract with "sensitivity loss systematically occurring to those cues which initially attract less attention" (p. 86). The effects of arousal therefore impair one's performance through a loss of sensitivity by interfering with one's capacity to process information.

According to Easterbrook (1959) the behavioral effects due to peripheral narrowing may appear as linear or curvilinear, depending on the degree of arousal and number of levels of stress manipulated. Recall that the inverted-U is merely a relationship which can be explained by Easterbrook's cue utilization theory. Given certain stimulus conditions, such as attentional conflict or the presence of fear cues in the immediate environmental surround, arousal will be heightened. This arousal, particularly if it is high, will often lead to anxiety reactions which are manifest in three general response components: cognitive, overt behavioral, and physiological.

Depending on one's learning history, individuals differ in their degree of reaction to a given stimulus condition. More importantly, Borkovec (1976) maintains that:

> individuals differ in terms of the learning history associated with each response component, resulting in individual differences in the intensity and/or functional importance of the response from each component in reaction to a particular feared or attentional conflict stimulus. Some individuals, for example, will report intense distress and display rapid avoidance when confronted with feared situations, but no evidence of increases in physiological arousal can be detected. Others may show such autonomic increases but differ in the degree to which they are aware of the arousal, the degree of avoidance behavior, the level of reported discomfort, etc. (p. 267)

For the majority of situations in sport and physical education most individuals will at least approach the activity, but often not without some degree of physiological or cognitive anxiety. As a result of heightened arousal in these response components, attentional narrowing occurs accompanied by a loss of sensitivity to environmental cues. Easterbrook's theory predicts that performance under these conditions will depend on the degree of arousal and the available number of task-relevant and irrelevant cues.

A person performing under low arousal has a broad perceptual range and therefore, either through lack of effort or low selectivity, irrelevant cues are accepted uncritically. Performance in this case is understandably low. When arousal increases up to a moderate or optimal level, perceptual selectivity increases correspondingly, and the individual's performance improves, presumably because he/she tries harder or is more likely to eliminate task-irrelevant cues. Arousal increases beyond this optimal point permit further perceptual narrowing and performance deteriorates, in accord with the inverted-U hypothesis. For example, the quarterback in football under high anxiety may be focused too narrowly to detect receivers open in the periphery.

There is some controversy concerning what is actually happening to the performer's attention under high arousal-anxiety. Easterbrook (1959) argues that the range of usable cues is further restricted to the point of eliminating relevant-task cues. High arousal, however, is associated with distractibility, which as Wachtel (1967) has correctly pointed out forces investigators to distinguish not only between the breadth of cues we attend to, but also the amount that we scan the environmental surround. Since the attentional narrowing effect is widespread spanning many different types of stimulus conditions, it is believed to be an adaptive response. Most people display this response but, dependent on their prior history and experience in the situation, they will exhibit it in varying degree. Weltman and Egstrom (1966), for example, detected marked individual differences among beginning divers' exposure for the first time to submergence in the open ocean environment.

The narrowing process is also influenced by the complexity of the task. Research showing variation in detecting environmental cues as a function of dual-task competition has led Easterbrook to suggest that the task difficulty differences are related to the Yerkes-Dodson Law. To establish this link he assumed that the range of essential task cues is narrower for simple than for complex tasks. Thus, with more relevant task cues to keep track of on a complex task, the probability is greater that a given amount of arousal will lead to a performance decrement on a complex task sooner than it would for a simple task. For simple tasks, the ability to tolerate higher levels of arousal without performance decrements has been empirically supported by research on animals (Broadhurst, 1957) and human motor-skill acquisition. Carron (1965), for instance, has demonstrated that chronically overaroused individuals perform more poorly on complex motor tasks and relatively better on simple motor tasks.

These relationships are not intended to indicate that attentional narrowing in fact causes the inverted-U relationship between arousal and performance. There is always a chance, however remote, that some other variable causes both attention and performance to change as arousal increases. Whatever the cause, the relationships are empirically supported (see Landers 1978 for a more complete review of this research). The attentional narrowing phenomenon is appealing because of its heuristic value and its ability to account for a wide range of findings from seemingly diverse areas. Geen and Gange (1977) have also suggested cognitively mediated cue-utilization effects as an explanation for a broad range of social facilitation findings. The rational for such an extension will be presented in the next section.

Social Facilitation and Cue Utilization

The area of social facilitation research is one of the few remaining strongholds for drive-theory explanations for performance effects. In the aftermath of Zajonc's (1965) application of drive theory to account for audience and coaction effects upon performance, there has been a fever of excitement as investigators have been attracted to this seemingly fertile area of research. This "herd effect" was short lived as many investigators became disillusioned with the weak performance effects and the inconsistent arousal effects which resulted from the presence of audiences and coactors (see Landers, Snyder-Bauer, & Feltz, 1978).

Part of this problem is perhaps due to the lack of well-designed field studies on social facilitation. This point of view has been expressed, perhaps to an extreme, by Martens (1979). Although field studies and field experiments may help to enhance the weak effects typically found in the laboratory (see Obermeier, Landers, & Ester, 1977 as an example), there is no guarantee that this approach will increase our understanding of the kind of effects on motor performance that have been the topic of discussion since Zajonc published his important review paper.

A more productive approach in confronting this problem is to use any theoretical or methodological approach (including various research settings) that will increase our understanding of this area. Above all, we must avoid giving up the problem by becoming shackled to a particular method or research setting (Dunnett, 1966; Platt, 1964).

In spite of what Geen and Gange concluded in their 1977 review of social facilitation research, I no longer believe that the best explanation for social facilitation is the drive theory formulation proposed by Zajonc. Recently, arousal-activation theorists have argued that two-factor theories (i.e., drive × habit) are too simplistic to predict performance. There is mounting evidence that subjects' attention must be considered and that this variable may be even more important than the concept of habit strength in predicting the effects of evaluative audiences upon performance.

There are two recent studies which support the conclusion that future research on social facilitation of motor behavior must investigate subjects' level of attention. The first is by Baron, Moore, and Sanders (1978), who found that people were distracted more often from the task in the audience condition than in the alone condition. To measure distraction they had subjects try to recall a "p" printed in red among the nonsense syllables they used for the performance tasks. This measure, more than other measures of distraction, suggests that task recall of subjects with an audience was low because they were attending to others in the situation. Baron et al. conclude that the social facilitation phenomenon is due at least partially to the distracting qualities of others. They propose that the drive-like effects occur because the presence of others creates an attentional conflict within subjects; that is, they must reconcile social comparison with the pressure of working diligently on the task. Their distraction-conflict theory does not predict that any form of irrelevant stimulation presented during a task will heighten drive. Drive is only created when conflict with task activity occurs; that is, it is only high when attempting to reconcile two mutually exclusive response tendencies. The distracting qualities of audiences have also been shown for other cognitive tests (Bruning, Capage, Kozuh, Young, & Young, 1968) as well as motor performance tasks (e.g., Gould, 1974).

The recognition that audiences and coactors do have distracting qualities brings us one step closer to Easterbrook's cue utilization theory and the attentional narrowing process outlined earlier. Although Baron et al. clarified why the evaluative aspects of audiences are arousing for some people but not others, they fall short of bringing the concept of "attentional conflict" in line with drive theory. Their data did not establish why distractions in the task setting produce drive.

I would suggest that the difficulty encountered by Baron et al. could only be alleviated by abandoning the drive theory explanation for social facilitation. I have already described evidence by Kushnir and Duncan (1978) which demonstrates that social facilitation effects are not due to response bias, as suggested by drive theory, but instead are due to sensitivity, or input bias, in the information presented. This of course is only one study and more replication is needed. However, this study was so carefully conceived and designed, à la Platt's (1964) strong inference approach, that it leaves little doubt that sensitivity in the receipt of environmental cues is where we need to search for an explanation for the social facilitation phenomenon.

These studies (Baron et al., 1978; Kushnir & Duncan, 1978) also explain why we have had so much trouble finding consistent and strong audience effects on arousal and motor performance. Our troubles have been precipitated not so much because of a failure to operationalize drive or habit, or because of lack of field studies; instead the problem has been in not understanding the phenomena well enough to know where to look for the effects on performance.

It should be clear from what I have presented that future social facilitation research must consider attention as a mediating factor in the arousal-performance relationship. I am also hypothesizing that the arousal created in those individuals who experience attentional conflict will lead to a loss of sensitivity to environmental cues. As with any other research area involving arousal/attention/performance, the performance effects will depend on the individual's past history, the level of arousal experienced, and the difficulty of the task. The latter factor, task difficulty, is where habit strength becomes important since well-learned, task-relevant cues are less likely to be overlooked. In the laboratory, subjects given feedback after numerous training trials can increase their sensitivity to peripherally presented lights as much as a hundred times above their initial threshold values (Abernathy & Leibowitz, 1968). This has practical significance for the teacher or coach because if through extensive training they can make the performer's response to essential task cues automatic, there will be less chance that the performer's sensitivity to these cues will be reduced.

Anxiety Measurement and Reduction

Up to this point the effects of arousal on attention and performance have been examined. An equally important problem of contemporary concern is understanding how to control higher levels of arousal or anxiety. Given the negative effects that anxiety has upon performance it is little wonder that this area has recently witnessed an increase in theoretical anxiety research as well as the development of self-regulation techniques.

Currently paper-pencil tests are the primary means of assessing situational anxiety (i.e., state anxiety) in sport and physical education settings. These state anxiety measures include Spielberger's A-state scale and Martens' Competitive Short Form of the State Anxiety Inventory (see Martens, 1977, for a comparative analysis of these measures). These self-report measures sample individuals' perceptions of their overall subjective feelings at a given point in time. Subjects are asked if they feel nervous, tense, secure, calm, etc. These items making up these scales primarily tap the physiological or behavioral dimensions of anxiety.

Unfortunately, most state anxiety questionnaires provide but a single, global score reflecting an unknown mixture of typologically different forms of anxiety. Some of these questionnaires may be designed to be situationally specific (e.g., Martens' Competitive SAI), but they still fail to differentiate between relevant physiological, behavioral, and cognitive components of anxiety. An implicit assumption of these global anxiety scales is that the arousal which is hypothesized to underlie such states as anxiety, is undifferentiated. This assumption by arousal-activation theorists (Duffy, 1972) is now being challenged.

The multidimensional nature of anxiety has been established through factor analytic studies of traditional anxiety questionnaires. For example, Barrett's (1972) analysis of anxiety items revealed two major subcomponents, one consisting of an awareness of somatic changes (e.g., "I blush often") and the other concerned with conscious awareness of unpleasant feelings about self or external stimuli (e.g., "I frequently find myself worrying about something"). Similar dimensions, labeled psychic (cognitive) and somatic anxiety, were derived from the self-ratings of psychiatric patients (Buss, 1962; Hamilton, 1959).

Recently, Schwartz, Davidson, and Goleman (1978) have developed an anxiety-symptom checklist with separate cognitive and somatic scales. They used this Cognitive-Somatic Anxiety Questionnaire to examine the differential effects of relaxation (physical exercises versus meditation) procedures designed to reduce anxiety in the somatic and cognitive mode, respectively. These investigators found that somatic relaxation through physical exercise was associated with less somatic and more cognitive anxiety than the cognitive relaxation technique of meditation. These studies amply demonstrate the importance of distinguishing between specific subcomponents of anxiety since they may be differentially associated with relaxation techniques engaging primarily cognitive versus somatic subsystems.

This evidence together with the psychophysiological evidence, which I will describe later, has prompted a number of contemporary investigators (e.g., Borkovec, 1976; Davidson & Schwartz, 1976; Smith, in press) to develop multidimensional models of anxiety and its reduction. Borkovec defines anxiety by the multiple measurements of three *separate but interacting* response components: cognitive, overt behavioral, and physiological. He maintains that there are individual differences in terms of learning history associated with cognitive behavior, motor behavior, and physiological reactions. In addition, these components may even be separately influenced by different environmental conditions at different points in time and may even obey different learning principles. However, these components may interact such that changes in one response component may ultimately affect subsequent changes in the remaining components.

Therapists are very much aware of this interaction. It is well known that if the physiological component is strongly present in the individual's immediate anxiety reaction, simple manipulation of the cognitive and behavioral components will be ineffective (Borkovec, 1976). This is just one example of how the independent assessment of the subcomponents of anxiety provides a better understanding of conditions which have implications for therapeutic practices for the maintenance or reduction of anxiety. From an applied standpoint, the therapist must also understand which response component is primarily affected since the anxiety coping technique selected should be based on the type of anxiety response displayed by the individual athlete or student.

Several common manipulations may be categorized in terms of which response components are their primary focus (Borkovec, 1976). For example, techniques which deal directly with physiological reactions to anxiety are: relaxation training, autogenic training, systematic desensitization, and biofeedback. Some of the coping techniques for the overt behavioral component are reinforcement of approach behavior and modeling, while cognitive restructuring therapies and thought stopping are specific intervention techniques for the cognitive component (see Meichenbaum, 1977, for a description of these therapeutic techniques).

With the existence of such a variety of recent evidence supporting the multidimensionality of anxiety, it is indeed curious that sport scientists have not considered this model. The reason that they have failed to recognize the merits of a multidimensional model is because of the low intersubject correlations which exist among physiological measures of arousal (Lacey & Lacey, 1958). Martens (1977), for example, maintains that "a general self-report measure of arousal is a better predictor of theoretically related constructs than physiological variables" (p. 104). Statements like these have encouraged most sport psychologists to abandon physiological measures and assess anxiety with a questionnaire which simply yields a single global score.

Although it is true that the correlations among physiological measures or between physiological measures and self-report measures are low, this pattern of findings does not necessarily lead to the assumption by some activation theorists (e.g., Duffy, 1972) that there is poor validity for the measures in question or inadequacies in the measurement procedures. When standard stimulus conditions are employed, some individuals may respond primarily with a specific physiological system (i.e., heart rate) whereas other individuals may respond with quite different physiological systems.

The fact that individuals display different patterns within the physiological component is not an insurmountable problem in the assessment of physiological anxiety. Mandler, Mandler, and Uviller (1958) have shown that the employment of the Autonomic Perception Questionnaire (APQ) provides a promising bridge between the cognitive and physiological subcomponents. Mandler and his associates have shown that subjects who were preselected for reporting high levels of autonomic perception displayed significantly greater autonomic reactivity (heart rate, respiration, etc.) during stress than low perceivers. This study and others (see Borkovec, 1976, for a review) support the view that autonomic perception is an important subject characteristic related to the anxiety process.

The APQ results from several studies have also been factor analyzed resulting in three distinct types of profiles for the female samples and two types for males. Type I males, for example, were characterized solely by high awareness of heart activity and low awareness of headaches and shallow breathing. On the other hand, Type II males were characterized by high stomach activity, perspiration, and frequency of noticing bodily reactions when anxious. Thus, the APQ can be used to indirectly tap, at least for subjects demonstrating high APQ scores, the physiological dimension of anxiety when (1) testing of large groups is required, (2) expensive physiological equipment is not readily available, and (3) the environmental context is not conducive to obtaining reliable physiological measures (e.g., movement artifacts). For the testing of small samples in the laboratory or limited field contexts, the APQ can be more appropriately used to determine which profile type the individual falls into so the appropriate physiological measures can be identified and subsequently used for research purposes.

The efficacy of the multidimensional nature of anxiety has also been demonstrated in the psychophysiological research. As a follow-up to their previous research, Davidson, Davison, and Freedland (Note 1) found that cognitive and somatic anxiety could be reliably distinguished on the basis of patterning of cardiovascular, electrodermal, and electromyographical measures. More sophisticated psychobiological partitions of anxiety include studies examining hemispheric asymmetry in emotion, patterning of facial muscle activity in different affective states, and desynchrony in different physiological dependent measures which all have considerable face validity (see Schwartz et al., 1978).

Perhaps the most devastating evidence against the undifferentiated nature of arousal has been the work by Orne and Paskewitz (1974). They examined the effect of learned control of alpha for reducing stress associated with an aversive stimulus. These investigators observed significant psychophysiological fractionation and specificity. When subjects were confronted with the possibility of receiving an electric shock, there was no significant decrement in learned control of occipital alpha presence, but heart rate and skin conductance responses were elevated. Based on their data, Orne and Paskewitz concluded "that it is possible for the subjects to report the experience of apprehension of fear as well as manifesting the autonomic concomitant of such experiences without associated changes in alpha density" (p. 460).

Because electroencephalogram recordings are considered by most activation theorists to be a *direct* measure of arousal, the findings by Orne and Paskewitz cast considerable doubt concerning the assumed undifferentiated nature of arousal. In referring to the Orne and Paskewitz findings, Schwartz et al. (1978) maintain that:

> Instead of assuming, as some activation theorists have occasionally done (Duffy, 1972), that such fractionation is indicative of poor validity for the measures in question or inadequacies in the measurement procedures, we can view such data as these as reflecting meaningful patterns of physiological processes that are associated with particular behavior and experiential states. (p. 323).

The evidence presented supports the conclusion that anxiety is a multidimensional phenomenon and that we should use multimethod procedures to examine it. In sport psychology research, situationally specific self-report measures are currently the rage! These questionnaires have been an improvement over the more general, nonsport-specific anxiety tests available in the field. Although these scales have enabled investigators to achieve slightly higher correlations than might have been obtained by nonsituationally specific scales, they are still global measures and thus have done little to increase our scientific understanding of the multidimensional anxiety process.

We need to use the situationally specific anxiety measures as one of several physiological, behavioral, and cognitive measures. In my opinion, a multimethod approach will go a long way to combat the "little studies" and "little papers" which abound in sport-anxiety research. This also has implications for graduate education. For students interested in anxiety, arousal, and sport performance, we need to discourage total reliance on a single instrument and encourage greater eclecticism in the choice of methods used to examine anxiety. I suspect that what will result from such a redirection of our research efforts will be of considerably greater consequence for furthering our understanding of an individual's anxiety in a sport context.

Reference Notes

1. Davidson, R. J., Davison, G. C., & Freedland, E. *Psychophysiological specificity and the self-regulation of cognitive and somatic anxiety.* Paper presented at the International Conference on Biofeedback and Self-Control. Tubingen, Germany, November 1977.

References

Abernathy, C. N., & Leibowitz, H. W. The effect of feedback on luminance thresholds for peripherally presented stimuli. *Perception and Psychophysics,* 1968, *10,* 172-174.

Bacon, S. J. Arousal and the range of cue utilization. *Journal of Experimental Psychology,* 1974, *103,* 81-87.

Baron, R. S., Moore, D., & Sanders, G. S. Distraction as a source of drive in social facilitation research. *Journal of Personality and Social Psychology,* 1978, *36,* 816-824.

Barrett, E. S. Anxiety and impulsiveness: Toward a neuropsychological model. In C. D. Spielberger (Ed.), *Anxiety: Current trends in theory and research* (Vol. 1). New York: Academic Press, 1972.

Borkovec, T. D. Physiological and cognitive processes in the regulation of anxiety. In G. E. Schwartz & D. Shapiro (Eds.), *Consciousness and self-regulation: Advances in research* (Vol. 1). New York: Plenum, 1976.

Broadbent, D. E. *Decision and stress.* London: Houghton Mifflin, 1971.

Broadhurst, P. L. Emotionality and the Yerkes-Dodson Law. *Journal of Experimental Psychology,* 1957, *54,* 345-352.

Broen, W. E., & Storms, L. H. A reaction potential ceiling and response decrements in complex situations. *Psychological Review,* 1961, *68,* 405-415.

Bruning, J. L., Capage, J. E., Kozuh, G. F., Young, P. F., & Young, W. E. Socially induced drive and range of cue utilization. *Journal of Personality and Social Psychology,* 1968, *9,* 242-244.

Burkun, M. M. Performance decrement under psychological stress. *Human Factors,* 1964, *6,* 21-30.

Buss, A. H. Two anxiety factors in psychiatric patients. *Journal of Abnormal and Social Psychology,* 1962, *65,* 426-427.

Carron, A.V. *Complex motor skill performance under conditions of externally-induced stress.* Unpublished master's thesis, University of Alberta, 1965.

Carron, A.V., & Bennett, B. The effects of initial habit strength differences upon performance in a coaction situation. *Journal of Motor Behavior,* 1976, *8,* 297-304.

Coleman, J. Normal stress reactions in shooting. *The Rifleman,* December 1977, 19-20.

Davidson, R. J., & Schwartz, G. E. The psychobiology of relaxation and related states. A multiprocess theory. In D. I. Mostofsky (Ed.), *Behavior control and modification of physiological activity.* Englewood Cliffs, N.J.: Prentice Hall, 1976.

Duffy, E. The psychological significance of the concept of "arousal" or "activation." *Psychological Review,* 1957, *64,* 265-275.

Duffy, E. Activation. In H.S. Greenfield & R.A. Sternbach (Eds.), *Handbook of psychophysiology.* New York: Holt, Rinehart & Winston, 1972.

Dunnett, M. Fads, fashions, and folderol in psychology. *American Psychologist,* 1966, *21,* 343-351.

Easterbrook, J. A. The effect of emotion on cue utilization and the organization of behavior. *Psychological Review,* 1959, *66,* 183-201.

Geen, R. G., & Gange, J. J. Drive theory of social facilitation: Twelve years of theory and research. *Psychological Bulletin,* 1977, *84,* 1267-1288.

Gould, D. R. *Arousal and attentional demands as intervening variables in social facilitation paradigms.* Unpublished master's thesis, University of Washington, Seattle, 1974.

Hamilton, M. The assessment of anxiety states by rating. *British Journal of Medical Psychology,* 1959, *32,* 50-55.

Hunt, P. J., & Hillary, J. M. Social facilitation in a coaction setting: An examination of the effects over learning trials. *Journal of Experimental Social Psychology,* 1973, *9,* 563-571.

Kahneman, D. *Attention and effort.* Englewood Cliffs, N.J.: Prentice Hall, 1973.

Klavora, P. An attempt to derive inverted-U curves based on the relationship between anxiety and athletic performance. In D. M. Landers & R. W. Christina (Eds.), *Psychology of motor behavior and sport.* Champaign, Ill.: Human Kinetics Publishers, 1978.

Kushnir, T., & Duncan, K. D. An analysis of social facilitation effects in terms of signal detection theory. *The Psychological Record,* 1978, *28,* 535-541.

Lacey, J., & Lacey, B. Verification and extension of the principle of autonomic response-stereotypy. *American Journal of Psychology,* 1958, *71,* 50-73.

Landers, D. M. Social facilitation and human performance: A review of contemporary and past research. In D. M. Landers (Ed.), *Psychology of sport and motor behavior II.* University Park, Pa.: College of HPER, 1975.

Landers, D. M. Motivation and performance: The role of arousal and attention factors. In W. Straub (Ed.), *Sport psychology: An analysis of athlete behavior.* Ithaca, N.Y.: Mouvement Publications, 1978.

Landers, D. M., Brawley, L., & Hale, B. Habit strength differences in motor behavior: The effects of social facilitation paradigms and subject sex. In D. M. Landers & R. W. Christina (Eds.), *Psychology of motor behavior and sport 1977.* Champaign, Ill.: Human Kinetics Publishers, 1978.

Landers, D. M., Snyder-Bauer, R., & Feltz, D. L. Social facilitation during the initial stage of motor learning: A reexamination of Martens' audience study. *Journal of Motor Behavior,* 1978, *10,* 325-337.

Mandler, G., Mandler, J. M., & Uviller, E. T. Autonomic feedback: The perception of autonomic activity. *Journal of Abnormal Social Psychology,* 1958, *56,* 367-373.

Martens, R. Arousal and motor performance. In J. H. Wilmore, *Exercise and sport science reviews* (Vol. 2). New York: Academic Press, 1974.

Martens, R. *Sport competition anxiety test.* Champaign, Ill.: Human Kinetics Publishers, 1977.

Martens, R. About smocks and jocks. *Journal of Sport Psychology,* 1979, *1,* 94-99.

Meichenbaum, D. H. *Cognitive-behavior modification.* New York: Plenum, 1977.

Miller, R. J., & Leibowitz, H. W. A signal detection analysis of hypnotically induced narrowing of the peripheral visual field. *Journal of Abnormal Psychology,* 1976, *85,* 446-454.

Murray, E. J. *Motivation and emotion.* Englewood Cliffs, N.J.: Prentice Hall, 1964.

Obermeier, G. E., Landers, D. M., & Ester, M. Social facilitation of speed events: The coaction effects in racing dogs and trackmen. In R. Christina & D. M. Landers (Eds.), *Psychology of motor behavior and sport 1976.* Champaign, Ill.: Human Kinetics Publishers, 1977.

Orne, M. T., & Paskewitz, D. A. Aversive situational effects on alpha feed-back training. *Science,* 1974, *186,* 458-460.

Oxendine, J. B. Emotional arousal and motor performance. *Quest,* 1970, *13,* 23-32.

Platt, J. R. Strong inference. *Science,* 1964, *146,* 347-352.

Schwartz, G. E., Davidson, R. J., & Goleman, D. Patterning of cognitive and somatic processes in the self-regulation of anxiety: Effects of meditation versus exercise. *Psychosomatic Medicine,* 1978, *40,* 321-328.

Smith, R. E. Development of an integrated coping response through cognitive-affective stress management training. In I. G. Sarason & C. D. Spielberger (Eds.), *Stress and anxiety* (Vol. 7). Washington, D.C.: Hemisphere, in press.

Spence, J. T., & Spence, K. W. The motivational components of manifest anxiety: Drive and drive stimuli. In C. D. Spielberger (Ed.), *Anxiety and behavior.* New York: Academic Press, 1966.

Wachtel, P. L. Conceptions of broad and narrow attention. *Psychological Bulletin,* 1967, *68,* 417-429.

Welford, A. T. Stress and performance. *Ergonomics,* 1975, *16,* 567-580.

Weltman, A. T., & Egstrom, G. H. Perceptual narrowing in novice divers. *Human Factors,* 1966, *8,* 499-505.

Zajonc, R. B. Social facilitation. *Science,* 1965, *149,* 269-274.

23 The Effects of Mental Practice on Motor Skill Learning and Performance: A Meta-analysis

DEBORAH L. FELTZ
Michigan State University

DANIEL M. LANDERS
Arizona State University

Before this Feltz and Landers review, more than 100 investigations tried to determine whether mental practice improved the physical performance of a task. The results of these investigations were equivocal and thus of little value to literature reviews in this area. The meta-analysis technique enabled researchers to examine the magnitude of differences between mental practice conditions as well as the probability of finding such differences. This allowed the investigators to review 60 studies and determine an overall effect size for these studies and provided researchers with a better representation of mental practice effects compared to the more limited and selective previous reviews. Feltz and Landers were able to generate four mental practice propositions, based on previous literature, in a more systematic manner using the meta-analysis technique. These four propositions are as follows:

1. *Mental practice effects are primarily associated with cognitive-symbolic rather than motor elements of the task.*
2. *Mental practice effects are not just limited to early learning. They are found in early and later stages of learning and may be task specific.*
3. *It is doubtful that mental practice effects are produced by low-gain innervation of muscles that will be used during actual performance.*
4. *Mental practice assists the performer in psychologically preparing for the skill to be performed.*

Another unique aspect of this review is that it compared published to unpublished investigations. The published studies generated much larger effect sizes. This finding may apply to other research areas since studies showing statistical significance are more often published.

This meta-analysis allowed mental practice researchers to determine systematic mental practice effects on performance. It also encouraged future researchers to examine the variables that may affect the relationship between mental practice and performance.

A longstanding research question in the sport psychology literature has been whether a given amount of mental practice prior to performing a motor skill will enhance one's subsequent performance. The research literature, however, has not provided any clear-cut answers to this question and this has prompted the present, more comprehensive review of existing research using the meta-analytic strategy proposed by Glass (1977). From the 60 studies yielding 146 effect sizes the overall average effect size was .48, which suggests, as did Richardson (1967a), that mentally practicing a motor skill influences performance somewhat better than no practice at all. Effect sizes were also compared on a number of variables thought to moderate the effects of mental practice. Results from these comparisons indicated that studies employing cognitive tasks had larger average effect sizes than motor or strength tasks and that published studies had larger average effect sizes than unpublished studies. These findings are discussed in relation to several existing explanations for mental practice and four theoretical propositions are advanced.

Since the 1930s there have been over 100 research studies on mental practice. The specific research question addressed in these studies has been whether a given amount of mental practice or rehearsal prior to performing a motor skill will enhance one's subsequent performance. Although this may seem like a relatively simple question, investigators have been slow in providing definitive answers. Sport psychologists have reviewed subsets of studies within the mental practice literature, but their conclusions have been contradictory. There is a need, therefore, to review the entire mental practice literature in a way that resolves these controversies. This article is an attempt to do so through the use of meta-analysis procedures.

The Mental Practice Paradigms

During the 1960s and early 1970s, the topic of mental practice held a conspicuously prominent place in the sport psychology literature. The typical research design involved a comparison of the performances of subjects who had

Adapted, by permission, from D.L. Feltz and D.M. Landers, 1983, "The effects of mental practice on motor skill learning and performance: A meta-analysis," *Journal of Sport Psychology* 5: 25-57.

previous mental practice to a control group that had not received mental instructions. Quite often, these groups were also contrasted to a physical practice group and a group receiving mental and physical practice. A practice period of varying lengths was then instituted in which all groups except the controls practiced a physical skill daily. Following this practice period, the subjects' skills were tested under standard conditions so that it could be determined whether their performance scores differed as a result of the practice condition administered. If the mental practice group surpassed the performance of the control group, mental practice was said to be effective in facilitating performance. Many studies have noted this finding, but it is sometimes found with this design that mental practice groups do not perform as well as physical practice groups and the groups with combined mental and physical practice (Corbin, 1972).

Although the relationship between mental practice and physical practice was once a comparison of interest, it no longer has the same fascination for researchers. By contrast, the comparison of groups having various types of mental practice to a control group has witnessed a resurgence of interest among behavior therapists and sport psychologists interested in understanding the bases for the numerous cognitive behavior therapies that are currently in vogue. For example, the recent work on internal-external imagery (Epstein, 1980), stress reduction techniques (Smith. 1981), "psyching-up" strategies (Gould, Weinberg, & Jackson, 1980; Sheldon & Mahoney, Note 1), coping skills (Meichenbaum, 1977), and techniques like visuo-motor behavioral rehearsal (Noel. 1980; Suinn, 1972), all depend upon some degree of mental practice which is assumed to have beneficial effects on performance.

To include this recent literature, the scope of the present review was limited to those studies containing a group that was given only mental practice and that had either pretest scores or a control group to which to be compared. This criterion for selection of studies permitted us to include (a) single group studies for which pre-and posttest scores were available and (b) multiple group studies having at least one comparison between mental practice and control groups. Following this criterion, the relationship of mental practice to physical practice is beyond the scope of this review. For a discussion of this relationship, the interested reader should consult previous reviews (Corbin, 1972; Richardson, 1967a, 1967b).

Previous Reviews

Research studies examining the effects of mental practice on motor learning and skilled performance have been reviewed on a selective basis. The reviews by Richardson (1967a) and Corbin (1972) included from 22 to 56 studies and provided contradictory conclusions. Richardson (1967a) concluded that in a majority of the studies reviewed, mental practice was associated with improved motor performance. Five years later, Corbin (1972) was much more cautious in his interpretation of the effects of mental practice on acquisition and retention of skilled motor behavior. In fact, he maintained that the studies were inconclusive and that a host of individual, task, and methodological factors used with mental practice produced different mental practice results.

It is not surprising that with all of the significant and nonsignificant findings in the numerous studies reviewed by Richardson (1967a) and Corbin (1972) it is exceedingly difficult to obtain any clear patterns. For example, if we were to examine only outcome (statistical significance) for the 60 studies currently meeting our criterion for acceptability as mental practice studies, 50% of them would show mental practice effects and 50% of them would not. This state of affairs has resulted in some investigators concluding that this is a "weak" or at least contradictory area of research and one that should be avoided until new, more objective research methodologies suitable for its study are available.

The insights about directions for future research that were provided in previous reviews by Richardson (1967a) and Corbin (1972) were helpful. However, the conclusion about mental practice effects may have been distorted in the above reviews for one or more of the following reasons: (a) too few studies have been included to accurately portray the overall empirical findings in the area; (b) only a subset of possible studies was included, leaving open the possibility that bias on the reviewers' part may have influenced them to include studies that support their position, while excluding those that may have contradicted their beliefs; (c) although the reviewers speculated about a range of variables that may influence the effectiveness of mental practice, the style used in these reviews was more narrative and rhetorical than technical and statistical, thus making it difficult to systematically identify the variables; and (d) the reviews have ignored the issue of relationship strength, which may have allowed weak disconfirmation, or the equal weighting of conclusions based on few studies with conclusions based on several studies (see Cooper, 1979). In other words, they had a smaller pool of studies, and at that time, more sophisticated tools for research integration were not widely available. Thus, some of their conclusions may no longer be tenable.

Given the current confusion that may have resulted from the basic limitations of previous reviews, there is a need for a more comprehensive review of existing research, using a more powerful method of combining results than summary impression. The methodology recommended for such a purpose is meta-analysis, which examines the magnitude of differences between conditions as well as the probability of finding such differences.

Meta-analysis

Meta-analysis is a way of statistically analyzing the findings of many individual analyses. A meta-analysis usually produces a significance level that gives the probability that a set of studies exhibiting the obtained results could have been generated if no actual relationship existed. Thus, when used to examine a complete survey of studies from a specific research area, meta-analysis procedures allow a characterization of the tendencies of the research and also yield information about the magnitude of any differences between conditions.

The research on mental practice is systematically compatible with the meta-analysis approach in that considerable research employs identical or conceptually similar variables, and therefore, statistical procedures can be reliably employed. This integrative technique should allow for more precise and confident statements to be made about the overall effectiveness of mental practice compared to a control group denied this opportunity. More importantly, it allows for a partitioning on the mental practice effect into sampling, design, and task characteristics used in these studies. An investigation of the covariation of mental practice effects for tasks classified as basically motor/cognitive or self-paced/reactive, or subject characteristics such as high/low ability or male/female, will perhaps reveal the conditions under which mental practice may have its greatest effect upon performance.

Method

Coding Characteristics of the Studies

Once the studies were obtained, various characteristics of the studies were coded into categories that were believed to moderate the effects of mental practice according to the literature reviews (cf. Corbin, 1972; Richardson, 1967a, 1967b). These characteristics were divided into three main areas: subject characteristics, task-type characteristics, and design characteristics.

Subject Characteristics. A paucity of research has concerned itself with differences between males and females in their ability to use mental practice. Thus, separate effect sizes were calculated, where possible, for males and females in order to examine possible differences between them.

Separate effect sizes were also calculated for subjects of elementary, high school, and college ages. Although some studies have been conducted with college-age subjects, some with high school-age subjects, and some with elementary-age subjects, only one study in our review concerned itself with differences among these three age groups in their ability to use mental practice (Wills, 1966). No consistent differences were found, however.

Finally, effect sizes were coded according to subjects' experience with the task because Richardson (1967a) and others (Clark, 1960[1]; Corbin, 1972) concluded that the degree of familiarity with the physical performance of a task was related to the efficiency of mental practice. Perhaps the physical practice experience is needed to form a perceptual trace or template that the learner can use as a reference against which to compare the mental practice. The research on this topic is inconclusive, however, because many studies have found mental practice effects with beginners.

Task-type Characteristics. One task-type comparison made was between motor, strength, and cognitive tasks. Some investigators (Morrisett, 1956; Richardson, 1967b; Ryan & Simons, 1981; Sackett, 1934) have questioned the efficacy of mental practice in tasks that are predominantly motor or strength in nature and have little symbolic control. If the task cannot be represented symbolically, it was thought that it would be difficult to practice in symbolic form. Additionally, studies investigating the effectiveness of mental practice for improving strength have been equivocal (Corbin, 1972). Thus, a need exists to resolve these inconsistencies by comparing the average effect sizes of these different task types.

We also compared findings using self-paced (closed-skill) tasks to those employing reactive (opened-skill) tasks. Because the environment in a self-paced or closed-skill task, such as foul shooting, is consistent and predictable, only one response need be learned and thus may be easier to practice mentally.

Design Characteristics. Richardson (1967b) suggested that motivation may be partly responsible for the effectiveness of mental practice. Specifically, mental practice groups may become more "ego-involved" when asked to mentally rehearse a task. To control for this motivational explanation, studies should include a no practice group that has the same number of scheduled experimental sessions as the mental practice group. If studies using motivational control groups have a combined effect size that is lower than those using a simple control, the motivational explanation may have some support.

The number of practice sessions given before the posttest and the length of each practice session (in trials or minutes) were also coded. Some researchers have suggested that the greater the number of mental rehearsals the greater the effect on performance (Sackett, 1935; Smith & Harrison, 1962; Smyth, 1975), whereas others have suggested that there may be an optimal number of practice sessions and length of practice at which mental practice is most effective for skill learning (Corbin, 1972; Twining, 1949). Thus, the linearity or curvilinearity between amount of practice and the effectiveness of mental practice needs to be tested.

Additionally, studies were coded as to whether the posttest was given immediately after mentally practicing

[1]Although Corbin (1972) reported that Clark (1960) concluded that novice performers used mental practice more effectively than junior varsity and varsity performers while learning a one-handed basketball shot, the original article by Clark (1960) concluded just the opposite; mental practice was more effective with varsity and junior varsity groups than it was with the novice group.

(within 10 min) or whether it was delayed. Mental practice may be most effective when done immediately prior to performance; however, the delay between mental practice and performance has not been systematically investigated.

Another variable included in the coding scheme was whether the study was published or unpublished. This comparison was made because published studies tend to be more biased toward statistical significance and this bias can yield overly optimistic estimates of the effectiveness of mental practice (Glass, 1977).

Meta-analysis Procedures

Effect sizes were calculated by dividing the differences between the means of the treatment and control groups by the within-group standard deviation. Where research reports did not contain the means and standard deviations of the experimental conditions, effect sizes could still be calculated in most cases using one of the formulas described by Glass (1977). The effect size for each finding of a study was treated as an observation and examined statistically in relation to the coding characteristics.[2]

Results

Studies (N = 98) using mental practice were identified. From these studies, 28 did not meet the criterion and 10 were not obtainable, leaving 60 with which to perform a meta-analysis. Because some studies measured the effect of mental practice on more than one task or under more than one condition, the number of effect-size measures exceeded the number of studies. Thus, from the 60 studies obtained, 146 effect sizes were calculated using the formulas by Glass (1977).

An overall average effect size yielded a value of .48 (SD = .67), amounting to almost one-half a standard deviation across all types of mental practice effects. This finding suggests, as did Richardson (1967a), that mentally practicing a motor skill influences performance somewhat better than no practice at all. However, because the type of skill, subjects used, and other conditions have been suggested to moderate this influence, additional comparisons were made according to the coding characteristics.

Behren's Fisher t' tests (Kohr, 1970) and F tests with Behren's Fisher t' test post hoc comparisons were employed to examine mean differences between effect sizes of the discrete variables. The large number of factors, all with unequal *ns*, eliminated the possibility of comparing more than one factor at a time. Due to the large number of analyses conducted, the alpha level was set at $p \leq .01$.

Results from these analyses indicated that the only significant comparisons were between cognitive and motor tasks, cognitive and strength tasks, and published and unpublished studies. Studies employing cognitive tasks had a larger average effect (M = 1.44) than motor tasks (M = .43) or strength tasks (M = .20). In addition, the average effect size in published studies (M = .74) is more than double the average effect size in unpublished studies (M = .32).

Because the linearity of the relationship is uncertain between the number/length of practice sessions and mental practice effects, three polynomial regression analyses were conducted (Blalock, 1972) for (a) number of practice sessions, (b) length of practice sessions in minutes, and (c) number of practice trials per session and their influence on effect size. Both length of practice and number of practice trials were included because some studies required subjects to mentally practice for a certain period of time, whereas others required them to practice a certain number of times.

A polynomial regression is conducted in a stepwise fashion. The original variable is entered on the first step (linear), the squared term on the second step (quadratic), and so on until no substantial improvement of fit is obtained. The null hypothesis that higher-degree polynomials are not significant is tested at each step by means of an F test (Blalock, 1972). Results indicated no significant linear or curvilinear relationships between number of practice sessions and effect size. There were, however, significant third degree polynomial relationships between length of practice sessions and effect size, $F(1,76) = 10.54, p < .005$, and between number of practice trials per session and effect size, $F(1,38) = 6.86, p < .025$. The amount of variance accounted for in these relationships was 14% for length of practice and 20% for number of practice trials. Practice sessions that were under 1 min or between 15 or 25 min produced the largest mental practice effects. It appears that studies that employed either less than 6 trials, or between 36 and 46 trials per practice session, demonstrated the largest effect sizes. Cognitive tasks were associated with very few trials (less than six) and motor and strength tasks generally required many more trials/min to achieve large effect sizes.

Discussion

The studies reviewed differ markedly in the types of tasks used, ages and background of subjects, as well as designs and methodologies employed. The results of this meta-analysis, therefore, have considerable generalizability. This generalizability has been achieved by considering all studies, even those that some may consider unworthy of attention. It could be argued that this type of averaging procedure may have masked problems in the mental practice literature (for a discussion of these, see Corbin, 1972; Richardson, 1967b; Weinberg, 1981). Our approach instead has been to examine some of the most frequently mentioned methodological considerations to determine

[2]Even though effect sizes could not be regarded legitimately as independent of each other, results were calculated under this assumption to allow the comparison of many interesting relationships within studies (Glass, 1977).

a posteriori if differences among studies using varying methods were apparent. At least for the methodological and subject characteristics examined in this meta-analysis, our results did not indicate that these differences made much of a difference in terms of outcome. It is certainly possible, however, that other design and subject characteristics not examined in this review may have been important factors. These could of course be looked at in follow-up meta-analyses, provided there were enough studies using a particular technique to statistically contrast it to other mental practice techniques.

In interpreting the findings of this review, it is important to bear in mind some of the limitations of applying meta-analysis to the population of studies dealing with mental practice. For example, the nonrandomness of the studies and the unequal distributions (*N*s) did not permit us to examine interaction effects among predictors. Thus, the results of the analysis of main effects on the variables lending themselves to this approach must be viewed primarily as suggestive of promising avenues of future research.

The advantage of meta-analysis is that it provides the investigator with an overall effect of a variable given a whole population of studies. In this case, the effect size was .48 for all types of mental practice effects. This effect, which amounts to about one-half of one standard deviation, is a better representation of the mental practice effects in general than the more limited and selective approach employed in previous reviews. It is our belief that much of the inconsistency in previous journal and book reviews of mental practice (e.g., Corbin, 1972; Richardson, 1967a, 1967b; Schmidt, 1982; Weinberg, 1981) originates from singling out published studies which may not be representative of mental practice effects that are typically achieved. This point was supported by the findings of the present review in which the effect size of published studies (M = .74) was more than twice as large as unpublished studies (M = .32). It is, of course, possible that the unpublished studies were not as well executed as those surviving the review process. Given that a high percentage of the unpublished studies were master's theses, however, it is much more likely that most of the unpublished studies were not submitted for review in the first place or that the investigator may have been discouraged from submitting due to relatively weak or nonsignificant results. Because the majority of studies are unpublished, their findings should perhaps receive greater weight in future reviews, at least until it can be convincingly demonstrated that a qualitative difference exists between published and unpublished studies.

Perhaps the major advantage of meta-analysis is the ability of the reviewer to break down the variables of interest to examine subject, task, and design characteristics thought to be important. Of all the coding characteristics examined, by far the most important was whether the task was primarily motor or cognitive, or whether it involved essentially strength. Cognitive tasks like dial-a-maze, card sorting, peg board test, symbol digit test, maze learning, and finger maze had much larger effect sizes than tasks that were essentially motor or involved strength. In addition, these large effects for cognitive tasks were most often achieved in a relatively short practice session (M = 3.17 min) and with only a few trials (M = 4.17) compared to motor (*M*s = 7.3 min and 17.97 trials) and strength tasks (*M*s = 7.5 min and 10.0 trials).

To help resolve some of the controversies concerning the efficacy of mental practice and to move debate toward a focus on the underlying mechanisms thought to be responsible for mental practice, we propose four theoretical propositions. We first state four of the major mental practice propositions that have been suggested in the contemporary motor behavior literature and then examine the evidence derived from the meta-analysis or, where necessary, from evidence not included in the meta-analysis.

Proposition I: Mental Practice Effects are Primarily Associated with Cognitive-symbolic rather than Motor Elements of the Task

One of the mechanisms by which the facilitory effects of mental practice have been explained was offered by Sackett (1934) and Morrisett (1956). This explanation, termed symbolic learning, posits that mental practice gives the performer the opportunity to rehearse the sequence of movements as symbolic components of the task. Thus, according to this notion, mental practice facilitates motor performance only to the extent that cognitive factors are inherent in the activity. According to Schmidt (1982), the learner practicing mentally "can think about what kinds of things might be tried, the consequences of each action can be predicted to some extent based on previous experiences with similar skills, and the learner can perhaps rule out inappropriate courses of action" (p. 520). The learner can also rehearse the temporal and spatial regularities of a skill. For example, after receiving instructions or having previewed the skill to be performed, subjects can choose to evoke images or subvocal responses which cue them of important temporal and spatial elements of a skill. Cues of this type have been systematically provided in the verbal pretraining (Adams & Creamer, 1962) and symbolic modeling (Bandura & Jefferies, 1973) literature, but as yet have not been directly examined in the mental practice literature.

Although the symbolic learning explanation of mental practice has been emphasized in some reviews (Corbin, 1972; Schmidt, 1982) and has been ignored in other recent reviews (e.g., Weinberg, 1981), it has received consistent support from empirical research designed to directly examine this question (Minas, 1978; Morrisett, 1956; Ryan & Simons, 1981; Wrisberg & Ragsdale, 1979). In these studies, mental practice improved performance on cognitive tasks, such as dial-a-maze, blocks test, or sequence learning, but did not effect "motor" tasks (e.g., stabilometer) that were low in cognitive or symbolic elements. The present meta-analysis of mental practice effects indicated that this trend was evident when comparisons were made across 60 studies having 146 different effect sizes. This suggests that in spite of different populations, designs, and methodologies employed in the mental practice studies, the distinction between symbolic and motor aspects of motor skill learning are very robust and provide very strong support for the symbolic learning explanation.

It should be pointed out that categorization of tasks into cognitive, motor, and strength categories presents a simplified and perhaps artificial view of task characteristics. More likely, motor tasks can be thought of as being on a continuum proceeding from tasks which have few cognitive elements to those that are primarily cognitive. The tasks that are classified as "cognitive" tasks in the present review are similar to "Eureka!" tasks used in problem solving (Steiner, 1972) in that they are primarily cognitive with the motor response merely being an appendage to carrying out the previously conceived principle which governs the action. Maze learning tasks, such as dial-a-maze, finger maze, and digit substitution, involve mainly cognitive solutions to the unique requirements imposed by the task before the correct motor response can be executed. Thus, the symbolic or cognitive elements of an unfamiliar task can be learned from task instructions, observational learning, or initial physical performance. Mental practice of these elements fosters subjects' retention of symbolized elements and their connections more so than for subjects denied the opportunity for mental rehearsal.

Although "cognitive" tasks typically have very large effect sizes (M = 1.44), other tasks lower on the cognitive continuum and therefore labeled as "motor" at times had large effect sizes (i.e., > .80). It may be that subjects mentally practicing motor tasks such as foul shooting, pursuit rotor, ball serving, and dart throwing may occasionally produce better performance results compared to subjects having no mental practice (Clark, 1960; Eideness, 1965; Kohl & Roenker, 1980; LaLance, 1974; Mendoza & Wichman, 1978; Rawlings & Rawlings, 1974; Shick, 1970; Hall, Note 2). It is not clear why for some "motor" tasks the effect sizes would be so large, but in other studies using the same task they are often much smaller. It may be that for motor or strength tasks having fewer or less obvious symbolic elements, success in mental practice depends upon the quality of instructional cues and the type of imagery engaged in by subjects. What is clear from this review, however, is that if larger effects are to be achieved in motor and strength tasks, more time needs to be spent in mental practice (both in minutes and number of trials) than for tasks that are high in cognitive elements. As we shall see later, small mental practice effects on motor and strength tasks may in addition be achieved by different processes and perhaps may supplement the effects brought about by symbolic learning (see Proposition IV).

Proposition II: Mental Practice Effects are not just Limited to Early Learning—They are Found in Early and Later Stages of Learning and may be Task Specific

An obvious extension of the symbolic nature of motor tasks is to relate mental practice to the stage of learning where cognitive elements are most prevalent (Fitts & Posner, 1967). This stage, of course, would be the initial verbal-motor stage of learning where Schmidt (1982) has suggested that mental rehearsal should have its greatest impact, Although some evidence supports this view (Wrisberg & Ragsdale, 1979), most reviews of the mental practice literature have arrived at the opposite conclusion; that is, mental practice is more effective following initial physical practice (e.g., Corbin, 1967b; Phipps & Morehouse, 1969) or for subjects preselected for having some prior experience on the task. This evidence suggests a counter-explanation to Schmidt's (1982) "initial learning hypothesis" such that prior task experience may aid performers in internalizing a very clear model of what good performance of the task is like, even though they cannot yet perform it this way (Richardson, 1967b).

The results of the meta-analysis do not provide a "clear-cut" winner for either of these alternative explanations. There were no significant differences (p > .18) between slightly experienced and novice performers when averaged across tasks varying in cognitive elements. Although the direction of the differences somewhat favored larger effect sizes for experienced subjects (M = .77), the effect size for the novice subjects was also quite large (M = .44). It appears then that mental practice effects are found in both the initial and later stages of learning. This conclusion, derived from the meta-analysis, suggests that it is too simplistic to think that mental practice operates at only one stage of learning. Based on these findings, it is more reasonable to infer that the processes affecting performance as a result of mental practice may be somewhat different at various stages of learning. In the early stages of learning, mental practice may give the performer a rough schema of the cognitive elements of the task and this could account for the mental practice effects in novice performers. With practice on the task, feedback from the muscles and sense develop the schema of cognitive elements more fully so that performance is enhanced for the mental practice group compared to the no mental practice group. This would be similar to effects found in the modeling literature (Landers, 1975) where observational learning (i.e., forming a schema) of key cognitive elements of the task was enhanced if observers saw the demonstration early as well as again later in their performance trials. It is also possible that attentional processes associated with mental practice may be operating to some degree throughout the stages of learning (see Proposition IV).

In examining mental practice effects early as well as later in learning, some potential methodological problems should be avoided. It would be important in future research examining mental practice effects to use scoring techniques (e.g., trials-to-criterion, percent transfer, etc.) or secondary tasks (e.g., decision-making, effort expenditure, etc.) to circumvent some of the problems in investigating mental practice effects in high level performers. For example, although nearly all of the studies in this review (Clark, 1960; Egstrom, 1964; Kuhn, 1971; Start, 1962) found somewhat greater mental practice effects for experienced as compared to novice subjects, Corbin (1967) found that the most proficient performers did not appear from their performance scores to show any additional gains due to mental practice than found for a moderately experienced group. It is obvious that during later stages of learning, performers having relatively few trials may show only small performance gains relative to the large gains achieved by novice performers. For subjects performing at high levels of proficiency, it would be better to use secondary task measures (see Schmidt, 1982, pp. 458–462, for a discussion) since performance scores may be insensitive to the small effects typically produced by mental practice.

It would also be important for future research to examine mental practice effects as a function of experience level together with task type (i.e., motor, cognitive, or strength).[3] Unfortunately, most studies in this review used novice subjects and thus examination of the experience level by task type interaction was not possible. In the absence of such a test, it is informative to discuss the Wrisberg and Ragsdale (1979) results. They examined, in their second experiment, mental practice effects following 30 practice trials on either a low cognitive task (stabilometer) or a high cognitive task (Blocks test). The percentage of transfer was then compared to the same measure in their first experiment where novice subjects having no practice trials were used. Wrisberg and Ragsdale (1979) found that with greater experience on the stabilometer, the percent of transfer decreased from 18% to 0%. Assuming that this performance measure was a sensitive measure for mental practice effects at this level of skill learning, these results would support the idea that mental practice effects are typically not found on motor tasks having few cognitive elements. However, on the Blocks test the opposite was observed, with experienced subjects having greater transfer than novice subjects (50% vs. 28%, respectively). These findings support the tentative conclusion that for tasks high in symbolic or cognitive elements, mental practice will be most effective when subjects have had some prior practice with the task.[4] Due to the paucity of studies examining the experience by task type interaction for mental practice effects on motor performance, the preceding conclusions should be regarded with caution until more research is available.

Proposition III: It is Doubtful that Mental Practice Effects are Produced by Low-gain Innervation of Muscles that will be Used during Actual Performance

A discussion of the mechanisms underlying mental practice would not be complete without devoting some attention to the most commonly mentioned alternative to the symbolic learning explanation for mental practice effects. This explanation, termed the psychoneuromuscular explanation, is an outgrowth of the ideo-motor principle (Carpenter, 1894), which posits that minimal or low-gain neuromuscular efference patterns during imagined movement should be identical to those patterns generated during the same overt movement, but reduced in magnitude. Although no overt movement takes place, this minute innervation, as indicated by EMG action potentials, is presumed to transfer to the physical practice situation. According to the theory, only a small, localized efferent outflow from imagery is required for visual and kinesthetic feedback to be available to the motor cortex in order for the motor schema to be further perfected (Hale, 1981) or for the priming of the corresponding muscle movement nodes (MacKay, 1981).[5]

The studies that have examined the psychoneuromuscular theory could not be included in the meta-analysis because very few quantitative studies existed and they did not include motor performance measures as a dependent variable. Instead, the paradigm used consisted of mental practice as an independent variable with muscle innervation as the dependent variable. Any changes in low gain muscle

[3]In future mental practice studies it may be advantageous to classify tasks as discrete, serial, and continuous since Fischman, Christina, and Vercruyssen (1981) have recently suggested that serial and discrete tasks "tend to have more of a verbal/cognitive component than do continuous tasks or gross motor repetitive skills, and thus they may be more prone to forgetting" (p. 183). Mental practice may therefore prove to be more beneficial for performance in discrete and serial tasks.

[4]The zero transfer for the low cognitive task may be due to the very limited practice (3 min). The present meta-analysis showed that at least 7.3 min were needed to produce large effect sizes in tasks labeled as "motor."

[5]There is some evidence that an internal orientation for imagery, sometimes called kinesthetic imagery, produces more muscle innervation than an external or strictly visual type of imagery (Hale, 1981; Jacobson, 1932; Lang, 1979). This latter type of imagery involves the subjects viewing themselves from the perspective of an external observer (as in a movie), whereas the former involves the person from his or her own internal perspective actually seeing and feeling those sensations which might be expected while participating in the actual situation. Although internal imagery has been shown to produce more muscle activity than external imagery (Hale, 1981), there is as yet no solid evidence to demonstrate that it results in better motor performance (Epstein, 1980).

tension were assumed to be responsible for the beneficial performance effects resulting from mental practice. Studies using this paradigm, however, have not typically compared task performance of groups previously demonstrating innervation of this type with groups not demonstrating it. Thus, lacking direct tests of this kind, it is difficult to assess the relevance of the psychoneuromuscular theory to the mental practice effects on motor performance noted in the present meta-analysis. Although the research support for the psychoneuromuscular theory is not an outgrowth of the present meta-analysis, a review would be incomplete without an examination of the few studies which have examined this frequently mentioned alternative explanation for mental practice effects (Corbin, 1972; Richardson, 1967b; Schmidt, 1982; Weinberg, 1981).

Although Jacobson (1930), Schramm (1967), and Suinn (1976) have reported that EMG activity obtained during imagery seemed to mirror the pattern revealed when a subject was asked to perform some act overtly, no controlled investigation has been attempted to quantify muscular activity and statistically test the mirror hypothesis. The early work by Jacobson is an example of research that is commonly cited in support of this theory. In addition to quantification problems there is no direct evidence in Jacobson's work that the muscle innervation was localized to the muscles used in an overt movement, such as a steady flexion of the right arm. Because electrodes were only placed in one location (the right arm), it is uncertain if other bodily sites were not also activated when imagining right arm flexion.

Shaw (1938) studied this more directly by recording action potentials in various body locations while subjects imagined squeezing a hand grip dynamometer with the right hand. As expected, he found heightened EMG activity in the right arm, but he unexpectedly found increased activity in the right leg. This nonlocalized effect was similar as well for imaging of typing, singing, and playing a musical instrument. Shaw (1938) concluded that although there were general increases in muscular action potentials from nearly all of the muscle groups tested, there was no evidence of localization to the muscle groups commonly thought to be involved in such performances.

More recently, Hale (1981) has similarly found that action potentials did not mirror the action of the agonists' and antagonists' muscles used in a biceps curl. When he placed electrodes on the right arm and had subjects image doing the curl, he found that in addition to biceps activity increasing as expected, triceps activity also increased from overt to covert conditions. This work, therefore, fails to support the psychoneuromuscular theory as well as other explanations for mental practice which assume that covert mental rehearsal mirrors the overt practice conditions (e.g., Jacobson, 1930; MacKay, 1981; Schramm, 1967; Suinn, 1976). Instead, it is more likely that these minute innervations associated with mental practice are more general throughout the whole body or a whole limb.

Proposition IV: Mental Practice Functions to Assist the Performer in Psychologically Preparing for the Skill to be Performed

If the muscle innervation as a result of mental practice is not localized to the action to be performed, it might be important to ask: What is the functional significance of the more general, minimal tension levels involved? Schmidt (1982) maintains that it is possible that the "performer is merely preparing for the action, setting the arousal level, and generally getting prepared for good performance" (p. 50).

It has been known for some time that submaximal muscular tension in the form of a preparatory set can facilitate reaction time (RT) (Freeman, 1933). This could improve performance in speed and strength tasks and could be one of the reasons why so many athletes mentally practice. In contrast to the deleterious performance effects associated with maximal tension levels (e.g., reduced accuracy of discrimination), the minimal tension levels accompanying mental practice would help to prime the coordinated hand movement (Johnson, 1928). Thus, this type of cognitive rehearsal can act to lower the sensory threshold of the performer and facilitate performance in a wide variety of motor tasks.

This "set" to perform probably involves much more than merely setting appropriate tension levels. Although not statistically significant ($p > .02$), the effects of mental practice tend to be greater when the posttest is administered later rather than immediately following mental practice. This delay in administering the posttest may give subjects a greater opportunity to mentally practice and perhaps perfect additional cognitive strategies that are advantageous in preparing for action on motor/strength tasks. For example, extended mental practice of the relevant aspects of the task can also develop a capacity for narrowed or focused attention. This capacity can facilitate performance by occupying the majority of the individual's attentional capacity so task-irrelevant thoughts and images are prevented from disrupting the on-going priming of the muscles for action. Although the role of mental practice in developing the proper attentional set has been ignored in the research literature, its role in this regard can be implied from the types of psychological states that have been found to be most conducive to producing mental practice effects on performance. Muscle action potentials, for example, are enhanced when subjects are allowed to select scenes with which they are most familiar (Jacobson, 1932) and if they are pretrained in imagery and relaxation (Hale, 1981; Jacobson, 1932). Electroencephalographic alpha pretraining has also been found to be more effective than regular mental practice in performing a tap dance skill (Browning, 1972). These techniques may enable the performer to concentrate more attention on the task while blocking disrupting thoughts, thereby permitting greater efference to the performer's muscles so as to better prepare for good performance.

This attentional-arousal set explanation may not be as limited as the symbolic learning explanation. It could conceivably be used by novice or experienced performers, with the only requirement being that performers have perfected psychological skills that enable them to set appropriate pretension levels and maintain their attention directed toward task-relevant cues. This explanation is also hypothesized to be of primary functional use of mental practice in activities having few symbolic elements (e.g., experienced weight lifters) and as a secondary facilitator of performance when mentally rehearsing tasks that are high in symbolic elements. The widespread use of mental practice among high-level athletes may be indicative of the necessity of setting tension levels and gearing their attention to the beginning of the upcoming task where attention demands are known to be the greatest (Posner & Keele, 1969). This explanation can be tested using a probe RT technique to determine if longer RTs would be evident for those engaging in mental practice as well as determining if too many probes may actually interfere with the development of the arousal-attentional state necessary for good performance.

Conclusion

We hope this meta-analysis will redirect the research efforts of those interested in mental practice away from simply empirical demonstrations of mental practice effects on performance toward an examination of the variables that may moderate or mediate the relations between mental practice and motor performance. The present meta-analysis has identified important task variables, and in light of these findings we have suggested other variables that likewise may be important. Such research may eventually help to verify if these determinants actually produce the suggested relations and thus move us toward a better theoretical understanding of mental practice. Only when this is done will sport psychologists be able to specify with confidence the exact type of mental practice that should be used for the specific conditions confronting the performer.

Reference Notes

1. Sheldon, A.O., & Mahoney, M.J. *Mental practice with varsity basketball players: Parameters of influence.* Paper presented at the Association for the Advancement of Behavior Therapy 14th Annual Convention—Symposium on Cognitive Behavior Therapy and Athletic Performance, New York, Nov. 21–23, 1980.
2. Hall, E.G. *The effect of positive visual imagery on free throw accuracy of intercollegiate women basketball players.* Unpublished manuscript, 1981. (Available from E.G. Hall, School of Health, Physical Education and Recreation, Louisiana State University, Baton Rouge, LA 70803.)

References

Adams, J.A., & Creamer, L.R. Anticipatory timing of continuous and discrete responses. *Journal of Experimental Psychology,* 1962, **63**, 84–90.

Arnold, E.L. *The relationship between physical and mental practice and initial ability in learning a simple motor skill.* Unpublished doctoral dissertation, Indiana University, 1965.

Bagg, E.J.K. *Effect of mental and physical practice on baseball batting.* Unpublished master's thesis, University of California at Los Angeles, 1966.

Bandura, A., & Jefferies, R.W. Role of symbolic coding and rehearsal processes in observational learning. *Journal of Personality and Social Psychology,* 1973, 26, 122–130.

Beckow, P.A. *A comparison of the effectiveness of mental practice upon the learning of two gross motor skills.* Unpublished master's thesis, University of Oregon, 1967.

Bissonette, R. *The relative effects of mental practice upon the learning of two gross motor skills.* Unpublished master's thesis, Springfield College, 1965.

Blalock, H.M., Jr. *Social statistics.* New York: McGraw-Hill, 1972.

Browning, G.S. *The influence of the alpha rhythm during mental practice while acquiring a specific tap dance skill.* Unpublished doctoral dissertation, Texas Woman's University, 1972.

Burns, P.L. *The effect of physical practice, mental practice, and mental-physical practice on the development of a motor skill.* Unpublished master's thesis, The Pennsylvania State University, 1962.

Carpenter, W.B. *Principles of mental physiology* (4th ed.). New York: Appleton, 1894.

Clark, L.V. Effect of mental practice on the development of a certain motor skill. *Research Quarterly,* 1960, 31, 560–569.

Cooper, H. Statistically combining independent studies: A meta-analysis of sex differences in conformity research. *Journal of Personality and Social Psychology,* 1979, 37, 131–146.

Corbin, C.B. The effect of covert rehearsal on development of a complex motor skill. *Journal of General Psychology,* 1967, 76, 143–150. (a)

Corbin, C.B. The effects of mental practice on skill development after controlled practice. *Research Quarterly,* 1967, 38, 534–538. (b)

Corbin, C.B. Mental practice. In W.P. Morgan (Ed.), *Ergogenic aids and muscular performance.* New York: Academic Press, 1972.

Cronk, J.M. *The effect of physical practice, mental practice, and physical-mental practice on the development of arm strength.* Unpublished doctoral dissertation, Florida State University, 1967.

Eggleston, D. *The relative value of actual versus imaginary practice in a learning situation.* Unpublished master's thesis, Columbia University, 1936.

Egstrom, G.H. Effect of an emphasis on conceptualizing techniques during early learning of a gross motor skill. *Research Quarterly,* 1964, 35, 472–481.

Eideness, C.L. *The effect of physical, mental-physical, and mental practice on the learning of a motor skill.* Unpublished master's thesis, South Dakota State University, 1965.

Epstein, M.L. The relationship of mental imagery and mental rehearsal to performance of a motor task. *Journal of Sport Psychology,* 1980, 2, 211–220.

Fischman, M.G., Christina, R.W., & Vercruyssen, M.J. Retention and transfer of motor skills: A review for the practitioner. *Quest,* 1981, 33, 181–194.

Fitts, P.M., & Posner, M.J. *Human performance.* Belmont, CA: Brooke/Cole, 1967.

Freeman, G.L. The facilitation and inhibitory effect of muscular tension upon performance. *American Journal of Psychology,* 1933, 45, 17–52.

Glass, G.V. Integrating findings: The meta-analysis of research. *Review of Research in Education,* 1977, 5, 351–379.

Glass, G.V. Reply to Mansfield and Busse. *Educational Researcher,* 1978, 7, 3.

Gondola, J.C. *A comparison of the effectiveness of programs of physical practice, mental practice, and a combined physical and mental practice on the performance of a selected test of balance.* Unpublished master's thesis, Purdue University, 1966.

Gould, D., Weinberg, R., & Jackson, A. Mental preparation strategies, cognitions, and strength performance. *Journal of Sport Psychology,* 1980, 2, 329–339.

Hale, B.D. *The effects of internal and external imagery on muscular and ocular concomitants.* Unpublished doctoral dissertation, The Pennsylvania State University, 1981.

Hall, E.G. The effect of positive visual imagery on free throw accuracy of intercollegiate women basketball players. *Journal of Sport Psychology,* in press.

Hamerslough, W.S. *The effectiveness of three methods of instruction, followed by mental rehearsal, in learning three complex gross motor tasks.* Unpublished doctoral dissertation, University of Oregon, 1971.

Harby, S.P. Comparisons of mental and physical practice in the learning of a physical skill. *U.S.N. Spec. Dev. Cen. Tech. Rep. S.D.C.,* 1952, 269, 7–25.

Howe, D.P. *The influence of five schedules of mental practice upon the physical performance of a novel gross motor skill after a criterion measure of skill has been attained.* Unpublished doctoral dissertation, Texas Woman's University, 1967.

Jacobson, E. Electrical measurement of neuromuscular states during mental activities. *American Journal of Physiology,* 1930, 94, 22–34.

Jacobson, E. Electrophysiology of mental activities. *American Journal of Psychology,* 1932, 44, 677–694.

Johnson, B. Changes in muscular tension in coordinated hand movements. *Journal of Experimental Psychology,* 1928, 11, 329–341.

Johnson, B.L. *An examination of some factors which might be related to effective utilization of mental practice in learning a gross motor skill.* Unpublished master's thesis, University of Oregon, 1967.

Kelly, D.A. *The relative effectiveness of selected mental practice techniques in H.S. girls' acquisition of a gross motor skill.* Unpublished master's thesis, University of Washington, 1965.

Kelsey, I.B. Effects of mental practice and physical practice upon muscular endurance. *Research Quarterly,* 1961, 32, 47–54.

Kohl, R.M., & Roenker, D.L. Bilateral transfer as a function of mental imagery. *Journal of Motor Behavior,* 1980, 12, 197–206.

Kohr, R.L. *A comparison of statistical procedures for testing $U_1 = U_2$ with unequal n's and variances.* Unpublished doctoral dissertation, Pennsylvania State University, 1970.

Kovar, S.V. *The relative effects of physical, mental, and combined mental-physical practice in the acquisition of a motor skill.* Unpublished master's thesis, University of Illinois, 1969.

Kuhn, W. *The effects of physical warm-up and mental rehearsal on the performance of experienced and nonexperienced soccer players in the soccer dribble test.* Unpublished doctoral dissertation, University of Oregon, 1971.

LaLance, R.C., Jr. *A comparison of traditional instruction, mental practice, and combined physical-mental practice upon the learning of selected motor skills.* Unpublished doctoral dissertation, Middle Tennessee State University, 1974.

Landers, D.M. Observational learning of a motor skill: Temporal spacing of demonstrations and audience presence. *Journal of Motor Behavior,* 1975, 7, 281–287.

Lang, P.J. A bio-informational theory of emotional imagery. *Psychophysiology,* 1979, 16, 495–512.

Levy, W.C. *The effects of three conditions of practice on the performance of the football center snap by college students.* Unpublished master's thesis, North Texas State University, 1969.

MacKay, D.G. The problem of rehearsal or mental practice. *Journal of Motor Behavior,* 1981, 13, 274–285.

Maxwell, J.M. *The effect of mental practice on the learning of the overhand volleyball serve.* Unpublished master's thesis, Central Missouri State College, 1968.

Meichenbaum, D.H. *Cognitive-behavior modification.* New York: Plenum, 1977.

Mendoza, D., & Wickman, H. "Inner" darts: Effects of mental practice on performance of dart throwing. *Perceptual and Motor Skills,* 1978, 47, 1195–1199.

Minas, S.C. Mental practice of a complex perceptual-motor skill. *Journal of Human Mouvement Studies,* 1978, 4, 102–107.

Moritani, T. *The effect of simulated movements on mental practice.* Unpublished master's thesis, California State University at Northridge, 1975.

Morrisett, L.N. *The role of implicit practice in learning.* Unpublished doctoral dissertation, Yale University, 1956.

Murphy, T.J. *The effects of mental warm-up on jump shooting accuracy among selected boys' high school basketball players.* Unpublished master's thesis, South Dakota State University, 1977.

Noel, R.C. The effect of visuo-motor behavior rehearsal on tennis performance. *Journal of Sport Psychology,* 1980, 2, 221–226.

Phipps, S.J., & Morehouse, C.A. Effects of mental practice on the acquisition of motor skills of varied difficulty. *Research Quarterly,* 1969, 40, 773–778.

Posner, M.I., & Keele, S.W. Attentional demands of movement. *Proceedings of the 16th Congress of Applied Psychology.* Amsterdam: Swets and Zeittinger, 1969.

Rawlings, E.I., & Rawlings, I.L. Rotary pursuit tracking following mental rehearsal as a function of voluntary control of visual imagery. *Perceptual and Motor Skills,* 1974, 38, 302.

Razor, J.E. *A comparison of the effects of mental and physical practice as a means of increasing strength.* Unpublished doctoral dissertation, Indiana University, 1966.

Richardson, A. Mental practice: A review and discussion (Part 1). *Research Quarterly,* 1967, 38, 95–107. (a)

Richardson, A. Mental practice: A review and discussion (Part 2). *Research Quarterly,* 1967, 38, 263–273. (b)

Rodriguez, G.J. *A comparison of the effects of mental and physical practice upon abdominal strength in high school girls.* Unpublished master's thesis, University of North Carolina at Greensboro, 1967.

Ryan, D.E., & Simons, J. Cognitive demand, imagery, and frequency of mental rehearsal as factors influencing acquisition of motor skills. *Journal of Sport Psychology,* 1981, 3, 35–45.

Sackett, R.S. The influences of symbolic rehearsal upon the retention of a maze habit. *Journal of General Psychology,* 1934, 10, 376–395.

Sackett, R.S. The relationship between amount of symbolic rehearsal and retention of a maze habit. *Journal of General Psychology,* 1935, 13, 113–128.

Schramm, V. *An investigation of the electromyographic responses obtained during mental practice.* Unpublished master's thesis, University of Wisconsin-Madison, 1967.

Schmidt, R.A. *Motor control and learning: A behavioral emphasis.* Champaign, IL: Human Kinetics, 1982.

Seaborne, T.C. *Effects of VMBR, relaxation and imagery on karate performance.* Unpublished master's thesis, North Texas State University, 1981.

Shappell, R.T. *The effects of three types of mental practice on performance and retention scores of a maze tracking task.* Unpublished doctoral dissertation, Florida State University, 1977.

Shaw, W. The distribution of muscular action potentials during imaging. *The Psychological Record,* 1938, 2, 195–216.

Sheldon, M.F. *An investigation of the relative effects of mental practice and physical practice in improving the efficiency of the breast stroke.* Unpublished master's thesis, University of Oregon, 1963.

Sheldon, A.O., & Mahoney, M.J. The content and effect of "psyching-up" strategies in weight lifters. *Cognitive Therapy and Research,* 1978, 2, 275–284.

Shick, M. Effects of mental practice on selected volleyball skills for college women. *Research Quarterly,* 1970, 41, 88–94.

Smith, L.E., & Harrison, J.S. Comparison of the effects of visual, motor, mental and guided practice upon speed and accuracy of performance of a simple eye-hand coordination task. *Research Quarterly,* 1962, 33, 299–307.

Smith, R.E. Development of an integrated coping response through cognitive-affective stress management training. In I.G. Sarson & C.D. Spielberger (Eds.), *Stress and anxiety* (Vol. 7). Washington, DC: Hemisphere, 1981.

Smyth, M.M. The role of mental practice in skill acquisition. *Journal of Motor Behavior,* 1975, 7, 199–206.

Spears (Alexander), C.L. *The effect of mental practice and physical practice in learning the running high jump for college women.* Unpublished master's thesis, Arkansas State College, 1966.

Standridge, J.O. *The effect of mental, physical, and mental-physical practice in learning the whip kick.* Unpublished master's thesis, University of Tennessee, 1971.

Start, K.B. The influence of subjectively assessed games ability on gain in motor performance after mental practice. *Journal of General Psychology,* 1962, 67, 169–172.

Stebbins, J. A comparison of the effects of physical and mental practice in learning a motor skill. *Research Quarterly,* 1968, 39, 714–720.

Steiner, I.D. *Group process and productivity.* New York: Academic Press, 1972.

Stephens, M.L. *The relative effectiveness of combinations of mental and physical practice on performance scores and level of aspiration scores for an accuracy task.* Unpublished master's thesis, University of North Carolina at Greensboro, 1966.

Suinn, R.M. Behavioral rehearsal training for ski racers. *Behavior Therapy,* 1972, 3, 519.

Suinn, R.M. Body thinking: Psychology of Olympic champs. *Psychology Today,* 1976, 10(2), 38–44.

Surburg, P.R. Audio, visual, and audio-visual instruction with mental practice in developing the forehand tennis drive. *Research Quarterly,* 1968, 39, 728–734.

Tufts, S.A. *The effects of mental practice and physical practice on the scores of intermediate bowlers.* Unpublished master's thesis, University of North Carolina at Greensboro, 1963.

Twining, W.E. Mental practice and physical practice in learning a motor skill. *Research Quarterly,* 1949, 20, 432–435.

Weinberg, R.S. The relationship between mental preparation strategies and motor performance: A review and critique. *Quest,* 1981, 33, 195–213.

Whitehill, M.P. *The effects of variations of mental practice on learning a motor skill.* Unpublished master's thesis, University of Oregon, 1964.

Whitehill, M.P. *The effects of mental practice on children's learning and retention of gross motor skills.* Unpublished doctoral dissertation, University of Oregon, 1965.

Wills, B.J. *Mental practice as a factor in the performance of two motor tasks.* Unpublished doctoral dissertation, University of Wisconsin-Madison, 1966.

Wills, K.C. *The effect of mental practice and physical practice on learning a motor skill.* Unpublished master's thesis, Arkansas State College, 1965.

Wilson, M. *The relative effect of mental practice and physical practice in learning the tennis forehand and backhand drives.* Unpublished doctoral dissertation, State University of Iowa, 1960.

Wrisberg, C.A., & Ragsdale, M.R. Cognitive demand and practice level: Factors in the mental rehearsal of motor skills. *Journal of Human Movement Studies,* 1979, 5, 201–208.

[1]Although Corbin (1972) reported that Clark (1960) concluded that novice performers used mental practice more effectively than junior varsity and varsity performers while learning a one-handed basketball shot, the original article by Clark (1960) concluded just the opposite; mental practice was more effective with varsity and junior varsity groups than it was with the novice group.

[2]Even though effect sizes could not be regarded legitimately as independent of each other, results were calculated under this assumption to allow the comparison of many interesting relationships within studies (Glass, 1977).

[3]In future mental practice studies it may be advantageous to classify tasks as discrete, serial, and continuous since Fischman, Christina, and Vercruyssen (1981) have recently suggested that serial and discrete tasks "tend to have more of a verbal/cognitive component than do continuous tasks or gross motor repetitive skills, and thus they may be more prone to forgetting" (p. 183). Mental practice may therefore prove to be more beneficial for performance in discrete and serial tasks.

[4]The zero transfer for the low cognitive task may be due to the very limited practice (3 min). The present meta-analysis showed that at least 7.3 min were needed to produce large effect sizes in tasks labeled as "motor."

[5]There is some evidence that an internal orientation for imagery, sometimes called kinesthetic imagery, produces more muscle innervation than an external or strictly visual type of imagery (Hale, 1981; Jacobson, 1932; Lang, 1979). This latter type of imagery involves the subjects viewing themselves from the perspective of an external observer (as in a movie), whereas the former involves the person from his or her own internal perspective actually seeing and feeling those sensations which might be expected while participating in the actual situation. Although internal imagery has been shown to produce more muscle activity than external imagery (Hale, 1981), there is as yet no solid evidence to demonstrate that it results in better motor performance (Epstein, 1980).

24 The Application of Sport Psychology for Performance Optimization

DANIEL GOULD AND ROBERT C. EKLUND
University of North Carolina at Greensboro

Since the earliest days of sport psychology, one of the most important issues addressed by sport and exercise psychologists has been related to the application of psychological techniques intended to aid people in making their performance more effective—in other words, psychological skills training (PST). That is, the way to achieve peak performance through appropriate psychological preparation has been a major focus of interest.

Psychological and physical skills are quite similar in the manner in which they are taught, learned, and practiced. However, for several reasons, including lack of time, insufficient knowledge, and misperceptions related to psychology, sport and exercise participants quite often apply psychological principles aimed at the enhancement of sport performance in an inappropriate manner, or even neglect such a possible application completely. Because of the increasing interest in systematic mental training techniques among elite athletes and their coaches alike, Gould and Eklund undertook the important task of reviewing the application of sport psychology principles for optimization of performance among elite athletes.

These authors begin by providing an overview of sport psychology and its applied relevance to athletic performance. They continue by identifying some core topics that are key areas of sport psychology to be contained in programs that enhance the performance of elite athletes. Finally, they present their approach as to the proper design and implementation of PST programs in elite athletic settings. Especially interesting is Gould and Eklund's discussion of several popular myths circulating about PST, which significantly contribute to the confusion around the issue of the sport psychology consultants' ability to help elite athletes through the application of PST. The authors correctly argue that if unchecked and unrefuted, such myths can cripple PST programs by diminishing their effectiveness.

This seminal review, based mainly on published scientific research and accumulating professional experience with elite athletes, provides important general guidelines that take into account central factors such as individual differences and cross-cultural variability and that applied sport psychologists can use in preparing elite athletes for optimizing their performances.

This review focuses on the application of sport psychology for elite athlete performance optimization. First, an overview of applied sport psychology and its role in athlete performance optimization is discussed. In particular, sport psychology is defined, general sport psychology research questions are delineated and common sport psychology myths are identified. Emphasis is placed on the need for an interdisciplinary sport science team approach to elite athlete preparation. Second, central or core sport psychology topics that are important to include in programs designed to facilitate elite athlete performance are discussed. Topics recommended for inclusion consist of anxiety and stress management, confidence enhancement, attention/concentration skills training, positive task oriented thought training, determination-motivation and commitment enhancement, goal setting, communication enhancement and imagery skills training. Finally, a general framework for designing and implementing psychological skills training programs is discussed. Steps contained in this framework include: (1) identifying psychological skill objectives; (2) operationally defining psychological skill objectives; (3) identifying strategies which can be used to develop specific psychological skills; (4) designing a psychological skills training schedule; (5) organizing a psychological skills training.

Applied Sport Psychology and Its Role in Athlete Performance Optimization

In terms of performance optimization sport psychologists are interested in understanding why some athletes rise to the occasion and have superior performances while others seem to buckle under the pressure and perform in a less than optimal fashion. Sport psychologists want to understand the factors and conditions that influence peak performance.

While there are many specific types of questions that can be posed in sports psychology, most of these questions can be categorized in two general areas. These general categories of questions include: (a) what effect does athletic participation have on the psychological make-up of the participant; and (b) what effect do psychological factors have on athletic performance?

Examples of specific questions of interest which fall within the first category include, what effect does participation in soccer have on the competitiveness of an

Adapted, by permission, from D. Gould and R.C. Eklund, 1991, "The application of sport psychology for performance optimization," *Thai Journal of Sports Science* 1(1): 10-21.

individual athlete or what effect does years of participation in competitive field hockey have on the self-esteem of the participant? In essence, questions in this category focus on whether sport participation initiates changes, for better or worse, in the psychological make-up of the athlete.

Specific questions which fall into the second category would include queries on the effects of negative statements or feedback from a coach on the performance of a weight lifter. Alternatively, how does confidence affect the track and field athlete's ability to put the shot? Or finally, how does group cohesion, the cement that holds the group together, affect the team. Does it facilitate performance or does it have a negative effect on performance?

Common Sport Psychology Myths

With the growth of applied sport psychology in recent years, a number of myths have developed relative to its role in assisting athletes in optimizing performance through mental training. It is important to recognize and refute these myths prior to initiating a psychological skills training program for athletes. If unchecked, these myths can diminish effectiveness by virtually crippling the program. Myths that are critical to address include:

Myth 1: Sport psychology consultants only work with "problem" or "sick" athletes. A commonly encountered myth in applied sport psychology is that sport psychology consultants only work with "problem" or "sick" athletes. This is not the case. In North America, for example, there are two distinct types of sport psychologists: clinical and educational (2). Clinical sport psychologists are typically licensed to practice clinical psychology in the state in which they practice. Their training is very specific and provides unique information which allows them to treat athletes with varying mental disorders. Specifically, clinical psychologists treat individuals who have demonstrated abnormal behavior that has been diagnosed in the clinical range. For example, the clinical sport psychologist could work with an athlete who is so severely depressed that he or she might contemplate suicide or an athlete that suffers from an eating disorder such as anorexia nervosa. The clinical sport psychologist works with individuals to resolve disorders of this nature.

Educational sport psychologists, on the other hand, can be thought of as mental coaches. Their training is usually in physical education or the sport sciences. They are much like a coach except that they specialize in the mental aspects of sport performance. Typically educational sport psychologists focus on teaching athletes strategies and techniques such as goal setting, anxiety management, relaxation training, imagery or in providing information to coaches about group cohesion enhancement or setting team goals. Hence, they focus their attention on mental skills development in athletes who are characterized by a normal range of functioning. They are not trained or qualified to treat athletes with mental disorders of a clinical nature.

Regardless of the distinctions between the two types of sport psychologists, it is important to recognize that one type of sport psychologist is not any more important that the other type. Rather, both the clinical and educational sport psychologist have important albeit distinct roles. Educational sport psychologists work with normal athletes in efforts to assist them in developing psychological skills which enable them to improve performance and achieve their goals. While clinical sport psychologists may help athletes educationally, they are also equipped to help athletes whose behavior is abnormal or maladaptive.

Myth 2: Sport psychology consultants focus only on elite athlete concerns. The second myth is that sport psychology consultants focus only on elite athlete concerns. This myth is false because a number of sport psychologists work with young, developing athletes who are not elite performers (3,4). Similarly, in the United States there are sport psychologists who work with mentally retarded Special Olympians. The children involved in the immensely successful Special Olympics Program would not fit the stereotypical view of an elite athlete. Sport psychology consultants involved in these types of programs are part of a team of dedicated individuals trying to provide excellent experiences for all sport participants and not just the elite athlete. However, media coverage seems to focus on sport psychology for only the elite athlete. Therefore, many people have been mislead into believing that sport psychology is just for the elite performer and not for the masses.

Myth 3: Sport psychologists will cause revolutionary changes in sport. The third myth we will address is that sport psychologists will provide revolutionary changes in sport. This myth was identified as being false in the mid 1920' s by America's first sport psychologist, Coleman Griffith at the University of Illinois (5). Griffith felt, and many sport psychologists would agree today, that while the sport psychology specialist can assist athletes to optimize their performance, they will not be radically changing the sport scene. Many coaches have been fairly good sport psychologists by themselves and, further, some have been outstanding intuitive sport psychologists. Indeed, research in this area has served to substantiate and reinforce many of the things that both coaches and athletes have already done (6, 7, 8). While sport psychologists can help coaches and athletes, it is unrealistic to think that they have all the answers or that they cause revolutionary changes.

Myth 4: "Magic pill" or "quick fix" psychological skill training methods exist. A fourth myth of interest is that "magic pill" or "quick fix" psychological skill training methods exist. This is a myth that is often encountered when one conducts interventions with athletes in educational programs. Athletes and coaches come in and expect very easy, quick solutions to difficult problems such as "teach me how to combat stress" or "teach me how to use imagery in twenty minutes or one day." This is intuitively appealing and consistent with the instant gratification cult in North American society however it is not consistent with what we know about the development of psychological skills. As Martens (1) has pointed out, psychological skills are like physical skills, the only way to improve psychological skills is through systematic practice. Just as complex physical skills require careful practice to acquire and further practice to maintain, psychological skills are acquired and maintained through consistent, considered effort.

Myth 5: Sport psychology is not useful. The final myth is that sport psychology is not useful. There is a substantial body of research published in scholarly journals and as well as anecdotal reports from athletes and coaches in the popular press indicating that sport psychology can and is having a positive effect in assisting those who want to achieve athletic excellence (9, 10). As has been indicated before, sport psychology is not going to have all of the answers or cause revolutions in the athletic domain. Regardless, sport psychologists can provide constructive criticism and educational ideas that will assist athletes in pushing the bounds of excellence.

The Need for a Team Approach to Sport Science Training

It is imperative to remember that sport psychology cannot exist in isolation from the other sport sciences or other personnel in the athletic environment. At minimum, we recommend considering a psychological skills personnel triad consisting of the athlete, coach and sport psychology consultant. This small work group is extremely important because if he or she is to have maximal effect, the sport psychology consultant needs to work with the coach as well as with the athlete. This ensures that everyone is working with the same priorities and using strategies that they think will help the athlete achieve those priorities.

Moving beyond the sport psychology personnel triad, the best approach for facilitating athletic excellence with elite performers is to use an integrated sport science team. This involves a sport science team made up of such specialists as an exercise physiologist, a sport psychology consultant, a biomechanist, and a sport medicine specialist working in concert to assist the coach and athlete in their daily training and routine. This integrated approach to science and practice offers the best possibility to enable the athlete to attain peak performance because it recognizes that athletic performance is psychobiological in nature. In this approach specialists from various subdisciplinary areas openly discuss various performance enhancement strategies and the relationships between strategies across subdisciplines.

Central or Core Sport Psychology Topics for Athlete Performance Optimization

Psychological Skills Training Knowledge Base

Once a common base for understanding the parameters of applied sport psychology has been established it is appropriate to identify what should be contained in a psychological skills training program. Specifically, what are the central or core psychological topics for elite athlete performance optimization?

The knowledge base used to derive the central or core sport psychology topics for performance optimization can be derived from three primary sources. These sources include general psychological research, sport psychology research, and experience (1). Each of these sources of knowledge make important contributions to our overall understanding. General findings in psychological research and the findings specific to the sport setting are crucial in identifying central or core topics for performance optimization. However, researchers often underestimate the critical contributions made to this knowledge base by the experiences of coaches, sport psychologists and athletes. It is judicious to blend these sources of knowledge in addressing this topic.

Elite Athlete Research

There have been a number of studies conducted throughout the years comparing successful and less-successful athletes on psychological skills and abilities. Williams (11) reviewed much of this research including studies utilizing a variety of diverse sports such as wrestling, racquetball, and gymnastics. She found that more successful athletes were characterized by higher levels of self confidence, better concentration, and more task-oriented thoughts (rather than thoughts oriented toward the score in the game or outcome.) In addition, these successful individuals had more positive thoughts in general and more often used imagery, specifically positive imagery. They were able to visualize success. Further, successful athletes tended to be more determined and to show more commitment. Finally, in some of the studies there was a trend for the successful athletes to exhibit less anxiety than their less-successful counterparts although this result was not as consistent as the previous findings.

The findings of Williams (11) were further verified and extended in a more recent investigation conducted by Mahoney, Gabriel and Perkins (12) comparing successful and less-successful athletes several important findings emerged. First, the successful athletes experienced fewer problems with anxiety. They were better able to concentrate and, in general, they were more self confident. These individuals also relied more on internal kinesthetic imagery; that is they would "feel" themselves performing from their own perspective (as opposed to the external perspective of an outsider). Further, these successful competitors focused more on their own performance rather than the performance of their opponent. Finally, they were more highly motivated.

There are striking similarities between the results of the Mahoney et al. (12), and Williams (11) studies. Specifically, it seems that successful athletes are better able to concentrate; are more self confident; exhibit different types of imagery and thought patterns; are more committed and motivated; and are better able to cope with their anxiety than their less-successful counterparts.

A second approach to identifying central or core sport psychology topics for performance optimization involves the assessment of those individuals served in these programs. Recently Gould, Murphy, Tammen and May (13) surveyed elite coaches and athletes associated with the United States Olympic Committee National Governing Body Sport Programs. In this study individuals were asked to rate the importance of various sport psychological topics for inclusion individual or group psychological skill training sessions. The elite coaches rated topics such as imagery and visualization, concentration and attention training, stress management, relaxation training and self-talk strategies as very important. These topics all received ratings of 8 or above on an 11 point Likert scale, with 11 signifying very important. Similarly, the athletes rated topics being most important as concentration-attention training, imagery and visualization techniques, relaxation, self talk, and arousal regulation. Hence, there was considerable consistency on the topics that coaches and athletes identify as worthy of emphasis.

Orlick and Partington's (14) recent landmark research on Mental Links to Excellence in Canadian Olympians provides a third source for determining core or central topics involved in performance optimization. These investigators individually interviewed 75 1984 Canadian Olympians. They also surveyed 160 other 1984 Canadian Olympic team members. The individual athletes surveyed and interviewed represented a wide variety of sports. The interviews and surveys conducted focused on the mental readiness of the athlete for participation in the 1984 Olympic games and conclusions were derived on the basis of comparing athletes that performed up to or exceeded their personal best with those athletes that did not perform up to their personal best or had a disappointing performance. Further, those athletes who performed up to or exceeded expectations were compared with those who did not perform up to expectations.

Orlick and Partington (14) found that athletes who performed up to their potential had quality mental preparation for competition. One of the most striking facets of this mental preparation was the extensive degree of planning leading to the optimal performance. The athletes achieving peak performance had developed competitive plans, a priori plans for performance evaluation, and plans and ideas for dealing with disruption. In the face of adversity or distraction, these individuals were able to overcome performance blocks by sticking with their plans. Through the extensive planning, these athletes knew how to deal with that adversity. They did not let adversity override them and cause tremendous anxiety, rather, they were prepared and able to channel that arousal.

The Olympians that achieved peak performance also demonstrated a total commitment to pursuing excellence while their counterparts did not show this total commitment. The athletes that optimized their performance had quality training. They had set daily training goals. They used simulation in practice to replicate the competitive environment. They used imagery in practice. In particular, the Olympians who achieved excellence were better able to focus their attention and better able to control performance imagery. These exceptional performers used positive imagery to visualize successful outcomes.

The Orlick and Partington study provides interesting qualitative and quantitative insights about highly skilled athletes who rose to the occasion and achieved excellence in Olympic competition versus those who did not. This information helps to clarify the kinds of mental preparation, mental readiness and mental coping skills involved in peak performance. As aptly described by Orlick and Partington (14), this study provides us with insight into mental links to excellence.

The final study that is relevant to address takes a different tact to the problem of identifying core or central topics in performance optimization. In 1987 Dr. Shane Murphy was the first sport psychologist assigned to provide psychological consulting services at the U.S. Olympic festival. Murphy detailed this experience in **The Sport Psychologist** (15). He noted the types of athlete problems encountered and the types of assistance provided. Coping with performance anxiety was the inquiry of highest incidence (23 athletes). The second area of concern involved 16 athletes asking for information about how to cope with training stress and fatigue. There were an additional five queries concerning both working on mental plans and visualization. Thus the top four issues identified by athletes seeking consultation at this event were coping with anxiety, coping with training stress and fatigue, information on mental plans and information on visualization. Other issues that were mentioned by either 3 or 4 athletes focused on dealing with injuries, handling interactions with families at the festival, communication problems with a coach, dealing with the media, communication problems with fellow athletes and team communication in general.

The importance of this study lies in the practical nature of the information. Specifically, this study identifies actual problems, frequency of inquiry, and concerns of athletes engaged in high level competition. This pragmatic approach contrasts with the earlier hypothetical or theoretical analyses of these problems.

In summary, research literature regarding the psychological characteristics of successful versus less-successful athletes, studies asking coaches and athletes about what kind of sport psychological information they desire, investigations examining mental links and plans associated with athletic excellence, and actual records of athletes who experience problems in high level competition have been examined. Core or central sport psychology issues consistently rising from this body of knowledge include anxiety and stress management, confidence enhancement, attention/concentration skills training, positive task oriented thoughts training (as opposed to negative and outcome oriented thoughts). Issues related to instilling determination, motivation, and commitment are relevant. Further, quality training and goal setting, simulation, imagery skills (specifically kinesthetic imagery and imagery control), and communication enhancement are prominent topics.

While these areas can be identified as central or core topics for performance optimization, it must be recognized that individual athlete differences must be the critical factor in determining program content. These topics are always dependent on the specific athlete, their orientations, their background experiences and other personal variables that they bring to the competitive situation. It is appropriate to use these central or core topics as a guide for determining what to include in a specific psychological skills training program but it must always be remembered that program organizers must meet the individual needs of athletes.

Designing and Implementing Psychological Skills Training Programs for Athlete Performance Optimization

The final purpose of this review is to examine how psychological skills training programs can be designed and implemented. To accomplish this objective, this section will provide a general blueprint for designing a psychological skills training program for a team or a group of athletes. Much of this blueprint is modeled after an excellent text by Rainer Martens entitled the **Coaches' Guide to Sport Psychology** (1). This book provides excellent information on how to structure a psychological skills training program.

Selling Psychological Skills

Before discussing what steps should be implemented to design psychological skills training programs, the first thing that must be understood is that practitioner has to "sell" the participants on the idea (16). Regardless of whether sport psychologist is working directly with athletes or indirectly through coaches, he or she needs to convince the parties involved that psychological skills training programs are important.

Competition is a test of both the athlete's physical and psychological skills. Providing salient examples of this contention is an excellent way to engage the athletes' attention. Greg Louganis' performance in the 1988 Summer Olympic Games is a powerful example of the physical and psychological demands of competition. During one of his dives, Louganis hit his head on the diving board. The resulting injury to his head required sutures. Then he had to come back and dive again. He had done those dives thousands of times and made one mistake. However, the fear, anxiety and worry caused by hitting the board and having to come back and not hit it again put tremendous stress on him. Further, Louganis was the defending Olympic champion and everyone was expecting him to win the gold medal. Indeed, Louganis must have been under a great deal of stress. Yet Louganis did rise to the occasion and successfully defend his Olympic title. This undoubtedly was one of the finest displays of psychological skill in controlling one's emotions that has ever been emitted in sport competition.

Another worthy example can be again be found in Olympic history. In the Montreal Olympics in 1976, a Japanese gymnast fractured his leg. He chose to compete in his last event and actually hit his dismount off of the rings. This gymnast demonstrated that psychological skills can even overcome pain. With even a meager effort, examples can be found to substantiate the contention that when athletes participate at the international level, the competition is a test of both their physical and psychological skills. Hence, psychological skills training is important because there is no room at the top for the partially prepared athlete.

In broaching the topic of psychological skills training, Martens (1) recommends asking athletes three questions. First, ask the athletes to identify how long they spend each day on average working on physical parameters, both conditioning and technique, for their sport. Second, ask those same athletes to rate how many minutes daily on average they work on psychological skills that will help them perform in competition. Finally, ask the athletes to rate how important psychological skills are to their performance on a 1-10 scale with 1 being not at all important and 10 being very important.

Typically, athletes spend a great deal of time working on physical skills. Elite athletes will report from two hours to six hours a day of physical training. Conversely, it is very typical for athletes to have very minimal daily time involvement for psychological skills; in the order of 5 or 10 minutes. Finally, athletes competing at the elite level will usually respond to the question posed on the importance of psychological skills with ratings of 8, 9, 10 on the scale. This indicates that they feel psychological skills are very important. The enormous disparity in time expenditure between physical and psychological provides an interesting counterpoint to the importance placed on psychological skills by these athletes.

This raises the important question of why athletes and coaches neglect psychological skills in their training. There are probably a number of answers. The most prevalent is the view that psychological skills are inherited characteristics much like being tall or short or being blue eyed or brown eyed. Many athletes have the misconception that they cannot do anything about their psychological skills. There is a feeling that they get anxious or they don't get anxious and that is just the way they are. Or they are confident or not confident and they cannot do anything about it. We know that this is not the case!

A further reason that psychological skills are neglected is that coaches and athletes often lack the knowledge about how to develop psychological skills. It is not uncommon for coaches to tell athletes that "you need to relax" or "you need to become more confident" but they do not specifically tell the athletes how to relax or how become more confident. In contrast, when an athlete over-rotates, the diving coach will usually identify the problem for the athlete and then give very specific instructional information on how to correct it. Many times coaches and athletes do not have knowledge to correct their psychological skills or further improve them.

In essence, most elite athletes intuitively know that psychological skills are important. It must be impressed upon them that they have to learn and train psychological skills very much as they learn and train physical skills. An excellent analogy can be made with weight training.

Coaches and athletes know that physical strength be developed if basic weight training principles are followed. If the body is systematically and progressively overloaded over time, adaptation will occur and strength is improved. However, not everyone responds exactly the same way. Some people become much stronger in a given time period than others, but everyone still gets stronger. So while there are individual differences, no one will become stronger unless they overload and practice. This is the important point we want to make with psychological skills. They are much like physical skills. There are individual differences in terms of how quickly and effectively athletes learn these skills. However, if athletes systematically practice, they can develop these skills. This point needs to be repeatedly emphasized to the athletes.

A final point in convincing athletes and coaches of the importance of psychological skills is to emphasize that psychological skills are only one component in a total package of training for peak performance. An athlete needs to maximize psychological skills, physical fitness, and physical skills to reach his or her full potential. It is not being suggested that it is just the psychological at the expense of the physical. It is the total package of psychological skills, physical skills, fitness and injury prevention that allows an athlete to increase the probability of having a peak performance.

Steps in Designing Psychological Skills Training Programs

There are a number of steps to consider in designing a psychological skills training program for teams or athletes for whom you work. The steps outlined here are not designed to be a very rigid, specific set of procedures that must be adhered to in developing an effective program. That is certainly not the case. Sport scientists have different ways of implementing programs just as they have different ways of coaching. However, these are seven very general steps that could be followed and would assist those sport scientists and coaches just becoming involved in setting up a psychological skills training program. These steps involve:

Step One: Identifying psychological skill objectives. One of the most difficult tasks for coaches, sport psychology consultants or even athletes to do when they are trying to develop a psychological skills training program is to decide what they do not want to focus on. For example, in various clinics or programs where we have worked with athletes and coaches on psychological skills development, we ask them to list the different psychological skills on which they would like to work. The variety of responses obtained includes such topics as self confidence, leadership, sportspersonship, independence, achievement, competitiveness, cooperativeness, anxiety management, character, personality, loyalty, teamwork, communication skills, positive mental attitude, mental toughness, assertive aggression, aggressiveness, self motivation, and respect for others. This list clearly shows that most coaches and athletes have a number of varied objectives that they could be trying to achieve. Moreover, most feel that all of these skills are important and should be further developed.

Knowing that all of these skills are important leads to a critical mistake that is often made when consultants, coaches and athletes first start to develop psychological skills training programs. They try to do everything as opposed to focusing on one or two psychological skill objectives. To be most effective it is best to focus on a few psychological skill objectives and design programs to achieve them.

Given this, the first thing that must be accomplished is to conduct a current assessment of the individual athlete or team to identify the current psychological strengths and deficits. Specifically, what are the areas that need to be improved? As an athlete, this could be a self assessment. For the coach, it could be an athlete or team assessment. As a sport psychology consultant, this assessment would entail the coach as well as his or her athletes.

Typically this evaluation will result in a list of five or six topics. The hardest part is to make a hierarchical listing of these specific skills. It may be difficult but list these topics in importance from 1 to 6 if six skills have been identified. From that list, no more than the first one or two concerns should be addressed. Commit your program to focusing on these one or two most important areas.

Keeping the program simple by focusing on only a few objectives has several advantages. First, it keeps the program manageable. Overwhelming the athlete and/or coach with too many objectives is not an effective approach. Second, a focused approach allows the athlete to see clear cut benefits in the areas of concentration. Results act as positive reinforcement and the athletes will be motivated to work harder in the future.

Step Two: Operationally defining psychological skill objectives. Once the psychological skills or objectives have been identified as the focus in the intervention program, these skills or objectives need to be precisely defined. This is extremely important. The social sciences, and particularly sport psychology, have a disadvantage relative to the physical sciences in that many of the terms used to define variables of interest have common every day meanings. For example, "positive mental attitude" may mean something different to the sport psychology consultant than it does to the coach and mean yet another thing to the athlete. Hence it is very valuable to very specifically identify for those involved in the program not only the objective (Step 1) but also the objective meaning.

To continue with the "positive mental" attitude" example, this concept can be operationally defined as no negative talk at practices and games, moving quickly between all drills, no complaining, and making supportive statements to teammates. This is not to say that everyone would define positive mental attitude this way. However, by precisely identifying the meaning of positive mental attitude for this particular situation, the athlete, coaches and sport psychology consultant will have a shared understanding of it. Hence, there should not be any inconsistency arising through one coach meaning one thing and another coach having a different understanding of the term. The consequence of failing to properly and fully define objectives is confusion on the athlete's part. Conflicting signals among the participants undermines progress and may ultimately lead to the program being abandoned by the athlete.

Step Three: Identify strategies which can be used to develop specific psychological skills. Step three focuses on identifying strategies which can be used to develop specific psychological skills. Many times when coaches and athletes decide to develop and implement a psychological skills training program, they have identified the skills they want to work on. They have even precisely defined the skills. However, they often fail by merely setting the goal and having no strategy by which to achieve the objective. It is extremely important for the individual implementing the psychological skills training program to develop very specific strategies to reach the desired objectives.

For example, in a recent study, Gould and his associates (7) asked elite coaches what strategies they used for developing self confidence in their athletes. The point we would like to make without discussing the relative merits of any of the strategies is that over 13 strategies that coaches use to develop self confidence in their athletes were identified. These included: instruction and drilling where athletes become more confident because their skills improve; positive talk where the athletes tell themselves they can do it; confidence modeling by the coach or other athletes; the coach using rewarding statements to build up the athletes' confidence; instituting extremely rigorous physical conditioning drills and emphasizing how the athlete will be in better physical condition than his or her competitors therefore he or she can be confident; goals setting programs; success imagery; and anxiety reduction strategies. Clearly there are a wide variety of strategies available. Careful consideration on specific strategy selection is required to ensure that the program is focused and, further, that the selected strategies are the ones that will be most efficient and effective with a particular individual or team in their particular setting.

A further advantage of specifically identifying the strategies to be employed is that it makes the whole program very systematic. It is not unusual for coaches to identify a number of psychological skills that athletes develop in their program. However, when asked how these skills are developed, coaches often respond with a blank look. Why? Because they have not specifically thought about strategies for developing those skills. Psychological skills are not typically "caught" by being in the practice environment the way one catches the common cold. Psychological skills are taught. Coaches and consultants need strategies to teach psychological skills. Teaching should be planned if it is to be most effective.

Step Four : Design a psychological skills training schedule. Once psychological skill objectives have been identified, defined and specific strategies have been delineated to achieve those objectives, it is appropriate to formulate a psychological skills training schedule. Similar to a strength training program, a psychological skills training program requires decisions on the number of meetings, the length of the meetings and the exercises or tasks to be employed.

For example, the consultant and coach might decide that there should be two meetings a week after practice. These might be viewed as a formal meetings where the athletes are educated about goal setting, confidence development or imagery. This is not a setting for individual consultation but rather a forum for group education, while the scheduling of meetings is subject to the constraints of the setting, it should be remembered that it is best to hold more frequent meetings of a shorter duration than meetings that are long.

It has been our experience that provision for a number of informal meetings is extremely valuable. For an example, if you were a consultant working with a team, you would want to be at the social events that the team attends. You might to stay in the team hotel on trips, to be at the venue and the places where they eat. Many times athletes will be hesitant to sign up for some kind of scheduled meeting but they will talk to the consultant or the coach for long periods of time informally. A tremendous amount of psychological skills training counseling can go on in these informal settings. Therefore a coach or a consultant might decide that he or she will meet with their athletes as a group two days a week formally. Then informally, perhaps without the athlete even knowing, he or she will make sure that individual meetings with each athlete on a team will occur every two weeks.

A very important point in deriving this type of training schedule is when and how long that schedule should last. It has been the experience of many North American sport psychologists that it is best to develop psychological skills training programs just before the season begins or in the off-season. During this period there is no pressure of competition and the coaches and athletes have a month or six weeks to work together developing these skills. In the competitive season the time available for formal and informal meetings is greatly reduced because of the athlete's or team's hectic schedule. However, if the psychological skills program was initiated in the off-season, the athletes will have skills developed for use in the competitive season. Further, the limited number of consulting meetings available during the competitive season are best focused on solving current problems.

Finally, the content of the meetings with the athletes must be determined. The content of the meeting depends a great deal on the scope and sequence of the program. Thus decisions need to be reached on appropriate exercises. Perhaps psychological tests are appropriate for use in assessing the athletes. The previously mentioned text by Rainer Martens (1) entitled the **Coaches' Guide to Sport Psychology** provides a number of excellent exercises coaches can use to help athletes learn and practice skills related to areas such as imagery, confidence and relaxation. Similarly, Orlick has developed packaged psychological skills training programs which can be implemented by coaches or consultants (17, 18).

Step Five: Organize your psychological skills training program. Once the schedule is derived it is necessary to organize the psychological skills program. Martens (1) has indicated that there are three general phases to any psychological skills training program. These phases are (a) an education phase, (b) an acquisition phase, and (c) a practice phase.

In the education phase, the goal is to help the athlete recognize the importance of learning psychological skills, and to facilitate their understanding of how these skills affect their performance. Further, it must be emphasized that athletes can learn and develop their psychological skills.

The education phase may last one day or a week. It may consist of anywhere from a one hour meeting to a two to three hour meeting. The discussion in this phase focuses on talking about psychological skills, the importance of psychological skills for competitive performance at the elite level and giving examples of how athletes have learned to develop their psychological skills.

The acquisition phase follows the education phase. In this phase the bulk of the formal and informal meetings would be devoted to teaching specific strategies to each athlete. For example, a formal meeting with a group of athletes may be focused on relaxation training. This session would involve specific relaxation technique instruction. This formal session would be followed up by sessions working with individual athletes to teach them how to use relaxation in their actual competitive environment. More specifically, a consultant working with a small group of 10,000 meter runners might conduct a one hour session on relaxation training where he or she teaches basic relaxation techniques. Following this general meeting, the consultant could meet individually with athletes on the track focusing on extending these relaxation skills into the actual race or practice condition.

During the acquisition phase specific strategies for each athlete must be developed which are tailored to each athlete's unique way of responding. As previously mentioned, psychological skills training is much like physical skills training in that there are tremendous individual differences in adaptation to training. Further, individual differences in terms of skill deficits must be taken into account.

Let us extend our relaxation example further. Some athletes will experience a mental worry type of anxiety or tension. Other athletes will experience a more somatic or body type anxiety. Knowing this individual difference variable may dictate the use of a different relaxation strategy for the individuals experiencing the different types of tension (19). It may be more appropriate to utilize a cognitively based strategy with an athlete who has primarily cognitive anxiety. Conversely, it may be more appropriate to use more of a deep muscle strategy or physical relaxation strategy for an athlete who has more somatic anxiety. Clearly, awareness of individual athlete characteristics is imperative to making these sorts of judgments.

After the athlete has assimilated the skill, they need to move into the practice phase. In this phase they adapt the specific acquired techniques into their own routine. For example, some athletes always use imagery before they compete while others would never use it before competition. Some athletes are actually able to use relaxation techniques while they compete, like a runner telling him or herself to "be loose", "stay loose", or "easy" Others will not utilize relaxation techniques this way. Some athletes have extensive, detailed goal systems while others have general goal systems. What is important in the practice phase is that these individual difference variables are allowed to surface. The skills must be tailored to the athlete's particular needs and personality.

An additional technique that is very helpful in the practice phase involves the maintenance of a log book. In the log book, the athletes should record their experiences with a particular skill application and rate the effectiveness. This systematic approach to skill development allows the athlete to chart his or her progress, evaluate the effectiveness of particular approaches, and select those strategies that are most effective. For example, after every practice the athlete could identity how tense they are, if their relaxation technique worked, and the precise relaxation technique employed. Through this methodical approach the relaxation techniques can be progressively evaluated and modified to maximize strategy effectiveness in helping the athlete to deal with stress in the competitive environment.

Step Six: Evaluation of changes in athlete psychological skills. The evaluation of psychological skills development or change is an important but often overlooked step. Some attempt should be made to ask the participants whether they feel the program is effective or ineffective in helping them. It may be the case that the programs are ineffective because the skills are not being presented in a way that is easily digested by the athlete. Conversely, the athletes may want to spend more time discussing an area than the consultant or coach thought. Some form of evaluation is necessary. It could be as simple as asking the athletes how the program is progressing, or having them complete some simple rating scales. This information can effectively facilitate the program development through knowledge of what is working and what is not.

Ideally it is best to identify ways to assess the effectiveness of the program prior to implementation. The a priori determination of indices for evaluation allows for an objective assessment of the program. Further, it allows for precise data collection to these ends. For example, if a strategy is devised for helping an athlete with low confidence to shoot better basketball free throws, it might be appropriate to evaluate this program on the percentage of shoots made in critical game situations. Normally free throw statistics are charted but not free throws in terms of critical game situations. This additional statistic could be kept to allow for evaluation of the program's effectiveness. This objective measure in combination with the athlete's subjective evaluation would provide a well rounded appraisal of the benefits of the enterprise.

Step Seven: Identify obstacles to psychological skills training and devise solutions to overcome them. This final step is important. Even though this step appears last in the planning sequence, it should permeate the entire process. Obstacles to psychological skills training must be identified and solutions for overcoming these obstacles must be developed. For example, a consultant may be very motivated to develop a goal setting program. He or she may work very hard with the athletes and get them into a program within a week or two. Suddenly the program comes to halt. Even though the consultant was very highly motivated to conduct the program perhaps the coaches were not. Consequently the coaches do not follow up on the goal setting sessions with feedback to the athletes on whether goals are being achieved. Perhaps the athletes were not as motivated as they could be or the consultant designed an ineffective program. Alternatively, there might have been a team in the facility immediately after the practice and thus program implementation was awkward and limited.

The key is to conduct an assessment with the personnel involved concerning likely obstacles to be faced prior to program implementation. These obstacles can range from athlete or coach motivation deficits to lack of facilities. There may be a lack of funds or insufficient time for the consultant to work with all of the athletes. Further, it may be the case that the consultant's personality may not interact well with the team or that the consultant does not demonstrate effective consultant characteristics (20, 21). While it is impossible to characterize all of the potential obstacles, the foreseeable obstacles should be identified. Once they are delineated, possible solution need to be derived.

For example, imagine that for some reason the consultant is constrained to four hours a week to spend with the team. Further, imagine that there are twenty athletes on the team and the coaches want individual meetings. This program would be doomed to failure because it is impossible to meet the coaches' expectations on only four hours a week. By anticipating this, the consultant can discuss an alternative viable schedule with the administrators and coaches. Perhaps they could decide on two group sessions a week and two individual sessions a week. The individual sessions could involve a total of three athletes. Further, the individual sessions could involve primarily the athletes that are most receptive or those the coaches feel need the program the most.

It is critical to identify obstacles ahead of time and to derive solutions for overcoming these obstacles. Waiting to be confronted with foreseeable obstacles only makes them more difficult to deal with. They will impair program effectiveness. Further, there is considerable potential for the consultant to lose credibility with the athletes. These obstacles are barriers to delivery on a promise given by the consultant regarding psychological skill development. To maximize his or her effectiveness in upholding this promise, the consultant must work to identify and derive solutions to these obstacles.

Summary

In conclusion, this review provides general guidelines that it is hoped will assist sport scientists in psychologically preparing elite athletes for optimizing their performance. It is of utmost importance to remember, however, that wide individual differences exist between athletes in terms of their particular psychological skills training program needs. Moreover, this review is based on research and professional experience with North American athletes. Hence, it would be best to use this information as a general guide, adapting and modifying it for the unique conditions and characteristics of Asian athletes. This also underscores the need for conducting research on the application of sport psychology for performance optimization in Asia. Only then will it be possible to identify what principles are universal across cultures and what principles are culture specific.

References

1. Martens A. *Coaches Guide to Sport Psychology.* Champaign,IL: Human Kinetics, 1987.
2. Nideffer RM. Current concerns in sport psychology. In : Silva JM.& Weinberg AS., eds. *Psychological foundations of sport.* Champaign. IL: Human Kinetics, 1984, 35–44.
3. Gould D. *Sport psychology : Future directions in youth sport research.* In Smoll FL., Magill RA. & Ash MJ. *Children in sport (3rd edition).* Champaign, IL: Human Kinetics, 1988, 317–344.
4. Weiss MR. *Who will take care of the children. Association for the Advancement of Applied Sport Psychology Newsletter,* 1989, *4* (3), 7.
5. Griffith C. Psychology and it's relations to athletic competition. *Amer. Phys. Educ. Rev.,* 1925, 30 193–199.
6. Gould D., Hodge K., Peterson K. & Petllchkoff, L. Psychological foundations of coaching : Similarities and differences among intercollegiate wrestling coaches. *The Sport Phychologist,* 1987, *1,* 293–308.

7. Gould D., Hodge K., Peterson K. & Giannini J. An exploratory examination of strategies used by elite coaches to enhance self-efficacy in athletes *Journal of Sport and Exercise Psychology,* 1989, *11*, 128–140

8. Kimiecik J. & Gould D. Coaching psychology : The case of James "Doc" Counsilman. *The Sport Psychologist,* 1987, *1,* 350–358.

9. Gould D., Tammen V., Murphy S. & May J. An examination of U.S. Olympic sport psychology consultants and the services they provide. *The Sport Psychologist.* In Press, *3* (4).

10. Orlick T. & Partington J. *Psyched : Inner views of winning.* Ottawa, Canada: Coaching Association of Canada. 1989.

11. Williams, JM. Psychological characteristics of peak performance. In : Williams JM. Ed. *Applied Sport Psychology: Personal Growth to Peak Performance.* Palo Alto, CA : Mayfield Publishing : 1986.

12. Mahoney MJ., Gabriel TJ. & Perkins, TS. Psychological skills and exceptional athletic performance. *The Sport Psychologist,* 1987, *1* (3), 181–199.

13. Gould D., Murphy S., Tammen V. & May J. *An assessment of psychological programs and personnel in U.S. amateur sports (1984 –1988)* A *report to the U.S. Olympic Committee.* Colorado Springs, Colorado, 1989.

14. Orlick T. & Partington J. Mental links to excellence. *The Sport Psychologist,* 1988. 2(2), 105–130.

15. Murphy, S. The on-site provision of sport psychology services at the 1987 U.S. Olympic Festival. *The Sport Psychologist, 1988,* 2(4),337–350.

16. Ravizza K. Gaining entry with athletic personnel for season-long consulting. *The Sport Psychologist,* 1988, 2(3), 243–254.

17. Orlick T. *Coaches training manual to psyching for sport.* Champaign, IL: Leisure Press, 1986.

18. Orlick T. *Psyching for sport : Mental training for athletes.* Champaign, IL: Leisure Press 1986.

19. Martens R., Burton D & Vealey R. *Competitive anxiety in sport* (3rd edition) Champaign. IL: In Press. (1989).

20. Orlick T. & Partington J. The sport psychology consultant: Analysis of critical components as viewed by Canadian Olympic athletes. *The Sport Psychologist,* 1987, *1*(1), 4–17.

21. Partington J. & Orlick T. The sport psychology consultant: Olympic coaches' views. *The Sport Psychologist,* 1987, *1*(2), 95–102.

25 Mental Training With Children for Sport and Life

TERRY ORLICK AND NADEANE MCCAFFREY
University of Ottawa

Children's sport participation has been a major focus of sport and exercise psychology. The issue of facilitating youngsters' psychological growth, development, and well-being through sport participation has been of particular importance not only in the relatively narrow domain of sport and exercise but also from a much broader sociocultural perspective. In this context, sport and exercise psychology includes a special emphasis on subjects such as children's experienced stress levels, self-esteem, and ineffective coaching.

For over three decades, Canadian sport psychologist Terry Orlick has been known for his ongoing contribution to the issue of helping child athletes to cope with stress. Orlick and his colleagues maintain that general directions related to mental training are not enough in this respect. According to their reasoning, to be adequately used with children, adult arousal regulation, stress management, and anxiety-reduction techniques (such as progressive relaxation, breath control, desensitization, biofeedback-based programs, cognitive-affective strategies, and autogenic training) should be modified and adapted to the specific requirements of this unique population. When such a strategy is appropriately applied, mental training becomes more relevant and even fun to kids. Moreover, Orlick argues that children's stress can be alleviated by reducing the significance of winning and the social evaluation embedded in their athletic surrounding. He claims that adults should make concerted efforts to facilitate the development of confidence in child athletes by expressing constructive attitudes toward mistakes and creating a positive, nonevaluative environment for children.

In this article, Orlick and McCaffrey present some key elements associated with this team's most successful mental training interventions with children of all age groups in and outside sport. The authors demonstrate how they have applied their philosophy of teaching children mental skills and positive perspectives, which will presumably contribute to the improvement of the general quality of their future lives far beyond the relatively narrow domain of sport and exercise.

In recent years we have applied mental skills training for child athletes, kindergarten and elementary school students, and children attempting to overcome serious illnesses. Key elements that have been associated with our most successful interventions include the use of simple, concrete strategies, an element of fun, positive individualized approaches, the use of role models, and involving parents. It is our belief that every child will experience growth, and some degree of success, if someone who cares devotes time to nurturing important mental skills related to personal development.

Mental training for children has been in effect in selected sport settings in Canada for approximately 20 years. These programs have been aimed primarily at helping children keep sport in perspective and teaching them basic mental skills for relaxation, imagery, focusing, and refocusing. Sweden has been implementing mental skills training programs with schoolchildren for a number of years and is the only country in the world where mental training is part of the normal elementary school curriculum. The focus of the Swedish program is on teaching relaxation skills, imagery, and stress control "triggers" (Solin, 1991).

Recently we have begun to introduce a mental training skills program to normal elementary school children through the medium of play and games (Cox, 1991; Orlick, 1992b). We have also been adapting mental skills successfully used in sport for children fighting to overcome life-threatening illnesses. Elements of mental training for life, sport, and illness will be the focus of this article.

In each of these arenas it is important to solicit the support of parents, teachers, coaches, and other caregivers. They are in a position to help prevent or reduce unnecessary stresses within the environment. They are also in a position to reinforce the healthy perspectives and mental skills we are attempting to teach. Wherever possible, they should be part of the process or at least be provided with appropriate readings that explain and support your perspective (Orlick, 1986a, 1992a, 1992b; Orlick & Botterill, 1975).

Cases in Point

A group of kindergarten children were asked whether they sometimes worry about things that have happened (like spilling paint or milk) or about things that might happen. They shared some of the things that worry them and we chatted about whether worrying really helps. We then shared ideas on how we might worry less or put our worries to rest.

Adapted, by permission, from T. Orlick and N. McCaffrey, 1991, "Mental training with children for sport and life," *Journal of Sport Psychology* 5: 322-334.

Later that same day we went outside and hiked to a nearby pond to observe clusters of frogs' eggs and other forms of aquatic life. To get a closer view, one of the little boys walked along a fallen log on the edge of the shallow pond. Before long he slipped off the log into the water, soaking his shoes and socks. His eyes darted up with a sheepish look, hinging on terror to see if I had noticed. I quickly looked away in an attempt to spare him unnecessary guilt. At almost the same instant one of the little girls blurted out, "Oh look, Alex got his feet wet." She hesitated for a second, and then continued by saying, "Oh, but it doesn't matter because it's already did, and we can't do magic."

She pointed out his predicament but also reminded him and the rest of us to keep things in perspective. Drawing upon the image of magic to clarify the concept of being unable to control the past was all hers. I had never mentioned the word magic. She was telling us in her own words that we cannot do magic and control the past, so we should not worry in vain, for we cannot do anything about it. Her comments seemed to calm Alex and he breathed a sigh of relief. Most gratifying for me was that my message had gotten through.

Andrew, a 9-year-old cancer patient with whom I had worked for over 2 years, was interviewed by a reporter about his treatment and his recovery. He was very forthright with his responses. He told the interviewer that when you are fighting for your life you have to be positive, look for good things, do some fun things, believe in yourself, and imagine yourself being strong and healthy. He informed her that it's not too hard to do if you really want to do it. His mother commented to me, "when he talks to the media about his illness and his recovery, he sounds just like you. It's like your thoughts are coming out of his mouth." The most important point here is that the message had gotten through.

Some specific mental approaches that Andrew commented on as being helpful to him included imagery and refocusing. With respect to imagery, he said, "Every time I got medicine I would think about a big lego spaceship [the medication] killing these small, bad lego guys [the cancer cells]." With respect to refocusing, he said, "I wanted to get my mind off everything that had happened and try to get started on what should happen, like going back to school and doing other things I wanted to do."

When asked what suggestions he had for other children facing a similar situation, Andrew said they shouldn't give up hope. His advice to them was to "think positive. Think 'I'm going to beat this'." He lived this perspective and it very likely influenced the fact that he has been off treatment for a number of years.

Each of these examples emphasizes the value of carrying a healthy perspective and points out the importance of being able to draw upon mental skills such as imagery and refocusing. Our work in providing mental training services for children in and out of sport has demonstrated to us that children are highly capable of learning and applying a variety of important mind/body skills (e.g., imagery, goal setting, relaxation, focusing, and refocusing). They can apply these mental skills in a multitude of settings, for example in play, games, sport, academics, school, music, dance, performing arts, at home, during conflicts, when experiencing fear, during treatments, or when recovering from illness or injury. The applications for mental training reach far beyond sport psychology.

Philosophy of Service

Our ultimate goal with children is to teach them relevant mental skills and positive perspectives that will enhance their quality of living. There is a great advantage in beginning this process at an early age to establish a concrete foundation of belief in themselves and in their capacity to directly influence the course of their own lives. Children who learn these mental skills early have more time to apply them to living their lives and pursuing their goals. For example, focusing and imagery skills can help children pursue anything they would like to accomplish.

With respect to stress control, it may seem ridiculous to teach stress control skills to children. In the perfect world they would not need these skills, but we do not live in the ideal world. So as we continue trying to improve the environment that children face, by intervening with adults, we must also place appropriate mental skills in the hands and minds of children.

Children are definitely a special group of people from whom we can learn a great deal. They are playful, imaginative, open, and also vulnerable. It is important to recognize and respect their unique qualities and be sensitive to their vulnerabilities. To be effective with children we must draw from their qualities and strengths, listen to their perspectives, use their input and, perhaps most important, care about them; otherwise we will never give them the special treatment they need and deserve. More than any other group, children want to know that you care before they care what you know.

Delivery of Service

Recently we developed a program of focusing and stress control activities specifically for preschool and elementary school children (Orlick, 1992a). The activities were designed to help children develop their mental strengths and stress control skills. One of the major objectives of developing these mental skills was to increase children's awareness of their capacity to control their own bodies, their own focus, and their own anxiety.

Our activities are presented to children in a fun-filled and supportive manner. They are introduced as "imagine" games or "focus" games and interspersed with more active cooperative games. Two sample activities from the program are presented below.

Spaghetti Toes. Before you introduce this activity, take out a piece of uncooked spaghetti. Let the children examine it. Let them see how stiff it is and how easily it breaks. Then take out a piece of cooked spaghetti. Let them examine it. Let them see how flexible it is and how easily it can curl up or change shape without breaking. The point you are trying to make here is that stiff, hard, tense spaghetti (uncooked) is much more fragile and breaks much more easily than flexible, soft, relaxed spaghetti (cooked). You emphasize that people are a bit like that too.

Leaf Connection. For the past 10 years, every autumn when the leaves are in full bloom I have gone out and gathered colorful leaves. I distribute one leaf to each student in my class and ask them to study their leaf very carefully. I want them to look for its designs and to connect totally with their leaf. I tell them in advance that after they have studied their leaf very closely, for a minute or two, we will mix all their leaves together and they will then each try to find their own leaf. Knowing they will have to find their leaf helps them focus. The amazing thing is that when they make an effort to really focus on their individual leaves, they all end up finding their leaf, even in large classes.

You can play this game with leaves from different trees, which makes it very easy, or take all the leaves from the same tree, which increases the need to focus well, but the children will still find their own leaf. You can even take fallen leaves from a single bush, where at first glance they all look exactly the same. If children look closely, they will discover that their leaf is distinct and they will be able to find it among many other leaves (Orlick, 1992a).

The overall program of focusing in stress control "games" has been very well received by classes from kindergarten through Grade 6. We found it to be a positive, fun way to introduce larger numbers of children to some basic mental skills (Cox, 1991). The children's assessments of these activities indicated that they "really liked them" and "felt relaxed" or "focused" while engaged in them. After playing some of these stress control games over a period of a week, a fourth grade girl wrote, "Thank you for teaching us how to relax because on Tuesday night I got mad at my sister and I got all tense. So I lay down and thought about drifting on a cloud. It worked. Thank you again. Suzy."

Individual Consultation

The basic procedure we follow in almost all our individual consulting work with children in sport and health enhancement is outlined below.

Consultation With Children in Sport. Our consulting with children in sport normally begins with a telephone call from a coach or parent. We ask what they hope to accomplish and discuss what we are able to provide. We then set a time to meet with the child (or team) before, during, or after their practice. We go to their sport environment, get a feel for it, and watch their practice. We then sit down with them and discuss their strengths and goals and whether they would like to be even stronger or more focused. We respect their input and follow their lead, much as we do with world class athletes.

We have found that many of the approaches we use with high performance athletes are relevant for children in sport, as long as the strategies and perspectives are explained, adapted, simplified, and presented in terms children understand. For example, most children enjoy doing imagery and simple relaxation procedures. They gain from developing simple individualized plans or routines for prepractice and precompetition situations and have some very creative ideas for dealing with hassles, stress, or distractions. We have also found that their mental skills improve dramatically with practice. For this reason we try to integrate mental skill refinement into their daily practice sessions. Children who are old enough and motivated in this direction can also read appropriate sections from relevant books (Orlick, 1986b, 1990, 1992a; Orlick & Partington, 1986).

The ideal situation is to incorporate mental skills (such as imagery or focusing) into the execution of every maneuver during practice sessions. Consistent input and reminders are often necessary to ensure that this happens on a daily basis. For example, a child diver can be encouraged to get into a routine of correctly "feeling" the takeoff and dive in his/her mind and body before doing every dive and then fully focus on executing it.

The ongoing integration of mental and physical skills with children is the key to mental skill refinement and personal excellence. When a particular mental skill or perspective is important to a child, we devise a way to ensure that it is integrated into his/her normal practice time in a natural way. This may require the cooperation of the child athlete and the coaching staff. It also helps when we spend time at practices, observe and monitor, and remind child athletes and coaches to implement their well-thought-out plans.

Reminders are a very important part of this learning process. If we are not available to serve as a reminder on a regular basis, we try to assign someone else to fulfill this role, for example an assistant coach who has the time and patience to help the child reach new heights and who has the child's best interests at heart. We also solicit input from children and coaches to fmd other good sources of positive reminders (e.g., videos, verbal reminders, signs on the wall or lockers, 3×5 reminder cards in gym bags, posters, key words on workout shirts, pictures with impact, a piece of tape on the wrist or finger, or a cue word on the shoe).

Applying Procedures to Other Areas. There are many areas in which our mental training teaching has proven extremely successful, but applying these principles to improving the quality of life for a seriously ill child has probably been the most rewarding. I got into this 7 years ago when a dear little friend was stricken with leukemia, and since then I have worked with a number of children and athletes with various forms of cancer and other major illnesses.

The parallels between our elite athletes going for gold and a child fighting for his or her life are numerous, and the bottom line is that neither is guaranteed success. Both have an overwhelming commitment to do whatever it takes to give themselves every opportunity to succeed, and their life revolves around achieving that goal. In pursuing their individual goals, both benefit from setting daily goals and long-term success goals, use of extensive imagery and various forms of relaxation, and planning for their respective "competitions." For the ill child this might include preparing for treatments (such as chemotherapy), torturous testing (such as bone marrow tests or lumbar punctures), the loss of control experienced in the clinic (hospital), or the ultimate, a bone marrow transplant, when the risk of death is real.

Both athlete and child need refocusing strategies when plans are not unfolding as hoped. Both need to leave the negatives behind and work on the positives, and both need to figure out how it can be better next time. The procedures we are teaching are very practical and simple, and when working with children, simple is best.

Imagery specifically related to healing includes seeing the treatment in a very positive light and knowing it has a specific beneficial purpose. Another important mental component of the treatment is not dwelling on the bad, negative, or painful elements (Ievleva & Orlick, 1991). Some of the treatments that children undergo, such as lumbar punctures or bone marrow tests, are best mentally blocked out completely because there are no lessons to be learned or easy ways to accept the painful procedures. The child, depending on age, may be given a "cocktail" (to induce a semiconscious state) or local anesthetic.

We try to teach them ways to detach themselves from their body through relaxation, music, or personalized scripts, all of which are tuned into on a walkman audiocassette. Since these particular treatments may be part of routine checkups for life, it is really valuable if early on you help them work out ways to survive the procedures while remaining unscarred mentally. The physical procedure, pain, and pressure remains the same, so something in the child's mind or focus must change. Incompetency or indifference that one sometimes encounters in the hospital delivery of the treatment procedure can be an added stressor for parent and child alike, for which both must be mentally prepared.

My work in the area of children with illnesses evolved by word of mouth. Parents would talk in a clinical waiting room or a social worker would refer a family because she recognized that a child could benefit from more one-on-one attention or more effective coping strategies. When I started in this area, in addition to applying the sportpsych principles of commitment, goal setting, plans of action, imagery, refocusing, and dwelling only on the positives, I also read relevant books related to self-directed healing (e.g., Achterberg, 1985; Cousins, 1979, 1989; Jaffe, 1980; Simonton & Matthews-Simonton, 1984; Simonton, Matthews-Simonton, & Creighton, 1978). I read anything I could find that related to taking charge of one's illness and asserting some control over it. Very little had been written specifically for children.

Children With a Serious Illness. The seriously ill children with whom we have worked are no different from many other children or child athletes of a similar age. They come from all walks of life, all income levels, and all sorts of family situations. Some are exceptionally bright, some are not. They have not been exposed to any more stress than other normal children, nor are their coping skills any less refined. The high stress profile normally associated with adults who are at a greater risk for disease (Achterberg, Matthews-Simonton, & Simonton, 1977; Siegel, 1986) does not seem to fit the children we have worked with. In almost all cases their illness or disease was totally unexpected and the source was unknown. Our purpose is to help these otherwise normal children to make the most of what they have and to control as much of their destiny as possible.

Initial contact is usually made through a telephone call from a social worker or parent. We set a time to meet the family. The parents may or may not be ready to talk freely, depending on how soon our meeting is after the disease has been diagnosed and the treatment protocol has been decided upon. Most of the time they are glad to talk with someone who knows the system, knows the drugs, is familiar with terminology and protocols, can relate to the doctors, nurses, and clinic setting, is sensitive and empathetic to the situation they face, and does not make glib offhand statements as to knowing their feelings or having simple answers.

The parents fill us in on the complete picture. This may take many hours and is not something one can break up into preset sessions. The initial introductions need a large block of time. We may start out by discussing how the child is coping and what are the real concerns. Some practical concerns may include finding a vein to administer the drugs, the child's fear and tension which restricts blood flow to the veins during the treatment session, the side effects of the drugs such as hair loss or vomiting, peer pressure, coping at school, panic that he/she may die, lack of trust of the staff at the clinic, or lack of empathy on the staff's part.

The discussion may then lead to siblings having to cope with the shift of attention, the added stress felt by the parents, guilt, or their own relationship because they have less time for each other. This is a normal family trying to cope with everyday concerns under very difficult circumstances. It is a family from any walk of life that has been dealt some very bad luck—their child being seriously ill. They want to talk about how they can survive this situation with the highest quality of living and the fewest disruptions to the family as a unit. Any of these parents would gladly trade places with their child so that their child would not have to suffer.

Our next meeting is with the child. We set aside a morning or an afternoon to get to know him or her, ask questions about his/her interests, and join the child in doing some things he/she likes to do. It could be painting, drawing, swimming, watching a movie or favorite TV program, or anything else a child of that age would do for fun. Even with a 3-year-old, you can make meaningful contact quite readily simply by playing with him/her. Another positive source of entry we have found effective for early interaction and acceptance with young children is a playful obedient dog who sometimes accompanies us.

It takes time and thought to make a real difference in the lives of children. We invest time in getting to know the child very well. It may take weeks of mornings or afternoons before we see some of our ideas registering. While we are engaged in play together, we suggest ways of dealing with a crisis as the child chatters about it in passing. We may ask, "How was treatment this week?" Sometimes it will be weeks before they are ready to share that particular topic with us. For children the treatment is undignified and a total loss of control. They feel abused and tortured.

To help them with treatment, we suggest they try certain things, such as feeling like jello or cooked spaghetti when the nurse is finding a vein. When a child is scared, tense, and highly stressed, it may require multiple attempts to find a vein (with a needle). During certain treatments it takes hours to administer the drugs, so we suggest alternatives to take their mind off the process. For example, we may suggest they listen to favorite music on a walkman, watch videos, bring games to play, or practice using various types of imagery. The imagery may relate to healing, being healthy, feeling how they want to be, perceiving the drug entering their body in a helpful way, or visualizing some goals they hope to attain.

One of the first questions we ask the children in a subtle way during play is to identify some goals. We don't ask what their goals are in life because most of them wouldn't know what we were talking about. We try to fmd out about some of their dreams or some things they would really like to do, or things that excite them. We find out what they're good at, what they want to be better at, what sports or activities they do well in, and why they feel good when engaged in these activities. We try to find out what they are up to this week: How is school going? What tests? What homework? Who are their friends? Why are they good friends?

Through this process we establish what is really important to them, set some goals, and set a plan for doing more of the things that make them feel great. A 7-year-old boy loved ice hockey, but because of his illness and treatment he did not have the stamina to skate with his teammates on the ice, but he was a great goalie. I suggested to his Dad that he do some extra work with the boy whenever possible to improve his goalie skills so that he would feel as much a part of the team as the best skaters out there.

One little girl said she loved clothes and enjoyed wearing all her nicest things to the clinic. I encouraged her to do this regularly so all the nurses would comment on how lovely she looked and would make a fuss over her. As a result she felt important and much more in control when she arrived at the clinic than would otherwise be the case. It was something positive.

I also suggest that the children take part in sport activities that don't involve too much wear and tear on the body or a great deal of intense activity. Swimming lessons that allow them to progress at their own pace, leisurely bike rides, horseback riding if they enjoy it, or cross-country skiing on easy terrain are some good examples. Other activities you can introduce include arts and crafts, sewing, constructing and building, music, or learning a musical instrument. The important point is that they should like the activity, have fun, see improvement or even success, and that it gives them joy, confidence, and belief in what they can do or produce.

For children who are having problems keeping up with a particular subject at school, I suggest a tutor to help them stay ahead of the game. Thus school won't become a burden or something that drags them down. Our goal is to help them experience more joy and to eliminate or reduce as many of the controllable stressors in their life as possible.

Our primary purpose is to give the children a sense of control and belief that when they set their mind to doing something, they can achieve it. This is accomplished by being very positive and by looking for ways to build their confidence and lift their spirits. The more positives you can add to a child's life, the more the child will be able to feel he/she can beat the illness and endure the treatment. The overall uplifting plan is usually discussed with the parents to create more opportunities to help the children feel good about themselves and to guide them toward some of their major goals.

Ultimately we are trying to create a very self-assured, cocky, totally full-of-him/herself individual who believes that anything is possible. You may not like the sound of this, but it is often essential for the child's wellness. At least internally the child must feel capable of beating anything in order to beat the illness and live.

We feel it is important to treat them as number one, the greatest, and to keep putting them in situations in which this is reinforced. If they are attending an oncology clinic for a number of years, they deserve whatever *special attention* they can get. The actual treatment is so horrendous for a child that without a tremendous amount of love and support it is impossible for the child to put it into the proper perspective.

Our mission is to allow children to have as much fun as possible and be able to control as much in their own life as they possibly can, outside of receiving treatment (over which they have little or no sense of control). They may gain a greater sense of control by pursuing subjects they love in or outside of school, by engaging in playful activities, and by doing more of the things that give them the most fun and pleasure.

Effectiveness

The fear of dying, and having so much to live for, combine to create a powerful motivation for survival. This is influenced by the extent to which a child has a support network of family and friends, how much pain she/he is experiencing, whether the treatment is working, and how much joy she/he is experiencing in life. If all of these components are working in the child's favor, the child may be able to develop a positive attitude that can prolong life. However, when a child is experiencing many setbacks and living through nonideal conditions, maintaining or instilling a positive attitude becomes progressively more difficult and critically important. This presents a real challenge. In the end all we can do is the best we can, given the conditions we face. Sometimes it is enough, sometimes it is not.

When we are effective with children, we have a meaningful impact with respect to enhancing life skills, coping skills, performance skills, self-confidence, and/or quality of living. This takes time and appears to occur most readily when the following conditions have been met:

Simple Strategies. Use simple approaches that allow the child to form a clear image or feeling of what he/she is attempting to accomplish. For example, a child can pretend he is a piece of cooked spaghetti to relax, imagine he is changing channels on a TV to change the focus in his mind, use a little marble bag ("stress bag") to place worries in, create internal performance images and feelings while watching a video of someone performing a skill, practice focusing with corn flakes by focusing on one flake and then finding it among a number of others (for additional examples, see Orlick, 1992a).

Keep it Fun. When working with children, it is important to keep an element of fun in your approach or integrate some fun into the strategy itself. A young child does not have fun going through a dry, matter-of-fact progressive muscle relaxation procedure. However, children do have fun pretending they are a piece of cooked spaghetti curling up on a plate, or wiggling and then relaxing their eyebrows, tongue, or toes. Turning an exercise into "playing a game" is the quickest way into a child's mind and heart.

Concrete, Physical Component. Strategies that allow a child to physically act out the removal of stress or physically act out an image seem to work best. For example, with respect to refocusing or shifting the focus away from worry, children relate well to putting "it" in a tree, in a match box, or in a stress bag. In a sport like gymnastics, putting the handgrips used for one event into a gym bag is an effective way to "put away" the last event and focus on the next.

Individualized Approach. Getting to know a child as a unique individual is very important. The better you get to know a child, the better you can understand her specific needs, draw upon her input, and adapt your approach to fit the reality of her situation. For example, we worked with a 4-1/2-year-old girl who was receiving treatment for a life-threatening illness. Her mother wanted a relaxation tape to help the child cope with the painful aspect of her treatment at the hospital. I spoke with the child about what she liked to watch on TV, what kinds of stories she liked and what pictures she drew, in an attempt to ascertain what kind of an image might work best for her. It turned out that she loved clouds, big white fluffy clouds. So her relaxation tape centered around floating on a big white fluffy cloud that she directed and controlled.

Multiple Approaches. If one approach does not work for a particular child, we simply try another. We do not view it as a failure but rather as another step on the way to success. As we get to know the children better and they begin to understand their options more clearly, approaches that fit the situation become more prevalent. This is also where our own creativity and persistence becomes important.

Be Positive and Hopeful. Whether you are working with children in sport or children with a serious illness, it is important that you project a positive belief in that child, in his/her strengths, and in his/her capacity to overcome obstacles and pursue personal goals.

Use Role Models. Most children respond well to the use of role models. If well chosen, a role model can set a positive example to emulate with respect to mental skills, physical skills, a healthy perspective, persistence, or anything else one might want to pursue. We often use videos of respected high performance athletes to help younger athletes form a clearer image of moves they might like to do.

We used a similar approach by drawing upon the recovery strengths of one of our best Olympic athletes. He had been stricken with cancer shortly before a world championship event and was told he had only a short time to live. He diligently applied all his sportpsych mental training skills toward his own healing; he set goals for wellness and listened to a personalized audiotape we made for him that included relaxation and imagery. His imagery was focused on seeing and feeling himself free his body from cancer, imagining successful outcomes, seeing himself fully recovered, and imagining himself competing stronger than ever before in his sport. He took charge of his disease in other ways by diet, vitamins, and herbal teas. He committed himself to wellness in the same diligent way that he pursued his goals in sport.

The extent to which his mental perspective influenced his complete recovery is difficult to determine, but it is clear that he took the responsibility for doing everything within his capabilities to heal himself; he freed his body from cancer and went on to compete successfully in the Worlds and the Olympics. We brought two children with cancer to watch him perform at a competition. He talked with them, showed them pictures of his bald head taken when he was undergoing chemotherapy, and set a quiet but strong example of persistence and success.

Involve Parents. One should draw upon all the support systems possible when working with children. Parents are central. Wherever possible, solicit their support for reinforcing the concepts, positive approaches, and healthy perspectives you are attempting to teach. Talk with parents about what you are attempting to do, explain why it is important, and request their ongoing assistance in encouraging these important objectives.

Conclusions

Key Ingredients

Some of the ingredients related to our best successes with mental training for children are outlined below. We have found that spending time with children in their environment is important. For children in sport this would normally mean attending some practices and competitions. For children pursuing wellness this would normally mean going to some of their treatments at the hospital clinic and spending some time at their home.

This is important for several reasons. First, it lets the child know you care enough about her to go to her place and spend time there. This generates a sense of trust and mutual caring. It allows you to see how the child functions in these important settings. It also enables you to see how she differs in one environment compared to the other with respect to focus, intensity, coping, interaction, or performance. It helps you get to know and understand the child, the sport or clinic, the coach or caregiver, and the real situation with which the child is faced. When strategies to improve personal control are suggested, being there allows you to see whether they are being implemented and the extent to which they are helpful. Being on site also facilitates interaction with children. When they trust you and know that you are there only for them, they sense that support and feel free to come up and talk to you.

Ongoing contact is another key to successful intervention with children. Ideally, contact should be made as often as possible to maintain a sense of trust, respect, and caring, and to keep updated on how things are progressing. This type of contact is often needed to guide the implementation of relevant mental skills, to monitor progress, and to give and receive feedback.

The use of daily goals is important and can be introduced in simple ways, for example by asking the child what he hopes to achieve today (at practice or at treatments) and how he will try to attain those goals today. For some children this can be extended to the use of simple logs, or diaries, to chart progress and draw out lessons. Mental skills or perspectives that are important must be integrated into the normal daily routine, whether in the gym or the clinic. Simple goals can help with this.

Reminding children of their strengths and their positive capacities is something that greatly benefits them. One must continue building upon the child's strengths and downplay negatives or perceived weaknesses. This is an important component of any mental training program, and for all those who work with children. Part of this process includes helping children to remember good things, reminding them to recall the times when something went well or when they had a good performance. Part of it involves reminding children to do things or think in ways that you have both agreed will help them achieve their personal goals and encouraging them to become responsible for their own thoughts and actions.

Guiding children into positive prepractice, precompetition, or pretreatment routines, encouraging them to think in positive or focused ways when going into these situations, and the frequent use of positive imagery on site have also been effective. In sport this includes "doing it" mentally before you do it physically, as well as correction imagery and success imagery. In clinics this includes positive imagery of treatment effects, success imagery, and imagery that mentally takes the child away from painful treatments.

Finally, we have to recognize and accept the fact that individual children have different goals and different ways of pursuing their goals. For child athletes and those pursuing higher levels of wellness, it is best if interventions are individualized to meet each child's preferences, goals, and needs.

If very young children enjoy your company, they will play with you and will respond to your initiatives. They will tell you by their actions and their responsiveness whether or not you are effective. You know you are getting through when they laugh and play and share their discoveries with you. With older children you know you are effective when they tell you they have been working on various strategies you have discussed and that a particular approach worked. They will be excited about that progress and will begin to feel a greater sense of personal control. Parents are also in a good position to give you feedback as to your effectiveness by sharing what they see the child doing and saying at home. You know they have arrived when you see children implementing strategies, talking about them, and sharing them with their parents or with other children.

We will never get rich through our consulting work with children, largely because of the time required to be effective. However, because we are committed to making a meaningful contribution to other human beings, we feel it is a great area to pursue. It is our belief that every child will experience growth, and some degree of success, if someone who cares devotes time to nurturing important mental skills related to human development.

For those who appreciate the qualities of childhood, consulting with children is extremely rewarding and lots of fun. Children continue to provide us with challenges to be creative and in the end we believe our greatest contributions will occur when we place in the hands of children some relevant mental skills for living.

References

Achterberg, J. (1985). *Imagery and healing: Shamanism and modern medicine.* Boston: New Science Library.

Achterberg, J., Matthews-Simonton, S., & Simonton, O.C. (1977). Psychology of the exceptional cancer patient: A description of patients who outlive predicted life expectancies. *Psychotherapy: Theory, Research and Practice,* 14, 416-422.

Cousins, N. (1979). *Anatomy of an illness.* New York: Bantam Books.

Cousins, N. (1989). *Headfirst: The biology of hope and the healing power of the human spirit.* New York: Penguin Books.

Cox, J. (1991). *Preliminary evaluation of Orlick's focusing and stress control games with elementary school children.* Unpublished manuscript, University of Ottawa.

Ievleva, L., & Orlick, T. (1991). Mental links to enhanced healing: An exploratory study. *The Sport Psychologist, 5,* 25-40.

Jaffe, D.T. (1980). *Healing from within.* New York: Simon & Schuster.

Orlick, T. (1986a). Evolution in children's sport. In M. Weiss & D. Gould (Eds.), *Sport for children and youth* (pp. 169-178). Champaign, IL: Human Kinetics.

Orlick, T. (1986b). *Psyching for sport.* Champaign, IL: Leisure Press.

Orlick, T. (1990). *In pursuit of excellence.* Champaign, IL: Leisure Press.

Orlick, T. (1992a). *Freeing children from stress: Focusing and stress control activities for children.* ITA Publications, PO Box 1599, Willits, CA.

Orlick, T. (1992b). *Nice on my feelings: Nurturing the best in children and parents.* ITA Publications, PO Box 1599, Willits, CA.

Orlick, T., & Botterill, C. (1975). *Every kid can win.* Chicago: Nelson Hall Publ.

Orlick, T., & Partington, J. (1986). *Psyched.* Ottawa: Coaching Association of Canada.

Siegel, B.S. (1986). *Love, medicine & miracles.* New York: Harper & Row.

Simonton, O.C., & Matthews-Simonton, S. (1984). A psychophysiological model for interventions in treatment of cancer. In J.S. Gordon, D.T. Jaffe, & D.E. Bresler (Eds.), *Mind, body, and health: Toward an integral medicine* (pp. 146-163). New York: Human Sciences Press.

Simonton, O.C., Matthews-Simonton, S., & Creighton, J.L. (1978). *Getting well again.* New York: Bantam Books.

Solin, E. (1991). *Mental training in the Swedish school systems.* Presented at the First World Congress on Mental Training, University of Orebro, Sweden.

26 The Coleman Roberts Griffith Address: Three Myths About Applied Consultancy Work

LEW HARDY
University of Wales, Bangor

Researchers in applied sport psychology have supported several tenets over the years. Their first recommendation is that cognitive anxiety is always detrimental to performance and should therefore be reduced whenever possible. However, Hardy advocates that when athletes experience cognitive anxiety without physiological arousal, these arousal symptoms may actually be facilitative.

The second recommendation is that outcome goals and ego orientation have a detrimental effect on performance-related variables, so performers should be encouraged to set performance rather than outcome goals. Hardy argues that elite athletes have a strong ego orientation and set outcome goals appropriately. Much of the research in this domain has used subjects in junior sport settings. One major limitation in applied sport psychology is a lack of research with elite athletes caused by a lack of access to these subjects. Hardy concludes this section by assimilating the literature on goal setting, and he purports four guiding principles for goal setting.

Hardy's third recommendation is that performers should not use internal visual imagery rather than external visual imagery. He suggests that one problem with previous research in this area is that internal imagery is inappropriately interpreted as kinesthetic imagery and there is no reason why performers would not be able to combine external visual images with kinesthetic images. A few other confounding effects include failure to consider the theoretical base for predictions of superiority for one visual perspective over another and the fact that performers often use a combination of imagery perspectives during mental rehearsal. Hardy suggests quite strongly that external visual imagery can be superior to internal visual imagery in at least some circumstances.

One major reason this is an essential reading is that it forces us to reconsider these tenets. As Hardy states, "It is only by constantly challenging what we think the research literature is telling us that we can ensure that our educated guesses are truly educated." His intention to question the way this literature is interpreted was achieved through this reading.

Three recommendations that are commonly made in the applied sport psychology literature are discussed. These three recommendations are: 1) cognitive anxiety is always detrimental to performance and should therefore be reduced whenever possible; 2) outcome goals and ego-orientations have a detrimental effect on a number performance-related variables, so that performers should be encouraged to set performance rather than outcome goals; 3) internal visual imagery is more beneficial to performance than external visual imagery, so performers should always be encouraged to use visual imagery from an internal perspective. For each of these recommendations, empirical and experiential evidence is presented which challenges the recommendation. Alternate refinements to the recommendations are discussed.

Myth 1: Cognitive Anxiety Is Always Detrimental to Performance

It is now generally well-established that anxiety responses can be divided into two relatively independent components: cognitive anxiety and somatic anxiety (see, for example, Jones & Hardy, 1990; or Martens, Vealey, & Burton, 1990). Cognitive anxiety has been defined as "the cognitive elements of anxiety, such as negative expectations and cognitive concerns about oneself, the situation at hand and potential consequences" (Morris, Davis, & Hutchings, 1981; p. 541), whereas somatic anxiety has been defined as "one's perception of the physiological-affective elements of the anxiety experience, that is indications of autonomic arousal and unpleasant feeling states such as nervousness and tension" (Morris et al., 1981; p. 541). Based on these definitions, cognitive anxiety is generally equated with worry, and somatic anxiety is generally equated with emotionality.

Many applied sport psychology practitioners appear to assume that cognitive anxiety, or worry, is necessarily detrimental to performance. For example, Harris and Harris (1984) stated that:

> Whenever we worry and become anxious we experience disruption and dysfunction to some degree. The more worried we become, the more anxiety we experience and the greater the degree of disruption to performance. (p. 29).

In fairness to applied practitioners, it is not difficult to see how they arrived at this assumption, since it is a basic tenet of multidimensional anxiety theory (Martens et al.,

1990). However, I would like to argue that, reasonable though the assumption might appear, it is in fact a myth. Evidence against this myth can be found as early as 1977, from Mahoney and Avener's classic study of Olympic trialists for the United States Gymnastics Team. Mahoney and Avener (1977) reported that:

> verbal interviews suggested that the more successful athletes tended to "use" their anxiety as a stimulant to better performance. The less successful gymnasts seemed to arouse themselves into near-panic states by self-verbalizations and images which belied self-doubts and impending tragedies. (p. 140).

Other examples of anecdotal evidence can also be found, but I would prefer to focus upon some of the more recent quantitative evidence that addresses this issue. A study by Hardy and Parfitt (1991) compares free throw performance of female basketball players. The players were tested on two occasions: one day prior to a major basketball tournament when they were cognitively anxious; and two days after the tournament when they were not cognitively anxious. On each of these two occasions, the basketball players attempted five free throws under ten different physiological arousal conditions. The results showed that, when subjects were cognitively anxious, their best free throw performance was significantly better, and their worst free throw performance significantly worse, than when they were not cognitively anxious.

Thus, high levels of cognitive anxiety were associated with either very good performance or very bad performance, depending upon the precise physiological arousal conditions pertaining. This finding has been replicated by Hardy, Parfitt, and Pates (1994) using crown green bowling. Crown green bowling is a peculiarly British game in which the players attempt to roll a handball-sized wooden ball as close as possible to a target ball (called the "jack"), possibly knocking the balls of opponents out of the way during the process. Other studies by Edwards and Hardy (1996), and Woodman, Albinson, and Hardy (1997), have also demonstrated interactive effects between cognitive and somatic anxiety which suggest that cognitive anxiety does not necessarily have a detrimental effect upon performance. In summary, then, there is ample evidence to question the assumption that cognitive anxiety is always detrimental to performance. It therefore seems reasonable to attempt to offer some sort of explanation as to *how* cognitive anxiety might be able to induce either beneficial or detrimental effects upon performance.

Potential Explanations of Mixed Positive and Negative Cognitive Anxiety Effects

It seems clear (to the present author, at least) that cognitive anxiety and somatic anxiety probably do *not* exert separate additive effects upon motor performance. Rather, they exert an interactive effect in which only the combination of high levels of both cognitive and somatic anxiety is particularly detrimental to performance. One possible explanation for these interactive effects can be found in the work of Jones, Swain, and associates (Jones, Hanton, & Swain, 1994; Jones and Swain, 1992; Jones, Swain, & Hardy, 1993; Swain & Jones, 1996). This has shown that the way in which performers interpret their anxiety symptoms is more important than the intensity of the symptoms that they experience. Furthermore, putting these two sets of results together, Hardy (1996) has argued that performers who are simultaneously experiencing high levels of cognitive anxiety and high levels of physiological arousal may interpret their anxiety symptoms as being detrimental to performance, so that they subsequently are detrimental. Conversely, performers who are experiencing high levels of cognitive anxiety without simultaneously high levels of physiological arousal may interpret their anxiety symptoms as being facilitative to performance, so that they subsequently are facilitative (see also Hardy, Jones, & Gould, 1996).

A rather more fine grained level of analysis is offered by Eysenck and Calvo's (1992) processing efficiency theory. Eysenck and Calvo review extensive evidence which suggests that cognitive anxiety may exert an influence upon performance via at least two different processes. First, cognitive anxiety may cause a reduction in the information processing resources which are available for the task at hand because vital resources are used up in worry, self-concern, and other task-irrelevant cognition. However, cognitive anxiety may also have a motivational effect upon performance by signaling to the performer the importance of the upcoming event, and the need to muster all available resources in order to perform the necessary actions at the required level. Thus, according to processing efficiency theory, cognitive anxiety may exert a beneficial effect upon performance, provided the cognitive demands of the task are not too great. Hardy (1996) has taken this proposal a stage further and argued that such (negative) cognitions may be precisely what is needed in order for performers to muster the very high levels of motivation and commitment that may be necessary in order to perform at the absolute limits of their capabilities.

In earlier formulations of processing efficiency theory, Eysenck (1982) also emphasized the role of self-confidence in the motivational effects of anxiety upon performance. More precisely, Eysenck proposed that cognitive anxiety only exerted a positive motivational effect if the performer was at least moderately confident of success. If the performer was not at least moderately confident of success, then Eysenck (1982) proposed that all effort would be withdrawn from the task. These proposals are consistent with the finding of Jones et al. (1993) that high levels of self-confidence were moderately associated with a positive interpretation of anxiety symptomatology. Thus, in the words of Revelle and Michaels (1976), "the tough get going when the going gets tough", but "wise men do not beat their heads against brick walls"! Similar arguments have also been proposed by Carver and Scheier (1988) except that they argue that the performer's perception of control is the crucial variable rather than the performer's self-confidence. The interested reader is referred to Hardy et al. (1996) where all these issues are discussed in more detail.

Applied Implications

A number of applied implications can be generated from the above line of reasoning. First, performers should be helped to understand that cognitive anxiety is a natural response to the circumstances in which they find themselves. To tell someone who is just about to perform in the Olympic Games that they should not be worried seems a trifle naive. Rather, performers should be encouraged to interpret their worries and concerns positively and believe that these same worries and concerns can help them to prepare better for the event, provided that they believe that they are "in with a good chance". For this reason, it seems a good idea to encourage performers to get cognitively anxious as early as possible before a major event so that they can use the worry to gain maximum motivational benefits during their training in the lead up to the event. Such a strategy also has the benefit of allowing the performer to get accustomed to their cognitive anxiety and get it under control (cf., Fenz & Epstein, 1967, 1968; Mahoney & Avener, 1977).

Second, the performer's training and competitive experiences during the lead-up to a major competition must be carefully organized and structured to maximize self-confidence. This might seem like a statement of the obvious, but I suspect that this ideal is rarely realized. For example, it is well known that physical experiences, imagery and self-talk can all be used to enhance self-confidence (Bandura, 1986), and that they all are used by elite performers (Hardy et al., 1996); yet it is also known that coaches usually make use of only the first of these mechanisms (physical experiences; Gould, Hodge, Peterson, & Giannini, 1989).

Other findings in the research which has been reviewed above suggests that when cognitive and somatic anxiety do interact to induce decrements in performance, these decrements are likely to be large, to occur suddenly, and to be difficult to recover from (for details, see Hardy, 1996; Hardy et al , 1996). This suggests that sport psychologists should use "psyche-up" strategies with caution because some performers could easily get "psyched-out", rather than psyched-up. It also suggests that performers should be encouraged to learn multiple relaxation strategies which enable them to independently control cognitive and somatic anxiety (cf., Burton, 1990). Finally, the same research suggests that controlled activation skills are an important, and possibly rather neglected, area of applied sport psychologists' work.

Myth 2: Performers should set Performance rather than Outcome Goals

At least three different types of goal can be distinguished in the sport psychology literature (Burton, 1992, 1993; Hardy et al., 1996). Outcome goals focus upon the end points of particular events and usually (but not always) involve interpersonal comparison of some kind; for example, finishing first in a half-marathon race. Performance goals also specify end products of performance, but this time the end product is usually expressed in terms of personal achievement and is relatively independent of other performers. They are often numeric in nature; for example, running the half-marathon race in under 70 minutes. Process goals, on the other hand specify the processes in which the performer will engage in order to perform satisfactorily; for example, maintain a given effort level or technique at different stages during the race. Similarly, at least two different types of goal orientation can be distinguished in the goal orientations literature (Duda, 1992; Nicholls, 1989). Ego-oriented performers formulate their perceptions of competence by comparing their own ability with that of others, whereas task-oriented performers base their perceptions of competence on absolute measures of performance or on personal improvement. Unfortunately, current conceptualizations of task orientation appear to confound "personal improvement" with "process".

A substantial proportion of the literature has invested in making comparisons between subjects who are encouraged to set outcome goals and subjects who are encouraged to set of performance goals. In general, these studies have shown that performers who doubt their own personal competence are likely to feel highly anxious, believe that they are unable to cope, and feel that there is little point in trying, when they are confronted with a situation that emphasizes the importance of the outcome (for example, winning). Other (correlational) studies have suggested that, compared with performers who are low in task orientation, performers who are high in task orientation are likely to practice more during their free time, and exert more effort in order to achieve high levels of performance. Finally, retrospective studies suggest that young drop-outs from sport may have stronger ego orientations than continuers (for a review of all these studies, see Duda, 1992). In light of these findings, many applied sport psychology consultants appear to concur with Weinberg's (1988) conclusion that athletes should be encouraged to "set performance goals instead of outcome goals" (p.153). Others have gone further than this. For example, following a review of athletes' views about sport, Duda (1992) concluded that high levels of ego orientation were associated with cheating. Such a view of ego orientation is very close to saying that people who want to compete (i.e., have a strong ego orientation) are "bad guys" and people who want to "play nicely" and not compete are "good guys". However, Hardy et al. (1996)

have presented a number of arguments which suggest that the issues surrounding ego orientation and outcome goals are not quite this simple.

First of all, the notion that high ego orientations are detrimental to performance and predispose one to drop out does not sit very comfortably with the notion that goals motivate and direct behaviour (Burton, 1992; Hardy et al., 1996; Locke & Latham, 1990). For, if goals really do motivate and direct behaviour, it is not easy to see how performers could become world champions without having strong ego orientations and setting outcome goals. In fact, there is very little evidence to suggest that ego-orientations *per se* have a detrimental effect upon performance-related variables. Rather, the available evidence suggests that it is the combination of ego-orientations with low perceptions of competence that leads to such effects. Furthermore, it seems reasonable to expect that elite performers might generally have higher, rather than lower, perceptions of their competence. Indeed, a lack of concern for issues involved in generalizing from one population to another seems to have been a defining feature of attempts to apply the goal orientations literature to high level sport. For example, much of the literature on goal orientations uses children in physical education and junior sport settings as subjects. Can these findings reasonably be expected to generalize to high level performers?

Second, although it may be interesting from an applied perspective to consider the effects of different motivational climates upon various performance-related variables, making comparisons of ego-orienting instructions against task-orienting instructions ignores an important distinction between task and ego orientations. Factor analytic studies on the Task and Ego Orientation in Sport Questionnaire (TEOSQ) have consistently demonstrated the orthogonality, as opposed to the bipolarity, of task and ego orientation (Duda, 1992). Thus, what is really required are studies that examine both the separate and the interactive effects of task and ego orientation. Making comparisons between subjects who are ostensibly high in task orientation against subjects who are ostensibly high in ego orientation amounts to a comparison of "apples with oranges" (cf., Hardy et al., 1996) and does not make a lot of sense theoretically. Rather, a number of different lines of research suggest that successful performers have multiple perceptions of competence and use outcome, performance, and process goals to good effect (Goudas, Fox, Biddle, & Armstrong, 1992; Jones & Hanton, 1996; Kingston & Hardy, 1994, in press, in preparation).

Jones and Hanton (1996) showed that high level athletes naturally set more than one type of goal for any particular event. The vast majority of the swimmers in their study set at least two different types of goal for the races in question, and almost half of them set all three types of goal. Similarly, Goudas et al., (1992) showed that the combination of high ego orientation plus high task orientation is associated with superior performance. Finally, a recent study by Kingston and Hardy (in preparation) compared the goal orientations of professional, county amateur, low handicap amateur, and high handicap amateur golfers across three different situational contexts. Of primary interest to the present discussion was the fact that, as competition approached, the professionals and high handicap amateurs significantly increased their ego orientation. The county amateur and low handicap amateur golfers maintained a stable ego orientation. However, the increase in ego orientation of the high handicap golfers was accompanied by a significant loss of task orientation. This was not the case for the professional golfers (or for either of the other two low handicap groups). Thus, it appears that professional, good amateur, and poor golfers may approach competition in radically different ways. The professional may try to use the competition as an additional source of motivation, while at the same time maintaining his or her process focus. The gifted amateur may try to treat the competition as though it were "just another round"; but the high handicap golfer focuses upon outcome goals to the detriment of his or her process focus.

In another study, Hardy and Pearce (in preparation) examined the effects of different goal orientations on the investment of effort in rock climbers attempting to lead a hard route. The results showed that task orientation and ego orientation interacted in such a way that the combination of high task and high ego orientation was particularly beneficial to on task effort. Taken together, the above findings suggest that strong ego orientations and outcome goals could have very beneficial effects under certain circumstances.

Finally, the suggestion that high ego orientations predispose performers to cheat does not sit very comfortably with Hemery's (1991) report that over 80% of the elite performers whom he interviewed reported that they would not intentionally foul or cheat. However, the study upon which Duda (1992) based her conclusion that ego orientations were associated with cheating (Duda, Olson, & Templin, 1991) asked subjects whether or not they would cheat in order to win. Winning is clearly not greatly relevant to someone who has a high task, but a low ego, orientation. It therefore remains quite possible that someone with a high task orientation might cheat in order to achieve something that was important to them. For example, as Hardy et al. (1996) postulate, "how many of us can honestly say that we have never 'cut corners' in order to achieve a new personal best? Yet such goals are clearly task oriented, and we are indeed only cheating on ourselves" (p.80).

Potential Explanations of the Goal Orientations and Goal-setting Literature

As reported above, it seems probable that high level performers have multiple conceptions of ability and make good use of all three different types of goal that have been discussed. Based on arguments similar to the ones that have been presented above, Hardy et al. (1996) concluded that:

> . . . elite performers may channel their ego orientation into long-term goals such as winning a World Championships or an Olympics in

> order to sustain their motivation over long and difficult training periods. Similarly, they may channel their task orientation into performance and process oriented goals for competitive performances.... Alternatively, elite performers may focus on outcome goals in certain situations, for example, during monotonous training sessions; but on performance and process goals in other situations, for example, during major competitions (p.79).

There is, of course, an extensive literature on goal-setting in sport and organizational settings. Unfortunately, this literature focuses almost exclusively on performance goals. The goal orientations literature does, at least, consider outcome goals, albeit somewhat indirectly. However, there is very little research which focuses directly upon the use of process oriented goals, and (as mentioned earlier) authors frequently confound process goals with performance goals. Some exceptions to this "rule" can be found in Kingston and Hardy (1994a, b) and Kingston, Hardy, and Markland (1992). Nevertheless, the general dearth of literature on process oriented goals remains surprising given that both applied practitioners and elite performers almost certainly make extensive use of them (see, for example, the whole of the section on quality training in Orlick and Partington, 1988). Furthermore, it is entirely plausible that one of the reasons for the contradictions that currently exist between the literature on goal-setting in organizational settings and the literature on goal-setting in sport is that performers are not being asked to set the most appropriate type of goal. For example, Burton (1992) has argued that for goal-setting to work with complex tasks, "strategy development is necessary to first develop a way to execute the technique correctly; then the motivational effects of goals can facilitate performance by focusing attention and increasing effort" (p 282). However, this conclusion ignores the possibility that process oriented goals might exert a very direct effect on strategy and technique development.

Applied Implications

One implication of the above discussion is that all goals have the potential to be both functional and dysfunctional. This notion of dysfunctionality is not new. Both Burton (1992) and Beggs (1990) discuss the possibility of goals acting as a "double-edged sword" such that the discrepancy between current and aspired to levels of performance can serve to positively motivate performance, but can also act as an additional source of pressure in certain circumstances. Burton (1992) appears to attribute this property solely to outcome goals, but Beggs (1990) more correctly ascribes it to both outcome and performance goals goals (cf., Deci & Ryan, 1985; Hardy et al., 1996).

Drawing firm conclusions from the literature that has been reviewed above is quite difficult. Nevertheless, if forced to make an "educated guess", the author would argue that the most important guiding principles for goal-setting are:

1. to maintain a balance between outcome, performance, and process orientations;
2. to strongly emphasize the outcome-performance-process link, so that the performer is able to elevate the status of process oriented goals when necessary (e.g., immediately prior to a major competition);
3. to practice maintaining a focus on process goals when under pressure {simulation training);
4. to encourage performers to use process oriented goals when performing complex tasks and when trying to enhance the quality of training.

Myth 3: Performers should use Internal Visual Imagery rather than External Visual Imagery

This myth grew out of Mahoney and Avener's (1977) pioneering study of Olympic gymnasts. Mahoney and Avener distinguished between internal and external imagery in the following way:

> [In] external imagery, a person views himself from the perspective of an external observer. . . . Internal imagery, on the other hand, requires an approximation of the real life phenomenology such that the person actually imagines being inside his/her body and experiencing those sensations which might be expected in the actual situation (p. 137).

Based on this distinction, Mahoney and Avener (1977) found that more successful elite gymnasts reported using internal imagery more frequently than less successful elite gymnasts. Other researchers (e.g., Hale, 1982; Harris & Robinson, 1986) have shown that internal imagery tends to produce stronger EMG activity in the muscles involved in the imaged activity. Consequently, the reader might feel that it is perfectly reasonable to conclude that internal imagery is more effective than external imagery. Certainly, this appears to be the received view of many applied sport psychology consultants.

So, where is the catch in all of this? Actually, there are several. First, not all studies have found internal imagery to be superior to external imagery. For example, replications of the original Mahoney and Avener (1977) study on different populations by Highlen and Bennett (1979), and Meyers, Cooke, Cullen, and Liles (1979), both failed to obtain the predicted effect. Similarly, experimental designs by Epstein (1980), and Mumford and Hall (1986), also failed to obtain it. Second, and perhaps most importantly, Mahoney and Avener's (1977) description of internal imagery confounds visual imagery from an internal perspective with kinesthetic imagery. Furthermore, this confounding has been replicated in all the empirical studies that have shown higher levels of EMG activity for internal imagery in comparison with external imagery (for a review, see Hale, 1994). It is not surprising that kinesthetic imagery produces higher levels of EMG activity than no kinesthetic imagery. Related to this confounding issue is the fact that many researchers appear to assume that kinesthetic imagery cannot be performed with an external visual image, or that it is at least easier to perform with an internal visual image. However, there is no logical reason why performers should not be able to combine external visual images with kinesthetic images, and empirical evidence from White and Hardy (1995), and Callow and Hardy (1997), suggests that they can in fact use kinesthetic images equally well with either internal or external visual images. Finally, there appears to be an assumption in the literature that task differences will not have any effect upon preferred visual imagery perspective. Evidence will be presented below which highlights the limitations of this assumption.

Not all previous researchers have fallen into the trap of believing that internal imagery is superior to external imagery; for example, Murphy has repeatedly argued that the evidence is inconclusive (see, for example, Murphy, 1990, 1994; Murphy & Jowdy, 1992). However, Murphy's position certainly seems to be a minority view. Fortunately, a recent series of studies conducted by the author with various associates does seem to clarify the issue somewhat. Using a wheelchair slalom task, White and Hardy (1995) found that internal visual imagery subjects completed a transfer trial with significantly fewer mistakes than external visual imagery subjects. In contrast, external visual imagery subjects completed all of the learning trials and the transfer trial significantly faster than the internal visual imagery subjects. In a second task, which required subjects to learn and precisely replicate certain arm and club positions with rhythmic gymnastics clubs, White and Hardy (1995) found external visual imagery to be significantly superior to internal visual imagery both during learning and in retention.

In a second study, Callow and Hardy (1997) required subjects to learn a short gymnastics routine comprising four moves in one of four different imagery conditions: external visual imagery with kinesthetic imagery; external visual imagery without kinesthetic imagery; internal visual imagery with kinesthetic imagery; and internal visual imagery without kinesthetic imagery. The results showed external visual imagery to be superior to internal visual imagery during acquisition, but produced a visual imagery perspective by kinesthetic imagery interaction in the retention trial. This interaction suggested that kinesthetic imagery enhanced the effects of external visual imagery upon performance, but impaired the effects of internal visual imagery upon performance.

Finally, in an attempt to clarify the latter interactive effect, Hardy and Evans (in preparation) examined the combination of different visual imagery perspectives with kinesthetic imagery on a bouldering (rock climbing) task. *Bouldering* is a form of training for rock climbing in which climbers attempt to link a sequence of very difficult moves together close to the ground so that they can fall off with relative impunity. Such technically difficult moves require the climber to be very precise in his or her body positioning. Performance was evaluated in three ways: self-assessed technical competence relative to personal norms; externally assessed technical competence by an expert who was blind to each subject's experimental condition; and objectively as the number of moves completed before the subject fell off. However, regardless of the performance measure considered, the results showed a significant main effect for kinesthetic imagery and a significant main effect for external visual imagery over internal visual imagery. Taken together, this evidence suggests quite strongly that external visual imagery can be superior to internal visual imagery in at least some circumstances.

Possible Explanations of Imagery Perspective Effects

In the author's opinion, at least three factors have contributed to the confusion which currently exists in the imagery perspective literature: first, the confounding of internal visual and kinesthetic imagery perspectives; second, the failure to seriously consider the theoretical bases of predictions of superiority for one visual perspective over another; and third, the failure to consider the different demands of different tasks (cf., Murphy, 1994). The first of these factors has already been discussed. The second and third are the central focus of the following discussion.

The theoretical driving force behind White and Hardy's (1995) study was a purely cognitive one; namely, that imagery should be beneficial to learning and performance only to the extent that the images generated contain information that would not otherwise be available to the performer. Thus, in gymnastics or rock climbing where body shape and the technical positioning of limbs are important, external visual imagery enables performers to mentally rehearse the precise movements and positions required for performance. This mental rehearsal is particularly effective when combined with kinesthetic imagery, because then the performer can see the desired shape and feel the sensations that should be experienced when attempting to perform the actual movements. Internal visual imagery could not provide this template because the required body shape cannot be seen in such an image, or if it can be seen the image is inadequate. Conversely, in a slalom type task internal visual imagery allows the performer to mentally rehearse the precise locations at which maneuvers need to be initiated. In this sort of task, the actual movements to be performed are relatively simple, well-learned and are not required to have particular shape. Thus, external imagery provides less useful information but may enhance competitive drives, hence the speed effects observed in the wheelchair slalom task. Kinesthetic imagery, on the other hand, might again be beneficial because it would enable the performer to match the timing and feel of the movement to the cues that need to be used to initiate the movement. The empirical studies that have been reported above provide support for all these contentions except the last one, which has yet to be examined.

Applied Implications

In light of the research reviewed above, some caution is clearly necessary when it comes to offering advice about ideal visual imagery perspectives. However, it is perhaps worth noting that in the studies reported, regardless of which visual imagery perspective is used, kinesthetic imagery always had a beneficial effect upon performance. Furthermore, the author would tentatively suggest that if the task places a strong emphasis upon form or body shape, then performers might be encouraged to try and combine external visual imagery with kinesthetic imagery. Conversely, if the task requires the performer to make relatively simple movements in which form is not particularly important, but the timing of the response relative to external cues is important, then the combination of internal visual imagery plus kinesthetic imagery may be optimal. Two qualifications to these recommendations may be added. First, the recommendations take no account of the imagery perspective preferences of performers. In the imagery perspective studies that the author has reported, subjects have always been selected on the basis that they were proficient in both internal and external visual imagery. Furthermore, as Jowdy, Murphy, and Durtschi, (1989) have observed, it appears that performers often use a combination of imagery perspectives during mental rehearsal.

Second, the above suggestions take no account of the use of imagery for motivational purposes (Moritz, Hall, Martin, & Vadocz, 1996; Paivio, 1985; Vadocz, Hall, & Moritz, in press). It is entirely plausible that internal and external visual imagery might exert qualitatively different motivational influences; for example, third person perspectives could enhance competitive drives, whereas first person visual perspectives could enhance self-efficacy because the performer can more easily identify with the image (cf., Bandura, 1986). Alternatively, as Murphy (1994) has suggested, internal and external imagery could exert differential effects upon the identification of technical errors. Many questions remain in this area.

Concluding Remarks

When I first started to work as an applied sport psychology consultant I was very impressed by the apparent ability of some consultants to know just exactly what to do in any given set of circumstances. Compared to these consultants my own strategy for survival seemed woefully inadequate. First, I would frequently ask the client if I could have some time to think about the issue that we were trying to address (an hour, a day, even a few days sometimes). Then, I would go away and try to brainstorm everything I could think of that might be of any relevance to the issue in question. Out of these ideas, I would pick half a dozen or so that looked like they might be of some use, and then repeatedly challenge them in my mind until I found something that I could describe as my best, educated, guess. I would then go back to my performer or coach and try to commit to this best guess with everything I had. I used to think that one day I would get better; but time went by and I did not. Then I learned that, for me, this was the best way to operate. Indeed, even when applied consultants are so experienced that they have some automatic solutions to problems and issues, there must be times when they question these solutions. Furthermore, it is only by constantly challenging what we think the research literature is telling us that we can ensure that our educated guesses are truly educated. My intention here was not to criticize other people's research. It was to question the way in which this work is interpreted, and it is my most sincere hope that this contribution to the debate which will undoubtedly ensue will be received in that spirit.

References

Bandura, A. (1986). *Social Foundations of Thought and Action: A Social Cognitive Theory.* Prentice-Hall, Englewood Cliffs, NJ.

Beggs, W. D. A. (1990). Goal setting in Sport. In J.G. Jones & L. Hardy (Eds.), *Stress and Performance in Sport* (pp.135–170). Wiley, Chichester.

Burton, D. (1990). Multimodal stress management in sport: Current status and future directions. In J.G. Jones & L. Hardy (Eds.), *Stress and Performance in Sport* (pp.171–201). Wiley, Chichester.

Burton, D. (1992). The Jeckyl/Hyde nature of goals : Reconceptualising goal setting in sport. In T.Horn (ed.), *Advances in Sport Psychology* (pp.267–297). Human Kinetics, Champaign, IL.

Burton, D. (1993). Goal setting in sport. In R.N. Singer, M. Murphey, & L.K. Tennant, *Handbook of Research in Sport Psychology* (pp.467–491). MacMillan, New York.

Callow, N., & Hardy, L. 1997. Kinaesthetic imagery and its interaction with visual imagery perspectives during the acquisition of a short gymnastics sequence. *Journal of Sport Sciences, 15*, 75.

Carver, C. S., & Scheier, M. F (1988). A control perspective on anxiety, *Anxiety Research, 1,* 17–22.

Deci, E. L., & Ryan, R. M. (1985). *Intrinsic Motivation and Self Determination in Human Behaviour*, Plenum Press, New York.

Duda, J. L. (1992). Motivation in sport settings : A goal perspective approach. In G. Roberts (ed.), *Motivation in Sport and Exercise* (pp57–91). Human Kinetics, Champaign, IL.

Duda, J. L., Olson, L. K., & Templin, T. (1991). The relationship of task and ego orientation to sportsmanship attitudes and the perceived legitimacy of injurious acts, *Research Quarterly for Exercise and Sport, 62*, 79–87.

Edwards, T., & Hardy, L. (1996). The interactive effects of intensity and direction of cognitive and somatic anxiety, and self-confidence upon performance. *Journal of Sport and Exercise Psychology, 18*, 296–312.

Epstein, M. L. (1980). The relationships of mental imagery and mental practice to performance of a motor task. *Journal of Sport Psychology, 2,* 211–220.

Eysenck, M. W. (1982). *Attention and Arousal: Cognition and Performance.* Springer, Berlin.

Eysenck, M. W., & Calvo, M. G. (1992). Anxiety and performance: the processing efficiency theory. *Cognition and Emotion, 6,* 409–434.

Fenz, W. D., & Epstein, S. (1967). Gradients of physiological arousal in parachutists as a function of an approaching jump. *Psychosomatic Medicine, 29,* 33–51.

Fenz, W. D., & Epstein, S. (1968). Specific and general inhibitory reactions associated with mastery of stress. *Journal of Experimental Psychology, 77,* 52–56.

Goudas, M., Fox, K., Biddle, S., & Armstrong, N. (1992). Children's task and ego goal profiles in sport : Relationship with perceived competence, enjoyment and participation. *Journal of Sport Sciences, 10, 6,* 606–607.

Gould, D., Hodge, K., Peterson, K., & Giannini, J. (1989). An exploratory examination of strategies used by elite coaches to enhance self-efficacy in athletes. *Journal of Sport and Exercise Psychology, 11,* 128–140.

Hale, B. D. (1982). The effects of internal and external imagery on muscular and ocular concomitants. *Journal of Sport Psychology, 4,* 379–387.

Hale, B. D. 1994. Imagery perspectives and learning in sports performance. In A. Sheikh & E. Korn (Eds.), *Imagery in Sports and Physical Performance* (pp. 75–96). Farmingdale, NY: Baywood.

Hardy, L. (1996). Testing the predictions of the cusp catastrophe model of anxiety and performance. *The Sport Psychologist, 10,* 140–156.

Hardy, L. & Evans, G. (in preparation). Combined effects of kinesthetic imagery with different visual imagery perspectives in experienced rock climbers. Manuscript in preparation.

Hardy, L., & Parfitt, C. G. (1991). A catastrophe model of anxiety and performance. *British Journal of Psychology, 82,* 163–178.

Hardy, L., & Pearce, R. (in preparation). Combined effects of ego and task orientation upon effort in experienced rock climbers. Manuscript in preparation.

Hardy, L., Jones, G., & Gould, D. (1996). *Understanding Psychological Preparation for Sport: Theory and Practice of elite performers.* Chichester: Wiley.

Hardy, L., Parfitt, C. G., & Pates, J. (1994). Performance catastrophes in sport: A test of the hysteresis hypothesis. *Journal of Sport Sciences, 12,* 327–334

Harris, D. V., & Harris, B. L. (1984). *The Athlete's Guide To Sport Psychology: Mental Skills For Physical People.* Leisure Press, Champaign, Illinois.

Harris, D. V., & Robinson, W. J. (1986). The effects of skill level on EMG activity during internal and external imagery. *Journal of Sport Psychology, 8,* 105–111.

Hemery, D. (1991). *Sporting Excellence: What makes a Champion* (2nd Ed.). Wiley, New York.

Highlen, P. S., & Bennett, B. B. (1983). Elite divers, wrestlers: A comparison between open and closed skilled athletes. *Journal of Sport Psychology, 5,* 390–49.

Jones, G., & Hanton, S. (1996). Interpretation of competitive anxiety symptoms and goal attainment expectancies. *Journal of Sport and Exercise Psychology, 18,* 144–157.

Jones, J. G., & Hardy, L. (1990b). *Stress and Performance in Sport.* Wiley, Chichester.

Jones, G., & Swain, A. B. J. (1992). Intensity and direction dimensions of competitive anxiety and relationships with competitiveness. *Perceptual and Motor Skills, 74,* 467–472.

Jones, G., Hanton, S., & Swain, A. B. J. (1994). Intensity and interpretation of anxiety symptoms in elite and non-elite sports performers. *Personality and Individual Differences, 17,* 657–663.

Jones, G., Swain, A. B. J., & Hardy, L. (1993). Intensity and direction dimensions of competitive state anxiety and relationships with performance. *Journal of Sport Sciences, 11,* 525–532.

Jowdy, D. P., Murphy, S. M., & Durtschi, S. (1989). *An Assessment Of The Use Of Imagery By Elite Athletes: Athlete, Coach And Psychological Perspectives.* United States Olympic Committee, Colorado Springs, CO.

Kingston, K. M., & Hardy, L. (1994b). Factors affecting the salience of outcome performance and process goals in golf. In A.J. Cochran and M.R. Farally (Eds.), *Science and Golf II* (pp.144–149). Chapman and Hall, London.

Kingston, K. M., & Hardy, L. (in press). Effects of different types of goals upon processes that support performance. *The Sport Psychologist.*

Kingston, K. M., & Hardy, L. (in preparation). Situational specificity in goal orientations amongst golfers of differing ability levels.

Kingston, K., Hardy, L. & Markland, D. (1992). A study to compare the effect of two different goal orientations and stress levels on a number of situationally relevant performance subcomponents. *Journal of Sports Sciences, 10,* 610–611.

Locke, E. A., & Latham, G. P. (1990). *A Theory Of Goal-Setting And Task Performance.* Prentice Hall, Englewood Cliffs, New Jersey.

Mahoney, M. J., & Avener, M. (1977). Psychology of the elite athlete: An exploratory study. *Cognitive Therapy and Research, 1,* 135–141.

Martens, R., Vealey, R. S., & Burton, D. (1990). *Competitive Anxiety in Sport.* Human Kinetics, Champaign, IL.

Meyers, A. W., Cooke, C. J., Cullen, J., & Liles, L. (1979). Psychological aspects of athletic competitors: A replication across sports. *Cognitive Therapy and Research,* 3, 361–366.

Moritz, S. E., Hall , C. R., Martin , K., & Vadocz, E. (1996). What are confident athletes imaging?: An examination of image content. *The Sport Psychologist, 10,* 171–179.

Morris, L. W., Davis, M. A., & Hutchings, C. H. (1981). Cognitive and emotional components of anxiety: Literature review and a revised worry-emotionality scale. *Journal of Educational Psychology, 73,* 541–555.

Mumford, P., & Hall, C. (1985). The effects of internal and external imagery on performing figures in figure skating. *Canadian Journal of Applied Sport Sciences, 10,* 171–177.

Murphy, S. M. (1990). Models of imagery in sport psychology: A review. *Journal of Mental Imagery, 14,* 153–172.

Murphy, S. M. (1994). Imagery interventions in Sport. *Medicine and Science in Sports and Exercise, 26,* 486–494.

Murphy, S. M., & Jowdy, D. P. (1992). Imagery and Mental Practice. In T.S. Horn (ed.), *Advances in Sport Psychology* (pp.222–250). Human Kinetics, Champaign, IL.

Nicholls, J. G. (1989). *The Competitive Ethos and Democratic Education.* Harvard University Press, Harvard.

Orlick, T., & Partington, J. (1988). Mental links to excellence. *The Sport Psychologist, 2,* 105–130.

Paivio, A. (1985). Cognitive and motivational functions of imagery in human performance *Canadian Journal of Applied Sport Sciences, 10*, 22–28.

Revelle, W., & Michaels, E. J. (1976). The theory of achievement motivation revisited: The implication of inertial tendencies. *Psychological Review, 83*, 394–404.

Swain, A., & Jones, G. (1996). Explaining performance variance: the relative contribution of intensity and direction dimensions of competitive state anxiety. *Anxiety, Stress, and Coping, 9,* 1–18.

Vadocz, E. A., Hall, C. R., & Moritz, S. E. (in press). The cognitive and motivational functions of images in the anxiety-performance relationship. *Journal of Applied Sport Psychology.*

Weinberg, R. S. (1988). *The Mental Advantage: Developing Your Psychological Skills In Tennis.* Human Kinetics, Champaign, IL.

White, A., & Hardy, L. (1995). Use of different imagery perspectives on learning and performance of different motor skills. *British Journal of Psychology, 86*, 169–180.

Woodman, T., Albinson, J.G., & Hardy, L. (1997). An investigation of the Zones of Optimal Functioning hypothesis within a multidimensional framework. *Journal of Sport and Exercise Psychology, 19*, 131–141.

27 Imagery Use by Athletes: Development of the Sport Imagery Questionnaire

CRAIG R. HALL, DIANE E. MACK, ALLAN PAIVIO, AND HEATHER A. HAUSENBLAS
University of Western Ontario, London, Canada

The use of imagery for enhancement of sport performance has been of central interest to applied sport psychologists. Methods of measuring imagery use in athletes have included questionnaires, self-report, and interview techniques. This reading discusses the development of the Sport Imagery Questionnaire (SIQ). What makes this investigation unique is the extensive psychometric properties used and the theoretical base that supports the development of this questionnaire.

The theoretical base is derived from Paivio's analytic framework of imagery effects (1985). This framework purports that there are four functions of imagery: motivation specific, motivation general, cognitive specific, and cognitive general.

The authors used three experiments to verify psychometric properties of this questionnaire. These properties include item reliability, item analysis, internal consistency, construct validity, and predictive validity. Through these experiments the authors support several findings that indicate a link between imagery use and successful performance and a link between imagery use and increased self-confidence and arousal control. The authors also indicated that the relationship between imagery use and successful performance varies with the skill level of the athlete; novice athletes use cognitive imagery for skill improvement and elite athletes use imagery to augment their motivation. This concept infers support for Hardy's premise in the previous reading.

The development and validation of the SIQ has benefited sport imagery researchers. This questionnaire is well respected and has thus become one of the most used research instruments in applied sport psychology.

The Sports Imagery Questionnaire (SIQ) was developed to assess the motivational and cognitive functions of imagery proposed by Paivio's Analytic Framework of Imagery Effects (1985). The present article reports three experiments designed to validate the content and construct properties of the SIQ. Initially, items were developed through a thorough literature review, other imagery questionnaires, and the expert evaluations of research professionals and elite athletes, In Experiments 1 and 2, the items on the SIQ were found to separate into distinct factors. These factors corresponded well with the functions of imagery proposed by Paivio. Experiment 3 was designed to assess construct and predictive validity in a sample of 271 athletes competing in individual and team sports. Again results revealed the existence of five distinct factors corresponding with the motivational and cognitive functions of imagery proposed. Predictive validity of the SIQ was supported in that greater imagery use was associated with successful performance. Finally, differences between individual and team sport athletes were observed with respect to the functions of imagery use. Overall, the results of these experiments indicate that the SIQ may be a useful tool for helping understand how athletes use different types of imagery.

The present studies focused on motivational and skill-oriented functions of imagery in athletic performance. The functional distinction was drawn in an analysis by Paivio (1985), who suggested that imagery plays both motivational and cognitive roles in mediating behavior, each capable of being targeted toward either general or specific behavioral goals. The relations were represented as a 2x2 orthogonal model with the motivational-cognitive contrast as one dimension and the general-specific contrast as the other. The functional distinctions are reflected in differences in imagery content. On the motivational side, imagery can represent emotion-arousing situations as well as specific goals and goal-oriented behaviors, without necessarily engaging cognitive processes aimed at directly improving performance. Conversely, on the cognitive side, imagery can be focused exclusively on performance-related aspects such as game strategies or specific motor skills.

The following summarizes and illustrates the four functions of imagery more explicitly. The motivational general function refers to images related to general physiological and emotional arousal, as in techniques designed to induce relaxation by "parking out" mentally or imaging a quiet place, or the converse, as in "turning anxiety into energy" or "psyching up" imagery. Motivational specific refers to goal oriented imagery — for example, imagining oneself winning an event, standing on a podium receiving a medal, being in the company of one's sports heroes, and so on. Cognitive general refers particularly to imagery strategies

Adapted, by permission, from C.R. Hall et al., 1998, "Imagery use by athletes: Development of the sport imagery questionnaire," *International Journal of Sport Psychology* 29: 73-89.

related to a competitive event. For example, Chris Evert Lloyd reported imagery rehearsal of strategies tuned to the style of a specific tennis opponent. Finally, cognitive specific refers to imagery directed at improving particular perceptual-motor skills. The central issue here is the functional reality of the framework — is it a performance model or simply an expository convenience? The examples used above imply that it is a performance model and that the two dimensions are functionally orthogonal. Thus, it is conceivable that we can image (a) emotional situations without thinking about behavioral goals, (b) goal directed activities without experiencing affect, (c) strategic behaviors independent of specific skills, or (d) skills without any of the other types of imagery content. We can also experience two or more types of imagery at once. For example, we can imagine an emotional "high" accompanying a successful performance.

The empirical implications of the model can be tested using one or more of three general classes of operational procedures that have been used in imagery research on memory and other cognitive phenomena (Paivio, 1971). These comprise (a) experimental procedures such as instructing participants to image, (b) varying the image-evoking value of words or other materials presented to participants, and (c) measuring individual differences in imagery abilities and habits, the latter referring to the frequency with which imagery is experienced or used in different contexts (cf. Paivio & Harshman, 1983). The present research focused on individual differences in imagery habits as measured by questionnaires.

Each functional category of the motivational/cognitive model implicates continuous dimensions related to the frequency with which a subject experiences or uses each type of imagery. If the imagery categories are orthogonal in the strong sense, all possible high-low imagery combinations would emerge when individual differences are measured. For example, a given athlete might indicate frequent use of general motivational imagery as well as specific goal oriented imagery, infrequent use of both, or frequent use of one and not the other, along with any frequency combination of general and specific performance-oriented (cognitive) imagery. Over participants, the four functional categories would then emerge as four independent factors. Another possibility is that the relevance of the categories would vary with the type of sport. For example, strategic use of imagery would be relevant in team sports and in any sport in which individuals are interactively engaged in competition-tennis, billiards, boxing, and the like. Competitive strategies (hence strategic imagery) are less relevant in non-interactive sports such as track and field, though a strategic component could be involved, as in pacing oneself in different ways in a race according to one's knowledge of the strengths and strategies of competitors. The results of earlier relevant studies provide some information on such possibilities.

Hall, Rodgers and Barr (1990a) developed a questionnaire to investigate the use of imagery by athletes in various sports. They found that all athletes reported using imagery but the higher the competitive level of the athletes the more often they reported using imagery. The athletes also reported using imagery more in conjunction with competition than with practice. Barr and Hall (1992) obtained similar results and additional specific findings in a study of imagery use by rowers. Salmon, Hall and Haslam (1994) developed an Imagery Use Questionnaire for Soccer Players (IUQ-SP), which was based partly on the questionnaire used by Hall et al. (1990a,b) and partly on the Paivio (1985) framework. In agreement with the earlier studies, Salmon et al. (1994) found that imagery was reportedly used more in relation to competition than practice, and that elite athletes reported greater use of imagery than non-elite athletes. Analyses of the questionnaire data also provided qualified support for the Paivio model, with the qualification that players generally reported using imagery more for its motivational function than its cognitive function. In addition, the use scores for the different functional categories varied as a function of the competitive level of the players.

Experimental manipulations of imagery also have produced results that bear on the motivational functions of imagery. Hall, Toews, and Rodgers (1990b; Experiment 1) found that athletes who were instructed to image a successful performance of a simple motor task in a laboratory environment voluntarily practised harder and longer than a control group. This is consistent with Paivio's (1985) suggestions regarding goal-oriented imagery. They found in addition, however, that skill-oriented imagery instructions were just as motivating as the goal-oriented instructions (Experiment 2). Martin and Hall (1995) instructed beginner golfers to practice by first imaging performance alone ("a perfect stroke") or performance plus a successful outcome (the golf ball rolling into the hole), followed by physical practice sessions. The measure of the motivational effect was the amount of time spent at voluntary practice at different stages of a series of experimental sessions. The results showed that the Performance Imagery subjects spent more time practising than either the Performance-plus-Outcome Imagery subjects or a non-imagery Control group. That the Performance-plus-Outcome Imagery group did not show the greatest motivational effect remains somewhat of a puzzle, particularly since their performance gains exceeded those of the other groups. Martin and Hall (1995) offer speculative suggestions that remain to be tested.

The present research extended the above studies by focusing on the development and predictive validation of a general Sport Imagery Questionnaire (SIQ) designed to measure individual differences in the extent to which imagery is used for the functions specified in the Paivio (1985) model.

Experiment 1

The purpose of Experiment 1 was to assess the motivational and cognitive functions of imagery through the development of the SIQ. In order to achieve this purpose, the psychometric properties of the items developed were examined using various analytic procedures. Of primary concern was (a) the individual-item characteristics, (b) the internal-consistency of each scale assessing each construct, and (c) the separation of the items into their respective scales following the use of factor analytic techniques.

Participants and Procedures

Item analysis required a pool of subjects large enough to examine item reliability, and a sample representing a broad range of areas (cf. Nunnally, 1978). Accordingly, 113 athletes competing in 10 different sports were administered the SIQ. Fifty percent of those surveyed competed in individual sports, 38% in team sports, and 12% were trained dancers (*). Fifty-three percent (n = 60) were female and 47% (n = 53) male. Subjects ranged in age from 11 to 32 years (M = 23.58 ± 6.40). On average, the athletes had competed in their respective sport for over 7 years (M = 7.54 ± .43), across a wide range of competitive levels, 46% competed at the high school level, 29.5% at the varsity level and 24.5% at the provincial/national level.

The first step was to develop an item pool that would form the basis for the SIQ. The SIQ was conceptualized as a general and improved version of the IUQ-SP employed by Salmon et al. (1994). The IUQ-SP provided valuable insight into how athletes use imagery, but it is a sport specific questionnaire.

Items representing each of the four constructs proposed by Paivio (1985) were developed based on constitutive definitions, reviews of the sport psychology and cognitive psychology literature, and an examination of other imagery use inventories such as the Psychological Skills Inventory for Sports (Mahoney, Gabriel, & Perkins, 1987) and the IUQ-SP (Salmon, Hall & Haslam, 1994). In the item generation process care was taken to ensure that no one construct was over represented in as much as biases in item representation could affect the results.

The content validity of this initial pool of items was assessed by four research experts, three in the area of sport psychology and a fourth in cognitive psychology, and four elite level athletes. The content, format, wording of the items, and usage within athletic populations were determined and evaluated by these individuals. Based on their recommendations, changes were made in the wording of the items and difficult or ambiguous items were dropped.

As a result of the above evaluation process, a total of 46 items were retained to represent the model's four constructs. The distribution of items in each of the four constructs was as follows: Motivational Specific (MS), 15 items; Cognitive General (CG), 12 items; Motivational General (MG), 11 items; and Cognitive Specific (CS), 8 items.

The SIQ was administered to all athletes following one of their regular practice sessions. Athletes were asked to respond to each item according to frequency of imagery use and concreteness (i.e., ease of imaging the item). Any item deemed to be difficult to image was considered for deletion from the SIQ. To assess the frequency with which athletes use the type of imagery implied in each item, a 7-point Likert-type scale was employed anchored at the extremes by 1 = "rarely" use that type of imagery and 7 = "often" use that type of imagery. Concreteness was rated on a 7-point Likert-type scale where 1 = "easy to image" and 7 = "difficult to image". The order in which athletes rated frequency and concreteness were counterbalanced across subjects to control for response bias.

The athletes were asked to participate in the study and were given the opportunity to freely decline. No time limit was imposed and the athletes were encouraged to ask questions should clarification be needed.

Results and Discussion

Means, standard deviations, and skewness were calculated for each item on the SIQ to evaluate individual item characteristics. All items were distributed within the tolerance levels of assumptions of normality except for one, "I image giving 100% during an event/game", which had a skewness of greater than -2.00. Examination of the standard deviations confirmed that response variability was satisfactory, as all standard deviations were greater than ±1.00. All items were rated as relatively easy to image, ranging from 2.09 to 4.13 on the 7-point concreteness scale. The pattern of results of the overall cell function means (MS = 5.41 ± .96, MG = 5.07± .84, CS = 4.74 ± 1.17, CG = 4.60 ± .88) was similar to that found by Salmon et al. (1994) with athletes using imagery more for its motivational function than its cognitive function.

The internal consistency of items measuring each construct was evaluated through a Cronbach's alpha. The criterion level for the definition of a scale was set at an alpha coefficient of .70 (Nunnally, 1978). All scales had acceptable internal consistencies: MS = .82, MG = .76, CS =.87, and CG = .77.

A principle components factor analysis was conducted on the frequency scores to determine if the items measured distinct factors as hypothesized. Maximum likelihood factor extraction with oblique rotation was employed. All items were entered and a four factor solution was specified. A criterion level of .35 was set for items loading on a factor {Tabachnick & Fidell, 1989). With all items entered into the analysis the subject-to-variable ratio was 2.5:1.

Results revealed that items reflecting CS (Factor 1) and MS (Factor 2) separated cleanly according to the model's constructs. The items reflecting MG separated on Factors 3 and 4. Examination of the specific items on the MG subscale suggested that items separated according to those representing "mastery" (MG-M) and those representing "arousal" (MG-A). Items designed to reflect CG did not

(*) Inclusion of the subsample of dancers did not change the factor structure of the SIQ, thus they were retained in the analysis.

load cleanly on a separate factor but were dispersed instead across the CS and MG factors. The eigenvalues ranged from 10.23 on Factor 1 to 1.42 on Factor 4. Multicollinearity between factors was not evidenced as correlations between the factors fell in the moderate to low range (-.46 to .23). A moderate relationship was found between CS (Factor 1) and MG-M (Factor 3). Low interfactor correlations were found between all other pairs. In sum, with the exception of the CG scale, the results indicated that the items separated into distinct factors that correspond generally with the functions of imagery proposed by Paivio (1985).

The use of factor analytic techniques to determine item retention and/or deletion provides a good indication of which items represent a construct and which do not (Clark & Watson, 1995). Based on the results of the content and construct validity of Experiment 1, many of the items were retained for further empirical evaluation. No new items were constructed to represent CS or MS. Items retained from these subscales were the six items with the highest loadings on their respective factors.

We decided it was necessary to make changes in the refinement of the other scales. However, item elimination should not be conducted without consideration as to why items did not load as expected (Clark & Watson, 1995). Thus, each item considered for elimination was examined. Some of the items were too wordy. For example, one item representing the subscale CG was "I image each step of my routine down to the last detail days prior to the actual performance". In addition to being wordy, another concern with this item was that it reflects two separate aspects, detail and time. It may be that some subjects responded to one but not both of these aspects. Not surprisingly, this item did not load above the set criterion. A second problem was that certain items could be interpreted to represent more than one subscale. For example, although the item "I imagine my performance to be a positive influence on others around me" was initially designed to represent CG, it could also conceivably represent MS. Thus, the items deleted from the SIQ were either too wordy/ambiguous, or they did not operationally define the subscale for which they were originally created.

The MG factor was found to represent two distinct subscales. Thus, two motivational-general scales were retained, one representing mastery (MG-M) imagery and the other representing arousal (MG-A) imagery. Two new items were constructed to measure MG-M and four new items for MG-A to strengthen these scales and compliment the original items retained.

The failure of Experiment 1 to provide clear support for the CG subscale is consistent with earlier findings. Salmon, Hall & Haslam (1994) also found the CG function to be less well-defined than the other functions of imagery in their factor analysis of the IUQ-SP, but all their items pertaining to the CG function loaded on the same cell. Even though the CG scale was internally consistent (.77) we reasoned that some of the items did not accurately represent the construct as defined. Thus, changes were made to the CG subscale. The only CG item found to load above criterion was retained and five new items were generated according to the same principles detailed earlier.

Experiment 2

While the results of Experiment 1 suggested good internal consistency and the division of the items into relatively distinct factors, the modifications made to the SIQ based on the results of Experiment 1 required independent evaluation. Thus, Experiment 2 was designed to examine the structure of the modified version of the SIQ, which consisted of 30-items with six items representing each of five constructs (i.e., CS, CG, MS, MG-M, and MG-A).

Participants and Procedures

Participants were 161 second year Kinesiology students. In contrast to Experiment 1, participants were asked to categorize each item according to the similarity of imagery use reflected in each statement. Participants were instructed to assign common letters of the alphabet to categorize similar types of items and were instructed to classify as many subgroups of imagery as they deemed appropriate.

A frequency table of subjects' classifications was constructed (i.e., the number of times subjects responded that item 1 represented a similar type of imagery as item 2, etc.). Factor analytic techniques were conducted on the frequency table.

Results and Discussion

A principle components factor analysis was conducted to determine if the modified version of the SIQ measured distinct factors. Maximum likelihood factor extraction techniques were employed and the factors were subjected to oblique rotation with a five factor solution specified. All items were entered into the solution, and the subject-to-variable ratio was acceptable (5.3:1).

The results of the factor analysis showed that the items loaded very cleanly onto five factors and all items loaded above the criterion level. These results indicated that the SIQ items developed to reflect Paivio's (1985) functions of imagery separate into the five unique constructs hypothesized. Thus, no changes were made to the SIQ for the next experiment.

Experiment 3

The primary purpose of Experiment 3 was to further assess the motivational and cognitive functions of imagery and the construct validity of the 30-item SIQ. The secondary purpose was to determine the predictive validity of the SIQ. Various researchers (Hall et al., 1990a,b; Vealey, 1986) have suggested there is a link between imagery use and successful performance. For example, elite athletes tend to use imagery more than non-elite athletes (Hall et al., 1990a,b; Salmon, Hall & Haslam, 1994) and how athletes use imagery (i.e., cognitively or motivationally) is related to how they perceive and feel (e.g., self-confident, anxious) about an upcoming performance (Moritz, Hall, Martin, & Vadocz, 1996; Vadocz, Hall, & Moritz, in press). Hall (1995) has recently argued that athletes use imagery to increase self-confidence and control arousal levels just before they perform, and the more they use imagery, the more beneficial it seems to be. It follows from these suggestions that SIQ scores should correlate positively with athletic performance. Finally, individual and team sport athletes were compared as to their reported levels of imagery use across the five subscales of the SIQ.

Participants and Procedures

A total of 271 male (n = 184) and female (n = 87) athletes competing in track and field (n = 180) and ice hockey (n = 91) participated in this study (**). Track and field athletes competed at either the high school (n = 94; 52%), varsity (n = 27; 15%) or national level (n = 59; 33 %). On average, the athletes had competed in track and field for over 5 years (M = 5.75 ± 2.73). They were categorized into events as follows: sprinters (n = 44; 24.4%), middle or distance runners (n = 47; 26.2%), field events (n = 64; 35.6%), hurdlers (n = 21; 11.6%), and decathletes or heptathletes (n = 4; 2.2%). Of the hockey players surveyed, over half competed at the varsity level (52.8%). Other levels included: 25% Junior B players; 18% played in the Ontario Hockey League and 4.2% played in the National Hockey League. Participants averaged over 13 years of playing experience (M = 13.74 ± 3.98).

To determine the relationship between imagery use (as assessed by the SIQ) and performance, track and field athletes were asked to indicate their personal best time/distance. An objective measure of performance (i.e., the Mercier Tables; Mercier & Beauregard, 1993) was used to test the above relationship. Points were awarded for performance according to the Mercier Tables. Points were based on an athlete's personal best time/distance. Points on the scale range from a low of 1 to a high of 1200 and are awarded differentially for male and female athletes.

The SIQ was administered to all athletes either prior to competition or following a regularly scheduled practice. Athletes were asked to respond to each item according to frequency of imagery use. Participation was voluntary and the experimenter was onsite in case clarification of items was necessary.

Results and Discussion

As in Experiment 1, the individual-item characteristics, the internal consistency of the scales, and factorial validity of the SIQ was assessed. Means, standard deviations, and skewness were calculated for each item to evaluate the individual item characteristics. One item assessing MG-M, I image giving 100% during an event/game, was found to have a skewness greater than – 2.00. Inspection of the mean for this item revealed that athletes indicated imaging giving 100% almost all the time (mean rating of 6.19 ± 1.27 on the 7-point scale). All other items were distributed within the tolerance levels for assumptions of normality. No limitation in item response was found upon examination of the standard deviations (i.e., all items had variances greater than one). An examination of the cell function means revealed that athletes generally reported using imagery most for its motivational general functions (MG-M = 5.48 ± 1.11, MG-A = 5.06 ± 1.09, CS = 4.98 ± 1.23, CG = 4.84 ± 1.12, MS = 4.33 ± 1.64). This finding was consistent with the results of Experiment 1 and Salmon, Hall & Haslam (1994).

Cronbach's alpha coefficient was again calculated to examine the internal consistency of each scale. Results indicated favorable internal consistency for the items designed to represent all 5 scales: MS = .88, CS = .85, MG-M = .83, CG = .75, and MG-A = .70.

A factor analysis was performed according to the procedures described in Experiment 1. All items were entered into the analysis and a five factor solution was specified. With 30 items, the subject-to-variable ratio was an acceptable 9.0: 1. In accord with Paivio's (1985) framework, results of the factor analysis revealed the existence of 5 distinct factors. In contrast to Experiment 1, the majority of items designed to represent CG loaded on a separate factor. Low to moderate interfactor correlations were revealed for the factor pairs ranging from -.45 to .32. Thus, it appears as though the SIQ adequately assesses the motivational and cognitive functions of imagery.

Separate regression analyses were conducted to determine whether imagery use, measured by the five subscale scores, could predict performance for the track and field athletes. Analyses were conducted separately across competitive level and gender. Results supported the proposed relationship between imagery use and performance. For the high school male sample, imaging skills (CS) accounted for 22% of the variance in performance and was statistically significant. Strategy use (CG) was found to predict performance significantly for varsity female athletes. Finally, MG-M and MS were found to predict performance significantly in national level females and males, respectively. Imagery use was not found to significantly predict performance for high school female athletes or varsity male athletes.

It is important to note that the motivational functions of imagery (i.e., goal-oriented imagery and arousal control) were more likely to predict performance for elite athletes compared to varsity or high school athletes. Conversely, the cognitive functions of imagery (i.e., skill acquisition and strategy use) were more likely to predict performance for athletes competing at lower competitive levels relative to elite athletes. Thus, it appears as though elite athletes

(**) All ice hockey players surveyed were male.

(who have already conquered many of the skills necessary to be successful) employ imagery primarily to keep themselves motivated.

A MANOVA was conducted to determine whether individual and team sport athletes report using the various functions of imagery differently. Results revealed significant differences in individual and team sport athletes reported use of imagery ($F(5,265) = 6.45, p < .001$). Results of univariate ANOVAs revealed significant differences between individual and team sport athletes on the subscales MS [$F(1,269) = 18.05, p < .001$] and MG-M ($F(1,269) = 10.97, p < .001$). Upon examination of the cell function means for these subscales, it was found that team sport athletes reported greater use of the MS and MG-M functions of imagery ($M = 4.90$ and $M = 5.78$, respectively) than did individual sport athletes ($M = 4.03$ and $M = 5.32$, respectively). This finding offers some indication that individual and team sport athletes employ the motivational and cognitive functions of imagery differently. This possibility warrants further investigation.

General Discussion

Paivio (1985) proposed that imagery serves two functions in athletic performance; athletes use imagery for both motivational and cognitive purposes. The present findings support this dual role. In all three experiments there was a clear distinction between motivational uses of imagery (e.g., imagining emotion-arousing situations) and cognitive ones (e.g., imagining the motor skills necessary for success). Furthermore, it is evident that MG imagery has two components, imagery associated with arousal and emotions (MG-A) and imagery associated with being in control, mentally tough, and confident (MG-M). This latter type of imagery represents an extension of Paivio's (1985) framework and in Experiment 3 athletes reported using MG-M imagery most often. Moreover, athletes consistently indicated using imagery more for its motivational function than its cognitive function, a finding previously reported by Salmon et al. (1994) for soccer players. This more extensive use of motivational imagery fits with the greater reported use of imagery in conjunction with competition than with practice (Barr & Hall, 1992; Hall et al., 1990a,b). At competitions athletes are concerned with performing well and achieving their goals and their imagery use reflects these concerns. It is too late to be concerned about getting better (i.e., learning), a primary reason for engaging in cognitive imagery.

The present findings also offer indirect support for recent research demonstrating a relationship between imagery use and sport confidence (Moritz Hall, Martin & Vadocz, 1996), and between imagery use and state anxiety (Vadocz, Hall & Moritz, in press). Moritz et al. found that MG-M imagery was the best predictor of state-sport confidence and suggested that when it comes to sport confidence, the imaged rehearsal of specific skills may not be as important as the imagery of sport-related mastery experiences and emotions. Vadocz et al. found that MG-A imagery use significantly predicted cognitive state anxiety and argued that imagery can be employed to help control competitive anxiety levels. Because most imagery research has considered the cognitive function of imagery, these results also point to the need for further examination of the motivational function of imagery.

Both motivational and cognitive imagery can be targeted toward either specific or general behaviors (Paivio, 1985). On the motivational side, this specific-general contrast was very evident in the present experiments. Athletes reported imagining specific goals such as winning a medal and being applauded or congratulated for a good performance (MS imagery). With respect to more general behaviors, they imagined mastering the competitive situation (e.g., being in control, being mentally tough, and staying focused; MG-M imagery) and the excitement and emotions of competing (MG-A imagery). While people readily conceptualize the difference between imagining skills (CS imagery) and imagining strategies (CG imagery), as shown by the results of Experiment 2, the distinction between skills and strategies is sometimes not as defined as that between MS imagery and MG imagery when athletes are actually using imagery. This was shown in Experiment 3 as two of the CG items loaded on the CS factor. Salmon, Hall & Haslam (1994) found support for the CG function with soccer players, and there are other sports (e.g., football, basketball) still to be examined in which the imagining of skills and strategies may be better differentiated than in the sports examined here.

Given the converging lines of evidence obtained from Experiments 2 and 3, we believe the SIQ to be a useful tool for further systematic studies of the use and functions of different types of imagery by athletes. There are numerous directions such research can take. While there has been some recent interest in motivational imagery (e.g., Martin & Hall, 1995; Moritz, Hall, Martin & Vadocz, 1996; Vadocz, Hall & Moritz, in press), the relationships between imagery and variables such as goal-setting, state anxiety, and self-confidence require additional investigation. The results of Experiment 3 provide an indication that imagery use is related to successful performance, but the exact relationship seems to vary with the skill level of the athlete and the sport. As suggested earlier, since novice athletes are primarily concerned with skill improvement, they would likely use cognitive imagery most. Elite athletes, however, are more concerned with winning and the use of motivational imagery would seem more appropriate. This issue needs to be explored further. Another possibility is to examine how imagery use changes over the course of a season. Measuring individual differences in how athletes use imagery has proven to be a worthwhile approach (e.g., Hall & Barr, 1992; Salmon, Hall & Haslam, 1994), and the development of the SIQ will improve and facilitate this type of research.

References

Barr, K., & Hall, C. R (1992). The use of imagery by rowers. *International Journal of Sport Psychology, 23*, 243–261.

Clark, L., & Watson, D. (1995). Constructing validity: Basic issues in scale development. *Psychology Assessment, 7*, 309–319.

Hall, C. R. (1985). Individual differences in the mental practice and imagery of motor skill performance. *Canadian Journal of Applied Sport Sciences, 10*, 17S–21S.

Hall, C. R (1995). The motivational function of mental imagery for participation in sport and exercise. In J. Annett, B. Cripps & H. Steinberg (Eds.), *Exercise addiction: Motivation for participation in sport and exercise* (pp. 17–23). Leicester: BPS Publications.

Hall, C. R., Rodgers, W. M., & Barr, K. A. (1990a). The use of imagery by athletes in selected sports. *The Sport Psychologist, 4*, 1–10.

Hall, C., Toews, J., & Rodgers, W (1990b). Les aspects motivationnels de l'imagerie en activities motrices. *Revue des Sciences et Techniques des Activities Physiques et Sportives, 11*, 27–32.

Mahoney, M.J., Gabriel, T.J., & Perkins, T.S. (1987). Psychological skills and exceptional athletic performance. *The Sport Psychologist, 1*, 181–199.

Martin, K.A., & Hall, C.R. (1995). Using mental imagery to enhance intrinsic motivation. *Journal of Sport and Exercise Psychology, 17*, 54–69.

Mercier, P., & Beauregard, M. (1993). *The Mercier tables.* Ottawa; Athletics Canada.

Mortiz, S.E., Hall, C.R., Martin, K.A., & Vadocz, E. (1996). What are confident athletes imaging?: An examination of image content. *The Sport Psychologist, 10*, 171–179.

Nunnally, J.C. (1978). *Psychometric theory.* (2nd ed.). New York: McGraw Hill.

Orlick, T., & Partington, J. (1986*). Psyched.* Ottawa: Coaching Association of Canada.

Paivio, A. (1971). *Imagery and verbal processes.* New York: Holt, Rinehart & Winston.

Paivio, A. (1985). Cognitive and motivational functions of imagery in human performance. *Canadian Journal of Applied Sport Sciences. 10*, 22S–28S.

Paivio, A., & Harshman, R.A. (1983). Factor analysis of a questionnaire on imagery and verbal habits and skills. *Canadian Journal of Psychology, 37*, 461–483.

Salmon, J., Hall, C., & Haslam, I. (1994). The use of imagery by soccer players. *Journal of Applied Sport Psychology, 6*, 116–133.

Tabachnick, B.G., & Fidell, L.S. (1989). *Using multivariate statistics.* New York: Harper & Row.

Vadocz, E.A., Hall, C.R., & Mortiz, S. (In press). The relationship between competitive anxiety and imagery use. *Journal of Applied Sport Psychology.*

Vealey, R.S. (1986). Mental imagery training for performance enhancement. In J.M. Williams (Ed.), *Applied sport psychology: Personal growth to peak performance* (pp. 209–234). Mountain View, CA: Mayfield.

28 Reliability and Validity of The Attentional and Interpersonal Style (TAIS) Inventory Concentration Scales

ROBERT M. NIDEFFER
Enhanced Performance Systems
San Diego State University

Robert Nideffer is renowned for his numerous publications and applied work in the areas of attention and concentration. The Attentional and Interpersonal Style (TAIS) inventory he first published in 1976 is still one of the most used questionnaires in applied sport psychology. The TAIS identifies an individual's concentration and interpersonal strengths and weaknesses. This information can then be used in developing performance-enhancement programs. TAIS originally assessed four attentional styles. Recent research has prompted the author to expand this to six attentional styles.

Over the years, some have questioned the reliability and validity of TAIS. Nideffer advocates that "the assumption of statistical independence of the attentional constructs, or of any performance-relevant cognitive or personality characteristic, is inappropriate . . . because attentional constructs are not and cannot be completely statistically independent of each other . . ." He specifically advocated that the TAIS internal consistency reliability coefficients are appropriate for applied basic research. The test–retest reliability coefficients are strong. The predictive validity is noteworthy especially since these data are derived from a large number of elite athletes and this level of athlete is underrepresented in most other research.

He also makes a case that different sports require different types of concentration, that there are gender differences for TAIS scales, and that concentration skills change over time. Nideffer's emphasis on the split between science and application brings to the surface problems that have plagued the field since its inception. He emphasizes the importance of conceptual independence of constructs as opposed to simply statistical independence. He concludes with some points about researchers' acceptable error variance and contrasts this with the practitioners' view. The author did an excellent job, in this original publication, of refuting the previous criticism of TAIS and emphasized the practical value of this commonly used inventory.

In 1976, I published a research article and a book that were to have a large impact on the field of sport psychology. The article appeared in the *Journal of Personality and Social Psychology* and described the development and validation of an instrument called "The Attentional and Interpersonal Style (TAIS) Inventory" (Nideffer, 1976a). TAIS was based on a theory I had developed about the relationship between an individual's concentration skills, their level of emotional arousal, and performance. The inventory was designed to measure those concentration skills and interpersonal characteristics that the theory suggested were the key components or "building blocks of performance."

The second publication was *The Inner Athlete,* a self-help book written for a lay audience that talked about the importance of concentration in sport, and presented parts of my theory (Nideffer, 1976b). The book included an abbreviated measure of the concentration skills measured by TAIS, along with information about how to use a variety of psychological procedures to improve one's ability to concentrate.

TAIS is a 144-item, self-report, paper and pencil inventory, and although publication of the inventory coincided with the release of a book on sport psychology, it is important to point out that TAIS was not developed as a sport psychology measure. Instead, TAIS was designed to be used to identify an individual's concentration and interpersonal strengths and weaknesses, independent of their particular performance arena. That information would then be used in the development of programs to help individuals improve their level of performance by either strengthening or better managing the concentration skills and interpersonal characteristics that proved to be most important to their particular job or performance objective.

Both *The Inner Athlete,* and TAIS, had an immediate impact on the field of sport psychology (Salmela, 1981; Snyder & Abernethy, 1992). What was of most interest within the sporting environment were those scales on TAIS, and those aspects of the theory, that dealt with concentration skills. The importance of concentration, the need to better define it, and the need to provide ways to help individuals improve was intuitively obvious to every coach, athlete, and psychological practitioneer who had ever been involved in sport. As a result, TAIS items and TAIS theory found their way in the Coaching Association of Canada's training and certification manuals for all their coaches at every level from youth sport to the Olympics (Coaching Association of Canada, 1981). The theory and test were incorporated into the development of athletes at the Australian Institute for Sport from the time it opened in the early '80s (Bond & Sargent, 1995). Both are being used at Olympic training centers in other parts of the world including Spain (Nideffer, 1989) and Italy (Selder, 1982; Cei, et. al., 1997). Finally, *The Inner Athlete* and TAIS were translated into Russian and Chinese and had an impact in Eastern European and Communist countries long before the Iron Curtain came down.

The interest in TAIS and in the theory weren't confined to the area of application. According to Fogarty (1995), the theory related to attentional styles was the third most heavily researched area within sport psychology between 1974, and 1992. Some of that research raised questions about the reliability and validity of one of the attentional constructs underlying the development of TAIS attentional scales (Van Schoyck & Grasha, 1981; Vallerand, 1983; Albrecht & Feltz, 1987; Dewey, Brawley, & Allard, 1989; Summers & Ford, 1990; Summers, Miller, & Ford, 1991). It is those questions that I want to address in this article. Before getting into the questions, however, I should review the constructs that TAIS is based on, and the concentration skills and interpersonal characteristics the instrument measures.

TAIS Attentional Constructs

- The intersection of the dimension of width and the dimension of direction of concentration leads to the identification of four distinct attentional styles: a broad-external style used to rapidly assess the environment; a broad-internal style used for problem solving and strategic thinking and planning; a narrow-internal style used to rehearse, systematize, and organize information; a narrow-external focus used for execution once an external performance-relevant target has been identified.
- Different performance situations require different amounts of shifting and/or place greater emphasis on particular concentration or attentional styles.
- Although the average individual has the ability to shift concentration along both dimensions the majority of the time, different individuals have different preferred or dominant concentration styles.
- Under pressure, shifting of attention breaks down as an individual's more highly developed or dominant concentration style begins to control the person, rather than the other way around. If the performance situation is one that plays to the person's dominant style, they perform well, if not, they lose their ability to make the adjustments needed in their focus of concentration to pick up performance-relevant cues and begin to make performance and/or decision-making errors.
- The specific type of mistake a person is most likely to make in what is for them a high-pressure situation will be mistakes related to their dominant concentration style.
- Choking, or a downward performance spiral, occurs when an individual's level of emotional arousal reaches the point that attention begins to involuntarily narrow and become increasingly focused on task-irrelevant internal thoughts and feelings. This is most likely to happen in those situations where the performance outcome is critical to the individual, where initial increases in emotional arousal causes them to rely too heavily on their particular strengths leading to mistakes, and as a result of the mistakes, the individual then loses confidence in their ability to achieve a successful outcome. This leads to a narrow internal focus on negative thoughts and feelings, a focus the individual is unable to break out of on his or her own.

When TAIS was developed, items were written to assess the ability to develop all four attentional styles. Items were also written to identify the types of mistakes, or the failure to make appropriate shifts in concentration. Subsequent item analyses revealed that items measuring the ability to narrow one's focus of concentration along both the external and internal dimensions were so highly inter-correlated that it was likely they were measuring the same thing. Thus, the items were combined into a single scale measuring focus. Likewise, correlations between items measuring errors because of a failure to shift from a narrow-external to a narrow-internal focus or vice versa, were combined into a single scale measuring errors of under-inclusion. This resulted in the development of the following six attentional scales:

- BET, a measure of the ability to develop a broad-external focus of concentration.
- BIT, a measure of the ability to develop a broad-internal focus of concentration.
- NAR, a measure of the ability to develop a narrow focus of concentration.
- OET, a measure of the tendency toward environmental distractibility or external overload.
- OIT, a measure of the tendency toward internal overload or distractibility.
- RED, a measure of a tendency toward a reduced focus of concentration, resulting in errors of under-inclusion.

TAIS Attentional Scale Reliability and Validity

There were two questions being raised by researchers. One had to do with whether or not TAIS scales designed to differentiate between an internal and an external attentional style were reliable and/or valid. The other, not unrelated to that question had to do with whether on not the attentional scales could reliably differentiate between levels of performance within sport.

Questions about the reliability and validity of the TAIS construct relating to the existence and measurement of a separate external and internal focus of concentration came from a few studies that used factor analysis of subjects' scores on the six TAIS attentional scales to see if the factor structure replicated the six TAIS scales (Van Schoyck & Grasha, 1981; Landers, 1982; Vallerand, 1983; Ford & Summers, 1992). This research was predicated on the belief that the attentional constructs being measured by TAIS should be uncorrelated with each other, or statistically independent.

What investigators found, and what I have found in countless studies with every kind of subject population from athletes, to CEOs, to special operations forces, is that factor analysis of the six TAIS attentional scales does not result in six factors. Instead, it results in two or three factors depending on the analysis, and/or the subject population being studied. The two factors that show up in virtually every analysis and account for about 70% of the variance are a factor reflecting the ability to narrow attention and avoid becoming distracted (NAR, –OET, –OIT), and a factor reflecting the ability to develop a broad focus of concentration avoiding the tendency to make mistakes of under-inclusion (BET, BIT, –RED). The three-factor solution accounts for 85% of the variance, pulling the RED scale away from factor 2 and combining it with the NAR scale which loads on both factor 1 and factor 3. This factor is more common with athletes and high scores on the factor suggest considerable attention to detail and a perfectionistic attitude on the part of the athlete. The conclusions drawn by these researchers based on the attentional factor structure was that there was support for the attentional construct of width of attention (broad to narrow focus), but not for the construct of direction of focus, internal to external (Abernethy, Summers, & Ford, 1998).

As I pointed out in an article in *The Sport Psychologist* (Nideffer, 1990), the assumption of statistical independence of the attentional constructs, or of any performance-relevant cognitive or personality characteristics is inappropriate. Using the attentional constructs as an example, the effective analysis of a problem (BIT) is dependent at least in part upon the individual's ability to gather or assess relevant external data (BET), and also dependent upon the individual's ability to organize that data and drive to a solution (NAR). The mutual interdependence of these attentional styles suggests they should be correlated with each other, and if they are, then factor analysis will not identify six factors reflecting the six different scales. Factor analysis will cluster scales together into factors around the constructs that seem to be accounting for the most variance. In this case, the variables accounting for the greatest amount of variance were those reflecting width of focus of concentration and effective and ineffective processing supporting these constructs. But because attentional constructs are not, and cannot be completely statistically independent of each other, factor analysis can not, or at least should not, be used to rule out constructs not supported by the factor structure.

Interestingly, factor analysis has been the tool of choice to demonstrate the inter-connectedness of various personality and cognitive behaviors, not their independence. Indeed, the definition of factor analysis provided in the American Psychological Association's Standards for educational and psychological testing is (APA, 1985): "Any of several methods of analyzing the intercorrelations or covariances among variables by constructing hypothetical factors, which are fewer in number than the original variables. It indicates how much of the variation in each original measure can be accounted for by each of the hypothetical factors" (pg. 91).

The fact that various intelligence subscales cluster together is seen by some as support for Spearman's theory of g, or general intelligence, and it is the inter-relatedness of personality characteristics as demonstrated by factor analysis that has led to the "Big Five" personality theory (John, 1990; Digman, 1997). What factor analysis of a broad range of personality inventories has shown, is that the literally hundreds of personality characteristics which make sense to us conceptually, and that we use to describe the behavior of others, typically cluster together into five broad personality factors (Barrack & Mount, 1991; Hough, 1992; Tett, Jackson, & Rothstein, 1991; Hogan, Hogan, and Roberts 1996).

The five broad or higher order factors identified by researchers include: 1) A leadership factor; 2) A factor reflecting emotional stability; 3) A factor reflecting conscientiousness; 4) A factor reflecting agreeableness, and; 5) A factor reflecting "intellectance," or being open, imaginative, broad minded, curious. Not surprising, when all twenty scales on TAIS are factor analyzed they typically result in five factors that to one degree or another can be related to the "big five" factors, and account for between 68 and 80% of the variance in subjects' test scores (Nideffer, 1990).

Does the fact that personality characteristics correlate with each other mean we have to abandon the use of the individual scales that make up those clusters, that they aren't valid and/or useful? No, in fact just the reverse. Although different personality characteristics share common variance with one or more of the five broad factors, they are each carving out a smaller portion of that larger factor, a portion that has relevance to a particular type of performance and/or situation (Hogan, Curphy, & Hogan, 1994). In other words, just because a personality characteristic is not completely statistically independent doesn't necessarily mean it is invalid or irrelevant. In fact, that characteristic may be much better as a predictor in certain situations than the broader behavioral category that it is associated with.

Reliability of TAIS Attentional Scales

The same group of researchers using factor analysis to examine the independence of TAIS attentional scales were the ones raising questions about the internal consistency or reliability of the scales (Van Schoyck & Grasha, 1981; Landers, 1982; Vallerand, 1983; Ford & Summers, 1992; Abernethy, Summers, & Ford, 1998). Internal consistency is a measure of the extent to which the items within a scale are measuring the same construct. The internal consistency or reliability coefficients found by these investigators for the six attentional scales averaged .645 and ranged from .57 to .72. These scores are statistically significant and do indicate the scales have a moderate level of internal consistency or reliability.

What is an appropriate level of reliability? Nunnally (1967), in his classic text on Psychometric Theory stated, "In the early stages of research one saves time and energy by working with instruments that have only modest reliability for which purposes reliabilities of .6 or .5 will suffice. . . . For basic research it can be argued that increasing reliability beyond .8 is often wasteful" (pg. 226).

If one examines the internal reliability coefficients for scales on the Wechsler Adult Intelligence Scale, and on the Minnesota Multiphasic Personality Inventory, they find a number of the scales on both instruments have reliability coefficients below .7 (Matarazzo, 1972; Dahlstrom, Welsh, and Dahlstrom, 1975).

Internal consistency of the items within a scale is going to vary for several reasons, other than "measurement error," depending on what the instrument has been designed to do. Internal consistency may vary because the items, although measuring a single construct, focus on the use of application of that attribute in different performance situations. Internal consistency of items may also vary because the construct the items are measuring is complex and different items are measuring different aspects of the construct.

It is true that the more narrowly defined the construct, the more easily understood the items, the less items range in difficulty, and the more situation-specific the focus of the items the higher you would expect the internal reliability coefficients to be. Investigators questioning the reliability of TAIS attentional scales were invested in the development of sport-specific versions of the TAIS attentional scales and were contrasting the reliability coefficients for those versions with the reliability coefficients they found for TAIS scales.

TAIS was not designed to be sport specific or situation specific. The goal was to create an inventory that would be useful for predicting behavioral predispositions in high-pressure performance situations, and for providing feedback about concentration skills to individuals involved in a variety of performance settings, feedback, that would help them improve performance. To this end, items within scales, although created to measure a specific construct like width of attention, differed from each other with respect to the performance arena they focused on. The theory underlying TAIS suggests that concentration and interpersonal skills have both state and trait components. Those skills and abilities that are more trait like for a given individual are the ones that dominate their behavior and define their "preferred style" of attending and interacting with others. To the extent a given subject's abilities are situation specific as opposed to being more trans-situational or trait like, the differences in the focus of items within scales acts to reduce internal reliability coefficients.

What becomes more important then than internal reliability coefficients for the attentional scales, is the stability of subjects' scores on those scales over time. Two-week test-retest reliability coefficients for all eighteen TAIS scales, on a group of 45 male and 45 female college students averaged .83 (Nideffer, 1976a). Eighteen-month test-retest reliability coefficients for a group of 776 elite level athletes at the Australian Institute for sport ranged from .52 to .74 with a mean and median of .64. It should be pointed out that athletes' scores on the first test were used to counsel them relative to steps they could take to improve concentration, and programs were developed which would be expected to cause positive changes in subjects' scores on the concentration scales. In spite of the variability introduced by training, TAIS test-retest reliability coefficients are well within the acceptable range for psychological inventories and clearly indicate subjects' scores are reasonably stable over time.

TAIS Predictive Validity

According to Moran (1996), studies of the predictive validity of TAIS attentional scales have had mixed, and at times confusing, results. High scores on the scale measuring a narrow focus, and correspondingly low scores on the external distractibility and internal distractibility scales have been found to predict performance in diving (Nideffer, 1987), and in rifle shooting (Landers, Furst, & Daniels, 1981). Those findings would be expected. The findings by Wilson, Ainsworth, & Bird (1985) that good concentrators in volleyball score higher on the narrow-focus scale and lower on the scales measuring a broad-external focus and a broad-internal focus are not so intuitively obvious. Nor is the finding by Kirshenbaum and Bale (1984), who discovered that expert golfers scored higher on both the narrow-focus scale and the TAIS scale measuring errors of under- inclusion than novice golfers. Finally, Summers, Miller, and Ford (1991) failed to find differences on the TAIS attentional scales between athletes with different levels of skill in the sports of cricket, basketball, and fencing.

For a long time, I was as confused about the results found by Wilson et al., and by Kirshenbaum and Bale, as others. Nor could I explain the failure of Summers et al. (1991) to find differences between athletes as a function of level of skill when other studies had. Over the past few years, however, through additional research, I have gained some insight that has helped refine my theoretical constructs, and at the same time explains some of the earlier, seemingly conflicting findings.

In what follows, I am going to first comment on some of the issues affecting the ability of researchers to find predicted relationships between test scores and outcome measures, and then review the construct and predictive validity of TAIS attentional scales in more detail. I will be adding new data to the literature and will relate that data to the theoretical constructs presented earlier in this paper.

Issues in Applied Research

In my 1987 article responding to questions about the predictive validity of TAIS, I identified a number of factors that make applied research difficult, especially when that research attempts to look at between-subject or between-group differences. I also offered some suggestions for reducing some of the error variance that interferes with the ability of many researchers to find hypothesized relationships (Nideffer, 1987). It is worth reviewing a couple of those here as they are related to the data that follows.

One problem researchers face involves gaining access to a large enough group of elite level performers. Because performance is complex and dependent upon a great many factors, it is difficult to get reliable, significant results with studies that only look at one or two predictor variables. Yet that is a compromise researchers often make when they cannot get a large enough group of subjects. One of the advantages I have over many other researchers, as the developer and distributor of TAIS, is access to a tremendous amount of data. That includes data on 239 world champion athletes, over a thousand corporate presidents and CEOs, all of the data from the Australian Institute for Sport from 1982 through 2005, as well as data from other Olympic training centers around the world.

Perhaps even more important than the numbers of elite level performers one has access to, however, are the conditions under which testing takes place. When data is collected strictly for research purposes and/or to make selection decisions, it affects the willingness of some subjects to cooperate, as well as the honesty of subjects' responses. This introduces considerable error variance into the data, dramatically increasing the number of subjects one needs to test for significance, and making between-subject comparisons of test data tenuous at best. Once again I am fortunate, in that I have access to data which was not collected for research purposes. All of the athlete and business data I will be talking about, including the data from the AIS, data on world champion athletes, and data on CEOs' of corporations throughout North America, was gathered to be used to provide feedback to those taking the inventory. The feedback was designed to help them improve their performance. Because testing conditions were non-threatening, and because the motivation to improve was extremely high among these individuals, responses tended to be more open and honest leading to less "error variance" in the data.

Construct Validity of TAIS Attentional Scales

What evidence is there to show: 1) that different individuals have different concentration strengths or styles; 2) that concentration skills have both state and trait components; 3) that different performance situations require different concentration skills; 4) that individuals gravitate toward and perform better in situations where the concentration demands match their particular skills; and 5) that the type of concentration error a person is most likely to make in pressure situations is directly related to his or her concentration strength?

When elite athletes' scores on TAIS concentration skills are standardized using the norms for the general population, athletes independent of gender, age, or level of performance are dominated by a narrow focus of attention. Not only that, but a comparison of elite-level performers at the AIS in Australia with a group of 142 athletes from around the world who had either won a world championship or an Olympic medal revealed that as the level of a performance for elite-level athletes increases scores on the narrow-focus scale on TAIS also increase, and scores on the broad-internal or analytical scale on TAIS decrease (Nideffer, Sagal, Lowry, and Bond, 2001; Nideffer & Bond 2003).

To investigate the phenomena further, we collected data on an additional 97 world champions bringing the total population to 239 athletes. Next, we divided them into two groups, a group that had won a single world championship or Olympic medal (N=152) and a group that had won multiple medals (N=87). Subjects' scores on the BET, BIT, and NAR scales were converted to standard scores and then to percentiles scores. The percentile scores reflect how the two groups of world champions compare to the general population, as well as to each other (Nideffer, Bond, Cei, & Manili, 2003).

For both groups, the dominant concentration style is focused. A Newman Keuls analysis of the significant interaction ($F = 7.38$, $df = 2, 474$, $p < .001$) shows that multiple medal winners are significantly more focused that single medal winners ($p < .01$), and significantly less analytical ($p = .038$). These results are consistent with those of Wilson, et al., (1985), in that they found elite performers to have lower scores on the BET and BIT scores and higher scores on the NAR or focus scale. The results provide additional support for TAIS 's ability to differentiate between athletes of different skill levels.

Although the results support the ability of TAIS attentional scales to differentiate between athletes as a function of level of performance, they seem to be inconsistent with the hypothesis that different types of sports or performance situations require different concentration strengths, and that athletes gravitate toward and/or perform better in those sports that play to their particular strengths. All elite athletes, when compared to the general population, are dominated by a narrow focus of concentration.

Concentration Skills as a Function of Type of Sport

By standardizing athletes' scores on TAIS based on their own means and standard deviations, instead of those of the general population, you remove the bias created by their exceptionally high NAR scores. When you do that, the "average" elite athlete scores at the 50th percentile on each of the attentional scales. Now when you separate athletes into groups based on the type of sport they participate in you begin to see the differences in concentration skills predicted by TAIS theory (Bond & Nideffer, 1992; Nideffer, 1993).

Recently, I went back to data collected on 4766 athletes at the AIS. There were 2535 athletes involved in team sports like hockey, soccer, baseball, 767 athletes involved in closed-skill sports like diving, archery, shooting, and 1464 athletes involved in open-skill sports like tennis, judo, and karate.

A Newman Keuls analysis revealed closed-skill sports participants continue to be dominated, as would be predicted, by a narrow focus of concentration, scoring significantly lower in both the aware and analytical areas ($p < .001$), and significantly higher than the other two groups on the focus scale ($p < .001$). Athletes participating in team sports and open-skill sports score significantly higher on the awareness scale than athletes in closed-skill sports ($p < .001$). The difference on the awareness scale between open-skill and team sports is also significant ($p = .03$). The differences between all three groups on the analytical scale are significant ($p < .01$). These results support the hypothesis that different sports require different types of concentration, and that athletes gravitate toward and perform better in sports that play to their particular concentration styles. These findings showing both between-subject and between-performance situation differences in concentration skills are not limited to athletes and/or to sport. These results provide additional support for the ability of TAIS scales to differentiate between groups based on level of performance and type of performance situation. They provide support for the construct of a broad-internal focus of concentration, and a focused concentration, and support for the hypothesis that high-level performers perform well because they find performance arenas that play to their strengths. The fact that scores on external awareness scale are significantly different from scores on the analytical scale indicates the two scales measure different constructs.

Concentration Errors

What TAIS theory would predict, given the ability to focus is a world champion's greatest strength, is that both world champion groups are significantly more likely to make errors of under-inclusion than they are to make either of the other errors ($p<.01$). In addition multiple medal winners are more likely to make errors of under-inclusion ($p<.01$) and less likely to make mistakes because they become internally overloaded than single medal winners ($p=.02$). Again, these results would be predicted by TAIS theory based on their respective scores on the TAIS scales measuring analytical skill and focus. The results are also consistent with those found by Kirshenbaum and Bale (1984), with elite golfers.

We might want to ask why multiple medal winners would score higher on the scale measuring under-inclusive errors than single medal winners. It isn't surprising that this is the highest error score, because that fits with the theory, but why would they be more likely than other elite athletes to be under-inclusive? I believe the answer to that can be found in what the RED scale on TAIS measures.

The scale measuring under-inclusive errors was designed to provide an indication of a breakdown in shifting between an external focus and an internal one. The individual either focuses too narrowly on internal thoughts and issues and ignores what is going on around him or her, or focuses too narrowly on the environment and fails to analyze situations when that is what is called for. Because TAIS was designed to measure general behavioral tendencies rather than situation-specific behavior, items ask things like, "I can become so involved in something I am doing that I lose awareness of things going on around me."

Because of the nature of the items on the scale whether or not a high score is seen as negative is at times a value judgment. For example, highly dedicated individuals may not pay attention to things going on around them, but they don't care because they are focused on what is important to them, and not on what others might like them to be paying attention to. They admit to making mistakes because they failed to shift attention when others wanted them to and/or didn't hear or react to things. These types of mistakes, however, instead of detracting from their performance actually contribute to their improvement because it is their performance-oriented focus (e.g., mentally rehearsing their sport, thinking about strategy, etc.) that prevents them from paying attention to others.

This fact makes it necessary to interpret an individual's score on the RED scale on TAIS within the context of his or her scores on other scales. Individuals who score high on the control scale and the self-confidence scale and also score high on the RED scale are perfectionists and highly focused. They make mistakes because they are focused but they don't see their behavior as a problem because it's helping them perform where in their mind it really counts. Those individuals who score high on the RED scale and score low on the scale measuring control and self-confidence do see their behavior, not just for themselves, but for others as well.

The relationship between the scale measuring errors of under-inclusion and the perfection of skills helps us understand the research findings of Kirshenbaum and Bale (1984). High scores for the elite golfers they tested on both the NAR and RED scale are consistent with the kind of dedication and perfectionism required to groove one's swing. The fact that narrowing of attention is an elite golfer's dominant concentration style is also consistent with the style required by closed-skill sports like golf. In addition, the fact that the errors of under-inclusion score was the highest error score is also consistent with the hypothesis that an athlete's greatest concentration skill will likely be his or her greatest weakness. What then happens to the types of mistakes athletes make when we standardize their scores based on their own means and standard deviations instead of the general population's?

There is significant interaction between type of concentration error and type of sport (F-7.129, df = 4,9520, $p < .001$) when subjects' scores are standardized based on their own means and standard deviations. Athletes involved in closed-skill sports, as we would predict based on the theory, are significantly more likely to make errors of under-inclusion than they are to become distracted or overloaded ($p < .01$), and they are more likely to make errors of under-inclusion than athletes in team sports ($p < .01$) and open-skill sports ($p = .05$). Athletes in open-skill sports scores in the three areas do not differ from each other, but they make significantly more mistakes because they become distracted than the other two groups ($p < .01$), and they make significantly more mistakes because they become overloaded than do athletes involved in team sports ($p < .01$). Athletes in team sports make fewer mistakes overall than the other two groups ($p < .01$), and are more likely to become distracted ($p < .01$), and/or overloaded ($p < .01$), than they are to become under-inclusive. Their scores on the distractibility and overload scales did not differ significantly from each other ($p = .2$).

These results provide additional support for the theoretical construct relating concentration errors to concentration strengths. It is interesting that athletes involved in team sports tend to make fewer errors than the other two groups. That may be due to the fact that teammates can serve as supports and reminders, helping them maintain an appropriate focus of attention.

Gender Differences

Another source of construct validity for TAIS comes from gender differences found when males and females are compared on both the test's attentional and interpersonal scales.

There is compelling neurobiological evidence to support the observations that from an information-processing standpoint, women appear to have more thought-linking capacity than men, whereas men have a greater capacity to inhibit information, to focus and process information in a logical, sequential way. Women's perceptual skills are oriented toward quick intuitive people reading, detecting thoughts and feelings, and absorbing contextual cues and responding in empathetic ways; men on the other hand are more oriented toward logical, sequential processing (Kimura, 2001; Marano, 2003; Cahill, 2005).

Studies that have looked at gender differences with respect to scores on the concentration scales on TAIS consistently find that males score significantly higher on the BIT (Analysis) scale, and on the NAR (focus) scale than women. With respect to the BET scale which measures environmental awareness, the results have been mixed, but there have been consistent differences showing that females are more externally distracted than males. These findings hold across cultures (Schmelzer, 1981), when looking at athletes across age levels and type of sport (Bond & Nideffer, 1992), when looking at differences between husbands and wives (LaMotte, 1981).

What is interesting when you look at the patterns of scores for males and females on the effective attentional scales is that there are some marked differences. For females external awareness is almost always either their highest or second-highest score and their score on the analytical scale is almost always their lowest. For males the pattern is the exact opposite. Scores on the analytical scale are almost always either the highest, or the second highest, and their score on external awareness is frequently the lowest.

One of the ways to examine these differences is to create an attentional efficiency score for each of the effective attentional scales by: 1) Standardizing scores based on the population being tested; 2) Taking each scale score once it has been standardized, doubling it, and then subtracting the other two scales in the group from it, for example, (BET×2)–(BIT+NAR); 3) The resulting efficiency scores are then standardized based on their respective means and standard deviations. It is these scores that are used in the data analysis instead of the regular BET, BIT, NAR scores.

The effect of this alteration in scores is to provide an indication of the relative position of subjects' attentional scales to each other. Thus, instead of just looking at between-subject differences, which are much more affected by response styles and response sets, you are looking at within-subject differences. It is the relative position of the attentional scales to each other, independent of the absolute elevation of the scale that defines a subject's, or a group's concentration strengths and weaknesses.

An analysis of variance was conducted to look at concentration efficiency scores as a function of both gender and vocation. To get a larger number of female CEOs, two CEO groups were combined into one (M = 910, F = 93). The Business Norm Group consisted of 1186 males and 522 females. The world champion group contained 171 males and 68 females. There is significant gender by concentration-efficiency scores interaction (F = 13.89, df = 2,5930, $p < .001$). It is important to keep in mind that the resulting analysis does not really show how males and females compare to each other with respect to the absolute elevation of their scores on the concentration scales. In other words, just because the analysis scale for males is higher than it is for females doesn't mean they actually had a higher percentile score on the scale. The data show the strength of the relative positions of the scales for the two different groups. What you are interested in is not the elevation of scores across groups, but the elevation of scores within each group. It is the pattern of each group's scores that is important.

Females score significantly higher on the scale measuring external awareness than they do on the scale measuring analytical skill ($p < .001$) and than they do on the scale measuring focused concentration ($p = .05$). Thus, their preferred style and their confidence is in their ability to read and react to the environment, and much less so in their ability to analyze and problem solve. Males on the other hand have relatively little confidence in their environmental awareness, and much more confidence in their ability to analyze ($p < .001$) and in their ability to focus ($P < .001$).

There are significant gender by groups by concentration-efficiency interaction ($F = 3.659$, $df = 4,5930$, $p = .005$). Once again, it is important to remember that you cannot with this analysis make comparisons across or between the different groups. What matters is each group's pattern of attention scores, as it is that pattern that tells you what they perceive their strengths and weaknesses to be.

Looking first at the male and female CEO groups, what you see is that the male CEOs perceive their greatest strength is their analytical skill ($p < .001$), followed by their ability to read and react to the environment, which is significantly higher than their ability to focus ($p < .01$). For females, their greatest strength seems to be their ability to read and react to the environment, which is significantly higher than their score on focus ($p < .001$) and marginally higher than their score on analysis ($p = .06$). It would appear as if women CEOs rely more on their ability to read people and situations than male CEOs do.

The basic concentration skills pattern found with female CEOs is also found with females in the business-norm group, though these differences are not statistically significant. What they continue to show, however, is the relative strength of awareness for women. For males in the business-norm group, the pattern relative to CEOs changes slightly in that focus is higher than BET. Once again, this pattern would be predicted based on the theory and on the differences in job demands that exist between levels of management. The lower a manager is in the hierarchy, the more focused and hands on he or she needs to be. The higher the manager goes, the less hands on, and the more strategic he or she needs to be.

With the world champion athlete groups, for both males and females it is the analytical area that is the area of relative weakness. For males focus is the preferred style and greatest strength ($p < .001$). The difference for males between aware and analytical is not significant. For females, focus is the strength relative to analytical ($p < .001$) and external awareness ($p = .04$). The external awareness efficiency score for female world champions, however, is significantly higher than their efficiency score for analytical ($p < .01$).

It is analyses like these that show both the state and trait component of the different concentration strengths. Although there appears to be room to move along the attentional dimensions in response to different environments, the consistency for women of the strength of BET in most settings and of BIT for men in most settings also supports the concept of a trait component, which may vary in intensity from group to group. An analytical focus is more critical and traitlike in the business environment, and a narrow focus appears to be more critical and trait-like at elite levels of sport. Additional evidence of the importance of being born with a predisposition toward and/or more of a trait-like component with respect to the ability to focus can be found in some test-retest data gathered at the AIS.

Changes in Concentration Skills Over Time

TAIS has been administered to athletes at the Australian Institute for Sport when they first enter the institute. The purpose behind the testing process is to assess existing concentration skills, and to then develop a program working with the Institute coaches to help athletes improve their ability to concentrate and avoid making mental errors. Frequently, athletes are re-tested as a part of their development process to see what changes, if any, have occurred, and/or to provide additional direction. The data that follows was collected on 776 athletes at the AIS. The subjects can be broken down in the following ways. There were 244 females, 90 between the ages of 11 and 16, 68 either 17 or 18 years old, 52 between 19 and 24, and 34 were 25 or older. Breaking those individuals up on the basis of their sport, 28 were involved in closed-skill sports, 104 in open-skill sports, and 112 in team sports. The breakdown for the 532 males was as follows. Seventy-three males were involved in closed-skill sports, 190 were involved in open-skill sports, and 269 were involved in team sports. Seventy-seven males were between the ages of 11 and 16, 121 were either 17 or 18, 211 were between 19 and 24, and the remaining 157 were 25 or older.

Independent of gender, age, or type of sport, when the athletes' scores are standardized based on the general norms for TAIS, their dominant concentration style is focus, and scores on that scale are significantly higher than scores on the other concentration scales. The fact that focused attention is a dominant score in elite athletes, from a very early age, suggests that this particular type of concentration is critical to high levels of performance in sport. It also suggests that for athletes, the ability to focus may be more trait like than it is for other groups.

The 776 athletes mentioned above were re-tested some eighteen months after their initial test. An analysis of the amount of change that occurred with respect to their concentration skills and tendency to make errors over that eighteen-month period is presented in table 28.1. What you will notice is that athletes' scores on the focused scale changed significantly less than their scores on the other five attentional scales ($p < .01$). The relatively small amount of change on the focus scale provides some additional support

Table 28.1 Changes in Athlete Concentration Skills Over Eighteen Months

TAIS Scale	% Change
BET	7.0%
BIT	8.7%
NAR	2.9%
OET	8.6%
OIT	8.7%
RED	8.4%

Both tables derived from Lachman (1960).

for the belief that this particular skill, at least for this group, has a large trait component to it.

Discussion

When is an instrument or a characteristic being measured by an instrument considered valid and reliable? What are the criteria we should be using to make that judgment? In this paper I have responded to the questions that have been raised about the internal consistency of the items within TAIS attentional scales, and about the construct and predictive validity of the instrument.

I have pointed out that the internal consistency coefficients being questioned are similar to those found with other psychological instruments whose reliability is not being questioned. I have discussed the fact that in the real world, performance-relevant psychological constructs are complex in themselves, and mutually interdependent. Highly respected multi-dimensional personality inventories and intelligence tests when factor analyzed result in solutions with far fewer factors than scales. That fact alone is not cause to question the construct validity of the scales being measured by the instruments.

I have provided additional evidence in this paper for the ability of TAIS attentional scales to differentiate between levels of performance at the highest levels in sport and in business (Nideffer, et al., 2001). In the process I have provided additional construct validity for scales measuring focused-concentration and analytical skills, and helped clarify earlier research findings that supported the predictive validity of the test, but were confusing based on our knowledge at the time.

I have added data to the earlier findings showing that elite athletes involved in different types of sports had higher scores on those particular concentration scales that according to the theory would be most important for their sport (Nideffer, 1990; Bond & Nideffer, 1992; Nideffer, 1993). I have shown how gender differences with respect to concentration skills are consistent with behavioral observations and with neuro-biological research, thus providing support and construct validity for the differentiation of external and internal attentional processes.

Will the additional data provided in this paper change the opinions of those researchers and reviewers questioning the validity and reliability of the inventory? I have responded to these same criticisms before, by pointing out the methodological problems associated with factor analysis, and by providing data to support the construct validity of the scales. The arguments and data have been brushed over and largely ignored. After challenging the construct validity and reliability of TAIS attentional scales Moran (1996) says, "but see Nideffer, 1990 for a rebuttal of these criticisms." Moran does not present the arguments, nor does he debate the arguments, he ignores them. In the review by Abnernethy, Summers, and Ford (1998), two of the articles I published that deal with methodological issues and provide data to support the constructs are cited in the text and bibliography, but none of the arguments or data are presented (Nideffer, 1987; Nideffer, 1990). Within the field of sport psychology, questions about the validity and reliability of the inventory are accepted without question and passed on. Why? I believe the following quote from Abnernethy, Ford, and Summers (1998), provides a clue to the answer to that question.

> "Although the TAIS was designed as both a research tool and feedback device, there is little strong empirical support for its use as a research instrument to examine the relationship between attentional abilities and sport performance. There is, however, some support for its use as a diagnostic tool for helping athletes to identify attentional problems that may be affecting performance." (pg. 188)

Notice the split between "science" and "application" contained in that quotation. Does it make sense? It doesn't to me. How does a test that is useful as a diagnostic tool, for helping athletes identify and work on the attentional problems the instrument was designed to measure, not have validity and reliability?

Both scientists and practioneers have a tendency to become wedded to their tools. So much so at times that our preconceived beliefs prevent us from seeing, believing, and even understanding arguments that run contrary to our particular philosophical and/or theoretical positions. In my rebuttal to critics, I challenged a methodology they believe in, a methodology that fits with their concept of what scientific research is about. I did not say the data they gathered was inaccurate, that the reliability coefficients they obtained were wrong. Instead, I argued with their interpretation of the meaning of the data. Believing in their methodology and in the need for assessment tools that measure statistically independent constructs, they could not accept my arguments. They would agree the tool is useful, and does what it was designed to do from an applied perspective, but couldn't or wouldn't allow that fact to cause them to call into question either their methodology, or the interpretations they were drawing.

Pure science seeks to increase the understanding, prediction, and control of nature by first, reducing everything to it's simplest form, and then slowly recombining the elements under highly controlled conditions to study their interactions. The goal is to increase our understanding and in the end to create a science that will allow us to make very specific predictions with an extremely high degree of accuracy, thereby increasing our control over ourselves, and the world around us.

Although I believe most of us would applaud the goal of pure science, and see tremendous value in the process, we often have problems with both the speed with which advances are made, as well as with the lack of immediate practical value obtained from that research. In my mind, the goal of applied research is to find a happy medium between basic laboratory research on the one hand, and faith in untested hypotheses about cause-effect relationships that on the surface appear to be important but when closely examined are found to be little more than superstitions.

As a scientist, unconcerned about the practical application of my research, but focused on identifying the purest, most basic aspects of human performance, I would focus as critics of TAIS have, on trying to purify measures, to identify constructs that are statistically independent and to then create measures of those constructs. I would use statistical tools similar to the ones those researchers have used, and I would draw the same conclusions they have drawn from the results they have achieved.

My ultimate goal would be to gain the understanding required to create an instrument that would measure those independent performance-relevant constructs with enough accuracy for me to be able to use test information to predict the specific behaviors and performance outcomes that would occur within highly specific performance settings. I would be trying to create an instrument that would take the human element, and the subjectivity that goes with that, out of the prediction equation.

Conceptual vs. Statistical Independence

As an applied researcher, as someone who is concerned both about the practical application of my research and the validity and reliability of the theoretical constructs and tools that I use, I have different expectations and different goals. First, I am more concerned with the conceptual independence of constructs than I am with their statistical independence.

I know that human performance is complex and that performance outcomes are determined on the basis of the interactions between a broad range of performance-relevant characteristics or behaviors. If I want to deal with real-life issues I have to accept this fact and for that reason realize there are serious limits to the extent to which I can create measures and/or design studies where relevant behaviors are completely statistically independent of each other.

Conceptual independence means there is sufficient statistical independence to talk about different constructs as if they were independent, even though correlations do exist between them. As an applied researcher, the key question I have to ask myself is, when the common variance measured by two conceptually independent constructs is extracted, do the constructs prove to be valid and reliable measures of what they were designed to measure?

If I am willing to accept conceptual independence as opposed to statistical independence, then the fact that factor analysis of TAIS scales doesn't result in the identification of statistically independent factors associated with those scales by itself doesn't trouble me. Not as long as the scales are still able to show different and predictable relationships with the conceptually independent behaviors they were designed to assess.

The rule of thumb you apply when evaluating the reliability and validity of a theoretical construct or tool is in part predetermined on the basis of your position relative to the importance of statistical vs. conceptual independence. So too, your judgment as to the required level of reliability and validity of a test will depend upon your ultimate goal and expectations for how the instrument will be used.

Testing vs. Assessment

Those psychologists who use psychological tests as a part of their practice for purposes of diagnosis, selection, counseling, or development, realize that there is sufficient error in the testing process to preclude the possibility of a test being used to make a decision about a person without that decision being consensually validated through other means (e.g., other tests, behavioral observations, past history, further exploration through the additional testing and/or questioning, etc.). Differences between people on some of the constructs we measure like speed of decision making, the willingness to take risks, the willingness to self-disclose, level of anxiety, and level of self-awareness are all examples of factors that will influence a subject's responses to tests and affect our ability to make accurate between-subject comparisons based on test data alone.

For this reason, psychologists do not test, they assess. Testing is an event that results in a set of scores. Assessment is a process that often includes testing as a part of the process. Tests are administered and the results from testing are then used to generate hypotheses not about behavior within specific contexts or time frames, but about behavioral predispositions or tendencies and the conditions likely to elicit these tendencies. We don't expect to be able to predict that person A will become distracted during the Olympic final and therefore lose the competition anymore than a geologist or seismologist expects to be able to predict a 7.0 magnitude earthquake in Southern California tomorrow.

The reason the American Psychological Association and test-publishing companies limit the sale of psychological tests to individuals who have had courses in statistics and in psychological testing and assessment is to ensure that they are aware of test limitations, of the need to consensually validate results. There is also the hope that they will have the skill sets necessary to engage in the consensual validation or entire assessment process.

Reliability and Predictive Validity Coefficients Are Often Low For Reasons Other Than Error Variance

Most psychological tests are not developed for research purposes. Tests are developed to provide answers to questions that are important to people. These are questions that don't have simple answers; if they did, there would be no need for the test. Especially when working with normal, healthy, and often very high-functioning individuals, the questions are not questions about "what," but instead are "why" and "how" questions. Coaches, athletes, business executives, don't need a psychologist to tell them what their mistakes are. More often than not their mistakes are painfully obvious to them and to everyone else. When they approach a psychologist it is because they have identified the issue but been unable to resolve it and want to know why it continues to be an issue and what to do about it. Psychologists develop tests to get at the root cause of issues and to help provide answers around what to do about those issues.

If you have been in the business of helping people get at the root cause of performance issues for any length of time, you recognize that problems are more complicated than they might seem on the surface. One of the first mistakes individuals within the field of sport psychology made with respect to TAIS was to ignore the scales measuring interpersonal characteristics and attitudes and focus exclusively on the concentration scales. They didn't realize that problems with concentration, like problems with anger or communication are multifaceted.

When people make mistakes, whether the mistakes manifest themselves as concentration or decision-making errors, or as inappropriate emotional expressions or insensitive interpersonal behaviors, to understand the mistakes you must determine the role concentration plays, the role emotions and interpersonal processes play, and the role the environment plays. To do this you have to assess all of these areas, not just concentration, not just emotions, and not just the situational variables. What you are looking for and what good tests help you find, when mistakes repeat themselves, are interactive patterns unique to the individual that increase the likelihood of the mistake. The same is true of exceptional performance; you look for patterns, for the coming together of concentration skills, personal and interpersonal variables within the context of specific situations that increase the likelihood of success. Where patterns do have some commonality across subjects, they can be identified with factor analysis. The factors show the particular combinations of attentional, personal, and interpersonal variables being measured by the instrument that are related within a given group of subjects. Two things to keep in mind, however, when looking at these patterns. First, as Hogan et al. (1994) indicated, just because some scales cluster together around a factor, does not mean they don't each contribute unique variance to that factor. The second thing to keep in mind is that the patterns found through factor analysis by no means represent the full range of patterns operating within different subjects!

You cannot separate concentration from emotions or emotions from concentration. Nor can you separate either of those from the environment. It is patterns of behavior that predict success, not individual variables. Because the patterns are complicated and it is difficult if not impossible to find enough subjects to examine all of these complex interactions researchers select the one or two variables they hope will have the most predictive power. The end result of ignoring many of the contributing factors is less predictive validity.

The Researchers Error Variance Is the Practitioneer's Gold

There are a couple of sources of "error" variance associated with the testing process that researchers attempt to eliminate. These are response set and response style influences. In sport, researchers tried to minimize these by making sport-specific versions of TAIS with some limited success. They did get slight increases in the internal item consistency coefficients when questions became sport specific. What the researchers failed to realize, however, is that response set and response style differences between subjects, along with differences in terms of self-awareness which affects test scores represents a gold mine of information to the applied psychologist who is trying to get at the root cause of developmental problems or issues.

When questions on an instrument are not situation- or sport-specific, and when subjects are not instructed to adopt a particular response set, respondents are free to relate to the items in any way they choose. Although it is true that in most instances, subjects take the testing situation into account and respond to the items in ways which are relevant to that situation, that is not always the case. This is especially true when there is a disconnect between an individual's emotional feelings about his performance or his life and the objective success or failure that outsiders would observe. It is not uncommon for example for highly self-critical performers to express lower self-esteem, to be more critical of their concentration skills than less-critical and less-skilled athletes (Nideffer, 1987). Likewise, problems of communication between individuals often result because one of them has a lack of self-awareness and simply doesn't have a clue as to how he is being perceived and can't understand the responses he is getting from others. Both of these issues would be seen as error variance for the researcher, but both of them provide absolutely critical information to the psychologist who is trying to get at the root cause of problems, and trying to determine the prognosis for change and/or to design an intervention. The more sport- or situation-specific you make a measure the more likely you are to prevent people from giving you information that will be far more valuable than any increase you might get in predictive validity coefficients from a research study.

I am not arguing that we should develop tests that don't have validity and/or reliability. Obviously, we want to create tests that have as much reliability and validity as we can, and the process of fine-tuning, refining, and improving our tools should be constant. However, when one recognizes that: 1) responsibility for the appropriate use and interpretation of tests resides with the test administrator; 2) test data is used not to make decisions but to generate hypotheses about probable behaviors and/or issues; 3) those behaviors are then consensually validated through the assessment process, and; 4) that some of what is considered error variance to researchers is of considerable importance to psychologists who are helping individuals understand and gain control over themselves and their behavior and improve performance, tolerance for less than perfect reliability and validity coefficients increases.

Bibliography

Abernethy, B., Summers, J.J. & Ford, S. (1998). Issues in the measurement of attention. In, J.L. Duda (Ed.) *Advances in sport and exercise psychology measurement* (pp. 173–193). Morgantown: Fitness Information Technology.

Albrecht, R.R. & Feltz, D.L. (1987). Generality and specificity of attention related to competitive anxiety and sport performance. *Journal of Sport Psychology,* 9, 231–248.

APA (1985). Standards for educational and psychological testing. Washington, DC: American Psychological Association.

Barrack, M.R. & Mount, M.K. (1991). The Big-Five personality dimensions in job performance: A meta-analysis. Personnel Psychology, 44, 1–26.

Bond, J.W., & Nideffer, R.M. (1992). Attentional and interpersonal characteristics of elite Australian Athletes. *Excell,* Australian Sports Commission, 8,2, 101–111.

Bond, J. & Sargent, G. (1995). Concentration skills in sport: An applied perspective. In T. Morris, & J.J. Summers (Eds.), *Sport psychology: Theory, applications and issues* (pp. 386–419) Brisbane: Wiley.

Cahill, L. (2005). His Brain, Her Brain, Scientific American, August, 2005.

Cei, A. & Manili, U. (1997). La consulenza psicologica nello sport di alto livello. In, P. Delfini & M. Pirritano (Eds.), *Psicologia per Lo Sport* (pp. 31–33.) Roma: Scuoa dello Sport.

Coaching Association of Canada (1981). Concentration, In, *Coaching Theory 3: National Coaching Certification Program* (pp. 10–7 to 10–18) Ottawa: Coaching Association of Canada.

Dahlstrom, G.W., Welsh, G.S. & Dahlstrom, L.E. (1975). *An MMPI Handbook Vol II Research Applications.* Minneapolis: University of Minnesota Press.

Dewey, D., Brawley, L.R. & Allard, F. (1989). Do the TAIS attentional style scales predict how visual information is processed? *Journal of Sport and Exercise Psychology,* 11, 171–186.

Digman, J. M. (1997). Higher-order factors of the Big Five. Journal of Personality and Social Psychology, 73, 1246–1256.

Fogarty, G.J. (1995) Some comments on the use of psychological tests in sport settings. *International Journal of Sport Psychology,* 26, 161–170.

Ford, S.K. & Summers, J.J. (1992). The factorial validity of the TAIS attentional-style subscales. *Journal of Sport & Exercise Psychology,* 14, 283–297.

Hogan R., Curphy, G.J., & Hogan J. (1994). What we know about leadership effectiveness and personality. American Psychologist, 49, 493–504.

Hogan R., Hogan, J. & Roberts B. W. (1996). Personality measurement and employment decisions, questions and answers. American Psychologist, 51, 469–477.

Hough, L.M.(1992). The "Big Five" personality variables-construct - Description versus prediction. Human Performance, 5, 139–155.

John, O. P. (1990). The "Big Five" factor taxonomy: Dimensions of personality in the natural language and in questionnaires. In L. A. Pervin (Ed.), *Handbook of personality. Theory and research* (pp. 66–100). New York: Guilford.

Kimura, D. (2001). Sex and Cognition, Badford Book, MIT Press.

Kirshenbaum, D.S. & Bale, R.M. (1984). Cognitive-behavioural skills in golf. In R.M. Suinn (Ed.), *Psychology of sports: Methods and application* (pp. 334–343). Minneapolis, MN: Burgess.

LaMotte, S.R. (1981). Attentional and interpersonal style in marital relationships. *Unpublished Doctoral Dissertation,* San Diego: California School of Professional Psychology.

Landers, D.M., Furst, D.M. & Daniels, F.S. (1981). Anxiety attention and ability level in open and closed shooting activities. Paper presented at a meeting of the *North American Society for the Psychology of Sport and Physical Activity,* Asilomar.

Landers, D.M. (1982). Arousal attention and skilled performance: Further considerations. *Quest,* 33, 271–283.

Marano, H.E. (2003),The new sex scorecard, Psychology Today, July-August, 2003.

Matarazzo, J.D. (1972). *Wechsler's Measurement and Appraisal of Adult Intelligence.* Baltimore: Williams & Wilkins.

Moran, A.P. (1996). *The Psychology of Concentration in Sport Performance: A Cognitive Analysis.* Exeter: BPC Wheatons Ltd.

Nideffer, R.M. (1976a). Test of Attentional and Interpersonal Style. *Journal of Personality and Social Psychology,* 34, 394–404.

Nideffer, R.M. (1976b). *The Inner Athlete,* New York: Thomas Crowell

Nideffer, R.M. (1987). Issues in the use of psychological tests in applied settings. *The Sport Psychologist,* 1, 18–28.

Nideffer, R.M. (1989). Adiestramiento Del Control De La Atencion, Ciencia E Intuicion. In, *Cuademos Tecnicos De Dporte* (pp. 17–51) Pamplona: Gobiemo de Navarra.

Nideffer, R.M. (1990). Use of the Test of Attentional and Interpersonal Style in Sport. *The Sport Psychologist,* 4, 285–300.

Nideffer, R.M. (1993). Attention Control Training. In, R.N. Singer, M. Murphey, and L.K. Tennant (Eds.), *Handbook of Research on Sport Psychology* (pp.542–556). New York: Macmillan

Nideffer, R.M., Sagal, M.S., Lowry, M. & Bond, J. (2001). Identifying and developing world class performers. In, Gershon Tenenbaum (Ed.), The practice of sport psychology (pp. 129–144). Morgantown, WV: Fitness Information Technology

Nideffer, R.M. & Bond, J. (2003). A Cross Cultural Examination of the Concentration Skills of Elite Level Athletes. http://www.taisdata.com/articles/xcult.php

Nideffer, R.M., Bond, J., Cei, A., and Manili, U., (2003). Building a psychologicial profile of Olympic Medalists and World Champions. http://www.epstais.com/articles/building.php

Nunnally, J.C. (1967). *Psychometric Theory.* New York: McGraw-Hill

Salmela, J.H. (1981). *The world sport psychology sourcebook.* Ithaca, NY: Mouvement.

Schmelzer, R.W. (1981). Comparisons of attentional and interpersonal style across two cultures, West Germany and the United States. Unpublished Doctoral Dissertation, San Diego, California School of Professional Psychology.

Selder, D. (1982). Psychological preparation of elite athletes. In, Atleticastudi, 5, 65–84.

Snyder, J. & Abernethy, B. (1992). *The Creative Side of Experimentation: Personal Perspectives From Leading Researchers in Motor Control, Motor Development, and Sport Psychology* (pp. 165–175) Champaign: Human Kinetics.

Summers, J.J. & Ford, S.K. (1990). The test of attentional and interpersonal style: An evaluation. *International Journal of Sport Psychology,* 21, 102–111.

Summers, J.J., Miller, K. & Ford, S.K. (1991). Attentional style and basketball performance. *Journal of Sport & exercise Psychology,* 8, 239–253.

Tett, R.P., Jackson, D.N. & Rothstein, M. (1991). Personality measures as predictors of job performance: A meta-analytic review. Personnel Psychology, 44, 703–742.

Vallerand, R.J. (1983). Attention and decision-making: A test of the predictive validity of the Test of Attentional and Interpersonal Style (TAIS) in a sport setting. *Journal of Sport Psychology,* 5, 449–459.

Van Schoyck, S.R. & Grasha, A.F. (1981). Attentional style variations and athletic ability: The advantage of a sport-specific test. *Joumal of Sport Psychology,* 3, 149–165.

Wilson, V., Ainsworth, M. & Bird, E. (1985). Assessment of attentional abilities in male volleyball players. *International Journal of Sport Psychology,* 16, 296–306.

29 Self-Confidence and Sports Performance

DEBORAH L. FELTZ
Michigan State University

Self-confidence (SC) is one of the most cited factors thought to affect athletic performance. SC is said to play a critical role in athletes' success; in contrast, lack of SC seems to be closely associated with athletic failure. Thus, confidence is an important factor that distinguishes successful athletes from unsuccessful ones in terms of both their mental states as well as their performances. However, the precise nature of SC was quite unclear until the publication of Feltz's seminal chapter on this issue.

The term self-confidence refers to one's belief that he or she can successfully execute a desired behavior (i.e., his or her belief of "I'll get the job done"). Feltz argued that the exact relationships of SC and performance in sport have not been scientifically clarified in a satisfactory manner. To promote our understanding of the precise nature of these relationships, she first presented several definitions of SC and briefly discussed them with reference to some related terms, such as perceived ability, self-concept, self-esteem, and performance expectancies. Feltz presented three of the major theoretical approaches available at that time for studying these relationships: Bandura's self-efficacy theory, Harter's perceived competence model, and Vealey's concept of sport confidence. She not only described the theoretical approaches but also provided extensive research evidence in sport and reviewed some relevant criticisms. Feltz summarized and compared these three approaches and derived some important conclusions referring to the (at that time) updated scientific status of the relationships between SC and sport performance.

This seminal chapter did not, of course, completely resolve the riddle of SC in sport. However, Feltz organized and presented the theoretical knowledge relevant to SC in sport at that time and undoubtedly had a profound influence on many researchers in this area, which is theoretically intriguing and has a substantial practical importance for those actively involved in sport.

Introduction

The cognitive approach to the study of achievement motivation assumes that strivings for achievement are mediated through several cognitive mechanisms. A growing body of evidence suggests that one's perception of ability or self-confidence is the central mediating construct of those achievement strivings [1, 13, 45, 72]. In sport, self-confidence is one of the most frequently cited psychological factors thought to affect athletic achievements. "Self-confidence," as the term is used here, is the belief that one can successfully execute a specific activity rather than a global trait that accounts for overall performance optimism. For example, one may have a high degree of self-confidence in one's driving ability in golf but a low degree of self-confidence in putting.

Although self-confidence is thought to affect athletic performance, its relationship with performance has not been clear in much of the sport science research. Self-confidence has been shown to be significantly correlated with skillful sport performance, but whether there is a causal relationship, and what the direction of that relationship is, cannot be determined from the correlational designs of the studies [33, 41, 50, 66].

This chapter focuses on the nature of the relationship between self-confidence and sport performance. First, definitions of self-confidence and related concepts are given. Second, the major theoretical approaches to studying this relationship are briefly described, research evidence from sport is provided, and general criticisms are reviewed. Third, a summary and comparison of the approaches are provided and the status of the relationship of confidence to sport performance is summarized. Finally, a conclusion is presented with suggestions for future research.

Definitions of Self-Confidence and Related Concepts

Various terms such as "self-confidence," "self-efficacy," "perceived ability," and "perceived competence" have been used to describe one's perceived capability to accomplish a certain level of performance. Bandura [1] uses the term "self-efficacy" to describe the conviction one has to execute successfully the behavior (e.g., a sports performance) required to produce a certain outcome (e.g., a trophy *or* self-satisfaction) and, thus, can be considered as a situationally specific self-confidence. In addition, as Bandura [5] notes, self-efficacy is not concerned with the skills an individual has but with the judgments of what an individual can do with the skills he or she possesses. He also distinguishes between perceived self-efficacy and self-confidence. Self-confidence, for him, refers to the strength of the belief or conviction but does not specify the level of perceived competence. Bandura prefers to use the term "self-efficacy" to specify the level of perceived competence and the strength of that belief.

"Perceived competence" and "perceived ability" are terms that have been limited in use to the achievement

Adapted, by permission, from D.L. Feltz, 1988, "Self-confidence and sports performance," *Exercise and Sport Science Reviews* 16: 423-457.

and mastery motivation literature, and indicate the sense that one has the ability to master a task resulting from cumulative interactions with the environment [45, 72]. In the specific area of sport and movement, Griffin and Keogh [42] use the term "movement confidence" to describe an individual's feeling of adequacy in a movement situation, whereas Vealey [87, p. 222] defines "sport confidence" as "the belief or degree of certainty individuals possess about their ability to be successful in sport."

Some terms are related to self-confidence but should not be confused with the construct. "Self-concept" represents a composite view of oneself that is developed through evaluative experiences and social interactions. As Bandura [5–7] has noted, however, a global self-concept will not predict the intra-individual variability in performance as well as self-confidence perceptions that vary across activities and circumstances.

"Self-esteem" is another concept related to self-confidence and pertains to one's personal judgment of worthiness. Although self-confidence and self-esteem may be related, certain individuals do not have high self-confidence for a given activity, but nevertheless still "like themselves"; by contrast, there are those who may regard themselves as highly competent at a given activity but do not have corresponding feelings of self-worth.

The concept of performance "expectancies" has been used to try to operationalize self-confidence in sport by asking subjects how well they expect to perform or whether they expect to beat their opponent [18, 19, 21, 71, 78, 79]. Most of the expectancy research in sport, however, is actually concerned with competitive efficacy expectations rather than outcome expectations. Bandura [1, 5] distinguishes judgments of personal efficacy from response-outcome expectations. Self-efficacy is a judgment of one's ability to perform at a certain level, whereas outcome expectancy pertains to one's judgment of the likely consequences of such a performance. For example, the belief that one can run a marathon in less than 2 hours is an efficacy judgment; the anticipated social recognition, money, and the self-satisfaction created by such a performance are the outcome expectancies. What Bandura refers to as the "outcome" should not be confused with the typical use of the term "sport outcome" in the sport psychology literature. "Sport outcome" refers to the performance accomplishment itself, not what follows from that accomplishment.

In this chapter, I will address the areas of the literature that conceptualize self-confidence as self-efficacy, perceived competence or ability, sport confidence, and movement confidence. Except when discussing a particular theoretical construct, I will use the term "self-confidence" to represent the perceived ability to accomplish a certain level of performance. The related areas of self-concept, self-esteem, and outcome expectancies are beyond the scope of this chapter and will not be considered. Readers interested in self-concept and self-esteem in sport are referred to recent reviews by Sonstroem [81] and by Weiss [93].

Theoretical Approaches to Studying Self-Confidence in Sport

Self-Efficacy

Bandura's [1] theory of self-efficacy has been the most extensively used theory for investigating self-confidence in sport and motor performance. Bandura originally proposed the theory to account for the different results achieved by the diverse methods used in clinical psychology for treating anxiety. It has since been expanded [3] and applied to other domains of psychological functioning, including motivation [8], achievement behavior [9, 80], career choice and development [11, 44], and health behavior [73], in addition to sport behavior.

This theory, developed within the framework of a social cognitive theory [5], poses self-efficacy as a common cognitive mechanism for mediating people's motivation and behavior. People's judgment of their capability to perform at given levels affect their behavior (i.e., choice of activities, effort expenditure, persistence), their thought patterns, and their emotional reactions in demanding or anxiety-provoking situations. Self-efficacy is a major determinant of behavior, however, only when proper incentives and the necessary skills are present.

Source of Information. According to Bandura's theory, expectations of personal efficacy are derived from four principal sources of information: performance accomplishments, vicarious experiences, verbal persuasion, and physiological arousal. These four categories of efficacy information are not mutually exclusive in terms of the information they provide, though some are more influential than others. For instance, performance accomplishments provide the most dependable source of efficacy information because they are based on personal mastery experiences. Bandura [1, p. 194] emphasized that the relationship between efficacy expectations and performance is reciprocal: "Mastery expectations influence performance and are, in turn, altered by the cumulative effects of one's efforts."

Performance accomplishments. As stated previously, performance accomplishments provide the most dependable source of information upon which to base self-efficacy judgments because they are based on one's mastery experiences. These experiences affect self-efficacy judgments through cognitive processing of such information. If these experiences have been repeatedly perceived as successes, they will raise efficacy expectations; if they have been perceived as failures, they will lower expectations. The influence that performance experiences have on perceived efficacy also depends on the perceived difficulty of the task, the effort expended, the amount of physical guidance received, and the temporal patterns of success and failure [3]. Performance accomplishments on difficult tasks, tasks independently attempted, and tasks accomplished early in learning with only occasional failures carry greater efficacy value than easy tasks, tasks accomplished with external aids, or tasks in which repeated failures are experienced early in the learning process.

Vicarious experiences. Efficacy information can also be obtained through observing or imagining others engaging in a task that observers themselves have never performed. Although vicarious sources of efficacy information are generally weaker than performance accomplishments, their influence on self-efficacy can be enhanced by a number of factors. The less experience one has had with a task or situation, the more one will rely on others to judge one's own capabilities. Similarities to the model in terms of performance or personal characteristics have been shown to enhance the effectiveness of modeling procedures on subjects' self-efficacy and performance [40].

Persuasion. Persuasive techniques are widely used by teachers, coaches, and peers in attempting to influence the learner's behavior. These techniques can include verbal persuasion and/or bogus performance feedback. Efficacy expectations based on this type of information are also likely to be weaker than those based on one's own accomplishments. In addition, persuasive techniques are effective only if heightened appraisal is within realistic bounds. The extent of persuasive influence on self-efficacy also depends on the credibility, prestige, trustworthiness, and expertise of the persuader.

Physiological states. The level and quality of physiological arousal also provide an indication of self-efficacy. Although other theorists [14, 28, 98] postulate that reduction in physiological arousal directly changes behavior through reinforcement, Bandura [1] states that arousal affects behavior through the cognitive appraisal (efficacy expectations) of the information conveyed by arousal. For example, some individuals may interpret increases in their physiological arousal as a fear that they cannot perform the skill successfully, whereas others may interpret this state as being psyched up and ready for performance. Bandura [5] also notes that physiological sources of self-efficacy are not limited to autonomic arousal. People use their levels of fatigue, fitness, and pain in strength and endurance activities as indicants of physical inefficacy [34, 82].

Anxiety or autonomic arousal is viewed not only as a source of efficacy information by Bandura [1] but also as a co-effect of behavior. This suggests another reciprocal relationship in self-efficacy theory: one between self-efficacy and physiological arousal.

Efficacy/behavior relationship. As mentioned previously, Bandura [1] states that self-efficacy is a major determinant of behavior only when people have sufficient incentives to act on their self-percepts of efficacy and when they possess the requisite subskills. He predicts that efficacy expectations will exceed actual performance when there is little incentive to perform the activity or when physical or social constraints are imposed on performance. An individual may have the necessary skill and high self-efficacy but no incentive to perform. Discrepancies will also occur when tasks or circumstances are ambiguous or when one has little information on which to base efficacy expectations.

How individuals cognitively process efficacy information will also influence the relationship between self-efficacy and behavior [1]. For instance, successes and failures may be perceived or distorted in importance. People who overweigh their failures will have lower levels of self-efficacy than those with the same performance levels who do not.

Measurement of Self-Efficacy. Bandura [1] advocates a microanalytic approach for testing propositions about the origins and functions of perceived self-efficacy. This requires a detailed assessment of the level, strength, and generality of perceived self-efficacy. "Level of self-efficacy" refers to people's expected performance attainments. "Strength" refers to the strength of people's beliefs that they can attain different levels of performance. "Generality" indicates the number of domains of functioning in which people judge themselves to be efficacious. Self-efficacy instruments are typically constructed by listing a series of tasks, usually varying in difficulty, complexity, or stressfulness. People are asked to designate the tasks they believe they can perform (efficacy level). For each task designated, they rate their degree of certainty (efficacy strength) that they can execute it on a 100-point probability scale ranging from high uncertainty to complete certainty.

According to Bandura [5], this method permits a microanalysis of the degree of congruence between self-efficacy and action at the level of individual tasks. However, this method also requires that one conduct a conceptual analysis of the subskills needed to perform a task and a contextual analysis of the level of situational demands. Bandura [5] uses the example of driving self-efficacy to show how the strength of perceived self-efficacy may vary for navigating through residential areas, arterial roads, congested city traffic, onrushing freeway traffic, and twisting mountain roads. In gymnastics, the subskills needed to perform competitively could be categorized by event (vault, beam, bars, floor exercise) and by the context of stunts within each event that vary in degree of difficulty.

In the sport literature, self-efficacy researchers have typically correlated aggregate self-efficacy scores with aggregate performance scores rather than examining the congruence between self-efficacy and performance at the level of individual tasks [102]. Perhaps this is due to the nature of the tasks used in sport. In most sports studies, subjects' efficacy expectations and performance have not been assessed in terms of the approach/avoidance to a series of tasks that increase in difficulty. Rather, subjects are asked about their confidence beliefs concerning a single task in terms of how long or at what height they can perform and then are asked to attempt that task in two or more trials.

Ryckman and his colleagues [77] developed the Physical Self-Efficacy Scale to provide an omnibus measure of perceived physical self-efficacy. The scale has two factors: a perceived physical ability factor and a physical self-presentation confidence factor that reflects confidence in the display of physical skills. The authors found significant correlations between total physical self-efficacy scores, perceived physical ability scores, and performance on a reaction-time task and a motor coordination task. Gayton and his colleagues [37] also found predictive validity for the scale with competitive marathon running performance. However, McAuley and Gill [70] found a task-specific measure of self-efficacy that measured expectations in the areas of vault, beam, bars, and floor exercise to be a much better predictor of gymnastics performance than the global measure of physical self-efficacy. This supports a growing body of evidence that particularized measures of self-efficacy have greater explanatory and predictive power than global measures [see 5, 6].

Research in Sport and Physical Activity. Much of the self-efficacy research in sport and motor performance has focused on examining (a) the effects of various methods used to create athletic competence in self-efficacy and performance and (b) the relationship between self-efficacy and performance. The various treatment techniques examined in these studies were based on one or more of the four major sources of efficacy information outlined by Bandura [1].

Sport and exercise research has examined the influence of techniques based on performance accomplishment and has shown them to be effective in enhancing both self-efficacy and performance [27, 33, 51, 54, 68, 89, 90, 91]. Studies have also supported the superiority of performance-based information over other sources of efficacy information [23, 33, 35, 68, 91]. For instance, participant modeling, which involves a model's demonstration plus guided participation of the learner, has been shown to produce superior diving performance and stronger expectations of personal efficacy than either live modeling or videotaped modeling techniques [33].

Information gained through vicarious experiences has been shown to increase perceived efficacy in muscular endurance tasks [34, 40], gymnastic performance [68], exercise activity [20], and competitive persistence [89]. These techniques have included modeling [20, 40], imagery [34], and information acquired about a competitor's competence [89]. Weinberg and his colleagues [89] manipulated subjects' efficacy expectations about competing on a muscular endurance task by having them observe their competitor (a confederate), who either performed poorly on a related strength task and was said to have a knee injury (high self-efficacy) or who performed well and was said to be a varsity track athlete (low self-efficacy). Results indicated that the higher the induced self-efficacy, the greater the muscular endurance. Subjects who competed against an injured competitor endured longer than those who competed against a varsity athlete.

The few studies that have investigated persuasive techniques such as positive self-talk [88, 97] and reinterpreting arousal [103] as a source of efficacy information report mixed results. Wilkes and Summers [97] were the only ones who found self-efficacy techniques (positive self-talk) to influence performance. However, efficacy-related cognitions did not seem to mediate the effect.

Few sport studies have investigated the influence of physiological or emotional states on self-efficacy [29, 35, 55]. In my work on diving [29, 35], I found that although actual physiological arousal did not predict self-efficacy expectancies, perceived autonomic arousal was a significant predictor, but not as strong a predictor as previous performance accomplishments. Kavanagh and Hausfeld [55], however, found that induced moods (happiness/sadness), as measured by self-report, did not alter efficacy expectations in any consistent manner using strength tasks.

In these studies that have examined non-performance-based sources of efficacy information, lack of effects may have been due to confounding with actual performance where multiple performance trials were used. Because personal experiences are so powerful, subjects' perceptions of their performance experience may overshadow any influence that the treatment variable may have on self-efficacy.

A number of studies have examined the relationship between self-efficacy and athletic and exercise performance [10, 29, 31, 33–35, 37, 40, 54, 55, 65, 68, 70, 77, 89, 91, 92, 99]. As Wurtele [102] noted, the results of these studies show a significant relationship between self-efficacy and performance across a number of sport tasks and physical activities. These correlational results do not necessarily demonstrate a causal relationship between self-efficacy and performance.

A few studies in the sport and motor performance area have been conducted to investigate the causal relationships in Bandura's theory [29, 31, 35, 68]. Using path analysis techniques, these studies found that although self-efficacy was indeed a major determinant of performance, direct effects of treatment on performance [68] and direct effects of past performance on future performance [29, 31, 35] were also present. These results indicate that performance-based treatments affect behavior through other mechanisms as well as perceived self-efficacy.

I conducted a study [29] that compared the influence of self-efficacy as a common cognitive mechanism with an alternative anxiety-based model [28] in the approach/avoidance behavior of college females attempting a modified back dive. The self-efficacy model in this study predicted that self-efficacy was the major predictor of performance and that a reciprocal relationship existed between self-efficacy and back-diving performance. The anxiety-based model included related performance experience, self-reported anxiety, and physiological arousal as causal influences on back-diving performance. Self-efficacy was hypothesized as merely an effect.

The results provided little support for the complete network of relationships in either model. Self-efficacy was neither just an effect nor the only significant predictor of performance, although it was the major predictor of performance on the first of four diving attempts. Physiological arousal and past related accomplishments also predicted approach/avoidance behavior on the first trial. After trial 1, however, performance on a previous trial was the major predictor of performance on the next trial. In other words, regardless of what subjects thought they were capable of performing after the first diving attempt, once they stepped to the end of the diving board, their next attempt or avoidance of the dive was determined more by what they did on the previous trial. In accord with Bandura's theory, I found a reciprocal relationship between self-efficacy and performance, although they were not equally reciprocal. As subjects progressed over trials, performance became a stronger influence on self-efficacy than self-efficacy became on performance.

Because I found little support for the complete network of relationships in either the self-efficacy or the anxiety-based model, I proposed a revised model that included both self-efficacy and previous performance as direct predictors of back-diving performance. This revised model was later tested with two different sample populations and found to be supported in terms of its major predictions [31, 35].

McAuley [68] also examined the self-efficacy and anxiety-based models of the relationship of anxiety, self-efficacy, and performance on a gymnastics task and found similar results. Neither model fit the data, though the self-efficacy model provided a better fit than the anxiety-based model. Although these findings, together with mine, suggest that self-efficacy, as a common cognitive mechanism, cannot account for all behavioral change in motor performance, self-efficacy has been found consistently to be an important and necessary cognitive mechanism in explaining motor performance, especially in an initial performance attempt. Furthermore, as Bandura [5–7] notes, commonality of mechanism does not imply exclusivity of mechanism; other mechanisms may also influence behavior. He would conclude, therefore, that McAuley's and my results are not at odds with self-efficacy theory.

Perhaps self-efficacy may have more of an effect on performance under more variable conditions than those used in the preceding studies. Predicting repetitive performance under the invariant conditions of these studies may not be the most informative paradigm for testing the relative contributions of self-efficacy, anxiety, and performance. In most real-life sport situations, people perform with some variation in circumstances (e.g., different meets, different settings) and temporal intervals. Under such conditions, there may be greater leeway for efficacy judgments to exert an effect on subsequent trial attempts. However, there are also occasions in sport where short-term trials under relatively invariant conditions do exist (e.g., archery) and are important to examine in relation to self-efficacy.

Weinberg's research [89, 90, 92] has also attempted to demonstrate the causal influence of self-efficacy on motor performance through experimental manipulation of self-efficacy. However, Biglan [12] has criticized this approach as leading to an arbitrary interpretation of self-efficacy's relationship to performance. He points out that when environmental variables are manipulated in order to manipulate self-efficacy ratings, performance behavior or other factors are also affected. Environmental manipulations may influence some other variable (e.g., anxiety) that influences self-efficacy and performance without any causal role for self-efficacy. "Third variable" causes must be considered. Regression and path analysis have been used to control for the contribution of other possible factors, including anxiety [29, 68].

Recovery and adherence efficacy. More recently, researchers have begun to study the significance of self-efficacy in explaining success of recovery from myocardial infarction and adherence to exercise regimens [23, 25, 27, 54, 82]. In the area of cardiac rehabilitation, Ewart and his colleagues [27] showed that perceived physical efficacy in patients with coronary artery disease was strengthened by having them master increasing exercise intensities on the treadmill and using persuasive medical counseling. Self-efficacy was found to be a good predictor of patients' activity levels after they returned to their home environment. In a subsequent study [25], perceived physical efficacy was used to identify successfully, in advance, coronary artery disease patients who overexerted by exercising at intensities above the prescribed heart rate range, thereby putting themselves at risk. In addition, Taylor and his colleagues [82] demonstrated the importance of raising the spouse's efficacy level regarding the patient's capabilities. Spouses who believed that their partners had a robust heart were more likely to encourage them to resume an active life than those who believed that their partner's cardiac capability was severely reduced.

Researchers have also begun to investigate the influence of self-efficacy in predicting adherence to exercise regimens. Kaplan and his colleagues [54] found that perceived self-efficacy mediated exercise compliance in patients with chronic obstructive pulmonary disease. Desharnais and his colleagues [23] examined the ability of self-efficacy and outcome expectancy (potential benefits from regular exercise) to predict adherence to exercise in an 11-week physical fitness program. Although both efficacy and outcome expectations were significant predictors of exercise adherence, self-efficacy best distinguished adherers from dropouts. Potential dropouts displayed less certainty than adherers about their capacity to attend the program regularly at the outset and expected more benefits from their participation. Efficacy research in this area is just beginning, but it appears to show consistent results in self-efficacy as a predictor of cardiac recovery and adherence to exercise.

Criticisms of Self-Efficacy Theory. Self-efficacy theory has been criticized for being so heavily based on self-report measures because of the demand and suggestion problems that may occur [14, 56]. However, Bandura [5] has presented evidence that in situations where individuals have no reason to distort their reports, self-reports can be quite representative of cognitions. Thus, efficacy judgments are best made when recorded privately. Weinberg et al. [92] compared public with private efficacy-expectation groups and found no differences between the two in terms of expectations or performance. Critics have suggested, however, that just making an efficacy statement, even privately, creates a demand or goal to match the performance with the efficacy judgment [12, 14]. Contrary to this presumption, Telch et al. [83] have shown that variation in social demand has little or no effect on congruence between self-efficacy and performance. If anything, social demand may encourage conservation and thus reduce the congruence between self-efficacy and performance.

Kazdin [56] has also criticized Bandura's measure of self-efficacy for being so closely related to the actual performance task that it ensured high correlations. But one can also be assured of finding low correlations if there is little similarity between the efficacy measure and what people are asked to perform [2]. Moreover, Kazdin was concerned about the possible reactivity occurring when the self-efficacy measure and the behavior test are administered so closely in time. Again, Bandura [2] points out that if the interval between efficacy judgments and performance is too great, efficacy expectations may be changed in the interim.

Self-efficacy, as a construct, has even been questioned as to its necessity in explaining behavior by those with strong behavioristic views [12, 14, 28, 98]. These theorists have argued that environmental events such as anxiety response "habit" were the direct cause of both self-efficacy expectations and behavioral change. Eysenck [28] considered efficacy expectations, as well as any other cognitive determinant of behavior, as merely a by-product of conditioned responses: In describing the role of self-efficacy in athletic performance, therefore, Bandura would argue that successful performance and reduced competitive anxiety are determined primarily by an athlete's self-efficacy expectations; by contrast, Eysenck and others would argue that an athlete's high degree of self-efficacy is merely an effect of reduced anxiety and that this reduced anxiety is the major determinant of successful performance and self-efficacy. However, path analysis studies have indicated that self-efficacy is not merely a by-product of conditioned anxiety [29, 68]. Indeed, evidence also shows that perceived self-efficacy accounts for a substantial amount of variance in behavior when anticipatory anxiety is controlled, whereas the relationship between anticipatory anxiety and behavior essentially disappears when perceived self-efficacy is partialled out [6]. Furthermore, a large body of evidence exists on the failure of conditioned anxiety responses to predict avoidance behavior [see 5].

On a related concern, Kirsch [60] has criticized the concept of "self- efficacy" as being merely old wine with a new label. He contends that self-efficacy is no different from Rotter's [76] concept of "expectancy for success." However, as Bandura [6] has countered, the label "expectancy for success" indicates an outcome expectancy. "Because self-percepts of efficacy are formed through acts of self-appraisal based on multidimensional information, perceived self-efficacy is more closely allied to the field of human judgment than to the subject of expectancy, which refers to an anticipation that something is likely to happen" [6, p. 362].

In summary, while some criticisms have focused on the methods by which self-efficacy ratings are made [12, 56, 59, 61], research on self-efficacy in numerous sport and physical activity settings has shown a consistent significant relationship between self-efficacy and performance. The studies that have been conducted to investigate the causal relationships in Bandura's theory of athletic activities [29, 31, 35, 68] have been consistent in showing that performance factors and perceived self-efficacy are both needed to explain performance.

Perceived Competence

"Perceived competence" and "perceived ability" are terms that have been limited in use to the achievement and mastery motivation literature and indicate the sense that one has the ability to master a task resulting from cumulative interactions with the environment [45, 72]. Harter [45] and Nicholls [72] have developed theories of achievement motivation incorporating the construct of perceived competence (or ability). Although both theoretical models are very similar in their predictions of perceived competence in achievement contexts, Nicholls uses attribution theory (a theory of causal judgment) to explain the cognitions involved in developing a sense of competence, whereas Harter bases her model on socialization and affective processes within a drive theory to explain the development of a child's sense of competence and subsequent behavior. These theories are not as well tested within the sport and physical activity areas as is self-efficacy theory, and where they have been employed, they have been used to explain participation motivation rather than specific task performance. Because Roberts [74] has described Nicholls' model in detail and has reviewed that literature in an earlier volume, I will provide only a brief overview of the model in this section. In addition, cognitive evaluation theory [22] includes perceived competence as a mediator of intrinsic motivation. However, this area was reviewed in the preceding volume of this series [85] and will not be reviewed here.

The concept of competence, as a psychological construct mediating achievement behavior, was first introduced by White [96]. White proposed "effectance" motivation (a global motive) to explain why an individual feels impelled to engage in mastery attempts. Individuals engage in mastery behaviors in order to have an effect on their environment. Being effective (or competent) results in a feeling of efficacy and intrinsic pleasure. White's model did not lend itself readily to empirical investigation, however, because of its global nature and lack of operational definitions. Harter [45], therefore, refined and extended White's model and also developed measurement procedures to test its components empirically.

Harter did not view perceived competence as a global trait or a unitary construct, but rather as a multidimensional motive, having specific domains in the areas of physical, social, and cognitive concerns. Cognitive competence emphasizes school or academic performance; social competence is defined in terms of popularity with one's peers; and physical competence reflects perceived ability at sports and outdoor games. This view of perceived confidence is more specific than the one overall trait view, but is still more global than Bandura's [1] microanalytic conception and is drive oriented rather than self-perception oriented. Harter also focused on the implications of failure as well as success; reconceptualized success as including a condition of "optimal degree of challenge"; considered the role of socializing agents in maintaining, enhancing, or attenuating competence motivation through reinforcement and modeling patterns; considered the effects of reinforcement history on the development of a self-reward system and the internalization of mastery goals; and addressed the relative influence of intrinsic and extrinsic motivation orientations.

According to Harter's [45] model, children's mastery attempts in specific domains result in successes or failures and are evaluated by significant others. If the successes are optimally challenging, this leads to perceived competence and intrinsic pleasure. Approval by significant others also leads to perceived competence, but the need for this approval diminishes with age. Perceived competence and intrinsic pleasure lead to increased motivation to be competent. A history of failure results in perceived lack of competence and anxiety in mastery situations, and decreases children's motivation to continue mastery attempts. In addition, the need for external approval persists developmentally, rather than diminishing.

Harter [45] suggested that perception of control, as well as significant others' approval or disapproval of mastery attempts, influences a child's perceived competence. Children who feel responsible for the outcome of their mastery attempts have a positive sense of competence. When children either do not know who is in control or view powerful others as responsible for their performance, they have a negative or lower sense of competence.

Harter's model is intuitively appealing to the study of motivation in youth sports. From this model, one would predict that young athletes who perceive themselves to be highly competent in a sport, who are oriented toward mastery in sport, and who identify themselves as primarily responsible for their performance persist longer at the sport and maintain interest in mastering the skills. In contrast, those who perceive themselves to have low competence in sport, who are oriented toward extrinsic mastery, and who believe that others are responsible for their performance do not maintain task performance and interest.

Competence motivation theory differs from self-efficacy theory on the origins of perceived efficacy or competence [5]. In Harter's framework, children's competence motives develop gradually through prolonged transactions with their surroundings and evaluative reinforcement of others. In Bandura's social cognitive framework, perceived efficacy is derived from diverse sources of information conveyed vicariously, as well as through social evaluation and direct experience. In addition, Harter has operationalized perceived competence based on a developmental approach; therefore, the measurement of perceived competence is valid only for children. Although Bandura [5] has provided an explanation of the developmental differences in perceived efficacy, its measurement has not been based on a developmental approach.

Nicholls' [72] theoretical model also relates perceived competence (ability) to effectance motivation. Like Bandura [1] and Harter [45], Nicholls believes that perceived competence is the critical mediator of performance and persistence. In addition, the basic assumption of Nicholls' theory is that people are motivated by a desire to demonstrate and/or develop high ability and avoid demonstrating low ability. Nicholls also conceptualizes two types of ability: ego-involved ability and task ability. Individuals may view competence relative to their peers or relative to their past performances or gains in knowledge. As Duda [24] explained, Harter's theory focuses on how much competence individuals perceive themselves to possess and the corresponding relationship to behavior, whereas Nicholls' theory considers the meaning of ability or how it is construed in relation to performance and persistence in achievement settings.

In sport, an athlete's goal would be to maximize the subjective probability of attributing high ability to the self and minimize the subjective probability of attributing low ability to the self. As long as the athlete is able to make high ability attributions to the self in a sport situation, participation will continue. In contrast, the athlete who makes low ability attributions will discontinue participation in that sport to avoid the unpleasant affect associated with feelings of failure.

Both Harter's [45] and Nicholls' [72] models provide the same explanation for children's discontinuation of an activity such as a sport. Nicholls proposes that athletes who realize that they do not possess enough ability to be successful will drop out. Harter also proposes that when athletes have a low perceived physical competence they will withdraw because this perception produces feelings of failure, anxiety, and sadness.

Measurement of Perceived Competence and Perceived Ability. Harter [45] developed the Perceived Competence Scale for Children to measure perceived competence in children from grades 3 through 9. Harter and Pike [49] later extended this scale to pictorial versions appropriate for pre-school-kindergarten and first-second grades. The original scale consists of 28 items, 7 in each of the three specific domains (cognitive, social, physical) and 7 that assess a child's general sense of self-worth. The structured alternative questionnaire format involves first asking the child to choose between one of two statements that was most descriptive of him or her as compared to other children of the same age. For instance, the child must choose between "Some kids do very well at all kinds of sports, BUT others don't feel that they are very good when it comes to sports." After choosing one of the two statements, the child is asked whether the statement is "sort of" or "really" true for him or her. This questionnaire format was designed to reduce social desirability effects. Both responses are worded so that they are perceived as socially legitimate. Each item is scored on a four-point scale, with 4 indicating the highest degree of perceived competence and 1 indicating the lowest. The scores are typically summed and then averaged for each subscale. Harter [46] found that girls consistently rated themselves as less competent than boys in the sports domain. However, if subjects are instructed to use same-sex children as their comparison peer group, these differences are eliminated [95].

Harter [48] has recently developed the Self Perception Profile for Children, which is a revision of the Perceived Competence Scale for Children. The revised scale contains two additional subscales: physical appearance and behavioral conduct. These new subscales assess self-adequacy rather than perceived competence in the form of actual skills. Several items from the original subscales also underwent revision.

In the sport literature, the physical subscale of Harter's Perceived Competence Scale for Children has been predominantly employed [32, 36, 52, 75, 95], and a few studies have employed sport-specific modifications [15, 32, 53, 84, 95]. In one study [32], I modified Harter's perceived physical competence subscale to apply to soccer in order to compare players' more specific perceived soccer competence with their perceived physical competence in predicting players' actual soccer ability. The results indicated that the perceived soccer competence subscale had higher internal consistency and was slightly more predictive of soccer ability than perceived physical competence. However, these sport-specific assessments are more representative of perceived general capacity in a particular sport than of self-efficacy as assessed by the microanalytic approach advocated by Bandura [1].

Harter has also developed scales to measure the construct of perceived control [Multidimensional Measure of Children's Perceptions of Control, 17] and the construct of intrinsic versus extrinsic motivational orientations [Intrinsic Versus Extrinsic Orientation in the Classroom, 47]. Harter's motivational orientations scale pertains only to classroom motivation; a modified version has been adapted for sports [94].

Nicholls [72] has not addressed the issue of how to measure perceived ability. Researchers have typically used a one-item Likert-type scale in which subjects are asked to rate their own ability for a particular task [16]. This type of assessment appears to be more situationally specific than Harter's assessment tool.

Research in Sport and Physical Activity. Despite the intuitive appeal of competence motivation theory to youth sports, relatively little research has been conducted to test Harter's model in sport and physical activity settings. The studies that have been conducted have examined (a) the relationship between perceived physical competence and participation in organized sports, (b) the sources of competence information and significant others' feedback, and (c) the relationship of perceived competence to actual competence, in addition to scale construction efforts [32, 84, 94].

Based on Harter's model, individuals who perceive themselves to be competent in sports should be more likely to participate, while those low in perceived physical competence should be more likely not to participate or to discontinue participation. A few studies in the area of youth sports have examined this hypothesis in terms of participant status [36, 63, 64, 75, 84]. These investigators found that older youth sport participants (9- to 11-year olds) were higher in perceived physical competence than same-age nonparticipants [75] but not higher than younger participants (5- to 9-year-olds) [84]. Interscholastic sport participants [36] and youth wrestlers [16] were found to be higher in perceived physical competence than dropouts, but elite young gymnasts did not differ in perceived physical competence compared to former gymnasts in the same program [63]. The fact that the former elite gymnasts had all experienced some degree of success may explain these contradictory findings. If former and current elite gymnasts are comparing perceptions of their own competence to those of other same-aged children in general, the scale is probably not sensitive enough to discern any differences.

As Klint and Weiss [64] have noted, the investigations just reported were based on the assumption that children participate in sports to demonstrate physical competence. However, children who have low perceptions of their physical competence may still participate in sports for affiliative reasons or to demonstrate social competence [84]. Klint and Weiss examined the relationship between perceptions of competence and particular motives for sport participation and found support for this assumption. Children high in perceived physical competence were more motivated to participate for skill development reasons, whereas those high in perceived social competence were more motivated to participate for the affiliative reasons. These results suggest that researchers should not assume that participation in an activity is due to a certain type of competence motivation or achievement goal.

Harter's model also suggests that the more experience a child has with a sport, the more opportunity that child has to develop a sense of perceived physical competence. Of course, mere participation in sports does not guarantee that a child will have a high sense of physical competence. The degree to which a child has been successful over the sport experience will have a greater influence on his or her perceived competence than will length of involvement. However, the longer a child has been involved in a sport, the more likely he or she has had more successful mastery experiences. Continual failures usually lead to discouragement.

Sport research has not supported this contention, however [32, 36, 75]. Only low [32, 36] or nonsignificant [75] relationships were found between years of playing experience and perceived physical competence. Roberts and his colleagues [75] suggested that the experience of sport participation may not influence children's perceptions of competence; rather, children with a higher perception of competence may select a sport as an activity to demonstrate their abilities. An alternative explanation for the low relationship found may lie in the questionnaire format used to measure perceived competence. Harter's questionnaire is constructed to measure perceived competence relative to one's peers rather than relative to one's own past performances. As children become older and gain more playing experience, their comparison peers change. Thus, they may not view themselves as becoming more competent in comparison to their peers as they gain playing experience, or more competent in absolute terms, because their peers are gaining competence, too. In fact, Ulrich [84] found that as children's age increased, perceived physical competence decreased while actual motor competence increased.

Harter [45] has not specified the sources of information available to children for making judgments about their competence to the same extent as Bandura [1]. Positive reinforcement or approval for independent mastery attempts from adults and optimal challenge plus success are the only two sources specified in the model. Horn and Hasbrook [53] examined what sources of competence information that children use in sport. They found younger children (8–11 years) tended to rate evaluative feedback from parents and game outcome (winning/losing) as more important sources of information about their competence than did older children (12–14 years), who rated social comparison sources as more important. However, adult feedback, especially from coaches, has been shown to be still influential in adolescent athletes' perceived physical competence [52].

Actual sports competence or sports achievement should likewise be a source of competence information, and studies have found significant relationships between perceived physical (or sport-specific) competence and actual skill [32, 52, 84, 95]. Weiss and her colleagues [95] predicted, however, that perceived competence was causally predominant over sports achievement and tested this assumption using causal modeling techniques. They also examined the interrelationships among Harter's contructs of perceived competence, perceived control, and motivational orientation. The results showed that perceptions of competence in sport causally influenced sports achievement and motivational orientation. Perceived control also influenced achievement and motivational orientation, as predicted.

These results do not mean that other competing models may not also fit the data equally well. Whether sports achievement causally influences perceived competence or whether there is a reciprocal relationship, as Bandura [1] would contend, must await additional research. This study was an important step, however, in determining the causal relationships among the constructs of perceived competence, perceived controls, motivational orientation, and actual achievement in the sport domain.

Criticisms of Competence Motivation. As with self-efficacy assessments, perceived competence is based on self-report and thus could suffer from demand and suggestion problems. Harter's [45] structured alternative format has reduced the likelihood of social desirability effects, however, and is regarded as a great advance in the measurement of children's self-confidence [62]. Nevertheless, as previously stated, the trait nature of the measurement reduces its predictive accuracy in relation to performance [5–7]. Sport researchers have used sport-specific measures to try to increase the predictive power of their tests [15, 53, 95], but some have still found this type of modification not to be specific enough [15].

The measurement of perceived competence has also been criticized for not taking the contextual factors of performance situations into account [5, 24]. For instance, children's perceived competence in a sport may change depending on the environmental pressure to compete, the competitiveness of the sport organization, or the peers with which children are comparing themselves [63]. Duda [24], therefore, has advocated more examination of children's perceived competence in actual sport and physical activity situations. The measurement of self-efficacy, on the other hand, involves a relational judgment between perceived capabilities and different task demands (e.g., can one jump 3 ft, 6 ft, 9 ft?) and thus builds contextual factors into the measurement format.

Bandura [5] has also criticized competence motivation conceptually as being difficult to verify because the motive is inferred from the mastery behavior it supposedly causes. One cannot tell, as Bandura points out, whether individuals engage in mastery behavior because of a competence motive to do so or for any number of other reasons without an independent measure of motive strength.

In summary, Harter's theory is developmentally oriented and thus well suited for studying children's competence motivation in sport. It is also trait oriented in its conception, even though the perceived competence construct is viewed as a multidimensional motive rather than as a global trait or unitary construct. Unfortunately, because perceived competence has been measured as a trait, the contextual factors of performance situations have not been considered and the research on perceived competence in youth sports has not been as consistent as the research on self-efficacy.

Sport Confidence

Vealey [87] was dissatisfied with the way self-efficacy and self-confidence had been operationalized in countless ways for every sport situation studied and noted that Harter's model of perceived competence was limited to children. Therefore, she developed a model and instrumentation for sport confidence (the belief in one's ability to be successful in sport) in an attempt to provide a parsimonious operationalization of self-confidence in sport situations. According to Vealey, this model and instrumentation allow for more consistent predictions of behaviors across different sport situations. Borrowing heavily from Nicholls' and Bandura's theories, she developed an interactional, sport-specific model of self-confidence in which sport confidence is conceptualized into trait (SC- trait) and state (SC-state) components, and also includes a competitive orientation construct to account for individual differences in defining success in sport.

SC-trait represents the perceptions that individuals usually possess about their ability to be successful in sport; SC-state represents the perceptions individuals have at a particular moment about their ability to be successful in sport. However, based on Nicholls' belief that success means different things to different individuals, Vealey recognized a need to include in her model a construct, competitive orientation, as a way to operationalize success. Competitive orientation is a dispositional construct that indicates one's tendency to strive toward achieving a certain type of goal in sport that will demonstrate competence and success. Vealey selected (a) performing well and (b) winning as the goals upon which competitive orientations are based. Performing well is similar in conceptualization to Nicholls' task ability orientation, and winning is similar to his ego-involved ability concept. Even though athletes may pursue both of these goals, through successive sport experiences they may become performance oriented or outcome oriented [87].

Although competitive orientation is not considered a primary construct in the model, both SC-trait and competitive orientation are predicted to influence how athletes perceive factors within an objective sport situation and how they respond with certain SC-state levels. Specifically, SC-state is hypothesized to be positively related to SC-trait and performance orientation and negatively related to outcome orientation. SC-state, in turn, is predicted to be the most important mediator of behavior.

SC-trait and competitive orientation are predicted to influence and be influenced by subjective outcomes. Vealey [87] has used causal attributions for performance, perceived past success, perceived performance rating, and performance satisfaction as measures of subjective outcomes. Performance satisfaction would be what Bandura [5] considers an outcome expectation. SC-trait and performance orientation are hypothesized to be positively related to internal attributions for performance, performance rating, performance satisfaction, and perceived success.

Measurement of Sport Confidence. Vealey [87] developed three instruments to test the relationships represented in her conceptual model: (a) the Trait Sport-Confidence Inventory (TSCI), (b) the State Sport-Confidence Inventory (SSCI), and (c) the Competitive Orientation Inventory (COI). Both the TSCI and SSCI use a five-point Likert scale for respondents to compare their own self-confidence with the most self-confident athlete they know. Similarly to Bandura [5], Vealey considered the conceptual areas of competence deemed important to sport performance in developing the TSCI and SSCI instruments. Besides physical ability, she noted [86] that abilities such as performing under pressure and being able to make critical decisions were also necessary competencies for success in sport. However, unlike Bandura's measurement of self-efficacy, Vealey considered the competency areas of sport in general in measuring sport confidence rather than conducting a conceptual analysis of each sport under investigation.

One might argue that because one of the dimensions of self-efficacy is generality, some measure of sport, athletic, or exercise self-confidence is warranted to assess how efficacy cognitions can be predictive of action across similar athletic activities. Bandura [6] points out, however, that the use of domain-linked efficacy scales does not mean that one cannot assess generality of perceived capability. He states that "one can derive the degree of generality from multidomain scales, but one cannot extract the patterning of perceived self-efficacy from conglomerate omnibus tests" [6, p. 372].

Researchers interested in sport confidence have also used the Competitive State Anxiety Inventory-2 (CSAI-2) [67] to measure self-confidence in sport situations. In the CSAI-2, self-confidence is viewed as a separate subcomponent of anxiety in addition to cognitive and perceived somatic anxiety. Specifically, self-confidence is thought of as the conceptual opposite of cognitive anxiety. This is in opposition to Bandura's [4] view of self-efficacy, which does not include anxiety in either the definition or the measuring devices. Just because three factors were found in a factor analysis does not mean that confidence is a subcomponent of anxiety or that anxiety is a subcomponent of confidence.

No consistent pattern of results has emerged from using the CSAI-2 measure of self-confidence to predict performance [39, 67, 69]. Gould and his colleagues [38] used an intraindividual analysis in an attempt to correct for the previous inconsistent findings and still did not find the predicted positive relationship between self-confidence and performance. These findings are in accord with a growing body of evidence that the convenience gained by trait approaches is at the cost of explanatory and predictive power [5, 6].

Research on the Sport Confidence Model. The only published research on the sport confidence model has been Vealey's own preliminary investigation and instrument development [87]. Her validation procedures included five phases of data collection involving 666 high school, college, and adult athletes. The TSCI, SSCI, and COI instruments demonstrated adequate item discrimination, internal consistency, test-retest reliability, content validity, and concurrent validity.

Vealey tested the construct validity of her model using 48 elite gymnasts who were participating in a national meet. The only results that supported her model were that SC-trait and competitive orientation were significant predictors of SC-state as well as of several subjective outcomes. Contrary to her model, precompetition SC-state did not predict performance, nor did a significant correlation emerge between performance and SC-trait. However, performance did predict postcompetition SC-state.

The explanations Vealey provided for SC-state's inability to predict performance were the elite nature of the sample, the importance of this particular competition, and the structure of the competition, which lasted for 2 days. The elite sample, as one might suspect, was very homogeneous and high in reported self-confidence. Vealey proposed that these athletes would not admit to feelings of diffidence. However, using a small and homogeneous sample, whether high or low in ability, makes it difficult to find any predictive relationships. A more heterogeneous group would have provided a better sample with which to test the hypothesized relationships within the model of sport confidence. The facts that the competition lasted for 2 days, and that sport confidence could not be assessed immediately prior to and throughout the competition, also made it difficult to get accurate assessments of SC-state.

Vealey [86] also suggested that perhaps sport performance is too complex to be predicted by SC-state. This is a very important point that sport psychology researchers sometimes fail to recognize in their attempts to explain sport performance solely by psychological variables [30]. In addition, as mentioned earlier, Bandura [1] contends that self-efficacy or confidence affects the choice of activities, effort expenditure, persistence in a given activity, and vulnerability to stress and depression. Competitive sport performance, however, includes more than approach/avoidance behavior, effort expenditure, and persistence; it also includes skills. Those researchers in sport and exercise who have measured self-confidence in terms of how it has influenced the performance behaviors outlined by Bandura have found significant relationships [23, 25–27, 29, 34, 65, 89, 90].

Criticisms of Sport Confidence. Vealey's measurement confidence represents an improvement over the physical self-efficacy scale [77] and Harter's physical subscale in that it assesses the generative capabilities necessary for successful performance in most sport situations. However, it does not consider specific sport contexts or assessments of those contexts in the microanalytic approach that will produce the most predictive power. For instance, in ice hockey, an important area of self-confidence is one's perceived ability in making power plays (scoring when the opponents are short-handed). Power play behavior can be assessed directly, which provides a measure that is especially relevant to the behavior being analyzed. As stated previously, measures that are tailored to the domain of functioning being studied have greater predictive power than general trait measures.

Also, in regard to the measurement of sport confidence, Vealey does not provide a rationale for instructing respondents to compare their self-confidence to that of the most self-confident athlete they know. Since people differ in terms of the athletes they know, such a rating procedure can create considerable unsystematic variance. Subjects could appear high or low in confidence, depending on whom they happen to select for comparison. Should the comparison athlete be one the respondent knows personally or a professional that the respondent reads about in the newspaper? Perhaps less variable results would occur if respondents were instructed to make comparisons to an age- and gender-appropriate athlete in terms of sport confidence.

The necessity for including SC-trait in the sport confidence model could be questioned, since the only variable it predicts is SC-state and is therefore redundant. Determining the important sources of SC-state may be more fruitful than assessing athletes' dispositional self-confidence.

In addition, inclusion of the concept of competitive orientation could be called into question. Vealey included the construct of competitive orientation in the model as a way to operationalize individual perceptions of success. However, how one perceives success in one situation may be different from how one perceives it in another. The definition of success may be situationally specific. In using the self-efficacy measurement approach, the questions can be structured to assess comparative confidence (how confident are you that you can beat your opponent?) and/or individual performance-oriented confidence (how confident are you that you can improve your last performance?). A dispositional competitive orientation is not needed.

To test fully the network of relationships hypothesized in the sport confidence model, a path analysis or causal modeling should have been conducted; however, this would have necessitated a larger sample. This type of analysis would better test the necessity for including SC-trait and competitive orientation in the model. In addition, even without a path analysis, a larger sample size is needed for any multivariate analysis.

Movement Confidence

Another model specific to sport and motor performance, one concerning movement confidence, was developed by Griffin and Keogh [42] to describe the feeling of adequacy in a movement situation as both a personal consequence and a mediator in that situation. This model is similar to the models previously reviewed. Griffin and Keogh claim, however, that their model expands these models to include evaluations that an individual makes of sensory experiences directly related to moving. Movement confidence is viewed as a consequence of this evaluation process, which then in turn mediates participation in a movement situation.

Movement confidence, as a consequence, involves the evaluation of a two-factor personal assessment: movement competence (MOVCOMP) and movement sense (MOVSENSE). MOVCOMP is an individual's perception of personal skill in relation to task demands, and MOVSENSE is an individual's personal expectations of sensory experiences related to moving. These sensory experiences can include muscle aches, breathing hard, sensing of speed, pain of injury, etc. Griffin and Keogh categorize these sensory experiences into two components: personal enjoyment of expected moving sensations and perceived potential for physical harm. Perceived movement competence and perceived movement sense thus interact to produce a sense or state of movement confidence.

Movement confidence as a mediator functions to influence participation choice, participation performance, and participation persistence in a fashion similar to that proposed by Bandura [1]. Participation, in turn, provides information that is added to an individual's experiences for future use in the personal evaluation process.

Measurement of Movement Confidence. Griffin and Keogh recognized that the difficulty of measuring movement confidence would be in measuring perceived movement competence, personal enjoyment of expected moving sensations, and perceived potential for physical harm as entities separate from each other and separate from movement confidence. They developed a Movement Confidence Inventory [43] in an attempt to identify these components as separate entities and as varying in their contribution to perceived levels of movement confidence. The inventory requires three different ratings to be made for any movement task: level of experience, level of confidence in performing the task, and extent to which each of 22 paired descriptor words (e.g., "safe/dangerous") contributes to one's perceived level of movement confidence. The descriptor words were organized into the three confidence components of competence, enjoyment, and physical harm. Unfortunately, factor analysis of the descriptor words did not reveal three factors organized around the three confidence components, rather, there were simply items loading on one factor, with the partner or opposite word loading on the second factor (e.g., "difficult/easy") [43].

The Movement Confidence Inventory does not provide an external criterion of movement confidence, which Griffin and Keogh [42] indicate is a difficult matter to resolve. One possibility they suggested is to identify observable behavioral manifestations of movement confidence. However, using behavior to measure self-beliefs would entangle one in hopeless circularity. Still, Keogh et al. [58] attempted to develop such an observational measure and appeared to end up measuring behavioral manifestations of fear rather than confidence. For instance, they identified behaviors such as shuffling feet, hesitation, reaching for support, and looking excessively at the instructor. Behavioral indicators of positive levels of movement confidence were much more difficult to observe. Bandura [1] would conceptualize these behavioral manifestations as anxiety or fear co-effects of avoidance behavior resulting from perceived inefficacy. Thus, there would be no fixed relationship between anxiety and actions. In fact, Keogh and his colleagues [58] found that some of the subjects who displayed these anxious behaviors were still able to perform adequately.

Criticisms of Movement Confidence. The only research conducted on movement confidence has been in instrumentation development. No research support for the model has been provided. The one study that tried to identify movement competence, personal enjoyment of expected moving sensations, and perceived potential for physical harm as separate entities failed to do so [43}.

On conceptual grounds, I see no need for this model in studying self-confidence in movement situations that could not be studied within Bandura's [1] theoretical framework of self-efficacy. Griffin and Keogh [42] believe that movement sense is the unique component that differentiates their model from other conceptions of self-confidence. However, in Bandura's model, expected sensory experiences are implied as a source of confidence information via physiological states. The personal enjoyment of such sensations appears to have more to do with having the incentive to perform the task than it does with having confidence. An increase in enjoyment may increase approach behavior and persistence, but not confidence in one's ability to perform the task more proficiently. In addition, perceived potential for physical harm may be viewed as part of the perceived task demands or task difficulty within Bandura's framework.

Summary and Comparison of Approaches

Self-efficacy theory [1], competence motivation theory [45], and the models of sport confidence [87] and movement confidence [42] have been reviewed in this chapter. All of these models view self-confidence as a critical mediator of motivation and behavior but differ on the origins of self-confidence and how it is measured.

Bandura [1] views self-confidence as specific to particular domains of functioning and as being derived from the cognitive appraisal of diverse sources of information, including enactive and vicarious experiences, social influences, and physiological information. A microanalytic procedure requiring a conceptual analysis of the required generative competencies for a given performance task is used and offers the most predictive power in explaining behavior. On the other hand, in Harter's [45] developmental framework, which is confined to children, self-confidence develops gradually through prolonged transactions with one's surroundings and evaluation reinforcement of others, and is considered to have a multidimensional trait orientation. Harter's measurement of the construct is psychometrically sound and derived from developmental theory, but it does not consider contextual factors within specific performance situations. Her measure also forces the child to assess self-confidence in relation to peers when, according to Nicholls [72] and evidence from sport research [53], the process by which children judge their capabilities changes with age.

Given Bandura's situationally specific model and Harter's developmental model, the models of sport confidence [87] and movement confidence [42] seem unwarranted for studying self-confidence in sport. Vealey's [87] constructs of trait sport confidence and competitive orientation, from which situational sport confidence is derived, do not add any new conceptual dimensions. Furthermore, the comparison "to the most confident athlete you know," used in the measurement of sport confidence, creates considerable unsystematic variance and thus does not provide the parsimonious operationalization of self-confidence that was intended. Regardless of the countless ways that self-confidence (or self-efficacy) has been operationalized for every sport situation studied, the results have been very consistent in finding situationally specific self-confidence to be significantly related to performance.

The research from the sport literature provides clear evidence that a significant relationship exists between self-confidence and performance. This evidence spans different tasks, measures of self-confidence, and major theoretical paradigms [1, 45]. In terms of causal interactions between self-confidence and performance, evidence from sport shows that self-confidence is both an effect and a cause in relation to performance [29, 31, 35, 68]. However, in the athletic domain, other factors, such as prior performance and behavior [29, 32, 35, 68], are also instrumental in influencing performance. Self-confidence, if considered as a common mechanism mediating behavior, should not be expected to fully explain human behavior [4], particularly the complex behavior of sport performance [86].

Conclusion

This chapter has compared the major theoretical frameworks used to examine self-confidence in sport and physical activity settings. Both Bandura's model and Harter's model (for studying motivational behavior in youth sports) appear to be viable theoretical frameworks in which to study self-confidence in sport, even though modifications will be required to explain the complex nature of sport performance. Variables such as previous performance, affective self-evaluation, goal setting, and physiological states (e.g., mood or fitness) may exert a direct influence on sport performance. In studying competence motivation in children, situational variables may need to be given greater consideration. The inclusion of these additional determinants should increase the amount of variance in athletic performance that can be explained as, was the case in my model on diving performance [29, 31, 35].

Much of the sport research has examined self-confidence in relation to actual sport performance in terms of skill rather than in terms of the motivational behavior actually specified by the theories, such as persistence or mastery attempts, choice of activities or skills, and effort expended. These behaviors are certainly contributors to skillful performance and should be given more attention in the study of self-confidence in sport.

Other areas that deserve attention in Bandura's model are the generalizability of self-confidence in terms of the number of domains of functioning within a sport (e.g., types of shots in golf) or within exercise, the nonmovement domains of confidence required in exercise and sport (e.g., psychological skills), how people process multidimensional confidence information, the study of self-confidence across a number of situations (e.g., over the course of a season), and the study of team confidence in relation to self-confidence. In terms of the generality of self-confidence, examination of the relative contributions of generality, level, and strength to overall performance would help determine where to focus intervention studies. In the nonmovement aspects of self-confidence, belief in control over one's intrusive thoughts, for instance, may be an important confidence component in the area of exercise behavior and sport performance. Bandura [5] proposes that self-confidence influences thought patterns, as well as behavior, and research has demonstrated its applicability in anxiety-provoking situations [57].

Scant research has been conducted on how people process multidimensional confidence information [5]. The importance of different types of information may vary across different types of activities and situations. In some sport and exercise situations, physiological information may be a more pertinent source of confidence information than previous performance. In processing multidimensional information, people may misjudge or ignore relevant information in trying to integrate it [5]. Results from this research may also have implications for the type and amount of confidence information provided to sport performers and exercise patients.

As mentioned earlier in this chapter, in many real-life sport situations, people perform with some variation in circumstances (e.g., different competitions) and temporal intervals. Studying confidence judgments across a number of competitions or situations may be the most informative paradigm for testing the relative contribution of self-confidence, performance, and other possible mediating variables.

All of the studies cited in this chapter have examined self-confidence in relation to individual athletic or exercise performance. In team sports, however, many of the challenges and difficulties athletes face reflect team problems requiring sustained team efforts to produce successful performance. Drawing from Bandura's [5] concept of collective efficacy, perceived team confidence should influence what athletes choose to do as a team, how much effort they put into it, and their staying power when team efforts fail to produce results. Confidence in one's team to be able to produce the required performance may be just as important as confidence in oneself. Similarly, coaches' perceived efficacy may have an important impact on team performance. Evidence that managerial self-efficacy affects organizational performance is especially relevant to this issue [100, 101].

Finally, in Harter's model, attention should be directed to examining children's self-confidence in actual sport and physical activity situations [24]. Bandura's concept of situationally specific self-confidence could be examined in relation to children's perceived physical competence. This interactional strategy may provide more power in explaining children's sport competence motivation.

References

1. Bandura, A. Self-efficacy: Toward a unifying theory of behavioral change. *Psychol. Rev.* 84:191-215, 1977.
2. Bandura, A. Reflections on self-efficacy. In S. Rachman, (ed.). *Advances* in *Behavior Research and Therapy,* Vol. 1. Oxford: Pergamon Press, 1978, pp. 237-269.
3. Bandura, A. Self-efficacy in human agency. *Am. Psychol.* 37:122-147, 1982.
4. Bandura, A. Recycling misconceptions of perceived self-efficacy. *Cog. Ther. Res.* 8:231-255, 1984.
5. Bandura, A. *Social Foundation of Thought and Action: A Social Cognitive Theory.* Englewood Cliffs, N.J.: Prentice-Hall, 1986.
6. Bandura, A. The explanatory and predictive scope of self-efficacy theory. J. Soc. Clin. Psychol. 4:359-373, 1986.
7. Bandùra, A. Self-efficacy mechanisms in physiological activation and health-promoting behavior. In J. Madden IV, S. Matthysse, and J. Barchas (eds.). *Adaptation, Learning and Affect.* New York: Raven Press, 1986.
8. Bandura, A., and D. Cervone. Self-evaluative and self-efficacy mechanisms governing the motivational effects of goal systems. *J. Pers. Soc. Psychol.* 45: 1017-1028, 1983.
9. Bandura, A., and D.H. Schunk. Cultivating competence, self-efficacy, and intrinsic interest through proximal self-motivation. *J. Pers. Soc. Psychol.* 41:586-598, 1981.
10. Barling, J., and M. Abel. Self-efficacy beliefs and tennis performance. *Cog. Ther. Res.* 7:265-272, 1983.
11. Betz, N.E., and G. Hackett. The relationship of career-related self-efficacy expectations to perceived career options in college women and men. *J. Counsel. Psychol.* 28:399-410, 1981.
12. Biglan, A. A behavior-analytic critique of Bandura's self-efficacy theory. *Behavior Analyst* 10:1-15, 1987.
13. Bird, A.M., and J.N. Brame. Self versus team attributions: A test of the "I'm ok, but the team's so-so" phenomenon. *Res. Q.* 49:260-268, 1978.
14. Borkovec, T.D. Self-efficacy: Cause or reflection of behavioral change. In S. Rachman (ed.). *Advances in Behavior Research and Therapy.* Oxford: Pergamon Press, 1978, pp. 163-170.
15. Brustad, R., and M.R. Weiss. Competence perceptions and sources of worry in high, medium, and low competitive trait-anxious young athletes. *J. Sport Psychol.* 9:97-105, 1987.
16. Burton, D., and R. Martens. Pinned by their own goals: An exploratory investigation into why kids drop out of wrestling. *J. Sport Psychol.* 8:183-197, 1986.
17. Connell, J.P. *A Multidimensional Measure of Children's Perceptions of Control.* Denver: University of Denver Press, 1980.
18. Corbin, C.B. Sex of subject, sex of opponent, and opponent ability as factors affecting self-confidence in a competitive situation. *J. Sport Psychol.* 3:265-270, 1981.
19. Corbin, C.B., D.M. Landers, D.L. Feltz, and K. Senior. Sex differences in performance estimates: Female's lack of confidence vs. male boastfulness. *Res. Q. Exerc. Sport* 54:407-410, 1983.
20. Corbin, C.B., D.R. Laurie, C. Gruger, and B. Smiley. Vicarious success experience as a factor influencing self-confidence, attitudes and physical activity of adult women. *J. Teach. Phys. Ed.* 4:17-23, 1984.
21. Corbin, C.B., and C. Nix. Sex-typing of physical activities and success predictions of children before and after cross-sex competition. *J. Sport Psychol.* 1:43-52, 1979.
22. Deci, E.L., and R.M. Ryan. *Intrinsic Motivation and Self-Determination in Human Behavior.* New York: Plenum Press, 1985.
23. Desharnais, R., J. Bouillon, and G. Godin. Self-efficacy and outcome expectations as determinants of exercise adherence. *Psychol. Rep.* 59:1155-1159, 1986.
24. Duda, J.L. Toward a developmental theory of children's motivation in sport. *J. Sport Psychol.* 9:130-145, 1987.
25. Ewart, C.K., K.J. Stewart, R.E. Gillilan, and M.H. Kelemen. Self-efficacy mediates strength gains during circuit weight training in men with coronary artery disease. *Med. Sci. Sports Exerc.* 18:531-540, 1986.
26. Ewart, C.K., K.J. Stewart, R.E. Gillilan, M.H. Kelemen, S.A. Valenti, J.D. Manley, and M.D. Kelemen. Usefulness of self-efficacy in predicting overexertion during programmed exercise in coronary artery disease. *Am. J. Cardiol.* 57:557-561, 1986.
27. Ewart, C.K., C.B. Taylor, L.B. Reese, and R.F. DeBusk. Effects of early postmyocardial infarction exercise testing on self-perception and subsequent physical activity. *Am. J. Cardiol.* 51:1076-1080, 1983.
28. Eysenck, H.J. Expectations as causal elements in behavioral change. In S. Rachman (ed.). *Advances in Behavior Research and Therapy.* Oxford: Pergamon Press, 1978, pp. 171-175.

29. Feltz, D.L. Path analysis of the causal elements in Bandura's theory of self-efficacy and an anxiety-based model of avoidance behavior. *J. Pers. Soc. Psychol.* 42:764-781, 1982.
30. Feltz, D.L. Future directions in theoretical research in sport psychology: From applied psychology toward sport science. In J. Skinner (ed.). *Future Directions in Exercise/Sport Research.* Champaign, Ill.: Human Kinetics Press, in press.
31. Feltz, D.L. Gender differences in the causal elements of self-efficacy on a high avoidance motor task. *J. Sport Psychol.* in press.
32. Feltz, D.L., and E.W. Brown. Perceived competence in soccer skills among young soccer players. *J. Sport Psychol.* 6:385-394, 1984.
33. Feltz, D.L., D.M. Landers, and U. Raeder. Enhancing self-efficacy in high avoidance motor tasks: A comparison of modeling techniques. *J. Sport Psychol.* 1:112-122, 1979.
34. Feltz, D.L., S. Marcotullio, and C. Fitzgerald. The effects of different forms of in vivo emotive imagery on self-efficacy and competitive endurance performance. Paper presented at the North American Society for the Psychology of Sport and Physical Activity, Gulfport, Miss., 1985.
35. Feltz, D.L., and D.A. Mugno. A replication of the path analysis of the causal elements in Bandura's theory of self-efficacy and the influence of autonomic perception. *J. Sport Psychol.* 5:263-277, 1983.
36. Feltz, D.L., and L. Petlichkoff. Perceived competence among interscholastic sport participants and dropouts. *Can. J. Appl. Sport Sci.* 8:231-235, 1983.
37. Gayton, W.F., G.R. Matthews, and G.N. Burchstead. An investigation of the validity of the physical self-efficacy scale in predicting marathon performance. *Percept. Mot. Skills* 63:752-754, 1986.
38. Gould, D., L. Petlichkoff, J. Simons, and M. Vevera. Relationship between Competitive State Anxiety Inventory-2 subscale scores and pistol shooting performance. *J. Sport Psychol.* 9:33-42, 1987.
39. Gould, D., L. Petlichkoff, and R.S. Weinberg. Antecedents of temporal changes in, and relationships between, CSAI-2 subcomponents. *J. Sport Psychol.* 6:289-304, 1984.
40. Gould, D., and M. Weiss. Effect of model similarity and model self-talk on self-efficacy in muscular endurance. *J. Sport Psychol.* 3:17-29, 1981.
41. Gould, D., M.R. Weiss, and R. Weinberg. Psychological characteristics of successful and nonsuccessful Big-Ten Wrestlers. *J. Sport Psychol.* 3:69-81, 1981.
42. Griffin, N.S., and J.F. Keogh. A model for movement confidence. In J.A.S. Kelso and J. Clark (eds.). *The Development of Movement Control and Coordination.* New York: Wiley, 1982, pp. 213-236.
43. Griffin, N.S., J.F. Keogh, and R. Maybee. Performer perceptions of movement confidence. *J. Sport Psychol.* 6:395-407, 1984.
44. Hackett, G., and N.E. Betz. A self-efficacy approach to the career development of women. *J. Vocat. Behav.* 18:326-339, 1981.
45. Harter, S. Effectance motivation reconsidered: Toward a developmental model. *Hum. Dev.* 21:34-64, 1978.
46. Harter, S. The development of competence motivation in the mastery of cognitive and physical skills: Is there still a place for joy? In G.C. Roberts and D.M. Landers (eds.). *Psychology of Motor Behavior and Sport—1980.* Champaign, Ill.: Human Kinetics Press, 1981, pp. 3-29.
47. Harter, S. A new self-report scale of intrinsic versus extrinsic orientation in the classroom: Motivational and informational components. *Dev. Psychol.* 17:300-312, 1981.
48. Harter, S. *Manual for the Self-Perception Profile for Children.* Denver: University of Denver Press, 1985.
49. Harter, S., and R. Pike. *The Pictorial Scale of Perceived Competence and Social Acceptance for Young Children.* Denver: University of Denver Press, 1983.
50. Highlen, P.S., and B.B. Bennett. Psychological characteristics of successful and non-successful elite wrestlers: An exploratory study. *J. SportPsychol.* 1:123-137, 1979.
51. Hogan, P.I., and J.P. Santomier. Effect of mastering swim skills on older adults' self-efficacy. *Res. Q. Exerc. Sport* 55:294-296, 1984.
52. Horn, T.S. Coaches' feedback and changes in children's perceptions of their physical competence. *J. Educ. Psychol.* 77:174-186, 1985.
53. Horn, T., and C. Hasbrook. Informational components influencing children's perceptions of their physical competence. In M. Weiss and D. Gould (eds.). *Sport for Children and Youth.* Champaign, Ill.: Human Kinetics Press, 1986, pp. 81-88.
54. Kaplan, R.M., C.J. Atkins, and S. Reinsch. Specific efficacy expectations mediate exercise compliance in patients with COPD. *Health Psychol.* 3:223-242, 1984.
55. Kavanagh, D., and S. Hausfeld. Physical performance and self-efficacy under happy and sad moods. *J. Sport Psychol.* 8:112-123, 1986.
56. Kazdin, A.E. Conceptual and assessment issues raised by self-efficacy theory. In S. Rachman (ed.). *Advances in Behavior Research and Therapy,* Vol. 1. Oxford: Pergamon Press, 1978, pp. 177-185.
57. Kent, G., and R. Gibbons. Self-efficacy and the control of anxious cognitions. *J. Behav. Ther. Exp. Psychiatry* 18:33-40, 1987.
58. Keogh, J.F., N.S. Griffin, and R. Spector. Observer perceptions of movement confidence. *Res. Q. Exerc. Sport* 52:465-473, 1981.
59. Kirsch, I. "Microanalytic" analyses of efficacy expectations as predictors of performance. *Cog. Ther. Res.* 4:259-262, 1980.
60. Kirsch, I. Self-efficacy and expectancy: Old wine with new labels. *J. Pers. Soc. Psychol.* 49:824-830, 1985.
61. Kirsch, I., and C. V. Wickless. Concordance rates between self-efficacy and approach behavior are redundant. *Cog. Ther. Res.* 7:179-188, 1983.
62. Kleiber, D.A. Of joy, competence, and significant others in children's sports. In G.C. Roberts and D.M. Landers (eds.). *Psychology of Motor Behavior and Sport—1980.* Champaign, Ill.: Human Kinetics Press, 1981, pp. 30-36.
63. Klint, K.A. Participation motives and self-perceptions of current and former athletes in youth gymnastics. Unpublished master's thesis, University of Oregon, Eugene, 1985.

64. Klint, K.A., and M.R. Weiss. Perceived competence and motives for participating in youth sports: A test of Harter's competence motivation theory. *J. Sport Psychol.* 9:55-65, 1987.

65. Lee, C. Self-efficacy as a predictor of performance in competitive gymnastics. *J. Sport Psychol.* 4:405-409, 1982.

66. Mahoney, M.T., and M. Avener. Psychology of the elite athlete: An exploratory study. *Cog. Ther. Res.* 1:135-141, 1977.

67. Martens, R., D. Burton, R.S. Vealey, L.A. Bump, and D. Smith. Cognitive and somatic dimensions of competitive anxiety. Paper presented at the North American Society for the Psychology of Sport and Physical Activity meeting, University of Maryland, College Park, Md., 1982.

68. McAuley, E. Modeling and self-efficacy: A test of Bandura's model. *J. Sport Psychol.* 7:283-295, 1985.

69. McAuley, E. State anxiety: Antecedent or result of sport performance? *J. Sport Behav.* 8:71-77, 1985.

70. McAuley, E., and D. Gill. Reliability and validity of the physical self-efficacy scale in a competitive sport setting. *J. Sport Psychol.* 5:410-418, 1983.

71. Nelson, L., and M. Furst. An objective study of the effects of expectation on competitive sport setting. *J. Psychol.* 81:69-72, 1972.

72. Nicholls, J.G. Achievement motivation: Conceptions of ability, subjective experience, task choice and performance. *Psychol. Rev.* 91:328-346, 1984.

73. O'Leary, A. Self-efficacy and health. *Behav. Res. Ther.* 23:437-451, 1985.

74. Roberts, G.C. Achievement motivation in sport. In R.L. Terjung (ed.). *Exercise and Sport Sciences Reviews.* Philadelphia: Franklin Institute Press, 1982, pp. 236-269.

75. Roberts, G.C., D.A. Kleiber, and J.L. Duda. An analysis of motivation in children's sports: The role of perceived competence in participation. *J. Sport Psychol.* 3:206-216, 1981.

76. Rotter, J.B. *Social Learning and Clinical Psychology.* Englewood Cliffs, N.J.: Prentice-Hall, 1954.

77. Ryckman, R.M., M.A. Robbins, B. Thornton, and P. Cantrell. Development and validation of a physical self-efficacy scale. *J. Pers. Soc. Psychol.* 42:891-900, 1982.

78. Scanlan, T.K., and M.W. Passer. Determinants of competitive performance expectancies of young male athletes. *J. Pers.* 49:60-74, 1981.

79. Scanlan, T.K., and M.W. Passer. Factors influencing the competitive performance expectancies of young female athletes. *J. Sport Psychol.* 1:212-220, 1979.

80. Schunk, D.H. Self-efficacy perspective on achievement behavior. *Educ. Psychol.* 19:48-58, 1984.

81. Sonstroem, R.J. Exercise and self-esteem. In R.L. Terjung (ed.). *Exercise and Sport Sciences Reviews.* Lexington, Mass.: Collamore Press, 1984, pp. 123-155.

82. Taylor, C.B., A. Bandura, C.K. Ewart, N.H. Miller, and R.F. Debusk. Raising spouse's and patient's perceptions of his cardiac capabilities following a myocardial infarction. *Am. J. Cardiol.* 55:635-638, 1985.

83. Telch, M.J., A Bandura, P. Vinciguerra, S. Agras, and A.L. Stout. Social demand and congruence between self-efficacy and performance. *Behav. Ther.* 13:694-701, 1983.

84. Ulrich, B.D. Perceptions of physical competence, motor competence, and participation in organized sport: Their interrelationships in young children. *Res. Q. Exerc. Sport* 58:57-67, 1987.

85. Vallerand, R.J., E.L. Deci, and R.M. Ryan. Intrinsic motivation in sport. In K.B. Pandolf (ed.). *Exercise and Sport Sciences Review,* Vol. 15. New York: Macmillan Co., 1987, pp. 389-425.

86. Vealey, R.S. The conceptualization and measurement of sport confidence. Unpublished Ph.D. dissertation, University of Illinois, 1984.

87. Vealey, R. Conceptualization of sport-confidence and competitive orientation: Preliminary investigation and instrument development. *J. Sport Psychol.* 8:221-246, 1986.

88. Weinberg, R. Relationship between self-efficacy and cognitive strategies in enhancing endurance performance. *Int. J. Sport Psychol.* 17:280-293, 1986.

89. Weinberg, R., D. Gould, and A. Jackson. Expectations and performance: An empirical test of Bandura's self-efficacy theory. *J. Sport Psychol.* 1:320-331, 1979.

90. Weinberg, R.S., D. Gould, D. Yukelson, and A. Jackson. The effect of preexisting and manipulated self-efficacy on a competitive muscular endurance task. *J. Sport Psychol.* 3:345-354, 1981.

91. Weinberg, R.S., M. Sinardi, and A. Jackson. Effect of bar height and modeling on anxiety, self-confidence and gymnastic performance. *Int. Gymnast.* 2:11-13, 1982.

92. Weinberg, R.S., D. Yukelson, and A. Jackson. Effect of public and private efficacy expectations on competitive performance. *J. Sport Psychol.* 2:340-349, 1980.

93. Weiss, M.R. Self-esteem and achievement in children's sport and physical activity. In D. Gould and M. Weiss (eds.). *Advances in Pediatric Sport Sciences,* Vol. 2: *Behavioral Issues.* Champaign, Ill.: Human Kinetics Press, 1987, pp. 87-119.

94. Weiss, M.R., B.J. Bredemeier, and R.M. Shewchuk. An intrinsic/extrinsic motivation scale for the youth sport setting: A confirmatory factor analysis. *J. Sport Psychol.* 7:75-91, 1985.

95. Weiss, M.R., B.J. Bredemeier, and R. Shewchuk. The dynamics of perceived competence, perceived control, and motivational orientation in youth sport. In M. Weiss and D. Gould (eds.). *Sport for Children and Youths.* Champaign, Ill.: Human Kinetics Press, 1986, pp. 89-102.

96. White, R. Motivation reconsidered: The concept of competence. *Psychol. Rev.* 66:297-323, 1959.

97. Wilkes, R.L., and J.J. Summers. Cognitions, mediating variables, and strength performance. *J. SportPsychol.* 6:351-359, 1984.

98. Wolpe, J. Self-efficacy theory and psychotherapeutic change: A square peg for a round role. In S. Rachman (ed.). *Advances in Behavioral Research and Therapy.* Oxford: Pergamon Press, 1978, pp. 231-236.

99. Woolfolk, R.L., S.M. Murphy, D. Gottesfeld, and D. Aitken. Effects of mental rehearsal of task motor activity and mental depiction of task outcome on motor skill performance. *J. Sport Psychol.* 7:191-197, 1985.

100. Wood, R.E., and A. Bandura. Impact of conceptions of ability on complex organizational decision-making. Unpublished manuscript, Stanford University, Stanford, Calif.

101. Wood, R.E., A. Bandura, and T. Bailey. Mechanisms governing organizational productivity in complex decision-making environments. Unpublished manuscript, Stanford University, Stanford, Calif.

102. Wurtele, S.K. Self-efficacy and athletic performance; A review. *J. Soc. Clin. Psychol.* 4:290-301, 1986.

103. Yan Lan, L., and D.L. Gill. The relationships among self-efficacy, stress responses, and a cognitive feedback manipulation. *J. Sport Psychol.* 6:227-238, 1984.

30 Future Directions in Psychological Skills Training

ROBIN S. VEALEY
Miami University

A variety of methods and skills have been included under the rubric of psychological skills training (PST). This reading assessed the trends in PST through content analysis of North American published works between 1980 and 1988. This was important since what had been included under the term PST was not standard. This content analysis systematically and objectively identified PST characteristics so it would be replicable by other researchers.

Six needs for the future direction of PST emerged: targeting more young athletes, identifying specific implementation procedures, differentiating between psychological skills and methods, adopting a more holistic approach, better defining the practice of sport psychology, and emphasizing a relationship between theory and practice through identifying PST methods and skills that are grounded in research-based principles. Traditional research methods, as well as idiographic and qualitative methods, are advocated when evaluating PST programs.

All these tasks were necessary so the field of sport psychology could better stand alone as a discipline by defining what makes it unique in terms of sport consumer needs. This reading assisted the field of sport psychology by showing its uniqueness without the constant desire to fall back on parent disciplines, which had been common in the past.

Content Analysis

To evaluate current PST approaches, a content analysis was conducted. Content analysis is "a research technique for making inferences by systematically and objectively identifying specified characteristics within a text" (Stone, Dunphy, Smith, & Ogilvie, 1966, p. 5). As with any scientific method, it is designed to be objective and systematic so as to be replicable for other researchers (Krippendorff, 1980).

The research design used in this study was based on Krippendorff's (1980) content analysis framework which includes six methodological steps. First, the data to be analyzed and population they are to be drawn from is clearly defined. Second, the context is made explicit to establish clear boundaries for the analysis. Third, the investigator's knowledge is taken into account in the evaluation of context. Fourth, the aim or target is clearly stated. Fifth, inferences are made from the data in relation to their context. Sixth, validity is assumed based on the a priori specifications of data, context, knowledge, and target. In the next section, the design of this study is discussed with regard to these six steps.

Design

Data. The data included all approaches to PST described in books published in North America between 1980 and 1988. Books that were included in the analysis focused on the application of psychological skills, techniques, and strategies for athletes, coaches, and/or sport psychologists. The analysis did not include books that cover the entire field of sport psychology or published conference proceedings, but rather books that explicitly outline applied PST approaches.

Context. Content of the books was analyzed in three areas. First, the target population was examined to ascertain type of consumer (athlete, coach, or sport psychologist) as well as the specificity of consumer (specific sport vs. general).

Second, content areas were examined regarding the types of methods and skills discussed. Four types of methods were examined in the content analysis: imagery, thought control (self-talk, affirmations), goal setting, and physical relaxation. These categories were chosen by the investigator as representative of most methods used in PST. Similarly, the investigator designated eight categories of psychological skills to be used in the content analysis: arousal control, attentional control, self-confidence, self-awareness, interpersonal skills, volition (motivation, commitment), self-esteem, and lifestyle management.

Third, specific format characteristics of the PST approaches were examined including the role of consumers and whether or not the PST approaches were research-based, systematic, and progressive. The analysis of the role of consumers examined whether provisions were made in the books to include consumers as active participants versus passive readers. Books were categorized as active if they included plans or exercises that encouraged self-evaluation and self-monitoring; they were categorized as passive if no exercises or activities designed to personalize the material were included. Books were categorized as research-based if the investigator felt the educational material presented and techniques offered were consistent with or supported by theory and research in psychology and sport psychology. Specifically, books were categorized as research supported (material is consistent with current literature),

Adapted, by permission, from R.S. Vealey, 1988, "Future directions and psychological skills training," *The Sport Psychologist* 2: 318-336.

research supported and presented (material is consistent with current literature and is presented to consumers), and unsupported by research (material is not consistent with or supported by existing literature). PST approaches in the books were categorized as systematic if provisions were made to help consumers move from an understanding of the material to the acquisition and implementation of PST techniques and skills into their behavioral routines. Finally, PST approaches in the books were categorized as progressive if specific, hierarchical sequences of skill mastery were established.

Investigator's Knowledge. The investigator was an educational and research sport psychologist whose credentials met the criteria established by the U.S. Olympic Committee (1983).

Target. The aim or target of this content analysis was to systematically examine the content of PST approaches published in books in North America between 1980 and 1988 with regard to target populations, content areas, and format characteristics.

Inference and Validity. Inferences were made about the data based on the specified context categories, and the validity of these inferences is supported by the context specifications, knowledge of the investigator, and specific target statement.

Results

Twenty-nine books meeting the established criteria of the content analysis were identified (see Appendix), but 27 were used in the content analysis because 2 books were unavailable for review.[1]

Target Population. With regard to type of consumer, 16 (59%) of the books were targeted for athletes, 8 (30%) were targeted for both athletes and coaches, and the remaining 3 books were targeted for coaches (Martens, 1987a), sport psychologists (Nideffer, 1981), and both coaches and sport psychologists (Williams, 1986). With regard to specificity of consumer, 20 (74%) books were targeted for athletes in general and 7 (26%) were targeted for athletes in specific sports. PST approaches targeted for specific sports included golf (Keogh & Smith, 1985; Rotella & Bunker, 1981), body building (Kubistant, 1988), skiing (Loudis, Lobitz, & Singer, 1986), running (Lynch, 1987), basketball (Mikes, 1987), and tennis (Weinberg, 1988).

Content Areas. With regard to methods, imagery was included in all of the books, with thought control and physical relaxation also used extensively. Goal setting was used in a majority of the books but less often than the other methods. Attentional control was the most highly represented skill, followed by arousal control and self-confidence. Less than half of the books included material on interpersonal skills, volition, lifestyle management, self-awareness, and self-esteem.

Format Characteristics. Fourteen books (52%) involved consumers as active participants, as opposed to 13 (48%) in which consumers were passive readers. Regarding research basis, 15 (56%) books were research supported, 8 (30%) were research supported and presented, and 4 (14%) were unsupported by research. Only 9 (33%) of the books were systematic in helping consumers acquire and implement PST methods and skills, and only 6 (22 %) were progressive in that a specific sequence of skill mastery was established.

Discussion and Conclusions

Overall, several conclusions may be drawn from the content analysis. First, most of the books were targeted for athletes, and although they were not written specifically for elite athletes they seemed to be geared to the elite level. Second, although 8 of the 27 books were targeted for both athletes and coaches, most of them did not provide information specific to coaches. The exception was Orlick (1986), who provided a separate coaches training manual to accompany his PST book. This manual was very specific in providing plans for coaches to systematically conduct PST with athletes including outlines of progressive mental training sessions, competition plans, and year-end evaluations. Only 2 books (Martens, 1987a; Williams, 1986) discussed psychological skills for coaches such as leadership behaviors, communication, and feedback effectiveness.

Third, the content areas of the books focused heavily on PST methods (imagery, thought control, physical relaxation, and goal setting) and the skills of attentional and arousal control. Thus the emphasis seemed to be on methods and psychological skills directly related to performance as opposed to psychological skills related to personal development such as self-esteem, interpersonal skills, and lifestyle management. Fourth, most of the PST approaches discussed in the books were research-based, indicating that the field is basing application on theory and research. However, consumers should be aware that some of the PST approaches being offered lack a research basis, and they should be cautious in choosing a PST approach to implement.

Finally, the analysis of the format characteristics indicated that most books written about PST simply present the information to the consumer about various psychological skills and techniques. Only about half of the books invite the consumer to be an active participant in the learning process, and most approaches lack a progressive approach and systematic implementation system. Based on these conclusions derived from the content analysis, six needs are set forth that represent viable future directions for PST.

Targeting Populations Other Than Elite Athletes

The first need identified for PST involves targeting consumers other than elite performers. Most PST programs are geared to elite athletes because their physical skills are well-developed and psychological factors are thought to play a major role in their performance. Yet it is important to realize that although young athletes are developing physically, they are also developing psychologically, and the argument can be made that they are more ripe for PST intervention than older athletes who have already internalized dysfunctional responses to competition. Thus, PST with younger athletes can be especially effective and rewarding as a means of helping youngsters develop appropriate psychological skills for sport competition. PST with young athletes could include the development of a positive approach to competition by teaching them to focus on personally controllable goals and helping them understand what is not within their control. Also, simple attentional skills such as verbal cues and positive imagery could easily be taught to help young athletes focus properly when competing. As Orlick (1982) states, if we expose youngsters to stressful situations such as organized competitive sport, we have a responsibility to teach them strategies to cope with that stress.

Coaches are potential consumers of PST who have been largely overlooked. They have long been viewed as a key in the PST process, as they must enthusiastically endorse the skills and techniques being taught and implemented with their athletes. In Eastern European countries, almost all coaches are trained in psychological techniques and strategies in order to incorporate PST into their regular training programs (Hahn, 1982; Harris & Harris, 1984; Williams, 1986). However, as is evident in the content analysis discussed previously, North American books on PST are almost entirely targeted for athletes. Clearly it is important that more information on psychological skills and methods be developed to help coaches implement PST with their athletes. Also, it is clear that coaches have special needs of their own and would benefit from PST programming specifically designed for them. Some potential areas to be addressed include communication and feedback effectiveness, empathy and social support skills, lifestyle and team management, and personal arousal regulation.

Moving Beyond Education to Implementation

Many PST programs examined in the content analysis present knowledge from various areas in sport psychology in useful and innovative ways. However, most of the books are designed to present information and educate consumers about PST but do not aid the consumer in actually implementing PST into behavioral routines. Although we assume that practitioners implement material learned in the educational phase based on individual needs, many times that does not occur. As is evident in the business world, not only must products be attractive to consumers but they must also be easy to use. Clearly PST is attractive and desired by many sport practitioners, but as consumers they are often frustrated by the lack of specific implementation procedures. It seems that an important future direction for PST is to change a passive audience into active participants. Several emerging delivery systems and approaches seem likely to precipitate this change.

Emerging Delivery Systems

Books and journals act as effective delivery systems to educate consumers about psychological skills and techniques. However, other vehicles are needed to move consumers beyond this initial education into the systematic utilization of PST techniques. Examples of these emerging delivery systems include implementation specialists, standardized training programs, and video technology.

Implementation Specialists. Most sport psychologists involved in PST implementation hold academic positions at universities or are clinical psychologists involved in private practice. These positions usually involve teaching, research, and professional service commitments in addition to PST intervention. Thus, a need has been created for implementation specialists, or people whose job entails implementing PST in different settings. Positions within athletic departments, similar to that of a physical strength and conditioning coach, would be ideal for PST implementation specialists. Athletic support networks that include staff for advising and counseling athletes is also an appropriate place to implement PST. Several graduate programs in sport psychology are instituting internship programs so that students can gain experience in PST implementation.

Budgetary limitations are usually cited as the reason these positions are unavailable, but a more opportunistic view can be advanced that we have not thoroughly convinced consumers that our product is important. If we can more effectively document positive results using PST, then administrators, parents, coaches, and athletes will become increasingly more interested in obtaining our services.

Standardized Training Programs. Another type of delivery system that may facilitate PST implementation is the emergence of standardized PST programs with a set format for teaching and/or learning psychological skills. The American Coaching Effectiveness Program[2] is an example of a standardized coaching education program using formatted materials and techniques to facilitate coaching behavior. A similar program could be developed for PST. Suinn (1985) has emphasized the need for standardized programs to facilitate greater precision and consistency in PST as well as to invite confirmatory research. It is ironic that we painstakingly outline methods and validate instrumentation in our research, but often fly by the seat of our pants in PST. This suggestion is not to induce rigid conformity but to emphasize the importance of standardized descriptions of steps in training and implementation to facilitate usage and evaluation of PST.

Video Technology. Approaches to PST have recently emerged on videotape (Jacobs, 1988; Porter & Foster, 1985) and with the growing popularity of this medium more are sure to follow. However, PST via videotape will not aid consumers in systematic implementation unless the approaches are specifically designed to do so. That is, PST on video is no different than PST outlined in books unless specific activities and plans are used to help consumers acquire and implement psychological skills and techniques. In fact, video PST may be less effective than written approaches, as far less material can be delivered in the short time of video programming (Gould, 1987). Thus, although videotape can enhance the delivery of PST by making these programs more visual, it is important that the video sequences be supplemented by written material to help the consumer with PST implementation. Another alternative technology for PST is the use of interactive video using microcomputers. In this medium, consumers not only view the video sequences but also interact by using a keyboard or touching the monitor screen to become an active participant in the program.

Emerging Approaches

In addition to the emergence of various delivery systems, newly developed approaches to PST may also facilitate moving beyond the initial education of consumers.

Sport-Specific PST Programs. Boutcher and Rotella (1987) emphasize that PST must be structured according to the specific characteristics and demands of a particular sport to be effective. Toward this end several authors have written PST books for specific sports, as was indicated in the content analysis (Keogh & Smith, 1985; Kubistant, 1988; Loudis et al., 1986; Lynch, 1987; Mikes, 1987; Rotella & Bunker, 1981; Weinberg, 1988). These sport-specific approaches aid the consumer in moving past an initial understanding of PST as they incorporate psychological practice into the physical practice techniques of specific sports. For example, Weinberg (1988) applies attentional control techniques to tennis by outlining service and service return mental routines as well as specific on-court concentration exercises for athletes. Mikes (1987) outlines psychological skills and techniques to facilitate shooting, ball-handling, defensive play, and rebounding in basketball.

Emphasis on Competition Plans. Another emerging approach that facilitates PST implementation is an emphasis on designing and focusing on mental competition plans. Orlick (1986) bases his PST approach on the development and use of mental plans in which athletes systematically use imagery, self-talk, and attentional techniques to focus appropriately during precompetition and competition. What is important here is not the specific methods that athletes use in their plan but the fact that developing and working their plan provides them with a systematic structure to utilize various PST techniques and skills.

Emphasis on Coping or Refocusing. Sport psychologists are fond of saying that psychological skills are similar to physical skills in that they must be acquired through systematic practice. Although that is true, this approach often misleads athletes into believing that once they gain proficiency in a skill then everything will go perfectly. Also, it is clear that athletes will not necessarily practice PST techniques and skills on their own. It is important that PST programs not only teach athletes how to develop skills but also how to sustain these skills under pressure and cope with problems that may arise. For example, Orlick (1986) helps athletes plan their competition focus but also has them plan refocusing techniques or ways of anticipating and coping with problems when they arise.

Martens (1987a) has divided PST into education, acquisition, and practice phases to emphasize a systematic approach. In this approach, athletes first learn the nature and basis of various psychological skills and how they influence performance (education). Then, because not all athletes are proficient in certain psychological skills and techniques (e.g., imagery), they follow a structured training program to acquire proficiency in these skills and techniques (acquisition). Once a certain level of proficiency is acquired, athletes then systematically integrate these skills into their practice routines (practice).

Similar to Martens' (1987a) approach, I work with athletes through the phases of attainment, sustainment, and coping. Using self-confidence as an example, we work on first attaining a positive level of self-confidence which would include Martens' education and acquisition phases. The athlete understands what self-confidence is and what it should be based on, and then works to acquire greater confidence using various techniques. We then plan how this confidence can be sustained over time (practice phase) by systematically incorporating techniques that facilitate confidence into daily and competition routines. Finally, we plan strategies for coping in times when confidence slips or is suddenly lost. This approach is useful in helping athletes move beyond the educational phase as it enables them to formulate a plan that can be implemented in their particular routines.

Differentiating Between Skills and Methods

The third need identified for PST is to differentiate between psychological skills and methods. Skills are qualities to be attained, as opposed to methods which are procedures or techniques athletes engage in to develop skills. The model of psychological skills breaks them into foundation skills, performance skills, and facilitative skills. In the next section, the rationale for the inclusion of these particular skills in the model is discussed. The basic PST methods include the four traditional techniques used in developing skills (also used as categories in the content analysis). Physical practice and education are included as foundation methods to emphasize that psychological skills are facilitated by productive physical practice and an understanding of the physical and mental processes that influence performance.

Clearly, sport psychologists utilize different models than those depicted here. Yet, whatever model is adopted, it seems useful to differentiate between skills, or target behaviors, and methods, which are the vehicles used to attain the target behaviors. This will encourage sport psychologists to focus on the skill to be attained and to choose any method or combination of methods to use toward attaining and enhancing that skill. Often sport psychologists become enamored of a particular method (e.g., imagery) and use it indiscriminately instead of focusing on a skill that an athlete needs to develop and then utilizing several methods to develop that skill. I have also noticed that athletes tend to get bogged down in learning all of the methods (imagery, relaxation, goal setting) and many times lose sight of the skills these methods are designed to facilitate. Orlick (1982) emphasizes that athletes often lose interest in PST unless the psychological training is directed specifically at meeting their individual needs.

An analogy to research is appropriate here. Research should be driven by the problem or question, with methodology being given a secondary role as the vehicle by which the question is asked. Problems occur when researchers let the method drive the question. The same problem can occur in PST. Sport psychologists are encouraged to focus on skills to be taught, and then to select appropriate methodology to teach these skills based on individual needs and situational influences.

Using a Holistic Approach

A fourth need identified for PST is the use of a holistic approach as an alternative to the narrow, unidimensional performance enhancement model currently being employed by many sport psychologists. The holistic approach views athletes as organisms constantly interacting with environmental stimuli and undergoing personal development.

Embracing the Interactional Paradigm

Danish and Hale (1981) emphasize the importance of accounting for both the individual and the environment in understanding sport performance and providing PST services. Most sport psychologists adhere to this model by preparing athletes for the environment as opposed to attempting to develop static traits. By focusing on attainment, sustainment, and coping, athletes learn to develop skills and also prepare to sustain these skills and cope with environmental stressors. Developing mental competition plans (Orlick, 1986) utilizes the interactional approach, as it forces athletes to actively focus on psychological skills within a specific context.

It is also important to understand that many personal factors are involved in the interaction of individuals with the environment. Personal factors that influence performance include physical fitness, physical skill, perceptual skill, and psychological skill. All of these interact with situational demands to influence behavior and performance. Many times athletes, coaches, and sport psychologists emphasize psychological factors to the exclusion of the other three areas. That is, although a performance slump may instigate a loss of concentration and increased anxiety, its etiology may include a flaw in technique, decreased fitness due to injury, or poor decision-making and use of strategy. Taylor (1988) supports this perspective by emphasizing that performance slumps in sport may often be caused by numerous environmental factors as well as by psychological factors.

Emphasizing Personal Development

My early work in PST was based on a narrow performance enhancement model that focused on teaching methods instead of skills. I taught athletes how to use imagery, how to physically relax, and how to set performance goals. However, I began to realize that these athletes' spheres of existence included much more than a narrow performance perspective. Their sport behavior was influenced by setbacks to their self-esteem, by a lack of life goals and plans, by their inability to communicate with teammates and coaches, and so forth. Thus, in addition to the interactional perspective, the second part of utilizing a holistic approach to PST is emphasizing personal development.

Danish and Hale (1981) were the first to recommend this approach by advocating a human development framework that focuses on human growth and change and assists athletes in gaining control of their lives. Other sport psychologists have supported Danish and Hale by emphasizing the need for personal intervention as well as performance enhancement (Brown, 1982; Suinn, 1985). The psychological skills model resulted from my dissatisfaction with the narrow performance enhancement approach. This framework is an example of a holistic, or personal development, approach that emphasizes a hierarchical progression and the attainment of different types of skills.

Foundation skills are those qualities that are basic and necessary psychological skills. The foundation skill progression begins with volition, which may be defined as internal motivation or the all-encompassing desire for success. If this skill is not developed and nurtured, there is no reason to continue with PST because the athlete will be unwilling to make the necessary commitment. Garfield (1984) begins his PST approach by having athletes identify their volition and then set personal goals to enhance the volition.

The second foundation skill, self-awareness, is based on the athlete understanding his or her behavior in sport. Ravizza (1986) emphasizes that athletes can only gain control and become more consistent by becoming more aware of their ideal performance state and behaviors that facilitate this state. Once athletes have developed the necessary motivation and self-awareness, they then can develop and/or nurture self-esteem and self-confidence. Athletes' self-worth or self-value (self-esteem) and perceptions of their ability (self-confidence) have been shown to critically influence sport behavior. It seems inappropriate to begin specific PST methods (e.g., relaxation or imagery) until athletes attain a certain level of proficiency in the foundation skills.

The performance skills in the model are the traditional PST skills that most sport psychologists address. The premise is that exceptional performance is based on the optimization of physical arousal, mental arousal, and attention. It can be argued that attention is part of mental arousal, but they are separate in the model to help athletes understand the components of optimal performance.

Facilitative skills are not directly influential on performance and sport behavior, but once acquired they facilitate behavior in sport as well as other areas of life. Interpersonal skill is an important facilitative skill as it allows athletes to communicate more effectively. Gauron (1984) as well as Harris and Harris (1984) address communication skills for athletes, Martens (1987a) discusses communication skills for coaches, and Orlick (1986) provides strategies to help athletes deal with the media more effectively. The inclusion of lifestyle management as a facilitative skill emphasizes the holistic, or personal development, approach to PST. Lifestyle management skill enables athletes to organize and manage their lives more effectively by becoming self-reliant, practicing effective time management, and focusing on career goals and priorities. Examples of PST approaches addressing lifestyle management include Orlick's (1980, 1986) and Ogilvie and Howe's (1986) guidelines for dealing with retirement from competitive sport as well as Bennett and Pravitz's (1982, 1987) strategies for effective time management.

Implementing the Personal Development Model

The adoption of a personal development model will not facilitate PST unless the model is implemented. To achieve this, several delivery systems and approaches discussed above can be utilized. One likely delivery system in the college setting would be to modify current academic advising programs for athletes to incorporate a personal development model of PST. A personal development program within a university setting has been implemented at Arizona State University that teaches psychological skills from a holistic perspective (Petruzzello, Landers, Linder, & Robinson, 1987). This program teaches lifestyle management skills along with the more traditional PST skills, and also provides services for coaches as well as athletes.

Lanning (1982) supports this type of delivery system based on the special needs of athletes such as time management skills, career goal planning, and self-image concerns. Brooks, Etzel, and Ostrow (1987) have shown that Division I academic advisors/counselors focus exclusively on academic performance (eligibility) as opposed to personal needs and development, yet Nelson (1982) documented higher academic performance and satisfaction for athletes who received personal counseling as compared to athletes in traditional academic advising programs. A personal development approach seems especially timely based on the growing schism between athletics and academics (Dubois, 1985; Purdy, Eitzen, & Hufnagel, 1985).

Defining the Sport Psychologist Based on a Personal Development Model

The fifth need identified for PST is to define our role as sport psychologists based on a personal development model. As mentioned previously, ethical and legal issues about the practice of PST and the definition of sport psychologist have commanded a great deal of attention in the literature, thus these arguments will not be reproduced here. However, based on rationale developed by Danish and Hale (1981, 1982) and supported by Brown (1982), it seems that a productive approach is to adopt a model of intervention from which respective roles and services may be derived.

With adherence to a personal development model such as the one outlined in this paper, educational sport psychologists as well as other sport scientists, coaches, and educators could provide personal development skills with no need for licensure. It may be argued that certification in counseling or clinical psychology is needed to work within this framework, but guidelines for service provision by educational versus clinic sport psychologists should be based upon the distinction between normal and abnormal behavior (Martens, 1987a), not the distinction between performance enhancement and personal development. Individuals adhering to the clinical model should be trained and credentialed to provide legal clinical service based on that model, and educational sport psychologists subscribing to the personal development model should be trained and credentialed with regard to the services derived from their particular model. It seems likely that the adoption of a model to serve as the basis for the practice of educational sport psychology may facilitate our attempts to define our profession.

Nurturing a Symbiotic Relationship Between Theory, Research, and Practice

The final need identified for PST is a balanced relationship between theory, research, and practice in sport psychology. Although the content analysis indicated that the majority of books on PST were consistent with the research literature, it is important to advocate continued consistency between theory and practice as well as the need to scientifically evaluate the effectiveness of PST. Readers may react ad nauseam to the worn-out cliché that theory, research, and practice must form a balanced interrelationship. This issue has been addressed at length in the sport psychology literature (Dishman, 1983; Landers, 1983; Martens, 1979; 1987b) with some concluding that an academic/professional (or theory/practice) separation is apparent (Dishman, 1983; Martens, 1987b). Rather than address the academic/professional issue here, it seems more useful to defuse it.

Clearly, many scholars in sport psychology engage in basic research as a "knowledge-making process" (Lachman, 1965, p. 97), which is "uninhibited by the requirement that it serve any need of practical application" (Henry, 1978, p. 24). Others seek solutions to practical problems via applied research. Finally, many sport psychologists engage in implementation or intervention with coaches and athletes in PST programs. These different thrusts should not be construed as rivalrous but rather as complementary. In fact, they should not be viewed as different approaches but rather as different levels based on whether the purpose of knowledge is to describe and explain or to apply and prescribe. Certainly many sport psychologists wear all three hats and perform at each level. Thus it seems important to avoid perpetuating an artificial distinction between theory and practice and get on with developing, applying, and utilizing knowledge in sport psychology.

Research-Based PST Programs

Toward this end, PST must be grounded in current theory and research. This is not to say that we should completely understand the underlying mechanisms of behavior before intervention is employed or that there is no room for experiential knowledge in PST programming. Martens (1987b) emphasizes that the development of PST programs should be based on experiential as well as scientific knowledge.

Examples of putting theory and research into practice are numerous. Based on the Yerkes-Dodson (1908) Law, or inverted-U relationship between arousal and performance, sport psychologists help athletes optimize arousal based on individual differences as well as the particular demands of their sport. Stress management techniques are divided into somatic and cognitive categories based on current theory and research indicating that anxiety is a multidimensional construct (Borkovec, 1976; Davidson & Schwartz, 1976). Achievement motivation theory and research has indicated the importance of teaching athletes to focus on factors within personal control (Deci & Ryan, 1980; Weiner, 1974). For the field to maintain credibility, it is important that PST approaches continue to utilize current thinking in the field which consists of theory and research as well as valuable experiential knowledge advanced by practitioners, coaches, and athletes.

Evaluation Research

The credibility of applied sport psychology is also based on our ability to develop effective ways of evaluating the outcomes of PST. Dishman (1983) argues that the professional model of sport psychology assumes that there is something to deliver that produces clearly defined and reliable results, but that the validity of this assumption is unclear. To provide accountability for PST, evaluation research incorporating various investigative strategies is needed (Martens, 1987b; Partington & Orlick, 1987).

Idiographic Methods. Martens (1987b) suggests that idiographic approaches to behavioral assessment are needed in conjunction with the more traditional and accepted nomothetic approaches. Gordon Allport (1961) is most often identified with the idiographic approach, in which individuality is stressed through the in-depth study of person. Nomothetic research focuses on establishing generalizations about behavior derived from the study of many persons (Sundberg, 1977). Sport psychologists are beginning to utilize idiographic methods such as case studies and single subject designs to tease out subtle behavioral change that perhaps would be undetected using nomothetic techniques (Bryan, 1987; Heyman, 1987; Smith, 1988; Zaichkowsky, 1980).

Qualitative Methods. Another important direction for PST evaluation research is the utilization of qualitative methods as an alternative to the traditional quantitative methods. Currently, research in sport psychology primarily employs quantitative methods based on what Martens (1987b) has termed orthodox science. The quantitative approach involves transforming psychobehavioral data gathered via questionnaires, interviews, or observations into numbers that are subjected to statistical analyses to determine their significance. The quantitative researcher stands apart from the research context to make inferences about behavior, and meaning is attributed to the behavior from the researcher's perspective.

Conversely, qualitative researchers enter the field as participant observers to understand behavior from the perspectives of the individuals being studied (Geertz, 1973; Patton, 1980). Qualitative data are usually gathered from the researcher's experiences in the field. These data may come from field notes, observations, and conversations with subjects. They are analyzed inductively, which allows concepts and categories to emerge from (versus being imposed on) the data. Examples of this type of investigation are Fine's (1987) study of the preadolescent subculture of Little League baseball, Dewar's (1987) study of a university physical education program, and Varpalotai's (1987) study of a girls' sporting subculture. This approach seems particularly useful for PST evaluation research, as it has been argued that qualitative researchers must understand and place themselves within the context they are studying (Hammersley, 1983; Patton, 1980). This means that sport psychologists can use qualitative methods to construct in-depth, personalized accounts of the sport experience and how PST influences that experience. Information such as this can facilitate the development of salient and appropriate PST approaches that truly meet the needs of athletes.

Multiple Criterion Measures. Another suggestion for future PST evaluation research is the use of multiple criterion measures. The research that has been conducted has focused primarily on performance change. Although performance is an important criterion, other target behaviors and cognitions are also worthy of evaluation such as effort, persistence, satisfaction, enjoyment, attitudes, and various personality constructs. For example, Burton (1983/1984) demonstrated that a systematic goal setting program used with a collegiate swimming team significantly decreased anxiety and increased concentration and self-confidence. If sport psychologists espouse that PST is designed to make sport more enjoyable for athletes (as well as to enhance performance), then it seems important to assess whether intervention is effective in that regard. Thus, PST should be viewed as important for everyone involved in sport to help them maximize their abilities as well as their enjoyment and satisfaction from sport participation.

Summary

To summarize, six needs that represent suggested future directions for PST have been outlined. These suggestions have included targeting populations other than elite athletes, moving beyond education to implementation, differentiating between psychological skills and methods, adopting a holistic approach, defining the sport psychologist based on a personal development model, and nurturing the theory/research/practice relationship. It is hoped that these suggested directions may facilitate productive growth and development in sport psychology. Sport consumers of all types should come to value psychological skill development and find programs targeted for them. PST should focus on the holistic development of consumers based on their interactions with the sport environment and their personal development as human beings. Sport psychology should define a unique role for itself based on the personal development of sport consumers and become recognized as a distinct and important profession. Sport psychology should gain credibility as our models and techniques are carefully and critically evaluated. And it is hoped that the pluralism in the field will cease as knowledge is interdependently developed and applied.

References

Allport, G.W. (1961). *Pattern and growth in personality.* New York: Holt.

Borkovec, T.D. (1976). Physiological and cognitive processes in the regulation of anxiety. In G. Schwartz & D. Shapiro (Eds.), *Consciousness and self regulation: Advances in research* (Vol. 1, pp. 261-312). New York: Plenum Press.

Boutcher, S.H., & Rotella, R.J. (1987). A psychological skills educational program for closed-skill performance enhancement. *The Sport Psychologist*, 1, 127-137.

Brooks, D.D., Etzel, E.F., & Ostrow, A.C. (1987). Job responsibilities and backgrounds of NCAA Division I athletic advisors and counselors. *The Sport Psychologist*, 1, 200-207.

Brown, J.M. (1982). Are sport psychologists really psychologists? *Journal of Sport Psychology,* 4, 13-18.

Bryan, A.J. (1987). Single-subject designs for evaluation of sport psychology interventions. *The Sport Psychologist*, 1, 283-292.

Burton, D. (1984). Evaluation of goal-setting training on selected cognitions and performance of collegiate swimmers (Doctoral dissertation, University of Illinois, 1983). *Dissertation Abstracts International,* 45, 116A.

Danish, S.J., & Hale, B.D. (1981). Toward an understanding of the practice of sport psychology. *Journal of Sport Psychology,* 3, 90-99.

Danish, S.J., & Hale, B.D. (1982). Let the discussions continue: Further considerations of the practice of sport psychology. *Journal of Sport Psychology*, 4, 10-12.

Davidson, R.J., & Schwartz, G.E. (1976). The psychobiology of relaxation and related states: A multi-process theory. In D. Mostofsky (Ed.), *Behavioral control and modification of physiological activity* (pp. 399-442). Englewood Cliffs, NJ: Prentice-Hall.

Deci, E.L., & Ryan, R.M. (1980). The empirical exploration of intrinsic motivational processes. In L. Berkowitz (Ed.), *Advances in experimental social psychology* (Vol. 13, pp. 39-80). New York: Academic Press.

Dewar, A.M. (1987). The social construction of gender in physical education. *Women's Studies International Forum,* 10, 453-465.

Dishman, R.K. (1983). Identity crisis in North American sport psychology: Academics in professional issues. *Journal of Sport Psychology*, 5, 123-134.

Dubois, P.E. (1985). The occupational attainment of former college athletes: A comparative study. In D. Chu, J.O. Segrave, & B.J. Becker (Eds.), *Sport and higher education* (pp. 235-248). Champaign, IL: Human Kinetics.

Fine, G.A. (1987). *With the boys: Little League baseball and preadolescent culture.* Chicago: University of Chicago Press.

Geertz, C. (1973). Thick description: Toward an interpretive theory of culture. In C. Geertz (Ed.), *The interpretation of cultures* (pp. 215-249). New York: Basic.

Gould, D. (1987). [Review of *The Mental Athlete* videotape]. *The Sport Psychologist*, 1, 364-365.

Hahn, E. (1982). The psychological preparation of Olympic athletes: East and west. In T. Orlick, J.T. Partington, & J.H. Salmela (Eds.), *Mental training for coaches and athletes* (pp. 156-158). Ottawa: Coaching Association of Canada.

Hammersley, M. (1983). *The ethnography of schooling: Methodological issues.* Driffield, England: Nafferton.

Henry, F.M. (1978). The academic discipline of physical education. *Quest,* 29, 13-29.

Heyman, S.R. (1982). A reaction to Danish and Hale: A minority report. *Journal of Sport Psychology,* 4, 7-9.

Heyman, S.R. (1987). Research and interventions in sport psychology: Issues encountered in working with an amateur boxer. *The Sport Psychologist*, 1, 208-223.

Jacobs, A.A. (1988). *Sports psychology: The winning edge in sports* [Videotape]. Kansas City: The Winning Edge.

Krippendorff, K. (1980). *Content analysis: An introduction to its methodology*. Beverly Hills, CA: Sage.

Lachman, S.J. (1965). *The foundations of science.* New York: Vantage.

Landers, D.M. (1983). Whatever happened to theory testing in sport psychology? *Journal of Sport Psychology*, 5, 135-151.

Lanning, W. (1982). The privileged few: Special counseling needs of athletes. *Journal of Sport Psychology*, 4, 19-23.

Martens, R. (1979). About smocks and jocks. *Journal of Sport Psychology*, 1, 94-99.

Martens, R. (1987b). Science, knowledge, and sport psychology. *The Sport Psychologist*, 1, 29-55.

Nelson, E.S. (1982). The effects of career counseling on freshman college athletes. *Journal of Sport Psychology,* 4, 32-40.

Ogilvie, B.C., & Howe, M. (1986). The trauma of termination from athletics. In J.M. Williams (Ed.), *Applied sport psychology: Personal growth to peak performance* (pp. 365-382). Palo Alto, CA: Mayfield.

Orlick, T. (1982). Beyond excellence. In T. Orlick, J.T. Partington, & J.H. Salmela (Eds.), *Mental training for coaches and athletes* (pp. 1-7). Ottawa: Coaching Association of Canada.

Partington, J., & Orlick, T. (1987). The sport psychology consultant evaluation form. *The Sport Psychologist*, 1, 309-317.

Patton, M.Q. (1980). *Qualitative evaluation methods.* Beverly Hills, CA: Sage.

Petruzzello, S.J., Landers, D.M., Linder, D.E., & Robinson, D.R. (1987). Sport psychology service delivery: Implementation within the university community. *The Sport Psychologist*, **1**, 248-256.

Porter, K., & Foster, J. (1985). *The mental athlete* [Videotape]. Eugene, OR: Westcom.

Purdy, D.A., Eitzen, D.S., & Hufnagel, R. (1985). Are athletes also students? The educational attainment of college athletes. In D. Chu, J.O. Segrave, & B.J. Becker (Eds.), *Sport and higher education* (pp. 222-234). Champaign, IL: Human Kinetics.

Ravizza, K. (1986). Increasing awareness for sport performance. In J.M. Williams (Ed.), *Applied sport psychology: Personal growth to peak performance* (pp. 149-161). Palo Alto, CA: Mayfield.

Smith, R.E. (1988). The logic and design of case study research. *The Sport Psychologist*, 2, 1-12.

Stone, P.J., Dunphy, D.C., Smith, M.S., & Ogilvie, D.M. (1966). *The general inquirer: A computer approach to content analysis.* Cambridge, MA: MIT Press.

Suinn, R.M. (1985). The 1984 Olympics and sport psychology. *Journal of Sport Psychology*, 7, 321-329.

Sundberg, N.D. (1977). *Assessment of persons.* Englewood Cliffs, NJ: Prentice-Hall.

Taylor, J. (1988). Slumpbusting: A systematic analysis of slumps in sports. *The Sport Psychologist*, 2, 39-48.

Varpalotai, A. (1987). The hidden curriculum in leisure: An analysis of a girls' sport subculture. *Women's Studies International Forum,* 10, 411-422.

Weiner, B. (Ed.). (1974). *Achievement motivation and attribution theory.* Morristown, NJ: General Learning Press.

Yerkes, R.M., & Dodson, J.D. (1908). The relation of strength of stimulus to rapidity of habit formation. *Journal of Comparative and Neurological Psychology,* 18, 459-482.

Zaichkowsky, L.D. (1980). Single case experimental designs and sport psychology research. In C.H. Nadeau, W.R. Halliwell, K.M. Newell, & G.C. Roberts (Eds.), *Psychology of motor behavior and sport-1979* (pp. 171-179). Champaign, IL: Human Kinetics.

Appendix—PST Books

Albinson, J.G., & Bull, S.J. (1988). *The mental game plan.* London, Ontario: Spodym.

Bell, K.F. (1983). *Championship thinking: The athlete's guide to winning performance in all sports.* Englewood Cliffs, NJ: Prentice-Hall.

Bennett, J.G., & Pravitz, J.E. (1982). *The miracle of sports psychology.* Englewood Cliffs, NJ: Prentice-Hall.

Bennett, J.G., & Pravitz, J.E. (1987). *Profile of a winner: Advanced mental training for athletes.* Ithaca, NY: Sport Science International.

Cratty, B.J. (1984). *Psychological preparation and athletic excellence.* Ithaca, NY: Mouvement.

Garfield, C.A. (1984). *Peak performance: Mental training techniques of the world's greatest athletes.* Boston: Houghton Mifflin.

Gauron, E.F. (1984). *Mental training for peak performance.* Lansing, NY: Sport Science Associates.

Harris, D.V., & Harris, B.L. (1984). *The athlete's guide to sports psychology: Mental skills for physical people.* Champaign, IL: Leisure Press.

Hendricks, G., & Carlson, J. (1982). *The centered athlete: A conditioning program for your mind.* Englewood Cliffs, NJ: Prentice-Hall.

Kappas, J.G. (1984). *Self-hypnosis: The key to athletic success.* Englewood Cliffs, NJ: Prentice-Hall.

Kauss, D.R. (1980). *Peak performance.* Englewood Cliffs, NJ: Prentice-Hall.

Keogh, B.K., & Smith, C.E. (1985). *Personal par: A psychological system of golf for women.* Champaign, IL: Human Kinetics.

Kubistant, T. (1986). *Performing your best.* Champaign, IL: Human Kinetics.

Kubistant, T. (1988). *Mind pump: The psychology of body building.* Champaign, IL: Leisure Press.

Loehr, J.E. (1982). *Mental toughness training for sports.* Lexington, MA: Stephen Green.

Loudis, L.A., Lobitz, W.C., & Singer, K.M. (1986). *Skiing out of your mind.* Champaign, IL: Leisure Press.

Lynch, J. (1987). *The total runner: A complete mind-body guide to optimal performance.* Englewood Cliffs, NJ: Prentice-Hall.

Martens, R. (1987a). *Coaches guide to sport psychology.* Champaign, IL: Human Kinetics.

Mikes, J. (1987). *Basketball fundamentals: A complete mental training guide.* Champaign, IL: Leisure Press.

Nideffer, R.M. (1981). *The ethics and practice of applied sport psychology.* Ithaca, NY: Mouvement.

Nideffer, R.M. (1985). *Athletes' guide to mental training.* Champaign, IL: Human Kinetics. Orlick, T. (1980). *In pursuit of excellence.* Champaign, IL: Human Kinetics.

Orlick, T. (1986). *Psyching for sport* and *Coaches training manual to psyching for sport.* Champaign, IL: Leisure Press.

Rotella, R.J., & Bunker, L. (1981). *Mind mastery for winning golf.* Englewood Cliffs, NJ: Prentice-Hall.

Scott, M.D., & Pellicioni, L., Jr. (1982). *Don't choke: How athletes can become winners.* Englewood Cliffs, NJ: Prentice-Hall.

Suinn, R.M. (1986). *Seven steps to peak performance: The mental training manual for athletes.* Lewiston, NY: Hans Huber.

Syer, J., & Connolly, C. (1984). *Sporting body, sporting mind: An athlete's guide to mental training.* New York: Cambridge University Press.

Weinberg, R.S. (1988). *The mental advantage: Developing your psychological skills in tennis.* Champaign, IL: Leisure Press.

Williams, J.M. (Ed.). (1986). *Applied sport psychology: Personal growth to peak performance.* Palo Alto, CA: Mayfield.

Notes

[1]Hendricks and Carlson (1982) and Kappas (1984) are out of print and unavailable at various libraries searched by the investigator.

[2]Information about the American Coaching Education Program is available from Human Kinetics Publishers, Box 5076, Champaign, IL 61820.

Acknowledgments

Appreciation is extended to Renee De Graff for her assistance in obtaining books used in the content analysis, and to Alison Dewar, Dan Gould, and two anonymous reviewers for helpful comments on an earlier version of this manuscript.

31 Effect of Goal Difficulty, Goal Specificity and Duration of Practice Time Intervals on Muscular Endurance Performance

MICHAEL BAR-ELI
Ben-Gurion University of the Negev
Wingate Institute

GERSHON TENENBAUM
University of Southern Queensland

JOAN S. PIE, YAACOV BTESH, AND ASHER ALMOG
Wingate Institute

Goal setting (GS) is one of the most commonly used performance-enhancement strategies in the behavioral sciences. In the late 1960s, Locke, later joined by Latham, proposed that intentions to work toward a goal should be considered a major source of work motivation; therefore, GS theory is now regarded as a process theory of motivation. The GS techniques that are derived from this theory rely on a series of propositions that allow us to explain and to predict a person's performance.

GS seems to work well. In fact, more than 90% of the studies that were conducted to test Locke's propositions (over 500 studies, with more than 40,000 participants sampled from a variety of populations from more than 10 different countries, who performed more than 90 different tasks) demonstrated that GS does indeed have a powerful and consistent effect on human performance.

Physical educators, coaches, and athletes have applied GS techniques in order to plan training programs. However, before 1985, such an application of GS techniques to physical education and sport and exercise was done on a more or less intuitive basis and with the use of unjustified extrapolations from research conducted primarily in the organizational domain, mainly because such an application did not have a sound scientific basis in studies conducted in the sport and exercise domain. In 1985, Locke and Latham offered several suggestions for the application of GS to sport. Many sport psychologists were inspired by these suggestions; as a result, GS research in sport and exercise has virtually exploded.

The most important GS principle is that of goal specificity, which contends that specific goals are much more effective than nonspecific (i.e., "do-your-best") goals in producing behavior change. Toward the mid-1990s, the evidence even for this central GS hypothesis was quite equivocal in the sport and exercise domain. When it came to the different kinds of specificity, however, the picture was even more complicated and unclear. For example, in line with the goal difficulty principle of GS, specific goals should be set that are difficult, yet realistic and attainable, in order to maximize human performance. Until the publication of Bar-Eli and colleagues' investigation, very few studies had tested this hypothesis in sport and exercise; moreover, these studies had failed to demonstrate any undermining effects of setting goals that are unreachable for the participants.

Bar-Eli and colleagues conducted a field experiment that can be considered very large in comparison to other GS studies in sport and exercise—346 participants (high school students) from 15 schools. The results provided strong support for the principle of goal specificity, including the importance of participants' accepting the specific goals set for them. But the major reason for including this article in this book is that it was the first investigation in the sport and exercise domain that quite consistently demonstrated that unattainable, improbable goals produced significantly lower performances than difficult and realistic goals—an important effect in the framework of Locke and Latham's GS theory.

The aims of this study were to explore the relationships between goal specificity, goal difficulty and performance, and to determine if setting unrealistic goals would produce decreases in performance. The subjects were high school students from 15 schools and an attempt was made to control for the effects of social comparison. The schools were randomly assigned to one of 15 conditions representing five levels of goal conditions—namely, 'do' (no goals), 'do your best', 'improve by 10%' (easy), 'improve by 20%' (difficult/realistic) and 'improve by 40%' (improbable/unattainable)—and three levels of practice duration (4, 6, and 8 weeks). This design consisted of nesting goal difficulty within practice duration, which enabled an examination of the goal specificity and goal attainability/difficulty hypothesis proposed by Locke and Latham (1985). A 5 x 3 factorial ANCOVA was applied to the post-baseline sit-up gain scores. The results indicated that all specific groups performed better than all non-specific groups. In addition, across practice durations, the difficult/realistic group exhibited the greatest increase in performance, followed by the easy group. The performance gains of the improbable/unattainable group were substantially less compared with the difficult/realistic group after 4 and 6 weeks, but not after 8 weeks of practice. These results are in line with both the goal specificity and goal difficulty hypotheses derived from the application of Locke's goal-setting theory to sport.

Introduction

One of the most powerful motivational techniques for enhancing performance and productivity is goal-setting. A number of reviews of the literature have produced overwhelming support for the effectiveness of setting goals in improving performance in business, industrial, organizational and educational settings (Locke *et al.,* 1981; Wood *et al.,* 1987; Locke and Latham, 1990). A goal is defined as the object, aim or endpoint of an action, or what an individual describes as an accomplishment being sought. Goals have been found to be effective in improving long-term self-motivation through eliciting commitment, perseverance, dedication and effort. They provide a focus and direction for one's activity, and permit an individual to measure performance continuously through internal processes of comparison, using subjective standards to evaluate ongoing pursuits (Locke and Latham, 1990; Weinberg, 1992).

Research on goal-setting has been influenced to a great extent by Locke's (1968) goal-setting model. This model, based on conscious goals and intentions, hypothesized that specific, difficult and challenging goals lead to higher levels of task performance compared with easy goals, do-your-best goals and no goals. These ideas generated intensive research, which demonstrated the robustness and replicable nature of this theory in a variety of tasks and settings (Locke and Latham, 1990). For example, Locke and co-workers' (1981) review indicated that 99 of 110 studies supported the goal difficulty/specificity proposition of Locke (1968). More recent meta-analytic reviews (Tubbs, 1986; Mento *et al.,* 1987) have also found a greater enhancement in performance and productivity (i.e. stronger mean effect size) with specific-difficult goals (in comparison to easy goals, no goals or do-your-best goals), thereby offering strong support for the effectiveness of setting specific, challenging goals.

Such consistent findings have led many coaches, athletes and physical educators to use goal-setting techniques in the domain of sport and exercise (Burton, 1992, 1993; Weinberg, 1992, 1994). Many sport psychologists have been influenced by Locke and Latham (1985), who offered a number of suggestions for the application of goal-setting to sports. One suggestion was that specific-difficult goals would produce significantly better performance than easy goals, general goals or no goals at all. Sport psychology studies concerning the effect of goal specificity and performance have been conducted in both field and laboratory settings, focusing on exercise and sport environments. Weinberg (1992, 1994) undertook extensive reviews of these studies and concluded that their results were equivocal, with only some of the studies supporting the hypothesis of Locke and Latham (1985) that specific hard goals produce higher levels of performance than no goals or do-your-best goals.

Another suggestion made by Locke and Latham (1985) is related to goal attainability. They hypothesized that performers should be encouraged to strive for goals that are difficult, yet realistic and attainable. They considered realistic, attainable and challenging goals to be motivationally superior, because unrealistic goals are too difficult and unreasonable, and would therefore result in continuing failure. This, in turn, leads to a drop in motivation, and a deterioration in subsequent performance. Few studies have tested the goal attainability hypothesis in sport and exercise settings (Weinberg *et al.,* 1987, 1990, 1991; Garland *et al.,* 1988; Bar-Eli *et al.,* 1993). These studies have failed to demonstrate undermining effects of setting goals that are seemingly unreachable. For example, Weinberg *et al.* (1991) conducted two experiments: one used an endurance task (sit-ups) with children, and the other used a basketball-shooting task with college students, assigned to one of several goal conditions (ranging from easy to unrealistically difficult). The results from both experiments revealed no significant differences between groups for either task, with the subjects placed in unrealistic goal conditions not producing any significant decrements in their motivation and performance (although perceiving their goal as being more difficult). Locke (1991, 1994) alluded to factors such as the setting of personal goals in the 'do-your-best' condition, as well as to the availability of feedback, when trying to explain some of the non-significant group differences for goal difficulty.

The lack of significant differences between realistic and unrealistic goal conditions in these investigations challenges the goal attainability hypothesis in the domain of sport and exercise behaviour. Thus although the importance of goal attainability has been repeatedly cited within the applied sport psychology literature, preliminary empirical findings do not support the notion that unrealistic goals are harmful to performance (for reviews, see Weinberg, 1992, 1994). This led Weinberg (1992, 1994) to offer the cognitive mediation theory of Garland (1985) as a possible alternative approach to the investigation of goal-setting in sport psychology. One reason for this suggestion is that Garland (1983, 1985; Garland *et al.,* 1988) has questioned the basis of the goal attainability hypothesis of Locke (1968), providing a conceptual framework and some empirical evidence to support his arguments.

Garland (1985) proposed a number of cognitive mechanisms to explain why higher goals may result in higher levels of self-efficacy (Bandura, 1982) and consequent performance. The positive link between individual task goals and performance, mediated by performance expectancies or self-efficacy, was supported by Garland *et al.* (1988) in an athletic context. Accordingly, Garland consistently maintained that the relationship between goal difficulty and performance is not a type of inverted-U (as predicted by Locke), but a monotonically positive one, with no evidence of a decline in either motivation or performance for subjects assigned to unrealistically difficult goal conditions.

In recent responses to the various challenges raised against his theory (e.g. Weinberg and Weigand, 1993, 1996), Locke (1991, 1994) has argued that the disappointing results of many goal-setting studies in the realm of exercise and sport psychology can be attributed to methodological flaws.

Locke (1991, 1994) has summarized some of the main errors in the methods used in this area of research and has suggested antidotes to solve the problems experienced when investigating his theory in sport. One methodological problem could be related to the goal attainability hypothesis (although not specifically discussed by Locke, 1991, 1994). Specifically, most previous studies have investigated the effect of goal difficulty on performance over the course of some designated time period where several experimental trials were completed. However, it is possible that the periods used were too short for the experimental effects to be revealed, especially in field settings. In the field experiment of Bar-Eli *et al.* (1993), a single performance trial was used; in contrast, Weinberg *et al.* (1991) used five trials in each of their field experiments. It is therefore possible that a number of experimental trials are required to detect the effects of goal difficulty manipulation on physical performance. In other words, the question of how long one has to work on attaining one's goals has yet to be investigated in the context of research on goal difficulty. Moreover, different levels of difficulty may interact with the time required for goal attainment.

As noted previously, empirical studies in sport and exercise settings, which have tested Locke and Latham's (1985) hypotheses, have yielded inconsistent results with regard to goal specificity and negative results with regard to goal attainability. It is possible, however, that the effects predicted by this essentially valid theory are blurred by definitional and methodological difficulties in the realm of sport and exercise, for example with regard to the question of goal difficulty and attainability (Kyllo and Landers, 1995). In the present study, an attempt was made to clarify the question of whether different levels of difficulty have different effects on performance over time. To this end, we manipulated relatively short, moderate and long practice time intervals, assigned three different levels of difficulty within each interval; and controlled social comparison via the use of intact groups rather than randomization. Accordingly, we investigated the effects of goal difficulty, goal specificity and duration of practice time intervals on muscular endurance performance. In line with Locke and Latham (1985), we hypothesized that specific goal conditions would produce higher levels of performance than non-specific goals, difficult and realistic goal conditions would produce higher levels of performance than easy or improbable/unattainable goals, and goal specificity or goal difficulty effects on performance would be affected by the duration of practice time.

Methods

Subjects

The subjects were 346 male grade 9 and 10 Israeli high school students from 15 schools (mean ± S.D.: age – 15.32 ± 0.21 years). The schools were randomly assigned to one of the following 15 conditions; 'improve by 10%' (4, 6, or 8 weeks); 'improve by 20%' (4, 6, or 8 weeks); 'improve by 40%' (4, 6 or 8 weeks); and three 'do' conditions, where the participants were simply told to do sit-ups (4, 6, or 8 weeks). The 'do' groups were included to act as a control, since it is possible that following 'do-your-best' instructions, subjects' motivation may increase. The 'do' condition, however, can be regarded as being more closely related to the classical concept of 'control', that is 'no treatment' (Kerlinger, 1973).

The students from the 15 urban schools were mostly of middle to high socio-economic status; 50% were of Western (European and American) and 50% of Eastern (Asian and African) family origin. These characteristics indicate that although the subjects were not selected at random, they did represent the ethnographic and socio-economic characteristics of the Jewish Israeli population. For technical reasons, female subjects were not available in sufficient numbers in all schools and, therefore, only males were recruited. In each of the 15 sample schools, physical education classes were offered to the students twice a week as part of the school curriculum. However, teachers were allowed to choose and emphasize specific aspects themselves.

Design

The goal-setting and control conditions were randomized among the 15 schools, with each school corresponding to only one condition to prevent any communication between subjects from different groups and to reduce between-group social comparison and competition (Hall and Byrne, 1988). Estimates of goal difficulty were made based on 10%, 20% or 40% improvement (gain) scores over the course of the study (4, 6, or 8 weeks), compared to the best score achieved at the end of the adaptation phase. The goal conditions were as follows:

- *Easy goals.* The subjects were given a goal of a 10% improvement on their own baseline sit-up score. Following the baseline measurements, the subjects were told the number of sit-ups that were required for a 10% improvement to be accomplished by the end of the study (4, 6, or 8 weeks). On each test occasion, the exact number of sit-ups expected of each subject was reiterated (also when a subject outperformed the given goal), to refresh the condition-specific goal instructions.
- *Difficult/realistic goals.* A 20% improvement was the goal in this condition. The instructions were as for the 10% improvement condition.
- *Improbable/unattainable goals.* A 40% improvement was the goal in this condition. Again the instructions given to the subjects were as for the 10% improvement condition.
- *Do your best.* On each test occasion, the subjects were instructed to perform as best they could without any further goal-setting.
- *Control group.* On each test occasion, the subjects were asked to perform sit-ups for 2 min without any further explanation.

The specific improvement scores (percent gain) were established based on two procedures. Weinberg *et al.* (1991) presented the 2 min sit-up performance means of their subjects. A simple calculation indicated an actual improvement of 17-19% over the course of the 5 week study in all goal conditions. It was therefore assumed that a 20% improvement can be viewed as difficult and realistic, in accordance with Locke and Latham's (1985) definition. Accordingly, it was assumed that 10% and 40% can be viewed as 'easy' and 'improbable/unattainable', respectively. To validate these assumptions, two experts in physical education were consulted, both of whom are high-ranking officers at the Combat Fitness Center of the Israel Defense Forces. Both experts have much experience working with youth in this area. The experts agreed independently with our assumptions, indicating the above-mentioned improvement percentages as 'easy', 'difficult/realistic' and 'improbable/unattainable', respectively. These estimations were further validated by the responses of the subjects to their perceived level of goal difficulty ratings (see Results section).

The design consisted of five levels of goal conditions ('do', 'do your best', 'improve by 10%', 'improve by 20%', and 'improve by 40%') and three levels of practice duration (4, 6 and 8 weeks), giving 15 conditions in total. The subjects were assigned to one condition only without being aware of the other conditions (intact gropus). Since there were three practice durations, the dependent variable was the difference in the number of sit-ups in the final session compared with at baseline. Thus the factorial design was 5 (goal conditions) x 3 (practice durations).

Procedure

A 2 min sit-up task was the primary dependent measure. The procedure for performing the sit-ups was modified from that described by Matthews (1978), in that the knees were bent rather than straight, and that the duration of the task was 2 min rather than 1 min. We believed that the extra time would help to alleviate any potential ceiling effect associated with a 1 min trial. Also, the extra time would provide an opportunity for the subjects to be motivated by their specific goal, rather than just perform sit-ups as quickly as is usually done over 1 min. A similar procedure has been used successfully in previous goal-setting studies (Weinberg *et al.,* 1988, 1991). Before the study commenced, the subjects were told that they would be practicing muscle endurance exercises over the next few weeks during their physical education classes. In addition to the subjects' informed consent, their parents' consent was also obtained.

The subjects first performed a maximal number of sit-ups once a week for 3 weeks. Thus three sessions were devoted to adaptation to the experimental task. This also enabled a more reliable estimation of the true ability of the students. At this stage, a sit-up baseline measure was recorded for each individual subject. This measure consisted of the best score achieved at the end of the adaptation phase. During the experimental phase, the subjects performed sit-ups twice a week for 4, 6 and 8 weeks, with the test taking place on the Thursday of each week. Each practice session consisted of one set of sit-ups. The subjects participated regularly twice a week in physical education classes in their schools. However, their teachers were asked to avoid performing sit-ups more than twice a week during the period of study. The subjects were also asked not to perform sit-ups in their free time, and their subsequent reports indicated that they had complied with this request. Within each condition, the subjects worked with a partner of their choice. At least 3 m separated each pair of students during both practice and assessment to reduce undesirable interactions and social comparisons (i.e. competition), as suggested by Hall and Byrne (1988).

For the 2 min sit-up assessment, one member of a pair held the feet of his performing partner and counted the number of successful sit-ups. On each test occasion, the instructors chose subjects at random and counted the number of sit-ups they performed. The instructors reported a complete agreement between their counts and those of the students. Following this assessment, the members of a pair switched over.

Each session was supervised by a professional instructor. The instructors were guided by the experimenters before the adaptation phase and between the adaptation and experimental phases. During performance, the instructor announced the time remaining at regular intervals. When only 10 s remained, a countdown began from 10 and ended with 'stop', thus concluding the assessment. At the end of each assessment, the instructor recorded the scores. Neither the teachers nor the students were given any information as to the purpose of the study. At the end of the experiment, the instructors were debriefed after goal-setting as a motivating factor in motor performance had been explained.

Questionnaire

The subjects in the three specific-goal conditions were asked to rate the perceived difficulty of their goals after completion of the practice and test sessions. This was done on a scale ranging from 'extremely easy' (1) to 'extremely difficult' (4). In addition, they were asked the following: 'Did you reach the goal set for you?' and 'Did you set any other goals besides the one given to you?' They answered 'yes' or 'no'. The questionnaire was used to ensure that the specific goals set were also perceived and accepted according to the various difficulty levels, in line with the propositions of Locke (1968) and Locke *et al.* (1981).

Results

Manipulation check

Non-parametric (χ^2) analyses of the subjects' perceptions relating to the goal conditions to which they were assigned revealed that, in all three specific-goal conditions, they differed significantly from each other in perceived goal difficulty ($\chi^2_6 = 48.68$, $P < 0.001$). They also differed in setting goals other than the one given to them ($\chi^2_2 = 33.28$, $P < 0.001$). However, goal achievement did not differ between the specific-goal conditions ($\chi^2_2 = 2.94$, $P > 0.05$).

Most subjects in the easy and difficult/realistic conditions (76% and 73%, respectively), and the improbable/unattainable condition (62%), felt that they reached their goals. In addition, most subjects (67%) given easy goals set themselves an additional goal to that set for them. The subjects in the difficult/realistic and improbable/unattainable conditions did not set themselves any additional goals (79% and 76%, respectively).

Most subjects in the easy goal condition (52%) felt that their goal was moderately difficult, whereas 36% thought it difficult. Of those in the difficult/realistic goal conditions, 44% thought it moderate, 32% thought it difficult and 15% thought it extremely difficult. Of those in the improbable/unattainable goal condition, 36% thought it difficult and 54% thought it extremely difficult.

Effects of goal condition and practice duration on sit-up performance

The numbers of sit-ups performed before the study (baseline measures) were compared using a one-way analysis of variance (ANOVA). The results indicated that the means of the 15 groups differed significantly ($F_{14,321} = 5.13$, $P < 0.001$). Because each of the five goal and control conditions was matched with three practice durations (4, 6 and 8 weeks), an ANCOVA procedure could not be applied to the performance (sit-up) scores at the end of the procedure, as a practice effect was inherent in the data. Therefore, to prevent any confounding of the results, gain scores were calculated for each subject within each condition, in line with the recommendation of Locke (1975). These gain scores were subjected to an ANCOVA procedure using the baseline scores as a covariate, and goal condition ($n = 5$) and practice duration ($n = 3$) as independent factors. The Bartlett procedure for testing normality of distribution (Kirk, 1968) indicated no violation of the homogeneity of variance assumptions in any of the treatment groups. Thus the assumptions underlying the subsequent analyses were met.

Statistical analysis was applied to the performance gains to assess whether goal difficulty and practice duration separately or in combination affected sit-up performance.

ANCOVA was applied to the gain scores because of the initial differences among the intact groups as well as the differences in practice durations nested within each condition. Though gain scores may mask the initial differences between the groups, this may not account for the possibility that a lower initial level in one group may result in a higher gain than a high initial level in another group. To ensure that differences in gain scores do not result from such a possibility, but from the manipulated conditions, the initial scores were used as a covariate.

Before applying the ANCOVA procedure to the gain scores, one should note that from a practical and perceptual point of view, the subjects who were given easy goals (10% gain) had improved much more at the end of the practice than was expected of them, particularly after 6 and 8 weeks. Similarly, the subjects assigned to difficult/realistic goals (20% gain) improved much more than was expected of them. However, those who were assigned to improbable/unattainable goals (40% gain) gained far less than expected, particularly after 4 and 6 weeks. The 5 x 3 (goal condition x practice duration) between-subjects ANCOVA applied to the sit-ups gain scores revealed highly significant effects of both goal condition ($F_{4,306} = 18.68$, $P < 0.001$) and practice duration ($F_{2,306} = 17.22$, $P < 0.001$). A less significant effect of the interaction between goal condition and practice duration was also found ($F_{8,306} = 3.21$, $P < 0.001$).

An examination of the mean performance gains by goal condition revealed a substantial improvement for all five goal conditions. However, the greatest gain in sit-ups (mean ± S.D. = 25.84 ± 10.82) was achieved by the difficult/realistic (20%) group, followed by the easy (10%) group (25.13 ± 19.67). The improbable/unattainable (40%) group demonstrated a smaller gain (19.26 ± 8.94) in sit-ups. The lowest gains were achieved by the 'control' and 'do-your-best' groups (10.15 ± 10.09 and 7.75 ± 11.99, respectively). Thus specific goals produced substantially higher performance gains compared with non-specific goals.

A Tukey *post-hoc* procedure applied to the five goal conditions means, with significance set at $P < 0.05$, indicated that the three specific groups gained significantly more sit-ups than the two control groups across the three practice durations. The 10%, 20% and 40% groups showed effect sizes of 1.03, 1.50, and 1.52 standard deviations respectively over the 'do' conditions, and 1.11, 1.59 and 1.07 respectively over the 'do-your-best' condition. The mean gains in sit-ups by goal conditions are presented in figure. 31.1.

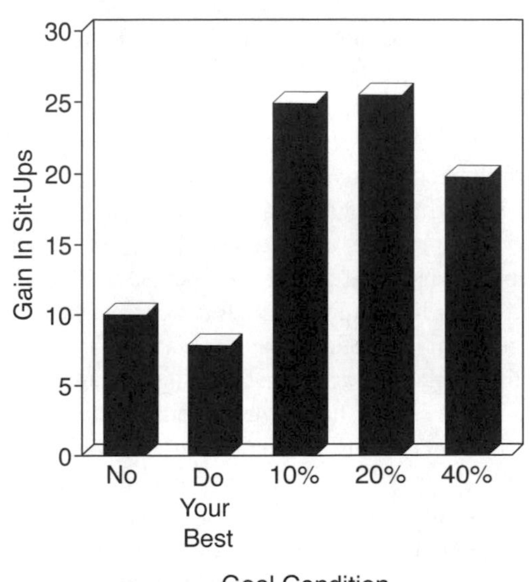

Figure 31.1 Mean gain in sit-ups by goal condition.

The significant effect of practice duration revealed that the 8 week condition resulted in the highest mean gain in sit-ups (23.06 ± 12.31), followed by the 6 week (20.55 ± 16.99) and 4 week (9.76 ± 11.37) conditions. Tukey *post hoc* comparisons showed that the 8 and 6 week durations resulted in significantly ($P < 0.05$) higher sit-up gains than after 4 weeks of practice. Compared with 4 weeks of practice, the 6 and 8 week durations resulted in effect sizes of 0.77 and 1.13, respectively.

The Tukey *post-hoc* procedure was applied to contrast the five means at each practice duration separately. This procedure was chosen because it is more conservative in controlling for Type I error with ANCOVA. This procedure revealed a number of significant ($P < 0.05$) effects. First, after 4 weeks of practice, setting 10%, 20% or 40% improvement goals resulted in higher sit-up gains than the two non-specific goal conditions. In addition, the 20% goal condition resulted in a significantly ($P < 0.05$) higher gain than the 10% and 40% goal conditions. Second, after 6 weeks of practice, the 10% and 20% goal conditions resulted in significantly ($P < 0.05$) higher sit-up gains than the 40% and the two non-specific conditions. However, the subjects in the 40% goal condition also gained significantly ($P < 0.05$) more sit-ups than those in the two non-specific conditions. Third, after 8 weeks of practice, the 10%, 20% and 40% groups were similar regarding sit-up gains, but all these groups gained significantly ($P < 0.05$) more than the two nonspecific groups.

Discussion

In this study, we tried to clarify the issues of goal specificity and goal attainability. Our gain was to determine the effectiveness of easy, difficult/realistic and improbable/unattainable goals in enhancing muscle endurance performance while trying to control for social comparisons. In addition, we varied the practice duration in the experimental trials to explore and facilitate goal difficulty effects.

Our results clearly support Locke and Latham's (1985) hypothesis that goal specificity produces higher levels of performance than no goals or 'do-your-best' goals. All nine specific-goal conditions consistently revealed substantially higher performance gains, at all times as well as across durations of practice, compared with the six non-specific goal conditions. That is, all 15 experimental groups performed according to the general pattern predicted by the goal specificity hypothesis.

Both popular and academic literature on sport psychology and goal-setting have cautioned that goals which are too difficult may result in a decline in motivation and performance. As noted earlier, only a small number of studies have tested this hypothesis in sport and exercise settings, each of which has failed to demonstrate the predicted negative effects of setting goals which are seemingly unreachable (Weinberg, 1992, 1994). In the present study, however, across all durations of practice, improbable/unattainable goals tended to produce lower gains in sit-ups compared with difficult/realistic goals. This important finding indicates that assigning individuals goals that are unrealistic and beyond their reach may have negative effects, such as a decrease in potential performance gain. However, whereas after 4 and 6 weeks of practice improbable/unattainable goals produced significantly lower performance gains than difficult/realistic goals, after 8 weeks this tendency was insignificant. These results are not in line with the prediction derived from Garland's (1983, 1985) cognitive mediation theory, which maintains that the relationship between goal difficulty and performance is a monotonically positive one, with no evidence of a decline in either motivation or performance for those assigned to unrealistically difficult goal conditions (Garland *et al.,* 1988).

In general, our results concur with Locke and Latham's (1985) goal specificity and goal attainability hypotheses. The only exception was the responses of the easy goals group, which outperformed all other groups in the 6 and 8 weeks conditions. That is, 13 of 15 groups—or 306 of 346 (88.4%) students—performed, in general, according to the predictions derived from both the goal specificity and attainability hypotheses; only 2 groups (namely, the 6 and 8 weeks easy goal conditions) performed in line with the predictions of goal specificity but not goal attainability. These results provide at least partial support for Kyllo and Landers' (1995) preliminary evidence in favour of an inverted-U type relationship between goal difficulty and performance, as indicated by the goal condition main effect (see Fig. 1) and by the three specific-goal groups in the 4 weeks condition.

A closer examination of the questionnaires revealed that, for some reason, the subjects in the 6 and 8 weeks easy goal conditions did not accept their specific goals, instead setting themselves other probably difficult (but reachable) goals. Thus, indirectly, this result is also in line with Locke and Latham (1985), because they maintain that goal acceptance is necessary for effective goal-setting. It is possible that this exception resulted from the specific nature of the 'easy' manipulation. The specific treatment conditions in the present study were based on the definition of a 20% improvement as difficult/attainable and realistic, yet challenging, with regard to Weinberg and co-workers' (1991) actual 17-19% improvement rates. Accordingly, we (correctly) assumed that 10% and 40% can be viewed as easy and improbable/unattainable, respectively. However, it is possible that when individuals are assigned a 10% improvement goal, they are substantially closer to a realistic possible improvement of 17-19% than individuals assigned a 40% improvement goal. Thus it is tempting for such individuals to 'break the rules' and strive for a somewhat more difficult but reachable goal (e.g. 17-19%). This needs to be examined in future research on goal-setting.

It should be noted that most subjects assigned difficult/realistic goals perceived them to be moderate to difficult, and that most who were assigned improbable/unattainable goals perceived them to be extremely difficult. As Weinberg and Weigand (1993) correctly indicated, it is virtually impossible to prevent any spontaneous goal-setting, both in specific and in non-specific goal conditions, with any attempt to define a 'minimally acceptable' amount of spontaneous goal-setting being viewed as arbitrary. In the present study, we found that all specific groups performed better than all non-specific groups even though the non-specific groups set spontaneous goals. According to Locke (1991), this should not have happened; according to Weinberg and Weigand (1993), it is unavoidable. Moreover, most subjects' perceptions in the specific conditions, at least in the improbable/unattainable and the difficult/realistic ones, were indeed in accordance with actual performance data. Those in the improbable/unattainable condition were way behind their expected performance and, therefore, many of them probably felt that the goals set for them were extremely difficult. In contrast, those assigned difficult/realistic goals gained more sit ups than expected (i.e., worked harder to exceed expectations) and, accordingly, tended to perceive their tasks as moderate to difficult. Thus Weinberg and Weigand (1993) are, in principle, correct in stating that when subjects set themselves their own goals, they may strive to reach these goals and ignore the ones set for them. However, in the present study, this occurred mainly in the 6 and 8 weeks 'easy' groups but not in the other groups, in which spontaneous goal-setting was kept to a reasonable, unavoidable minimum, which did not impair the experimental manipulation, as the performance data clearly shows.

Improbable/unattainable goals tended to produce lower gains in sit-ups and were also viewed as much more difficult, in comparison to all other specific-goal conditions. However, 62% of the subjects assigned improbable/unattainable goals reported that they believed they reached their goals, even if this was not actually the case. We believe that this has more to do with the way people would like to present themselves (e.g., 'Despite the fact that it was extremely difficult, I feel I did it'), than with the way the goal difficulty conditions were defined. It is possible, therefore, that goals which vary in their difficulty level may lead individuals to different strategies of spontaneous goal-setting, as well as to different subjective perceptions related to the various levels of goal difficulty. In future research, this possibility should be explored within the framework of relevant theories, such as Locke and Latham's (1990) theory of goal-setting and task performance in combination with Bandura's (1982) theory of self-efficacy. From a more general perspective, crucial variables such as personal goals, self-efficacy and commitment should be incorporated into the research on goal attainability, to investigate their potential mediating effects on motor performance (Locke, 1994; Lerner and Locke, 1995). For example, Locke (1968) originally hypothesized that goal commitment would moderate the relationship between level of difficulty and performance. In the present study, we assumed that within all goal conditions, the distribution of such crucial variables was similar. However, this methodological consideration does not preclude the theoretical need to investigate the moderating effects of variables such as goal commitment or self-efficacy in future goal-setting research in sport.

Duration of practice resulted in an overall improvement across weeks, from the 4 to the 6 and 8 week conditions which corresponds to a simple practice effect. A closer examination reveals a minor reduction in performance gains in the 10% and 20% groups from the 6 to the 8 week conditions, which is the only exception to the consistent increase over time revealed for all other groups. This can be attributed to the subjects in the easy and difficult/realistic groups being quite close to their maximal performance after 6 weeks, and thus they could not improve much more compared with the other three groups. In addition, in the 8 week conditions, the difference between groups was somewhat less (with the specific groups still demonstrating the highest gains in performance). These results might be explained by the fact that, in the 8 week condition, the specific goals were too far removed in time to most effectively direct the subjects' actions. In other words, after 8 weeks, it may be that specific goals result in quite similar performance gains, but still somewhat different perceptions of the various goal conditions.

Eminent psychologists, including Bandura (1982) and Carver and Scheier (1982), have argued that short-term (proximal) goals, which provide immediate feedback about an individual's progress, should produce larger improvements in performance compared with long-term (distal) goals, which are often perceived to be too abstract and too distant to affect performance substantially. Preliminary evidence from the sport and exercise domain indicates that subjects assigned a short-term goal improve significantly more than those assigned a long-term goal (e.g., Tenenbaum *et al.,* 1991). Thus Locke and Latham's (1985) goal proximity hypothesis (reviewed by Weinberg, 1992, 1994; Kyllo and Landers, 1995) should be investigated in conjunction with their goal attainability hypothesis, to examine such combined effects. Such research would also provide a better indication of the duration of practice necessary to produce the greatest improvements in performance over time.

At a methodological level, the decision to randomize the goal-setting and control conditions among schools, with each school corresponding to only one condition to prevent any exchange of communication among students in the different groups and to reduce between-group social comparison and competition, was found to be very efficient. This design, based on the propositions of Hall and Byrne (1988), seems to have provided rigid controls to reduce social comparison and between-group competition. Thus the random assignment of schools, rather than classes, to specific-goal or control conditions appears to have prevented comparisons of performance or competition, thus eliminating the possibility of the subjects in the experimental treatment groups encouraging those in the control groups to set goals for themselves. A similar design was used successfully by Tenenbaum *et al.* (1991) when investigating goal proximity. Such a design is recommended for future research on goal-setting in general, although some statistical considerations related to the use of intact groups should be taken into account (Tabachnick and Fidell, 1989). Moreover, despite the potential problems of such designs (e.g., social comparisons that may occur outside classes, specific teacher/school characteristics), Kyllo and Landers (1995) regard them as useful and recommend their use in future research to enhance methodological rigour.

In conclusion, our findings provide some support for the notion that difficult goals, when improbable and unreachable, can produce significant effects on muscular endurance performance, causing the smallest performance gains among all specific-goal conditions. It would appear that future research should focus on understanding the various conditions under which goal-setting affects motor performance. This might include an investigation of potential mediating variables, including feedback, rewards, participation and supportiveness (Tenenbaum *et al.,* 1991). Because having male subjects only of middle to high socio-economic status may have limited the generalizability of our findings, the task of future research is to determine how unrealistic goals affect different types of individuals (for example, in terms of personality styles, such as goal orientation and self-motivation; see Duda, 1992, 1993) when performing a variety of motor tasks (e.g., aerobic, anaerobic and power tasks; see Bar-Eli *et al.,* 1993) in different situations and social environments. Such research could provide more generality to the findings concerning the effects of goal difficulty on athletic performance (Kyllo and Landers, 1995). Hence, more empirical support could be provided for the notion that setting unrealistically high goals is detrimental to motivation and performance, a notion which has previously been suggested in the applied sport psychology literature, but with insufficient empirical support (Weinberg, 1992, 1994).

References

Bandura, A. (1982). Self-efficacy mechanism in human agency. *American Psychologist,* 37, 122-147.

Bar-Eli, M., Levy-Kolker, N., Tenenbaum, G. and Weinberg, R.S. (1993). Effect of goal difficulty on performance of aerobic, anaerobic and power tasks in laboratory and field settings. *Journal of Sport Behavior,* 16, 17-32.

Burton, D. (1992) The Jekyll/Hyde nature of goals: Reconceptualizing goal setting in sport. In *Advances in Sport Psychology* (edited by T.S. Horn), pp. 267-297. Champaign, IL: Human Kinetics.

Carver C.S. and Scheier, M.F. (1982). Control theory: A useful conceptual framework for personality, social, clinical, and health psychology. *Psychological Bulletin,* 92, 111-135.

Duda, J.L. (1992). Motivation in sport settings: A goal perspective approach. In *Motivation in Sport and Exercise* (edited by G.C. Roberts), pp. 57-91. Champaign, IL: Human Kinetics.

Duda, J.L. (1993). Goals: A social-cognitive approach to the study of achievement motivation in sport. In *Handbook of Research on Sport Psychology* (edited by R.N. Singer, M. Murphey and L.K. Tennant), pp. 421-436. New York: Macmillan.

Garland, H. (1983). Influence of ability, assigned goals and normative information on personal goals and performance: A challenge to the goal attainability assumption. *Journal of Applied Psychology,* 68, 20-30.

Garland, H. (1985). A cognitive mediation theory of task goals and human performance. *Motivation and Emotion,* 9, 345-367.

Garland, H., Weinberg, R.S., Bruya, L.D. and Jackson, A. (1988). Self-efficacy and endurance performance: A longitudinal field test of cognitive mediation theory. *Applied Psychology: An International Review,* 37, 381-394.

Hall, H. and Byrne, T. (1988). Goal setting sport: Clarifying anomalies. *Journal of Sport and Exercise Psychology,* 10, 184-198.

Kerlinger, F.N. (1973). *Foundations of Behavioral Research.* New York: Holt, Rinehart and Winston.

Kirk, R.E. (1968). *Experimental Design: Procedures for the Behavioral Sciences.* Belmont, CA: Brooks/Cole.

Kyllo, L.B. and Landers, D.M. (1995). Goal setting in sport and exercise: A research synthesis to resolve the controversy. *Journal of Sport and Exercise Psychology,* 17, 117-137.

Lerner, B.S. and Locke E.A. (1995). The effects of goal setting, self-efficacy, competition and personal traits on the performance of an endurance task. *Journal of Sport and Exercise Psychology,* 17, 138-152.

Locke, E.A. (1968). Toward a theory of task motivation incentives. *Organizational Behavior and Human Performance,* 3, 157-189.

Locke, E.A. (1975). Personnel attitudes and motivation. *Annual Review of Psychology,* 26, 457-480.

Locke, E.A. (1991). Problems with goal-setting research in sports – and their solutions. *Journal of Sport and Exercise Psychology,* 13, 311-316.

Locke, E.A. (1994). Comments on Weinberg and Weigand. *Journal of Sport and Exercise Psychology,* 16, 212-215.

Locke, E.A. and Latham, G.P. (1985). The application of goal setting to sports. *Journal of Sport Psychology,* 7, 205-222.

Locke, E.A. and Latham, G.P. (1990). *A Theory of Goal Setting and Task Performance.* Englewood Cliffs, NJ: Prentice-Hall.

Locke, E.A., Shaw, K.N., Saari, L.M. and Latham, G.P. (1981). Goal setting and task performance:1969-1980. *Psychological Bulletin,* 19, 125-152.

Matthews, D.K. (1978). *Measurement in Physical Education.* Philadelphia, PA: W.B. Saunders.

Mento, A.J., Steel, R.P. and Karren, R.J. (1987). A meta-analytic study of the effects of goal setting on task performance: 1966-1984. *Organizational Behavior and Human Decision Processes,* 39, 52-83.

Tabachnick, B.G. and Fidell, L.S. (1989). *Applied Multivariate Statistics.* New York: Harper and Row.

Tenenbaum, G., Pinchas, S., Elbaz, G, Bar-Eli, M. and Weinberg, R. (1991). Effect of goal proximity and goal specificity on muscular endurance performance: A replication and extension. *Journal of Sport and Exercise Psychology,* 13, 174-187.

Tubbs, M.E. (1986). Goal setting: A meta-analytic examination of the empirical evidence. *Journal of Applied Psychology,* 71, 474-483.

Weinberg, R.S. (1992). Goal setting and motor performance: A review and critique. In *Motivation in Sport and Exercise* (edited by G.C. Roberts), pp. 177-197. Champaign, IL: Human Kinetics.

Weinberg, R.S. (1994). Goal setting and performance in sport and exercise settings: A synthesis and critique. *Medicine and Science in Sports and Exercise,* 26, 469-477.

Weinberg, R.S. and Weigand, D.A. (1993). Goal setting in sport and exercise: A reaction to Locke. *Journal of Sport and Exercise Psychology,* 15, 88-96.

Weinberg, R.S. and Weigand, D.A. (1996). Let the discussions continue: A reaction to Locke's comments on Weinberg and Weigand. *Journal of Sport and Exercise Psychology,* 18, 89-93.

Weinberg, R.S., Bruya L.D., Jackson, A. and Garland, H. (1987). Goal difficulty and endurance performance: A challenge to the goal attainability assumption. *Journal of Sport Behavior,* 10, 82-92.

Weinberg, R.S., Bruya L.D., Longino, J. and Jackson, A. (1988). Effect of goal proximity and specificity on endurance performance of primary-grade children. *Journal of Sport and Exercise Psychology,* 10, 81-91.

Weinberg, R.S., Bruya, L.D., Garland, H. and Jackson, A. (1990). Effect of goal difficulty and positive reinforcement on endurance performance. *Journal of Sport and Exercise Psychology,* 12, 144-156.

Weinberg, R.S., Fowler, C., Jackson, A., Bagnall, J. and Bruya, L.D. (1991). Effect of goal difficulty on motor performance: A replication across tasks and subjects. *Journal of Sport and Exercise Psychology,* 13, 160-173.

Wood, R.E., Mento, A.J. and Locke, E.A. (1987). Task complexity as a moderator of goal effects: A meta-analysis. *Journal of Applied Psychology,* 72, 416-425.

PART VI

Enhancing Health and Well-Being

The studies of the influence that psychological factors have on exercise, health, and wellness has increasingly caught the attention of exercise and health psychologists during the last four decades. Rejeski and Thompson (1993) provide an overview of the historical and conceptual roots of exercise psychology and its visible interface with health psychology. Dishman and Buckworth (1996), who used meta-analysis to conduct a quantitative review, were pioneers in systematically studying the synthesized, integrative influence of various exercise settings on the effectiveness of supervised, programmed interventions intended to increase physical activity. Another meta-analysis conducted in the same year (Carron, Hausenblas, & Mack, 1996), which was intended to investigate promotional strategies aimed at increasing exercise adherence, reviewed the effects that various sources of social influence have on various manifestations of exercise involvement (e.g., behaviors, cognitions, and affect). These two early meta-analyses not only reviewed the limited research in the area at the time but also set the direction for future research on exercise adherence. Based mainly on studies conducted in the United Kingdom, Biddle (1995) suggested some important theoretical concepts, which should be applied in order to promote public health across the life span through understanding and enhancing the motivation for physical activity and exercise in different age groups.

Athletic and exercise participation may also have potential negative consequences. Bahrke (2000), for example, reviewed the studies conducted on the psychological and behavioral effects of endogenous testosterone and anabolic-androgenic steroids. The issue of steroid use for performance enhancement in sport has gained much notoriety. In Smith's (1986) article, his well-known cognitive-affective model of athletic burnout is presented, which has had a substantial effect on later research conducted on this important yet quite neglected topic in sport and exercise psychology. Finally, in the classic article by

Andersen and Williams (1988), their famous theoretical model of stress and athletic injury is presented. This comprehensive model, which substantially helped in clarifying the effects of psychosocial factors on athletic injury, has been the most influential approach developed in sport and exercise psychology to account for the antecedents of sport injury.

32 Toward a Cognitive-Affective Model of Athletic Burnout

RONALD E. SMITH
University of Washington

The phenomenon of job burnout appeared for the first time as a substantial subject of research in psychology in the mid-1970s, especially with regard to human employees in service professions. In essence, burnout, a process that illustrates some of the negative long-term psychological and behavioral effects of work-related stress, is a serious problem in the work world. Not only does it lead to increased tardiness and absenteeism as well as decreased work performance, but it can also lead to complete withdrawal from the organization. The effects of burnout eventually can spill over to an individual's other spheres of life, including possible health-related consequences.

In general (i.e., organizational) psychology, there has been some debate among researchers about the definition of the complex burnout phenomenon. For instance, researchers have disagreed on the number and qualitative characteristics of the components of the burnout syndrome. In sport, the concept of burnout has too often been confused with the concepts of overtraining and staleness. Partly because of this conceptual confusion, empirical, theory-based research on burnout in sport has been quite rare.

Coaches' burnout was investigated mainly in the late 1980s and early 1990s. At that time, despite the inherent interest in athletes' burnout, empirical studies investigating burnout in athletes were rare. In the mid-1990s, empirical research on burnout in athletes was still in its infancy. In the last decade, some relatively infrequent yet serious attempts were made to fill the void in empirical research on athletic populations. Much of this research was directly and indirectly affected by Smith's pioneering cognitive-affective model, which was the first attempt to provide a comprehensive theory that would help in stimulating further thought and research on the neglected topic of burnout in sport.

Although athletic burnout is a frequent topic of discussion and speculation, little in the way of a conceptual model or empirical data currently exists. An attempt is made to incorporate what is known about the nature, causes, and consequences of burnout within a cognitive-affective model of stress and to note the parallel situational, cognitive, physiologic, and behavioral components of stress and burnout. Thibaut and Kelley's social exchange model is used to define the conditions under which withdrawal from a sport can be attributed to burnout. Empirical findings concerning the causes and consequences of burnout derived from nonathletic populations are incorporated within the athletic burnout model, and its implications for preventing and coping with burnout are discussed. A number of conceptual and methodological issues are discussed, including operationalizing and measuring athletic burnout, the need for epidemiological research, and the assessment of causal and moderator variables. Based upon the literature on burnout in nonsport environments and the literature on sources and consequences of athletic stress, a number of testable hypotheses are advanced.

In recent years, the term *burnout* has also begun to appear with increasing frequency in athletics. Coaches at all levels have begun to discuss the dangers of burnout in their profession. Elite athletes have dropped out of sports at the peak of their careers, maintaining that they are "burned out" and that participation has become too aversive for them to continue. Concern about the large number of athletes who drop out of sports during the adolescent years has been fueled by speculation that years of inappropriately intense competitive pressures during childhood may cause some youngsters to bum out and abandon sport participation (Martens, 1978; Orlick & Botterill, 1975). Burnout among athletic trainers and team physicians has also been addressed (Gieck, Brown, & Shank, 1982).

Burnout is typically viewed as a response to job-related stress, and several investigators have noted the desirability of relating burnout to the theoretical and research literature on stress and coping (Jones, 1981; Shinn, Rosario, Morch, & Chestnut, 1984). The present discussion is an attempt to incorporate the phenomenon of burnout—as well as what is known about its antecedents and consequences—within a cognitive-affective model of stress (Smith, 1980, 1985), to explore the implications of this model for preventing and coping with burnout, and to address a number of conceptual

Adapted, by permission, from R.E. Smith, 1986, "Toward a cognitive-affective model of athletic burnout," *The Journal of Sport Psychology* 8: 36-50.

issues, methodological problems, and empirical questions concerning athletic burnout.

The Burnout Syndrome

Burnout is a reaction to chronic stress (Cherniss, 1980; Freudenberger, 1980). The burnout syndrome has physical, mental, and behavioral components, and its development represents complex interactions between environmental and personal characteristics. Its most notable feature is a psychological, emotional, and at times a physical withdrawal from a formerly pursued and enjoyable activity. However, not all withdrawal from such activities can be attributed to burnout. To differentiate between withdrawal patterns that reflect burnout and those that do not, it is necessary to consider factors that govern involvement and persistence in activities.

A theoretical formulation advanced by Thibaut and Kelley (1959) provides a useful framework within which to differentiate between burnout-induced withdrawal from sport participation and other determinants of withdrawal. In their social exchange model, Thibaut and Kelley begin with the assumption that human behavior is governed primarily by the desire to maximize positive experiences and to minimize negative ones. From this perspective, people participate in relationships and activities only so long as the outcomes of participation are sufficiently favorable. Favorability is determined by the balance between rewards and costs.

Rewards and costs are generic terms referring to a variety of potential consequences. Rewards may involve tangible consequences such as money, property, or trophies, as well as psychological ones such as the achievement of desired goals, feelings of competence and mastery, the admiration and esteem of others, the experiencing of closeness in interpersonal relationships, or the opportunity to perform behaviors that are intrinsically motivated or enjoyable in their own right. Costs also encompass a range of experiences, including the amount of time and effort expended, feelings of failure or the disapproval of others, negative emotions such as anxiety or depression, feelings of helplessness or lack of control, or the inability to engage in other activities or relationships. It is important to note that some of the most important psychological rewards and costs are self-administered in the form of self-approval or self-derogation consequent to success or failure in meeting internal standards of performance (Bandura, 1977).

According to Thibaut and Kelley, the decision to enter or remain in a relationship or activity is not based solely on the outcome (reward minus costs). Outcomes are evaluated in relation to two standards, the comparison level and the comparison level for alternatives. The comparison level is essentially the neutral point for the person on a scale of goodness or badness of outcome. Outcomes above the comparison level are experienced as satisfying or pleasant, those below it as unsatisfying or unpleasant. The comparison level is a function of the person's past outcomes, observation of other people's outcomes, and momentary need states.

The relationship of outcome to comparison level determines how satisfying a person will find an activity, but it does not in itself determine whether the person will continue in the activity. Sometimes, for example, athletes continue to participate even though they find the outcomes unsatisfying. Persistence is instead determined by the relationship of the outcome to the comparison level for alternatives, defined as the lowest outcome level a person will accept in the light of outcomes thought to be available in alternative activities (including nonparticipation). Thus, even if the outcome of participation is above the comparison level (i.e., satisfying), the person will choose to leave the activity if that outcome falls below the comparison level for alternatives and a choice must be made. The more similar the outcomes of the two courses of action are, the more conflict the person will experience. If the outcomes are above the comparison level, the conflict will be of the approach-approach variety; if below it, the person will experience avoidance-avoidance conflict.

This formulation seems applicable to the results of research on factors related to sport participation, nonparticipation, and dropout. Studies of participation motivation have shown that people are attracted to sport by a variety of rewards, including skill improvement, the excitement of competition, increased physical fitness, affiliation with others, feelings of mastery, and recognition and approval from significant others (Gill, Gross, & Huddleston, 1981; Gould, 1983; Wankel & Kreisel, 1985). Studies of nonparticipants and dropouts, on the other hand, have identified factors that apparently increase costs of participation to the point that outcomes can drop below both the comparison level and the comparison level for alternatives. These include fear of failure, excessive competitive pressures, dislike for the coach, interpersonal difficulties with teammates, excessive time and energy demands, and boredom (Gould, Feltz, Horn, & Weiss, 1982; Orlick & Botterill, 1975).

We might be tempted to conclude, therefore, that stress-inducing factors typically underlie the decision of children to discontinue participation. However, this does not appear to be the case. Instead it appears that the most prevalent reason youngsters drop out of sport is because they are attracted to other activities. For example, a study of youngsters who had dropped out of competitive swimming revealed that most of them quit because of interest in other activities, not because of excessive pressure, a lack of fun, or training demands (Gould et al., 1982). Gould (1983) reviewed nine other studies of athletic dropouts. In six of the studies, the desire to participate in different activities (including different sports) was found to be a prominent reason for dropping out of a sport. In Thibaut and Kelley's terms, this would imply that the outcomes expected in the other activities raised the comparison level for alternatives above the participation outcome for the current sport. It would be inappropriate to attribute withdrawal to burnout in such cases.

In contrast to withdrawal based on a change in interests or a value reorientation, burnout results from an increase in stress-induced costs, and the theoretical model advanced here is restricted to the latter. From this perspective, burnout seems applicable to the decision of former Philadelphia Eagles head coach Dick Vermeil to resign several years ago. Vermeil's public statements indicated that the inordinate work demands to which he had subjected himself for many years resulted in physical and emotional exhaustion as well as a lowered level of functioning. When at last he found himself decompensating and unable to cope with the pressures, he resigned as head coach. There was no indication that the reward value of coaching had decreased; rather, it appeared that the positives became outweighed by the stress-induced costs to the point that the outcome dropped below the comparison level for the alternative of discontinuing the activity. It is unclear at this point how frequently burnout prompts retirement from sports. Emerging theoretical and empirical interest in athletic retirement (e.g., Coakley, 1983; Greendorfer & Blinde, 1985) may help to clarify the potential role of burnout in this form of withdrawal from participation.

Burnout thus involves a psychological, emotional, and sometimes a physical withdrawal from an activity in response to excessive stress or dissatisfaction (Cherniss, 1980; Freudenberger, 1980). When burnout occurs, a previously enjoyable activity becomes an aversive source of stress. People suffering burnout experience low energy, chronic fatigue, and an increased susceptibility to illness. They may feel exhausted during the day, yet sleep poorly at night. At an emotional level, feelings of depression, helplessness, and anger are frequently reported. Tension and irritability occur even though the person may feel emotionally depleted in other respects, and increasingly negative attitudes toward the activity may generalize to other areas of life as well. Everything seems like it is too much to deal with, and resentment may be experienced toward anyone who makes demands. At a behavioral level, decreased efficiency and inconsistent performance occurs, and at extreme levels, inappropriate behavior and withdrawal may result.

Burnout is a complex phenomenon, and this complexity has prevented investigators from arriving at a uniform and coextensive definition of the syndrome. One element common to all definitions, however, is an emphasis on burnout as a response to chronic stress. In the discussion to follow, an attempt will be made to incorporate the phenomena of stress and burnout within a common conceptual framework that emphasizes relationships among situational, cognitive, physiological, and behavioral components and to specify the parallel interactions among these four sets of factors. The model will be related to what is currently known about factors that contribute to and reduce burnout, and a number of methodological issues and empirical questions concerning athletic burnout will be addressed.

Parallel Models of Stress and Burnout

A conceptual model showing the dynamics of and relationships between stress and burnout includes a stress model that encompasses relationships among situational factors, cognitive appraisal of various aspects of the transaction between the person and the situation, physiological responses, and behavioral responses. Each of these components is in turn influenced by motivational and personality variables. The application of this cognitive-affective model to athletic stress has been discussed in detail elsewhere (Smith, 1985) and will be merely summarized here.

The first component of the model, the situation, involves interactions between environmental demands and personal and environmental resources. Stress results from an imbalance between demands and resources. Demands can be external, as when an athlete confronts a strong opponent in an important contest, or they can have an internal origin in the form of desired goals, personal standards of behavior relating to values or commitments, or unconscious motives and conflicts. When demands are not met, costs in the form of anxiety, guilt, anger, and self-derogation may occur.

Typically we think of stress as occurring in situations in which demands exceed resources ("overload"). However, stress can also result when resources greatly exceed demands, or when the person is not challenged to use his or her resources. Feelings of stagnation and boredom are common responses to this state of affairs, and a condition of "underload" may also take its toll.

Although people often view their emotions as direct responses to situations, in most instances situations exert their effects through the intervening influence of thought (Lazarus, 1982; Smith & Ellsworth, 1985). Through their own thought processes, people create the psychological reality to which they respond. Cognitive appraisal processes play a central role in understanding stress because the nature and intensity of emotional responses are a function of at least four different appraisal elements: appraisal of the demands, appraisal of the resources available to deal with them, appraisal of the nature and likelihood of potential consequences if the demands are not met, and the personal meaning of those consequences for the person. The meanings attached to the consequences derive from the person's belief system.

Smith (1985) has discussed how excessive or inappropriate stress responses can result from errors in any of these appraisal elements. For example, an athlete with low self-confidence or self-efficacy may misappraise the balance between demands and resources so that failure seems imminent. Likewise, an athlete who believes that his or her self-worth depends on success will attach a different meaning to athletic outcomes than will an athlete who can divorce self-worth from success or failure. Many people appear to be victimized by irrational beliefs concerning the meaning and importance of success and social approval, and such beliefs predispose them to inappropriate stress reactions (Ellis, 1962; Rohsenow & Smith, 1982).

When appraisal indicates the threat of harm or danger, physiological arousal occurs as part of the mobilization of resources to deal with the situation. Arousal in turn provides feedback concerning the intensity of the emotion being experienced, thereby contributing to the process of appraisal or reappraisal (Lazarus, 1966; Schachter, 1966).

The fourth component of the model consists of the output behaviors that constitute the person's attempt to cope with the situation. These include task-oriented, social, and other classes of coping behaviors that are affected by the demands of the situation, cognitive appraisal processes, and whatever physiological responses occur.

Each of these four components can be affected by motivational and personality factors. Motivational and personality variables can be viewed as predispositions to seek out certain situations and goals and to perceive, think, and respond emotionally and behaviorally in certain ways. Personality probably has its greatest effects at the level of cognitive appraisal. Indeed, most of the personality variables that are the focus of psychological research (e.g., self-concept, locus of control, repression-sensitization) are basically cognitive appraisal styles.

Within a parallel cognitive-affective framework, burnout represents the manifestations or consequences of the situational, cognitive, physiological, and behavioral components of stress.

At the situational level, a number of factors have been shown to contribute to burnout (Beehr & Newman, 1978; Berkeley Planning Associates, 1977; Pines & Aronson, 1981; Shinn et al., 1984). Though generally assessed in work environments, these factors can readily be extrapolated to the athletic environment as well. Studies of young athletes indicate that such factors as difficulties with coaches and interpersonal difficulties with peers (low social support), high competitive demands, time and energy demands, insufficient skills, and boredom can be sources of athletic stress (Gould, 1983; Gould et al., 1982; Orlick & Botterill, 1975). In young adults, regimentation and lack of personal autonomy can be a major reason for dropping out of sports (Jones & Williamson, 1979; Meggyssey, 1970). Similarly, lack of autonomy created by autocratic coaches and low solidarity and social support are among the factors associated with dropout in high school athletes (Robinson & Carron, 1982). All of these factors are capable of increasing the demands and costs of athletic participation for athletes, and these factors may also relate in a direct manner to the stresses experienced by other members of the athletic community such as coaches, administrators, and trainers. On the other hand, low levels of success and accomplishment clearly can reduce the reward value of participation (Gould et al., 1982).

Imbalance between demands and resources over a long period of time can give rise to a number of cognitions that have been identified in burnout victims. Cognitive appraisal of demands, resources, and consequences results in perceived overload. In most cases of burnout, the person feels outweighed by the demands of the situation, although boredom experienced when resources greatly exceed demands can also be involved. There is often a perception of low accomplishment (Caccese & Mayerberg, 1984; Maslach & Jackson, 1981) which, if extended over a sufficient period of time, results in low perceived control over the situation. A state of learned helplessness can result that undermines still further the person's motivation and ability to cope (Seligman, 1975). Perhaps the most pernicious aspect of learned helplessness is a loss of ability to discriminate between those aspects of the situation that are under control and those that are not. Eventually the person may conclude that nothing can be changed.

A final cognitive characteristic of burnout is a loss of meaningfulness concerning what one is doing and a subsequent devaluation of the activity (Freudenberger, 1980; Pines & Aronson, 1981). We would expect that burned out athletes, coaches, trainers, and administrators would begin to question the value and significance of their efforts and begin to perceive their situation as an aversive treadmill.

At the physiological level, chronic stress produces tension, fatigue, and irritability. Victims of burnout begin to feel emotionally depleted and have difficulty experiencing positive emotions. Sleep-related disorders, increased susceptibility to physical illness, and lethargy tend to occur (Freudenberger, 1980). As in the case of stress, the model assumes a reciprocal relationship between the cognitive and physiological components. That is, the physiological responses are largely elicited by the kinds of appraisals the person makes, but these bodily responses are also part of a feedback loop that affects appraisal and reappraisal. Thus, bodily sensations of arousal, fatigue, or illness serve to prompt and reinforce appraisals of overload, helplessness, and so on. At the physical and emotional levels, the term burnout aptly captures the subjective experience of those who suffer from it; it conveys the image of energy dampened, the fire of enthusiasm extinguished.

The behavioral consequences of burnout involve a decreased level of efficiency and a psychological if not physical withdrawal from the activity. A commonly noted response to stress is rigidity in behavior (Lazarus, 1966). The person appears to get into a behavioral rut that does not permit the degree of flexibility needed for effective coping, task performance, or interpersonal functioning. As a result of this rigidity, the person's behavior may be viewed as inappropriate and may be the source of interpersonal difficulties as well as lowered task efficiency. Another possible response to excessive stress is behavioral disorganization. Whether rigidity or disorganization occurs, the result is often alienation of others and a further reduction in the amount of social support available to the person.

The erosion of social support serves to remove important buffers against the stressful demands of the situation and to decrease an important environmental resource (Cherniss, 1980; Shinn et al., 1984).

As in the case of stress, certain individual difference variables increase the risk of burnout by influencing the balance of rewards and costs. To this point researchers have been more concerned with situational factors than with individual difference variables predictive of increased burnout potential. In the next section, some hypotheses concerning potentially important personal factors will be discussed.

Methodological and Empirical Issues

Conceptualizing stress and burnout within a common framework has the advantage of clarifying the parallel processes that seem to comprise these related phenomena. Moreover, it is possible to relate the theoretical and empirical literature on stress and coping to burnout and, indeed, to view burnout as a particular type of stress response. In a practical vein, this also implies that principles of prevention and amelioration that have been applied in the area of stress might be applicable to burnout as well.

Although burnout has been discussed in relation to athletics for a number of years, only recently have empirical studies begun to appear (e.g., Caccese & Mayerberg, 1984). Most of what is known about burnout is derived from studies of other populations, such as health professionals, teachers, and business people. Athletic burnout may share many of the features identified in these populations, but there may also be important differences. Clearly, the topic of athletic burnout needs and deserves more empirical attention. It is my hope that this conceptual model will help stimulate further thinking and research on this neglected topic. With that purpose in mind, I should like to discuss several conceptual and methodological issues and suggest a few testable hypotheses.

Conceptual Issues

The conceptual model of burnout must be regarded as a tentative one, at least in terms of the specifics within the four basic components (situational, cognitive, physiological, and behavioral). Too little is known at this point about the nature, causes, and consequences of athletic burnout to assume a perfect fit with the factors derived from research on other populations.

For example, research with subjects working in the helping professions led Maslach and Jackson (1981) to conceptualize burnout as comprising three major dimensions: emotional exhaustion, depersonalization, and feelings of low accomplishment. Do these factors also comprise athletic burnout? If so, are the three factors equally important? If not, what is the nature of athletic burnout? Does athletic burnout have some different or additional dimensions, such as staleness? Do its components differ in nature or importance for different roles within the athletic establishment (e.g., athletes, coaches, administrators, trainers)? What are its consequences in terms of performance, illness and injury susceptibility, and attitudes toward the sport and toward physical activity in general? How does athletic burnout affect other areas of functioning, such as social relationships, academics, and job performance? How transitory or long-lasting are its effects? These and other questions have yet to be answered.

The need for some degree of prudence in extrapolating burnout in the helping professions to athletics is suggested by the results of a large-scale study of job stress reported by Caplan, Cobb, French, Harrison, and Pinneau (1975). Their study of 23 different occupations showed that several major effects of job demands on stress responses held across occupations, but that particular stressors, and to some extent relationships between demands and stress reactions, varied from occupation to occupation. A logical question then is the extent to which the nature, causes, and consequences of athletic burnout are unique and to what extent they are shared by those who suffer burnout in other domains of activity.

The Measurement of Athletic Burnout

The intimate relationship between constructs and their operational definitions immediately raises the next issue: How is athletic burnout to be measured? In the final analysis, measurement issues are the most basic ones in any area of psychological research, and athletic burnout is no exception. Although established measuring instruments like the Maslach Burnout Inventory (Maslach & Jackson, 1981) can result in interesting and useful data (e.g., Caccese & Mayerberg, 1984), studies of the nature of athletic burnout can result in the development of sport-specific measures that assess with high content validity (i.e., in a representative fashion) the components of burnout most applicable to athletics. We need look only as far as the related area of stress and anxiety to witness the increment in precision and validity that domain-specific measures of test anxiety (Sarason, 1980) and competitive trait anxiety (Martens, 1977) have provided over more general measures of trait anxiety.

How should the development of such measures proceed? Since the development of valid measures presupposes the determination of the nature of athletic burnout, the interview might serve as a very useful starting point. Open-ended interviews with athletes and others identified or self-defined as burned out could provide useful information on the perceived causes, cognitive and physiological reactions, and behavioral consequences they have experienced. Indeed, this is one of the ways Maslach and her co-workers proceeded in their initial explorations of burnout in the helping professions. Not only is the interview a potentially useful starting point, but more structured interview methods that are amenable to quantitative scoring could provide valid measures in their own right, making possible, in conjunction with objective questionnaires, a multimethod approach to measuring athletic burnout. A reasonably comprehensive conceptual model of burnout could serve as a basis for the development of both interview and objective measures.

Epidemiological Issues

Our earlier application of Thibaut and Kelley's social exchange model to the existing research on participation motivation and dropouts led to the conclusion that the majority of those who drop out of sports are not appropriately defined as burned out. It appears that young athletes are more likely to cease participating because of greater interest in other activities than because of stress-induced costs. Undoubtedly, however, an unknown number of athletes do experience burnout. The question is, how many and under what conditions? Badly needed are epidemiological studies of the incidence and severity of burnout.

One of the very few attempts to study burnout in an athletic population was recently reported by Caccese and Mayerberg (1984). They administered the Maslach Burnout Inventory to a sample of 231 male and female college coaches. Although females scored significantly higher than males did on the emotional exhaustion and low personal accomplishment subscales, the mean scores on all of the subscales were fairly similar to the means of the helping professions norm group studied by Maslach and Jackson. Unfortunately, however, only means and standard deviations were reported. In order to establish the incidence of burnout among the sample of coaches, frequency data are needed. That is, we need to know how many of the coaches obtained scores that would place them above the point on the scale that we would define as the lower limit of burnout. In future research, it is important that frequency data as well as measures of central tendency and dispersion be reported if we wish to answer basic epidemiological questions. Epidemiological studies done with different athletic populations can provide important information not only on the incidence of burnout among various subgroups but also on possible causal factors, a topic to which we now turn.

Causal and Moderator Variables

Once the nature of athletic burnout is established and reliable and valid measures developed, causal and moderator variables need to be explored. The model components that relate directly to such variables are the situational component and the personality and motivational variables that are assumed to affect each of the four basic components.

Most existing research on the causal factors in burnout relates to situational variables (Berkeley Planning Associates, 1977; Farber, 1983; Shinn et al., 1984). Organizational climate and workload variables that increase demands, and lowered autonomy, role definition, and social support, which decrease available resources, are clearly implicated. Analogously, we might expect that such variables as training and competitive demands, poor coach-player relationships, and low levels of social support from peers would be related to athletic burnout. Thus, burnout might be expected to occur with higher frequency in highly competitive and individual sports such as tennis, skating, or gymnastics. The rationale for this hypothesis is that such sports are unusually demanding in terms of time and effort requirements, the repetitive nature of training (particularly in the latter two sports) can produce boredom, and the individual nature of the sport reduces the level of social support received from peers. We might further predict that in such sports the nature of the coach-athlete and parent-athlete relationships would assume paramount importance because of the lack of potentially compensatory social support from peers.

The public nature of the sport environment offers an important advantage in the study of situational variables related to burnout: It is possible to directly observe and measure such factors. One of the weaknesses of burnout research is that situational factors are often measured in terms of self-reports of those who are burned out. Given the reciprocal nature of physiological and appraisal processes, there is the possibility that ratings of causal factors are affected in unknown ways. Such measures, though valid in terms of reflecting the perceptions of the workers, may not be totally accurate representations of the actual situation. Independent assessment of situational factors may be accomplished through the use of unobtrusive measures such as statistics of various types (number of competitive events, length of practices, performance statistics, etc.) and by direct situational and behavioral assessment. For example, coach-player relationships may be studied directly through the use of behavioral coding systems (e.g., Horn, 1985; Smith, Zane, Smoll, & Coppel, 1983). Likewise, level of social support on a team may be measured by behavioral assessment of interaction patterns among players.

Individual difference variables have received less empirical attention than situational factors in burnout research, and few consistent relationships have been established (Perlman & Hartman, 1982). Burnout is but one potential response to stressors, yet we know little about individual difference factors that predict burnout as opposed to other possible responses, such as somatic problems or aggressive outbursts. Caccese and Mayerberg (1984) found higher mean scores for females than for males on the emotional exhaustion and low personal accomplishment subscales of the Maslach inventory, but other studies have reported more burnout among males (e.g., Metz, 1979), and still others have found no notable gender differences (Shinn et al., 1984). Age is often negatively related to burnout, but this may be because survivors or renewed workers are being studied at more advanced ages.

An important question concerns developmental variables related to burnout. At what developmental/maturational and experimental stages is burnout most likely to occur? What are the personal characteristics (including coping styles) of those who survive burnout? A related issue for the researcher concerns the developmental stages at which it is most profitable to study burnout.

We might assume that certain individual characteristics can alter the reward/cost relationship of sport activity and increase the likelihood of burnout. Such factors might include low frustration tolerance, an external locus of control, unrealistic performance standards, poor social and problem-solving skills, fears of failure and/or disapproval, anxiety-proneness, athletic ability limitations, low physical vitality, the Type A behavior pattern, and depressive tendencies. Although none of these factors have been established as moderators of the relationship between situational variables and burnout, they might serve as initial foci of exploration.

Coping and Prevention

Implications of the cognitive-affective model of stress for coping and stress management have been discussed elsewhere (Smith, 1984; Smith & Smoll, 1982). Coping and prevention strategies may occur at the situational, cognitive, physiological, or behavioral levels of the model. A similar approach might be taken to conceptualizing coping and intervention strategies in the case of burnout.

Assuming that the situational factors listed in the model are found to contribute to athletic burnout, a variety of approaches that affect the balance between demands and resources might be indicated. On the demand side, some degree of stress is endemic to the sport setting. But additional and unnecessary sources of stress can be created by coaches, parents, and peers. Programs directed at modifying problematic coaching and parent behaviors and at helping coaches to structure practices and game experiences in ways that are more rewarding to athletes could be effective. Training methods that result in feelings of accomplishment and the prevention of tedium and boredom should help to enhance the reward/cost equation.

On the resource side, both individual and situational resources can be enhanced. The learning of athletic, social, and problem-solving skills can positively alter the demands/resources balance. At the situational level, the availability of social support has been shown to be an important buffer against burnout (Shinn et al., 1984). Programs designed to increase social support, such as coach training, team building, and social skills and communication training, could have significant promise in reducing athletic burnout.

Research has generally suggested that individual coping strategies are either unrelated or positively related to burnout (Pearlin & Schooler, 1978; Pines & Aronson, 1981; Shinn et al., 1984). This may be due to the fact that many of the strategies examined in these studies were attempts to cope with stress and burnout through avoidance of feelings and the work situation. In contrast, Shinn et al. (1984) found that problem-focused strategies such as seeking to increase competence and changing one's approach to the job were related (though not significantly) to lower levels of experienced stress. The present model of burnout would predict that coping skills directed at modifying cognitions that produce maladaptive emotional responses and at controlling somatic arousal could help to reduce burnout. Such skills could also help to counteract the learned helplessness that seems to be a core factor in the burnout syndrome. Rosenbaum and Ben-Ari (1985) have found that subjects who report having self-control skills are more resistant to experimental conditions designed to produce learned helplessness. Moreover, stress management training programs designed to teach people cognitive and somatic coping skills have been found to be promising methods for reducing stress and increasing feelings of self-efficacy in a variety of populations (Holtzworth-Munroe, Munroe, & Smith, 1985; Meichenbaum, 1977).

Studies of coping and prevention strategies related to athletic burnout could make substantial contributions to what is known about burnout in general. The athletic environment offers unusual opportunities to study the interaction of situational and personal factors and to relate them to a variety of meaningful response measures, including performance and physiological indices.

The history of psychology has shown that empirical progress tends to occur most rapidly within the context of theoretical models that guide the development of methodology and the formulation of testable hypotheses, and which invite revision in the event of disconfirmatory findings. Hopefully, the present attempt at a conceptualization of athletic burnout will help to focus needed empirical attention on this phenomenon.

References

Bandura, A. (1977). *Social learning theory.* Englewood Cliffs, NJ: Prentice-Hall.

Beehr, T.A., & Newman, J.E. (1978). Job stress, employee health, and organizational effectiveness: A facet analysis, model, and literature review. *Personnel Psychology,* 31, 665-699.

Berkeley Planning Associates. (1977). *Evaluation of child abuse and neglect demonstration projects* 1974-1977: *Vol.* 9. *Project management and worker burnout: Final report.* Springfield, VA: National Technical Information Service. (NCHSR 78-72)

Caccese, T.M., & Mayerberg, C.K. (1984). Gender differences in perceived burnout of college coaches. *Journal of Sport Psychology,* 6, 279-288.

Caplan, R.D., Cobb, S., French, J.R.P., Harrison, R.V., & Pinneau, S.R., Jr. (1975). *Job demands and worker health* (HEW Publication No. NIOSH 75-160). Washington, DC: U.S. Government Printing Office.

Cherniss, C. (1980). *Staff burnout: Job stress in the human services.* Beverly Hills, CA: Sage.

Coakley, J.J. (1983). Leaving competitive sport: Retirement or rebirth? *Quest,* 35, 1-11.

Ellis, A. (1962). *Reason and emotions in psychotherapy.* Secaucus, NJ: Lyle Stuart.

Farber, B. (Ed.) (1983). *Stress and burnout in human service professions.* New York: Pergamon.

Freudenberger, H.J. (1980). *Burnout.* New York: Doubleday.

Gieck, J., Brown, R.S., & Shank, R.H. (1982). The burnout syndrome among athletic trainers. *Athletic Training,* August, pp. 36-41.

Gill, D.L., Gross, J.B., & Huddleston, S. (1981). Participation motivation in youth sports. In G.C. Roberts & D.M. Landers (Ed.), *Psychology of motor behavior and sport-1980* (p. 111). Champaign, IL: Human Kinetics.

Gould, D. (1983). Future directions in youth sports participation research. In L. Wankel & R. Wilberg (Eds.), *Psychology of sport and motor behavior: Research and practice.* Edmonton: University of Alberta Faculty of Physical Education and Recreation.

Gould, D., Feltz, D., Horn, T., & Weiss, M. (1982). Reasons for attrition in competitive youth swimming. *Journal of Sport Behavior,* **5,** 155-165.

Greendorfer, S.L., & Blinde, E.M. (1985). *"Retirement" from intercollegiate sports: Theoretical and empirical considerations.* Unpublished manuscript, University of Illinois.

Holtzworth-Munroe, A., Munroe, M.S., & Smith, R.E. (1985). Effects of a stress management training program on first- and second-year medical students. *Journal of Medical Education,* 60, 417-419.

Horn, T.S. (1985). Coaches' feedback and changes in children's perceptions of their physical competence. *Journal of Educational Psychology,* 77, 174-186.

Jones, J.M., & Williamson, S.A. (1979). Athletic Profile Inventory: Assessment of athletes' attitudes and values. In J.H. Goldstein (Ed.), *Sports, games, and play: Social and psychological viewpoints* (pp. 157-188). Hillsdale, NJ: Erlbaum.

Jones, J.W. (Ed.) (1981). *The burnout syndrome.* Park Ridge, IL: London House Management Press.

Lazarus, R.S. (1966). *Psychological stress and the coping process.* New York: McGraw-Hill.

Lazarus, R.S. (1982). Thoughts on the relation between emotion and cognition. *American Psychologist,* 37, 1019-1024.

Martens, R. (1977). *Sport competition anxiety test.* Champaign, IL: Human Kinetics.

Martens, R. (Ed.) (1978). *Joy and sadness in children's sports.* Champaign, IL: Human Kinetics.

Maslach, C., & Jackson, S.E. (1981). The measurement of experienced burnout. *Journal of Occupational Behavior,* 2, 99-113.

Meggyssey, D. (1970). *Out of their league.* Berkeley, CA: Ramparts Press.

Meichenbaum, D. (1977). *Cognitive-behavior modification.* New York: Plenum.

Metz, P. (1979). An exploratory study of burnout and renewal among educators. Unpublished doctoral dissertation, University of Colorado-Boulder.

Orlick, T.D., & Botterill, C. (1975). *Every kid can win.* Chicago: Nelson-Hall.

Pearlin, L.I., & Schooler, C. (1978). The structure of coping. *Journal of Health and Social Behavior,* 19, 2-21.

Perlman, B., & Hartman, E.A. (1982). Burnout: Summary and future research. *Human Relations,* 35, 283-305.

Pines, A.M., & Aronson, E. (1981). *Burnout: From tedium to personal growth.* New York: Free Press.

Robinson, T.T., & Carron, A.V. (1982). Personal and situational factors associated with dropping out versus maintaining participation in competitive sport. *Journal of Sport,* 4, 364–372.

Rohsenow, D., & Smith, R.E. (1982). Irrational beliefs as predictors of negative affective states. *Motivation and Emotion,* 6, 299-314.

Rosenbaum, M., & Ben-Ari, K. (1985). Learned helplessness and learned resourcefulness: Effects of noncontigent success and failure on individuals differing in self-control skills. *Journal of Personality and Social Psychology,* 48, 198-215.

Sarason, I.G. (Ed.) (1980). *Test anxiety: Theory, research, and applications.* Hillsdale, NJ: Erlbaum.

Schachter, S. (1966). The interaction of cognitive and physiological determinants of emotional state. In C.D. Spielberger (Ed.), *Anxiety and behavior* (pp. 193-224). New York: Academic Press.

Seligman, M.E.P. (1975). *Helplessness: On depression, development, and death.* San Francisco: Freeman.

Shinn, M., Rosario, M., Morch, H., & Chestnut, D.E. (1984). Coping with job stress and burnout in the human services. *Journal of Personality and Social Psychology,* 46, 864-876.

Smith, C.A., & Ellsworth, P.C. (1985). Patterns of cognitive appraisal in emotion. *Journal of Personality and Social Psychology,* 48, 813-838.

Smith, R.E. (1980). Development of an integrated coping response through cognitive-affective stress management training. In I.G. Sarason & C.D. Spielberger (Eds.), *Stress and anxiety* (Vol. 7, pp. 265-280). Washington, DC: Hemisphere.

Smith, R.E. (1984). Theoretical and treatment approaches to anxiety reduction. In J.M. Silva & R.S. Weinberg (Eds.), *Psychological foundations of sport* (pp. 157-170). Champaign, IL: Human Kinetics.

Smith, R.E. (1985). A component analysis of athletic stress. In M. Weiss & D. Gould (Eds.), *Competitive sports for children and youths: Proceedings of the Olympic Scientific Congress* (pp. 107-112). Champaign, IL: Human Kinetics.

Smith, R.E., & Smoll, F.L. (1982). Psychological stress: A conceptual model and some intervention strategies in youth sports. In R.A. Magill, M.J. Ash, & F.L. Smoll (Eds.), *Children in sport* (2nd ed.) (pp. 178-195). Champaign, IL: Human Kinetics.

Smith, R.E., Zane, N.W.S., Smoll, F.L., & Coppel, D.B. (1983). Behavioral assessment in youth sports: Coaching behaviors and children's attitudes. *Medicine and Science in Sports and Exercise,* 15, 208-214.

Thibaut, J.W., & Kelley, H.H. (1959). *The social psychology of groups.* New York: Wiley.

Wankel, L.M., & Kreisel, P.S.J. (1985). Factors underlying enjoyment of youth sports: Sport and age group comparisons. *Journal of Sport Psychology,* 7, 51-64.

33 A Model of Stress and Athletic Injury: Prediction and Prevention

MARK B. ANDERSEN AND JEAN M. WILLIAMS
University of Arizona

Epidemiological studies on athletic injuries conducted in various countries in the last four decades have indicated an increasingly alarming situation that has underscored the need for delving into the nature of sport injuries and the mechanisms underlying their occurrence. Of course, physical factors play a major role in causing athletic injuries; psychosocial factors can be a factor as well and should not be disregarded in this context.

Early studies on the connection between athletic injuries and relevant psychosocial variables were influenced by the literature on life events, which became popular in psychoneuroimmunology since the late 1960s. It was claimed and empirically established that the association between stress from life events and sport injuries is quite strong. However, a comprehensive, sport-specific model for injury antecedents was still absent, which could better clarify these findings from a theoretical perspective.

For the first time in sport and exercise psychology, Andersen and Williams proposed a comprehensive theoretical model that helped in clarifying the role that psychosocial factors play in athletic injuries. More specifically, the authors focused on the relationship between stress and athletic injury along with some important mechanisms said to underlie that relationship. They incorporated various factors related to a potentially stressful athletic situation: Personality factors, the history of stressors, coping resources, and psychological skill interventions interactively affected athletes' stress response and, in turn, their probability of injury.

Andersen and Williams' model has thus far been the most influential framework in sport and exercise psychology to account for the antecedents of athletic injury. Over the years, this complex, interactional stress–injury model has proven to be a viable theoretical foundation for conducting research on the psychology of athletic injuries, with only few minor revisions required in later versions of the model in light of the accumulating supporting empirical evidence.

The purpose of this paper is to propose a framework for the prediction and prevention of stress-related injuries that includes cognitive, physiological, attentional, behavioral, intrapersonal, social, and stress history variables. Development of the model grew from a synthesis of the stress–illness, stress–accident, and stress–injury literatures. The model and its resulting hypotheses offer a framework for many avenues of research into the nature of injury and reduction of injury risk. Other advantages of the model are that it addresses possible mechanisms behind the stress–injury relationship and suggests several specific interventions that may help diminish the likelihood of injury.

There are myriad factors that may contribute to injury, many of which are primarily physical (e.g., overtraining, equipment failures, poor field conditions, weather, the nature of the sport). Many psychological and social factors may also influence injury occurrence. This paper will address the interconnections of psychosocial factors and stress and their impact on injury outcome. First a brief review of the research conducted on psychosocial and stress factors in injury will be presented, followed by a detailed explication of a model for stress and the prediction and prevention of athletic injury.

Early studies of psychological factors and athletic injury stemmed from clinical or coaching experiences (e.g., Ogilvie, 1966). More recently, better controlled studies on personality and athletic injury have been conducted, but unfortunately the results have been inconsistent. Jackson et al. (1978) found that Factor I (tough-minded vs. tender-minded) of Cattell's Sixteen Personality Factor Questionnaire (16 PF) discriminated injured from noninjured football players, with the tender-minded players being more likely to incur injury than the tough-minded ones. Valiant (1981) obtained similar results with runners. Irvin (1975), however, found no differences between injured and noninjured football players on Factor I but did find differences on Factor A. Injured players were more reserved (vs. outgoing) than noninjured players. Brown (1971), on the other hand, using the California Psychological Inventory, found no differences between injured and noninjured football players on any personality variable. The above trait approaches to studying behavior have been criticized for rigidity, over-simplification, and low explanatory value. See Fischer (1984) for a critique of the trait approach and an appeal for an interactional (Person × Situation) model of sport behavior.

Adapted, by permission, from M.B. Andersen and J.M. Williams, 1988, "A model of stress and athletic injury: Prediction and prevention," *Journal of Sport and Exercise Psychology* 10: 294-306.

The personality and athletic injury research recently has been overshadowed somewhat by stress–injury research, the results of which appear to be more consistent, at least for football. Much of the stress and athletic injury research has centered on the influence of stressful life events. Life events are major changes in an individual's life (e.g., marriage, death of a close friend, change in financial status). Initial interest in life events stems from the work of Holmes and Rahe (1967), who developed the Social Readjustment Rating Scale (SRRS) to measure stressful life events. Using the SRRS, they found that individuals with high life stress seemed generally to be at greater risk of disease than those with low life stress. Later a similar relationship was found for accident occurrence (e.g., Selzer & Vinokur, 1974; Stuart & Brown, 1981).

From the evidence supporting a relationship of life stress with illness and accidents, it was reasoned that life stress might influence another form of "disease," that is, athletic injury. An early and rarely cited study (Holmes, 1970) using the SRRS found that football players who experienced high life stress were more likely to incur injury than players who were rated low on life stress. Later, Bramwell, Masuda, Wagner, and Holmes (1975) modified the SRRS to better fit an athletic population by deleting some items and adding items relevant to athletics (e.g., troubles with head coach, difficulties with eligibility, being dropped from team). The new tool was called the Social and Athletic Readjustment Rating Scale (SARRS). Bramwell et al.'s results were consistent with the previous Holmes (1970) study. Coddington and Troxell (1980) and Cryan and Alles (1983) also found greater incidence of injury in high stress high school and college football players compared to low stress players.

In another study on football injuries, Passer and Seese (1983) adapted Sarason, Johnson, and Siegel's (1978) Life Experiences Survey (LES) to athletics, creating the Athletic Life Experiences Survey (ALES). The original LES was designed to separate positive and negative life events and test the influence of each on illness. Holmes and Rahe (1967) assumed that any major change, whether positive or negative, would be stressful and deleterious to health, but evidence from Vinokur and Selzer (1975) indicated that only negative events were associated with negative outcome.

Passer and Seese (1983) also broadened the scope of the research on stressful life events and injury by including three possible moderator variables of the life events–injury relationship (i.e., trait anxiety, competitive trait anxiety, and locus of control). The life events–injury relationship was again demonstrated, only for negative events, but Passer and Seese failed to detect any influence from the moderator variables. However, a recent study found that the moderator variable of social support contributed directly to the likelihood of injury. Subjects with low social support were more likely to become injured than those with high social support, regardless of life stress levels (Hardy, Prentice, Kirsanoff, Richman, & Rosenfeld, 1987).

All of the initial research that identified a life stress and athletic injury relationship was conducted on football players. In recent studies of collegiate volleyball players (Williams, Tonymon, & Wadsworth, 1986) and basketball and cross-country athletes (Williams, Haggert, Tonymon, & Wadsworth, 1986), a subject's score on a life events scale had no relationship to injury occurrence. In the study with basketball and cross-country athletes, too small of a sample size may have influenced the results; similar problems did not occur in the volleyball study. In another study with nonfootball athletes, high life stress physical education students involved in a variety of sports were more likely to experience an acute injury than low life stress physical education students (Lysens, Auweele, & Ostyn, 1986). These inconsistent results illustrate the need for theory development and refinement in methodology and measurement.

Most of the research on stress and athletic injury has been conducted on a narrow scope, minimally considering the complexity of stress and the broad array of factors that might moderate stress and injury outcome. Also, much of this research has been conducted without the benefit of an adequate framework to explain the relationships between psychosocial factors and injury. The purpose of the present paper is to propose an interactional theoretical model of injury and the cognitive, physiological, attentional, behavioral, intrapersonal, social, and stress history variables that may influence injury occurrence and prevention. The model and its resulting hypotheses offer a framework for many avenues of research into the identification of the injury-prone athlete and the reduction of injury risk. This model of stress and athletic injury was proposed recently (Williams & Andersen, 1986) and has since had minor modifications. The model includes not only stressful life events but other aspects of stress as well as psychosocial factors that may influence injury occurrence. Other advantages of the model are that it addresses possible mechanisms behind the stress–injury relationship and suggests several specific interventions that may help diminish the likelihood of injury.

The general model and its conceptual foundation will be briefly described, followed by a closer examination of the model's subcomponents and the rationale for their inclusion. An initial perusal of the model reveals four major components in the central portion: The potentially stressful athletic situation, the cognitive appraisal of various aspects of that situation, the physiological and attentional responses, and the potential injury outcome. This conceptual foundation for the model was derived from Smith' s (1980) mediational model of stress. Smith's model addresses the external situation, the bidirectionally connected core of cognitive appraisal and emotional (physiological) response, and the outcome behavior. Smith's model also proposes interventions aimed at the stress response core. Similar models may be found in health (e.g., Allen, 1983; Pelletier, 1977) and in other areas of sport psychology (see Martens' 1975 model of the competition process).

Above the stress response core of the model are three major areas (i.e., personality factors, the history of stressors, and coping resources). It is hypothesized that one's stress history contributes directly to the stress response while personality factors and coping resources may act on the stress response either directly or through the effects of the history of stressors. Most of the health literature has viewed these moderator variables as merely buffering the effects of life stress. But such a view may be too narrow in that personality factors and coping resources may moderate the stress response regardless of the levels of life stress or daily hassles.

The model is predicated on the assumption that the two basic mechanisms behind the stress–injury relationship are increases in general muscle tension and deficits in attention during stress. It is hypothesized that individuals with a lot of stress in their lives who have personality traits that tend to exacerbate the stress response and few coping resources will, in a stressful situation, be more likely to appraise the situation as stressful, exhibit greater muscle tension and attentional changes, and thus be at greater risk of injury compared to individuals who have the opposite profile.

Below the stress response are two groups of interventions that are hypothesized to lessen the stress response by addressing either the cognitive appraisal or the physiological/attentional aspects. In addition, these interventions and others may be used to directly influence the moderator variables of coping resources and personality factors. A closer examination of the model's subcomponents will follow.

The Stress Response

The present model and its components was developed primarily from an examination of the stress–illness, stress–accident, and stress–injury literatures (e.g., Passer & Seese, 1983; Smith, 1980; Stuart & Brown, 1981). Other factors are included not because of empirical evidence that they influence accident, illness, or injury outcome but because of demonstrated moderating effects on the stress response.

Cognitive Appraisal

Cognitive appraisal and the potentially stressful athletic situation may be logically, but not experientially, separable. As athletic situations develop, and the process may take weeks or months, there is a continual appraisal and reappraisal. In response to stressful situations (e.g., competition, practice, selection to first or second strings), the athlete appraises the demands of the situation and his or her ability to meet those demands (resources). If the athlete perceives his or her resources as exceeding demands, the stress response to the situation may be minimal. On the other hand, if perceived demands exceed perceived resources, the stress response to the situation may be pronounced. Also, appraisal of the consequences of the event may influence the stress response. If the consequences, whether actual or perceived, are crucial to the athlete's career or self-esteem, the stress response may be extreme.

Whether or not one's cognitive appraisal of potentially stressful situations reflects reality is of little importance in generating a stress response. The cognitive portion of the model owes much to Ellis' (1962) work concerning the influence of perceptions, attributions, and irrational beliefs on the generation of inappropriate or maladaptive emotional responses. These responses, if extreme, may predispose an individual to be at risk of injury because of the attentional and physiological changes that accompany negative cognitive appraisals.

Physiological/Attentional Aspects

The cognitive appraisal of demands, resources, and consequences is connected bidirectionally to physiological and attentional aspects of the stress response. Just as cognitive appraisal of a situation can influence attention and physiological arousal, arousal and attentional patterns can act as feedback information for the continual appraisal and reappraisal of the external situation and one's performance.

Many physiological changes occur during stress, but increases in generalized muscle tension (bracing) may be one of the mechanisms behind the stress–injury relationship (Nideffer, 1983). Generalized muscle tension can disturb motor coordination and reduce flexibility, thus contributing to strains, sprains, and other musculoskeletal injuries. A research issue that needs to be addressed is whether certain individuals will, under stress, exhibit greater increases in generalized muscle tension than others (e.g., high life stress vs. low life stress subjects), and whether these "tenser" persons are more likely to become injured.

The most frequently cited culprit in the stress–injury relationship, however, is change in attention (e.g., Bramwell et al., 1975; Cryan & Alles, 1983; Williams, Tonymon, & Wadsworth, 1986). During stress, narrowing of the visual field may occur, leading to a failure to pick up vital cues in the periphery and thus increasing the likelihood of injury (e.g., getting blind-sided). Also, attention may become scattered under stress, causing the athlete to attend to stimuli not relevant to the task at hand and thus failing to detect vital cues. Research has addressed attentional changes during stress (see Hancock, 1984, for a review), but studies are needed of those attentional changes as they relate to sport and the variables that may influence attentional processes (see below).

If the core of the stress response (i.e., cognitive appraisals and attentional and physiological changes) can be positively modified during a potentially stressful situation, then the likelihood of injury may also be lowered. The literature is replete with studies of variables that may moderate the responses to and consequences of stress. Three broad areas that may influence the response to specific stressful situations, either directly or through interactions with other factors, are presented below.

History of Stressors

An individual's history of stressors (i.e., major life events, chronic daily problems, and previous injuries) should have a substantial impact on the stress response, and thus on injury risk. A thorough assessment of the stressors in an athlete's life may give the coach, trainer, or sport psychologist a good estimate of how much at risk of injury that athlete is, at least from a history-of-stressors standpoint.

Life Events

Although the stress–athletic injury literature is not as substantial as the stress–illness research, there is support for a life event/stress–injury relationship. This relationship has been particularly well established for football but, as noted earlier, attempts to test the effects of life stress outside of football have been somewhat equivocal. Perhaps the nature of the sport is a major determinant of injury outcome. Football is a full-contact sport whereas basketball, volleyball, and cross-country running move, respectively, from moderate to minimal to almost no contact. Future research must determine whether the relationship between stress and injury is more likely to occur in sports that have a naturally higher incidence of injury due to physical contact.

Several measurement issues in the assessment of stressful life events (e.g., confounding nature of some items, time frames, item weighting schemes, positive vs. negative events, scales for special populations) also need to be addressed. Resolution of these issues and the refinement of stress scales may help elucidate the present inconsistencies in the stress–injury literature. For thorough reviews of major measurement issues, see Christensen (1981) and Creed (1985).

Daily Hassles

One weakness of earlier stress–injury studies is that they only examined stress within the framework of life events scales; a weakness of such scales is that they measure only major stressful events. Stress also may stem from the minor daily problems, irritations, or changes an individual encounters. These chronic daily stressors may have nothing to do with a major life event (e.g., job dissatisfaction, loneliness) or they may be a direct consequence of the adaptation required by major life events. For example, moving to a new city also involves a lot of daily problems such as getting used to a new school, new neighbors, new streets, new climate, and so forth.

Kanner, Coyne, Schaefer, and Lazarus (1981) developed the Daily Hassles Scale (DHS), which was designed to measure minor chronic stressors rather than major life events. The scale demonstrated an ability to predict illness as well as life events scales. In fact, in one study daily hassles were found to be better predictors of psychological distress than were major life events (Monroe, 1983). The relationship of daily hassles to athletic injury needs to be investigated, but it may be necessary to develop an athletic daily hassles scale since the generalizability of the DHS to athletes is probably questionable.

Previous Injury

An assessment of previous injuries (and their severity) incurred by an individual would seem crucial for the prediction of future injury. If the athlete has not recovered enough to return to the sport but does anyway, the probability of reinjury is high. Also, if the athlete is physically but not psychologically prepared to return to sport participation, problems may arise due to negative cognitive appraisals. Fear of reinjury may lead to a considerable stress response and may actually increase the probability of reinjury. The history of previous injuries, and the psychological and physical rehabilitation of the athlete, are extremely important as their role in reinjury may outweigh other contributing factors in the model.

Measurement of life events, daily hassles, and previous injuries may produce a more complete assessment of an individual's history of stressors. Future research will help determine which of these stress factors, or combination of factors, are the best predictors of injury. Also, the nature of each sport and its training procedures probably interacts with stress factors. Studies of stress and injury in many different sports are needed in order to test for generalizability and to provide potential theoretical explanations for differences in the stress–injury relationship between sports.

Personality

Any comprehensive model of the relationship of stress to athletic injury would not be complete without considering certain personality differences. The stress–illness literature has identified many personality and psychosocial factors for their roles in moderating the stress–illness relationship (see Garrity & Marx, 1985; Jenkins, 1979). These personality differences may make some individuals less likely to perceive situations and events as stressful or may predispose one to be less susceptible to the effects of stressors. The personality factors that follow have been shown to be such moderator variables, and some have been examined in the stress–injury literature. These factors do not constitute an exhaustive list and there is surely considerable overlap among the variables, but they are all presented here as suggestions for future research in identifying who is most at risk of injury. See Bergandi (1985), and Crossman (1985) for reviews of other psychological and personality factors related to athletic injury.

The trait of psychological hardiness has been shown to moderate the stress–illness relationship in several studies (e.g., Kobasa, Maddi, & Puccetti, 1982). Psychological hardiness is really a constellation of characteristics such as curiosity, willingness to commit, seeing change as a challenge and stimulus to development, and having a sense of control over one's life (Kobasa, 1979). Recently the hardiness concept has come under close scrutiny (Hull, Van

Treuren, & Virnelli, 1987) and some refinement is needed. Although the relationship between hardiness and injury has not been established, the Jackson et al. (1978) finding that tough-minded football players were less likely to be injured than tendered-minded ones seems to be addressing issues very similar to hardiness.

Locus of control (Rotter, 1966) and Antonovsky's sense of coherence (1985) were included in the list of personality factors because of their resemblance to the hardiness concept and because both constructs have demonstrated their usefulness in stress–illness research. Other personality factors such as sensation seeking, achievement motivation, and competitive trait anxiety are included because they are variables common to the world of athletics and appear to be related to stress.

Research is needed to determine if these personality factors influence the stress response and injury rate directly. For example, do high sensation seekers see competition as challenging rather than anxiety provoking? Also, do individuals with a high need to avoid failure experience a greater stress response when in a potentially stressful athletic situation, thus placing themselves at greater risk of injury? Do personality factors interact with the history of stressors (e.g., high sense of coherence seems to buffer the deleterious effects of high life stress; Antonovsky, 1985), thus modifying stress through that pathway? Many of these factors could be used in longitudinal studies as predictor variables in regression equations to determine which personality variables are helpful in identifying the high-risk-of-injury athlete. Sport-specific instruments for measuring these variables may be necessary to best determine the usefulness of the variables in predicting injury (e.g., an athletic locus-of-control scale).

Coping Resources

Coping resources comprise a wide variety of behaviors and social networks that help the individual deal with the problems, joys, disappointments, and stresses of life. The role of coping resources in the stress–illness literature is extensive. See Billings and Moos (1981) for a review of the interactions of coping resources and life stress. What constitutes coping has long been debated and is surely multifaceted. The coping resources presented in the model probably do not comprise a complete list and must be considered only as suggestions for future research in the stress–injury field.

General coping behavior is a category containing several diverse behaviors that may influence an athlete's overall stress level. Their relationship to athletics and injury has not been clearly demonstrated and their inclusion here is only suggestive. This category might include the assessment of such coping behaviors as sleep patterns, nutritional habits, time management, general self-esteem and, if the athlete is a student, study skills. Lack of good general coping behaviors in this category may easily lead to higher stress and thus greater risk of injury. In the area of athletic injury, Williams, Tonymon, and Wadsworth (1986) found that general coping resources—measured by the Miller and Smith (1982) Vulnerability to Stress subscale of their Stress Audit Questionnaire—were directly related to injury. Athletes who had low coping resources were more likely to be injured than those with better coping resources.

In much of the stress and health literature, coping resources have been viewed as moderating the effects of life stress, and by that route influencing illness outcome. As stated earlier, this may be too narrow a view. Some coping factors may act on the stress response and injury rate directly. One major source of coping resources is the extent and kind of social support system an athlete has. Agreement on what constitutes social support and how to measure it has been lacking in the stress literature. Social support usually is considered to be the presence of others whom we know value and care for us and on whom we can rely (Sarason, Levine, Basham, & Sarason, 1983).

One study (Coddington & Troxell, 1980), although it did not specifically examine social support, found that football players who experienced family instabilities (e.g., separations, divorces, deaths) were more likely to become injured than those who did not. This could be interpreted as a disruption of the athlete's social support system.

Evidence for social support's role in athletic injury also comes from Williams, Tonymon, and Wadsworth (1986). Half of the items on their coping resource questionnaire dealt with social support and, as stated above, coping resources was the only variable related to athletic injury. Hardy et al. (1987) also found a direct influence of social support on injuries. Again, athletes with high levels of social support had a lower incidence of injury, but the notion that social support buffers the effect of life stress by serving as a mediating variable in the life stress–injury relationship was not supported.

The presence of a supportive social network (family, friends, coach, sports medicine staff, and teammate support) may directly inoculate the athlete against injury or may attenuate the stressfulness of life events and daily hassles as well as the stressfulness of athletic participation. Although initial athletic injury research suggests only a direct influence, more research is needed before we can determine whether social support only directly influences the risk for injury or whether it also buffers the negative effects of stress, as suggested in the general health literature. Also, see Sarason, Sarason, and Johnson (1985) for a discussion of the myriad problems of assessing and defining social support.

The stress management techniques and other mental skills an athlete possesses may influence athletic performance and responses to stress. These techniques are not only coping resources but also interventions and will be discussed briefly in the next section.

Drug use is prevalent in athletics for legitimate as well as illegitimate reasons. An extensive pharmacopoeia is employed for performance enhancement, injury treatment, pain management, and recreation. Many of these substances have the ability to influence the stress response, perception, and performance, and thus the probability of injury. Assessment of an athlete's drug use other than those drugs that are prescribed is often difficult if not impossible, due to the clandestine nature of drug use. The health and welfare of the athlete needs to be of paramount importance to athletic directors, coaches, trainers, teammates, family, and health care professionals. Identification of substances used or abused by the athlete and programs for drug use modification should help not only in injury prevention but in most aspects of the athlete's life.

The above list of coping variables that may moderate stress and the stress response is surely incomplete and in some places redundant. The variables are offered here as a springboard for research that will lead to a better picture of the coping factors involved in athletic injury. Single variables mentioned above may not be very useful, but when combined with others and with personality and history-of-stressors variables, may prove to be moderately strong predictors of injury risk and outcome.

Interventions

Not only do we wish to identify the factors that may predispose an athlete to injury but also the potential interventions for preventing injury. Following Smith's (1980) suggestion, the stress response's two major components invite a two-pronged offensive directed at attenuating the negative cognitive and physiological/attentional aspects of the stress response.

Interventions for the cognitive appraisal side of the stress response include cognitive restructuring to eradicate thinking patterns that lead to maladaptive responses (see Heyman, 1984). Other techniques such as thought stoppage and confidence training may enhance an athlete's ability to appraise the athletic situation (see Bunker & Williams, 1986). Improving team cohesiveness (a way of manipulating social support) and fostering and communicating realistic expectations are the responsibilities of the coaches, trainers, sport psychologists, and sports medicine staff (see Carron, 1986). If the athlete feels the team is behind him or her and knows what is expected, then the athlete's cognitive reactions to stressful situations may be tempered.

Interventions for the attentional/physiological aspects of the stress response would be aimed at lowering arousal and enhancing concentration. Harris (1986) offers several techniques for lowering arousal levels (e.g., autogenics, progressive relaxation, meditation, breathing exercises). Concentration training can lead to lower distractibility and help keep the athlete on task (see Schmid & Pepper, 1986). Finally, modifying an athlete's use of drugs is an obvious step to improving the stress response and the quality of the athletic experience. All these interventions are aimed at reducing the stress response, either by modifying cognitions or lowering physiological arousal, and thus reducing the likelihood of injury.

Summary and Conclusions

Past research on injury and stress has been atheoretical and too narrow in scope, focusing on a limited conceptualization of stress and a restricted consideration of the interaction of personal and situational variables that may influence the stress response and, ultimately, injury. The present model provides a broad theoretical foundation for future investigations into the prediction and prevention of injury and the many psychosocial variables to be considered in the stress–injury relationship. The model also suggests some probable mechanisms behind the as yet unexplained correlation between stress and injury.

References

Allen, R.J. (1983). *Human stress: Its nature and control.* Minneapolis: Burgess.

Antonovsky, A. (1985). The sense of coherence as a determinant of health. In J.D. Matarazzo, S.M. Weiss, J.A. Herd, & N.E. Miller (Eds.), *Behavioral health: A handbook of health enhancement and disease prevention* (pp. 37–50). New York: Wiley.

Bergandi, T.A. (1985). Psychological variables relating to the incidence of athletic injury: A review of the literature. *International Journal of Sport Psychology,* 16, 141–149.

Billings, A.G., & Moos, R.H. (1981). The role of coping resources and social responses in attenuating the stress of life events. *Journal of Behavioral Medicine,* 4, 139–157.

Bramwell, S.T., Masuda, M., Wagner, N.N., & Holmes, T.H. (1975). Psychological factors in athletic injuries: Development and application of the Social and Athletic Readjustment Rating Scale (SAARS). *Journal of Human Stress,* 1, 6–20.

Brown, R.B. (1971). Personality characteristics related to injuries in football. *Research Quarterly for Exercise and Sport,* 42, 133–138.

Bunker, L., & Williams, J.M. (1986). Cognitive techniques for improving performance and building confidence. In J.M. Williams (Ed.), *Applied sport psychology: Personal growth to peak performance* (pp. 235–255). Palo Alto, CA: Mayfield.

Carron, A.V. (1986). The sport team as an effective group. In J.M. Williams (Ed.), *Applied sport psychology: Personal growth to peak performance* (pp. 75–91). Palo Alto, CA: Mayfield.

Christensen, J.F. (1981). Assessment of stress: Environmental, intrapersonal, and outcome issues. In P. MacReynolds (Ed.), *Advances in psychological assessment.* Vol. 5 (pp. 62–123). San Francisco: Jossey-Bass.

Coddington, R.D., & Troxell, J.R. (1980). The effect of emotional factors on football injury rates: A pilot study. *Journal of Human Stress,* 6, 3–5.

Creed, F. (1985). Invited review: Life events and physical illness. *Journal of Psychosomatic Research,* 29, 113–123

Crossman, J. (1985). Psychosocial factors and athletic injury. *Journal of Sports Medicine and Physical Fitness,* 25, 151–154.

Cryan, P.O., & Alles, E.F. (1983). The relationship between stress and football injuries. *Journal of Sports Medicine and Physical Fitness,* 23, 52–58.

Ellis, A. (1962). *Reason and emotion in psychotherapy.* New York: Lyle Stewart.

Fischer, A.C. (1984). New directions in sport personality research. In J.M. Silva & R.S. Weinberg (Eds.), *Psychological foundations of sport* (pp. 70–80). Champaign, IL: Human Kinetics.

Garrity, T.F., & Marx, M.B. (1985). Effects of moderator variables on the response to stress. In S.R. Burchfield (Ed.), *Stress: Psychological and physiological interactions* (pp. 223–240). New York: Hemisphere.

Hancock, P.A. (1984). Environmental stressors. In J.S. Warm (Ed.), *Sustained attention and human performance* (pp. 103–142). New York: Wiley.

Hardy, C.J., Prentice, W.E., Kirsanoff, M.T., Richman, J.M., & Rosenfeld, L.B. (1987, June). Life stress, social support, and athletic injury: In search of relationships. In J.M. Williams (Chair), Psychological factors in injury occurrence. Symposium conducted at the meeting of the NASPSPA, Vancouver.

Harris, D.V. (1986). Relaxation and energizing techniques for regulation of arousal. In J.M. Williams (Ed.), *Applied sport psychology: Personal growth to peak performance* (pp. 185–207). Palo Alto, CA: Mayfield.

Heyman, S.R. (1984). Cognitive interventions: Theories, interventions, and cautions. In W.F. Straub & J.M. Williams (Eds.), *Cognitive sport psychology* (pp. 289–303). Lansing, NY: Sport Science Associates.

Holmes, T.H. (1970). Psychological screening. In *Football injuries: Papers presented at a workshop* (pp. 211–214). (Sponsored by Subcommittee on Athletic Injuries, Committee on the Skeletal System, Division of Medical Sciences, National Research Council, Feb. 1969). Washington, DC: National Academy of Sciences.

Holmes, T.H., & Rahe, R.H. (1967). The Social Readjustment Rating Scale. *Journal of Psychosomatic Research,* 11, 213–218.

Hull, J.G., Van Treuren, R.R., & Virnelli, S. (1987). Hardiness and health: A critique and alternative approach. *Journal of Personality and Social Psychology,* 53, 518–530.

Irvin, R.F. (1975). Relationship between personality and the incidence of injuries to high school football participants. *Dissertation Abstracts International,* 36, 4328-A.

Jackson, D.W., Jarrett, H., Barley, D., Kausch, J., Swanson, J.J., & Powell, J.W. (1978). Injury prediction in the young athlete. *American Journal of Sports Medicine,* 6, 6–14.

Jenkins, C.D. (1979). Psychosocial modifiers of response to stress. *Journal of Human Stress,* 5, 3–15.

Kanner, A.D., Coyne, J.C., Schaefer, C., & Lazarus, R.S. (1981). Comparison of two modes of stress measurement: Daily hassles and uplifts versus major life events. *Journal of Behavioral Medicine,* 4, 1–39.

Kobasa, S.C. (1979). Stressful life events, personality and health: An inquiry into hardiness. *Journal of Personality and Social Psychology,* 37, 1–11.

Kobasa, S.C., Maddi, S.R., & Puccetti, M.C. (1982). Personality and exercise as buffers in the stress–illness relationship. *Journal of Behavioral Medicine,* 5, 391–404.

Lysens, R., Auweele, Y.V., & Ostyn, M. (1986). The relationship between psychosocial factors and sports injuries. *Journal of Sports Medicine and Physical Fitness,* 26, 77–84.

Miller, L.H., & Smith, A.D. (1982, December). Stress audit questionnaire. *Bostonia: In-depth,* pp. 39–54.

Monroe, S.M. (1983). Major and minor life events as predictors of psychological distress: Further issues and findings. *Journal of Behavioral Medicine,* 6, 189–205.

Nideffer, R.M. (1983). The injured athlete: Psychological factors in treatment. *Orthopedic Clinics of North America,* 14, 373–385.

Ogilvie, B.C. (1966). *Problem athletes and how to handle them.* London: Pelham.

Passer, M.W., & Seese, M.D. (1983). Life stress and athletic injury: Examination of positive versus negative events and three moderator variables. *Journal of Human Stress,* 9, 11–16.

Pelletier, K.R. (1977). *Mind as healer, mind as slayer.* New York: Delacorte Press/Seymour Lawrence.

Rotter, J.B. (1966). Generalized expectancies for internal versus external control of reinforcement. *Psychological Monographs,* 80 (1, Whole No. 609).

Sarason, I.G., Johnson, J.H., & Siegel, J.M. (1978). Assessing the impact of life changes: Development of the Life Experiences Survey. *Journal of Consulting and Clinical Psychology,* 46, 932–946.

Sarason, I.G., Levine, H.M., Basham, R.B., & Sarason, B.R. (1983). Assessing social support: The Social Support Questionnaire. *Journal of Personality and Social Psychology,* 44, 127–139.

Sarason, I.G., Sarason, B.R., & Johnson, J.H. (1985). Stressful life events: Measurement, moderators, and adaptation. In S.R. Burchfield (Ed.), *Stress: Psychological and physiological interactions* (pp. 241–261). New York: Hemisphere.

Schmid, A., & Pepper, E. (1986). Techniques for training concentration. In J.M. Williams (Ed.), *Applied sport psychology: Personal growth to peak performance* (pp. 271–284). Palo Alto, CA: Mayfield.

Selzer, M.L., & Vinokur, A. (1974). Life events, subjective stress, and traffic accidents. *American Journal of Psychiatry,* **131**, 903–906.

Smith, R.E. (1980). A cognitive affective approach to stress management for athletes. In C.H. Nadeau, W.R. Halliwell, K.M. Newell, & G.C. Roberts (Eds.), *Psychology of motor behavior and sport* (pp. 54–72). Champaign, IL: Human Kinetics.

Stuart, J.C., & Brown, B.M. (1981). The relationship of stress and coping ability to incidence of diseases and accidents. *Journal of Psychosomatic Research,* 25, 255–260.

Valiant, P.M. (1981). Personality and injury in competitive runners. *Perceptual and Motor Skills,* 53, 251–253.

Vinokur, A., & Selzer, M.L. (1975). Desirable versus undesirable life events: Their relationship to stress and mental distress. *Journal of Personality and Social Psychology,* 32, 329–337.

Williams, J.M., & Andersen, M.B. (1986, June). The relationship between psychological factors and injury occurrence. In J. Heil (Chair), Psychological aspects of sport injury. Symposium conducted at the meeting of the NASPSPA, Scottsdale, AZ.

Williams, J.M., Haggert, J., Tonymon, P., & Wadsworth, W.A. (1986). Life stress and prediction of athletic injuries in volleyball, basketball, and cross-country running. In L.E. Unestahl (Ed.), *Sport psychology in theory and practice.* Orebro, Sweden: Veje Publishers.

Williams, J.M., Tonymon, P., & Wadsworth, W.A. (1986). Relationship of stress to injury in intercollegiate volleyball. *Journal of Human Stress,* 12, 38–43.

34 Historical and Conceptual Roots of Exercise Psychology

W. JACK REJESKI AND AMY THOMPSON
Wake Forest University

In the past four decades, knowledge in sport psychology has virtually exploded. Unlike their forerunners, current sport psychologists can hardly be experts in every area of this rapidly expanding field. From a historical perspective, this state of affairs led to the distinction between sport psychology and motor learning and control as separate domains in sport science. Later on, new subspecializations emerged in sport psychology. Toward the end of the 1980s, the most visible growth could be registered in the area of exercise psychology.

In 1988, Rejeski and Brawley wrote an article in which they attempted to define the boundaries of sport psychology. These authors noted the definitional ambiguity that was inherent with regard to the subspecialty of exercise psychology. According to these authors, this ambiguity caused serious problems, such as failure to recognize several legitimate areas of research and lack of agreement regarding appropriate academic professional training. It was argued that there was no proper specification of what the term exercise denotes. Without such a specification, the discussion of exercise psychology and its health-related outcomes would be futile.

In continuation of the aforementioned article, Rejeski and Thompson undertook the task of providing an overview of the historical and conceptual roots of exercise psychology, a field existing now for about four decades, and the visible interface between this discipline of sport science and health psychology. They begin their chapter by defining the terms exercise and exercise psychology; then they discuss how exercise psychology and health psychology differ. After making this important distinction, the authors present the historical roots of exercise psychology, making a special reference to significant issues such as fitness and mental health, body image and self-esteem, physical self-concept, physical anxiety, stress reactivity, in-task emotional responses, fatigue and exertion, exercise motivation, exercise metabolism, and performance. Finally, the authors discuss some important issues, such as the modification of the scope of empirical inquiry and professional involvement, as well as the historical lessons to be learned with regard to experimental methods applied and conceptual frameworks used in this area.

In their conclusion, Rejeski and Thompson predicted that significant advancements would be made in the field of exercise psychology. Their prediction (that to avoid repetition of failures made, understanding of the past is necessary) has come to fruition.

Introduction

The information presented in this chapter is based on two key beliefs shared by the editor and the authors. First, it is important that the reader appreciate the relationship of the research presented in this text to the field of study known as "exercise psychology." Such a perspective reveals limitations in our current knowledge base and provides direction for future study. Second, there are historical events, conceptual directions, and technological developments that either have served as or continue to constitute either barriers or facilitating forces in the development of exercise psychology and related fields of study. Awareness of these can elevate the quality of research, creating a more systematic, productive science.

Defining Exercise Psychology

To some, *exercise* includes just about any form of physical exertion, from walking to work to planting the garden. Others, however, believe that the term *exercise* is reserved for vigorous aerobic activity or vigorous resistance training. Indeed, even in the scientific literature, the word *exercise* is used freely without qualification. Are we to assume that this refers to aerobic training conducted according to standards published by the American College of Sports Medicine? Would a circuit training program in a local health spa serve the same purpose?

To understand what the word *exercise* entails, and thus the breadth and boundaries of the subspecialty of exercise psychology, it behooves us to reflect momentarily on the field of exercise physiology. Typically, exercise physiologists define the content of their field around the parameters of physical fitness. These include muscular strength, muscular endurance, cardiopulmonary endurance, flexibility, and body composition. Also, exercise physiologists have a role in science, education, and clinical programs, such as cardiac rehabilitation and corporate fitness. Parallel to the insightful work of Matarazzo (1980) in health psychology, it is also important to note that exercise physiologists contribute knowledge that is important to the explanation, promotion, and maintenance of strength, flexibility, aerobic

Adapted, by permission, from W.J. Rejeski and A. Thompson, 1993, Historical and conceptual roots of exercise psychology. In *Exercise psychology: The influence of physical exercise on psychological processes,* edited by P. Seraganian (Hoboken, NJ: John Wiley and Sons, Inc.), 3-35.

power, and body composition. What then are the implications of the historical basis of exercise physiology for the developing field of exercise psychology?

First of all, it is important to have consistency across fields of study. For example, if exercise psychology was defined in a manner that placed restrictions on the content already established by exercise physiology, it would create problems in the design of curricula. Moreover, professionals would be inadequately trained, and important areas of study would remain underdeveloped. Second, exercise psychology is not limited to the study of aerobic fitness, which was the craze of the 1980s. It also involves exercise forms that enhance strength and range of motion. Moreover, consideration needs to be given to psychological factors that influence perceptions related to physique, as well as actual changes in body composition. In 1988, Rejeski and Brawley, following the lead of Matarazzo (1980) in health psychology, suggested that exercise psychology represented "the application of the educational, scientific, and professional contributions of psychology to the promotion, explanation, maintenance, and enhancement of behaviors related to physical work capacity" (p. 239). The only modification we are suggesting is to replace the words "behaviors related to physical work capacity" with the phrase "the parameters of physical fitness." Thus, *exercise psychology* is the "application of the educational, scientific, and professional contributions of psychology to promoting, explaining, maintaining, and enhancing the parameters of physical fitness." It is concerned with cognitions, emotions, and behaviors that are related to the perception of and/or objective changes in muscular strength and endurance, range of motion, cardiopulmonary endurance, and body composition.

How Exercise and Health Psychology Differ

At this point, a logical question is how to distinguish exercise psychology from health psychology. After all, a major area of research for the past decade has been the role of exercise in enhancing various aspects of psychological well-being. Does this type of research rightfully fall under the umbrella of exercise or of health psychology? Rejeski and Brawley (1988) proposed that a very simple yet effective means of resolving this problem is to further define boundaries through the identification of the primary dependent variables. Hence, if one examined the role of self-efficacy in exertional responses during exercise, it is clearly a study within the field of exercise psychology because the dependent measure in question is exercise based. On the other hand, if the experimental hypothesis was that exercise training enhanced physical self-efficacy, then the study would be more appropriately labeled as health psychology.

In a general exercise psychology course, content would probably include investigations in which exercise is considered as both an independent and a dependent variable. This arrangement is similar to that found in health psychology. For example, health psychologists would want to understand compliance to exercise in order to maximize the efficacy of this health behavior. Additionally, properly trained exercise psychologists can make important contributions to the study of how exercise influences psychological well-being. In particular, most health psychologists do not have formal training in exercise physiology and lack the measurement expertise that is critical to understanding and interpreting exercise manipulations. The interface of exercise and health psychology is essential to the future development of both fields. This is precisely the belief that motivated Seraganian to invite both exercise and health scientists as contributing authors to this text. The outcome should be rewarding for everyone involved.

The Historical Roots of Exercise Psychology

According to our reconstruction, the case study of a female subject in 1884 represents the first published work in exercise psychology. The investigator, C. Rieger, suggested that hypnotic catalepsy greatly facilitated muscular endurance (see Morgan, 1972). Several years later, Norman Triplett (1897), in the *American Journal of Psychology,* published the first experimental study in exercise. In an intriguing paper, Triplett recounted trends that were observed from bicycle records obtained from the Racing Board of the League of American Wheelman. Triplett was fascinated by the apparent facilitative effects of interpersonal competition, and the second part of his paper described an experimental study in which he developed the first hand ergometer to evaluate the performance effects of working alone versus working in competition with another. In his concluding remarks, Triplett noted, "we infer that the bodily presence of another individual contestant participating simultaneously in the race serves to liberate latent energy not ordinarily available" (p. 533). Although not mentioned in the summary, Triplett partitioned his data on the basis of difference scores computed between the alone and the dyadic conditions. He noted that not all individuals experienced a facilitative effect with competition; for some, the competitive environment was debilitating. He described these individuals as overstimulated, exhibiting a feature described as "rigidity of the arms" (p. 523). It would appear that Triplett was the first investigator to observe the adverse effects of competitive anxiety.

Despite this auspicious beginning, between the years 1897 and the late 1970s, the growth of exercise psychology—and of research in which exercise had been treated as an independent variable—was relatively slow. We believe the explanation for this secular trend is the fact that the early part of the twentieth century was a period of history in which attitudes toward sport and exercise were, at best, mixed. For certain, the enhancement of physical skills and physiological potentials were viewed as secondary to intellectual activity. This *competition* between mind and body was also evident in the field of medicine, a perspective that can be traced to the concept of dualism fostered by Plato, Galen, and Descartes, among others (Sarafino, 1990). This split between mind and body in medicine is painfully evident in the biomedical model—the view that all diseases and physical disorders are linked to disturbances in physiological processes. Interestingly, as late as 1986, Taylor argued that the biomedical model continued to be the dominant force in medicine, despite significant challenges to the contrary from contemporary study within the fields of psychosomatic medicine, behavioral medicine, and health psychology.

Despite Taylor's (1986) position, she readily admits that since the late 1970s, there has been a growing awareness on the part of the medical community, and within the general population at large, that dualism is neither a correct nor a constructive philosophical position. Additionally, escalating health-care costs have spawned considerable interest in life-style modification as a means of primary intervention. Coupled with increased leisure time in our society, the past 15 years or so have resulted in new meaning being attributed to exercise and other forms of physical activity. Indeed, exercise is not only linked to physical well-being. As can be seen in this text, there is ample evidence that physical abilities and physical conceptions of the self play an integral role in mental health. The mind-body distinction has slowly, but noticeably yielded to the concept of biopsychosocial interactions—the position that the body, the mind, and the social context of human existence are reciprocally interdependent on one another.

It should not come as a surprise then to find that the 1980s gave rise to a surge of scientific interest in exercise, particularly work in which exercise was studied for its potential therapeutic value in the arena of mental health. Historically, exercise-related investigations fall into 1 of 10 categories: (1) fitness and mental health, (2) body image/esteem, (3) stress reactivity, (4) fatigue/exertion, (5) motivation, (6) exercise performance and metabolic responses, (7) sleep, (8) cognition, (9) the corporate/industrial environment, or (10) exercise addiction.

In the following pages, we provide a selective historical overview of this literature. We have attempted to be particularly sensitive to early investigations, yet provide a contemporary perspective on the field (1983-1990) through the use of a PsychINFO computer search. Although it was impossible to be comprehensive in a single chapter, we have attempted to include key developments and weaknesses that have characterized various lines of research. Additionally, due to restrictions in the length of individual chapters and the focus of the present text, we elected to concentrate on the areas of research that have clear implications for the interface between exercise and mental health. We have omitted research from the final four of the preceding categories: sleep, cognition, the corporate/industrial environment, and exercise addiction. Deleting these areas of study did not hinder the historical sketch we sought to provide.

Fitness and Mental Health

One of the earliest reports in the psychological literature to discuss a connection between exercise and mental health appeared in the 1926 issue of *Occupational Therapy and Rehabilitation*. In this journal, Vaux proposed that exercise helps to relieve cases of depression by promoting nervous-system stimulation and improving glandular secretion. In 1934, Linton, Hamelink, and Hoskins compared the cardiovascular fitness of a group of schizophrenics to a control group drawn from the hospital staff. The mean score of the psychiatric group (Schneider test) was 19% lower than the control group, a finding that was attributed to inactivity of the mental patients. A review paper by Morgan (1969) critiqued six other preexperimental investigations conducted between the years 1936 and 1962. Collectively, these empirical studies suggested that individuals with personality dysfunction also have weakness in their physical-fitness profile. Furthermore, in his review, Morgan (1969) reported on data that were initially quite striking. He found a moderate negative correlation (-0.50) between physical work capacity and depth of depression. We should remember, however, that physical inactivity may be a *consequence* rather than an *antecedent* of poor mental health. Also, the research cited by Morgan involved a very small sample of depressed patients ($n = 7$).

The most comprehensive and informative review of the pre-1980 literature dealing with exercise and mental health appeared in the *American Psychologist* (Folkins & Sime, 1981). Based on an analysis of study designs, these authors concluded that physical fitness training leads to improved mood, self-concept, and work behavior (i.e., reduced absenteeism, reduced errors, and improved output). There was no evidence that exercise interventions altered personality or psychotic symptomatology. Folkins and Sime also noted that the interpretation of published data was complicated by variation across studies in both the intensity and the duration of activity. Moreover, subjects employed in most exercise interventions were volunteers. If individual differences such as preferred coping styles or beliefs in the efficacy of exercise as a therapeutic tool mediate mental health outcomes, then there may well be a positive bias in this literature.

Finally, Folkins and Sime (1981) were highly critical of the theoretical positions evoked to explain the effects of fitness on depression; in fact, as they pointed out, a significant segment of this research literature has been atheoretical. When theoretical explanations were present, it was criticized as being too mechanistic or simplistic. Examples of these include (a) the endorphin hypothesis, (b) the position that exercise exerts a positive effect on mental health through reductions in resting muscle-action potential, (c) the fact that exercise may compete with anxiety-provoking stimuli for limited channel capacity, (d) the impact of exercise on an improved sense of control or mastery, and (e) the meditative experience provided by exercise through altered states of consciousness (see Morgan, 1985a, for a review of the literature pertinent to most of these hypotheses). One alternative offered by Folkins and Sime was to conceptualize exercise as a self-regulatory (coping) process similar to Lazarus's (1975) interpretation of biofeedback. Such a model places cognitive appraisal in a central position for understanding why and how exercise has positive affective consequences. For example, for an executive who is having to deal with occupational stress, acute exercise may have the immediate effect of increasing vigor and decreasing negative affect. However, in such a context, it is likely that exercise serves two purposes: (1) An immediate effect is enhanced affect, and (2) awareness of being able to curb stress responses (secondary appraisal) effectively then strengthens self-efficacy toward coping with job strain.

Through a psychINFO computer search covering 1983 to 1990, we located 23 investigations dealing with the antidepressive effects of exercise and 42 related to anxiety, mood, and various other self-reported symptoms. It is to the credit of those investigating exercise and depression that we have seen increased attention given to groups with documented depressive disorders (≈40%). Across the general area of mental health there has been an interest in women (25%), gender comparisons (57%), and groups with diverse subject characteristics. In addition, significant additions to the mental health literature have been meta-analyses in the areas of depression (North, McCullagh, & Vu Tran (1990), anxiety (Petruzzello, Landers, Hatfield, Kubitz, & Salazar, 1991), and self-concept (McDonald & Hodgdon, 1991).

The quantitative review on depression by North and his colleagues (1990) led to the conclusion that both chronic and acute exercise significantly reduce both state and trait depression, but that the combined effect of exercise and psychotherapy is greater than exercise alone. While the efficacy of exercise as a treatment for depression appears robust across various populations, the largest decreases are seen in medical and psychological rehabilitation settings and in studies that demonstrate sound internal validity. To the surprise of some, anaerobic work (weight training) was found to be an effective form of therapy, and there was evidence that changes in depression occurred early in several programs of research, at a time before physiological training effects had occurred. At the same time, however, it does appear that length of time spent in exercise therapy correlates positively with the decreases seen in depression.

The meta-analysis by Petruzzello et al. (1991) revealed a general anxiolyic effect for aerobic exercise on state anxiety, trait anxiety, and the psychophysiological correlates of anxiety (blood pressure, heart rate, muscle tension, skin responses, brain-wave activity, and the Hoffman reflex). There was some support for the proposition that at least 20 minutes of activity is required to reduce state and trait anxiety; however, this effect was confounded by the fact that a significant number of the investigations that employed 20 minutes of exercise or less compared exercise to other treatments, as opposed to no-treatment controls, possibly creating a negative bias. When the authors restricted their analyses to exercise versus no-treatment control comparisons, there was no support for the proposed 20-minute cut point. Also of interest was an analysis of how duration of activity influenced psychophysiological correlates of anxiety. The largest effect sizes were found for exercise of 30 minutes or less. In other words, it appears that the psychophysiological correlates of anxiety are adversely affected by duration of each training session.

Finally, McDonald and Hodgdon's (1991) review of the self-concept literature found that exercise leads to improved conceptions of the self across diverse psychometric measures that differ both in the construct being assessed and in the measure's level of specificity (e.g., body cathexis vs. global self-esteem). There was no evidence for gender differences; however, the largest effect size was obtained for senior citizens. It is also interesting to note that aerobic dance was found to be as effective in improving self-concept as standard aerobic exercise (i.e., jogging or running). It is also important to emphasize that recent theoretical developments in this area call for a hierarchical structure of concepts, based on level of specificity. For example, Sonstroem and Morgan (1989) have hypothesized that changes in physical self-efficacy enhance more general levels of physical competence and physical acceptance, which jointly contribute to global self-esteem. Indeed, research in cardiac rehabilitation has shown that resistance training can substantially improve patients' confidence in strength-related abilities, consequences that have ramifications for both mental health and physical recovery (Ewart, 1989). Also, Fox and Corbin (1989), in developing the Physical Self-perception Profile, have provided preliminary data to support the position that conceptions of the physical self are related in a hierarchical fashion to more global aspects of self-esteem. It is surprising, however, that these new developments have failed to incorporate important conceptual distinctions into their models. For example, self-esteem and body image do not simply differ in their degree of specificity. This problem is addressed in greater detail in the following section on body image and related constructs.

In summary, it is unfortunate that 50% of the empirical studies on exercise and mental health issues identified in our search employed preexperimental designs. There is very restricted information on how depressive symptoms are influenced by acute bouts of physical work, and most studies involving chronic exercise continue to provide insufficient information concerning the intensity of the exercise stimulus. Interestingly, one study in the literature on the chronic effects of physical work manipulated the intensity of exercise (Blumenthal, Emery, & Rejeski, 1988). In that study, cardiac patients exercised for 3 months at either 65–75% of heart rate reserve (HRR) or below 45% HRR. Contrary to expectations, both groups made significant improvements in cardiovascular function; however, there was no main effect of time in relation to psychosocial status. It is worth noting that individuals who were clinically depressed at the onset of the study did appear to derive some therapeutic value from exercise; however, due to the absence of a no-treatment control, the possibility of regression to the mean cannot be ignored. Parenthetically, not all literature reviews have placed the same degree of confidence in the antidepressive effects of exercise as the North et al. (1990) meta-analysis. For example, Dunn and Dishman (1991) have argued that the existing research is too weak and varied for any firm consensus statement.

An additional concern we have with the mental-health literature pertains to the assessment of mood in acute exercise settings. In our own laboratory (Rejeski, Hardy, & Shaw, 1991), we have shown that traditional psychometric measures, when they are used either during or in close proximity to exercise, may be confounded by somatic changes induced by the accompanying physical stress. Quite frankly, in this area of exercise psychology, research is needed to verify the construct validity of measures such as the State-Trait Anxiety Inventory (STAI) and the Profile of Mood States (POMS). A simple example of interpretational problems that can exist is found in an abstract published by Morgan and Horstman (1976). Using the STAI, these investigators described an increase in anxiety with exercise. When we attempted to replicate these data using the short form of the STAI (Rejeski et al., 1991), we found that increased anxiety during exercise was due to elevation in two STAI items. Other measures taken permitted us to verify that these changes were due to elevated biological responses that had nothing whatsoever to do with cognitive or somatic anxiety. In fact, the internal consistency of the STAI during exercise was totally unacceptable (0.33). Another study conducted by Steptoe and Cox (1988) is subject to similar problems. These investigators reported that high-intensity exercise has negative effects on mood when assessments are taken immediately following exercise. The concern here is that it is incorrect to assume that all changes in arousal denote negative psychological states. For example, is it any surprise that subjects report feeling more tense or shaky after they just exercised at 100 watts for 8 minutes? Is this the same tension that people feel when they are under job strain? Along these same lines, the meta-analysis by Petruzzello et al. (1991) is characterized as a review of the anxiety literature. However, their work does not acknowledge differences between tension and anxiety. Furthermore, they found that the psychophysiological correlates of anxiety were adversely affected by duration of activity. It is important to underscore the fact that physiological measures alone cannot be taken as evidence that anxiety is present or absent, a point that was made earlier in our discussion of the STAI.

Finally, a major challenge that remains in the literature on exercise and mental health is teasing out the conceptual basis for observed effects. Although, it is beyond the scope of this chapter to explore this point in any detail, from a historical perspective, several comments seem relevant. First, there is considerable evidence that psychological outcomes of exercise therapy need not be contingent on changes in physiological parameters. As one example, Rodin (1988) found that consistent high-efficacy feedback to exercisers (e.g., "You are doing something you should be proud of") greatly facilitated a variety of positive mental-health outcomes when contrasted with a group of exercisers who received no such feedback. Second, both human and lower-animal research leave open the possibility that enhanced aminergic synaptic transmission plays a role in at least some cases where exercise has antidepressant effects (Dunn & Dishman, 1991; Ransford, 1982). It seems judicious to encourage the study of both biological and social cognitive variables simultaneously. Third, in chronic programs of exercise, it may well be the repeated acute bouts of exercise that explain positive mental-health outcomes. Training effects may or may not be necessary. Rather than simply using a pretest/posttest design, previous research suggests that psychological outcomes should be monitored using continuous assessments. Along these lines, the comments of Lise Gauvin and Lawrence Brawley's concerning experiential sampling are particularly relevant.

Body Image, Physical Self-Concept, Body Esteem, and Physique Anxiety

In 1935, Schilder first defined the concept of body image as "the picture of our body which we form in own mind" (p. 11). Another related concept, *body affect* (also called "body esteem"), refers to how satisfied or dissatisfied individuals are with various aspects of their body (Secord & Jourard, 1953). In fact Secord and Jourard (1953) originally used the term *body cathexis* to separate feelings that people had about their body from perceptions concerning its objective size and shape.

Early research on body image and affect focused on body-image disturbances that were evident in clinical populations, such as individuals with neurological impairment (Kolb, 1959) or physical deformities (Schonfeld, 1962). However, it was soon realized that perceptual distortions of body image were more ubiquitous and were present in normal populations as well (Cappon & Banks, 1968). For instance, Miller, Linke, and Linke (1980) reported that 54% of college undergraduates were dissatisfied with their weight, a trend that has been found to be gender dependent. In particular, women tend to consistently overestimate their body size when compared to men (e.g., Clifford, 1971) and to express a desired weight that is 14 pounds lighter than their actual weight (Miller et al. (1980). An intriguing fact about the work of Miller and his colleagues (1980) is that only 39% of the women could be classified as overweight by objective standards, yet 70% reported that they were at least slightly overweight. It should be noted, however, that a significant portion of the variance in dysfunctions of body image/esteem frequently has an objective basis. That is to say, individuals with a higher percentage of body fat are particularly prone to disturbances in body image (Young & Reeve, 1980) and body-esteem (Mendelson & White, 1985).

An important finding is that disturbances in body image/esteem are related to general conceptions and feelings about the self (Rosen & Ross, 1968; Rohrbacker, 1973). For both males and females, dissatisfaction with body image has been found to correlate with low self-esteem, (Hawkins, Turrell, & Jackson, 1983), insecurity (Hurlock, 1967), and depression (Marsella, Shizuru, Brennan, & Kameoka, 1981). Tucker (1983a) studied the relationships between muscular strength and mental health in college men. After covarying body weight, he found that strength was positively related to body esteem, emotional stability, facets of extroversion, and confidence. In a related training study, Tucker (1983b) evaluated the impact of weight training on the self-concept of college males. Although there are limitations in the design due to static group comparisons, he did find that individuals enrolled in weight-training classes experienced significant improvements in self-concept when contrasted with subjects taking coursework in personal health. Also of interest was the finding that improvements in self-concept were related to changes in neuroticism, body cathexis, and muscular-strength scores.

Since 1984, several studies have examined the relationship between various physical activities and changes in women's body image/esteem. For example, Skrinar, Bullen, Cheek, and McArthur (1986), using a single-group preexperimental design, reported that aerobic exercise improves middle-aged women's perception of internal body consciousness and enhances feelings of body competence. Riddick and Freitag (1984) suggested that exercise has a positive influence on the body image of elderly women; however, the design of this study was also preexperimental. The best study to date was conducted by Ben-Shlomo and Short (1985-1986). They randomized middle-aged women into one of three conditions: 6 weeks of arm training, 6 weeks of leg training, or no-treatment control. Those who exercised had improved physical self-concepts and showed marginally significant improvement in body cathexis.

An important development in the body-image/esteem literature has been the gradual realization that critical gender differences exist. Specifically, Franzoi and Shields (1984) found that dimensions of body esteem for male college students consist of physical attractiveness, upper-body strength, and physical condition. Conversely, for college women, the dimensions of esteem were sexual attractiveness, weight concern, and physical condition. An independent report by Silberstein, Striegel-Moore, Timko, and Rodin (1988) found that men were as likely to want to be heavier as thinner, whereas virtually no women wished to be heavier. These two studies suggest that men and women have different motives for and will seek different outcomes from physical training. Based on these data, it is odd to discover that the recent development of a physical self-perception profile (Fox & Corbin, 1989) appears not to have considered gender differences in the development of the subscales. Moreover, investigators in exercise science have not been careful in their use of constructs such as "self-efficacy," "body image," "body-concept," "body esteem," and so forth. For example, Sonstroem and Morgan (1989) have offered a hierarchical model of self-perceptions that are influenced by exercise. The model's hierarchy ascends from the specific to the general and proposes that "self-efficacy statements relative to particular physical tasks represent the lowest generality level of the competence dimension" (p. 333). Moreover, self-efficacy is proposed to feed a higher level of physical competence (the general evaluation of physical fitness), which combines with physical acceptance (i.e., body cathexis) to determine global self-esteem. One problem with this model is the lack of congruence among the levels of construction. For example, self-efficacy toward specific physical tasks need not translate into more general feelings of competence about *one's level of physical fitness.* A single bout of exercise via a treadmill exam can bring cardiac patients to the realization that they were not as disabled as they once thought. While this may increase their physical competence, there need not be (and probably is not) a change in the evaluation of their physical fitness per se. Similarly, increasing coordination through aerobic dance has important ramifications for physical competence and more global conceptions of the self, yet these increases are unrelated to fitness.

There is an enormous amount of literature on body-image/esteem. Several hundred entries were located across a 7-year period. Unfortunately, many studies published during the past decade continue to be correlational, and there has been limited interest in the interface between these topics and exercise behavior. Hart, Leary, and Rejeski (1989) have suggested that an interesting and neglected area of study is the socially based anxiety that people have regarding their physiques. They constructed a social-physique anxiety measure and argued that self-presentational motives related to this form of anxiety have implications for (a) the physical activities in which people engage, (b) where and with whom they do so, and (c) the enjoyment they derive from such involvement. "Research should begin to explore the impact of physique anxiety on recreational activities, particularly on the degree to which concerns with others' evaluations inhibit people from participating in physical activities that would be beneficial to them. Ironically, individuals who have the greatest need for aerobic exercise may be the most reluctant to engage in it because of their concerns with others' impressions of them" (p. 102).

Exercise as a Buffer to Stress Reactivity

In the past decade, there has been substantial interest in the potential effects that exercise may have on reducing the biological consequences of stress. Although most of the attention has been directed toward the effects of fitness training on reactivity, there has been some work on the effects that acute bouts of exercise have on subsequent responses to psychological stress. Even though most of the research activity is recent, there are traces of work in this area as early as the 1950s. For example, in 1957, Michael published a review on "Stress Adaption Through Exercise." He cited Van Liere as one of the first investigators to study the effects of exercise and the autonomic nervous system. Van Liere had found that exercising rats manifested increased propulsive motility of the small intestine, as compared to a group of nonexercising rats. This was attributed to the positive influence of exercise on the parasympathetic nervous system. Michael (1957) also reviewed work on stress and the adrenal glands, concluding—largely from indirect evidence—that "the increased adrenal activity resulting from repeated exercise seems to cause an increase in the reserve of steroids available to counter stress" (p. 53).

In 1987, Crews and Landers conducted "A Meta-analytic Review of Aerobic Fitness and Reactivity to Psychosocial Stressors." From examining their data and the research published over the past 3 years, a fairly clear historical picture emerged. First, despite the early efforts of Michael (1957), research on this topic really did not blossom until the late 1970s (Cantor, Zillman, & Day, 1978; Cox, Evans, & Jamieson, 1979; Sime, 1977). Up until 1987, 74% of the studies conducted dealt with chronic exercise, and the majority were correlational (77%). For the most part, dependent measures have focused on cardiovascular function via blood pressure and heart rate; however, recent publications suggest that this trend may be changing. In their conclusion, Crews and Landers (1987) stated that "the mean ES was 0.48 which was significantly different from zero (P<.0l). Thus, the effect of aerobic exercise on psychosocial stress response amounts to approximately one-half of a standard deviation above that of the control group or baseline value" (p. S118). We should add, however, that recent longitudinal studies have challenged the conclusions reached by Crews and Landers (1987). For example, a carefully executed investigation by de Geus, Lorenz, vanDoornen, de Visser, and Orlebeke (1990) has compared cross-sectional and training data in the same study. Interestingly, they found support for the proposition that exercise buffers stress reactivity using a cross-sectional approach; however, they failed to support this hypothesis using a 7-week training program. It is possible, of course, that there is a dose-response relationship involved. In other words, subjects may have to train for 3 months or more before exercise has a noticeable effect on stress reactivity. Perhaps this explains why the stress-buffering hypothesis of exercise is supported by cross-sectional data. On the other hand, de Geus and his colleagues (1990) point out that the "concurrent effects of constitution on both aerobic exercise and diastolic or vagal reactivity cannot be excluded by correlational analyses" p. 473.

There are three points that we would like to consider from a historical perspective. First, until recently, much of the research addressed the therapeutic value of chronic as opposed to acute exercise. More important, in Crews and Landers's review, the mean effect size for investigations involving acute bouts of activity (0.11) was considerably lower than that reported for chronic training effects (0.59). Regrettably, however, previous studies involving acute exercise and stress reactivity have been poorly designed (see Rejeski, Gregg, Thompson, & Berry, 1991). For example, one shortcoming in early work was the heavy emphasis placed on the use of heart rate (HR) as an index of stress reactivity. The dilemma facing investigators is that HR remains elevated for an extended period following exercise, a condition that confounds its use as an index of change in subsequent stress manipulations. Moreover, there has been some indication that researchers would benefit from focusing on peripheral, as opposed to central, factors. In particular, vanDoornen, de Geus, and Orlebeke (1988) argue that "the effect of fitness on adrenoceptor sensitivity suggests that the most important effect of fitness might be found in the vascular part of the stress response" p. 303). A second problem is that many of the early studies on acute exercise elected to use very low doses of work. It is not uncommon to find intensities lower than 60% of maximum aerobic capacity and durations less than 15 minutes. Interestingly, we (Rejeski et al., 1991) produced evidence in support of a positive dose-response relationship between acute exercise and subsequent blood-pressure reactivity to stress.

Second, the recent availability of reliable ambulatory blood pressure devices now makes it possible to examine how long the effects of acute exercise persist. In fact, data from a paper delivered by Ebbesen, Prkachin, and Mills (1989) suggest that exercise may buffer blood-pressure responses to some stressors for as long as 3 hours postexercise. This same technology can be used to track the effects of fitness training on responses to daily stress or to examine the influence of acute and chronic physical activity on average responses across different phases of daily living. It is also worth noting that the data reported by Ebbesen et al. revealed a potential confound in studies involving chronic exercise and stress reactivity. That is, if investigators do not ensure that subjects have refrained from acute exercise for as long as 3 or 4 hours prior to psychophysiological studies, it is possible that significant findings are inappropriately attributed to training.

Third, we question the suitability of the conceptual model that has dominated this line of empirical inquiry. Typically, investigators rely exclusively on physiological mechanisms to explain the positive effects that exercise—either acute or chronic—has on various biological stress responses. In our view, this historical trend has created a number of methodological shortcomings and ignores the possibility that a broader social-psychobiological framework is required to understand the problem at hand. For example, far too many experiments now in the literature have failed to provide documentation that their stress manipulations were successful. It is well recognized in the psychological literature that stress is an interactive process between individuals and their environments. It is inappropriate to *assume* that an objective demand selected by the experimenter places subjects in a position of threat or challenge. Furthermore, we might ask whether the effects of exercise on stress reactivity are similar for perceptions of threat versus challenge and how other features of the stressor (e.g., whether an active coping response is elicited) influence various outcomes. A broader conceptual model integrating social, psychological, and biological variables is also essential to teasing out potential cognitive and/or emotive-based causal networks. For example, as mentioned earlier in this chapter, work by Lazarus (1975) places exercise in the realm of *secondary appraisal*; that is, once the threat of challenge or harm is realized, a major determinant of physiological reactivity is subjects' cognitive evaluation of skills and resources that they have to combat the demand. The perception that exercise is beneficial or that it has enhanced an individual's hardiness in some way could constitute critical mediating variables.

The Study of Fatigue/Exertion and In-Task Emotional Responses

It is beyond the scope of this chapter to provide a detailed historical treatise on fatigue. Its importance as a psychological construct can be traced to the work of Thorndike at the beginning of the twentieth century (e.g., Thorndike, 1912), but the term has been used to describe various forms of incapacitation, including such diverse topics as (a) cellular activity, (b) x-ray irradiation, (c) changes in the visual and auditory systems, (d) deterioration in intellectual functioning, and (e) studies of exertion in various work situations (Bartley, 1976). It is this lack of specificity that made the work of Gunnar Borg particularly appealing. In 1962, he published a monograph on "Physical Performance and Perceived Exertion." Although Borg had conducted research as early as 1960, it was his publications from 1962 through 1968 that appear to have served as the impetus for the large volume of exercise research that followed in the 1970s and 1980s. Indeed, a significant feature of Borg's work is that in addition to presenting a clearly defined construct, he offered a simple and psychometrically sound approach to reliably assess ratings of perceived exertion (RPE).

From a conceptual viewpoint, it is instructive to track the history of this construct. Borg is a psychophysicist whose assumptions place RPE within a unidirectional sensory model. What this means is that, much like motor reflexes, subjective estimates of exertion are believed to be automatic, the function of direct sensory input (Borg, 1985, personal communication). Thus, for the first decade or so, RPE existed as a construct independent of emotion and conscious thought processes. Most of the attention was directed toward investigating the physiological correlates of RPE and documenting the manner in which individual differences such as disease or level of fitness moderated such responses. Much like B. F. Skinner's (1990) position, there was no need for theory.

There were, however, three important exceptions to this exclusive physiological orientation. Specifically, in the early 1970s, Morgan (1973) published a paper on the role of personality in perceived exertion. He demonstrated that anxious neurotics and depressives at moderate workloads and extroverts at heavy workloads tend to underestimate RPE. These conclusions, however, were based on data from very small sample sizes and had to be viewed cautiously. In a second line of research, Morgan and his colleagues (e.g., Morgan, Raven, Drinkwater, & Horvath, 1973) studied the effect of hypnotic suggestion on ratings of perceived exertion. Their data provided the first indication that a cognitive manipulation (i.e., suggestion) could alter perceptual responses.

In that same year, Weiser and his colleagues (Weiser, Kinsman, & Stamper, 1973), working with bicycle ergometry, demonstrated that subjective responses during exercise could be differentiated into local, central, and general fatigue. More important, they offered a conceptual model, which introduced the proposition that subjective factors such as motivation contributed to the fatigue experience. It is important to note that the work of these researchers represented a departure from Borg's conception of perceived exertion. Unfortunately, their model was reductionistic; that is, the origin of all subjective experience was proposed to be rooted in physiological substrata. Furthermore, despite two chapters dedicated to the "Introspective Aspects of Work and Fatigue," which appeared in a 1976 text (Simonson & Weiser), the main influence of this work on RPE research was that it led to the measurement of specific, as well as generalized, responses. For example, in a typical experiment, subjects might be asked to provide local (e.g., ratings of the legs) as well as general RPEs. As one might suspect, research in the late 1970s was designed to evaluate the physiological basis of these differentiated ratings (cf. Pandolf, 1977).

A paper in the early 1980s (Rejeski, 1981) was designed to integrate the RPE research that had been conducted during the 1960s and 1970s. The major objective of this review was to underscore the fact that exertional responses are *not* analogous to muscle reflexes or amenable to a strict psychophysical paradigm. Rather, psychological dispositions and social-cognitive variables constitute potent mediating mechanisms in the perceived sense of effort. Morgan's work (Morgan 1973, Morgan et al., 1983) certainly offered support for this supposition, as did research in our own laboratory (Rejeski & Ribisl, 1980), which had demonstrated that RPEs given at a particular point in exercise are affected by the expected duration of a task. In the 1981 review, I also proposed (Rejeski, 1981) that the relative contribution of subjective and objective input to perceptions of exertion will depend on the intensity and duration of the exercise stimulus. For example, when a physical demand is excessive, powerful metabolic changes may preclude cognitive manipulations from enabling someone to continue an activity.

In the mid-1980s, a conceptual paper appeared (Rejeski, 1985), which reinforced the idea that self-reported exertion involves an "active" rather than a "passive" subject. In this report, discussion and empirical support was provided for Leventhal and Everhart's (1979) parallel process model of pain. For example, we have published data indicating that preconscious cognitive and emotional schemas influence that extent to which subjects rate the difficulty of physical work (e.g., Hochstetler, Rejeski, & Best, 1985). Moreover, in an experimental context (Rejeski & Sanford, 1984), we have shown that emotional schemas concerning exercise can be primed and altered using social models. That is, RPEs are influenced by how negatively subjects view physical activity. In 1986, in an independent laboratory, Hardy, Hall, and Presholdt demonstrated that RPEs can be influenced by self-presentational motives. This position was corroborated by the work of Boutcher, Fleischer-Curtian, and Gines (1988), who found that males gave lower RPEs with female than with male experimenters.

When we examined the trends in the RPE research since 1985, 20 entries were found, 10 of which involved college students. There was a fairly even split on gender and a propensity toward the study of social cognitive variables (35%). Moreover, 50% of the study designs were experimental or quasi-experimental. Overall, these date are quite encouraging. In contrast to earlier work, more of the contemporary research is theory driven, with a balance of attention now being given to the study of both men and women. For the future, it is important to build on the social-psychobiological framework that was precipitated by the psychometric contributions of Borg and the early research on cognition by Morgan (see Rejeski, 1985). We would encourage more experimental work on the possible social basis of schemata that are pertinent to the processing of exercise-induced changes in various biological systems. Based on recent date from our own laboratory, we suspect that aversion to exercise symptoms profoundly influence responses both to acute episodes of work and to chronic patterns of physical activity.

The concern that we have for subjects' both preconscious and conscious affective responses toward exercise symptoms (see Rejeski, 1985) motivated us to study a central in-task dimensional feature of affect—that is, how good or bad a person feels when involved in exercise (Hardy & Rejeski, 1989; Rejeski, Best, Griffith, & Kenney, 1987). It has become quite clear that the measurement of RPE and positive or negative "feelings" are distinct enough from a measurement perspective to warrant individual instruments (Hardy & Rejeski, 1989). For example, Boutcher and Trenske (1990) found that the introduction of music to controlled bouts of exercise did not alter RPE; however, subjects reported a better feeling about working under these conditions. Similarly, Kenney, Rejeski, and Messier (1988) reported that distress-management training provided for novice women runners resulted in improved feelings but no change in the RPEs of fixed workloads. Because data also indicate that feminine-typed men (e.g., submissive, emotional, dependent) are, in general, less positive toward exercise symptoms (Rejeski et al., 1987), it appears that both dispositional and situational variables can influence the feelings that subjects experience during exercise. We think that an interesting area of study for the future is the manner in which in-task feelings contribute to motivational states, as well as to the acute and chronic effects of exercise on various mental-health outcomes. Finally, we would encourage investigators to further explore the subjective realm of exercise behavior because we readily admit to the limitations inherent in a single-item affect measure.

Exercise Motivation

An issue that is interconnected with nearly every topic discussed in this opening chapter is the problem of motivating people to exercise. What is the key to keeping depressed patients involved in exercise therapy? How are subjective responses to exercise-related symptoms related to participant motivation? Do concerns regarding peer evaluation of physique or feelings of low self-efficacy serve as deterrents to physically active life-styles? These and related questions suggest that the topic of exercise motivation may be the most important of all. However, other than Kenyon's (1968) work in the mid-1960s, interest in this facet of exercise psychology did not blossom until the late 1970s and early 1980s.

Rod Dishman and his colleagues (Dishman, 1982, 1986, 1988; Dishman, Sallis, & Orenstein, 1985) have provided extensive reviews of research on factors that correlate with the initiation of and compliance with programs of exercise.

What we wish to emphasize in this chapter is how various conceptual/theoretical models may have limited what we know and why some of the conclusions reached may be misdirected.

It is our impression that the growth of interest in exercise motivation during the late 1970s was precipitated, in part, by the increased popularity of applied programs in behavioral medicine (e.g., cardiac rehabilitation), which relied on exercise therapy as its principal mode of intervention. As one would expect, the early research was characterized by descriptive investigations that were largely atheoretical (e.g., Andrew & Parker, 1979; Oldridge & Jones, 1983). Despite this limitation, these data brought to our attention the potential importance of both individual differences and situational/environmental barriers as determinants of exercise behavior. The following decade gave rise to several different lines of research that were designed to increase the systematic study of compliance. For example, Dishman, Ickes, and Morgan (1980) introduced the self-motivation inventory as an individual difference measure of behavioral persistence. There were investigations based on the health-belief model (e.g., Lindsey-Reid & Osborn,

1980), social-learning theory (e.g., Long & Haney, 1986), and self-efficacy theory (e.g., Dzewaltowski, 1989). Fishbein and Ajzen's theory of reasoned action was touted as an improved conceptual model for studying the combined effects of attitudes, beliefs, and intentions (e.g., Riddle, 1980), while a number of investigators examined various facets of cognitive-behavioral modification (see Martin & Dubbert, 1984).

On the bright side, researchers employing different conceptual models have consistently found that compliance to organized exercise programs is significantly related to perceived barriers such as the physical demands of exercise and the time required for training (Dzewaltowski, 1989; Godin, Shephard, & Colantonio, 1986; Sonstroem, 1982). There is evidence that various forms of social support play a significant part in exercise motivation (King, Taylor, Haskell, & Debusk, 1988; Wankel, 1984), and a number of different studies have reinforced the value of various cognitive-behavioral interventions (Martin & Dubbert, 1984). Furthermore, McAuley (1992) recently reviewed research on self-efficacy and was very optimistic about research from both primary and secondary preventive perspectives. By implication, he argued that self-efficacy is a common mechanism that can be employed to explain the effects of seemingly diverse processes such as goal setting and social support. The movement toward parsimonious theoretical explanations ought to be viewed as a step in the right direction; however, according to Rejeski (1992), there are several characteristics of the historical record that create confusion and will continue to cause problems if left uncorrected.

Take for example, the conclusion that "attitudes toward physical activity have not predicted who will eventually adhere or drop-out" (Dishman, 1982, p. 240). Dishman is correct about the studies reviewed; yet, if you examined these investigations, you would find several different operational definitions of *attitudes,* none of which reflected contemporary theory or established measurement protocols. In short, in 1982, it was premature to suggest that attitudes were unrelated to either initiation of or continued involvement in physical activity. Another more complex problem surfaces in the conclusion that "high self-motivation reliably predicts compliance" (Dishman, 1986, p. 143). First of all, not all published results on the self-motivation inventory (SMI) have been positive (see Wankel, 1984). More important, however, are current limitations in the SMI, created by the fact that it was developed independent of any systematic theory. Our point here is simple. Self-motivation may be an important psychological construct; however, the history of psychology tells us that general levels of construction (e.g., "I seldom work to my full capacity") and reliance on single constructs will yield disappointing levels of behavioral prediction (Rotter, 1954). This would suggest that even research on self-efficacy—a situation-specific theory—must be reexamined. For example, freedom from barriers may yield high levels of self-efficacy, yet this cognitive set is unlikely to lead to persistence if the individual involved does not value the outcomes associated with exercise. To reiterate, single constructs are ineffective in providing stable behavioral predictions. We believe that investigators— ourselves included—need to step back and closely reexamine the integrity of conceptual models and theories that serve as the basis for hypothesis testing (see Rejeski, 1992).

Psychological Influences on Exercise Performance and Metabolic Parameters

Exercise Performance. As indicated in the opening paragraph of this section, the earliest recorded investigations in exercise psychology can be traced to the performance research of Reiger and Triplett in the late 1880s. Unfortunately, Triplett's pioneering work did not stimulate systematic study of how social factors influence exercise behavior. In fact, other than studies by Ayres (1911) and Voor, Lloyd, and Cole (1969), there was practically no interest in the social psychology of exercise prior to the late 1970s.

The earlier of the two studies (i.e., Ayres, 1911), utilized an annual bicycle race in Madison Square Garden to test the hypothesis that music enhances performance. It so happened that part of the competition involved routine play by a military band; they would play a musical selection, rest, and repeat this cycle throughout 46 miles of competition. Although there were no statistical comparisons of the two experimental conditions (music vs. no music), Ayres reported that the average speed of the group while the band played was 19.6 mph, whereas when the band stopped, the speed decreased to 17.9 mph! Voor and his colleagues (1969) brought the study of social facilitation to the laboratory. In their study, male college students who participated on intramural teams were tested in one of two conditions: individually or in a group ostensibly involving team competition ($25 was given to the winning team). All subjects were required to hold a submaximal isometric contraction for as long as possible. In the group condition, three individuals performed one at a time, with the average score taken as the team score. During each subject's performance, the two remaining team members were present, to provide whatever encouragement they desired. Contrary to expectations, social facilitation did not improve performance. However, the team atmosphere did lead to higher electromyographic (EMG) responses, which was interpreted as an index of increased stress.

Throughout the early twentieth century and into the 1970s, the principal focus of performance-based research in psychology centered around the *ergogenic* (performance-enhancing) properties of hypnosis (Barber, 1966; Hull, 1933; Morgan, 1972); however, in recent years there have been several lines of research emphasizing the active role that subjects may play in performance enhancement. Shelton and Mahoney (1978), for example, have been able to show that emotional "psych-up" prior to a weightlifting task dramatically increases performance, a finding that has been replicated since in several laboratories (see Weinberg, Gould, Yukelson, & Jackson, 1981). Nelson and Furst (1972) manipulated perceived superiority in a muscular strength/endurance competition and found that objectively weaker opponents who thought they were stronger won 83% of their bouts. Along similar lines, Weinberg et al. (1981) have shown that preexisting and manipulated self-efficacy significantly influence muscular endurance. Yet another direction of empirical inquiry has been the role of active coping in managing exercise distress. Several investigators have reported that distracting attention from the distress of exercise can result in enhanced performance (e.g., Gill & Strom, 1985; Morgan, Horstman, Cymerman, & Stokes, 1983; Weinberg, Smith, Jackson, & Gould, 1984); however, the term *distraction* has been used to describe several different methods that are not conceptually equivalent. Also, no systematic attention has been given to individual differences. This may well be an important consideration, given Rejeski and Kenney's (1987) data, which suggest that cognitive complexity is an important determining factor in the effectiveness of cognitively involved dissociative strategies.

Like other areas of research in exercise psychology, there are general lessons to be learned from the historical footprints left by research on cognition and performance. Morgan (1972) mentioned several methodological problems in his review on hypnosis, which have implications for other programs of research. Most significant, we believe, are the concerns that he expressed regarding confounds between hypnosis and suggestion. Frequently, independent variables in the exercise-psychology literature are too broad and combine variance from multiple sources. For example, in a paper on dissociative cognitive strategies by Morgan and his colleagues (1983), the manipulation of dissociation involved suggestions of "psych-up" and reduced distress in conjunction with some aspects of noncultic relaxation. In reflecting on these data, one is compelled to ask, "Just what was responsible for the observed effect?" This criticism could also be lodged against chronic exercise interventions because they typically involve more than exercise alone. For example, subjects in rehabilitation programs are frequently praised for their performance and typically gain social support from other group members. How then can one be confident that it is the exercise that buffers stress or reduces depression?

A second point related to the first, which was made less explicit by Morgan (1972), is that across investigations, there is substantial variation in the operational definition of *suggestion,* a problem that increases the difficulty of synthesizing information from different laboratories. This concern reminds us of a study in the cognitive-behavioral literature, which examined the relative efficacy of association versus dissociation in improving the attendance rates of males and females in a 12-week exercise program (Martin et al., 1984). The authors reported that dissociation yielded better compliance than association.

> Close inspection of the cognitive strategies, however, suggests that their operational definitions of association and dissociation were inconsistent with contemporary theory (cf. Rejeski, 1985). Normally, association is used to refer to a focus on physical sensations, the attempt is to tune subjects into physiological input so that less cognitive capacity is available for negative affective processing of sensory cues. In contrast, dissociation refers to attentional strategies designed to cover-up or distract subjects from the fatigue-producing effects of exercise. In the Martin et al. study, subjects who associated did focus on physiologic cues, but they were encouraged to "be their own coach," to set high personal standards, and to reemphasize in their own minds that they could do better than they had in the past. By contrast, those in the dissociation condition were told to attend to the environment and pleasant stimuli, to set realistic goals, and to replace self-defeating thoughts with positive coping statements. Thus, at best, their results imply that positive realistic cognitive restructuring is superior to cognitive sets in which performance is the focal point and continued improvement is the mark of success. (Rejeski, 1992, p. 154)

A third point made by Morgan concerns the importance of establishing stable baseline data. As he noted, stable baselines are crucial to drawing inferences about the effects of hypnosis or cognitive manipulations on performance. This is another problem with broad implications. For example, an investigator may employ a field test of cardiovascular fitness as a manipulation check of aerobic conditioning. Let us suppose that an experimental group trained for 15 minutes, twice weekly for 12 weeks, whereas a control group remained sedentary. Improvement in pacing alone would create group differences on the posttest. Parenthetically, such a confound may even exist on submaxirnal tests, where HR is employed as the criterion, or in measuring baseline blood pressure when one is attempting to study the influence of exercise on resting hemodynamics. As reported in a subsequent section, metabolism can be altered by mental processes.

As a final lesson from history, research in cognition and performance reaffirms the importance of emphasizing theory-based research. In light of this, it is unfortunate that work on dissociative strategies has proceeded largely independent of formal theory. Trial and error has yielded some important lessons; however, conceptual models from the pain literature provide the starting point for a much more systematic plan of inquiry (cf. Rejeski, 1985). Additionally, after reading the research in hypnosis, one cannot help but wonder why this technique should enhance performance. Actually, there are several possible hypotheses, yet no agreed-upon theoretical structure to guide research. If this does not change, our sense is that a decade from now, another review on hypnosis will conclude similar to Morgan's (1972): "Hull stated in 1933 that the literature in this area was contradictory, and unfortunately the present review suggests that 40 years of research have failed to provide any clarification" (p. 216).

Psychological Factors and Exercise Metabolism. An interesting area of study, with a 60-year history is the influence that cognition, affect, and the perceived intensity of physical work have on metabolic responses. This body of literature offers strong support to the position that anticipatory reactions to an exercise stimulus and the manner in which subjects process information during exercise significantly alter metabolism. As early as 1939, two Russian scientists, Nemtzova and Shatenstein, reported that hypnotic suggestions of heavy work increased ventilation 14.5 L/ min^{-1} and elevated oxygen uptake by 409 mL/min^{-1} (reported in Morgan 1985b). In a clever comparison, Dudlye and his colleagues (Dudlye, Holmes, Martin, & Ripley, 1964), using hypnotic suggestion, contrasted the metabolic effects of thinking about active and passive behavior/emotions. When subjects were given suggestions of exercise, anxiety, or anger (active responses), their ventilation and oxygen consumption increased, whereas carbon dioxide decreased. The opposite was true for relaxation and depression (passive responses): Ventilation and oxygen consumption decreased while carbon dioxide increased. As Morgan (1985b) stated in a recent review of psychogenic factors in metabolism, data support the position that the mere image of exercise—like other action-oriented responses (e.g., anxiety)—can elevate HR, cardiac output, ventilation, and oxygen uptake.

As noted previously, research also indicates that metabolic responses *during exercise* can be influenced by the way in which exercise stimuli are processed. A demonstration of this effect was published by Morgan (see 1985b review). Subjects in this investigation were required to exercise on a bicycle ergometer in a control waking state and in several hypnotic states. During the control condition, subjects were given the suggestion that the work was of moderate intensity, whereas in the hypnotic states, subjects exercised under the suggestion of light, moderate, or heavy exercise. The principal finding, according to Morgan, was the pattern in the ventilatory data. The suggestion of heavy exercise resulted in a ventilatory response that was 15 L/min higher than the suggestion of moderate work in the waking state. Also, the observed effect for suggestions of heavy work in a hypnotic state was accompanied by increases in both carbon dioxide and the respiratory exchange ratio. Incidentally, an interesting pattern in Morgan's data was the similarity in responses between the suggestion of moderate work, which was given in either a waking or a hypnotic state. In other words, it seems highly probable that suggestion rather than hypnosis is responsible for many effects attributed to the hypnotic trance (Barber, 1966).

The position that conscious cognitive processes can alter metabolic responses has garnered some interesting, yet limited support (Morgan, 1985b). In particular, research suggests that relaxation training (Benson, Dryer, & Hartley, 1978) and stress-management training (Ziegler, Klinzing, & Williamson, 1982) can increase the efficiency with which oxygen is utilized during exercise. Benson and his colleagues studied subjects who had had a minimum of 6 months training in noncultic relaxation. Compared to a control run, the use of relaxation improved oxygen consumption by 4%. Ziegler and her associates (1982) found similar effects with stress-management training; however, these investigators used collegiate cross-country runners. This latter finding has particular significance, in that it is believed to be more difficult to find support for cognitive manipulations in trained, as compared to untrained populations (Morgan, 1972). Finally, there is some indication that the physiological effects of physical warm-up are, in part, psychologically based (see Franks, 1972). Unfortunately, to our knowledge, no additional attention has been given to the study of this important topic.

Modifying the Scope of Empirical Inquiry and Professional Involvement

In the very beginning of this chapter, we defined *exercise psychology* as "the application of the educational, scientific, and professional contributions of psychology to promoting, explaining, maintaining, and enhancing the parameters of physical fitness." We also argued that exercise psychologists should concern themselves with research questions where exercise is treated as an independent variable. For example, properly trained exercise psychologists can make significant contributions to the study of exercise therapy in enhancing mental health. Moreover, mental-health outcomes are closely connected with exercise topics such as compliance and subjective responses to exercise symptoms. From a historical viewpoint, a major consequence of not having a formally defined field of study is that the scope of empirical inquiry has been restricted. There are only a handful of studies on strength, not a single investigation involving range of motion, most exercise psychologists do not even consider body image to be a part of the field, and investigators have chosen to essentially ignore topics such as the psychology of warm-up. Moreover, psychologists have not been extensively involved in national educational programs such as the committee for Preventive and Rehabilitative Exercise Programs within the American College of Sports Medicine. There are national certifications for fitness instructors and program directors, yet little input from the profession of psychology. If, as a field of study, we are to experience significant change in the future, then it is critical to define what we are about and to promote a broad-based educational, scientific, and professional growth.

Historical Lessons in Experimental Methods

The historical sketch of exercise psychology presented in this chapter has provided some valuable lessons in the realm of experimental methods. First, much of the chronic-exercise research in mental health suffers from a common problem: There are multiple sources of variance in experimental manipulations. Truthfully, when we say that exercise programs can provide an effective means of combating depression, the word *program* should probably be taken to mean exercise, social support, performance feedback, and so on. Unfortunately, in many published investigations it is not even possible to discern what the term *exercise therapy* meant. Along these same lines, a second limiting factor has been the failure both to quantify treatment effects (i.e., ensure that subjects' physiology has been modified as a function of training) and to verify that subjects complied with therapeutic protocols. Third, across several areas of study, it has become apparent that investigators should consider both alternative endpoints and novel approaches to assessment. For example, experiential sampling and ambulatory blood pressure monitoring enable researchers to increase the ecological validity of research. Fourth, we are quick to look toward tightly designed experiments for verification of theory yet largely ignore external validity. How can we rule particular constructs or entire theoretical approaches as invalid in the absence of random samples? Attitudes may be unimportant when you deal with volunteer populations; however, they might well have a lot to do with explaining the behavior of individuals who normally would not choose to exercise. Fifth, construct validity is an ongoing process that is extremely critical to the study of acute exercise. Exercise symptoms can be easily misinterpreted by investigators. Whereas changes in HR and muscle activity may imply the onset of anxiety or feelings of fatigue—the presence of depression—these same sensations can signify energetic arousal and, as one power lifter has described, "the positive cathartic effects of a good pump."

Issues Related to Theory

The final comments in the chapter, those related to theory, may be the most significant historical lessons of all. Our initial challenge in the future is to define research problems concisely and unambiguously, to seek theoretical frameworks that combine input from social, psychological, and biological perspectives. We will have to fight to resist recurring historical setbacks created by reductionism and dualism. As we have seen in the physical-exertion literature and in the study of exercise with stress reactivity, it is easy to be lured by the concrete nature of objective measures; it has been tempting for investigators who work with RPE to attempt to discover the single critical physiological cue that determines perceived sense of effort (cf. Mihevic, 1981). However, in doing so, the fact is ignored that social cognition and human biological responses are reciprocal systems that cannot be studied in isolation—not if we are to reject dualistic thinking as we attempt to understand phenomena such as aversion to physical work or the role of exercise in mediating responses to threat and challenge.

The study of explanatory concepts/processes in exercise psychology underscores the importance of considering theoretical models that cut across multiple disciplines and diverse measurement strategies. For example, research in depression (North et al., 1990) has shown that some of the therapeutic benefits of exercise programs occur before training effects are realized; yet, among these same data, there is evidence that changes in depression covary with length of time in training. Rodin (1988) has shown that efficacy feedback in conjunction with exercise yields more favorable psychological outcomes than exercise alone; however, there are some indications that the ability of exercise to buffer subsequent physiological responses to stress are dose dependent (Rejeski et al., 1991). In reality, positive psychological outcomes attributed to exercise are probably determined by multiple causes, the specific factors varying with the nature of the disorder and the needs of the individual. A nomothetic approach treats this source of variance as error.

Finally, our choice of theories and conceptual frameworks has been as much of a problem to exercise psychology as was the atheoretical stance found in early research. Put differently, there are ample instances where constructs, theories, and conceptual models have been inappropriately applied; moreover, some theories and models offer very poorly articulated blueprints for the construction of knowledge. As a gold standard, theories that guide our research programs ought to (a) involve multiple levels of construction, (b) include content-related as well as process-oriented constructs, and (c) offer clear, systematic operational definitions of constructs (cf. Rejeski, 1992). The problem of not having multiple levels of construction is that historically single constructs used in isolation have offered very poor behavioral prediction (Rotter, 1954). The distinction between content-related and process-oriented constructs implies that theories must recognize individual differences (i.e., content-related constructs), yet include constructs that assist in explaining why behavior occurs and how it is changed. The recent success of self-efficacy theory is a testimony to the value inherent in this level of construction. Finally, we have mentioned several times how vague operational definitions have confused rather than assisted research in exercise psychology. Ideally, constructs within a theory, via their operational definitions, should be systematically tied to one another (see Rotter, 1954).

References

Andrew, G.M., & Parker, J.O. (1979). Factors related to dropout of postmyocardial infarction patients from exercise programs. *Medicine and Science in Sports, 11*, 376–378.

Ayres, L. P. (1911). *American Physical Education Review, 16*, 321.

Barber, T. X. (1966). *British Journal of Social and Clinical Psychology, 5*, 42.

Bartley, S.H. (1976). Visual fatigue. In E. Simonso & P. C. Weiser (Eds.), *Psychological aspects and physiological correlates of work and fatigue.* Springfield, IL: Charles C. Thomas.

Ben-Shlomo, L. S., & Short, M. A. (1985–1986). The effects of physical conditioning on selected dimensions of self-concept in sedentary females. *Occupational Therapy in Mental Health, 5*, 27–46.

Benson, H., Dryer, B. A., & Hartley, H. H. (1978). Decreased $\dot{V}0_2$ consumption exercise with elicitation of the relaxation response. *Journal of Human Stress, 4*(2), 38–42.

Blumenthal, J. A., Emery, C. F., & Rejeski, W. J. (1988). The effects of exercise training on psychosocial functioning after myocardial infarction. *Journal of Cardiopulmonary Rehabilitation, 8*, 183–193.

Borg, G. (1962). *Physical performance and perceived exertion.* Lund: Gleerup, 1962.

Boutcher, S. H., & Trenske, M. (1990). The effects of sensory deprivation and music on perceived exertion and affect during exercise. *Journal of Sport & Exercise Psychology, 12*, 442–447.

Boutcher, S. H., Fleischer-Curtian, L. A., & Gines, S. D. (1988). The effects of self-presentation on perceived exertion. *Journal of Sport and Exercise Psychology, 10*, 270–280.

Cantor, J. R., Zillman, D., & Day, K. D. (1978). Relationship between cardiovascular fitness and physiological responses to films. *Perceptual Motor Skills, 46*, 1123–1130.

Cappon, D., & Banks, R. (1968). Distorted body perception in obesity. *Journal of Nervous and Mental Disorders, 46*, 465–467.

Clifford, E. (1971). Body satisfaction in adolescence. *Perceptual and Motor Skills, 33*, 119–125.

Cox, J. P., Evans, J. F., & Jamieson, J. L. (1979). Aerobic power and tonic heart rate responses to psychosocial stressors. *Personality and Social Psychological Bulletin, 5*, 160–163.

Crews, D. J., & Landers, D. M. (1987). A meta-analytic review of aerobic fitness and reactivity to psychosocial stressors. *Medicine and Science in Sports and Exercise, 19*, 114–120.

de Geus, E. C. J., Lorenz, J. P., van Doornen, L. J. P., de Visser, D. C., & Orlebeke, J. F. (1990). Existing and training induced differences in aerobic fitness: Their relationship to physiological response patterns during different types of stress. *Psychophysiology, 27*, 457–478.

Dishman, R. K. (1982). Compliance/adherence in health related exercise. *Health Psychology, 1*, 237–267.

Dishman, R. K. (1986). Exercise compliance: A new view for public health. *The Physician and Sports Medicine, 14*, 127–145.

Dishman, R. K. (1988). *Exercise adherence: Its impact on public health.* Champaign, IL: Human Kinetics.

Dishman, R. K., Ickes, W., & Morgan, W. P. (1980). Self-motivation and adherence to habitual physical activity. *Journal of Applied Social Psychology, 2*, 115–132.

Dishman, R. K., Sallis, J. F., & Orenstein, D. R. (1985). The determinants of physical activity and exercise. *Public Health Report, 100*, 158–171.

Dudlye, D. L., Holmes, T. H., Martin, C. J., & Ripley, H. S. (1964). Changes in respiration associated with hypnotically induced emotion, pain, and exercise. *Psychosomatic Medicine, 26*, 46–57.

Dunn, A. L., & Dishman, R. K. (1991). Exercise and the neurobiology of depression. In J. O. Holloszy (Ed.), *Exercise and sport science reviews* (pp. 41–98). Baltimore, MD: Williams & Wilkins.

Dzewaltowski, D. A. (1989). Toward a model of exercise motivation. *Journal of Sport and Exercise Psychology, 11*, 251–269.

Ebbesen, B. L., Prkachin, K. M., & Mills, D. E. (1989). *Effects of acute exercise on cardiovascular reactivity.* Paper presented at the tenth annual meeting of the Society of Behavioral Medicine, San Francisco.

Ewart, C. K. (1989). Psychological effects of resistive weight training: Implications for cardiac patients. *Medicine and Science in Sports and Exercise, 21*, 683–688.

Folkins, C. H., & Sime, W. E. (1981). Physical fitness training and mental health. *American Psychologist, 36*, 373–389.

Fox, K. R., & Corbin, C. B. (1989). The physical self-perception profile: Development and preliminary validation. *Journal of Sport and Exercise Psychology, 11*, 408–430.

Franks, D. (1972). Physical warm-up. In W. P. Morgan (Ed.), *Ergogenic aids and muscular performance* (pp. 159–191). New York: Academic Press.

Franzoi, S. L., & Shields, S. A. (1984). The Body Esteem Scale: Multidimensional structure and sex differences on a college population. *Journal of Personality Assessment, 48*, 173–178.

Gill, D., & Strom, E. H. (1985). The effect of attentional focus on performance of an endurance task. *International Journal of Sport Psychology, 16*, 217–223.

Godin, G., Shephard, R. J., & Colantonio, A. (1986). The cognitive profile of those who intend to exercise but do not. *Public Health Reports, 101*, 521–526.

Hardy, C. J., Hall, E. G., & Presholdt, P. H. (1986). The mediational role of social influence in the perception of exertion. *Journal of Sport and Exercise Psychology, 8*, 88–104.

Hardy, C.J., & Rejeski,W. J. (1989). Not what, but how one feels: The measurement of affect during exercise. *Journal of Sport and Exercise Psychology, 11*, 304–317.

Hart, E. A., Leary, M. R., & Rejeski, W. J. (1989). The measurement of social physique anxiety. *Journal of Sport and Exercise Psychology, 11*, 94–104.

Hawkins, R. C., Turell, S., & Jackson, L. J. (1983). Desirable and undesirable masculine and feminine traits in relation to students' dieting tendencies and body image dissatisfaction. *Sex Roles, 9*, 6.

Hochstetler, S. A., Rejeski, W. J., & Best, D. L. (1985). The influence of sex-role orientation on ratings of perceived exertion. *Sex Roles, 12*, 825–835.

Hull, C. L. (1933). *Hypnosis and suggestibility.* New York: Appleton.

Hurlock, E. B. (1967). *Adolescent development.* New York: McGraw-Hill.

Kenney, E. A., Rejeski, W. J., & Messier, S. P. (1988). Managing exercise distress: The effect of broad spectrum intervention on affect, RPE, and running efficiency. *Canadian Journal of Sport Sciences, 12*, 97–105.

Kenyon, G. S. (1968). A conceptual model for characterizing physical activity. *Research Quarterly, 39*, 96–105.

King, A. C., Taylor, C. B., Haskell, W. L., & Debusk, R. F. (1988). Strategies for increasing early adherence to and long-term maintenance of home-based exercise training in healthy middle-aged men and women. *American Journal of Cardiology, 61*, 628–632.

Kolb, L. C. (1959). Disturbances of body image. In S. Arieti (Ed.), *American handbook of psychiatry* (Vol. 1, pp. 749–769). New York: Basic Books.

Lazarus, R S. (1975). A cognitively oriented psychologist looks at biofeedback. *American Psychologist, 30*, 553–561.

Leventhal, H., & Everhart, D. (1979). Emotion, pain, and physical illness. In C. E. Izard (Ed.), *Emotions in personality and psychopathology* (pp. 263–298). New York: Plenum.

Lindsey-Reid, E., & Osborn, R. W. (1980). Readiness for exercise adoption. *Social Science Medicine, 14*, 139–146.

Linton, J. M., Hamelink, M. H., & Hoskins, R. G. (1934). Cardiovascular system in schizophrenia studied by the Schneider method. *Archives of Neurological Psychiatry, 32*, 712–722.

Long, B. C., & Haney, C. J. (1986). Enhancing physical activity in sedentary women: Information, locus of control, and attitudes. *Journal of Sport Psychology, 8*, 8–24.

Marsella, A. J., Schizuru, L., Brennan, J., & Kameoka, J. (1981). Depression and body image satisfaction. *Journal of Cross-Cultural Psychology, 12*, 360–371.

Martin, J. E., & Dubbert, P. M. (1984). Behavioral management strategies for improving health and fitness. *Journal of Cardiac Rehabilitation, 4*, 200–208.

Martin, J. E., Dubbert, P. M., Kattell, A. D., Thompson, J. K., Raczynski, J. R., Lake, M., Smith, P.O., Webster, J. S., Sisora, T., & Cohen, R. A. (1984). Behavioral control of exercise in sedentary adults: Studies 1 through 6. *Journal of Consulting and Clinical Psychology, 52*, 795–811.

Matarazzo, J. D. (1980). Behavioral health medicine: Frontiers for a new health psychology. *American Psychologist, 42*, 893–903.

McAuley, E. (1992). Understanding exercise behavior: A self-efficacy perspective. In G. C. Roberts (Ed.), *Motivation in sport and exercise* (pp. 107–128). Chicago, IL: Human Kinetics.

McDonald, D. G., & Hodgdon, J. A. (1991). *Psychological effects of aerobic fitness training.* New York: Springer-Verlag.

Mendelson, B. K., & White, D. R. (1985). Development of self- body-esteem in overweight youngsters. *Developmental Psychology, 21* (1), 90–96.

Michael, E. D. (1957). Stress adaptation through exercise. *Research Quarterly, 28*, 50–54.

Mihevic, P. M. (1981). Sensory cues for perceived exertion: A review. *Medicine and Science in Sports and Exercise, 13*, 150–163.

Miller, T. M., Linke, J. G., & Linke, R. A. (1980). Survey on body image, weight, and diet of college students. *Journal of the American Dietetic Association, 77*, 561–566,

Morgan, W. P. (1969). Physical fitness and emotional health: A review. *American Correctional Therapy Journal, 23*, 124–127.

Morgan, W. P. (1972). Hypnosis and muscular performance. In W. P. Morgan (Ed.), *Ergogenic aids and muscular performance* (pp. 193–231). New York: Academic Press.

Morgan, W. P. (1973). Psychological factors influencing perceived exertion. *Medicine and Science in Sports, 5*, 97–103.

Morgan, W. P. (1985a). Affective beneficence of vigorous physical activity. American College of Sports Medicine Symposium: Exercise and endorphins (1983, Montreal, Canada). *Medicine and Science in Sports and Exercise, 17*, 94–100.

Morgan, W. P. (1985b). Psychogenic factors and exercise metabolism: A review. *Medicine and Science in Sports and Exercise, 17*, 309–316.

Morgan, W. P., & Horstman, D. H. (1976). Anxiety reduction following acute physical activity. *Medicine and Science in Sports, 8*, 62.

Morgan, W. P., Horstman, D. H., Cymerman, A., & Stokes, J. (1983). Facilitation of physical performance by means of a cognitive strategy. *Cognitive Therapy and Research, 7*, 251–264.

Morgan, W. P., Raven, P. B., Drinkwater, B. L., & Horvath (1973). Perceptual and metabolic responsivity to standard bicycle ergometry following various hypnotic suggestions. *International Journal of Clinical and Experimental Hypnosis, 21*, 86–101.

Nelson, L. R., & Furst, M. L. (1972). An objective study of the effects of expectation on competitive performance. *Journal of Psychology, 81*, 69–72.

Nemtzova, O. L., & Shatenstein, D.I. (1939). The effect of the central nervous system upon some physiological processes during work. (From *Psychological Abstracts,* p. 422.)

North, C. T., McCullagh, P., & Vu Tran, W. (1990). Effect of exercise on depression. In R. Terjung (Ed.), *Exercise and Sport Science Reviews, 19*, 379–415.

Oldridge, N. B., & Jones, N. L. (1983). Improving patient compliance in cardiac exercise rehabilitation: Effects of written agreement and self-monitoring. *Journal of Cardiac Rehabilitation, 3*, 257–262.

Pandolf, K. B. (1977). Psychological and physiological factors influencing perceived exertions. In G. Borg (Ed.), *Physical work and effort.* New York: Pergamon.

Petruzzello, S. J., Landers, D. M., Hatfield, B. D., Kubitz, K. A., & Salazar, W. (1991). A meta-analysis on the anxiety reducing effects of acute and chronic exercise: outcomes and mechanisms. *Sports Medicine, 11*, 143–180.

Ransford, C. P. (1982). A role for amines in the antidepressant effect of exercise: A review. *Medicine and Science in Sports and Exercise, 14*, 1–10.

Rejeski, W. J. (1981). The perception of exertion: A social psychophysiological integration. *Journal of Sport Psychology*, *4*, 305–320.

Rejeski, W. J. (1985). The perception of exertion: An active or passive process? *Journal of Sport Psychology, 7*, 371–378.

Rejeski, W. J. (1992). Motivation for exercise behavior: A critique of theoretical directions. In G. C. Roberts (Ed.), *Motivation in sport and exercise* (pp. 129–158). Chicago, IL: Human Kinetics.

Rejeski, W. J., Best, D. L., Griffith, P., & Kenney, E. (1987). Sex-role orientation and the responses of men to exercise stress. *Research Quarterly for Exercise and Sport, 58*, 260–264.

Rejeski, W. J., & Brawley, L. R. (1988). Defining the boundaries of sport psychology. *The Sport Psychologist, 2*, 231–242.

Rejeski, W. J., Gregg, E., Thompson, A., & Berry, M. (1991). The effects of varying doses of aerobic exercise on psychophysiological stress responses in highly trained cyclists. *Journal of Sport and Exercise Psychology*, *13*, 188–199.

Rejeski, W. J., Hardy, C. J., & Shaw, J. (1991). Psychometric confounds of assessing state anxiety in conjunction with bouts of vigorous exercise. *Journal of Sport and Exercise Psychology, 13*, 65–74.

Rejeski, W. J., & Kenney, E. (1987). Distracting attentional focus from fatigue: Does task complexity make a difference? *Journal of Sport Psychology, 9*, 66–73.

Rejeski, W. J., & Ribisl, P. M. (1980). Expected task duration and perceived effort: An attributional analysis. *Journal of Sport Psychology, 2*, 227–236.

Rejeski, W. J., & Sanford, B. (1984). Feminine-typed females: The role of affective schema in the perception of exercise intensity. *Journal of Sport Psychology, 6*, 197–207.

Riddick, C. C., & Freitag, R. S. (1984). The impact of aerobic fitness programs on the body image of older women. *Activities, Adaptation, and Aging, 6*, 59–70.

Riddle, P. K. (1980). Attitudes, beliefs, behavioral intentions, and behaviors of women and men toward regular jogging. *Research Quarterly for Exercise and Sport, 51*, 663–674.

Rodin, J. (1988). *The psychological effects of exercise.* Unpublished manuscript, Yale University.

Rohrbacker, R. (1973). Influence of special camp program for obese boys on weight loss, self-concept, and body image. *Research Quarterly, 44*, 150–157.

Rosen, G. M., & Ross, A. D. (1968). Relationship of body image to self-concept. *Journal of Consulting and Clinical Psychology, 32*, 100.

Rotter, J. B. (1954). *Social learning and clinical psychology.* Englewood Cliffs, NJ: Prentice-Hall.

Sarafino, E. P. (1990). *Health psychology: Biopsychosocial interactions*. New York: Wiley.

Schilder, P. (1935). *The image and appearance of the human body.* New York: International Universities Press.

Schonfield, W. A. (1962). Gynecomastia in adolescence: Effect on body image and personality adaptation. *Psychosomatic Medicine, 24*, 379–389.

Secord, P. F., & Jourard, S. M. (1953). The appraisal of body cathexis: Body cathexis and the self. *Journal of Consulting Psychology, 17*(5), 343–347.

Shelton, T. O., & Mahoney, M. J. (1978). The content and effect of "psyching-up" strategies in weight lifters. *Cognitive Therapy and Research, 2*, 275–284.

Silberstein, L. R., Striegel-Moore, R. H., Timko, C., & Rodin, J. (1988). Behavioral and psychological implications of body dissatisfaction: Do men and women differ? *Sex-Roles, 19*, 291–232.

Sime, W. E. (1977). A comparison of exercise and meditation in reducing physiological responses to stress. *Medicine and Science in Sports and Exercise, 9*, 55.

Simonson, E., & Weiser, P. C. (1976). Psychological and physiological correlation of work and fatigue. Springfield, IL: Charles C. Thomas.

Skinner, B. F. (1990). Can psychology be a science of mind? *American Psychologist, 45*, 1206–1209.

Skrinar, G. S., Bullen, B. A., Creek, J. M., McArthur J. W., et al. (1986). Effects of endurance training on body-consciousness in women. *Perceptual and Motor Skills, 62*, 485–490.

Sonstroem, R. J. (1982). Attitudes and beliefs in the prediction of exercise participation. In R. C. Cantu & W. J. Gillespie (Eds.), *Sports medicine, sports sciences: Bridging the gap.* Lexington, MA: Collamore Press.

Sonstroem, R. J., & Morgan, W. P. (1989). Exercise and self-esteem: Rationale and model. *Medicine and Science in Sports and Exercise, 21*, 329–337.

Steptoe, A., & Cox, S. (1988). Acute effects of aerobic exercise on mood. *Health Psychology, 7*, 329–340.

Taylor, S. E. (1986). *Health psychology.* New York: Random House.

Thorndike, E. (1912). The curve of work. *Psychological Reviews, 19*, 165–194.

Triplett, N. (1897). The dynamogenic factors in pacemaking and competition. *American Journal of Psychology, 9*, 507–553.

Tucker, L. A. (1983a). Effect of weight training on self-concept: A profile of those influenced most. *Research Quarterly for Exercise and Sport, 54*, 389–397.

Tucker, L. A. (1983b). Muscular strength and mental health. *Journal of Personality and Social Psychology, 45*, 1355–1360.

van Doornen, L. J. P., de Geus, E. J. C., & Orlebeke, J. F. (1988). Aerobic fitness and the physiological stress response: A critical evaluation. *Science and Medicine, 26*, 303–307.

Vaux, C. L. (1926). A discussion of physical exercise and recreation. *Occupational Therapy and Rehabilitation, 5*, 329–333.

Voor, V. H., Lloyd, A. J., & Cole, R. J. (1969). *Journal of Motivational Behavior, 1*, 210.

Wankel, L. M. (1984). Decision-making and social support strategies for increasing exercise involvement. *Journal of Cardiac Rehabilitation, 4*, 124–135.

Weinberg, R. S., Gould, D., Yukelson, D., & Jackson, A. (1981). The effect of preexisting and manipulated self-efficacy on a competitive muscular endurance task. *Journal of Sport Psychology, 4*, 345–354.

Weinberg, R. S., Smith, J., Jackson, A., & Gould, D. (1984). Effect of association, dissociation and positive self-talk strategies on endurance performance. *Canadian Journal of Applied Sport Sciences, 9*, 25–32.

Weiser, P. C., Kinsman, R. A., & Stamper, D. A. (1973). Task specific symptomatology changes resulting from prolonged submaximal bicycle riding. *Medicine and Science in Sports, 5*, 79–85.

Young, M., & Reeve, G. (1980). Discrimination analysis of personality and body image factors of females differing in percent body fat. *Perceptual and Motor Skills, 50*, 547–552.

Ziegler, S. G., Klinzing, J., & Williamson, K. (1982). The effects of two stress management training programs on cardiorespiratory efficiency. *Journal of Sport Psychology, 4*, 280–289.

35 Increasing Physical Activity: A Quantitative Synthesis

ROD K. DISHMAN AND JANET BUCKWORTH
University of Georgia, Athens

It is widely accepted in the scientific community as well as in the general public that regular physical activity contributes to people's well-being, both physically and psychosocially. As a consequence, sedentariness is viewed as a substantial problem to the public's health in many Western countries. Experts in clinical and community medicine are often expected to facilitate healthful changes in the population's physical activity habits. However, their (at least partial) failure (evident, for example, by the status of widespread physical inactivity in many Western societies) is explained, among other things, by the limited understanding of available intervention programs that are intended to increase physical activity or maximize its positive consequences.

Several theories and models that can help us in understanding the processes that underlie the adoption of exercise and its maintenance have been suggested to the field of exercise psychology. Another way of attempting to learn about exercise adherence has been through examining the various determinants of exercise behavior. Rod Dishman has been a prominent researcher in the field of exercise adherence. With his colleague Buckworth, he systematically addressed and investigated numerous factors associated with participation in and dropout from exercise programs.

In this seminal article, these researchers used meta-analysis, which is a statistical method of review presented in the late 1970s, with which researchers can integrate the findings of many studies conducted on a specific topic in order to arrive at general, quantitative derivations related to that topic. In fact, Dishman and Buckworth were among the pioneers in systematically studying the role of the exercise setting in relation to the effectiveness of programmed interventions. For example, it was found that although successful interventions took place at different settings such as at home, in school, at work, or in the community, community-based interventions were the ones that produced the most positive effects. It was also found that behavior-modification approaches to improving exercise adherence consistently produced very positive effects, probably through their impact on the physical environment that acts as a cue for exercise behavior.

Overall, Dishman and Buckworth concluded that interventions intended to increase physical activity have had a moderately large effect. However, beyond this general finding, the identification and quantitative synthesis of numerous factors that moderate the success of supervised exercise programs have been important to the science of medicine as well as to exercise and health psychology.

National policy for increasing leisure physical activity in the United States is impeded by a poor understanding of interventions that can be implemented by community and clinical medicine. To clarify the literature in this area, we conducted a quantitative, meta-analysis of 127 studies that examined the efficacy of interventions for increasing physical activity among ~131,000 subjects in community, worksite, school, home and health care settings; 445 effects were expressed as Pearson correlation coefficient (r) and examined as they varied according to moderating variables important for community and clinical intervention. The mean effect was moderately large, $r = 0.34$, approximating three-fourths of a standard deviation or an increase in binomial success rate from 50% to 67%. The estimated population effect weighted by sample size was larger, $r = 0.75$, approximating 2 standard deviations or increased success to 88%. Contrasts between levels of independent moderating variables indicated that effects weighted by sample size were larger when the interventions: 1) employed the principles of behavior modification, 2) used a mediated delivery, 3) target groups, 4) of combined ages, 5) sampled apparently healthy people, or 6) measured active leisure, or 7) low intensity, 8) by observation. Independently of sample size, effects were larger when interventions 1) used behavior modification, 2) employed a pre- or quasi-experimental design, or 3) were of short duration, regardless of features of the people, setting, or physical activity. Our results show that physical activity can be increased by intervention. The optimal ways for selecting intervention components, settings, and population segments to maintain increases in physical activity and the relative contributions by community and clinical medicine toward successful physical activity intervention require experimental confirmation, warranting accelerated attention in clinical trials.

Adapted, by permission, from R.K. Dishman and J. Buckworth, 1996, "Increasing physical activity: A quantitative synthesis," *Medicine and Science in Sport and Exercise* 28: 706-719.

Our purpose for the analysis reported herein is to provide a quantitative synthesis of the literature examining the effects of interventions used to increase physical activity. Our goals are to describe the efficacy of such interventions and the factors that moderate their success in order to guide public health policy, form hypotheses testable by further experimentation, and inform physicians and other health care providers about interventions that increase physical activity in communities and patients.

Methods

One-hundred twenty-seven published studies and 14 dissertations were located from 1965 through August, 1995, by computer searches of literature in the English language using *Medline, Current Contents, Psychinfo, SOCIAL SCISEARCH, ERIC,* and *Dissertation Abstracts International* data bases, bibliographic searches, and a personal retrieval system, cross-referenced with expert colleagues. Index words were behavior modification, health promotion, health education adherence, compliance, physical activity, fitness, and exercise. Five redundant publications were excluded. A quantitative synthesis then was conducted using standard meta-analytic procedures (23,25,27,49) with the aid of two statistical software programs: Meta 5.3 (56) and SPSS/PC- 6.0 (39).

Criteria for including a study were: 1) The dependent variable was a measure of physical activity consistent with consensus definitions used in public health (13,43) or a measure of physical fitness that is a surrogate of physical activity (1). 2) The independent variable was an intervention designed to increase habitual physical activity. 3) Outcomes of the intervention were quantified and could be compared with a variance estimate of the outcome from a control group or condition in the absence of the intervention. 4) An effect size could be expressed as a Pearson correlation coefficient r (50), permitting effects to be calculated from studies that used diverse statistical presentations including frequencies, percentages, graphs, *t*-tests, and chi-square- and *F*-tests with a single *df*, when means and standard deviations were not reported (49,50). Sixty located studies were excluded. Commonly used statistical guideposts for evaluating the size of r as a small, moderate, or large effect are 0.10, 0.30, or 0.50 (15,50).

The use of r also permitted a binomial effect size display (51) of the interventions' effects, interpreted as a practical measure of the success of an intervention. An r equaling 0.00 equates to a binomial effect of zero, reflecting a 50% chance for success in the absence of intervention. This approximates the mean success rate of nearly 50% reported for adherence to supervised (19,22) or community-based (54) exercise programs in the absence of intervention. An r of 0.20 is equivalent to an increase in success from 50% to 60%, whereas an r of 0.40 indicates an increase to 70%. When possible, effect sizes were calculated by subtracting the mean change for a control group or condition from the mean change for an experimental group or condition, and dividing this difference by the initial standard deviation of the control scores (15,23). This procedure reduced bias from pooling experimental variance and from the correlated variance of repeated measures (4). For multiple-baseline studies, intervention effects were compared to the initial baseline using the mean of each subject's effects. Interrater agreement for r was determined by intraclass correlation (R_I computed from ANOVA of r judged by four pairs of raters. Each rater pair blindly retrieved effects from 10 to 15 articles selected separately from among the 127 articles. R_I ranged from 0.89 to 0.96. We also examined variation in effects according to moderating variables deemed practically important for understanding and optimizing effective interventions.

We retrieved 445 effects from 127 studies based on ~131,156 people. Fisher's z transformation of r (z_r) was used for analyses to adjust for the nonnormal distribution of r, protecting against small sampling bias in estimates of the population r. The reported values of r are back transformations from z. Factors relevant for community and clinical medicine that might moderate the estimated population effect of the interventions were considered by comparing effects among features describing subjects, interventions, settings, and physical activity. Most studies reported multiple effects owing to separate effects derived according to age, race, or gender, concurrent estimates of physical activity using different measures, or follow-up measures of physical activity after an intervention ended. The mean effect was used when a study reported multiple measures of physical activity using the same method (e.g., multiple self-reports). The number of effects and the mean effect size per study were unrelated (r (125) = –0.07, P = 0.45), but we adopted a conservative statistical criterion ($P < 0.001$) to protect against Type I error when using several effects per study in analyses of moderators (49,53). Small sample sizes can increase Type II error (25). Hence, individual effects also were weighted by sample size (25,27) to adjust for sampling errors in r, giving more credence to studies with large samples.

Results

A stem-and-leaf display of the 445 effects indicates a nearly normal distribution of effects, with a negative skewness. The mean value of r was 0.34 (95% CI, 0.26–0.42), or 0.75 (95% CI, 0.70–0.79) after weighting by sample size. The effect r = 0.34 approximates an effect of three-fourths standard deviation (50). The effects were heterogeneous (49,56). A correlation of 0.25 between sample size and z_r contributed to the larger weighted estimate of r. The corresponding binomial effect represents a potential increase in success rates after intervention from 50% to 67%, or to 88% for the weighted analysis. The estimated population value of r was 0.64, or 0.76 for the weighted analysis, after adjustment (25,27) for a reliability of r = 0.80 among the measures of physical activity (1).

In contrast to results from the published sources, 14 unpublished doctoral dissertations reporting 55 effects for 668 subjects yielded a mean r of 0.17 (95% CI, –0.10 to 0.41), or 0.09 (95% CI, –0.18 to 0.35) when effects were weighted by sample size. Hence, we estimated the impact of unpublished null findings upon the population value of r derived from the published studies using the fail-safe *N* (41); a reduction of r to 0.20 from the observed values of 0.34 and 0.75 requires 317 and 1219 null findings, respectively.

Focused contrasts (49,52), each tested as Z at $P < 0.001$, subsequently were conducted to determine if moderators describing subjects, settings, or features of interventions and physical activity important for understanding and implementing interventions in community and clinical medicine might account for variability in the mean effect size. Effects for each moderator include a mean r with a 95% confidence interval. Variables that were significant moderators also were entered into a linear multiple regression model to clarify their independent effects for explaining variation in z_r. Moderators with more than two nonordinal levels were dichotomized based on results from the contrasts.

Moderating Variables Weighted by Sample Size

Subject attributes. Effect sizes did not differ between males and females, between age groups, or between whites and non-whites, but studies that reported on samples combining race or ages reported effects that were larger than those for specific race or age groups. The effect among healthy subjects was larger contrasted with all groups of patients. Small effects were observed in studies of people who had CHD, high risk for CHD, or other chronic diseases or physically or developmentally disabling conditions, but there were relatively few studies of interventions with patients.

Intervention type and setting. Effect sizes differed by intervention type, whereby behavior modification approaches were associated with effects that were larger compared with the other approaches. There were differences according to the manner of delivery of the intervention; effects were larger among studies using mediated approaches contrasted with face-to-face delivery. Interventions in community settings and interventions delivered to groups reported larger effects, contrasted with those in schools and other settings or with delivery to individuals, the family, and to an individual combined within a group, respectively. Effects were larger when the physical activity was not supervised compared with a supervised physical activity program. Effects were unrelated to the number of weeks the intervention, r (443) = –0.07, or the follow-up period, r (171) = –0.06, $P > 0.05$, lasted.

Physical activity features. Effect sizes differed according to the mode of physical activity. Effects for active leisure time were larger contrasted with exercise programs prescribing strength, aerobic exercise, or aerobic exercise combined with other fitness activities. Effect sizes did not differ according to the weekly frequency or daily duration, but studies that observed physical activities carried out at a low intensity reported larger effects compared with studies using estimates of physical activities conducted at higher intensities. Effects from studies using an objective measure of attendance or direct observation were larger compared with those using self-reports by participants or surrogate measures of physical activity based on changes in physiological responses to exercise testing or strength. Only about 25% of the studies reported follow-up measures of physical activity to determine if increases in physical activity were maintained after the intervention ended, but followup effects generally were small.

Multiple regressions analysis. Direct entry of the significant moderating variables into a multiple linear regression analysis indicated that 9 variables independently accounted for variation in z_r: age, physical activity mode, intervention delivery, health status, physical activity measure, physical activity intensity, social context, intervention type, and research design, $P < 0.05$. Reentry of these variables into the regression model yielded a multiple R of 0.66, adjusted $R^2 = 0.42$, $F(9,435) = 36.9$, $P < 0.0001$. Research design did not add to the final model.

Weighting versus Not Weighting by Sample Size?

Weighting by sample size yields a better estimate of the true effect of interventions in the population, which is especially important when hypotheses or policy judgments are formed about interventions to increase physical activity in a community. Nonetheless, sampling bias in the relationship between z_r and sample size can create anomalies confounding the interpretation of moderators. Examples presently are the larger effects for samples comprised of several age categories or more than one race in the weighted analysis, contrasted with the small effects for studies that reported separate effects for specific age groups or for whites and non-whites. Numerous studies intervening with large samples did not report analyses separately based on age or race, focusing on mediated approaches with community-based groups participating in unsupervised physical activity of low intensity.

Hence, weighting z_r by sample size can obscure important effects observed in studies of smaller groups of people that may prove to be good estimates of population effect upon further sampling. This concern particularly applies when comparing the effects among interventions applied in clinical health care settings where the mean sample was about 50 people, contrasted with community-based interventions where the mean sample was about 925 people. Several of the aforementioned moderators are important features of clinical applications of physical activity. Thus, additional contrasts were focused on the moderator variables using z_r without weighting by sample size.

Moderating Variables Not Weighted by Sample Size

Subject attributes. In contrast with the weighted analysis, effects from samples of more than one race did not differ from the effects for specific races. Also, effects from studies sampling patients who were obese or who had developmental or physical disabilities and a chronic illness other than cardiovascular disease were larger than effects of studies of healthy people, all of which were larger than effects from studies of people with, or at risk for, cardiovascular disease.

Intervention type and setting. Behavior modification again had larger effects contrasted with the other interventions. In contrast to the weighted analysis, effects did not differ according to social context, the method of delivering the interventions, or according to the intensity of the physical activity, or whether the physical activity was supervised or free-living without supervision. Also, in contrast to the weighted analysis, effects of interventions conducted in community settings were similar to those applied in home, school, worksite, and health care settings. Effects were related inversely to the number of weeks in the intervention, r (443) = –0.20, $P < 0.001$ and the follow-up, r (171) = –0.18, $P < 0.01$, periods.

Physical activity features. In contrast with the weighted analysis, effects did not differ according to mode or intensity of physical activity. As was the case for the weighted analysis, effects at follow-up generally were small.

Multiple regression analysis. Direct entry of the significant moderating variables into a multiple linear regression analysis indicated that intervention type, intervention length, and research design accounted for variation in z_r, $P < 0.05$. The regression model yielded a multiple R of 0.48, adjusted $R^2 = 0.23$, F (3,441) = 44.4, $P < 0.0001$. Health status did not contribute to the model.

Research Design

Effects derived from a pre- or quasi-experimental design (11) (N = 169) were larger (mean ± 95% CI (0.87 ± 0.82–0.90 and 0.53 ± 0.41–0.64) than those from randomized experiments (N = 276) (0.10 ± 0.00–0.21 and 0.21 ± 0.09–0.32) in the weighted and unweighted analyses, respectively, $P < 0.001$. Though research design did not independently influence effect size in the weighted analysis, we further examined the impact of lowered internal validity on the moderator analyses by adjusting z_r for the quality of the research design using fractional weights (49) for effects from studies employing a pre- or quasi-experimental design. Contrasts within the moderators then were repeated. The quality of the research design generally did not interact with the moderator variables. Exceptions were that, without weighting by sample size, the studies using pre- or quasi-experimental designs yielded larger effects for low-intensity physical activity and for health care settings, contrasted with the studies using experimental designs, whereas research design in the weighted analysis did not moderate the pattern of effects for physical activity intensity or the intervention setting. Interventions in health care settings, contrasted with those in a community, typically used pre- or quasi-experimental designs, studying supervised physical activity after shorter intervention periods. Otherwise, clinical and community interventions did not differ in the gender, age, or race of subjects or in the features of the interventions and physical activity studied. Hence, the differences in the impact of moderators observed for the weighted vs unweighted analyses were not biased by differing distributions of the moderating variables, but can be partly attributed to the manner by which community versus clinical intervention studies were conducted or reported.

Discussion

A conservative interpretation of our quantitative synthesis of the literature, gauged by statistical guideposts (15), is that interventions for increasing physical activity have a moderately large effect. The effect also is large practically, equivalent to improving success from the typical rate of 50% without intervention to about 70% –88% (51). Though summaries from a meta-analysis require experimental confirmation, our aforementioned results suggest directions about the best ways to implement effective interventions for increasing physical activity in community and clinical medicine. The analysis of effects weighted by sample size suggests that interventions based on the principles of behavior modification, delivered to healthy people in a community, are associated with large effects, particularly when the interventions are delivered to groups using mediated approaches or when the physical activity is unsupervised, emphasizing leisure physical activity of low intensity, regardless of the duration or frequency of participation. The multiple linear regression model of the moderating variables supported that the larger effects reported for combined ages, behavior modification, and the delivery of the interventions using media, to groups or to healthy subjects, describing low-intensity, active leisure physical activity measured by observation, were independent of each other; whereas the influences on effect size by community setting, combined races, and a pre- or quasi-experimental research design found in the univariate analysis by contrasts was not independent of the other moderating variables.

Since the mean effect for each level of the significant moderating variables was heterogeneous (49,56), interactions among the moderators or their levels will better explain the findings suggested by our independent analysis of moderators. Not all studies reported information on each of the moderators we examined. Hence, there were not enough studies and effects to permit a statistically powerful analysis of interactions among the moderators, a limitation to inferring causality by moderators that is common among meta-analyses.

Our quantitative analysis provides some support for consensus opinions (8,18,28) that modifying traditional guidelines for exercise programming (3) to accommodate moderately intense physical activities of varied type (8,18) in a community using mediated (28), as well as face-to-face, approaches will increase participation among segments of the sedentary population (43). The maintenance of successful physical activity after the conclusion of an intervention has been less encouraging implying a need for sustained or repeated implementation of interventions. Though past studies have reported little success in increasing physical activity among people representing racial or ethnic minorities or older ages, these groups have been underrepresented in past studies and should receive more attention by researchers in the future.

The aforementioned findings imply an influential role by community medicine for increasing physical activity. Nonetheless, clinical uses of physical activity applied toward the secondary prevention of health problems also are important for public health. When the size of the studies' samples was ignored, interventions in health care settings and schools were similarly effective compared with interventions in the community, regardless of the features of the physical activity. Sample size ignored, interventions were most effective when they employed behavior modification approaches, often combining reinforcement- and stimulus-control. In addition to behavior modification, interventions that altered the physical education curriculum in schools or combined two or more types of interventions were effective. Also, interventions targeting patient groups, other than those with cardiovascular disease or high risk, were more effective compared with interventions targeting apparently healthy people. Though the effects of setting or health status were not independent influences on intervention effectiveness, they warrant experimental testing.

The absence of effects by interventions using health education or health risk appraisals is consistent with a narrative review of the literature (16). In contrast, the apparent ineffectiveness of cognitive-behavior modification and the supervised prescription of moderate exercise is not consistent with previous narrative reviews (18,28). The large confidence intervals surrounding the mean effect, usually including zero, for interventions other than behavior modification, coupled with the smaller number of effects, makes it premature to conclude that interventions other than behavior modification are ineffective for increasing physical activity. This caveat also applies to interventions with heart patients for whom few effects were reported. Also, it appears that interventions other than behavior modification have been implemented in widely varying ways, especially in the case of cognitive-behavior modification. Cognitive-behavior modification techniques often were combined with other interventions, precluding a determination of their independent effects in many studies. These combination interventions had the same effect size as interventions using cognitive-behavior modification, alone. Moreover, most studies using cognitive-behavior modification did not base the interventions on a broader theoretical model of behavior change (29,47).

When weighted by sample size, the effect for pre- and quasi-experimental studies was markedly larger compared with randomized experimental studies, including those using a minimally effective intervention condition (i.e., a placebo). However, a randomized research design is extremely difficult and costly to implement in community- or population-based studies. The use of a placebo for control comparisons was rare, and usually it is not feasible for a population-based study. Scientific quality notwithstanding, whether the research design was experimental versus pre- or quasi-experimental was not an independent influence on the size of effects when weighted by sample size and, ignoring sample size, had little impact on the pattern of moderating effects other than in health care settings, where effects were larger for pre- or quasi-experimental designs. Nonetheless, it is important to not infer prematurely that a moderator implied by our meta-analysis is a causal determinant of variations in effects when the studies we reviewed did not experimentally manipulate levels of the moderator.

Few studies verified self-reported physical activity by measuring increases in fitness expected to result from increased physical activity or by concomitantly using an objective measure of activity such as a motion sensor or observation. While increases in physical activity typically were largest when an objective measure of attendance or observation was used, the failure of interventions to increase physical activity when it was estimated by a surrogate measure of physical fitness indicates that the validity of physical activity measures other than observation remains an important methodology dilemma for the study of physical activity in public health. Furthermore, it is important to determine whether the absolute levels of increased activity were adequate to increase physical fitness (3) or decrease the risk for disease morbidity or all-cause mortality (6,31,42). Only about one-fourth of the studies reviewed herein reported a follow-up to the intervention, but those studies typically showed that increases in physical activity or fitness associated with the interventions were diminished as time passed after the intervention ended. Many of the community studies that reported large effects did not report on the maintenance of physical activity after the intervention's conclusion, or reported a return near to the pre-intervention activity level within a few weeks after the intervention.

Two implications of our literature analysis especially are important for understanding the roles of community and clinical medicine in promoting physical activity. One arises from the larger effects by interventions using media, or applied in large groups, contrasted with smaller effects by interventions to small groups or in a clinical setting, or using face-to-face delivery. Though the larger effects reported in community settings were not independent of the other moderators, the pattern of moderator influences suggested influential roles by public health initiatives and community-based medicine for increasing physical activity. Until around 1990, most intervention studies used single dimensional approaches with small numbers of people of similar gender, race, ethnicity, education, and economic and health status (16,18). More recently, community-based interventions applying psychological and behavioral theories for behavior change have predominated (18,28). These approaches extend beyond the traditional practice of face-to-face counseling to include changes in organizational (community recreation centers, churches, diffusion strategies through schools), environmental (e.g., facility planning), and social (e.g., family interventions) factors or they use cost effective or convenient vehicles (e.g., mailings, telecommunication) for reaching many people who are not accessible or amenable to traditional interventions based in clinical settings. Such interventions are appropriately part of community medicine, but they do not depend upon a direct physician-patient encounter. They warrant further experimental testing for effectiveness.

Another implication of our analysis is that previous interventions for increasing physical activity applied in health care settings, including cognitive-behavior modification, were not implemented optimally. Our qualitative evaluation of the studies suggests this may be explainable because the studies did not use standardized approaches based on newer theories about how health behavior, specifically physical activity, changes. Recently, a successful clinical trial (10) based in the physician's office used a theoretical model grounded in cognitive-behavior modification (47) that triages patients into stages of readiness for changing their physical activity habits, then introducing standardized counseling by the physician, supported by nurses and staff, that is stage-appropriate. Such an approach offers more promise for increasing physical activity than the counseling approaches traditionally used by physicians (33,36,61) and deserves evaluation by clinical research. About 80% of the U.S. population has annual contact with a physician, with 65% of patient contacts involving primary-care specialties (38). Nearly 50% of practicing physicians in the U.S., about 245,000 physicians, are in primary-care specialties of family or general practice, internal medicine, pediatrics, and obstetrics-gynecology (48) which permit physical activity intervention during patient counseling. Similarly, there are approximately 250,000 nurses in primary care (9) who can support physical activity interventions applied in the medical office. Hence, exploiting more fully the impact of the physician-patient encounter remains an important area for experimental tests of effective interventions for increasing the nation's level of physical activity.

The relative contributions by community and clinical medicine to successful interventions for increasing physical activity warrant accelerated testing by clinical trials. This is important particularly among people with high risk for cardiovascular disease, whereby physical activity exerts its greatest influence in reducing premature death (6,42), yet few interventions for increasing physical activity have been conducted with success in that group. An emphasis also is needed for understanding the ways by which cognitive-behavior modification can be uniformly applied to increase physical activity, since it is theoretically superior to health education, health risk appraisal, and exercise prescription which, though easily implemented, have not proved effective for increasing physical activity.

Controlled experiments are required to confirm the varying effects of interventions suggested by the foregoing analysis and how intervention components, settings, and population segments can be combined to optimally increase and maintain physical activity in the largely sedentary U.S. population. Nonetheless, our quantitative synthesis of the literature demonstrates that the use of behavior modification has efficacy for increasing physical activity, providing a basis for optimism among professionals in public health and medicine that physical activity can be increased.

References

1. Ainsworth, B. E., H. J. Montoye, and A. S. Leon. Methods of assessing physical activity during leisure and work. In: *Physical Activity, Fitness, and Health: International Proceedings and Consensus Statement,* C. Bouchard, R. Shephard, and T. Stephens (Eds.). Champaign, IL: Human Kinetics, 1994, pp. 146–159.
2. American College of Sports Medicine. Physical activity, physical fitness, and hypertension. *Med. Sci. Sports Exerc.* 25:i–x, 1993.
3. American College of Sports Medicine. Position statement on the recommended quality and quantity of exercise for developing and maintaining fitness in healthy adults. *Med. Sci. Sports Exerc.* 22:265–274, 1990.
4. Becker, B. J. Synthesizing standardized mean-change measures. *Br. J. Math. Stat. Psychol.* 41:257–278, 1988.
5. Berlin, J. A. and G. A. Colditz. A meta-analysis of physical activity in the prevention of coronary heart disease. *Am. J. Epidemiol.* 132:612–628, 1990.
6. Blair, S. N., H. W. Kohl III, C. E. Barlow, R. S. Paffenbarger, L. W. Gibbons, and C. A. Macera. Changes in physical fitness and all-cause mortality. A prospective study of healthy and unhealthy men. *J.A.M.A.* 273:1093–1098, 1995.
7. Blair, S. N., H. W. Kohl III, R. S. Paffenbarger, Jr., D. G. Clark, K. H. Cooper, and L. W. Gibbons. Physical fitness and all-cause mortality: a prospective study of healthy men and women. *J.A.M.A.* 262:2395–2401, 1989.
8. Blair, S. N., K. E. Powell, T. L. Bazzarre, et al. Physical inactivity. Workshop V. AHA Prevention Conference III. Behavior Change and Compliance: Keys to improving cardiovascular health. *Circulation* 88:1402–1405, 1993.
9. Bureau of Health Professions. *Factbook: Health Personnel,* U.S. HRSA-P-AM-93-1, 1993, pp. 1–76.
10. Calfas, K. J., B. J. Long, J. F. Sallis, W. J. Wooten, M. Pratt, and K. Patrick. A controlled trial of physician counseling to promote the adoption of physical activity. *Prev. Med.* (in press).

11. Campbell, D. T. and J. C. Stanley. *Experimental and Quasi-Experimental Designs for Research.* Chicago: Rand McNally & Company, 1966, pp. 1–84.

12. Caspersen, C. J., R. K. Merritt, and T. Stephens. International physical activity patterns: a methodological perspective. In: *Advances in Exercise Adherence,* R. K. Dishman (Ed.). Champaign, IL: Human Kinetics, 1994. pp. 73–110.

13. Caspersen, C. J., K. E. Powell, and G. M. Christenson. Physical activity, exercise, and physical fitness: definitions and distinctions for health-related research. *Public Health Rep.* 100:126–130, 1985.

14. Centers for Disease Control and Prevention. Behavioral risk factor surveillance, 1986–1990. MMWR 1991;40(SS-4):1–23.

15. Cohen, J. *Statistical Power Analysis for the Behavioral Sciences,* 2nd Ed. New York: Academic Press, 1988, pp. 1–567.

16. Dishman, R. K. Increasing and maintaining exercise and physical activity. *Behav. Ther.* 22:345–378, 1991.

17. Dishman, R. K. Medical psychology in exercise and sport. *Med. Clin. North Am.* 69:123–143, 1985.

18. Dishman, R. K. and J. F. Sallis. Determinants and interventions for physical activity and exercise. In: *Physical Activity, Fitness, and Health: International Proceedings and Consensus Statement,* C. Bouchard, R. J. Shephard, and T. Stephens (Eds.). Champaign, IL: Human Kinetics Publishers, 1994, pp. 214–238.

19. Dishman, R. K., J. F. Sallis, and D. Orenstein. The determinants of physical activity and exercise. *Public Health Rep.* 100:158–171, 1985.

20. Drinkwater, B. L. Physical activity, fitness, and osteoporosis. In: *Physical Activity, Fitness, and Health: International Proceedings and Consensus Statement,* C. Bouchard, R. J. Shephard, and T. Stephens (Eds.). Champaign, IL: Human Kinetics Publishers, 1994, pp. 724–736.

21. Fletcher, G. P., S. N. Blair, J. Blumenthal, et al. Statement on exercise: benefits and recommendations for physical activity programs for all Americans. *Circulation* 86:2726–2730, 1992.

22. Franklin, B. A. Program factors that influence exercise adherence. In: *Exercise Adherence: Its Impact on Public Health,* R. K. Dishman (Ed.). Champaign, IL: Human Kinetics, 1988, pp. 237–258.

23. Glass, G. V., B. McGraw, and M. L. Smith. *Meta-analysis In Social Research.* London: Sage Publications, 1981, pp. 1–279.

24. Harris, S. S., C. J. Caspersen, G. H. Defries, and E. H. Estes. Physical activity counseling for health adults as a primary preventive intervention in the clinical setting. *J.A.M.A.* 264:2654–2659, 1989.

25. Hedges, L. V. and I. Olkin. *Statistical Methods for Meta-analysis.* San Diego: Academic Press, 1985, pp. 1–369.

26. Helmrich, S. P., D. R. Ragland, R. W. Leung, and R. S. Paffenbarger, Jr. Physical activity and reduced occurrence of noninsulin-dependent diabetes mellitus. *N. Engl. J. Med.* 325:147–152, 1991.

27. Hunter, J. E. and F. L. Schmidt. *Methods of Meta-analysis: Correcting Error and Bias in Research Findings.* Newbury Park, CA: Sage Publishers, 1990.

28. King, A. C., S. N. Blair, D. Bild, et al. Determinants of physical activity and interventions in adults. *Med. Sci. Sports Exerc.* (Suppl. 24):S221–5236, 1992.

29. Knapp, D. N. Behavioral-management techniques and exercise promotion. In: *Exercise Adherence: Its Impact on Public Health,* R. K. Dishman (Ed.). Champaign, IL: Human Kinetics, 1988, pp. 203–236.

30. Kriska, A. M., S. N. Blair, and M. A. Pereira. The potential role of physical activity in the prevention of non-insulin-dependent diabetes mellitus. *Exerc. Sport Sci. Rev.* 22:121–143, 1994.

31. Lakka, T. A., J. M. Venaliainen, R. Rauramaa, R. Salonen, J. Tuomilehto, and J. T. Salonen. Relation of leisure-time physical activity and cardiorespiratory fitness to the risk of acute myocardial infarction. *N. Engl. J. Med.* 330:1549–1554, 1994.

32. Lewis, C. E., C. Clancy, B. Leake, and J. S. Schwartz. The counseling practices of internists. *Ann. Intern. Med.* 114:54–58, 1991.

33. Lewis, B. S. and W. D. Lynch. The effect of physician advice on exercise behavior. *Prev. Med.* 22:110–121, 1993.

34. Mann, K. V. and R. W. Putnam. Physicians' perceptions of their role in cardiovascular risk reduction. *Prev. Med.* 18:54–58, 1985.

35. Manson, J. E., E. B. Rimm, M. J. Stampfer, et al. Physical activity and incidence of non-insulin-dependent diabetes mellitus in women. *Lancet* 338:774–778, 1991.

36. Mullen, P. and G. R. Tabak. Patterns of counseling techniques used by family practice physicians for smoking, weight, exercise and stress. *Med. Care* 27:694–704, 1989.

37. Nader, P. R., H. L. Taras, J. F. Sallis, and T. L. Patterson. Adult heart disease prevention in childhood: A national survey of pediatricians' practices and attitudes. *Pediatrics* 79:843–850, 1987.

38. National Center For Health Statistics. *Health, United States, 1989,* (DHHS Publication No. PHS 90-1232). Hyattsville, MD: U.S. Department of Health and Human Services, 1990.

39. Norusis, M. J. *SPSS for Windows 6.0.* Chicago: SPSS Inc., 1993, pp. 1–828.

40. Orleans, C. T., L. K. George, J. L., Houpt, and K. H. Brodie. Health promotion in primary care: a survey of U.S. family practitioners. *Prev. Med.* 14:636–647, 1985.

41. Orwin, R. G. A fail safe N for effect size in meta-analysis. *J. Ed. Stat.* 8:157–159, 1983.

42. Paffenbarger, R. S., Jr., R. T. Hyde, A. L. Wing, I-M. Lee, D. L. Jung, and J. B. Kampert. The association of changes in physical activity level and other lifestyle characteristics with mortality among men. *N. Engl. J. Med.* 328:538–545, 1993.

43. Pate, R., M. Pratt, S. B. Blair, et al. Physical activity and health: a recommendation from the Centers for Disease Control and Prevention and the American College of Sports Medicine. *J.A.M.A.* 273:402–407, 1995.

44. Pavlou, K. N., S. Krey, and W. P. Steffee. Exercise as an adjunct to weight loss and maintenance in moderately obese subjects. *Am. J. Clin. Nutr.* 49:1115–1123, 1989.

45. Powell, K. E. and S. N. Blair. The public health burdens of sedentary living habits: theoretical but realistic estimates. *Med. Sci. Sports Exerc.* 26:851–856, 1994.

46. Prince, R. L., M. Smith, I. M. Dick, et al. Prevention of postmenopausal bone osteoporosis. A comparative study of exercise, calcium supplementation, and hormone-replacement therapy. *N. Engl. J. Med.* 325:1189–1195, 1991.

47. Prochaska, J. O. and B. H. Marcus. The transtheoretical model: applications to exercise. In: *Advances in Exercise Adherence,* R. K. Dishman (Ed.). Champaign, IL: Human Kinetics, 1994, pp. 161–180.

48. Roback, G., L. Randolph, and B. Seidman. *Physician Characteristics and Distribution in the U.S.* Chicago: American Medical Association, 1993.

49. Rosenthal, R. *Meta-analytic procedures for social research.* Beverly Hills, CA: Sage, 1991, pp. 1–155.

50. Rosenthal, R. Parametric measures of effect size. In: *The Handbook of Research Synthesis,* H. Cooper and L. V. Hedges (Eds.). New York: Russell Sage Foundation, 1994, pp. 231–244.

51. Rosenthal, R. and D. B. Rubin. A simple, general purpose display of magnitude of experimental effect. *J. Ed. Psychol.* 74:166–169, 1982.

52. Rosenthal, R. and D. B. Rubin. Comparing effect sizes of independent studies. *Psychol. Bull.* 92:500–504, 1982.

53. Rosenthal, R. and D. B. Rubin. Multiple contrasts and ordered Bonferroni procedures. *J. Ed. Psychol.* 76:1028–1034, 1984.

54. Sallis, J. F., W. L. Haskell, S. P. Fortmann, K. M. Vranizan, C. B. Taylor, and D. S. Solomon. Predictors of adoption and maintenance of physical activity in a community sample. *Prev. Med.* 15:331–341, 1986.

55. Schwartz, J. S., C. E. Lewis, C. Clancy, M. S. Kinosian, M. H. Radany, and J. P. Koplan. Internists' practices in health promotion and disease prevention: a survey. *Ann. Intern. Med.* 114:46–53, 1991.

56. Schwarzer, R. *Meta: programs for secondary data analysis, 5.3.* Berlin: Free University of Berlin, 1991, pp. 1–46.

57. Sternfeld, B. Cancer and the protective effect of physical activity: the epidemiological evidence. *Med. Sci. Sports Exerc.* 24:1195–1209, 1992.

58. St. Jeor, S. T., K. D. Brownell, R. L. Atkinson, et al. Obesity. Workshop III. AHA Prevention Conference III. Behavior change and compliance: keys to improving cardiovascular health. *Circulation* 1993, pp. 88:1391–1396.

59. U.S. Department of Health and Human Services. *Healthy People 2000: National Health Promotion and Disease Prevention Objectives* (DHHS Publication No. [PHS] 91-50212). Washington, DC: U.S. Government Printing Office, 1991.

60. Wechsler, H., S. Levine, R. K. Idelson, M. Rohman, and J. O. Taylor. The physician's role in health promotion—a survey of primary care practitioners. *N. Engl. J. Med.* 308:97–100, 1983.

61. Wells, K. B., C. E. Lewis, B. Leake, M. K. Schleiter, and R. H. Brook. The practice of general and subspecialty internists in counseling about smoking and exercise. *Am. J. Public Health* 76:1009–1013, 1986.

62. Williford, H. N., B.R. Barfield, R.B. Lazenby, and M. Scharff Olson. A survey of physicians' attitudes and practices related to exercise promotion. *Prev. Med.* 21:630–636, 1992.

36 Psychological Effects of Endogenous Testosterone and Anabolic-Androgenic Steroids

MICHAEL S. BAHRKE
Human Kinetics Publishers

Some athletes are ready to do whatever it takes to gain a competitive advantage over their opponents. Accordingly, it is no secret that, for many years, the use of performance-enhancing substances, such as forbidden drugs, has been widespread among Olympians and other world-class athletes. Despite the fact that it is often difficult to obtain an accurate picture of substance abuse in sport because of the sensitive and often private nature of the subject, it is quite clear that abuse of performance-enhancing drugs appears to be on the upswing. This is remarkable since drug abuse may have serious negative consequences that sometimes go far beyond the sport domain itself (e.g., disqualification). Some former top athletes are now experiencing serious negative consequences of taking these drugs; even an early death has not been infrequent among such drug users.

Bahrke undertook the challenge of reviewing nearly 50 reports concerning the psychological and behavioral effects of endogenous testosterone and anabolic-androgenic steroids. He began with discussing the effects of anabolic steroids on aggressive behavior in animals. Then he presented the relationships between levels of endogenous testosterone and moods and behavior in humans, with a special reference to aggressive behavior and to responses to winning and losing. He discussed estrogen-related aggression and described different effects of the clinical use of anabolic steroids on moods and behavior in human male contraceptive studies. Bahrke continued by presenting how the use of anabolic steroids affects athletes' mental health, including important issues such as psychological dependence and withdrawal. Finally, he concluded the chapter by discussing selected methodological issues related to the assessment of psychological and behavioral effects of anabolic steroids.

Drugs per se should not be considered a problem, because not all substances are out of place in physical activity and sport settings. For example, antibiotics and even simple painkillers may be viewed as useful medical tools in sport. The use of harmful, illegal, and banned substances is considered the major problem in the exercise and sport domain. Bahrke's seminal review chapter makes a substantial contribution to the clarification of this important and sometimes delicate issue.

Interest in the psychological and behavioral aspects of using anabolic-androgenic steroids was heightened during the late 1980s due to the interaction of several events: (1) use of anabolic-androgenic steroids by professional, Olympic, and collegiate athletes was increasingly reported by the media (Blackwell, 1991; Pearson & Hansen, 1990); (2) use among children and adolescents was documented (Buckley et al., 1988; Johnson, Jay, Shoup, & Rickert, 1989); (3) anecdotal reports and testimonials of violent behavior associated with anabolic-androgenic steroid use were presented by the media ("The Insanity of Steroid Abuse," 1988); and (4) studies examining the psychiatric effects of anabolic-androgenic steroid abuse began to appear in the scientific literature (Brower, Blow, Beresford, & Fuelling, 1989; Pope & Katz, 1988). Nearly 50 reports examining the psychological and behavioral effects of using endogenous testosterone and anabolic steroids have been published since this chapter was first published (Bahrke, 1993). This new chapter extends the analysis of the previous chapter to include studies published since 1993.

From the late 1930s to the late 1970s, anabolic steroids were used in clinical settings to successfully treat depression, melancholia, and involutional psychoses (Bahrke, Yesalis, & Wright, 1990). It is unclear why the use of anabolic steroids to treat certain psychiatric disorders diminished over time, but presumably it was due to the development of other, more efficacious drugs. Recently, however, in contrast to the previously successful use of these drugs to treat psychiatric disorders, a number of scientific and clinical reports have suggested that affective and psychotic syndromes, some of violent proportions and including suicide (Elofson & Elofson, 1990; "NHL Tough Guy Kordic," 1992), may be associated with the use of anabolic steroids in individuals seeking to enhance their performance or appearance (Bahrke et al., 1990). Citing an association between steroid abuse and violent behavior, Orchard and Best (1994) have recommended that violent offenders be tested for anabolic steroid use at the time of arrest in order to document the possible association between steroid abuse and violent acts, and that the information obtained be used to develop additional tactics to control steroid abuse.

Anabolic Steroids and Aggressive Behavior in Animals

Rejeski, Gregg, Kaplan, and Manuck (1990) examined the effects of anabolic steroids on behavior, baseline heart rate, and stress-induced heart rate responses in cynomolgus

Adapted, by permission, from M.S. Bahrke, 2000, Psychological effects of endogenous testosterone and anabolic-androgenic steroids. In *Anabolic steroids in sport and exercise*, edited by C.E. Yesalis (Champaign, IL: Human Kinetics), 247-278.

monkeys who were assigned to one of four mixed social groups of both steroid- and sham-injected control animals. Hormone administration resulted in increases in dominant behavior in dominant animals and increased submission in subordinate animals. Behavior returned to pretreatment levels 8 weeks after cessation of drug administration. Affiliative behaviors decreased in all steroid-treated animals and, with the exception of play behavior, failed to return to pretest levels after an 8-week recovery period. Testosterone appeared to have a relatively long lasting suppressive influence on most affiliative responses. Minkin, Meyer, and van Haaren (1993) administered an anabolic steroid, nandrolone decanoate, for 8 weeks to six groups of normal and castrated male rats and also found a decrease in spontaneous behavior.

To determine if long-term exposure to high doses of anabolic steroids increases aggression and sexual activity in gonadally intact male rats, Lumia, Thorner, and McGinnis (1994) administered testosterone propionate 3 times per week for 10 consecutive weeks. Long-term treatment did not alter any parameter of male copulation. However, testosterone propionate-treated males were significantly more dominant and less submissive toward gonadally intact opponents than were control males. Using a high-dose cocktail of anabolic steroids (testosterone cypionate, nandrolone deconate, and boldenone undecylenate), Melloni, Connor, Hang, Harrison, and Ferris (1997) have also demonstrated increased aggressive behavior in adolescent male hamsters. Clark and Barber (1994) utilized the resident-intruder paradigm of aggression to evaluate the aggression-inducing properties of two anabolic steroids (methyltestosterone and stanozolol) in castrated male rats. Castrated male rats treated with methyltestosterone displayed levels of aggression equivalent to the levels displayed by castrated males treated with testosterone propionate on most of the behavioral indices assessed. In contrast, treatment with stanozolol produced no changes in aggressive behavior. Nor were any effects observed with either steroid treatment on the levels of locomotor behavior. Likewise, Martinez-Sanchis, Brain, Salvador, and Simon (1996), using high, moderate, and low doses of stanozolol over 21 days, have reported no significant effects on aggression and motor activity in young and adult intact male mice. These findings highlight the heterogeneity of anabolic steroid effects on the nervous system and behavior and indicate that the psychological effects reported by human anabolic steroid users may likewise depend upon the distinct chemical structures of the anabolic steroids used.

With regard to the behavioral and neurochemical effects of anabolic steroids and the neural mechanisms that may mediate the adverse effects of anabolic steroids on mental health, Bitran, Kellog, and Hilvers (1993) have reported that 1 week of treatment with testosterone propionate in intact male rats resulted in anxiolytic behavior that was accompanied by an increase in the sensitivity of cortical gamma-aminobutyric acid (GABA) receptors. However, observed changes were no longer present in a second group after 2 weeks of testosterone propionate exposure, indicating that tolerance to this may have developed.

To study the short-term effect of an anabolic steroid on behavior, Agren, Thiblin, Tirassa, Lundeberg, and Stenfors (1999) administered Metenolon three times, at a low dose, to rats. The steroid-treated rats showed less fear or anticipatory anxiety when compared with control animals, leading the researchers to conclude that Metenolon produced an anxiolytic drug effect at a low dose in rats. Similarly, Salvador, Moya-Albiol, Martinez-Sanchis, and Simon (1999), using several different steroids (testosterone propionate, nandrolone decanoate, and a mixture of both steroids), and single or repeated injections, found no effect of the steroids on spontaneous locomotor activity in intact, male rats. These results emphasize the importance of duration of treatment, the interaction with endogenous androgen levels, and specific type of activity (spontaneous or forced). Previous investigation by Martinez-Sanchis, Salvador, Moya-Albiol, Gonzalez-Bono, and Simon (1998) also found 10 weeks of treatment with various doses of testosterone propionate had little effect on aggression levels in intact male mice.

Anabolic steroid effects on brain reward have been investigated by Clark, Lindenfeld, and Gibbons (1996) using the rate-frequency curve shift paradigm of brain stimulation reward in male rats with electrodes implanted in the lateral hypothalamus. In the first experiment, treatment for 2 weeks with methandrostenolone had no effect on either the reward or performance components of intracranial self-stimulation. In a second experiment, treatment for 15 weeks with an anabolic steroid "cocktail" (testosterone cypionate, nandrolone decanoate, boldenone undecylenate) did not alter brain reward, but did produce a significant change in bar-press rate. In addition to the steroid treatment in the second study, animals were administered a single injection of dexamphetamine before and after 15 weeks of steroid exposure. The rate-frequency curve shift was significantly greater in animals after 15 weeks of steroid cocktail treatment. Results indicate that anabolic steroids may influence the sensitivity of the brain reward system.

Research by Le Greves, Huang, Johansson, Thornwall, Zhou, and Nyber (1997) demonstrates that chronic high doses of nandrolone decanoate affect the mRNA expression of NMDA receptor units in certain areas of the brain. Some of these areas may relate to a mechanism involved in the recently suggested steroid-induced stimulation of the brain reward system.

Bronson, Nguyen, and de la Rosa (1996) exposed adult female mice to a combination of four anabolic steroids for 9 weeks at doses that were either the same or 5 times the level of the androgenic maintenance level for male mice, in an investigation designed to examine the effects of anabolic steroids on the behavior and physiological characteristics of female mice. Behaviorally, steroid exposure decreased activity in an open field, increased aggressiveness, and eliminated one type of sexual behavior. Overall, there was little or no difference in the effect of high and low steroid dose, suggesting a threshold effect. In a related study by Bronson (1996), adult male and female mice were treated with the same combination of four anabolic steroids at pharmacological doses for 6 months to determine the effects of prolonged exposure to steroids on behavior. Males were exposed to either 5 or 20 times androgenic maintenance levels, and females were exposed to either the same or 5 times the maintenance level for males. Steroids increased aggressiveness in females, but not in males. Results of this experiment suggest no enhancement of normal androgenic-mediated behavior in males, but significant effects on female behavior.

In summary, these recent investigations, demonstrating behavioral changes associated with the administration of exogenous testosterone, support previous reports documenting a relationship between endogenous testosterone levels and behavioral changes in animals (Bahrke, Yesalis, & Wright, 1990). However, conclusions drawn from animal models must be applied cautiously to humans. For example, it is difficult to show that animals experience emotional states that are qualitatively similar to human experiences, such as euphoria, depression, and anger. Also, humans cannot be subjected to many of the same stringent controls and manipulations used in animal research. Finally, the effects of sex hormones vary considerably among individuals as well as species.

Effect of Endogenous Testosterone Levels on Human Moods and Behaviors

Relative to the animal literature, fewer studies have assessed the relationship of endogenous or exogenous androgens to aggression or violent behavior in humans. Although a pattern of association between testosterone levels and both subjectively perceived and observed aggressive behavior in humans has been revealed in many earlier studies, the relationships between plasma testosterone and psychometric indices of aggression and hostility have been less consistent (Albert, Walsh, & Jonik, 1993; Archer, 1991, 1994; Bahrke, Yesalis, & Wright, 1990; Bahrke, Wright, Strauss, & Catlin, 1992; Gray, Jackson, & McKinlay, 1991; Rubinow & Schmidt, 1996).

Aggressive Behavior

Gladue (1991a) assessed aggressive behavioral characteristics in a large group of college men ($N = 517$) and women ($N = 43$) using a self-report instrument and found significant gender differences, with men reporting more physical and verbal aggression than women. Gladue (1991b) has also reported on the relationship of resting levels of testosterone and estradiol and self-reported aggressive behavior in men and women, including those who differed in sexual preferences. Adult men reported more physical and verbal aggression than did women. Men also had higher scores on measures of impulsivity and lack of frustration tolerance than did women, while women were more likely to avoid confrontation. Homosexual men were indistinguishable from heterosexual men on all measures of aggression. Homosexual women differed from heterosexual women on only physical aggression, in which homosexual women had lower scores. Total testosterone and estradiol were positively correlated with several indices of aggressive behavioral characteristics in men, but were negatively correlated with those same measures in women.

Data from a study designed to examine the relationship between testosterone and antisocial behavior in a sample of 4,462 U.S. male military veterans were reported by Dabbs and Morris (1990). They found that testosterone was correlated with a variety of antisocial behaviors among all individuals; however, socioeconomic status proved to be a moderating variable, with weaker testosterone-behavior relationships among individuals with high socioeconomic status. In another study, Booth and Dabbs (1993) found that men producing more testosterone are less likely to marry; once married, they are more likely to leave home because of troubled marital relations, extramarital sex, hitting or throwing things at their spouses, and experiencing a lower quality of marital interaction.

Dabbs, Jurkovic, and Frady (1991) have also examined the relationship of salivary testosterone and cortisol concentrations to personality, criminal violence, prison behavior, and parole decisions among 113 late-adolescent male offenders. Offenders high in testosterone had committed more violent crimes, were judged more harshly by the parole board, and violated prison rules more often than those low in testosterone. A significant interaction between testosterone and cortisol was found, in which cortisol moderated the correlation between testosterone and violence of crime. As cortisol concentrations increased, the correlation between testosterone and violent behavior dropped. Dabbs, Jurkovic, and Frady (1991) concluded that cortisol may be a biological indicator of psychological variables that moderate the testosterone-behavior relationship. Likewise, in a more recent study examining testosterone levels, crime, and prison misbehavior among 692 prison inmates, Dabbs, Carr, Frady, and Riad (1995) found that inmates who had committed personal crimes of sex and violence had higher testosterone levels than inmates who had committed property crimes of burglary, theft, and drugs. Inmates with higher testosterone levels also violated more prison rules, especially those involving confrontation.

Lindman, von der Pahlen, Ost, and Eriksson (1992), however, found no relationship between violent behavior and the serum concentrations of testosterone, cortisol, glucose, and ethanol obtained from 16 adult men taken into police custody after incidents of spouse abuse when concentrations were compared with sober state levels and data from equally intoxicated but nonviolent men. Similarly, measures of testosterone and concurrent self-ratings of aggression in 100 adolescent males over a 3-year period provide little evidence of a systematic relationship between aggression and concurrent or earlier measures of testosterone (Halpern, Udry, Campbell, & Suchindran, 1993).

Berman, Gladue, and Taylor (1993) found a significant positive relationship between endogenous testosterone levels in 38 male college students and direct aggression. Although individuals were also classified as either Type A or Type B behavior pattern, observations gave little evidence for the moderating effects of hormones on the level of aggression expressed by Type A behavior.

Responses to Winning and Losing

Gladue, Boechler, and McCaul (1989) have examined hormonal response to competition in men. Winners had higher testosterone levels than losers, with no significant difference between close and decisive contests. Cortisol levels did not differ between winners and losers, nor between close and decisive contests. Mood was depressed in decisive losers. The results indicate that the perception of winning or losing, regardless of actual performance, differentially influenced testosterone levels but not cortisol levels, and that changes are not simply general arousal effects but are related to mood and status change.

Findings from two experiments by McCaul, Gladue, and Joppa (1992) suggest that winning, even by luck or chance, can alter testosterone levels in men, and that mood may mediate such changes. In experiments in which male college students either won or lost money on a task controlled entirely by chance, winners reported more positive mood change than did losers. Winners also reported a more positive mood change and higher testosterone levels than did a neutral group that did not win or lose money. In both cases, winners exhibited significantly higher testosterone levels than losers. Likewise, Mazur, Booth, and Dabbs (1992) have observed that in nonphysical face-to-face competition, tournament winners show higher testosterone levels than losers. In addition, under certain circumstances such as closeness of competition, competitors show increases in testosterone before their games.

Conclusions

In summary, although several recent studies reveal a significant positive association between endogenous testosterone levels and aggressive behavior, other investigations do not. Additional research suggests that humans may undergo specific endocrine changes in response to victory or defeat and that mood may influence the degree of change.

Estrogen-Related Aggression

Research findings from animal studies have shown that aggressive behavior can be developed by estrogen as well as androgen administration (Simon & Whalen, 1986). In adolescent boys and girls, Susman, Dorn, and Chrousos (1991) have shown fewer emotional effects for gonadal hormones compared to adrenal androgens and other hormones. Although testosterone has been linked with aggression for many years, particularly in males, recent research indicates that estrogen, and not testosterone, may be partly responsible for increased aggression. Since testosterone, through the enzyme aromatase, can be converted in the brain to estrogen, higher levels of estrogen can act directly on brain cells.

Ogawa, Luban, Korach, and Pfaff (1995), in a study of the behavioral consequences of loss of functional estrogen receptors in male estrogen receptor knockout mice, have shown that a lack of estrogen receptors in the central nervous system modifies male emotional behavior in a manner not restricted to simple reproductive behaviors, demonstrating the relative importance of estrogen receptors in the regulation of male aggression.

In a study to assess the effects of sex steroids on aggressive behavior, Finkelstein and colleagues (1997) administered either depo-testosterone to hypogonadal boys or estrogen to girls at three physiological doses using a double-blind, placebo-controlled, 3-month, crossover design. Responses to placebo were compared with responses to hormones at specific doses. At the low dose, scores for aggressive impulses and physical aggression against peers significantly increased only for girls. At mid-dose, the scores for girls significantly increased for aggressive impulses, physical aggression against peers, and physical aggression against adults. The scores for boys significantly increased for physical aggression against adults. At the high dose, physical aggression against peers significantly increased only for boys. These results suggest that sex steroids affect aggressive behavior in adolescents. Girls showed larger and earlier increases than boys, suggesting that estrogen has a significant role in the change in aggression scores during puberty and that testosterone may exert its effect via conversion to estrogen.

The relationship between aggressive behavior and hormone levels appears to be more complex than just the result of elevated levels of testosterone. Taken together, these studies suggest an increased role for estrogen in aggressive behavior.

Male Contraceptive Studies and Moods

In addition to the above studies, which have examined the relationship between endogenous testosterone levels and aggression, others have been carried out over the past three decades to assess the contraceptive efficacy of testosterone-induced azoospermia.

In an investigation conducted by the World Health Organization Task Force on Methods for the Regulation of Male Fertility (1990), 157 of 271 men became azoospermic following weekly injections of testosterone enanthate (200 mg/wk), and were followed over a 1-year efficacy phase. Although many participants withdrew from the study, only 3 reported increased aggressiveness and libido resulting from the injections as the cause for their discontinuation.

Problems of increased aggressiveness or libido, if there were any, for men who remained in the study were not reported by the authors. Wu, Farley, Peregoudov, and Waites (1996), in a recent follow-up report to the original study, confirm the low overall incidence of adverse reactions and other side effects leading to discontinuation from the study. Increased fatigue, aggression, and cyclical changes in mood were among the most common reasons for discontinuation given by the participants.

Of the 399 healthy, male participants in a similar, but more recent investigation conducted by the World Health Organization Task Force on Methods for the Regulation of Male Fertility (1996), only 10 participants discontinued due to mood, aggression, or libido change.

Anderson, Bancroft, and Wu (1992), using a single-blind, placebo-controlled design and daily mood ratings, found no alteration in any of the mood states studied, including those associated with increased aggression, in 31 healthy men injected with testosterone enanthate (200 mg/wk) for 8 weeks. Bagatell, Heiman, Matsumoto, Rivier, and Bremner (1994) also found no significant change in self-reported sexual and aggressive behaviors (although some individuals complained of increased irritability) in 19 healthy men given testosterone enanthate (200 mg/wk) for 20 weeks and followed for several months thereafter.

In a study examining the effect of testosterone replacement therapy on mood changes in 54 hypogonadal males, Wang and colleagues (1995) found significant decreases in anger, irritability, sadness, tiredness, and nervousness and significant improvement in energy level, friendliness, and well/good feelings.

These studies suggest that concerns about adverse effects of moderate doses (200 mg/wk) of exogenous testosterone on male sexual and aggressive behavior have perhaps been overstated, particularly by the media. This dose (200 mg/wk), while less than that used by most serious competitive bodybuilders and strength athletes, equals or exceeds that used by many athletes in other sports (Yesalis & Bahrke, 1995).

Effects of Anabolic Steroids on Athletes' Moods and Behavior

Psychological and behavioral changes, such as increased aggressiveness and irritability, have been reported on an anecdotal basis by anabolic steroid users as well as their families and friends for many years. However, a previous review had determined that objective evidence documenting the short-term psychological and behavioral changes accompanying and following anabolic steroid use by athletes was extremely limited and inconclusive (Bahrke et al., 1990). Since then, several case, survey, and research studies addressing these issues have been published.

Case Reports

Leckman and Scahill (1990) have described two male athletes whose Tourette's syndrome symptoms uncharacteristically acutely worsened rather than improved in young adult life. Both were abusing high doses of anabolic steroids when, two weeks into a course of increasing androgen dosage, they noted worsened tic symptoms, heightened irritability, and aggressiveness. Both improved after withdrawal of exogenous androgens. According to Leckman and Scahill, the association between abuse of anabolic steroids and increased tic symptoms in these two patients may have been a chance event or a nonspecific response.

Pope and Katz (1990) have described three men who impulsively committed violent crimes, including murder, while taking anabolic steroids. Structured psychiatric interviews of each man suggested that steroids played a role in the etiology of the violent behavior. Pope and Katz suggest that the aggressive behavior associated with the use of anabolic steroids may pose a significant public health problem. Several other cases of apparent steroid-induced crimes have also been reported by Pope and colleagues (1996), suggesting that steroid use may occasionally be a significant, although uncommon, factor in criminal behavior. Corrigan (1996) has commented on two recent violent murders in which anabolic steroid use was implicated. In one case, a 29-year-old male bodybuilder used a hammer to batter his wife to death, and then shot himself through the head. In the second case, a 22-year-old male bodybuilder murdered a female companion by repeatedly bashing her head against a wall and then kicking her. However, Byrne (1997) has pointed out the presence of other psychoactive drugs (benzodiazepines and alcohol), in addition to anabolic steroid use, in these two murder cases.

A case in which brief exposure to a low dose of anabolic steroid resulted in a significant detrimental change in behavior, culminating in armed robbery, has been reported by Dalby (1992). The patient, a 20-year-old man, reported irritability, depression, and violent rages following a 5-week cycle of anabolic steroids. A 1-year jail sentence was imposed by a judge who ruled that steroid use was a mitigating factor in the commission of the robbery.

Schulte, Hall, and Boyer (1993) have described the case of child abuse and spouse battery by a 19-year-old male college football player who had been using multiple anabolic steroids over a 4-month period. No previous steroid use or aggressive and violent behavior was reported. However, during steroid use, the man became increasingly irritable and "rough" with his wife, both physically and sexually, and more impatient and punitive with their 2-year-old son. In an effort to discipline the child, the child's buttocks were scalded with boiling water. Upon cessation of steroid use, the man's irritability and violent outbursts resolved within a 2-month period. There was no recurrence at follow-up 18 months later. Repeated child sexual abuse and hypomanic episodes associated with anabolic steroid use and moderate cannabis intake has been reported in a 25-year-old male bodybuilder by Driessen, Muessigbrodt, Dilling, and Driessen (1996). Choi (1993) has also described several cases of violent criminal behavior, including rape and murder, associated with the use of anabolic steroids.

Stanley and Ward (1994) have recently described a case that relates anabolic steroid abuse to the development of psychiatric illness and violent crime in a 27-year-old male bodybuilder. He was treated with an anti-psychotic drug, ceased anabolic steroid use, and his psychotic symptoms and mood improved without further treatment. Increased self-reported aggression and libido has also been reported by Wemyss-Holden, Hamdy, and Hastie (1994) as an undesirable effect in a pilot study evaluating the effects of exogenous anabolic steroids on prostatic volume, reduction in urine flow rate, and alteration in voiding patterns in a 49-year-old male bodybuilder.

Cross-Sectional Studies

In addition to case reports, many cross-sectional studies documenting the psychological and behavioral effects of anabolic steroids have been published recently.

Lindstrom and colleagues (1990) surveyed 138 male bodybuilders from a local gym to determine the prevalence of anabolic steroid use, the relationship of health risks to use, medical knowledge of steroids, social background, and current socioeconomic status of users and found that 38% had used anabolic steroids and 81% had experienced undesired effects. Changes in mood (51%) and increased libido (34%) were two of the more frequently self-reported effects among steroid users.

Parrott, Choi, and Davies (1994) administered an aggression inventory and a mood questionnaire to 21 steroid-using male amateur athletes attending a needle-exchange clinic and found individuals reporting significantly higher levels of aggression, alertness, irritability, anxiety, suspiciousness, and negativism while using steroids compared with periods of nonuse.

Silvester (1995) interviewed 22 former elite male shot put and discus throw athletes to determine self-perceptions of the acute and long-range effects of anabolic steroids. Among other acute effects while on the drugs, an increase in aggressiveness and irritability was reported by 13 athletes, distinct feelings of well-being were reported by 10, and quicker recovery from workouts was reported by 5. Twenty athletes reported no long-range psychological effects attributed to steroid use, while 2 believed that their occasionally elevated level of aggressiveness or irritability stemmed from their past use of steroids.

In an investigation examining the effects of long-term, relatively high dose anabolic steroid use on hostility and aggression in 6 male strength athletes, Choi, Parrott, and Cowan (1990) reported significantly more self-rated aggression in the 3 steroid users during periods of use compared with periods of nonuse. Users, however, were also significantly more hostile and aggressive than nonusers during periods of nonuse. Violence toward women during periods of anabolic steroid use has also been reported by Choi and Pope (1994), who found significantly more verbal aggression and violence in steroid-using athletes toward their wives and girlfriends during periods of steroid use than in nonuser athletes.

In an investigation to determine psychiatric symptoms associated with anabolic steroid use, Perry, Yates, and Andersen (1990) compared 20 male weightlifters who were currently using anabolic steroids with 20 male weightlifters who had never used steroids. The steroid users reported significantly more somatic, depressive, anxiety, hostility, and paranoid complaints when using steroids than when they were not using the drugs and significantly more complaints of depression, anxiety, and hostility during cycles of steroid use than did nonusers. The absence of significant differences in the frequency of major mental disorders between the two groups led Perry, Yates, and Andersen to conclude that the organic affective changes associated with abuse of anabolic steroids usually present as a subsyndromal depressive disorder were not severe enough to be classified as a psychiatric disorder.

In another study, Perry, Andersen, and Yates (1990) used two self-report instruments and a verbal interview to examine mental status changes in 20 competitive and noncompetitive anabolic steroid–using weightlifters. Based on responses to the questionnaire, significant percentages of individuals admitted to increased hostility and aggression, depression, paranoid thoughts, and psychotic features during steroid use. The steroid users displayed more personality disturbances overall compared with a control group of 20 weightlifters who did not use anabolic steroids and with a sex- and age-matched control group from the local community. However, no individual personality disorder or trait differences were significant between steroid users and the weightlifter control group, and both the steroid-user and nonsteroid-user weightlifter groups exhibited more flamboyant features than the community controls. The verbal interview was unable to identify any psychiatric diagnoses that were occurring more frequently in either the weightlifter control group or the steroid group. No cases of panic disorder, major depressive episode, grief reaction, mania, or atypical bipolar disorder were found. Interestingly, there were two cases of major depression in the control group and one in the steroid users. Alcohol abuse was diagnosed in 65% of the weightlifter control group, while seven (35%) cases of abuse and two (10%) cases of dependence were recognized in the steroid users. Drug abuse was observed in one individual in the control group and in one steroid user, while drug dependence was seen in one of the steroid users.

Malone, Dimeff, Lombardo, and Sample (1995), using a demographic survey, psychological testing, and psychiatric diagnosis, examined the psychiatric effects of anabolic steroid use and the frequency of other psychoactive substance use in 164 participants. Current and past steroid users did not differ on psychological testing, but past steroid users had a significantly higher incidence of psychiatric diagnoses than nonuser and current user groups. Hypomania was associated with steroid use and major depression with steroid discontinuation. Past steroid dependence was observed in 13% of current users and 15% of past users. Current psychoactive substance abuse or dependence was relatively low in all user groups. Malone and colleagues concluded that anabolic steroid use may lead to psychiatric disorders in certain individuals, and the concurrent use of psychoactive drugs, other than steroids, does not appear to be common in weightlifters and bodybuilders who are training intensively.

Yates, Perry, and Andersen (1990) evaluated a series of illicit anabolic steroid users and compared them with a control group of age-matched alcoholics and two control groups. Using a self-report measure, anabolic steroid users were found to have increased risk for personality psychopathology compared with one of the control groups, although this risk appeared to be partially explained by a group membership effect, as weightlifter controls also had higher rates of psychopathology. Additionally, similar to the alcoholic groups, illicit anabolic steroid users demonstrated significant antisocial traits.

Lefavi, Reeve, and Newland (1990) used two questionnaires to compare present steroid users with nonusers and former users, and concluded that anabolic steroid use may be associated with more frequent episodes of anger that are of greater intensity and duration and are characterized by a more hostile attitude toward others.

In an investigation similar to the study by Lefavi and colleagues, Bahrke and colleagues (1992) examined the psychological characteristics and subjectively perceived behavioral and somatic changes accompanying steroid usage in current anabolic steroid users. The results were compared with those obtained from previous users and nonusers. Although both current and former users reported subjectively perceived changes in enthusiasm, aggression, irritability, insomnia, muscle size, and libido when using anabolic steroids, these changes were not confirmed in comparisons across groups using standardized psychological inventories. No relationship was found between steroid dose and psychological moods in steroid users. More recently, Galligani, Renck, and Hansen (1996) assessed personality traits in three groups of strength athletes who self-administered anabolic steroids at the time of testing, had stopped using steroids for at least 6 months, or had never used steroids. Current steroid users were significantly more verbally aggressive than past steroid users and nonusers. No other statistically significant group differences were found for the other 14 personality factors that included somatic anxiety, muscular tension, psychic anxiety, psychasthenia, inhibition of aggression, socialization, social desirability, impulsiveness, monotony avoidance, detachment, indirect aggression, irritability, suspicion, and guilt.

In one of the few investigations examining the psychological changes accompanying anabolic steroid use by female athletes, Bahrke and Strauss (1992) found lower hostility among female steroid users in comparison with nonuser female athletes. A significant decrease in hostility among steroid users following 14 weeks of steroid use was also reported. These findings both conflict with and confirm earlier research with male and female athletes and emphasize the need to further delineate the relationship between anabolic steroid use and psychological changes in female athletes.

Yates, Perry, and Murray (1992) compared the aggression and hostility levels of current and recent steroid-using weightlifters with a nonuser weightlifter control group. Significantly elevated scores were found for active steroid users compared with both former and nonusers. These researchers were unable to demonstrate a relationship between dosage and psychometric scores in users.

Moss, Panazak, and Tarter (1992) have examined the relationship between the use of anabolic steroids and specific personality dimensions in 50 male bodybuilders who were current or past users in comparison with a sample of 25 age-matched, "natural" bodybuilders who never used steroids. No personality differences were found. Current steroid users scored higher than nonusers only on psychometric scales measuring hostility, aggression, and somatization. No statistical differences were found for the numerous other scales, including, among others, anxiety, depression, confidence, vigor, confusion, obsessiveness, and sensitivity.

Two questionnaires were used by Burnett and Kleiman (1994) in a cross-sectional study to assess a broad range of psychological characteristics in adolescent athletes who reported anabolic steroid use. Similar data were obtained from adolescent athletes who did not use steroids and from non-athletic adolescents. Although some personality variables differentiated between athletes and nonathletes, no personality variables significantly differentiated between athletes who used steroids and athletes who did not use steroids. However, steroid users who were currently on a steroid-use cycle had significantly more depression, anger, psychic vigor, and total mood disturbance than those who were not on a cycle.

Using a structured interview, Pope and Katz (1994) compared athletes who were using steroids with nonusers and found 23% of the users experienced major mood syndromes in association with steroid use. In addition, steroid users displayed mood disorders during steroid exposure significantly more frequently than in the absence of steroid exposure, and significantly more frequently than nonusers. Significant positive relationships were found between total weekly dose of steroids used and the prevalence of mood disorders. Approximately 25% of the users appeared to show a syndrome of dependence on steroids.

Bond, Choi, and Pope (1995) used an aggression scale, three scales of current feelings (alertness, contentment, and calmness), and a color-word conflict task containing sets of neutral, verbally aggressive, and physically aggressive words to measure the effects of anabolic steroids on mood and attentional bias to aggressive cues in current users, former users, and nonusers. Attention bias did not significantly differ between groups, but current users took longer to name the colors of all three sets. Nonusers rated themselves as more affable on the only significantly different item of the aggression scale. There were no significant differences between the groups on the three scales of current feelings.

The relationship between anabolic steroids and psychiatric symptoms, including aggressiveness and violent behavior, among steroid users has been examined by Thiblin, Kristiansson, and Rajs (1997). Using retrospective evaluation based on information from forensic psychiatric evaluations, police reports, and court records, violent offenders were evaluated for current or previous use of steroids. Results suggest that steroids may produce violent behavior and other mental disturbances, including psychosis. According to Thiblin, Kristiansson, and Rajs, steroids may lead to violent acts in vulnerable persons not only during current use, but also after withdrawal. In a similar investigation, but with a considerably different outcome, Isacsson, Garle, Ljung, Asgard, and Bergman (1998) screened for anabolic steroids in the urine of individuals in a Stockholm jail who had been arrested for violent crimes. No steroids were detected in the urine samples of 50 prisoners who had volunteered to participate in the study. However, 2 of the participants admitted steroid abuse and 16 prisoners refused to participate. Consequently, no conclusions can be drawn regarding the relationship between steroid use and violent crime.

In summary, investigations reviewed in this section have been cross-sectional in design. Unfortunately, retrospective studies rely on recall, the accuracy of which depends upon the honesty and ability of the individual to provide information on both the frequency and type of psychological and behavioral disturbances as well as on the training and skills of the researchers responsible for the assessments. To recall psychological and behavioral problems, individuals must have specific memories about the disturbances and be able to retrieve the information. Some may lack the ability to recall incidents, some may have little awareness of what has happened, and others may tend to "blow" incidents out of proportion to the actual events. In addition, some events may be selectively forgotten or reported. Investigations reviewed in this section have not reported on the validity and reliability of an individual's ability to recall psychological and behavioral disturbances. While cross-sectional studies of the psychological and behavioral effects encountered by anabolic steroid users are generally easier to perform than longitudinal studies, they require considerable care in sampling so that the participants selected accurately reflect the population being studied. Methods of participant selection are significant limitations to many of the studies reviewed in this section. Cross-sectional studies are also limited in that the only information they provide is an indication of current status, with information regarding previous conditions generally missing.

Longitudinal Investigations

Although a considerable number of cross-sectional or retrospective studies have examined the psychological and behavioral effects of anabolic steroids, only a small number of longitudinal or prospective investigations have been conducted.

Hannan and colleagues (1991) found significant increases in hostility, resentment, and aggression after administering nandrolone decanoate and testosterone enanthate in a 6-week, double-blind study using healthy men. During the study, one participant reported an incident of unprovoked anger and another participant was treated in an outpatient clinic for a transient episode of confusion and uncontrolled crying. No other problems were reported by participants during this study. However, the failure to include control or placebo treatments and the small sample size were serious limitations in the design of this investigation. Note that these problems encountered by participants in this investigation have not been seen in the male contraceptive studies using similar doses and much larger participant groups (World Health Organization Task Force, 1990; Wu, Farley, Peregoudov, and Waites, 1996).

Su and colleagues (1993) used a 2-week, double-blind, fixed-order, placebo-control, crossover trial of methyltestosterone to evaluate the neuropsychiatric effects of an anabolic steroid in normal male volunteers. A sequential trial for 3 days each of placebo, lower dose, higher dose, and placebo was administered to participants. Significant increases in symptom scores were observed during higher-dose administration compared with baseline in positive mood, negative mood, and cognitive impairment. An acute manic episode was observed in one of the participants. Another participant became hypomanic. Based on these results, these researchers concluded that an anabolic steroid had a significant impact on mood and behavior in normal male volunteers during what they labeled as a "relatively low dose," short-term period of administration. The results of this study confirm anecdotal reports by steroid users of the aggressive effects of methyltestosterone (Duchaine, 1989). As Clark and Barber (1994) and Martinez-Sanchis and colleagues (1996) have pointed out, the psychological effects of steroids may depend upon the distinct chemical structure of the steroids used.

The personality traits of bodybuilders using high doses of anabolic steroids were observed over a period of 5 months and compared with a control group of nonusers by Cooper and Noakes (1994). Personality traits of users before the onset of steroid use, as assessed retrospectively, were not significantly different from those of the control group. However, users scored significantly higher than the control group on seven personality traits when using steroids. Also, users scored significantly higher on the same seven personality traits during periods of steroid use than during periods of nonuse. It is interesting to note that this study was able to document significant changes in personality traits that, by their very nature, are considered to be enduring and generally unchangeable characteristics.

Increased aggressive responding (button pressing) in male volunteers following experimenter-administered, gradually increasing doses of testosterone cypionate or placebo, using a double-blind, randomized, crossover design, has been recently reported by Kouri, Lukas, Pope, and Oliva (1995) in a prospective study examining the effects of anabolic steroids on level of aggression.

Bhasin and colleagues (1996) examined the effects of supraphysiologic doses of testosterone enanthate, administered for 10 weeks, on muscle size and strength. They randomly assigned healthy men to one of four groups: placebo with no exercise, testosterone with no exercise, placebo plus exercise, and testosterone plus exercise. Men in the exercise groups performed standardized weight training exercises 3 times per week. Standardized questionnaires were administered during the first week of a 4-week control period and after 6 and 10 weeks of treatment. For each man, a live-in partner, spouse, or parent answered the same questions about the man's mood and behavior. Neither mood nor behavior was altered in any group. In addition to increased fat-free mass and muscle size and strength in the strength-training men, the results of this prospective, double-blind, placebo-controlled study indicate that supraphysiologic doses of testosterone, with or without exercise, did not increase the occurrence of angry behavior. However, these researchers note, "the possibility exists that still higher doses of multiple steroids may provoke angry behavior in men with pre-existing psychiatric or behavioral problems." (p. 6)

In a long-term, 3-year, physician-managed, harm-reduction program for 169 anabolic steroid-using weight trainers, Millar (1996) reported that side effects were minimal, including aggression, which "was not a problem at any time." (p. 7)

The psychosexual effects of 3 doses of testosterone cycling in normal men have been studied by Yates, Perry, Maclndoe, Holman, and Ellingrod (1999). A sequential trial of 2 weeks of placebo injections, 14 weeks of 1 of 3 weekly doses of testosterone cypionate, and 12 weeks of placebo injections, was administered to the participants. All doses of testosterone demonstrated only minimal effects on measures of mood and behavior. There was no evidence of a dose-dependent effect on any measure and only 1 high-dose participant developed a brief syndrome with symptoms similar to an agitated and irritable mania. Ellingrod, Perry, Yates, Maclndoe, Watson, Arndt, and Holman (1997) have also reported that high doses of testosterone cypionate do not increase aggressive driving behavior, nor result in increased aggression among normal men.

Using a double-blind study design, Fingerhood, Sullivan, Testa, and Jasinski (1997) have evaluated the subjective and physiological effects of 3 single, increasing doses of testosterone; 1 dose of morphine; and placebo over 5 consecutive days. Testosterone produced no significant changes in self-reported or observed measures, unlike morphine, which produced significant changes in several measures, including "feel the drug," "like the drug," and "feel high." There were no adverse effects of administering high doses of testosterone, leading the researchers to conclude that single doses of testosterone do not result in the usual pharmacologic effects that are associated with abuse.

Finally, in a double-blind experiment, Bjorkqvist, Nygren, Bjorklund, and Bjorkqvist (1994) administered testosterone undecanoate, placebo, or no treatment to men over a 1-week period. Subjective and observer-assessed mood estimations were conducted before and after treatment. The results revealed a significant placebo effect. After treatment, the placebo group scored higher than both the testosterone and control groups on self-estimated anger, irritation, impulsivity, and frustration. Observer-estimated mood scores yielded similar results. The results suggest that androgen use causes expectations of, rather than an actual increase of, aggressiveness. As previously noted (Bahrke, Yesalis, & Wright, 1990), many of the psychological and behavioral changes reported by, and observed in, anabolic steroid users may be a direct result of expectancy, imitation, or role modeling. And, as Bjorkqvist and colleagues (1994) have so adroitly pointed out, "Dissemination of the myth of the steroid-aggressiveness connection may lead to anticipation (a placebo effect) of aggressiveness among steroid abusers and, in turn, to actual acts of violence. It may, in fact, work as an excuse for aggression." At least one investigation has noted the physiological and psychological placebo effects of anabolic steroids (Ariel & Saville, 1972).

In summary, while several recently published reports reveal a pattern of association between use of anabolic steroids by athletes and increased levels of irritability, aggression, personality disturbance, and psychiatric diagnoses, other reports do not. Several reports also document significant alterations in users' moods and, at times, violent behavior. One study indicates a relationship between total weekly steroid dose and the prevalence of mood disorders; several other studies do not.

Effects of Anabolic Steroids on Body Image

In addition to studies examining the psychological and behavioral effects of anabolic steroids, several investigations have examined the relationship between anabolic steroid use and body image (Wroblewska, 1997).

Using structured interviews with steroid-using bodybuilders and nonuser controls, Pope, Katz, and Hudson (1993) found two disorders of body image. Three of the 108 participants reported a history of anorexia nervosa. Nine of the participants, 2 of whom were former anorexics, described a "reverse anorexia" syndrome, in which they believed that they appeared small and weak even though they were actually large and muscular. All 9 reverse anorexia cases occurred among steroid users. Four participants reported that their reverse anorexia symptoms contributed to their decision to begin using steroids.

Pope, Gruber, Choi, Olivardia, and Phillips (1997) also have presented preliminary observations, including several case studies, suggesting that a substantial number of men and women may have a particular subtype of body dysmorphic disorder which they have termed "muscle dysmorphia." This condition may cause severe subjective distress, impaired social and occupational functioning, and abuse of anabolic steroids and other substances.

Blouin and Goldfield (1995) also have examined the association between body image and steroid use among male bodybuilders, runners, and martial artists. The bodybuilders in the study self-reported the greatest use of steroids and had significantly greater body dissatisfaction, with a high drive for bulk, high drive for thinness, and greater bulimic tendencies than either of the other two athletic groups. Bodybuilders also reported significant elevations on measures of perfectionism, ineffectiveness, and lower self-esteem. The results suggest that male bodybuilders who use anabolic steroids may be at risk for body image disturbance. Conversely, male bodybuilders may be more susceptible to anabolic steroid use.

Contrary to the researchers' expectations, anabolic steroid use was rare (0.6%) and was not associated with a desire for weight gain in a cross-sectional survey by Drewnowski, Kurth, and Krahn (1995) that examined body image, dieting and exercise variables, and steroid use in 2,088 male high school graduates. Steroid users were more likely to engage in running and swimming than football.

In an effort to construct a psychological profile of anabolic steroid users, Porcerelli and Sandler (1995), in a cross-sectional study, compared weightlifters and bodybuilders who did or did not use anabolic steroids on an objective measure of narcissism and on clinical ratings of empathy. Steroid users had significantly higher scores on dimensions of pathological narcissism and significantly lower scores on clinical ratings of empathy.

Effects of Anabolic Steroids on Psychological Dependence and Withdrawal

Previous research concerning the withdrawal effects encountered by some anabolic steroid users has led to a hypothesis that anabolic steroid use may result in psychological dependence (Bahrke, Yesalis, & Wright, 1990).

In 1991, Brower, Blow, Young, and Hill published their findings from the anonymous, self-administered questionnaire they used to investigate addiction patterns in male steroid-using weightlifters. At least one symptom of dependence was reported by 94% of the participants. Three or more symptoms, consistent with a diagnosis of dependence, were reported by 57%. Dependent users were distinguished from nondependent users by their use of large doses, more cycles of use, more dissatisfaction with body size, and more aggressive symptoms. Multiple regression analysis revealed that dosage and dissatisfaction with body size were the best predictors of dependent use. Patterns of other substance use, although not predictive of anabolic steroid dependence, revealed very low cigarette use but high alcohol consumption. Results from this study support the hypothesis that anabolic steroids can be addictive and suggest that dissatisfaction with body size may lead to dependent patterns of use.

The use of fluoxetine in treating depression associated with anabolic steroid withdrawal has been examined by Malone and Dimeff (1992). All four patients suffering from anabolic steroid withdrawal depression treated with fluoxetine responded in a time-course consistent with the response of major depression to antidepressant medications. Further study is needed to confirm these results.

In an investigation designed to determine factors undermining the success of prevention and harm-reduction strategies for anabolic steroid abuse, Cooper (1994) found that 10 of 12 steroid-using bodybuilders satisfied the diagnostic number of criteria for at least 1 of 11 standard personality disorders. All 12 users satisfied criteria for psychological substance abuse and 9 for psychoactive substance dependence on anabolic steroids.

Allnut and Chaimowitz (1994) have described the case of anabolic steroid withdrawal depression that was resistant to antidepressant therapy, but responded to electroconvulsive treatment. The patient had been using anabolic steroids for a period of approximately 2 years. During his steroid use, the patient noticed feelings of aggression and aggressive behavior. After reading about anabolic steroids, he became concerned and discontinued their use. Two months later he presented at the psychiatric emergency room with complaints of depression and suicidal ideation, which he related to the discontinuation of anabolic steroids 2 months earlier. He was treated with desipramine and haldol. A 4-week washout period followed an 8-week trial of fluoxetine. At this time, the patient received seven electroconvulsive treatments, after which he showed marked improvement in his depressive symptomatology and was discharged on desipramine.

Cowan (1994) has also reported a similar case of severe depression, in which a male bodybuilder that had been using steroids on and off for 2 years, as well as other drugs, presented to his physician with suicidal ideation following withdrawal from anabolic steroids. The patient also experienced loss of energy, deteriorated concentration, insomnia, and appetite impairment accompanied by weight loss. There was a family history of affective disorder. Following treatment and a partial recovery the man was discharged to an outpatient program. Cowan proposed that prolonged exposure to anabolic steroids and a biological vulnerability to affective disorder would explain the severity of the episode.

Previously only men have been reported as dependent on anabolic steroids. However, recently, the first case of steroid dependence in a woman has been reported by

Copeland, Peters, and Dillon (1998). A 30-year-old woman was prescribed methenolone acetate and oxymetholone tablets by her general practitioner. This was followed by her purchase and use of another illicit steroid (stanozolol). The patient reported various adverse effects, including increased aggression, as a result of her steroid use. She also qualified for the diagnosis of substance dependence. Copeland and colleagues recommend advising all patients of the potential for dependence when using anabolic steroids.

Methodological Issues

Although a number of reports documenting the occurrence of behavior changes, mood swings, and depression following cessation of steroid use have been published, most of these reports are case studies or studies involving small numbers of participants (Bahrke, Yesalis, & Wright, 1990). Case studies are limited in their representativeness. They do not necessarily allow valid generalizations to the population from which they came, and they are vulnerable to subjective biases. Cases may be selected because of their dramatic, rather than typical, attributes, or because they neatly fit an observer's preconceptions.

Methodological shortcomings of previously reviewed investigations designed to examine the psychological and behavioral effects of anabolic steroids have included (Bahrke, Yesalis, & Wright, 1990) inappropriate sampling strategies; lack of adequate control and placebo groups; failure to report the types, dosage, and length of administration of anabolic steroids; use of several types, doses, and lengths of administration of anabolic steroids; failure to assess and report other drug use; not measuring free testosterone levels and not measuring testosterone at appropriate times; not confirming anabolic steroid use by urinalysis; limitations of drug testing; the veracity of self-reports of aggression and drug use (Ferenchick, 1996); and a variety of techniques used to assess the psychological and behavioral outcomes. Unfortunately, despite attempts to reduce and eliminate these methodological limitations over the past few years, many of the same problems persist (Bahrke, Yesalis, & Wright, 1996).

Only three prospective, blinded studies documenting aggressive or adverse overt behavior resulting from anabolic steroid use have been reported (Hannan et al., 1991; Kouri et al., 1995; Su et al., 1993), and these studies have limitations. Additional methodological problems that have arisen recently include

- the impurity and content of anabolic steroids, especially those available through the black market,
- not differentiating between anabolic steroids and corticosteroids in prevalence surveys with adolescent participants, and
- the failure to consider weight training as a confounding variable when examining the psychological and behavioral effects of anabolic steroids.

Weight Training as a Confounding Variable

The idea that weight training must be considered a confounding factor when examining the psychometric and behavioral effects of anabolic steroids has been raised by Bahrke and Yesalis (1994). While psychological and behavioral changes are reportedly associated with anabolic steroid use, changes in personality, moods, and self-esteem following weight training have also been documented. However, the fact that many steroid users are also dedicated weight trainers has been overlooked in most studies examining the relationship between steroid use and behavioral changes. A triad may exist between steroid use, weight training as part of a "lifestyle" or commitment, and behavioral change (including dependence). Weight training and related practices must be considered potential confounding factors in future studies designed to examine the psychological and behavioral effects of steroids.

It is also possible that changes frequently attributed to steroid use may also reflect changes resulting from the concurrent use of other substances, such as alcohol, cocaine, amphetamines, or other stimulants such as ephedrine and caffeine, and from dietary manipulations, including nutritional supplements (McBride, Williamson, & Petersen, 1996; Newton, Hunter, Bammon, & Roney, 1993). The long-term effects of alcohol abuse include depression, psychosis, and hallucinations. Insomnia, confusion, anxiety, and psychosis, characterized by paranoia and hallucinations, are some of the long-term consequences of cocaine use. Chronic, high-dose use of amphetamines also can produce hallucinations, delusions, and disorganized behavior (Donatelle & Davis, 1996).

Distinguishing Between Anabolic Steroids and Corticosteroids

Recently, scientists have become aware that it is necessary in their surveys to differentiate between anabolic steroids and corticosteroids (Edbauer, Levine, & Stapleton, 1992). As a result of widespread media coverage of the adverse effects of anabolic steroids, many people now confuse anabolic steroids with corticosteroids that are frequently used in the treatment of many common medical disorders, including acute inflammatory conditions. "Steroidophobia" has become a legitimate concern in asthma management, because asthma patients and the general public frequently confuse anabolic steroids with corticosteroids ("Steroidophobia," 1993).

In a related issue, Higgins (1993) has described the confusion of a bodybuilder over the use of prednisone (a corticosteroid) and anabolic steroids. Perry and Hughes (1992) have also described the problems encountered by a bodybuilder taking a substance (haldol decanoate) he mistakenly thought was an anabolic steroid (nandrolone decanoate).

Purity and Content of Anabolic Steroids

It has been estimated that as much as 50 to 80% or more of the anabolic steroids used by athletes may have been obtained from black-market sources (Office of Diversion Control, 1994). Many of the anabolic steroids found in the illegal market often do not contain the ingredients or dose indicated on the label.

Conclusions

Nearly fifty reports concerning the psychological and behavioral effects of endogenous testosterone levels and anabolic steroids have been published in the past few years. In addition to their traditional medical uses, anabolic steroids are now beginning to be used as male contraceptives and to supplement declining testosterone levels in aging males. Unfortunately, information concerning the legitimate adverse behavioral effects of anabolic steroids has often been inaccurate and wildly speculative. As a result, the frequent and often hysterical references by the media to the unsubstantiated adverse behavioral effects of anabolic steroids has resulted in the loss of both media and medical/scientific credibility, deterring research on beneficial and legitimate uses, and stimulating litigation against physicians (Kochakian, 1989). Significant positive effects resulting from anabolic steroid administration also may have been overlooked. Also, it is quite possible that the lack of accurate and balanced reporting by the media has hindered efforts to prevent and reduce the use of anabolic steroids. Despite enactment of legislation to restrict the use of anabolic steroids, use to promote muscular strength development and improve physical appearance continues among a diverse population.

Previous and current research documents an association between levels of endogenous testosterone and behavioral changes in animals. Although fewer studies have examined the relationship between endogenous androgens and aggressive and violent behavior in humans, a pattern of association between endogenous testosterone levels and aggressive behavior in males has been increasingly established. While studies using moderate doses of exogenous testosterone for contraceptive and clinical purposes reveal few adverse effects on male sexual and aggressive behavior, other investigations, and case reports of athletes using higher doses, suggest the possibility of affective and psychotic syndromes (some of violent proportions), psychological dependence, and withdrawal symptoms.

Aggression is defined on a broad spectrum. The fact that a steroid user feels more aggressive and self-reports more aggression does not necessarily indicate increased violent behavior or a psychiatric disorder.

The prevalence and symptomology of anabolic steroid dependence is difficult to reliably establish because of the small number of cases. In addition to small sample sizes, the variety of anabolic steroids used, and the diversity of techniques used to assess the psychological and behavioral changes associated with anabolic steroid use, other factors such as the purity and content of steroids and the concomitant use of other drugs further complicate an already complex area. Unfortunately, despite attempts to reduce and eliminate the number of methodological limitations associated with investigating the psychological and behavioral effects of anabolic steroids, these problems persist.

Although anabolic steroid dependency may be a problem, its prevalence and symptomology is difficult to reliably establish based upon the existing literature. With present estimates of 300,000 yearly anabolic steroid users in the United States (Yesalis, Kennedy, Kopstein, & Bahrke, 1993), an extremely small percentage of users appear to experience psychological dependence requiring clinical treatment. Additional research with larger and more heterogeneous samples will be needed.

Only three prospective, blinded studies documenting aggression and adverse overt behavior resulting from steroid use have been reported (Hannan et al., 1991; Kouri et al., 1995; Su et al., 1993). As Bjorkqvist and colleagues (1994) point out, much of the psychological and behavioral effect of steroid intake may be placebo. Anticipation of the aggressiveness related to steroid use may lead to actual violent acts and become, in effect, an excuse for aggression. Again, it is interesting to note that with a million or more steroid users in the United States (Yesalis et al., 1993), only an extremely small percentage of users appear to experience mental disturbances that result in clinical treatment. Also, of the small number of individuals who do experience significant changes, most apparently recover without additional problems when the use of steroids is terminated.

References

Agren, G., Thiblin, I., Tirassa, P., Lundeberg, T., & Stenfors, C. (1999). Behavioural anxiolytic effects of low-dose anabolic androgenic steroid treatment in rats. *Physiology and Behavior, 66*, 503–509.

Albert, D.J., Walsh, M.L., & Jonik, R.H. (1993). Aggression in humans: What is its biological foundation? *Neuroscience and Biobehavioral Reviews, 17*, 405–425.

Allnutt, S., & Chaimowitz, G. (1994). Anabolic steroid withdrawal depression: A case report. *Canadian Journal of Psychiatry, 39*, 317–318.

Anderson, R.A., Bancroft, J., & Wu, F.C.W. (1992). The effects of exogenous testosterone on sexuality and mood of normal men. *Journal of Clinical Endocrinology and Metabolism, 75*, 1503–1507.

Archer, J. (1991). The influence of testosterone on human aggression. *British Journal of Psychology, 82*, 1–28.

Archer, J. (1994). Testosterone and aggression. *Journal of Offender Rehabilitation, 21*(3/4), 3–39.

Ariel, G., & Saville, W. (1972). Anabolic steroids: The physiological effects of placebos. *Medicine and Science in Sports, 4*(2), 124–126.

Bagatell, C.J., Heiman, J.R., Matsumoto, A.M., Rivier, J.E., & Bremner, W.J. (1994). Metabolic and behavioral effects of high-dose exogenous testosterone in healthy men. *Journal of Clinical Endocrinology and Metabolism, 79*, 561–567.

Bahrke, M.S. (1993). Psychological effects of endogenous testosterone and anabolic-androgenic steroids. In C.E. Yesalis (Ed.), *Anabolic steroids in sport and exercise* (pp. 161–192). Champaign, IL: Human Kinetics.

Bahrke, M.S., & Strauss, R.H. (1992). Selected psychological characteristics of female anabolic-androgenic steroid (AAS) users. *Medicine and Science in Sports and Exercise, 24*, S136.

Bahrke, M.S., Wright, J.E., Strauss, R.H., & Catlin, D.H. (1992). Psychological moods and subjectively perceived behavioral and somatic changes accompanying anabolic-androgenic steroid usage. *American Journal of Sports Medicine, 20*, 717–724.

Bahrke, M.S., & Yesalis, C.E. (1994). Weight training: A potential confounding factor in examining the psychological and behavioral effects of anabolic-androgenic steroids. *Sports Medicine, 18*, 309–318.

Bahrke, M.S., Yesalis, C.E., and Wright, J.E. (1990). Psychological and behavioural effects of endogenous testosterone levels and anabolic-androgenic steroids among males: A review. *Sports Medicine, 10*, 303–337.

Bahrke, M.S., Yesalis, C.E., & Wright, J.E. (1996). Psychological and behavioural effects of endogenous testosterone levels and anabolic-androgenic steroids: An update. *Sports Medicine, 22*, 367–390.

Berman, M., Gladue, B., & Taylor, S. (1993). The effects of hormones, Type A behavior pattern, and provocation on aggression in men. *Motivation and Emotion, 17*(2), 125–138.

Bhasin, S., Storer, T.W., Berman, N., Callgari, C., Clevenger, B., Phillips, J., Bunnell, T.J., Tricker, R., Shirazi, A., & Casaburi, R. (1996). The effects of supraphysiologic doses of testosterone on muscle size and strength in normal men. *New England Journal of Medicine, 335*(1), 1–7.

Bitran, D., Kellog, C.K., & Hilvers, R.J. (1993). Treatment with an anabolic-androgenic steroid affects anxiety-related behavior and alters the sensitivity of cortical $GABA_A$ receptors in the rat. *Hormones and Behavior, 27*, 568–583.

Bjorkqvist, K., Nygren, T., Bjorklund, A-C., & Bjorkqvist, S-E. (1994). Testosterone intake and aggressiveness: Real effect or anticipation. *Aggressive Behavior, 20*, 17–26.

Blackwell, J. (1991). Discourses on drug use: The social construction of a steroid scandal. *Journal of Drug Issues, 21*(1), 147–164.

Blouin, A.G., & Goldfield, G.S. (1995). Body image and steroid use in male bodybuilders. *International Journal of Eating Disorders, 18*(2), 159–165.

Booth, A., & Dabbs, J.M. (1993). Testosterone and men's marriages. *Social Forces, 72*, 463–477.

Bond, A.J., Choi, P.Y.L., & Pope, H.G. (1995). Assessment of attentional bias and mood in users and non-users of anabolic-androgenic steroids. *Drug and Alcohol Dependence, 37*(3), 241–245.

Bronson, F.H. (1996). Effects of prolonged exposure to anabolic steroids on the behavior of male and female mice. *Pharmacology, Biochemistry and Behavior, 53*, 329–334.

Bronson, F.H., Nguyen, K.Q., & de la Rosa, J. (1996). Effect of anabolic steroids on behavior and physiological characteristics of female mice. *Physiology and Behavior, 59*(1), 49–55.

Brower, K.J., Blow, F.C., Beresford, T.P., & Fuelling, C. (1989). Anabolic-androgenic steroid dependence. *Journal of Clinical Psychiatry, 50*(1), 31–33.

Brower, K.J., Blow, F.C., Young, J.P., &Hill, E.M. (1991). Symptoms and correlates of anabolic-androgenic steroid dependence. *British Journal of Addiction, 86*, 759–768.

Buckley, W.E., Yesalis, C.E., Friedl, K.E., Anderson, W.A., Streit, A., & Wright, J. (1988). Estimated prevalence of anabolic steroid use among male high school seniors. *Journal of the American Medical Association, 260*, 3441–3445.

Burnett, K.F., & Kleiman, M.E. (1994). Psychological characteristics of adolescent steroid users. *Adolescence, 29*(113), 81–89.

Byrne, A.J. (1997). Anabolic steroids and the mind. *Medical Journal of Australia, 166*, 224.

Choi, P.Y.L. (1993, June). Alarming effects of anabolic steroids. *The Psychologist*, 258–260.

Choi, P.Y.L., Parrott, A.C., & Cowan, D. (1990). High-dose anabolic steroids in strength athletes: Effects upon hostility and aggression. *Human Psychopharmacology, 5*, 349–356.

Choi, P.Y.L., & Pope, H.G. (1994). Violence toward women and illicit androgenic-anabolic steroid use. *Annals of Clinical Psychiatry, 6*(1), 21–25.

Clark, A.S., & Barber, D.M. (1994). Anabolic-androgenic steroids and aggression in castrated male rats. *Physiology and Behavior, 56*, 1107–1113.

Clark, A.S., Lindenfeld, R.C., & Gibbons, C.H. (1996). Anabolic-androgenic steroids and brain reward. *Pharmacology, Biochemistry and Behavior, 53*, 741–745.

Cooper, C. (1994). Factors undermining the success of prevention and harm reduction strategies for anabolic-androgenic steroid abuse. In D. Adey, P. Steyn, N. Herman, et al. (Eds.), *State of the art in higher education* (Vol. I, pp. 133-142). Pretoria, South Africa: University of South Africa.

Cooper, U., & Noakes, T.D. (1994). Psychiatric disturbances in users of anabolic steroids. *South African Medical Journal, 84*, 509–512.

Copeland, J., Peters, R., & Dillon, P. (1998). Anabolic-androgenic steroid dependence in a woman. *Australian New Zealand Journal of Psychiatry, 32*, 589.

Corrigan, B. (1996). Anabolic steroids and the mind. *Medical Journal of Australia, 165*(4), 222–226.

Cowan, C.B. (1994). Depression in anabolic steroid withdrawal. *Irish Journal of Psychological Medicine, 11*(1), 27–28.

Dabbs, J.M., Carr, T.S., Frady, R.L., & Riad, J.K. (1995). Testosterone, crime, and misbehavior among 692 male prison inmates. *Personal and Individual Differences, 18*, 627–633.

Dabbs, J.M., Jurkovic, G.J., & Frady, R.L. (1991). Salivary testosterone and cortisol among late adolescent male offenders. *Journal of Abnormal Child Psychology, 19*, 469–478.

Dabbs, J.M., & Morris, R. (1990). Testosterone, social class, and antisocial behavior in a sample of 4,462 men. *Psychological Science, 1*(3), 209–211.

Dalby, J.T. (1992). Brief anabolic steroid use and sustained behavioral reaction. *American Journal of Psychiatry, 149*(2), 271–272.

Donatelle, R.J., & Davis, L.G. (1996). *Access to health.* Boston: Allyn & Bacon.

Drewnowski, A., Kurth, C.L., &. Krahn, D.D. (1995). Effects of body image on dieting, exercise, and anabolic steroid use in adolescent males. *International Journal of Eating Disorders, 17*, 381–386.

Driessen, M., Muessigbrodt, H., Dilling, H., & Driessen, B. (1996). Child sexual abuse associated with anabolic androgenic steroid use. *American Journal of Psychiatry, 153*, 1369.

Duchaine, D. (1989). *Underground steroid handbook II.* Venice, CA: HLR Technical Books.

Edbauer, M.J., Levine, A.M., & Stapleton, F.B. (1992). The importance of differentiating between anabolic steroids and glucocorticoids. *New York State Journal of Medicine, 92*(8), 365.

Ellingrod, V.L., Perry, P.J., Yates, W.R., MacIndoe, J.H., Watson, G., Arndt, S., & Holman, T.L. (1997). The effects of anabolic steroids on driving performance as assessed by the Iowa Driver Simulator. *American Journal of Drug and Alcohol Abuse, 23*, 623–636.

Elofson, G., & Elofson, S. (1990). Steroids claimed our son's life. *The Physician and Sportsmedicine, 18*(8), 15–16.

Ferenchick, G.S. (1996). Validity of self-report in identifying anabolic steroid use among weightlifters. *Journal of General Internal Medicine, 11*, 554–556.

Fingerhood, M.I., Sullivan, J.T., Testa, M., & Jasinski, D.R. (1997). Abuse liability of testosterone. *Journal of Psychopharmacology, 11*, 59–63.

Finkelstein, J.W., Susman, E.J., Chinchilli, V.M., Kunselman, S.J., D'arcangelo, M.R., Schwab, J., Demers, L.M., Liben, L.S. Lookingbill, G., & Kulin, H.E. (1997). Estrogen or testosterone increases self-reported aggressive behaviors in hypogonadal adolescents. *Journal of Clinical Endocrinology and Metabolism, 82*, 2423–2438.

Galligani, N., Renck, A., & Hansen, S. (1996). Personality profile of men using anabolic androgenic steroids. *Hormones and Behavior, 30*, 170–175.

Gladue, B.A. (1991a). Qualitative and quantitative sex differences in self-reported aggressive behavioral characteristics. *Psychological Reports, 68*, 675–684.

Gladue, B.A. (1991b). Aggressive behavioral characteristics, hormones, and sexual orientation in men and women. *Aggressive Behavior, 17*, 313–326.

Gladue, B.A., Boechler, M., & McCaul, K.D. (1989). Hormonal responses to competition in human males. *Aggressive Behavior, 15*, 409–422.

Gray, A., Jackson, D.N., & McKinlay, J.B. (1991). The relation between dominance, anger, and hormones in normally aging men: Results from the Massachusetts Male Aging Study. *Psychosomatic Medicine, 53*, 375–385.

Halpern, C.T., Udry, J.R., Campbell, B., & Suchindran, C. (1993). Relationship between aggression and pubertal increases in testosterone: A panel analysis of adolescent males. *Social Biology, 40*(1/2), 8–24.

Hannan, C.J., Friedl, K.E., Zold, A., Kettler, T.M., & Plymate, S.R. (1991). Psychological and serum homovanillic acid changes in men administered androgenic steroids. *Psychoneuroendocrinology, 16*, 335–342.

Higgins, G.L. (1993). Adonis meets Addison: Another potential cause of occult adrenal insufficiency. *Journal of Emergency Medicine, 11*, 761–762.

The insanity of steroid abuse. (1988, May 23). *Newsweek,* 75.

Isacsson, G., Garle, M., Ljung, E-B., Asgard, U., & Bergman, U. (1998). Anabolic steroids and violent crime—an epidemiological study at a jail in Stockholm, Sweden. *Comprehensive Psychiatry, 39*(4), 203–205.

Johnson, M.D., Jay, S., Shoup, B., and Rickert, V.I. (1989). Anabolic steroid use in adolescent males. *Pediatrics, 83*, 921–924.

Kochakian, C.D. (1989, July 30–31). *The steroids in sports problem.* Paper presented at the National Steroid Consensus Meeting.

Kouri, E.M., Lukas, S.E., Pope, H.G., & Oliva, P.S. (1995). Increased aggressive responding in male volunteers following the administration of gradually increasing doses of testosterone cypionate. *Drug and Alcohol Dependence, 40*(1), 73–79.

Leckman, J.F., & Scahill, L. (1990). Possible exacerbation of tics by androgenic steroids. *New England Journal of Medicine, 322*, 1674.

Lefavi, R.G., Reeve, T.G., & Newland, M.C. (1990). Relationship between anabolic steroid use and selected psychological parameters in male bodybuilders. *Journal of Sport Behavior, 13*(3), 157–166.

Le Greves, P., Huang, W., Johansson, P., Thornwall, M., Zhou, Q., & Nyberg, F. (1997). Effects of anabolic-androgenic steroid on the regulation of the NMDA receptor NR1, NR2A subunit mRNAs in brain regions of the male rat. *Neuroscience Letters, 226*, 61–64.

Lindman, R., von der Pahlen, B., Ost, B., & Eriksson, C.J.P. (1992). Serum testosterone, cortisol, glucose, and ethanol in males arrested for spouse abuse. *Aggressive Behavior, 18*, 393–400.

Lindstrom, M., Nilsson, A.L., Katzman, P.L., Janson, L., & Dymling, J-F. (1990). Use of anabolic-androgenic steroids among bodybuilders—frequency and attitudes. *Journal of Internal Medicine, 227*, 407–411.

Lumia, A.R., Thorner, K.M., & McGinnis, M.Y. (1994). Effects of chronically high doses of the anabolic androgenic steroid, testosterone, on intermale aggression and sexual behavior in male rats. *Physiology and Behavior, 55*, 331–335.

Malone, D.A., & Dimeff, R.J. (1992). The use of fluoxetine in depression associated with anabolic steroid withdrawal: A case series. *Journal of Clinical Psychiatry, 53*(4), 130–132.

Malone, D.A., Dimeff, R.J., Lombardo, J.A., & Sample, R.H.B. (1995). Psychiatric effects and psychoactive substance use in anabolic-androgenic steroid users. *Clinical Journal of Sports Medicine, 5*(1), 25–31.

Martinez-Sanchis, S., Brain, P.F., Salvador, A., & Simon, V.M. (1996). Long-term chronic treatment with stanozolol lacks significant effects on aggression and activity in young and adult male laboratory mice. *General Pharmacology, 27*(2), 293–298.

Martinez-Sanchis, S., Salvador, A., Moya-Albiol, L., Gonzalez-Bono, E., & Simon, V.M. (1998). Effects of chronic treatment with testosterone propionate on aggression and hormonal levels in intact male mice. *Psychoneuroendocrinology, 23*(3), 275–293.

Mazur, A., Booth, A., & Dabbs, J.M. (1992). Testosterone and chess competition. *Social Psychology Quarterly, 55*(1), 70–77.

McBride, A.J., Williamson, K., & Petersen, T. (1996). Three cases of nalbuphine hydrochloride dependence associated with anabolic steroids use. *British Journal of Sports Medicine, 30*, 69–70.

McCaul, K.D., Gladue, B.A., & Joppa, M. (1992). Winning, losing, mood, and testosterone. *Hormones and Behavior, 26*(4), 486–504.

Melloni, R.H., Connor, D.F., Hang, P.T.X., Harrison, R.J., & Ferris, C.F. (1997). Anabolic-androgenic steroid exposure during adolescence and aggressive behavior in golden hamsters. *Physiology and Behavior, 61*, 359–364.

Millar, A.P. (1996). Anabolic steroids--a personal pilgrimage. *Journal of Performance Enhancing Drugs, 1*(1), 4–9.

Minkin, D.M., Meyer, M.E., & van Haaren, F. (1993). Behavioral effects of long-term administration of an anabolic steroid in intact and castrated male Wistar rats. *Pharmacology, Biochemistry and Behavior, 44*, 959–963.

Moss, H.B., Panazak, G.L., & Tarter, R.E. (1992). Personality, mood, and psychiatric symptoms among anabolic steroid users. *American Journal on Addictions, 1*(4), 315–324.

Newton, L.E., Hunter, G., Bammon, M., & Roney, R. (1993). Changes in psychological state and self-reported diet during various phases of training in competitive bodybuilders. *Journal of Strength and Conditioning Research, 7*(3), 153–158.

NHL tough guy Kordic dies of lung failure at 27. (1992, August 10). *USA Today*, p. 15C.

Office of Diversion Control. (1994). *Report of the International Conference on the Abuse and Trafficking of Anabolic Steroids.* Washington, DC: United States Drug Enforcement Administration Conference Report.

Ogawa, S., Luban, D.B., Korach, K.S., & Pfaff, D. W. (1995, June 14–17). *Behavioral characteristics of transgenic estrogen receptor knockout male mice: Sexual aggressive and open-field behaviors.* Paper presented at the Seventy-Seventh Annual Meeting of the Endocrine Society, Washington, DC.

Orchard, J.W., & Best, J.P. (1994). Test violent offenders for anabolic steroid use. *Medical Journal of Australia, 161*(3), 232.

Parrott, A.C., Choi, P.Y.L., & Davies, M. (1994). Anabolic steroid use by amateur athletes: Effects upon psychological mood states. *Journal of Sports Medicine and Physical Fitness, 34*(3), 292–298.

Pearson, B., & Hansen, B. (1990, February 5). Survey of U.S. Olympians. *USA Today*, p. CI0.

Perry, H.M., & Hughes, G.W. (1992). A case of affective disorder associated with the misuse of "anabolic steroids." *British Journal of Sports Medicine, 26*(4), 219–220.

Perry, P.J., Andersen, K.H., & Yates, W.R. (1990). Illicit anabolic steroid use in athletes: A case series analysis. *American Journal of Sports Medicine, 18*, 422–428.

Perry, P.J., Yates, W.R., & Andersen, K.H. (1990). Psychiatric symptoms associated with anabolic steroids: A controlled, retrospective study. *Annals of Clinical Psychiatry, 2*(1), 11–17.

Pope, H.G., Gruber, A.J., Choi, P., Olivardia, B.A., & Phillips, K.A. (1997). Muscle dysmorphia: an unrecognized form of body dysmorphic disorder. *Psychosomatics, 38*, 548–557.

Pope, H.G., & Katz, D.L. (1988). Affective and psychotic symptoms associated with anabolic steroid use. *American Journal of Psychiatry, 145*, 487–490.

Pope, H.G., & Katz, D.L. (1990). Homicide and near-homicide by anabolic steroid users. *Journal of Clinical Psychiatry, 51*(1), 28–31.

Pope, H.G., & Katz, D.L. (1994). Psychiatric and medical effects of anabolic-androgenic steroid use. *Archives of General Psychiatry, 51*(5), 373–382.

Pope, H.G., Katz, D.L., & Hudson, J.I. (1993). Anorexia nervosa and "reverse anorexia" among 108 male bodybuilders. *Comprehensive Psychiatry, 34*, 406–409.

Pope, H.G., Kouri, E.M., Powell, K.F., Campbell, C., & Katz, D.L. (1996). Anabolic-androgenic steroid use among 133 prisoners. *Comprehensive Psychiatry, 37*, 322–327.

Porcerelli, J.H., & Sandler, B.A. (1995). Narcissism and empathy in steroid users. *American Journal of Psychiatry, 152*, 1672–1674.

Rejeski, W.J., Gregg, E., Kaplan, J.R., & Manuck, S.B. (1990). Anabolic steroids: Effects on social behavior and baseline heart rate. *Health Psychology, 9*, 774–791.

Rubinow, D.R., & Schmidt, P.J. (1996). Androgens, brain, and behavior. *American Journal of Psychiatry, 153*, 974–984.

Salvador, A., Moya-Albiol, L., Martinez-Sanchis, S., & Simon, V.M. (1999). Lack of effects of anabolic-androgenic steroids on locomotor activity in intact male mice. *Perceptual and Motor Skills, 88*, 319–328.

Schulte, H.M., Hall, M.J., & Boyer, M. (1993). Domestic violence associated with anabolic steroid abuse. *American Journal of Psychiatry, 150*, 348.

Silvester, L.J. (1995). Self-perceptions of the acute and long-range effects of anabolic-androgenic steroids. *Journal of Strength and Conditioning Research, 9*(2), 95–98.

Simon, N.G., & Whalen, R.E. (1986). Hormonal regulation of aggression: Evidence for a relationship among genotype, receptor binding, and behavioral sensitivity to androgen and estrogen. *Aggressive Behavior, 12*, 255–267.

Stanley, A., & Ward, M. (1994). Anabolic steroids--the drugs that give and take away manhood. A case with an unusual physical sign. *Medicine, Science and the Law, 34*(1), 82–83.

Steroidophobia: Public misperceptions of steroid medications. (1993). *Pharmacy Times, 59*, 42, 44.

Su, T-P., Pagliaro, M., Schmidt, P.J., Pickar, D., Wolkowitz, O., & Rubinow, D.R. (1993). Neuropsychiatric effects of anabolic steroids in male normal volunteers. *Journal of the American Medical Association, 269*, 2760–2764.

Susman, E.J., Dorn, L.D., & Chrousos, G.P. (1991). Negative affect and hormone levels in young adolescents: Concurrent and predictive perspectives. *Journal of Youth and Adolescence, 20*(2), 167–190.

Thiblin, I., Kristiansson, M., & Rajs, J. (1997). Anabolic androgenic steroids and behavioural patterns among violent offenders. *Journal of Forensic Psychiatry, 8*(2), 299–310.

Wang, C., Alexander, G., Berman, N., Salahain, B., Davidson, T., McDonald, V., Callegori, C., & Swerdloff, R.S. (1995, June 14–17). Effect of testosterone replacement therapy on mood changes in hypogonadal men. Paper presented at the Seventy-Seventh Annual Meeting of the Endocrine Society, Washington, DC.

Wemyss-Holden, S.A., Hamdy, F.C., & Hastie, K.J. (1994). Steroid abuse in athletes, prostatic enlargement and bladder outflow obstruction—is there a relationship? *British Journal of Urology, 74*, 476–478.

World Health Organization Task Force on Methods for the Regulation of Male Fertility. (1990). Contraceptive efficacy of testosterone-induced azoospermia in normal men. *Lancet, 36*, 955–959.

World Health Organization Task Force on Methods for the Regulation of Male Fertility. (1996). Contraceptive efficacy of testosterone-induced azoospermia and oligozoospermia in normal men. *Fertility and Sterility*, *65*, 821–829.

Wroblewska, A-M. (1997). Androgenic-anabolic steroids and body dysmorphia in young men. *Journal of Psychosomatic Research, 42*(3), 225–234.

Wu, F.C., Farley, T.M.M., Peregoudov, A., & Waites, G.M.H. (1996). Effects of testosterone enanthate in normal men: Experience from a multicenter contraceptive efficacy study. *Fertility and Sterility, 65*, 626–636.

Yates, W.R., Perry, P.J., & Andersen, K.H. (1990). Illicit anabolic steroid use: A controlled personality study. *Acta Psychiatrica Scandinavica, 81*, 548–550.

Yates, W.R., Perry, P.J., MacIndoe, J., Holman, T., & Ellingrod, V.L. (1999). Psycho-sexual effects of three doses of testosterone cycling in normal men. *Biological Psychiatry, 45*, 254–260.

Yates, W.R., Perry, P., & Murray, S. (1992). Aggression and hostility in anabolic steroid users. *Biological Psychiatry, 31*, 1232–1234.

Yesalis, C.E., & Bahrke, M.S. (1995). Anabolic-androgenic steroids: Current issues. *Sports Medicine, 19*, 326–340.

Yesalis, C.E., Kennedy, N.J., Kopstein, A.N., & Bahrke, M.S. (1993). Anabolic-androgenic steroid use in the United States. *Journal of the American Medical Association, 270*, 1217–1221.

37 Social Influence and Exercise: A Meta-Analysis

ALBERT V. CARRON, HEATHER A. HAUSENBLAS, AND DIANE MACK
University of Western Ontario

An increased public and scientific interest in exercise and health psychology has been evident during the past three decades. Attempts to understand the role that psychological factors play in exercise and health have focused on two major issues: the psychological benefits of exercise and exercise motivation. In the first category, exercise is investigated in the context of its positive effects on various facets of exercisers' well-being, such as personality, tension, anxiety, depression, self-esteem, mental health, and cognitive functioning. If regular physical activity does indeed improve people's well-being, then the second category becomes highly important. Here, the focus is on the ways of keeping people exercising consistently. Various determinants of exercise involvement, which can be used to promote exercise adherence, have been investigated.

To implement intervention programs based on various promotional strategies intended to enhance or maximize participants' exercise adherence, the impact of social influence on exercise involvement must be fully understood. Albert Carron, a prominent social sport psychologist, and his team undertook the challenge of reviewing the effects of various sources of social influence on manifestations of exercise involvement, such as behaviors, cognitions, and affect. To do that, they chose to use meta-analysis, a statistical review method presented in the late 1970s, which quantitatively integrates the findings of many studies conducted on a particular topic and enables the researchers to arrive at general conclusions on that domain.

Overall, the results obtained by Carron and his associates supported the general conclusion that social influence positively affects these manifestations of exercise involvement, but with a varying magnitude of effect sizes. This quantitative review provided an appropriate scientific picture of the state of the art of this social psychological domain at that time. It also identified some unexplained findings and unexplored issues that have been significant to our psychological understanding of social influence on exercise involvement.

Using meta-analysis, the impact of a number of manifestations of social influence (important others, family, class leaders, coexercisers, social cohesion, and task cohesion) on exercise behaviors (adherence and compliance), cognitions (intentions and efficacy), and affect (satisfaction and attitude) was examined. The results showed that social influence generally has a small to moderate positive effect (i.e., effect size [ES] from .20 to .50). However, four moderate to large effect sizes (i.e., ES from .50 to .80) were found: family support and attitudes about exercise, task cohesion and adherence behavior, important others and attitudes about exercise, and family support and compliance behavior.

An ongoing concern in the exercise sciences has been identifying effective promotional strategies at the societal level and intervention strategies at the group level to enhance adherence, compliance, or both in exercise programs (cf. Carron & Spink, 1993; Quinney, Gauvin, &Wall, 1994; Wankel & Mummery, 1994).

Research has shown that regular participation in physical activity is associated with a large number of psychological, physical, and physiological benefits.

Among the psychological benefits, for example, are reductions in state anxiety, decreases in the levels of mild to moderate depression, positive changes in personality for the traits of anxiety and neuroticism, and improvements in various stress indices (International Society of Sport Psychology, 1991). In addition, exercise has positive emotional effects for both sexes across all ages and can be a positive adjunct in the professional treatment of severe depression (International Society of Sport Psychology, 1991).

Among the positive physical and physiological changes identified are improvements in maximum oxygen uptake, decreases in percent body fat, decreases in body weight, decreases in blood pressure, improvements in flexibility, reductions in orthopedic spinal problems, changes toward a lower resting heart rate, and decreases in stress-related indicators such as cholesterol and triglyceride levels in the blood (cf. Hill, Glassford, Burgess, & Rudnicki, 1988).

Despite the substantial benefits associated with involvement in physical activity, epidemiological studies have shown that 41 to 51% of individuals between the ages of 18 and 65 are sedentary (National Center for Health Statistics, 1980). It also has been well-documented that exercise programs have difficulty in retaining participants. Typically, there is a 20 to 50% withdrawal rate in participation in the first 6 months of an exercise program (Dishman, 1988; Oldridge, 1984; Ward & Morgan, 1984).

Adapted, by permission, from A.V. Carron, H.A. Hausenblas, and D. Mack, 1996, "Social influence and exercise: A meta-analysis," *Journal of Sport and Exercise Psychology* 18: 1-16.

As indicated above, the question of how to alleviate problems associated with nonadherence is viewed as important. How can we effectively intervene to enhance adherence? One of the principal strategies used to address this question has been to identify the profile of correlates associated with nonadherence. Franklin (1988) has conveniently categorized the factors that correlate with nonadherence under three profile headings: personal, program, and other.

Components of the *personal* profile include smoker, inactive in leisure time, blue-collar occupation, type-A personality, increased physical strength, poor credit rating, overweight or overfat, low self-esteem, depression, hypochondria, anxiety, and low ego strength. The *program* factors found to be associated with exercise nonadherence are inconvenient time/location, excessive cost, lack of exercise variety, high intensive exercise, exercise alone, lack of positive feedback or reinforcement, inflexible exercise goals, low enjoyability ratings for running, and poor leadership. And, finally, under the category of *other* factors, Franklin identified lack of spouse support, inclement weather, excessive job travel, injury, medical problems, and job change/move.

Although the personal factors listed by Franklin might be useful to reliably describe, predict, or explain exercise adherence, it should be apparent that, ultimately, these factors will be of little or no value in any intervention program. Personality traits, for example, are very resistant to change, and influencing economic factors (e.g., blue collar, poor credit rating) is outside the domain of the sport scientist, medical practitioner, health promotion professional, or exercise leader.

An examination of the list of *other* factors summarized by Franklin contributes to a suggestion that most of these are not subject to intervention—the weather, job travel, injury, medical problems, and job change/move, for example. The sole exception is spousal support.

Subsequent research has contributed to the suggestions that social influence is positively linked to exercise involvement. Social influence is "either real or imagined pressure to change one's behavior, attitudes or beliefs" (Alcock, Carment, & Sadava, 1991, p. 195). Many of the program factors (as well as spousal support) identified by Franklin (1988) are a manifestation of social influence. And, as Baron and Byrne (1991) pointed out, "Perceptions, attitudes, and actions are strongly affected by other persons, either individually or collectively. In short, our behavior and thoughts are very different from what they would be if we lived in total isolation" (p. 311).

The general purpose of the present study was to quantify, through the use of meta-analysis, the impact of social influence on exercise involvement. When we initiated the literature search for the meta-analysis, it became apparent that exercise involvement (considered a dependent variable) has been operationally defined in a variety of ways. For example, one general line of research has examined the impact of others' influence on individual exercise *behavior* including both adherence (e.g., Massie & Shephard, 1971) and compliance (e.g., Daltroy & Godin, 1989). (The distinction between these two is that *adherence* is behavior that is self-selected and initiated, whereas *compliance* is behavior that is required or prescribed by others, such as a health-care professional.) Other research has provided evidence relating to the impact of others' influence on individual *cognitions* about exercise including intention (e.g., Wankel & Mummery, 1994) and self-efficacy (e.g., Yordy & Lent, 1993). Finally, other research has examined the impact of others' influence on individual *affect* associated with exercise, including attitudes about exercise (e.g., Godin, Vezina, & Leclerc, 1989) and satisfaction with the exercise experience (e.g., Carron & Spink, 1993).

Similarly, it became apparent that social influence as an independent variable has been operationally defined in a variety of ways in the exercise literature. The six major sources of social influence examined include important others such as physicians or work colleagues (e.g., Anderssen & Wold, 1992), family members (e.g., Miller, Johnson, Garrett, Wickoff, & McMahon, 1982), exercise instructors or other in-class professionals (Atkins, Kaplan, Timms, Reinsch, & Lofback, 1984), other coexercisers (e.g., Clifford, Tan, & Gorsuch, 1991), and social and task cohesive exercise groups (e.g., Spink & Carron, 1994).

Given the breadth of the operational measures of exercise involvement and social influence, a decision was made to examine the various combinations in a series of independent meta-analyses. Thus, the specific purpose of the study was to examine independently the impact of six sources of social influence (important others, family, exercise leaders, coexercisers, social cohesion, and task cohesion) on two manifestations of exercise behavior (adherence and compliance), two types of cognitions associated with exercise (intention and self-efficacy), and two types of affect associated with exercise involvement (satisfaction and attitude).

Method

Selection of the Data

The data for the study were generated through three principal sources: computer searches, manual searches, and journal searches. The computer searches used PsychLIT, MEDLINE, and SPORTdiscus. Manual searches were conducted using the reference lists from recent comprehensive empirical and narrative reviews (e.g., Dishman, 1988, 1994; Godin, 1994; Quinney et al., 1994). Finally, 12 journals considered likely to have pertinent research were examined from at least 1975 to the present (i.e., some of the journals did not publish prior to 1975): *Canadian Journal of Applied Sport Sciences, Health Psychology, International Journal of Sport Psychology, Journal of Applied Sport Psychology, Journal of Behavioral Medicine, Journal of Sport & Exercise Psychology, Journal of Sport Behavior, Journal of Sport Medicine and Physical Fitness, Journal of Sport Sciences, Perceptual and Motor Skills, Research Quarterly for Exercise and Sport,* and *The Sport Psychologist.*

The criteria for initial selection was the presence of key words: adherence, compliance, social support, dropout, aerobic, spousal support, motivation, satisfaction, exercise, physical activity, exercise behavior, attendance, attitude, and intention. Studies were discarded from further consideration if they either failed to compare the effect of at least one level of social influence on individual behavior, cognitions, or affect, or if they failed to provide usable statistics to compute an effect size. Five studies identified as consistent with the purpose of the study were not used because they failed to include statistics usable for meta-analysis.

Considerable discussion has revolved around the question of how many results should be used from the same study (cf. Wolf, 1986). In analyzing studies for the present meta-analysis, it became apparent that in some studies comparisons were made on more than one dependent variable. In those cases, a separate effect size (ES) was computed for each dependent variable. Thus, for example, if a study focused on the impact of a supportive family on adherence (behavior), efficacy for exercise (cognition), and satisfaction with the exercise experience (affect), three ESs were computed.

In other studies, multiple results pertaining to the same dependent variable were available. In those cases, an average ES was computed. Thus, for example, if a study examined the relationship between family support and exercise behavior at 1 month and 6 months, one (average) ES was computed from the two results.

Finally, in other studies, multiple results pertaining to different levels of the independent variable were available. In those instances, an ES was computed for each result. Thus, for example, a study might have evaluated the influence of social support provided by spouses, children, exercise partners, physicians, and exercise leader. Because of the coding scheme utilized (which is discussed subsequently), an average ES was computed from the spouse and children data, and three separate ESs were calculated from the exercise partners, physician, and exercise leader data.

A total of 87 studies containing 49,948 participants with 224 ESs were included in the meta-analysis.

Coding of the Data

Initially, each study was coded on the basis of the nature of the social influence and the dependent measure examined. The nature of the *social influence* was coded according to whether the study examined the impact of (a) important others (e.g., physicians, work colleagues), (b) family (e.g., spouse, children), (c) instructors or other professionals within the exercise environment, (d) the presence of other exercise participants, (e) social cohesion in the exercise group, or (f) task cohesion in the exercise group.

In some studies, a broad operational definition of social influence was used that incorporated both family members and important others. In those instances, the nature of the social influence was categorized as family support.

In some studies, the influence of others on the participant's exercise involvement was assessed through the use of psychological inventories. Although the results derived from these psychological inventories were not directly relevant to the purpose of the study, these data were also coded and examined. Two categorizations of results were coded. The first came from studies in which a psychological test assessed the need for affiliation (i.e., Is a high need for affiliation related to exercise adherence?). The second came from studies in which a psychological test assessed the degree to which powerful external others represented the locus of control for exercise involvement (i.e., Are nonadherers to exercise programs characterized by an external locus of control?).

The dependent measure—*exercise involvement*—was comprised of three general types of outcomes: behavior, cognitions, and affect. Two behaviors were recorded: adherence and compliance. Two cognitions were recorded: intention to exercise and self-efficacy for exercise. Finally, two measures of affect were recorded: attitude toward exercise and satisfaction with exercise.

Given that six measures of social influence (important others, family, class members, instructors, social cohesion, task cohesion) and six types of exercise involvement (adherence, compliance, efficacy, intention, attitude, satisfaction) were coded, it was theoretically possible to carry out 36 analyses. Following the lead of Thomas and French (1985), a meta-analysis was undertaken only in those instances where three or more ESs were available. For adherence behavior, it was possible to calculate an ES for each type of social influence. However, for compliance behavior, efficacy, intention, and attitude, all types of social influence were not sufficiently represented in every category. Only three studies (across two categories of exercise involvement) were found in which satisfaction was examined, so a decision was made to combine satisfaction and attitude into one category that was relabeled *affect.*

Computation of ES

The statistical techniques used to compute ES were those outlined by Hedges (1981, 1982) and Hedges and Olkin (1985) and summarized by Thomas and French (1986). That is, because ESs are positively biased in small samples, a correction factor was used on each ES prior to subsequent analyses. Also, each ES was then weighted by the reciprocal of its variance prior to combining ESs. An overall weighted mean estimate was then obtained using the formula provided by Hedges and Olkin (1985). Finally, an estimate of the variance of ES was obtained, again using the formula provided by Hedges and Olkin (1985). The designation ES is used in the present report (rather than ES') to represent effect sizes that underwent all of the above transformations.

Results

General Analyses

Initially, our interest was in determining whether there was homogeneity in ES within the total sample. The *H* statistic was computed using the weighted sum of squared deviations of ES from the overall weighted mean ES (Hedges & Olkin, 1985). The results showed that the distribution of ES was not homogeneous. $\chi^2(223, N = 224) = 50.14, p < .01$.

Given Cohen's (1969, 1992) suggestion that .20, .50, and .80 represent small, medium, and large effect sizes, respectively, it is apparent that the majority of the ESs are in the small to medium range. There are four exceptions—all of which are in the medium to large range. These are associated with the impact of (a) family support on affect associated with exercise involvement (ES = .59), (b) task cohesion in the exercise class on adherence behavior (ES = .62), (c) important others on affect associated with exercise involvement (ES = .63), and (d) family support on compliance behavior (ES = .69).

There is a marked contrast between the impact of family support on adherence (ES = .36) versus the impact of family support on compliance (ES = .69). This difference was statistically significant $t(57) = 5.32, p < .001$. Support from family members is almost twice as important when the individual is complying to an exercise prescription set out by a health professional than when the individual is exercising in a self-selected and initiated program.

The 95% confidence intervals associated with the ES for the influence of class members, class leaders, and social cohesion on adherence behavior include zero. Thus, these effects should be considered zero-order.

A number of authors have discussed the file drawer issue—the question of how many unlocated studies with null effects would have to be found to reduce the ES to a zero-order or minimal level (cf. Hunter & Schmidt, 1990; Rosenthal, 1979; Wolf, 1986). This question is particularly relevant in the present study given the relatively small number of studies that contributed to the computations of some of the average ESs. Consequently, a fail-safe *N* was computed to determine the number of unlocated, unpublished, or currently uncompleted studies that would be needed to reduce the average ES to a critical value of .10—the smallest ES that we would consider theoretically and practically important. We used a formula outlined by Hunter and Schmidt (1990), which is relatively conservative. As they noted, using their formula, "the number of missing studies averaging null results needed to reduce the effect size to [ES = .10] is usually much smaller than the number required to reduce the combined probability value to $p = .05$" (Hunter & Schmidt, 1990, p. 513).

Although the fail-safe *N*s are quite conservative, when they are considered in concert with the data pertaining to the 95% confidence intervals, it is reasonable to suggest that many of the ES should be viewed with caution.

Analyses From Psychometric Tests of Social Influence

Sufficient studies were available to examine the impact of social influence assessed through the use of psychometric tests on adherence behavior only. The results showed that powerful (external) others have a small negative impact on adherence behavior (ES = –.18, *SD* = .12; 95% confidence interval [CI] = .05 to –.42; fail-safe *N* = 1). In short, when the exercise participant holds the perception that the locus of control resides in the hands of powerful others, adherence behavior suffers, but the effect is small.

Psychological tests that assess affiliation motives/incentives appear to have no utility in accounting for adherence behavior; the ES is zero-order (ES = –.06, *SD* = .14; CI = .55 to –.69; fail-safe *N* = 1). As was the case above, however, the magnitude of the ESs in concert with the confidence interval and fail-safe *N* contribute to a suggestion that any conclusion about the relationship of psychological tests to adherence behavior must be viewed with caution.

Discussion

The results of the meta-analysis support an overall conclusion that social influence has a positive influence on exercise behavior (both adherence and compliance), cognitions about exercise involvement (both intentions to exercise and efficacy for exercise), and attitudes associated with the exercise experience. Paper-and-pencil tests of social influence show that powerful (external) others have a small negative impact, whereas affiliation motives/incentives appear to have no utility in accounting for adherence behavior.

One of the strongest ESs obtained was for the relationship of social influence of the family on compliance behavior. As was pointed out above, family members have almost twice as much impact when the individual is complying to an exercise prescription set out by a health professional than when the individual is adhering to a self-selected, personally initiated program. At the least, these results have strong implications for the implementation of programs involving exercise compliance. Spouses and other family members of individuals entering into a exercise compliance program should be instructed prior to the onset and throughout the course of the program to provide constant encouragement. The present results clearly show that compliance will be enhanced.

However, an examination of other ESs shows that the family does not represent the strongest source of social influence for adherence behavior. The influence of important others is slightly larger, and the presence of a task-cohesive group has almost twice the social impact of family. We were unable to examine the impact of important others or task cohesion on compliance in our meta-analysis—no data were available. It could be hypothesized, however, that the support of important others and the presence of a highly cohesive group would have at least the same impact on compliance as on adherence. If that is the case, there are implications for the implementation of intervention programs. One possible implication is that encouragement from important others (such as friends, physicians, or employers) at the onset and throughout a program is likely to have a strong impact on compliance. A second possible implication is that developing a highly cohesive group that is focused on the exercise task and the outcomes it can produce is likely to have a strong impact on compliance. The impact of both cohesion and important others on compliance should be addressed through future research.

The superiority of important others over family support insofar as both adherence behavior and attitudes associated with exercise involvement was somewhat surprising. Intuitively, it seemed reasonable to predict that family members (spouses, parents, children) would possess greater social influence than friends, physicians, or employers. Possibly the present results can be interpreted in light of research which has indicated that social reinforcement (e.g., praise, criticism, favorable gestures, frowns, smiles) contains both informational and motivational components. Also, social reinforcement contains more information and, therefore, has more social influence when it is administered infrequently or by an individual who is less well known (cf. Carron, 1984; Stevenson, 1965). Consequently, support from important others may be superior to support from family for two reasons. First, support from others may provide more information that the individual is engaged in a worthwhile activity. Second, social reinforcement from friends is received relatively less frequently than from family. Thus, it may serve as a stronger source of motivation and lead to more positive attitudes in the exercise participant.

The effect of family and important others on affect associated with exercise involvement is in the medium to large range. In fact, family and important others have more impact on affect than they do on either intention to exercise or exercise adherence itself. This is not surprising. As Wilson, Lisle, Kraft, and Wetzel (1989) noted, when individuals hold an expectation about how they will react to a situation, these expectations shape both their cognitions and their subsequent affect. Thus, with the positive endorsement (i.e., support) of exercise from family and important others, it is likely that individuals will prejudge the experience as more favorable. And, in a self-fulfilling prophecy, they will derive more enjoyment or satisfaction.

The negative effect size for the relationship between powerful others (as measured by psychological inventories) and adherence behavior is consistent with our conceptual understanding of intrinsic motivation. Deci (1975) has proposed that intrinsically motivated behavior is founded on the need to feel competent and self-determining. When perceptions of competence or self-determination are undermined, intrinsic motivation diminishes and persistence in voluntary activities is reduced (cf. Lepper & Greene, 1975; Lepper, Green, & Nisbett, 1973). If powerful others are considered the locus of control for exercise behavior, perceptions of self-determination may be undermined and adherence would deteriorate. When others (family, important others, class members, exercise leaders) provide support without exerting control over behavior, the individual has retained a perception of self-determination, and adherence should be enhanced.

Social influence can come from varied sources (family, important others, coexercisers, the class leader) and can have an impact on numerous manifestations of exercise involvement: behavior, cognitions, and affect. Our results showed that the social influence of others does make a difference in exercise involvement. However, our search for empirical data also showed that there are still numerous unexplored issues and unexplained findings. For example, insofar as both efficacy for exercise and compliance to exercise prescriptions are concerned, some relationships that either have not been explored or for which there is less than three studies concern the impact of important others, other class members, exercise leaders, and task and socially cohesive groups. Insofar as both intention to exercise and affect associated with the exercise experience are concerned, only two forms of social influence have been examined: important others and family. The field of social psychology provides testimony to the impact of social influence on human behavior, cognitions, and affect. Continued research is necessary for us to understand the broad impact of social influence on exercise involvement.

References

Alcock, J.E., Cannent, D.W., & Sadava, S.W. (1991). *A textbook of social psychology* (2nd. ed.). Scarborough, ON: Prentice Hall.

Anderssen, N., & Wold, B. (1992). Parental and peer influences on leisure-time physical activity in young adolescents. *Research Quarterly for Exercise and Sport,* 63, 341–348.

Atkins, C.J., Kaplan, R.M., Timms, R.M., Reinsch, S., & Lofback, K. (1984). Behavioral exercise programs in the management of chronic obstructive pulmonary disease. *Journal of Consulting and Clinical Psychology,* 52, 591–603.

Baron, R.A., & Byrne, D. (1991). *Social psychology: Understanding human interaction* (6th. ed., Instructor's ed.). Boston, MA: Allyn & Bacon.

Carron, A.V. (1984). *Motivation: Implications for coaching and teaching.* London, ON: Sports Dynamics.

Carron, A.V., & Spink, K.S. (1993). Team building in an exercise setting. *The Sport Psychologist,* 7, 8–18.

Clifford, P.A., Tan, S.Y., & Gorsuch, R.L. (1991). Efficacy of a self-directed behavioral health change program: Weight, body composition, cardiovascular fitness, blood pressure, health risk, and psychosocial mediating variables. *Journal of Behavioral Medicine,* 14, 303–323.

Cohen, J. (1969). *Statistical power analysis for the behavioral sciences.* New York: Academic Press.

Cohen, J. (1992). A power primer. *Psychological Bulletin,* 112, 155–159.

Daltroy, L.H., & Godin, G. (1989). The influence of spousal approval and patient perception of spousal approval on cardiac patient participation in exercise programs. *Journal of Cardiopulmonary Rehabilitation,* 9, 363–367.

Deci, E.L. (1975). *Intrinsic motivation.* New York: Plenum Press.

Dishman, R.K. (1988). Preface. In R.K. Dishman (Ed.), *Advances in exercise adherence* (pp. vii–viii). Champaign, IL: Human Kinetics.

Dishman, R.K. (1994). Epilogue and future directions. In R.K. Dishman (Ed.), *Exercise adherence: Its impact on public health* (pp. 417–426). Champaign, IL: Human Kinetics.

Franklin, B.A. (1988). Program factors that influence exercise adherence: Practical adherence skills for the clinical staff. In R.K. Dishman (Ed.), *Exercise adherence: Its impact on public health* (pp 237–258). Champaign, IL: Human Kinetics.

Godin, G. (1994). The theories of reasoned action and planned behavior: Overview of findings, emerging research problems, and usefulness for exercise promotion. *Journal of Applied Sport Psychology,* 5, 141–157.

Godin, G., Vezina, L., & Leclerc, O. (1989). Factors influencing intentions of pregnant women to exercise after giving birth. *Public Health Reports,* 104, 188–195.

Hedges, L.V. (1981). Distribution theory for Glass's estimator of effect size and related estimators. *Journal of Educational Statistics,* 6, 107–128.

Hedges, L.V. (1982). Fitting categorical models to effect sizes from a series of experiments. *Journal of Educational Statistics,* 7, 119–137.

Hedges, L.V., & Olkin, I. (1985). *Statistical methods for meta-analysis.* New York: Academic Press.

Hill, R., Glassford, G., Burgess, A., & Rudnicki, J. (1988). Employee fitness and lifestyle programs, Part One: Introduction, rationale, and benefits. *Journal of the Canadian Association for Health. Physical Education and Recreation,* 54(1), 10–14.

Hunter, J.E., & Schmidt, F.L. (1990). *Methods of meta-analysis: Correcting error and bias in research findings.* Newbury Park, CA: Sage Publications.

International Society of Sport Psychology. (1991). Physical activity and psychological benefits. *Newsletter,* 2, 1–2.

Lepper, M.R., & Greene, D. (1975). Turning play into work: Effects of adult surveillance and extrinsic rewards on children's intrinsic motivation. *Journal of Personality and Social Psychology,* 31, 479–486.

Lepper, M.R., Greene, D., & Nisbett, R.E. (1973). Undermining children's intrinsic interest with extrinsic rewards: A test of the "overjustification hypothesis." *Journal of Personality and Social Psychology,* 28, 129–137.

Massie, J.F., & Shephard, R.J. (1971). Physiological and psychological effects of training: A comparison of individual and gymnasium programs, with characteristics of the exercise "drop out." *Medicine and Science in Sport,* 3, 110–117.

Miller, P., Johnson, N.L., Garrett, M.J., Wikoff, R., & McMahon, M. (1982). Health beliefs of and adherence to the medical regimen by patients with ischemic heart disease. *Heart and Lung,* 11, 332–339.

National Center for Health Statistics. (1980). *Health United States, 1977–1978.* Washington, DC: U.S. Government Printing Office.

Oldridge, N.B. (1984). Compliance and drop-out in cardiac exercise rehabilitation. *American Journal of Cardiology,* 4, 166–177.

Quinney, H.A., Gauvin, L., & Wall, A.E.T. (1994). *Toward active living: Proceedings of the International Conference of Physical Activity, Fitness, and Health.* Champaign, IL: Human Kinetics.

Rosenthal, R. (1979). The "file drawer" problem and tolerance for null results. *Psychological Bulletin,* 86, 638–641.

Spink, K.S., & Carron, A.V. (1994). Group cohesion effects in exercise classes. *Small Group Research,* 25, 26–42.

Stevenson, H.W. (1965). Social reinforcement of children's behavior. In L.P. Lipsitt & C.C. Spiker (Eds.), *Advances in child development and behavior* (Vol 2). New York: Academic Press.

Thomas, J.R., & French, K.E. (1986). The use of meta-analysis in exercise and sport: A tutorial. *Research Quarterly for Exercise and Sport,* 57, 196–204.

Wankel, L.M., & Mummery, W.K. (1994). Using national survey data incorporating the theory of planned behavior: Implications for social marketing strategies in physical activity. *Journal of Applied Sport Psychology,* 5, 158–177.

Ward, A., & Morgan, W.P. (1984). Adherence patterns of healthy men and women enrolled in an adult exercise program. *Journal of Cardiac Rehabilitation,* 4, 143–152.

Wilson, T.D., Lisle, D.J., Kraft, D., & Wetzel, C.G. (1989). Preferences as expectation-driven inferences: Effects of affective expectations on affective experience. *Journal of Personality and Social Psychology,* 56, 519–530.

Wolf, F.M. (1986). *Meta-analysis: Quantitative methods for research synthesis.* London: Sage.

Yordy, G.A., & Lent, R.W. (1993). Predicting aerobic exercise participation: Social cognitive, reasoned action, and planned behavior models. *Journal of Sport & Exercise Psychology,* 15, 363–374.

38 Exercise Motivation Across the Life Span

STUART J.H. BIDDLE
University of Exeter

The idea of a European federation that would accelerate the integration of sport and exercise psychologists acting in the continent began in 1968 and 1969 at the two first European sport psychology congresses held in Varna, Bulgaria, and Vittel, France, under the leadership of Ema Geron (then from Bulgaria, later Israel). In 1987, Stuart Biddle from the UK was elected as a member of the managing council of the European Federation of Sport Psychology (FEPSAC). In 1991 he became president of the organization and served in that role until 1999. Toward the late 1980s, Biddle thought that a greater representation of European work in the international sport and exercise psychology literature was needed. He decided to produce, under the umbrella of FEPSAC, a forum for the dissemination of ideas and research from European authors in the form of an edited book titled European Perspectives on Exercise and Sport Psychology. In this pioneering book, key themes in European exercise and sport psychology were systematically presented from the European perspective for the first time.

In the first part of the book, key areas of the (at that time) rapidly developing field of exercise psychology, to which Biddle himself has made a substantial contribution over the years, were reviewed. These areas involved mainstream psychological aspects of exercise participation, such as antecedent factors, consequences of exercise, and the promotion of physical activity. Biddle argued that, even in countries that were previously focused on elite sport performance, interest in exercise psychology was on the increase (caused by the changes in the political conditions in Eastern Europe during the late 1980s and early 1990s). Issues such as health-related public policy and motivation for and conduct of a positive health behavior became appealing in European countries.

In the first chapter of his book, Biddle discussed exercise motivation across the life span. After the presentation of some general issues, the definition of the term motivation is discussed. Then it presents the results of descriptive research conducted mainly in the UK on children, youth, and adults on participation motives and reasons for ceasing participation. Biddle argued that much of this research has been atheoretical in nature; therefore, he suggested some theoretical concepts that could be used to understand exercise motivation: competence, attributions, achievement goals, self-confidence, self-efficacy, decision making, and enjoyment.

This chapter stresses the importance of studying motivation toward exercise from a life-span perspective. Biddle maintained that most of the research previously conducted on exercise motivation was biased toward the younger ages; therefore, he argued that to promote public health through an effective policy toward physical activity and exercise, much more should be known about exercise motivation among older adults and about changes across the life span. This chapter, representative of Biddle's own yearlong work in this area, is not only a substantial contribution in promoting theory and research in this sociocultural domain but also a pillar for a significant period in the development of FEPSAC under the leadership of Stuart Biddle.

For this chapter the subject of motivation will focus on participation in exercise and physical activity. In this context, *physical activity* is defined as all human musculoskeletal movement resulting in energy expenditure; it includes all aspects of movement, such as walking and manual labour. *Exercise* refers to structured forms of physical activity usually engaged in to gain, maintain or improve fitness (Caspersen, Powell, & Christenson, 1985). Although this could include sport, I will be referring not to motivation in elite high-performance sport but to participation in exercise and physical activity at a recreational, or health-related, level.

Physical activity is considered important in contemporary European society. For example, the World Health Organization (WHO, 1985) published its targets for the European regional strategy for Health for All for the year 2000, including these:

> ensure equality in health, by reducing the present gap in health status between countries and groups within countries;
>
> add life to years, by ensuring the full development and use of people's . . . capacity to derive full benefit from and to cope with life in a healthy way;
>
> add health to life, by reducing disease and disability;
>
> add years to life, by reducing premature deaths, and thereby increasing life expectancy. (p. 23)

Current research evidence strongly supports the efficacy of exercise and physical activity in the last three of these aims (Bouchard, Shephard, Stephens, Sutton, & McPherson,

---

Adapted, by permission, from S.J.H. Biddle, 1995, Exercise motivation across the life span. In *European perspective on exercise and sport psychology*, edited by S.J.H. Biddle (Champaign, IL: Human Kinetics), 3-35.

1990). In addition, more specific objectives particularly relevant to physical activity were included in Target 15 on 'knowledge and motivation for healthy behaviour' and Target 16 on 'positive health behaviour'.

Target 15 points to the need to help people 'change habits that have become routine' (p. 62). Such habits will include physical inactivity in many cases. Similarly, WHO (1985), in statements associated with Target 16, suggest that 'positive health behaviour constitutes a conscious effort by individuals to actively maintain their health' (p. 64). However, they contend that 'positive health behaviour is by far the most challenging field for a health promotion policy' (p. 65). Clearly these targets and associated statements make implicit and explicit reference to motivation and the problems of changing health behaviours. This is also reflected in national documents on health promotion.

Society faces a difficult problem. Although it is acknowledged that exercise and physical activity contribute significantly to an individual's healthy lifestyle, many people appear to face considerable difficulties when they attempt to start or maintain such activities. The study of human motivation, therefore, appears to be an area of more than academic interest.

Recent reviews of research on motivational determinants of people's involvement in exercise and physical activity show that much of it has centred on children and young adults (see Biddle & Mutrie, 1991). For obvious reasons, greater attention has been given to the young and active. The difficulties of studying nonparticipants, or those outside places where research is more convenient to conduct, such as schools, universities and sports clubs, have resulted in a biased profile of research on motivation and exercise (Biddle, 1994).

This bias is more than just a problem for researchers. First, the greatest challenge in exercise and public health promotion is to motivate nonexercisers to start regular exercise. However, this subpopulation has rarely been studied (Sallis & Hovell, 1990). Second, a great deal of discussion has centred on the importance of promoting physical activity in childhood so that such positive habits will persist in later life. However, very little is known about such 'tracking effects', even at a cross-sectional level. A life-span perspective is important for a fuller understanding of the processes involved in exercise motivation. In particular, there is a need to study older adults (over 50 years of age) as this age-group is almost totally missing from contemporary research in exercise psychology, although a few studies have appeared recently in the European literature (Ashford & Rickhuss, 1992; Codina, Jimenez, & Rufat, 1991).

Defining Motivation

The study of human motivation has remained at the heart of psychology since the earliest days of the discipline (Weiner, 1992). The roots of motivation research are firmly European (e.g., Freud, Lorenz), although recent dominant perspectives have been influenced greatly by North Americans (e.g., Bandura, Weiner). For Weiner (1992) the subject matter of the field of motivation concerns why people think and behave as they do.

In this context or exercise, *direction* refers to the extent to which an individual might choose exercise in preference to other behaviours; persistence refers to concentration of attention on a task, or duration of exercise; *continuing motivation* is the extent to which the individual returns on a regular basis to exercise; intensity is the effort put into exercise. Finally, inferences about motivation can be made from performance.

Historically, human motivation has been viewed from the perspectives of 'people as machines' (e.g., drive theory), personality (e.g., achievement motivation theory), and social cognition (e.g., self-efficacy and attribution theories) (Weiner, 1991, 1992). Contemporary motivation theory is no longer based on the notions of drives or instincts but more on social perception and cognitive perspectives espoused in approaches such as attribution theory and achievement goal orientations (see Roberts, 1992a; Weiner, 1992). To use Weiner's (1992) metaphorical approach, psychologists have moved from 'the machine metaphor' to 'Godlike metaphors' whereby humans are seen to act as evaluating judges of their own behaviour through cognitive and emotional processes.

This chapter will review the current state of knowledge of the role of motivation in exercise across an individual's life span. Research will be reviewed in two main areas: descriptive findings and findings based on more theoretical foundations or models. Emphasis will be placed on European research, but, where appropriate, other relevant research will be discussed.

Descriptive Research on Children and Youth

Much of the research on sport and exercise motivation has been atheoretical or descriptive in nature. Such studies have often simply asked participants or nonparticipants why they have chosen their preferred course of action. In addition, many studies have ascertained reasons for ceasing participation.

Much of the research on children's participation motivation tends to focus on competitive sport rather than more diverse aspects of exercise and physical activity. However, this is not surprising, because children are less likely to participate in fitness pursuits currently favoured by adults.

Motives for Participation

Research in Wales on youth and young adults 16 to 24 years of age (Heartbeat Wales, 1987) found that nonparticipants would find the following to be incentives to become active in sport: improved fitness or weight loss, having more free time, and maintenance of good health.

Incentives decline with age, although the relative strength of the main incentives remains fairly constant within each age-group. Similarly, Ashford, Biddle, and Goudas (1993) found, in a survey of 336 participants in six English leisure centres, that subjects 16 to 25 years of age were significantly less interested in the motives associated with sociopsychological well-being than subjects over 25 years. Younger subjects appeared to be more motivated by the pursuit of physical development, either through skills and competition or fitness. Ashford and Rickhuss (1992) also found age-group differences in sport participation motives. Sports mastery motives were rated significantly higher by younger children (aged 6-9 years), whereas social status was an important motive for youth aged 10 to 14 years.

A study in Finland (Telama & Silvennoinen, 1979) of over 3,000 youths aged 11 to 19 years, showed clear differences in motivation for physical activity as a function of age and gender. Boys of all ages and younger subjects of both sexes were more interested in achieving success in competition, but by late adolescence very few girls showed interest in this factor. This pattern was reversed for motives associated with relaxation and recreation. Also of interest, given the current focus on children's exercise and fitness (Armstrong & Biddle, 1992), was that fitness motivation was strongest among subjects who often thought about sport and took part in sports club activities. This fitness motive was unimportant for those 18 to 19 years old and for those uninterested or inactive in sport. This has important implications for the way we promote fitness in youth and illustrates the need to distinguish between sport and exercise.

Another study from Finland (Saarinen, 1987) found that boys 16 to 17 years old rated fitness, experiencing success and developing skills as the most important motives for physical activity. Girls likewise rated the factors of fitness and experiencing success highest but also strongly endorsed the motive of recreation. In a large study in Italy by Buonamano, Cei, and Mussino (1993), on over 2,500 participants in youth sports, enjoyment was reported as the main reason for participation by 49.2% of the sample. This was followed by physical (health or fitness) motives (32%), social reasons (8.9%), competition (4.2%), skill motives (2.9%), and social visibility or status (2.8%). A factor analysis of the questionnaire used by Buonamano et al. (1993) revealed factors of success and status, fitness and skill, extrinsic rewards, team factors, friendship and fun, and energy release.

German research (Brettschneider, 1992) has shown that the participation of adolescents in sport has increased in recent years. Activities now featuring more often compared with the 1950s are 'new individual sports such as bodybuilding, jogging and surfing as well as the Eastern movement forms and the different forms of aerobic dancing' (Brettschneider, 1992, p. 541). Similarly, Brettschneider (1992) reports on research on 2,000 adolescents and young adults in which distinctive profiles of adolescent lifestyle could be seen. For example, 5% of the group were categorised as a 'no sports group' since they preferred other leisure-time pursuits. Another 4% were motivated by body image and general image promotion, whereas 13% were characterised by individuality and self-expression and 'are disposed to health-related hedonism' (p. 548). Such typologies were confirmed by both quantitative and qualitative data.

The findings reported so far might have important implications for physical education curricula if one objective is to educate children and youth for an active lifestyle as adults. However, our own research (Biddle & Brooke, 1992) has shown that 12-year-old British children have a strong intrinsic interest in physical education and sport. For example, using the Motivational Orientation in Sport Scale (Weiss, Bredemeier, & Shewchuk, 1985), we found that all five dimensions of intrinsic motivation were rated above the scale midpoint, thus showing moderate to high intrinsic motivation in physical education and sport. Indeed, these scores were much higher than those reported for a comparable scale constructed for classroom settings. However, boys were found to have higher intrinsic motivation than girls for physical education and sport. In a related study, we found that such differences were also related to the higher activity levels of boys than girls (Biddle & Armstrong, 1992). Similarly, data from children in Northern Ireland (Van Wersch, Trew, & Turner, 1992) have shown that interest in physical education remains relatively constant in boys from age 11 to 19 years, whereas during the same period girls' interest declines sharply. Interest was assessed by questionnaire items pertaining to attitude, behaviour, motivation and perceptions of fun in the physical education setting.

North American research (Canada Fitness Survey, 1983; Gould & Petlichkoff, 1988; Wankel & Kreisel, 1985) confirms reports from Europe that children are motivated for a variety of reasons. Reviews by Biddle (1992c), Biddle and Fox (1988) and Gould and Petlichkoff (1988) concluded that children are motivated for diverse reasons, including fun and enjoyment, learning and improving skills, being with friends, success and winning, and physical fitness and health. The latter factor might also include weight control and body appearance for older youth. However, more research is needed to understand the differences in motives across activities, levels of participation and developmental stages, although the research so far shows some similarity in motives across settings and groups.

Reasons for Ceasing Participation

Various surveys are available on the reasons children and youth give for nonparticipation or ceasing involvement in sport and exercise (Canada Fitness Survey, 1983; Heartbeat Wales, 1987). However, one of the problems is that many studies classify those who cease activity as 'dropouts', yet it is possible that they have switched their interest to another activity. Indeed, White and Coakley (1986), in a study of adolescents in southeast England, stated that the terms `nonparticipant' and 'dropout' were inappropriate descriptors for young people who no longer participated in organised sport.

Gould and Petlichkoff (1988) make the important distinction between sport-specific dropout (ceasing participation in one sport) and domain-general dropout (ceasing sport participation altogether). This distinction may need to be incorporated into future studies.

As with motives for participation, there appear to be numerous reasons why children and youth cease their involvement. For example, White and Coakley (1986) conducted 60 in-depth interviews with 13- to 23-year-olds, half of whom had decided to participate in one of five different sports initiatives in their local town (see also Coakley & White, 1992). The others had either ceased involvement or had decided not to participate at all. The decision to participate or not appeared to be influenced by perceptions of competence, by external constraints (such as money and friends of the opposite sex), degree of support from significant others, and past experiences, including school physical education. Negative memories of school physical education included feelings of boredom and incompetence, lack of choice and negative evaluation from peers. These results are supported by Saarinen (1987) with Finnish school students. Here it was found that those who had had negative experiences in school physical education also expressed a negative attitude to physical activity outside school. Such attitudes centred on an overemphasis on competition and performance results, and the compulsory nature of the programme, with its lack of personal choice of activities.

Similarly, Heartbeat Wales (1987) found that youngsters aged 12 to 17 years did not participate in physical activity for the practical reasons of time, money and facilities, whereas Gould (1987) summarised the reasons for childrens' nonparticipation as conflicts of interest, lack of playing time, lack of fun, limited improvement in skills or no success, boredom, and injury. Competitive stress and dislike of the coach have also been cited in sport settings. Children, therefore, appear to have multiple motives for involvement and noninvolvement in sport, although less research is available on more diverse physical activity settings.

Descriptive Research on Adults

The literature on children and youth has focused mainly on participation in competitive sport, whereas research on adults has focused generally on reasons for participation or nonparticipation in exercise and recreation (Biddle, 1992c).

Motives for Participation

Ashford, Biddle, and Goudas (1993) studied participants in 14 activities in six English public sports centres. Subjects were divided into 5-year age-groups from 16 to 19 years up to 65 years and over. Fifteen motives for participation were rated on a questionnaire. A factor analysis produced four clear factors, two being related to performance ('assertive achievement' and 'sports mastery and performance'), with two related to fitness and health ('physical well-being' and 'sociopsychological well-being'). Males rated higher than females on the two performance factors. Also, as reported earlier, younger subjects were less interested than older participants in the factor of sociopsychological well-being. This supports findings in the literature on the relationship between exercise and mental health, which suggest that the beneficial psychological effects of exercise are more pronounced in older subjects (North, McCullagh, & Tran, 1990; Stephens, 1988). Similarly, research in Portugal (Serpa, 1986) has also shown that motivation to participate in exercise ('leisure sport') is strongly health-oriented, the main motives being associated with psychological well-being.

An instrument to assess motivation for exercise has been developed in Britain by Markland and Hardy (1993). The 'Exercise Motivations Inventory' (EMI) consists of 12 subscales labelled stress management, weight management, re-creation, social recognition, enjoyment, appearance, personal development, affiliation, ill-health avoidance, competition, fitness and health pressures. An initial study revealed that men aged 18 to 25 years reported that they exercised more for competition and social recognition and less for weight management than women of the same age. The most strongly endorsed factors for women were re-creation, fitness, enjoyment and weight management, whereas for men they were re-creation, competition, fitness and personal development.

The English 'Allied Dunbar National Fitness Survey' (ADNFS, 1992) was an ambitious study of over 4,000 people aged 16 to 74 years from 30 parliamentary constituencies. Home interviews took place with 1,840 men and 2,109 women for up to 1.5 hours. Physical measures were taken subsequently, mostly in mobile laboratories. The physical tests involved anthropometry, blood pressure, lung function, joint flexibility, muscle function and cardiorespiratory response to exercise.

The home interview included questions on involvement in physical activities as well as health, lifestyle and health-related behaviours, barriers and motivation to exercise, social background, personal attributes, and general attitudes. The most important motivational factors for physical activity were 'to feel in good shape physically', 'to improve or maintain health' and 'to feel a sense of achievement'. Physical appearance was also an important factor for women.

Participants in the ADNFS also rated highly the importance of exercise for health. The level of importance declined slightly across the age groups of 16 to 34 years, 35 to 54 and 55 to 74. Surprisingly, however, relatively little is known about changes in motives through the adult life cycle, although Mihalik, O'Leary, McGuire, and Dottavio (1989) did study 6,720 subjects from the cross-sectional

Nationwide Recreation Survey in the USA. They found that there was a decline in participation of 29- to 36-year-olds, which was attributed to changes in job and family circumstances. However, motivational factors in changes in activity patterns through the life cycle have yet to be systematically investigated. Initial results reported by Ashford and Rickhuss (1992) suggest that British adults aged 23 to 39 are more interested in sport and exercise for reasons of physical fitness, 'getting exercise' and fun, whereas adults aged 40 years and over report health improvement as a strong motive, alongside getting exercise and fun. Physical fitness was less important for this age group.

British research has also shown interesting differences in the motivation of subjects within the same type of activity. Schlackmans (1986) studied nearly 2,000 women in 10 English towns. Exercise and fitness classes were studied, which included traditional keep-fit, jazz-dance, and 'aerobics' (aerobic exercise-to-music). Through qualitative analyses, six main types of participants were identified. These were 'sporty socialisers', 'weight conscious', keen exercisers', 'modern mothers', 'social contact' and 'get out of the house'.

The study by Schlackmans (1986) shows that motivation for exercise is diverse and not just related to factors associated with the exercise itself. A number of social and environment factors are also important and should be recognised by those wishing to promote exercise participation. For example, some individuals may use exercise as the most convenient way of meeting people or 'getting out of the house'. Exercise may serve a purpose unrelated to fitness, health or other such factors.

One salient dimension that is likely to affect motives for participation is the intensity of the exercise. For example, the anxiety-reducing effects of exercise, so keenly promoted in the popular and research literature, have been shown to be much less likely at higher levels of exercise intensity (see Steptoe & Bolton, 1988; Steptoe & Cox, 1988). This suggests that motives other than, or in addition to, psychological well-being might be found in studies of vigorous exercise. Clough, Shepherd, and Maughan (1988), for example, investigated the reasons for participation of 500 runners taking part in a marathon in Scotland. They found that 70 stated reasons for running could be reduced to six main factors after factor analysis. These factors were well-being, social, challenge, status, addiction and health fitness. Similarly, Barrell, High, Holt, and MacKean (1988) also found challenge, well-being, social factors and fitness to be important motives for participation in marathons and half-marathons in England. These studies suggest that psychological well-being motivates those participating in more vigorous exercise, but, as expected, the motive of challenge is also prominent. Perhaps motivation for these runners is associated with the interaction between challenge and the well-being associated with meeting, or trying to meet, that challenge.

Reasons for Ceasing Participation

Dropping out of exercise should not be seen as an all or none phenomenon (Sonstroem, 1988) but as an ongoing process of change. For example, Sallis and Hovell (1990) have proposed a process model of exercise in which at least two different routes could be taken by adults who cease participation. One route is to become sedentary; the other is to cease participation temporarily, but to return at a later date. Motivational factors affecting these routes may be different (Biddle, 1992a, 1992b; Biddle & Smith, 1991; Sallis & Hovell, 1990). Indeed, why some adults resume participation after a period of inactivity is poorly understood.

The English National Fitness Survey (ADNFS, 1992) reported the reasons given for stopping regular participation in moderate to vigorous sport, exercise and active recreation. The three most frequently cited reasons were associated with work, loss of interest and the need for time for other things. The factors of marriage or change in partnership and having or looking after children were also important factors, but more so for women. Reported barriers preventing adults from taking more exercise were classified into five main types: physical, emotional, motivational, time and availability. Time barriers appeared to be the most important for both men and women, although women were likely to report emotional barriers to exercise more than men. These barriers referred to perceptions of not being 'the sporty type' or being too embarrassed about involvement in physical activity. Predictably, the physical and emotional barriers increased across the age-groups, while time barriers decreased, at least for those over 55 years of age.

In the Heartbeat Wales (1987) survey lack of time and loss of interest were cited frequently as reasons for ceasing participation in sport. In an interview study of 250 adults in the north of England, Boothby, Tungatt, and Townsend (1981) found that the most frequently stated reasons for stopping sport participation were loss of interest, lack of facilities, physical problems (such as low fitness or disability), moving away from an area and lack of spare time. Similar results were obtained by Lee and Owen (1985) in a study of adults ceasing participation in aerobic exercise programmes in Australia.

Perceived lack of time is frequently cited as the major reason for nonparticipation. Owen and Bauman (no date) reported on just over 5,000 sedentary Australians and found that the reason 'no time to exercise' was much more likely to be reported by those in the 25 to 54 age-group compared with those over 55 years. This confirms the results from the ADNFS (1992). The barrier of time in the Australian study was not reported as often by those with higher education levels. Those who had children, however, reported a perceived lack of time more than others. Again, these data show the need to study motives and barriers in a wider social context.

A final comment on nonparticipation concerns the growing interest of some European researchers in sport retirement and career transition (Dupont & Schilling, 1992; Patriksson, 1991; Strahlman, 1991). This has implications not only for sport, but also for participation in health-related exercise after competition has ceased. We need to develop our understanding of the effects of prolonged or intense involvement, such as motivational effects, on activities pursued in later life. This clearly is an avenue for future work.

Theoretical Approaches

Some authors (e.g., Klint & Weiss, 1987) have suggested that the study of participation motives at a descriptive level needs to progress towards a more theoretical approach. Similarly, Gould and Petlichkoff (1988) have proposed that reported motives ('surface level' motivation) are underpinned by more theoretical explanations of why people do or do not participate. Certainly the understanding of exercise motivation will be furthered by our ability to provide theoretically-based models. However, the current state of knowledge gleaned from surface participation motives is important for practical applications in exercise promotion. We now know in what ways children, youth and adults are motivated to participate, although information on changes through the life span is sparse (see Ashford & Rickhuss, 1992; Brodkin & Weiss, 1990). Nevertheless, we do not understand fully *why* people are motivated in these ways, *how* these motivations are derived or developed, or *what* the underlying processes are, whether psychological or otherwise. This is where the development and testing of theoretical models become important.

It is likely that the distinction between descriptive individual motive constructs and more theoretically driven models of motivation is one of time proximity. For example, the participation motives reviewed so far could be viewed as proximal, or immediate, motivational determinants whereas integrated theoretical models of, say, goal orientations or perceived competence might be more distal (remote) factors in the motivational chain.

The diversity of the theoretical approaches to exercise motivation makes them difficult to summarise. However, Gould and Petlichkoff (1988) suggest three broad headings under which to conceptualise theories for sport motivation in children: achievement orientations, competence motivation and cognitive-affective stress. While the competence- or achievement-oriented models are wholly appropriate and important, they provide but one perspective on the issue of exercise motivation.

The purpose of this section, therefore, is to provide an overview of theoretical perspectives currently popular in exercise psychology, as well as other perspectives that might be important for future research. Discussion will centre on competence perceptions, goal orientations and attributions, self-confidence, decision-making theories, and enjoyment. In addition, extensive discussion of expectancy-value models and health-related behaviour theories can be found in Biddle and Mutrie (1991).

The excellent historical picture of human motivation theory drawn by Weiner (1991, 1992) has shown that the same trends have been mirrored in the sport psychology literature (Biddle, 1994; Roberts, 1992b). Early attempts at explaining sport motivation (exercise was rarely a topic in the early days of sport psychology) were characterised by a recognition of drive theory and relatively mechanistic views of humans. For example, Butt (1976) states that 'motivation may be seen as evolving from two major sources: a biologically-based fund of energy, and all secondary or environmental influences, each with positive and negative pulls' (p. 3). This approach is not widely researched in the contemporary literature, although Butt herself has persisted (Butt & Cox, 1992). Similarly, Alderman (1974) said 'motivated behaviour is the sum total of instincts and needs, motives and drives, conscious and unconscious forces, and a function of what one expects to gain from participation in sport' (p. 202). Both Butt and Alderman recognise other factors in human motivation, but their approach gives greater emphasis to mechanistic factors ('Man as machine'; Weiner, 1992) than contemporary approaches favour. Psychology and sport psychology have witnessed a paradigmatic shift towards cognitive and social cognitive approaches ('Man as Godlike'; Weiner, 1992). This shift emphasises the importance of individuals' perceptions within the context of sport and exercise, and how cognitions and emotions affect and interact reciprocally with behaviour.

This is confirmed through a content analysis I conducted of two main sport and exercise psychology journals, the *International Journal of Sport Psychology* and the *Journal of Sport (and Exercise) Psychology (JSEP;* the word 'exercise' was added in 1988). The content analysis (Biddle, 1994) involved entering details of 224 articles on motivation into a computer data base. Articles between 1979 and 1991 were considered because 1979 was the first year of publication of *JSEP.* These were then sorted by fields for analysis. The most frequently studied topics were attributions, self-confidence, achievement motivation (including goal orientations), group cohesion and goal-setting. Attribution research showed a decline in the number of papers from the period 1980-85 to 1986-91, although a shift of focus towards goal orientations could partly account for this. The areas of self-confidence, achievement motivation and goal-setting showed increases across time. The content analysis also revealed a bias towards the study of younger participants, with only 6% of studies involving adults over 50 years of age. Similarly, many studies used what appeared to be convenience samples of students. Coaches, officials or physical education teachers were rarely the subject of investigation.

Finally, the methods adopted in these sport and exercise motivation studies reflected a strong bias in favour of survey (50%) and experimental (30.8%) methods.

Qualitative methods (0.89%) and longitudinal designs (1.3%) were rare. Such results are further evidence of the narrow approaches adopted in research on sport and exercise motivation and highlight the need for a life-span approach utilising a wide variety of methods, theories and samples.

Harter's Competence Motivation Theory

Attempts at explaining human behaviour through individuals' desire to seek situations where they can display competence are not new in psychology. White's (1959) seminal paper on 'effectance' (competence) motivation argued against the mechanistic explanations of the time in favour of a more cognitive approach. This was followed by a comprehensive interpretation of competence motivation by Susan Harter in the USA (see Harter, 1978; Harter & Connell, 1984). Many sport psychologists have followed the lead of Harter and tested her theory, or parts of the theory, in physical activity settings (see Ommundsen & Vaglum, 1991; Weiss, 1987). The concept of perceived competence underpins many currently favoured approaches, such as attributions, goal orientations and intrinsic motivation.

Harter's theory suggests that individuals are motivated in achievement domains where their competence can be demonstrated, particularly if they also feel intrinsically motivated in that area and see themselves as having an internal perceived locus of control. Successful mastery attempts under such conditions are associated with positive emotion and low anxiety.

Harter has specified at least three achievement domains: cognitive, physical and social. However, self-perception domains are likely to become more differentiated with age. Harter's measures of self-perception and competence reflect this. For example, Harter and Pike (1983) have developed a pictorial scale for young children reflecting the domains of perceived competence and social acceptance, whereas the 'Self-Perception Profile for Children' (Harter, 1985) assesses the specific domains of scholastic competence, social acceptance, athletic competence, physical appearance and behavioural conduct. This is expanded further to 12 domains in the 'Self-Perception Profile for College Students' (Neemann & Harter, 1986) and 11 domains for the 'Adult Self-Perception Profile' (Messer & Harter, 1986).

Harter's theory predicts that those high in perceived physical competence will be more likely to participate in physical activity. Such a relationship has been found, although it is not strong, probably due to the influence of other variables (Roberts, 1992b).

Ommundsen and Vaglum (1991) studied a representative sample of 223 Norwegian boys from a soccer league in Oslo. In testing Harter's theory, they found that higher perceptions of ability in soccer were related to higher levels of enjoyment. In addition, enjoyment was also predicted by perceived coach and parental behavlours, and perceived soccer-related self-esteem. These findings support the view that socialisation factors are also important in competence perceptions and motivation (see Brustad, 1992).

The strength and attraction of Harter's theory centre on the development of psychometrically sound and developmentally-based instruments for the testing of her model, However, in sport and exercise psychology the following points can be offered in discussion and critique of the theory:

1. The complete model has not been tested. Only parts of the model, such as motivational orientation, or domain-specific perceptions of competence, have been tested against behaviour and related variables.
2. Harter's theory has been tested almost exclusively on children and youth in North American volunteer sport settings. Little work has been done on the testing of Harter's scales in European populations (see Biddle & Brooke, 1992), nor has the cross-cultural validity of the theory received a great deal of attention (Ommundsen & Vaglum, 1991; Ponkko, 1992).
3. The focus of research into competence motivation has generally been on sport rather than more diverse settings of health-related exercise. It remains to be seen how relevant Harter's model is to such settings.
4. Harter's scale for the assessment of perceived competence adopts a comparative, or ego, orientation where children are asked to rate themselves relative to others. There appears to be a need, therefore, to also include mastery, or self-related, judgements of competence (Roberts, 1992b).

Attributions and Achievement Goals

The study of attribution theories in sport psychology was dominant in the 1980s, and such approaches are still popular in the 1990s (see Biddle, 1993). From a motivational standpoint, much has been written about attributions which will not be repeated here (for extensive reviews see Weiner, 1986, 1992). It is sufficient for now just to say that attributions given after participation in exercise may have important behavioural and motivational implications, although much of the research has centred on competitive sport of young adults and youth, and little on health-related exercise for older adults (Biddle, 1993).

One approach related to theories of attribution that has received a great deal of attention recently is that of achievement goal orientations (Duda, 1992, 1993; Roberts, 1992b). Such an approach might prove to be an important step towards finding a theoretically integrating framework for exercise motivation.

Dissatisfied with traditional approaches to achievement motivation, Maehr and Nicholls (1980) suggested that achievement could only be considered in the light of the personal meaning individuals attached to achievement. Subsequent research by Maehr, Nicholls and others established that two main goals for educational achievement could be identified: mastery or task goals, and ego goals. Individuals adopting the mastery or task perspective define success in terms of personal improvement and task mastery, whereas those adopting the ego orientation define success as winning or demonstrating superior ability relative to others. Research has shown that these two goal orientations are largely uncorrelated and thus individuals can be high in both, low in both or high in one and low in the other.

Extensive research in the USA, led by Joan Duda (see Duda, 1992 and 1993 for reviews), has revealed that 'conceptually coherent relationships have emerged with respect to the interdependencies between goal perspectives and motivational processes, achievement-related behaviours, and values and beliefs in the sport domain' (Duda, 1992, p. 84). For example, our own research with 11- to 12-year-old children in England has revealed consistent relationships between goal orientations and motivational variables. Duda, Fox, Biddle, and Armstrong (1992) found that a task orientation in sport, measured by Duda's Task and Ego Orientation in Sport Questionnaire (TEOSQ), was associated with a focus on cooperation and. the belief that success in sport results from effort. An ego orientation, however, was accompanied by an emphasis on work avoidance and the view that success in sport is related to ability. Factor analysis revealed a 'task dimension' (task orientation, cooperation and effort belief) and an 'ego dimension' (ego orientation, work avoidance, ability and deception beliefs). The task dimension was quite strongly correlated with sport enjoyment whereas the ego dimension was slightly related to sport boredom. However, Fox, Goudas, Biddle, Duda, and Armstrong (1994) have shown that the children with the most positive motivational profile and greatest involvement in physical activity are those high in both task and ego orientation. The group with high task and low ego scores had the second most positive profile.

Given the orthogonal relationship of the task and ego constructs, it might be more important to investigate the differences between the four groups (high task/high ego, low task/low ego, etc.), rather than look at correlations between each goal and selected variables. Nevertheless, taken overall, a task orientation does appear to have certain motivational advantages, but the above cautionary note about the need to look at both goals in combination is still valid. For example, we have shown that intrinsic motivation after physical fitness testing in children is highest in the group with a high task and low ego orientation (Goudas, Biddle, & Fox, 1994).

Research by Jean Whitehead in England has shown that children are likely to have more than two achievement goal orientations. Developing the work of Ewing (1981) in the USA, she confirmed that children may have goals of ability (ego), mastery (task) and social approval, but she also found other goals. Whitehead (1992) considered that the goals could be grouped into three categories: personal progress (goals of breakthrough and mastery), beating others (victory, ability), and pleasing others (social approval, teamwork). Clearly, the goals of task and ego are likely to be too restrictive to explain the achievement behaviours of sport or exercise participants, particularly the latter, for whom achievement may not be too important. However, it remains to be seen whether task and ego goals are the most important from a motivational perspective.

Papaioannou suggests that it is also necessary to study the motivational climate of physical activity settings in conjunction with individual goal orientations (Ames, 1992). For example, in a study of English adolescents, Lloyd and Fox (1992) found that girls in a 6-week aerobic fitness programme, taught as part of their normal physical education curriculum, reported higher levels of enjoyment and motivation to continue participation when placed in a class emphasising a mastery, as opposed to a competitive, climate, regardless of their initial level of ego orientation. Similarly, we have found that intrinsic motivation towards physical education was significantly enhanced by perceptions of the class's mastery climate beyond the motivation accounted for by perceived competence. Pupils perceiving their class to be high in both mastery and performance climate had the highest intrinsic motivation and perceived competence (Goudas & Biddle, 1994).

Self-Confidence and Self-Efficacy

The important variable of self-confidence in exercise has been studied mainly in terms of Bandura's (1977, 1986) self-efficacy theory. This theory is recognised as an important milestone in cognitive motivational research in exercise and sport psychology (Biddle, 1994). Our own review of research on self-confidence and health-related exercise identified nine studies (Biddle & Mutrie, 1991), and more have been published since. This review will not be repeated here. In summary, we found that much of the early work was on male patients in rehabilitation from chronic heart disease, that some evidence showed that self-efficacy could generalise to a limited extent from one exercise mode to another, and that generalised expectancies predict behaviour less effectively than do specific perceptions of efficacy.

In summarising our findings, we identified the following key needs in the study of self-efficacy and exercise (Biddle & Mutrie, 1991):

1. The need to study how self-efficacy influences behaviour in diverse exercise and physical activity settings, such as habitual 'free-living' activity
2. The need for more integration between theories of efficacy and attribution (see McAuley, 1992)
3. The need for further research on the nature and extent of gender differences in self-efficacy
4. The need to study self-efficacy in situations of prolonged effort

5. The need to study the longevity of self-efficacy
6. The need to study the relation of self-efficacy to other theoretical constructs

Self-efficacy is a popular area of motivational research in sport and exercise (Biddle, 1994), but further work is required to place it alongside other perspectives and to expand the exercise contexts that have been studied so far.

Decision-Making Theories

Motivated behaviour involves making decisions. Two theoretical perspectives based specifically on decision-making principles are Subjective Expected Utility Theory (Edwards, 1954) and Action Control Theory (Kuhl, 1985).

Edwards's theory suggests that exercise behaviour is based on the value or importance attached by the subject to the outcomes of exercise and the subject's estimate of the probability that such outcomes will occur. To this extent it is rooted firmly in expectancy-value theories of motivation (see Weiner, 1992). In addition, however, the theory states that the behaviour chosen will be influenced by the subject's perception of the alternative courses of action available and the values and probabilities he or she attaches to these. This is an important point often missing from the literature on exercise psychology—the choice to exercise is made in the context of other possible health and nonhealth behaviours (Smith & Biddle, 1990).

Related to the notion of competing alternatives is Kuhl's Action Control Theory. Action control perspectives have been favoured a great deal by German sport psychologists (see Hackfort, 1989; Kunath & Schellenberger, 1991), but have attracted less attention elsewhere.

Kuhl (1985) states that 'action control . . . will be used here . . . to denote those processes which *protect* a current intention from being replaced should one of the competing tendencies increase in strength before the intended action is completed' (p. 102). Kendzierski (1990; Kendzierski & LaMastro, 1988) studied both Subjective Expected Utility and Action Control Theories in the context of exercise. In her 1988 study, Subjective Expected Utility Theory was found to predict interest in weight training, but not actual participation. Her 1990 study investigated both theories. Specifically, she classified individuals on Kuhl's 'action control scale', which assesses whether the individual is action oriented or state oriented. Those who plan for the future and focus on it are classified as action oriented. State-oriented individuals are those who focus more on the present or past. The results showed that Subjective Expected Utility Theory predicted intention to exercise but not adherence, but the correlation between intention and behaviour was stronger for action-oriented individuals. However, Kuhl (1985) suggests that state-oriented individuals may have cognitions related to a 'catastatic' mode of control (change-preventing) or a 'metastatic' mode of control (change-inducing). 'As long as an individual is in a catastatic mode of control, the enactment of action-oriented intentions seems to be more difficult than when the individual is in a metastatic mode of control' (Kuhl, 1985, p. 102).

Decision-making theoretical perspectives may prove to be important for the study of exercise motivation through the life span. Perceptions of control and planning strategies require some investigation in the future.

Enjoyment in Exercise

A number of researchers have noted the importance of enjoyment as a factor in exercise motivation (Biddle & Mutrie, 1991; Scanlan & Simons, 1992). However, currently enjoyment is still a relatively elusive construct that does not have a strong theoretical or empirical base. I have included it in this section of the chapter, however, as it has started to feature quite prominently in the literature, and no discussion of motivation would be complete without some mention of enjoyment.

Although there can be little doubt that enjoyment is important for exercise motivation, it has been studied mainly in the sports context with children (see Wankel & Kreisel, 1985). Much more needs to be known about adults through the life span and the potential sources of exercise enjoyment. For example, Ashford et al. (1993) found that the best predictor of enjoyment for participants in English sport centres was the motive factor of sociopsychological well-being. However, this factor accounted for only 8.5% of the variance in enjoyment ratings.

Perhaps the nearest we have to a theory of enjoyment is that of Csikszentmihalyi' s (1975) 'flow' model. This suggests that high levels of enjoyment and intrinsic satisfaction ('flow') are more likely to be experienced under conditions of optimal challenge; that is to say when personal abilities match the challenge at hand. An imbalance could create anxiety or boredom.

There is little doubt that the construct of enjoyment has high ecological validity in motivation. However, the proximal and distal determinants of enjoyment in exercise through the life span require investigation (see Csikszentmihalyi & Csikszentmihalyi, 1988).

Conclusion

In this chapter I have argued for the importance of studying motivation towards exercise from a life-span perspective. However, the current state of knowledge is biased towards the younger end of the age scale. If significant effects on public health are to accrue from physical activity and exercise, we need to know more about the motivation of older adults and changes between stages of the life span.

The chapter has tackled motivation from two angles: descriptive research and perspectives based on integrated theories or models. Many researchers have criticised the descriptive approach and called for greater emphasis on theoretically-based explanations of motivated behaviour. Although I have some sympathy with this view, I also believe that it is important to know the 'surface' motives of individuals adopting, maintaining or ceasing participation in exercise. It is an approach that is likely to have high ecological validity and relevance to psychological factors close to the behaviour itself (proximal determinants). Nevertheless, further research efforts are also needed to establish conceptually coherent models of exercise motivation. These are likely to provide a better explanation of more distal determinants, although the temporal importance and relationship of these factors remain to be clarified.

References

Aldennan, R.B. (1974). *Psychological behaviour in sport.* Philadelphia: W.B. Saunders.

Allied Dunbar National Fitness Survey. (1992). *Allied Dunbar National Fitness Survey main findings*. London: Sports Council and Health Education Authority.

Ames, C. (1992). Achievement goals, motivational climate and motivational processes. In G.C. Roberts (Ed.), *Motivation in sport and exercise* (pp. 161–176). Champaign, IL: Human Kinetics.

Armstrong, N., & Biddle, S.J.H. (1992). Health-related physical activity in the National Curriculum. In N. Armstrong (Ed.), *New directions in physical education: Vol. II. Towards a national curriculum* (pp. 71–110). Champaign, IL: Human Kinetics.

Ashford, B., Biddle, S.J.H., & Goudas, M. (1993). Participation in community sports centres: Motives and predictors of enjoyment. *Journal of Sports Sciences,* 11, 249–256.

Ashford, B., & Rickhuss, J. (1992). Life-span differences in motivation for participating in community sport and recreation. *Journal of Sports Sciences,* 10(6), 626. (Abstract)

Bandura, A. (1977). Self-efficacy: Toward a unifying theory of behavioral change. *Psychological Review,* 84, 191–215.

Bandura, A. (1986). *Social foundations of thought and action: A social cognitive theory.* Englewood Cliffs, NJ: Prentice Hall.

Barrell, G., High, S., Holt, D., & MacKean, J. (1988). Motives for starting running and for competing in full and half marathon events. In *Sport, Health, Psychology and Exercise Symposium proceedings* (pp. 226–241). London: The Sports Council/Health Education Authority.

Biddle, S.J.H. (1992a). Adherence to physical activity and exercise. In N. Norgan (Ed.), *Physical activity and health* (pp. 170–189). Cambridge, England: Cambridge University Press.

Biddle, S.J.H. (1992b). Exercise psychology. *Sport Science Review,* **1**(2), 79–92.

Biddle, S.J.H. (1992c). Sport and exercise motivation: A short review of antecedent factors and psychological outcomes of participation. *Physical Education Review,* 15, 98–110.

Biddle, S.J.H. (1993). Attribution research and sport psychology. In R.N. Singer, M. Murphey, & L.K. Tennant (Eds.), *Handbook of research on sport psychology* (pp. 437–464). New York: Macmillan.

Biddle, S.J.H. (1994). Motivation and participation in exercise and sport. In S. Serpa, J. Alves, & V. Pataco (Eds.), *International perspectives on sport and exercise psychology* (pp. 103–126). Morgantown, WV: FIT.

Biddle, S.J.H., & Armstrong, N. (1992). Children's physical activity: An exploratory study of psychological correlates. *Social Science and Medicine,* 34, 325–331.

Biddle, S.J.H., & Brooke, R. (1992). Intrinsic versus extrinsic motivational orientation in physical education and sport. *British Journal of Educational Psychology,* 62, 247–256.

Biddle, S.J.H., & Fox, K.R. (1988). The child's perspective in physical education: II. Children's participation motives. *British Journal of Physical Education,* 19(2), 79–82.

Biddle, S.J.H., & Mutrie, N. (1991). *Psychology of physical activity and exercise: A health-related perspective.* London: Springer-Verlag.

Biddle, S.J.H., & Smith, R.A. (1991). Motivating adults for physical activity: Towards a healthier present. *Journal of Physical Education, Recreation and Dance,* 62(7), 39–43.

Boothby, J., Tungatt, M.F., & Townsend, A.R. (1981). Ceasing participation in sports activity: Reported reasons and their implications. *Journal of Leisure Research,* 13, 1–14.

Bouchard, C., Shephard, R.J., Stephens, T., Sutton, J.R., & McPherson, B.D. (Eds.) (1990). *Exercise, fitness, and health: A consensus of current knowledge.* Champaign, IL: Human Kinetics.

Brettschneider, W.-D. (1992). Adolescents, leisure, sport and lifestyle. In T. Williams, L. Almond, & A.C. Sparkes (Eds.), *Sport and physical activity* (pp. 536–550). London: Spon.

Brodkin, P., & Weiss, M.R. (1990). Developmental differences in motivation for participation in competitive swimming. *Journal of Sport and Exercise Psychology*, 12, 248–263.

Brustad, R.J. (1992). Integrating socialisation influences into the study of children's motivation in sport. *Journal of Sport and Exercise Psychology*, 14, 59–77.

Buonamano, R., Cei, A., & Mussino, A. (1993, July). *Participation motivation in Italian youth sport.* Paper presented at the 8th World Congress of Sport Psychology, Lisbon, Portugal.

Butt, D.S. (1976). *Psychology of sport.* New York: Van Nostrand Reinhold.

Butt, D.S., & Cox, D.N. (1992). Motivational patterns in Davis Cup, university and recreational tennis players. *International Journal of Sport Psychology*, 23, 1–13.

Canada Fitness Survey. (1983). *Canadian youth and physical activity.* Ottawa, ON: Author.

Caspersen, C.J., Powell, K.E., & Christenson, G.M. (1985). Physical activity, exercise and physical fitness: Definitions and distinctions for health-related research. *Public Health Reports,* 100, 126–131.

Clough, P.J., Shepherd, J., & Maughan, R.J. (1988). Motivations for running. In *Sport, Health, Psychology and Exercise Symposium proceedings* (pp. 242–246). London: The Sports Council/Health Education Authority.

Coakley, J.J., & White, A. (1992). Making decisions: Gender and sport participation among British adolescents. *Sociology of Sport Journal,* 9, 20–35.

Codina, N., Jimenez, M.J., & Rufat, M.J. (1991, September). *Benefits of sport activities in old age: A psychosocial view.* Paper presented at the 8th European Congress of Sport Psychology, Köln, Germany.

Csikszentmihalyi, M. (1975). *Beyond boredom and anxiety.* San Francisco: Jossey-Bass.

Csikszentmihalyi, M., & Csikszentmihalyi, I.S. (Eds.) (1988). *Optimal experience: Psychological studies of flow in consciousness.* Cambridge, England: Cambridge University Press.

Duda, J.L. (1992). Motivation in sport settings: A goal perspective approach. In G.C. Roberts (Ed.), *Motivation in sport and exercise* (pp. 57–91). Champaign, IL: Human Kinetics.

Duda, J.L. (1993). Goals: A social-cognitive approach to the study of achievement motivation in sport. In R.N. Singer, M. Murphey, & L.K. Tennant (Eds.), *Handbook of research on sport psychology* (pp. 421–436). New York: Macmillan.

Duda, J.L., Fox, K.R., Biddle, S.J.H., & Armstrong, N. (1992). Children's achievement goals and beliefs about success in sport. *British Journal of Educational Psychology, 62,* 313–323.

Dupont, J.B., & Schilling, G. (1992, July). *Career transition for professional athletes and dancers.* Paper presented at the Olympic Scientific Congress, Benalmadena, Málaga, Spain.

Edwards, W. (1954). The theory of decision making. *Psychological Bulletin,* 51, 380–417.

Ewing, M.E. (1981). *Achievement orientations and sport behaviour of males and females.* Unpublished doctoral dissertation, University of Illinois, Urbana.

Fox, K.R., Goudas, M., Biddle, S.J.H., Duda, J.L., & Armstrong, N. (1994). Children's task and ego goal profiles in sport. *British Journal of Educational Psychology,* 64, 253–261.

Goudas, M., & Biddle, S.J.H. (1994). Perceived motivational climate and intrinsic motivation in school physical education classes. *European Journal of Psychology of Education,* 9, 241–250.

Goudas, M., Biddle, S.J.H., & Fox, K.R. (1994). Achievement goal orientations and intrinsic motivation in physical fitness testing with children. *Pediatric Exercise Science,* 6, 159–167.

Gould, D. (1987). Understanding attrition in children's sport. In D. Gould & M. Weiss (Eds.), *Advances in pediatric sport sciences: Vol. II. Behavioural issues* (pp. 61–85). Champaign, IL: Human Kinetics.

Gould, D., & Petlichkoff, L. (1988). Participation motivation and attrition in young athletes. In F.L. Smoll, R.A. Magill, & M.J. Ash (Eds.), *Children in sport* (3rd ed., pp. 161–178). Champaign, IL: Human Kinetics.

Hackfort, D. (1989). Action regulation and self presentation in sports. In C.K. Giam, K.K. Chook, & K.C. Teh (Eds.), *Proceedings of the 7th World Congress in Sport Psychology* (pp. 205–206). Singapore: Singapore Sports Council.

Harter, S. (1978). Effectance motivation reconsidered: Toward a developmental model. *Human Development,* 21, 34–64.

Harter, S. (1985). *Manual for the Self-Perception Profile for Children.* Denver: University of Denver.

Harter, S., & Connell, J.P. (1984). A model of children's achievement and related self-perceptions of competence, control and motivational orientation. In J.G. Nicholls (Ed.), *Advances in motivation and achievement: Vol. III. The development of achievement motivation* (pp. 219–250). Greenwich, CT: JAI Press.

Harter, S., & Pike, R. (1983). *Procedural manual to accompany the Pictorial Scale of Perceived Competence and Social Acceptance for Young Children.* Denver: University of Denver.

Heartbeat Wales. (1987). *Exercise for health: Health-related fitness in Wales.* Cardiff, Wales: Author.

Kendzierski, D. (1990). Decision making versus decision implementation: An action control approach to exercise adoption and adherence. *Journal of Applied Social Psychology,* 20, 27–45.

Kendzierski, D., & LaMastro, V.D. (1988). Reconsidering the role of attitudes in exercise behaviour: A decision theoretic approach. *Journal of Applied Social Psychology,* 18, 737–759.

Klint, K.A., & Weiss, M.R. (1987). Perceived competence and motives for participating in youth sports: A test of Harter's competence motivation theory. *Journal of Sport Psychology,* 9, 55–65.

Kuhl, J. (1985). Volitional mediators of cognition-behaviour consistency: Self-regulatory processes and action versus state orientation. In J. Kuhl & J. Beckmann (Eds.), *Action control: From cognition to behaviour* (pp. 101–128). New York: Springer-Verlag.

Kunath, P., & Schellenberger, H. (Eds.) (1991). *Tatigkeits-orientierte sportpsychologie: Eine einfuhrung fur sportstudenten und praktiker.* Frankfurt, Germany: Verlag Harri Deutsch.

Lee, C., & Owen, N. (1985, March). Reasons for discontinuing regular physical activity subsequent to a fitness course. *The ACHPER National Journal,* 7–9.

Lloyd, J., & Fox, K.R. (1992). Achievement goals and motivation to exercise in adolescent girls: A preliminary intervention study. *British Journal of Physical Education Research Supplement,* 11, 12–16.

Maehr, M.L., & Nicholls, J.G. (1980). Culture and achievement motivation: A second look. In N. Warren (Ed.), *Studies in cross-cultural psychology* (Vol. 2, pp. 221–267). New York: Academic Press.

Markland, D., & Hardy, L. (1993). The Exercise Motivations Inventory: Preliminary development and validity of a measure of individuals' reasons for participation in regular physical exercise. *Personality and Individual Differences,* 15, 289–296.

McAuley, E. (1992). Self-referent thought in sport and sport activity. In T. Horn (Ed.), *Advances in sport psychology* (pp. 101–118). Champaign, IL: Human Kinetics.

Messer, B., & Harter, S. (1986). *Manual for the Adult Self-Perception Profile.* Denver: University of Denver.

Mihalik, B.J., O'Leary, J.T., McGuire, F.A., & Dottavio, F.D. (1989). Sports involvement across the life span: Expansion and contraction of sports activities. *Research Quarterly for Exercise and Sport,* 60, 396–398.

Neemann, J., & Harter, S. (1986). *Manual for the Self-Perception Profile for College Students.* Denver: University of Denver.

North, T.C., McCullagh, P., & Tran, Z.V. (1990). Effect of exercise on depression. *Exercise and Sport Sciences Reviews,* 18, 379–415.

Ommundsen, Y., & Vaglum, P. (1991). Soccer competition anxiety and enjoyment in young boy players: The influence of perceived competence and significant others' emotional involvement. *International Journal of Sport Psychology,* 22, 35–49.

Owen, N., & Bauman, A. (no date). *Determinants of physical inactivity and of reasons for inactivity.* Unpublished manuscript, University of Adelaide, Adelaide, Australia.

Patriksson, G. (1991, September). *Retirement from elite sport: Psychological aspects.* Paper presented at the 8th European Congress of Sport Psychology, Köln, Germany.

Ponkko, A. (1992, July). *The perceived competence of 5–6 year old kindergarten children and its connections to motor ability and experiences from sports.* Paper presented at the Olympic Scientific Congress, Benalmadena, Málaga, Spain.

Roberts, G.C. (Ed.) (1992a). *Motivation in sport and exercise.* Champaign, IL: Human Kinetics.

Roberts, G.C. (1992b). Motivation in sport and exercise: Conceptual constraints and convergence. In G.C. Roberts (Ed.), *Motivation in sport and exercise* (pp. 3–29). Champaign, IL: Human Kinetics.

Saarinen, P. (1987). Not all students take an interest in sports. In *Proceedings of the 7th Congress of the European Federation of Sport Psychology* (pp. 563–566). Leipzig, Germany: Deutsche Hochschule für Korperkultur.

Sallis, J.F., & Hovell, M.F. (1990). Determinants of exercise behaviour. *Exercise and Sport Sciences Reviews,* 18, 307–330.

Scanlan, T.K., & Simons, J.P. (1992). The construct of sport enjoyment. In G.C. Roberts (Ed.), *Motivation in sport and exercise* (pp. 199–215). Champaign, IL: Human Kinetics.

Schlackmans. (1986). *Women's fitness and exercise classes: Vol. I. Summary and conclusions.* London: Author.

Serpa, S. (1986). Motivation and 'gymnastique de maintien.' In L-E. Unestahl (Ed.), *Contemporary sport psychology: Proceedings from the 6th World Congress of Sport Psychology* (pp. 261–262). Orebro, Sweden: Veje.

Smith, R.A., & Biddle, S.J.H. (1990, September). *Exercise adherence: A theoretical perspective.* Paper presented at the annual conference of the British Association of Sports Sciences, Cardiff, Wales.

Sonstroem, R.J. (1988). Psychological models. In R.K. Dishman (Ed.), *Exercise adherence: Its impact on public health,* (pp. 125–153). Champaign, IL: Human Kinetics.

Stephens, T. (1988). Physical activity and mental health in the United States and Canada: Evidence from four population surveys. *Preventive Medicine,* 17, 35–47.

Steptoe, A., & Bolton, J. (1988). The short-term influence of high and low intensity physical exercise on mood. *Psychology and Health,* 2, 91–106.

Steptoe, A., & Cox, S. (1988). Acute effects of aerobic exercise on mood. *Health Psychology,* 7, 329–340.

Strahlman, O. (1991, September). *Motivation-related issues on sport retirement.* Paper presented at the 8th European Congress of Sport Psychology, Köln, Germany.

Telama, R., & Silvennoinen, M. (1979). Structure and development of 11 to 19 year olds' motivation for physical activity. *Scandinavian Journal of Sports Sciences,* 1, 23–31.

Van Wersch, A., Trew, K., & Tumer, I. (1992). Post-primary school pupils' interest in physical education: Age and gender differences. *British Journal of Educational Psychology,* 62, 56–72.

Wankel, L.M., & Kreisel, P.S.J. (1985). Factors underlying enjoyment of youth sports: Sport and age group comparisons. *Journal of Sport Psychology,* 7, 51–64.

Weiner, B. (1986). *An attributional theory of motivation and emotion.* New York: Springer-Verlag.

Weiner, B. (1991). Metaphors in motivation and attribution. *American Psychologist,* 46, 921–930.

Weiner, B. (1992). *Human motivation: Metaphors, theories and research.* Newbury Park, CA: Sage.

Weiss, M.R. (1987). Self-esteem and achievement in children's sport and physical activity. In D. Gould & M.R.Weiss (Eds.), *Advances in pediatric sport sciences: Vol. II. Behavioural issues* (pp. 87–119). Champaign, IL: Human Kinetics.

Weiss, M.R., Bredemeier, B.J., & Shewchuk, R.M. (1985). An intrinsic/extrinsic motivation scale for the youth sport setting: A confirmatory factor analysis. *Journal of Sport Psychology,* 7, 75–91.

White, A., & Coakley, J.J. (1986). *Making decisions: The response of young people in the Medway towns to the 'Ever Thought of Sport?' campaign.* London: Greater London and South East Region Sports Council.

White, R. (1959). Motivation reconsidered: The concept of competence. *Psychological Review,* 66, 297–333.

Whitehead, J. (1992, July). *Toward the assessment of multiple goal perspectives in children's sport.* Paper presented at the Olympic Scientific Congress, Benalmadena, Málaga, Spain.

World Health Organization. (1985). *Targets for Health for All.* Copenhagen: Author.

PART VII

Facilitating Psychological Growth and Development

Part VII focuses on the ways in which psychological development, growth, and well-being occur or may be facilitated as a consequence of sport and exercise participation. Early sport experience has the potential to promote character development in young athletes. However, the potential is also there for this early sport experience to be detrimental to character development. Coaches are usually influential in the direction of this development. These readings describe an instrument for measuring coaching behavior. They have assisted coaches and youth sport researchers in molding appropriate youth sport development.

Smith, Smoll, and Curtis (1979) present the Coaching Behavior Assessment System (CBAS), which has become the most commonly applied measurement instrument of coaching behavior. They also discuss the major dos and don'ts—guidelines intended to improve coach–player interactions—which have become milestones in promoting effective coaching and leadership behaviors in organized sport for children and youth. However, not only do coaches affect children's and teenagers' psychosocial development in and through sport; friends also have a profound influence. Weiss, Smith, and Theeboom (1996) investigated friendships in youth sport, contending that peer relations establish a fruitful context for moral development. Indeed, sport and physical activity are expected to promote young participants' moral values, such as sportspersonship, and build character. However, the definition of these terms has been quite imprecise, at least until Vallerand, Deshaies, Cuerrier, Briere, and Pelletier (1996) proposed their multidimensional and ecologically valid definition of sportspersonship, and Shields and Bredemeier (2005) substantially contributed to the clarification of the relationship between sport and character building. Danish, Pepitas, and Hale (1990) demonstrated how sport can be used as a context or medium through which young people can learn and develop psychosocial skills, such as personal and social competence, and transfer those skills to other domains of life (e.g., home, school, and workplace).

Sport involvement may not always be beneficial for young participants. When that is the case, attrition is evident. Gould's (1987) chapter presents an integrated process model of youth sport withdrawal, which has affected much of the later work on this important subject.

39 Coach Effectiveness Training: A Cognitive-Behavioral Approach to Enhancing Relationship Skills in Youth Sport Coaches

RONALD E. SMITH, FRANK L. SMOLL, AND BILL CURTIS
University of Washington

Toward the mid-1970s, sport psychologists, in particular in North America, became increasingly interested in the developments in children's sport. More specifically, in the preceding decades, youth sport had been formalized and organized, with an evidently broadening range of community participation. Parents, coaches, and other relevant adults had also become more involved in youth sport, and the level of complexity steadily increased around this sociocultural system. However, the desirability of the growing number of organized youth sport programs had also been subject to substantial controversy. The central issue of debate had been whether the outcomes of children's athletic experiences gained through their participation in organized sport is indeed favorable (e.g., for their psychosocial development). As a result, sport psychologists started to direct their attention and effort to promoting the psychological welfare of young athletes involved in organized sport.

In a series of classic investigations, two sport psychologists with a background in clinical psychology, Ron Smith and Frank Smoll, made an immense contribution in this area. They first developed a system for the behavioral assessment of athletic coaches, widely known as CBAS (Coaching Behavior Assessment System). CBAS is an observationally based instrument, which directly observes and codes overt coaching behavior. It has well-established psychometric properties (i.e., reliability and validity) gained through extensive empirical research. Over the years, CBAS has become the most commonly used instrument for measuring coaching behavior. It involves assessing the quality, frequency, and type of feedback provided to athletes by their coaches in contests and practices.

After the development of CBAS, Smith, Smoll, and their associates presented and examined the effectiveness of a training program for coaches. This program was derived from the principles of the cognitive-behavioral approach and was intended to assist coaches in improving their relationship skills and make the entire training process more effective for both children and coaches. In this framework, Smith and Smoll presented a list of behavioral guidelines for coaches in youth sport, which were formulated in terms of "dos and don'ts," and constituted the basis of the to-be-developed positive approach to coaching.

This article presents both the CBAS and the major guidelines for enhancing the positive interactions between coaches and players. After about three decades, in which it has become a milestone in understanding coaching behavior in particular and sport leadership in general, Smith and Smoll's work seems to have lost nothing from its relevance to the current reality of children and youth in organized sport both in and outside North America.

Little League Baseball coaches were exposed to a preseason training program designed to assist them in relating more effectively to children. Empirically derived behavioral guidelines were presented and modeled, and behavioral feedback and self-monitoring were used to enhance self-awareness and to encourage compliance with the guidelines. Trained coaches differed from controls in both overt and player-perceived behaviors in a manner consistent with the behavioral guidelines. They were also evaluated more positively by their players, and a higher level of intrateam attraction was found on their teams despite the fact that they did not differ from controls in won-lost records. Children who played for the trained coaches exhibited a significant increase in general self-esteem compared with scores obtained a year earlier; control group children did not. The greatest differences in attitudes toward trained and control coaches were found among children low in self-esteem, and such children appeared most sensitive to variations in coaches' use of encouragement, punishment, and technical instruction.

The present investigation involved the development and assessment of an experimental training program designed to enhance the ability of Little League Baseball coaches to relate more effectively to their players. The behavioral guidelines communicated to coaches in the training program were empirically derived from a preliminary investigation which involved 51 Little League coaches and 542 of their players (Smith, Smoll, & Curtis, 1978). In this investigation, a behavioral assessment system was used to categorize the behaviors of the coaches during an

Adapted, by permission, from R.E. Smith, F.L. Smoll, and B. Curtis, 1979, "Coach effectiveness training: A cognitive-behavioral approach to enhancing relationship skills in youth sport coaches," *Journal of Sport Psychology* 1: 59-75.

average of nearly four complete games. At the conclusion of the season, the children were interviewed individually in their homes to obtain measures of their perception and recall of their coaches' behaviors and of their evaluative reactions to the coach, teammates, and other aspects of their athletic experience. On the basis of empirical relationships between observed coaching behaviors, players' perceptions and recall of such behaviors, and player attitudes, a series of behavioral guidelines were developed (Smoll, Smith, & Curtis, 1977). In the present study, an attempt was made to transmit these guidelines to coaches and to promote their utilization.

The intervention program was conceptualized within a cognitive-behavioral framework (cf. Bandura, 1977). The techniques chosen were designed to make coaches more aware of their behaviors, to create expectancies concerning the likely consequences of various coaching behaviors, to increase their desire to generate certain consequences rather than others, and to develop or enhance their ability to perform desirable behaviors effectively. It was expected that cognitive changes of this nature would promote and mediate positive changes in overt coaching behaviors.

The training package involved a number of techniques. In addition to verbal and written presentation of behavioral guidelines, modeling, behavioral feedback, and self-monitoring were employed. These methods, singly and in combination, have proven to be effective behavior change procedures in a variety of intervention contexts (e.g., Edelstein & Eisler, 1976; Gottman & McFall, 1972; McFall & Twentyman, 1973). The effects of the training program on coach behaviors and player perceptions, attitudes, and self-esteem were assessed. Additionally, the role of self-esteem as a moderator variable affecting children's reactions to trained and untrained coaches was investigated. In a previous investigation (Smith, Smoll, & Curtis, 1978), it was shown that children low in general self-esteem were most responsive to differences in coaching behaviors in terms of their attitudes toward their coaches. Since the behavioral differences to which they were responsive were an explicit focus of the training program, it was hypothesized that differences in attitudes toward trained versus untrained coaches would be most pronounced for low self-esteem children.

Method

Subjects

The initial sample consisted of 34 Seattle-area male Little League Baseball coaches. All of the coaches were involved at the major (10- to 12-year-olds) and senior (13- to 15-year-olds) levels of the program. They coached in three leagues that had participated in the earlier investigation of relationships between coaching behaviors and players' reactions to their Little League experience (Smith et al., 1978). Eighteen coaches were randomly assigned to an experimental group and 16 were assigned to a no-treatment control condition. The unequal group sizes were to allow for a sufficiently large experimental group in case of no-shows for the training program. All of the experimental coaches attended the training session. However, three coaches in the control condition were lost during the course of the season due to team mergers or changes in residence. The final design, therefore, consisted of an experimental group of 18 coaches and a no-treatment control group of 13. The mean age of the coaches was 36.10 years (*SD* = 9.99). They had an average of 8.37 years of coaching experience (*SD* = 6.11).

Training Procedures

The coaches in the experimental group were contacted by telephone and invited to participate in an evening training session. They were told that the results of the previous study conducted within their leagues would be described and that coaching guidelines would be presented and discussed.

The training session lasted approximately 2 hours and was conducted by the authors. The relationships that had been found between specific coaching behaviors and children's attitudes toward their coach, teammates, and other aspects of their sport involvement were described, as was the relationship that had been found between winning and player attitudes. The research results had shown that winning percentage was essentially unrelated to liking for the coach and desire to play for him again, but that certain coaching behaviors were highly related to these measures. The coaches were told that these behavioral findings were the basis for the guidelines.

The behavioral guidelines were presented both verbally and in written materials given to the coaches. The verbal presentation was supplemented by modeling of both desirable and undesirable methods of responding to specific situations (e.g., player mistakes) by the experimenters. In general, the guidelines stressed the desirability of reinforcement, encouragement, and technical instruction designed to elicit and strengthen desirable behaviors. The explicit goals of the guidelines were to increase positive interactions between coach and players, as well as among teammates, and to reduce fear of failure among players. The following, excerpted from the written materials given to the coaches, summarizes the major guidelines:

I. Reactions to player behaviors and game situations:

A. Good plays

Do: REWARD!! Do so immediately. Let the players know that you appreciate and value their efforts. Reward *effort* as much as you do results. Look for positive things, reward them, and you'll see them increase. Remember, whether the kids show it or not, the positive things you say and do stick with them.

Don't: Take their efforts for granted.

B. Mistakes, screw-ups, boneheaded plays, and all the things the Cincinnati Reds seldom do

Do: ENCOURAGE immediately after mistakes. That's when the kid needs encouragement most. Also, give corrective INSTRUCTION on how to do it right, but *always* do so in an encouraging manner. Do this by emphasizing not the bad thing that just happened, but the good things that will happen if the kid follows you instruction (the "why" of it). This will make the player positively self-motivated to correct the mistake rather than negatively motivated to avoid failure and your disapproval.

Don't: PUNISH when things are going wrong. Punishment isn't just yelling at kids; it can be any indication of disapproval, tone of voice, or action. Kids respond much better to a positive approach. Fear of failure is reduced if you work to reduce fear of punishment.

C. Misbehaviors, lack of attention

Do: Maintain order by establishing clear expectations. Emphasize that during a game *all* members of the team are part of the game, even those on the bench. Use REWARD to strengthen team participation. In other words, try to prevent misbehaviors from occurring by using the positive approach to strengthen their opposites.

Don't: Get into the position of having to constantly nag or threaten the kids in order to prevent chaos. Don't be a drill sergeant. If a kid refuses to cooperate, quietly remove him from the bench for a period of time. Don't use physical measures (e.g., running laps).

The idea here is that if you establish clear behavioral guidelines early and work to build team spirit in achieving them, you can avoid having to repeatedly KEEP CONTROL. Remember, kids want clear guidelines and expectations, but they don't want to be regimented. Try to achieve a healthy balance.

II. Getting positive things to happen:

Do: Give INSTRUCTION. Establish your role as a teacher. Try to structure participation as a learning experience in which you're going to help the kids develop their abilities. Always give INSTRUCTION in a positive fashion. Satisfy your players' desire to become the best ball players they can be. Give instruction in a clear, concise manner and, if possible, demonstrate how to do it.

Do: Give ENCOURAGEMENT. Encourage effort, don't demand results. Use it selectively so that it is meaningful. Be supportive without acting like a cheerleader.

Do: Concentrate on the game. Be "in" the game with the players. Set a good example for team unity.

Don't: Give either INSTRUCTION or ENCOURAGEMENT in a sarcastic or degrading manner. Make a point, then leave it. Don't let "encouragement" become irritating to the players.

To supplement these guidelines, a written brochure given to the coaches contained concrete suggestions for communicating effectively with players, gaining their respect, and relating to parents. The importance of sensitivity and being responsive to individual differences among players was also stressed.

In addition to the information-modeling portion of the training program, behavioral feedback and self-monitoring procedures were employed to increase self-awareness and to encourage compliance with the coaching guidelines. Both procedures were designed to increase the coaches' awareness of their own behavioral patterns and to repeatedly focus their attention on the guidelines. Behavioral feedback was provided in terms of a 12-category behavioral assessment system known as the Coaching Behavior Assessment System (CBAS) (Smith, Smoll, & Hunt, 1977a). The CBAS is described in greater detail below. The coaches were observed during the first 2 weeks of the season by trained coders and were then mailed behavioral profiles reflecting their behavioral patterns during two complete games. The profiles, based on a mean of 219 behaviors per game, indicated the percentage of behaviors falling into each of the 12 CBAS categories. The feedback sheet also included norms derived from the previous year's behavioral data of 51 coaches across 202 games. One explicit behavioral goal was communicated: Coaches were urged to increase their reinforcement rate to 25% of their responses.

In addition to receiving behavioral feedback, coaches also monitored their own desirable behaviors, Given the impracticality of asking coaches to monitor and record their behaviors during games, the coaches were given a brief self-monitoring form which they completed immediately after each of their first 10 games of the season. On these forms, they indicated approximately what percentage of the time they engaged in the recommended behaviors in relevant situations. Self-monitoring was restricted to desired behaviors in light of evidence that the tracking of undesired behaviors can be detrimental to effective self-regulation (Cavior & Marabotto, 1976; Gottman & McFall, 1972; Kirschenbaum & Karoly, 1977). The self-monitoring forms were returned in stamped envelopes provided by the experimenters. The coaches were contacted periodically to remind them to complete and return the self-monitoring forms. All of the coaches returned their completed forms.

Evaluation Procedures

In order to assess the effects of the training program on coaches and their players, the experimental and control coaches were compared in terms of observed behaviors during games, players' perceptions of their behaviors, and player attitudes toward themselves, the coaches, teammates, and the sport.

Observed behaviors: Overt coaching behaviors were assessed by means of the CBAS. This behavioral assessment procedure was developed to permit the direct observation and coding of coaches' behavior during practices and games.

The CBAS encompasses two major classes of behaviors. *Reactive* behaviors are responses to immediately preceding player or team behaviors, whereas *spontaneous* behaviors are initiated by the coach and are not a response to an immediately preceding event. These classes are roughly analogous to the distinction between elicited behaviors (responses to identifiable stimuli) and emitted behaviors (behaviors that do not have clear-cut antecedents). Reactive behaviors are responses to either desirable performances, mistakes, or misbehaviors on the part of the players, while the spontaneous class is subdivided into game-related and game-irrelevant behaviors initiated by the coach. The system thus involves basic interactions between the situation and the coach's behavior.

In utilizing the CBAS, observers stationed themselves at a point from which they could observe the coach in an unobtrusive manner. Observers did not introduce themselves to the coach, nor did they indicate in any way that they would be observing him. They were unaware of which coaches were trained and which were controls. Observations were recorded by writing the behavioral codes (e.g., *R, P, TIM*) on code sheets designating half-innings as the behaviors occurred. Each coach was observed during four complete regular season games.

Although CBAS data may be utilized in a number of ways, we have found the most useful and reliable behavioral index to be the percentage of behaviors within each coding category. The mean percentages across all observations (games) served as the units of analysis.

The observers were 16 undergraduates who were trained over a 4-week period. The training program included: (a) extended study of a training manual containing instructions for use of the CBAS and a programmed learning module (Smith, Smoll, & Hunt, 1977b); (b) group instruction in use of the scoring system, including viewing and discussion of an audio-visual training module (Smith, Smoll, Hunt, & Clarke, 1976); (c) written tests in which trainees were required to define the CBAS categories and score behavioral examples; (d) the scoring of videotaped sequences of coaching behaviors; and (e) extensive practice in the use of the CBAS in actual field settings. A high degree of demonstrated expertise in the use of the CBAS was required before an observer was permitted to collect research data. In their field codings, the observers demonstrated a median inter-rater reliability coefficient of .94.

Player, perceptions and attitudes. The players' perception/recall of the coaches' behaviors and their attitudes toward the coach and other aspects of their participation were assessed in structured interviews conducted at the conclusion of the season. A total of 325 male players (82% of those who played for the experimental and control coaches) were individually interviewed in their homes by trained interviewers who had not been involved in the behavioral observations of the coaches and who were unaware of the experimental conditions. Children and their parents were assured that their data were confidential and that coaches would be given no information about the data obtained from their teams.

The measure of the players' perception of the coach's behavior was presented as a recall test in the hope of minimizing distortions in reporting: "We've observed your coach, and now we want to see how well you and your teammates can remember what he did." The player was given a description and examples of each of the 12 CBAS behaviors and indicated on a 7-point scale ranging from *Never* to *Almost always,* how frequently his coach had engaged in that behavior in situations like those described.

Following the recall section of the interview, the children indicated reactions to their participation and ability-related perceptions. The children were given a clipboard and recorded their own responses on a series of 7-point scales in such a way that the interviewer could not see them. The following questions were asked:

1. How much do you like playing baseball?
2. How much did you like playing for your coach?
3. How much would you like to have the same coach again next year?
4. How much does your coach know about baseball?
5. How good a baseball teacher is your coach?
6. How well did the players on your team get along?
7. How good are you in sports?
8. How good are you in baseball?
9. How good does your coach think you are in baseball?
10. How good do your teammates think you are in baseball?
11. How good do your parents think you are in baseball?

The scales relating to liking ranged from *Dislike a lot* to *Like a lot.* Item 4's scale ranged from *Almost nothing* to *Almost everything*, item 5's from *Very poor* to *Excellent,* and that for item 6 from *Very poorly* to *Very well.* Items 7 through 11 were rated on scales ranging from *Very poor* to *Excellent.*

Assessment of self-esteem. As part of the postseason interview, the players were administered an adaptation of Coopersmith's (1967) Self-Esteem Inventory as a measure of general or "global" self-esteem. It consisted of 14 descriptive statements, each of which was rated on a 5-point scale ranging from *Not at all like me* to *Very much like me.* Six of the items referred to positive attributes (e.g., "I'm pretty sure of myself"; "I'm proud of myself'), whereas 8 were negative self-evaluative statements (e.g., "I have a low opinion of myself'; "I'm a failure"). The scale was designed to provide a maximum range of scores (14 to 70) with a relatively small number of items. The scale has adequate interitem reliability (alpha coefficients ranging from .63 at ages 10 to 12 to .70 at ages 13 to 15). Test-retest reliability coefficients over 12 months were .60 at ages 10 to 12 and .74 at ages 13 to 15.

Results

Comparability of Experimental and Control Coaches

In order to assess the preseason comparability of the experimental and control group coaches, they were compared on a number of variables which might possibly affect their behavior and their players' perceptions and attitudes. No significant differences were found between the two groups of coaches in age, number of years of total coaching experience, and number of years coaching baseball. Data were also available from the previous season on all the dependent variable measures for 13 coaches in the experimental group and 6 members of the control group. At the level of observed CBAS behaviors, the two groups of coaches did not differ on any of the behaviors except General Communication, in which the experimental coaches engaged relatively more frequently ($p < .05$). On the corresponding player-perceived behaviors, there were no significant differences between the experimental and control coaches on any of the 12 behavior categories. Finally, the two coach groups did not differ significantly on any of the player attitude measures from the previous season or on won-lost record. Given that the remaining coaches on whom previous year's data were not available were also randomly assigned to the treatment conditions, we may assume that the experimental and control groups were quite comparable.

Observed CBAS Behavior Differences

A total of 26,412 behaviors were coded during four game observations of the experimental and control coaches. Each coach averaged 213.19 codable behaviors per game. Since the time duration of the games varied, an initial analysis of rate scores was conducted. The frequency data within the CBAS categories were converted to rate scores by dividing the total behavior frequencies by the number of minutes observed across the four games. The rate scores for the experimental and control group coaches did not differ significantly on any of the 12 behavior categories, nor did they differ on the total of the combined categories. Because the two groups did not differ in their level of activity, subsequent analyses focused on the distribution of behaviors within the categories.

In order to identify the combination of behaviors which discriminated optimally between the experimental and control coaches, a stepwise discriminant analysis was conducted (Cooley & Lohnes, 1971). Behavior categories were thus entered into the analysis on the basis of their discriminating power. Maximum separation between the group centroids (multivariate group composite scores) occurred with a weighted linear combination of the following seven behaviors: Reinforcement, General Communication, Keeping Control, Nonreinforcement, Mistake-contingent Encouragement, Organization, and Punishment (Wilks' Lambda = .52, $p < .02$). However, it is worth noting that after Reinforcement was entered on the first step and significance was attained, differences between group centroids were not significant for the step-down multivariate F ratios on Steps 2 through 5. Given the small number of subjects relative to the number of variables being combined thereafter, the most conservative and appropriate conclusion is that Reinforcement was the major discriminator between the two groups. This conclusion is consistent with the results of univariate F tests which yielded a significant group difference only for the Reinforcement category.

Differences in Players' Perceptions of Coaching Behaviors

A stepwise discriminant analysis of the behavioral ratings made by the two groups of children revealed a significant difference in group centroids based on the 12 behaviors (Wilks' Lambda = .91, $p < .002$). Follow up univariate ANOVAs yielded significant group differences on six of the perceived behavior categories. Experimental group coaches were rated as more frequently engaging in Reinforcement, Mistake-contingent Encouragement, and General Technical Instruction, and as less frequently engaging in Nonreinforcement, Punishment, and Punitive Technical Instruction. All of these differences were consistent with the behavioral guidelines.

Player Attitudes and Self-esteem

Evaluative reactions to coach and teammates. These data indicate that the children who played for the trained coaches did not differ in liking for baseball. On the other hand, they indicated greater enjoyment in having played for their coaches and a stronger desire to play for them in the future. They also rated the trained coaches as better teachers of baseball. Finally, children who played for trained coaches evaluated the relationships which existed among teammates more positively.

Postseason self-evaluations. Postseason measures of general self-esteem and athletic self-evaluations of children who played for trained and untrained coaches were compared by means of one-way ANOVAs. On the measure of general self-esteem, no significant group difference was found, $F(1, 323) = .78$. Likewise the children's evaluations of their own baseball ability did not differ, $F(1, 316) = .01$. There were, however, significant differences in the children's perceptions of their coaches' and teammates' evaluation of their skills. Children who played for the trained coaches felt that both their coach $F(1, 317) = 4.73$, $p < .05$, and their teammates, $F(1, 315) = 6.05$, $p < .02$, evaluated their skills more highly. No difference was found in the children's perception of their parents' evaluations of their skills.

Pre-post self-esteem changes. As reported above, the total samples of children ($N = 325$) who played for the trained and untrained coaches did not differ in postseason self-esteem scores. However, self-esteem data obtained in similar interviews conducted the previous year were available for 75 of the children who played for the control group coaches and 112 of those who played for the trained coaches. It was therefore possible to examine changes in self-esteem scores for these subsamples.

An analysis of covariance of the posttreatment scores, using baseline self-esteem scores as covariate, revealed a significantly higher level of self-esteem in the children who had played for the trained coaches, $F(1, 184) = 6.43$, $p < .01$. As an additional test of treatment effects, changes in self-esteem scores for the two groups were assessed separately by means of *t* tests for correlated means. These tests revealed a significant increase in scores for the children who played for the trained coaches, $t(111) = 2.07$, $p < .05$. The control group children exhibited no significant change in scores, $t(74) - 1.70$.

Self-esteem as a moderator variable. A question of both applied and theoretical significance concerns the impact of the trained and untrained coaches on the evaluative reactions of children who differ in general self-esteem. Given that the *total* groups (including the subsamples on whom scores from the previous year were available) of children who played for the two groups of coaches did not differ in postseason self-esteem, the use of the self-esteem scores as a moderator variable was statistically justifiable. Likewise, within the total sample self-esteem was unrelated to any of the attitudes toward the coach.

The mean self-esteem score for the entire player sample was 51.87 ($SD = 6.79$). The total player sample was divided into high, moderate, and low self-esteem groups; the low self-esteem group was comprised of players having scores of less than 48, while the highs had scores of 55 or above. The numbers of low, moderate, and high self-esteem children who played for the trained coaches were 44, 71, and 70, respectively. The corresponding cell sizes for the untrained coaches were 46, 41, and 52. The self-esteem levels were crossed with the coach groups to create a 3 x 2 factorial design. Because of unequal cell sizes, ANOVAs for unweighted means were computed.

The four attitude items concerning enjoyment in playing for the coach, desire to play for him again, and evaluation of his knowledge and teaching skill all intercorrelated above .80 and were therefore combined into a single dependent variable measure reflecting overall evaluation of the coach. The ANOVA yielded a significant main effect for coach groups, $F(1, 317) = 11.84$, $p < .001$. Neither the main effect for self-esteem nor the self-esteem x coach groups interaction was significant. Because of the a priori prediction that attitudinal differences between children who played for trained as opposed to untrained coaches would be greatest at the low self-esteem level, *F* tests of simple group effects were computed at each self-esteem level using the procedure recommended by Winer (1971, p. 387). These analyses revealed a significant groups effect only at the low self-esteem level, $F(1, 88) = 8.54$, $p < .01$. It is interesting to note that a corresponding pattern of results occurred on the player-perceived measures of Mistake-contingent Encouragement, Punishment, and General Technical Instruction. That is, as noted above, significant main effects for coach groups were obtained for all three perceived behavior categories. But the simple effects at each self-esteem level were significant only in the case of the low self-esteem groups ($p < .01$ for Mistake-contingent Encouragement; p's $< .05$ for Punishment and General Technical Instruction when tested with the Newman-Keuls procedure).

ANOVAs of the other attitudinal items (intrateam attraction and liking for baseball) yielded significant effects only on the intrateam attraction variable. On the measure of how well teammates got along with one another, significant main effects were found for both coach groups, $F(1, 318) = 9.33$, $p < .01$, and self-esteem, $F(2, 318) = 3.72$, $p < .05$. Children who played for the trained coaches rated their teams as higher in intrateam attraction, as did children high in self-esteem. The coach group x self-esteem interaction was not significant. However, Newman-Keuls comparisons of the intrateam attraction means for the two coach groups at each level of self-esteem disclosed that the ratings of the children who played for the trained coaches were significantly higher than were those of children who played for untrained coaches only at the low self-esteem level ($p < .05$).

Team Records

Given the strong attitudinal differences found between children who played for the two groups of coaches, it seemed important to examine the potential influence of won-lost records. The trained coaches had a mean winning percentage of 54.5% ($SD = 24.72$), whereas the control coaches won 44.7% of their games ($SD = 26.91$). The difference in winning percentages did not approach statistical significance. As the large standard deviations indicate, both groups contained both successful and unsuccessful coaches in terms of winning games.

Discussion

The results of the present study indicate that the experimental training program exerted a significant and positive influence on overt coaching behaviors, player-perceived behaviors, and children's attitudes toward their coach, teammates, and other aspects of their athletic experience. There is also evidence that positive changes in self-esteem occurred in children who played for the trained coaches and on whom previous scores were available.

Despite the fact that there was no significant difference between the won-lost records of trained and untrained coaches, children who played for the trained coaches evaluated their coach and the interpersonal climate of their teams more positively. These evaluative differences were related to observed and player-perceived behavioral differences between the two groups of coaches which were consistent with the behavioral guidelines and with coaching behavior-attitude relationships found in earlier research (Smith et al., 1978). The fact that the trained and untrained coaches on whom data from the previous year were available did not differ at that time on any of the guideline behaviors (either observed or player-perceived) or on player attitudes strongly suggests that the training program was responsible for the group differences obtained in the present study.

Of the observed behavioral differences between the trained and untrained coaches, only the relative frequency of Reinforcement was significant. This was the behavior that was most highly emphasized and urged in the training program. As noted above, maximum discrimination between the trained and untrained coaches occurred with a combination of seven behaviors, six of which were directionally consistent with the training guidelines. However, because of the large number of variables being combined and the relatively small number of coaches, these latter results are best viewed as suggestive and deserving of replication with a larger coach sample.

The player-perception data yielded more imposing group differences, perhaps because they were based on a far larger sample of the coaches' behavior. In line with the behavioral guidelines, trained coaches were seen by their players as more reinforcing in response to desired behaviors, more encouraging and less punitive in response to mistakes, and as more technically instructive. All of these behaviors have previously been shown to relate to attraction toward coach and teammates (Smith et al., 1978). In the present study, players who played for the trained coaches evaluated both the coach and the team's interpersonal climate more positively. The latter finding suggests that the "positive approach" to relating to players and developing team cohesion resulted in more positive interactions among players. It is also interesting to note that the children who played for the two coach groups did not differ in liking for baseball. Evidently, attitudes toward the sport were fairly well established and not readily affected by coaching behaviors.

Self-esteem was found to be an important moderator of attitudinal responses to coaching behaviors. Consistent with predictions derived from previous research (Smith et al., 1978), low self-esteem children exhibited by far the greatest difference in attitudes toward the trained and untrained coaches. They also perceived the greatest difference between trained and untrained coaches in frequency of Mistake-contingent Encouragement, Punishment, and General Technical Instruction, suggesting that low self-esteem children may be particularly sensitive to variations in such behaviors. Whether these perceived differences reflect more sensitive perception of such behaviors or greater impact of such behaviors upon them, or both, is a question worthy of future empirical attention. Whatever the factors involved, we find this pattern of results to be noteworthy, since it is the low self-esteem child who is probably in greatest need of a positive athletic experience and who appears to respond most favorably to desirable coaching practices and most unfavorably to negative practices. The role of self-esteem in mediating responses to coaching (and other adult) behaviors and the manner in which specific kinds of athletic experiences affect self-esteem are issues deserving of further inquiry.

Previous research (Smith et al., 1978) has shown that children who have played for highly reinforcing and encouraging coaches have significantly higher levels of postseason self-esteem that do those exposed to coaches who do not behave in this manner. In the present study, it was shown that children who played for coaches trained to behave in this fashion evidenced significant increases in self-esteem scores as opposed to those who played for untrained coaches. Given that these changes were shown only in a subsample on whom scores from the previous year were available, replication of these results is highly desirable, as is an assessment of the stability of such changes. Nonetheless, these results suggest that training programs designed to assist coaches, teachers, and other adults occupying leadership roles in creating a positive and supportive environment can influence children's personality development in a positive manner.

The cognitive-behavioral approach used in the present study had a number of treatment components—information, modeling, self-monitoring, and behavioral feedback. As noted above, each of these individual components has been demonstrated in other research to be an effective means of producing positive behavior change and skill acquisition with a wide range of populations in diverse settings. The present attempt was to develop a potentially effective training package and to assess its effects. Thus, the training components are necessarily confounded. Future research is needed to assess the relative efficacy of the components singly and in combination with one another as well as the cognitive processes which underlie their effects. From a practical point of view, for example, it would be desirable if behavioral feedback were not a necessary training component, since this was the most costly (in time and effort) aspect of the present program.

Practical considerations (namely, the limited number of coaches available to study) precluded the use of an attention-placebo control condition in the present study. Thus, we cannot know the extent to which nonspecific factors might have combined with the treatment components to produce the obtained differences. In future studies, credible attention-placebo control conditions in combination with unconfounding of treatment components would permit more definitive and theoretically meaningful conclusions to be drawn concerning the efficacy of the treatment components. However, the lack of an attention-placebo control group does not detract from the practical reality that the training program produced desirable behavior and attitudinal effects.

References

Bandura, A. *Social learning theory.* Englewood Cliff, N.J.: Prentice-Hall, 1977.

Cavior, N., & Marabotto, C.M. Monitoring verbal behaviors in a dyadic interaction. *Journal of Consulting and Clinical Psychology,* 1976, 44, 68–76.

Cooley, W.W., & Lohnes, P.R. *Multivariate data analysis.* New York: Wiley, 1971. Coopersmith, S. *The antecedents of self-esteem.* San Francisco: Freeman, 1967.

Edelstein, B.A., & Eisler, R.M. Effects of modeling and modeling with instructions and feedback on the behavioral components of social skills. *Behavior Therapy,* 1976, **7**, 382–389.

Gottman, J.M., & McFall, R.M. Self-monitoring effects in a program for potential high school dropouts: A time series analysis. *Journal of Consulting and Clinical Psychology.* 1972, 39, 273–281.

Kirschenbaum, D.S., & Karoly, P. When self-regulation fails: Tests of some preliminary hypotheses. *Journal of Consulting and Clinical Psychology,* 1977, 45, 1116–1125.

Little League Baseball. *Official rules.* Williamsport, Pa.: Author, 1977.

McFall, R.M., & Twentyman, C.T. Four experiments on the relative contribuations of rehearsal, modeling, and coaching to assertion training. *Journal of Abnormal Psychology,* 1973, 81, 199–218.

Smith, R.E., & Smoll, F.L. Sport and the child: Conceptual and research perspectives. In F.L. Smoll & R.E. Smith (Eds.), *Psychological perspectives in youth sports.* Washington, D.C.: Hemisphere, 1978.

Smith, R.E., Smoll, F.L., & Curtis, B. Coaching behaviors in Little League Baseball. In F.L. Smoll & R.E. Smith (Eds.), *Psychological perspectives in youth sports.* Washington, D.C.: Hemisphere, 1978.

Smith, R.E., Smoll, F.L., & Hunt, E. A system for the behavioral assessment of athletic coaches. *Research Quarterly,* 1977, 48, 401–407. (a)

Smith, R.E., Smoll, F.L., & Hunt, E.B. Training manual for the Coaching Behavior Assessment System. *JSAS Catalog of Selected Documents in Psychology*, 1977, **7**, 2. (Ms. No 1406) (b)

Smith, R.E., Smoll, F.L., Hunt, E.B., & Clarke, S.J. *CBAS audio visual training module.* Seattle: University of Washington, 1976. (Film)

Smoll, F.L., Smith, R.E., & Curtis, B. Coaching roles and relationships. In J.R. Thomas (Ed.), *Youth sports guide for parents and coaches.* Washington, D.C.: American Alliance for Health, Physical Education, and Recreation, 1977.

Winer, B.J. *Statistical principles in experimental design* (2nd ed). New York: McGraw-Hill, 1971.

40 Understanding Attrition in Children's Sport

DANIEL GOULD
University of Illinois

During the past three decades, pediatric sport psychologists have investigated the problem of attrition in organized youth sport. Research related to children's and youth's motivation to participate and drop out has been considered important because of concerns related both to the subjective psychological experiences of young athletes and the structure of organized sport, which may contribute to increased probability of attrition. Thus, research in this area has not only substantial scientific significance but great practical importance as well.

In the late 1970s and early 1980s, several investigations were devoted to the identification of young athletes' motives for participation in and withdrawal from sport. Most of this research was descriptive but was at the same time also helpful in empirically providing a useful basis for the study of these phenomena from a perspective that is more theoretical in nature. Three major theoretical concepts have been applied in an attempt to understand young athletes' sport involvement and dropout: achievement orientation, competence motivation, and cognitive-affective social exchange. All these concepts have been incorporated into Gould's integrated process model of youth sport withdrawal, which has affected much of the current research in this domain.

To date, the question of understanding attrition in youth sport is far from resolved. As physical activity and sport have become major facets of current society and culture, studying the determinants of youth sport participation and dropout is important not only for pediatric sport and exercise scientists but also for policy makers trying to develop organized sport and promote public health. In this framework, Gould's work presented in this chapter is expected to continue to play an influential role in the future, as it has done in the past.

Pediatric sport scientists studying reasons for attrition in children's sport have arrived at different conclusions. Some (Feigley, 1984; Orlick, 1973; Orlick & Botterill, 1975; Pooley, 1981) have concluded that the high attrition rates result from an overemphasis on competition, burnout from overtraining, and inadequate organization and instruction. Others, such as Nettleton (1979), have suggested that few organizations can retain the interest of even 25 to 30% of their clientele over time and that the high attrition rates in youth sports are not unexpected. Still others (Gould & Horn, 1984; Guppy as cited in McPherson, Guppy, & McKay, 1976) have concluded that most children are not discontinuing sport involvement completely but are either discontinuing on a short-term basis or dropping out of one sport and entering another. Given the infancy of this line of research, a need exists to examine these issues.

The present review examines the children's sport attrition research and has a four-fold purpose. First, the descriptive studies assessing reasons for youth sport withdrawal will be reviewed to determine the current state of knowledge in the area. Second, the newly emerging studies designed to identify theoretically based motives for sport withdrawal will be examined. Third, a conceptual framework or model of youth sport withdrawal will be developed. This model will organize and integrate the previously discussed descriptive and theoretical research and show that by integrating these findings our understanding of attrition in children's sport is enhanced. Finally, based on an examination of the model, future research directions and practical implications will be outlined.

Descriptive Studies of Youth Sport Withdrawal

Assessing children's motives for sport withdrawal is a relatively new area of research, with the first studies on the topic appearing in the early 1970s. Since the publication of these initial studies, however, more investigators have become interested in the area, and a body of literature has begun to evolve. More importantly, consistent patterns of findings have begun to emerge across studies.

The first investigation of the youth sport dropout was conducted by Orlick (1973). In this study, 32 Canadian children, aged 8 to 9 and who had withdrawn from organized sports, participated in open-ended interviews. Orlick concluded that lack of participation, fear of failure, disapproval by significant others, and psychological stress were the underlying factors for the children's decisions to withdraw from competitive sport. He also suggested that when children of this age discontinue sport participation, they are reacting to a negative environment created from the emphasis of coaches and the structure of the sports themselves.

Orlick and Botterill conducted a second investigation (Orlick, 1974; Orlick & Botterill, 1975), designed to examine further reasons for children's sport withdrawal.

Adapted, by permission, from D. Gould, 1987, Understanding attrition in children's sport. In *Advances in pediatric sport sciences*, edited by D. Gould and M.R. Weiss (Champaign, IL: Human Kinetics), 61-85.

They extensively interviewed 60 former sport participants ranging in age from 7 to 19 years and representing baseball, cross-country skiing, ice hockey, soccer, and swimming. The findings revealed that 40 of the 60 subjects (67%) withdrew because of program emphasis. Thirty of these 40 children discontinued because of the competitive nature of the program, citing their lack of enjoyment, the seriousness of the sport, and the emphasis on winning as major motives for withdrawal. The remaining 10 children indicated that they had discontinued because of coaches' actions, which included such things as leaving players out of contests, criticizing players frequently, and pushing the athletes too hard. Twenty-one percent of the 60 former participants indicated that they discontinued participation because of conflicts of interest with nonsport activities, 10% because of interest in other sports, and 2% because of injury. Finally, reasons for discontinuing were found to be age-related as 60% of the high school-aged dropouts withdrew because of conflicting sport and nonsport interests, whereas all the elementary school-aged dropouts discontinued either because of little success (60%) or a lack of playing time.

The studies by Orlick and Orlick and Botterill provided valuable initial information about children's motives for sport withdrawal. These initial efforts, however, were characterized by small samples and focused exclusively on qualitative data analyses. In contrast, Sapp and Haubenstricker's (1978) and Robertson's (1981) investigations of the youth sport dropout were much larger in scope, whereas Petlichkoff (1982) used both descriptive and inferential statistics in her investigation of the youth sport dropout.

In the Sapp and Haubenstricker (1978) investigation, 1,183 male and female active athletes aged 11 to 18 years and parents of 418 athletes aged 6 to 10 years completed a survey assessing both participation motives and reasons for sport withdrawal. These young athletes and parents represented a wide variety of sports including baseball, softball, basketball, bowling, tackle football, golf, figure skating, gymnastics, ice hockey, soccer, swimming, synchronized swimming, tennis, track and field, and wrestling. Thirty-five percent of the older athletes and 24% of the parents of the younger athletes indicated that they or their children did not plan to participate in the next season. Of the athletes who indicated that they did not plan to participate next season, 64% rated involvement in other activities, 44% rated working, and 34% rated disinterest as the major motives for dropping out. Less than 15% of the athletes rated lack of participation, dislike of the coach, injury, expense, and dislike for teammates as important. Sixty-five percent of the parents of younger athletes who indicated that their children would no longer participate also reported involvement in other activities as the most frequent reason for their children discontinuing involvement, whereas 43% indicated that their children were not interested in the sport.

Robertson's (1981) study involved the assessment of reasons for discontinuing sport participation in 405 male and 353 female 12-year-old, Australian former athletes. The results revealed that 51% of the boys and 39% of the girls discontinued because of the program emphasis (e.g., "boring," "no fun," "never played", "too rough", "not interested"); 14% of the boys and 17% of the girls rated general life conflicts (e.g., "no free time", "social life", "got a job"); and 12% of the boys and 1% of the girls rated other sport conflicts as major motives for withdrawal.

In her study, Petlichkoff (1982) surveyed 46 former junior high and high school athletes aged 12 to 18 and found that having other things to do (78%); being injured (58%); not improving skills (52%); not being as good as wanted to be (52%); and not having enough fun (52%) were the motives rated as being most important for discontinuing involvement. Younger dropouts were found to differ significantly from older dropouts, in that they rated different factors as more important for discontinuing. These included no teamwork, did not meet new friends, did not feel important enough, not challenged enough, and skills did not improve. Thus, the younger dropouts were suggested to be more socially oriented and hopeful their participation would lead to meeting new friends and gaining recognition. Follow-up interviews also revealed that 59% of the dropouts had not participated in any organized sport since discontinuing involvement.

The investigations reviewed thus far have focused on the assessment of motives for sport withdrawal in young athletes representing a variety of sports. Other investigators, however, have focused on assessing motives for sport withdrawal in former athletes from specific sports. In particular, Pooley (1981) examined dropouts in soccer; Fry, McClements, and Sefton (1981) in ice hockey; Gould, Feltz, Horn, and Weiss (1982) and Sefton and Fry (1981) in swimming; Robinson and Carron (1982) in football; Burton and Martens (1986) in wrestling; and Klint and Weiss (1986) in gymnastics.

Pooley (1981) conducted extensive interviews with 50 youth soccer dropouts, 10 to 15 years old. His results revealed that 54% of the children reported that they stopped playing because of conflicts of interest; 33% cited the overemphasis on competition (e.g., the coach shouted when errors were made); and 10% cited poor communication. Younger (10- to 12-year-old) as compared to older (13- to 15-year-old) participants were also found to withdraw more often because of the overemphasis on competition.

In an extensive study of youth hockey participants and dropouts, Fry, McClements, and Sefton (1981) surveyed 200 dropouts, aged 8 to 16. When asked why they stopped playing hockey these children indicated conflicts of interest (31%); lack of skill (15%); dislike of coach (14%); rough play (10%); and organizational difficulties (10%; e.g., inconvenient game times) as major motives for their decision to withdraw. Young players (under age 9) were also found to rate a lack of skill and no fun or boredom as more important motives for discontinuing than the older players. Dropouts were also found to demonstrate a lower achievement orientation than the active participants.

Gould et al. (1982) examined motives for attrition in 50 former swimmers 10 to 18 years old. Important motives for discontinuing were "other things to do" (rated as important by 49% of the respondents), "not enough fun" (28%), "wanted to participate in another sport" (24%), "not as good as wanted to be" (24%), "dislike of the coach" (20%), "did not like the pressure" (16%), "boredom" (16%), and "training too hard" (16%). Based on these findings, the researchers concluded that these former swimmers most often discontinued because of conflicts of interest (84% of the respondents rated this as an important or very important motive). However, a lack of ability, dislike of the coach, dislike of the pressure, boredom, and training too hard were, at times, important factors affecting the young swimmers' decision to withdraw from the sport.

Sefton and Fry (1981) also examined children's motives for discontinuing swimming in a cross-sectional study of active ($n = 72$) and former swimmers ($n = 86$), ranging in age from 6 to 22 years. The findings revealed that major motives for withdrawal included too much time (rated as important by 31% of the former swimmers); dissatisfaction with practices (27%); conflicts with other activities (14%); favoritism displayed by coaches (12%); an overdemanding coach (12%); injuries (9%); and work (9%). Sixty-seven percent of the former swimmers also reported that they achieved what they had hoped from competitive swimming, whereas 30% said they did not. Fifiy-eight percent of the former swimmers indicated that they would never swim competitively again, whereas 42% thought they would. Finally, when asked what changes they would make in competitive swimming before participating again, 19% of the former swimmers cited reduced practice time; 8% a more understanding coach; and 6% more variety in practices.

One of the best designed studies examining youth sport dropouts was conducted by Robinson and Carron (1982). These investigators adopted a Lewinian interactionist framework where dropout behavior was viewed as a product of both personal and environmental factors (Lewin, 1935). A variety of personal and situational factors was then selected as variables thought to influence sport withdrawal. These included competitive trait anxiety, achievement motivation, self-motivation, self-esteem, causal attributions, attitudes toward competition, sportsmanship, communication measures, parental and group sport involvement, coach leadership, and group cohesion. These variables were assessed in 98 high school football players who were classified as either football dropouts ($n = 26$), football starters ($n = 33$), or football survivors or nonstarters ($n = 39$). The results supported the interactionist model as both situational and personal factors discriminated between the groups. In particular, dropouts were found to feel less a part of the team, enjoyed participation less, felt they had less support from their fathers for participation, more often attributed poor performance to ability, less often attributed success to effort, and more often viewed the coach as an autocrat than the other groups, who also differed from one another.

Robinson and Carron's (1982) investigation is important as it further supports the notion that the youth sport attrition process is a complex phenomenon influenced by a variety of personal and situational variables. Based on these findings and those of the previously reviewed studies, an interactionist framework must be adopted if attrition in children's sport is to be fully understood.

Youth wrestlers and former wrestlers aged 7 to 17 were the focus of a recent investigation by Burton and Martens (1986). Eighty-three youth wrestlers, 83 parents of these wrestlers, 26 former wrestlers, 26 parents of the former wrestlers, and 69 coaches were asked to rate reasons why children discontinue wrestling. The results revealed that "other things to do" was the major motive cited for discontinuing by all five groups. Other motives rated as important included "doesn't care any more," "no fun," and "isn't motivated any more." Although certain patterns of attrition motives were evident over all groups, considerable variation occurred between the groups in their ratings of motives for sport withdrawal.

Finally, Klint and Weiss (1986) examined participant motives in 43 competitive gymnasts, 26 recreational gymnasts, and 37 former competitive gymnasts. Each of these groups were surveyed regarding their reasons for participating in gymnastics, and the former gymnasts were also interviewed regarding why they discontinued gymnastics involvement. When motives for participation were examined, the competitive gymnasts most often cited fitness and challenge; the recreational gymnasts cited fun and situational factors (e.g., like to use the equipment); and the former gymnasts cited fun, challenge, and action as the most important motives for involvement. The former gymnasts also indicated that they most often discontinued involvement because they had other things to do, did not like the pressure, did not have enough fun, and felt gymnastics required too much time. When asked to indicate the single most important reason for withdrawing from gymnastics, 19% of the former gymnasts cited injury; 14% not enough fun, 11% dislike of the pressure, and 11% too much time. Only 2 of the 37 former gymnasts studied discontinued sport participation completely. After initially dropping out, the remaining 35 individuals either returned to gymnastics at a different level or became involved in other sports.

A number of general conclusions can be derived from these descriptive studies examining motives for youth sport withdrawal. Former youth sport participants cite a number of varied personal and situational reasons for sport withdrawal. These include such diverse motives as interest in other activities, conflicts of interest, lack of playing time, lack of success, little skill improvement, lack of fun, boredom, and injury. Conflicts of interest and interest in other activities have been found to be the most consistently cited motives for sport withdrawal. Other more negative motives such as a lack of playing time, overemphasis on competition, boredom, competitive stress, dislike of the coach, and no fun have been rated as major motives for sport withdrawal by a smaller number of former participants. Some evidence reveals that these more negative motives play a more important role in the discontinuation of younger as compared to older dropouts. Several studies have shown that most young athletes who discontinue participation do not totally withdraw from sport. In contrast, they reenter the same sport or participate in other sports at some time in the future.

Theoretical Attempts to Examine Youth Sport Withdrawal

This review has shown that the majority of the youth sport attrition studies conducted to date have been descriptive in nature. These studies helped to identify important trends and variables influencing the attrition process. However, descriptive studies alone will not further advance knowledge in the area. Theoretical or conceptual models are needed that allow researchers to explain and predict behavior. For example, the descriptive research has clearly shown that large numbers of children discontinue involvement because of interest in or conflicts of interest with other activities. What has not been shown in these studies, however, is whether the changing of children's interests from one sport to another or from sport to nonsport activities results from a normal trial-and-error sampling process that allows children to identify activities that they most like, or whether it reflects the inability of organized sport programs to meet the psychological needs of a high percentage of children (Burton & Martens, 1985). This question has prompted investigators to begin to search for various theoretical constructs that may underlie a child's decision to discontinue sport involvement.

Thus, the time has come to go beyond descriptive studies of attrition in youth sports and to begin to develop theoretical models to explain the attrition process. To date, three theoretical frameworks have been identified as possible explanations of the underlying causes of attrition in children's sport. These include the achievement orientation, competence motivation, and social exchange/cognitive-affective frameworks.

Achievement Orientation Theory

Ewing (1981) and Roberts (1984) were two of the first investigators to examine attrition in children's sport from a conceptual framework. These investigators used Maehr and Nicholls's (1980) cognitive interpretation of achievement motivation theory to explain youth sport persistence and withdrawal. They contended that in order to fully understand achievement behavior, the child's perception of success and failure, as well as his or her achievement goals, must also be understood. In essence, three orientations or goals of achievement behavior are said to exist: (a) an ability orientation where a child participates in an activity in an effort to demonstrate high ability and minimize low ability, usually by winning; (b) a task orientation where the child participates in an effort to perform the task as well as possible, regardless of any competitive outcome; and (c) a social approval orientation where the child participates in an effort to seek approval from significant others, usually by exhibiting maximum effort. These multiple goals of achievement are important because the extent to which a child will be motivated and remain active in an achievement context (e.g., sport) depends on his or her perception of whether his or her achievement goals are satisfied. Thus, to predict sport persistence and withdrawal, researchers must determine the salient achievement orientations of the child and the degree to which the child perceives that these achievement goals are fulfilled.

Based on this achievement orientation framework, Ewing (1981) predicted that individual differences in achievement orientations will emerge in children and that these differences in orientation will be related to both youth sport participation and withdrawal. Specifically, ability, task, and social approval orientations were predicted to emerge when young athletes were asked to identify their motives for participation. Children who were more ability oriented were expected to persist longer in sport (be athletes) than children who were not as high on ability orientation (nonparticipants or dropouts). In order to test these predicted achievement goals, perceived sport success, perceived sport failure, and attributions were assessed in 452 males and females who were 14 to 15 years old and who had been identified as sport participants, nonparticipants, or dropouts. The results supported the theory's prediction that multiple achievement goals would exist, in that ability and social approval orientations clearly emerged on a factor analysis, although no clear task orientation was identified. In addition, a relationship was found between achievement orientations, sport persistence, and sport withdrawal. Contrary to the predictions, however, the active sport participants did not display a higher ability orientation than the dropouts or the nonparticipants. Instead, the active sport participants were characterized by a social approval orientation and dropouts by an ability orientation. It was suggested that social approval–oriented children persist longer in sport because the organized sport structure provides ample opportunities for social support (e.g., coaches, parents, and teammates reward their expenditure of maximum effort). For the ability-oriented dropouts, however, the organized sport structure exposed their performance limits (they demonstrated "low" ability by failing) or did not allow them ample opportunity to test their abilities (they sat on the bench). Consequently, the ability-oriented children's goal of demonstrating high ability by winning was not fulfilled, so they were more likely to discontinue participation.

Although Ewing's (1981) study provides some initial support for Maehr and Nicholls's (1980) theoretical contentions, to date it has been the only empirical study conducted on the topic, and its utility therefore cannot yet be judged. It has much intuitive appeal, however, in that it specifies that individual differences exist in achievement orientations of young athletes and that sport persistence is dependent on the fulfillment of these objectives. Additionally, this theoretical framework is parsimonious because it contends that children can be characterized by three general achievement orientations.

Competence Motivation Theory

A second theoretical approach that has been used to explain attrition in youth sport is Harter's (1978) theory of competence motivation. Based on White's (1959) earlier theory, Harter (1978, 1981) predicted that children are motivated to experience mastery or competence feelings when dealing with their environment and because of this, they seek to demonstrate or acquire competencies by engaging in mastery attempts. When mastery is attained (e.g., they are successful), perceived competence is enhanced, which in turn increases competence motivation. Increased competence motivation then causes the child to seek out other situations where competence can be developed. Thus, young athletes who perceive themselves to be highly competent or confident at a particular skill will persist longer at the skill and maintain interest in mastering the skill. In contrast, individuals who perceive themselves to have low competence at a particular skill will not maintain task persistence and interest. Harter does not view perceived competence as being a global trait or unitary construct but rather as having specific domains in the areas of physical, social, and cognitive concerns. Quite possibly, then, a child could show variations in motivation across these competence domains depending on his or her history of experiences and socialization.

Not only does Harter's (1978) model explain the perceived competence and task persistence/performance relationship, but it also accounts for the development of competence. A history of success in mastering skills leads to perceived competence, which in turn leads to increased motivation to be competent. On the other hand, children who have had a history of unsuccessful mastery attempts in a given activity usually experience feelings of low competence. This perception of low competence in turn decreases their motivation to continue participation in that activity. Harter's model also suggests that children who have little experience in a given type of activity will not have had the opportunity to develop a sense of competence in that domain.

Harter's theory is not only intuitively appealing, but it seems directly applicable for researchers studying participation motivation in young athletes. Unfortunately, research has only begun to test its contentions in the athletic domain, although preliminary support for its predictions have been generated in academic classroom situations (Harter, 1978). Evidence also indirectly supports Harter's hypothesis that one's participation motivation is related to a history of successful mastery attempts, in that former young athletes indicated that a lack of success and a lack of skill improvement were important reasons for discontinuing their participation in competitive sports. No direct link can be made between these variables, however, because these studies have not directly assessed perceived competence as the possible mediating variable.

One of the few studies designed to directly test Harter's (1978) model in the area of sports was conducted by Roberts, Kleiber, and Duda (1981). Roberts and his colleagues used Harter's (1979) Perceived Competence Scale for Children to compare male and female fourth and fifth graders who were either participants or nonparticipants in organized sport. They hypothesized that children who participate in organized sport programs would be higher in perceived physical competence than nonparticipants. Their results revealed that the youth sport participants were not only higher in perceived physical competence, but in social competence and general self-worth as well. These findings suggested that either the experience of sport participation influences perceptions of competence or that children with high perceptions of competence are attracted to and persist in sport. To address this issue, Roberts and his associates examined the relationship between years of experience in sport and perceived competence. The nonsignificant correlations between perceived competence and years of experience suggested that individuals with higher perceptions of competence select sport as an activity to demonstrate their abilities. In using only fourth- and fifth-grade students, however, the limited range of years of experience in these subjects may have masked the possible influence that sport experience may have on the development of perceived competence.

A second study designed to examine perceived competence in a youth sport setting was conducted by Feltz, Gould, Horn, and Weiss (1982). This study examined the effects that gender and years of competitive swimming experience had on the perceived competence of young swimmers ($n = 349$) and former swimmers ($n = 50$). Differences between swimmers and former swimmers in perceived competence were also studied. Unlike the results of Roberts and his colleagues, significant (but low) correlations were found between length of swimming involvement and perceived physical and social competence. In addition, male dropouts were found to exhibit higher levels of perceived physical competence and general self-esteem than female dropouts. A limitation of the statistical analyses employed prohibited the desired comparison of participants and former participants.

Feltz and Petlichkoff (1983) examined the relationship among perceived physical competence, participation status (active athlete or dropout), years of athletic experience, and gender. The sample studied included 239 participants and 43 dropouts representing a number of school-sponsored sports. A significant but low relationship existed between perceived physical competence and length of sport participation. Moreover, active participants were found to exhibit significantly higher levels of perceived competence than dropouts and males higher levels of competence than females.

Finally, in a study related to competence motivation, Burton and Martens (1986) examined the relationship between young athletes' perception of their ability and the decision to drop out of sport. Unlike previous theorists who focused solely on the competence-persistence relationship, however, these investigators hypothesized that this relationship can only be understood if other factors are examined, such as the child's perception of success and failure, activity importance, and expectations of parents and coaches. A preliminary test of their hypotheses was conducted using the previously discussed sample of active youth wrestlers, parents of active wrestlers, wrestling dropouts, parents of wrestling dropouts, and coaches. Their results supported the notion that dropouts turn to other activities when wrestling no longer allows them opportunities to perceive themselves high in ability. Specifically, participants reported higher levels of perceived ability, were characterized by more positive future performance expectancies, and exhibited more realistic minimal acceptable standards of performance than the dropouts. Perceived ability, then, when examined in conjunction with these external factors, proved to be a strong predictor of persistence.

The studies examining the relationship between perceived competence (or ability) and sport persistence are encouraging. Dropouts have been consistently found to demonstrate lower levels of perceived competence than participants, and perceived competence seems to be related to years of experience. Additional studies are needed, however, to determine definitely whether children characterized by high levels of competence are drawn to sport in efforts to demonstrate mastery or whether sport participation fosters competence. Moreover, Weiss, Bredemeier, and Shewchuk (1986) have indicated that the competence-persistence relationship is mediated by three interrelated variables. These include the child's intrinsic-extrinsic motivational orientation, perceived control (the child's perception of who or what is responsible for success-failure), and actual achievement. The athletic dropout can only be better understood when the complex interaction among these variables is studied.

Social Exchange and Cognitive-Affective Theories

Smith (1986) has proposed the most recent theoretical framework to explain the process of sport withdrawal. In this framework the important distinction is made between sport burnout and sport dropout. Specifically, burnout-induced withdrawal is defined as the psychological, emotional, and physical withdrawal from sport resulting from chronic stress, whereas dropping out results from a change of interests and/or value reorientation. Thus, all sport dropouts are not necessarily burnouts.

The distinction between the dropout and burnout is central to the conceptual framework forwarded by Smith (1986), who convincingly argues that the dropout and burnout syndromes have differing theoretical explanations. That is, a social exchange model best explains dropout forms of withdrawal, whereas a cognitive-affective model best explains athletic burnout.

Smith (1986) uses the classic social exchange framework developed by Thibaut and Kelly (1959) to explain the process of dropping out of sport. According to this theory, the decision to participate and persist in sport is a function of costs (e.g., time and effort, anxiety, disapproval of others) and benefits (e.g., trophies, feelings of competence) with the athlete constantly trying to maximize benefits and minimize costs. Thus, interest and participation is maintained when the benefits outweigh the costs, and withdrawal occurs when costs outweigh benefits. However, behavior is not fully explained by a simple rewards-minus-costs formula. The decision to participate and persist is mediated by the athlete's minimum comparison level (the lowest criteria one used to judge something as satisfying or unsatisfying) and the comparison level of alternative activities. Consequently, someone may choose to stay involved in sport even if costs are exceeded by rewards because no alternative opportunities are available. Similarly, an athlete who perceives that the rewards outweigh costs in a program may discontinue involvement because a more desirable alternative activity is available.

Although a direct empirical test for the social exchange interpretation of youth sport withdrawal has not been conducted, this formulation seems to readily explain the existing findings in the area (Smith, 1986). Participation motivation studies show that children are attracted to sport because of a variety of benefits and awards. Dropping out of sport occurs when children perceive costs to outweigh benefits and have other, desirable activities available. Hence, the most prevalent motive cited for discontinuing involvement is interest in other activities or conflicts of interest.

In contrast to the vast majority of individuals who drop out of sport, Smith (1986) argues that burnout does occur in a substantial minority of these athletes (and coaches). Athletes who burn out are often very successful, but the previously pleasurable activity becomes a source of undue stress as performance demands are perceived to outweigh one's capabilities. A lack of energy, exhaustion, sleeplessness, depression, tension, irritability, and anger often result. The situation becomes unbearable, and the athlete discontinues involvement as a method of coping with stress.

Smith (1986) has proposed a cognitive-affective model to explain the burnout process. This theoretical framework parallels his general model of athletic stress (Smith, 1986) and draws heavily upon the burnout literature from the social service professions. Situational factors alone, however, do not create stress. The athlete cognitively appraises the demands of the situation and resources available. A negative appraisal results in the perception of threat, which in turn influences one's physiological responses (e.g., tension, fatigue). Finally, the athlete attempts to cope with the situation in any number of ways, possibly including rigid behavior, decreased performance, and withdrawal from sport.

Unfortunately, Smith's cognitive-affective theory of athletic stress has not been empirically tested because of its recent development. It has great intuitive appeal, however. In addition, in outlining the model, Smith provides specific guidelines for empirically examining it.

An Integrated Model of Youth Sport Withdrawal

One of the difficulties facing those trying to understand attrition in children's sport is the lack of a unifying model or framework. Like many new research areas, unrelated studies are conducted, and theoretical models are developed and tested independently of one another. For example, investigators studying possible theoretical explanations that may underlie attrition have often ignored important descriptive findings (e.g., that a high percentage of children who withdraw from sport enter other sports). Similarly, investigators conducting descriptive studies have failed to consider theoretical constructs that may underlie frequently cited, surface-level responses for withdrawal (e.g., low perceived ability feelings may cause a child to lose interest in sport). A need exists to integrate these diverse findings and theoretical approaches into a general model that describes and helps explain the attrition process in children's sport. An integrated model will not only serve as a guide for future research but will also better organize the existing findings and in turn facilitate practical implications. A model of youth sport withdrawal based on an analysis of the literature described earlier is divided into four interrelated components, each focusing on a different aspect of the attrition process. Each of these components is discussed next.

Component 1—Sport Withdrawal

The attrition process ends when a child stops participating in an organized sports program. It is a mistake to assume, however, that when young athletes discontinue participation in one sport, they never participate again. Recent research reveals that many children discontinue involvement in one sport only to initiate involvement in another. Still other children discontinue involvement in one sport only to reenter the same sport at a different level. For example, Gould et al. (1982) found that 80% of the competitive youth swimming dropouts interviewed reentered or planned to reenter the sport, whereas Klint and Weiss (1986) found that 35 of 37 of the dropouts they surveyed reentered gymnastics or other sports. This is not to say that some children who drop out of sport never participate again. Petlichkoff (1982) found that 59% of the high school dropouts she interviewed had not participated in any organized sport since discontinuing involvement. Consequently, in Component 1 of the model, sport withdrawal is viewed on a continuum ranging from an activity-specific or program-specific withdrawal (e.g., drop out of baseball or a specific baseball program) to a domain-general withdrawal (e.g., drop out of all competitive sports permanently).

Component 2—Child- or Externally Controlled Withdrawal

Working back from the actual decision to withdraw, the second component of the model focuses on whether young athletes control the decision to withdraw. In some cases, the decision to withdraw is externally controlled. For example, children who are cut from teams, can no longer afford the costs of some sports, or suffer such severe injuries that they are no longer able to participate have little choice about the decision to withdraw. Unfortunately, few studies have focused on this aspect of the attrition process, although Ogilvie and Howe (1982) have speculated that the ramifications of such withdrawal can be devastating. Especially significant would be studies examining the effects of "cutting" on the perceived competence and intrinsic motivation of the child.

Child-controlled withdrawal occurs more frequently than externally controlled withdrawal and has been the focus of most of the research conducted to date. In the case of child-controlled withdrawal, the young athlete makes the ultimate decision to discontinue participation. Even though the child makes the ultimate decision to discontinue, however, this decision can be markedly influenced by outside sources like the actions of coaches and parents and success or failure received in the program.

Component 3—Costs-Benefits Analysis

The costs-benefits analysis that the child uses in making the decision to discontinue involvement is contained in Component 3. Based on Smith's (1986) application of the social exchange framework, the young athlete weighs the perceived benefits of participation against the costs, relative to his or her minimal comparison level (the minimum criteria he or she uses to define success or benefits) and the attractiveness and availability of alternative sport and nonsport activities (the comparison level for alternatives). In essence, when the child athlete perceives costs to outweigh benefits and alternative activities to be more attractive, he or she discontinues participation.

Smith's (1986) costs-benefits application of social exchange theory was separately incorporated in this component of the model because it provides a general theoretical framework that integrates both surface-level explanations cited for sport withdrawal, as well as underlying theoretical motives (see Component 4). Specifically, this framework predicts that children withdraw from sport when costs outweigh benefits, whether costs-benefits be defined as a young athlete's perceived competence, satisfaction of ability, task and social approval goals, psychological stress, or other varied personal and situational factors.

Component 4—Motivation for Sport Withdrawal

Component 4 of the model is subdivided into two highly interrelated subcomponents. Subcomponent 4a depicts the surface-level explanations or self-ratings of program costs that children cite for discontinuing involvement. An interactionist paradigm is employed in this component, as the attrition research has shown that both personal and situational factors are cited as variables influencing the decision to withdraw. Personal reasons include psychological factors like interest in other activities, no fun, and competitive stress. Physical factors include such items as a lack of skill improvement and injury, and situational factors include things like program emphasis, poor organization, and social support from significant others. Finally, although the reasons cited for withdrawal are subdivided into categories, they do overlap considerably.

Subcomponent 4b of the model contains theoretical motives that underlie and affect the stated reasons for sport withdrawal. For example, a child may be unable to express whether she or he is task-, socially, or ability-oriented, yet individual differences exist on these achievement orientations and have been linked to participation persistence (Ewing, 1981). Similarly, the child's competence motivation or perceived competence has been shown to be an important variable affecting the attrition process, with dropouts being characterized by lower levels of competence than active participants. Finally, Smith's (1986) cognitive-affective model of athletic burnout seems especially appropriate for explaining attrition in a specific subclass of youth sport dropouts—those burnouts who suffer from the effects of chronic stress.

In summary, this model has the advantage of integrating both the descriptive and theoretical findings on attrition in children's sport. It is also broad in scope, integrating the social exchange, achievement orientation, perceived competence, and cognitive-affective theoretical frameworks. Finally, it emphasizes precisely defining the generality of youth sport withdrawal and the important distinction between dropouts and burnouts.

Future Directions in Youth Sport Attrition Research and Practice

This review has clearly shown that much has been learned from the youth sport attrition research conducted to date. If further improvements are to be made, however, a number of theoretical, methodological, and measurement concerns must be addressed. Moreover, the conceptual model outlined in this review can serve as a guide for examining these research issues, as well as a guide for implementing practices designed to curtail attrition.

Future Research Directions

The youth sport attrition model clearly shows that to understand youth sport withdrawal, investigators must integrate the descriptive responses children give for dropping out of sport with possible underlying motivational constructs. In particular, Component 4 of the model shows that the achievement orientation, competence motivation, and cognitive-affective burnout theories all contain likely motives that may underlie sport withdrawal. Merely testing each theory's predictions with samples of active and former participants is not enough, however. Critical studies are needed in which these theories are tested simultaneously.

The need for designing critical investigations is especially noteworthy because the theories contained in the model are similar in many ways. For example, they are all cognitively oriented and focus on the child's perceptions of specified psychological or environmental states (e.g., perceived competence). Quite possibly, then, these theories are not comprised of independent psychological constructs and may at times discuss the same constructs under the guise of different labels. Thus, simultaneous tests of the various theories will determine if explanatory and predictive overlap exists.

Not only must varying theoretical constructs be simultaneously examined, but the model suggests that investigators should assess both theoretical and descriptive explanations for sport withdrawal. Investigators too often assume that the specific theoretical construct in which they are interested accounts for 100% of the variance in young athletes' decisions to withdraw. The research clearly shows, however, that the attrition process is complex and influenced by several factors. What is needed are studies that show how important various theoretically and practically grounded measures are in predicting withdrawal and when, in what situations, and with whom these measures explain and predict behavior.

Investigators utilizing this model will not only need to identify the underlying explanations for attrition in children's sport, but they must also stress the most advanced elements of theory—behavioral prediction and control. Yet, this review has shown that the majority of studies conducted to date have utilized a traditional field study paradigm where variables are observed but causal relationships not pursued. Consequently, causal inferences cannot be made. A need exists to conduct field experiments in which investigators test causal links between variables and behavior or to design studies that use path and structural-analytic statistical techniques that can be used to test causal links in nonexperimental settings. For example, Smith, Smoll, Hunt, Curtis, and Coppel (1979) have conducted a systematic series of studies that focus on how coaching behaviors influence the affective states of young athletes. A logical extension of this line of research would involve the assessment of young athletes' participation motives or achievement orientations. Coaching behaviors hypothesized to influence the various motives could also be assessed. The predicted correspondence between participation motives, coaching behaviors, attrition rates, and attrition motives could then be examined.

Components 1 and 2 of the model focus on identifying the extent and type of withdrawal that occur in youth sport. Future investigators must consider these components further because the lack of appropriate operational definitions has plagued the previous research. For example, little consistency has occurred across studies in regard to the definition of an athlete or dropout. Many of the previous studies have simply defined a dropout as a child who no longer participates in a particular sport. Component 1 of the model, however, reflects the finding that many of these children reenter sport. A dropout who reenters sport (an activity-specific dropout) may be considerably different from one who never returns (a domain-general dropout). Smith (1986) has also shown that an athletic burnout is substantially different from a dropout. Consequently, future investigators must heed the advice of investigators like Robinson and Carron (1982) and Smith (1986) and better define the participation-persistence continuum, including such levels as active athlete (starter), survivor (active athlete who receives little playing time), dropout, and burnout.

The model also reveals that two types of withdrawal can exist (see Component 2). Unfortunately, most of the existing research has focused solely on examining child-controlled withdrawal. Examining externally controlled withdrawal and its effects on future sport involvement is an important area for additional study.

The previous research has also been characterized by small, nonrandom samples. A need exists to ensure that minimal sample sizes and, when appropriate, random samples are obtained. Similarly, if many moderator variables are to be examined (e.g., gender, sport played, age, years of experience), samples should be selected that provide an adequate range of these variables.

Lastly, when conducting future investigations designed to assess costs and benefits of participation, as well as motives for sport withdrawal, a number of measurement concerns face the youth sport attrition researcher (Gould, 1983). These include the need to develop valid and reliable measures of achievement orientations and motives for withdrawal. In addition, methods of overcoming problems associated with giving socially desirable responses are needed. In the Petlichkoff (1982) study on high school dropouts, for instance, some of the former athletes indicated that injury was the major motive underlying the decision to discontinue. In some cases, however, further probing by the interviewer revealed that injury was used as a socially accepted reason, with the true reason for discontinuing (e.g., not as good as wanted to be) not initially cited. The social desirability problem can be overcome by using multiple assessment techniques (both self-report scales that make quantitative assessments and in-depth qualitative interviews where investigators can probe for additional responses) or designs where psychological data are collected before the season and prior to the decision to discontinue.

Practical Implications for Preventing Attrition in Young Athletes

Although additional and improved research is needed, this does not imply that lack of practical implications characterizes the existing youth sport attrition research. In contrast, the existing research as summarized in this model has a number of important implications for those directly involved in children's sport.

A number of varied explanations exist for the high rate of attrition in youth sports. Some investigators have suggested that the high rate of attrition reflects a normal trial-and-error sampling process, in which children identify those activities they like best. Other reviewers contend that the high attrition rate results from inappropriate coaching and emotional stress. Neither of these views seems totally correct. Conflict of interest or interest in alternative activities was clearly the motive cited most often for discontinuing. Moreover, many children were found to leave one sport only to enter another. Some normal trial-and-error sport sampling is therefore occurring. At the same time, a substantial minority (15 to 20%) of young athletes discontinue because of more negative, adult-controlled motives such as an overemphasis on competition, lack of playing time, and excessive competitive stress. This supports the view that adult-controlled factors are related to attrition patterns in young athletes. Additionally, recent evidence reveals that various psychological constructs, such as low perceived ability, may underlie the change of interest in some children. An important implication of the research, then, is that trial-and-error sport sampling occurs on the part of some young athletes, whereas some children leave because of low perceived competence, lack of skill improvement, little fun, and an overly competitive environment (see Component 4).

A second important implication resulting from the model focuses on the finding that children have multiple motives for participating in sports and in turn for discontinuing involvement. Major participation motives include developing skill, experiencing fun and excitement, achieving success, and being with friends. When these motives are not achieved, children weigh the costs versus benefits of participation (Component 3) and often withdraw citing other things to do as the reason. Knowing this, Gould and Horn (1984) have suggested that adult leaders structure the athletic environment so that these motives are fulfilled. Special emphasis should be placed on skill instruction for children of all ability levels. Excitement and fun must be maintained in practices and competitions by keeping young athletes active and by allowing all children the opportunity to participate. Special efforts should be made to meet the affiliation needs of young athletes. Finally, success should be more broadly defined as personal improvement, in contrast to competitive outcome.

A third implication generated from the model is that perceived competence and ability play important roles in the youth sport attrition process. The development of perceived competence is influenced by the child's history of successes and failures at the activity. Efforts must be made to develop realistic but positive perceptions of competence in young athletes. This can be accomplished by (a) equalizing competitive settings so that all children will experience some success, (b) providing positive but contingent evaluative feedback, (c) enhancing skill development, and (d) emphasizing the attainment of individual performance goals. Coaches working directly with young athletes must implement these procedures, as should additional significant others such as parents (Gould, in press).

Summary

The high rate of attrition in children's sport programs is one of the most significant issues facing those involved in youth sports. Fortunately, pediatric behavioral scientists have begun to study the area. The results of these investigations have shown that the attrition process is complex and is influenced by a variety of personal and situational variables. In particular, descriptive studies have revealed that conflicting and changing interests are the most often cited motives for youth sport withdrawal, with adult-controlled negative factors being cited by a much smaller but significant number of former athletes. The more recent theoretical literature supports these findings but also shows that various psychological constructs such as perceived competence, achievement orientations, and stress may at times underlie these changes in interest. A theoretical model of youth sport withdrawal integrating the descriptive findings in the area with initial theoretical explanations has been derived from this research. This model serves as both a guide for future research and as a means of organizing existing knowledge for practical application.

References

Burton, D., & Martens, R. (1986). Pinned by their goals: An exploratory investigation into why kids drop out of wrestling. *Journal of Sport Psychology*, 8(3), 183–197.

Ewing, M.E. (1981). *Achievement orientations and sport behavior of males and females.* Unpublished doctoral dissertation, University of Illinois, Urbana.

Feigley, D.A. (1984). Psychological burnout in high-level athletes. *The Physician and Sportsmedicine*, 12(10), 108–119.

Feltz, D.L., Gould, D., Horn, T.S., & Weiss, M.R. (1982, June). *Perceived competence among youth swimmers and dropouts.* Paper presented at the meeting of the North American Society for the Psychology of Sport and Physical Activity, College Park, MD.

Feltz, D.L., & Petlichkoff, L. (1983). Perceived competence among interscholastic sport participants and dropouts. *Canadian Journal of Applied Sport Science,* 8(4), 231–235.

Fry, D.A.P., McClements, J.D., & Sefton, J.M. (1981). *A report on participation in the Saskatoon Hockey Association.* Saskatoon, Canada: SASK Sport.

Gould, D. (1983). Future directions in youth sports participation motivation research. In L. Wankel & R. Wilberg (Eds.), *Psychology of sport and motor behavior: Research and practice* (pp. 137–145). Edmonton: University of Alberta, Faculty of Physical Education and Recreation.

Gould, D. (in press). Promoting positive sport experiences for children. In M.J. Ash & J. May (Eds.), *Sport psychology: The psychological health of the athlete.* Jamaca, NY: SP Medical and Scientific Books.

Gould, D., Feltz, D., Horn, T., & Weiss, M.R. (1982). Reasons for discontinuing involvement in competitive youth swimming. *Journal of Sport Behavior,* 5, 155–165.

Gould, D., & Horn, T. (1984). Participation motivation in young athletes. In J.M. Silva & R.S. Weinberg (Eds.), *Psychological foundations of sport* (pp. 359–370). Champaign, IL: Human Kinetics.

Harter, S. (1978). Effectance motivation reconsidered: Toward a developmental model. *Human Development,* 21, 34–64.

Harter, S.P. (1979). *Perceived competence scale for children.* (Manual: Form O). Denver, CO: University of Denver.

Harter, S. (1981). The development of competence motivation in the mastery of cognitive and physical skills: Is there still a place for joy? In G.C. Roberts & D.M. Landers (Eds.), *Psychology of motor behavior and sport—1980* (pp. 3–29). Champaign, IL: Human Kinetics.

Klint, K., & Weiss, M.R. (1986). Dropping in and dropping out: Participation motives of current and former youth gymnasts. *Canadian Journal of Applied Sport Sciences,* 11(2), 106–114.

Lewin, K. (1935). *A dynamic theory of personality.* New York: McGraw-Hill.

Maehr, M.L., & Nicholls, J.G. (1980). Culture and achievement motivation: A second look. In N. Warren (Ed.), *Studies in cross-cultural psychology* (pp. 221–267). New York: Academic Press.

McPherson, B.D., Guppy, L.N., & McKay, J.P. (1976). The social structure of the game and sport milieu. In J.G. Albinson & G.M. Andrews (Eds.), *Children in sport and physical activity* (pp. 161–200). Baltimore, MD: University Park.

Nettleton, B. (1979, June). *The social institution of sport today and tomorrow.* Paper presented at the "Sport Today: Health or Disability" seminar, Lincoln Institute of Health Sciences, Melbourne, Australia.

Ogilvie, B.C., & Howe, M.A. (1982). Career crisis in sport. In T. Orlick, J.T. Partington, & J.H. Salmela (Eds.), *Mental training for coaches and athletes* (pp. 176–183). Ottawa, Canada: Coaching Association of Canada.

Orlick, T.D. (1973, January/February). Children's sport—A revolution is coming. *Canadian Association for Health, Physical Education and Recreation Journal,* pp. 12–14.

Orlick, T.D. (1974, November/December). The athletic dropout—A high price of inefficiency. *Canadian Association for Health, Physical Education and Recreation Journal,* pp. 21–27.

Orlick, T.D., & Botterill, C. (1975). *Every kid can win.* Chicago, IL: Nelson-Hall.

Petlichkoff, L.M. (1982). *Motives interscholastic athletes have for participation and reasons for discontinued involvement in school sponsored sport.* Unpublished master's thesis, Michigan State University, East Lansing.

Pooley, J.C. (1981). *Drop-outs from sport: A case study for boys age-group soccer.* Paper presented at the meeting of the American Alliance for Health, Physical Education, Recreation, and Dance, Boston, MA.

Roberts, G.C. (1984). Achievement motivation in children's sport. *Advances in Motivation and Achievement,* 3, 251–281.

Roberts, G.C., Kleiber, D.A., & Duda, J.L. (1981). An analysis of motivation in children's sport: The role of perceived competence in participation. *Journal of Sport Psychology*, 3, 203–211.

Robertson, I. (1981, January). *Children's perceived satisfactions and stresses in sport.* Paper presented at the Australian Conference on Health, Physical Education and Recreation Biennial Conference, Melbourne.

Robinson, T., & Carron, A. (1982). Personal and situational factors associated with dropping out versus maintaining participation in competitive sport. *Journal of Sport Psychology*, 4, 364–378.

Sapp, M., & Haubenstricker, J. (1978). *Motivation for joining and reasons for not continuing in youth sport programs in Michigan.* Paper presented at the meeting of the American Alliance for Health, Physical Education, Recreation, and Dance, Kansas City, MO.

Sefton, J.M.M., & Fry, D.A.P. (1981). *A report on participation in competitive swimming.* Saskatoon, Canada: Canadian Amateur Swimming Association (Saskatchewan Section).

Smith, R.E. (1986). Toward a cognitive-affective model of athletic burnout. *Journal of Sport Psychology*, 8, 36–50.

Smith, R.E., Smoll, F.L., Hunt, E., Curtis, B., & Coppel, D.B. (1979). Psychology and the bad news bears. In G.C. Roberts & K.M. Newell (Eds.), *Psychology of motor behavior and sport—1978* (pp. 109–130). Champaign, IL: Human Kinetics.

Thibaut, J.W., & Kelly, H.H. (1959). *The social psychology of groups.* New York: Wiley.

United Nations. (1982). *United Nations 1982 demographic yearbook.* New York: United Nations Publications.

Weiss, M.R., Bredemeier, B.J., & Shewchuk, R.M. (1986). The dynamics of perceived competence, perceived control, and motivation orientation in youth sport. In M.R. Weiss & D. Gould (Eds.), *Sport for children and youths* (pp. 89–102). Champaign, IL: Human Kinetics.

White, R.W. (1959). Motivation reconsidered: The concept of competence. *Psychological Review,* 66, 297–333.

41 Sport as a Context for Developing Competence

STEVEN J. DANISH
Virginia Commonwealth University

ALBERT J. PETITPAS
Springfield College

BRUCE D. HALE
Pennsylvania State University

Morality is an important issue in everyday life and sport alike. In the public domain, controversial questions such as the values of youth are often discussed, and frequent references are made to the subject of moral development in the domain of sport and physical activity. Traditionally, sport involvement has been viewed as contributing to the development of moral virtues, such as fair play, honesty, and respect, which could eventually generalize to important life skills, such as coping with stress, learning to compete, or using social cooperation. In short, sport is intended to build character, but this tenet has come under serious critique because of the immorality often revealed in athletic activities.

To enhance the morality of sport participants, educators, politicians, and business people interested in the welfare of children and teenagers in the family setting and in society in general have revealed increasing interest in various school- and community-based intervention programs proposed to children and youth, which were aimed at educating them about moral values and character. They thereby promote their moral development in and outside the context of physical activity and sport. In this framework, Steven Danish and his team devoted substantial efforts toward using sport as a context through which young people can develop personal and social competence. He assumed that psychosocial skills learned on the athletic field will, at least in part, transfer to other domains, such as home, school, and the workplace. However, for this approach to succeed, the child's or teenager's experiences should be purposefully designed and implemented, taking into account the characteristic developmental life periods, including their unique skills and needs.

On this tenet, Danish built his popular Life Skill Development Model. In this model, life skills were defined as essential competencies that should be learned, transferred across domains, and maintained throughout one's development. Among the life skills suggested in Danish's programs, goal setting and self regulation through imagery, positive self-talk, self-control, and decision making can be found, as well as seeking social support, which is necessary for increasing the probability of goal attainment. In this chapter, Danish and colleagues first present the concept of competence and its relation to sport. Then they demonstrate how, and under what conditions, sport can be applied with adolescents in order to promote and enhance the development of competence through specific programs designed for this purpose (in this case, Athletes Coaching Teens and Success 101). Most important is their concluding discussion of how the skills learned through sport participation can be applied in adolescents' later life.

Danish's life skills intervention programs, which were applied in various sport settings, are well grounded in the developmental needs and skills of the participating children and adolescents and are therefore targeted to their characteristic social and moral growth process. Despite the fact that more evaluation research is still required to empirically examine the impact of these programs, there is no doubt about their immense value for youth in terms of improving their mastery, autonomy, personal identity, respect for others, and social responsibility, which are essential for improving their chances of living a better life.

American culture places high value on sports. It is a major source of entertainment and provides heroes for the young and old (Reppucci, 1987). More than 20 million children ages 6–15 participate in one or more extraschool sports yearly (Magill, Ash, & Smoll, 1978) at a cost of $17 billion (Martens, 1978). Only family, school, and television involve children's time more than sport (Institute for Social Research, 1985). Not only has sport become a major influence on the development of children, it has become a cultural phenomenon that permeates all of society (Nelson, 1982). It is a social institution comparable to other social institutions such as religion, law, government, politics, education, and medicine.

The status sport has attained in our society enhances its importance to youth. But even before children understand sport as a cultural phenomenon, the development of their self-esteem is influenced by their participation in sport. Despite its immediate value to children, the importance of sport as a vehicle to enhance personal development is in question. Psychologists have lined up on both sides of the discussion. Some have argued that sport builds character; others say it promotes character disorders.

In this chapter, we will briefly review the empirical literature that examines the relationship between sport and competence. Following the review a framework will be developed for understanding how, if, and under what conditions sport contributes to personal competence. This framework is based on our belief that sport has the potential either to enhance or to inhibit development among adolescents. For sport to promote competence, the sport experience must be designed specifically with such a purpose in mind. Examples of sport programs that enhance personal and social competence will be described. Finally, we will consider how the skills learned through sport participation can be applied in later life.

The Concept of Competence

One of the inherent problems in understanding competence has been the difficulty of developing a definition with which both theorists and researchers can agree and that has validity across the life span. The issue of whether experience in one period of life affects an individual's behavior at a later point in life is critical to the understanding of this concept. If it is possible to show continuity over time and across situations, we will have a better understanding of the roots of competence and the nature of human development. As such the work of stage theorists such as Erikson (1950) is important for understanding the development of competence. Competence viewed developmentally is not an end state but a process related to an individual's particular stage of life.

White (1959, 1963) has been credited by many with introducing the concept of competence. He considered competence to be an innate need of infants to master their environment that exists independent of the instinctual drives for food, sex, or avoidance of pain. Observations of infants and young children at play reveal that they will stay actively involved with objects on which they can have some effect (Piaget, 1954). The more possibilities for manipulation, the longer the infant will explore. White felt that infants develop feelings of satisfaction and enjoyment in being able to influence their world. This independent energy is referred to as "effectance" and the emotional satisfaction as "feelings of efficacy" (White, 1963).

These feelings of efficacy experienced at one stage of the life span have an impact on subsequent stages. As described by Havighurst (1953), developmental tasks are encountered at each stage. These tasks are a set of skills that are acquired as individuals gain mastery over different areas of intellectual development, social and interpersonal skills, and emotionality. The recognition that competence is not a unitary concept but refers to several areas of mastery has resulted in a stronger construct (Harter, 1978). The mastery of skills associated with later stages of development is enhanced by competence in skills acquired at earlier life stages. However, mastery in one area, for example motor skills, does not necessarily transfer to another area. The issue of transferability is a critical one in our discussion of whether competence in sport relates to personal competence; it will be considered in more detail later.

As one progresses through the stages, certain demands or social expectations are placed upon the individual by society. The effort to adjust to these demands produces a state of tension that provokes action. This action is the use of the set of developmental skills just recently acquired. Successful achievement or learning of a task promotes happiness and suggests that the individual is likely to be successful at mastering other developmental tasks. Failure to acquire the skills necessary for task mastery can lead to personal unhappiness, societal disapproval, and difficulty in achieving later developmental tasks. Thus with age individuals begin to adopt external assessments of their perceptions of their competence.

For the purposes of this chapter, the definition of *competence* developed by Danish, D' Augelli, and Ginsberg (1984) will be used. This definition is based, in part, on White's (1974) perspective on coping, which involves the ability to (a) gain and process new information, (b) maintain control over one's emotional state, and (c) move freely in one's environment. Danish, D' Augelli, and Ginsberg (1984, p. 531) define "competence" as "the ability to do life planning, to be self reliant, and to seek the resources of others in coping." At different stages or levels of development, these skills relate to different behaviors.

Sport and the Development of Personal Competence

The process whereby individuals acquire attitudes, behaviors, values, and skills through sport participation has been a topic of increasing interest and debate. Almost every coach, athlete, and sport psychologist believes that participation in sports can have a beneficial effect on the psychosocial development of children and adolescents. Further, many supporters of youth sports programs believe that what is learned "on the playing field" is directly transferable to "the classroom" and "the boardroom."

In this section we will examine the literature from three perspectives: historical, empirical, and conceptual.

A Historical Perspective

The belief that sport provides "training for life" has its roots in the turn-of-the-century movement to legitimize athletics and physical education. It was assumed that through sports children learned good sportsmanship and other values and skills necessary in a competitive society. At the same time participation in sports was viewed as an important means of maintaining social control over children. Youth could be taught to accept the norms and rules of the existing culture, use their free time constructively, and conform to the status quo. For many decades this philosophy prevailed.

By the 1960s and 1970s the philosophy concerning the value of sport had changed. Professionals began to worry that sport participation, especially for youth, had the potential of limiting rather than enhancing individual development. Ogilivie and Tutko (1971) discussed the potential for sport to produce "characters" as opposed to character. They contended that the environment of competitive athletics is not conducive to the development of prosocial behavior. Orlick and Botterill (1975) questioned the overly competitive nature of organized athletics with its unhealthy atmosphere of overbearing parents and the continuing opportunity for repeated failure and resulting loss of self-esteem. Martens (1983) warned that the emphasis on performance rather than learning was potentially dangerous. He noted that youth were being pushed toward unrealistic goals and that playing for extrinsic rewards was reducing intrinsic motivation.

What is most striking about this brief review is that the positions adopted by the writers seem to parallel the prevailing social philosophies of the day. Thus it is not surprising that writers differ on the value of sport during these different periods. Expectations concerning what constitutes appropriate behavior for a child have varied dramatically during this century. During the first half of the century, children were viewed as miniature adults and the activities in which they engaged were expected to prepare them to be hardworking, competitive adults. In recent years child rearing has emphasized the development of prosocial behavior and "doing things for oneself rather than always being concerned with how others see us." The expectations for sport then have mirrored society's present definition of competence.

Therefore, defining competence is a critical first step. The definition we have proposed is developmentally based and process-oriented rather than related to a particular end state. As a result, our review of the empirical literature will focus on the process behaviors specific to various developmental stages. For example, the psychosocial stage theory of development developed by Newman and Newman (1979) seems especially relevant. This theory is based on five organizing concepts: stages of development, developmental tasks, the psychosocial crisis, the central processes for resolving the crisis, and coping behaviors. Such a theory applied to children, adolescents, and young adults aged 8 to 20 could serve as the orienting framework for examining the empirical literature on the value of sport for developing competence.

An Empirical Perspective

Unfortunately, there is little empirical evidence on the relationship between participation in sport and competence. Much of the literature that does exist seems to be more opinion, speculation, and subjective observation than empirical research (Burchard, 1979). Furthermore, researchers who have reviewed the empirical studies conducted to examine the effects of athletic participation on psychosocial development have concluded that the literature consists largely of correlational findings, little experimental manipulation, few longitudinal studies, and a high probability of biased self-selectional effects (Browne & Mahoney, 1984; Morgan, 1980). In other words, few, if any, causal relationships have been established.

The most comprehensive review to date has been conducted by Iso-Aloha and Hatfield (1986). In their examination of correlational studies concerning sport involvement and development, they conclude that self-concept is likely to improve through involvement in activities highly valued by the participants. The basis for this conclusion was drawn from several studies: Koocher (1971) reported that learning to swim (a new skill) enhanced self-concept; Kay, Felker, and Varoz (1972) reported that those with higher athletic competence had higher self-concept; Sonestroem (1982) concluded that fitness training can enhance self-esteem not just merely by participating but by interpreting the experience as personal success and growth in competence; and Duke, Johnson, and Nowicki (1977) noted that increased fitness was associated with a sense of increased personal control.

Not all of the findings are so positive. The "Robbers Cave" experiments (Sherif, Harvey, White, Hood, & Sherif, 1961, Sherif & Sherif, 1953; Sherif, White, & Harvey, 1955) are examples of how competitive sports can be either destructive or constructive depending on their purpose and management. Competitive failure led to impaired interpersonal behavior whereas winning tended to increase aggressive tendencies. However, the inclusion of superordinate goals did reduce conflict and increase cooperation. Burchard. (1977) found that losing reduced the enjoyment and produced a less positive attitude toward oneself and others among 11- and 12-year-old hockey players. Finally Landers and Landers (1978) found that participation in sport may hinder academic performance and that failure in sport may accelerate movement toward increased delinquent behavior.

Following an examination of the considerable empirical literature in the area, Iso-Aloha and Hatfield (1986) concluded that early athletic participation may contribute to later success through reinforcement of the critical behaviors necessary for success. One recent study provides support for this perspective. Seidel and Reppucci (1989) assessed changes in self-perception of various kinds of competence and global self-worth after a season of participation in organized youth sports. Results revealed that, across all groups, children's perceptions of their athletic and scholastic competence, physical appearance, and global self-worth increased from pre- to postseason. The authors concluded that the activities at best promoted the children's psychological development and, at worst, were not psychologically damaging.

All in all, however, the empirical literature does not support a cause-and-effect relationship between sport participation and competence. To address this question, specific experimental studies including the random assignment of participants must be designed. The effect of participating in different sports, the different skill levels of the participants, the different reasons for participating, and the different ages at which participants start must be assessed, as should the impact of different expectations by family, coaches, and teachers, and friends. Finally, it will be important to be sensitive to the individual differences of the participants. Serious participation in sport may have different payoffs for girls than for boys in terms of self-actualization and achievement (Crandell & Battle, 1970; Kleiber & Kane, 1984).

Thus it is not possible to conclude definitively that sport participation enhances competence, largely because of the lack of well-designed studies and an understanding of the different variables that must be considered. However, before we reject a causal relationship, let's examine the issue from a conceptual perspective.

A Conceptual Perspective

If we adopt White's (1963) framework as described earlier, feelings of efficacy should motivate effort in the neophyte athlete. A sense of competence originates from subjective feelings of confidence in one's ability to master the environment. Preschoolers who are more coordinated interact more quickly and in a more extended manner with their environment and gain a better sense of trust in their environment and themselves. Better developed physical abilities enhance the acquisition of a sense of autonomy, achievement, and initiative and promote stronger family and peer relationships. As children continue to explore and play, they learn what they can do. Their feelings of competence result from their successful experiences with the world.

Effectance prompts manipulation and exploratory behavior. It can be observed in the child who engages in solitary practice of a specific sport skill. He or she spends hour after hour working on a jump shot or a headstand. This solitary effect is motivated by the intrinsic satisfaction of mastering the environment.

Children who are more physically coordinated seem to have a head start at developing self-esteem and the potential to reach higher levels of physical skills. Equally important is the likelihood that they will also develop more effective interpersonal and intrapersonal skills. Because of these accomplishments (achieving age-appropriate developmental tasks) by the age of 10, athletic children are often seen as leaders (Ambron & Brodzinsky, 1979). Participation in sports then is rewarded by peers and adults at very early ages.

If children are not impeded by the competency needs of over-involved parents or coaches, they will continue to explore, take risks, and learn strategies to affect their environment. Children who are taught to fear failure or mistakes may develop self-imposed restrictions that can severely compromise further opportunities for the development of feelings of efficacy. Play then ceases to be meaningful and rewarding.

White (1963) felt that an initial sense of competence was necessary or children would not be able to benefit from the process of identification. Children identify with those individuals whose competence they admire. They imitate basketball players, such as Michael Jordan, or tennis stars, such as Steffi Graf, in the hope of developing their own levels of competence. Like simpler forms of imitation, identification requires that children feel confident that the skills they want to improve or refine are already part of their repertoire. Through trial and error children discover which identifications will work and which are doomed to failure. Without an initial foundation of feelings of efficacy, it is doubtful whether children would be able to gain maximum benefits from the process of identification. White (1963) contends that identification must be viewed in terms of "attempted action." Clearly people can dream of acquiring skills beyond their present range, but it is action and its consequences that provide children with feedback on which identifications might succeed and which might fall.

Sports become a logical testing ground for levels of personal competence once children move outside the home environment, in part because of its value in society. Moreover, the mastery of the intricacies of sport requires considerable mental and physical skill. The intrinsic rewards of being able to master one's environment are quickly matched by the external reinforcements that also accrue from being the strongest, fastest, or simply the best player. Even in the sandlots children quickly learn that the most competent in the sport will get to choose the other players to make up the teams for the pickup games. On the other hand, the least competent will be the last one selected, often with comments like, "I guess that leaves me with Jimmy." For some children being the last one picked can become so traumatic that they will avoid the athletic field and never participate in the sport again. Other children will take the initial rebuff as a challenge and practice on their own until their level of competence matches or surpasses that of their playmates. Subsequent action depends on the child's appraisal of the meaning of the situation. A situation perceived as a threat will often result in avoidance; an appraisal of a situation as challenging will more likely result in approach (Lazarus & Folkman, 1984).

As children progress through the early school years, they are introduced to the more formal sports structure. Youth sports and school teams provide more clearly defined rules and criteria for measuring personal competence. Although numerous reasons for sports participation have been cited in the literature, Gould and Horn (1984) have identified six motives that are the most consistently listed by young athletics between the ages of 8 and 19.These are improving skills, having fun, being with friends, experiencing thrills and excitement, achieving success, and developing fitness. Gould (1987) concludes that children will continue to participate in sport if their motives are being fulfilled but will discontinue participation if their interests change or if they feel they are having little success in the activity. At the youth sport and school levels of experience, children continue to compare their skills with those of their peers. The most skillful will become identified as the star athletes. In addition to intrinsic rewards from the mastery of increasingly more difficult skills and competitions, they also accrue considerable external reinforcement for their athletic accomplishments. With increased levels of competition, sport becomes one of the most important proving grounds for personal competence. Sport provides clear, immediate feedback. Elite performers continue to develop confidence in their abilities and a stronger identification with the sport. The less gifted athletes often become victims of the athletic system that tends to reward success rather than simply participation. In a "win at all costs" sports environment, athletes with lesser skills are unlikely to get opportunities to develop feelings of competence from the sport due to lack of playing time and limited reinforcement for their efforts.

As athletes move into adolescence, their developmental focus shifts from a need to maintain a sense of industry (Erikson, 1959) to a quest for personal identity. As outlined by Erikson, all adolescents must synthesize childhood identifications in such a manner that they can establish a reciprocal relationship with society while simultaneously maintaining a sense of continuity within themselves. What a person thinks he or she can be is a product of past experiences and the feedback of significant others.

Although research (Coleman, 1961; Eitzen, 1975) has shown that athletic success in high school accrues more status than academic achievement, to fully examine the impact of sport on the development of competence among adolescents, we must consider the influence of sports in later adolescence. It is during this period that the need to acquire a personal identity becomes critical. Ironically it is the same sport system that apparently provides so many benefits for the young athlete that may later interfere with opportunities for optimal identity development during this period and in early adulthood.

Chickering (1969) describes late adolescence and early adulthood as periods during which a number of developmental tasks must be confronted. These include achieving competence, managing emotions, becoming autonomous, establishing relationships, developing more mature interpersonal relationships, clarifying purpose, and developing integrity. The psychosocial crisis (Erikson, 1950) of these periods is individual identity versus role diffusion and the central process is role experimentation. As can be seen, this is a period in which the focus is on broadening one's horizons. If the individual continues to invest all his or her energies in sport, he or she may be impeded in engaging in a quest for personal identity (Petitpas & Champagne, 1988). The immediate result may be role strain and frustration (Chartrend & Lent, 1987); the long-term consequences may be foreclosure of the search for an identity (Marcia, 1966).

Stein and Hoffman (1978) delineate a number of role strains athletes experience that are related to their development. Among these conflicts are (a) the demands of simultaneously being a student, athlete, friend, and son or daughter and the concomitant role overloads associated with these demands; (b) the increasing need to compete to meet the expectations of others as opposed to the desire to adopt a more cooperative posture consistent with the appropriate developmental tasks for this period; (c) anxiety about being physically injured while at the same time needing to take risks to excel and to play in pain when necessary; and (d) the increasing external rewards associated with high-level performance at the same time that the need for a sense of internal satisfaction becomes paramount.

Marcia (1966) describes foreclosure as occurring when a commitment to an occupation is made prematurely and without sufficient exploration of one's needs or values. Foreclosure is often brought on by the demands of the environment. However, it may also be the result of the individual choosing to forgo engaging in exploratory behaviors and instead opting to commit to the activity in which he or she has previously been rewarded. In other words, adolescents rewarded for their athletic endeavors may choose not to commit to seeking success in academic activities or other career opportunities. By avoiding exploration a sense of security is gained at the expense of one's search for identity. It should be pointed out that identity foreclosure is not in itself harmful. In fact, many professions require early and relatively complete commitments. Foreclosure becomes problematic when individuals fail to develop adequate coping skills. It is through the process of exploration that individuals learn more about themselves. They acquire additional social competencies through their interactions with others. They receive feedback about their strengths and weaknesses by testing themselves in a variety of situations. Without such exploration it is likely that one's self-esteem can be too narrowly defined and subject to severe threat in the face of possible loss (Petitpas, 1978).

Two types of foreclosure have been identified: psychological and situational (Henry & Renaud, 1972). In psychological foreclosure individuals avoid change at all cost. They rigidly hold to original commitments and avoid all challenges to their views as a means of maintaining their security. Although in situational foreclosure individuals appear resistant to change, it is a result of a lack of exposure to new ideas, information, or life-styles rather than resistance to change. It is our belief that some adolescents become so involved in sport that identity foreclosure may result.

From this review several conclusions can be drawn: (a) It is not possible to determine empirically that participation in sport contributes to the development of competence because of a paucity of well-designed studies in this area; (b) although we cannot say that sport enhances competence, we can conclude that more interpersonal and intrapersonal youth are more likely to become involved in sport, especially during early adolescence; and (c) for sport to have a positive impact on the development of competence during adolescence and beyond, sport activities must be more developmental in nature. In the next section sport activities designed to enhance the development of the participants will be considered.

Designing Sport Activities to Enhance Development

Two aspects seem critical in determining developmentally appropriate sport activities: understanding why an adolescent is participating in a sport and ensuring that the activity is intrinsically rewarding. As noted earlier, Gould and Horn (1984) identified improving skills, having fun, being with friends, experiencing thrills and excitement, achieving success, and developing fitness as motives for youth sport participation. Which of these six actually motivates a particular child or adolescent is partially dependent on the individual's age. Therefore, at a minimum, knowing why a child begins an activity and what he or she gains from continuing to participate is necessary for designing appropriate activities.

For an activity to be intrinsically rewarding, it must be enjoyable and challenging. Csikszentmihalyi (1975) posits that the experience of self-rewarding involvement in play and work is a key to optimal development. He has proposed an empirically derived model of enjoyment titled the Flow Model. In the Flow Model *enjoyment* is defined as a balance between the challenges of an activity and the skills of the participant. When the individual perceives challenges to be greater than his or her skills, anxiety results. Boredom results when an individual appraises his or her skills as being greater than the perceived challenges. When the perceived challenges are equal to an individual's sense of skills, the experience is optimal and is labeled *flow*. Whether in work or play, feedback from activities wherein competence is extended to meet expanding challenges contributes significantly to self-concept and the sense of well-being. Moreover, because greater challenges are sought as abilities expand, the activity becomes growth producing (Danish, Kleiber, & Hall, 1987).

Csikszentmihalyi and his colleagues (Chalip, Csikszentmihalyi, Kleiber, & Larons, 1984; Csikszentmihalyi & Larson, 1984) used an approach called "experience sampling" to examine the subjective experiences associated with various activities of adolescents. The authors found that the combination of challenge, concentration, intrinsic motivation, and positive affect was best reflected in arts, hobbies, sports, and games. They called these activities "transitional" because they require discipline and concentration while still being enjoyable. For this reason they serve as a template for adult activities.

The advantage of tasks that are intrinsically rewarding is that attention to the task is given more readily and intensity is governed more naturally. The individual does not have to struggle to raise or lower arousal if his or her abilities are well matched with, and effectively employed in relation to, the demands of an activity. The challenge for a coach then is to arrange or control circumstances to provide and protect that match.

This is an ongoing process; as abilities improve, greater challenges are required to maintain the intensity. If greater challenges are not present, intensity drops and the individual becomes bored. Of course, the opposite can also occur; a mentor's zeal for providing greater challenges or the individual's own ambitiousness can result in a situation of excessive demand, which is anxiety producing and makes concentration and investment extremely difficult (Danish, Kleiber, & Hall, 1987).

For a coach to understand what motivates an athlete to participate in sport and/or to be able to match the athlete's level of ability with the appropriate task requires not only a knowledge of coaching techniques but the ability to understand and communicate effectively with the athlete. Although adult coaches usually know their sports quite well, the real issue is whether they understand and can relate to their athletes (Singer, 1972). Intervention with the coach, and secondarily with the parents, is likely to have an immediate and significant impact on the motivation and enjoyment level of the athlete.

One program developed to train coaches was designed by Smith and his colleagues (Smith, Smoll, & Curtis, 1978, 1979). First, the authors identified a number of coach and player measures. The coach measures included (a) a system of assessment of observed behaviors, (b) the recall of behaviors by the coaches, (c) the coaches' goals, and (d) their perception of the player's motives. Among the player measures were (a) the players' perception of the coaches, (b) their attitudes toward the coaches, (c) participation and teammates, and (d) both general and athletic self-esteem.

In designing the program the authors collected behavioral observations on 51 Little League coaches and 542 players. At different age levels players were found to be sensitive to punitive comments by coaches. Children who played for supportive, encouraging coaches had significantly higher self-esteem scores at the end of the season. Finally, the technical proficiency of the coaches was more important to older players than to younger ones.

As a result of their initial research, Smith and his colleagues developed a Coaching Effectiveness Training module for coaches. During the two-hour clinic coaches were taught techniques for interacting with players. They were also given feedback on how they behaved during the games in which they coached. Compared with control group coaches, trained coaches were rated as giving more reinforcement, more encouragement after a mistake, and more general technical instruction. Trained coaches were seen as engaging in less punishment, less punitive technical instruction, and less nonreinforcement. Finally, children who played for trained coaches liked their coaches more, felt they were better teachers of the game, and felt that their teams were more cooperative (Smith, Smoll, & Curtis, 1979).

Other researchers and practitioners have developed coaching programs. Perhaps the best known is the certification designed by Martens (1982). The American Coaching Effectiveness Program (ACEP) is a comprehensive educational program for coaches of youth aged 6 to 18. ACEP consists of two parts: (a) sport-specific information and (b) sport medicine and science information.

Each of the coaching training programs has a segment on player-coach communication. Smoll and Smith (1984) make the following recommendations: provide plenty of praise and encouragement and make sure it is sincere; develop realistic expectations; reward effort and correct technique as much as outcome; and provide effective feedback. From our perspective, what is missing from these recommendations as well as the other training programs is the teaching of listening skills that reflect an empathic understanding of the player and his or her concerns (Danish, D' Augelli, & Hauer, 1980). Without the development of these skills, the coach is less able to understand the unique needs and goals of each player.

Although the programs described increase the likelihood that sport activities will enhance development among adolescents, especially younger ones, a significant problem remains. As adolescents are exposed to other activities and experiences and recognize the need to become adept at new developmental tasks, the sport experience may hinder rather than promote development.

Designing Sport-Related Life Skills Training Programs

Each year 35% of youth sport participants drop out (Gould, 1987). Some may drop out because the experience is not a positive one. Others stop participating because it no longer meets their needs. For example, for some youth what was once a pleasurable activity may have become a source of stress as performance demands outweigh perceived capabilities. Yet others have identified alternative means that are more rewarding and intrinsically motivating to reach the developmental tasks on which they are working. For still other youth their participation in sports remains positive and they have identified that much of their self-esteem is based on their level of athletic performance. Consequently they may be unable to develop alternative sources of satisfaction because they fear that they will not be successful in other areas. For this last group their situation can be characterized as an example of "selective optimization" (Baltes & Baltes, 1980). Individuals have a limited amount of time and energy. Based on an assessment of environmental demands and motivation, skills, and biological capacities, individuals select a pathway upon which to focus. Giving up a rewarding activity is difficult when there are no assurances that rewards will be available in the new activity.

Both for those youth who choose to drop out as well as for those who remain, it is reasonable to question whether their experience with sports has facilitated or impeded their competence. In other words, does skill mastery or lack of it transfer and generalize from one area to another? For those youth who have not felt competent in sports, do they begin their new pursuits with a lack of confidence about their ability to be successful? For those youth whose goals have changed, will they transfer and generalize what they have learned to their new activities? Finally, will those youth who persist in sport foreclose the opportunity to expand their identities and thus limit their competence?

Although mastery of skills in later adolescence is enhanced by mastery of related skills early in adolescence, what is not clear is how mastery in one area affects mastery in other areas. For example, Havighurst (1953) identifies developmental tasks related to intellectual development, social and interpersonal skills, and emotional development. What effect will competence in sport have on these various areas?

It would appear that, for competence to be generalized across the various domains and tasks identified by Harter and Havighurst, several factors must be present. First, the adolescent must understand what set of skills is required to be competent in each of the areas. Second, the adolescent must believe that he or she possesses these skills. Third, the adolescent must know how the skills were learned and how they can be transferred to a different domain or task. When an individual possesses the skills but cannot identify them, he or she is not likely to be able to apply them in another setting and may be unsuccessful in developing a generalized sense of competence.

For competence to be attained, or to have the skills related to competence transfer across domains and tasks and be maintained throughout development, the essential skills must be identified and taught. These skills called "life skills" include (a) learning to set and develop plans to reach goals; (b) acquiring the necessary knowledge to attain the goal; (c) developing the sufficient skills (e.g., decision making, relaxation, imagery, positive self-talk, self-control) to attain the goal; (d) learning to assess the risks involved in goal attainment; and (e) identifying and obtaining the needed social support to reach the goal (Danish & D' Augelli, 1983). The Life Development Intervention Program developed by Danish and D'Augelli is designed to teach these skills. This program has been used in a number of contexts and has been described in considerable detail elsewhere (Danish & D'Augelli, 1980; Danish, D'Augelli, & Ginsberg, 1984; Danish & Hale, 1983; Danish, Smyer, & Nowak, 1980).

When taught to athletes, the general goal of the intervention is to assist them in gaining control over their lives by providing them with skills to direct their future. As a result a sense of empowerment and efficacy develops. The teaching of these skills also enables the athlete to perform better athletically.

Two examples of life skills programs used with adolescents will be described. The first, Athletes Coaching Teens, uses sport as a vehicle to motivate high-risk, inner-city early adolescents to reduce their health-compromising behaviors and increase their health-enhancing behaviors (Jessor, 1984; Perry & Jessor, 1985). The second, Success 101, is a one-credit course designed to ease the transition from high school to college for freshmen student-athletes.

(1) Athletes Coaching Teens (ACT) is a school-based program implemented with selected high school students serving as peer teachers for seventh-grade students in the Richmond City Public Schools. ACT was developed as part of a three-year substance abuse prevention demonstration project funded by the Office of Substance Abuse Prevention. ACT is a comprehensive program based on a life span developmental and critical life events model (Danish, D' Augelli, & Ginsberg, 1984; Danish, Smyer, & Nowak;

1980). The focus of ACT is on developing the student's potential and competence as a means to avoid health-compromising behaviors such as drug use, unsafe sexual activity, violent behavior, and dropping out of school. The ACT program teaches students "what to say yes to" as opposed to "just saying no."

The program is targeted at middle school students in the Richmond City Public Schools. These students are largely from minority and economically disadvantaged families who live in neighborhoods where the incidence of crime and drug use is high. In 1988 the ACT staff conducted a citywide study of seventh-grade students in the school system (N = 1,350). The majority of these students were black (87%), lived with the mother only (60%), and qualified for the free or reduced school lunch program (60%). Moreover, these seventh graders reported a high rate of health-compromising behaviors including drug use, sexual activity, and violence. Based on this survey, 30% of these students had smoked cigarettes, 38% had used beer, 15% had used marijuana, 4% had used cocaine/crack, 32% had shoplifted, 15% had threatened a teacher, and 59% had sexual intercourse (mostly without ever using contraception). More important, 11% of these students regularly (i.e., at least once a month) used cigarettes, 13% regularly used beer, 7% regularly used marijuana, 2% regularly used cocaine/crack, 6% regularly shoplifted, 6% regularly threatened a teacher, and 36% regularly had sexual intercourse (Farrell et al., in press).

The ACT project is conducted by the Department of Psychology at Virginia Commonwealth University (VCU) in collaboration with the Office of Planning and Development of the Richmond City Public Schools. In addition to the VCU staff, professional, college, and high school athletes are involved in various stages of program implementation. Professional and college athletes present school assemblies where they discuss excellence through goal setting and attainment as well as the problems associated with drug involvement and other problem behaviors such as teen pregnancy and dropping out of school. The college athletes also assist in training the selected high school students to be ACT leaders. These students are chosen by their schools for their academic performance, leadership qualities, and athletic involvement. They receive special training provided by the ACT staff with the assistance of VCU college athletes. Because these high school students are regarded as positive role models and have grown up in Richmond, they are in a unique position to be effective teachers for middle school youth. Once high school athletes have completed the ACT training program, they implement a seven-session program within middle school health classes.

The purpose of the seven sessions is to teach five skills: (a) to learn to dream and set goals; (b) to learn to develop plans to attain the goals; (c) to identify and overcome roadblocks to reaching the goals; (d) to learn to problem-solve; and (e) to learn to rebound from temporary setbacks. It is our belief that, when students know what they want and how to attain it, they are more likely to feel a sense of personal control and confidence about the future. As a result they will make better decisions and ultimately become better citizens (Danish, Mash, & Howard, in press).

(2) Success 101 is a 10-week course designed to enhance the transition of student-athletes from high school to college. It also serves as a means of preventing the likely involvement of student-athletes with drugs. Research on drug use among adolescents suggests that two factors contribute to drug use among adolescents: (a) needing to cope with the frustrations and stresses of life and (b) wanting to be involved in social activities with friends (Johnston & O'Malley, 1986).

When students arrive at college they experience new stresses and demands on their lives, whether or not they are athletes. Two of these stressors revolve around the increased work load and more difficult academic demands they encounter as well as the social pressures of making new friends and understanding new social norms. The first year, and especially the first semester or term, is a difficult one and more students drop out or decide not to return to school at this time than at any time afterward.

Student-athletes have additional demands. The demands involved in playing intercollegiate athletics are now almost year-round. Athletes must make an extensive time commitment. Athletes can spend as much as two to four hours per day or about 15 to 30 hours per week during the competitive season. Such a commitment is a drain on a student-athlete's time and energy. In addition to the time constraints, the pressures of travel and expectations of coaches, friends, family, fans, and the student him- or herself, as well as dealing with the media, increase the student-athlete's feelings of stress. These athletic-related demands, when added to the normal stresses a new student faces, place the student-athlete under considerable pressure and require the development of new coping strategies. Sometimes the coping is positive to the student-athlete's development; other times it is negative. The student-athlete may decide to focus on athletics rather than on academics. This may result in the student cutting corners in academic work, either taking easy courses and deciding to "major" only in staying academically eligible or doing poorly. The reverse may happen and the student-athlete may drop intercollegiate sports to concentrate on academics. This may leave the student-athlete feeling lost and purposeless if sports have been a major part of his or her life. This may also be financially difficult if the student-athlete is on scholarship.

It is more than likely that the student-athlete will try to cope with both demands. Effective coping requires goal setting, effective time management, good decision-making skills, and learning to relax. If successful in learning to cope, the student-athlete will achieve both academically and athletically. The result will be increased self-confidence. Ineffective coping, on the other hand, could lead to substance use, inappropriate control of emotions, lack of concentration, and other behaviors associated with a lack of academic and athletic success.

From Competence in Sports to Competence in Life

When children begin to participate in sport, their physical prowess determines their athletic performance. With age the physical abilities of the adolescent athlete become less important and his or her level of mental preparation becomes increasingly more important. Thus by the time he or she reaches later adolescence, it is the quality and level of mental preparation that determines success as an athlete. Better athletes concentrate more, talk more positively to themselves, set clearer goals, develop more well-defined plans to reach their goals, and deal more effectively with the stress of competition. We believe that, for athletes to attain excellence in sport, they must not only possess these skills but know that they do. In other words, it is not enough for the athlete to be a good goal setter, or to concentrate well or to be able to relax under pressure; he or she must be able to recognize that he or she possesses these skills.

As life circumstances and developmental tasks change for young athletes, and they begin to focus on new domains to meet their needs, their efforts must be redirected. The skills necessary for effective mental preparation are not athletic in nature. These skills are life skills and they are what determines the level of excellence reached, regardless of whether they are applied to sport, business, politics, the arts, or the sciences. So for the skills to be transferred to the new setting, the athlete must recognize not only the existence of these skills but their transferability to other settings. Assuming that athletes will automatically recognize the existence and transferability of these skills is naive. Interventions must be designed to facilitate this understanding. The ACT program and Success 101 are examples of such interventions. As developmental psychologists, community psychologists, and sport psychologists gather more information about the relationship of sport and personal competence, more and better programs will be developed.

In 1983 the senior author of this chapter noted:

> Sport has taken on new meaning for many individuals as they discover new meaning in the experience of participation. Sport need not be a place where one continues to have to prove oneself, it can be a place where one begins to know oneself. When knowing becomes as important as proving, sport becomes an essential vehicle for developing personal competence. Sport can provide participants with immediate and specific feedback about their performance. There is a clear beginning and end and an opportunity to evaluate one's progress toward a goal. This opportunity is infrequent in our life experiences for we rarely have the criteria for evaluation. In sum, sport provides an environment which is more *personal, concrete, time-limited,* and *intense* than the rest of society. (Danish, 1983, pp. 237-238)

It is our belief that, although this statement is accurate, it is incomplete. The understanding it describes will not be developed without specific efforts designed to teach the athlete how to know him- or herself. Sport participation should not be seen as an end point but as a point of departure for developing personal competence across settings.

References

Ambron, S. R., & Brodzinsky, D. (1979). *Lifespan human development.* New York: Holt, Rinehart, & Winston.

Baltes, P. B., & Baltes, M. M. (1980). Plasticity and variability in psychological aging: Methodological and theoretical issues. In G. Gurski (Ed.), *Determining the effects of aging on the central nervous system.* Berlin: Shering.

Browne, M. A., & Mahoney, M. J. (1984). Sport psychology. *Annual Review of Psychology, 35*, 605–625.

Burchard, J.D. (1977). *Competition and social competence.* Paper presented at the Canadian Psychomotor Learning and Sports Psychology Symposium, Banff, Canada.

Burchard, J. D. (1979). Competitive youth sports and social competence. In M. W. Kent & J. E. Rolf (Eds.), *The primary prevention of psychopathology: Vol 3. Promoting social competence and coping in children.* Hanover, NH: University Press of New England.

Chalip, L., Csikszentmihalyi, M., Kleiber, D., & Larson, R. (1984). Variations of experience in formal and informal sport. *Research Quarterly for Exercise and Sport, 55*,109–116.

Chartrand, J., & Lent, R. (1987). Sports counseling: Enhancing the development of the student-athlete. *Journal of Counseling and Development, 66*, 164–167.

Chickering, A. W. (1969). *Education and identity.* San Francisco: Jossey-Bass.

Coleman, J. S. (1961). *The adolescent society.* New York: Free Press.

Crandell, V., & Battle, E. (1970). The antecedents of adult correlates of academic and intellectual achievement efforts. In J. Hill (Ed.), *Minnesota Symposium on Child Psychology* (Vol. 4). Minneapolis: University of Minnesota Press.

Csikszentmihalyi, M. (1975). *Beyond boredom and anxiety.* San Francisco: Jossey-Bass.

Csikszentmihalyi, M., & Larson, R. (1984). *Being adolescent.* New York: Basic Books.

Danish, S. J. (1983). Musing about personal competence: The contributions of sport, health, and fitness. *American Journal of Community Psychology, 11*(3), 221–240.

Danish, S., & D' Augelli, A. R. (1980). Promoting competence and enhancing development through life development intervention. In L. A. Bond & J. C. Rosen (Eds.), *Competence and coping during adulthood* (pp. 105–129). Hanover, NH: University Press of New England.

Danish, S., & D' Augelli, A. R. (1983). *Helping skills II: Life development intervention.* New York: Human Sciences.

Danish, S., D' Augelli, A. R., & Ginsberg, M. (1984). Life development intervention: Promotion of mental health through the development of competence. In S. Brown & R. Lent (Eds.), *Handbook of counseling psychology* (pp. 520–544). New York: John Wiley.

Danish, S. J., D'Augelli, A. R., & Hauer, A. L. (1980). *Helping skills: A basic training program* (2nd ed.). New York: Human Sciences Press.

Danish, S. J., & Hale, B. D. (1983). Sport psychology: Teaching skills to athletes and coaches. *Journal of Physical Education, Recreation, and Dance, 11–13*, 80–81.

Danish, S., Kleiber, D., & Hall, H. (1987). Developmental intervention and motivation enhancement in the context of sport. In *Advances in motivation and achievement: Enhancing motivation* (Vol. 5, pp. 211–238). Greenwich, CT: JAI.

Danish, S., Mash, J. M., & Howard, C. W. (in press). "But will it play in Peoria?": The problem of technology transfer in alcohol and other drug use prevention programs. In J. Swisher & B. McColgan (Eds.), *Experiences in prevention with high risk youth.*

Danish, S., Smyer, M. A., & Nowak, C. A. (1980). Developmental intervention: Enhancing life-event processes. In P. B. Baltes & O. G. Brim, Jr. (Eds.), *Life-span development and behavior* (Vol. 3, pp. 339–366). New York: Academic Press.

Duke, M., Johnson, T. C., & Nowicki, S., Jr. (1977). Effects of sports fitness camp experience on locus of control orientation in children, ages 6 to 14. *Research Quarterly, 48*, 280–283.

Eitzen, D. S. (1975). Athletics in the status system of male adolescents: A replication of Coleman's The adolescent society, *Adolescence, 10*, 267–276.

Erickson, E. H. (1950). *Childhood and society.* New York, Norton.

Erickson, E. H. (1959). Identity and the life cycle. *Psychological Issues, 1*, 1–171.

Farrell, A. D., Howard, C. W., Danish, S. J., Smith, A. F., Mash, J. M., & Stovall, K. L. (in press). Athletes coaching teens for substance abuse prevention: Substance use and risk factors in urban middle school students. In J. Swisher & B. McColgan (Eds.), *Experiences in prevention with high risk youth.*

Gould, D. (1987). Promoting positive sport experiences for children. In J. R. May & M. J. Asken (Eds.), *Sport psychology: The psychological health of the athlete.* New York: PMA.

Gould, D., & Horn, T. S. (1984). Participation motivation in young athletes. In J. M. Silva & R. S. Weinberg (Eds.), *Psychological foundations of sports.* Champaign, IL: Human Kinetics.

Harter, S. (1978). Effectance motivation reconsidered, toward a developmental model. *Human Development,* 21, 34–64.

Harter, S. (1981). The development of competence motivation in the mastery of cognitive and physical skills: Is there still a place for joy? *Psychology of Motor Behavior and Sport—1980,* 3–29.

Harter, S. (1983). The development of the self-system. In M. Hetherington (Ed.), *Handbook of child psychology: Social and personality development* (Vol. 4). New York: John Wiley.

Havighurst, R. (1953). *Developmental tasks and education.* New York: John Wiley.

Henry, M., & Renaud, H. (1972). Examined and unexamined lives. *Research Reporter,* 7(1), 5.

Institute for Social Research. (1985). *Time, goods & well-being.* Ann Arbor: University of Michigan.

Iso-Aloha, S., & Hatfield, B. (1986). *Psychology of sports: A social psychological approach.* Dubuque, IA: William C. Brown.

Jessor, R. (1984). Adolescent development and behavioral health. In J. D. Matarazzo et al. (Eds.), *Behavioral health: A handbook of health enhancement and disease prevention.* New York: John Wiley.

Johnston, L., & O'Malley, P. (1986). Why do the nation's students use drugs and alcohol: Self-reported reasons from nine national surveys. *Journal of Drug Issues, 16*, 29–66.

Kay, R. S., Felker, D. W., & Varoz, R. O. (1972). Sports interests and abilities as contributors to self-concept in junior high school boys. *Research Quarterly, 43*, 208–215.

Kleiber, D. A., & Kane, M. (1984). Sex differences and the use of leisure as adaptive potentiation. *Society and Leisure, 7*, 165–173.

Koocher, G. P. (1971). Swimming, competence, and personality change. *Journal of Personality and Social Psychology, 18*, 275–278.

Landers, D. M., & Landers, S. (1978). Socialization via interscholastic athletics: Its effects on educational attainment. *Research Quarterly, 47*, 75–83.

Lazarus, R. S., & Folkman, S. (1984). *Stress, appraisal and coping.* New York: Springer.

Magill, R. A., Ash, M. J., & Smoll, F. L. (Eds.). (1978). *Children in sports: A contemporary anthology.* Champaign, IL: Human Kinetics.

Marcia, J. E. (1966). Development and validation of ego-identity status. *Journal of Personality and Social Psychology, 3*, 551–558.

Martens, R. (Ed.). (1978). *Joy and sadness in children's sports.* Champaign, IL: Human Kinetics.

Martens, R. (1982). *The American coaching effectiveness program.* Champaign, IL: Human Kinetics.

Martens, R. (1983). Coaching to enhance self-worth. In T. Orlick, J. Partington, & J. Salmela (Eds.), *Mental training for coaches and athletes.* Ottawa: Coaching Association of Canada.

Michener, J. A. (1976). *Sports in America.* New York: Random House.

Morgan, W. P. (1980). The trait psychology controversy. *Research Quarterly Exercise Sports, 51*, 50–76.

Nelson, J. (1982, Winter). Sport in America: New directions and new potentials. In S. W. White (Ed.), *Sports in America* [Special issue] *National Forum,* pp. 5–6.

Newman, B., & Newman, P. (1979). *Development through life.* Homewood, IL: Dorsey.

Ogilivie, R., & Tutko, T. (1971). Sport: If you want to build character, try something else. *Psychology Today*, *5*, 61–63.

Orlick, T. D. (1972). *A socio-psychological analysis of early sports participation.* Unpublished doctoral dissertation, University of Alberta.

Orlick, T. D., & Botterill, C. (1975). *Every kid can win.* Chicago: Nelson-Hall.

Perry, C. L., & Jessor, R. (1985). The concept of health promotion and the prevention of adolescent drug abuse. *Health Education Quarterly, 12*, 169–184.

Petitpas, A. (1978). Identity foreclosure: A unique challenge. *Personnel and Guidance Journal, 56*, 558–561.

Petitpas, A. L., & Champagne, D. E. (1988). Developmental programming for intercollegiate athletes. *Journal of College Student Development, 29*(5), 454–460.

Piaget, J. (1954). *The construction of reality in the child.* New York: Basic Books.

Reppucci, N. D. (1987). Prevention and ecology: Teenage pregnancy, child sexual abuse and organized youth sports. *American Journal of Community Psychology, 15*, 1–22.

Seidel, R. W., & Reppucci, N. D. (1989). *The psychological development of nine year old males participating in youth sports.* Unpublished manuscript, University of Virginia.

Sherif, M., Harvey, O. J., White, B., Hood, W., & Sherif, C. (1961). *Inter-group conflict and cooperation: The Robbers Cave experiment.* Norman: University of Oklahoma Press.

Sherif, M., & Sherif, C. W. (1953). *Groups in harmony and tension.* New York: Harper & Row.

Sherif, M., White, B. J., & Harvey, O. J. (1955). Status in experimentally produced groups. *American Journal of Sociology, 60*, 370–379.

Singer, R. N. (1972). *Coaching, athletics, and psychology.* New York: McGraw-Hill.

Smith, R. E., Smoll, F. L., & Curtis, B. (1978). Coaching behaviors in Little League baseball. In F. L. Smoll & R. E. Smith (Eds.), *Psychological perspectives in youth sports.* New York: Hemisphere.

Smith, R. E., Smoll, F. L., & Curtis, B. (1979). Coach effectiveness training: A cognitive-behavioral approach to enhancing relationship skills in youth sport coaches. *Journal of Sport Psychology, 1*, 59–75.

Smoll, F. L., & Smith, R. E. (1984). Leadership research in youth sports. In J. M. Silva & R. S. Weinberg (Eds.), *Psychological foundations of sport.* Champaign, IL: Human Kinetics.

Sonestroem, R. J. (1982). Exercise and self esteem: Recommendations for expository research. *Quest, 33*, 124–139.

Stein, P.J., & Hoffman, S. (1978). Sports and male role strain. *Journal of Social Issues, 34*(1), 136–150.

White, R. (1959). Motivation reconsidered: The concept of competence. *Psychological Review, 66*, 297–323.

White, R. (1963). Ego and reality in psychoanalytic theory: A proposal regarding independent ego energies. *Psychological Issues, 3*(3), Monograph 11. New York: International University.

White, R.W. (1974). Strategies of adaptation: An attempt at systematic description. In G.V. Coehlo, D.A. Hamburg, & J.E. Adams (Eds.), *Coping and adaptation.* New York: Basic Books.

42 Can Sports Build Character?

DAVID LIGHT SHIELDS AND BRENDA LIGHT BREDEMEIER
University of Missouri at St. Louis

Participation in sport and physical activity is said to contribute substantially to the development of moral values and to the building of character. For example, participants may benefit from sport by learning to compete, overcome obstacles, cope with stress, persist in the face of defeat, develop self-control, cooperate with teammates, and act according to virtues such as fair play, honesty, respect, integrity, and compassion, thereby enjoying the character-developing advantages of sport. However, many well-known negative occurrences in elite sport (such as bribery, violence, racism, and cheating) raise the question of whether sport participation does indeed build character, and if so, what role, if any, can sport psychologists play in athletes' character development. As a result, the field of sport psychology has become increasingly interested in the relationship between sport participation and sociomoral functioning, development, and education, with many applied interventions available (e.g., physical education programs) aimed at promoting the sociomoral development of sport participants.

For over two decades, Brenda Bredemeier and David Shields have contributed to the advancement of this domain. For example, in a series of studies (conducted together with other colleagues) mainly in the 1980s, they extensively examined the hypothesis that moral reasoning levels are related to legitimacy of and behavioral tendencies toward unfair or aggressive play. In the mid-1990s, they proposed a model of moral action in sport, which has provided a custom framework for investigating personal and social factors that affect moral sensitivity, judgment, choice, and behavior. In the present chapter, Shields and Bredemeier, building on their extensive experience in this field, discuss the very question of whether sport can indeed build character, by reviewing several important theoretical and empirical foundations relevant for the successful promotion of effective sociomoral practices in sport psychology. They survey the empirical literature on sports and morality (i.e., moral reasoning development, situational moral reasoning, and game reasoning) and suggest that an integrative conceptual framework is required in order to bring together different constructs related to moral functioning and development.

Shields and Bredemeier present two novel ideas in this chapter. In the first one, an Aristotelian perspective is suggested within an achievement ethic approach to game reasoning to promote appropriate moral reasoning in sport settings. In the second, they describe the "communities of character" approach as a useful way of promoting appropriate dimensions of character among sport teams. It is expected that, as with the previous work of these authors, these intriguing ideas will also become milestones in future research on sport and the development of character.

For the purposes of this chapter, we will limit our empirical review of the sports literature to the relationship between sports involvement and two aspects of individual moral character: the *development* of moral reasoning and the *form* of moral reasoning used in sports. Thus, in our review of the empirical research, we reword the question of whether sports build character to two related questions. Is sports participation related to moral reasoning development? Do people use similar patterns of moral reasoning in sports as they do in other domains? The rationale for limiting the empirical review to these two questions is as much practical as theoretical. These are questions that have received significant empirical attention.

In the conceptual section of the chapter, we discuss two related issues that will help to broaden our focus. The first concerns an achievement ethic. We suggest that an Aristotelian perspective on virtue can be useful in suggesting how current theories of achievement motivation can shed light on dynamics of moral reasoning in sport contexts. Finally, we close the chapter with a discussion of how sports can be made more conducive to character development. Here, we introduce the idea of promoting sport teams as *communities of character*.

Sports and Morality: An Empirical Review

By way of preview, we suggest that the relationship between sports participation and moral reasoning development is an ambiguous one, but that when differences between athletes and nonathletes are found, the results do not favor a positive role for sports in character education. With regard to the second question, we suggest that sports tend to elicit a pattern of moral reasoning that is different from the one used in most other contexts.

Sports and Moral Reasoning Development

Sports are socially rich environment that provide participants with many opportunities to interact with others in ways that have moral significance. There are ample opportunities to nurture and practice capacities for role taking, empathy, conflict resolution, and various subskills

Adapted, by permission, from D.L. Shields and B.L. Bredemeier, 2005, Can sports build character? In *Character psychology and education* (Notre Dame, IN: University of Notre Dame Press), 121-139.

related to moral judgment. It is plausible, then, that active involvement in sports might provide the kind of cognitive and social stimuli needed to promote moral reasoning development. On the other hand, some would point to the heteronemous way that most sport teams are run, and the all too frequent instances of flagrant cheating and aggression, to suggest that rather than promote moral development, sports might actually impede moral growth.

Most of the research that has been done on sports and moral development has utilized one or another theory in the structural developmental tradition associated with the pioneering work of Piaget and Kohlberg (see, especially, Haan,1978, 1983, 1991; Haan, Aerts & Cooper, 1985; Kohlberg, 1981; 1984; Piaget, 1932; Rest, 1979). There are important theoretical differences among these approaches, but they share in common the view that children undergo regular age-related changes in the underlying structure of their moral reasoning, and that with age and appropriate experience comes increasing moral reasoning competence. Progression toward moral reasoning maturity is typically described in terms of a hierarchical sequence of stages, levels, or phases.

For those who look to sports to provide a positive stimulus to moral growth, the research has not been encouraging. Utilizing Kohlberg's interview technique with 65 male Division I intercollegiate basketball players, Hall (1986) found that her sample scored lower on moral judgment than reported college norms. Similarly, Bredemeier and Shields (1984b), using Rest's *Defining Issues Test*, found that their sample of 24 male and 22 female intercollegiate basketball players scored lower than reported norms of college students. Both of these findings were reported in studies that had other primary research goals, and the negative relationship between sports participation and moral judgment maturity were based on comparing the experimental samples to results reported by others. In the first study to compare athletes and nonathletes directly on moral reasoning maturity, Bredemeier and Shields (1986c) utilized Haan's interactional model of morality (Haan, Aerts & Cooper, 1985; Haan, 1977, 1983, 1991) to assess the moral reasoning of 30 male and female intercollegiate basketball players and 10 nonathletes. They found that the athletes had significantly less mature moral reasoning than their peers. However, a follow-up study that added 20 swimmers to the sample concluded that there were no statistically significant differences in moral reasoning development between the swimmers and the nonathletes (Bredemeier & Shields, 1986c). In sum, the basketball players, but not the swimmers, scored lower on moral reasoning than nonathlete peers. Since athletes from only two sports were assessed, it was unclear whether the observed differences were due to factors internal to some types of sports (e.g., team sports vs. individual sports, contact sports vs. noncontact sports) or factors extrinsic to the actual sport experience (for example, the study did not control for GPA).

Similar results were obtained by Stevenson (1998) who employed a measure of cognitive moral reasoning developed specifically for his study of 213 Division I student-athletes and 202 general student peers. Tapping a broader cross-section of sports, he found that the team sport athletes, both male and female, had significantly lower moral judgment scores than did either the nonathletes or the individual sport athletes. Similarly, Priest, Krause, and Beach (1999), in a longitudinal study of 631 U.S. Military Academy cadets, reported a negative impact of sports participation, especially in intercollegiate team sports, on moral judgment. Their study used the Hahm-Beller Values Choice Inventory in the Sports Milieu (HBVCISM) (Hahm, Beller & Stoll, 1989), an instrument that reportedly correlates at .82 with Rest's *Defining Issues Test*.

Overall, the results from these studies suggest that there is a negative correlation between participation in some sports at the intercollegiate level, especially team sports, and moral reasoning maturity. However, none of these studies controlled for the fact that recruited athletes, on average, enter college with lower academic test scores (Shulman & Bowen, 2001). The longitudinal methodology employed by Priest, Krause, and Beach (1999) provides the best evidence of a potential negative effect of sports involvement, but the measure employed in that study has not undergone adequate peer review (see Bredemeier & Shields, 1998).

Results are mixed at the high school level. Beller and Stoll (1995) used the HBVCISM in a study of 1,330 male and female high school students, finding that the nonathletes scored significantly higher than the team athletes. However, in the Bredemeier and Shields (1986c) study, mentioned above, no difference was found between high school athletes and nonathletes. Rulmyr (1996) administered the *Defining Issues Test* to 540 students in southern Arizona high schools and also found no differences between the athletes and nonathletes. Until the validity and reliability of the HBVCISM is further assessed, the Beller and Stoll (1995) results should probably be treated with caution.

Finally, in a study of children in the 4th through 7th grade, it was found that boys who participated in high contact sports and girls who participated in medium contact sports were significantly less mature in their distributive justice reasoning than children who had participated in other sports or had not participated in any organized sport program (Bredemeier et al., 1986). Level of physical contact may be an important variable because of the type of attributions elicited. Young athletes in relatively high contact sports may believe that opponents are intentionally seeking to inflict pain or harm, even when they are not. Children may have a difficult time distinguishing between aggression and non-aggressive but physically forceful play. This, in turn, may impede the development of conceptions of fairness and just distribution of goods and rewards. The reason girls in medium contact sports paralleled boys in high contact sports may simply reflect the fact that girls do not have access to high contact sports, and, therefore, may make similar attributions in the highest contact sports allowed them.

Taken together, the results from these studies suggest that it is important not to lump all sport participants together. Though inconsistencies may relate to different methodologies and tools of assessment (cf. Bredemeier & Shields, 1998), it is also true that not all sport experiences share similar moral qualities. Not only do the rule structures of the various sports promote different types of social interaction, each sport tends to have its own subculture and implicit moral norms, and each individual sport team develops its own unique moral microculture. Methodologically, it is also important to emphasize that all of the studies reported here, with the exception of the Priest, Krause, and Beach (1999) investigation, were cross-sectional in design and, therefore, no cause-effect relationships can be inferred. In those cases where athletes were found to be less mature in their moral reasoning, it may be that they were differentially attracted to those sports or, alternately, were selected to participate because of some attribute that itself correlates with less mature moral reasoning (e.g., aggressiveness).

The potential impact of sports on moral reasoning development and/or its differential appeal to individuals with preexisting differences, is far from inconsequential. Within sports, moral reasoning development level has been shown to relate to such important moral variables as aggression (Bredemeier, 1985, 1994; Bredemeier et al., 1986, 1987; Bredemeier & Shields, 1984a, 1986a; Stephens, 2000; Stephens & Bredemeier, 1996), sportspersonship (Horrocks, 1979), and beliefs about fair play (Stephens, Bredemeier & Shields, 1997).

Sports and Situational Moral Reasoning

The research reported above focused on the relationship between sports involvement and participants' stage or level of moral reasoning. Another line of research relevant to the sports involvement/moral reasoning relationship focuses on how people think about, process, or organize moral situations in sports. Do they do so in the same way, through the same reasoning structures, as they do in other contexts?

Structural developmental theorists have traditionally held that a person's moral reasoning level will remain fairly constant across different types of contents and situations (e.g., Colby & Kohlberg, 1987; cf. Krebs et al., 1991). Stages are thought to reflect structured wholes or integrated cognitive systems. While the content of a person's moral thinking may shift from one situation to another, the underlying pattern of reasoning has been said to be relatively constant. This premise of structural consistency across situations, in fact, is central to a stage model of moral development (Kohlberg, 1981).

While consistency in moral stage usage across situations is expected, a few highly irregular situations have been shown to significantly alter the person's level of moral reasoning. Research conducted in prisons (Kohlberg, Hickey, & Scharf, 1972), for example, has demonstrated that inmates use lower stages of moral reasoning in response to prison dilemmas than when they attempt to resolve standard hypothetical dilemmas. To explain this divergence from theoretical expectations, Kohlberg hypothesized that when a group's collective norms reflect a low stage of moral reasoning, then the constraining "moral atmosphere" may inhibit more advanced moral functioning, even among those individuals capable of higher stage thought (see Power, Higgins, & Kohlberg, 1989). Elsewhere, we (Bredemeier & Shields, 1985, 1986b; Shields & Bredemeier, 1984, 1995) have hypothesized that sports are among those contexts where moral reasoning is dissimilar to the pattern of reasoning typically employed. This hypothesis was generated in light of two complementary sets of observations, one theoretical, the other empirical.

The theoretical observation draws from a social science tradition that posits that play, games, and sports are often seen by participants and observers alike as "set aside" or "set apart" from everyday life (e.g., Bateson, 1955; Corsaro, 1981; Firth, 1973; Giffin, 1982; Handelman, 1977; Huizinga, 1955; Schmitz, 1976; Sutton-Smith, 1971). Sports are set apart from everyday life spatially, through clearly marked boundaries, and temporally, by designated playing periods replete with "time outs." A variety of symbols – such as whistles, buzzers, flags, uniforms, and special rituals and ceremonies – are used to create and reinforce the "world within a world" character of sports. The separate world of sports is governed by artificial rules and roles, and sport activities are directed toward goals with no intrinsic meaning or value. Handelman (1977) suggests that entry into this separated realm requires "a radical transformation in cognition and perception" (p. 186). Similarly, Schmitz (1976) has suggested that entry into play involves participants in a world with new forms of space, time, and behavior, "delivering its own values in and for itself" (p. 26). Given this literature, it seemed reasonable to hypothesize that moral reasoning within sports would depart from moral reasoning in everyday life.

The empirical observation comes from several of our studies mentioned earlier. In multiple studies, we used moral interviews that included both standard *life* dilemmas and a second set of *sport* dilemmas. When we analyzed moral reasoning maturity scores, we found that the *life* scores were significantly higher than the *sport* scores (Bredemeier and Shields, 1984a). This finding was quite robust, holding for athletes and nonathletes, swimmers and basketball players, college students and high school students, males and females.

Similar analyses were conducted with 110 girls and boys in grades 4 through 7 (Bredemeier, 1995). It was found that 6th and 7th graders' "sport" reasoning was significantly lower than their "life" reasoning, and that this life-sport reasoning divergence was significantly greater than that for the younger children. The children below grade 6 did not demonstrate context-specific reasoning patterns.

Selman (1980) suggests that it is roughly during the 6th and 7th grades that children develop the capacity to take the generalized perspective of a third party which may be a prerequisite skill to adopting a context-specific reasoning pattern. It was also the case that the younger children were predominantly preconventional in their everyday life moral reasoning, leaving little room for a drop in moral reasoning level in response to sport dilemmas.

Game Reasoning

Based on these findings, we proposed a theory of *game reasoning* (Bredemeier & Shields, 1985, 1986a,b; Shields & Bredemeier, 1984, 1995). The theory holds that the context of sport elicits a temporary adaptation in moral reasoning such that egocentrism, typically the hallmark of immature morality, becomes a valued and acceptable principle for organizing the moral exchange. In terms of moral reasoning, we hypothesized that sports offer contexts for a "legitimated regression" (Bredemeier & Shields, 1986b; Shields & Bredemeier, 1984) to a form of moral reasoning that is similar to less mature moral reasoning. It is important to emphasize, however, that the term *regression* is not meant literally. Individuals in sports do not lose touch with their everyday moral capacities, and the egocentric reasoning that flourishes in sports is not identical to the preconventional reasoning of young children. It is playful egocentrism more than genuine egocentrism. This point needs further elaboration.

Sports, in our view, allow for the temporary suspension of the typical moral obligation to equally consider the immediate interests of all parties, in favor of a more lenient, egocentric style of moral engagement. Most of the time, this egocentric reasoning reflects an implicit consensual agreement among the participants, and there is, thus, an informal social contract allowing for it. Game reasoning can serve as an enjoyable and non-serious moral deviation that is consensually embraced.

There may be several reasons why such a moral adaptation is culturally sanctioned and viewed as appropriate within the limits of sports. First, competition is premised on each party or team seeking self gain. There is little room in sports for equally considering the desires, goals, and needs of opponents. While competition demands a degree of egocentrism, the unique protective structures of sports function to legitimate it. The carefully planned and rigorously enforced rules protect participants from many of the negative consequences that would typically ensue from egocentric morality. Furthermore, the continual presence of officials and coaches allows for the temporary and partial transference of moral responsibility.

The theory of game reasoning adds one more level of complexity. The theory holds that sports may encourage two types of moral "regression". Thus far, we have been addressing a *legitimated regression* in which an egocentric morality is embraced. But, of course, sports are not devoid of moral concerns. Players remain people and moral responsibility cannot be completely set aside. To remain legitimate, one can only *play* at egocentrism. When the play character of game reasoning is lost, sports can (and too often do) deteriorate into breeding grounds of aggression, cheating, and other moral defaults. Thus, game reasoning can take the form of an *illegitimate regression*.

The criterion of internal consistency can be used to distinguish legitimate from illegitimate forms of game reasoning (Bredemeier & Shields, 1986b). Two examples can serve to illustrate. First, since game reasoning is itself legitimated by the set aside character of sports, game reasoning ceases to be legitimate if used to justify actions with game-transcending implications. For example, the use of egocentric morality to justify injuring another person is no more legitimate in sports than elsewhere. Second, game reasoning ceases to be legitimate if it is used to justify actions that undercut the contest structure of sports. Thus, game cheating represents an illegitimate regression. Again, to use the egocentric quality of game reasoning to justify cheating behavior is self-contradictory since cheating undermines the conditions that allow for game reasoning in the first place.

The elaboration and validation of the theory of game reasoning awaits future research and at this point we can only speculate about potential implications for the theory. If sports do elicit their own special form of moral reasoning, it may help to shed light on some of the earlier findings. Consider, for example, the finding that for some college athletes participation in sports is associated with lower levels of moral reasoning maturity. Perhaps for some college athletes, game reasoning may begin to lose its "set aside" character and have undue influence on moral reasoning beyond the bounds of sports. Several factors may account for why this is more true for participants in some sports than in others. Participation in elite sports, particularly those for which professional opportunities are available, often include external rewards contingent on performance. The infusion of "daily life" rewards (e.g., money or educational opportunity) into sport experiences may encourage a blurring of the distinction between sports and everyday life. Additionally, some sports allow for a high level of physical contact which is inherently ambiguous with regard to moral significance. Was the "cheap shot" intentional or accidental? Was the opponent trying to intimidate me or just play hard? High levels of investment in these sports may habituate a moral attribution pattern that is difficult to leave behind once the game is over.

Sports and Character: A Conceptual Framework

We noted earlier that character is a multidimensional construct. In our view, morality is central to what is meant by character. But the development of moral judgment is only one dimension of character. In addition, character involves harnessing such nonmoral skills as emotional regulation and persistence for moral aims. In addition, character involves conceptions of the good, as well as the right. To further flesh out the concept of character, we have found Rest's Four Component Model of moral action to be a useful starting place (Bredemeier & Shields, 1994; Shields, Bredemeier, Power, 2002).

Rest (1983, 1984) hypothesized that every moral action necessarily entails the activation of four conceptually distinct but interrelated sets of processes: moral interpretation (which draws upon moral sensitivity), moral judgment (which draws upon moral reasoning), moral choice (which reflects moral motivation), and moral implementation (which reflects self-regulation skills). In later works, Rest gave the word *character* to the fourth component of the model (Rest, Narvaez, Bebeau & Thoma, 1999).

The model is quite useful for identifying psychological processes tethered to the production of moral behavior. What the model lacks, however, is an integrative, core. It lacks any conception of personal agency that can animate the processes and gives them coherence and coordination. We have proposed (Shields, Bredemeier & Power, 2002) that the concept of character is centered in what Blasi (1983, 1984, 1985, 1988) refers to as the *moral self* and that it serves as the integrative, agentic center out of which the moral processes come.

What sports help make clear is that the concept of character, while tethered to the moral, is not limited to the moral narrowly conceived. Character also connotes virtues that stem from pursuit of the good, as well as the right. This ties character to the area of achievement and pursuit of worthy goals. Typically in sports, the athlete with character is thought of as the athlete who does not give up, who persists regardless of difficulties or odds, who endures and perseveres. A sport team that has character exemplifies teamwork and courage, loyalty and dedication. To account for these dimensions of character, we have developed the concept of an *achievement ethic*. In the next section, we elaborate on this concept and relate it to our previous discussion of game reasoning.

An Achievement Ethic Approach to Game Reasoning

We noted above that sports tend to encourage a more egocentric style of moral reasoning. This *game reasoning* can take two forms: a playful, legitimated regression or an illegitimate regression. The consequences are dramatically different for the two. Playful game reasoning may enhance the enjoyment of sports by providing an experience of freedom and release. On the other hand, under the cloak of play, egocentric moral reasoning can, metaphorically speaking, break loose from its moral moorings and justify an "anything goes" morality. This would seem to be implied, for example, in a comment by former heavyweight boxing champion Larry Holmes. In a 60 Minutes interview, he was asked how he mentally prepared for a fight. In response, he said, "I have to let all the good out and bring all the bad in, like Dr. Jeykll and Mr. Hide" (quoted in Bredemeier & Shields, 1985). Comments such as Holmes' are frequent in the world of sports.

As yet we do not understand well what causes a person to employ an illegitimate as opposed to legitimate form of game reasoning. One avenue that we are pursuing relates to what we are calling an *achievement ethic* (Bredemeier, Power & Shields, 2002).

Sports are achievement contexts. They are goal-directed activities involving competition and a quest for excellence or mastery. They are contexts in which success matters. Psychologists have generally avoided treating achievement issues in ethical terms. In this, they differ markedly from Aristotle (1985) who, in his classical treatment of ethics, located the striving for excellence at the heart of virtue and drew on sports as well as the crafts to illustrate his theory. Aristotle posited that humans achieve happiness when they exercise their capacities, physical and intellectual, to the fullest. Sports provide a rich opportunity for individuals to excel and to experience the happiness intrinsic to excelling. From an Aristotelian view, the ethical value of sports is not that sports participation leads to the rewards associated with success, but that sports participation brings with it, potentially at least, the happiness intrinsic to human striving. Correspondingly, the great danger in sports is that the emphasis on winning can undermine what makes sports virtuous in the first place – the desire to develop one's capacities in pursuit of worthy ends.

Aristotle's ideas can be connected to contemporary achievement motivation theory. Over the past decades, Nicholls (1984, 1989) and Duda (1987, 1989, 1993, 1996) have proposed that individuals can approach achievement contexts in two distinct ways; they can adopt a *task* and/or an *ego* orientation. While all people are motivated to develop and display competence, people differ with regard to how success is understood. The person who has a *task* orientation feels successful when he or she meets or exceeds self-referenced goals. In contrast, the *ego*-oriented person evaluates success through social comparison; thus, an ego-oriented person feels competent only to the extent that his or her performance is better than that of peers. Research conducted in the U.S. has provided support for the existence of task and ego orientations in the educational domain (Nicholls et al., 1989; Nicholls et al., 1990; Thorkildsen, 1988), as well as in sport contexts (see Duda & Whitehead, 1998, for a review).

Nicholls explicitly linked the task and ego motivational orientations to moral motivations. He suggested that a high *task* orientation would lead to greater weight being given to moral concerns. The focus on performance outcome, in Nicholls view, will lead to less concern for the moral dimensions of achievement experiences (Nicholls, 1989). Evidence within sport domains supports this contention of a link between motivational orientation and moral priorities (Duda, Olson & Templin, 1991; Dunn & Dunn, 1999; Guivernau & Duda, 1998; Kavussanu & Ntoumanis, 2001;

Kavussanu & Roberts, in press; Stephens & Bredemeier, 1996). However, the two orientations are not mutually exclusive, and high task orientation does not necessarily imply low *ego* orientation.

Blasi (2005) has suggested that experiences of intrinsic value (whether of music, of art, of relationship, etc.) are likely precursors to the development of moral desire. An achievement ethic suggests that intrinsic value inheres within striving for excellences. Learning to take pleasure in striving toward excellence in worthy pursuits is itself part of character development. Placed in the context of contemporary achievement motivation theory, we suggest that a task motivational orientation, because it is focused on the intrinsic value of striving within achievement contexts, is to be preferred to an ego orientation.

Though the empirical evidence is not yet available, we hypothesize that a task motivational orientation is closely associated with the legitimated regression of game reasoning and that an ego motivational orientation is linked to illegitimate regression. As noted earlier, a legitimated regression can enhance the intrinsic quality of the sport involvement through allowing for an experience of freedom and release. When connected with the multidimensional quest for excellence (excellence of performance, excellence of character), this experience of freedom and release is placed in the service of an experience of *the good*. The appreciation of the intrinsic good within sports keeps the moral "regression" from straying into illegitimate forms. In contrast, the focus on defeating others that is the hallmark of an ego motivational orientation does not contain a limiting element that would keep the moral regression within legitimate bounds. The only limiting element is an external one – what one can get away with – and does not carry moral force.

Sport Teams as Communities of Character

In our view, character encompasses what is usually meant by morality as well as an achievement ethic. Character is an *ethical self* that reflects moral and achievement virtues, integrating them into a coherent sense of self. When we say a person *has character* we mean that they have a coherent sense of themselves, together with those personal competencies that enable them to act consistently with regard to moral and achievement virtues. Moral reasoning is related to character and, in fact, provide the touchstone for the moral dimension. But character involves virtues and reasons beyond the moral. Character entails a view of the good, as well as a commitment to the right.

For coaches and sport educators, the question becomes how to create a sport environment that facilitates the development of character. Clearly, this is a highly complex question, but we think a good starting point is to ask two related questions. How can sport experiences be made conducive to the development of moral judgment? How can they be made conductive to the adoption of a task motivational orientation?

Though the literature reviewed above suggests that sports may not be good contexts for promoting moral reasoning, several studies have also demonstrated that sport experiences can be designed effectively to promote moral growth (Bredemeier, Weiss, Shields & Shewchuk, 1986; Romance, Weiss & Bockoven, 1986; Wandzilak, Carroll & Ansorge, 1988). Thus, when moral development is adopted as an explicit goal and appropriate strategies implemented, sport experience can stimulate the development of moral reasoning.

In our own work, we seek to incorporate insights from the *just community* approach to moral and character education in the schools (e.g., Power, Higgins & Kohlberg, 1989), together with insights stemming from our research on game reasoning and a motivational ethic. We have labeled our approach a *communities of character* approach to character education through sports.

The *communities of character* approach recognizes that people develop their character in the context of social relations and that the shared norms and values of the group are important influences on what the individual comes to value and how they act. Those sport teams, for example, in which collective norms are lenient when it comes to the use of aggression are more likely to have players who accept aggression as legitimate (Guivernau & Duda, 1998; Shields, Bredemeier, Gardner & Bostrom, 1995; Stephens & Bredemeier, 1996).

The *communities of character* approach to sports has two critical dimensions. First, it attempts to build a sense of community within the team that features shared norms for ethical behavior. From a pragmatic standpoint, the heart of the approach is democratic leadership exercised through the team meeting. In team meetings, rules and goals are established, strategies are taught, and performances are assessed, all with the aim of accentuating the moral dimension of the sport experience. The *communities of character* approach requires that players participate to the fullest extent possible in such meetings by discussing and deciding upon disciplinary rules and punishments and offering suggestions and feedback about strategies and performances. Participation in such team meetings should help players to develop shared norms that express and realize ideals of cooperation, fair play, and respect for officials and opponents. In team meetings, players learn the democratic skills of self-expression, listening, and deliberating about the common good.

A second critical element of the *communities of character* approach is the promotion of a mastery-oriented achievement climate. A *mastery climate* encourages or augments task motivation, in contrast to a *performance climate,* which encourages or augments ego motivation. Mastery climates are associated with participants' use of effective learning strategies, preference for challenging tasks, positive attitudes, and the beliefs that effort leads to success (Ames, 1992; Ames & Archer, 1988; Burton, 1989; Hall; 1988; Newton, 1994; Newton & Duda, 1998;

Seifriz, Duda, & Chi, 1992; Treasure, 1993; Treasure & Roberts, 1994, 1998; Walling, Duda & Chi, 1993). Mastery climates nurture an achievement ethic that places value on the intrinsic quality of the experience.

Pedagogically, coaches can learn to develop mastery climates through paying careful attention to the structuring of the environment, and through adopting a communication style that focuses on relationship and process (Ames, 1992; Duda, 1987; Epstein, 1988, 1989; Nicholls, 1989; Nicholls & Miller, 1984). The means by which a mastery climate is created have been summarized by Epstein in his TARGET acronym (Epstein, 1988, 1989). Mastery climates can be created through attention to Task, Authority, Recognition, Grouping, Evaluation, and Timing. Though initially developed for educational settings, the framework is readily adaptable to sports. In brief, to create a mastery climate, tasks need to entail variety and diversity; authority should be shared; recognition ought to focus on effort; groupings for drills should be varied and heterogeneous; evaluation should be based on improvement, participation, and effort; and the allotment of time for skill development needs to be flexible and adaptive.

Fortunately, promoting a mastery climate is very congruent with forming a sense of moral community. By emphasizing mastery goals, each participant is empowered to be an active participant in the community and the deleterious effects of an over-emphasis on social comparison is mitigated. As a sport community develops its own unique character, rooted in morality and conceptions of the good, it can make a positive contribution to the character development of each of its participants. Future research will determine whether this and/or other models of character education through sports can be efficacious in benefiting our youth.

References

Ames, C. (1992). Achievement goals, motivational climate, and motivational processes. In G. Roberts (Ed.), *Motivation in sport and exercise* (pp. 161-176). Champaign, IL: Human Kinetics.

Ames, C., & Archer, J. (1988). Achievement goals in the classroom: Students' learning strategies and motivation processes. *Journal of Educational Psychology, 80*, 260-267.

Aristotle (323 B.C./1985). *Nicomachean Ethics*. (T. Irwin, Trans.) Indianapolis: Hacket.

Bateson, G. (1955). A theory of play and fantasy. *Psychiatric Research Reports*, *2*, 39-51.

Beller, J., & Stoll, S. (1995). Moral reasoning of high school student athletes and general students: An empirical study versus personal testimony. *Pediatric Exercise Science, 7*, 352-363.

Blasi, A. (1983). The self and cognition: The roles of the self in the acquisition of knowledge, and the role of cognition in the development of the self. In B. Lee and G. Noam (Eds.), *Psychological theories of the self* (Vol. 2, pp. 1-25). New York: Plenum.

Blasi, A. (1984). Moral identity: Its role in moral functioning. In W. Kurtines & J. Gewirtz (Eds.), *Morality, moral behavior, and moral development* (pp. 128-39). New York: Wiley.

Blasi, A. (1985). The moral personality: Reflections for social science and education. In M. Berkowitz & F. Oser (Eds.), *Moral education: Theory and application* (pp. 433-444). Hillsdale, N.J.: Lawrence Erlbaum.

Blasi, A. (1988). Identity and the development of the self. In D. K. Lapsley and F. C. Power (Eds.), *Self, ego, and identity: Integrative approaches* (pp. 226-242). New York: Springer-Verlag.

Blasi, A. (2005). Moral character: A psychological approach. In D. Lapsley & F.C. Power (Eds.), *Character psychology and character education* (pp. 67-100). Notre Dame, IN: University of Notre Dame Press.

Bredemeier, B.J. (1985). Moral reasoning and the perceived legitimacy of intentionally injurious sport acts. *Journal of Sport Psychology, 7*, 110-124.

Bredemeier, B. J. (1994). Children's moral reasoning and their assertive, aggressive, and submissive tendencies in sport and daily life. *Journal of Sport and Exercise Psychology, 16*, 1-14.

Bredemeier, B. J. (1995). Divergence in children's moral reasoning about issues in daily life and sport specific contexts. *International Journal of Sport Psychology, 26*, 453-463.

Bredemeier, B, Power, F.C., & Shields, D. (2002, April). *Sport teams as communities of character*. Workshop offered at the American Alliance for Health, Physical Education, Recreation and Dance convention, Cincinnati, Ohio.

Bredemeier, B.J. & Shields, D.L. (1984a). Divergence in moral reasoning about sport and life. *Sociology of Sport Journal, 1*, 348-357.

Bredemeier, B.J. & Shields, D.L. (1984b). The utility of moral stage analysis in the investigation of athletic aggression. *Sociology of Sport Journal, 1*, 138-149.

Bredemeier, B.J. & Shields, D.L. (1985). Values and violence in sport. *Psychology Today, 19*, 22-32.

Bredemeier, B.J. & Shields, D.L. (1986a). Athletic aggression: An issue of contextal morality. *Sociology of Sport Journal, 3* 15-28.

Bredemeier, B.J. & Shields, D.L. (1986b). Game reasoning and interactional morality. *Journal of Genetic Psychology, 147*, 257-275.

Bredemeier, B.J. & Shields, D.L. (1986c). Moral growth among athletes and nonathletes: A comparative analysis. *Journal of Genetic Psychology, 147*, 7-18.

Bredemeier, B.L., & Shields D.L. (1994). Applied ethics and moral reasoning in sport. In J. Rest & D. Narvaez (Eds), *Moral development in the professions* (pp. 173-187). Hillsdale, NJ: Lawrence Erlbaum.

Bredemeier, B., & Shields, D. (1998). Moral assessment in sport psychology. In J.L. Duda (Ed.), *Advances in sport and exercise psychology measurement* (pp. 257-276). Morgantown, WV: Fitness Information Technology.

Bredemeier, B., Weiss, M., Shields, D., & Cooper, B. (1986). The relationship of sport involvement with children's moral reasoning and aggression tendencies, *Journal of Sport Psychology, 8*, 304-318.

Bredemeier, B., Weiss, M., Shields, D., & Cooper, B. (1987). The relationship between children's legitimacy judgments and their moral reasoning, aggression tendencies and sport involvement. *Sociology of Sport Journal, 4*, 48-60.

Bredemeier, B., Weiss, M., Shields, D., & Shewchuk, R. (1986). Promoting moral growth in a summer sport camp: The implementation of theoretically grounded instructional strategies. *Journal of Moral Education, 15*, 212-220.

Burton, D. (1989). Winning isn't everything: Examining the impact of performance goals on collegiate swimmers; cognitions and performance. *The Sport Psychologist, 2,* 105-132.

Colby, A., Kohlberg, L. (1987). *The measurement of moral judgment* (Two volumes). Cambridge, MA: Cambridge University Press.

Corsaro, W. A. (1981). Friendship in the nursery school: Social organization in a peer environment. In S. R. Asher & J. M. Gottman (Eds.), *The development of children's friendships*. Cambridge: Cambridge University Press.

Duda, J. L. (1987). Toward a developmental theory of achievement motivation in sport. *Journal of Sport Psychology, 9*, 130-145.

Duda, J.L. (1989). Goal perspectives and behavior in sport and exercise settings. In C. Ames & M. Maehr (Eds.), *Advances in motivation and achievement* (Vol. 6, pp. 81-115). Greenwich, CT: JAI Press.

Duda, J.L. (1993). Goals: A social cognitive approach to the study of motivation in sport. In R.N. Singer, M. Murphey, & L.K. Tennant (Eds.), *Handbook on research in sport psychology* (pp. 421-436). New York: Macmillan

Duda, J.L. (1996). Maximizing motivation in sport and physical education among children and adolescents: The case for greater task involvement. *Quest, 48*, 290-302.

Duda, J.L., Olson, L.K., & Templin, T.J. (1991). The relationship of task and ego orientation to sportsmanship attitudes and the perceived legitimacy of injurious acts. *Research Quarterly for Exercise and Sport, 62*, 79-87.

Duda, J.L., & Whitehead, J. (1998). Measurement of goal perspectives in the physical domain. In J. Duda (Ed.), *Advances in sport and exercise psychology measurement* (pp. 21-48). Morgantown, WV: Fitness Information Technology.

Dunn, J.G.H., & Dunn, J.C. (1999). Goal orientations, perceptions of aggression, and sportspersonship in elite male youth ice hockey players. *The Sport Psychologist, 13*, 183-200.

Epstein, J. (1988). Effective schools or effective students? Dealing with diversity. In R. Haskins & B. MacRae (Eds.), *Policies for America's public schools* (pp. 89-126). Norwood, NJ: Ablex.

Epstein, J. (1989). Family structures and student motivation: A developmental perspective. In C. Ames & R. Ames (Eds.), *Research on motivation in education* (Vol. 3, pp. 259-295). New York: Academic Press.

Firth, R. (1973). *Symbols public and private*. New York: Cornell University Press.

Frankl, D. (1989). Sport participation and moral reasoning: Relationships among aspects of hostility, altruism, and sport involvement. Unpublished doctoral dissertation, Southern Illinois University at Carbondale.

Giffin, H. L. N. (1982). *The metacommunicative process in a collective make-believe play*. Unpublished doctoral dissertation, University of Colorado, Boulder.

Guivernau, M., & Duda, J. (1998). Integrating concepts of motivation and morality: The contribution of norms regarding aggressive and rule-violating behavior, goal orientations, and the perceived motivational climate to the prediction of athletic aggression. *Journal of Sport and Exercise Psychology, Supplement, S13*.

Haan, N. (1977). *A manual for interactional morality*. Unpublished manuscript. Berkeley: Institute of Human Development, University of California.

Haan, N. (1978). Two moralities in action contexts: Relationship to thought, ego regulation, and development. *Journal of Personality and Social Psychology, 36,* 286-305.

Haan, N. (1983). An interactional morality of everyday life. In N. Haan, R. Bellah, P. Rabinow, & W. Sullivan (Eds.), *Social science as moral inquiry* (pp. 218-250). New York: Columbia University Press.

Haan, N. (1991). Moral development and action from a social constructivist perspective. In W. Kurtines & J. Gewirtz (Eds.), *Handbook of moral behavior and development, Vol.1: Theory*, (pp. 251-273). Hillsdale, NJ: Lawrence Erlbaum Associates, Inc.

Haan, N., Aerts, E. & Cooper, B. B. (1985). *On moral grounds: The search for a practical morality.* New York: New York University.

Hahm, C.H., Beller, J.M., & Stoll, S.K. (1989). *The Hahm-Beller values choice inventory in the sport mileau*. Moscow: University of Idaho, The Institute for ETHICS.

Hall, E.R. (1986). Moral development levels of athletes in sport-specific and general social situations. In L. Vander Velden & J.H. Humphrey (Eds.), *Psychology and sociology of sport: Current selected research* (Vol. 1), (pp. 191-204). New York: AMS Press.

Hall, K. H. (1988). *A social-cognitive approach to goal setting: The mediating effects of achievement goals and perceived ability*. Unpublished doctoral dissertation, University of Illinois at Urbana-Champaign.

Handelman, D. (1977). Play and ritual: Complementary frames of metacommunication. In A.J. Chapman & H.C. Foot (Eds.), *It's a funny thing, humour*. Oxford: Pergamon Press.

Horrocks, R.N. (1979). The relationship of selected prosocial play behaviors in children to moral reasoning, youth sports, participation, and perception of sportsmanship. Unpublished doctoral dissertation, University of North Carolina, Greensboro.

Huizinga, Johan. (1955). *Homo ludens: A study of the play element in culture*. Boston: Beacon Press.

Kavussanu, M. & Ntoumanis, N. (2001, May). Participation in sport and moral functioning: The mediating role of ego orientation. Paper presented at the10th World Congress of Sport Psychology, Skiathos Island, Greece.

Kavussanu, M., & Roberts, G. (In press). Moral functioning in sport: An achievement goal perspective. *Journal of Sport and Exercise Psychology*.

Kohlberg, L. (1981). *Essays on moral development: Vol. 1: The philosophy of moral development*. San Francisco: Harper & Row.

Kohlberg, L. (1984). *Essays on moral development: Vol. 2: The psychology of moral development*. San Francisco: Harper & Row.

Kohlberg, L., Hickey, J., & Scharf, P. (1972). The justice structure of the prison: a theory and intervention. *The Prison Journal, 51*, 3-14.

Krebs, D., Vermeulen, S., Carpendale, J., & Denton, K. (1991). Structural and situational influences on moral judgment: The interaction between stage and dilemma. In W. Kurtines & J. Gewirtz

(Eds.), *Handbook of moral behavior and development. Vol. 2: Research* (pp. 139-169). Hillsdale, NJ: Lawrence Erlbaum.

Newton, M. (1994). *The effect of differences in perceived motivational climate and goal orientations on motivational responses of female volleyball players*. Unpublished Doctoral dissertation. Purdue University.

Newton, M., & Duda, J. L. (1998). The interaction of motivational climate, dispositional goal orientations, and perceived ability in predicting indices of motivation. *International Journal of Sport Psychology, 29*, 1-20.

Nicholls, J.G. (1984). Achievement motivation: Conceptions of ability, subjective experience, task choice, and performance. *Psychological Review, 91*, 328-346.

Nicholls, J.G. (1989). *The competitive ethos and democratic education*. Cambridge, MA: Harvard University Press.

Nicholls, J.G. Cobb, P., Wood, T., Yackel, E., & Patashnick, M. (1990). Assessing students' theories of success in mathematics: Individual classroom differences. *Journal for Research in Mathematics Education, 21,* 109-122.

Nicholls, J.G., Cheung, P.C., Lauer, J., & Patashnick, M. (1989). Individual differences in academic motivation: Perceived ability, goals, beliefs, and values. *Learning and Individual Differences, 1(1)*, 63-84.

Nicholls, J., & Miller, A. (1984). Development and its discontents: The differentiation of the concept of ability. In J. Nicholls (Ed.), *Advances in Motivation and Achievement: The Development of Achievement Motivation* (pp. 185-218). Greenwich, CT: JAI Press.

Piaget, J. (1932/1965). *Moral judgment of the child*. New York: Free Press.

Power, F.C., Higgins, A. & Kohlberg, L. (1989). *Lawrence Kohlberg's approach to moral education*. Columbia University Press. New York.

Priest, R.G., Krause, J.V., & Beach, J. (1999). Four-year changes in college athletes' ethical value choices in sports situations. *Research Quarterly for Exercise and Sport, 70*, 170-178.

Rest, J.R. (1979). *Development in judging moral issues*. Minneapolis: University of Minnesota Press.

Rest, J. R. (1983). Morality. In P. Mussen (Gen. Ed.), *Manual of child psychology*, volume *Cognitive development* (pp. 556-629), J. Flavell & E. Markman (eds), 4th ed. New York: John Wiley & Sons.

Rest, J. R. (1984). The major components of morality. In W. Kurtines & J. Gewirtz (eds.), *Morality, moral behavior, and moral development* (pp. 356-629). New York: John Wiley & Sons.

Rest, J., Narvaez, D., Bebeau, M., & Thoma, S. (1999). *Post-conventional moral thinking: A neo-Kohlbergain approach*. Mahwah, NJ: Erlbaum.

Romance, T.J., Weiss, M.R., & Bockoven, J. (1986). A program to promote moral development through elementary school physical education. *Journal of Teaching in Physical Education, 5,* 126-136.

Rulmyr, R. (1996). *Interscholastic athletic participation and the moral development of adolescents in Arizona high schools.* Unpublished doctoral dissertation, Northern Arizona University.

Schmitz, K. (1976). Sport and play: Suspension of the ordinary. In M. Hart (Ed.), *Sport in the sociocultural process*. Dubuque: W.C.: Brown.

Seifriz, J. J., Duda, J. L., & Chi, L. (1992). The relationship of perceived motivational climate to intrinsic motivation and beliefs about success in basketball. *Journal of Sport and Exercise Psychology, 14,* 375-391.

Selman, R. (1980). *The growth of interpersonal understanding: Developmental and clinical analyses.* New York: Academic Press.

Shields, D.L., & Bredemeier, B.J. (1984). Sport and moral growth: A structural developmental perspective. In W. Straub & J. Williams (Eds.), *Cognitive sport psychology* (pp. 89-101). Lansing, NY: Sport Science Associates.

Shields, D., & Bredemeier, B. (1995). *Character development and physical activity*. Champaign, IL: Human Kinetics.

Shields, D., Bredemeier, B., Gardner, D., & Bostrom, A. (1995). Leadership, cohesion and team norms regarding cheating and aggression. *Sociology of Sport Journal, 12*, 324-336.

Shields, D., Bredemeier, B., & Power, F.C. (2002). Moral development and children's sport. In F. Smoll & R. Smith (Eds.), *Children and youth in sport: A biopsychosocial perspective* (2nd ed) (pp. 537-559), Indianapolis: Brown & Benchmark.

Shulman, J., & Bowen, W. (1991). *The game of life: College sports and educational values*. Princeton, NJ: Princeton University Press.

Stephens, D. (2000). Predictors of likelihood to aggress in youth soccer: An examination of coed and all-girls teams. *Journal of Sport Behavior, 23*, 311-325.

Stephens, D., & Bredemeier, B. (1996). Moral atmosphere and judgments about aggression in girls' soccer: Relationships among moral and motivational variables. *Journal of Sport and Exercise Psychology, 18*, 158-173.

Stephens, D., Bredemeier, B., & Shields, D. (1997). Construction of a measure designed to assess players' descriptions and prescriptions for moral behavior in youth sport soccer. *International Journal of Sport Psychology, 28*, 370-390.

Stevenson, M. J. (1998). *Measuring the cognitive moral reasoning of collegiate student-athletes: The development of the Stevenson-Stoll Social Responsibility Questionnaire.* Unpublished doctoral dissertation, University of Idaho.

Sutton-Smith, B. (1971a). Boundaries. In R. E. Herron & B. Sutton-Smith (Eds.), *Child's play*. New York: John Wiley & Sons.

Thorkildsen, T. (1988). Theories of education among academically precocious adolescents. *Contemporary Educational Psychology, 13*, 323-330.

Treasure, D.C. (1993). *A social-cognitive approach to understanding children's achievement behavior, cognitions and affect in competitive sport*. Unpublished Doctoral dissertation. University of Illinois. Urbana-Champaign.

Treasure, D. C., & Roberts, G. C. (1994). Cognitive and affective concomitants of task and ego goal orientations during the middle school years. *Journal of Sport and Exercise Psychology, 16,* 15-28.

Treasure, D. C., & Roberts, G. C. (1998). Relationship between female adolescents' achievement goal orientations, perceptions of the motivational climate, belief about success and sources of satisfaction in basketball. International *Journal of Sport Psychology, 29*, 211-230.

Walling, M. D., Duda, J. L., & Chi, L. (1993). The Perceived Motivational Climate in Sport Questionnaire: Construct and predictive validity. *Journal of Sport and Exercise Psychology, 15,* 172-183.

Wandzilak, T., Carroll, T., & Ansorge, C.J. (1988). Values development through physical activity: Promoting sportsmanlike behaviors, perceptions, and moral reasoning. *Journal of Teaching in Physical Education, 8*(1), 13-22.

43 Toward a Multidimensional Definition of Sportsmanship

ROBERT J. VALLERAND
Université du Québec à Montréal
PAUL DESHAIES AND JEAN-PIERRE CUERRIER
Université de Sherbrooke
NATHALIE M. BRIÈRE
Gaspe, Québec
LUC G. PELLETIER
University of Ottawa

Sport and physical activity are said to build character and develop moral values in participants. However, it is not easy to provide a precise definition of the terms character and sportsmanship. Whereas it is quite clear that, in general, these two terms have to do with people's perceptions and actions as to right (ethical) versus wrong (unethical) (i.e., morality) in the sport context, no universally accepted definitions of these terms are available in the sport and exercise scientific literature.

In line with the social psychological approach, Robert Vallerand, a Canadian sport psychologist, and his associates made an extensive attempt to identify a meaningful definition of sportspersonship. In fact, they investigated athletes' definition of the term sportspersonship (at that time, sportsmanship). They conducted a large empirical study with 1056 French-Canadian child and adolescent athletes who participated in seven different sport disciplines. Factor analysis of the sportspersonship survey administered to these 10- to 18-year-old athletes revealed five factors involved in the athletes' definition of this concept. In line with these five factors, Vallerand defined sportspersonship in terms of respect and concern for rules and officials, social conventions, and opponents, as well as a person's full commitment to his or her sport and the relative absence or avoidance of a negative approach (i.e., poor attitudes) toward participation in sport.

This study was important in proposing, for the first time, a multidimensional definition of sportspersonship that is ecologically valid. Although the problem of providing a universally accepted definition for this term is not yet solved through this study, it has been significant in helping not only to guide later research in this area but also to improve the knowledge base related to sport environments and to promote sportspersonship in young athletes.

One major problem with research conducted on sportsmanship is the absence of an accepted definition. The purpose of this study was to attempt to derive a definition of sportsmanship by applying premises from social psychological theories and research. A major assumption of this perspective is that sportsmanship meanings and labels attached to given behaviors are learned through interpersonal interactions with various sport participants and that eventually a consensual agreement develops regarding the nature of sportsmanship. It thus follows that a meaningful definition of sportsmanship should be obtained through the athletes themselves. In this study, 1056 male and female athletes completed a questionnaire which contained various items pertaining to sportsmanship. Results from a factor analysis revealed the presence of 5 factors corrresponding to the respect and concern for: a) one's full commitment toward sport participation, b) the rules and officials, c) social conventions, d) the opponent, as well as e) a negative approach toward sport participation. Implications of this multidimensional definition for future sportsmanship research are drawn.

Much research has focused on the concept of sportsmanship (see Bredemeier & Shields, 1993; Shields & Bredemeier, 1995; Weiss & Bredemeier, 1986, for reviews). While research on sportsmanship has progressed, it has been plagued by a major problem, namely a definition problem (Weiss & Bredemeier, 1986). A host of different definitions have been proposed without consensus on what would be the most appropriate one. Thus, sportsmanship has been conceptually defined as a general attitude toward certain sport behaviors (Haskins, 1960; Kistler, 1957; McAfee, 1955), as respect for prescribed and proscribed norms from an ethics code (Kroll, 1976), as positive social interaction related to game play (Giebnink & McKenzie, 1985), and as "the tendency to behave in accordance with one's most mature moral reasoning patterns, even when conventional dictates or success strategies would encourage alternative behaviors" (Weiss & Bredemeier, 1986).

Several issues need to be addressed with respect to the definition of sportsmanship. We will focus on two. A first point concerns the fact that up until now, there has not been any agreement with respect to the content of sportsmanship. In other words, researchers are still looking for the conceptual domain of sportsmanship, for what it is as well as for what it is not. Thus, is violent behavior (such as fighting in ice hockey) part of the sportsmanship concept or the aggression concept? Without a proper definition of sportsmanship, it is impossible to answer this question. Furthermore, without a clear definition of the content of sportsmanship, it becomes impossible to further our knowledge on three key aspects of sportsmanship, namely sportsmanship behavior (behavior pertaining to the content of sportsmanship as scientifically defined), sportsmanship orientations (i.e., individual differences in the propensity to act in a sportsmanlike fashion), and sportsmanship development (the processes that lead to these individual differences). By providing a definition of sportsmanship, however, it would become feasible to clearly delineate the proper domain of application of sportsmanship and to unite research on the concept on all fronts (sportsmanship behavior, orientations, and development).

The second issue dealing with the definition of sportsmanship pertains to the processes through which athletes come to learn what behaviors are related to sportsmanship and which ones are not. Much social psychological research reveals that moral meaning and labels attached to situations and behaviors are learned through interpersonal interactions (Backman, 1985; Damon, 1988; Graziano, 1987). We believe that the same process applies to sportsmanship (see Vallerand, 1991; Vallerand, Deshaies, & Cuerrier, in press; Vallerand & Losier, 1994). It is through interactions with not only coaches, referees, parents, and other adults, but also through communication with their peers (see Fine, 1987) that children come to learn what sportsmanship is and what it is not. It is the social context, and more specifically the various interactions and observations it allows, which provides participants with the necessary background with which to define the various behaviors emitted (Damon, 1988; Shweder & Much, 1987). Eventually, through repeated interactions in given sport settings, athletes develop a consensual agreement regarding the nature of sportsmanship.

An important implication of this proposition is that athletes should be in a prime position to identify the nature of the sportsmanship concept. In fact, it may even be posited that the most meaningful and ecological understanding of the nature of sportsmanship should be obtained from the very individuals who participate in sport settings: the athletes themselves. A similar position has been espoused by Quinn, Houts, and Graesser (1994). These researchers proposed and showed that a meaningful definition of morality can be obtained by asking subjects' perceptions of morality in naturally occurring situations. It thus appears that such an approach might be useful in leading to an ecological definition of sportsmanship.

In light of the importance for the field to propose a valid definition of sportsmanship, it was the purpose of this study to test the above proposition and to identify athletes' definition of sportsmanship. In the present study, athletes were presented with items (collected in a previous pilot study) describing various behaviors and attitudes toward sport situations and were asked to rate each item regarding its pertinence to sportsmanship. Subjects' assessments were then subjected to a factor analysis. It was hypothesized that a meaningful conceptualization of sportsmanship would be obtained.

Method

Subjects

A total of 1056 French-Canadian athletes from 10 to 18 years of age (M= 14.8 years) participating in seven different sports (track and field, hockey, gymnastics, volleyball, badminton, swimming, and basketball) were recruited from lists of teams and sport clubs provided by Quebec sport organizations. Participants were from four different areas of the Province and were representative of Quebec sport participants for this age group. All athletes were participating in competitive leagues at various levels as a function of their age (e.g., Pee-Wee, Bantam, Midget etc.) and were representing their schools or civic clubs depending on the sport.

The sampling procedures were as follows. First, it was decided to subdivide the Province of Quebec into four regions representing the largest possible portion of the Quebec population. Second, 7 individual and team sports were identified (see above). Third, lists of teams for these 7 sports were obtained for each of the 4 regions from the provincial sport bodies. Fourth, both male and female teams were then selected at random. Finally, coaches of these teams were contacted and asked to participate in the study. When a coach refused to participate, another team from the same region and sport was randomly selected. Overall, these procedures ensured that approximately the same number of male (n = 563) and female (n = 492) athletes participated in the study and that each sport was equally represented. Furthermore, these procedures also ensured that athletes who participated in the study were representative of athletes from the Province of Quebec participating in these sports for these age groups.

Questionnaire

Before presenting the questionnaire, we emphasized the fact that subjects should not put their name down and that anonymity would thus be preserved. Subjects were then presented the questionnaire which was made up of various parts. On the first page, it was explained that we were interested in finding out how athletes perceive various sport situations or behaviors. It was underscored that we wanted subjects to indicate how they *themselves* perceived these various situations or behaviors. It was emphasized that we did not want to know how subjects felt personally regarding these situations, but rather if they perceived these situations to be related to the concept of sportsmanship or not. On the following pages, subjects were asked to indicate the extent to which they felt that each item was related to the concept of sportsmanship on a 4-point scale ranging from 1 (not related at all to the notion of sportsmanship) to 4 (greatly related to the notion of sportsmanship). An example of an item (different from the ones used in the actual study) and how it could be scored by subjects was presented. Following this example, the 21 items to be rated were presented.

These items were selected from two major sources. First, the major part of the items were selected from results of a pilot study. In this study, 10 males and 10 females for each of the following age groups: 10-14 years, 15-18 years, and 19 and over (n = 60;) with a mean age of 18.3 years were asked to complete a questionnaire. All subjects had been (or were still) involved in a variety of competitive sports, including those performed by subjects of the main study. Subjects were asked to present their definition of the "sportsmanship" concept. They were then told to provide as many examples of their definition as they wished (see Bovyer, 1963 for a similar strategy). This procedure assured that different aspects of the definition would be highlighted through examples. Similar examples were coded into a category and one item per category was selected to create the items that would be presented to the subjects of the main study. Second, 3 items were added by the researchers. This was because some of the definitions presented by subjects of the pilot study were not translated into examples. Doing so might allow some aspects of the sportsmanship concept as perceived by subjects to come out more clearly. Overall, 21 items were included in the questionnaire and rated by subjects of the main study.

Finally, on the last page of the questionnaire, subjects were asked to indicate their sex, age, as well as the number of years of participation in competitive sports, and the number of hours of training per week.

Procedures

Prior to the testing sessions, the experimenters phoned the head coaches of the various randomly selected teams in order to sollicit their collaboration in the study. Coaches were told that participation was important because it could lead to a better understanding of sport competition as it can be found in their respective sports.

Only one team was assessed per meeting. Athletes completed the questionnaire either in a classroom near the gymnasium (if applicable), or in the locker room. Subjects were thanked for agreeing to participate in the study. It was explained that "this study is not a test but rather some kind of survey on sport competition". They were told that their answers would not serve for selection purposes and that their coach would not see their individual answers. Subjects were told, however, that their answers were important as they could contribute to a better understanding of their sport. Subjects were finally told that they should not put their names down and were thus assured of confidentiality. Following these instructions, the questionnaire was verbally described and distributed. Athletes then completed the questionnaire on their own. It should be noted that for athletes 14 years old and under, items were read to them. Subjects were encouraged to ask questions at any time. These overall procedures ensured that the questionnaire was clear for all subjects. Following completion of the questionnaire, subjects were told the purpose of the study, thanked for their cooperation, and dismissed.

Results

A factor analysis was performed on the 21 items using the maximum likelihood approach (Jöreskog & Lawley, 1968). Results revealed the presence of 5 factors with eigenvalues greater than 1 and explaining 50% of the variance. An oblique rotation was used because it was expected that the factors would be correlated. Factor 1 reflects respect and concern for one's full commitment toward sport participation. Such a commitment is displayed through behaviors such as obeying the coach and showing up (and working hard) during practices and games (i.e., not letting the team down and always offering the best opposition). In Factor 2, the approach toward sportsmanship is negative wherein the athlete takes a win at all costs approach toward playing, ridicules opponents, and shows a temper after losing. In Factor 3, the emphasis is on respect and concern for the rules and officials: respecting the rules even when the opponent cheats, not criticizing the referee when he or she makes mistakes, not retaliating against opponents' cheap shots, and remaining calm after making a mistake. Factor 4 reflects respect for social conventions to be found in sports: shaking hands after the game, encouraging teammates, and being a good loser. Finally, in Factor 5, the emphasis is on true respect and concern for the opponent. This form of sportsmanship is evidence through lending one's equipment to the opponent (and thereby allowing him or her to compete), agreeing to play even if the opponent is late (rather than winning by default), refusing to take advantage of an injured opponent, and informing the referee when the latter has made a mistake in one's favor. Overall, the 5-factor structure reflects a readily interpretable multidimensional definition of sportsmanship.

Inspection of the mean for each factor reveals that subjects perceived that five sportsmanship dimensions somewhat differently. While all factors were perceived as being part of the sportsmanship concept, subjects perceived Factor 4 (social conventions) as reflecting sportsmanship the most and Factor 2 (negative approach toward sport participation) the least.

Cronbach alphas of each factor, as well as the factor correlations were also computed. Results revealed that each factor was somewhat reliable, especially in light of the low number of items per factor. Nevertheless, results also revealed that there was somewhat more consensus with respect to the content of Factors 1, 2, and 4 (which had alpha values of .71, .72, and .66, respectively) than with respect to Factors 3 and 5 (which had alpha values of .59). Thus, findings with these last two factors must be interpreted with caution. In addition, results from the factor correlations revealed the presence of positive and moderate values (ranging from .24 to .42), except for the values involving Factor 2 (a negative approach toward sport participation) where correlations with the other factors ranged from -.25 to .02. Thus, these 5 factors are only moderately correlated and can be perceived as somewhat independent of one another.

Finally, correlations were also conducted between the 5 factors and the socio-demographic variables assessed in this study (sex, age, number of years of participation in competitive sports, and number of hours of training per week). Results revealed that correlations were very small (the average correlation was r= + .01). Only one correlation exceeded 12. It involved age and Factor 2. The older the subjects, the higher the tendency to perceive items pertaining to Factor 2 as reflecting sportsmanship (r= .23). Thus, socio-demographic variables had little impact on how sportsmanship items were assessed.

Discussion

The purpose of this study was to identify a meaningful definition of sportsmanship. In line with much social psychological research, this was done by asking athletes to rate the extent to which various items, previously obtained from other athletes, pertained to the concept of sportsmanship. The results from the factor analysis revealed the presence of 5 factors corresponding to the respect and concern for: a) one's full commitment toward sport participation, b) the rules and officials, c) social conventions, d) the opponent, as well as e) a negative (win at all costs) approach toward sport participation. The present findings have important implications for sportsmanship research.

A first major implication of this study is that the present findings represent the first preliminary step toward an ecologically valid definition of sportsmanship. Three points should be underscored in this respect. First, sportsmanship is essentially multidimensional in nature. This entails that sportsmanship can be perceived as a core concept which encompasses a certain number of related and more specific dimensions. From this conceptualization, it appears that sportsmanship reflects a general or core tendency toward the respect of and the concern for the sport environment, the rules, and its participants (coaches, teammates, referees and officials, and the opponent), and a concomittant avoidance of a negative win-at-all-costs approach toward participation in sports.

Second, the present definition underscores the fact that if we are to make sense of sportsmanship as it exists in sports, we need to go beyond the justice dimension as postulated by certain theorists (e.g., Kohlberg, 1981, 1984). In fact, it would appear that justice is only one element of the concept of sportsmanship. Rather, it may be posited that the main characteristic of the concept is the concern and respect for others, social conventions, as well as oneself. This is not to say that the notion of justice is not important for an understanding of sportsmanship. It is indeed important especially as pertains to the respect of the rules. However, in line with suggestions from other researchers in the moral area (e.g., Gilligan, 1977), to base the concept of sportsmanship only on the dimension of justice would lead to a limited view of sportsmanship and phenomena related to it.

In line with the second point above, a third and final point concerning the definition of sportsmanship leads to the suggestion that the change of focus from a justice to a social concern approach should have profound consequences for which theories should be used in future research to scrutinize the sportsmanship concept. Up to now, research has been largely atheoretical (see Weiss & Bredemeier, 1986). The few studies conducted from a theoretical perspective have adopted a structural-developmental perspective focusing largely on age, individual stages, and other intrapersonal variables (e.g., moral reasoning) as the cause of various types of behaviors such as aggression (Bredemeier, 1985, 1994; Shields & Bredemeier, 1986).[1] By putting the emphasis on the social component of sportsmanship, the present position underscores the fundamental importance of contextual and interpersonal variables in the display of sportsmanship behavior and the development of sportsmanship orientations. Thus, social psychological theories and concepts, such as equity (Adams, 1976), social comparison (Masters & Keil, 1987), relative deprivation (Cosby, 1976; Folger, 1987), competition (Gelfand & Hartmann, 1978), altruism and prosocial behavior (Latané & Darley, 1970), conformity (Asch, 1956), obedience (Milgram, 1974), observational learning (Bandura, 1986), social justice (Lerner, 1977; Reis, 1987), and intergroup bias (Tajfel, 1982) known to explain interpersonal behaviors, now become relevant to the understanding of sportsmanship. The present definition of sportsmanship puts the focus back on the interpersonal aspect of sportsmanship and this should serve to reorient future research in this direction.

A second contribution of the present findings is that the 5-component definition of sportsmanship may allow an integration of the extant literature on sportsmanship. Indeed, some of the factors uncovered in the present study have been previously postulated or used by sport researchers. For instance, the factors dealing with the respect for one's full commitment toward sport participation, and the negative approach toward sport participation bear similarity with the "Play" and "Professional" orientations proposed by Webb (1969) where the athlete plays with either a positive or a negative (a win at all costs) approach toward the game. The respect for the opponent dimension is similar to

[1]Recently, Shields and Bredemeier (1995) have acknowledged the role of the social context in their 12-component model of moral action. However, the impact of the social context on sportsmanship behavior has yet to be empirically tested from this perspective.

the concept of Fairplay, wherein the athlete strives to assure that the opponent can compete on equal footing (International Committee for Fairplay, 1981; McIntosh, 1979). Similarly, various types of behaviors subsumed under the "social conventions" and the "rules and officials" factors have also been studied in sportsmanship research (see Bovyer, 1963; Kistler, 1957; McAfee, 1955). By reviewing previous research in relation to the 5 sportsmanship dimensions, it may become possible to make sense of a literature which at present appears in a state of disarray.

A third major implication from the findings of this study deals with the measurement of sportsmanship orientations. Previous measures of sportsmanship orientations (e.g., Haskins, 1960) and moral reasoning (e.g., Bredemeier, 1985) are largely unidimensional in nature. Based on the present findings, it appears that it is feasible to devise a sportsmanship orientations questionnaire that would capture the multidimensional nature of this sportsmanship definition. Such a questionnaire should be comprised of 5 scales assessing each of the 5 sportsmanship components. Because the 5 dimensions are only moderately related among themselves, individuals can be expected to show intraindividual differences on the 5 scales. For instance, an athlete could be high on the "Respect for the rules and officials" orientation but low on the "Respect and Concern Toward the Opponent" orientation. The use of such a questionnaire would be useful in research because it could lead to very specific hypotheses. We (Vallerand, Brière, & Provencher, 1995) have recently constructed such a questionnaire (the Multidimensional Sportsmanship Orientations Scale; MSOS) and preliminary results are very encouraging. For instance, the five-factor structure of the MSOS was supported by confirmatory factor analyses and each of the MSOS subscales related to specific behavioral intention and psychological measures. In addition, it was possible to predict young athletes' intention to use steroids from their scores on the MSOS. Thus, it would appear that the MSOS which makes use of the present sportsmanship definition should lead to fruitful research in the area.

Finally, a fourth contribution of the proposed definition of sportsmanship is that it provides a clear operationalization of the concept of sportsmanship behavior to be studied in future research. While past research did not distinguish among the various types of sportsmanship behavior, it is suggested that future sportsmanship research clearly spell out which dimension of sportsmanship is being studied because the 5 dimensions may not be subjected to the same influences or yield the same results. In addition, because sportsmanship is now clearly operationalized into 5 dimensions, it becomes possible to study behaviors corresponding to these dimensions and to tease out the personal and contextual determinants of such behaviors.

In closing, we should identify certain limitations of this study that point to the need of future research in order to assess the generalization of the present findings. First, only French-Canadian athletes were used. It remains to be seen whether their definition of sportsmanship corresponds to that of other cultures. Second, only athletes' definition was assessed. It is not clear how their definition of sportsmanship would compare to that of other sport participants such as coaches and parents. Third, athletes of the present study were rather young and performed at low to moderate levels of the competition hierarchy. It would be important to test whether similar findings would be obtained with older athletes that perform at elite levels (i.e., members of national, olympic, and professional teams).

In sum, an ecologically valid definition of sportsmanship is proposed. This multidimensional definition delineates for the first time the domain of sportsmanship. It also promises to lead to a better integration of the field as well as to redirect future research toward fruitful avenues. It is believed that a better understanding of the concept of sportsmanship offered by the definition should lead to greater knowledge of the processes involved in the display of sportsmanship behavior, and hopefully to the design of sport environments conducive to the development of sportsmanship orientations in athletes.

References

Adams, J.S. (1976). Equity revisited: Comments and annotated bibliography. In L. Berkowitz (Ed.), *Advances in experimental social psychology* (vol. 9, pp. 43–90). New York: Academic Press.

Asch, S. (1956). Studies of independence and conformity: 1. A minority of one against a unanimous majority. *Psychological Monographs, 70* (9) (whole number 416).

Backman, C.W. (1985). Identity, self-presentation, and the resolution of moral dilemma: Towards a social psychological theory of moral behavior. In B.R. Schlenker (Ed.), *The self and social life* (pp. 261–289). New York: McGraw-Hill.

Bandura, A. (1986). *Social foundations of thought and action: A social cognitive theory.* Englewood Cliffs, NJ: Prentice-Hall.

Bovyer, G. (1963). Children's concepts of sportsmanship in the fourth, fifth, and sixth grades. *Research Quarterly, 34,* 282–287.

Bredemeier, B.J. (1984). Sport, gender, and moral growth. In J. Silva & R. Weinberg (Eds.), *Psychological foundations of sport* (pp. 400–413). Champaign, IL: Human Kinetics.

Bredemeier, B.J. (1985). Moral reasoning and the perceived legitimacy of intentionnally injurious acts. *Journal of Sport Psychology, 7,* 110–124.

Bredemeier, B.J. (1994). Children's moral reasoning and their assertive, aggressive, and submissive tendencies in sport and daily life. *Journal of Sport and Exercice Psychology, 16,* 1–14.

Cosby, F. (1976). A model of egoistical relative deprivation. *Psychological Review, 83,* 85–113.

Damon, W. (1988). *The moral child.* New York: Free Press.

Fine, G.A. (1987). *With the boys: Little league baseball and preadolescent culture.* Chicago: University of Chicago press.

Folger, R. (1987). Reformulating the preconditions of resentment: A referent cognitions model. In J.C. Masters & W.P. Smith (Eds.), *Social comparison, social justice, and relative deprivation* (pp. 183–215). Hillsdale, NJ: Erlbaum.

Gelfand, D.M., & Hartmann, D.P. (1978). Some detrimental effects of competitive sports on children's behavior. In R. Magill, M. Ash, & F. Smoll (Eds.), *Children in sport: A contemporary anthology* (pp. 165–173). Champaign, IL: Human Kinetics.

Giebnink, M.P., & McKenzie, T.L. (1985). Teaching sportsmanship in physical education and recreation: An analysis of interventions and generalization effects. *Journal of Teaching in Physical Education, 4*, 167–177.

Gilligan, C. (1977). In a different voice: Women's conceptions of self and morality. *Harvard Educational Review, 47*, 481–517.

Graziano, W.G. (1987). Lost in thought at the choice point: Cognition, context, and equity. In J.C. Masters & W.P. Smith (Eds.), *Social comparison, social justice, and relative deprivation* (pp. 265–294). Hillsdale, NJ: Erlbaum.

Haskins, M.J. (1960). Problem solving test of sportsmanship. *Research Quarterly, 31*, 610–616.

International Committee for Fairplay (1981). *Manifeste de l'entente international pour un sport sans violence et pour le Fair Play.* Paris: C.I.F.P.

Jöreskog, K.G., & Lawley, D.M. (1968). New methods in maximum likelihood factor analysis. *British Journal of Mathematical and Statistical Psychology, 21*, 85–96.

Kistler, J.W. (1957). Attitudes expressed about behavior demonstrated in certain specific situations occurring in sports. *National College Physical Education Association for Men Proceedings, 60*, 55–58.

Kohlberg, L. (1981). *The philosophy of moral development: Moral stages and the idea of justice.* New York: Harper & Row.

Kohlberg, L. (1984). *Essays of moral development: Vol. 2. The psychology of moral development.* New York: Harper & Row.

Kroll, W. (1976). Psychological scaling of the AIWA code-of-ethics for players. *Research Quarterly, 47*, 126–133.

Latané, B., & Darley, J.M. (1970). *The unresponsive bystander: Why doesn't he help?* New York: Appleton-Century-Crofts.

Lerner, M.J. (1977). The justice motive: Some hypotheses as to its origins and forms. *Journal of Personality, 45*, 1–52.

Masters, J.C., & Keil, L.J. (1987). Generic comparison processes in human judgment and behavior. In J.C. Masters & W.P. Smith (Eds.), *Social comparison, social justice, and relative deprivation* (pp. 11–54). Hillsdale, NJ: Erlbaum.

McAfee. R.A. (1955). Sportsmanship attitudes of sixth, seventh, and eighth grade boys. *Research Quarterly, 26*, 120.

McIntosh, P. (1979). *Fairplay: Ethics in sport and education.* London: Heinemann.

Milgram, S. (1974). *Obedience to authority: An experimental view.* New York: Harper & Row.

Quinn, R.A., Houts, A.C., & Graesser, A.C. (1994). Naturalistic conceptions of morality: A question-answering approach. *Journal of Personality, 62*, 239–262.

Reis, H.T. (1987). The nature of the justice motive: Some thoughts on operation, internalization. and justification. In J.C. Masters & W.P. Smith (Eds.), *Social comparison, social justice, and relative deprivation* (pp. 131–150). Hillsdale, NJ: Erlbaum.

Shields, D.L., & Bredemeier, B.J. (1986). Morality and aggression: A response to Smith's critique. *Sociology of Sport Journal, 3*, 65–67.

Shields, D.L., & Bredemeier, B.J. (1995). *Character development and physical activity.* Champaign, IL: Human Kinetics.

Shweder, R.A., & Much, N.C. (1987). Determinations of meaning: Discourse and moral socialization. In W.M. Kurtines & J.L. Gewirtz (Eds.), *Moral development through social interaction* (pp. 197–244). New York: Wiley.

Tajfel, H. (1982). Social psychology of intergroup relations. *Annual Review of Psychology, 33*, 1–39.

Vallerand, R.J. (1991). Une analyse psycho-sociale de l'esprit sportif (A social psychological analysis of sportsmanship). In J. Bilard & M. Durand (Eds.), *Sport et psychologie* (Sport and psychology) (pp. 289–299). Montpellier, France: Ed. Revue EPS.

Vallerand, R.J., Brière, N.M., & Provencher, P. (1995). *On the development and validation of the Multidimensional Sportsmanship Orientations Scale (MSOS).* Manuscript submitted for publication.

Vallerand, R.J., Deshaies, P., & Cuerrier, J.-P. (in press). On the Effects of the Social Context on Behavioral Intentions of Sportsmanship. *International Journal of Sport Psychology.*

Vallerand, R.J., & Losier, G.F. (1994). Self-determined motivation and sportsmanship orientations: An assessment of their temporal relationship. *Journal of Sport and Exercise Psychology, 16*, 229–245.

Webb, H. (1969). Professionalization of attitudes toward play among adolescents. In G.S. Kenyon (Ed.), *Aspects of contemporary sport sociology* (pp. 161–187). Chicago: The Athletic Institute.

Weiss, M.R., & Bredemeier, B.J. (1986). Moral development. In V. Seefeldt (Ed.), *Physical activity and human well-being* (pp. 374–390). Reston, VA: AAHPERA.

44 "That's What Friends Are For": Children's and Teenagers' Perceptions of Peer Relationships in the Sport Domain

MAUREEN R. WEISS AND ALAN L. SMITH
University of Oregon

MARC THEEBOOM
University of Brussels, Belgium

Children's psychological development through sport participation is substantially affected by the role of friends. In fact, children participate in sports to make new friends and to be with existing ones. In other words, affiliation is an important motive for participation; however, it seems that friends and peer groups also have other major effects on young athletes with regard to their psychological development. For example, peer relations are associated with important psychosocial variables, such as children's motivation, perceived self-esteem, and subjective sense of acceptance.

Maureen Weiss, one of the leading developmental sport psychologists, believes that although the structural features of and the social agents acting in children's athletic environments may affect group norms, group norms and their formation can be understood by focusing on peer relationships. Peers are highly relevant to moral development, as the studies conducted on young athletes' perceptions of teammates demonstrate. Weiss and colleagues extensively investigated youth sport friendships and highlighted the importance of prosocial behavior, conflict, and conflict resolution with young athletes, arguing that peer relationships can be conceived as a context for moral development. In this particular study, in-depth interviews with 19 male and 19 female sport participants aged 8 to 16 years were conducted with the purpose of learning how children perceive friendship in sport. Weiss and colleagues made an attempt to identify both positive and negative dimensions of friendship, as conceived by the interviewed young athletes. In fact, the researchers did not have any specific prior hypotheses, but they designed the study to be exploratory in nature, thereby extending previous research on children's friendship conceptions conducted in schools. Indeed, perceived positive and negative dimensions of sport friendship were identified, including some significant gender- and age-related differences.

Weiss and Smith used the results of this seminal study as the basis for further investigations in this domain. For example, they later developed the Sport Friendship Quality Scale to measure different aspects of sport friendships, and they studied peer relationships and participation in physical activity among early adolescent male and female middle school children. The development of the scale enabled a more extensive research on peer relations in sport, whereas the results of such research indicated that promoting positive peer relationships may indeed enhance sport participation among young people. This includes its substantial implications for children's and adolescents' psychosocial development. Without this pioneering study, this entire endeavor would have been difficult.

The influence of peer groups on children's psychosocial development is highlighted in the sport psychology literature in areas such as motivation, self-perceptions, and affect. However, scant research has been devoted to examining children's and teenagers' conceptions of friendships within the physical domain. Current and former sport program participants ($N = 38$) took part in an in-depth interview that concerned their best friend in sports. An inductive content analysis revealed the existence of 12 positive friendship dimensions: companionship, pleasant play/association, self-esteem enhancement, help and guidance, prosocial behavior, intimacy, loyalty, things in common, attractive personal qualities, emotional support, absence of conflicts, and conflict resolution. Four negative friendship dimensions were extracted: conflict, unattractive personal qualities, betrayal, and inaccessible. These conceptions of friendship were both similar and unique to friendship conceptions found in mainstream developmental research. Future research directions include measurement efforts, relationships among important constructs, and intervention techniques in the sport setting.

Educators, parents, and researchers have long regarded children's involvement in physical activity and sport as a means of deriving beneficial outcomes such as competence in motor skills, self-confidence, sportspersonship, and interpersonal skills (Weiss, 1995; Wiggins, 1996). Of particular interest has been the role of sport as a socializing vehicle for teaching children how to effectively interact with peers in terms of leadership skills, cooperative behaviors, and building cohesive relationships. However, despite the widespread study of peer relations among children and adolescents in developmental psychology (e.g., Asher & Coie, 1990; Belle, 1989a; Berndt & Ladd, 1989; Newcomb & Bagwell, 1995), little research has been conducted in the area of peer relations in the physical domain, and more

Adapted, by permission, from M.R. Weiss and A.L. Smith, 1996, "That's what friends are for": Children's and teenagers' perceptions of peer relationships in the sport domain," *Journal of Sport and Exercise Psychology* 18: 347-379.

specifically about the quality of friendships, peer acceptance, and the development of social competence (Brustad, 1996; Weiss & Duncan, 1992).

The importance children and teenagers place on peer relationships in sport has frequently been mentioned in related literatures in pediatric sport psychology. For example, the literature on sport participation motivation has consistently cited affiliation opportunities as being just as important as learning and improving skills, experiencing the excitement of competition, and enjoying being physically active (Weiss, 1993). Specifically, being with and making new friends are salient to youths' sport involvement, and reductions of positive affiliation contribute to ceasing participation. Moreover, the sport context is riddled with examples of peer interactions that impinge upon children's enjoyment of and attraction to physical activity (Kunesh, Hasbrook, & Lewthwaite, 1992; Scanlan, Carpenter, Lobel, & Simons, 1993; Weiss, 1991). These include the social context surrounding arguments among or negative treatment from peers, negotiation and resolution of these conflicts, and feelings of self-worth that emanate from peer evaluation.

Research of a developmental nature conducted within the physical domain has also provided insight into the salience of peer influences in sport. Horn and her colleagues (Horn & Hasbrook, 1986; Horn & Weiss, 1991) have shown that peer comparison and evaluation (a) serve as important sources of physical competence information beginning in early childhood, and (b) increase markedly between the ages of 8 and 14 years. The peer group continues to be a central source of judging personal competence in the physical domain throughout the teenage years (Horn, Glenn, & Wentzell, 1993). Thus, an understanding of peer relations within the sport context is important from the perspective of continued physical activity, as well as children's psychological well-being and health.

In addition to empirical research in sport psychology, most theories of motivation highlight perceived social regard as a central antecedent of self-perceptions, affect, activity choice, effort, and persistence (for reviews, see Weiss & Chaumeton, 1992; Weiss & Ebbeck, 1996). The notion of perceived social regard emanates from Cooley's (1902) writings and his coining of the phrase "looking-glass self." This phrase implies that significant others serve as mirrors through which we judge ourselves: our self-worth, competence, and liking of ourselves as a person. Perceived social regard includes the feedback and evaluation from parents, coaches, and peers within a specific achievement domain. Although the literatures addressing parental influences (e.g., Brustad, 1993; Dempsey, Kimiecik, & Horn, 1993; Duda & Horn, 1993) and coaching behaviors (e.g., Black & Weiss, 1992; Horn, 1985; Smoll, Smith, Barnett, & Everett, 1993) have multiplied rapidly over the last decade, concomitant research on peer relationships within the sport social context pales in comparison. This dearth of literature is surprising given the number of theoretical and narrative articles about the role of sport as a socializing vehicle for the development of quality friendships and supportive peer relationships (e.g., Weiss, 1987, 1993; Wiggins, 1996).

The few studies that have been conducted on peer relations in the sport context have provided insight into the importance of friendships as social support mechanisms and the need for continued research in this area. A review of the sport-related literature on children's peer relations indicates two general categories of studies: peer acceptance and friendship. Peer acceptance usually refers to two attributes: peer status and popularity (Bukowski & Hoza, 1989). Status refers to one's social standing or worthiness within one's peer group, and popularity reflects the degree to which one is liked or gets along with peers. Friendship, in contrast, refers to aspects of a particular dyadic relationship, such as quality or supportive functions (Belle, 1989a; Newcomb & Bagwell, 1995). Peer acceptance and friendship represent qualities of peer relationships that merit research attention. To date, however, only a handful of studies have examined peer status and popularity (i.e., peer acceptance) and friendship quality in the physical domain.

Peer status was investigated in a study by Evans (cited in Evans & Roberts, 1987), who was especially interested in the phenomenon of team selection or "choosing up sides," one of the grueling rituals of childhood. Evans employed interview and observational methods to study a group of third- through sixth-grade boys, and found a consistent relationship between sport ability and peer status (i.e., order of team selection) in playground settings. He found that the boys who assumed leadership roles were the most athletically skilled players, and that team selection proceeded based on a "pecking order" of better to lesser ability. Moreover, the more skilled boys were more likely to attain higher peer status (i.e., played central positions in the game), which enhanced their abilities even further, and had more opportunities to develop and strengthen friendships (i.e., maintained their status).

An early study by Buchanan, Blankenbaker, and Cotten (1976) surveyed fourth- through sixth-grade boys and girls about what qualities were most important for being popular with their peers. They found that boys ranked being good at sports first, followed by making good grades, whereas girls ranked these in the reverse order. In a replication and extension of this study, Chase and Dummer (1992) found a shift in popularity preference for both boys and girls. They found that boys ranked being good at sports as most important, followed by being handsome and getting good grades, whereas girls ranked being pretty as most important, followed by being good in sports and getting good grades. Thus, features of popularity in middle childhood changed considerably over a 16-year time period. In a more recent study, Weiss and Duncan (1992) examined the relation between physical competence and peer acceptance (i.e., popularity) among 8- to 13-year-old children in a sports camp. They found that actual physical ability and beliefs about one's athletic ability were strongly related to actual peer acceptance and beliefs about being accepted by one's peer group. Some other studies have also looked at peer status and popularity (e.g., Eitzen, 1975; Feltz, 1978; Kane, 1988).

Only a few studies have investigated the nature of children's friendships in sport-related contexts. Zarbatany, Ghesquiere, and Mohr (1992) were interested in children's expectations of their friends across a variety of activity contexts such as watching television, participating in sports, and engaging in academic activities. They found that friendship expectations varied considerably as a function of the social context: friends were expected to engage in self-esteem reinforcement and character admiration in the sport context, whereas helping was the most important friendship expectation for academic activities, and common interests and considerateness were essential for watching television. The researchers concluded that friendship provisions must be studied within the specific social context in which they occur.

Duncan (1993), in a large-scale study of 12- to 14-year-old youth in physical education classes, examined structural relationships among friendship support, affect, and motivated behavior. She found that teenagers who reported greater levels of companionship and esteem support also reported greater positive affect about their physical activity experiences, verbalized future expectancies of success, and expressed greater interest in activity participation outside of the school setting. Finally, Bigelow, Lewko, and Salhani (1989) examined children's expectations of their friendships within the sport context. Results revealed that children agreed with the notion that playing on a sport team contributes to making and developing new friendships, and more specifically in nurturing specific friendship expectations such as intimacy, ego reinforcement, acceptance, loyalty, altruism, stimulation value, and source of humor.

It is apparent from this literature review that insufficient research exists to fully understand the role of peer influence and friendship provisions on children's cognitive, affective, and behavioral responses in sport and physical activity. This literature is especially devoid of studies on children's conceptions of friendship or friendship support functions in the sport domain. Thus, the present study was designed to extend the knowledge base about children's peer relationships. First, we conducted an exhaustive review of the developmental psychology literature on children's peer relationships and friendship quality, which has been generally studied within the school context (e.g., Asher & Coie, 1990; Belle, 1989a; Berndt & Ladd, 1989). The literature on children's friendship support was especially relevant to our purpose (e.g., Berndt, 1989; Berndt & Perry, 1986; Furman & Bierman, 1983; Furman & Buhrmester, 1985; Parker & Asher, 1993).

These researchers, among others, investigated children's and adolescents' perceptions of friendships and identified several types of social support or qualitative aspects of friendships. The number of friendship dimensions and their specific names vary from study to study, but there is considerable similarity in the types of friendship support that exist in children's social networks. These include esteem enhancement (i.e., validation of self-worth), loyalty, companionship, help and guidance, intimate exchange (e.g., disclosing personal information), emotional security (i.e., caring about each other), absence of conflict, conflict resolution, affection, and similarity (i.e., values, interests). Children who report a higher quality of friendship support on these dimensions score higher on peer acceptance, social satisfaction, and general psychological well-being.

Contemporary issues regarding the study of children's and adolescents' peer networks have recently been identified (Hartup, 1996; Newcomb & Bagwell, 1995; Zarbatany et al., 1992). One important area is the nature of the social context in which peer interactions and friendship support occur. Specifically, the vast majority of peer relations research has been conducted within school environments, but the question arises as to whether friendships serve the same functions in other contexts such as sport, music, or child care. A second issue in need of more research is the negative side of friendship. The positive contributions of peer relations to psychosocial development have predominated, but little attention has focused on the influence of negative interactions such as conflict, teasing, and betrayal. Finally, Newcomb and Bagwell (1995) contend that gender differences in the nature and functions of friendships have not been given the attention they deserve. This is somewhat surprising given the rather consistent data base on gender differences in peer relations.

Findings from the research on children's friendships indicate that gender is a key variable in shaping social networks and in relating to peer group members (Berndt & Perry, 1986; Feiring & Lewis, 1989). Gender differences are not usually found until early adolescence (about Grade 5 or 6), and these differences have traditionally been in the friendship support dimensions of intimacy, emotional support, affection, and esteem enhancement (e.g., Belle, 1989b; Berndt & Perry, 1986; Furman & Buhrmester, 1985), with girls assigning higher importance to these dimensions than boys. Age variations in friendship support and expectancies have also been documented. Younger children (i.e., under 10 years) tend to focus on overt, behavioral characteristics such as help and guidance, prosocial behavior, and physical features of individuals (Berndt, 1989; Berndt & Perry, 1986; Newcomb & Bagwell, 1995). Older children and adolescents (i.e., 10 to 14 years), in contrast, rely more frequently on dimensions that characterize psychological concepts (e.g., intimacy, loyalty, emotional support, esteem enhancement).

Given this vantage from the developmental and sport psychology literatures, the specific purpose of the present study was to extend previous research on friendship support conducted within the school context to the context of sport participation. That is, what positive dimensions of friendship are perceived by children and adolescents within the social context of sport (Newcomb & Bagwell, 1995; Zarbatany et al., 1992)? Do age- and gender-related variations in conceptions of friendship exist (Kunesh et al., 1992; Newcomb & Bagwell, 1995)? What negative aspects, if any, do children perceive about their friendships (Newcomb & Bagwell, 1995)? Finally, what are children's expectations of their sport friendships (Zarbatany et al., 1992)? Our study was designed to be descriptive and exploratory regarding children's friendship conceptions in sport. Thus, we did not forward specific research hypotheses; rather we focused on answering the previously stated questions.

Method

Participants

The sample ($N = 38$) consisted of 19 females and 19 males ranging in age from 8 to 16 years ($M = 12.0$, $SD = 2.53$). The children interviewed included three 15-year-olds; four each of 8-, 9-, 10-, 12-, and 16-year-old youth; and five 11-, 13-, and 14-year-old youth. Individuals were either current or former participants in a university summer sports program, and primarily represented White, middle-class families. In general, these children and adolescents were active in sports and physical activity, and had been so for some time. They were currently and had previously participated in a wide range of team (e.g., baseball, basketball, soccer) and individual (e.g., ballet, skating, swimming, horseback riding) activities (usually multiple) at both competitive and recreational levels. Participation experience within each sport ranged from 1 to 10 years.

Participants were selected based upon several criteria. First, because conceptions of friendship have been found to vary developmentally (see Newcomb & Bagwell, 1995), we drew upon participants who spanned middle childhood through adolescence. Second, our methodology depended upon children's willingness to disclose their thoughts and feelings about a best friendship. Therefore, we selected participants who were familiar with the first author (who had been program director for 12 years) or with the second or third author (who were program instructors) to increase the likelihood the participants would be comfortable expressing their opinions. Finally, we selected youth who represented the spectrum of peer acceptance and friendship qualities. The youths ranged from those who were popular and had many friends to those who were less popular and had few friends. Thus, we did not constrain our sample to only the most popular or rejected children; instead we increased the variability with which conceptions of friendship might be viewed. In sum, our sample was selected to represent a heterogeneous group based on gender, age, and quality of friendships.

Interview Schedule

An in-depth interview that prompted children's thoughtful responses to open-ended questions about their best friend in sport was selected as the methodology for this initial phase of the project. Thus, an interview schedule was devised based on methodology sources (e.g., Erlandson, Harris, Skipper, & Allen, 1993), the developmental psychology literature, the authors' experience in working with children and teenagers, and insights gained from a pilot study. The interview schedule consisted of three parts. The first portion contained questions about the participant's personal background (e.g., age, grade level, school of attendance) and sport participation history, including types of sports played, length of involvement, favorite sports, and sports that have been discontinued. These questions were designed as a "warm-up" to subsequently more difficult questions, and to facilitate rapport between the interviewer and participant:

1. What grade will you be going into? What school do you go to?
2. What sports do you play where you have coaches and organized practices? For how long have you been playing?
3. What is your favorite sport(s)? Why?
4. What sports have you done before that you no longer do? Why don't you play anymore?

The second part of the interview schedule consisted of questions about the participant's best friend in sport, and were intended to tap their conceptions of friendship:

1. Where did you meet your best friend?
2. How do you know when you have a best friend?
    - Probe: Why do you consider [friend's name] your best friend?
    - Probe: What does a best friendship mean to you?
3. What are some of the differences between [friend], whom you consider to be your best friend, and other kids who you do not consider to be your best friends?
    - Probe: What does your best friend sometimes do for you that others don't?
    - Probe: What does your best friend sometimes say to you that others don't?
4. What are some of the best things about your friendship with [friend]?
    - Probe: What do you like best about your friendship?
    - Probe: If [friend] 's family suddenly moved from Eugene, what would you miss most about your friendship?
5. Are there any things about your friendship with [friend] that you don't like?
    - Probe: Are there things that he or she sometimes does that you don't like?
    - Probe: Are there things that he or she sometimes says that you don't like?

6. So far I have been asking about you and your best friend in a general way. Now I want you to think about you and your best friend, [friend's name], while doing sports together.
   - What does your best friend sometimes do for you that others don't?
   - What does your best friend sometimes say to you that others don't?
7. Imagine that you're playing sports with your best friend, [friend's name]. What kinds of things would you like her or him to say or do?
   - Probe: What kinds of things could she or he say to make you like her or him more?
   - Probe: What kinds of things could she or he do to make you like her or him more?
8. Do you have friends who do not do sports? Is a best friend in sports different from a friend that you have outside of sports?
   - Probe: Are there different things that they do for you or with you?
   - Probe: Are there different things that they say to you or not say to you?

In order to help children respond to these questions, we asked them to identify their "best friend in sports" to establish a frame of reference, rather than attempt the more difficult task of averaging across multiple friends (Parker & Asher, 1993). "Best friend in sports" was defined as someone with whom the participants do sports frequently—someone at the university sports program, on their community sports team (e.g., YMCA), on their school sports team, or someone with whom they simply do sports. Specifically, we contextualized "sport" in two ways: (a) by having the participants select who they consider to be their "best sports friend," and (b) asking questions specific to the sport social context (e.g., "While doing sports, what does your best friend sometimes do for you that others don't?") as well as questions of a more general nature about their best sports friend (e.g., "Why do you consider [friend] to be your best friend?"). Each question contained specific follow-up probes to elicit more detailed responses from the participants. Also, clarification probes ("What do you mean by . . . ?") and elaboration probes ("Can you give an example of . . . ?") were used generously to encourage richness in the respondents' descriptions of their best friendships in sport.

The concluding portion of the interview schedule allowed the participant an opportunity to make additional comments about her or his best friend, as well as ask questions to the interviewer. At the completion of the interview, the participant was thanked for sharing her or his thoughts and feelings, and was provided a short debriefing about the nature of the study.

A pilot study was conducted with 6 children (4 boys, 2 girls; 8 to 10 years old) to determine the effectiveness of the interview schedule in terms of comprehension of questions and probes, order of questions, and effectiveness of questions to elicit in-depth responses. The pilot study also provided an opportunity for the authors to practice their interviewing skills. Specifically, interviewers rehearsed and received feedback about their interaction style with children, use of probes to elicit responses, time management (i.e., about 30 minutes), and audiotaping and videotaping procedures. Results of the pilot study were used to rearrange the order of questions, modify the wording of questions, and delete questions that were perceived as redundant by the children.

Interview Procedure

Early in the sports program, parents received a letter about the nature and purpose of the study, and what their child's participation would entail. The sports program has been routinely used as a field laboratory for the first author's research, and parents were aware that research projects were conducted each summer. Follow-up phone calls were made about one week after the letters were mailed. Only 2 of the 40 youth contacted declined to participate in the study. Upon arrival at the sport and exercise psychology laboratory, parents were asked to read and sign the consent form informing them of the benefits, risks, and voluntary nature of their child's participation. During this time, the individual who was responsible for the interview familiarized the participant with the interview room that adjoined the main laboratory and engaged in rapport-building conversation. The interview room was designed to be "child-friendly" by containing art prints of children placed at a child's eye level, comfortable chairs, and a relatively short round table for the interview itself, an air conditioner for the hot summer days, and a portable easy-to-run microcassette dictator and transcriber {Sony M-2020; Park Ridge, NJ) with a built-in microphone.

After signing the consent form, the parent remained in the outer laboratory room while the interviewer and participant interacted in the interview room. The child or teenager was asked to sit in an upright position and close to the table for audible recording. The interviewer also modeled the appropriate posture (upright, leaning toward the microphone and table). Some children brought balls, Transformers, and hats with them into the interview room; these were potential distractors, and the children were asked to place these aside until the interview was completed. Then the interviewer read aloud the child's assent form (teenagers read on their own) and asked the child to sign her or his name. Some children and adolescents were also videotaped; a separate form and signature were required for this protocol.

Upon completion of these preliminary procedures, the audiotape (and videotape) machine was turned on, and the participant was given general instructions about the interview (i.e., three sections, estimate of interview time). After completing Part 1 (background and sports history), the child or teenager was introduced to Part 2 of the interview schedule through the following script:

> The questions I am going to ask you now have to do with you and a person you consider to be *your best friend in sports* (for example, at KidSports, YMCA). I would like you to think about this best friend as you answer the questions. So you can remember to always think of this friend when we're talking, I'd like you to *write the first name* of this person on this sheet of paper and keep it in front of you. Okay. Remember, think of [friend's name] when you answer the questions.

The second and third authors were trained in interviewing techniques by the first author, according to guidelines outlined by several research methodologists (Backstrom & Hursh-Cesar, 1981; Erlandson et al., 1993; Patton, 1990). A one-age sheet was generated, detailing preparation and guidelines for interviewing, and was reviewed prior to each interview. Among the items emphasized on this sheet were the preparation of the interview room, the general procedures described previously, and specific strategies for eliciting detailed responses.

Several interview techniques were emphasized to enhance the likelihood of a positive interaction between interviewer and participant, and to obtain coherent, in-depth responses to questions about conceptions of a best friendship. These included using effective communication techniques such as eye contact, paraphrasing, restating, and probing for clarification and elaboration; being open and friendly to every response made by the child or teenager; and emphasizing that all answers were helpful, that there were no right or wrong answers. The use of probes was emphasized (i.e., at least one for every question) by gently but persistently encouraging participants to elaborate upon or clarify their answers.

Data Analysis

Inductive Content Analysis. The interview data on positive aspects of friendship (Questions 1–4 and 6 on the Part 2 of the interview schedule) were first subjected to an inductive content analysis. The procedure for this type of analysis followed guidelines set forth by methodologists (e.g., Patton, 1990) and employed in previous qualitative investigations in sport psychology (e.g., Gould, Eklund, & Jackson, 1992; Scanlan, Stein, & Ravizza, 1989; Weiss, Barber, Sisley, & Ebbeck, 1991). At all stages of analysis, the first and second author worked independently and then came together to reach consensus prior to advancing to the next stage of analysis. Consensual validation decreases experimenter bias and allows for greater accuracy in the depiction of the participants' experience (Scanlan, Stein, & Ravizza, 1989).

The 344 single-spaced pages of verbatim transcription were first read thoroughly by the first and second author. The researchers then extracted raw data quotations, phrases, or paragraphs that represented salient examples of conceptions of friendship. Following this step, the researchers discussed and reached consensus on which raw data quotations to include as the basic units of analysis. Raw data quotations with similar meaning were combined into groups. These groups represented *lower order themes* and were labeled so as to highlight their underlying meaning. A total of 216 lower order themes were identified in this way. The grouping process was repeated with the lower order themes so that a greater degree of abstraction was obtained. This resulted in the identification of 47 *higher order themes*, which in turn were combined into 12 groupings representing the highest level of abstraction. These groupings were labeled *dimensions* of friendship. The inductive process was considered completed at the dimension level because no further meaningful groupings could be inductively formed.

When the data analysts were in agreement on the raw data quotations, lower and higher order themes, and dimensions of friendship, a flow diagram was developed. In an effort to cross-validate the inductive process, the higher order themes and dimensions of friendship were given to the third author in a random order, and he was asked to try to correctly assign the higher order themes to their respective dimensions. His groupings yielded a percentage agreement of 81% (i.e., 38/47 higher order themes). Inductive content analyses were also conducted for the questions concerning negative aspects of best sport friendships (see Question 5) and friendship expectancies (see Question 7). Data analysis for Question 8, which dealt with differences between sport and nonsport friendships, was abandoned after encountering several unusable responses from the youths (e.g., no response; responses specific to individuals, not friendships).

Frequency Analysis. For positive aspects of friendship, frequency analysis was employed to examine the percentage of the total sample citing higher order themes and dimensions, as well as whether gender and age variations existed on positive friendship dimensions. The age categories for analysis (8–9 years, 10–12 years, 13–16 years) were determined based on the developmental sport psychology literature (see Weiss & Ebbeck, 1996, for a review). Frequency analysis was also used to analyze questions related to negative dimensions of friendship, and friendship expectations.

Results and Discussion

Positive Dimensions of Friendship

Inductive content analysis yielded 12 friendship dimensions: companionship, pleasant play/association, self-esteem enhancement, help and guidance, prosocial behavior, intimacy, loyalty, things in common, attractive personal qualities, emotional support, absence of conflicts, and conflict resolution. Table 44.1 contains the percentage and number of participants who cited the 47 higher order themes and 12 dimensions. Each dimension is described below and discussed with reference to previous research findings.

Companionship. The companionship dimension was cited by the largest percentage of participants (95%) and was defined as "hanging out together," spending time together, and doing things together. Higher order themes included (a) we do many things together, (b) I've known him or her a long time, (c) we go to each others' houses, (d) he or she is available and willing to do things, and (e) he or she was my only option. These higher order themes were derived from lower order themes and raw data quotations such as "play together a lot," "going places together," "invite each other over," "he or she is willing to do or try things," "she or he is available to do sports with me," and "I've known her or him for a long time."

With the exception of the higher order theme of "he or she was my only option," the sport friendship dimension of companionship was consistent with developmental psychology research on quality of relationships with friends (e.g., Furman & Buhrmester, 1985), although it is sometimes referred to as companionship and recreation (Parker & Asher, 1993), play/association (Berndt & Perry, 1986), or common activities (Furman & Bierman, 1983). The higher order theme of "he or she was my only option" was cited by 2 children and would seem to imply a low quality of friendship for these individuals.

Pleasant Play/Association. The pleasant play/association dimension was distinguished from the companionship dimension in terms of a positive valence attached to being together or spending time together, as well as enjoying an association with one's best friend. A total of 89% of the sample cited pleasant play/ association in their interviews. Higher order themes within this dimension were the following: (a) we enjoy doing things together; (b) mutual liking/affection; (c) we joke around together; (d) we compete in a positive way; (e) we work together well; and (f) he or she is fun-oriented in sports. These higher order themes were verbalized by 87% of the study sample, and comprised the following higher order themes: (a) we positively reinforce each other; (b) she or he is accepting of my mistakes; (c) we respect each other; (d) she or he makes me feel good; (e) we say nice things to each other; and (f) he or she motivates me in sports. These higher order themes

Table 44.1 Percentage and Frequency of Positive Friendship Dimensions and Higher Order Themes

DIMENSION	DIMENSION		HIGHER ORDER THEME	
Higher order theme	%	n	%	n
Companionship	95	36		
We do many things together.			94	34
I've known him or her a long time.			31	11
We go to each others' houses.			28	10
He or she is available and willing to do things.			14	5
He or she was my only option.			6	2
Pleasant play/association	89	34		
We enjoy doing things together.			56	19
Mutual liking/affection.			53	18
We joke around together.			29	10
We compete in a positive way.			29	10
We work together well.			21	7
He or she is fun-oriented in sports.			15	5
Self-esteem enhancement	87	33		
We positively reinforce each other.			58	19
She or he is accepting of my mistakes.			33	11
We respect each other.			30	10
She or he makes me feel good.			18	6
We say nice things to each other.			15	5
He or she motivates me in sports.			12	4
Help and guidance	79	30		
We help each other in sports.			73	22
We help each other to learn sport skills.			53	16
We help each other in general.			40	12
We help each other with school.			30	9
Prosocial behavior	76	29		
We do nice things for each other.			76	22
He or she shares things.			41	12
She or he doesn't say negative things to me.			31	9
She or he doesn't do mean things to me.			21	6
Intimacy	71	27		
We disclose our thoughts/feelings to each other.			56	15
We feel comfortable with each other.			52	14
We understand each others' feelings/thoughts.			44	12
We trust each other.			41	11
We have a bond with each other.			37	10
Loyalty	71	27		
He or she sticks up for me.			78	21
We pick each other to do things.			37	10
We can depend on each other.			33	9

(continued)

Table 44.1 *(continued)*

DIMENSION	DIMENSION		HIGHER ORDER THEME	
Higher order theme	%	*n*	%	*n*
Things in common	63	24		
Similar beliefs and activities.			71	17
We have a similar interest in sports.			42	10
We have similar school/ability interests.			12	3
Attractive personal qualities	58	22		
I like her or his personality in general.			36	8
Her or his attractive personal attributes.			27	6
He or she gets along with my family.			23	5
His or her physical features.			18	4
She or he is other-oriented.			14	3
Emotional support	45	17		
We care about each other.			94	16
He or she fills a void in my life.			24	4
Absence of conflicts	39	15		
We rarely argue/fight.			73	11
We're accepting of each other.			33	5
We're agreeable with one another.			27	4
Conflict resolution	16	6		
We resolve our conflicts.			100	6

Note: $N = 38$. The value listed under each dimension represents the percentage of the total sample, while the value listed for each higher order theme represents the percentage of individuals citing the particular dimension.

were linked with many examples of positive affect when describing one's best friend. Lower order themes included, "we like being partners," "we're excited about doing things together," "we get along well," and "she or he helps ease frustration in sports." An 11-year-old girl summed it up this way: "She's funny. She makes it more of a game for fun than a game for we gotta win kind of thing."

This sport friendship dimension was closely aligned with ones found in the nonsport friendship literature. For example, positive interactions have been subsumed under companionship and recreation (Parker & Asher, 1993), play/association (Berndt & Perry, 1986), or social contact (Newcomb & Bagwell, 1995), whereas our higher order theme of mutual liking/affection has often been regarded as a distinct friendship feature that characterizes children's positive relationships with one another (Furman & Bierman, 1983; Furman & Buhrmester, 1985; Newcomb & Bagwell, 1995). At this early stage of our research on conceptions of sport friendships, we believed there was merit in not combining companionship and pleasant play/association.

Self-Esteem Enhancement. Self-esteem enhancement was characterized as saying or doing things to boost one's feelings of self-worth. This dimension was verbalized by 87% of the study sample, and comprised the following higher order themes: (a) we positively reinforce each other; (b) she or he is accepting of my mistakes; (c) we respect each other; (d) she or he makes me feel good; (e) we say nice things to each other; and (f) he or she motivates me in sports. These higher order themes subsumed an acceptance among friends (i.e., accepting of my mistakes, we respect each other), as well as behaviors that specifically enhanced one's feelings of competence (e.g., we say nice things to each other, she or he makes me feel good). The "acceptance" higher order themes included such lower order themes as, "he or she is patient when I make mistakes," "he or she is not judgmental of me in sports," and "he or she has confidence in me in sports." Self-enhancing behaviors included, "she or he gets me pumped up," "he or she cheers me up," and "she or he positively reinforces me for doing sports well."

The friendship support of self-esteem enhancement has been prevalent in the developmental literature under the labels of ego reinforcement, esteem support, self-esteem enhancement, validation and caring, and enhancement of worth (Berndt & Perry, 1986; Furman & Buhrmester, 1985; Parker & Asher, 1993). However, unique findings emerged at the higher order level, with an emphasis on acceptance and self-enhancing behaviors while doing sports, watching one another play sports, and motivating each other. These results suggest that the social context of sport may provide opportunities for developing and strengthening friendship bonds via the important vehicle of self-esteem enhancing behaviors and attitudes.

Help and Guidance. Providing instrumental assistance and tangible support defined the help and guidance dimension that was mentioned by 79% of the sample. Higher order themes consisted of the following: (a) we help each other in sports; (b) we help each other to learn sport skills; (c) we help each other in general; and (d) we help each other with school. Three of these themes were informational, such as giving advice or guidance (i.e., we help each other in general; we help each other learn sport skills; and we help each other with school), while "we help each other in sports" was more instrumental, such as providing resources. For example, "we help each other in general" included lower order themes such as "he or she informs me on things," "she or he solves problems," and "she or he is someone I can seek advice from." A 10-year-old male participant provided a quotation for "we help each other learn sport skills": "When I can't do something very well, like hit the ball in baseball or something, he'll help me hit the ball. And he'll show me the right and wrong way to hit the ball." The higher order theme of "we help each other in sports" included lower order themes of "he or she does favors for me in sport," "she or he gives me a second chance to perform a skill," and "he or she is the first to help me in sports."

Help and guidance as a dimension of friendship support has been prevalent in the developmental literature, varying in labeling as tangible aid, instrumental help, advice and information, help and guidance, and cooperation (Furman, 1989; Furman & Buhrmester, 1985; Newcomb & Bagwell, 1995; Zarbatany et al., 1992). As with the self-esteem enhancement dimension, unique findings with help and guidance were found at the higher and lower order theme levels with numerous examples in the sport context given by respondents.

Prosocial Behavior. Prosocial behavior was defined as saying or doing things that conform to social convention and was cited by 76% of the youth who were interviewed. Higher order themes composing this dimension were the following: (a) we do nice things for each other; (b) he or she shares things; (c) she or he doesn't say negative things to me; and (d) she or he doesn't do mean things to me. These higher order themes, in contrast to the previously discussed help and guidance dimension, mostly revolved around nonsport contexts as reflected by the lower order themes (e.g., "she or he is thoughtful," "he or she lends me personal possessions," "he or she doesn't get me in trouble"). One of the few exceptions is exemplified in this quotation from an 8-year-old girl: "She shares with me . . . a lot of things . . . like the soccer ball, the basketball."

In the developmental psychology literature on peer relations, prosocial behavior has often been subsumed under helping behaviors or cooperation (Newcomb & Bagwell, 1995; Parker & Asher, 1993), but has also been included as a separate category of sharing (e.g., Bigelow et al., 1989; Zarbatany et al., 1992). The dimension of prosocial behavior found in this study, with its emphasis on sharing resources and behaving in ways that conform to social expectations, was kept separate from the more informational or instrumental forms of support such as the help and guidance dimension.

Intimacy. The intimacy dimension was defined as interactions or mutual feelings of a close personal nature. A total of 71% of the study sample discussed this friendship support in one or more ways. Higher order themes within this dimension included the following: (a) we disclose our thoughts/feelings to each other; (b) we feel comfortable with each other; (c) we understand each others' feelings/thoughts; (d) we trust each other; and (e) we have a bond with each other. This dimension clearly invoked a more abstract quality of friendship than previous dimensions such as prosocial behavior, companionship, and help and guidance.

A clearer understanding of some of the higher order themes is obtained from examination of the lower order themes used to derive a catch-all label. "We have a bond with each other" included such lower order themes as "we connect with each other," "we click with each other," and "it's an intangible feeling." The higher order theme of "we understand each other's feelings/thoughts" included examples such as "we know each other well," "we understand each other's feelings in sport," and "she or he acts the way I feel." Finally, lower order themes such as "we can talk about anything," and "he or she is easy to talk with" defined the higher order theme of "we feel comfortable with each other."

The friendship support of intimacy, closeness, intimacy potential, or intimate exchange has been a consistent finding in the friendship literature (Newcomb & Bagwell, 1995; Parker & Asher, 1993; Zarbatany et al., 1992). When we asked children to describe their relationship with a best sports friend, perceptions of a strong, emotional bond of caring and disclosure were also evident. These findings suggest that sport has the potential to maintain as well as provide opportunities for close, intimate friendships.

Loyalty. The loyalty dimension was defined as a sense of commitment to one another, or "being there" for each other, and was cited by 71% of the children and teenagers. Higher order themes producing this dimension included the following: (a) he or she sticks up for me; (b) we pick each other to do things; and (c) we can depend on each other. These themes were reflected by lower order themes such as "we don't let each other down," "she or he is there to back me up," and "he or she is the first person I pick to play with." The following quotation, from an 11-year-old female participant (the only participant to nominate an opposite-sex friend), falls within this dimension: "If he's team captain, he'll like pick me first, and some of the people thought that was crazy, picking me first.... You know, they got kind of upset."

Loyalty, reliable alliance, or faithfulness has been a consistent type of friendship support in the developmental psychology literature (see Newcomb & Bagwell, 1995). Along with intimacy, this theme characterizes a deep emotional bond, one of depending upon one another and the understanding that "I'll be there for you."

Things in Common. Things in common was defined as similarity of interests, activities, and values, and was cited by 63% of the sample. The higher order themes within this dimension were the following: (a) similar beliefs and activities; (b) we have a similar interest in sports; and (c) we have similar school ability/interests. The higher order theme of similar beliefs and activities included "we have common interests" and "we have the same values," and lower order themes for similar interest in sports included examples like "he or she is a good athlete," "someone to talk to about sports," and "we inform each other about our sport achievement." Specific quotations such as "We like doing the same things" and "We like to believe the same way" by a 16 year-old female participant exemplify the types of commonalities perceived by these individuals.

Things in common is comparable to relationship properties such as similarity and equality found in the developmental psychology literature (Newcomb & Bagwell, 1995). Similarity has typically referred to similarity in activities, interests, and values, as well as similarity in educational aspirations, self-concept, and physical attractiveness, whereas equality ensures a balanced relationship among friends (i.e., similar school ability, he or she is a good athlete). Our findings suggest that a best sports friend is not only one who is similar in his or her valuing of physical activities and physical abilities but also one who is similar in school ability and general values.

Attractive Personal Qualities. Positive personal characteristics or descriptors were discussed by 58% of the study sample. Attractive personal qualities included both physical and psychological characteristics: (a) I like her or his personality in general; (b) she or he has attractive personal attributes; (c) he or she gets along with my family; (d) his or her physical features; and (e) she or he is other-oriented. Physical features included raw data quotations such as liking a friend's hair or facial features, while attractive personal attributes included things such as, "he or she is an energetic person," "she or he is adventurous," and "he or she is more open-minded." Contrasting quotations that exemplify this friendship dimension include, "I would miss her long hair, she has really long hair; I would miss her eyes" (8-year-old girl) and, "She just watches out for people....She makes sure they don't get hurt. She doesn't like do really stupid stuff that could really easily get them hurt" (11-year-o1d girl).

The developmental literature has sometimes separately included friendship dimensions such as physical characteristics, admiration of physical traits, character admiration, and stimulation value (i.e., the extent that a friend is perceived as interesting and imaginative) (Bigelow et al., 1989; Furman & Bierman, 1983; Zarbatany et al., 1992). In other instances, "attractive personal qualities" has been subsumed under the similarity dimension as in a resemblance in physical attractiveness and personality (Newcomb & Bagwell, 1995). In either case, the existence of this dimension invokes a question of how it functions to facilitate or support a best friendship.

Emotional Support. Emotional support was defined as feelings or expressions of concern for one another, and was comprised of two higher order themes: (a) we care about each other, and (b) he or she fills a void in my life. This dimension was mentioned by about half the study sample (45%). The first higher order theme was characterized by lower order themes such as, "he or she looks out for me," "he or she is supportive," and "he or she takes care of me." The higher order theme of "she or he fills a void in my life" was exemplified by "It would be a harder life without him or her," and "I feel empty without her or him."

Emotional support has been frequently identified as a friendship dimension in the developmental psychology literature, although it has often been subsumed under loyalty and commitment, closeness, or nurturing (Bigelow et al., 1989; Furman & Buhrmester, 1985; Zarbatany et al., 1992). It is conceivable that emotional support, loyalty, and intimacy dimensions within our study are perceived similarly by respondents. Given the differences in underlying higher and lower order themes, however, our strategy was to keep these dimensions distinct at this stage of sport friendship research.

Absence of Conflicts. Refraining from arguments, fights, or judgmental attitudes defined the absence of conflicts dimension. This dimension was cited by 39% of the study sample and contained the following higher order themes: (a) we rarely argue/fight; (b) we're accepting of each other; and (c) we're agreeable with one another. Two short quotations exemplify this dimension: "We've never really got into an argument" (9 year-old boy) and, "We don't get mad at each other but we might disagree about a few things" (11 year-old boy). This dimension and the next one, conflict resolution, are discussed together.

Conflict Resolution. The conflict resolution dimension (mentioned by 16% of the sample) consisted of one higher order theme that could not be meaningfully combined with any others (we resolve our conflicts). This dimension was defined as getting over fights or arguments.

The issues of conflict and conflict management are prevalent in the literature on peer relations (Hartup, 1989; Newcomb & Bagwell, 1995). An age-related phenomenon has been suggested, with younger children believing that friendship and conflict are incompatible events, while older children and adolescents understand that friends can argue and still be friends (i.e., agree to disagree). The topic of conflict resolution is one that is of particular interest in the sport context, and is intimately related to contemporary moral development research (see Shields & Bredemeier, 1995, for a review).

Frequency Analysis of Positive Dimensions

The qualitative analysis provided rich responses from children and adolescents concerning their conceptions of friendship. To determine whether there were any gender or age similarities and differences in these conceptions, the percentage of boys and girls, as well as those who comprised the age groups of 8–9 (n = 8), 10–12 (n = 13), and 13–16 (n = 17), who cited the various dimensions were compared. These findings should be interpreted with some caution given the small numbers of male and female participants, as well as participants in each age group.

Approximately equal numbers of girls and boys mentioned 11 of the 12 conceptions of friendship (see table 44.2). The only conspicuous difference was in the dimension of emotional support, where 71% of females and 29% of males were quoted as saying something related to this area. The finding that emotional support distinguished males and females is consistent with previous research, but lack of differences on friendship conceptions such as

Table 44.2 Positive Friendship Dimensions by Gender

Dimension	Female (n = 19) %	Male (n = 19) %
Companionship	47	53
Pleasant play/association	50	50
Self-esteem enhancement	52	48
Help and guidance	50	50
Prosocial behavior	48	52
Intimacy	56	44
Loyalty	48	52
Having things in common	54	46
Attractive personal qualities	59	41
Emotional support	71	29
Absence of conflicts	47	53
Conflict resolution	50	50

Note. The value listed for females and males represents the percentage of those citing the friendship dimension.

intimacy and self-esteem enhancement were surprising because gender differences in these areas have also been documented (e.g., Belle, 1989b; Berndt & Perry, 1986; Furman & Buhrmester, 1985).

It is conceivable that contextualizing friendship conceptions to the sport domain minimized the emergence of gender differences. Our participants were all physically active and valued the importance of sport and physical activity. Because the sample was homogeneous in terms of activity level and value toward sport, conceptions of sport friendships were likely to be similar for both girls and boys. This possibility is substantiated by research conducted by Lever (1976, 1978) on gender differences in the way children play sports, and by Lewko and Ewing (1980), who compared low- and high-active boys and girls on significant others' influence.

Lever (1976, 1978) documented large differences between an activity-heterogeneous group of elementary-age boys and girls in size of play group, game complexity, player interdependence, and member role differentiation. These differences, Lever contended, carried implications for the development of social skills with peers, such as opportunities for boys to learn leadership skills and competitiveness, and girls to enhance their interpersonal communication and affective expression. Our sample of boys and girls, in contrast, were homogeneous with regard to activity involvement, types of sports, and importance of being actively involved in sports—perhaps contributing to the nonsignificant differences on the majority of friendship dimensions.

Lewko and Ewing (1980) divided girls and boys ages 9–11 years on extent of sport participation (i.e., years in sport) and examined gender by sport involvement differences on perceptions of parental, sibling, and peer influence on their sport involvement. They found much larger differences in perceived social influence between children who varied in activity level rather than gender. This suggests that activity level and value toward sport may help explain the minimal gender differences in conceptions of friendship found with our sample.

The frequency analysis for age resulted in some interesting findings (see table 44.3). First, similarities across age groups occurred for the dimensions of companionship, pleasant play/association, self-esteem enhancement, and help and guidance, which all recorded high percentages (range = 71–100%). Similarity also occurred for things in common, emotional support, absence of conflicts, and conflict resolution, with the latter three dimensions showing a smaller percentage of individuals (range = 12–47%). The lack of age-related differences on the conflict dimensions is contrary to some of the developmental research previously mentioned, and is likely due to the small sample size or the context in which these age-related findings were examined.

Table 44.3 Positive Friendship Dimensions by Age Group

	AGE GROUP		
Dimension	8–9 (n = 8) %	10–12 (n = 13) %	13–16 (n = 17) %
Companionship	88	100	94
Pleasant play/association	88	85	94
Self-esteem enhancement	75	92	88
Help and guidance	88	85	71
Prosocial behavior	100	92	53
Intimacy	38	69	88
Loyalty	75	85	59
Things in common	50	69	65
Attractive personal qualities	38	62	65
Emotional support	38	46	47
Absence of conflicts	50	38	35
Conflict resolution	25	15	12

Note. Values listed represent the percentage of participants within each age group citing the friendship dimension.

Age group differences emerged for the dimensions of prosocial behavior, intimacy, loyalty, and attractive personal qualities. Specifically, the two younger groups (8–9, 10–12) cited prosocial behavior and loyalty dimensions more frequently than the 13–16 year-olds, while the 10–12 and 13–16 year-olds recorded higher frequencies of attractive personal qualities. For intimacy, there was a progressive increase in percentage from younger to older age group.

Higher order themes of the prosocial behavior dimension represent overt behavioral characteristics that have been associated with younger as compared to older youth (see Newcomb & Bagwell, 1995). In contrast, older children and adolescents tend to describe their friendships in terms of psychological constructs such as intimacy, which was corroborated by our data. However, adolescents discussed loyalty as a friendship dimension less frequently than did the two younger age groups, a finding in opposition to previous developmental research. The qualities defining loyalty appear to portray overt characteristics of peer support in the sport setting, which may be a possible explanation for the higher percentage of younger children citing this dimension.

The dimension of attractive personal qualities was also cited more often by older children and adolescents. This was a function of the youngest group discussing physical characteristics (e.g., eye and hair color) while the older participants were attracted to personality attributes (e.g., "She is other-oriented"). Thus, the younger children identified more overt qualities, while older youth selected psychological characteristics in relation to attractive personal qualities. It is conceivable that the qualities cited by older children and adolescents may represent a form of "character admiration" that has been previously cited as a friendship dimension (Bigelow et al., 1989; Zarbatany et al., 1992).

Negative Dimensions of Friendship

The inductive analysis unveiled four negative dimensions of friendship discussed by 25 of the 38 youth (66%). These dimensions were labeled conflict, unattractive personal qualities, betrayal, and inaccessible. These dimensions comprised 9 higher order and 55 lower order themes. It should be noted that children and adolescents who disclosed negative sides of their friendship did so in a qualified manner; that is, negative events occurred sometimes or infrequently. After all, these were their best friendships. Moreover, 13 (34%) participants did not identify negative features about their friendship. Thus, the following discussion should be considered in this light. An individual not involved with the study was asked to replicate a portion of our analysis, and 71% agreement was obtained for matching lower to higher order themes.

Conflict. The dimension of conflict was defined as negative behaviors that cause disagreement, disrespect, or dissension between friends. Conflict was discussed by 16 of the 38 youth (42%), and included higher order themes of (a) verbal insults, (b) argumentation, (c) negative competitiveness, and (d) physical aggression. A quotation that depicts verbal insults was, "The only times that he says stuff that I don't like is when he's trying to make me mad. But I do that to him too . . . we like make each other mad on purpose a lot." Physical aggression was quoted by one boy as, "Sometimes he like jumps on me and stuff when I'm hurt or . . . he'll always like pick at me."

Unattractive Personal Qualities. This dimension was defined as undesirable personality or behavioral characteristics and was cited by 37% of the sample. It consisted of the following higher order themes: (a) negative characteristics, (b) different views, and (c) self-centered. Negative characteristics comprised such lower order themes as "she's afraid of things," "she's indecisive," and "she can be moody." The higher order theme of self-centered was concentrated on personal qualities of a more specific nature: "acts bossy," "he's egotistical," "he's immature," and "he thinks he's cool." Finally, the higher order theme of different views comprised qualities that suggested differences between the two friends such as "she thinks the opposite of me," "we have different opinions," and "he cares less about schoolwork than I do."

Betrayal. Betrayal was defined as actions of disloyalty or insensitivity on the part of the friend, and was cited by 16% of the interviewees. Betrayal consisted of one higher order theme that subsumed lower order entries, such as "she says she'll stop being my friend," "he pays more attention to another friend," "he tells others personal information about me," and "he'll ignore me." According to an 11-year-old girl, "Once in a while he'll just kind of like ignore me if he's . . . with some of his other friends." A 12-year-old boy put it this way; "Sometimes he goes off and plays with different people, and I ask him to play, and he goes, 'No, I don't want to,' and he goes and plays with somebody else."

Inaccessible. This dimension and higher order theme was cited by 3 participants, and was defined as infrequent opportunities to interact together. Three lower order themes defined inaccessible: "we don't play much together," "she has friends other than me," and "he's away a lot." An 11-year-old girl said, "We don't play much together, though, because she has kind of her group of friends, and I kind of have my group."

According to Newcomb and Bagwell (1995), the study of peer relations has been dominated by examination of the positive side of friendship. However, empirical data from school (e.g., Hartup, 1989; Parker & Asher, 1993; Shantz & Hobart, 1989) and sport contexts (Evans & Roberts, 1987; Kunesh et al., 1992; Weiss, 1991), demonstrate that friendships can have their down side in the form of negative competition, verbal and physical aggression, disloyalty, and unfair play. These areas revolve around the two dimensions of conflict and betrayal. These negative friendship aspects have been discussed in the peer relations literature (e.g., Parker & Asher, 1993), but mostly as they relate to interactions among peers who *are not* best friends (e.g., Hartup, 1989). As Furman and Buhrmester (1985) point out, frequent conflicts among good friends would most likely result in termination of such a friendship. Negative interactions among peers has been generally explored in sport psychology from a moral development perspective (see Shields & Bredemeier, 1995), but should be the focus of future research to determine their effects on psychosocial development and adjustment.

Friendship Expectations

One of the questions posed in the interview was, "Imagine that you're playing sports with your best friend, [friend's name]. What kinds of things would you like her or him to say or do?" This line of questioning was adopted from the study by Zarbatany et al. (1992) who examined whether expectations children had of their friendships varied depending upon the social context. Our intent was to determine whether youths' *expectations* of their best sport friendship were synonymous with or diverged from the positive friendship dimensions extracted from the first several interview questions and discussed in detail previously.

Children readily discussed expectancies of their best sport friendship. This was reflected by the extraction of raw data quotations from 30 of the 38 (79%) participants that resulted in 64 lower order themes, 14 higher order themes, and 7 dimensions. The percentage of youth who discussed each of the particular dimensions is considerably smaller than that for positive friendship dimensions, suggesting that they are relatively happy with their best sport friendships the way they are. Nevertheless, children identified characteristics that they would like to see more often in their friends. The dimensions of friendship expectations were labeled positive reinforcement/encouragement, attractive personal qualities, prosocial behavior, loyalty, instrumental guidance, emotional support, and spend time together. These dimensions are very similar to the dimensions or higher order themes of positive friendship conception.

Summary and Conclusions

This study extends previous research on children's conceptions of friendships. Specifically, we extended research conducted within school contexts to the context of sport by asking children to identify and describe their best sports friendship. Most of the positive friendship dimensions that emerged through inductive analysis were similar to those cited in the developmental literature. However, many of the underlying higher and lower order themes that composed these dimensions were unique to the physical domain. The quantity and diversity of responses suggests that the sport domain is intimately linked to the development, maintenance, and enhancement of peer relationships. Future research is needed to examine these critical linkages.

Moreover, we extended previous research by examining negative friendship dimensions as well as children's expectations of their best sport friendships. These data provided additional insight into our understanding of children's conceptions of friendship. Some age-related trends were uncovered in the frequency analysis of positive friendship dimensions. These data support previous research conducted in the academic domain and point to future research directions that can more precisely determine the mechanisms underlying these trends. Few gender differences were found on friendship dimensions, which does not support previous research. It is possible that few differences emerged because we included activity homogenous boys and girls who were prompted for their perceptions of peer relations in the sport domain. Future research is warranted to continue to explore age and gender trends in friendship dimensions.

Based on the findings of the present study and the abundance of research pointing to the importance of peer relations in other achievement domains, it is clear that the relation between perceptions of peer acceptance and psychosocial development has been ignored long enough. From both theoretical and practical perspectives, this is an area of research that merits our future attention as we explore the influence of all significant others on children's social and psychological development through sport and physical activity participation. The emotional experiences associated with friendship quality can be encapsulated in the words of a 9-year-old female: "1 would like her to, like, pass to me in a game and stuff. Usually no one passes.... I'm like just one acre of land and there's like a million acres of land left, and I feel really small sometimes." Sport psychologists and educators should certainly be able to empathize with this young girl's sentiments, but most importantly, they should be in a position to make a difference in children's and teenagers' sport experiences by implementing strategies to enhance sport-specific peer relationships!

This study represents the first phase of a series of interrelated investigations that we hope will contribute to the development and refinement of current theoretical models within sport psychology that focus upon the role of social influences on self-perceptions, affect, and motivation in youth (Gould, 1996; Weiss & Bredemeier, 1983). Having identified dimensions of friendship support in the physical domain, our subsequent research phases will involve: (a) developing and validating measurement instruments; (b) examining relationships among salient theoretical constructs such as friendship quality, self-perceptions, and motivated behavior in sport; and (c) employing intervention techniques to enhance friendship quality in the physical activity setting. In embracing the steps of descriptive to correlational to experimental research, we believe that we can contribute to a further understanding and explanation of peer relationship processes in the physical domain.

References

Asher, S.R., & Coie, J.D. (Eds.) (1990). *Peer rejection in childhood.* Cambridge: Cambridge University Press.

Backstrom, C.H., & Hursh-Cesar, G. (1981). *Survey research.* New York: Wiley.

Belle, D. (Ed.) (1989a). *Children's social networks and social supports.* New York: Wiley.

Belle, D. (1989b). Gender differences in children's social networks and supports. In D. Belle (Ed.), *Children's social networks and social supports* (pp. 173–190). New York: Wiley.

Berndt, T.J. (1989). Obtaining support from friends during childhood and adolescence. In D. Belle (Ed.), *Children's social networks and social supports* (pp. 308–331). New York: Wiley.

Berndt, T.J., & Ladd, G.W. (Eds.) (1989). *Peer relationships in child development.* New York: Wiley.

Berndt, T.J., & Perry, B. (1986). Children's perceptions of friendships as supportive relationships. *Developmental Psychology,* 5, 640–648.

Bigelow, B.J., Lewko, J.H., & Salhani, L. (1989). Sport-involved children's friendship expectations. *Journal of Sport and Exercise Psychology,* 11, 152–160.

Black, S.J., & Weiss, M.R. (1992). The relationship among perceived coaching behaviors, perceptions of ability, and motivation in competitive age group swimmers. *Journal of Sport & Exercise Psychology,* 14, 309–325.

Brustad, R.J. (1993). Who will go out and play? Parental and psychological influences on children's attraction to physical activity. *Pediatric Exercise Science,* 5, 210–223.

Brustad, R.J. (1996). Parental and peer influence on children's psychological development through sport. In F.L. Smoll & R.E. Smith (Eds.), *Children and youth in sport: A biopsychosocial perspective* (pp. 112–124). Madison, WI: Brown & Benchmark.

Buchanan, H.T., Blankenbaker, J., & Cotten, D. (1976). Academic and athletic ability as popularity factors in elementary school children. *Research Quarterly*, 47, 320–325.

Bukowski, W.M., & Hoza, B. (1989). Popularity and friendship: Issues in theory, measurement, and outcome. In T.J. Berndt & G.W. Ladd (Eds.), *Peer relationships in child development* (pp. 15–45). New York: Wiley.

Chase, M.A., & Dummer, G.M. (1992). The role of sports as a social status determinant for children. *Research Quarterly for Exercise and Sport*, 63, 418–424.

Cooley, C.H. (1902). *Human nature and the social order.* New York: Scribner.

Dempsey, J.M., Kimiecik, J.C., & Horn, T.S. (1993). Parental influence on children's moderate to vigorous physical activity participation: An expectancy-value approach. *Pediatric Exercise Science,* 5, 151–167.

Duda, J.L., & Hom, H. (1993). Interdependencies between the perceived and self-reported goal orientations of young athletes and their parents. *Pediatric Exercise Science,* 5, 234–241.

Duncan, S.C. (1993). The role of cognitive appraisal and friendship provisions in adolescents' affect and motivation toward activity in physical education. *Research Quarterly for Exercise and Sport,* 64, 314–323.

Eitzen, D.S. (1975). Athletics in the status system of male adolescents: A replication of Coleman's The Adolescent Society. *Adolescence,* 10, 267–276.

Erlandson, D.A., Harris, E.L., Skipper, B.L., & Allen, S.D. (1993). *Doing naturalistic inquiry: A guide to methods.* Newbury Park: Sage.

Evans, J., & Roberts, G.C. (1987). Physical competence and the development of children's peer relations. *Quest,* 39, 23–35.

Feiring, C., & Lewis, M. (1989). The social networks of girls and boys from early through middle childhood. In D. Belle (Ed.), *Children's social networks and social supports* (pp. 119–150). New York: Wiley.

Feltz, D.L. (1978). Athletics in the status system of female adolescents. *Review of Sport and Leisure*, 3, 98–108.

Furman, W. (1989). The development of children's social networks. In D. Belle (Ed.), *Children's social networks and social supports* (pp. 151–172). New York: Wiley.

Furman, W., & Bierman, K.L. (1983). Developmental changes in young children's conceptions of friendship. *Child Development,* 54, 549–556.

Furman, W., & Buhrmester, D. (1985). Children's perceptions of the personal relationships in their social networks. *Developmental Psychology,* 21, 1016–1024.

Gould, D. (1996). Sport psychology: Future directions in youth sport research. In F.L. Smoll & R.E. Smith (Eds.), *Children and youth in sport: A biopsychosocial perspective* (pp. 405–422). Madison, WI: Brown & Benchmark.

Gould, D., Eklund, R.C., & Jackson, S.A. (1992). 1988 U.S. Olympic wrestling excellence: I. Mental preparation, precompetitive cognition, and affect. *The Sport Psychologist,* 6, 358–382.

Hartup, W.W. (1989). Behavioral manifestations of children's friendships. In T.J. Berndt & G.W. Ladd (Eds.), *Peer relationships in child development* (pp. 46–70). New York: Wiley.

Hartup, W.W. (1996). The company they keep: Friendships and their developmental significance. *Child Development,* 67, 1–13.

Horn, T.S. (1985). Coaches' feedback and changes in children's perceptions of their physical competence. *Journal of Educational Psychology,* 77, 174–186.

Horn, T.S., Glenn, S.D., & Wentzell, A.B. (1993). Sources of information underlying personal ability judgments in high school athletes. *Pediatric Exercise Science,* 5, 263–274.

Horn, T.S., & Hasbrook, C.A. (1986). Informational components influencing children's perceptions of their physical competence. In M.R. Weiss & D. Gould (Eds.), *Sport for children and youths* (pp. 81–88). Champaign, IL: Human Kinetics.

Horn, T.S., & Weiss, M.R. (1991). A developmental analysis of children's self-ability judgments in the physical domain. *Pediatric Exercise Science,* 3, 310–326.

Kane, M.J. (1988). The female athletic role as a status determinant within the social system of high school adolescents. *Adolescence,* 23, 253–264.

Kunesh, M.A., Hasbrook, C.A., & Lewthwaite, R. (1992). Physical activity socialization: Peer interactions and affective responses among a sample of sixth grade girls. *Sociology of Sport Journal,* 9, 385–396.

Lever, J. (1976). Sex differences in the games children play. *Social Problems*, 23, 478–487.

Lever, J. (1978). Sex differences in the complexity of children's play and games. *American Sociological Review,* 43, 471–483.

Lewko, J.H., & Ewing, M.E. (1980). Sex differences and parental influence in sport involvement of children. *Journal of Sport Psychology,* 2, 62–68.

Newcomb, A.F., & Bagwell, C.L. (1995). Children's friendship relations: A meta-analytic review. *Psychological Bulletin,* 117, 306–347.

Parker, J.G., & Asher, S.R. (1993). Friendship and friendship quality in middle childhood: Links with peer group acceptance and feelings of loneliness and social dissatisfaction. *Developmental Psychology,* 29, 611–621.

Patton, M.Q. (1990). *Qualitative evaluation and research methods.* Newbury Park, CA: Sage.

Scanlan, T.K., Carpenter, P.J., Lobel, M., & Simons, J.P. (1993). Sources of enjoyment for youth sport athletes. *Pediatric Exercise Science,* 5, 275–285.

Scanlan, T.K., Stein, G.L., & Ravizza, K. (1989). An in-depth study of former elite figure skaters: II. Sources of enjoyment. *Journal of Sport & Exercise Psychology,* 11, 65–83.

Shantz, C.U., & Hobart, C.J. (1989). Social conflict and development: Peers and siblings. In T.J. Berndt & G.W. Ladd (Eds.), *Peer relationships in child development* (pp. 71–94). New York: Wiley.

Shields, D.L.L., & Bredemeier, B.J.L. (1995). *Character development and physical activity.* Champaign, IL: Human Kinetics.

Smoll, F.L., Smith, R.E., Barnett, N.P., & Everett, J.J. (1993). Enhancement of children's self-esteem through social support training for youth sport coaches. *Journal of Applied Psychology,* 78, 602–610.

Weiss, M.R. (1987). Self-esteem and achievement in children's sport and physical activity. In D. Gould & M.R. Weiss (Eds.), *Advances in pediatric sport sciences: Vol. 2. Behavioral issues* (pp. 87–119). Champaign, IL: Human Kinetics.

Weiss, M.R. (1991). Psychological skill development in children and youth. *The Sport Psychologist,* 5, 335–354.

Weiss, M.R. (1993). Psychological effects of intensive sport participation children and youth: Self-esteem and motivation. In B.R. Cahill & A.J. Pearl (Eds.), *Intensive participation in children's sports* (pp. 39–69). Champaign, 1L: Human Kinetics.

Weiss, M.R. (1995). Children in sport: An educational model. In S.M. Murphy (Ed.), *Sport psychology interventions* (pp. 39–69). Champaign, IL: Human Kinetics.

Weiss, M.R., Barber, H., Sisley, B.L., & Ebbeck, V. (1991). Developing competence and confidence in novice female coaches: II. Perceptions of ability and affective experiences following a season-long coaching internship. *Journal of Sport & Exercise Psychology,* 13, 336–363.

Weiss, M.R., & Bredemeier, B.J. (1983). Developmental sport psychology: A theoretical perspective for studying children in sport. *Journal of Sport Psychology,* 5, 216–230.

Weiss, M.R., & Chaumeton, N. (1992). Motivational orientations in sport. In T.S. Horn (Ed.), *Advances in Sport Psychology* (pp. 61–99). Champaign, IL: Human Kinetics.

Weiss, M.R., & Duncan, S.C. (1992). The relationship between physical competence and peer acceptance in the context of children's sports participation. *Journal of Sport & Exercise Psychology,* 14, 177–191.

Weiss, M.R., & Ebbeck, V. (1996). Self-esteem and perceptions of competence in youth sport: Theory, research, and enhancement strategies. In O. Bar-Or (Ed.), *Encyclopaedia of sports medicine. Vol. 5: The child and adolescent athlete* (pp. 364–382). Oxford: Blackwell Scientific.

Wiggins, D.K. (1996). A history of highly competitive sport for American children. In F.L. Smoll & R.E. Smith (Eds.), *Children and youth in sport: A biopsychosocial perspective* (pp. 15–30). Madison, WI: Brown & Benchmark.

Zarbatany, L., Ghesquiere, K., & Mohr, K. (1992). A context perspective on early adolescents' friendship expectations. *Journal of Early Adolescence,* 12, 111–126.

PART VIII

Understanding Professional Issues

Professional issues are critical to any developing academic organization. Three of the readings in part VIII are from past presidents of the Association for the Advancement of Applied Sport Psychology (AAASP) formed in 1986. Four of the readings discuss certification issues and three discuss the importance of applied research methodologies. The issue of certification threatened to divide the field in the late 1980s and early 1990s, and some people are still sensitive to these issues. These readings impelled us to give additional thought to professional issues and to see alternative viewpoints. These views enabled the leadership of AAASP to appease both those members from psychology and those from physical education–related disciplines. This understanding of others' views has enabled the membership, for the most part, to stick together and has facilitated the consistent growth of the organization.

Rainer Martens, the keynote speaker at the first AAASP Conference, focuses on the conflict between academic and practicing sport psychology, along with suggested methods for studying the phenomena of the field. His discontent with the direction of the field of sport psychology was evident. This reading encouraged sport psychology researchers to rethink how knowledge can be obtained through experiential, not only experimental, methods.

John Silva, the founding president of AAASP, focuses on major issues he perceived had limited the progress of AAASP over the years: the training of graduate students, the accreditation of graduate programs, the job market, and the establishment of systematic educational outreach programs.

In his presidential address, Bob Weinberg brought out the critical issues facing the young AAASP organization and the anticipated challenges. These critical issues included certification, applied research, professional practice, and interdisciplinary cooperation.

In his AAASP keynote address, Carron attempted to introduce a conceptual framework for AAASP in which research and theory, application and intervention, and quality of life should be regarded as equal, compatible, complementary, and mutually interdependent elements in a continuous cycle of professional activity.

Petitpas, Brewer, Rivera, and Van Raalte surveyed the ethical beliefs and behaviors of AAASP members. Most were in line with the APA ethical standards. Since the report of these survey results, ethical issues have remained at the forefront of AAASP concerns.

Finally, Zizzi, Zaichkowsky, and Perna discussed several issues surrounding the certification process, how sport psychology consultants should be trained, and who should provide those services. This reading addresses the issues by providing the background to AAASP certification, exploring the criticism of it, and promoting future improvements to this certification.

Despite the professional concerns, it is important to note that, over the years, AAASP has developed into the premier academic and professional organization of applied sport psychology.

45 Science, Knowledge, and Sport Psychology

RAINER MARTENS
University of Illinois

This reading is from a paper presented at the first annual meeting of the Association for the Advancement of Applied Sport Psychology (AAASP). The major sport psychology organization at the time was the North American Society for the Psychology of Sport and Physical Activity (NASPSPA). NASPSPA had taken a stance against encouraging applied research to be presented at their conference. Thus, most of the professionals in this new AAASP organization were applied researchers. The conflict between academic sport psychology and practicing sport psychology was at its peak. Many thought that academic sport psychology and practicing sport psychology were mutually exclusive.

Rainer Martens, a respected researcher with an extensive publication record, expressed his discontent with the direction of the field of sport psychology. Specifically he was dissatisfied with the methods of studying the phenomena of the field. He advocated a heuristic paradigm for sport psychology, emphasizing ideographic, introspective, and field study methodologies. He seemed less than optimistic about the future direction of the field in using these three methodologies, mostly because the "gatekeepers of knowledge" (the journal editors) tend to subscribe to orthodox scientific methods that are limited due to their reductionist approach to studying human behavior.

This reading made sport psychology researchers rethink how knowledge can be obtained through experiential, not only experimental, methods. It is interesting to note that the new AAASP organization flourished from that stage onward, expanding to become the largest sport psychology organization.

Two sport psychologies have emerged—academic sport psychology and practicing sport psychology—which presently are on diverging courses because of an unjustified belief in orthodox science as the primary source of knowledge. To support this contention, the basic assumptions of orthodox science are examined, with the doctrine of objectivity singled out as fallacious and especially harmful in that it attempts to remove the person from the process of knowing. Polanyi's (1958) heuristic philosophy of knowledge, which places humans in the center of the process of knowing, is recommended as an alternative approach for the study of human behavior. This alternative approach reveals the inadequacy of the laboratory experiment which has been invented primarily to pursue the doctrine of objectivity. Next, the Degrees of Knowledge theory is proposed as an alternative way to view the reliability of knowledge. This view, within the heuristic paradigm, places great significance on experiential knowledge. Recommendations for an improved science of human behavior emphasizes the idiographic approach, introspective methods, and field studies. Also, recommendations are made for a more progressive approach to applied research, and the significance of knowledge synthesis from applied research. The two sport psychologies will converge when orthodox science and the doctrine of objectivity are replaced with the heuristic paradigm and its emphasis on experiential knowledge.

For about 15 years I studied sport psychology using the methods of science that had been taught to me in graduate school. As the years passed I became increasingly discontent with these methods, not because of lack of interest in the phenomena I was studying, for I am today even more fascinated with the subject matter of sport psychology. Instead, I became dissatisfied with the *methods* for studying the phenomena of our field, but I did not fully understand why. I could not explain it intellectually, but emotionally these methods just did not "seem right" for wanting to truly understand human behavior.

Over the years I have sought intellectual answers regarding this emotional discontent. What did not seem right, I discovered, went to the very core of the scientific enterprise. It has led me to a new, evolving philosophy of science. The purpose of this paper is to present this philosophy of science and to express the reasons for my change in views about the scientific method of acquiring knowledge about human behavior.

As I look back, I now realize how inadequate my knowledge of the philosophical underpinnings of the scientific method were. I briefly studied them, accepted them, and applied them in my sport psychology research. I suspect I was no different from many other sport psychologists. Recently, though, I have revisited the basic assumptions upon which the scientific method is based. In this paper I will question several of these assumptions and show why one—the objectivity of knowledge assumption—is false, and that the effects this assumption has had on the behavioral sciences have been harmful.

Adapted, by permission, from R. Martens, 1987, "Science, knowledge, and sport psychology," *The Sport Psychologist* 1: 29-55.

This leads me to an alternative view of what knowledge is and some ideas for a better scientific paradigm for the study of human behavior. Throughout this paper I attempt to relate my views to current events in sport psychology.

Two Sport Psychologies

Sport psychologists rightfully take pride in the development of their field. The quality of research has improved, at least by current standards of excellence, and more recently we have witnessed a tremendous increase in the sports public's interest in applied sport psychology. Yet, peculiarly, these two elements of sport psychology—the research and the practice—are diverging rather than converging, an anomaly of serious consequences.

I have come to know quite intimately two very different sport psychologies—what I term *academic sport psychology* and *practicing sport psychology*. They have caused me to lead two very different lives. One is academic, scientific, and abstract; the other practical, applied and, as seen by some, mystical. Why are these two sport psychologies on diverging courses? The answer, I contend, lies in sport psychologists' perceptions of what constitutes legitimate knowledge.

In the early 1960s Bruce Ogilvie attracted considerable attention in North America for his pioneering work in offering clinical services to athletes with psychological problems and for his observations about these problems. He did so not because there was tremendous academic interest in the field, but because he was asked to help coaches and athletes with the practical psychological problems that athletes encounter. Thus began the modem era of practicing sport psychology in North America.

In the mid-1960s several young physical educators, including myself, exhumed a sport psychology that Coleman Griffith had fathered at the University of Illinois in the 1920s. We began by studying the discipline of social psychology for the purpose of applying the theory and methods of this field to sport.

I recall well how we were enraptured with the American social psychological experimental paradigm, devoured the theories of the day, and charged into our laboratories to lift the field of sport psychology to a true science. With timers, sudorimeters, contrived motor tasks, and of course our smocks, we created unique, controlled, and artificial environments to observe people compete, imitate, be reinforced, cheat, and cope with stress. (We never once thought that these studies might in turn produce artificial, contrived behavior unique to the environment we created.) With strong convictions based on our ability to use the scientific method, we saw ourselves as the new generation of sport psychologists who were going to build a solid foundation of scientific facts for the field of sport psychology. Thus began the modem era of the academic discipline of sport psychology in North America.

Today academic sport psychology is characterized by its concern with applying the rules of science in a way considered acceptable among behavioral researchers. I will call it *orthodox* science, what Thomas Kuhn (1962) calls normal science. It embraces the accepted scientific paradigm—a set of generally accepted assumptions and rules regarding the nature of problems in a given discipline and the appropriate means for addressing them. It focuses on *nomothetic research,* comparing differences between groups to arrive at generalizations or abstractions about people. It rarely focuses on *idiographic methods,* the in-depth study of one person. It is the type of research that is reported in the *Journal of Sport Psychology* exclusively, and it is the type of activity that young sport psychologists must conduct to survive in academe today. It has been likened to a game—the game of science—and if you don't play by the rules, you are out. And who are the referees? The editors and editorial board members of the scholarly journals in the field, and the organizers of conferences who select the papers to be presented.

So this was my first life, an academic sport psychologist. My second life was as a practicing sport psychologist with the U.S. Ski Team. Practicing sport psychology is characterized by its concern with helping athletes and coaches, and with the need to focus on the whole person in order to do so. Its emphasis is not on knowledge gained from the experimental method, but on knowledge gained from any method that helps to understand the person. Most often these are experiential methods. These experiential methods, I contend, may also be scientific, and they include case studies, introspectionism, observation, and clinical experience.

This second life as a practicing sport psychologist led me and several excellent doctoral students to develop a program that I call Psychological Skills Training, or PST. The focus of PST is on helping athletes learn such psychological skills as emotional control, especially for anxiety and anger, attentional skills, goal-setting skills, and interpersonal skills. The knowledge base we used for developing the PST program originated from our collective experience, the experience shared by coaches, athletes, and fellow sport psychologists, and then later from field research my students conducted. It also was developed with an awareness of the existing scientific research in sport psychology, and in social and clinical psychology.

I consider my second life as a practicing sport psychologist to have been far more productive, not because I got a special satisfaction from helping people directly, although it is very satisfying, but because I gained more knowledge by practicing sport psychology than by using the orthodox scientific method to study sport psychology.

This dual life as an academic and practicing sport psychologist required that I live by two mutually exclusive rules and speak two different languages. It struck me, though, that this was not entirely the way it should be. Indeed, I believe it is imperative that these two sport psychologies marry, and I am quite certain they will. *The major reason they have not is the unjustified belief in orthodox science as the only source of true knowledge.*

I shall attempt to justify this statement in the following sections of this paper, and then I will close by once again looking at the schism between academic and practicing sport psychology. But first let me declare that I am not anti-science. I am pro-science—very pro-science. I simply contend that the methods of orthodox science are too limited for the study of human behavior. Thus I shall go beyond mere criticism of orthodox science and outline some alternatives which, in my opinion, will make for a better behavioral science in general and sport psychology in particular.

Axioms and Conceptions of Orthodox Science

In this section I briefly review some of the assumptions of orthodox science as it is practiced today. According to Lachman (1960, p. 13), "Science refers primarily to those systematically organized bodies of accumulated knowledge concerning the universe which have been derived exclusively through techniques of *objective observation*" (my emphasis). The scientist's objective is to explain these phenomena. Their explanations are to be accurate and objective descriptions of antecedent conditions and specifications of the intermediate (directly unobservable) influences that operate between the observable antecedent conditions and the observable subsequent phenomena.

Orthodox science holds that we can observe, know, and understand the universe in which we live; that by means of objective, inductive-empirical methods of science, we can fully comprehend the natural influences in our universe. The six general steps of the scientific method are these:

1. Formulation of specific hypotheses or specific questions for investigation;
2. Design of the investigation;
3. Accumulation of the data;
4. Classification of the data;
5. Development of generalizations;
6. Verification of the results, both the data and generalizations.

The goal of orthodox science is not the mere accumulation of highly precise and specific data, although this is a necessary step, but rather the development of generalizations. Thus the building of theory is the scientist's ultimate objective.

The scientific method, as it has evolved over the past 300 years, is based on a number of fundamental axioms and operating conceptions. Table 45.1 contains the basic axioms of science, and the basic operating conceptions of science are summarized in table 45.2.

Each time we use the orthodox scientific method to study the phenomena of sport psychology, we implicitly accept these axioms and conceptions of science. Viewed from the other end, it is these axioms and conceptions which determine the methods we use that are considered to be "good science." Do you understand the full meaning of these axioms and conceptions? Do you agree with all of them? If you disagree with any, what are the implications for your use of the scientific method?

I agree with all of the axioms in table 45.1 except determinism and empiricism. With regard to human behavior, I believe most events are determined or caused, but I also believe some events are random and thus unpredictable. What this means to me is that the study of human behavior cannot be an exact science; at best we will be able only to understand and predict behavior imperfectly.

Nor can I subscribe to the axiom of empiricism. How we come to know our world is a much more complex and involved process than the simple view expressed by the doctrine of empiricism. I shall develop this position much more fully later in this paper.

I also question several of the conceptions of science in table 45.2, especially the conception of objectivity. Science at its best has been likened to a firm but gentle hand

Table 45.1 Fundamental Axioms of Science

Axiom	Scientists' belief
Reality of space	Belief that space is real
Reality of time	Belief that time is real
Reality of matter	Belief that matter is real
Quantifiability of matter	What exists, exists in some amount; what exists, and even relationships between existing phenomena, are amenable to observation and measurement
Consistency in the university	The universe is organized in an orderly manner; there is regularity, constancy, consistency, and uniformity in the operation of the universe
Intelligibility of the universe of mankind	Science holds that we can observe, know, and understand the universe in which we live
Determinism	All events are determined or caused
Empiricism	Knowing is the result of first-hand, direct original observation

Derived from Lachman (1960).

Table 45.2 Operating Conceptions of Science

Concept	Scientists' belief
Conception of objectivity	Scientists must remain impersonal, impartial, and detached in making observations and in interpreting data; the scientists must maintain a disinterested attitude
Conception of amorality	Science is not moral or immortal, it is amoral
Conception of caution	Scientsist must maintain meticulous caution and painstaking vigilance in their methods
Conception of skepticism	Scientists reject the notion of absolutism; scientists refuse to acknowledge authoritarianism or dogmatism as a source of knowledge; even the data of science are viewed as tentative
Conception of theory construction and utilization	Science strives to build and test theory
Conception of parsimony	Science should be conservative in stating the implications of its data; the data should be inerpreted in the simplist, most succinct form possible
Conception of reductionism	Science strives to reduce specific data to succinct statements of consistency; ultimately, reductionism demands that generalizations be specified in terms of precise mathematical formulae

Derived from Lachman (1960).

that holds a butterfly without crushing it. For the physical sciences, orthodox science has elegantly caressed many butterflies, but for the study of human behavior it has nearly annihilated the species. The major reason for this is our dogmatic belief in the concept of scientific objectivity. In the following section of this paper I shall argue that the conception of objectivity is fallacious and that it calls into question all of orthodox science when studying human behavior.

Conception of Objectivity

This concept or doctrine seems on the surface to be highly desirable and beyond question. Scientists' measurements and statements should be free of bias and extraneous influence. Their statements should be candid reflections of the data. This is the only way to true, objective knowledge. Of course, all scientists recognize that this is an ideal and that no one is ever completely free from bias. The scientist, though, works hard at being aware of and attempting to control for the contamination of facts, or inferences derived from personal bias. To meet the objective of objectivity, scientists' observations are checked with instruments and their theories are checked by several investigators independently.

From Bacon to Kuhn

When the scientific method was first formulated, objectivity, according to Francis Bacon and his inductionist friends, was possible because nature's laws were absolute and clear. Consequently human reason could discover these laws as long as scientists observed things clearly. Scientists' biases did not make any difference because nature's laws were impervious to influence by humankind. However, this view was seriously challenged by the emergence of the theory of relativity and the quantum theory, which showed that nature's laws were not impervious to influence by humankind. Instead the way the world is depends greatly upon how we perceive it. In science this means the laws discovered through research are entirely dependent upon the scientific paradigm that currently influences the perceptions of scientists. This challenge to the principle of objectivity sent tremors of uncertainty throughout the scientific community because it questioned the entire scientific enterprise.

Karl Popper (1972), an Austrian-born philosopher, rescued the orthodox scientific method by reformulating the doctrine of objectivity to mean that objectivity is possible because of science's willingness to test anew even the most accepted theory. This is accomplished, according to Popper, not by proving theories true but by proving them false. This view had great influence on orthodox science and continues to be widely espoused today..

Along came Thomas Kuhn, a historian of science, who observed in *The Structure of Scientific Revolutions* (1962) that science does not really practice what it preaches about proving theories false. In reality theories are difficult to prove false, primarily because any one experiment involves a range of possible errors, and so there is always room to question the validity of the experiment rather than the validity of the theory. Thus Kuhn teaches us that the falsifiablity of theory is not a standard that assures objectivity. In fact, we see that the very thing we believe so fundamental to the practice of science—the objectivity of knowledge—does not exist at all. Briggs and Peat (1984) comment on Kuhn's observations:

> If Kuhn's analysis is true, it also demolishes one of the primary underpinnings of the scientific method. The whole idea of a scientific experiment rests on the assumption that the observer can be essentially separate from his experimental apparatus and that the apparatus "tests" the theory. Kuhn shows that the observer, his theory, and his apparatus are all essentially expressions of a point of view—and the results of the experimental test must be expressions of that point of view as well. (pp. 32–33)

Polanyi on Objectivity

The ideal of objective knowledge is also rejected by Michael Polanyi in his magnum opus, *Personal Knowledge* (1958). More than any other philosopher of science, Polanyi has identified the fatal error of adopting orthodox science as it has developed in the physical sciences for the study of human behavior. "I start by rejecting the ideal of scientific detachment," writes Polanyi. "In the exact sciences, this false ideal is perhaps harmless, for it is in fact disregarded there by scientists. But . . . it exercises a destructive influence in biology, psychology and sociology and falsifies our whole outlook far beyond the domain of science" (p. vii).

In *Personal Knowledge*, Polanyi provides overwhelming evidence, much of it from the physical sciences, demonstrating that this is not the way science really works. His book convincingly ousts three centuries of epistemology that was built upon a structure of knowledge in which humans were not part of the knowledge process. As we all know, at every step of the scientific method are personal judgments that demand insight and understanding. A good hypothesis, for example, is more a creative act and more an art than it is a formalized procedure defined by a set of rules.

More Evidence

In a provocative work titled *Scientist as Subject,* Michael Mahoney, a clinical and sport psychologist (1976), presents evidence that scientists are a long way from being value-free, objective, or neutral about the phenomena they study. Instead, scientists are often extremely biased, less objective than other members of society, and not as honest as we would assume. According to Mahoney, it is a psychological imperative that we begin to study the behavior of scientists. Quite amazingly, he observes we have studied about every known phenomenon on this earth, and yet rarely studied how the scientist goes about doing science!

Significance of the Implausibility of the Doctrine of Objectivity

From the analyses of several scholars, from observation of what scientists actually do, and from logical reasoning, the case against the doctrine of objectivity is overwhelming. It is an unmet assumption of science. But can this ideal of objective knowledge be so important as to call into question all of orthodox science? The answer is yes, especially in the behavioral sciences, because this distorted ideal blocks us from abandoning orthodox science and moving to a better scientific paradigm for studying human behavior. Orthodox science exerts a comprehensive power over most of us today, not unlike religion once did. To be branded "unscientific," especially in academe, is likely to lead to excommunication from the hallowed halls and ivoried towers.

It is ironic that science espouses the rejection of dogma but has failed to recognize that the doctrine of objectivity is dogma itself—very firmly entrenched dogma. Polanyi (1958) contends that it is the central dogma of the scientific age; it is the foundation attitude for rationalism, empiricism, positivism, and reductionism.

Scientific Revolutions

If scientists don't really prove theories false, if they don't adhere to the doctrine of objectivity, just how do scientists do science? How have the great discoveries of science been made over the past 300 years? Kuhn's analysis of the history of science led him to a unique discovery.

Kuhn says when a theory has major influence on the field of study by attracting a number of scientists to it, and the theory inspires many provocative problems to be studied, it is a paradigm. This paradigm becomes a way of looking at the world: It is the scientist's spectacles. Kuhn observes that after normal science has prevailed for a while, anomalies in findings begin to surface. That is, studies obtain results that do not fit the predictions of the theory. Eventually a search is made for a better theory to explain the phenomena under study. Kuhn terms this a *paradigm* crisis.

This search is seldom undertaken by those who have spent years doing normal science within a given paradigm, because they have invested too much in this paradigm and are usually unable to see alternatives by removing the spectacles through which they view the world. In short, they are unable to be entirely objective about the phenomena they study. The leaders of what Kuhn terms the paradigm revolution are usually young, maverick scientists. As they break away, these leaders of the new paradigm create their own organizations, their own journals, their own rules for how the game of science is played. As they do, they attract their followers who are taught the ways of the new paradigm, and normal science returns—but only until the next paradigm crisis. (It is worth speculating that sport psychology may presently be experiencing a "micro" paradigm revolution of its own.)

What Kuhn tells us is that the paradigms don't change; the paradigms are buried only when the scientists who nurtured them to life are buried. Instead, science progresses by revolution—by young, maverick scientists breaking away and replacing the old paradigms. The doctrine of objectivity is simply not reality.

The problem of objectivity is especially exacerbated in the behavioral sciences. While orthodox science has worked wonderfully in the physical and biological sciences despite the failure to fulfill the doctrine of objectivity, orthodox science has worked miserably in the study of human behavior, and therefore in sport psychology. Consequently, orthodox science, which itself is a paradigm and not sacrosanct, is a paradigm in crisis. So if science is not objective, is it subjective? Certainly not. Reality is not all in our minds. But what is science if it is neither objective nor subjective? What is the scientist's relationship to this universe he or she observes? Briggs and Peat (1984) propose a most intriguing answer to this question based on Kuhn's analysis of scientific paradigms:

> Between the lines of Kuhn's analysis we push through the gap in the traditional view of science and down a narrow tunnel. We now stick our heads out into a fog-shrouded landscape—shimmering, infinitely subtle, and new. In this landscape we see scientists as they move from paradigm to paradigm like rabbits in a magic show, seeming to discover in their movement that the very jaws of nature are protean, changing with each new paradigm. As the scientists shift paradigms, even the data change . . . And as it unfolds, a paradigm seems to generate (not just uncover) anomalies which destroy it, leading to others. Thus here, through the steaming mist, we seem to glimpse the strange possibility that the changeableness of nature's laws may be relative somehow to the activity of scientists' looking. Observer and observed appear to influence one another, the scientist like a whirlpool trying to study the flow of water. Here we have left behind, with Bacon and Descartes and Popper, a universe where the observer observes the observed and have entered a looking-glass, a universe where, in some way (we can only see this part very dimly now) the observer is the observed. We may reflect that if this is so, then we may have discovered a universe that is whole. (p. 33)

A Capsulation

Science is one method for acquiring knowledge. Orthodox science is a paradigm of knowledge derived from the 15th- and 16th-century scientific revolution in astronomy, physics, and mathematics. It has been enormously successful in the physical and biological sciences, and even in the study of part processes in humans. It has failed miserably, however, when studying the behavior of people, especially the more complex functions of people, because it has clung to the doctrine of objectivity. This doctrine has prevented behavioral scientists from developing alternative ways of knowing that are more suitable for the study of human behavior.

So if you find any credibility in the notion that scientists play an active role in what they observe, that the reality they report is shaped by their perceptions, then we must bury orthodox science and replace it with a scientific paradigm better suited to studying human behavior in all its complexities. Such a paradigm is not yet fully developed, but I believe some of the ingredients for a better paradigm are known.

A New Philosophy of Knowledge

Gelwick (1977) proposes that Polanyi has provided us with the beginning of a new paradigm of science, an alternative philosophy of knowledge. Although Polanyi's "heuristic philosophy of knowledge" gained prominence in the 1960s, his impact on the behavioral sciences has been limited to date, perhaps because he is difficult to understand and the paradigm crisis in the behavioral sciences was not as great then as it is today.

Nevertheless, I believe he provides us with a philosophical basis that is much more appropriate for the study of human behavior. The origin and full meaning of Polanyi's philosophy are complex, and I do not fully grasp all that is implicated by his heuristic philosophy of knowledge. However, my own tacit knowledge, tacit knowledge being a critical feature of Polanyi's philosophy, tells me that a philosophy that gives central importance to humans in understanding humans is worthy of further study. Thus I present here a synopsis of Polanyi's heuristic philosophy of knowledge as the basis for a new philosophy of science. It is only a synopsis, and I highly recommend Polanyi's *Personal Knowledge* (1958) and *The Tacit Dimension* (1966), as well as Gelwick's excellent interpretation of Polanyi titled *The Way of Discovery* (1977).

The Heuristic Paradigm of Knowledge

The key concept in Polanyi's heuristic paradigm is that all knowledge revolves around the responsible person, unlike orthodox science that attempts to establish knowledge, with certainty, independent of the person. When studying how scientific discoveries were really made, Polanyi found that scientists work with clues that can mean different things to different scientists. Scientists pay attention to clues by seeking to find meaningful pattern in what seems to be random data. They are more or less skilled at this ability and perceive patterns differently, depending greatly on their experiences. Zajonc's (1965) reformulation of social facilitation data and Schmidt's (1982) development of schema theory both come to mind as examples of scientists seeing new patterns in existing data.

What is it that provides scientists with the ability to see pattern in seemingly random data? Polanyi describes it as tacit knowledge and credits it with great importance in science. We can understand what Polanyi means by tacit knowledge by looking at how he describes the fundamental structure of all knowing.

The fundamental structure of all knowing is a triad. The focal target is the problem; it is what we direct our efforts toward. Next we have clues of which we are only subsidiarily aware. At times we can identify some of them, but at other times we cannot. This subsidiary awareness is the tacit dimension of knowledge. The third part of the triad that forms our knowledge is the person who links our focal target with our subsideary clues.

Polanyi says *knowing* is a type of tacit integration of clues into meaning. We move from clues or particulars to wholes. An example of tacit knowledge is the identification of a physiognomy used by police in developing descriptions of criminals. Victims are often unable to describe a criminal's facial features bur can respond to a selection of various facial features that create a composite that can be quite accurate. In the same way, athletes often cannot articulate how they execute skills so exquisitely, yet they know how to do them "We know more than we can tell," is Polanyi's (1966) aphorism about the tacit dimension.

Subsidiary awareness guides us to the integration of a coherent pattern. Without tacit integration of data and ideas into wholes, theories or laws cannot be perceived. The doctrine of objectivity denies the existence of two major areas of knowing—our subsidiary reliance upon clues and our integration powers as persons.

Not only is tacit knowledge important in the business of science, those who study the science of business have found it equally important. While in the business world tacit knowledge is commonly referred to as "intuition," business executives today are being trained not only to use facts and figures when engaging in strategic planning but to also use their subsidiary awareness—their tacit knowledge—in decision-making.

Harlan Cleveland (1985) provides a complementary way of looking at knowledge. He says there are four key words about knowledge: data, information, knowledge, and wisdom. Data are undigested observations, unvarnished facts. Information is organized data. Knowledge is organized information, internalized by me, integrated with everything else I know from experience or study or intuition, and therefore useful in guiding my life. "Wisdom," Cleveland states, "is integrated knowledge, information made superuseful by theory, which relates bits and fields of knowledge to each other, which in turn enables me to use the knowledge to do something" (p. 23). This is what Polanyi calls the tacit dimension.

Significance of Tacit Knowledge

Why so much fuss about finally giving recognition to our subsidiary awareness, our tacit knowledge? Because the old paradigm, orthodox science, dictates methods that do not incorporate tacit knowledge, and because we are so committed to the doctrine of objectivity that it has prevented us from developing a new scientific paradigm. Polanyi gives us reason and evidence to abandon orthodox science and build a new science—one that puts the person back into the study of people. "The separation of the knower and the known is no longer convincing even though that separation is institutionalized in our habits of thought, our ideals, and our organization of life," writes Gelwick (1977, p. 82). "Instead of arguing further for it, the task seems to be one of understanding the new paradigm that has emerged and beginning to live within it. It is at this juncture that the work of Polanyi is important to us. He is not the first to criticize scientific objectivism. He is the first to provide a comprehensive alternative commensurate with the problems we face."

Psychology and Orthodox Science

Most academic sport psychologists have accepted the imposed doctrine that the only source of knowledge, true knowledge, is orthodox science. We continually try to make this paradigm work even though we know from our tacit knowledge that it works badly when we want to understand the person.

Before looking at the implications of the heuristic paradigm for sport psychology, we should consider more specifically how psychology and sport psychology have been influenced by orthodox science. With this background we can better proceed to develop a science of sport psychology within the heuristic paradigm.

Assumptions of Orthodox Psychology

The study of psychology as it evolved from the paradigm of orthodox science is based on the following assumptions:

1. The nature of cognitive processes is individualistic, static, and passive.
2. These processes can be broken down into elements.
3. The elements of these processes can be conceived of and investigated in their pure form unaffected by other elements.

This orthodox science has a methodological commitment to the laboratory experiment, or its variants. Its goal is to find common properties among the subjects being studied through the discovery of cause-effect relationships or correlations between independent and dependent variables. The experiments strive for external validity, but only to the extent they do not sacrifice internal validity. Studies without internal validity are unpublishable; studies without external validity are readily publishable but practically insignificant. At present orthodox psychology prefers publishability to practical significance.

Alternatively, a heuristic paradigm would hold the following assumptions:

1. Cognitive processes are social, developing, and active.
2. Cognitive processes are wholes that cannot be broken down into discrete elements.
3. Cognitive processes can be studied only in their relationship to one another.

The acceptance of these alternative views prescribe the development of different methods for the study of cognitive processes. The use of a factorial design with manipulation of variables would contradict these assumptions and would be an inappropriate tool for investigation.

What happens often in psychology is that researchers will readily acknowledge that cognitive processes are social and dynamic and must be understood in relation to one another, but they cling to their methods of orthodox science by studying one or a few variables at a time. They do so because they know no other way. And why? Because it is the only way to objectively study these phenomena.

As Maslow (1966) observed, "It is tempting, if the only tool you have is a hammer, to treat everything as if it were a nail" (pp. 15–16).

People as Experimental Artifacts

It became obvious in the 1960s that we could not study people in the same way orthodox science studies inanimate objects. Thus psychology responded by working harder to eliminate what are called subject and experimenter errors. Psychologists recognized that subjects are not just passive participants in an experiment. They interpret the experimental situation, guess at hypotheses, and try to be either good or devious subjects, depending on their interpretation. We also learned that the characteristics of the experimenter, and his or her actions, can introduce unwanted variables into the experiment and thus "ruin" it.

Kuhn (1962) observes that when a paradigm is not working well, efforts are made initially to remedy the problem within the existing paradigm. This has happened in reaction to the discovery that subjects and experimenters introduce artifacts into the experiment that contaminate the *objectivity* of the study. (If only we could find a way to get rid of the people in people experiments!) Some of the ways psychologists have sought to minimize human influence in laboratory experiments include the use of placebos, double-blind experiments, deception, control groups who are given a plausible hypothesis unrelated to the experiment, tape-recorded instructions, the use of multiple experimenters, and so on. Unfortunately, none of these remedies within orthodox psychology has been found satisfactory (Brenner & Bungard, 1981). And the reason is that the problem cannot be solved using the assumptions of orthodox science, especially the assumptions of objectivity and reductionism. The problem calls for a radically new philosophy of science.

Why Laboratory Experiments Fail

As psychologists are confronted daily with the fact that the people they study are active, whole individuals and respond in the experimental environment as active, whole individuals, the methodology of orthodox science becomes totally inadequate. Although I invested many years in using the laboratory experiment, I now have little faith in it as a useful means for answering questions about complex human behavior in the sport context. I have grave doubts that isolated psychological studies that manipulate a few variables, attempting to uncover the effects of X on Y, can be cumulative to form a coherent picture of human behavior. I know of no line of research in the behavioral sciences that has accomplished this yet. The external validity of laboratory studies is at best limited to predicting behavior in other laboratory studies.

Laboratory studies also frequently lead to an erroneous specification of causality. We assume that if we manipulate X and it significantly affects Y, then X caused Y to change. Laboratory studies, however, usually impose a directional model of causality. In unconstrained natural settings, Y may also cause X, or X and Y may cause changes in each other.

Reductionism

Related to the problems of the laboratory experiment, orthodox science assumes that the complex is composed of simple elements or can be explained at a more basic level, an atomistic view of the world. Thus scientists try to reduce the complex to the so-called simple. Then, through models and theory, the parts are put back together to understand the whole. It is essential in investigating complex phenomena to focus the problem on the more pertinent variables. No one can adequately study all the factors that influence behavior simultaneously. However, I believe sport psychology research has often erred by reducing complex behavior to such a small set of components that we destroy the phenomenon to be studied. You cannot understand human interactions by looking at the isolated behavior of the people interacting. You must also look at the dynamic process of the interaction itself. Yet sometimes sport psychologists reduce a problem to its simplest components or a lower level in order that the study meets the assumption of objectivity.

The miserable failures in social psychology, especially in the field of group dynamics, are testimonies to the inadequacy of orthodox science, not of the scientists who sought to understand these phenomena. We will not come to understand motivation, self-esteem, peak experiences, imagery, values, beliefs, and personality by reducing them to their simplest components.

The reductionistic approach of orthodox science narrows our vision in searching for complex explanations of human behavior. Some movement is now developing to reverse this trend by placing more emphasis on studying complete systems, seeking pattern in whole organisms or groups, and looking for synthesis rather than for reductionistic explanations (see Briggs & Peat, 1984; Maslow, 1966).

Is reductionism an issue in sport psychology? It most certainly is. Some of the gatekeepers of sport psychology knowledge ascribe to a reductionistic view regarding the legitimate study of certain phenomena. For example, some sport psychologists hold the view that to study state anxiety, physiological measurements must corroborate behavioral or cognitive measurements. Yet there is no convincing evidence that physiological variables are closely associated with anxiety states. On the contrary, there is considerable evidence that physiological variables are poor predictors of anxiety states. Because physiological variables can be more reliably measured, even though using them for the study of anxiety states is without validity, they are advocated by those who endorse a reductionistic view.

Significance of These Issues for Sport Psychologists

It is not an inconsequential matter that some people hold the view that knowledge from orthodox science is the only legitimate knowledge in sport psychology. Given the current system in academe, those who hold this view inevitably become the gatekeepers of knowledge for the field. Those who do orthodox science are those who get published because the editors of scientific journals will accept only this type of research. In turn, those who get published are invited to serve on editorial boards which then apply the standards of their craft to others. Change tends to occur only in the direction of more conservative science, more statistics, more control—in short, supposedly greater objectivity.

I recall discussing the weaknesses of orthodox science with a group of my graduate students a few years ago. Shortly thereafter, one of those students, a first-year doctoral candidate, expressed to me his consternation about what he had heard. In his words, “It’s obvious that lab studies can’t get at the real richness of athletes’ behavior in sport. It doesn’t take a genius to figure that out. But what am I supposed to do? I want to work in academe; I want to be respected in the field. If I don’t play the game according to their rules, I won’t be permitted to play at all.” Unfortunately, at the present time, he is right!

My graduate students had little choice but to listen to my views about philosophy of science, but I have found it much more difficult to discuss these issues with sport psychologists, especially academic sport psychologists. There is something so sacred about the orthodox scientific method that when I raise these issues, some sport psychologists adamantly refuse to discuss them. I don’t mean accept them, or consider them, just discuss them! Apparently, to them orthodox science is sacrosanct and its assumptions cannot be questioned.

Perhaps for those who respond this way, science is a defense. It provides them a security system. It provides order and thus stability. It provides easy-to-apply rules for making decisions in a complex world. I recall a prominent sport psychologist, who had been responsible for selecting papers for a major symposium in the field, telling me how disappointed he was for being criticized because he had rejected so many papers. With pride he asserted, “I used two criteria for selecting papers. They had to have data and a control group.” He was imbued with confidence that those were reasonable rules for determining whether a paper contained sufficient knowledge to warrant time on the program. Think about that for a moment. Are papers that report the results of orthodox science using the experimental method in order to have a control group the only source of knowledge? Is that the quintessence of science?

The lunacy goes a step further. Those who believe in orthodox science as the only source of knowledge reason that practicing sport psychology, without full knowledge derived from orthodox science, should not occur and is unethical. This view totally denies the existence of other sources of knowledge, and exalts knowledge gained from orthodox science to a position of supremacy.

I have been asked by academic sport psychologists, “How can you offer your services to athletes when we don’t have a scientific base for doing so?” I have two answers. First, recognize that none of the helping professions have much of a scientific base for the services they offer. Medicine, education, all aspects of clinical psychology, even engineering rely heavily on experience. Experience is even institutionalized in many professions in the form of internships. Second, we now see that those who criticize practicing sport psychologists on the grounds that they are unscientific falsely assume that their orthodox science is producing reliable knowledge. It is not difficult to develop a thesis that practicing sport psychologists who use tacit knowledge derived from experience have a stronger knowledge base than academic sport psychologists who rely exclusively on orthodox science.

Conclusion

In this section, I have shown how orthodox science influences assumptions about cognitive processes that are widely recognized to be untenable. Efforts to eliminate some of the biases introduced into experiments by subjects and experimenters, thus attempting to make the study of behavior more objective, have failed. I then presented the reasons why the laboratory experiment is entirely inadequate for acquiring knowledge about human behavior, and concluded by showing how orthodox science prevents the development of a more fruitful sport psychology by restricting the activities of sport psychologists in undesirable ways.

Degrees of Knowledge

As we move toward the development of a new paradigm of knowledge, and hence toward better methods of science, we can benefit by conceptualizing knowledge on a continuum of reliability. Some years ago I came upon the Degrees of Knowledge theory, or DK theory, which has been helpful in my conceptualization of knowledge. The DK theory, indicates the range of knowledge reliability from “Damn Konfident” to “Don’t Know.” I have arbitrarily indicated various sources of knowledge along this continuum to illustrate the idea of “degrees” of knowledge. At this point, it is unimportant whether or not you agree with their placement on the continuum; what is important here is the concept of degrees of knowledge.

Knowledge is more reliable or less reliable, but it is still knowledge as long as its probability of being correct is greater than chance. Knowledge, like humans, has an embryology and goes through various developmental stages; it cannot be limited to its fully matured forms alone. Less reliable knowledge is also part of knowledge, and is the infant through which we nurture more reliable knowledge. Subjective experiences, intuition, hunches, observations based on insufficient samples, are essential parts of our knowledge base, and a healthy science must incorporate these sources of knowledge into its theories. The tacit dimension of Polanyi’s philosophy does so.

The first stages of knowledge are sloppy and ambiguous, just as the first days of practice in a sport are less than adroit demonstrations of skill. But this is a stage through which knowledge must pass. Our current system in academe of rewarding only those who play the orthodox game of science denies players the right to pursue other more beneficial and enjoyable games.

We are often criticized in sport psychology for our use of paper-and-pencil tests, for our personality inventories, and for our observations made without any instrumentation other than fallible human observers. Of course, we all would delight in being able to study competitive anxiety or motivation, for example, with such reliable instruments as a dynamometer, barometer, or galvanometer. If only we had PET scans to measure peak experiences, an X-ray machine for monitoring vivid mental images, or a photometer for recording group interactions.

When we invent such external and publicly observable instruments that measure psychological phenomena reliably and validly, then a new era will have begun in our field. But the development of such reliable instrumentation is a long way off. Certainly physiological and biochemical measures have not been the answer, not for a lack of trying to make them work. But in the absence of such instrumentation we must press on with the best we have. Peak experiences, vivid images, and interpersonal interactions continue to play an essential part of the psychology of sport. And we have an obligation to understand these phenomena to the best of our ability, using the best methods available. If we cannot use more reliable methods, then we must use less reliable methods.

But this is not at all what happens today. Those who use orthodox science simply avoid studying difficult questions that do not lend themselves easily to orthodox science methods. Or alternatively, they impose the orthodox scientific method on the phenomenon, generating research findings that have high internal validity but virtually no external validity.

We need to broaden our concept of science. We should not limit our search for the understanding of human behavior in sport to those things we can study using orthodox science. We should be able to ask any question, raise any problem. Once raised, we can go from there and do our best to get the answer to that particular question. Presently we are hampered from developing a more mature sport psychology by our conceptual and methodological pieties about scientism.

"A scientist's first duty," says Maslow (1966), "is to describe the facts. If these conflict with the demand for a 'good system' then out with the system" (p. 79). Methods must be created as necessary. There are no rules as such. The only requirement is to do the best you can with the problem at the time and under the circumstances. "The scientific method," writes Percy Bridgman (1959), "as far as it is a method, is nothing more than doing one's damndest with one's mind, no holds barred."

It is imperative that we understand this as a field. It is especially imperative that the gatekeepers of knowledge apply these types of criteria when evaluating articles submitted to journals and papers for presentation at conferences. They will, of course, find it a much more difficult task than the comparatively simple rules of orthodox science, but the alternative is worse.

I sense a tendency on the part of those sport psychologists who have a need for neatness, exactness, and simplicity to stay away from the humanistic and complex problems of humans in sport. Their criticism of those who undertake the study of these tough problems with less reliable methods is not so much a criticism of the methodology as it is a criticism for asking that particular question. This indicates a preference for neatness over new knowledge about human behavior.

Orthodox scientists dichotomize knowledge into true or false, significant or nonsignificant, reliable or unreliable. This is unwise. Reliability of knowledge, as we have seen, is a matter of degree. So is truth and falsehood, significance and pertinence. In the absence of more reliable knowledge we must rely on less reliable knowledge.

For these reasons, I have difficulty accepting the way we use inferential statistics in the behavioral sciences. Because an observation fails to be statistically significant at the .05 level but instead has a significance level of .06, we feel compelled either not to report the results or to reject them on the grounds that they lack significance. Here we confuse statistical significance with practical significance. When we recognize that knowledge falls on a continuum varying in degrees of reliability, then all findings, whether statistically significant or not, provide us with some knowledge (see Bakan, 1967, and Meehl, 1978, for more about these problems).

The Heuristic Paradigm and Sport Psychology

Let's say that I have convinced you: We need a better scientific paradigm. "How do I do science within the heuristic paradigm?" you justifiably ask. In this section I shall identify some general strategies for acquiring knowledge about human behavior based on the heuristic paradigm. If you are looking for specific prescriptions for conducting your research, you will be disappointed. The new paradigm will not likely lend itself to the construction of a precise, highly standardized, elegantly controlled science. While the heuristic paradigm will continue to follow the six basic steps of the scientific method, which are logical steps for solving any problem, the specific procedures for implementing any of these steps will not be as clearly defined as they are within orthodox science.

The heuristic paradigm certainly will not abandon all the methodologies that have been developed over the last hundred years for the study of human behavior. Gradually, psychologists have been modifying the methods of orthodox science anyway because of the problems discussed in this paper. *The major change in the heuristic paradigm is that the knower (the scientist) has a central position in the process of knowing because of Polanyi's recognition of the significance of tacit knowledge.*

Experiential Knowledge

Knowledge from experience, it seems to me, rises to new prominence in the heuristic paradigm because it is the basis of tacit knowledge.

Maslow (1966) in *The Psychology of Science* gives great significance to experiential knowledge and identifies some of the strategies for implementing the heuristic paradigm. He states,

> There is no substitute for experience, none at all. All the other paraphernalia of communication and of knowledge—words, labels, concepts, symbols, theories, formulas, sciences—all are useful only because people already know experientially. The basic coin in the realm of knowing is direct, intimate, experiential knowing. Everything else can be likened to banks and bankers, to accounting systems and checks and paper money, which are useless unless there is a real wealth to exchange, to manipulate, to accumulate, and to order. (pp. 45–46)

So how can we best acquire experiential knowledge? We can of course experience the world ourselves, we can study systematically the experiences of others, and we can observe others in field studies. I would like to focus on three aspects of experiential knowing: (a) the idiographic approach, (b) introspectionism, and (c) field studies.

Idiographic Approach. If we want to know why an athlete behaves as he or she does, what is the best way to go about doing that? Orthodox science is helpful only to the extent that we can reach some generalizations about athletes, or about specific categories of athletes, in order to place a particular athlete into a crude classification. The statement that high trait anxious athletes tend to perform less well in highly competitive situations than do low trait anxious athletes is an example.

As a coach, knowing this may make me more alert to performance problems of those athletes on the team who are highly anxious. And yet all this nomothetic or generalized knowledge is useful only if it can help me know a particular person better. Maslow (1966) writes, "To the seeker of knowledge about persons, abstract knowledge, scientific laws and generalizations, statistical tables and expectation are all useful if they can be humanized, personalized, individualized, focused into a particular interpersonal relationship" (p. 11).

To understand the person, to gain real knowledge about the person, the sport psychologist must view the person as a whole, as a unique being. Maslow observes, "By far the best way we have to learn what people are like is to get them, one way or another, to tell us about themselves. Of course you all know this, and you use this method of knowing in your daily lives" (p. 12).

This means that as scientists we must first approach the subject not as an object but as a unique entity. No other person is exactly like this person. Next, we will have to gain the confidence of our subject so that he or she will cooperate in sharing experiences. We will have to come to know this unique being intimately through in-depth study. Consequently, we will need to place much greater emphasis on the idiographic approach of studying humans. Case studies, in-depth interviews, extended participant observation studies, and comprehensive content analyses of a person's oral or written records are examples of the idiographic approach.

A call for more idiographic research is not a suggestion that the demise of nomothetic research is imminent, but that a shift in emphasis is needed. In a review of the *Journal of Sport Psychology,* I could not find a single study using the idiographic approach. Why is this? Because academic sport psychologists have subscribed to the doctrine of objectivity and have viewed idiographic methods as being nonobjective, and thus unscientific. Within the heuristic paradigm, however, the idiographic approach provides us with knowledge that is just as useful, if not more so, than knowledge gained through the nomothetic approach.

Idiographic research, just like nomothetic research, can be done well or not so well. A call for the idiographic approach is not a call for sloppy, careless research, even though it may in some cases have less reliability on the DK continuum. Acquiring knowledge through close acquaintance with the person places a great burden on us as scientists. We can no longer be the detached, objective scientists we have eulogized. Instead, we must rely to a much greater extent on the integration of the knowledge triad elucidated by Polanyi (1958). Ultimately, idiographic research must be judged by fellow scientists on the following criterion: *Is it the best that can be done given the problem being studied?*

Introspectionism. Introspectionism is a valuable means of understanding certain human experiences, when we approach the people we study with an element of trust, good will, and honesty. We must take the view that the study of human behavior is a cooperative venture between scientist and subject, with a lack of cooperation by either destroying the study's validity. Orthodox science taught us to manipulate objects, poke at them, take them apart. If we attempt to do this to people, they won't let us know them and they may take a poke back!

The much maligned method of introspection was abandoned by psychologists as a reaction to the radical behaviorism of the 1950s and 60s. Introspective methods certainly have weaknesses; just because people say they experienced some thought or emotion by no means proves they did. And some subconscious processes cannot be studied by this method. Such methods have their place, however, especially in the early stages of acquiring knowledge about some psychological phenomena. Lieberman (1979) writes, "If introspective reports are sometimes wrong or misleading, however, there is equally compelling evidence that in some instances they may provide information of truly impressive accuracy and reliability" (p. 319). Lieberman reviews considerable evidence within psychology to support this statement. When used wisely, introspective reports will be a valuable method in the heuristic paradigm.

One means of acquiring knowledge through introspective methods is advocated by Maslow (1966), who states, "A knowing of the other [person] comes about through becoming the other, that is, it becomes experiential knowledge from within. I know it because I know myself, and it has now become part of myself. Fusion with the object of knowledge permits experiential knowledge" (p. 103). This approach is certainly in accord with the type of knowledge that Polanyi tells us is essential for good science. Indeed, I believe that when I conducted research using orthodox science I learned more from simply being immersed in the phenomenon of study then from the study's actual, formal results. Because I was engrossed with the problem, I not only studied it experimentally but I thought about it frequently, I observed it, I experienced it. These experiences formed my tacit knowledge, which gave me more useful insights into the problem than did the study's findings.

Another means for sport psychologists to acquire knowledge through introspective methods is by helping those who have a great deal of experiential knowledge direct their own awareness and focus it on a given problem. Thus while a coach or athlete may "know more than he or she can tell," to use Polanyi's aphorism, those who study sport psychology for a living can help them tell it. It seems to me an enormous loss of knowledge that coaches and athletes with many years of experience are permitted to retire and never record, in some systematic way, their experiences. While the more famous may write their autobiographies, how much more could we learn if someone spent a month interviewing John Wooden, for example, to discover what he has learned about the psychology of sport? With your ability as a sport psychologist to ask probing questions, with your tacit knowledge to search for patterns, how much more would you learn by such an interview than by conducting another 2 × 2 factorial study in your laboratory? Most of us would delight in pursuing such knowledge because the yield would be so great. Yet at present we deny ourselves this approach because it does not fulfill the doctrine of objectivity, and thus is deemed unscientific.

Field Studies. Field studies and their variants have the potential to overcome many problems of the laboratory experiment. Moreover, sport is an ideal context for conducting field studies because of the somewhat controlled environment. Field studies that approach the problem from the orthodox science perspective, however, are no better than laboratory experiments. For example, some sport psychologists have attempted to remove the investigator from field research in order to make the study adhere more to the doctrine of objectivity. When this occurs, field studies are typically as sterile as laboratory experiments, or nearly so. The field studies that gather the richest knowledge are those in which the investigators are an active part of the study and in which their tacit knowledge plays a vital role in problem formation, methodology, and interpretation of results. The Robber's Cave experiments (Sherif & Sherif, 1961) and the classic study of William Foot Whyte (1943) are examples.

Some years ago in an article titled *From Smocks to Jocks* (Martens, 1979), I suggested that we needed more field research to overcome the inherent weaknesses of the laboratory experiment and the reductionist approach to studying human behavior. Field research, I am pleased to report, has increased significantly in sport psychology. Most of these studies have been descriptive field studies—surveys, comparisons between intact groups, and a few observational studies. Unfortunately, though, my appeal for field studies was incomplete in the 1979 article. It is not just the study of behavior in the field setting but the adoption of the heuristic paradigm in field research that is essential.

Some researchers contend that we need to return to controlled laboratory studies, especially studies that test theories—these theories, I assume, being the existing ones in social psychology since sport psychology is theory poor. I could not disagree more. We have been so eager to test theories of the larger field of psychology in order to confirm our scientific respectability that we have not adequately observed, described, and theorized about our own thing—SPORT. We clearly need to spend more time observing behavior in sport and building our own theories unique to sport. We not only need more field studies but also competent sport psychologists who put themselves into the heart of these studies by being intimate, participant observers.

Conclusion

The heuristic paradigm, which gives the knower (the scientist) a central place in the process of knowing, elevates experiential knowledge to prominence. Those methods that help us arrive at knowledge by recording our own experiences and those of others become more significant because they are not falsely judged by the doctrine of objectivity. If the heuristic paradigm is embraced by sport psychologists, a shift from the almost exclusive reliance on nomothetic, abstract research to the use of idiographic methods would most assuredly occur. We would find greater emphasis on case studies, clinical reports, and other introspective methods of acquiring knowledge. Also, we would expect to see many more field studies in which the investigator integrated his or her tacit knowledge with the behaviors of those observed.

For certain, it will be much more difficult to evaluate the quality of this kind of research; and yet as the heuristic paradigm develops, it will need to find ways of distinguishing more reliable from less reliable knowledge. As it does, and as this paradigm matures, I have little doubt that it will lead to a much better sport psychology.

From Two Sport Psychologies to One

I began this paper by making the observation that we currently have two sport psychologies traveling divergent courses. Academic sport psychology subscribes to and is governed by orthodox science. Practicing sport psychology relies mostly upon experiential knowledge, although it does integrate experimental knowledge into its practice when such is available and applicable.

A Road to Convergence

The schism between academic and practicing sport psychology is largely the result of different epistemologies concerning the nature of legitimate knowledge. In this paper I have demonstrated the inadequacy of orthodox science and the potential that lies in Polanyi's heuristic paradigm. If we can embrace this latter paradigm, we will be back on the road to convergence. Rather than view knowledge as being either scientific or unscientific, reliable or unreliable, we will have a richer sport psychology if we view knowledge as a continuum—the Degrees of Knowledge theory. From this perspective, those who study problems in their embryonic state using less reliable methods will be rewarded equally with those who study more mature problems using more reliable methods.

If academic sport psychologists will adopt this perspective, they will begin acquiring knowledge that is far more useful to practicing sport psychologists. Furthermore, practicing sport psychologists will be more inclined to conduct research that will contribute to the body of knowledge in the field. At present, few practicing sport psychologists bother to do research using the available "embryonic" methods because they have been discouraged from such activity by the academic sport psychologists who condemn these as unscientific.

All of sport psychology will gain by recognizing that orthodox science's doctrine of objectivity is fallacious and has inhibited the development of more appropriate methods for the study of human behavior, especially the more complex, higher functions of humans. When we recognize the importance of experiential knowledge, we will see that practicing sport psychologists can contribute as equally to the acquisition of knowledge as do academic sport psychologists. Indeed, the distinction between academic and practicing sport psychologist becomes blurred.

Basic and Applied Research

Up to this point I have avoided the quagmire of distinguishing between basic and applied research in our field. While sport psychology is primarily an applied field because it focuses on human behavior within a particular context, sport psychologists may certainly pursue some problems from a basic research perspective. Basic science is concerned with discovering how something works, and applied science is concerned with solutions to practical problems. Typically, we would expect that most basic research would be conducted in the mother discipline of psychology, not in sport psychology. The applied research in sport psychology would draw upon this basic research and experiential knowledge to find solutions to the practical problems in the field. In turn, the knowledge acquired about solutions in practical problems may be very helpful in acquiring more basic knowledge about how something works.

At least, this is the way I think it should be. Some believe, mistakenly in my opinion, that to find solutions to practical problems we must completely understand the principles of human behavior. There is considerable evidence in every field that this is nonsense. For example, we can readily enough learn how to ride a bicycle without understanding the principles of how we stay up on a bicycle when riding it. In turn, we can readily enough develop programs for helping athletes manage their anxiety without fully knowing the causes of anxiety. We undoubtedly would be able to develop more effective stress management programs if we understood the causes of stress fully, but even without this knowledge we can design some useful programs. How do we do this? Largely from our experiential knowledge.

I believe we are spending too many of our resources in sport psychology attempting to answer questions that are basic research issues and not applied issues. Our primary mission in sport psychology is to help people enjoy sports more and to perform better when participating in sports, as well as to design the sport experience so that people come closer to reaching their potential through optimal personal development. To accomplish these objectives, I believe we should leap ahead with the development and testing of innovative techniques and programs rather than continue the traditional atomistic approach so many are now following.

Leap and Creep Strategies

From the study of what scientists do, we have learned that inference based on many observations is a myth. We have seen that what Platt (1964) has called strong inference is not an approach widely used in science, even in the physical sciences, and that it is not economical. There are too many disconfirming hypotheses to be tested. Furthermore, most scientists are biased toward confirming, not disconfirming, their hypotheses. Polanyi (1958) and Kuhn (1962) have shown us that science progresses by conjecture, by jumping to conclusions, often after a single observation.

I believe sport psychologists can acquire knowledge much more rapidly by developing solutions to practical problems, such as psychological training programs for athletes, if these solutions are based on experiential knowledge combined with any experimental knowledge that has some degree of external validity. Then sport psychologists can determine through good evaluation research the efficacy of these techniques and programs. If they are found to be effective, then more detailed study of the programs will be warranted.

I believe we will acquire far more knowledge by using this "leap strategy" rather than the present "creep strategy," which is based on the flawed atomistic doctrine. I see little hope from example or reason that eventually we will develop comprehensive theories to guide the development of new techniques and training programs by using the creep strategy.

From Applied Research to Applied Knowledge

It also is useful to distinguish between basic and applied knowledge in another sense. Today, academe rewards only the creation of original research, both basic and applied, but does not give much recognition to the synthesis of research into applied knowledge. In Harlan Cleveland's terms, academe rewards the generation of data and information, but gives less recognition to the development of knowledge and wisdom. Cleveland (1985) tells of someone asking Isaac Stern, one of the world's great violinists, why all professional musicians seem able to play the same notes in the same order, yet some sound wonderful and others do not. Stern thought for a moment and then replied, "But it isn't the notes that are important. It's the intervals between the notes" (p. 11). This is not only true about music but also about our research and its transformation into useful knowledge.

Applied *knowledge,* in contrast to applied research, involves sifting through all the research available on a problem, using one's tacit knowledge regarding the problem, and developing creative programs for how to solve it. Applied research alone often does not directly reveal how the research can be used to help solve a problem. The process of synthesizing research and developing knowledge that can be directly applied to solving problems requires enormous intellectual skill and considerable creativity. We need to recognize the value of this contribution, especially when viewed from the perspective presented in this paper. Those who practice sport psychology and those who teach sport psychology often are the synthesizers of research into knowledge. Therefore, they contribute equally to the creation of knowledge in our field and thus should be admired and rewarded equally for their contribution to the field. With this perspective, we once again will have one sport psychology.

A Final Note

Although the heuristic paradigm is a better paradigm, it is not an easier one than orthodox science. It is far less developed at this point and does not provide precise rules for problem solving. Nevertheless, the heuristic paradigm is not a license for doing sloppy or careless research. Asking insignificant questions, using poor problem-solving procedures, introducing unnecessary bias, failing to be thorough, and using faulty logic to interpret results are just as much eschewed when using the heuristic paradigm as when using the orthodox science paradigm. Consequently the heuristic paradigm places far greater responsibility on the scientist to do the best with the problem being studied. In turn, it places equally more responsibility on fellow scientists, especially reviewers and editors, to judge the research on the basis of its being the best that can be done given the problem at hand.

References

Bakan, D. (1967). *On method: Toward a reconstruction of psychological investigation.* San Francisco: Jossey-Bass.

Brenner, M., & Bungard, W. (1981). What to do with social reactivity in psychological experimentation? In M. Brenner (Ed.), *Social method and social life* (pp. 187–214). New York: Academic Press.

Bridgman, P. W. (1959). *The way things are.* Cambridge, MA: Harvard University Press.

Briggs, J.P., & Peat, F.D. (1984). *Looking glass universe: The emerging science of wholeness.* New York: Simon & Schuster.

Cleveland, H. (1985). *The knowledge executive.* New York: Dutton.

Gelwick, R. (1977). *The way of discovery: An introduction to the thought of Michael Polanyi.* New York: Oxford University Press.

Kuhn, T.S. (1962). *The structure of scientific revolutions.* Chicago: University of Chicago Press.

Kuhn, T.S. (1963). In A. Crombie (Ed.), *Scientific change.* New York: Basic Books.

Lachman, S.J. (1960). *The foundations of science.* New York: Vantage Press.

Lieberman, D.A. (1979). Behaviorism and the mind: A (limited) call for a return to introspectionism. *American Psychologist,* 34, 319–333.

Mahoney, M.J. (1976). *Scientist as subject: The psychological imperative.* Cambridge, MA: Ballinger.

Martens, R. (1979). From smocks to jocks. *Journal of Sport Psychology,* 1, 94–99.

Maslow, A.H. (1966). *The psychology of science.* Chicago: Henry Regnery.

Meehl, P.E. (1978). Theoretical risks and tabular asterisks: Sir Karl, Sir Ronald, and slow progress of soft psychology. *Journal of Consulting and Clinical Psychology,* 46, 806–834.

Platt, J.R. (1964). Strong inference. *Science,* 146, 347–353.

Polanyi, M. (1958). *Personal knowledge: Towards a post-critical philosophy.* Chicago: University of Chicago Press.

Polanyi, M. (1966). *The tacit dimension.* Garden City, NY: Doubleday.

Popper, K. (1972). *Objective knowledge.* Oxford: Clarendon Press.

Schmidt, R.A. (1982). *Motor control and learning.* Champaign, IL: Human Kinetics.

Sherif, M., & Sherif, C. (1961). *Intergroup conflict and cooperation.* Norman: University of Oklahoma Book Exchange.

Whyte, W.F., Jr. (1943). *Street corner society.* Chicago: University of Chicago Press.

Zajonc, R. (1965). Social facilitation. *Science,* 149, 269–274.

46 Critical Issues Confronting the Advancement of Applied Sport Psychology

JOHN M. SILVA III
University of North Carolina at Chapel Hill

DAVID E. CONROY
University of Utah

SAMUEL J. ZIZZI
West Virginia University

John Silva, the lead author of this reading, was the founding president of the Association for the Advancement of Applied Sport Psychology (AAASP). Since the inception of this organization, 12 years prior to the publication of this journal article, major issues were perceived to have limited the progress of AAASP and also the progress of the field of sport psychology: the training of graduate students, the accreditation of graduate programs, the job market, and the establishment of systematic educational outreach programs. Furthermore, the authors purport that the lack of AAASP movement on these critical issues has slowed the economic and employment developments in the field.

Most graduate programs in sport psychology are housed in exercise science and related university departments. Most have more of a research than an applied orientation, and few have practical internship programs. The three major challenges listed by the authors are establishing a formal and recognized program identity, establishing a graduate program composed of a critical mass of faculty trained in sport psychology, and developing and establishing supervised practicum experiences. Graduate sport psychology programs have a wide scope of emphasis with little individual program identity. Few programs have enough faculty to generate the necessary depth of perspectives and diversity. Also, few graduate programs include systematic practicum experiences.

For years the issue of accreditation of graduate programs was discussed among the AAASP membership. It was first thought by most that AAASP, in its infancy, should not take on the daunting task of accreditation. These authors make a strong argument for the appropriateness of implementing accreditation. These authors also state that the common view in AAASP that no jobs exist in sport psychology is a myth. They liken it to the job market in clinical psychology.

For years AAASP included educational and outreach committees with little effect on the field. These authors advocated an increased emphasis on this committee through systematic marketing and outreach efforts toward private individuals and groups interested in utilizing sport psychology practitioners. AAASP certification of sport psychology practitioners is well under way at the time of this reading. These authors advocate that "AAASP must commit to educating coaches, sport administrators, national governing bodies (NGBs) and other sport organizations on the current status of certification." Few sport organizations to this point even know about sport psychology certification, let alone use the registry of certified consultants when selecting sport psychology professionals.

Despite considerable progress over the last 10 years, applied sport psychology confronts several persistent issues that continue to limit the growth and development of the field. Specifically, issues requiring more comprehensive and proactive attention and initiatives include: the training of graduate students, the accreditation of graduate programs, the job market, and the establishment of systematic educational outreach programs. Suggestions are offered regarding how enhancements in each of the aforementioned issues can be initiated, and potential benefits gained by students, faculty, and the general public are identified and discussed. Given the climate in many academic institutions emphasizing program downsizing, sport psychology may be approaching and confronting one of the most crucial crossroads in its existence. Without direct efforts to assure academic credibility and public confidence in the standards of training and practice, sport psychology may fail to actualize a meaningful future role in the competitive field of allied health service provision.

A decade ago Silva (1989) identified four defining issues confronting sport psychology: accreditation, information dissemination, interorganizational collaboration, and use of title. With the establishment of the Sport Psychology Council (SPC) the challenge of interorganizational collaboration has been acted upon, however to date the SPC remains a relatively untapped resource. AAASP certification has the potential for alleviating some concerns about title, however, issues of title will persist until awareness of certification standards reaches beyond the AAASP membership and into relevant professional groups involving athletic directors, administrators in professional sports, coaches, the Association of State and Provincial Psychology Boards, and the American Board of Professional Psychology. The persistence of debate regarding title has continued to retard the growth of the field and this debate has caused considerable confusion for prospective students interested in becoming sport psychologists. From direct correspondence with students interested in applying to a graduate program in sport psychology, it is obvious that many students are often misinformed and are initially under the impression that what department they receive their degree from is more important in the development of their professional future than the specific type and depth of training they will receive as a student interested in specializing in sport psychology! Professionals and students alike must realize that receiving a degree in psychology or even being licensed in psychology does not in and of itself permit one to label themselves as a sport psychologist and engage in practice outside of their area(s) of competence. Similarly, repeated delays in initiatives designed to disseminate information have inhibited the growth and professionalization of sport psychology (Alford, 1997). The authors maintain that the lack of organizational movement toward training enhancement and accreditation has slowed economic and employment developments in the field. This is evidenced by the current lack of recruitment initiatives by professional sport teams of certified sport psychology consultants.

A number of students and professional have expressed concerns at AAASP meetings (Murphy, 1996; Silva, 1996a, 1996b, 1997a, 1997b, 1997c; Students', 1997), and via the internet, that the organizational leadership of AAASP must facilitate meaningful initiatives in a timely manner that enhance training programs and the practice of sport psychology. Whether the current leaders in sport psychology choose to address professional training issues now, or in the immediate future, these are the issues that will impact how sport psychology presents itself to the academic and athletic communities and the public consumer. The major critical issues presented in this paper require not only reflection but a course of systematic action.

Training in Applied Sport Psychology

Sport psychology has its roots as an applied science! Since Coleman Griffiths' early science-practice efforts in his work with the Chicago Cubs, sport psychology has been positioned to apply knowledge to participants (Wiggins, 1984). Similar to other helping professions, sport psychologists face an ever-present social mandate to demonstrate the efficacy of their methods and techniques. In response to this demand, the contemporary job market for sport psychologists supports the science-practice training model. Students without skills in both the research and application of sport psychology will continue to be challenged to find full-time employment in sport psychology. Since the majority of career opportunities in applied sport psychology are academic positions, mentoring in research skills and grantsmanship will be required for career advancement (Andersen, Williams, Aldridge, & Taylor, 1997). Formal training in the application of sport psychology principles will also be necessary to address inquiries from athletes and coaches who inevitably bring forward questions, concerns, and requests for services from professionals familiar with sport psychology. Unfortunately, while research training has been and continues to be accessible in sport psychology graduate programs, applied training and supervised applied experiences are underdeveloped in contemporary programs (Andersen et al., 1997; Silva, 1996b, 1997a, 1997b).

Existing deficits in applied sport psychology graduate training must be eliminated if science and practice are to be integrated in training programs. Three challenges stand out as primary tasks for applied sport psychology program directors and faculty. These challenges are: (a) establishing a formal and recognizable program identity, (b) establishing a graduate program composed of a critical mass of faculty specifically trained in sport psychology, and (c) developing and establishing supervised practicum experiences.

A primary source of frustration for students has been the discrepancy between the experiences expected upon application and enrollment and the experiences actually received while participating in the program. Programs should consider constructing specific, formal written profiles that clarify their training goals and methods for prospective students. Equally concerning is the fact that many sport psychology graduate programs are represented by a single faculty member specifically trained in sport psychology. A master's or doctoral program in a specialty area simply cannot provide students with comprehensive graduate training experiences or a context of perspectives on the field with only one faculty member. Student-to-faculty ratios and faculty numbers need to be considered more closely to ascertain the minimum number of graduate faculty required to establish a critical mass and provide adequate breadth and depth of training. Mass and diversity in faculty is needed to further nurture the interdisciplinary interaction of sport psychology graduate students with faculty in psychology, counseling, and allied health professions.

Contemporary applied sport psychology training programs can also benefit from the establishment and enhancement of formal supervised practicum experiences available for graduate students that involve consulting with athletes, teams, and exercise participants under the direct supervision of an AAASP certified sport psychology consultant. More programs must offer formal supervised practica or internships in order to enhance graduate student training in the practice of sport psychology. It is unfortunate than many students continue to learn through trial and error just as previous generations of sport psychologists have learned how to practice. This training model is inefficient and outdated and no longer reflects the current evolution of the profession. Graduate programs must be reviewed carefully by faculty and a decision must be made regarding the identity of the program and the ability of a program to properly educate and train future generations of sport psychologists.

Evaluating Program Identities

An interesting phenomenon has occurred in recent years whereby the term "applied sport psychology" has taken on two very different meanings. One interpretation focuses on training students to conduct applied research while the second interpretation describes training in the application of sport psychology principles with clients. The majority of graduate programs do not specify their interpretation of "applied sport psychology" for prospective students. Too often students discover these divergent interpretations only after entering a program and subsequently experience dissatisfaction with the type and level of training received. To alleviate this concern, each program should form a clear program identity and delineate how that identity translates into a specific training model with specific training experiences for students. For example, if the training in a program is primarily centered around science (research), the orientation should be clearly conveyed in writing to students interested in the program before they apply to the program. If a program is based on a science-practice model, students should understand the nature of research and applied training experiences offered before applying to that program. The 5th edition of the Directory of Graduate Programs in Applied Sport Psychology (Sachs, Burke, & Gomer, 1998) has provided an opportunity for programs to self-rate their orientation on a research to practice continuum. This may provide prospective students with some general information, however, the actual research/practice orientation of any program should be carefully investigated by a prospective student. Clarifying program identities, training goals, and training procedures will enable students to select programs which address their emerging professional interests.

Unfortunately, requests to clarify a program's identity can be mistaken for a threat to a program's uniqueness and the faculty's academic freedom. Some faculty may fear that establishing formal program identities and training models will lead to a loss of program diversity or a loss of academic freedom in constructing a program. The primary goal of a comprehensive graduate program review should not be to create a "standardized" identity to which each program must conform. Rather, a review of graduate programs would be desirable to stimulate the development of a host of unique programs, each of which is designed to provide the minimal experiences necessary for competency in the science and/or practice of applied sport psychology. Beyond minimum training criteria, programs would be free to form their own unique identities within sport psychology by providing specialized experiences in areas such as rehabilitation counseling, group or team dynamics, and individual-athlete performance enhancement. A comprehensive program review or self-study will help clarify existing program identities and establish a basis for organized program development across the field.

Core Faculty and Course of Study

Once a program identity has been established, the composition of the program should be carefully examined. Faculty that compose programs at each university should evaluate the diversity and depth of perspectives feasible given their specializations and training. This self-evaluation will allow each program to realize how narrow or broad its focus should be (e.g., research only or research and practice). This decision will of course significantly influence the course of study offered to students. A quality program should involve faculty members with expertise in complementary areas of sport psychology such as health psychology, social psychology of sport, and intervention/performance enhancement. Having a critical mass of sport psychology faculty with complementary interests and training allows students to be educated and trained beyond the fundamentals of sport psychology and thus receive knowledge and adequate mentoring once a specialized focus is selected during training in the graduate program.

The responsibility for offering breadth and depth in training perspective requires both intra- and inter-departmental cooperation. Intra-departmental coursework should include a core of courses in sport psychology, performance enhancement interventions, exercise and health psychology, and social psychology of sport. In order to properly prepare the student for AAASP certification, coursework in motor learning, motor control, information processing, exercise physiology, psychophysiology, clinical psychology, counseling psychology, social psychology, and developmental psychology must be available to the student.

The need for inter-disciplinary cooperation in a sport psychology training program has been addressed by many authors (Lutz, 1990; Petrie & Watkins, 1994; Silva, 1989; Taylor, 1991). Of particular importance for students interested in the practice of applied sport psychology are courses on counseling theories and skills, individual and group dynamics, psychopathology, the psychological requirements of sport performance, psychometrics, and psychological assessment.

Without a balance of interdisciplinary coursework and specific training experiences in applied sport psychology, students will be limited in their approaches to both research and practice. Applied sport psychology consultants (with clinical, counseling, or exercise science backgrounds) who do not possess the necessary background and experiences in exercise science, counseling, and behavior change issues may rely on a "cookbook" approach dependent on "psychological skills training." Reliance on technique-driven approaches to service provision will be inherently limiting for the consultant and the client (Corlett, 1996). Behavior change is a very difficult process that requires an ability to identify and conceptualize complex dynamics and contingencies that generally result in overt behavior. The student who receives interdisciplinary training will be more likely to achieve a level of knowledge and training that will facilitate effective intervention and promote desirable behavior change. The complexity of meaningful behavior change will be reinforced for the student through supervised practicum and internship experiences. Thus, balanced intra- and inter-disciplinary training in sport psychology has the potential to prepare students to provide valuable consultation services and to produce scholarly inquiry to support the further development of professional practice. Although many student graduate programs appear to acknowledge the importance of balanced training, very few appear to have formal mechanisms in place to facilitate this type of training for their students.

Supervised Practicum Experiences

It is unfortunate that student interest in applied sport psychology has not been matched by the development of appropriate applied training models. Several professionals have discussed the need for specialized applied experiences in sport psychology as a necessary component of training if a student is interested in developing a consultative practice (e.g., Murphy, 1988; Silva, 1984, 1996a, 1996b, 1997a, 1997b, 1997c; Simons & Andersen, 1995; Taylor, 1991). Not suprisingly, the AAASP Graduate Tracking Committee found that an unacceptably high number of advanced degree recipients whose course of study focused primarily on sport performance enhancement consulting did not have any practicum or internship experiences in their graduate programs (Andersen et al., 1997). In addition to experience working with sport groups and individual athletes on typical performance enhancement concerns, it may also be worthwhile to provide opportunities for students in the form of rotations in relevant areas such as academic advising, career transition, injury rehabilitation, and substance abuse education. Faculty and students have publically addressed the fact that supervised training opportunities are very limited in most contemporary applied sport psychology graduate programs (Cogan, Petrie, Richardson, & Martin, 1998; Conroy, 1997; Murphy, 1996; Silva, 1997b, 1998; Students', 1997; Wiechman, 1998; Yukelson, 1998; Zaichowski, 1997). To develop a standard for applied training in sport psychology, it will be necessary to develop a more formal model through which students may obtain supervised experiences. Faculty resources will be required to accommodate the supervised practicum experiences that are crucial to quality applied training. This type of one-on-one supervised experience is the cornerstone of counselor training and should have already become an integral part of the standard training model for programs in applied sport psychology. The supervised intervention experience provides an excellent learning environment in which trainees can develop their general counseling skills and learn to apply specific sport psychology knowledge and techniques in a "safe environment" for both the client and the trainee.

Few graduate programs at either the masters or doctoral levels appear to be meeting students' needs for training in the application of sport psychology principles through formal supervised practicum and internship experiences (Andersen & Williams-Rice, 1996). Student experience has indicated that, when questioned about the absence of supervised practica and structured internships in "applied" sport psychology training programs, graduate program directors and faculty have provided many explanations, ranging from a maze of perceived bureaucratic and ethical obstacles to a lack of resources and even a lack of interest (Conroy, 1996). It should be noted that none of these explanations have been compelling enough to prevent other helping professions from advancing the training models provided to their students. Students will continue to be unduly challenged to develop competencies in applied sport psychology without the development of training programs which are designed and supervised by trained and experienced sport psychology consultants. The limited applied experiences which most students acquire are often the products of their own efforts to assemble "an experience" to fill that void in their training and to develop a "competency" in applied sport psychology. Unfortunately, these experiences are usually unorganized and inadequately-supervised experiences for students. Consequently, learning is not systematic and the benefits for students are unpredictable at best. Andersen et al. (1997) found that the average graduate with a doctorate in sport psychology has not acquired enough applied experience to meet the AAASP certification guidelines. Andersen et al. (1994) documented that most sport psychology students received fewer than 200 contact hours of *supervised* applied experiences during their graduate training. This total does not represent half of the contact time required for AAASP certification! Obviously, many students are not receiving sufficient supervised experiences. Rather than passively waiting for a legal procedure (fraud, negligence, malpractice) to stimulate advancement in applied sport psychology training, students and professionals alike would be prudent to assume a proactive orientation toward enhancing quality supervision in applied sport psychology training. Such an approach in any profession increases the likelihood of competent practice being offered to consumers of services.

The casualties of the deficits in contemporary applied training programs are widespread and significant. The students who receive incomplete training leave graduate programs with a superficial understanding of the complexities involved in establishing consulting relationships in sport. These young professionals often do not know how to design and implement an intervention program with an athlete or a team or may grossly underestimate the challenge involved in facilitating *meaningful* behavior and performance enhancement. Coaches and athletes who obtain the services of a poorly-trained sport psychology consultant place themselves, and the quality of their personal and team performance at risk. Institutions and agencies which employ improperly trained consultants assume liability for mistakes. The probability of making such mistakes is greater in the professional who has received limited supervised experiences in applied sport psychology training. Finally, the reputation of sport psychology as a practicing profession is at risk when untrained individuals (young or established professionals) are allowed to represent themselves to the public as competent sport psychology consultants. This is of particular concern from an ethical perspective given that many sport psychology consultants are very aware of the lack of adequately supervised sport psychology consulting experiences either in their retooling process or in their original graduate training. The consequences of deficits in the applied area of training programs are significant and worthy of collective reflection, attention and action by the leaders of the field.

One of the most effective means of enhancing applied sport psychology training is graduate program accreditation. Accreditation is defined as a "voluntary self-regulatory process of quality assessment and enhancement among institutions and professional programs of higher education and training" (APA, 1986, p. 1).

A Cost-Benefit Analysis of Accreditation in Sport Psychology

Despite the tremendous success of the APA accreditation process in regulating and enhancing standards of graduate training, the initiation of accreditation in the specialty of sport psychology has been slow to develop. Many arguments used against accreditation are outdated and/or unfounded and appear to be grounded in fundamental misunderstandings of the accreditation process. Common concerns voiced in opposition to accreditation in sport psychology will be reviewed and contrasted against benefits documented by other fields which have implemented formal training standards via program accreditation.

Perceived Obstacles to Accreditation in Sport Psychology. Commonly cited arguments against accreditation in sport psychology relate to the cost of accreditation for the institution, the effects of accreditation on the smaller graduate programs in sport psychology, the larger impact of accreditation on the growth of the field, especially in academic settings, and the impact of accreditation on the academic freedom of faculty. Concerns about the cost of accreditation are largely overstated. Graduate programs which are interested in seeking accreditation are generally held responsible for an application fee to cover administrative costs, a two-day site visit from a group of two to three visitors, the cost of any program enhancements which the accreditation committee and site visit team recommend, and an annual fee to cover administrative costs in reviewing annual reports. The application fee for APA accreditation as of January 1998 for new doctoral programs is $2,000. Most organizations also establish an annual fee for maintaining accredited status. While APA charges $4,500 for a site visit, a two-day site visit by two individuals can be liberally estimated at $2,000 for all travel and lodging expenses. Given the cost of program enhancements not withstanding, the total cost of accreditation over a five-year cycle could be set by AAASP at approximately $5,000 or an average of $1,000 per year. Obviously, the greatest cost in the implementation phase for any professional organization moving in this direction is in the human resource investment required.

Despite the financial costs and other university resources required for accreditation, outcome studies have indicated that faculty and administrators generally perceive accreditation to be a "cost-effective" measure in view of the consequential benefits and program enhancements (Zellman, Johansen, & Van Winkle, 1994). Interestingly, a separate study of the effects of accreditation on athletic training graduate programs indicated that accredited programs actually increased their resources following accreditation (Roth, 1989). Specific increases in resources included the addition of new faculty lines, an increased ration of full- to part-time employees, a decreased supervision ratio, the reallocation of departmental funding to support the accredited program, more computers, more support personnel, an increase in library holdings, and the establishment of a departmental professional library (Roth, 1989). In view of these facts, it becomes difficult to understand how programs committed to training sport psychology students could not find a way to afford the cost of accreditation!

Opponents of accreditation also fear that financial crises will force universities to eliminate graduate programs which fail to earn accredited status. Rather than lose faculty positions and jobs, these opponents argue that the field would be better off postponing training regulation and enhancement until the field becomes more well-established. In reality, inadequate graduate programs are likely to be terminated by cost-conscious administrators regardless of whether accreditation procedures are enacted. Programs which fear unfavorable evaluations by an accreditation committee and are not able or willing to upgrade their programs to develop needed competencies in their students should reflect upon the question of whether they should be in the business of training future professionals. Programs with one faculty member or lacking in critical training experiences may find that Deans eliminate their programs prior to the initiation of any accreditation process by the field of sport psychology. On the other hand, the accreditation process can serve as an objective index of program quality for administrators. Thus, accredited programs should be better able to protect themselves from administrative elimination or down sizing than unaccredited programs.

Unfortunately, some professionals seem to fear that program accreditation will stifle individual creativity in structuring a graduate training program. In reality, accreditation facilitates greater program diversity. Accredited programs would cover the core training areas and students and faculty would have the freedom to further specialize their program of study with the security that they have met the minimum requirements for training sport psychologists. Accreditation and academic freedom are interdependent forces which complement and protect rather than oppose each other (Elman, 1994). The fact remains that not every existing applied sport psychology program will be accredited and enhancements will be necessary in many existing programs. This process of self-enhancement will require the critical and creative efforts of faculty as well as institutional support. Fortunately, accreditation procedures in other fields have demonstrated a history of short- and long-term benefits which greatly outweigh the costs of the process.

Consequences of Accreditation in Sport Psychology. The consequences of accreditation are far-reaching and seem fairly consistent regardless of the setting being accredited. Selden and Porter (1977) have identified internal, external, professional, and societal benefits of accreditation. With regard to documented internal benefits, accredited programs have gained prestige (Zellman et al., 1994) and "stature on campus" (Roth, 1989, p. 35). Additionally, the faculty's involvement in and awareness of the program increased in the process of evaluation and planning (Roth, 1989). Program goals became clarified (Roth, 1989; Zellman et al., 1994) and faculty morale (Zellman et al., 1994) and program cohesion (Roth, 1989) have been shown to increase as a consequence of the accreditation process. Selden and Porter (1977) also identify the benefit of a general raising of standards among educational institutions (p. 8). Zellman et al. (1994) documented student-oriented innovations in curricula, enhanced cultural diversity in curricula, and enhanced student performance in accredited programs. Notably, Roth (1989) found that accreditation in athletic training programs led to an increased applied training component and better integration of research into the program.

Selden and Porter (1977) identified external benefits of accreditation as a useful reference for students researching programs in a specialization as well as a measure of quality for external granting agencies. Professionally, accreditation can be linked to and thus strengthen certification and licensure criteria. Accredited specialty programs are also able to gain increased support (Selden & Porter, 1977) and add resources (such as faculty) to their programs (Roth, 1989). Roth (1989) also found that accredited programs were able to increase their interdisciplinary involvement and collaboration. Finally, Selden and Porter (1977) argue that accreditation is valuable protection "against harmful external and internal pressures" (p. 14-15), such as politically-motivated influences from legislators and administrators. Thus, accreditation will help to secure the academic freedom of graduate programs and the faculty contributing to those programs.

There are a number of specific consequences of accreditation which would be probable in applied sport psychology. First, accreditation is likely to stimulate greater inter-disciplinary interaction in training programs. As a result, applied sport psychology will gain greater recognition "across campus." A public commitment to enhancement and self-regulation should afford the field an increased degree of respect in academia. By raising the standard of training for future professionals, the field will also be better able to articulate its social relevance both to service populations and funding agencies. Subsequent impressions of applied sport psychology should contribute to professional growth and within a few years, the impact of well-trained young professionals may be actualized as additional markets open for individuals trained in applied sport psychology because of increased recognition of competency by professional sport teams and the general public.

The job market should become more fertile as programs desiring accredited status seek to add faculty. It is true that adding faculty to sport psychology programs will be a challenge for many programs and not all programs will be successful in adding new faculty. Fortunately, accreditation will provide programs with some leverage in requesting additional faculty, especially for establishing a critical mass to meet minimum training standards. Faculty and administrators will nevertheless need to be creative and resourceful as they broach the issue of adding faculty. It may be worthwhile to examine the potential for dual or adjunct appointments between exercise science, psychology, and athletic departments. The utilization of dual appointments should also facilitate the development of formal, supervised applied experiences for students. Several Exercise and Sport Science (ESS) departments may have to make some difficult decisions regarding the focus of the department. Currently, many Exercise and Sport Science departments attempt to offer several specialization degrees without the faculty to support these so-called "Ph.D.'s" in sport psychology, exercise physiology, motor learning, etc. Exercise and Sport Science departments may need to streamline to one or two Ph.D. specializations and different universities will become known for their exceptional programs in one or two areas. This approach will be a significant improvement over having 4 or 5 mediocre "Ph. D." specializations in one academic department. Despite the short-term challenges inherent in adding faculty positions, conscientious and resourceful efforts to add faculty will ultimately contribute to a larger job market for well-trained applied sport psychologists which should last beyond the initial stage of program growth.

Voluntary accreditation would be likely to stimulate much-needed graduate training advancements by enhancing the diversity of program offerings, especially as they relate to supervised, applied training experiences. At the same time, programs would have to formulate identities and thus acquire a greater clarity of focus. This enhanced program focus will help prospective students to identify training programs suited to their interests. Consequently, students who are interested in learning how to practice will be less likely to find themselves in research-only sport psychology programs and vice-versa. Furthermore, by endorsing an integrative science-practice model, programs will be more likely to prepare students with the skills which are required in the contemporary job market.

Administrative Responses to Accreditation. From the perspective of graduate program directors, Skinner, Berry, and Jackson (1994) reported that over 80% of the training directors who went through the APA accreditation process perceived the accreditation standards in a favorable light and at least 75% of the training directors valued the accreditation committees input as "educational" (p. 297).

Based on the athletic training accreditation process, Roth (1989) advised that the accreditation process was best approached from a "vision of excellence" (p. 38) perspective. This comment is important because accreditation is often misconceptualized as a concrete standard for curriculum design to which programs are bound. On the contrary, accreditation is actually a *voluntary,* dynamic process of self-enhancement among educational programs. Earning accredited status demonstrates an ongoing commitment to self-regulation and enhancement (Bender, 1983). This commitment to the future of the field is desperately needed in contemporary applied sport psychology.

An Action Proposal for Accreditation in Sport Psychology

Despite the lag in organizational attention to an obvious training need, there have been no definitive arguments put forth to oppose the development and implementation of a voluntary accreditation procedure for applied sport psychology graduate programs. Similar to Rogers' insightful perception over fifty years ago (Report, 1947), a failure to regulate training in applied sport psychology today will be an abuse of whatever public trust currently exists in the profession. It is no longer possible to dodge accreditation under the pretense that "the field isn't ready for it." Students are asking for a more advanced training model. At the 1997 AAASP Conference in San Diego, CA, a vote was taken in the student meeting on the need for accreditation of graduate programs in sport psychology. Of the over 80 students present for the vote, fewer than 5 students voted in opposition with the remainder voting in support for program accreditation (Students', 1997). Accreditation can both stimulate and guide much needed enhancements in sport psychology graduate programs. The job market is demanding a more advanced training model and it is time to embrace the issue and establish training standards and accreditation criteria in applied sport psychology. Faculty must allay their personal fears and objectively assess the benefits of program development that will be initiated and sustained by the accreditation process. Furthermore, sport psychology must remember that psychology, a much larger field even in the 1940s, started with only 18 accredited programs (Sears, 1947).

The Role of AAASP

AAASP can address the accreditation issue by advocating the benefits of accreditation for the field of sport psychology. This process will require the formation of an AAASP Graduate Training Standards and Accreditation Committee. A recommended committee composition of two student members, one Past President, the current President, and three at-large members would provide diversity, experience, and perspective. This committee would be charged with developing a model and process to systemically advance the state of graduate training in applied sport psychology. It may be helpful to initiate this process in two stages thus making the process more accessible to the programs which are upgrading to meet the accreditation standards. The first step in the review process would involve the formation of a committee to develop the specific accreditation standards, a review protocol, and a registry of programs. The second step in the process would involve a transition from a registry of programs into the formal accreditation of programs in applied sport psychology. While this process would require some organizational resources, its culmination would indeed mark a historical advancement in the field. Furthermore, as a non-profit organization, AAASP is chartered to return its resources to the membership. Investing AAASP funds in a process that has the potential to advance the field as a whole is an investment that will pay professional dividends that can not be quantified by dollars and cents.

Step I: A Graduate Program Registry

The first step in the process of voluntary program accreditation would begin with the systematic development of criteria proposed for admission into the registry. Programs would engage in a comprehensive self-study to determine how effectively they meet the registry criteria. To create a Sport Psychology Graduate Program Registry, AAASP would need to develop a Sport Psychology Standards and Review Protocol for Master's and Doctoral programs that would allow for an initial, informational review of three areas within each program: (a) the core academic content should be reviewed for evidence that the available interdisciplinary coursework develops the competencies required for certification, (b) a critical faculty mass and faculty-to-student ratios should be established so that doctoral programs in particular are able to manage the advising and supervised practicum experiences essential to comprehensive training in applied sport psychology, and (c) because it is recommended that the field first pursue the accreditation of a science-practice model, a review of both the research training and practicum experiences provided within the course of a program will be essential. A balance of research and applied experiences would increase the probability of producing competent professionals, who are then adequately qualified for certification *and* available faculty positions in sport psychology.

Once the criteria for review are established and interested programs have completed a self-study, program folios would be submitted to AAASP for review. An AAASP committee would either initially approve these programs for the registry or provide the programs with specific recommendations for program enhancement. After this first stage, those programs which were unable to demonstrate their ability to develop the defined competencies in students would notify AAASP of their intent (or lack thereof) to meet the registry standards, and project the year in which they realistically expected to meet those standards. Concurrently, AAASP would establish the Graduate Program

Registry and publish the universities which meet the standards in the *Directory of Graduate Programs in Applied Sport Psychology* (Sachs, Burke & Gomer, 1998) and in the *Journal of Applied Sport Psychology.* The programs which are listed on the Registry would also be the first programs eligible for accreditation since they should be the most prepared for full accreditation. The compilation of a Graduate Program Registry would mark the completion of the first step in graduate program accreditation for applied sport psychology.

Step II: Graduate Program Accreditation

As graduate schools submit their programs for review, approval of the accreditation standards by the AAASP Fellows will merge with the registration process. A committee coordinated with the Standards committee would be charged with the task of developing a procedure for program accreditation. The procedures used by APA for program accreditation are well-established and may be worth considering as a model for applied sport psychology accreditation. The APA requires that programs seeking accreditation declare the specific training model being used to train students and then demonstrate the program's fit with the declared model. Since accreditation is a voluntary process, it is the programs responsibility to establish the burden of proof that it meets or exceeds the accreditation criteria. Science-practice training programs often demonstrate their compliance with the model by providing outcome measures related to research productivity, teaching involvement, service delivery, professional service, degree completion rates, and job placement success (Gaddy, Charlot-Swilley, Nelson, & Reich, 1995). The presentation of this evidence in the form of a comprehensive self-study is followed by a site visit from a team representing the accreditation committee. The APA allows programs to have some input in selecting the site visitors. This site visit is usually funded by the department seeking accreditation. Shortly after the site visit, the site visit team files its report with both the department seeking accreditation and the accreditation committee. The department then has an opportunity to review the team's findings and address how they will respond to the perceived weaknesses in their program. Based on the information gathered through the self-study, the site visit, and the program's response to the site visit team's report, the accreditation committee makes a decision regarding the status of the program's application. Programs may be granted either full or provisional accreditation status. Fully accredited programs must file an annual report in subsequent years detailing any modifications in the training program and the program's continued compliance with the training model. Assuming that the program is relatively stable and does not provide the committee with any reason for premature reevaluation, future self-studies and site visits would be scheduled to take place at five years intervals following the initial accreditation. Provisionally accredited programs must file annual reports and also document their efforts to address program weaknesses.

Programs which are not satisfied with the committee's decision regarding their status are entitled to appeal that decision. In any case, the committee reserves the right to place fully- or provisionally-accredited programs on probationary status for significant changes that impair the program's ability to provide the minimal educational experiences for students. It is recommended that the AAASP committee charged with developing procedures for sport psychology base their approach on the APA model since it has been met with favorable reviews from the programs involved in the process (Skinner et al., 1994). This general model would be tailored to match the determined criteria for the field of sport psychology. Psychology and other disciplines in ESS (e.g., athletic training, sport management) have embraced such standards. What makes applied sport psychology so different that movement toward program enhancement has not been embraced and enacted?

The accreditation of graduate programs in applied sport psychology can take many forms and one such proposal has been advanced in this paper. It is a sad but accurate reflection of the level of training in contemporary applied sport psychology that when the accreditation process is initially implemented, few programs will likely meet the proposed guidelines. However, this position is not an acceptable rationale for failing to pursue accreditation at the present time. If only a few programs meet the preliminary guidelines, at least there will be a few programs in which students can be confident that they will get quality, comprehensive training in applied sport psychology. A few high quality programs are better than none, and far better than many not properly training future professionals. These accredited schools will become the prototypes for a developing network of accredited programs in the near future. As noted, psychology started out with only 18 accredited programs; sport psychology should be realistic and place quality before quantity.

The Job Market

Persistent misconceptions continue to exist regarding employment in the field of applied sport psychology. Students interested in pursuing the specialization of applied sport psychology are often misinformed concerning the nature of job availability, and continually discouraged by the myth that there are no jobs in sport psychology. The reality of the situation indicates the ratio of jobs to new Ph.D.s graduating with specialized training in sport psychology compares favorably with other academic disciplines in the social sciences. Students need only read *On the Market* (Boufis & Olsen, 1997) to understand the extraordinary level of competition for jobs in other fields and how the competition for jobs in sport psychology pales in comparison to many of these fields. As an example, consider the number of students coming out of doctoral programs in sport psychology to those graduating from clinical psychology programs. Clinical psychologists flood the field each year with new Ph.D.s searching for positions, whereas the production of young professionals in applied sport psychology is very limited. Thus, the number of available sport psychology jobs is quite small in comparison to the number of clinical psychology jobs offered each year, however, the relative placement rate for sport psychologists is favorable. Recently, the AAASP Graduate Tracking Committee indicated that for the last five years, approximately 30 new Ph.D.s have entered the market each year (Andersen et al., 1997). Consider that in 1996, over 20 sport psychology-related jobs were available at universities in North America (Stevens, 1996). A fairly fertile employment situation appears to exist for recent graduates seeking sport psychology positions in academia. Additionally, this example assumes each new graduate plans on pursuing a career in academia and excludes the possibility of independent employment in the consulting market or employment in another related area (e.g., athletic academic advising, university counseling centers). Results of the AAASP Graduate Tracking Committee (Andersen et al., 1997) support this claim since the vast majority of sport psychology doctoral graduates who were interested in academic careers were placed in academic jobs with an emphasis on sport psychology. Thus, it appears that jobs do exist in sport psychology and students must become more informed regarding the type of training that will best prepare and position the young professional for academic sport psychology.

A major source of the confusion over the viability of the sport psychology job market may be the type of training received by job applicants. As the field exists today, individuals seeking to become sport psychologists are best served by getting a broad-based, science-practice training within the interdisciplinary specialization of sport psychology. Consider, for example, the persistent myth that a doctoral degree from a general clinical or counseling psychology program will prepare an individual for a career in sport psychology. The reality of the job market is that if a student seeks a university position in sport psychology in the United States, well over 90 percent of these positions are in ESS departments. Further, these departments have traditionally hired Ph.D.s from ESS programs with specializations in sport psychology and interdisciplinary training in clinical or counseling psychology. Individuals with pure clinical or counseling training are naturally at a competitive disadvantage for these position searches and this situation will continue until either psychology departments demonstrate an interest in hiring sport psychologists or a standard training model is developed for sport psychologists that makes it possible for students trained in either psychology or ESS to be able to compete for these academic positions. Critically examining the reality of the sport psychology job market provides a more optimistic employment outlook than is currently portrayed, especially for graduates of exercise and sport science programs. Several recommendations are offered below to promote more accurate representations of the field with respect to employment opportunities.

AAASP's Role in Promoting Job Opportunities

AAASP should create a job database that can be updated by sending out a form or e-mail notice twice a year to universities requesting information on sport psychology related jobs that are available. This information would allow AAASP to stay abreast of employment opportunities within the field. AAASP could then promote these sport psychology job openings in the AAASP Newsletter and on the AAASP homepage on the World Wide Web. These advertisements would centralize information for those attempting to locate employment opportunities and, in addition, send the implicit message that there is a strong desire from the organization for *competent* professionals to fill the available positions. While AAASP is seeking information on, and promoting available sport psychology jobs, administrators at North American universities should be formally contacted by e-mail or a mailing that informs them of AAASP certification and encourages the requirement of certification or application for certification as a basic component of job announcements for sport psychology faculty positions. As a part of this outreach, AAASP should annually contact ESS and Psychology department chairs with a mailing to update them on relevant training issues such as accreditation and certification. This last effort should contribute to enhancing public awareness of the minimum level of training necessary for an individual to be considered competent in sport psychology.

After encouraging students to develop broader skills within the specialization of sport psychology and communicating certification standards to the academic community, other branches of the university and relevant non-academic organizations will need to be contacted and informed about the potential role of sport psychology professionals in their work. Communicating openly with university counseling centers, academic advising units, and independent sport organizations/leagues will assist in clarifying the nature of the job market in sport psychology. Such initiatives increase the overall awareness of the profession of applied sport psychology in the public domain, and enhance the field's professional reputation. Educating professionals about sport psychology will help tap into more new and existing job markets for sport psychology than ever before, a necessary step in the fields ongoing development.

Educational Outreach

The logical extension of communicating with academic units regarding the nature of applied sport psychology would involve a systematic marketing and outreach effort toward private individuals and groups who may desire contact with sport psychology practitioners. To effectively facilitate the education of individuals and sport organizations regarding the current status of applied sport psychology, however, would demand a very efficient use of AAASP's resources. This educational outreach process would have the benefit of informing national organizations regarding the qualifications of sport psychologists and stimulating the development of greater career opportunities for sport psychologists. Ultimately, such contact will be influential in increasing student placement in diverse fields related to sport psychology.

The primary outreach issue challenging the field's growth is a general lack of communication with external sources regarding the nature of applied sport psychology and the qualifications necessary for the proper preparation of a sport psychologist. Andersen et al. (1997) note that consulting opportunities have not increased for sport psychology graduates in recent years. Potential outreach efforts should be directed at, but not limited to, athletes, coaches, athletic directors, NCAA, professional organizations, and the public. The educational process for these groups would involve both promoting AAASP Certification standards as the minimum criteria for practice and addressing general misconceptions surrounding sport psychology. By clarifying the nature of sport psychology and the minimum training requirements for sport psychology service provision, AAASP may contribute to expanding the opportunities available for work in applied sport psychology.

Certification should be promoted and used more as a tool to educate those in positions to hire sport psychologists. Many individuals in administrative positions continue to hire practitioners who are not specifically trained in sport psychology, preferring to base their decisions on personal networks and referrals from associates. Too often this practice results in the hiring of former athletes with no formal training in sport psychology or clinical psychologists with no specific training in sport psychology. Knowledge of AAASP certification would provide administrators, coaches, and organizations with a basis on which to judge candidates for employment, ideally leading to an increased number of competent professionals working with athletes. To affect change on a national level, AAASP must commit to educating coaches, sport administrators, National Governing Bodies (NGBs) and other sport organizations on the current status of certification. Enhancing awareness of the minimum standards for sport psychology service provision will also enhance understanding of the nature of applied sport psychology. When individual and organizational levels of sport become aware of the necessary qualifications of an applied sport psychologist, increased employment opportunities for competent sport psychologists may be enhanced. Misconceptions about sport psychology are sufficiently wide-spread to suggest that significant time and energy will be required for comprehensive outreach efforts to be successful.

AAASP Outreach Consultant Proposal. One possible means for directing organizational attention and effort to outreach without placing an undue demand on individual AAASP members would involve creating the new position of AAASP Outreach Consultant. This position could be a two-year paid internship, and the individual would be responsible for formally and informally educating athletic organizations at all levels. The minimum qualifications should include a Master's Degree with a specialization in sport psychology. This position would provide a unique opportunity for a student in the field to gain experience within the organization and to develop a vast network of sport psychology connections nationwide. The outreach consultant would be the impetus for the educational process and, after some time in the position, be able to return to AAASP with tremendous feedback regarding the experience. This individual could present her/his realistic assessment of the state of the field at each AAASP conference. Creating a position for an AAASP Outreach Consultant would be an excellent step toward reducing practice outside of one's competencies and increasing awareness in the public domain regarding the qualifications of applied sport psychologists.

AAASP must adopt a more proactive role in disseminating information and creating a public awareness of applied sport psychology. The existing financial resources of the organization can be used to generate and distribute informational materials on the profession of applied sport psychology and to fund an internship to advocate applied sport psychology at the national level. These educational efforts should subsequently increase employment opportunities for qualified professionals, improve understanding of applied sport psychology on a national level, and stimulate a more efficient entry process for students interested in careers in applied sport psychology. The AAASP Outreach Consultants position would be one of the most progressive uses of AAASP funds imaginable!

Sport Psychology: Advancement is the Goal

A central purpose of AAASP has been to develop and promote the professional and scientific aspects of applied sport psychology. The authors have provided a description of several issues which confront the advancement of the field. Specific action plans for progress on these issues have been proposed (Silva, 1996b, 1997a, 1997b) and it is anticipated that colleagues will recognize the urgency of these issues in determining the future existence and quality of the field of sport psychology. As the field moves toward the 21st century, AAASP must continue to adopt a proactive role in facilitating advancement. The AAASP leadership and professional membership must mobilize together to place meaningful issues at the forefront of the Association's agenda. Students and young professionals, the future of the field, must also assume a more proactive role in the advancement of the field and thus facilitate the emergence of sport psychology as a worthy and notable discipline *and* profession in the 21st century.

References

AAASP passes certification criteria. (1990, Winter). *AAASP Newsletter, 5*, 3, 8.

AAASP (1995, Winter). Ethical principles of AAASP. *AAASP Newsletter, 10*, 15, 21.

Alford, L. (1997, Winter). Organization and Outreach and Education Committee Report, *AAASP Newsletter, 12*, 9, 25.

American Psychological Association (1986). *Accreditation handbook.* Washington, DC: APA.

Andersen, M. B., Van Raalte, J. L., & Brewer, B. W. (1994). Assessing the skills of sport psychology supervisors. *The Sport Psychologist, 8*, 238–247.

Andersen, M. B., Williams, J. M., Aldridge, T., & Taylor, J. (1997). Tracking the training and careers of advanced degree programs in sport psychology, 1989 to 1994. *The Sport Psychologist, 11*, 326–344.

Andersen, M. B., & Williams-Rice, B. T. (1996). Supervision in the education and training of sport psychology service providers. *The Sport Psychologist, 10*, 278–290.

Bender, L. W. (1983). Accreditation: Its misuses and misconceptions. In K. E. Young, C. M. Chambers, H. R. Kells, & Associates (Eds.), *Understanding accreditation: Contemporary perspectives on issues and practices in evaluating educational quality.* San Francisco, CA: Jossey-Bass Publishers.

Boufis, C., & Olsen, V. C. (1997). *On the market: Surviving the academic job search.* New York: Riverhead Books.

Cogan, K. D., Petrie, T., Richardson, P., & Martin, S. (1998, September). Applied sport psychology training at the University of North Texas Center for Sport Psychology. In K. D. Cogan (Chair), *Interdisciplinary approaches to applied sport psychology training.* Symposium conducted at the Annual Conference of the Association for the Advancement of Applied Sport Psychology.

Conroy, D. E. (1996). Science-practice and accreditation in applied sport psychology. *Journal of Applied Sport Psychology, 8*, S51.

Conroy, D. E. (1997, September). A cost-benefit analysis of graduate program accreditation in sport psychology. In J. M. Silva (Chair), *Initiating program accreditation in sport psychology.* Symposium conducted at the Annual Conference of the Association for the Advancement of Applied Sport Psychology.

Corlett, J. (1996). Sophistry, Socrates, and sport psychology. *The Sport Psychologist, 10*, 84–94.

Elman, S. E. (1994). Academic freedom and regional accreditation: Guarantors of quality in the academy. *New Directions for Higher Education, 88*, 89–100.

Gaddy, C. D., Charlot-Swilley, D., Nelson, P. D., & Reich, J. N. (1995). Selected outcomes of accredited programs. *Professional Psychology: Research and Practice, 26*, 507–513.

Lutz, D. J. (1990). An overview of training models in sport psychology. *The Sport Psychologist, 4*, 63–71.

Murphy, S. M. (1988). The on-site provision of sport psychology services at the 1987 U.S. Olympic Festival. *The Sport Psychologist, 2*, 337–350.

Murphy, S. M. (1996, September). Wither certification? In J. M. Silva (Chair), *Current issues confronting the advancement of applied sport psychology.* Symposium conducted at the Annual Conference of the Association for the Advancement of Applied Sport Psychology.

Petrie, T. A., & Watkins, C. E. (1994). A survey of counseling psychology programs and exercise/sport science departments: Sport psychology issues and training. *The Sport Psychologist, 8*, 28–36.

Report of the Committee on Training in Clinical Psychology of the American Psychological Association submitted at Detroit meeting of the American Psychological Association, September 9–13, 1947 (1947). Recommended training program in clinical psychology. *American Psychologist, 2*, 539–558.

Roth, R. A. (1989). NCATE: Institutional perspectives from the pilot studies. *Action in Teacher Education, 11*, 33–38.

Sachs, M., Burke, K., & Gomer, S. (1998). *Directory of graduate programs in applied sport psychology.* Morgantown, WV. Fitness Information Technology Inc.

Selden, W. K., & Porter, H. V. (1977). *Accreditation: Its purposes and uses.* Washington, DC: Council on Postsecondary Accreditation.

Silva, J. M. (1984). The emergence of applied sport psychology: Contemporary trends—Future issues. *International Journal of Sport Psychology, 15*, 40–51.

Silva, J. M. (1989). Establishing professional standards and advancing applied sport psychology research. *Journal of Applied Sport Psychology, 1*, 160–165.

Silva, J. M. (1996a). Current issues confronting the advancement of applied sport psychology. *Journal of Applied Sport Psychology, 8*, S50–S52.

Silva, J. M. (1996b). A second move: Confronting persistent issues that challenge the advancement of applied sport psychology. *Journal of Applied Sport Psychology, 8*, S52.

Silva, J. M. (1997a). Initiating program accreditation in sport psychology. *Journal of Applied Sport Psychology, 9*, S47–S49.

Silva, J. M. (1997b, August). Advancing progressive training models in applied sport psychology. In C. M. Janelle (Chair), *Training, employment, and accreditation issues in sport psychology—Student perspectives.* Symposium conducted at the meeting of the American Psychological Association, Chicago, IL.

Silva, J. M. (1997c, September). Accreditation: A process designed to enhance preparatory and professional standards. In J. M. Silva (Chair), *Initiating program accreditation in sport psychology.* Symposium conducted at the Annual Conference of the Association for the Advancement of Applied Sport Psychology.

Silva, J. M. (1998, September). Interdisciplinary approaches to training in applied sport psychology at the University of North Carolina at Chapel Hill. In K. D. Cogan (Chair), *Interdisciplinary approaches to applied sport psychology training.* Symposium conducted at the Annual Conference of the Association for the Advancement of Applied Sport Psychology.

Simons, J. P., & Andersen, M. B. (1995). The development of consulting practice in applied sport psychology: Some personal perspectives. *The Sport Psychologist, 9*, 449–468.

Skinner, L. J., Berry, K. K., & Jackson, T. L. (1994). Accreditation of doctoral psychology training programs: Results of a nationwide survey. *Professional Psychology: Research and Practice, 25*, 296–299.

Stevens, D. E. (1996) Personal Communication with J. M. Silva, September 1996.

Students' Vote on Graduate Training Accreditation Issue. (1997, September 25). The Annual Conference of the Association for the Advancement of Applied Sport Psychology.

Taylor, J. (1991). Career direction, development, and opportunities in applied sport psychology. *The Sport Psychologist, 5,* 266–280.

Wiechman, S. (1998, September). Applied sport psychology training at the University of Washington. In K. D. Cogan (Chair), *Interdisciplinary approaches to applied sport psychology training*. Symposium conducted at the Annual Conference of the Association for the Advancement of Applied Sport Psychology.

Wiggins, D. K. (1984). The history of sport psychology in North America. In J. M. Silva and R. S. Weinberg (Eds.), *Psychological foundations of sport.* Champaign, IL: Human Kinetics.

Yukelson, D. (1998, September). Applied sport psychology training at Penn State University. In K. D. Cogan (Chair), *Interdisciplinary approaches to applied sport psychology training.* Symposium conducted at the Annual Conference of the Association for the Advancement of Applied Sport Psychology.

Zaichkowsky, L. D. (1997, September). *Initiating program accreditation in sport psychology: A reaction.* Symposium conducted at the Annual Conference of the Association for the Advancement of Applied Sport Psychology.

Zellman, G. L., Johansen, A. S., & Van Winkle, J. (1994). *Examining the effects of accreditation on military child development center operations and outcomes.* Santa Monica, CA: RAND.

47 Applied Sport Psychology: Issues and Challenges

ROBERT S. WEINBERG
University of North Texas at Denton

This reading was the presidential address delivered by Bob Weinberg at the third annual conference of the Association for the Advancement of Applied Sport Psychology (AAASP). This young organization had experienced rapid growth, and Weinberg addressed the critical issues facing the organization and the challenges anticipated. One of his goals for AAASP was for it to take the lead in critical applied issues for sport psychology.

These critical issues included certification, applied research, professional practice, and interdisciplinary cooperation. Certification had been a major goal of AAASP since its inception three years prior. The perception by many AAASP members was that there were too many unqualified individuals calling themselves sport psychologists. Inappropriate methodologies used by these individuals were creating a negative perception about the field. However, the AAASP certification committee had run into a variety of problems that delayed the implementation of the certification process. This committee could not even agree on what title to use to refer to a certified individual. The author advocated that this AAASP certification should be respected by consumers of their services and that AAASP should promote this certification. This prophetic recommendation has been an AAASP challenge for at least the subsequent 18 years. AAASP is still trying to determine the best way to promote its certified consultants to consumer groups, individuals, and organizations.

In the infancy of the AAASP, Weinberg was an advocate for the development of cooperation with professional organizations that had common goals and missions. These interrelationships could augment the growth and development of this young AAASP organization. Some efforts were made along those lines, but the rapid growth and development of AAASP over the ensuing years probably had little to do with the interrelationships.

Many graduate students, at that time, did not think that they received the best possible education at their universities because of the lack of interdisciplinary programs in applied sport psychology. For example, graduate students in physical education had difficulty enrolling in some counseling and clinical psychology courses since the courses tended to be reserved for graduate students in those specific programs. Over the years some graduate programs have achieved this cooperation in interdisciplinary enrollment, but it remains an issue.

Weinberg suggests a distinction in which practicing sport psychologists are also researchers. He recognizes that this scientist-practitioner model had proved unsuccessful in other similar disciplines (e.g., clinical psychology). Part of the challenge in this model is that, from an academic perspective, the practitioner is usually perceived as a second-class academician by researchers. Applied sport psychologists have actually done a fairly good job over the years of maintaining a research orientation as well as sharing expertise with coaches and athletes through workshops, presentations, and interventions with athletes. It is interesting to view how these issues played out over the years for AAASP.

Development and Accomplishments of the AAASP

Taking a closer look at our membership, the AAASP has the unique distinction of being, to my knowledge, the only professional society to have an equal mix of professionals from physical education and psychology backgrounds. This mix is essential if we are to move forward as an integrative and interdisciplinary field. To date, by and large, sport psychologists trained in psychology vs. physical education have led virtually separate lives with minimal interaction on an academic and professional level. As I will discuss later concerning certification issues, it is imperative that we start to close the artificial gap that has evolved between sport psychologists from physical education and psychology. The AAASP can play an instrumental role in developing and fostering these relationships by getting input and feedback from the membership. I believe that one of the reasons that in a few short years the AAASP has become a strong positive force in the evolving field of sport psychology is that it has attracted a talented and interdisciplinary membership. However, we need your continued help to aid us in identifying what mechanisms and strategies might help bring us closer together rather than tear us apart. This could be accomplished, for example, by presenting a symposium in which members from physical education and psychology can voice their opinions and suggestions concerning ways to achieve greater harmony, cooperation and integration in teaching, research, and application of sport psychology

Another unique aspect of our membership is the large contingent of students that regularly attend our conferences. In fact, approximately 45% of our membership are students which demonstrates to me that the new generation of sport psychologists is keenly interested in the applied

---

aspects of our field. It also signals to me that the students can play an important role in the development of our field and your input is critical in helping to identify the needs and concerns of students currently trying to study the field of sport psychology. Along these lines, I for one, have been very impressed by the dedication and personal commitment exhibited by our student members. Your attendance at the conferences, usually at considerable financial expense, is a testimony to your involvement and professional growth and development in the field of applied sport psychology. I would encourage the student membership (in conjunction with professional members) to submit symposium and panel discussions that might highlight some of your concerns as budding professionals and offer possible solutions or directions that may help better meet the academic and professional needs of the students. How can your training as sport psychologists in the area of research, teaching and practice be improved so that you are better prepared to meet the challenges that await you upon graduation? Your input in answering these questions is crucial for the development of applied sport psychology as we try to tackle the many problems of an emerging profession.

The success of our infant organization can also be seen in a number of different areas but all of these in some way reflect the interest and enthusiasm about the field of applied sport psychology. First of all, although this is only the third conference, we already have attendance and membership either rivaling or surpassing many sport science professional organizations that have been in existence for many years. Most professional organizations usually take many years to get off the ground and receive the recognition from professionals already in that field of endeavor. However, the 1st Annual AAASP Conference held in Jekyll Island was attended by over 200 participants and we have consistently been increasing our numbers in the last two years.

A second way to evaluate the success of an organization is to take a close look at the type of programs that are offered to their membership at their annual conventions. I think you will agree that the AAASP has been extremely successful in putting together a wide array of presentations including workshops, panel discussions, free communications, interactive poster presentations, invited speakers, informal conversation hours and symposium. In fact, the program committee is already hard pressed to find time for all the presentations in our 3 1/2 days of conference. The willingness on your part to share your research, ideas, professional concerns and practical applications in applied sport psychology with your colleagues has provided us with a forum to grow professionally and personally from our involvement in the AAASP.

The AAASP is also taking the next step forward with disseminating new information and ideas to our membership and other individuals interested in applied sport psychology by the publication of the *Journal of Applied Sport Psychology* (JASP). The JASP is designed to advance thought, theory and research on applied aspects of sport psychology. John Silva is the editor and Joan Duda, Larry Brawley and myself are section editors for social psychology, health psychology and intervention/performance enhancement, respectively. The journal will offer several topic issues that will take an indepth look at a particular area of applied sport psychology and should serve as a valuable resource for teaching, research and practice. I encourage you to submit your work to the journal because it will be a reflection of our association and we want to put forth the highest standards of scholarship possible.

A final aspect of the AAASP that is indicative of an emerging professional society is the Newsletter. Most professional societies have newsletters that keep the membership informed on upcoming conferences, activities of the membership, and other items of interest to the profession. But I think that those of you that have been receiving the AAASP newsletter will wholeheartedly agree with me that it is nothing short of first class, already exceeding the newsletters of many sport science professional organizations. It goes way beyond what a traditional newsletter usually tries to accomplish with many added features such as conversations with different members, issues and answers, the applied sport psychology forum and other interesting columns.

Future Challenges for Applied Sport Psychology

The rapid growth of AAASP is in part a reflection of the recent development of applied sport psychology. This development can be seen in the appearance of new scientific and professional journals, the increased number of professionals offering psychological services to individual athletes and teams in promoting health as well as performance enhancement, the increased funding of research by federal and state organizations, as well as the creation of Division 47 (Exercise and Sport Psychology) within the American Psychological Association. While this is an exciting time in applied sport psychology, it is also a time when we must bear the increased burden of making sure that sport psychology develops in a manner that encourages the highest levels of scholarship and ethical standards. In last year's thought provoking presidential address, Ron Smith (1987) underscored the notion that the AAASP should exercise leadership in enhancing and protecting the welfare of the public. In essence we as sport psychologists need to be accountable to the public that we serve and the AAASP as an organization can serve as a vehicle to help insure that consumers are getting the best professional information and help that is available.

In short, there are many challenges that await us as the emerging field of applied sport psychology continues to flourish in the 1980's and into the 1990's. Along these lines, I feel that the AAASP has the potential to lead the field of applied sport psychology in the areas of ethical standards, certification, applied research, professional practice, and interdisciplinary cooperation.

Certification

Probably the issue that has been utmost in most people's minds has been the idea of certification (Silva, 1987). In fact, one of the most important activities that the AAASP is involved in is the development and implementation of a certification program for sport psychology consultants who offer educational services to the public. The certification process should not only help promote quality control by certifying individuals who have the training and experience necessary to deliver psychological services in an ethical and competent manner, but it should also help us to take the initiative in defining and identifying the specific training experiences and competencies that a certified professional in our field needs to have in order to provide quality psychological services in applied sport and exercise settings. These competencies and training experiences will undoubtedly come from both sport science and psychology departments, but hopefully in a more integrated and interdisciplinary fashion than in the past where separatism and independent programs have been the status quo.

As many of you know, the certification committee, chaired by Dan Kirschenbaum, has been working very hard the past two years in attempting to formulate a certification process that will help us define who we are and maybe more importantly, who we need to be. As a member of that committee I have come to realize how complex and intricate a process it really is trying to put together a certification program. Some of the major parts of the certification program include ethical standards and enforcement of ethical violations, training, experiential and knowledge competencies in applied sport psychology, the title of this certified professional, and grandparenting individuals already working in the area of applied sport psychology. All of these areas require an enormous amount of thought as decisions made today will probably help shape the field of applied sport psychology for years to come. However, when the certification package is finally brought to the AAASP Fellows for a vote, undoubtedly it will spark some controversy and debate (as it did in the committee itself). However, I think that all of you can be confident that these issues have been extremely well researched and thought out by the committee as literally hundreds of hours have been collectively spent hashing out the pros and cons of different alternatives.

Once the certification procedure is passed, I think it is extremely important that all of us look to the future in terms of what this will mean for our field instead of only what this will mean for me as an individual. I would like to focus on some potential ramifications that certification might have on the field of applied sport psychology and how you as members of the AAASP can play a central role in this process.

First, a certification in any field of endeavor is only as good as the people who stand behind it. Certification in itself means very little if that certification is not respected by the consumers of our services as well as professionals in our field. In other words, how important will it be to an individual practicing applied sport psychology to be certified by the AAASP? My sincere hope and expectation is that it will be a certification that is sought out by members of our field and be respected by the consumers of our services. Your dedication and commitment in defining the field of applied sport psychology in the years ahead will allow us to forge ahead as a respected and influential profession. This will mean in part that the AAASP needs your help in getting the word out concerning the certification procedures as well as supporting them. As an organization, we must stand united in our efforts to bring some stability and definition to our field through our certification program. If certification is to make an impact on the field of applied sport psychology in the years to come, we must be committed to making it important for individuals administering psychological services in exercise and sport settings to seek out the AAASP certification. In essence, the public and consumers (and certainly professionals in our field) must be made aware that receiving the AAASP certification in applied sport psychology is akin to receiving APA certification in clinical psychology. That is, certification needs to mean something more than just another title. This of course takes time, but we are at that exciting point where we have a chance to influence in a positive manner the direction of our field and I urge all of you to help us achieve this goal.

One way that the AAASP can support the certification program is through the development of continuing education workshops and possibly self-study courses that relate to their certification requirements. In this way, the Association can help its members develop new knowledge competencies and gain new experiences which will contribute to their professional growth. In addition, special invited speakers who can help us address many of the difficult questions which will most certainly arise as we attempt to implement the certification process would be extremely helpful and informative. A good example was the invitation to David Mills from the American Psychological Association to speak at this convention concerning specific and unique ethical issues that applied sport psychologists face in working with athletes, coaches and sport organizations (Mills, 1988). These types of opportunities will allow our membership to keep abreast of the latest developments in our field and help educate all of us regarding different professional issues.

Looking into the future, I would hope that down the line the AAASP can turn its attention to certifying programs in addition to individuals along the lines of APA accreditation. It would add a great deal to the reputation and visibility of applied sport psychology if we can set up standards and criteria that PhD programs need to have in order to be accredited by the AAASP. At the same time, this might facilitate cooperation between Psychology and Physical Education Departments in the creation of interdisciplinary programs. It would also put some pressure on universities offering sport psychology specializations to maintain high standards. Finally, it would give prospective graduate students a clearer picture of choosing the right type of program for their special needs and interests. In essence, if the AAASP can successfully administer the certification of individuals practicing applied sport psychology, then the next logical step might be the certification of graduate programs in sport psychology.

Interorganization Cooperation

A future direction that is related to certification but also incorporates other areas as well revolves around interorganization cooperation. At present there are several professional societies and organizations that are concerned with sport psychology in North American Society for Sport Psychology and Physical Activity, the Canadian Society for Psychomotor Learning and Sport Psychology, the Sport Psychology Academy of the American Alliance for Health, Physical Education, Recreation and Dance, the Division of Exercise and Sport Psychology of the American Psychological Association, and the United States Olympic Committee's Sport Psychology Department.

At this point in time, to my knowledge, there has been little interaction between these organizations concerning how we can work together more effectively although a move in this direction was made with a symposium at the 1987 NASPSPA conference which was devoted to exploring the implications of the growth in the number of professional sport psychology organizations including ways in which we can facilitate more cooperative efforts. I think that the AAASP needs to take a leadership role in helping to facilitate cooperation within the field of sport psychology. For example, the AAASP could sponsor a one day meeting where representatives from the different sport psychology organizations would be invited to share their views on how to consolidate our efforts toward the advancement of the field. In fact, this might be developed into a yearly meeting so that continual interaction is insured and long-term planning can be facilitated. We are a relatively young and small field and it is imperative that we are united as we face the challenges of the 1990's.

In terms of certification, at the present time the Canadians have developed a certification procedure and the United States Olympic Committee has developed the Sport Psychology Registry. This registry was developed to provide some structure and control for the use of sport psychologists with U.S. Olympic teams and athletes with its goal being to insure that our Olympic athletes receive psychological services, both educational and clinical, from highly qualified individuals. And of course, the AAASP is currently attempting to develop a broader based certification program in applied sport psychology which will potentially encompass all individuals providing psychological services that are educational in nature for exercise and sport settings. Finally, it is anyone's guess what the other sport psychology organizations might do in terms of certification in the years to come although it's clear that the AAASP has taken the lead in working toward certification in applied sport psychology. It is my guess that the AAASP is being watched very carefully by the other sport psychology groups to see what kind of certification program is endorsed.

I think, however, the larger and more important issue is not what specific form the certification program might take, but rather how is the field and profession of applied sport psychology going to be affected by a certification process. Along these lines it is imperative that the various sport psychology organizations work together in helping to present a unified front to the consumers and other professionals concerning the certification of individuals in applied sport psychology. In essence, I think that we need just one certification program that represents the field of sport psychology just as APA has one certification and licensing procedure for clinicians and clinical programs. There may need to be modifications and compromises as the years go by as we try to test out and refine our certification so that we meet the needs of the rapidly evolving field of applied sport psychology. Although, at the same time it is critical that there is consensus, support and adherence within the sport psychology community for the certification program.

On a more global level, we need to enhance interorganizational cooperation in working toward the common goals of generating new knowledge and disseminating that knowledge to the public. The AAASP is just one of many professional organizations that is interested in human movement, health and sport science. I am sure that most of you are associated with at least one other professional organization and in many cases several organizations. Unfortunately, most of these professional societies have traditionally either worked totally independently of each other or at times even at cross purposes concerned only about their own small worlds and spheres of influence. This lack of interaction has led to a fractionated field in the sport and exercise sciences both in terms of research and professional issues.

However, there is a move under way to help us start to open up the lines of communication and encourage more cooperative activities. Specifically, the Research Consortium and the National Association for Physical Education in Higher Education which are under the auspicies of the American Alliance for Health, Physical Education, Recreation and Dance have organized 15 different physical education, sport and exercise organizations to meet to discuss ways in which we can facilitate our interactions. I have been the AAASP's official representative at these meetings which took place last year in Ft. Worth and last month in Washington, D.C. Although we are still in the preliminary planning stages, I feel that many positive outcomes are possible through these cooperative efforts. For example, one direction the group is taking is to map out some strategies for obtaining long-term extramural funding for research programs. One such idea would be that the exercise/sport groups together might develop a statement and rationale of major research directions that need attention in the next decade, and then take this around to various agencies to seek major funding. As we envision it, agencies would not be asked at this initial stage to fund specific research projects, but rather they would be asked to earmark an overall fund from which individual exercise/sport researchers might receive grants. The interorganizational liaison group would play the major role in securing the overall fund, and it might play a continuing role in establishing and implementing a mechanism for evaluation of grant proposals. Hopefully, we might be able to sell agencies on the multidisciplinary thrusts of our overall exercise/sport research efforts and on the multidisciplinary nature of some of the specific projects within the overall effort. These types of meetings present a window of opportunity for a new organization such as the AAASP to get involved with other sport and exercise science organizations in cooperative endeavors and provide enhanced visibility to the field of applied sport psychology.

Sport Science/Psychology Interface

Another area that will continue to have a large impact on the field of applied sport psychology is the integration and interface of the sport and psychological sciences. This integration is not only going to be important as we continue to refine our research perspectives in applied sport psychology but also in terms of developing curricula to meet the needs of the sport psychologist of the 1990's. At present, the vast majority of programs specializing in sport psychology are housed in physical education departments with just a couple of formal programs administered within psychology departments. In a typical physical education curriculum, aspiring sport psychologists usually take a variety of sport science and sport psychology courses and then venture into the psychology departments to pick up additional coursework in such areas as social psychology, personality, physiological psychology, measurement, and other related areas. However, since they are not psychology PhD students, they often have difficulty or are blocked from taking some potentially important courses for an applied sport psychologist in the areas of clinical and counseling psychology as well as assessment. On the other hand, students in clinical or counseling psychology programs usually have to find their own way in terms of getting the coursework and experiences that would prepare them for a career in sport psychology. In addition, these students are usually without a mentor whose specialization is sport psychology since most psychology departments do not consider sport psychology part of mainstream psychology. Consequently, in many cases the prospective clinical and counseling students in psychology departments have difficulty in getting specific courses in sport psychology, as well as receiving the benefit of a mentor who can guide and direct then in research in applied sport psychology.

In essence, both physical education and psychology graduate students are not receiving the best possible education and training to prepare them for careers in sport psychology. This of course is an unfortunate and untenable state of affairs. What is needed is the establishment of interdisciplinary programs in applied sport psychology that would meld the talent, expertise and resources of faculties in psychology and physical education. We need to work together to tear down the artificial barriers that have been built up between the two disciplines of we want our future sport psychologists to acquire the knowledge, competencies, experiences and skills necessary to provide quality services in applied sport psychology. A spirit of cooperation will facilitate such programs and this cooperation needs to be of an active rather than passive nature. Specifically, we must go and seek out our physical education and psychology colleagues and initiate some dialogue that will stimulate the interface of the two disciplines.

I know that I, as well as many of you, are constantly asked by prospective graduate students interested in studying in sport psychology the following question, "Should I get my PhD in psychology or should I get it in physical education?" At this point in time that is a very difficult question to answer for many of us since there are many factors to consider. However, it is my hope that with your help this will become an irrelevant question in the future if we can start to develop interdisciplinary programs in sport psychology. Along these lines, the forthcoming certification committee report will undoubtedly provide some guidelines and directions for developing such programs. In any case, it will take a concerted effort from this membership to realize this goal and we need the help of all of you.

Research/Practice Distinction

Another challenge that we all face in the future is to help erase the artificial boundary between research and practice in sport psychology. This separation or distinction is one that is divisive to the field of applied sport psychology if we are to make positive strides in expanding our body of knowledge and then disseminating this knowledge. In last year's insightful presidential address, Ron Smith touched upon the history of the scientist-practitioner model in clinical psychology and drew some analogies to the development of applied sport psychology. The essence of the model is that the clinical psychologist should be trained as both a researcher and clinician, and that even those clinicians who work in applied settings should contribute to the body of scientific knowledge by also doing research. I am in agreement with Ron, in that I also believe that this model has much to recommend it. But although this idea seems to have some merit, studies have indicated that only a small percentage of clinicians working in applied settings ever publish anything including their dissertations (Kelly, Goldberg, Fiske, & Kilkowski, 1978).

Presently, in applied sport psychology, there has been a tremendous increase in the provision of psychological services with athletes and teams with the primary goal being performance enhancement. If your experiences are anything like mine, you would then concur that most individuals now entering the field of sport psychology are interested in working with athletes. Along these lines, psychological techniques such as relaxation, imagery, attentional control, goal setting and self-regulation are typically part of the psychological skills that are used to enhance performance. The question then becomes, "How effective are these techniques in enhancing athletic performance?" This is where the distinction between research and practice becomes critical since it has been argued by some sport psychologists that there are not sufficient empirical data in applied settings that demonstrate the effectiveness of these psychological techniques and therefore we should not be promising athletes something we can't deliver.

Although one can certainly argue against this point of view, it does emphasize the importance of the scientist-practitioner model. Specifically, it is those sport psychologists working in applied settings who are the most likely candidates to be able to document the effectiveness of their interventions. But, if we are to follow the history of clinical psychology, these individuals are the least likely to carry out such research (Borenstein & Wollersheim, 1978). Furthermore, the term applied research has often been depicted as an inferior classification of research inherently inferior to other forms of scientific inquiry. I think this distinction is an artificial one which has contributed to the field becoming more fractionated instead of integrative. The practice of sport psychology should be based on sound scientific principles tested in research settings. The AAASP, as an organization and we as individuals need, to work to refine and improve research in applied settings so that applied research is not seen as an inferior approach to scientific inquiry. As Martens (1987) has pointed out, there are many idiographic techniques that are available to us in addition to the traditional nomothetic approaches to document the effectiveness of our interventions. The key thing is that all of us working in applied settings should strive to live up to the spirit of the scientist-practitioner model by not only providing the best psychological services possible but also putting the outcome of our work under rigorous scientific scrutiny. In this manner we will not only enhance our credibility as a profession but also expand the knowledge base of applied sport psychology.

Another challenge for us in the future in terms of the split between research and practice revolves around the dissemination of sport psychology knowledge and principles. A common complaint that I hear from practitioners such as coaches, athletes and exercise leaders is that research findings are not being conveyed in a manner that is conducive to comprehension by individuals not well versed in scientific terminology and jargon. If we are going to interface with the consumers of sport psychology services, then it is our responsibility to help educate them concerning the basic principles, research and applications of our discipline. It is not enough to restrict ourselves to writing scholarly articles in professional journals that only a handful of people can understand and even less will actually take the time to read. We must also make a concerted attempt to reach out to the public so that they can be more knowledgeable and educated about sport psychology. Unfortunately, I am sure you are all well aware that there have been many abuses of sport psychology which have turned many people off to our field. I recently read a newspaper article which reported that a new hotline in New York was created where athletes could call up 24 hours a day. The creator of the service said that he was "pioneering the field of sport psychiatry."

Many coaches and athletes are thirsting for sport psychology information to give them "the winning edge." With the pressures of competitive sports, it is not unusual for athletes and coaches to look at sport psychology as a "quick fix" and thus they are often easy prey for charlatans who are willing to promise them instant success through the use of some psychological gimmick. Hopefully, our certification process will alleviate some of these problems but I think we would be naive to think that it will eliminate them. We need to also make the public aware of the latest developments in sport psychology both in terms of research and practice. We can do this in a variety of ways.

First we can start publishing some applied articles in various coaching and athletic journals. Almost all sport organizations have a journal solely devoted to their sport in which basic how-to articles are published. Most of these types of journals are very open, and in fact actively looking for articles in the area of sport psychology. Of course, those of us in the academic community will not receive much acknowledgement and support for these types of articles in terms of scholarly achievement but we are providing an important service to our consumers by keeping them abreast of the latest knowledge in sport psychology. I am pleased to note that it appears that we are doing a better job in this regard but we still have a way to go.

Another avenue to share our expertise with coaches and athletes and other consumers of sport psychology services is through workshops and presentations. These would optimally occur not at scholarly meetings, but rather at the meetings of the respective sport and coaching associations. For example, at the most recent meeting of the Texas Coaching Association, over 7,000 coaches from junior high, high school and colleges attended. We can reach a lot of people if we can get involved with these organizations and provide them with a good exposure to the area of applied sport psychology. Many of the school districts have in-service workshops for all of their teachers and I have recently given several of these to coaches and physical educators on various topics with sport psychology. The coaches are generally eager to learn about our area and we need to make sure that they are receiving the most up-to-date information that is available. It should be noted that I am not implying that we should be forsaking our empirically based research efforts and the reporting of their results in scholarly publications. In fact, the information disseminated to these coaching and sport publications should be based on research that has undergone the highest standards of scientific scrutiny. It is only with this research foundation that we can enhance the credibility of our applied services. Research and application do not have to be separate endeavors or entities; rather they should both be seen as integral and complementary facets of the field of applied sport psychology. In addition, coaches and athletes are rich sources of information as demonstrated by some of the work of Terry Orlick and his colleagues (1986, 1987, 1988) with Canadian elite athletes. We should use them as valuable resources in our development of psychological intervention programs as they have much to teach us. In essence we need to respect their knowledge and expertise just as they need to be open and receptive to what we have to offer them.

Defining Applied Sport Psychology

A final area that we as sport psychologists will have to come to grips with is defining the boundaries of our field. As with other scientific areas within physical education departments, there has been a rapid growth in both the quantity and quality of available information under the general rubric of sport psychology. To date, articles dealing with such diverse topics as exercise adherence, psychological aspects of sport injury, perceived exertion and exercise tolerance, psychological factors and performance enhancement, psychological effects of participation in sport and exercise, and Type A behavior and sport have all been seen as being part of sport psychology. This broad perspective is not surprising, given the sociocultural complexity of sport, the numerous factors that can impinge on sport performance, and its use as a health promotion modality. However, this broad conception of sport psychology can carry with it certain liabilities which may stunt our growth as a scientific field of inquiry.

For example, in a recent article by Larry Brawley and Jack Rejeski (1988), they argue that there are really four different areas that up to this point in time have mostly been subsumed under the title of sport psychology. Specifically, these areas might be termed sport psychology, health psychology, rehabilitation psychology and exercise psychology. The authors present some cogent arguments and examples why these can be considered four distinct areas of inquiry. Although each of the areas has an important link to the parent discipline of psychology, they are all independent yet they share important interrelations with one another. Finally, within each of the areas basic research, applied research and application should be acknowledged.

It is not my purpose to propose what the exact definition of sport psychology should be or to argue for specific content areas that the AAASP as an organization should foster. Obviously, up to this point in time we have separated out three areas under the general rubric of applied sport psychology: health psychology, intervention/performance enhancement and social psychology. Rather, I would hope that as an organization, we should give some serious thought as to how we want to define our discipline since if we don't do it then someone else might. There are some advantages from a research and methodological standpoint as well as from a professional point of view to providing more clarity as to how we define the field of sport psychology. Since we are an evolving and emerging discipline it is not unusual that there should be some definitional ambiguity and global conceptions of sport psychology. But I feel that as we move into the future we should take a more reflective look into who we are and who we want to become. This will involve us all asking some serious questions about the direction of the field of applied sport psychology.

Summary

In closing, I would like to borrow a famous quote from the beginning of Charles Dickens' *A Tale of Two Cities*: "It was the best of times, it was the worst of times." Although this quote might be slightly overstating the case, I feel that it captures the present state of applied sport psychology.

It can be seen as the worst of times because of all the uncertainty and confusion that is often characteristic of an evolving field. For example, graduate students are unsure of what course of study is most appropriate for them (i.e., psychology or physical education) as well as what kind of jobs will be available for them when they finally graduate; nobody really knows how the certification process will eventually shake out and what ramifications this might have for applied sport psychologists; the development of curriculum in sport psychology appears at this moment to be somewhat fragmented; and acceptance of applied sport psychology in both academic and applied settings is often tenuous, just to name a few. Consequently, especially for those of you considering entering the field of sport psychology, there is much uncertainty and ambiguity which impacts greatly on the important decisions you must make concerning your training and involvement in the field. It is a field that is characterized by rapid change and thus it becomes difficult to predict the state of affairs even a few years into the future. What is a sport psychologist?, who can practice sport psychology?, what is the best preparation for a sport psychologist?, are all questions that need further clarification and thus make this period a potentially unsettling one for most of us.

However, it can be seen as the best of times because of the opportunity all of us have for helping shape the field of applied sport psychology. It's an exciting time where the field is emerging and there are many opportunities for growth and development. I think that 10 years from now we will all be able to look back to the early development of the AAASP and realize that we were involved with a ground breaking effort of an association that will be providing leadership and direction to the field of applied sport psychology. It is not often that professionals have the unique opportunity to help develop and shape their field of study. But we all can make our mark in sport psychology because it is a rapidly evolving field which requires our enthusiasm, creativity, dedication and involvement. As a body of professionals committed to this field of endeavor we have the responsibility in helping establish sport psychology as an academic profession. We owe this responsibility to the founders of the field, to future generations of sport psychologists, to the consumers of our services, and perhaps most importantly to ourselves. It is certainly an exciting time in our development and we all have the opportunity to share in that excitement as we prepare to meet the challenges ahead. It may not be an easy journey but I sincerely believe it will be a fulfilling and worthwhile one. The field of applied sport psychology is depending on all of us.

References

Borenstein, P. H., & Wollersheim, J. P. (1978). Scientist-practitioner model activities among psychologists of behavioral and nonbehavioral orientations. *Professional Psychology: Research and Practice*, *9*, 659–664.

Brawley, L. R., & Rajeski, W. J. (1988). Defining the boundaries of sport psychology. *The Sport Psychologist*, *2*, 231–242.

Kelly, E. L., Goldberg, L. R., Fiske, D. W., & Kilkowski, J. M. (1978). Twenty-five years later: A follow-up study of the graduate students in clinical psychology assessed in the VA selection research project. *American Psychologist*, *33*, 746–755.

Martens, R. (1987). Science, knowledge and sport psychology. *The Sport Psychologist*, *1*, 29–55.

Mills, D. (1988). *Potential ethical dilemma faced by sport psychologists.* Paper presented at the annual meeting of the Association for the Advancement of Applied Sport Psychology, Nashua, New Hampshire.

Orlick, T., & Partington, J. (1988). Mental links to excellence. *The Sport Psychologist*, *2*, 105–130.

Orlick, T., & Partington, J. (1987). The sport psychology consultant: Analysis of critical components as viewed by Canadian Olympic athletes. *The Sport Psychologist*, *1*, 4–17.

Orlick, T., & Partington, J. (1986). *Psyched: Inner views of winning.* Coaching Association of Canada.

Silva, J. (1986). *AAASP: Committed to enhancing professional standards and enhancing applied research.* Presidential Address presented at the annual meeting of the Association for the Advancement of Applied Sport Psychology. Jekyll Island, Georgia.

Smith, R. (1987). *Applied sport psychology in the age of accountability.* Presidential Address presented at the annual meeting of the Association for the Advancement of Applied Sport Psychology. Newport Beach, California.

48 The Coleman Roberts Griffith Address: Toward the Integration of Theory, Research, and Practice in Sport Psychology

ALBERT V. CARRON
University of Western Ontario

In this inaugural Coleman Griffith address (the keynote presentation at the annual AAASP Conference), Albert Carron, a prominent sport social psychologist, undertakes the task of advancing some ideas that are relevant for the promotion of integration of research, theory, and intervention. He argues that an integration of these three activities was actually a central component in Griffith's original legacy. In line with this tradition, he objects to considering these three elements as mutually exclusive and independent, which was the direction in which the field was progressing at the time.

Carron introduces a conceptual framework for AAASP in which research and theory, application and intervention, and quality of life should be regarded as equal, compatible, complementary, and mutually interdependent elements in a continuous cycle of professional activity. Through his own experience with research and intervention in the social psychological areas of coach–athlete dyads, motivation in coaching and teaching, and group cohesion in exercise classes, Carron vividly illustrates his ideas. Finally, he discusses some additional considerations to be viewed as prerequisites for the facilitation of a successful integration of the proposed concept, to be regarded as a goal for AAASP to strive for. This has set a precedent for professionals in the field in their quest to integrate research, theory, and intervention in their research and professional activities.

There were three general purposes in the present paper. One was to introduce a conceptual framework which provides a useful way to consider the activities and purposes of AAASP. This conceptual framework presents research/theory, application and the quality of life as equal, mutually interdependent components of continuous cycle of professional activity. A second was to illustrate through personal research and intervention experiences how the integration of theory/research and application is logically and professionally consistent. The third was to advance additional considerations for the integration of theory, research, and intervention with AAASP.

Historically, concerns that research, theory, and intervention might be treated as mutually exclusive activities have had a rich long-standing tradition in mainstream psychology. And, professionals in psychology have cautioned against this possibility. For example, Kidd and Saks (1980) pointed out: "within social psychology, whose founder, Kurt Lewin . . . expressed the unity of knowledge and application . . . devoted adherence to the distinction borders on the absurd" (p. 2).

From a somewhat different perspective, both Fisher (1980) and Mayo and La France (1980) argued that theory, research, and intervention are mutually dependent upon one another. For example Fisher (1980) stated that "these three areas of scientific and practical endeavor are highly complementary if not essential to each other. Theory guides research and practice and is in turn informed by them. Research evaluates practice, and action concerns direct research toward relevance and utility" (Fisher, 1980, 188–189). And, Mayo and La France (1980) observed that "perhaps it is possible in the physical sciences to conceive of two disparate spheres, one devoted to basic knowledge, the other to application. In the social sciences, and in social psychology in particular, such bifurcation yields sterile principles and inept application" (p. 81).

And, finally, Lewin (1951) commented on what he considered to be an underlying problem—the attitudes held by researchers and practitioners—when he stated: "many psychologists working today in an applied field are keenly aware of the need for close cooperation between theoretical and applied psychology. This can be accomplished . . . if the theorist does not look toward applied problems with a high-brow aversion or fear of social problems, and if the applied psychologist realizes that there is nothing so practical as a good theory" (p. 169).

Even within the relatively young discipline of sport psychology, concerns have been expressed that research, theory, and intervention might be treated as mutually exclusive activities. Illustrative of this point is the fact that each of the presidents of AAASP, in their presidential address, has cautioned against this possibility. For example,

---

Weinberg (1989) noted that "a challenge that we all face in the future is to help erase the artificial boundary between research and practice in sport psychology. This separation or distinction is one that is divisive to the field of applied sport psychology if we are to make positive strides in expanding our body of knowledge and then disseminating this knowledge" (p. 190).

Similarly, Smith (1989) and Gould (1990) addressed this issue from the perspective of individuals with a primary focus on intervention. Smith (1989) pointed out that "accountability in applied sport psychology, as in clinical psychology, is best fostered by a continuous integration of basic research, application, and evaluation of application outcomes" (p. 168). And, Gould (1990) argued that "we need a research base to guide professional practice and AAASP has to facilitate this research base" (p. 107).

Finally, in his presidential address, Brawley (1992) stated that in social psychology the integration of intervention and research is occurring. He urged more interaction and communication in sport psychology between those individuals primarily engaged in intervention and those primarily engaged in research before asking the question: "will AAASP . . . learn from [social psychology's] integration or will it take another 10 years after making all the same errors as scientist-practitioners from other fields? The latter scenario could easily become reality if our science and practice are not encouraged to merge to a greater degree and if sport psychology leaders at either end of the science-practice continuum do not moderate their positions toward learning from each other" (Brawley, 1992, p. 18).

There is good reason for the cautions expressed in the above quotations by social psychologists and AAASP presidents. Theory development, research, and intervention are not (and cannot be approached as) independent activities. They are compatible, complementary, and interdependent. Each is essential to the growth and development of the others. Theory development is of minimal value if it occurs in a vacuum; ultimately evaluations through research and application are required. Intervention is of minimal value if it occurs in a vacuum; ultimately evaluation and theory development are required. And, finally, research is of minimal value if it occurs in a vacuum; ultimately theory development and application are required.

Purpose

One purpose in this paper is to introduce a conceptual framework which provides a useful way to consider the activities and purposes of AAASP. This conceptual framework, which was developed by Mayo and La France (1980), presents research/theory, application and the quality of life as equal, mutually interdependent components of a continuous cycle of professional activity.

A second purpose is to illustrate through personal research and intervention experiences how the integration of theory/research and application is logically and professionally consistent. The final purpose is to provide some additional considerations that might be adapted in order to facilitate the integration of theory, research, and intervention within AAASP.

The Mayo and La France (1980) Conceptual Model

Mayo and La France (1980) consider knowledge building (theory and research), utilization and intervention, and improvement in the quality of life as three equally important activities interdependently linked in a cyclical fashion. Thus, an issue of concern relative to the quality of life might emerge such as, for example, the smoking behavior of adolescent females. In an attempt to obtain insight into this issue, research programs might be initiated and theories based on that research could be proposed. Ultimately, through the increased insights provided from research and theory development, it would then be possible to implement programs of intervention. These interventions, in turn, would impact on the quality of life, and the cycle would be completed.

Or, similarly, an issue of concern pertaining to the quality of life might be perceived as sufficiently severe that programs of intervention would be introduced immediately. Subsequently, through research, evaluation, and analysis of those intervention programs, theories could be proposed to explain the phenomenon of interest. In short, Mayo and La France emphasized that depending upon circumstances, different issues may result in an initial focus at any one of the three points of the cycle. And, most importantly, independent of the starting point, a subsequent focus on each of the other two activities is logical.

There are numerous published reports in sport psychology which illustrate the interdependent nature of the three activities highlighted by Mayo and La France. Consider, for example, the transition from theory and research to intervention. Brewer and Shillinglaw (1992) developed a psychological skills training program containing elements shown to be effective through research (e.g., goal setting, relaxation, imagery, cognitive restructuring). This psychological skills training program was then introduced (and found to be beneficial) with intercollegiate lacrosse players.

The work of Orlick and McCaffrey (1991) provides an excellent example of the transition from intervention to improving the general quality of life. Orlick and McCaffrey reported how mental skills found to be effective in sport settings (e.g., imagery, goal setting, relaxation, etc.) were introduced to kindergarten and elementary school students as well as children attempting to overcome serious illnesses. As they pointed out, children "can apply these mental skills in a multitude of settings . . . . The applications for mental training reach far beyond sport psychology" (Orlick & McCaffrey, 1991, 324).

And, finally, the transition from quality of life to theory and research is illustrated in the Eccles and Harold (1991) work on gender differences. Concern over the differences between females and males in achievement and participation in sport stimulated the development of a conceptual model and a 10-year program of research designed to gain a greater understanding of the issues. In the sections which follow, I have used my personal research and intervention experiences (which were almost always carried out in collaboration with colleagues) as examples of the interdependent nature of the activities.

Theory/Research to Intervention: Compatibility in Coach-Athlete Dyads

The first program of activity which illustrates my thesis—that the integration of theory/research and application is logically and professionally consistent—proceeded from theory and research to intervention. The focus was on compatibility in coach-athlete dyads (cf. Carron & Bennett, 1977; Carron & Chelladurai, 1978; 1981).

The Theory

A three-dimensional theory of interpersonal behavior—Fundamental Interpersonal Relations Orientation (FIRO)—has been developed by Schutz (1958, 1966). A fundamental axiom in Schutz's theory is that *people need people.* That is, in much the same way that we have biological needs that must be satisfied in order to sustain personal health, it is necessary for us to satisfy specific interpersonal (social) needs. These interpersonal needs are fulfilled through the establishment and maintenance of relationships with others. According to Schutz, interpersonal needs are reflected in three broad dimensions of behavior: *inclusion, control*, and *affiliation.*

Inclusion represents behaviors relating toward association, communication, and companionship. Control represents behaviors associated with the decision-making process between people; it is related to power, authority, dominance, influence, and control. Finally, affection represents behaviors related to love and affection.

Schutz postulated that each of us manifests these three interpersonal dimensions in two ways. That is, we *express* each of these three behaviors toward others (i.e., by actively including others, exerting control, and providing affection). And, we *want* others to extend each of these three behaviors toward us (i.e., by including us, exerting some control over us, and providing us with affection). There are individual differences in the degree to which different individuals want and express control, affection, and inclusion.

The Research

Over the course of approximately seven years, Schutz's theory and questionnaire (Fundamental Interpersonal Relations Orientation Behavior, FIRO-B) were used by my colleagues and me to explore a number of questions pertaining to coach-athlete relationships. For example, Carron and Bennett (1977) investigated the interpersonal needs associated with compatibility and incompatibility between intercollegiate coaches and athletes. When the results for coach-athlete dyads categorized as compatible and incompatible were compared, inclusion behavior emerged as the critical factor; control and affection did not differentiate between incompatible and compatible coach-athlete dyads. It was found that the former dyads were characterized by relatively withdrawn, detached, isolated behavior on the part of both the coach and athlete.

Our subsequent research focused on athlete and coach perceptions of the interpersonal role behaviors expected of coaches and athletes (Carron, 1978), the relationship between coach-athlete interpersonal compatibility, and athlete success (Carron & Garvie, 1979; Horne & Carron, 1985).

The Intervention

In 1980, a Canadian sport association was interested in enhancing coach-athlete relationships for principals participating at the international level. My colleague, Chella Chelladurai and I were approached and invited to evaluate the dynamics of the athletic environment, provide input to coaches and athletes, and suggest strategies to improve coach-athlete interpersonal relations.

Initially, we administered a sport-specific version of the FIRO-B questionnaire as well as Chelladurai's Leadership Scale for Sports (LSS) (Chelladurai, 1984; Chelladurai & Carron, 1981) to both the athletes and their coaches. The athletes in this study completed a version of the LSS which assesses leadership behaviors preferred by a subordinate. The coaches complete a version which assesses a leader's self-described actual behaviors.

Following an analysis of the responses to the questionnaires, coaches and athletes were brought in independently. Using normative data and graphs, an explanation was provided to each coach and athlete pertaining to his/her self-described interpersonal needs and specific preferences for or actual leadership behaviors. Following these consultations, the combined results for each coach-athlete dyad were plotted schematically to illustrate the "compatibility" of the dyad. Consultation then occurred with each dyad to provide insight into the nature of each individual's interpersonal needs as well as his/her coaching leadership preferences and behaviors. Potential sources of incompatibility or conflict were outlined and discussed with the dyad. For example, if both an athlete and a coach had a high need for control, it was pointed out that this was a potential source of strain in the athletic situation. Similarly, if an athlete preferred a high level of positive feedback and her coach manifested this behavior infrequently, again, it was pointed out that this would be a potential source of strain in the sport setting. We did not evaluate the program directly. Nonetheless, the feedback received from coaches and athletes indicated that the consultations were perceived to be highly beneficial in terms of providing insight into (a) personal needs, preferences, and behaviors, (b) the needs, preferences, and behaviors of the other principal in the dyadic relationship, (c) the sources of potential strain in the dyadic relationship, and (d) possible strategies to enhance interpersonal compatibility.

Thus, in summary, Schutz (1958, 1966) advanced a three-dimensional theory of interpersonal behavior. Considerable research by Schutz and others (cf. Schutz, 1958) in a non-sport context demonstrated the utility of his theory in describing, explaining, and predicting interpersonal compatibility. The research of my colleagues and I demonstrated the utility of the theory in a sport context (e.g., Carron & Bennett, 1977). Subsequently, the theory and research provided the basis for our applied work (i.e., intervention) (i.e., Carron & Chelladurai, 1981).

Certainly, our experiences in this context served to highlight the claim advanced by Lewin (1951) which was introduced earlier: namely, that "there is nothing so practical as a good theory" (Lewin, p. 169). Our experiences also serve to illustrate the contention that theory development, research, and intervention are compatible, complementary, and interdependent.

Intervention to Theory: A Conceptual Model for Motivation in Coaching and Teaching

The second program of activity proceeded from intervention to theory (or more accurately, from intervention to conceptual development). The general focus was on motivation in sport and physical activity (cf. Carron, 1984).

The Intervention

Most individuals who teach sport psychology at the university level receive numerous requests from athletes, coaches and/or parents to present information on their area of expertise. I am no exception. And, rather early in my career it became apparent to me that the most popular, frequently requested topic was motivation (Carron, 1974, 1975a, 1975b, 1982a). As the resident university sport psychologist, I was constantly presented with questions such as:

"How can I motivate my athletes?"

"We're having problems with kids leaving sport. Can you discuss some strategies to overcome this problem?"

"Johnny doesn't seem to try [followed by a detailed description of young Johnny]. Any ideas?"

After accepting many of the invitations to address sport groups, it also become apparent to me that I faced three dilemmas. (In order to facilitate communication, I borrowed and/or assigned labels to these three dilemmas, Carron, 1984.) The first can be referred to as a *fish in the fish market* dilemma. Because I like almost all types of fish and seafood, I am always faced with difficult choices in a fish market. In the same manner, because motivation is a complex phenomenon, it was difficult for me to choose one aspect or motivational approach—such as token economies, goal setting, intrinsic interests, for example—and highlight it to the exclusion of the others.

I also experienced what has been referred to as a *bricks in the brickyard* dilemma. Bricks in a brickyard become most useful when they are organized—set out in some overall structure such as a wall, house, driveway. Thus, in a similar fashion, because each of us has a limited ability to process and utilize information, it seemed to me to be of little value to provide a comprehensive list of motivational approaches without some meaningful framework to tie them all together. Otherwise, my information would have simply represented another brick in the coaching brickyard. To be truly useful, information must be presented within an overall schema, framework or model. The units or categories of that schema or model will then represent smaller more manageable informational packages.

Finally, I also experienced what can be referred to as a *ivory tower dilemma*. When I was approached by a coaching association to speak to their membership about motivation, I was politely warned to avoid an ivory tower approach—to make sure my material was practical, was useful, was applicable (actually, I was warned not to get into that research bull excrement). The request for practicality from any coach, athlete, or parent is legitimate. However, as a university professor committed philosophically to the belief that coaching and teaching in sport and physical activity will only develop fully through the establishment of a sound, research-based foundation, I was loathe to short circuit research and simply rely on my experiences.

In an attempt to resolve these dilemmas, I developed a lecture package for my talks with coaches (which ultimately became the foundation for my undergraduate class as well as a textbook, Carron, 1984). In that lecture package, I attempted to accomplish three things: (1) provide a comprehensive picture of the more important motivational factors which influence performance in physical education, sport, and physical activity; (2) provide a frame-of-reference (conceptual model) within which these motivational factors can be more readily understood; and (3) draw upon research findings as the basis for any claims or generalities advanced.

The Conceptual Model

The conceptual model had as its foundation the well-accepted premise in psychology that human behavior (e.g., motivated behavior) is a result of contributing factors from within the individual and from within the individual's environment (situation). A second fundamental cornerstone for the model was the premise that many contributors to overall athlete motivation—within the situation and within the athlete—are outside the coach's direct control or intervention. Thus, for example, an audience is a situational factor which influences athlete motivation; it cannot be manipulated readily (if at all) by the coach. On the other hand, the nature of the practice situation also can influence the athlete's motivation but it is directly under the coach's control. Similarly, the personality trait of need for achievement is a personal factor which influences athlete motivation. Because personality changes very slowly over time, it cannot be manipulated readily by the coach. Conversely, intrinsic interest is a powerful source of information within the individual athlete that can be directly influenced by the coach.

Having placed each of the principal motivational factors within this conceptual framework, it was then necessary to derive a series of propositions or generalizations from available research. Thus, for example, one research-based generalization pertaining to intrinsic motivation is that *perceptions of competence and self determination enhance the selectivity, intensity, and duration of individual behavior* (Deci, 1975).

The final step was to draw out implications for coaches, athletes, and parents from the research-based generalizations. Thus, for example two implications emanating from the above generalization would be (1) the coach should provide opportunities for athlete input into decision-making in order to enhance self-determination and consequent intrinsically motivated behavior; and (2) the coach should make rewards contingent on performance in order to enhance perceptions of competence and consequent intrinsically motivated behavior.

Thus, in summary, applied work with coaches, athletes and parents highlighted the need to develop a conceptual model for motivation. That conceptual model helped to simplify the complex phenomenon of motivation and facilitated the instructional process for me in my role as a communicator, and for the recipients (i.e., coaches, athletes, and students). Again, my experiences in this context served to highlight Lewin's (1951) comment that "there is nothing so practical as a good theory" (p. 169). Intervention, theory development, and research are compatible, complementary, and interdependent.

Theory and Research to Intervention: Group Cohesion in Exercise Classes

The third program of activity proceeded from theory and research to intervention. The general focus in this instance was on adherence in exercise classes (cf. Carron & Spink, 1993; Carron, Widmeyer, & Brawley, 1988; Spink & Carron, 1993).

The Conceptual Model

Approximately 10 years ago, my colleagues and I initiated a program to develop an instrument for the measurement of cohesiveness in sport groups (Brawley, Carron, & Widmeyer, 1987; Carron, Widmeyer, & Brawley, 1985; Widmeyer, Brawley, & Carron, 1985). In terms of our constitutive definition, we viewed cohesion as "a dynamic process reflected in the tendency for a group to stick together and remain united in the pursuit of its goals and objectives (Carron, 1982b, 124).

The conceptual model which represented the foundation for the development of the operational measure, The Group Environment Questionnaire, emanated from research and writing in the group dynamics literature. This body of information led us to the view that cohesiveness is a group property which exists in the minds of individual members. That is, each individual group member has perceptions about the task and social aspects of the group. Further, each individual holds a perception of the attractiveness of the group from a personal perspective as well as a perception of the group as a totality. The result is four manifestations of cohesiveness: group integration-task, group integration-social, individual attractions to the group-task and individual attractions to the group-social.

The Research

After modifying the Group Environment Questionnaire for an exercise setting, my colleagues and I examined the relationship between perceptions of cohesiveness and adherence behavior. One project showed that individuals who had dropped out of an exercise class held significantly lower perceptions of their former group's cohesiveness than individuals still actively involved (Carron et al., 1988). A second project showed that individuals who were high in absenteeism and lateness—two other measures of adherence behavior—during a 13-week exercise program held significantly lower perceptions of their group's cohesiveness than individuals never absent or late (Spink & Carron, 1992). A third project showed that perceptions of cohesiveness secured in the third week of a 13-week exercise session were a reliable predictor of subsequent dropout behavior (Spink & Carron, in press).

The Intervention

On the basis of these findings, we attempted to determine whether a team building program (a) could be implemented in a minimal group setting such as an exercise class, and, if so, (b) would positively influence perceptions of cohesiveness and exercise adherence (Carron & Spink, 1993; Spink & Carron, 1993). For the team building program, the positive benefits of cohesiveness for exercise groups were outlined for fitness instructors. Then a series of factors considered to be contributors to an enhanced sense of group unity were introduced. These included: (1) being distinctive as a collective, (2) having stable group norms, (3) insuring that members retain stable positions in class, (4) providing for interaction and communication among members, and 5) having members make sacrifices for the collective. The fitness instructors then developed a number of specific strategies within each of these five categories that they could implement in their class. The classes were monitored to insure that the instructors did implement and maintain these team building strategies throughout the 13-week class. A comparison of fitness classes where the team building strategies were implemented with general fitness classes showed that both cohesion and adherence were significantly improved through the intervention program.

Thus, in summary, a conceptual model for group cohesion led to the development of a questionnaire, The Group Environment Questionnaire. Subsequently, that questionnaire was used in research with exercise classes to investigate the relationship between perceptions of cohesiveness and adherence behavior. A series of investigations established that the cohesion-adherence relationship was reliable. Therefore, an intervention program was developed which had a positive effect on both cohesiveness and adherence behavior. So, once again, these experiences served to illustrate the contention that theory development, research, and intervention are compatible, complementary, and interdependent.

Additional Considerations

It is important to emphasize that we should continue to strive for an integrated AAASP—an AAASP where research/theory, intervention, and the quality of life are considered to be compatible, complementary and interdependent activities. If this is to occur, one important prerequisite is an appreciation of the interrelatedness of the broad spectrum of activities in which our membership is involved throughout the research, intervention, quality of life cycle. As Louis Pasteur pointed out over a 100 years ago, "no, a thousand times no; there does not exist a category of science to which one can give the name applied science. There are science and application of science, bound together as the fruit of the tree which bears it" (*Revue Scientifique,* 1871; quoted in Kidd & Saks, 1980). AAASP would not be well served if our membership focused on research/theory or intervention or quality of life exclusively. And, of course, the problems we explore—through intervention, research, or theory development—would not be well understood.

A second important consideration concerns the need for conceptual models to guide our research and interventions. Conceptual models serve four functions. First, complex issues can be simplified and more readily explained and understood. Secondly, it is possible to more readily draw assumptions about how the components are related to each other. Third, the more important correlates of the phenomenon—the aspects to be emphasized—can be more readily identified. And, finally, it is easier to determine what is known and unknown about the phenomenon and what subsequent actions should be taken (McGrath, 1984).

A third important consideration is the need for greater tolerance within AAASP toward students and professionals who present work that might be judged to be below the normative standard. None of us deliberately presents an inferior product. But if that happens, we learn from the experience when the feedback is constructive. On the other hand, if a climate develops in which tolerance is not the rule, a climate in which only a limited number of members have the confidence to submit their work, AAASP will be the loser over the long term. Every presentation has the potential to serve two functions—education of the audience and growth and development of the presenter. The growth and development of a knowledgeable, broad-based constituency contributes to AAASP's strength as an association.

As another aspect of the attitude issue, it is also important for us to remember that the activities of science do not fall along a hierarchy of respectability. So-called qualitative and quantitative methods, pure and applied research, and/or research and application are simply alternate approaches—not superior versus inferior strategies. Although he was discussing the locus rather than the process of research, a caution by Deutsch (1980) is also pertinent here: "research of no theoretical significance can be done anywhere—in the laboratory, a school or a factory. Similarly, research of considerable theoretical significance can be done in a school, a factory, or a community as well as in the laboratory" (p. 98). The development of hierarchies—either real or contrived—is divisive, and nonproductive for AAASP.

References

Brawley, L. R. (1992). Dealing with reality in order to develop AAASP's future. *Journal of Applied Sport Psychology, 4,* 102–118.

Brawley, L. R., Carron, A. V., & Widmeyer, W. N. (1987). Assessing the cohesion of sport teams: Validity of the Group Environment questionnaire. *Journal of Sport Psychology, 9,* 275–294.

Brewer, B. W., & Shillinglaw, R. (1992). Evaluation of a psychological skills training workshop for male intercollegiate lacrosse players. *The Sport Psychologist, 6,* 139–147.

Carron, A. V. (1974). The football coach as a psychologist. Invited presentation at The University of Western Ontario Basketball Coaches Clinic, London, Ontario.

Carron, A. V. (1975a). The basketball coach as a psychologist. Invited presentation at the University of Western Ontario High School Coaches Clinic, London, Ontario.

Carron, A. V. (1975b). Motivating the athlete. Invited presentation at The Art and Science of Coaching Seminar, York University, Downsview, Ontario.

Carron, A. V. (1978). Role behavior and coach-athlete interaction. *International Review of Sport Sociology, 13,* 51–65.

Carron, A. V. (1982a). Motivating the athlete. Invited presentation at the Ontario Olympic Wrestling Federation Coaching Seminar, London, Ontario.

Carron, A. V. (1982b). Cohesiveness in sport groups: Interpretations and considerations. *Journal of Sport Psychology, 4,* 123–138.

Carron, A. V. (1984). *Motivation: Implications for coaching and teaching.* London, Ontario, Sport Dynamics.

Carron, A. V., & Bennett, B. B. (1977). Compatibility in the coach-athlete dyad. *Research Quarterly, 48,* 671–679.

Carron, A. V., Brawley, L. R., & Widmeyer, W. N. (1985). The development of an instrument to measure cohesion in sport teams: The Group Environment Questionnaire. *Journal of Sport Psychology, 7,* 244–266.

Carron, A. V., & Chelladurai, P. (1981, May). An analysis of factors associated with coach-athlete interaction. Report to the Canadian Amateur Diving Association, Ottawa, Ontario.

Carron, A. V., & Chelladurai, P. (1978). Psychological factors and athletic success: An analysis of coach-athlete interpersonal behavior. *Canadian Journal of Applied Sport Sciences, 3*, 43–50.

Carron, A. V., & Garvie, G. T. (1978). Compatibility and successful performance. *Perceptual and Motor Skills, 46*, 1121–1122.

Carron, A. V., & Spink, K. S. (1993). Team building in an exercise setting. *The Sport Psychologist, 7*, 8–18.

Carron, A. V., Widmeyer, L. R., & Brawley, L. R. (1988). Group cohesion and individual adherence in physical activity. *Journal of Sport and Exercise Psychology, 10*, 127–138.

Chelladurai, P. (1984). Leadership in sports. In J. M. Silva & R. S. Weinberg (Eds.), *Psychological foundations of sport* (pp. 329–339). Champaign, IL: Human Kinetics.

Chelladurai, P., & Carron, A. V. (1981). Applicability to youth sports of the Leadership Scale for Sports. *Perceptual and Motor Skills, 53*, 361–362.

Deci, E. L. (1915). *Intrinsic motivation.* New York: Plenum Press.

Deutsch, M. (1980). Socially relevant research: Comments on "applied" versus "basic" research. In R. F. Kidd & M. J. Saks (Eds.), *Advances in applied social psychology, Vol. 1* (pp. 97–112). Hillsdale, NJ: Erlbaum.

Eccles, J. S., & Harold, R. D. {1991). Gender differences in sport involvement: Applying the Eccles' expectancy-value model. *Journal of Applied Sport Psychology*, *3*, 7–35.

Fisher, R. J. (1980). Touchstones for applied social psychology. In R. F. Kidd & M. J. Saks (Eds.), *Advances in applied social psychology, Vol. 1* (pp. 187–190). Hillsdale, NJ: Erlbaum.

Gould, D. (1990). AAASP: A vision for the 1990's. *Journal of Applied Sport Psychology*, *2*, 99–116.

Horne, T., & Carron, A. V. (1985). Compatibility in coach-athlete relationships. *Journal of Sport Psychology, 7*, 137–149.

Kidd, R. F., & Saks, M. J. (1980). What is applied social psychology? An introduction. In R. F. Kidd & M. J. Saks (Eds.), *Advances in applied social psychology, Vol. 1* (pp. 1–24) Hillsdale, NJ: Erlbaum.

Lewin, K. (1951). *Field theory in social science.* New York: Harper.

Mayo, C., & La France, M. (1980). Toward an applicable social psychology. In R. F. Kidd & M. J. Saks (Eds.), *Advances in applied social psychology, Vol. 1* (pp. 81–96). Hillsdale, NJ: Erlbaum.

McGrath, J. E. (1984). *Groups: Interaction and performance.* Englewood Cliffs, NJ: Prentice-Hall.

Orlick, T., & McCaffrey, N. (1991). Mental training for children for sport and life. *The Sport Psychologist*, *5*, 322–334.

Schutz, W. C. (1958). *FIRO: A three-dimensional theory of interpersonal behavior.* New York: Holt, Rinehart & Winston.

Schutz, W. C. (1966). *The interpersonal underworld, 5th ed.* Palo Alto, CA: Science and Behavior Books.

Smith, R. E. (1989). Applied sport psychology in an age of accountability. *Journal of Applied Sport Psychology, 1*, 166–180.

Spink, K. S., & Carron, A. V. (1992). Group cohesion and adherence in exercise classes. *Journal of Sport and Exercise Psychology, 14*, 78–86.

Spink, K. S., & Carron, A. V. (1993). The effects of team building on the adherence patterns of female exercise participants. *Journal of Sport and Exercise Psychology, 15*, 39–49.

Spink, K. S., & Carron, A. V. (in press). Group cohesion effects in exercise classes. *Small Group Behavior.*

Weinberg, R. S. (1989). Applied sport psychology: Issues and challenges. *Journal of Applied Sport Psychology*, *1*, 181–195.

Widmeyer, W. N., Brawley, L. R., & Carron, A. V. (1985). *Measurement of cohesion in sport teams: The Group Environment Questionnaire*. London, Ont.: Spodym Publishers.

49 Ethical Beliefs and Behaviors in Applied Sport Psychology: The AAASP Ethics Survey

ALBERT J. PETITPAS, BRITTON W. BREWER, PATRICIA M. RIVERA, AND JUDY L. VAN RAALTE
Springfield College

This reading surveyed the ethical beliefs and behaviors of applied sport psychologists. At the time this survey was administered to Association for the Advancement of Applied Sport Psychology (AAASP) members, certification of AAASP-certified consultants was in full swing. The AAASP executive board was concerned with ethical issues and the development of ethical guidelines for the newly certified sport psychology consultants. Thus an AAASP ethics committee was established and a subgroup of this committee developed this survey to assess the membership's ethical beliefs and behaviors. Numerous ethical issues had surfaced in sport psychology literature, including concerns about boundaries of competence, public statements, the welfare of clients, and dual relationships. This survey was mailed to the entire professional and student membership of AAASP, which included 508 members at that time.

The AAASP ethics committee sought to determine if the APA ethical standards were appropriate for AAASP. In addition, the survey sought to determine the levels of supervision and income for sport psychology consultants. The survey results indicated that the ethical beliefs and behaviors of most AAASP members were in line with APA ethical standards. Surprisingly few of the respondents were committing much time to applied consulting, and the consulting that was taking place was for little or no pay. Another problematic issue that surfaced in the survey results related to the supervision of applied work by others. In general, few consultants received adequate supervision, and few supervisors received training in how to supervise others. Since the report of these survey results, ethical issues have remained at the forefront of AAASP concerns.

AAASP members (N = 508) were surveyed to obtain preliminary data on ethical beliefs and behaviors specific to the practice of applied sport psychology. Completed surveys were received from 165 individuals. On the structured response portion of the survey, there were few differences in ethical beliefs and behaviors as a function of gender, professional/student status, and academic discipline. Nevertheless, a large number of controversial behaviors (N = 24) and difficult judgments (N = 8) were identified. Results of the open-ended portion of the survey indicated that most of the questionable ethical practices cited by respondents corresponded to violations of American Psychological Association (APA) Ethical Standards. The findings lend initial support for AAASP to adopt the APA Ethical Standards and suggest the need for ethics training specific to applied sport psychology.

Ethical issues are of paramount importance in an emerging interdisciplinary field such as applied sport psychology (Berger, 1993; Biddle, Bull, & Seheult, 1992; Nideffer, 1981; Sachs, 1993; Singer, 1993; Zeigler, 1987). In the Fall of 1991, the Executive Board of the Association for the Advancement of Applied Sport Psychology (AAASP) charged the newly created AAASP Ethics Committee with the task of developing "ethical guidelines" for the organization. Unfortunately, sport psychologists' beliefs about and compliance with ethical principles had not been investigated systematically. The members of the Ethics Committee believed that it would be ill-advised to recommend adoption of the American Psychological Association's "Ethical Principles for Psychologists" (APA, 1992) or to develop a new code of ethics without first gathering data specific to the practice of applied sport psychology.

A subgroup of the Ethics Committee was assigned the task of developing a survey that would assess the membership's beliefs and behaviors related to a number of situations that could arise in the practice of applied sport psychology. AAASP had adopted APA's (1977) Ethical Standards (Smith, 1989), but the development of a new revised ethical code (APA, 1992) and the push for the "professionalization" of applied sport psychology (Gould, 1990; Silva, 1989; Smith, 1989; Weinberg, 1989) suggested the need for careful consideration of ethical issues. These issues included concerns about boundaries of competence (Gardner, 1991; Silva, 1989), public statements (Smith, 1989), the welfare of clients (Heyman, 1990; Rotella & Murray, 1991), and dual relationships (Buceta, 1993; Burke & Johnson, 1992; Ellickson & Brown, 1990; Smith, 1992).

Discussions of the ethical issues identified in the literature led the committee to seven general questions that eventually provided a framework for the survey. These questions were identified by applied sport psychology professionals as critical issues for the field to address (e.g., Andersen, 1992; Rotella, 1992). The first four questions concerned the appropriateness of the revised APA (1992) "Ethical Standards" for the membership of AAASP.

1. Are there differences in beliefs and behaviors of AAASP members related to the ethical practice of applied sport psychology as a function of the academic discipline from which the individual received his or her degree?
2. Are there specific sport psychology related behaviors that are difficult to judge or highly controversial in terms of ethical practice?
3. Do members of AAASP observe sport psychologists engaging in behaviors that would be considered ethically questionable?
4. If ethically questionable behaviors are observed, what actions do the observers take?

The remaining three questions centered on issues related to the development of applied sport psychology as a profession and the role of an ethics committee.

5. What is the extent of supervision received by student and professional members of AAASP for their applied work in sport psychology?
6. What percentage of the professional membership of AAASP "makes a living" exclusively through the practice of applied sport psychology?
7. What does the membership of AAASP believe the role of the Ethics Committee should be?

To obtain preliminary data addressing these seven general questions, the AAASP Ethics Committee surveyed the membership.

Method

The AAASP Ethics Survey, a cover letter, and a return envelope were mailed to 508 professional and student members of AAASP in April of 1992. These individuals constituted the entire paid membership of AAASP at that time.

Items on the AAASP Ethics Survey were adapted from previous surveys of ethical issues in a variety of subfields within psychology (Pope, Tabachnick, & Keith-Spiegel, 1987; Pope & Vetter, 1992; Tabachnick, Keith-Spiegel, & Pope, 1991). Original items pertaining to ethically challenging sport situations were also developed. Items were designed to identify common ethical dilemmas in applied sport psychology and difficulties in applying the APA Ethical Standards to the practice of sport psychology. Both quantitative and qualitative approaches were used in the questionnaire.

In the structured response portion of the questionnaire, following the protocol of Pope et al. (1987) and Tabachnick et al. (1991), respondents were asked to rate each of 47 behaviors in terms of: (a) the extent to which they had engaged in the behavior in their work as a sport psychologist; and (b) the extent to which they considered the behavior ethical. Interpretation of the term "sport psychologist" was left up to the individual respondents. Response options for the first category of ratings were *never* (1), *rarely* (2), *sometimes* (3), *fairly often* (4), and *very often* (5). Response options for the second category of ratings were *unquestionably not* (1), *under rare circumstances* (2), *don't know/not sure* (3), *under many circumstances* (4), and *unquestionably yes* (5).

In the open-ended response section of the questionnaire, respondents were asked to: (a) ". . . describe, in a few words or more detail, an incident that you or a colleague have faced in the past year or two that was ethically challenging or troubling to you." (b) ". . . list questionable ethical practices in applied sport psychology that you have observed" and ". . . mention any actions that you may have taken in response to these questionable practices." and (c) describe their beliefs about the role and function of the AAASP Ethics Committee (i.e., education, enforcement) and provide recommendations on how to implement these beliefs.

Participants were asked to respond to items requesting demographic information (e.g., gender, age, degree, AAASP membership status, AAASP certification status, discipline, specialization, primary work setting, hours per week in applied sport psychology work, average monthly income derived from *non-teaching* applied sport psychology activities, membership in professional organizations). Additional items addressed respondents' exposure to ethical standards and supervision in applied sport psychology. Copies of the questionnaire are available from the first author.

Results

Demographic Characteristics

A 28% response rate was obtained, as 165 (113 professional members, 52 student members) questionnaires were returned. Demographic characteristics of the respondents (and of AAASP members in March 1994) are presented in table 49.1. It is clear from the data shown in table 49.1 that the respondents are largely representative of those who belong to AAASP. Professional members and members in disciplines other than physical education/exercise science and psychology appear to be slightly overrepresented and student members and members in psychology appear to be slightly underrepresented in the current sample.

Respondents reported engaging in an average of 6.04 (SD = 8.62, median = 2) hours per week of direct applied sport psychology service. This distribution was positively skewed, as over 70% (N = 116) of respondents reported

Table 49.1 Demographic Characteristics of Respondents to the AAASP Ethics Survey

Characteristic	N	%[a]	AAASP %[b]
Sex			
Female	64	38.8	40.7
Male	101	61.2	59.3
Age group			
35 and under	75	45.5	—
36 to 50	71	43.0	—
Over 50	12	7.3	—
AAASP membership status			
Professional	113	68.5	52.2
Student	52	31.5	47.8
AAASP certification status			
Certified	18	10.9	9.8
Not certified	147	89.1	90.2
Discipline			
Physical education/ exercise science	70	42.4	44.5
Psychology	54	32.7	49.2
Other	41	24.9	6.5

[a]May not sum to 100% due to missing data.

[b]Percentages refer to AAASP membership figures in March 1994. AAASP does not record the age of its members.

5 or fewer hours per week and over 90% (N = 149) of respondents reported 17 or fewer hours per week. In terms of average monthly income derived from *non-teaching* applied sport psychology activities, the modal response (N = 101, 61%) was $0. Eighteen respondents (11%) reported monthly incomes of greater than $1,000.00.

Exposure to Ethical Standards

Nearly a third of the sample (30%, N = 49) indicated that they had taken a specific course in ethics (e.g., ethics course in psychology or counseling). Seventy respondents (42%) reported that they had taken one or more courses in which ethics were covered. A small portion of the sample (22%, N = 36) indicated that they had gained information on ethical standards in a workshop context (e.g., at professional conferences). Approximately half of the respondents (46%, N = 76) reported that they had been exposed to ethical standards through independent study (e.g., reading journal articles, textbooks, ethical guidelines).

Supervision

Overall, 50 respondents (30%) indicated that they were being supervised in their applied sport psychology work. Most of the students (62%, N = 32) and only a small portion of the professionals (16%, N = 18) reported that their work was being supervised. Of the respondents who indicated that they were receiving supervision, students tended to report being supervised by faculty members (88%, N = 28) and professionals tended to report being supervised by peers (100%, N = 18). Patterns of supervision were similar for both students and professionals, as approximately half of the respondents who reported receiving supervision (47% [N = 15] of students and 56% [N = 10] of professionals) indicated that they obtained supervision on a regular basis. Reports of "as needed" supervision were common for both students (63%, N = 20) and professionals (83%, N = 15). Of the 49 respondents who stated that they were supervising the applied work of others, 28 (57%) reported that they had received training in supervision. The most commonly cited source (N = 21) of supervision training was a specific course in supervision (N = 10 in counseling/psychology, N = 3 in physical education, N = 1 in teacher supervision, N = 7 in an unspecified area).

Ethical Beliefs and Behaviors

Chi-square analyses were performed on responses to the 47 items to examine differences in ethical beliefs and behaviors as a function of gender, AAASP membership status (professional vs. student), and discipline (physical education/exercise science vs. psychology). Because of the large number of comparisons in these analyses, $p < .001$ was used as the criterion for statistical significance. No significant gender differences in ethical beliefs and behaviors were found. No differences in ethical beliefs between AAASP professional members and student members were obtained, but professional members were significantly more likely than student members to acknowledge "Publicly claiming to be a sport psychologist," "Practicing without supervision or peer consultation," and "Omitting significant information when writing a letter of recommendation for a student." Respondents in physical education/exercise science differed from respondents in psychology in only one belief and one behavior. Respondents in physical education/exercise science were more likely than those in psychology to report believing it ethical to accept "goods/services in exchange for sport psychology consultation" and to report "Serving concurrently as college instructor and psychologist for a student-athlete."

Procedures developed by Pope et al. (1987) and Tabachnick et al. (1991) were used to examine the relationship between beliefs and behaviors and to identify rare behaviors, nearly universal behaviors, difficult judgments, and controversial behaviors.

Relationship between Beliefs and Behaviors. Because "the frequency with which the respondents reported engaging in a behavior was less than the frequency of instances in which the behavior was ethical in their judgment" (Pope et al., 1987, 998) for all 47 items, the data suggest that the AAASP members in this sample are practicing largely in accordance with their beliefs.

Rare Behaviors. A rare behavior was defined as one acknowledged by less than 5% of the respondents. Only four behaviors met this criterion: "Including unverified claims in promotional materials," "Claiming affiliation with organizations that falsely implies sponsorship or certification," "Becoming sexually involved with a client *after* discontinuing a professional relationship," and "Betting on a team or individual with which or whom you are working."

Nearly Universal Behaviors. In accord with Pope et al. (1987) and Tabachnick et al. (1991), the criterion for a nearly universal behavior was to be acknowledged by at least 90% of the respondents. None of the 47 behaviors met this criterion.

Difficult Judgments. Tabachnick et al. (1991) defined a difficult judgment as "one in which 25% of the respondents indicated "don't know/ not sure" in terms of whether the behavior was ethical" (pp. 512–513). Applying this definition to the current study, eight behaviors were identified as difficult judgments. These items are shown in table 49.2.

Controversial Behaviors. Tabachnick et al. (1991) defined a controversial item as "one in which the ethical judgments were so diverse that the SD > 1.25" (p. 513). Using this criterion, over half of the 47 items were identified as controversial. These 24 controversial behaviors are displayed in table 49.3.

Table 49.2 Items Identified as Difficult Judgements

Item
14. Reporting recruiting violations to appropriate officials.
18. Reporting an athlete's gambling activity.
20. Reporting an athlete who acknowledged committing rape in the past.
24. Consulting with athletes in a sport that you find morally objectionable (e.g., boxing).
37. Socializing with clients (e.g., partying with the team).
42. Allowing out-of-town clients to reside in your home while services are being provided.
46. Working with an athlete who uses steroids.
47. Refusing to continue consulting with a client after you discover that he or she is involved in illegal activity.

Table 49.3 Items Identified as Controversial Behaviors

Item
1. Publicly claiming to be a sport psychologist.
2. Advertising sport psychology services.
3. Including athlete testimonials in advertising.
7. Practicing without supervision or peer consultation.
9. Accepting goods/services in exchange for sport psychology consultation.
14. Reporting recruiting violations to appropriate officials.
15. Reporting an athlete who uses cocaine.
16. Reporting an athlete who uses steroids.
17. Reporting abusive coaching practices.
18. Reporting an athlete's gambling activity.
19. Reporting an athlete who committed burglary.
20. Reporting an athlete who acknowledged committing rape in the past.
21. Working with an athlete whose sexual or religious practices you oppose.
24. Consulting with athletes in a sport that you find morally objectionable (e.g., boxing).
29. Using profanity in your professional work.
36. Serving concurrently as coach and sport psychologist for a team.
38. Serving concurrently as college instructor and psychologist for a student-athlete.
40. Being sexually attracted to a client.
41. Becoming sexually involved with a client after discontinuing a professional relationship.
42. Allowing out-of-town clients to reside in your home while services are being provided.
44. Using institutional affiliation to recruit private clients.
45. Entering into a business relationship with a client.
46. Working with an athlete who uses steroids.
47. Refusing to continue consulting with a client after you discover that he or she is involved in illegal activity.

Ethical Dilemmas

Eighty-four respondents identified 89 ethically challenging or troubling incidents that they or a colleague had faced in the past year or two. In accord with procedures outlined by Strauss and Corbin (1990), responses were categorized by three independent raters using the APA Ethical Standards (APA, 1992) as categories. Frequencies of incidents corresponding to the 8 ethical standards are displayed in table 49.4. Most of the incidents pertained to General Standards and Confidentiality. Frequently cited issues in the general standards category included providing services without proper training, having students working with athletes without supervision, engaging in dual role relationships, and failing to make appropriate referrals. Frequently cited issues in the confidentiality category included dealing with coaches who want information about their athletes and responding to coaches who verbally and/or physically abuse their athletes.

Seventy-five respondents identified 136 questionable ethical practices. As shown in table 49.5, the majority of these responses pertained to General Standards and Advertising and Other Public Statements. Frequently cited issues in the General Standards category included practicing outside of areas of competence, serving as both course instructor and sport psychology consultant to the same person, and failing to refer appropriately. Frequently cited issues in the Advertising and Public Statements category

Table 49.4 Frequencies of Ethically Challenging or Troubling Incidents Identified by Respondents

Ethical standard	N
General standards	40
Evaluation, assessment, or intervention	1
Advertising and other public statements	5
Therapy	3
Confidentiality	38
Teaching, training, supervision, research, and publishing	1
Forensic issues	0
Resolving ethical issues	1

Table 49.5 Frequencies of Questionable Ethical Practices Identified by Respondents

Ethical standard	N
General standards	56
Evaluation, assessment, or intervention	2
Advertising and other public statements	52
Therapy	4
Confidentiality	14
Teaching, training, supervision, research, and publishing	8
Forensic issues	0
Resolving ethical issues	0

included claiming responsibility for client success and identifying clients during professional presentations.

The leading action reported in response to the questionable ethical practices was to do nothing (N = 57, 35%), followed by talking with or confronting the person involved (N = 39, 24%). Other actions listed were talking with colleague or supervisor (N = 10, 6%), reporting the questionable ethical practice (N = 9, 5%), educating prospective consumers about ethical practices (N = 8, 5%), and referring to a qualified professional (N = 2, 1%).

Respondents were split regarding their beliefs about the role and function of the AAASP Ethics Committee. Fifty-eight respondents (35%) advocated that the committee perform both education and enforcement functions, while 46 respondents (28%) suggested that the committee provide only education. Recommendations for education focused primarily on promoting awareness of APA standards (tailored specifically to sport psychology) through such avenues as workshops/group supervision at professional meetings, continuing education, increased coverage of ethical issues in sport psychology courses, and a workbook/casebook highlighting ethical dilemmas in applied sport psychology. Respondents advocated that educational efforts present formalized ethical standards, define competencies in sport psychology (i.e., *who* can practice *what*?), and address client–practitioner boundary issues. The need for consumer education (of athletes, coaches, parents, etc.) on ethical issues was also noted.

Regarding the role of AAASP in the enforcement of ethical standards in sport psychology, responses ranged considerably. Some respondents strongly opposed AAASP's involvement in enforcing ethical standards, while others argued fervently for AAASP to adopt an active role in monitoring the professional conduct of its members. Several respondents noted that avenues for enforcing ethical standards already exist for APA members and for unlicensed or uncertified practitioners violating title restrictions. AAASP-specific options suggested for enforcement of ethical standards included installation of a peer review board that could recommend disciplinary action for ethical violations, arbitration of alleged ethical violations by unbiased parties, and creation of a reporting system for victims of ethical violations (e.g., athletes, coaches). Some respondents, citing the financial and logistical difficulties in establishing enforcement mechanisms, argued instead for such options as peer enforcement, ethics hotlines, and educational programs providing proactive recommendations for change in identified problem areas.

Discussion

Major Questions

The purpose of this survey was to assess the ethical beliefs and behaviors of the AAASP membership specific to the practice of applied sport psychology. In particular, the AAASP Ethics Committee was interested in two main questions: 1) Are the APA Ethical Standards (APA, 1992) appropriate for the membership of AAASP?; and 2) How is sport psychology developing as a profession, particularly with regard to levels of supervision and income of AAASP members?

In general, the results of this survey indicate that the ethical beliefs and behaviors of AAASP members are consistent with the APA Ethical Standards. The overall lack of differences by gender, professional/student status, and academic discipline offers initial support for the adoption of the APA Ethical Standards. However, the relatively large number of "controversial behaviors" (N = 24) and "difficult judgments" (N = 8) indicates a need for continuing education in identifying and discussing appropriate conduct related to these so-called "grey areas."

All of the 89 ethically challenging or troubling incidents and the 136 questionable ethical practices that were identified by respondents fell within the general categories outlined in the APA Ethical Standards. In particular, the respondents identified many incidents related to dual role relationships, limits of competence, confidentiality, and public statements that are sport specific and beg further clarification. This lack of clarity may also have accounted for some members (35%, N = 57) taking no action in response to questionable ethical practices that they observed.

In examining the Ethics Committee's second general question related to aspects of the "professionalization" of applied sport psychology, the survey data are alarming. Over 70% of the respondents reported 5 or fewer hours of direct applied sport psychology services offered per week and 61% reported a monthly income of $0 derived from *non-teaching* applied sport psychology activities. Only 18 respondents (11%) reported monthly incomes of greater than $1,000. These data call into question the ethics of continuing to accept large numbers of students into a field that may not have an adequate number of non-teaching employment possibilities (Waite & Pettit, 1993).

Equally troubling is the finding that only 30% of the respondents reported that they were receiving supervision for their applied sport psychology work. Regular supervision is an important element of the learning process in the overall preparation of applied sport psychologists (Sachs, 1993). It is during supervision that individuals often learn the specifics of "how" to consult with athletes, exercisers, and coaches that are necessary supplements to the theories and techniques taught in the classroom. Supervision is not just for students. It should be an important element in the continuing education of all sport psychologists. Yet only 16% of the professionals reported that they received any type of supervision. This apparent lack of "quality control" can create a negative image for an evolving field like sport psychology. In addition, failure to adequately protect the consumer by neglecting to provide supervision can have both legal and ethical ramifications for students' advisors and affiliated institutions.

Another concern regarding supervision is the lack of training reported by those individuals who are supervising the applied work of others. AAASP now requires a supervised experience with a "qualified person" as one of the criteria to become a Certified Consultant. It would seem imperative for AAASP to provide continuing education to insure that these "qualified persons" gain training in providing *sport psychology* supervision.

Respondents were split regarding their beliefs about the functions of the Ethics Committee, with slightly more respondents (N = 58, 35%) advocating both education and enforcement functions than education only (N = 46, 28%), but both groups clearly advocating the provision of sport psychology specific information. AAASP appears to be committed to fulfilling this need, as evidenced by the three invited "Ethics" presentations at the 1993 AAASP Conference and the inclusion of a specific ethics continuing education requirement for renewal of Certified Consultant status within AAASP.

Validity and Interpretation Issues

First, it should be noted that a 28% response rate is relatively low for a within organization survey on an important topic, but it is consistent with the return rates of ethics surveys of other professional groups (e.g., Percival & Striefel, 1994). It is possible that the survey length may have discouraged participation in the study. Second, it is impossible to determine if the 6.04 hours per week of direct applied sport psychology consultation reported by respondents is typical of most professionals in the field. The sample in this study appears to have been made up largely of faculty members and private practice clinicians who do applied sport psychology work "on the side." Third, the same individuals rated both the frequency of their own behaviors and their judgments about the ethicality of those behaviors. There is some evidence that this procedure does not bias results (Borys & Pope, 1989), but caution in interpreting these findings needs to be exercised. Fourth, many of the 47 items represent complex issues that may not be best represented by the brief descriptions provided. Finally, this survey contained items pertaining to ethically challenging sport situations that were generated by the authors to gather initial data about the ethical beliefs and behaviors of AAASP members. This survey should be replicated and expanded to include other examples of ethically challenging and questionable behaviors, such as those identified by respondents in the open-ended response section of the survey.

Conclusion

It is understandable that members of AAASP not affiliated with APA might be skeptical about having their sport psychology practices regulated by a code of ethics that was developed for psychologists, who typically work in traditional clinical settings. Unfortunately, this skepticism may lead some AAASP members to reject the APA Ethical Guidelines before they have thoroughly examined the document. As pointed out by Tabachnick et al. (1991), "A crucial aspect of the maturation and moral development of any profession is the collective openness and dedication of its membership to study and critically examine itself" (p. 515). Based on the results of this survey, the APA Ethical Guidelines appear to provide an excellent framework for AAASP's self-evaluation process.

The APA Guidelines can provide a vehicle to more closely examine the similarities and differences between sport psychology practices and psychological interventions in more traditional settings. For example, many sport psychology consultants work in settings with high public visibility and environmental expectations that are much different than those typically associated with seeing a client in a private professional office (Danish, Petitpas, & Hale, 1993). Just as the nature of a student-professor relationship may violate traditional "clinical boundaries" (Tabachnick et al., 1991), so too might the sport psychologist-athlete relationship, which frequently requires more time spent interacting with athletes and coaches in a variety of settings (e.g., Dorfman, 1990; Ravizza, 1990; Rotella, 1990).

The APA Ethical Guidelines provide a framework for self-evaluation that is generally comprehensive but open to interpretation. The Ethical Guidelines are subject to both external influence, as evidenced by the recent Federal Trade Commission rulings on the legality of APA's standards for public statements, and internal modification, as witnessed by the adoption of "Specialty Guidelines for the Delivery of Services" for Clinical, Counseling, Industrial/Organizational, and School Psychologist subgroups (APA, 1981). AAASP may best be served by adopting and using the current APA Ethical Standards while discussing the "grey areas" specific to the practice of applied sport psychology through a process of critical self-examination.

References

American Psychological Association. (1977). *Standards for providers of psychological services.* Washington, DC: APA.

American Psychological Association. (1981). Specialty guidelines for the delivery of services. *American Psychologist, 36,* 640–681.

American Psychological Association. (1992). Ethical principles of psychologists and code of conduct. *American Psychologist, 47,* 1597–1611.

Andersen, M. B. (1992). Sport psychology and procrustean categories: An appeal for synthesis and expansion of service. *AAASP Newsletter, 7*(3), 8–9, 15.

Berger, B. G. (1993). Ethical issues in clinical settings: A reaction to ethics in teaching, advising, and clinical services. *Quest, 45,* 106–119.

Biddle, S. J. H., Bull, S. J., & Seheult, C. L. (1992). Ethical and professional issues in contemporary British sport psychology. *The Sport Psychologist, 6,* 66–76.

Borys, D. S., & Pope, K. S. (1989). Dual relationships between therapist and client: A national study of psychologists, psychiatrists, and social workers. *Professional Psychology: Research and Practice, 20,* 283–293.

Buceta, J. M. (1993). The sport psychologist/athletic coach dual role: Advantages, difficulties, and ethical considerations. *Journal of Applied Sport Psychology, 5,* 64–77.

Burke, K. L., & Johnson, J. J. (1992). The sport psychologist-coach dual role position: A rebuttal to Ellickson and Brown. *Journal of Applied Sport Psychology, 4,* 51–55.

Danish, S. J., Petitpas, A. J., & Hale, B. D. (1993). Life development interventions for athletes: Life skills through sports. *The Counseling Psychologist, 21,* 352–385.

Dorfman, H. A. (1990). Reflections on providing personal and performance enhancement consulting services in professional baseball. *The Sport Psychologist, 4,* 341–346.

Ellickson, K. A., & Brown, D. R. (1990). Ethical considerations in dual relationships: The sport psychologist-coach. *Journal of Applied Sport Psychology, 2,* 186–190.

Gardner, F. L. (1991). Professionalization of sport psychology: A reply to Silva. *The Sport Psychologist, 5,* 55–60.

Gould, D. (1990). AAASP: A vision for the 1990's. *Journal of Applied Sport Psychology, 2,* 99–116.

Heyman, S. R. (1990). Ethical issues in performance enhancement approaches with amateur boxers. *The Sport Psychologist, 4,* 48–54.

Nideffer, R. M. (1981). *The ethics and practice of applied sport psychology.* Ithaca, NY: Mouvement.

Percival, G., & Striefel, S. (1994). Ethical beliefs and practices of AAPB. *Biofeedback and Self-Regulation, 19,* 67–93.

Pope, K. S., Tabachnick, B. G., & Kieth-Spiegel, P. (1987). Ethics of practice: The beliefs and behaviors of psychologists as therapists. *American Psychologist, 42,* 993–1006.

Pope, K. S., & Vetter, V. A. (1992). Ethical dilemmas encountered by members of the American Psychological Association. *American Psychologist, 47,* 397–411.

Ravizza, K. (1990). SportPsych consultation issues in professional baseball. *The Sport Psychologist, 4,* 330–340.

Rotella, R. J. (1990). Providing sport psychology consulting services to professional athletes. *The Sport Psychologist, 4,* 409–417.

Rotella, R. J. (1992). Sport psychology: Staying focused on a common and shared mission for a bright future. *AAASP Newsletter, 7*(3), 8–9.

Rotella, R. J., & Murray, M. (1991). Homophobia, the world of sport, and sport psychology consulting. *The Sport Psychologist, 5,* 355–364.

Sachs, M. L. (1993). Professional ethics in sport psychology. In R. N. Singer, M. Murphey, & L. K. Tennant (Eds.), *Handbook of research on sport psychology* (pp. 921–932). New York: Macmillan.

Silva, J. M. (1989). Toward the professionalization of sport psychology. *The Sport Psychologist, 3,* 265–273.

Singer, R. N. (1993). Ethical issues in clinical services. *Quest. 45,* 88–105.

Smith, D. (1992). The coach as sport psychologist: An alternative view. *Journal of Applied Sport Psychology, 4,* 56–62.

Smith, R. E. (1989). Applied sport psychology in an age of accountability. *Journal of Applied Sport Psychology, 1,* 166–180.

Strauss, A., & Corbin, J. (1990). *Basics of qualitative research: Grounded theory procedures and techniques.* Newbury Park, CA: Sage.

Tabachnick, B. G., Keith-Spiegel, P., & Pope, K. S. (1991). Ethics of teaching: Beliefs and behaviors of psychologists as educators. *American Psychologist, 46,* 506–515.

Waite, B. T., & Petit, M. E. (1993). Work experiences of graduates from doctoral programs in sport psychology. *Journal of Applied Sport Psychology, 5,* 234–250.

Weinberg, R. S. (1989). Applied sport psychology: Issues and challenges. *Journal of Applied Sport Psychology, 1,* 181–195.

Zeigler, E. F. (1987). Rationale and suggested dimensions for a code of ethics for sport psychologists. *The Sport Psychologist, 1,* 138–150.

50 Certification in Sport and Exercise Psychology

SAMUEL ZIZZI
West Virginia University

LEONARD ZAICHKOWSKY AND FRANK M. PERNA
Boston University

Since the inception of certification in the Association for the Advancement of Applied Sport Psychology (AAASP), several criticisms have been leveled at the requirements, the process, and the certification itself. Zizzi, Zaichkowsky, and Perna discussed several issues surrounding not only the certification process but also how sport psychology consultants should be trained and who should provide these services. This reading addresses these issues by providing the background on AAASP certification, exploring the criticisms of it, and promoting potential improvements to this certification.

At the time of this writing AAASP certification of sport psychology consultants had become the gold standard for sport psychology certification. In fact, both the USOC and the British Association of Sport and Exercise Sciences (BASES) had formed a certification partnership with AAASP.

Despite the benefits of certification, which include accountability and professionalism, recognition, credibility, professional preparation, and public awareness, many in the field had remained disillusioned with this program and process. Some of this criticism was brought to the surface by Anshel (1992, 1994). Anshel's key criticisms are vague language in the guidelines, the over-exclusionary process, the fact that it is discriminatory toward individuals trained in the sport sciences, and its potential for harm. Since few clients refer to the registry when selecting consultants, the value of securing this certification is also questioned.

Many sport psychology consultants think that certification is unnecessary and that the market will determine the quality of the consultant. Others think that certification is vital and, if left to the market, would create a professional disaster. Despite the fact that certification had been around for more than 10 years, there were still only 143 certified consultants. This inadequate number is due to several reasons. Many have difficulty attaining the 400 supervised hours and new methods of supervision. Others see little value in certification since few clients refer to this registry when selecting a consultant. Many graduate students in psychology have difficulty accessing the required kinesiology courses, and kinesiology graduate students find access to the clinical psychology courses problematic. The authors did an excellent job of explaining these various points of view surrounding certification.

Similar to other applied disciplines in an early stage of development, sport and exercise psychology faced the task of generating a mutually accepted mode of professional training, code of practice, and espoused core knowledge base. Perhaps no other area in an applied profession generates as much attention and controversy as codifying standards for professional preparation and practice because the practice of a profession serves as the primary interface of the field with the general public and encompasses both legal and professional issues (see Brooks & Gerstein, 1990, on the credentialing of counselors; see Cummings, 1990; Fretz & Mills, 1980, on credentialing of professional psychologists). Fairly or unfairly, the general public views the educational background and professional behavior of those who practice as the model for the field. The field of sport and exercise psychology is no exception. Issues surrounding the provision of sport and exercise psychology services have generated considerable debate about whether services should be provided (Kirschenbaum, 1994; Morgan, 1988), how individuals should be trained, and who should provide those services (Anshel, 1992, 1994; Danish & Hale, 1981; Dishman, 1983; Gardner, 1991; Harrison & Feltz, 1979; Heyman, 1993; May, 1993; Monahan, 1987; Silva, 1989; Zaichkowsky, 1993; Zaichkowsky & Perna, 1992).

Certification is a function of a professional organization that attempts to codify a common standard of preparation and practice. At a beginning stage, these standards must serve the dual purpose of recognizing the experience of members currently in the field as well as setting guidelines for those newer members who wish to pursue sport and exercise psychology. This chapter (a) defines terminology associated with certification, which has been at the root of much controversy; (b) provides a brief history of international certification; (c) provides a rationale for the existence of the certification process; (d) presents AAASP certification criteria; (e) outlines and responds to criticisms that have been levied against certification and the associated criteria in sport and exercise psychology; and (f) explores future improvements in certification that could further develop the field.

Defining Certification and Related Terms

Clearly, there is a need to clarify the terminology associated with the credentialing process in general and in sport and exercise psychology in particular. For instance, confusion exists regarding statutory versus nonstatutory designations and regarding certification versus licensure.

From S. Zizzi, L. Zaichkowsky, and F.M. Perna, 2002, "Certification in sport and exercise psychology. In *Exploring sport and exercise psychology* (Washington, DC: American Psychological Association), 459-477.

• *Credentialing.* This is a broad, generic term that is commonly defined as a process of giving a title or claim of competence. Credentialing includes statutory designations that are protected by law and enacted by a legislative body, as well as nonstatutory designations, such as recognition by organizations and registries, that are not protected by law.

• *Certification.* This is generally a nonstatutory designation granted by an organization rather than by a legislative body. However, some states use the label in reference to statutory designations (e.g., certified teacher, certified psychologist). Certification is usually a transitional designation that may serve as a preliminary step toward statutory standards for that profession (Smith, 1986).

• *Registry.* This term is generally a nonstatutory designation indicating "that an individual has been publicly identified as meeting qualifications as specified by the organization and is eligible for formal listing" Smith, 1986, p. 13).

• *Licensure.* This is a statutory process and is the most restrictive of all these terms. The statutory designation of licensure indicates a state or provincial process that is designed to regulate professional conduct within a particular field. At times, a state may adopt a professional organization's admission standards or code of ethics, and it may even relegate the monitoring of the field to a professional board of the organization. However, the state legislature retains legal authority and determines the professional organization's involvement.

• *Psychologist.* This title is restricted in many states and provinces in the United States and Canada. Use is generally restricted to those who are licensed or certified to offer services to the public. Psychologists generally have a doctoral degree in counseling or clinical psychology. Exceptions to this restricted use of title include individuals who teach and conduct research in psychology and individuals from selected states and provinces that recognize master's-level psychologists.

• *Counselor.* This is a term that appears to apply to literally a cast of thousands. Any person who is helping another is in fact offering counseling services. For instance, there are academic counselors, drug and alcohol counselors, career counselors, marriage counselors, and so forth. In many cases, little or no training is provided for these "lay" counselors; however, in other cases, counselors undergo rigorous training, making them eligible for statutory designation such as "licensed mental health counselor" or "licensed counseling practitioner."

• *Accredited or approved program.* These terms generally refer to an educational, training, or service program that has met certain standards that may or may not be related to certification or licensure. Accreditation is usually the result of a review of relevant documentation (of curriculum and practicum offerings) and a site visit by a team of reviewers from the accreditation agency. The American Psychological Association (APA) has an accreditation program that approves training programs in counseling, school, and clinical psychology. It should be emphasized, however, that by participating in an APA-approved program, one does not automatically become licensed to practice psychology. This point is particularly confusing to aspiring young professionals, because they may be unaware of the fact that licensing is a state function and not a function of APA. Typically, state licensing boards require applicants to complete a standardized exam and a set number of clinical hours (usually 2,000 hours), along with graduation from a doctoral-level program.

A Brief History of Sport Psychology Certification

The question of who is qualified to be a "sport psychologist" has been an issue ever since the field of sport psychology expanded from being primarily a topic for research and teaching in universities to providing "professional services" to athletes and coaches. Several position papers have been written on the topic, beginning in the late 1970s (Harrison & Feltz, 1979) and continuing to the present (Anshel, 1992; Danish & Hale, 1981; Dishman, 1983; Nideffer, Feltz, & Salmela, 1982; Silva, Conroy, & Zizzi, 1999; Zaichkowsky & Perna, 1992).

The USOC initiated the first systematic attempt in North America to credential sport and exercise psychologists. In the early 1980s, the USOC chose to improve the provision of sport science services to athletes. The USOC Sports Medicine Council was comfortable with identifying qualified biomechanists and exercise physiologists but thought that the standards for quality control in sport psychology were "elusive." In August 1982, the USOC brought together 12 individuals with established expertise and experience with the differing orientations of sport psychology to develop an approach to standards and identify organizational and referral processes and relationships. Guidelines proposed by this committee were subsequently published (USOC, 1983). The main recommendation made by the committee was that a sport psychology registry be established that would include the names of qualified workers in three separate categories of sport psychology: (a) clinical/counseling sport psychologists, (b) educational sport psychologists, and (c) research sport psychologists. The committee provided criteria for the three categories (USOC, 1983) and invited sport psychologists to apply for membership in the registry. From 1983 to 1995, a total of 67 sport psychologists were listed on the USOC registry.

In 1989, after several years of committee deliberations, AAASP approved a certification program. The AAASP Executive Board, Certification Committee, and Fellows focused particular attention on matters pertaining to role definition (i.e., what can "sport and exercise psychologists" do?) and title (i.e., what is the most appropriate legally acceptable title for members working in sport and exercise psychology?). Numerous experts in law and psychology were consulted regarding the issue of title. After extensive deliberation, it was concluded that if AAASP certified individuals as "sport psychologists," the association might be in violation of state and provincial laws. Because of this legal issue, AAASP Fellows voted to use the title "Certified Consultant, AAASP" rather than a title supported by many members—"certified sport psychologist." The criteria for AAASP certification are presented below. A total of 143 AAASP members have been certified through 2000. In 1995, the USOC and AAASP formed a certification partnership (AAASP, 1995). All AAASP-certified consultants who are also members of APA are considered to have met the criteria for acceptance to the registry.

Criteria for AAASP Certification

1. Completion of a doctoral degree from an institution of higher education accredited by one of the regional accrediting bodies recognized by the Council of Postsecondary Accreditation. In Canada, an institution of higher education must be recognized as a member in good standing of the Association of Universities and Colleges of Canada. Programs leading to a doctoral degree must include the equivalent of three full-time academic years of graduate study, two years of which are at the institution from which the doctoral degree is granted and one year of which is in full-time residence at the institution from which the doctoral degree is granted.

2. Four hundred hours of supervised experience with a qualified person (i.e., one who has an appropriate background in applied sport psychology), during which the individual receives training in the use of sport psychology principles and techniques (e.g., supervised practicums in applied sport psychology in which the recipients of the assessments and interventions are participants in physical activity, exercise, or sport).*

3. Knowledge of professional ethics and standards. This requirement can be met by taking one course on these topics or by taking several courses in which these topics comprise parts of the courses or by completing other comparable experiences.

4. Knowledge of the sport psychology subdisciplines of intervention/performance enhancement, health/exercise psychology, and social psychology as evidenced by three courses or two courses and one independent study in sport psychology (two of these courses must be taken at the graduate level).

5. Knowledge of the biomechanical and/or physiological bases of sport (e.g., kinesiology, biomechanics, exercise physiology).

6. Knowledge of the historical, philosophical, social behavior, or motor behavior bases of sport (e.g., motor learning/control, motor development, issues in sport/physical education, sociology of sport history, and philosophy of sport/physical education).

7. Knowledge of psychopathology and its assessment (e.g., abnormal psychology, psychopathology).

8. Training designed to foster basic skills in counseling (e.g., graduate coursework on basic intervention techniques in counseling, supervised practica in counseling, clinical psychology, or industrial/organizational psychology).*

9. Knowledge of skills and techniques within sport or exercise (e.g., skills and techniques courses, clinics, formal coaching experiences, or organized participation in sport or exercise).

10. Knowledge and skills in research design, statistics, and psychological assessment. At least two of the following four criteria must be met through educational experiences that focus on general psychological principles (rather than sport-specific ones).

11. Knowledge of the biological bases of behavior (e.g., biomechanics/kinesiology, comparative psychology, exercise physiology, neuropsychology, physiological psychology, psychopharmacology, sensation).

12. Knowledge of the cognitive-affective bases of behavior (e.g., cognition, emotion, learning, memory, motivation, motor development, motor learning/control, perception, thinking).

13. Knowledge of the social bases of behavior (e.g., cultural/ethnic and group processes, gender roles in sport, organization and system theory, social psychology, sociology of sport).

14. Knowledge of individual behavior (e.g., developmental psychology, exercise behavior, health psychology, individual differences, personality theory).

*Graduate-level work only.

International Developments in Sport and Exercise Psychology Certification

Canada

In 1987, under the leadership of Dr. Murray Smith, Canada instituted the Canadian Registry for Sport Behavioral Professionals. This national registry was a part of the Canadian Association of Sport Sciences (CASS) and was designed to provide a list of names of providers who were qualified to provide professional services to the sport community, including athletes, coaches, parents, teams, administrators, agencies, and sport governing bodies. The registry was similar to the USOC registry in that it listed qualified professionals in three categories: (a) licensed psychologists, (b) sport educators or counselors, and (c) sport researchers. For a variety of reasons, this version of the registry ceased to function and was replaced by the Canadian Mental Training Registry (CMTR) in 1994.

The CMTR, which lists 26 active members (Coaching Association of Canada, 1999), states two purposes: (a) to identify people in Canada who may be able to assist athletes and coaches with mental training and performance enhancement and (b) to promote the continued development of effective mental training services for athletes and coaches in Canada. The Registry Review Committee is a subcommittee of the High Performance Sport Committee (HPSC) of the Canadian Society for Exercise Physiology. The HPSC identified the following areas of preparation and experience as important applied sport psychology training: (a) academic training that generates an appropriate knowledge base with respect to mental links to excellence, applied mental training consulting, and applied sport sciences; (b) demonstrated personal experience in sport as a participant/athlete/performer or teacher/coach; (c) mental training supervised internship or demonstrated experience in mental training consulting; and (d) favorable client evaluations (CASS, 1994). The CMTR review committee indicates that most registrants acquire a master's or doctoral degree with specialization in sport psychology or mental training, as well as participate in a supervised internship with athletes and coaches. The recommended length for an internship is 30 weeks of supervised consulting experience.

In addition, the CMTR is careful to state what registrants do not do. Mental training consultants do not "conduct psychometric testing for the purpose of diagnosing or treating psychiatric disorders; nor do they provide psychotherapy, prescribe drugs, deal with deep-seated personality disorders or mental illness" (CASS, 1994, p. 4). The treatment of patients with mental disorders clearly falls outside the scope of ongoing mental training consulting work with athletes or others pursuing excellence. This is a distinctly different role from the mental strengthening role that mental training consultants engage in with athletes and coaches.

Australia

Like their colleagues in North America, Australians have struggled with the question of who can be a sport psychologist. Jeffrey Bond was appointed as the first "applied" sport psychologist at the Australian Institute of Sport in 1982. Since then, educational programs as well as opportunities in the field of sport and exercise psychology have grown at a rapid rate. After many years of debate regarding credentialing of sport psychologists, the Australians have determined that, to be called a sport psychologist, one needs to be a full member in the Australian Psychological Society (APS) and accepted as a member of the Board of Sport Psychologists. The board has been sanctioned by and held directly accountable to the APS. As such, sport and exercise psychology is closely linked to the profession of psychology (Chairperson's Report, 1993).

In Australia, psychologists do not have to complete a doctoral degree to call themselves psychologists. Individuals can provide psychological services to the public if they are full members of APS. The criteria for full membership, in the absence of a graduate psychology degree from a certified APS university program, include a record of research publications, letters of endorsement from current APS members, and successful completion of supervised field experience. Recent changes within APS require future psychologists to have six years of university training plus two years of supervised clinical experience. Several universities have recently instituted master's degree programs in psychology in sport psychology to provide the type of interdisciplinary training that is needed for preparing professionals with a specialization in sport and exercise psychology.

United Kingdom

The British Association of Sport and Exercise Sciences (BASES) has accreditation criteria for sport and exercise scientists (psychology section) that are designed to outline and regulate the standards for professionals in the sport and exercise sciences (BASES, 1994). Accreditation is available in two categories: (a) research accreditation (i.e., carrying out research in sport and exercise science) and (b) support accreditation (i.e., providing appropriate guidance and service to client groups). To be accredited as a "researcher," one has to make presentations and publish articles on sport and exercise psychology. For "support accreditation," a candidate must submit a portfolio that demonstrates involvement in the scientific study of sport and exercise and the ability to transpose relevant scientific knowledge into effective work in the field with clients. The accreditation process also requires supervised experience to be accredited as a sport and exercise psychologist. BASES does not require a specific number of hours of supervision for accreditation, but applicants must submit three nonconsecutive annual reports of supervised experience in a period of six years.

Benefits of Certification

In every instance in which certification has been instituted, the sponsoring organization has written about the benefits of certification. The statement issued by AAASP captures much of what other organizations have said

> Because the Association for the Advancement of Applied Sport Psychology (AAASP) and its membership are committed to the promotion of applied sport psychology, its members strive to maintain high standards of professional conduct while rendering consulting service, conducting research, and training others. AAASP has made a commitment to promoting excellence in sport psychology by instituting a certification program. (AAASP, 1991, p. 5)

This was followed by a statement of the benefits of a certification program, including accountability and professionalism, recognition, credibility, professional preparation, and public awareness. In addition to these, another benefit to certification not listed by the AAASP but stated by Smith (1987) in the Canadian registry document is that of "proactive self-determination." There is clearly an advantage to having the sport and exercise psychology profession proactively define education/training roles, ethical standards, and so forth, rather than having external professional organizations define conditions in possibly unacceptable ways.

Accountability and Professionalism

The primary objective of a certification program is to provide a standard by which sport administrators, coaches, psychologists, other health care professionals, the media, and the public accept as reliable evidence that an individual has attained specified professional competency. In this way, AAASP is assuming accountability for high standards of performance in sport and exercise psychology. Certification also attests to the professionalism of the individual, thereby serving to protect the public interest.

Recognition

Individuals certified as consultants are listed in a registry of accredited specialists. They are recognized for having fulfilled prescribed standards of performance and conduct. This registry is made available to all amateur and professional sport organizations as well as other professional groups. In this way, certification provides a vehicle for identifying qualified practitioners.

Credibility

The certification process affords credibility because certification procedures for identifying qualified professionals are rigorous and based on peer review. The public can be assured that sport and exercise psychology is maintaining high standards of performance because of the recertification procedure, which requires the continuing education of consultants.

Professional Preparation

By specifying what is considered to be appropriate preparation of professionals, the AAASP certification process provides colleges and universities with guidelines regarding programs, courses, and practicum experiences in the field of sport and exercise psychology.

Public Awareness

Certification serves to raise awareness and understanding about sport and exercise psychology for all members of the sport community as well as the public at large.

Criticisms of AAASP Certification

Considering that sport and exercise psychology and AAASP are relative newcomers as an applied science and professional organization, it is not surprising that the organization's attempt to codify guidelines for professional practice has been met with both favorable and unfavorable reactions. It is our position that division in opinion is not only understandable but also desirable. In this section, a rationale for AAASP certification is presented, and the major criticisms levied against it are addressed. See Anshel (1992, 1994) and Zaichkowsky and Perna (1992) for a full discussion of these issues.

In brief, Anshel (1992, 1994) has suggested that vague language permeates the certification guidelines. He has also asserted that the process and criteria associated with AAASP certification are flawed with respect to three primary areas: (a) Certification is overexclusionary; (b) the criteria are discriminatory toward individuals trained in the sport sciences; and, perhaps most important, (c) certification is sport and exercise psychology has greater potential for harm than for good.

Generic and Specific Language

Some of the AAASP guidelines clearly identify many specific behaviors, whereas other guidelines describe the practice of sport and exercise psychology in generic terms. Guidelines specifically address required preparatory coursework, educational degrees, and field experiences, as well as identify professional behaviors that are outside the scope of practice for AAASP-certified consultants. Although it is true that some guidelines are left to interpretation, this is the case for most professional codes of conduct. Broad language is necessary because guidelines attempt to convey heuristics to govern practice rather than concretely specify a wide array of behaviors constituting either wrongful or desirable practice. This type of language provides a document with longevity and sensitivity to the organization membership's views that may change as a function of new information such as legal statutes and public feedback. The Constitution of the United States is based on the same principle that provides citizens with both the specific letter of the law and an opportunity for an interpretative review of the spirit of the law. Similarly, AAASP certification guidelines allow professional peers to determine whether adherence to the spirit of the guidelines is followed and whether a particular guideline is appropriate.

Overexclusionary

Anshel (1994) stated that AAASP certification "fails to recognize the expertise of individuals who meet many, but not all, of the criteria for certification" (p. 345). Anshel presented the scenario of an émigré to the United States who had been recognized by his or her country as a sport psychologist and the case of a licensed, but not AAASP-certified, U.S. psychologist who provides clinical services to athletes with eating disorders as examples of competent individuals who would be excluded from AAASP certification or precluded from providing clinical services.

When the AAASP certification process was in the early stages, certification guidelines stated that current professionals desiring certification were not expected to meet all of the stated educational criteria, particularly if they could document applied experience or expertise by training, research, or continuing education. A five-year grandparenting provision was instituted specifically to recognize such individuals and to serve as an appeals process that provided a forum for professionals to state their case. No statement in AAASP certification guidelines should be construed to preclude professionals from practicing within a protected scope of practice in their recognized areas of expertise. Grandparenting is no longer in effect and, as such, all applicants must now meet the minimum requirements in all areas to achieve certification.

Returning to the first scenario, a sport psychologist from a country other than the United States would be eligible for AAASP certification; however, the burden of proof would lie with the individual seeking certification, regardless of his or her country of origin. In addition, AAASP certification does not require U.S. citizenship. In the case of the psychologist, AAASP certification guidelines do not govern the practice of professionals other than certified consultants. Furthermore, although statutes from state to state may vary, the use of psychological methods and testing to diagnose and treat psychological disorders; disorders of habit or conduct; and psychological aspects accompanying physical illness, injury, or disability are but a few of the functions protected by law. Therefore, psychologists could not be preempted from providing services that are within their legal scope of practice and areas of expertise even if their clients were athletes. It is important to note, however, that licensure as a psychologist is not sufficient to qualify for AAASP-certified consultant status.

Discriminatory Against the Sport Sciences

A major criticism of AAASP certification suggests that biased representation of the certification committee existed and that the ensuing guidelines favor individuals with psychology over sport science backgrounds. However, no data support this view. During the development of AAASP certification standards, experts from psychology, sport science, and the legal and medical disciplines as well as the AAASP membership contributed input at the inception of proposed guidelines and in ensuing years. In addition, an empirical analysis comparing the educational backgrounds of applicants accepted or rejected for AAASP-certified consultant status revealed that significantly more individuals with sport science training than individuals with psychology training achieved certification (Zaichkowsky & Perna, 1992). In recent years, this gap has narrowed, although sport science professionals achieving certification still outnumber psychology professionals achieving certification (AAASP, 2000; D. Burton, Chair of Certification Committee, University of Idaho, personal communication, September 26, 2000).

Potential for Harm

It has been suggested that credentialing an individual as a certified consultant may diminish rather than promote quality service. This criticism is based largely on the premise that certification may create the illusion of sanctioning fraudulent practice (Anshel, 1992; Zaichkowsky & Perna, 1992). Fraudulent practices in sport and exercise psychology primarily include practitioners who misrepresent the efficacy of sport and exercise psychology interventions and those who engage in practice without proper training. Although it is true that certified consultants who make fraudulent claims, misapply techniques, and generally practice outside of their area of expertise would likely damage the field of sport and exercise psychology, no evidence exists to suggest that certification promotes this occurrence. More arguments can be made supporting the opposite view—that certification likely minimizes unethical practice.

An ample knowledge base exists supporting the efficacy of many interventions used in the provision of sport and exercise psychology services (Druckman & Bjork, 1991; Greenspan & Feltz, 1989; Kendall, Hrycaiko, Martin, & Kendall, 1990; Meyers, Schleser, & Okwumabua, 1982; Meyers, Whelan, & Murphy, 1996; Zaichkowsky & Fuchs, 1988). The coursework and supervised practica required for certification are intended to document that applicants for certification are not only exposed to these techniques but also demonstrate proficient skill and judgment in their application. Present AAASP-certified consultants, similar to other applied professionals, are encouraged to regularly apprise themselves of new developments through journals, conferences, workshops, and consultation. To maintain certified status, consultants are also required to complete continuing education credits to keep abreast of new information and applications within the field.

It is true that certification, similar to all credentialing processes, can only minimally define competent practice. Whether consultants seek to adjust their practice as new evidence accumulates or engage in consultation and referral where appropriate is not an issue of certification but rather an issue of professional integrity. However, we contend that certification standards serve to promote competent practice by providing a structure and training guidelines for students and professionals seeking to expand their practice.

A related criticism that often arises concerns the belief that licensed mental health practitioners without requisite experience in the practice of sport and exercise psychology, specifically psychologists, would be eligible for AAASP-certified consultant status. This is simply not the case. Nor is it appropriate to assume that a psychologist, without demonstrated expertise, may opt to advertise and practice as a sport and exercise psychologist without the potential for censure. Although state statutes typically protect the title of psychologist and permutations thereof, state regulatory boards prohibit psychologists and other mental health professionals from practicing and advertising in areas outside of their expertise. Professionals may be reported to their respective certifying or licensing boards for practicing outside of their area of expertise. Therefore, although AAASP has no legal jurisdiction over professionals who practice unethically, having publicly stated AAASP certification criteria, individuals and sport and exercise psychology organizations are in a better position to curtail practice that is detrimental to the field of sport psychology.

It is our view that certification, as designed by AAASP, provides the public with standard criteria that certified consultants have met and a means by which certified and noncertified professionals can be compared. With time, professional sport and exercise psychology organizations and the public will decide whether distinction by AAASP certification is important. In the interim, the public is protected, to the greatest extent possible, from fraud. However, as is the case with credentialing in other professional fields, certification does not, and never was intended to, guarantee expertise or personal integrity. All professional organizations contain some individuals who have engaged in unethical, and at times criminal, conduct. To allege that certification promotes inappropriate behavior detrimental to the field is unsubstantiated. On the contrary, to dispense with certification and let "the market" determine quality, as has been suggested (Anshel, 1992), would likely be a professional disaster.

Future Developments in AAASP Certification

For certification credentialing to significantly improve the quality of training and services provided within applied sport psychology, it must be supported by a large number of professionals within the field. Currently, there are approximately 570 professional members of AAASP, which includes 295 trained in psychology, 247 trained in the sport sciences, and 28 trained in other disciplines (AAASP, 2000). Yet, there are only 143 certified consultants, which represents just 25% of the professional membership. Furthermore, based on the most recent statistics from the certification committee, AAASP certifies an average of only 9 to 10 new consultants per year, which will not substantially increase the certified consultant pool in years to come.

The following section addresses several alternative approaches to meeting AAASP certification that, if adopted, would provide a more flexible model of credentialing while maintaining the standard of training. The overall goal of these alternative approaches would not be to simply increase the *quantity* of certified consultants but rather to facilitate the application process to allow for *qualified* consultants to become certified more efficiently.

Meeting the Practicum Hours Requirements

Many applicants struggle to meet the 400 supervised hours working in sport and exercise settings, and this struggle includes candidates from both sport science and psychology backgrounds. One key issue involves acquiring qualified supervision for applied work with sport and exercise clients. To provide support for those seeking certification, AAASP may need to establish a clearinghouse, wherein certified consultants could offer supervision by telephone and e-mail to those consultants who are unable to acquire personal supervision in their geographic area. This indirect supervision model may be effective in encouraging applicants to complete their hours and would establish a more direct mentoring relationship beyond the boundaries of graduate programs.

Aside from supervision issues students also often struggle to get diversity of experience across sport and exercise settings. To ensure comprehensive training, opportunities need to be developed within graduate programs to ensure that students have access to high school and college athletes, youth sport participants, adult and older adult exercisers and, possibly, populations with chronic diseases (e.g.. diabetes, heart disease). For instance, some sport psychology or counseling programs have already developed relationships with other academic units (e.g., community medicine, exercise physiology) to provide practicum opportunities for their students. It would be useful for AAASP to establish a formal outlet for communicating new and creative practicum opportunities to all applied sport psychology programs. This outlet could come in the form of a committee within AAASP charged with collecting and disseminating ideas for applied experiences or in the form of a Web site focused on applied experience within graduate programs. Not only would the development of new applied opportunities increase the likelihood that students could meet the minimum hour requirements for AAASP certification, it would also allow them to gain experience in providing sport psychology interventions to several different populations.

Meeting the Coursework Requirements

In addition to their struggles with practicum hours, students preparing to apply for AAASP certification often have difficulty in meeting all of the 12 curriculum areas as well. According to the current certification committee chair, students from sport science backgrounds have the most difficulty with ethics courses, a graduate counseling class, and various psychology classes in the last four areas (Areas 11–14 on page 507). Those with a psychology background also have difficulty, but these applicants struggle to fill the three sport psychology courses and the sport science courses such as biomechanics, motor learning, and exercise physiology (D. Burton, personal communication, September 26, 2000). Two general approaches may help students get the courses they need for certification.

The first approach involves encouraging programs to develop coursework that mirrors the requirements for AAASP certification. This coursework would be especially beneficial to students with a sport psychology specialization at the graduate level. A recent study of online course catalogs revealed that the majority of graduate programs in sport psychology are not offering the necessary courses for students interested in pursuing AAASP certification (Van Raalte et al., 2000). Some authors have argued that certification will not be able to sustain itself in the future without the support of quality graduate training programs (Silva et al., 1999). Thus, in addition to support from AAASP members, certification also needs the support of sport psychology graduate programs to help produce a greater number of consultants who have the requisite training to become certified consultants.

Second, on an institutional level, and regardless of programmatic change (which can be slow and costly), the minimal involvement for faculty advisers and department chairs interacting with sport psychology students should include teaching students about the requirements of certification early in their careers and considering the 12 coursework components of AAASP certification when developing plans of study with their students. Then, if the program or department does not offer a particular class, students can proactively seek out their remaining requirements in other departments before graduation.

Another idea related to curriculum improvements is the possibility of meeting some of the coursework requirements for certification through continuing education workshops or Web-based courses. These options may be particularly appealing to those individuals who have already completed a degree and are working in the field. The current inflexibility of AAASP certification coursework criteria may have deterred these applicants from becoming certified consultants. Internet-based and workshop-centered training methods could create a more efficient model through which professionals who are lacking only a few classes or competencies could be eligible for certification.

References

Anshel, M. H. (1992). The case against the certification of sport psychologists: In search of the phantom expert. *The Sport Psychologist, 6*, 265–286.

Anshel, M. H. (1994). *Sport psychology: From theory to practice.* Scottsdale, AZ: Gorsuch, Scarisbrick.

Association for the Advancement of Applied Sport Psychology. (1995). A New USOG-AAASP Partnership. *AAASP Newsletter, 10*(3), 9.

Association for the Advancement of Applied Sport Psychology. (2000). 1999 membership report. *AAASP Newsletter, 15*(2), 43.

British Association of Sport and Exercise Sciences. (1994). *Accreditation criteria for sport and exercise scientists—Psychology section.* Unpublished manuscript.

Brooks, D. K., & Gerstein, L. H. (1990). Counselor credentialing and interprofessional collaboration. *Journal of Counseling & Development, 68*, 476–490.

Canadian Association of Sport Sciences. (1994). *Canadian Mental Training Registry.* [Brochure]. Gloucester, Ontario, Canada: Author.

Chairperson's report. (1993). *Australian Sport Psychology Association Bulletin, 2*, 4–6.

Coaching Association of Canada. (1999). Canadian Mental Training Registry. Retrieved from http:/ /www.coach.ca/cmtr/home.htm.

Cummings, N. A. (1990). The credentialing of professional psychologists and its implication for the other mental health disciplines. *Journal of Counseling & Development, 68*, 485–490.

Danish, S. J., & Hale, B. D. (1981). Toward an understanding of the practice of sport psychology. *Journal of Sport Psychology, 3*, 90–99.

Dishman, R. K. (1983). Identity crisis in North American sport psychology. *Journal of Sport Psychology, 5*, 123–134.

Druckman, D., & Bjork, R. A. (1991). *In the mind's eye: Enhancing human performance.* Washington, DC: National Academy Press.

Fretz, B. R., & Mills, D. H. (1980). *Licensing and certification of psychologists and counselors: A guide to current policies, procedures and legislation.* San Francisco: Jossey-Bass.

Gardner, F. L. (1991). Professionalization of sport psychology: A reply to Silva. *The Sport Psychologist, 5*, 55–60.

Greenspan, M. J., & Feltz, D. L. (1989). Psychological interventions with athletes in competitive situations: A review. *The Sport Psychologist, 3*, 219–236.

Harrison, R P., & Feltz, D. L. (1979). The professionalization of sport psychology: Legal considerations. *Journal of Sport Psychology, 1*, 182–190.

Heyman, S. (1993, August). *The need to go slowly: Educational and ethical issues in proposed sport psychology certification.* Paper presented at the annual meeting of the American Psychological Association, Toronto, Ontario, Canada.

Kendall, G., Hrycaiko, D., Martin, G. L., & Kendall, T. (1990). The effects of imagery rehearsal, relaxation and self-talk package on basketball game performance. *Journal of Sport and Exercise Psychology, 12*, 157–166.

Kirschenbaum, D. S. (1994, August). *Helping athletes improve sport performance—Best guesses.* Division 47 Presidential Address at the annual meeting of the American Psychological Association, Los Angeles, CA.

May, J. (1993, August). *Issues concerning certification of sport psychologists.* Paper presented at the annual meeting of the American Psychological Association, Toronto, Ontario, Canada.

Meyers, A. W., Schleser, R., & Okwumabua, T. M. (1982). A cognitive-behavioral intervention for improving basketball performance. *Research Quarterly for Exercise and Sport, 53*, 344–347.

Meyers, A. W., Whelan, J. P., & Murphy, S. M. (1996). Cognitive-behavioral strategies in athletic performance enhancement. In M. Hersen, R. M. Eisler, & P. M. Miller (Eds.), *Progress in behavior modification: Vol. 30* (pp. 137–164). Pacific Grove, CA: Brooks Cole.

Monahan, T. (1987). Sport psychology: A crisis identity? *The Physician and Sportsmedicine, 15*, 203–212.

Morgan, W. P. (1988). Sport psychology in its own context: A recommendation for the future. In J. S. Skinner, C. B. Corbin, D. M. Landers, P. E. Martin, & C. L. Wells (Eds.), *Future directions in exercise and sport science* (pp. 97–110). Champaign, IL: Human Kinetics.

Nideffer, R. M., Feltz, D., & Salmela, J. (1982). A rebuttal to Danish and Hale: A committee report. *Journal of Sport Psychology, 2*, 2–4.

Silva, J. M. (1989). Toward the professionalization of sport psychology. *The Sport Psychologist, 3*, 265–273.

Silva, J. M., Conroy, D. C., & Zizzi, S. J. (1999). Critical issues confronting the advancement of applied sport psychology. *Journal of Applied Sport Psychology, 11*, 298–320.

Smith, M. F. R. (1986, October). *Background to the proposal for a Canadian registry for sport psychology.* Paper presented at the annual meeting of the Canadian Association of Sport Science, Ottawa, Ontario, Canada.

Smith, M. F. R. (1987). *Canadian Association of Sport Sciences: Registry for Sport Behavioral Professionals.* Unpublished manuscript.

U.S. Olympic Committee. (1983). U.S. Olympic Committee establishes guidelines for sport psychology services. *Journal of Sport Psychology, 5*, 4–7.

Van Raalte, J. L., Brown, T. D., Brewer, B. W., Avondoglio, J. B., Hartmann, W. M., & Scherzer, C. (2000). An on-line survey of graduate course offerings satisfying AAASP certification criteria. *The Sport Psychologist, 14*, 98–104.

Zaichkowsky, L. D. (1993, August). *Certification program of AAASP.* Paper presented at the annual meeting of the American Psychological Association, Toronto, Ontario, Canada.

Zaichkowsky, L. D., & Fuchs, C. Z. (1988). Biofeedback applications in exercise and athletic performance. In K. Pandolf (Ed.), *Exercise and sport science reviews* (pp. 381–421). New York: Macmillan.

Zaichkowsky, L. D., & Perna, F. M. (1992). Certification of consultants in sport psychology: A rebuttal to Anshel. *The Sport Psychologist, 6*, 287–296.

Index

Note: The italicized *f* and *t* following page numbers refer to figures and tables, respectively.

Q

R

About the Editors

Daniel Smith, PhD, has been an active sport psychology professional for 25 years. Currently he is instructional dean and professor at Cerritos College in Norwalk, California. Dr. Smith served as a sport psychology consultant and faculty member at the National Institute of Education at Nanyang Technological University in Singapore. He is coauthor of the Competitive State Anxiety Inventory (CSAI-II). He was the first full-time sport psychologist in a major university athletic program, the University of Illinois. Smith has been a sport psychology consultant to professional sport teams, including the Chicago Bulls, Chicago White Sox, Indiana Pacers, and Buffalo Sabres.

Dr. Smith was on the executive board of the Asian-South Pacific Association of Sport Psychology and was a member of the National Association of Basketball Coaches. He earned a PhD in physical education and sport psychology from the University of Illinois.

He has published extensively in the field of sport psychology and is a certified consultant of the Association for Applied Sport Psychology, where he has an international reputation in this field of study. He has also conducted performance-enhancement workshops for East Singaporean, German, Russian, Japanese, Swedish, French, and Taiwanese elite coaches and athletes.

Michael Bar-Eli, PhD, is a professor in the department of business administration, and Nat Holman chair in sports research, at Ben-Gurion University of the Negev, Israel. He studied psychology and sociology at universities in Israel and Germany. Bar-Eli has published more than 135 international refereed journal articles and book chapters as well as numerous publications in Hebrew and has served as associate editor and section editor of leading sport psychology journals. He held senior psychology positions in the Israel Defense Forces and is psychological consultant to elite athletes and teams in various sports. Bar-Eli is senior vice president of ASPASP (Asian-South Pacific Association of Sport Psychology).